Lecture Notes in Computer Science 8186

Commenced Publication in 1973
Founding and Former Series Editors:
Gerhard Goos, Juris Hartmanis, and Jan van Leeuwen

Yan Tang Demey   Hervé Panetto (Eds.)

On the Move to Meaningful Internet Systems: OTM 2013 Workshops

Confederated International Workshops:
OTM Academy, OTM Industry Case Studies Program,
ACM, EI2N, ISDE, META4eS, ORM, SeDeS, SINCOM,
SMS, and SOMOCO 2013
Graz, Austria, September 9-13, 2013
Proceedings

 Springer

Volume Editors

Yan Tang Demey
European Space Agency
Systems, Software
and In-Orbit Demonstration Department
Noordwijk, The Netherlands
E-mail: yan.tang@esa.int

Hervé Panetto
University of Lorraine
CRAN
Vandoevre-les-Nancy, France
E-mail: herve.panetto@univ-lorraine.fr

ISSN 0302-9743   e-ISSN 1611-3349
ISBN 978-3-642-41032-1   e-ISBN 978-3-642-41033-8
DOI 10.1007/978-3-642-41033-8
Springer Heidelberg New York Dordrecht London

Library of Congress Control Number: Applied for

CR Subject Classification (1998): I.2.4, I.2.6, H.3.3-5, J.1, I.6.3-5, H.5.3, H.4.1-3, C.2, D.2

LNCS Sublibrary: SL 3 – Information Systems and Application, incl. Internet/Web and HCI

Typesetting: Camera-ready by author, data conversion by Scientific Publishing Services, Chennai, India

Printed on acid-free paper

Springer is part of Springer Science+Business Media (www.springer.com)

General Co-Chairs' Message
for OnTheMove 2013

The OnTheMove 2013 event, held 9–13 September in Graz, Austria, further consolidated the importance of the series of annual conferences that was started in 2002 in Irvine, California. It then moved to Catania, Sicily in 2003, to Cyprus in 2004 and 2005, Montpellier in 2006, Vilamoura in 2007 and 2009, in 2008 to Monterrey, Mexico, to Heraklion, Crete in 2010 and 2011, and to Rome in 2012. This prime event continues to attract a diverse and relevant selection of today's research worldwide on the scientific concepts underlying new computing paradigms, which, of necessity, must be distributed, heterogeneous, and supporting an environment of resources that are autonomous and yet must meaningfully cooperate. Indeed, as such large, complex, and networked intelligent information systems become the focus and norm for computing, there continues to be an acute and even increasing need to address the implied software, system, and enterprise issues and discuss them face to face in an integrated forum that covers methodological, semantic, theoretical, and application issues as well. As we all realize, email, the Internet, and even video conferences are not by themselves optimal nor even sufficient for effective and efficient scientific exchange.

The OnTheMove (OTM) Federated Conference series has been created precisely to cover the scientific exchange needs of the communities that work in the broad yet closely connected (and moving) fundamental technological spectrum of Web-based distributed computing. The OTM program every year covers data and Web semantics, distributed objects, Web services, databases, information systems, enterprise workflow and collaboration, ubiquity, interoperability, mobility, grid, and high-performance computing.

OnTheMove does not consider itself a so-called multi-conference event but instead is proud to give meaning to the "federated" aspect in its full title: it aspires to be a primary scientific meeting place where all aspects of research and development of internet- and intranet-based systems in organizations and for e-business are discussed in a scientifically motivated way, in a forum of loosely interconnected workshops and conferences. This year's event provided, for the 11th time, an opportunity for researchers and practitioners to understand, discuss, and publish these developments within the broader context of distributed and ubiquitous computing. To further promote synergy and coherence, the main conferences of OTM 2013 were conceived against a background of three interlocking global themes:

- Cloud Computing Infrastructures emphasizing Trust, Privacy, and Security
- Technology and Methodology for Data and Knowledge Resources on the (Semantic) Web
- Deployment of Collaborative and Social Computing for and in an Enterprise Context.

Originally the federative structure of OTM was formed by the co-location of three related, complementary, and successful main conference series: DOA (Distributed Objects and Applications, held since 1999), covering the relevant infrastructure-enabling technologies, ODBASE (Ontologies, DataBases, and Applications of SEmantics, since 2002) covering Web semantics, XML databases, and ontologies, and of course CoopIS (Cooperative Information Systems, held since 1993), which studies the application of these technologies in an enterprise context through, e.g., workflow systems and knowledge management systems. At the 2011 event, security issues, originally started as topics of the IS workshop in OTM 2006, became the focus of DOA as secure virtual infrastructures, further broadened to cover aspects of trust and privacy in so-called Cloud-based systems.

Each of the main conferences specifically seeks high-quality contributions and encourages researchers to treat their respective topics within a framework that simultaneously incorporates (a) theory, (b) conceptual design and development, (c) methodology and pragmatics, and (d) application in particular case studies and industrial solutions.

As in previous years we again solicited and selected quality workshop proposals to complement the more "archival" nature of the main conferences with research results in a number of selected and emergent areas related to the general area of Web-based distributed computing. This year this difficult and time-consuming job of selecting and coordinating the workshops was brought to a successful end by Yan Tang, and we were very glad to see that six of our earlier successful workshops (ORM, EI2N, META4eS, ISDE, SOMOCO, and SeDeS) re-appeared in 2013, in some cases for the fifth or even ninth time, and often in alliance with other older or newly emerging workshops. Two brand-new independent workshops could be selected from proposals and hosted: ACM and SMS. The Industry Track, started in 2011 under the auspicious leadership of Hervé Panetto and OMG's Richard Mark Soley, further gained momentum and visibility.

The OTM registration format ("one workshop buys all") actively intends to stimulate workshop audiences to productively mingle with each other and, optionally, with those of the main conferences. In particular EI2N continues to so create and exploit a visible synergy with CoopIS.

We were most happy to see that in 2013 the number of quality submissions for the OnTheMove Academy (OTMA) again increased. OTMA implements our unique interactive formula to bring PhD students together, and aims to carry our "vision for the future" in research in the areas covered by OTM. It is managed by a dedicated team of collaborators led by Peter Spyns and Anja Metzner, and of course by the OTMA Dean, Erich Neuhold. In the OTM Academy, PhD research proposals are submitted by students for peer review; selected submissions and their approaches are to be presented by the students in front of a wider audience at the conference, and are independently and extensively analysed and discussed in front of this audience by a panel of senior professors. One will readily appreciate the effort invested in this by the OTMA Faculty...

As the three main conferences and the associated workshops all share the distributed aspects of modern computing systems, they experience the application pull created by the Internet and by the so-called Semantic Web. For DOA-Trusted Cloud 2013, the primary emphasis remained on the distributed object infrastructure and its virtual and security aspects. For ODBASE 2013, the focus continued to be the knowledge bases and methods required for enabling the use of formal semantics in web-based databases and information systems. For CoopIS 2013, the focus as before was on the interaction of such technologies and methods with business process issues, such as occur in networked organizations and enterprises. These subject areas overlap in a scientifically natural fashion and many submissions in fact also treated an envisaged mutual impact among them. As with the earlier editions, the organizers wanted to stimulate this cross-pollination by a program of famous keynote speakers around the chosen themes and shared by all OTM component events. We were quite proud to announce this year

- Richard Mark Soley, OMG, USA;
- Manfred Hauswirth, DERI, Ireland;
- Herbert Zimmerman, Metasonic, Germany;
- Ainhoa Uriarte, European Commission.

And additionally, an inspiring dinner keynote by justly famous Prof. Dr. Em. Hermann Maurer, H.C. mult., allowed participants to put everything past, present, and future into a coherent context.

In spite of a general downturn in submissions observed this year for almost all conferences in computer science and IT, we were fortunate to receive a total of 137 submissions for the three main conferences and 131 submissions in total for the workshops. Not only may we indeed again claim success in attracting a representative volume of scientific papers, many from the USA and Asia, but these numbers of course allowed the Program Committees to compose a high-quality cross-section of current research in the areas covered by OTM. In fact, the Program Chairs of the CoopIS and ODBASE conferences decided to accept only approximately one full paper for each four submitted, not counting posters. For the workshops and DOA-Trusted Cloud 2013 the acceptance rate varied but the aim was to stay consistently at about one accepted paper for two to three submitted, this rate as always subordinated to proper peer assessment of scientific quality. As usual we have separated the proceedings into two volumes with their own titles, one for the main conferences and one for the workshops and posters, and we are again most grateful to the Springer LNCS team in Heidelberg for their professional support, suggestions, and meticulous collaboration in producing the files and indexes ready for downloading on the USB sticks. This year, a number of high-quality international journals will select best papers from the conferences and workshops to be extended and further submitted for a few special issues of their journal. This is also a great opportunity for some researchers to disseminate their results worldwide.

The reviewing process by the respective OTM Program Committees was as always performed to professional standards: each paper in the main conferences was reviewed by at least three referees (four for most ODBASE papers), with arbitrated email discussions in the case of strongly diverging evaluations. It may be worth emphasizing once more that it is an explicit OnTheMove policy that all conference Program Committees and Chairs make their selections completely autonomously from the OTM organization itself. As in recent years, proceedings on paper are now only available to be ordered separately.

The General Chairs are once more especially grateful to the many people directly or indirectly involved in the setup of these federated conferences. Not everyone realizes the large number of persons that need to be involved, and the huge amount of work, commitment, and in the uncertain economic and funding climate of 2013 certainly also financial risk, that is entailed by the organization of an event like OTM. Apart from the persons in their roles mentioned above, we wish to thank in particular explicitly our nine main conference PC Co-Chairs:

- CoopIS 2013: Johann Eder, Zohra Bellahsene, Rania Y. Khalaf;
- ODBASE 2013: Pieter De Leenheer, Dejing Dou, Haixun Wang;
- DOA-Trusted Cloud 2013: Norbert Ritter, Makoto Takizawa, Volkmar Lotz.

And similarly we thank the 2013 OTMA and Workshops PC (Co-)Chairs (in order of appearance on the website): Irina Richkova, Ilia Bider, Keith Swenson, Alexis Aubry, Georg Weichhart, J. Cecil, Kasuhiko Terashima, Alok Mishra, Jürgen Münch, Deepti Mishra, Ioana Ciuciu, Anna Fensel, Rafael Valencia García, Mamoun Abu Helu, Stefano Bortoli, Terry Halpin, Herman Balsters, Avi Wasser, Jan Vanthienen, Dimitris Spiliotopoulos, Thomas Risse, Nina Tahmasebi, Fernando Ferri, Patrizia Grifoni, Arianna D'Ulizia, Maria Chiara Caschera, Irina Kondratova, Peter Spyns, Anja Metzner, Erich J. Neuhold, Alfred Holl, Maria Esther Vidal, and Omar Hussain.

All of them, together with their many PC members, performed a superb and professional job in managing the difficult yet existential process of peer review and selection of the best papers from the harvest of submissions. We all also owe a serious debt of gratitude to our supremely competent and experienced Conference Secretariat and technical support staff in Brussels and Guadalajara, respectively Jan Demey and Daniel Meersman.

The General Co-Chairs also thankfully acknowledge the academic freedom, logistic support, and facilities they enjoy from their respective institutions, Vrije Universiteit Brussel (VUB), Belgium, Université de Lorraine, Nancy, France and Latrobe University, Melbourne, Australia without which such a project quite simply would not be feasible. We do hope that the results of this federated scientific enterprise contribute to your research and your place in the scientific network... We look forward to seeing you at next year's event!

July 2013

Robert Meersman
Hervé Panetto
Tharam Dillon
Yan Tang

Organization

OTM (On The Move) is a federated event involving a series of major international conferences and workshops. These proceedings contain the papers presented at the OTM Academy 2013, the OTM Industry Case Studies Program 2013, the OTM 2013 federated workshops and the OTM 2013 federated conferences poster papers.

Executive Committee

General Co-Chairs

Robert Meersman	VU Brussels, Belgium
Hervé Panetto	University of Lorraine, France
Tharam Dillon	La Trobe University, Melbourne, Australia
Yan Tang	European Space Agency, Noordwijk, The Netherlands

OnTheMove Academy Dean

Erich Neuhold	University of Vienna, Austria

OnTheMove Academy Organizing Chairs

Peter Spyns	Vrije Universiteit Brussel, Belgium
Anja Metzner	University of Applied Sciences Augsburg, Germany

Industry Case Studies Program Chair

Hervé Panetto	University of Lorraine, France

ACM 2013 PC Co-Chairs

Irina Rychkova	Centre de Recherches en Informatique, Paris 1, France
Ilia Bider	Ibissoft, Sweden
Keith Swenson	Fujitsu America, USA

EI2N 2013 PC Co-Chairs

Alexis Aubry	University of Lorraine, France
Georg Weichhart	Johannes Kepler Universität, Austria
J. Cecil	Oklahoma State University, USA
Kasuhiko Terashima	Toyohashi University of Technology, Japan

ISDE 2013 PC Co-Chairs

Alok Mishra   Atilim University, Turkey
Jürgen Münch   University of Helsinki, Finland
Deepti Mishra   Atilim University, Turkey

META4eS 2013 PC Co-Chairs

Ioana Ciuciu   Joseph Fourier University, France
Anna Fensel   STI Innsbruck and FTW Telecommunications
                               Research Center Vienna, Austria

ORM 2013 PC Co-Chairs

Terry Halpin   INTI International University, Malaysia
Herman Balsters   University of Groningen, The Netherlands

SeDeS 2013 PC Co-Chairs

Avi Wasser   University of Haifa, Israel
Jan Vanthienen   LIRIS, Katholieke Universiteit Leuven,
                               Belgium

SMS 2013 PC Co-Chairs

Dimitris Spiliotopoulos   Innovation Lab, ATC, Greece
Thomas Risse   L3S Research Center, Hannover, Germany
Nina Tahmasebi   L3S Research Center, Hannover, Germany

SOMOCO 2013 PC Co-Chairs

Fernando Ferri   IRPPS, National Research Council, Italy
Patrizia Grifoni   IRPPS, National Research Council, Italy
Arianna D'Ulizia   IRPPS, National Research Council, Italy
Maria Chiara Caschera   IRPPS, National Research Council, Italy
Irina Kondratova   IIT, National Research Council, Canada

Logistics Team

Daniel Meersman
Jan Demey

OTM Academy 2013 Program Committee

Galia Angelova   Alfred Holl
Christoph Bussler   Frédéric Le Mouël
Philippe Cudré-Mauroux   Marcello Leida

Erich J. Neuhold   Fatiha Saïs
Hervé Panetto   Andreas Schmidt
Erik Proper   Maria Esther Vidal

Industry Case Studies 2013 Program Committee

Sinuhe Arroyo   Roger Roberts
Ian Bayley   François B. Vernadat
Arne Berre   Steve Vinoski
Serge Boverie   Alex Wahler
Dennis Brandl   Georg Weichhart
Christoph Bussler   Detlef Zühlke
David Cohen   Peter Benson
Francesco Danza   Dennis Brandl
Piero De Sabbata   Marc Delbaere
Marin Dimitrov   Laurent Liscia
Donald Ferguson   Richard Martin
Kurt Fessl   Richard Soley
Albert Fleischmann   Martin Zelm
George Fodor   Luis Camarinha-Matos
Jean-Luc Garnier   J. Cecil
Pascal Gendre   Vincent Chapurlat
Ted Goranson   Yannis Charalabidis
Matthew Hause   Michele Dassisti
Florian Kerschbaum   Andres Garcia Higuera
Harald Kuehn   Ricardo Gonçalves
Antoine Lonjon   Peter Loos
Juan-Carlos Mendez   Arturo Molina
Silvana Muscella   Yasuyuki Nishioka
Yannick Naudet   Lawrence Whitman
Ed Parsons   Milan Zdravkovic

ACM 2013 Program Committee

Birger Andersson   Colette Rolland
Judith Barrios Albornoz   Gregor Scheithauer
Karsten Böhm   Rainer Schmidt
Rebecca Deneckere   Lars Taxén
Paul Johannesson   Alain Wegmann
Erik Perjons   Jelena Zdravkovic
Gil Regev

EI2N 2013 Program Committee

Hamideh Afsarmanesh
Rafael Batres
Giuseppe Berio
Peter Bernus
Xavier Boucher
Nacer Boudjlida
Pierre Brimont
Prasad Calyam
Luis M. Camarinha-Matos
Vincent Chapurlat
Yannis Charalabidis
David Chen
Adrian Curaj
Michele Dassisti
Eduardo de Freitas Rocha Loures
Claudia Diamantini
Antonio Dourado Correia
Andres Garcia Higuera
Ronald Giachetti
Virginie Goepp
Ted Goranson
Geza Haidegger
Tran Hoai Linh
Ricardo Jardim-Goncalves
Uma Jayaram
Ulrich Jumar
John Krogstie
Georghe Lazea
Mario Lezoche
Qing Li
Peter Loos
Juan-Carlos Mendez
Istvan Mezgär
Pierre-Alain Millet
Takanori Miyoshi

Nejib Moalla
Arturo Molina
Yannick Naudet
Shimon Nof
Ovidiu Noran
Angel Ortiz Bas
Hervé Panetto
Jinwoo Park
Michaël Petit
Erik Proper
Rajiv Ramnath
David Romero Diaz
Hubert Roth
Antonio Ruano
Irina Rychkova
Ryo Saegusa
Klaus Schilling
Czeslaw Smutnicki
Richard Soley
Aurelian M. Stanescu
Lawrence Stapleton
Kamelia Stefanova
Janusz Szptyko
Ryosuke Tasaki
Miroslav Trajanovic
Bruno Vallespir
François B. Vernadat
Agostino Villa
Marek Wegrzyn
Lawrence Whitman
Esma Yahia
Milan Zdravkovic
Martin Zelm
Yun-gui Zhang
Xuan Zhou

ISDE 2013 Program Committee

Adam Wojciechowsk
Adel Taweel
Amar Gupta
Allen E. Milewski
Alexander Norta

Anil Kumar Tripathi
Barbara Carminati
Bernard Wong
Cagatay Catal
Charles Wallace

Cigdem Gencel
Deo Prakash Vidyarthi
Ian Allison
Ita Richardson
Jeffrey Carver
Juan Garbajosa
Jukka Kääriäinen
Marco Kuhrmann
June Verner

Kassem Saleh
Liguo Yu
M. Ali Babar
Mahmood Niazi
Orit Hazzan
Qing Yao
Ricardo Colomo-Palacios
Silvia Abrahao

META4eS 2013 Program Committee

Adrian M.P. Brasoveanu
Alberto Messina
Alina Dia Miron
Ana Roxin
Andrea Kö
Andreas Harth
Christophe Debruyne
Christophe Roche
Cosmin Lazar
Cristian Vasquez
Davor Meersman
Doina Tatar
Dumitru Roman
Efstratios Kontopoulos
Erik Mannens

Fouad Zablith
Georgios Meditskos
Irene Celino
Jutta Mülle
Koen Kerremans
Magali Séguran
Maria-Esther Vidal
Marta Sabou
Mike Matton
Ozelín Lopez
Paolo Ceravolo
Peter Spyns
Stamatia Dasiopoulou
Yan Tang
Yuri Katkov

ORM 2013 Program Committee

Herman Balsters
Linda Bird
Anthony Bloesch
Peter Bollen
Andy Carver
Matthew Curland
Dave Cuyler
Necito Dela Cruz
Ken Evans
Pat Hallock
Terry Halpin
Clifford Heath
Stijn Hoppenbrouwers
Mike Jackson

Mustafa Jarrar
Inge Lemmens
Dirk van der Linden
Tony Morgan
Maurice Nijssen
Baba Piprani
Erik Proper
Gerhard Skagestein
Peter Spyns
Serge Valera
Theo van der Weide
Jos Vos
Jan Pieter Wijbenga

SeDeS 2013 Program Committee

Alessandro Antonucci
Chiara Verbano
Daniela Grigori
Dean Vucinic
Gregor Grambow
Ioana Ciuciu
Issachar Gilad
Jiehan Zhou
José-Fernán Martínez-Ortega
Kazuya Haraguchi
Mati Golani
Maya Lincoln
Michael Adams
Moe Wynn

Peter Spyns
Piotr Paszek
Rantham Prabhakara
Ricardo Colomo Palacios
Roman Goldenberg
Saiful Akbar
Sergio España
Seunghyun Im
The Anh Han
Wilfried Lemahieu
Yan Tang
Ying Liu
Zhiwen Yu

SMS 2013 Program Committee

Ismail Altingövde
Cosmin Cabulea
Bogdan Cautis
Jonathon Hare
Bernhard Haslhofer
Amin Mantrach
Diana Maynard
Georgios Petasis

Wim Peters
Volha Petukhova
Pierre Senellart
Marc Spaniol
Yannis Stavrakas
Pepi Stavropoulou
Michael Wiegand
Xuan Zhou

SOMOCO 2013 Program Committee

Kevin C. Almeroth
Frederic Andres
Richard Chbeir
Karin Coninx
Juan De Lara
Anna Formica
Rajkumar Kannan
Nikos Komninos

Stephen Marsh
Rebecca Montanari
Nitendra Rajput
Tommo Reti
Nicola Santoro
Thanassis Tiropanis
Riccardo Torlone
Adam Wojciechowski

Keynotes

Streams, Semantics and the Real World

Manfred Hauswirth

Digital Enterprise Research Institute (DERI),
Galway, Ireland

Short Bio

Manfred Hauswirth is the Vice-Director of the Digital Enterprise Research Institute (DERI), Galway, Ireland and a professor at the National University of Ireland, Galway (NUIG).

His research current research focus is on linked data streams, semantic sensor networks, sensor networks middleware, large-scale semantics-enabled distributed information systems and applications. Manfred has also worked extensively in peer-to-peer systems, Internet of things, self-organization and self-management, service-oriented architectures and distributed systems security.

He has published over 160 papers in these domains, he has co-authored a book on distributed software architectures and several book chapters on data management and semantics.

Manfred is an associate editor of IEEE Transactions on Services Computing, has served in over 180 program committees of international scientific conferences and was program co-chair of the Seventh IEEE International Conference on Peer-to-Peer Computing (IEEE P2P) in 2007, general chair of the Fifth European Semantic Web Conference (ESWC) in 2008, program co-chair of the 12th International Conference on Web Information System Engineering (WISE) in 2011, and program co-chair of the 10th International Conference on Ontologies, DataBases, and Applications of Semantics (ODBASE) in 2011.

He is a member of IEEE and ACM and is on the board of WISEN, the Irish Wireless Sensors Enterprise Led Network, the scientific board of the Corporate Semantic Web research center at FU Berlin, and the Scientific Advisory Board of the Center for Sensor Web Technologies (CLARITY) in Dublin, Ireland.

Talk

"Streams, Semantics and the Real World"

Until recently the virtual world of information sources on the World Wide Web and activities in the real world have always been separated. However, knowledge accessible on the Web (the virtual world) may influence activities in the real world and vice versa, but these influences are usually indirect and not immediate. We still lack general-purpose means to interconnect and link this information in a meaningful and simple way. Additionally, information comes in the form of streams which complicates the data management at all levels - from the Internet of Things (IoT) up to the backend information systems. The increasingly popular Linked Data paradigm provides a great model for data integration. However, supporting this approach from resource-constrained sensors on the IoT to (stream) databases and (stream) reasoning systems, possibly as hosted solutions in the cloud, opens up many genuine research problems that require well-orchestrated and synchronized research efforts in and across research communities. In this talk I will discuss these problems and possible solutions.

Empowering Process Participants – The Way to a Truly Agile Business Process Management

Herbert Kindermann

Metasonic AG, Germany

Short Bio

Since August 2009, Herbert Kindermann, has been the sole member of the Executive Board and CEO of Metasonic AG and responsible for all operative units, from marketing to software development. Kindermann focus on the company's customer orientation and the internationalization of sales and services around Metasonic® Suite. Before joining Metasonic in June 2007 as a member of the board of directors, Herbert held the position of a Member of the Executive Board at IDS Scheer with responsibility for all international business of the IDS Scheer AG. Previously, Herbert held various positions at COMSOFT GmbH (project manager, department manager and building up the SAP consulting business), IBCS S.A. (founder and CEO, building up business with subsidiaries in Germany, Czech Republic and Slovakia). In the beginning of the year 2000, IBCS became a member of the IDS Scheer group, taking over business responsibility for the region of Central and Eastern Europe. In 2003 Herbert Kindermann became a Member of the Extended Board of IDS Scheer AG.

Talk

"Empowering process participants - the way to a truly agile business process management"

Business process management (BPM) is widely adapted in large and mid-sized companies. While the focus is shifting more and more from the modelling of business processes for documentation reasons towards IT-backed business process support for the end-users there are still some open spots to consider to bring real business process management to the business departments of those companies. Herbert Kindermann will shed some light on current tool support for business process participants with respect to BPM, the actual needs of the business departments, the gap in between and how current technologies and trends, like a strong focus on KPIs, semantically enabled user interfaces, big data analytics, gamification and flexible workflow technology could lead to fundamental organizational changes and provide more enterprise agility in the future.

Long-Range Forecasting: Important Yet Almost Impossible

Hermann Maurer

TU Graz, Austria

Short Bio

Professor Dr. Hermann Maurer is Professor Emeritus at Graz University of Technology. He started his career at the University of Calgary as Assistant and Associate Professor, was appointed full professor at Karlsruhe just before he turned 30, and has been now Professor and Dean in Computer Science at Graz University of Technology since 1978, with some interruptions, like guest-professorships of more than a year at Denver University, University of Auckland, and shorter visits to Edith Cowan University in Perth, SMU in Dallas, Waterloo, Brasilia and others. Chair of the Informatics Section of Academia Europaea, "The Academy of Europe" since April 2009, and receiver of many national and international distinctions, Professor Maurer is author of over 650 papers and 20 books, founder of a number of companies, supervised some 60 Ph.D. and over 400 M.Sc. students and was leader of numerous multi-million Euro projects

Talk

"Long-range forecasting: important yet almost impossible"

In this talk I will first explain why we desperately need long range forecasts; then I present arguments (far beyond what comes to ones mind immediately) why such forecasts are in general impossible. Some of the arguments are also important for our own life and for society in general. I conclude this section, however, with one dramatic long range prediction. In the rest of the talk I discuss some important aspects of WWW, smart phones and e-Learning and conclude by showing why the main 5 theses of Spitzer's book "Digital dementia: how we ruin us and our children" are (fortunately) only partially correct, but why the impact of this book (in German, no translation exists so far) is potentially dangerous.

The Model-Driven (R)evolution

Richard Mark Soley

OMG

Short Bio

Dr. Richard Mark Soley is Chairman and Chief Executive Officer of OMG®.

As Chairman and CEO of OMG, Dr. Soley is responsible for the vision and direction of the world's largest consortium of its type. Dr. Soley joined the nascent OMG as Technical Director in 1989, leading the development of OMG's world-leading standardization process and the original CORBA® specification. In 1996, he led the effort to move into vertical market standards (starting with healthcare, finance, telecommunications and manufacturing) and modeling, leading first to the Unified Modeling Language TM (UML®) and later the Model Driven Architecture® (MDA®). He also led the effort to establish the SOA Consortium in January 2007, leading to the launch of the Business Ecology Initiative (BEI) in 2009. The Initiative focuses on the management imperative to make business more responsive, effective, sustainable and secure in a complex, networked world, through practice areas including Business Design, Business Process Excellence, Intelligent Business, Sustainable Business and Secure Business. In addition, Dr. Soley is the Executive Director of the Cloud Standards Customer Council, helping end-users transition to cloud computing and direct requirements and priorities for cloud standards throughout the industry.

Dr. Soley also serves on numerous industrial, technical and academic conference program committees, and speaks all over the world on issues relevant to standards, the adoption of new technology and creating successful companies. He is an active angel investor, and was involved in the creation of both the Eclipse Foundation and Open Health Tools. Previously, Dr. Soley was a cofounder and former Chairman/CEO of A.I. Architects, Inc., maker of the 386 HummingBoard and other PC and workstation hardware and software. Prior to that, he consulted for various technology companies and venture firms on matters pertaining to software investment opportunities. Dr. Soley has also consulted for IBM, Motorola, PictureTel, Texas Instruments, Gold Hill Computer and others. He began his professional life at Honeywell Computer Systems working on the Multics operating system.

A native of Baltimore, Maryland, U.S.A., Dr. Soley holds bachelor's, master's and doctoral degrees in Computer Science and Engineering from the Massachusetts Institute of Technology.

Talk

"The Model-Driven (R)evolution"
All sorts of promises of a revolution in software development accompany the phrase "model-driven" these days. Model Driven Architecture, Model Driven Development, Model Driven Enterprise – there must be something to these ideas, but is "model driven" the key to a revolution, or just the newest buzz word? Will we have to completely change the way we develop systems? Is code dead?

Richard Soley, Chairman of the Object Management Group (stewards of the Model Driven Architecture Initiative) will dispel some rumors about the model driven approach, and put it in the context of computing history. While there are some important implications for how complex systems are built, like most revolutions in software, Model Driven Architecture has straightforward underpinnings and represents a direct evolution from where we have been.

Overview of European Commission R&D Activities on Net Innovation

Ainhoa Uriarte

Short Bio

Ainhoa Uriarte is Project Officer in the unit "Net Innovation" of the Communications Networks, Content and Technology Directorate General in the European Commission. She has a degree in Industrial Engineering and a Postgraduate diploma in Business and Management. Previous to working for the Commission Mrs. Uriarte hold a position as research programme manager in the Spanish National Research Council (CSIC) and she has over eight years of experience working as a research project manager in several public and private institutions. She joined the European Commission in 2012 where she contributes to the implementation of the Net Innovation domain of the Information and Communication Technologies area of the 7th Framework Programme for research and technological development.

Talk

"Overview of European Commission R&D activities on Net Innovation"

The talk will give an overview of the research projects funded by the European Commission on Sensing Enterprises. Also future relevant activities under the next H2020 Framework Programme for Research and Innovation will be presented. The aim of the Future Internet challenge in the new programme is three fold; addressing the limitations of an Internet which was not designed to support the very large set of requirements imposed by an ever more diversified usage; supporting the advent of more efficient computational and data management models that respond to the challenges posed by increased device / object connectivity and data-intensive applications; and leveraging the Internet to foster innovative usages of social and economic value.

Table of Contents

Platforms and Frameworks

Interoperability Case Studies and Issues

Enterprise Systems

International Workshop on Adaptive Case Management and Other Non-workflow Approaches to BPM (ACM) 2013

Experience Based Papers

Research and New Theoretical Ideas

Position Papers

Workshop on Enterprise Integration, Interoperability and Networking (EI2N) 2013

Architectures and Platforms

Engineering and Modelling

Sustainable Interoperability and Interoperability for Sustainability

International Workshop on Information Systems in Distributed Environment (ISDE) 2013

Architecture, Knowledge Management and Process in Distributed Information System

Quality Management in Distributed Information System

Distributed Information Systems Applications

Workshop on Methods, Evaluation, Tools and Applications for the Creation and Consumption of Structured Data for the e-Society (META4eS) 2013

Business Process Models and Semantics for the e-Society

Structured Data Consumption for the e-Society

Ontology Evolution and Evaluation

Workshop on Fact-Oriented Modeling (ORM) 2013

ORM Formal Foundations and Transforms

Extensions to ORM

Demonstrations of Fact-Oriented Modeling Tools

Combining Data, Process and Service Modeling

Conceptual Query and Verbalization Languages

Workshop on Semantics and Decision Making (SeDeS) 2013

Workshop on Social Media Semantics (SMS) 2013

Workshop on SOcial and MObile COmputing for Collaborative Environments (SOMOCO) 2013

Social Networking and Social Media

Methods, Models and Applications in Web and Mobile Computing

Cooperative Information Systems (CoopIS) 2013 Posters

Ontologies, DataBases, and Applications of Semantics (ODBASE) 2013 Posters

The 10th OnTheMove Academy Chairs' Message

The term 'academy', originating from Greek antiquity, implies a strong mark of *quality and excellence in higher education and research* that is upheld by its members. In the ten past editions, the OTM Academy has yearly innovated its way of working to uphold its mark of quality and excellence. OTMA Ph.D. students students publish their work in a highly reputed publication channel, namely the Springer LNCS OTM workshops proceedings. The OTMA faculty members, who are well-respected researchers and practitioners, critically reflect on the students' work in a positive and inspiring atmosphere, so that the students learn to improve not only their research capacities but also their presentation and writing skills. OTMA participants learn how to review scientific papers. They also enjoy ample possibilities to build and expand their professional network thanks to access to all OTM conferences and workshops. And last but not least, an ECTS credit certificate rewards their hard work.

Crucial for the success of OTM Academy is the commitment of our other OTMA faculty members whom we sincerely thank:

- Erich J. Neuhold (University of Vienna, Austria), OTMA Dean
- Alfred Holl (University of Applied Sciences, Nuremberg, Germany)
- Maria Esther Vidal (Universidad Simon Bolivar, Caracas, Venezuela)
- Josefa Kumpfmüller (Vienna, Austria), Student Communication Seminar

The OTMA submissions were reviewed by an international programme committee of well-respected experts. We thank them for their effort and time:

- Galia Angelova (Bulgarian Academy of Science, Sofia, Bulgary)
- Christoph Bussler (XTime Inc., USA)
- Philippe Cudré-Mauroux (Massachusetts Institute of Technology, USA)
- Marcello Leida (Khalifa University, Abu Dhabi, United Arabic Emirates)
- Frédéric Le Mouël (University of Lyon, Lyon, France)
- Hervé Panetto (Nancy University, Nancy, France)
- Erik Proper (Public Research Centre - Henri Tudor, Luxembourg)
- Fatiha Saïs (Université Paris-Sud XI, France)
- Andreas Schmidt (Karlsruhe University of Applied Sciences, Germany)

We also express our thanks to Christophe Debruyne (Vrije Universiteit Brussel) who again volunteered to be the OTMA 2013 "social media master" and to Danai Symeonidou and Nathalie Pernelle (Université Paris-Sud) and Milan Zdravkovic and Mario Lezoche (Nancy University) as additional reviewers.

This year, eight papers were submitted by students from six countries. Three submissions have been accepted as regular papers and one as a poster. We hope that you find the papers promising and inspiring for your research.

July 2013

Peter Spyns
Anja Metzner

Y.T. Demey and H. Panetto (Eds.): OTM 2013 Workshops, LNCS 8186, p. 1, 2013.
© Springer-Verlag Berlin Heidelberg 2013

On the Likelihood of an Equivalence

Giovanni Bartolomeo[1], Stefano Salsano[1], and Hugh Glaser[2]

[1] University of Rome Tor Vergata,
Via del Politecnico 1, 00133 Rome, Italy
{Giovanni.Bartolomeo,Stefano.Salsano}@uniroma2.it
[2] Seme4, Ltd.
18 Soho Square, London, W1D 3QL, UK
Hugh.Glaser@seme4.com

Abstract. Co-references are traditionally used when integrating data from different datasets. This approach has various benefits such as fault tolerance, ease of integration and traceability of provenance; however, it often results in the problem of entity consolidation, i.e., of objectively stating whether all the co-references do really refer to the same entity; and, when this is the case, whether they all convey the same intended meaning. Relying on the sole presence of a single equivalence (owl:sameAs) statement is often problematic and sometimes may even cause serious troubles. It has been observed that to indicate the likelihood of an equivalence one could use a numerically weighted measure, *but the real hard questions of where precisely will these values come from arises.* To answer this question we propose a methodology based on a graph clustering algorithm.

Keywords: Equivalence Mining, Co-references, Linked Data.

1 Introduction

Co-references (i.e. reference to the same resource) are widely used in Linked Data to integrate data from different datasets. The simplest and usual way of representing co-references is to state the explicit equivalence between two RDF nodes connecting them through the owl:sameAs property. Hu [1] noted that despite other properties such as inverse functional properties, functional properties and maximum cardinality that may indirectly confirm the equivalence of two resources, the bulk of equivalence relationships in Linked Data are traditionally given by explicit owl:sameAs statements (henceforth also called equivalence statements or simply equivalences). Using co-references is probably unavoidable in a distributed environment[1] and brings various benefits such as fault tolerance, ease of integration and traceability of provenance [2]. However, it often results in the open problem of objectively stating whether all the co-references do really refer to the same entity (a well known problem sometimes called object identification, entity consolidation, etc.) and, most

---

[1] Attempts to provide single unique identifiers, such as [14, 15], at the end result in centralized systems.

Y.T. Demey and H. Panetto (Eds.): OTM 2013 Workshops, LNCS 8186, pp. 2–11, 2013.
© Springer-Verlag Berlin Heidelberg 2013

importantly, whether all co-references convey the same intended meaning, as OWL specifications[2] would require. owl:sameAs statements do not always honor this rigorous semantics. For example, [3] reports four very different typologies of use of owl:sameAs they actual found in Linked Data (contextualization, referential opacity, similitude, and reference misplacement). While these different uses appear to be acceptable and sometimes even useful for some applications (e.g. surfing the web of Linked Data for general knowledge, such as finding that Berlin is a city in Germany, together with a number of other cities), for others, especially for those using automatic reasoning, a higher degree of precision is indeed needed [4].

Looking at existing properties in well known vocabularies conveying the meaning of equivalence and similitude, one could think of a classification of the strength of this kind of relationship. For example, [5] points out that rdf:seeAlso is much "weaker" than owl:sameAs; and [3] that the SKOS vocabulary has a number of "matching" predicates that are close in meaning to owl:sameAs without however implying full identity (skos:broadMatch, skos:narrowMatch, skos:closeMatch, etc.). However, their use may be subjective and even if *one is tempted to engage with some sort of numerically weighted uncertainty measure of identity, the real hard questions of where precisely will these real values come from* [3] arises. Our first question to answer.

2   Related Works

At the time of writing there are two main ways of creating equivalence relationships: automatic and manual. Automatically generated equivalences[3] depend on the effectiveness of various adopted algorithms in detecting similar property values presented by candidate equivalent resources (and obviously on the public availability of such property values). Many of these algorithms are domain-independent and – as opposite to humans – tend to disregard semantic nuances in favour of the sought similitude. Thus, reliable links are often established after manual inspections of candidate resources.

Manually established equivalence links depends on the publisher's knowledge about the referent, the meaning they intend to convey, their understanding of the candidate equivalent resources in other datasets and her knowledge about contextual aspects (for instance, when linking data from medical domains, a publisher might be well aware that a high precision is needed).

As equivalence is a transitive and symmetric property, sets of resources that convey the same meaning, seen as nodes connected by owl:sameAs arcs, should form

---

[2] According to OWL specifications, two RDF subjects stated to be equivalent should be identical, and thus perfectly interchangeable in all the statements they appear.

[3] Examples of these tools include Silk (http://wifo5-03.informatik.uni-mannheim.de/bizer/silk/) and LIMES (http://aksw.org/Projects/LIMES.html). In addition, the Ontology Alignment Evaluation Initiative website (http://oaei.ontologymatching.org/) contains articles and reports about several methods which have been compared in various schema matching campaigns starting from 2004.

a complete directed graph, in which every pair of distinct nodes is connected by a pair of unique arcs, one in each direction.

"Consistent Reference Service" (CRS) is a concept that has been proposed in the past to deal with equivalences [12]. A CRS is a framework that aggregates "real" co-references into bundles. A user can look for a reference and get all the co-references belonging to the same bundle (a well-known instantiation of a CRS is "sameAs.org", which is exposed both as a web site and a web API[4]).

The genesis for CRS deployment was to cope with the questions of how to deal with nodes related by owl:sameAs predicates which should form a complete directed graph, either explicitly or by inference. In combining different graphs where equivalences have been defined or identified, a CRS takes the only safe action and asserts all the (N^2) individual owl:sameAs links connecting all the possible pairs of nodes. In practice, however, other topologies are observable. In 2010, working on equivalence links connecting RDF nodes from the BTC2010 corpus, Ding [6,7] found that their distribution exhibits the power law pattern characteristic of scale-free networks, i.e. few nodes have many incoming arcs while others have much fewer ones.

3   Method

We observe [8] that co-references coming from different datasets show a dynamic tendency to aggregate into groups of graph nodes within which edges are much more dense than between them. In literature, these groups are known as "clusters" [9]. These empirical findings led us to a second question: why does this happen?

Answering this question means analyzing equivalence network using cluster detection techniques. In general, the graph clustering problem is NP-hard, therefore no algorithm exists to solve it in polynomial time; at the time of writing only heuristics are available. Newman and Girvan [10] propose the concept of modularity as a measure of the degree of clustering of a graph. The modularity is defined as the fraction of edges falling in the resulting disjoint connected components minus the expected value that the same quantity would have if the graph had random connections between nodes. They also describe an iterative procedure to identify possible clusters based on betweenness centrality of each edge[5] (number of shortest paths passing through the edge) in the graph. At each step, the edge with the highest betweenness is removed; as edges with high betweenness are likely to be the ones connecting *different* clusters, the modularity increases until a maximum value is reached. The remaining connected components are likely to represent the sought clusters. In [8] we illustrate the results obtained applying this algorithm to a subset of equivalence relationships taken from the Linked Open Data cloud. Despite Newman and Girvan's algorithm, and other similar ones, actually being able to detect clusters,

---

[4] Whereas sameAs.org maintains its own CRS, it also hosts several others maintained by different organizations.

[5] Many cluster detection algorithms work on undirected graphs, thus on edges, not on arcs. To account for arcs that mutually connect two nodes, we assume that the corresponding edge connecting the two nodes has a double weight.

unfortunately they often tend to overestimate their number; due to the choice of edge betweenness as a criterion, some topologies (e.g. star-like structures) are not seen as clusters and are thus decomposed into single nodes. A different approach recently proposed by Noack [11] seems to overcome this behavior. In Noack's approach, a graph is seen as a metaphor of a mechanical system where each node is a particle whose "position" is determined by the "forces" acting on it. Close particles tend to repulse each other; edges, which can vary their "length", provide attractive forces that tie particles together. At the equilibrium the fraction between the average edge length and the average node distance is minimized. By making edges short and distances between not connected nodes long, this approach tends to highlight clusters.

Noack identifies a whole class of "clustering" energy models which satisfy these properties and differ only for the law used in the mathematical formulation of the attractive and the repulsive forces between particles. Two relevant models of this class are "LinLog" and "QuadLin"; both of them are below discussed.

LinLog Energy Model. Let $N(G)$ be the set of nodes in the graph G, x, y two arbitrary nodes, p_x and p_y their own position in a spatial system R^n. Given two disjoint non empty sets of nodes U, V such that $U \cup V = N(G)$ we denote with $E(U,V)$ the set of pairs of nodes connected by edges (x,y) with $x \in U$ and $y \in V$. We call the pair (U,V) a bipartition of G, and define its density as

$$d_{U,V} = |E(U,V)| / (|U| \cdot |V|) \tag{1}$$

where $| \cdot |$ is the cardinality of a set. The LinLog energy model is then defined by the formula

$$E = \sum_{x,y \in E(U,V)} \|p_x - p_y\| - \sum_{x \in N(G),\, y \in N(G),\, x \neq y} \ln(\|p_x - p_y\|) \tag{2}$$

where E is the energy associated to the system. In LinLog, initially, the position of each node is set using a random function; the position then evolves according to the forces acting on each node determined by the energy model. Noack demonstrates that, when the system reaches a stable equilibrium, the *harmonic* mean of the distance between any pair of nodes x, y belonging to an arbitrary bipartition U, V is inversely proportional to the density of the bipartition $d_{U,V}$:

$$\text{harmdist}(U,V) = |U| \cdot |V| / (\sum_{x \in U,\, y \in V} 1 / \|p_x - p_y\|) = 1 / d_{U,V} \tag{3}$$

Because the harmonic mean distance weights small distances much higher than large distances, this energy models is particularly useful when drawing graphs. In fact, the well known graph visualization toolkit Gephi[6] uses LinLog to produces nice graph layouts (Figure 2).

QuadLin Energy Model. The QuadLin energy model is defined by the formula

$$E = \sum_{x,y \in E(U,V)} \tfrac{1}{2}\|p_x - p_y\|^2 - \sum_{x \in N(G),\, y \in N(G),\, x != y} \|p_x - p_y\| \tag{4}$$

---

[6] Gephi, an open source graph visualization and manipulation software, https://gephi.org/

where symbols have the usual meaning. QuadLin makes the *arithmetic* mean of the distance between any pair of nodes of an arbitrary bipartition inversely proportional to the density of the bipartition $d_{U,V}$:

$$\text{arithdist } (U,V) = \sum_{x \in U, \, y \in V} \|p_x - p_y\| \, / \, (|U| \cdot |V|) = 1 \, / \, d_{U,V} \qquad (5)$$

At the equilibrium, nodes belonging to the same cluster tend to stay very close, much closer than in any other clustering energy model. This makes QuadLin particularly appealing for solving our original problem. In fact, the inverse of the distance between two nodes could be used a measure of the strength of their connection; which – in the case of an equivalence network – can be taken as an indication of the likelihood of their equivalence.

The previous equation could be written as

$$\sum_{x \in U, \, y \in V} \|p_x - p_y\| = (|U| \cdot |V|)^2 \, / \, |E(U,V)| \qquad (6)$$

which should hold for any possible bipartition of the original graph, i.e. it is an over-determined system of linear equations which, in principle, could be solved using the linear least squares approach. Unfortunately, the total number of possible bipartitions of a graph G is the cardinality of the power set of N(G), $2^{|N(G)|}$, minus two (the empty set and N(G) itself). Thus, the most efficient existing way of solving such a system for non trivial graphs is by simulation.

4   Implementation

To illustrate the effectiveness of clustering energy model when applied to our original problem, we implemented a simple demonstrator system based on the QuadLin energy model.

The system is made up of a front-end and a back-end (Figure 1). The front-end client runs in a Web browser as an AJAX application. After the user specifies a reference to a corresponding resource, the client connects to the back-end server, retrieves all known equivalences for that resources and displays them in the form of a 2D animation. Equivalent resources are presented as floating bubbles (Figure 2). The size of each bubble is proportional to its degree, i.e. the number of equivalences for the corresponding resource. The position of a bubble is finally determined by the composition of forces acting on it, forces derived from the energy model. Their relative positions provide an indication of the strength of the equivalence. The bubbles also react to pointing device gestures, as if they altered their stable equilibrium. Clusters may be easily detected by looking at the different sets of nearby bubbles.

The back-end server performs two functions: retrieving equivalences from a RDF triplestore and providing a corresponding graph model, which, serialized, is sent to the client. The triplestore acts a cache server for RDF data extracted from Sindice.

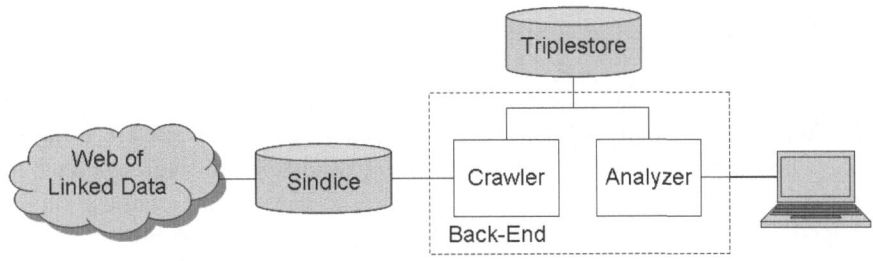

Fig. 1. System architecture. The system is made up of a front-end, running in a Web browser, and a back-end, implemented as a Java 2 Enterprise application.

The back-end is implemented as a Java 2 Enterprise application running on Apache Tomcat 6.0 servlet container. The triplestore is Aduna Sesame server v2.60 powered by Gentoo Linux MySQL server v5.1. All the server-side software is hosted into a i686 Intel Xeon CPU 3060 machine, 2.40GHz processor, 1,048,772kB RAM, featured Gentoo Linux Base System 1.12 OS, kernel 2.6.18-xen.

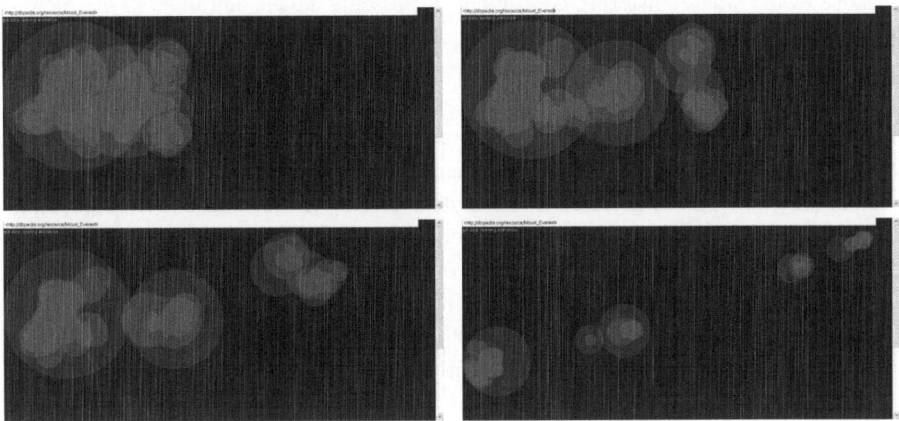

Fig. 2. Front-end. Equivalent resources presented as floating bubbles. The size of each bubble is proportional to the number of its equivalence links. The position is determined by the composition of forces acting on it, according to the QuadLin energy model.

The client part is implemented using Google Web Toolkit, and is suitable to run on a variety of HTML 5 enabled browsers. The client runs a porting of the program originally developed by Noack[7]; but, differently from the original software, the porting uses the QuadLin energy model.

---

[7] The original program by Noack is available at
`http://code.google.com/p/linloglayout/`

5   Evaluation

Figure 3 shows the equivalence network obtained starting from the resource <http://rdf.freebase.com/ns/en.mount_everest>. We generated this picture using the Gephi framework which adopts the LinLog energy model. In this representation, the harmonic (not the arithmetic) mean of the length of the edges connecting two clusters is proportional to the inverse of the inter-cluster density; this feature provides a more readable layout, suitable, e.g., for this article's format, but reduces the inter-cluster nodes distance and increase the intra-cluster one. If QuadLin were used instead, nodes in the same cluster would be much closer and clusters more distant, as in Figure 2. Through the use of colours, Figure 3 also illustrates clusters as detected by Newman and Girvan's algorithm (section 2): nodes with different colours belong to different clusters.

Inspecting this figure, we see that LinLog (as well as QuadLin) recognizes the star-like topology around the resource <http://rdf.freebase.com/ns/en.mount_everest> and places all nodes belonging to this structure closer each others (bottom left of the picture). Newman and Girvan's algorithm fails in recognizing this topology, probably because of the small clustering coefficient[8] it presents: nodes and links in the picture are in fact marked with dozens of different colours, each meaning a potential different cluster. The star-like structure, also reported in [7], reflects the asymmetric use of owl:sameAs by the Freebase community: their nodes link many resources in DBpedia that however do not represent the very same concept (and in fact are not interlinked with each other, lowering the cluster coefficient).

A second structure is detected in the middle of the picture. This structure develops around the DBpedia resource <http://dbpedia.org/resource/Mount_Everest> and connects nodes belonging to a number of other domains. This structure has indeed a higher cluster coefficient and is correctly recognized by all the algorithms (LinLog, QuadLin and Newman and Girvan's algorithm).

The top right corner of the picture clearly shows a third cluster, connected to the previously described one by one single arc. The cluster is well separated from the other two, although not reflected by LinLog – the same distance measured out after applying the QuadLin algorithm is about 130% of the distance between the two previous structures. This is not surprising: because of one single arc connecting the two structures, the density of the corresponding bipartition is small and the nodes on the two sides are far. In our method, a great spatial distance implies a marked semantic difference. Looking at this third cluster, we realize that all its nodes refer to a different entity: Sun Valley in Blaine County, Idaho, US.

---

[8] The clustering coefficient is a local property of a node and is defined as the fraction between the average number of edges between the neighbors of a node and the average number of possible edges between these neighbors.

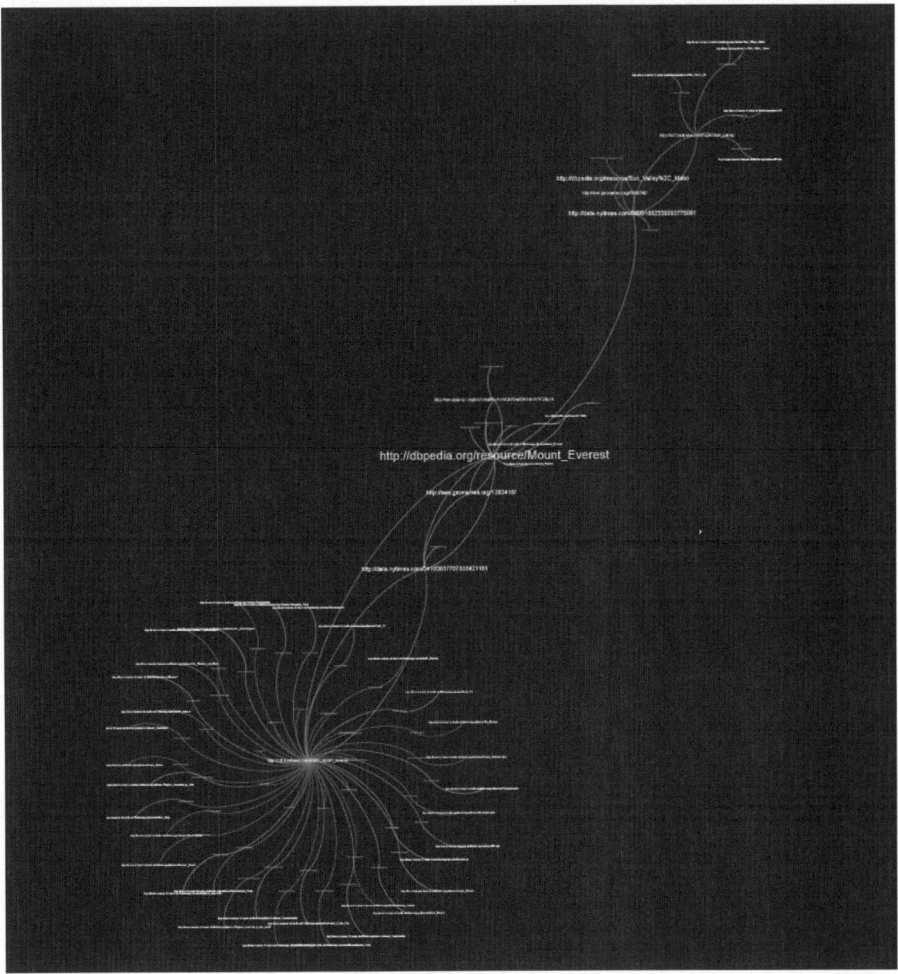

Fig. 3. The equivalence network for the entity "Mount Everest" (picture generated using the Gephi framework which adopts the LinLog energy model).

6   Discussion

Question #1 – (from section 1) Where could a possible weighted uncertainty measure of identity come from? Experimental evidences show that co-references coming from different datasets show a tendency to aggregate into star-like structures, and more in general into clusters. Missing intra-cluster arcs can be probably interpreted as omitted equivalences and isolated inter-cluster arcs are likely to represent wrongly stated equivalences. To distinguish the two case, we assume two thresholds, m and M, run a simulation, and calculate the edge length $\|p_x - p_y\|$ between each pair of connected nodes (x,y). If $\|p_x - p_y\| < m$, then nodes are in the same cluster and likely to be equivalent; if $\|p_x - p_y\| > M$, probably the two nodes are different from each other and would be better characterized by the owl:differentFrom relationship. Therefore the edge length could be used as a possible uncertainty measure.

The difference between clusters and non-clusters lies purely in the density of the links connecting a given group of nodes, and in the density of the links connecting this group with the rest of the graph. This "vague" definition does not provide any canonical value to distinguish a cluster from a weaker group of nodes. Therefore the aforementioned thresholds have to be evaluated for each equivalence network. Are there advantages in shifting the original dilemma of evaluating the strength of a single equivalence link to the (maybe as difficult) problem of finding global thresholds for the equivalence network the link belongs to? We think so. First, a metric has been defined, enabling ranking of the strength of different equivalence links. Second, statistics could help in defining canonical or typical values like thresholds. We expect to mine these values from massive batch processing we are currently carrying on.

Question #2 – (from section 2) Why do nodes aggregate into clusters? In our interpretation, this phenomenon typically reflects the partition of linked data publishers into communities, where nodes representing similar concepts inside the two different communities of publishers are loosely coupled. The communities may have different purposes, degree of specialization and ways of defining equivalences. For instance, DBpedia provides lots of hyponyms (i.e. more specialized terms, finer granule definitions) while other data providers – including Freebase – publish more generic definitions. Nodes from Freebase usually link hyponyms in DBPedia, semantic nuances are not captured during the linkage and are flattened as "equivalences" with the corresponding hyperonym (i.e. the more generic tem). Though a mistake when considering the formal semantics, this way of establishing equivalences is not always annoying; sometimes it is even helpful end users who might want to follow links to discover slightly different meanings and thus increase their knowledge about a subject.

On the other hand, the raising of new communities and addition of new nodes and links in the future might create new specialized clusters "detached" from the parent ones and reflecting hyponyms more closely. This phenomenon probably mirrors the way knowledge specializes, beginning from a rough level of definition and getting structured when interests from members of domain-specific communities start developing. Cluster detection techniques may provide effective insights for this investigation.

7   Conclusions

Equivalence links connecting co-references may be seen as a graph known as "equivalence network". In this paper we introduced a method to rank equivalence links based on the contextual knowledge of the topology of this graph. The rank provides an estimation of the strength of each equivalence link. The method can be used either in batch processing mode (suitable to provide analysis of massive datasets and to extract canonical values) or interactively; here we presented a simple prototype which exploits the latter option. As a tool, it may help Linked Data engineers to better understand and "debug" equivalence networks and, indirectly, to unveil different emerging communities of publishers, their different goals and linking strategies.

References

1. Hu, W., Qu, Y., Sun, X.: Bootstrapping object coreferencing on the semantic web. Journal of Computer Science Technology 26(4), 663–675 (2011)
2. Bizer, C., Health, T.: Linked Data: Evolving the Web into a Global Data Space. Synthesis Lectures on the Semantic Web: Theory & Technology 1(1), 1–136 (2011)
3. Halpin, H., Hayes, P.J., McCusker, J.P., McGuinness, D.L., Thompson, H.S.: When owl:sameas isn't the same: An analysis of identity in linked data. In: Patel-Schneider, P.F., Pan, Y., Hitzler, P., Mika, P., Zhang, L., Pan, J.Z., Horrocks, I., Glimm, B. (eds.) ISWC 2010, Part I. LNCS, vol. 6496, pp. 305–320. Springer, Heidelberg (2010)
4. McCusker, J., McGuinness, D.: owl:sameas Considered Harmful to Provenance. In: Proceedings of the ISCB Conference on Semantics in Healthcare and Life Sciences (2010)
5. Hayes, P., Halpin, H.: In defense of ambiguity. International Journal of Semantic Web and Information Systems 4(3) (2008)
6. Ding, L., Shinavier, J., Finin, T., McGuinness, D.: owl:sameAs and Linked Data: An Empirical Study. In: Proceedings of the WebSci 2010: Extending the Frontiers of Society On-Line (2010)
7. Ding, L., Shinavier, J., Shangguan, Z., McGuinness, D.: SameAs Networks and Beyond: Analyzing Deployment Status and Implications of owl:sameAs in Linked Data. In: Patel-Schneider, P.F., Pan, Y., Hitzler, P., Mika, P., Zhang, L., Pan, J.Z., Horrocks, I., Glimm, B. (eds.) ISWC 2010, Part I. LNCS, vol. 6496, pp. 145–160. Springer, Heidelberg (2010)
8. Bartolomeo, G., Salsano, S.: A Spectrometry of Linked Data. In: Proceedings of the Linked Data on the Web Workshop (2012)
9. Strogatz, S.H.: Exploring complex networks. Nature 410, 268–276 (2001)
10. Newman, M.E., Girvan, M.: Finding and evaluating community structure in networks. Physical Review E 69(2) (2004)
11. Noack, A.: Energy Models for Graph Clustering. Journal of Graph Algorithms and Applications 11(2), 453–480 (2007)
12. Jaffri, A., Glaser, H., Millard, I.: URI disambiguation in the context of linked data. In: Proceedings of the 1st International Workshop on Linked Data on the Web (2008)
13. Halpin, H., Presutti, V.: An ontology of resources: Solving the identity crisis. In: Aroyo, L., Traverso, P., Ciravegna, F., Cimiano, P., Heath, T., Hyvönen, E., Mizoguchi, R., Oren, E., Sabou, M., Simperl, E. (eds.) ESWC 2009. LNCS, vol. 5554, pp. 521–534. Springer, Heidelberg (2009)
14. Bouquet, P., Stoermer, H., Niederee, G., Mana, A.: Entity Name System: The Backbone of an Open and Scalable Web of Data. In: Proceedings of the IEEE International Conference on Semantic Computing, ICSC 2008, pp. 554–561. IEEE Computer Society (2008)
15. Bouquet, P., Palpanas, T., Stoermer, H., Vignolo, M.: A Conceptual Model for a Web-scale Entity Name System. In: Proceedings of 9th the Asian Semantic Web Conference (2009)

Development of Information Systems for Transparent Corporate Sustainability Using Data-Driven Technologies

Lisa Madlberger

Vienna University of Technology, Vienna, Austria
lisa.madlberger@tuwien.ac.at

Abstract. Corporations, as influential players in a global environment, face increased pressure of the society and governments to assume responsibility for the consequences of their corporate actions. Although information technologies advance rapidly, data collection still heavily relies on manual input, static reports and to a broad extent the integration of stakeholders is not yet the general rule. Data-driven technologies like Participatory Sensing methods, Linked Open Data practices or Geographical Information Systems are useful methods to collect, aggregate and disseminate information. This paper outlines the problem scope, the solution approach and the research plan for my doctoral thesis which explores the potential of these technologies to improve the transparency of corporate sustainability using a design-science based approach. Experiences gained by designing and evaluating IT artifacts are expected to bring new insights about the relation of IT and corporate sustainability where existing research is still sparse.

Keywords: Corporate Sustainability, Participatory Sensing, Linked Data, GIS.

1 Introduction

The world has never faced greater challenges: over-consumption of finite natural resources, climate change, and the need to provide clean water, food and a better standard of living for a growing global population [26]. In the last decades, the term "Sustainability" has become increasingly popular, as a strategy to tackle these challenges. In 1987, the Brundtland Commission, a UN world commission on environment and development, coined the term "sustainable development" as "development that meets the needs of the present without compromising the ability of future generations to meet their own needs" [4].

1.1 Corporate Sustainability

Corporations, as main players in a global environment, face increased pressure of the society and governments to assume responsibility for the consequences of their corporate actions. As a result, companies started to integrate next to

Y.T. Demey and H. Panetto (Eds.): OTM 2013 Workshops, LNCS 8186, pp. 12–21, 2013.

economic, also social and environmental aspects into their visions, missions and goals [22].

However, many companies still rely on purely reactive strategies and understand sustainability as an opportunity to enhance their company reputation, save resource costs, address new customer groups, attract employees or to gain easier access to capital [18,9]. It is still not common knowledge that corporate sustainability is also important beyond the business case, as a vital requirement for companies' long-term existence established on a secure resource base [5].

Sustainability drivers are strongly related to the interests of different stakeholder groups, therefore it is essential for companies to integrate their opinions into business considerations and to provide stakeholders with a transparent view on the company's sustainable behavior. Following this premise, companies increasingly initiate stakeholder dialogues and publish Corporate Social Responsibility Reports. Since these actions require time and resource intensive processes, results are commonly published only on an annual basis in form of static, textual reports. However, in times of significant progress in the field of information technologies, stakeholders' demands for real-time information is a logical consequence. This leads to the presumption, that sustainability reporting practices are still more aligned with reactive strategies focused on accountability rather than on proactive value-adding strategies [28].

1.2 Data-Driven Technologies

Innovative data-driven technologies provide useful methods for the effective collection, dissemination and visualization of information. These technologies are the main enablers to improve stakeholder integration and communication and help companies to develop a more transparent picture of their corporate sustainable behavior.

With increasing access to the internet, we can state an emerging trend to outsource different tasks to "the crowd". More and more people are equipped with a smart phone, which possesses a number of different sensors which can be utilized for collecting data about its environment. These devices can not only be used for automatic sensing but they can serve as input facility for human observations, a concept referred to as "People as Sensors" [23]. These new forms of data collection can be applied in companies to monitor environmental and social aspects which they have not been able to monitor before or not in an efficient manner. For example, employees or people living around a production site could be questioned about environmental conditions in the firm, e.g. odor or smoke emissions. Responses can be tracked and visualized automatically, which provides other stakeholders, e.g. decision makers with insights about very remote production sites. The utilization of these participatory sensing methods, enables collection of observations and measurements in real-time through mobile devices and we are able to systematically integrate stakeholders into the sustainability data collection process.

Another recent important approach in the area of data-driven technologies is the Linked Open Data initiative. The term Linked Data refers to a set of best practices for publishing and connecting structured data on the Web best preserving its semantics [2]. The adoption of these practices has lead to the extension of the Web with a global data space connecting data from diverse domains such as governments, companies or scientific publications [2]. Linked Open Data could be applied in the corporate sustainability domain in two ways (1) as possible data source to integrate data from stakeholders, e.g. information about social indicators from local governments, regional data on climate change from the world bank and (2) as a channel to disseminate sustainability information in a structured format, e.g. for the exchange with other companies like business customers.

A further technology with a large potential to support stakeholder demands is the integration of Geographic Information Systems (GIS), to capture, store and analyze spatial information. Obviously, especially in the case of environmental information related to physical locations, a spatial representation of corporate sustainability information is very promising to provide an intuitive understandable format of information, e.g. resource usage or air quality information. One specific type of GIS, namely "Participatory GIS", aim to utilize GIS technology in the context of the needs and capabilities of communities that will be involved with, and affected by, development projects and programs [1]. In a corporate sustainability context, these systems could enable a more interactive representation of sustainability reports, by giving stakeholders the opportunity to not only exploit, but also add information, e.g. by pinning concerns, comments or questions to the same map. mes [1]. In a corporate sustainability context, these systems could enable a more interactive representation of sustainability reports, by giving stakeholders the opportunity to not only exploit, but also add information, e.g. by pinning concerns, comments or questions to the same map.

1.3   Research Question

In academic research, a central role is attributed to Information Technology and Systems in the quest for advanced corporate sustainability, as these have been the greatest force for productivity improvement in the last half of the 20th century [6,16,27]. Nevertheless, research in the field of Information Systems on corporate sustainability is still not widely distributed. My doctoral thesis, aims at a contribution to close this gap and specifically focuses on how data-driven technologies can increase the transparency of corporate sustainability.

In particular, I will address the following research questions:

1. How can participatory sensing methods be applied to monitor environmental and social sustainability in companies?
2. Which role can Linked Open Data play for the collection of corporate sustainability data? How can corporate sustainability information be published in the Linked Open Data Cloud?
3. How can GIS be utilized for interactive sustainability reporting?

As the research outlined in this paper is in an early stage, listed research questions are rather broad and will have to be refined in a later phase. In general, the problem area to be investigated is clearly neither a purely technical, nor a purely economic one. Instead, a solution has to integrate technical, economic as well as social aspects. Existing literature in this context is sparse, accordingly requirements in this area are not clear yet. Therefore, this paper proposes to classify this as a "wicked problem", best solved by applying a design-science based approach (See Hevner et al [10]). Design science relies on the development and evaluation of IT artefacts, to be able to better analyze the problem domain and to deliver steps towards the problem solution. Therefore, the main objective of the thesis is the development and evaluation of software prototypes based on selected data-driven technologies with the goal to examine the potential of these technologies to increase the transparency of corporate sustainable behavior.

The expected contributions include on the one hand, identified requirements regarding the functionality and design of corporate sustainability information systems based on experiences gained during the design and evaluation process, and, on the other hand, the description of the developed design variants and according advantages and limitations identified.

2   Related Work

The problem studied in this paper resides at the intersection of two domains: Corporate Sustainability and Information Technology and Systems.

In IS literature, the area of IS support for corporate sustainability has been recently structured by various researchers. Melville [16] develops a conceptual framework and a research agenda to expedite development and adoption of information systems for environmental sustainability. Elliot et al. [6] compile a holistic, trans-disciplinary, integrative framework for IT-enabled business transformation as a research agenda. Watson et al. [27] create a research agenda to establish a new sub field of energy informatics, which applies Information Systems' thinking and skills to increase energy efficiency frameworks. However, there is no clear notion about the role of Information Systems with regard to corporate sustainability yet.

As this thesis will adapt a more technology-oriented approach the most relevant work is related to the three technologies in the focus of this study:

2.1   Participatory Sensing

Participatory Sensing systems have been developed for various application scenarios with relation to environmental sustainability in general. Mun et al. [17] developed a participatory sensing application that uses location data sampled from everyday mobile phones to calculate personalized estimates of environmental impact and exposure. Peterova and Hybler propose a "Do-It-Yourself Environmental Sensing" approach, which enables citizens to measure pollution with immediate feedback [21]. The application "BudBurst" enables citizens to monitor flowers and plants as the seasons change and thereby help scientists to monitor the regional impacts of climate change [8]. There are also non-academic endeavors to use participatory sensing methods to collect data from voluntary citizen scientists e.g. Save-the-Redwood [24] users can add their observations about the location and condition of redwood which helps conservation agencies to understand climate change related impacts to redwood. However, no research has been found which applies participatory sensing methods in a corporate context.

2.2 Linked Open Data

In the domain of sustainability, the work of Phuoc et al. [14] can be mentioned as an effort to publish environmental sensor data in the LOD-cloud. Furthermore, Zapico et al. [29] developed a web service that delivers life cycle assessment information about different products openly, linked and reusable. The project Sourcemap [3] integrates linked open data to display supply-chain information of products. In the corporate context, some approaches demonstrate how to link enterprise data. Garcia and Gil [7] demonstrate how corporate financial reports present in XBRL-format can be published and linked to the LOD-cloud. Hondros [11] describes a content architecture based on OWL, RDF and XHTML that is used to build a standard representation of legal content, allowing publishable assets to be integrated across the enterprise.

2.3 GIS

Geographical Information Systems, and especially Participatory Geographical Information Systems have been widely applied in the area of environmental sustainability (e.g. for community-based natural Resource Planning [15], [25] or community carbon monitoring [13]). One of the most successful projects in the area of participative mapping is the Ushahidi project [19], which enables citizens to report an incident, event or observation for a specified location. In the enterprise context, Keating et al. [12] discuss challenges of the application of GIS in enterprises from a management-perspective.

2.4 Synthesis

Data-driven technologies have been applied in various areas to collect or disseminate sustainability data. Existing research mostly focuses on sustainability in a broader context, e.g. on country or city level. Little of the existing work approaches the topic of sustainability from a company-internal perspective, accounting for the specific information flows, sustainability aspects and information needs in the context of corporate sustainability.

3   Research Hypotheses

According to the stated research questions, the thesis should more concretely evaluate the following hypotheses:

1. Participatory Sensing methods can be applied to integrate stakeholders into the collection of data about social and environmental aspects (RQ 1)
2. The Linked Open Data Cloud is a possible Data Source for monitoring environmental and social aspects in a company's environment (RQ 2)
3. Linked Open Data practices can be utilized to publish and link corporate sustainability information (RQ 2)
4. GIS support companies to represent sustainability information in a dynamic, interactive and stakeholder-specific format (RQ 3)

4   Methods / Work Plan

Each of the hypotheses follows a four step process: (1) Problem understanding (2) Design (3) Evaluation (4) Communication (adapted from Hevner et al. [10]). As depicted in figure 1, this process is not linear, but it involves iterations (See also Pfeffers [20]).

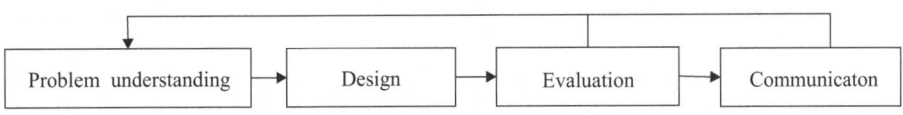

Fig. 1. The Design Science Process [10,20]

In this thesis, the design science process applies on both a macro-level and a micro-level.

On a macro-level the problem to be studied is more generally, how data-driven technologies can be applied to increase the transparency of corporate sustainable development. From that perspective, an evaluation of different technologies can be seen as an assessment of possible design alternatives. These would be evaluated separately and in comparison to the other design alternatives, and eventually results are communicated in form of a PhD-thesis (See figure 2).

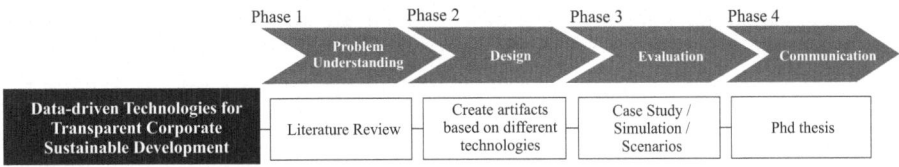

Fig. 2. Research Plan - Macro-Perspective

However, each of these design alternatives address different sub-scopes of the main problem scope and can thereby be seen as independent problems on a micro-level perspective. Therefore, each of the alternatives and according hypotheses will be evaluated separately by going through the main phases of the design science process (See figure 3).

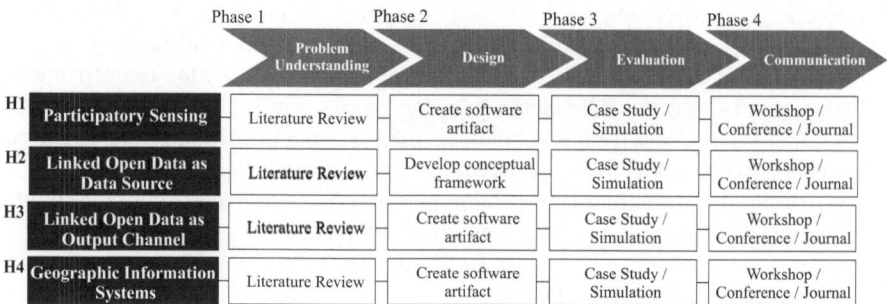

Fig. 3. Research Plan - Micro-Perspective

4.1   Problem Understanding

For all three hypotheses, the task of problem understanding will be mainly based on existing literature from different domains. Previous findings in the field of stakeholder-management, corporate sustainability and enterprise reporting will help to understand the problem and requirements from a business perspective. Existing knowledge in the fields of sensing, semantic technologies and GIS will provide important fundamentals from a technical perspective.

4.2   Design and Evaluation

Depending on the investigated technology, we will have differentiated design and evaluation phases:

Participatory Sensing (H1). In the design phase, the IT artifact to be created, is a prototypical software system that can be used in companies to collect data about environmental and social aspects from observations reported by stakeholders via their mobile devices (e.g. employees, residents around production sites). According to our plan, this prototype will be evaluated in a real-life application scenario with an industry partner in a case study. Alternatively, a simulation with artificial data or a descriptive evaluation based on scenario construction could be applied. Thereby, we expect to learn about business requirements to the design of data collection mechanisms for corporate sustainability data.

Linked Open Data as Data Source (H2). We will develop a technological framework to study in depth the potential of the LOD-cloud to serve as a data source for the collection of social and environmental aspects about the company's environment. A critical factor to be investigated is data source reliability, which still is an open problem in the Linked Data Project. The resulting framework should outline both a process for the identification of relevant Linked Open Data and mechanisms to integrate this information with other sustainability data. It will be evaluated descriptively by illustrating how this framework could be applied in exemplary scenarios.

Linked Open Data as Output Channel (H3). A software artifact will be designed which facilitates publishing of corporate sustainability information (e.g. corporate sustainability reports) in RDF format and linking it to existing information present in the LOD-cloud. This prototype can be evaluated by a simulation involving open corporate data, which is freely available on many company websites in form of reports. Expected outcomes include lessons learned about possibilities to represent sustainability data using ontologies and to link it to existing data sources.

Geographic Information Systems (H4). Based on available Open Source systems a prototype will show that participatory GIS can be used to integrate stakeholders into the mapping of spatial data in sustainability management tasks. The artifacts' utility should be demonstrated by a simulation relying on artificial data and descriptively by illustrating detailed application scenarios. It is expected to learn about the potential to represent corporate sustainability data using maps and about requirements of internal and external stakeholders towards a corporate sustainability GIS.

4.3 Communication

Intermediate findings and results from evaluating different technologies, will be reported on workshops, conferences and journals. Feedback from peers can lead to changes in developed design alternatives and repeated evaluation activities.

5 Conclusion

Adapting a design-science approach, in my PhD thesis, I want to analyze how innovative data-driven technologies can be utilized to increase the transparency of corporate sustainability. Specifically, the potential of participatory sensing methods (RQ1), Linked Open Data practices (RQ2 & RQ3) and Geographic Information Systems (RQ 4) to be applied for sustainability data collection and dissemination, should be investigated. The thesis aims to contribute by providing lessons learned from the development and evaluation of IT artifacts about business requirements and design principles for information systems solutions in the corporate sustainability domain. Applied evaluation methods include observational (case study), experimental (simulation) and descriptive (scenarios) approaches.

Acknowledgments. The author of this paper is financially supported by the Vienna PhD School of Informatics (http://www.informatik.tuwien.ac.at/teaching/phdschool).

References

1. Abbot, J., Chambers, R., Dunn, C., Harris, T., de Merode, E., Porter, G., Townsend, J., Weiner, D.: Participatory gis: opportunity or oxymoron? PLA Notes-International Institute for Environment and Development (1998)

2. Bizer, C., Heath, T., Berners-Lee, T.: Linked data-the story so far. International Journal on Semantic Web and Information Systems (IJSWIS) 5(3), 1–22 (2009)
3. Bonanni, L., Ebner, H., Hockenberry, M., Sayan, B., Brandt, N., Csikszentmihàlyi, N., Ishii, H., Turpeinen, M., Young, S., Zapico Lamela, J.L.: Sourcemap. org: First application of linked and open lca data to support sustainability (2011)
4. Brundtland, G.H.: Report of the World Commission on environment and development: "our common future". United Nations, New York (1987)
5. Dyllick, T., Hockerts, K.: Beyond the business case for corporate sustainability. Business Strategy and the Environment 11(2), 130–141 (2002)
6. Elliot, S.: Transdisciplinary perspectives on environmental sustainability: a resource base and framework for it-enabled business transformation. MIS Quarterly 35(1), 197–236 (2011)
7. García, R., Gil, R.: Publishing xbrl as linked open data. In: CEUR Workshop Proceedings, vol. 538. Citeseer (2009)
8. Goldman, J., Shilton, K., Burke, J., Estrin, D., Hansen, M., Ramanathan, N., Reddy, S., Samanta, V., Srivastava, M., West, R.: Participatory sensing: A citizen-powered approach to illuminating the patterns that shape our world. Foresight & Governance Project, White Paper (2009)
9. Hansen, U., Schrader, U.: Corporate social responsibility als aktuelles thema der bwl. Betriebswirtschaft-Stuttgart 65(4), 373 (2005)
10. Hevner, A.R., March, S.T., Park, J., Ram, S.: Design science in information systems research. MIS Quarterly 28(1), 75–105 (2004)
11. Hondros, C.: Standardizing legal content with owl and rdf. In: Linking Enterprise Data, pp. 221–240. Springer (2010)
12. Keating, G.N., Rich, P.M., Witkowski, M.S.: Challenges for enterprise gis. URISA Journal 15(2), 25–39 (2003)
13. Larrazábal, A., McCall, M.K., Mwampamba, T.H., Skutsch, M.: The role of community carbon monitoring for redd+: a review of experiences. Current Opinion in Environmental Sustainability 4(6), 707–716 (2012)
14. Le-Phuoc, D., Hauswirth, M.: Linked open data in sensor data mashups. In: Proc. Semantic Sensor Networks, p. 1 (2009)
15. McCall, M.K., Minang, P.A.: Assessing participatory gis for community-based natural resource management: claiming community forests in cameroon. The Geographical Journal 171(4), 340–356 (2005)
16. Melville, N.: Information systems innovation for environmental sustainability. Management Information Systems Quarterly 34(1), 1–21 (2010)
17. Mun, M., Reddy, S., Shilton, K., Yau, N., Burke, J., Estrin, D., Hansen, M., Howard, E., West, R., Boda, P.: Peir, the personal environmental impact report, as a platform for participatory sensing systems research. In: Proceedings of the 7th Int. Conference on Mobile Systems, pp. 55–68. ACM (2009)
18. Münstermann, M.: Corporate Social Responsibility: Ausgestaltung und Steuerung von CSR-Aktivitäten, vol. 48. Gabler Verlag (2007)
19. Okolloh, O.: Ushahidi, or'testimony': Web 2. 0 tools for crowdsourcing crisis information. Participatory Learning and Action 59(1), 65–70 (2009)
20. Peffers, K., Tuunanen, T., Gengler, C.E., Rossi, M., Hui, W., Virtanen, V., Bragge, J.: The design science research process: a model for producing and presenting information systems research. In: Proceedings of the First International Conference on Design Science Research in Information Systems and Technology (DESRIST 2006), pp. 83–106 (2006)
21. Peterová, R., Hybler, J.: Do-it-yourself environmental sensing. Procedia Computer Science 7, 303–304 (2011)

22. Petrini, M., Pozzebon, M.: Managing sustainability with the support of business intelligence: Integrating socio-environmental indicators and organisational context. The Journal of Strategic Information Systems 18(4), 178–191 (2009)
23. Resch, B.: People as sensors and collective sensing-contextual observations complementing geo-sensor network measurements. In: Krisp, J.M. (ed.) Progress in Location-Based Services. Lecture Notes in Geoinformation and Cartography, pp. 391–406. Springer, Heidelberg (2013),
    http://dx.doi.org/10.1007/978-3-642-34203-5_22
24. Save the Redwoods League: About save the redwoods (2013),
    http://www.savetheredwoods.org/
25. Tripathi, N., Bhattarya, S.: Integrating indigenous knowledge and gis for participatory natural resource management: state of the practice. The Electronic Journal of Information Systems in Developing Countries 17 (2004)
26. UN Global Compact: Formation of the international integrated reporting committee (iirc) (2010), http://www.unglobalcompact.org/news/57-08-02-2010
27. Watson, R., Boudreau, M., Chen, A.: Information systems and environmentally sustainable development: energy informatics and new directions for the is community. Management Information Systems Quarterly 34(1), 23–38 (2010)
28. Wheeler, D., Elkington, J.: The end of the corporate environmental report? or the advent of cybernetic sustainability reporting and communication. Business Strategy and the Environment 10(1), 1–14 (2001)
29. Zapico Lamela, J.L., Sayan, B., Bonanni, L., Turpeinen, M., Steve, Y.: Footprinted. org–experiences from using linked open data for environmental impact information. In: Proceedings of the 25th EnviroInfo Conference–Innovations in Sharing Environmental Observations and Information, pp. 1–9. Schaker-Verlag (2011)

Cooperative and Fast-Learning Information Extraction from Business Documents for Document Archiving

Daniel Esser

Technical University Dresden
Computer Networks Group, 01062 Dresden, Germany
daniel.esser@tu-dresden.de

Abstract. Automatic information extraction from scanned business documents is especially valuable in the application domain of document management and archiving. Although current solutions for document classification and extraction work pretty well, they still require a high effort of on-site configuration done by domain experts or administrators. Especially small office/home office (SOHO) users and private individuals often do not use such systems because of the need for configuration and long periods of training to reach acceptable extraction rates. Therefore we present a solution for information extraction out of scanned business documents that fits the requirements of these users. Our approach is highly adaptable to new document types and index fields and uses only a minimum of training documents to reach extraction rates comparable to related works and manual document indexing. By providing a cooperative extraction system, which allows sharing extraction knowledge between participants, we furthermore want to minimize the number of user feedback and increase the acceptance of such a system.

A first evaluation of our solution according to a document set of 12,500 documents with 10 commonly used fields shows competitive results above 85% F1-measure. Results above 75% F1-measure are already reached with a minimal training set of only one document per template.

Keywords: Document Layout Analysis, Information Extraction, Cooperative Extraction, Few-Exemplar-Learning.

1 Introduction

Today a huge amount of communication between business partners is done in a textual manner. The movement towards paperless offices all over the world and the need for archiving due to legal regulations will further increase this tendency. To handle the wealth of information, companies need fast and accessible technologies for document management and archiving. Existing solutions like smartFIX [1] and OpenText [2] automate this process. They provide functionality to scan paper documents, classify them according to business processes and

Y.T. Demey and H. Panetto (Eds.): OTM 2013 Workshops, LNCS 8186, pp. 22–31, 2013.

extract relevant information. This index data can later on be used for improving document search, automatical handling of correspondences or attaching them to existing ERP systems or internal databases.

While current solutions work pretty well for large and medium-sized companies, it still requires a high effort of on-site configuration to adapt such a system to the own requirements. Depending on the domain of the institution, new document types and index fields have to be considered and specialized extraction mechanisms have to be added. Especially for SOHO users and private individuals, the need for configuration and long periods of training to archive high classification and extraction rates constrain the usage of such systems. The goal of this work is the reduction of configuration efforts in business document extraction to make such kind of systems more attractive and suitable for small companies. Therefore we plan a solution, which combines highly adaptable and fast-learning classification and extraction algorithms adapted to the domain of business documents with a cooperative approach to share extraction knowledge with other participants. While specialized algorithms reduce the need for locally available pre-annotated documents, the cooperative approach minimizes feedback by improving the system performance using foreign extraction knowledge. Altogether the combination of both procedures lowers necessary user interaction and ends up in minimal effort for manual configuration.

The local algorithms will mainly focus on incremental few-exemplar learning and work purely training-based without a need for generating rules or pre-annotated example documents. Relevance feedback provided by the user, i.e. new document types and fields or corrections of wrong extractions, is taken into account for the classification and extraction of the next document. The cooperative approach is based on a pool of common extraction knowledge every user can contribute to. This allows to include individual extraction knowledge and profit from annotations and corrections another user has already done. Especially in the domain of business correspondences, where similar documents are exchanged between many companies, the probability for finding another participant having information on how to extract a given document is quite high. The idea of such collaborative solutions is not new at all [3]. Therefore we want to focus on problems coming along when connecting thousands of local systems to a huge distributed one. While the size of such a global pool increases very fast, we want to explore the relation between size and extraction performance and give solutions for separating distributed extraction systems.

2   Related Work

The classification of business documents and the extraction of relevant information has been tackled by a lot of researches in the last twenty years.

The categorization according to the document type is nearly solved. As an evidence for that, one can see the high spread of this functionality within commercial products from ABBYY[1], Insiders Technologies[2] and OpenText[3]. Therefore a lot of novel works focus on the categorization of documents according to their template. Current solutions either use the document's text [4] or different levels of layout [5,6,7] as feature base. While [6,7] only work on the density of pixels, more sophisticated approaches like [5,8] try to transform a document into a high-level representation, i.e. trees or graphs that can later on be used by matching or learning algorithms. The machine learning approaches used in current solutions are manifold and vary from symbolic algorithms [5] over artificial neuronal networks [9] to statistical [7] and instance-based [10] techniques.

The extraction of information is mostly done on top of a classification. Knowing the type and template of a document allows to draw a conclusion on the existing index fields within that document. Solutions in the field of document extraction differ in the level of granularity of extracted information. While some authors only try to identify single field values [11,12] – this is the kind of fields we are going to extract – other works focus on finding multiple value fields like contents of lists or tables [13,14]. The applied techniques do not differ a lot from categorization. Current solutions either use text or layout to find relevant index data. Textual solutions try to find patterns and are mostly built upon some pattern matching [15]. Layout-based solutions try to include position and font effects into their extraction decision [12,13].

Although current solutions produce acceptable results, [16] criticizes the high level of manual effort that is necessary to train machine learning approaches to reach good classification and extraction rates. Future research should attend to mechanisms that allow learning from very few examples. The best-case scenario will be a one-shot learning, whereby only one example of the same class will be sufficient for learning to classify and extract other documents of that class.

[17,18] did first empirical studies on the field of few-exemplar learning. The authors compare different algorithms from Weka[4] using changing sizes of training documents. While both works are a first step towards the improvement of few-exemplar learning algorithms, they only focus on general implementations. In context of document classification and extraction only a small number of related works evaluate their approaches according to the ability to learn from few examples. [5,8] use a minimum of ten documents per class as a training set for classification. As this size is almost too high for our requirements, a user would not accept to correct ten or more documents per class or template to reach good results, [10,7] present approaches with one and two training documents per class. Both solutions rely on low-level layout features, which makes it hard to differentiate between very similar types of templates. [13] used only ten documents for training and reach impressive extraction rates of 92%. While this approach focuses on multiple values and uses repeating structures within a document, it is not fully comparable to our goal of single value extraction.

---

[1] http://www.abbyy.com

[2] http://www.insiders-technologies.com

[3] http://www.opentext.com

[4] http://www.cs.waikato.ac.nz/ml/weka

Altogether we could not find a solution that completely fulfills our requirements for adaptive and fast-learning document processing. Although some solutions were tested according to small training sets, there currently exists no solution that provides a real one-shot learning within this domain.

3 Research Hypotheses

The proposed system is based on following hypotheses:

Hypotheses 1 - Self-learning template detection: Because of the clear structure of business documents and company workflows, self-learning systems can instantly and successfully classify documents according to their template with classification rates above 95% F1-measure. In case of using self-learning approaches users will be relieved by the abolition of manual configuration.

Hypotheses 2 - Few-exemplar extraction: The usage and combination of specialized algorithms allow comparative extraction results and an improvement of learning speed especially in the starting period of an extraction system. This reduces the need for feedback and enhances the user acceptance. Altogether we want to reach a one-shot learning ensuring common extraction rates upon 80%.

Hypotheses 3 - Scalability of distributed knowledge pools: The usage of distributed knowledge pools and the combination of foreign and self-generated extraction results can improve the performance of local systems. This influence decreases with the number of training documents in the distributed knowledge pool because of a missing differentiation between similar documents. A fragmentation and specialization of the distributed knowledge pool into a hierarchical system compensates this effect.

4 Methods

To prove the hypotheses described in the previous section, we developed an information extraction process containing the single steps that can be seen in Figure 1. Until today we already implemented a prototype according to this process. Unfortunately the usage of distributed knowledge bases is not yet integrated. Nevertheless first evaluation results of template detection and few-exemplar extraction are presented in Section 5.

Template Detection: While relevant information within a document are highly dependent on the document's template, the first step of our methodology is a classification according to the template, the document was built on. Starting with such a model, the creator of a document adds relevant index data and gets a new document instance. Due to corporate identity and standardizations, companies are influenced to produce their business documents in a consistent manner. A first analysis on our set of real-world business correspondences has

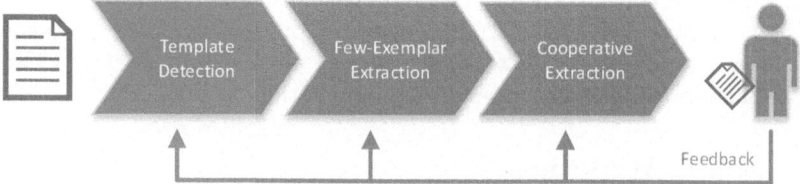

Fig. 1. The information extraction process

shown that 97% of all documents were generated in such a way. The goal of our template detection is the classification of a document according to its template without configuration effort. Therefore we use an adapted feature generation in combination with a kNN algorithm to label a document with the template used by its nearest neighbors. To ensure fast classification behavior, we avoid to analyze the structure of a document, but rather use only word tokens and their coordinates within the documents as features. The usage of an instance-based algorithm ensures an online processing of documents and a nearly instant integration of user feedback, which either can be acknowledgments on system results or corrections for wrong classification and extraction decisions. Details on our template detection so far can be found in [19].

Few-Exemplar Extraction: The extraction of index data is mainly based on templates which were identified in the previous step. The existence of templates indicates a clear structure within documents generated out of it. This structure can be used to extract relevant information. For illustration, Figure 2 shows three instances created on top of the same template. Relevant information like sender, customer identifier, and amount share nearly the same positions within each document. Based on the information from template detection, we identify documents using the same template within the training set. On this similar looking documents, three types of extraction steps are currently executed. First, we try to identify fields with similar value across the set of similar looking documents which often apply for document type and sender. Second, we try to identify index fields with values at nearly the same position using bounding boxes. Third, we use context words in the surrounding of tagged fields in the training documents. Altogether each of these algorithms needs at least one document of the same template within the training set to produce extraction results. The combination of template detection, usage of similar documents and instant integration of feedback guarantees a very low number of training documents and allows a high adaptivity for new document types, templates and fields via user feedback.

Cooperative Extraction: To further reduce the amount of manual annotations and improve the performance of our system especially in the starting period, we focus on a cooperative approach. Therefore local knowledge pools are defined, where extraction knowledge from each individual user can be securely stored. Each of them is connected to a common distributed knowledge pool. Depending on the quality of local results, a document is forwarded to the common pool

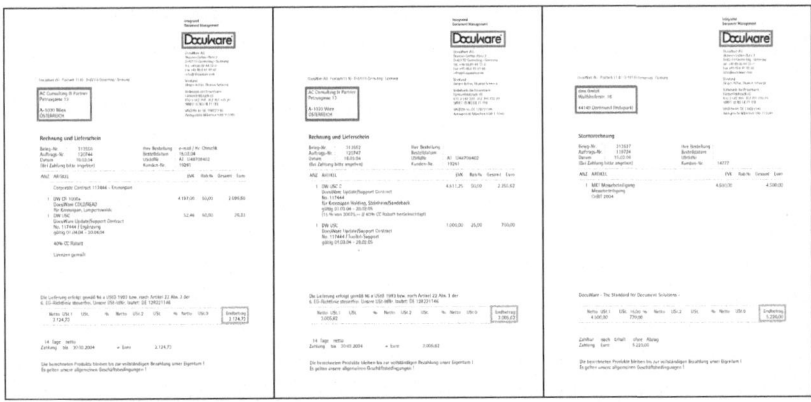

Fig. 2. Business documents using the same template. Bounding boxes show the nearly constant positions of index data over all documents.

for extraction. Afterwards distributed and local results will be combined and delivered back to the user. In order to enhance the effectivity of the common knowledge base, feedback given by the user will also be passed. For customization purposes the number of common knowledge pools and possible communication paths can be adopted to business domains and workflows.

Security and privacy issues play an important role within a distributed approach. Although they are not the main aspect of our work, we want to discuss solutions like obfuscation of documents and feedback.

Altogether the cooperation approach limits the amount of feedback by avoiding the manual tagging of documents that already have been seen and tagged by another user. While first results indicate an improvement of systems performance in the starting period, we expect limitations of this approach with a larger amount of training documents within the distributed knowledge pool. Coupling thousands of local extraction systems to interact with a distributed knowledge base will highly increase the number of documents within this pool. By implementing such a scenario, we plan to identify limits of this kind of distributed approaches and give solutions for solving such problems, i.e. finding thresholds for splitting decision and dividing a distributed knowledge pool into several specialized parts, communicating with each other to ensure constantly high extraction rates.

5   Evaluation

Our document corpus consists of 12,500 real-world business documents from the archive of our project partner DocuWare. Due to international business relations, our corpus includes German, English, and Spanish documents. We captured each with a customary scanner and tagged and corrected it according to commonly

used fields in document archiving. Beside a minimal set of fields to enable structured archiving (*document type, recipient, sender, date*), we added further popular fields like *amount, contact, customer identifier, document number, subject,*
and *date to be paid* based on an inedited survey carried out by DocuWare.

To evaluate our system we use common metrics precision, recall and F1-
measure. For classification we rely on the definition by Sebastiani [20]. For
extraction we evaluate according to the metrics presented by Chinchor and Sundheim [21] for MUC-5. As the user expects only correct results, we ignore error
class "partial" and tackle this kind of extractions as wrong. Overall values are
calculated using a micro-averaging approach by averaging single results over all
recognized labels.

For evaluation of learning behavior and speed we use an iterative testing procedure. To underline the highly adaptive character of our approach, we test our
solutions with what we call "cold start metrics", i.e. a gold standard evaluation
starting with an empty learning model and adding each document not recognized
correctly as a training example. The system performance is evaluated depending
on the current size and structure of the training set. By calculating the area
under this curve, we get a single value, which represents the learning speed and
allows a comparison between algorithms.

To test the performance of our template detection, we evaluated it against
the document set of 12,500 documents using our "cold start metrics" approach.
Therefore we manually tagged each document according to the template that
was used for creation. Altogether we identified 399 different templates within
our document set. The first prototype of our template detection reaches 95%
F1-measure, which is already comparable to the state of the art.

Afterwards we tested our local extraction algorithms against our document
set. Again we used our iterative "cold start metrics" approach. The overall and
field-by-field results are shown in Figure 3. The dotted line represents the minimal rate a user reaches doing manual index data extraction. [22] identified by

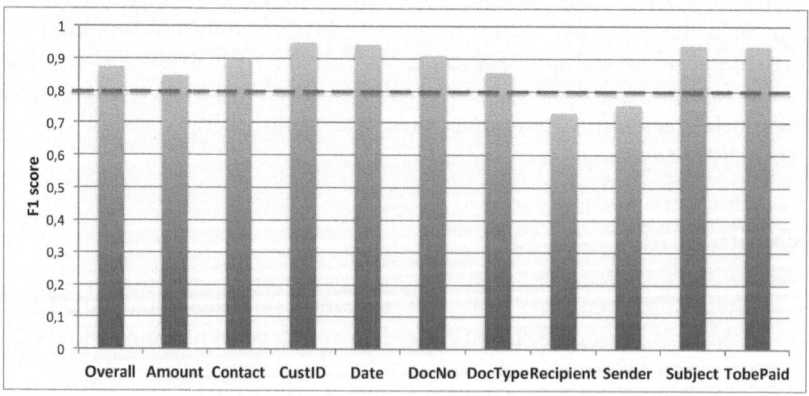

Fig. 3. Overall and field-by-field extraction results of our local extraction approach

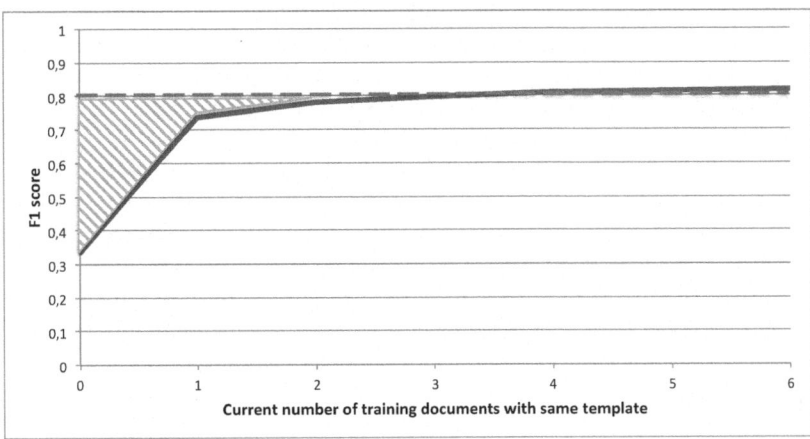

Fig. 4. Learning behavior of our local extraction approach in relation to the number of documents with same template within the current training set

interviewing several companies an error rate up to 20% for manual indexing. As one can see, our overall result for extraction reaches 87%.

To test the learning behavior of our system, we determined for each processed document the number of training examples with the same template in the current training set and calculated our evaluation metrics upon this number. Figure 4 shows the results. Having only one document of the same template within the training set, our system produces overall extraction results upon 74%. With three documents of the same template we already pass the threshold of 80%.

6   Discussion and Future Work

Our first evaluations have shown the ability of our system to reach good results on basis of a minimal set of training documents. Although we pass 80% F1-measure with three documents of the same template within our training set, a user will get frustrated, if he has to provide feedback for documents of a new template multiple times. Therefore we have to increase the learning speed furthermore to reach this limit with only one similar document or in best case with no similar document in training (see shaded area in Figure 4).

A first step into this direction is the further improvement of our template detection and extraction algorithms. While they are not yet perfect, we want to analyze typical error cases, i.e. extraction and OCR errors, and improve the performance of the local system. Possible solutions are the optimization of our feature generation and modifications on our instance-based learning algorithms. Even without collaboration we want to reach a level in learning speed that lies above existing solutions.

A second step is the integration of our distributed approach. We expect to get a much higher performance in the starting period by coupling local systems following our cooperative approach. Ideally the threshold of 80% F1-measure will often already be passed without any similar document in the local training set, only by using extraction knowledge from other participants. Therefore we plan to repeat our evaluations for learning speed using the proposed distributed approach.

To get significant results for scalability, we also have to enlarge the size of our document set. While 12,500 documents are enough for local system evaluation, we want to detect the influence of very large sets of training documents in a distributed knowledge pool according to our cooperative extraction approach. Therefore we plan to reach a much higher number of business documents (i.e. 1,000,000) by generating new ones based on our current document set.

7   Conclusion

In this paper we propose a distributed information extraction system to identify index terms from scanned business documents using a highly adaptable and fast-learning approach that needs nearly no effort in on-site configuration. For that reason it is especially suitable for SOHO users and private individuals. The combination of local and distributed knowledge pools improves the learning behavior of local systems and enhances the user acceptance. First evaluations on our local system have proven the ability of our methodology to reach acceptable extraction results with a minimal amount of training documents. Further work will mainly focus on integration and evaluation of our distributed approach.

Acknowledgments. This work is a result of my research efforts in the context of the ModelSpace project, which was funded by the German Federal Ministry of Education and Research (BMBF) within the research program "KMU Innovativ" (fund number 01/S12017). My special thanks to my colleagues for insightful discussions and careful prove reading and our project partners from DocuWare for providing us with the document corpus used for evaluation.

References

1. Klein, B., Dengel, A., Fordan, A.: smartfix: An adaptive system for document analysis and understanding. In: Reading and Learning, pp. 166–186 (2004)
2. Opentext, Opentext capture center (2012),
   http://www.opentext.com/2/global/products/
   products-capture-and-imaging/products-opentext-capture-center.htm
3. Schulz, F., Ebbecke, M., Gillmann, M., Adrian, B., Agne, S., Dengel, A.: Seizing the treasure: Transferring knowledge in invoice analysis. In: 10th International Conference on Document Analysis and Recognition, pp. 848–852 (2009)
4. Sako, H., Seki, M., Furukawa, N., Ikeda, H., Imaizumi, A.: Form reading based on form-type identification and form-data recognition. In: Seventh International Conference on Document Analysis and Recognition, pp. 926–930 (2003)
5. Appiani, E., Cesarini, F., Colla, A.M., Diligenti, M., Gori, M., Marinai, S., Soda, G.: Automatic document classification and indexing in high-volume applications. International Journal on Document Analysis and Recognition 4(2), 69–83 (2001)

6. Sorio, E., Bartoli, A., Davanzo, G., Medvet, E.: Open world classification of printed invoices. In: Proceedings of the 10th ACM Symposium on Document Engineering, DocEng 2010, pp. 187–190. ACM, New York (2010)
7. Vila, M., Bardera, A., Feixas, M., Sbert, M.: Tsallis mutual information for document classification. Entropy 13(9), 1694–1707 (2011)
8. Diligenti, M., Frasconi, P., Gori, M.: Hidden tree markov models for document image classification. IEEE Transactions on Pattern Analysis and Machine Intelligence 25(4), 519–523 (2003)
9. Belaïd, A., D'Andecy, V.P., Hamza, H., Belaïd, Y.: Administrative Document Analysis and Structure. In: Biba, M., Xhafa, F. (eds.) Learning Structure and Schemas from Documents. SCI, vol. 375, pp. 51–71. Springer, Heidelberg (2011)
10. Alippi, C., Pessina, F., Roveri, M.: An adaptive system for automatic invoice-documents classification. In: IEEE International Conference on Image Processing, ICIP 2005, vol. 2, pp. II-526–II-529 (2005)
11. Adali, S., Sonmez, A.C., Gokturk, M.: An integrated architecture for processing business documents in turkish. In: Gelbukh, A. (ed.) CICLing 2009. LNCS, vol. 5449, pp. 394–405. Springer, Heidelberg (2009)
12. Cesarini, F., Francesconi, E., Gori, M., Soda, G.: Analysis and understanding of multi-class invoices. IJDAR 6(2), 102–114 (2003)
13. Bart, E., Sarkar, P.: Information extraction by finding repeated structure. In: Proceedings of the 9th IAPR International Workshop on Document Analysis Systems, DAS 2010, pp. 175–182 (2010)
14. Belaid, Y., Belaid, A.: Morphological tagging approach in document analysis of invoices. In: Proceedings of the 17th International Conference on Pattern Recognition, ICPR 2004 (2004)
15. Likforman-Sulem, L., Vaillant, P., Yvon, F.: Proper names extraction from fax images combining textual and image features. In: Seventh International Conference on Document Analysis and Recognition, vol. 1, pp. 545–549 (2003)
16. Saund, E.: Scientific challenges underlying production document processing. In: Document Recognition and Retrieval XVIII, DRR (2011)
17. Salperwyck, C., Lemaire, V.: Learning with few examples: An empirical study on leading classifiers. In: The International Joint Conference on Neural Networks, IJCNN (2011)
18. Forman, G., Cohen, I.: Learning from little: Comparison of classifiers given little training. In: Boulicaut, J.-F., Esposito, F., Giannotti, F., Pedreschi, D. (eds.) PKDD 2004. LNCS (LNAI), vol. 3202, pp. 161–172. Springer, Heidelberg (2004)
19. Esser, D., Schuster, D., Muthmann, K., Berger, M., Schill, A.: Automatic indexing of scanned documents - a layout-based approach. In: Document Recognition and Retrieval XIX, DRR, San Francisco, CA, USA (2012)
20. Sebastiani, F.: Machine learning in automated text categorization. ACM Comput. Surv. 34(1), 1–47 (2002)
21. Chinchor, N., Sundheim, B.: Muc-5 evaluation metrics. In: Proceedings of the 5th Conference on Message Understanding, MUC5 1993, pp. 69–78 (1993)
22. Klein, B., Agne, S., Dengel, A.R.: Results of a study on invoice-reading systems in germany. In: Marinai, S., Dengel, A.R. (eds.) DAS 2004. LNCS, vol. 3163, pp. 451–462. Springer, Heidelberg (2004)

Sustainable Supply Chain Management: Improved Prioritization of Auditing Social Factors, Leveraging Up-to-Date Information Technology

Andreas Thöni

Vienna University of Technology, Vienna, Austria

1 Introduction

For companies, sustainability issues in the supply chain can cause severe problems and reputational damage. Especially social sustainability is of a problem (e.g. human rights) and has only been narrowly addressed in academic literature [1].

In business, the increased risk of issues in supply chains has amplified the need for the auditing of social responsibility at supplier locations [2]. As supply chains can include hundreds of suppliers, it seems impossible for companies to evaluate all factors in depth and even lesser in first-hand [3]. Because no interaction would require too much trust, a prioritized approach to the auditing of suppliers appears necessary.

The thesis addresses this prioritization problem of social sustainability auditing in international goods supply chains based on a design science approach to reduce risk and save costs [4]. Thus, the thesis' core question is: *How can the prioritization of auditing activities of socially sustainable supply chain management be improved, leveraging up-to-date information technology?* Hence, a new prioritization software toolset could be an answer.

2 Related Work and Research Hypotheses

Existing academic work relates to selecting and measuring suppliers as well as specific supply chains (e.g. [5]). However, it lacks aspects for improved prioritization of social auditing such as automatic and quick data-integration, real-time event inclusion and data integrating necessary for a complete, up-to-date picture of supplier locations.

In recent years LOD has grown as an instantly-accessible data pool allowing to derive rating-relevant statistical and meta data (e.g. corruption indexes). Moreover, as a method, it allows a simple representation of supply chains, leading to the first hypothesis: (H1) *LOD can leverage the prioritization of auditing activities of socially sustainable supply chain management (SSSCM) by improving data-update efficiency.* Unstructured text mining has already been applied to multiple fields. In the specific context it allows analyzing news for risk evidences (e.g. geographically close events): (H2) *Text mining with a focus on companies/industries/geographies can further leverage auditing prioritization of SSSCM by generating real-time sustainability risk events.* Bayesian networks and Dempster-Shafer's belief-function formalism are

Y.T. Demey and H. Panetto (Eds.): OTM 2013 Workshops, LNCS 8186, pp. 32–33, 2013.

related approaches to integrate uncertain data from multiple sources. In order to combine supplier-related indicators, punctual evidence and history, a third hypothesis is connected: (H3) *Bayesian networks or Dempster-Shafter theory can improve auditing prioritization of SSSCM by facilitating the integration of multiple data sources.*

3   Methods, Work Plan and Evaluation

In order to show the usefulness of the approaches described above for social sustainability auditing, the thesis follows a design science approach (i.e. a software artifact will be developed and evaluated) and is built in several steps. First, an overarching literature review will be performed followed by detailing H1 to H3. Each step will include specific literature work followed by data gathering, model building and evaluation. The thesis will focus on one aspect of social sustainability (e.g. corruption, to be defined). A prototypical implementation will be based on an artificially created supply chain first. For evaluation, multiple techniques (experimental/observational evaluation; experimental simulation) will be combined and artificial data will be pooled with real data from an international goods sourcing supply chain (case study).

4   Discussion and Conclusion

Publicly discussed social sustainability issues can cause severe damage to a company. Existing approaches to limit risk appear to offer insufficient inclusion of dynamically available and real-time data in an integrated way while respecting uncertainty. By applying new sources and methods this thesis aims at closing this presumed gap. Thus, the software artifact of the design science approach has the potential to save costs in social sustainability auditing by increasing its effectiveness and efficiency.

References

1. Seuring, S., Müller, M.: From a literature review to a conceptual framework for sustainable supply chain management. Journal of Cleaner Production 16, 1699–1710 (2008)
2. Klassen, R.D., Vereecke, A.: Social issues in supply chains: Capabilities link responsibility, risk (opportunity), and performance. International Journal of Production Economics 140, 103–115 (2012)
3. Kogg, B., Mont, O.: Environmental and social responsibility in supply chains: The practise of choice and inter-organisational management. Ecological Economics 83, 154–163 (2012)
4. Hevner, A.R., March, S.T., Park, J., Ram, S.: Design science in information sys-tems research. MIS Quarterly 28, 75–105 (2004)
5. Govindan, K., Khodaverdi, R., Jafarian, A.: A fuzzy multi criteria approach for measuring sustainability performance of a supplier based on triple bottom line approach. Journal of Cleaner Production 47, 345–354 (2013)

Industry Case Studies Program 2013
PC Co-Chairs Message

Cloud computing, service-oriented architecture, business process modelling, enterprise architecture, enterprise integration, semantic interoperability-what is an enterprise systems administrator to do with the constant stream of industry hype surrounding him, constantly bathing him with (apparently) new ideas and new "technologies"? It is nearly impossible, and the academic literature does not help solving the problem, with hyped "technologies" catching on in the academic world just as easily as the industrial world. The most unfortunate thing is that these technologies are actually useful, and the press hype only hides that value. What the enterprise information manager really cares about is integrated, interoperable infrastructures that support cooperative information systems, so he can deliver valuable information to management in time to make correct decisions about the use and delivery of enterprise resources, whether those are raw materials for manufacturing, people to carry out key business processes, or the management of shipping choices for correct delivery to customers.

The OTM conference series have established itself as a major international forum for exchanging ideas and results on scientific research for practitioners in fields such as computer supported cooperative work (CSCW), middleware, Internet/Web data management, electronic commerce, workflow management, knowledge flow, agent technologies and software architectures, to name a few. The recent popularity and interest in service-oriented architectures & domains require capabilities for on-demand composition of services. Furthermore, cloud computing environments are becoming more prevalent, in which information technology resources must be configured to meet user-driven needs. These emerging technologies represent a significant need for highly interoperable systems.

As a part of OnTheMove 2013, the Industry Case Studies Program on "Industry Applications and Standard initiatives for Cooperative Information Systems for Interoperable Infrastructures", supported by OMG, IFAC TC 5.3 "Enterprise Integration and Networking" and the SIG INTEROP Grande-Région, emphasized Research/Industry cooperation on these future trends. The focus of the program is on a discussion of ideas where research areas address interoperable information systems and infrastructure. 9 short papers have been presented, focusing on industry leaders, standardization initiatives, European and international projects consortiums and discussing how projects within their organizations addressed software, systems and architecture interoperability. Each paper has been reviewed by an international Programme Committee composed of representatives of Academia, Industry and Standardisation initiatives. We thank them for their dedication and interest. We hope that you find this industry-focused part of the program valuable as feedback from industry practitioners, and we thank the authors for the time taken to contribute to the program.

July 2013   Hervé Panetto

Y.T. Demey and H. Panetto (Eds.): OTM 2013 Workshops, LNCS 8186, p. 34, 2013.

A Cooperative Social Platform to Elevate Cooperation to the Next Level – The Case of a Hotel Chain

Short Paper

Emmanuel Kaldis[1], Liping Zhao[1], and Robert Snowdon[2]

[1] University of Manchester, CS, Manchester, UK
{E.Kaldis@postgrad.,Liping.Zhao@}manchester.ac.uk
[2] University of Manchester, CS, Manchester, UK
robert@casaram.demon.co.uk

Abstract. This paper presents a cooperative social platform which was developed to accommodate the needs of a hotel chain. The web-based platform aims at interconnecting strategic functions that previously required the use of various tools that lacked interoperability. The platform encourages isolated managers of the hotel chain to interact and actively participate in the strategy formation and implementation. It provides novel functions that enhance the collective intelligence within the hotel chain, as well as enables the dynamic 'sensing' and 'acting' upon customer feedback. Results from the case study show that the platform enhanced bottom-up change and increased the pace of innovation, while the hotel chain became more cohesive and demonstrated evidence of 'self-organization'.

Keywords: Cooperative social platform, self-organization, collaborative strategy formulation and implementation, collective intelligence, synergy.

1   Introduction

Having well entered the globalized networked era, business organizations are confronted with new challenges. Obstacles to entering new markets have been reduced and thus organizations can expand their operations into new regions more easily. Given though the continuous pressure for change at all levels of the organization, centralized control gives place to more decentralized organizational structures. At the same time, the increased turnover rate of managers makes organizational knowledge increasingly vulnerable. The experience and knowledge obtained through the years, unless captured, can be lost. Hence, the role of an Information System (IS) in terms of supporting the cooperation and knowledge transfer among the members of geographically distributed organizations has become critical.

In the last decades, a specific class of ISs referred to as "Cooperative Information Systems" (CISs) has emerged to tackle the challenges of the contemporary business environment and the lack of interoperability among ISs. As Lezoche et al. [1] note, CISs "provide a backbone for the integrated information infrastructure". Given the

Y.T. Demey and H. Panetto (Eds.): OTM 2013 Workshops, LNCS 8186, pp. 35–41, 2013.
© Springer-Verlag Berlin Heidelberg 2013

development of the web, a number of cloud-based applications usually referred to as corporate social networks or platforms have emerged aiming at integrating the parts of the decentralized organization.

This paper discusses the impact of a cooperative social platform (CSP) which was developed and applied in the case of a hotel chain. The remaining of this paper is structured as follows: Section 2 presents the challenges faced in the case study of a hotel chain and the limitations of the ISs in place. Subsequently, section 3 describes the functionalities of a web-based cooperative platform that was developed and the benefits from its application in the hotel chain. The last section discusses the conclusions from this research and areas for further research.

2   Background

A hotel chain in Greece was used as the main case of this research. The initial phase of the empirical study began with an investigation of the existing strategic businesses processes and the supporting ISs in place over a one-year period. Subsequently, interviews were conducted with key stakeholders of the hotel chain with the aim to identify possible limitations of the ISs in place. The hotel chain consists of six geographically distributed hotels, five of which have been established in the last ten years. During the study of the hotel chain and based on interviewees' input, it became apparent that the hotel chain was facing new challenges. The level of competition in all regions where the hotels of the chain resided was unprecedented. Hence, hotel managers were given more autonomy in order to respond more effectively to the local market needs. However, this meant that the hotel chain as a whole was becoming less cohesive and internal knowledge transfer was becoming a challenge. At the same time, the hotel chain was experiencing an increased turnover rate of employees, which was often affecting business continuity.

Given the above challenges, the hotel chain was using a number of IS to support its nation-wide business processes. More strategic functions for supporting the managers of the hotel chain were addressed by a number of synchronous and asynchronous tools that existed within the corporate intranet. Asynchronous functions included an Announcements area, a Calendar, a File Management System, a Discussion Forum, a Search functionality, a Brainstorming tool and a Project Management tool. Synchronous functions included Chat, Google Voice and Video Chat. Finally, further to the corporate intranet, knowledge was frequently transferred internally or from the external environment through the use of email communication.

By critically examining the ISs in place in terms of supporting cooperation within the hotel chain, three main limitations were identified. First, it was noticed that the various tools which were used lacked interoperability. For example, if a manager of a hotel unit was interested to find all the knowledge related to a particular change undertaken in the past, he or she would be required to search in various sources such as the discussion forum, the brainstorming and project management tool, within electronic files or email conversations. As a result, valuable knowledge was typically disintegrated and therefore could not be easily traced, queried and reused. The second limitation was the fact that the existing ISs treated the hotel chain as a hierarchical organization which was led from the top, rather than an organization consisting of self-organizing communities. More specifically, a hotel unit was typically treated as belonging only to a certain hotel and not as being part of a larger community consisting of other hotel units that had similar structural characteristics and purpose. For example, a restaurant unit was typically treated as only being part of a hotel and not as being part of a wider community which consists of all the restaurant units across the chain. This meant that structurally similar hotel units operated in isolation and that cooperation among them was limited. Thirdly, the existing ISs in place did not support effectively the interaction of the hotel chain with external parties such as business partners (suppliers), customers and job candidates. The key processes with external parties were not well supported and took place usually through email communication. For example, requests towards suppliers such as a purchase order or a corrective action due to a non-conformity of a product usually occurred through email. Similarly, the application process of job candidates was typically communicated through email. Also, feedback received by customers and the corrective actions undertaken in relation to the feedback provided constituted valuable knowledge which was not effectively managed.

To summarize, the variety of tools used by the hotel chain, the fact that such tools had not truly conceived the organization as a set of self-organizing communities as well as the limitations in terms of interacting efficiently with external parties delimited the potential of collaboration and knowledge exchange within the hotel chain. As a consequence, the prevailing approach to change was the top-down approach where change and knowledge was driven from the top, either by the hotel manager or the top-management at the headquarters.

3   The Adoption of a CSP

Given the above limitations, the management of the hotel chain explored the possibility of installing a CSP for enhancing further the cooperation and knowledge flows within the hotel chain. The adoption of CSPs has been recently widespread. The key characteristic of such platforms is that they incorporate functions provided by common social media tools (i.e. Facebook) such as microblogging, dynamic commenting, "liking" and an activity feed. A number of commercial CSPs exist such as Yammer [2], Saba Cloud People [3] and Jive Software [4]. However, the application of such tools in the hospitality sector is limited.

The management of the hotel chain preferred the solution of a custom platform in order to address the more specific needs of a hotel chain. Further to the standard functions of a CSP, the platform would also support typical processes with external parties such as business partners, customers and job candidates, as well as would structure the knowledge created within the platform in a more organized manner. All posts would be categorized based on the relevant topic and would be easily filtered based on their popularity or date published.

The platform has been developed using PHP5 and MySQL 5.5 and has responsive design which enables access from any mobile device. The platform provides the standard social functions and further groupware functions such as the grouping of users into communities of practice. Moreover, it provides typical synchronous functions such as chatting, file transfer, screen-sharing and voice and video communication.

Further to these functions, the platform provides five main features which have aimed to elevate cooperation within the hotel chain to a new level. At first, the "Ideas" function acts as a collaborative strategy formulation process which allows any community member to propose ideas or suggestions and receive feedback by any interested party. All ideas are classified according to the relevant community and are automatically ranked based on the ratings received by their community members. Next, the "Initiatives" function provides to the members of a community the possibility to share the implementation plan of their actions and receive feedback by their peers, giving rise to a participatory form of strategy implementation. Upon completion of a change, community members can rate the impact of the implemented change and provide feedback, as well as share their thoughts and lessons learnt from the action. The platform provides functions for cooperation with external parties too. The "Business Partners Center" is a function that enables the members of every community within the hotel chain to create a directory of preferred partners (suppliers), supports typical business processes such as purchasing orders as well as provides the possibility for evaluating the business partners. The "Applicant Center" is another collaborative function that enables the community members to create a pool of candidates in combination with their evaluation during interviews performed. Applicants can be notified about the status and outcome of their application.

Last but not least, the "Feedback" function provides to the members of a community the possibility to receive feedback by customers who had stayed in any hotel of the chain with the use of an online questionnaire. The platform then provides comparisons of the performance of every community within the hotel chain (i.e. the restaurant units across the hotel chain), giving rise to the phenomenon of "coopetition" [5] which implies simultaneously cooperative and competitive behavior. The Feedback function in fact acts as an alert to those community members that are performing below average, thus promoting corrective action and self-organization.

The study of the application of the platform adopted by the hotel chain lasted fourteen months. Access to the platform was not restricted to the managerial level but included all members of staff that were IT literate. Access rights to the content posted within the platform were carefully assigned. At the same time, both an individual and a group incentive were provided to motivate the users to share their knowledge, ideas and initiatives within the platform. The individual reward was non-monetary. The member of staff who posted the knowledge obtained upon undertaking initiatives for change would be appointed as the "Member of the Year" and would be awarded a complimentary three days stay in one of the hotels of the chain. Moreover, the members of the most active group (i.e. restaurant members of staff across the hotel chain) in terms of knowledge creation would be rewarded with a complimentary daily excursion.

The follow-up interviews that were conducted with the same stakeholders that were interviewed before the application of the platform demonstrated significant benefits for the hotel chain. Knowledge was not anymore fragmented within various sources-silos but could be easily traceable within a single and easily searchable platform. Furthermore, by capturing and sharing systematically every change within the Initiatives area, it became possible for the members of a community to reapply successful changes which have been implemented by their peers. The transfer of horizontal knowledge -directly among the members of a community- became possible and thus it was not only top-management that solely led change. For example, as Fig. 1 shows, knowledge was transferred horizontally between the hotels or the similar departments residing within the hotel chain. As a consequence, successful actions could be reapplied more easily since community members had all the necessary knowledge related to a particular initiative.

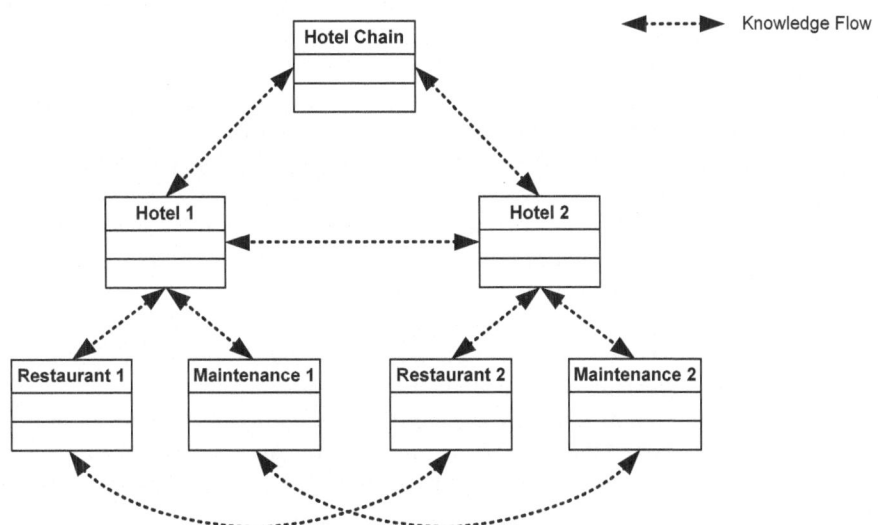

Fig. 1. Horizontal knowledge transfer between hotels and hotel departments for self-organization

More specifically, over the fourteen months application period, the total number of initiatives for change recorded in the platform was ninety-two (92). Twenty nine changes were initiated from the headquarters (top) and sixty three were initiated from the bottom, either from the hotel managers or the members of a hotel unit. Eighty one initiatives were implemented, while the rest were either abandoned or postponed for the future. Most of the changes were considered as incremental improvements to the existing processes. Out of the ninety-two initiatives for changes, twenty six were reapplied within the period of the study, while the reapplication of another seven changes had started but their implementation had not been completed by the end of this study. In all twenty six changes which were reapplied, the managers found easily all the relevant knowledge created upon the brainstorming, implementation and evaluation phase of the change within the CSP. In fact, the headquarters were mostly involved in terms of authorizing decisions for change that initiated considerable expenditure. It can be said that the role of the headquarters was gradually changing from "leading" to "listening".

Another characteristic which was noticed during the period of application of the platform in the hotel chain was the improved pace of innovation and cohesion. Changes are now reapplied faster across the hotel chain as the members interested in a certain change don't have to "reinvent the wheel". All the details related to a particular initiative such as the implementation plan and obstacles faced during the change have now been well documented. In fact, in four cases of change it was also noticed that the members of a group collaborated actively in order to decide jointly about the best course of action of an initiative for change. This was achieved through the asynchronous functions Ideas and Initiatives.

Another aspect which demonstrated the improved ability of the hotel chain to self-organize was the possibility for new members to integrate in their role easier. A smooth integration of new managers would mean that top management would not be required to put significant effort into training and explaining the rationale of past initiatives for change which were now recorded in the platform. In fact, the users and particularly the members that had recently joined the hotel chain considered this as the biggest asset of the CSP.

The extranet that was created for organizing and collaboratively evaluating the suppliers as well as the job candidates of the hotel chain proved useful too. Such functions enhanced synergies among the hotel chain as the knowledge obtained from the evaluation of the suppliers was not anymore kept distributed across the hotel chain. The same applied for HR functions such as the selection and evaluation of candidates, a process which was typically performed by the headquarters.

Finally, self-organization was also enhanced by the ability of the CSP to project dynamic views that enabled the comparison of the performance between the members of a group. Such comparison acted as a mechanism for motivating managers to be more alert and undertake more initiatives which shall improve the sustainability of their units. With the new KMS in place, managers now needed to be more alert, to monitor the initiatives of their colleagues and reapply them when found applicable.

4   Conclusions

This paper aimed to demonstrate how CISs such as a CSP can elevate cooperation to a new dimension: namely that of self-organization. The adoption of a CSP by a hotel chain has been used as a case study. As the follow-up interviews with key stakeholders of the hotel chain indicated, the platform brought considerable benefits to both the members of the communities and higher management. The findings suggest that the application of the CSP, which is extensively used by the hotel chain up to today, reduced top management's intervention to promote change, while organizational cohesion and the pace of change increased.

A number of areas for further research are suggested. To name a few, a potentially interesting area to explore would be the application of a platform in global organizations operating in different sectors and for a longer period of time. Finally, a socio-technical factor such as the use of incentive systems for motivating the users to contribute their knowledge is another element that requires further research.

References

1. Lezoche, M., Yahia, E., Aubry, A., Panetto, H., Zdravković, M.: Conceptualising and structuring semantics in cooperative enterprise information systems models. Computers in Industry 63, 775–787 (2012)
2. Yammer, http://www.yammer.com
3. Saba Cloud People, http://www.sabapeoplecloud.com
4. Jive Software, http://www.jivesoftware.com
5. Tsai, W.: Social Structure of "Coopetition" within a Multiunit Organization: Coordination, Competition, and Intraorganizational Knowledge Sharing. Organization Science 13, 179–190 (2002)

Applying BPM 2.0 in BPM Implementation Projects
Short Paper

A practice report demonstrating the opportunities and limitations of BPM 2.0 in a
BPM implementation project and an ISO 9001 certification at Eisen-Fischer GmbH

Matthias Kurz[1], Manfred Scherer[2], Angelika Pößl, Jörg Purucker[3],
and Albert Fleischmann[4]

[1] DATEV eG, Nuremberg, Germany
[2] Eisen-Fischer GmbH, Nördlingen, Germany
[3] BIK GmbH, Nuremberg, Germany
[4] Metasonic GmbH, Pfaffenhofen, Germany

Abstract. Businesses today have to adapt their business process models to new
market changes instantaneously. New social BPM approaches leverage collaborative Enterprise 2.0 methods and tools in order to empower the process participants to improve their business processes continuously. By enabling those
who are running the processes to adapt "their" processes, businesses can respond to new market demands faster. A well-tested example of such an approach is BPM 2.0. This contribution reports about a BPM implementation
project conducted at Eisen-Fischer GmbH, which uses BPM 2.0 as the underlying methodology. It provides insights in the potentials and limitations of social
BPM approaches like BPM 2.0. As a major objective of the BPM implementation project is to retain the existing ISO 9001 certification, this report assists
businesses in a similar situation to assess the potentials social BPM may
provide for their individual situation.

Keywords: BPM 2.0, Social BPM, Practices Report, ISO 9001, Enterprise 2.0.

1 Introduction

Business processes are subject to ever-increasing flexibility requirements, as businesses have to adapt to more dynamic and complex business environments [1]. In
order to address these issues, Enterprise 2.0 approaches towards business process
management (BPM) like *Business Process Management 2.0* (BPM 2.0; [2]) or *Decentralized Business Process Management* [3] are becoming more popular.

BPM 2.0 has the objective to adapt business processes more quickly to new requirements by empowering employees participating in the respective business process
as part of their daily routine to adapt the processes by themselves. BPM 2.0 combines
elements from self-organization and empowerment and applies them to business
process management (BPM). The approach has three key principles:

Y.T. Demey and H. Panetto (Eds.): OTM 2013 Workshops, LNCS 8186, pp. 42–46, 2013.
© Springer-Verlag Berlin Heidelberg 2013

1. When redesigning businesses processes, employees may actively contribute to the redesign project.
2. The operational employees can adapt or improve "their" business processes by themselves as well.
3. Several facilitator and expert roles ensure that methodical knowledge is available to the employees when needed.

This contribution can only provide a brief overview of BPM 2.0. The approach is documented in greater detail in [4] and [5]. BPM 2.0 has been applied to a number of companies [4]: A plant construction company successfully utilized the approach for improving business processes. Furthermore, BPM 2.0 has been used for documenting selected business processes at a European defense company. This contribution reports from a BPM 2.0 related project at the German wholesaler Eisen-Fischer.

2   Eisen-Fischer GmbH

The Eisen-Fischer GmbH (short Eisen-Fischer) is a medium-sized wholesaler with three sites. The company was founded 1874 and has about 400 employees. Its customers primarily comprise craftsmen, specialist dealers, industrial companies, and the public sector.

In 2007, the company introduced an enterprise resource planning (ERP) system based on SAP R/3. This system automates the company's core processes, increases their efficiency, and reduces the number of errors. However, the ERP system can only benefit the processes supported by the system. Therefore, Eisen-Fischer initiated a project for further improving the management of business processes not supported by the ERP system. This project established BPM using the BPM 2.0 method and tools.

With certified quality management increasingly gaining significance in business-to-business commerce, Eisen-Fischer's customers are increasingly asking for a certified quality management of their suppliers. Therefore, it is essential for Eisen-Fischer to extend the existing ISO 9001 certification.

At the time of the certification, the implementation of BPM has not been completed entirely. Instead, the following most important components have been in place:

- **Process map:** All top-level processes are identified and structured in a single process map. Eisen-Fischer focused on order management, inventory management, and delivery processes.
- **Responsibilities:** The BPM 2.0 role concept serves as a foundation for assigning the responsibilities. In order to reduce the initial resource requirements for establishing BPM 2.0, the BPM project manager is responsible for the main supporting and facilitating roles as well.
- **Conventions and notation:** A radically reduced subset of BPMN 2.0 (business process model and notation 2.0; [7]) is used as the modeling notation. This subset is based on the descriptive conformance subclass of BPMN [7]. Special attention has been paid to ensure that only the most important elements are part of this

subset. Therefore, this notation distinguishes no task types and supports only a single pool within a diagram.

- **Tool:** The Microsoft Sharepoint based BPM 2.0 modeling environment is used as the central instrument for documenting and optimizing the process models.
- **Training:** In order to spread the modeling knowledge across the company, a small group of key multipliers is selected for in-depth training. This group is trained using two ways: Web based trainings of a university convey the methodical and conceptual knowledge. In-house trainings complement this foundation and tailor it to the specifics of Eisen-Fischer.
- **Process analysis and optimization:** As BPM 2.0 is not yet completely established, the business processes are primarily improved by the process owners. On the other hand, the collaborative nature of BPM 2.0 increased the acceptance for the modeled processes.
- **Process automation:** In order to analyze changes to the ERP system more efficiently, change requests are required to describe the changes in the process model. This has proven useful for discovering unplanned implications of change requests.

3   Certification Result

Based on the current state of the BPM implementation, Eisen-Fischer was successfully certified according to ISO 9001. In the report for the certification, three aspects were applauded in particular:

- Using the BPM 2.0 approach as well as the web based modeling tool for documenting and optimizing business processes.
- Measuring and analyzing key performance indicators for the business processes.
- The efficient and standardized order management automation using the ERP system.

4   Discussion of the Findings

While the foundation for BPM and BPM 2.0 is laid, encouraging a larger share of the process participants to actively develop or improve new processes appears to be a more time-consuming endeavor. This can be attributed primarily to three factors: (1) The process participants find it difficult to find enough time to actively improve their processes. (2) This reluctance is reinforced by the lack of modeling knowledge of many process participants. (3) The process participants see limited use in formalizing the daily routine in a process model. The last factor is particularly surprising, as the lack of formal and standardized processes was a major cause for issues in the past.

In this case, starting a BPM project by an IT department appears to be a sound strategy as it is vital for this department to understand and standardize business processes before they are automated by the ERP system. As a gatekeeper for changes to the central ERP system, IT departments are in a good position to provide a business case for establishing BPM in small companies. However, once established, the responsibility for managing the processes should move over to the organizational units responsible for the processes as soon as possible.

Despite the low number of proactive process innovations from the process participants, the respective process owners receive substantial feedback and improvement suggestions during workshops that use both the platform and the simplified modeling notation. In other words, it appears as if using Enterprise 2.0 methods and tools supports classical workshops well. Improvement suggestions from process participants primarily occur in contexts where the participants are already documenting, analyzing, or discussing "their" business processes.

This observation is in line with the case study presented in [5; 6]. In this case study, processes of a large European plant construction company were improved using both the BPM 2.0 approach and the web-based modeling platform. While there were substantial improvements to the processes during the project, there were only few ad-hoc improvements to the processes from outside the project. However, contrary to the experience at Eisen-Fischer, the process participants at the plant construction company contributed to the process improvements without attending to workshops. This can be attributed to the fact, that the plant construction company already had a working BPM implementation. Therefore, the process innovations at the plant construction company were more incremental when compared to the situation at Eisen-Fischer, which just began establishing BPM. This observation is well in line with the finding that BPM 2.0 works well for process optimizations with limited complexity yet proves to be inefficient for more complex scenarios [5; 6].

5   Summary

While the findings are based on the experience gained at Eisen-Fischer and therefore not necessarily generalizable, small and medium sized companies considering to establish BPM may wish to consider the following lessons learned.

- BPM 2.0 methods and tools assist in the initial discovery and documentation of a company's business processes even if discovery and documentation happen as part of workshops.
- BPM 2.0 works well for incremental improvements to business processes. However, complex changes are difficult to tackle using pure Enterprise 2.0 instruments. In these cases, experienced BPM practitioners should be consulted.
- Ensuring the continuous improvement of processes requires organizational structures like working groups or projects. However, contributions during such projects are simpler for process participants using web-based modeling tools.
- By starting with simple tools and notations, the learning curve is less steep for process participants without prior BPM knowledge. If necessary, more complex notational elements may be introduced later.
- IT departments are a candidate for being the driving force behind the effort to establish BPM within a company, as their work depends on well-defined processes. Still, in the long run, the responsibility for managing the processes should move to the businesses departments.

References

1. Schreyögg, G.: Organisation. Grundlagen moderner Organisationsgestaltung. Mit Fallstudien. Gabler, Wiesbaden (2008)
2. Kurz, M.: BPM 2.0. Selbstorganisation im Geschäftsprozessmanagement. Bayerischer Forschungsverbund Dienstorientierte IT-Systeme für Hochflexible Geschäftsprozesse (forFLEX), Bericht-Nr. forFLEX-2011-05 (2011a)
3. Turetken, O., Demirors, O.: Business Process Modeling Pluralized. In: Fischer, H., Schneeberger, J. (eds.) S-BPM ONE 2013. CCIS, vol. 360, pp. 34–51. Springer, Heidelberg (2013)
4. Kurz, M.: BPM 2.0. Selbstorganisation im Geschäftsprozessmanagement. In: Bartmann, D., Bodendorf, F., Ferstl, O.K., Sinz, E.J. (eds.) Dienstorientierte IT-Systeme für Hochflexible Geschäftsprozesse. University of Bamberg Press, Bamberg (2011b)
5. Kurz, M., Fleischmann, A.: BPM 2.0. Business Process Management meets Empowerment. In: Fleischmann, A., Schmidt, W., Singer, R., Seese, D. (eds.) S-BPM ONE 2010. CCIS, vol. 138, pp. 54–83. Springer, Heidelberg (2011)
6. Kurz, M.: BPM 2.0. Geleitete Selbstorganisation im Geschäftsprozessmanagement. forFLEX-Bericht, Bamberg, Erlangen-Nürnberg, Regensburg (2011)
7. Object Management Group, Business Process Model and Notation (BPMN) (2011) (formal/2011-01-03), http://www.omg.org/spec/BPMN/2.0/PDF/ (accessed July 13, 2013)

Information Centric Engineering (ICE) Frameworks for Advanced Manufacturing Enterprises

J. Cecil

Associate Professor, School of Industrial Engineering & Management
Center for Information Centric Engineering (CICE),
Oklahoma State University, Stillwater, Oklahoma, USA

Abstract. As revolutionary advances in Next Generation Internet technologies continue to emerge, the impact on industrial manufacturing practices globally is expected to be substantial. Collaboration among enterprises is becoming more commonplace. The design of next generation frameworks based on Information Centric Engineering (ICE) principles holds the potential to facilitate rapid and flexible collaboration among global industrial partners. This paper outlines the key components of such a framework in the context of an emerging industrial domain related to micro devices assembly. Discussions of pilot demonstrations using Next Generation and Future Internet frameworks related to the GENI and US Ignite initiatives are also provided.

1   Introduction

The recent advances in Information Technology (IT) especially the development of next generation Internet frameworks including cloud computing technologies holds the potential of catalyzing the next revolution in advanced global manufacturing that relies heavily on information centric engineering (ICE) principles. The adoption of ICE principles in manufacturing lays the foundation for industrial manufacturing and other organizations to form virtual partnerships to collaborate in response to fast changing customer requirements. The 3 core facets of an Information Centric Engineering (ICE) framework include functions, principles and technologies related to:

(i)   Modeling of Information
(ii)   Simulation and Visualization of Information
(iii)   Exchange of Information

A brief discussion of these 3 facets follows.

Modeling of Information (the role of information models): The role of information models assumes significance in any industrial engineering collaboration. Creating such 'information models' (or information intensive process models) at various levels of abstraction within an enterprise is key to understanding an existing or new process. The modeling abstraction can be at the process, factory or enterprise levels (or a combination of them). Such models provide a foundation for designing software

Y.T. Demey and H. Panetto (Eds.): OTM 2013 Workshops, LNCS 8186, pp. 47–56, 2013.

systems to support manufacturing or other engineering activities as well as can be used to propel a large cross section of engineering activities in a product development life cycle (from product conceptualization to assembly, shipping, etc.). Such information models can be created by a variety of existing languages. For example, Activity diagrams can be built using the Unified Modeling Language UML; enterprise models can be created using engineering Enterprise Modeling Language (eEML). These models can capture a range of attributes such as critical information or physical inputs, constraints, performing mechanisms and physical or information outcomes. The major benefit of using such information models is that they provide a detailed understanding of the functional relationships between the various activities and sub-activities. While some of them (such as UML based activity) provide only functional dependencies, other models (such as those built using eEML, for example) capture both the functional relationships and the temporal precedence constraints among the modeled entities. When a virtual enterprise needs to be created, in response to an existing or emerging need, the creation of such information models for a given collaborative context becomes essential to designing, modifying and implementing such collaborations.

Simulation and Visualization of Information: The second major facet of ICE relates to simulation and visualization of information. Such information can be both in the product and process design contexts within a product development life cycle. The motivating force behind adopting such principles is the benefit accrued from simulating product and process design attributes. In today's global environment, when cross-functional engineering teams are distributed, the need for advanced 3D virtual reality based simulation techniques becomes as essential part of any collaborative effort. While CAD/CAM tools are widely used in industry, the next generation of simulation techniques rely substantially on Virtual Reality based simulation tools. The adoption of such Virtual Reality based prototypes (sometimes referred to as Virtual Prototypes) in design, manufacturing, assembly, testing, service and other life cycle activities enables engineers involved in downstream activities (even though they are in a different location) to be involved in upstream 'conceptual' design activities. The primary benefit to a collaborative enterprise lies in being able to identify design problems early in the design, discarding infeasible designs from downstream perspectives (such as assembly, testing, etc.) and providing a powerful collaborative medium (through Virtual Reality technology) for engineers to communicate effectively. Such virtual prototypes can be physics or non physics based depending on the process or product design context. For example, a virtual assembly based analysis approach can be adopted by a team of distributed manufacturing engineers collaborating on studying assembly alternatives.

Exchange of Information: The third major facet of ICE deals with the exchange of information which is essential to collaboration at any level. In general, the 'exchange' facet underscores the importance of exchanging information seamlessly across heterogeneous platforms among distributed partners. Such an information exchange can be accomplished by using Cyber networks which can be our existing Internet, the more advanced Internet2 (which is available to a limited number of universities and hospitals) and the emerging GENI network (which is the next generation of Internets under development by various countries as part of the next generation Global Environment for Network Innovation GENI initiative).This information exchange can be between physical resources, or software (cyber) resources or between cyber physical resources involved in a product development life cycle (including design, planning, simulation based analysis and physical assembly tasks, service, etc.). Under exchange, enterprises will also need to address semantic interoperability issues to ensure seamless exchange of information between software and other resources belonging to various engineering partners or enterprises.

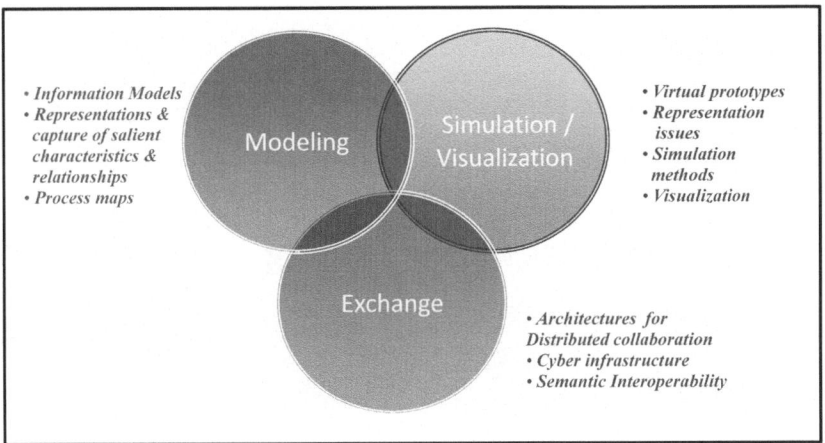

Fig. 1. The 3 core facets of an Information Centric Engineering (ICE) Framework

2   ICE Framework for Micro Devices Assembly

For emerging industrial domains such as the field of micro devices assembly, the adoption of an ICE framework will facilitate collaboration among distributed partners. A brief note about the domain of micro assembly is relevant. Micro Devices Assembly (MDA) refers to the assembly of micron sized devices for various engineering and other application contexts. When a micro sized part design has complex shapes and varying material properties, then the existing MEMS technologies will not be able to produce such a design. In such contexts, the individual micro parts need to be assembled using micro devices assembly techniques and technology. MDA is an emerging domain with a significant economic potential in various fields such as biomedicine (sensors and monitors), semiconductor and electronics manufacturing and surveillance/imaging devices (micro cameras, monitors), and safety products (to detect leak of contaminants).

Most of the existing MDA approaches are cumbersome, time consuming and costly. In most scenarios MDA resources are not available at a single organization; resources are very expensive and distributed among different organizations across different locations. This underscores the necessity for engineering collaborations among enterprises with expertise in micro design, planning, simulation and assembly. The adoption of an ICE based framework linking distributed teams, their software and physical resources assumes significance. The role of information models (to propose and formulate collaborative approaches between teams as well as to understand existing micro assembly processes and systems), virtual prototypes (to conduct simulation and analysis of proposed assembly approaches prior to physical assembly) as well as next generation Internet based exchange strategies (to exchange information between collaborating partner enterprises) become an intrinsic aspect of any collaborative framework developed to respond to changing customer requirements. Figure 2 illustrates such an ICE framework for the domain of micro devices assembly.

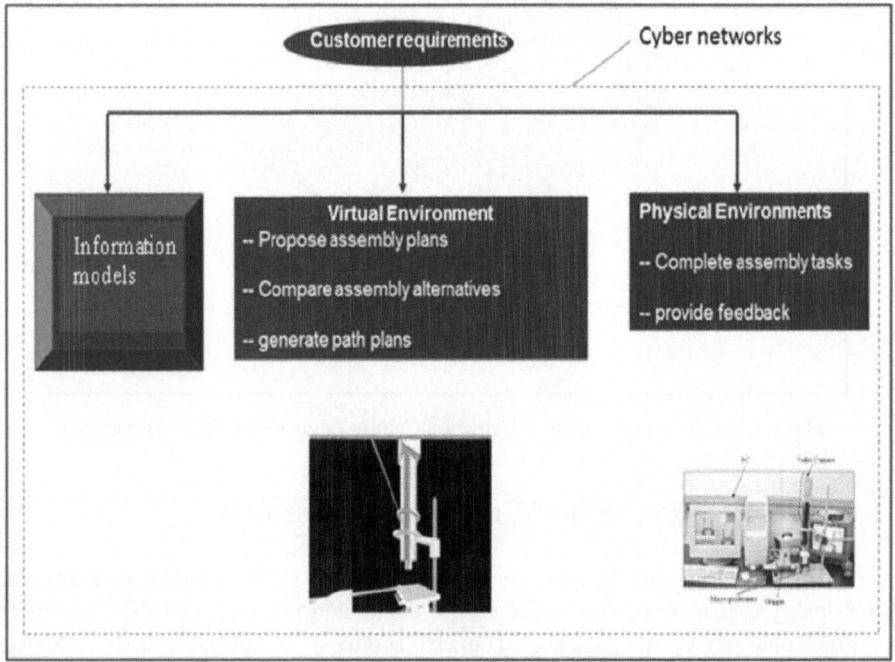

Fig. 2. An Information Centric Engineering (ICE) Framework for micro devices assembly

A discussion of the ICE framework for advanced manufacturing follows. This framework (outlined in figure 2) emphasizes 4 key components: (i) *role of information models, (ii) virtual environments and (iii) physical assembly resources which are linked through (iv) information exchange frameworks and cyber infrastructure.* Together, these components in this ICE framework facilitate distributed enterprise partners operating as a Virtual Enterprise (VE) to respond to emerging micro assembly needs. When a set of requirements to assemble a set of micro devices is provided by a customer (through the Internet), the ICE framework seeks to facilitate this accomplishment using these collaborative resources (figure 2). An overview of these components follows. In our framework, users (through a user interface), provide the information about a target micro device to be assembled.

Information Models: An array of information models (for various process contexts and needs) can capture the functional dependencies and temporal precedence constraints (for various needs such as formulating the collaboration among partners, for mapping the process steps within micro assembly, etc.). These models can also be used to propel manufacturing level simulations as they capture the sequence of events as well as identify driving inputs (from collaborators or partners), enterprise or process constraints, performing mechanisms (responsible for assigned tasks) and WIP or final outcomes. These models were built for the domain of micro assembly using the engineering Enterprise Modeling Language (eEML); they were used to design the collaborative environments (the virtual environments) as well as lay the foundation for the information exchange approaches among the distributed partners and resources.

Virtual Reality Based Simulation Environments: These virtual reality based simulation environments were designed and developed to enable distributed teams of engineers to rapidly study assembly alternatives for varying part designs; they can be used to generate (propose), compare and evaluate assembly plans to assemble a target set of micro devices (figure 3). Subsequently, assembly path plans including micro gripping approaches for assembly were proposed and validated using virtual environments (figure 3). Semi immersive and fully immersive VR environments allow teams of users to collaborate cross-functionally through Internet or other cyber infrastructure (eg. Extranets). The simulation of the assembly activities were linked using cloud computing technologies as part of a Future Internet / Next Generation Initiatives involving the GENI test bed and the US Ignite initiative.

Physical MDA Resources: To be able to respond to diverse micro designs, a diverse range of physical micro assembly resources are needed to complete a target assembly. These resources include micro assembly grippers, sensors, fixtures and work cells, which will be needed to complete various target assembly tasks (as an implementation of selected assembly alternatives studied using the VR environment). In a virtual enterprise context, these resources are distributed but linked through cyber infrastructure. In our demonstration, we used two different work cells to assemble a variety of millimeter and micron sized parts (figure 3 a and 3 b provide views of the virtual work cell and the physical work cell for micro assembly activities).

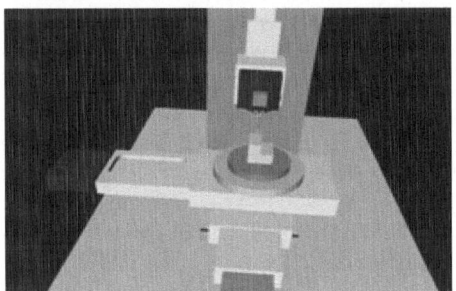 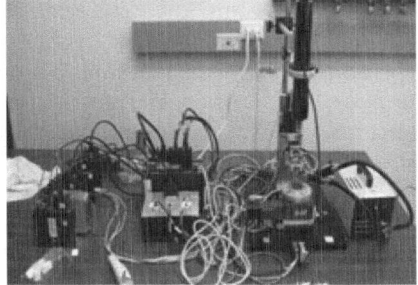

Fig. 3. (a) A Virtual Assembly environment (b) A Physical micro assembly work cell

Advanced Cyber Infrastructure: This is needed to support the information exchange (or the "exchange of information" identified in figure 2 in the ICE framework) among the cyber physical resources to accomplish various planning, simulation based analysis and physical assembly tasks using the distributed resources. Recently, the use of cloud based technologies is becoming widespread.

In our pilot demonstration aimed at demonstrating the feasibility of such an ICE framework, we used distributed resources and modules for generating the assembly plan, 3D path plan, conducting the simulation of target assembly/path plans, and finally completing physical assembly of target parts. These resources were linked using the next generation (GENI) network using a cloud computing approach. An array of micro devices were assembled using this ICE framework (one of them is shown in figure 5). A part of this demonstration was accomplished as part of the US Ignite initiative. A brief discussion of both these initiatives follows.

The GENI (www.geni.net) initiative is an NSF initiative in the US which focuses on the design of the next generation of Internets including the deployment of software designed networks (SDN) and cloud based technologies (as part of a long term Future Internet initiative). In the context of advanced manufacturing (such as micro assembly), such networks will enable distributed VE partners to exchange high bandwidth graphic rich data (such as the simulation of assembly alternatives, design of process layouts, analysis of potential assembly problems as well as monitoring the physical accomplishment of target assembly plans). In the European Union (EU) and Japan (as well as other countries), similar initiatives have also been initiated; in the EU, the Future Internet Research and Experimentation Initative (FIRE) is investigating and experimentally validating highly innovative ideas for new networking and service paradigms (http://cordis.europa.eu/fp7/ict/fire/).

Another important initiative is the US Ignite (http://us-ignite.org/) which seeks to foster the creation of next-generation Internet applications that provide transformative public benefit using ultrafast high gigabit networks. Advanced Manufacturing is one of the six national priority areas (the other five are Health, Public Safety, Education & Workforce, Energy, and Transportation). Both these initiatives herald the emergence of the next generation computing frameworks which in turn have set in motion the next Information Centric revolution in Advanced Manufacturing (and Engineering) that is expected to impact global practises in a phenomenal manner.

The simulation of target micro devices using Virtual Assembly environments (figure 6) has also been posted at this Youtube site: https://www.youtube.com/watch?v=pwxXZqn7R34. The related physical assembly activities can be found at this web location (https://www.youtube.com/watch?v=OC0WpoeA7Ck). The general approach to exchange information and sharing of resources from the advanced manufacturing domain discussed in this paper was also used to demonstrate feasibility of linking educational resources and learning modules among K-12 and engineering students. One of these demonstrations involved children with autism interacting with their teacher at another location using haptic device (which enabled them to "feel" the objects they touched virtually inside a computer); this collaborative framework was used to teach science and math concepts to autistic students in grades 1 and 2 from a local school (Sangre Ridge Elementary) in Stillwater, Oklahoma; this was part of a project aimed at supporting learning activities for children with autism; a part of these activities have been recorded and can be found at https://www.youtube.com/watch?v=BAfd2ax6tk4. Another recording of interactions among middle school students (from Stillwater Middle School) can be found at http://youtu.be/ EIlNqpCAIu4. The important conclusion from the latter demonstrations involves recognizing the potential of using such next generation frameworks for supporting educational activities when it involves sharing of distributed resources as well as supporting interaction between teachers and children at different locations.

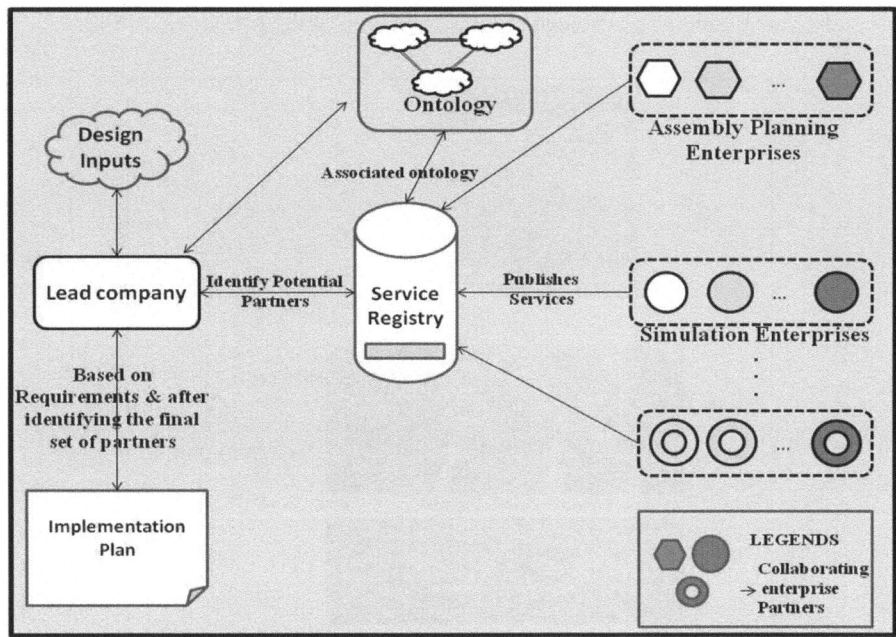

Fig. 4. A Semantic Test Bed to demonstrate collaboration among distributed VE partners

In a different demonstration, a Semantic Test Bed was created to demonstrate an approach aimed at addressing semantic interoperability. In this Test Bed, our emphasis was to highlight an innovative approach which would allow VE partners to collaborate based on the user requirements. This approach can be described using figure 4, which outlines the main interactions among the distributed VE partners and their resources. There are 3 phases:

(i) Understanding user design requirements: Based on this understanding, an enterprise level plan is developed which identifies the main engineering tasks to be completed to assemble the target micro design (this can range from assembly planning path planning, analysis of assembly alternatives, simulation of assembly alternatives and finally physical assembly)

(ii) Identification of VE partners: This phase involves selecting enterprise partners based on capabilities of VE partners and enterprise level plan. If there are more than one enterprise who can perform a given task in the enterprise plan, then based on their performance capabilities, cost of involvement and history of prior activities, the most feasible partner is identified. Each enterprise interested in being of a VE needs to publish their services in a services directory (see figure 4).

Ontology of micro assembly activities were created using the OWL (Web Ontology Language); the services of each potential enterprise partner were described using OWL-S (where S is for services)

(iii) Implementation of enterprise plan: In this last phase, the enterprise manager module initiates completion of enterprise level plan including assembly plan development, simulation and finally physical assembly. This is executed by interacting with the distributed modules and tools at the partner enterprises.

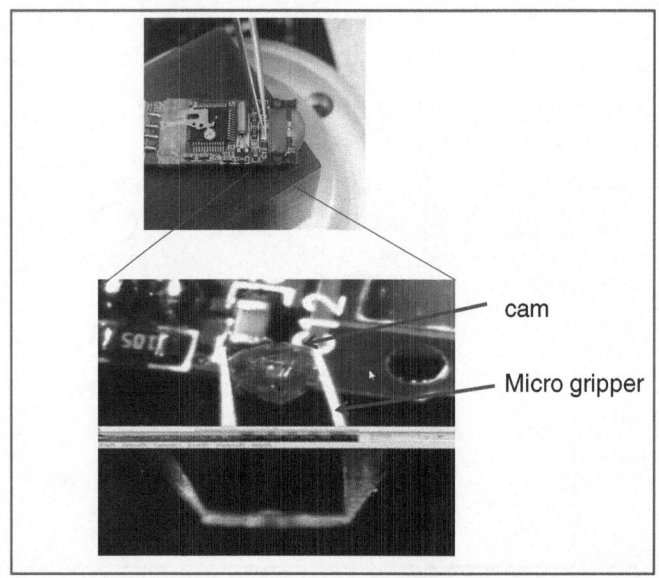

Fig. 5. Two views of a micro assembly process in progress

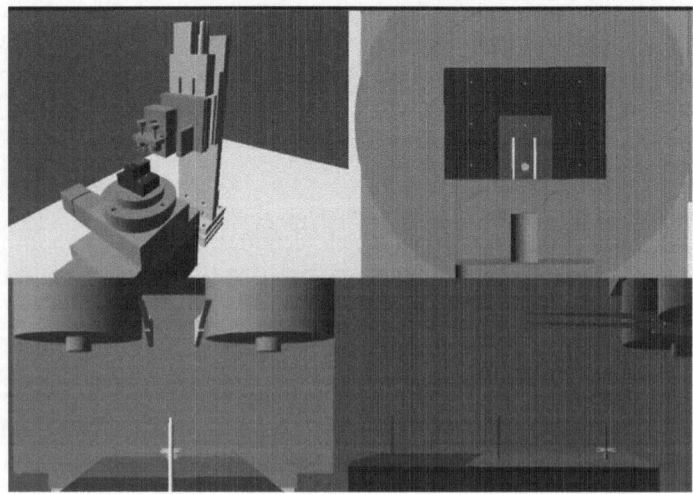

Fig. 6. Views of a virtual environment to study micro assembly alternatives

3   Conclusion

This paper outlined an Information Centric Engineering (ICE) to support collaborations among distributed partners in manufacturing contexts. An overview of the 3 core facets of ICE (which emphasized the role of information models, virtual prototyping frameworks and information exchange approaches) was provided. This ICE framework was used as basis to develop a more comprehensive framework for the emerging domain of micro assembly. The collaborative framework emphasized the 3 facets of ICE which was used to support collaboration among enterprise partners (and their software and physical resources) using advanced cyber infrastructure (to support the information exchange necessary for collaboration). In most situations, micro devices assembly (MDA) resources are not located at a single organization; resources will be distributed among different organizations across different locations. For this reason, an ICE framework is needed to support the collaborative and rapid assembly of micro devices.

Our ICE framework enabled the sharing of engineering resources using next generation Internet technologies (as part of pilot demonstrations involving use of GENI frameworks and as part of the US Ignite initiative); a discussion of an innovative semantic framework to support collaboration among potential partner enterprises was also provided; this demonstration focused also on the domain of micro assembly and included enterprise planning, resources discovery, selection of identified partner for relevant services and finally execution of the enterprise plan which ended in the assembly of target micro part designs. Such ICE frameworks facilitate the realization of global virtual enterprises where collaboration between with distributed partners is possible especially when responding quickly to changing customer requirements.

Acknowledgment. Funding for this research was obtained through grants from the National Science Foundation (NSF Grant 0965153, 1256431, 1257803), Sandia National Laboratories, Los Alamos National Lab, the Mozilla Foundation, and Oklahoma State University (as part of the Interdisciplinary Planning Grants program, the Office of the Provost). Their assistance is gratefully acknowledged.

References

[1] Alex, J., Vikramaditya, B., Nelson, J.B.: A Virtual Reality Teleoperator Interface for Assembly of Hybrid MEMS Prototypes. In: ASME Design Engineering Technical Conference (1998)

[2] Boettner, Scott, S., Cecil, J., Jiao, Y.: An Advanced Collaborative Framework for Micro Assembly. In: IEEE Conference on Automation Science and Engineering, pp. 806–811 (2007)

[3] Cecil, J., Kanchanapiboon, A.: Virtual Engineering Approaches in Product and Process Design. International Journal of Advance Manufacturing and Technology 31, 846–856 (2007)

[4] Cecil, J., Powell, D., Gobinath, N.: Micro devices assembly using Virtual environments. Springer Journal of Intelligent Manufacturing 18, 361–369 (2007)

[5] Cecil, J., Gobinath, N.: A Cyber Physical Test Bed for Collaborative Micro Assembly Engineering. In: 2010 International Symposium on IEEE Collaborative Technologies and Systems (CTS), pp. 430–439 (2010)

[6] Chang, R.J., Lin, C.Y., Lin, P.S.: Visual-Based Automation of Peg-in-Hole Microassembly Process. ASME Journal of Manufacturing Science and Engineering 133, 1–12 (2011)

[7] Gobinath, N., Cecil, J.: Development of a Virtual and Physical work cell to assemble micro-devices. In: International Conference on Flexible Automation and Intelligent Manufacturing, vol. 21, pp. 431–441 (2005)

[8] Ferreira, A., Cassier, C., Hirai, S.: Automatic Microassembly System Assisted by Vision Servoing and Virtual Reality. IEEE/ASME Transactions on Mechatronics 9 (2004)

[9] Rabenorosoa, K., Clevy, C., Lutz, P., Bargiel, S., Gorecki, C.: A Micro-Assembly Station used for 3D Reconfigurable Hybrid MOEMS Assembly. In: Proceedings of IEEE International Symposium on Assembly and Manufacturing, pp. 17–20 (2009)

[10] Paolo, V.P.: Interactive Virtual Assembling in Augmented Reality. International Journal of Interactive Design Manufacturing 3, 109–119 (2009)

[11] Wason, D.J., Wen, T.J., Choi, Y., Gorman, J.J., Dagalakis, G.N.: Vision Guided Multi-Probe Assembly of 3D Microstructures. In: IEEE International Conference on Intelligent Robots and Systems, pp. 5603–5609 (2010)

[12] Cecil, J. (ed.): Virtual Engineering, New Jersey, Viii (preface). Momentum Press,

[13] Calyam, P., Sridharan, M., Xu, Y., Zhu, K., Berryman, A., Patali, R., Venkataraman, A.: Enabling Performance Intelligence for Application Adaptation in the Future Internet. Journal of Communications and Networks (JCN) (2011)

A Cross-Scale Models Interoperability Problem: The Plate-Form(E)3 Project Case Study

Short Paper

Alexis Aubry[1,2], Jean Noël[3], Daniel Rahon[4], and Hervé Panetto[1,2]

[1] Université de Lorraine, CRAN, UMR 7039, Campus Sciences, BP 70239,
Vandœuvre-lès-Nancy Cedex, 54506, France
[2] CNRS, CRAN, UMR 7039, France
{alexis.aubry,herve.panetto}@univ-lorraine.fr
[3] CETIAT, 25 Avenue des arts, BP 52042, 69603 Villeurbanne, France
jean.noel@cetiat.fr
[4] IFP Energies nouvelles, 1 & 4 avenue de Bois-Préau, 92852 Rueil-Malmaison, France
daniel.rahon@ifpen.fr

Abstract. This paper presents the Plate-Form(E)3 project which is funded by the French National Research Agency (ANR) as a case study highlighting cross-scale models interoperability problems. This project involves public and private French organisations. It deals with the specification of a software platform for computing and optimising the energetic and environmental efficiency for industries and territories. Its aim is the integration of specialised tools for analysing sustainability of any processes. One important topic addressed by this project concerns the interoperability issues when interconnecting these tools (for modelling, simulating, and optimising) into the platform at different modelling scales (territory/plant/process/component). This paper proposes to highlight the interoperability issues led by the heterogeneity of the related tools in the energetic and environmental efficiency context.

Keywords: interoperability, energetic and environmental efficiency.

1 From Energy and Environmental Efficiency Needs to Cross-Scale Models Interoperability Needs

The current context of increasing scarcity of fossil fuels and the associated price volatility strongly encourage our society for energy saving. Although significant efforts have been made in the industrial sector since 1973, according to estimation from the French institute CEREN[1], the potential power saving could be up to 12 Mtoe[2] (about 23% of energy consumption in the industrial sector). These savings could be made on the following basis:

---

[1] CEREN, French Centre for Studies and Economic Research on energy.
[2] Mtoe = Million Tonnes of Oil Equivalent.

Y.T. Demey and H. Panetto (Eds.): OTM 2013 Workshops, LNCS 8186, pp. 57–61, 2013.
© Springer-Verlag Berlin Heidelberg 2013

- About 2/3 of the savings can be made on plants using local optimisation approach, using conventional or experimental technologies.
- The remaining 1/3 of the savings can be achieved by conducting cross-cutting actions, using technology for recovery and transport of residual energy.

The local optimisation approach (process/plant scale) is already extensively studied, while the global optimisation approach (territorial area) is not addressed in the literature. In fact, it does not exist any tool able to achieve a cross-scale optimization of energy and environmental efficiency. The Plate-Form(E)3 project proposes to address this problem.

2   The Plate-Form(E)3 Project

The ANR Plate-form(E)3[3] project: Digital Platform for computation and optimization of Energy and Environmental Efficiency at different scales for industry (component/process/plant/territory) must contribute to the optimization of energy and environmental efficiency of industry and territories. Plate-form(E)3 will be realized by a prototype for assessing the impact of new technologies on a large scale. This framework will propose the integration of any energy sources and sinks across the territory, seeking potential interconnections between industries (territory scale), to optimise process efficiency (plant/process scale) and to facilitate the optimal design of new technologies (component level).

This prototype will enable validating the concept through different scenarios that must be defined by end-users. We can cite as potential end-users of the platform industrials such as Lafarge, INEOS, Arcelor Mittal who want to reduce their energy and environmental impact.

The platform will interconnect some existing tools (open-source or proprietary) implementing different specialised methods, models and algorithms. The issue of interoperability is thus important.

3   Interoperation Problems and Scientific Questions

The tools that must be interconnected in Plate-Form(E)3 do not operate at the same scale, with the same business knowledge and on the same models but they must always be able to share information and models that they produce, ensuring the overall coherency of the whole. That means that these tools must be interoperable. [1] defines interoperability as the ability of a collection of communicating entities to (i) share specified information and (ii) operate on that information according to a shared operational semantics (iii) in order to achieve a specified purpose in a given context.

---

[3] http://www.agence-nationale-recherche.fr/en/anr-funded-project/?tx_lwmsuivibilan_pi2[CODE]=ANR-12-SEED-0002

The above context will be defined through three generic scenarios that must be realised within two classical interoperability levels (technical and conceptual) [2]. Some scientific questions then arise when intersecting those scenarios with the interoperability levels.

3.1   Generic Scenarios

In order to highlight the underlying problems in setting interoperation between the specialised tools for modelling physical systems and their optimisation, it is important to identify the generic scenarios that realize this interoperation. We have identified the following scenarios: cross-scale interoperation, cross-domain interoperation, cross-feature interoperation (see Fig. 1).

1. Cross-scale interoperation: the different scales concern the component (optimal design of new technologies), the process/plant (optimization of energy efficiency) and the territory (optimization of potential interconnections between industries). The tools that will potentially be connected with the platform will be used at these different scales, producing models that need to be exchanged compromising the overall performance.
2. Cross-domain interoperation: for modelling/simulating/optimising the physical systems through the platform, users use knowledge and domain-dependant tools that are specialised. Thus experts' knowledge covers broad areas of physics for modelling thermal, thermodynamics, chemistry and energetics processes. We must also add the experts' knowledge related to optimization.
3. Cross-feature interoperation: physical systems modelled in Plate-Form(E)3 will be simulated and optimized through these models. Tools for modelling, simulation and optimization tools need to be interconnected.

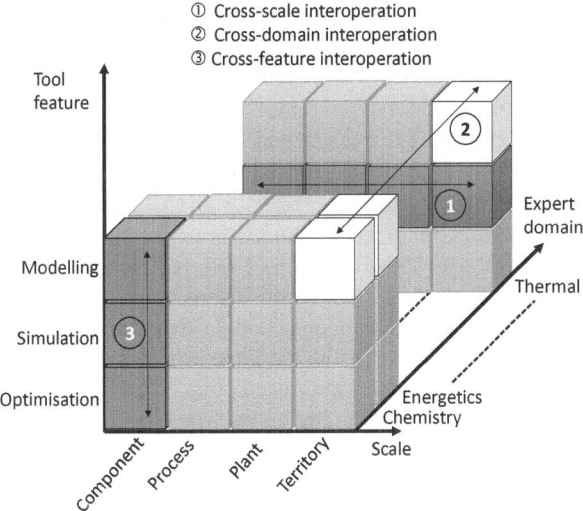

Fig. 1. Plate-Form(E)3 interoperation framework

3.2 Interoperability Levels

For making the previous scenarios effective, there exist some barriers (conceptual, technological and organisational) that define levels of interoperability to be studied. While organisational barriers are an issue mainly from governmental and privacy perspectives, the project will focus on technical and conceptual barriers defined in [2] as follows:

- Technical barriers are related to the incompatibility of information technologies (architecture & platforms, infrastructure...).
- Conceptual barriers are related to the semantic mismatches of information to be exchanged. These barriers concern the modelling at the high level of abstraction.

3.3 Scientific Questions and Discussion

For highlighting the scientific questions linked to the Plate-Form(E)3 project, we propose to intersect the different generic scenarios with the interoperability levels.

Technical interoperability problems appear in each scenario. Solving these technical barriers is now easier and partly achieved by standard techniques and implemented interfaces. We can cite, for instance, XML (eXtensible Mark-up Language) and linked applications: SOAP (Simple Object Access Protocol) and WSDL (Web Services Description Language). We must therefore assess whether the candidate tools for integration into Plate-Form(E)3 use existing standards (CAPE-OPEN[4], ...) or we must define such a standard. When connecting a new tool, we must be able to assess quickly its ability to interoperate with Plate-Form(E)3 at the technical level.

Conceptual interoperability problems concern:

- for the cross-scale interoperation scenario, the dynamics and the granularity of the used models that are not the same. Indeed, the models have not the same time scale when considering a territory or a component. Moreover, the different models represent heterogeneous aggregates of information depending of the scale of the modelled system (from territory to component). It is therefore necessary to formalize and finally assess the correlation between models outputs at a given scale and their use as inputs at another scale (with the same tool or not).
- for the cross-domain or cross-feature interoperation scenarios, the knowledge of several specific domains that are managed by the different tools to be connected through the platform. These heterogeneous knowledge produce semantically heterogeneous models that must be exchanged, stored, processed consistently with the purposes for which they have been built. Moreover, this raises the issue of the a priori evaluation of the ability to exchange ad-hoc models (related to a specific domain or a particular tool feature) without knowing in advance the tools that will be connected to the platform to process these models (and thus the business semantics of the related models that are shared through the platform).

---

[4] http://www.colan.org

We propose in Table 1 below, a synthesis of the highlighted scientific questions that raised from the scenarios.

Table 1. Table Interoperation Scenario/Interoperability levels

Interoperability level / Interoperation scenario	Technical level	Conceptual level
Cross-scale interoperation	Representation of knowledge	Assesment of the dynamics and granularity compatibility of models
Cross-domain interoperation		A priori evaluation of semantic interoperability between models
Cross-feature interoperation		

Acknowledgement. This work has been partially funded by the program SEED 2012 from the French National Agency for Research ANR in the frame of the Plate-Form(E)3 project.

References

1. Carney, D., Fisher, D., Place, P.: Topics in Interoperability: System-of-Systems Evolution. Technical Note, University of Pittsburgh, Software Engineering Institute (2005)
2. INTEROP, Enterprise Interoperability-Framework and knowledge corpus - Final report, INTEROP NoE, FP6 – Contract n° 508011, Deliverable DI.3 (May 21, 2007)

Integrated Management of Automotive Product Heterogeneous Data: Application Case Study

Massimo D'Auria[1], Marialuisa Sanseverino[2], Filippo Cappadona[3],
and Roberto d'Ippolito[1]

[1] Noesis Solutions N.V., Gaston Geenslaan 11, B4 – B3001 Leuven, Belgium
{massimo.dauria,roberto.dippolito}@noesissolutions.com
[2] Pininfarina S.p.A., Via Nazionale, 30, Cambiano, Italy
f.cappadona@pininfarina.it
[3] Screen 99, Largo Re Umberto 104, Torino, Italy
marialuisa.sanseverino@gmail.com

Abstract. The product development process (PDP) in innovative companies is becoming more and more complex, encompassing many diverse activities, and involving a big number of actors, spread across different professions, teams and organizations. One of the major problems is that development activities usually depend on many different inputs and influencing factors, and that the information that is needed in order to make the best possible decisions is either not documented or embodied in data that is spread over many different IT-systems. In this context a suitable knowledge management approach is required that must ensure the integration and availability of required information along with the federation and interoperability of the different Enterprise tools.

This paper presents a description of an industrial use case application where the innovative methodology researched in the iProd project is adopted. This methodology aims at improving the efficiency and quality of the Product Development Process (PDP) by means of a software ontological framework. The methodology is first briefly outlined and then its application is illustrated with an automotive application case developed together with Pininfarina. This case demonstrates how it is possible to capture and reuse the knowledge and design rationale of the PDP.

Keywords: Enterprise integration, Enterprise interoperability, PDP, ontologies.

1 Introduction

A reduction of the development time for new products and an improvement in productivity and quality together with a reduction of costs are key objectives for company competitiveness. These objectives are achieved through three fundamental elements: corporate strategy, processes optimization and computer support technologies.

The nature of the Product Development Process (PDP) within modern organizations has altered dramatically over the past decade as the products themselves became more complex. The engineering of such complex products as automobiles, airplanes and appliances of any type is highly knowledge-intensive. Vast amounts of very

Y.T. Demey and H. Panetto (Eds.): OTM 2013 Workshops, LNCS 8186, pp. 62–69, 2013.

different kinds of information and knowledge have to be managed in a precise way. The product and process complexity in these industries is steadily increasing. The life cycles tend to get shorter, and the time and cost pressure are increasing. The Product Development Process (PDP) is therefore becoming more and more distributed and networked – not just within an enterprise but even between professions and teams along supply and design chains in a globalized economy [3].

In this context data and knowledge management technologies are of fundamental importance for industrial innovation, provided they are integrated in the enterprise processes, in the organizational structure, and can be flexibly adapted to company evolution. Present ICT solutions address parts of product development separately, but an integrated approach that includes data and services required for the whole PDP does not yet exist.

This paper presents a real case study in the field of automotive where the innovative solution researched in the iProd project [1] is adopted. iProd aims at improving efficiency and quality of the PDP of innovative products in the aerospace, automotive and home appliances industries by developing a flexible and service oriented ontology-based software framework. This framework, reasoning and operating on a well-structured knowledge, will be the backbone of the computer systems associated with current and new product development processes.

2   iProd Methodology

The iProd project has the objective to develop a software platform which addresses the high amount of heterogeneous information involved in all activities associated with current and new product development processes, from the definition of subjective goals from customer viewpoint (and subsequent description in the form of technical goals), to the drawing of a Test Plan (physical and virtual) and its monitoring, to final approval and product validation. This Process involves most company departments, such as Marketing, Quality, Experimentation & Design, Experimental Constructions, Technologies and Suppliers. Control of such a wide-ranging process, however, necessarily requires the introduction of computing tools able to acquire, analyze and structure large, rapidly evolving and often conflicting amount of information, with the objective to rapidly adapt the flow of knowledge to the operational flow of the activities, keeping employees and stakeholders up-to-date with the progress of the work, helping in performing complex tasks and taking decisions. More in detail, iProd addresses the activities related to requirement definition(part in product conception and part in user needs), requirements specification, test planning and optimization, system integration testing and acceptance testing (product delivery).

According to the main concepts of systems engineering and to ISO15288 standard (which establishes a common framework for describing the life cycle of "systems created by human") the main sub-processes managed by the iProd framework are:

- System requirements (customer view)
- Requirement Analysis (technical view)
- Verification Plan Management
- Virtual & Physical verification execution
- System Validation

More details on the methodology implemented in iProd can be found at [2]. To achieve these goals, iProd applies knowledge management (KM), reasoning engine (RE) and process integration and automation technologies.

The heart of the iProd framework is in its ontological foundations: in contrast to typical database driven software tools, iProd is based on a set of ontologies that map design engineering domains like product structure, requirements, processes, design rationales, optimization and creates links between them. The resulting consistent, domain independent, set of ontologies is complemented by a set of domain specific ontologies that capture the specific characteristics of the domains of application (like automotive or aerospace). This ontological framework and its design approaches are not in the scope of this paper, but more details can be found in [7, 8]. Their main goal is to capture the knowledge related to the PDP and reuse it as much as possible.

3   Application to the Automotive Context: Pininfarina Case Study

Being iProd focused on capturing, reusing and operationalizing the knowledge related to the product development process, the application context selected for the present paper puts its attention first to the PDP of one of the major European industrial markets: automotive. iProd can be generally applied to all type of markets that can formalize their PDP, including (but not limited to) aerospace, home appliances, electronics, embedded systems and services.

The PDP in automotive industry is affected by a close collaboration of OEM(s), tier 1 to n-suppliers, and engineering service providers with many interfaces within the development networks, not only between the different companies but also between the diverse stakeholders within the different PDP steps, from product design via prototyping, testing, production ramp-up to production. The main PDP steps are separated by special milestones, so-called Stage Gates [4] or Quality Gates (with a stronger risk management approach) [5]. The same milestones must be passed in each development project, requiring a set of criteria that must all be fulfilled for successfully passing to the next step. The automotive PDP is strongly focused on specifications that are based on functional requirements that can be experienced by customers. The required criteria at each gate are thus often derived from these functional requirements. The automotive PDP has strong emphasis on keeping the functional requirements consistent and valid for testing, particularly when they are transferred to technical specifications for components and modules.

During the development of a car, huge amounts of data are handled. The recent Mercedes-Benz C-class has more than 2 Terabytes of product data [6]. The complexity of the PDP is largely reflected by the amount and distribution of different IT systems used all across the development network, but these tools are frequently not fitting together, using different data sources and file formats, resulting in fragmented process chains with island-like software systems and discontinuous information flows. In summary, the main deficiencies that can be identified in the automotive PDP are:

- Communications among the supply chain (OEM, TIER 1, 2 and 3)
- Complexity of the design and development methodologies
- The use of experimentation in the PDP

In this context iProd provides a solution that allows an integrated management of this heterogeneous data (as explained in section 2). This approach has been applied to the PDP of the italian leading design and engineering company Pininfarina.

The use case presented in this paper is focused on the design and optimization of a car door structure. For the sake of simplicity (and data confidentiality), this use case is not covering the entire PDP, but only part of it and only the higher level details. Doors are complex structures that contain just about everything that a car as a whole contains except for power train elements. Customers directly interact with car doors and they are aware of their characteristics called "dimensions" by Pininfarina, or called "attributes" by Ford.

The door that has been taken into consideration as a use case for the iProd project refers to the NIDO concept car (Fig. 1) which was first presented to the public in September 2004 at the Paris Motor-show.

Fig. 1. Pininfarina "NIDO" (Paris 2004)

The core business process that Pininfarina uses to develop and take products to market is called "Shape". This process is used from styling through design development and production projects (in Pininfarina or at the OEM) and combinations of these areas. All Pininfarina projects use the same "stage-gate" approach: it is so simpler for a Core team to understand what to focus on as a project progresses. Also, "stage-gate" makes it possible to standardized and simplify the project review process though the use of gate reviews at which all areas of the project can be assessed. The process of Shape is showed in Fig. 2 and it is divided into six phases, each phase is called Stage that is divided into different sub-activities.

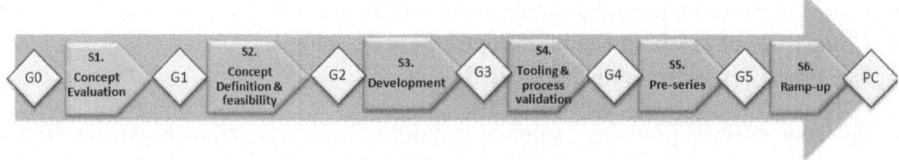

Fig. 2. Pininfarina "Shape" PDP diagram

iProd covers essentially the phases S1-S4 and is able to capture all the knowledge related to product structure, requirements, competitors management, tests planning and verification as shown in Fig. 3. However, for the present case, focus will be put only on steps S3 and S4 for the sake of simplicity. In order to apply the iProd methodology, a number of steps are needed to capture process and product knowledge associated with the car door. These steps require the acquisition of the following knowledge As such, a number of items need to be considered:

- The performance tree, which represents a hierarchical decomposition of the requirements for the new product. The first three levels of the tree define the performance requirements that have been further detailed in technical specifications
- The list of requirements, which is derived from market analysis, voice of customer, customer needs, state and safety regulations and deficiencies in earlier series of the product.
- A subjective target value, which ranges between 1 and 10 and is adopted to measure the performance requirements and also for making an analysis of the competitors.
- Technical specifications, which are engineering parameters that have to be specified in order to satisfy a particular performance. For each technical specification one or more tests can be associated that enable to verify the achievement of the specified target.

For all of them, specific ontologies have been developed and illustrated in [7]. As shown in Fig. 3, the correlation between the requirements and the different subsystems impacted is captured by creating nodes in a correlation matrix. Each node can be associated with a set of tests called Performance Drivers and related target engineering values that if satisfied allow to deliberate the subsystems of the product. Once the list of requirements and tests is completed iProd provide an initial work breakdown that can be further elaborated by the users to create a first plan of the task assigning timing schedule and responsibilities to the activities involved in the product development process.

An optimized task planning is then computed and suggested in real time by iProd to the designer to support them in making the best decisions possible on the base of the current situation of the on-going activities. Strategic key performance indicators are indeed available to monitor the evolution of the plan. This platform enables the engineers to address also the critical phases of the PDP when redesign loop are necessary due to test failures or significant delays in the execution of the tasks.

Performance Tree	Subjective T.S Competitor_1	Competitor_2	New project	Objective T.S. PTS Target	Test code	(SS) - FRONT LEFT DOOR INNER PANEL	(SS) - FRONT LEFT DOOR EXT. SKIN	(SS) - ACOUSTIC PANEL	(S) - DOOR HINGE	(S) - BOLT M8X30	(SS) - INTERIOR DOOR HANDLE	(SS) - EXTERIOR DOOR HANDLE	(S) - DOOR CATCHER
[TLR1] - ERGONOMICS													
[TLR2] - EXTERIOR ERGONOMICS													
[TLR3] - FRONT DOOR - OPENING/CLOSING	7	8	9										
[PTS] - opening load				35N	7N8087				X			X	X
[PTS] - handle dimensions				200 x 30 x 25 mm	2P1							X	
[PTS] - handle distance from the ground				10Nm	3P1							X	
[PTS] - available hand space				...	4P1							X	
[PTS] - interior Sag test				...	5	X							
[PTS] - feed-back of the opening pressure				300N	7N8087				X			X	X
[PTS] - opening angles in different opening position				...	9D				X				
[PTS] - opening angles in different closing position				...	10D				X				
[TLR3] - FRONT ACCESSIBILITY	6	8	8										
[PTS] -				...									
[PTS] -				...									
[TLR3] - ERGONOMIC/FUNCTIONALITY OF DOOR OPENING DEVICES	8	8	8										
[PTS] -				...									
[PTS] -				...									
[TLR2] - INTERIOR ERGONOMICS													
[TLR3] - FRONT DOOR - OPENING/CLOSING	7	8	9										
[PTS] - Timing for up and down in glass operation													
[PTS] - handle dimensions				...	12D							X	
[PTS] - opening load				...	11D				X			X	
[PTS] - available hand space				...	13D							X	
[PTS] - feed-back of the closing operation				...	14D				X			X	
[TLR1] - VEHICLE BIW													
[TLR2] - FRONT LEFT DOOR BIW													
[TLR3] - FRONT LEFT DOOR BIW - OPENING/CLOSING													
[PTS] - Door YIELDING UNDER LOAD				15 mm	7N9312				X				
[PTS] - Door PERMANENT YIELDING				5 mm	7N9312				X				

Fig. 3. Correlation Matrix between Product structure and Requirements for Pininfarina use case

A typical virtual test performed in car door design and illustrated in this section is represented by the door sag test. This activity is positioned in Stage 3 "Development" of the Pininfarina "SHAPE" PDP when product engineers carry out engineering development activities and CAE experts carry out virtual and physical engineering validation. The objective of the analysis conducted is to predict the vertical sag behavior of the door assembly.

The complete virtual design process is described in Fig. 4 and involves four main simulation tasks: CAD model creation; meshing of the created CAD model; finite element analysis preparation and virtual test execution. These simulation tasks are performed by different tools and are integrated in a seamless way in a simulation workflow that allows automating the execution of this process.

In this specific process different versions of hinges have been designed and need to be tested on the virtual prototype of the door. The virtual test definition and its associated simulation workflow are shown in Fig. 4 and Fig. 5 (implemented by using Noesis Optimus). The simulation workflow is dynamically generated from knowledge base by means of reasoning on its ontologies [9].

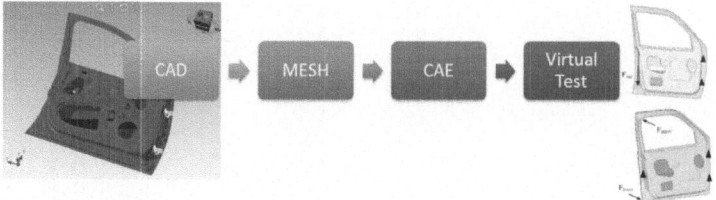

Fig. 4. Virtual design process of a new car door in Pininfarina

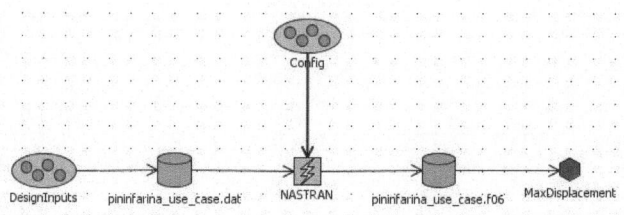

Fig. 5. Simulation workflow that performs the virtual door sag test in Pininfarina case study

The main result achieved by the application of the iProd approach for this use case can be quantified in terms of:

- Reduction of the number of physical tests by accessing, relating and comparing the physical and virtual tests and their historical results by means of the Correlation Matrix and on this basis replacing a physical test by a virtual test if repeated historical comparisons of their results demonstrates their equivalence
- Reduction of test re-planning time and corresponding cost by replacing current internal meetings procedures for test result evaluation and test activities rescheduling by automatic identification of required new tests and real-time rescheduling
- Reduction of time for project set-up, project status review and assessment and project reset-up after test verification failure by re-using knowledge by means of the Correlation Matrix
- Reduction of the time and costs of test result management (knowledge reuse and feedback) by giving feedback to the designer the test results and by reusing test knowledge for subsequent projects

All these results constitute benefits that produce an increase of efficiency and product quality with a reduction of time to market.

4 Conclusion

In this paper an industrial application case from the automotive supplier Pininfarina has been presented, where the innovative methodology proposed in the EC 7th Framework joint research project iProd have been adopted. First an introduction on the product development process is given and then the iProd solution able to address the complexity, semantic diversity and richness of content PDP is described.

A detailed description of the application case related to the development of a new car door was provided. In that a proof-of-concept of the methodology was developed and the potential benefits that iProd may provide in the product development process was shown: drastic reduction of product development costs by means of an optimized testing process with a higher and more intelligent use and integration of virtual testing models; support for knowledge and competencies extraction, structuring, reusing and sharing also with suppliers; improved focus of new product development with a fast and structured management of competitor and market analysis data and possibility to make more reliable decisions by exploiting structured indicators along product development activities.

Acknowledgement. The research leading to these results has been supported by the iProd collaborative research project, which has received funding from the European Community's Seventh Framework Programme (FP7/2007-2013) under grant agreement number 257657. The authors are solely responsible for its content. It does not represent the opinion of the European Community and the Community is not responsible for any use that might be made of the information contained therein.

References

1. http://www.iprod-project.eu/
2. http://www.iprod-project.eu/2-1-common-methodology-for-pdp-analysis
3. Payne, K.H., Deasley, P.J.: Cultural issues is aerospace engineering design teams. Design management Process and Information Issues. In: Proceedings of the International Conference on Engineering Design, pp. 417–424 (2001)
4. Cooper, R.G.: Product leadership - Creating and launching superior new products. Perseus Books, Cambridge (2002)
5. Spath, D., Scharer, M., Nesges, D.: Quality Gate Concept with integrated Risk Management. Production Engineering 10(1), 73–76 (2003)
6. Virtuelle Entwicklung am Beispiel der C-Klasse, http://www.heise.de/autos/artikel/Virtuelle-Entwicklung-am-Beispiel-der-C-Klasse-792668.html (last visit October 4, 2009)
7. Woll, R., Geißler, C., Hakya, H.: Modular Ontology Design For Semantic Data Integration. In: Proceedings of the 5th International Conference on Experiments/Process/System Modeling/Simulation/Optimization, 5th IC-EpsMsO, Athens, July 3-6 (2013)
8. Spasojevic, P., Sanseverino, M., d'Ippolito, R., Xirouchakis, P.: A General Model of The Product Development Process Correlated With The Architecture of A Semantic Software Support System. In: Proceedings of the 5th International Conference on Experiments/Process/System Modeling/Simulation/Optimization, 5th IC-EpsMsO, Athens, July 3-6 (2013)
9. D'Auria, M., d'Ippolito, R.: Process Integration and Design Optimization Ontologies for Next Generation Engineering. In: Proceedings of the 5th International Conference on Experiments/Process/System Modeling/Simulation/Optimization, 5th IC-EpsMsO, Athens, July 3-6 (2013)

iFeel_IM!: A Cyberspace System for Communication of Touch-Mediated Emotions

Dzmitry Tsetserukou[1], Alena Neviarouskaya[2], and Kazuhiko Terashima[3]

[1] EIIRIS, Toyohashi University of Technology
tsetserukou@eiiris.tut.ac.jp
[2] Department of Computer Science and Engineering, Toyohashi University of Technology
alena@kde.cs.tut.ac.jp
[3] Department of Mechanical Engineering, Toyohashi University of Technology,
Toyohashi, Japan
terasima@syscon.pse.tut.ac.jp

Abstract. The paper focuses on a cyberspace communication system iFeel_IM!. Driven by the motivation to enhance social interactivity and emotionally immersive experience of real-time messaging, we proposed the idea of reinforcing (intensifying) own feelings and reproducing (simulating) the emotions felt by the partner through specially designed system iFeel_IM!. Users can not only exchange messages but also emotionally and physically feel the presence of the communication partner (e.g., family member, friend, or beloved person). The paper will also describe a novel portable affective haptic system iTouch_IM!. The motivation behind the research is to provide the emotional immersive communication regardless the location. This system has a potential to bring a new level of immersion for mobile on-line communication.

Keywords: Affective haptics, affective computing, 3D world, emotional communication, haptic device, touch gestures.

1   Introduction

Touch communication is an essential part of our social life as it conveys our emotions and attitude toward people and helps with socialization. The physical touch is also very important to the health and development of infants and babies. It is considered that touch is the intensifier of emotion-related communication. It augments the emotional displays from other modalities [1].

Companies providing media for remote online communications place great importance on live communication and immersive technologies. Such internet services as Skype, Facebook, Twitter, Instagram let us keep in touch with friends in real time over multiple networks and devices. 3D virtual worlds (for example, Second Life and OpenSim) with embedded chat and IM bring rich communication experience.

Such systems encourage people to establish or strengthen interpersonal relationships, share ideas, gain new experiences, and feel genuine emotions during their VR adventures. However, conventional mediated systems usually:

Y.T. Demey and H. Panetto (Eds.): OTM 2013 Workshops, LNCS 8186, pp. 70–77, 2013.
© Springer-Verlag Berlin Heidelberg 2013

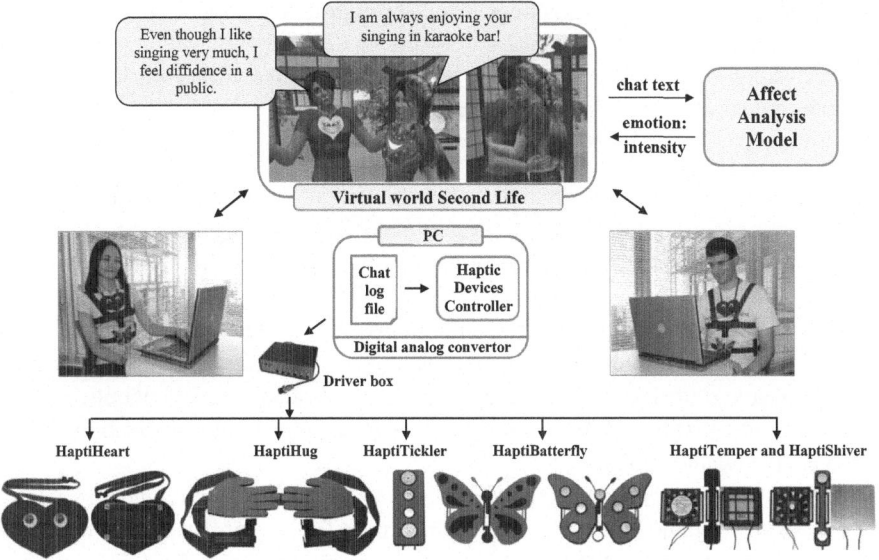

Fig. 1. Architecture of the real-time communication system iFeel_IM!

- support only simple textual cues such as emoticons,
- lack visual emotional signals such as facial expressions and gestures,
- support only manual control of the expressiveness avatars, and
- ignore such important social-communication channel as the sense of touch.

Tactile interfaces could let users enhance their emotional-communication abilities by adding a new dimension to mobile communications. When person stays in hospital for a long time, works abroad, or immigrates, they experience the emotional pressure because of not being able to share their experiences with family members, close friends, spouse as if they were conversing face-to-face. Several research groups have proposed to communicate messages with haptic effect (vibration pattern) to substitute the emoticons [2-4].

Here, we describe iFeel_IM!, a system that employs haptic devices and visual stimulation to convey and augment the emotions experienced during online conversations [5]. iFeel_IM! stands for Intelligent System for Feeling Enhancement Powered by Affect-Sensitive Instant Messenger.

2 Architecture of the System

Fig. 1 shows the structure of the affective haptic communication system.   iFeel_IM! stresses:

- automatic sensing of emotions conveyed through text messages (artificial intelligence),
- visualization of the detected emotions through avatars in a virtual world,
- enhancement of the user's affective state, and
- reproduction of social touch through haptic stimulation in the real world.

We use Second Life as the communication platform. With Second Life, users can flexibly create their online identities (avatars) and play various animations (for example, facial expressions and gestures) of avatars by typing special abbreviations in a chat window.

We implement control of the conversation through EmoHeart, a Second Life object attached to an avatar's chest. EmoHeart communicates with the Affect Analysis Model (AAM), a system for textual affect sensing [6]. It also senses symbolic cues or keywords in the text that indicate a hug and generates a hugging visualization (that is, it triggers the related animation).

The haptic-device controller analyzes the data in real time and generates control signals for the digital/analog converter, which then feeds control cues for the haptic devices to the driver box. On the basis of the transmitted signal, iFeel_IM! activates the user's corresponding haptic device.

3   The Affect Analysis Model

The AAM senses nine emotions conveyed through text: anger, disgust, fear, guilt, interest, joy, sadness, shame, and surprise. The affect recognition algorithm, which takes into account the specific style and evolving language of online conversation, consists of five main stages: (1) symbolic-cue analysis; (2) syntactical-structure analysis; (3) word-level analysis; (4) phrase-level analysis; and (5) sentence-level analysis.

The AAM is based on the compositionality principle. According to this principle, we determine the emotional meaning of a sentence by composing the pieces that correspond to lexical units or other linguistic constituent types, governed by the rules of aggregation, propagation, domination, neutralization, and intensification, at various grammatical levels.

Empirical testing showed promising results regarding the AAM's ability to accurately classify affective information. Employing the Connexor Machinese Syntax parser (www.connexor.eu/technology/machinese/machinesesyntax), the AAM achieves 81.5 percent accuracy.

4   EmoHeart

The EmoHeart object listens to its owner's messages and sends each message to the AAM's Web-based interface. After receiving the results (the dominant emotion and intensity), it visually reflects the sensed affective state through:

- animation of the avatar's facial expression,
- EmoHeart's texture (its expression, shape, and color, which indicate the type of emotion), and
- EmoHeart's size (indicating the emotion's strength—low, medium, or high).

Fig. 2 shows avatar facial expressions and EmoHeart textures.

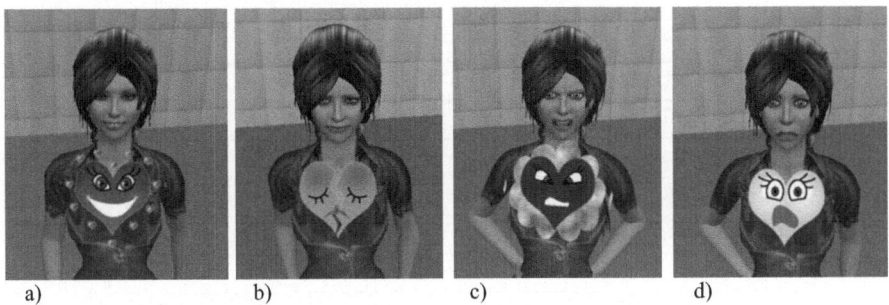

a)   b)   c)   d)

Fig. 2. Avatar facial expressions with the corresponding EmoHeart: (a) joy, (b) sadness, (c) anger, and (d) fear. EmoHeart's texture (its expression, shape, and color) indicates the type of emotion; its size indicates the emotion's strength

During the experiment, 89 Second Life users became owners of EmoHeart; 74 actually communicated using it. The AAM categorized 20 percent of the sentences as emotional and 80 percent as neutral. The most frequent emotion conveyed was joy (68.8 percent of all emotional sentences), followed by surprise (9.0 percent), sadness (8.8 percent), and interest (6.9 percent). We believe that this dominance of positivity is due to the nature and purpose of online communication media (to establish or strengthen interpersonal relationships).

5   Affective Haptic Devices

Physiological changes controlled by autonomous nervous system play the fundamental role in emotional experience [7]. According to the James-Lange theory, the conscious experience of emotion occurs after the cortex receives signals about physiological-state changes. That is, certain physiological changes precede feelings. The research suggests the existence of multiple, physiologically distinct positive emotions [8]. To support affective communication, iFeel_IM! incorporates three types of haptic devices:

- HaptiHeart, HaptiButterfly, HaptiTemper, HaptiShiver implicitly elicit emotion.
- HaptiTickler directly evokes emotion.
- HaptiHug uses social touch to influence mood and provide a sense of physical copresence.

Each emotion is characterized by a specific pattern of physiological changes. We selected four distinct emotions having strong physical features: anger, fear, sadness, and joy. Table 1 lists the emotions that each haptic device induces.

Table 1. The iFeel_IM! affective haptic devices with the emotions they stimulate

Device	Stimulated Emotion			
	Joy	Sadness	Anger	Fear
HaptiHeart	—	Yes	Yes	Yes
HaptiButterfly	Yes	—	—	—
HaptiShiver	—	—	—	Yes
HaptiTemper	Yes	—	Yes	Yes
HaptiTickler	Yes	—	—	—
HaptiHug*	Yes	—	—	—

HaptiHug also simulates social touch.

HaptiHug. Online interactions rely heavily on vision and hearing, so a substantial need exists for mediated social touch. Of the forms of physical contact, hugging is particularly emotionally charged; it conveys warmth, love, and affiliation [9], [10].

We developed HaptiHug to create a wearable haptic display generating forces similar to those of a human hugging another human [11]. Our approach's significance is that it integrates both active haptics (HaptiHug) and pseudohaptics (the animation) [12]. Thus, it produces a highly immersive experience.

HaptiHeart. Of the bodily organs, the heart plays a particularly important role in our emotional experience. Research has proven that false heart rate feedback can change our emotional state [13]. We developed HaptiHeart to produce heartbeat patterns corresponding to the emotion to be conveyed or elicited. A low-frequency prerecorded sound generates pressure on the human chest through speaker vibration. We exploit the fact that our heart naturally synchronizes with the heart of the person we're hugging or holding.

HaptiButterfly. We developed HaptiButterfly to evoke joy. It reproduces "butterflies in your stomach" (the fluttery or tickling feeling felt by people experiencing love) through arrays of vibration motors attached to the user's abdomen. We conducted an experiment to see which patterns of vibration motor activation produce the most pleasurable and natural sensations on the abdomen.

HaptiShiver and HaptiTemper. To boost fear, we developed HaptiShiver and HaptiTemper. HaptiShiver sends "shivers up and down your spine" through a row of vibration motors. HaptiTemper sends "chills up and down your spine" through both cold airflow from a fan and the cold side of a Peltier element.

HaptiTickler. The reflex explanation of our inability to tickle ourselves suggests that tickling requires the element of unpredictability or uncontrollability [14]. Research also shows that the social and emotional factors of ticklishness can affect the tickle response greatly. We developed HaptiTickler to directly evoke joy by tickling the user's ribs. It includes four vibration motors reproducing stimuli similar to human finger movements.

6   User Study

We selected six participants and conducted a preliminary user study to evaluate the effectiveness of emotion elicitation and hug reproduction. The results revealed that the devices successfully generated the corresponding emotion (see Table 2, in which 100 percent stands for six positive replies).

Table 2. Results of a six-user study evaluating the effectiveness of emotion elicitation and hug reproduction

Device	Percentage of participants experiencing the emotion.			
	Joy	Sadness	Anger	Fear
HaptiHeart	—	83.3	66.7	100
HaptiButterfly	83.3	—	—	—
HaptiTickler	100	—	—	—
HaptiHug*	100	—	—	—

100 percent of the HaptiHug users experienced social touch.

7   iTouch_IM!

iTouch_IM! is a novel portable communication system with direct haptic avatar-mediated communication (Fig. 3). A user wearing the affective haptic devises and holding the tablet computer interacts with an avatar by finger gestures. The avatar represents the user's communicating partner.

A special gesture language Haptish is designed to trigger the avatar's emotions. The examples of basic touch gestures are given in Fig. 4. The user can hug the avatar by touching the avatar's body on the surface of display with two fingers and performing the pinching. The heartbeat is generated through rapid touch of surface with fingertips. The time between consequent touches defines the frequency of the heartbeat. The tickling of avatar is driven by quick brushing of the surface with fingertips continuously engaging in the process. To make avatar feel afraid, the user touches the surface by five fingertips continuously. The wearable affective robot developed by user evokes the emotion shown by avatar through haptic stimuli. The idea behind the Haptish was not only to provide communication language but also to deliver the capability of designing the own emotional expressions to the user.

The animation of hugging and tickling is played on the screen. The effect of affective haptic feedback (force, tickling sensation) is augmented by visual stimuli. The user can also evoke avatar's emotions by drawing a finger on the screen. The shape, speed, and duration of strokes trigger a particular emotion of the avatar.

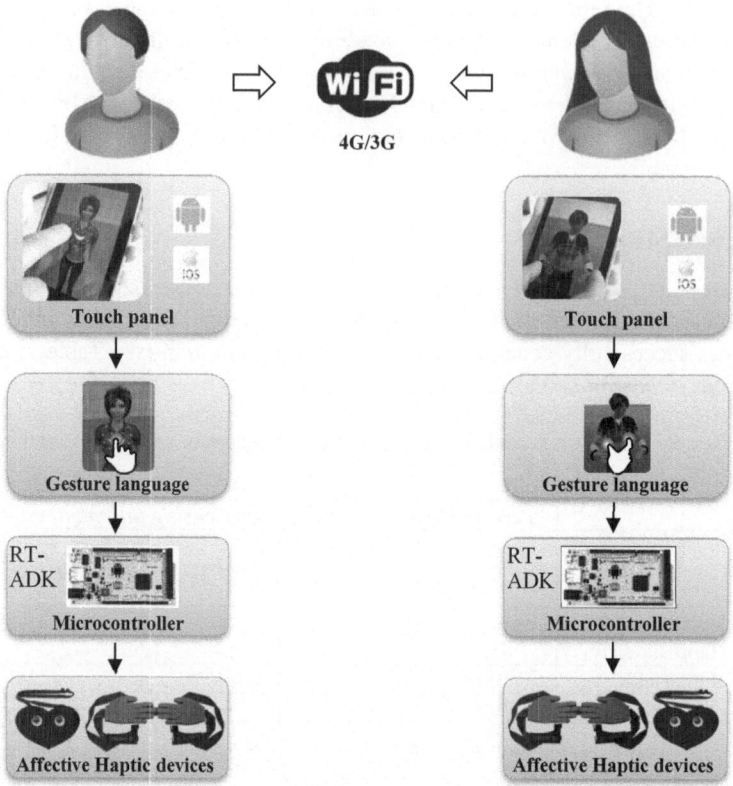

Fig. 3. iTouch_IM!: mobile affective haptic system for emotional communication

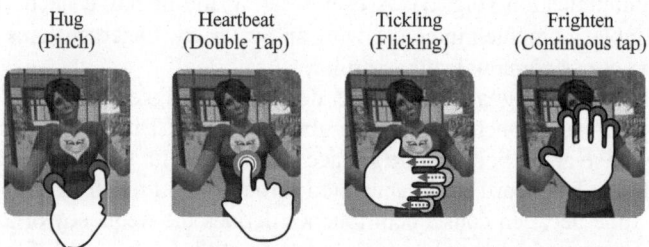

Fig. 4. Tactile gestures of communication language Haptish

8   Discussion and Conclusions

The combination of physical stimulation of emotions, remote touch, and visual stimuli increase immersion in the 3D environment and maintain the illusion of being there. We also presented a novel mobile affective haptic system iTouch_IM! that allows the emotional rich communication far and wide.

The examples of the possible applications of iFeel_IM! for future research include:

- treating depression and anxiety (problematic emotional states),
- supporting communication of person staying long time in hospital with severe disease,
- controlling and modulating moods on the basis of physiological signals,
- affective and collaborative games, and
- psychological testing.

We believe that iFeel_IM! and iTouch_IM! could greatly enhance communication in online virtual environments that facilitate social contact. They could also improve social life in terms of both interpersonal relationships and the character of community.

References

1. Knapp, M.L., Hall, J.A.: Nonverbal Communication in Human Interaction, 4th edn. Harcourt Brace College, Fort Worth TX (1997)
2. Rovers, A.F., Van Essen, H.A.: HIM: a Framework for Haptic Instant Messaging. In: ACM International Conference on Human Factors in Computing Systems, pp. 1313–1316. ACM Press, New York (2004)
3. Shin, H., Lee, J., Park, J., Kim, Y., Oh, H., Lee, T.: A Tactile Emotional Interface for Instant Messenger Chat. In: International Conference on Human-Computer Interaction, pp. 166–175. Springer Press, Heidelberg (2007)
4. Chang, A., O'Modhrain, S., Jacob, R., Gunther, E., Ishii, H.: ComTouch: Design of a Vibrotactile Communication Device. In: ACM Designing Interactive Systems Conference, pp. 312–320. ACM Press, New York (2002)
5. Tsetserukou, D., Neviarouskaya, A.: iFeel_IM!: Augmenting Emotions During Online Communication. IEEE Computer Graphics ad Applications 30(5), 72–80 (2010)
6. Neviarouskaya, A., Prendinger, H., Ishizuka, M.: Compositionality Principle in Recognition of Fine-Grained Emotions from Text. In: AAAI International Conference on Weblogs and Social Media, pp. 278–281. AAAI Press, Melno Park (2009)
7. Damasio, A.: The Feeling of What Happens: Body, Emotion and the Making of Consciousness. Vintage, London (2000)
8. Hertenstein, M., Keltner, D., App, B., Bulleit, A., Jakolka, A.R.: Touch Communicates Distinct Emotions. Emotion 6(3), 528–533 (2006)
9. Haans, A., Ijsselsteijn, W.I.: Mediated Social Touch: A Review of Current Research and Future Directions. Virtual Reality 9(2), 149–159 (2006)
10. Mueller, F.F., Vetere, F., Gibbs, M.R., Kjeldskov, J., Pedell, S., Howard, S.: Hug Over a Distance. In: ACM Conference on Human Factors in Computing Systems, pp. 1673–1676. ACM Press, New York (2005)
11. Tsetserukou, D.: HaptiHug: a Novel Haptic Display for Communication of Hug Over a Distance. In: Kappers, A.M.L., van Erp, J.B.F., Bergmann Tiest, W.M., van der Helm, F.C.T. (eds.) EuroHaptics 2010, Part I. LNCS, vol. 6191, pp. 340–347. Springer, Heidelberg (2010)
12. Lecuyer, A., Coquillart, S., Kheddar, A., Richard, P., Coiffet, P.: Pseudo-haptic feedback: Can Isometric Input Devices Simulate Force Feedback? In: IEEE Virtual Reality, pp. 403–408. IEEE Press, New York (2000)
13. Decaria, M.D., Proctor, S., Malloy, T.E.: The Effect of False Heart Rate Feedback on Self reports of Anxiety and on Actual Heart Rate. Behavior Research & Therapy 12, 251–253 (1974)
14. Harris, C.R., Christenfeld, N.: Can a machine tickle? Psychonomic Bulletin & Review 6(3), 504–510 (1999)

Interoperability Assessment Approaches for Enterprise and Public Administration

Short Paper

José Marcelo A.P. Cestari, Eduardo R. Loures, and Eduardo Alves Portela Santos

Pontifical Catholic University of Paraná, Curitiba, PR, Brazil
{jose.cestari,eduardo.loures,eduardo.portela}@pucpr.br

Abstract. The need for collaboration among organizations is a reality with which systems, managers and other stakeholders must deal. But this is not an exclusive concern of private administrations, once the increasing need for information exchange among government agencies, the supply of online services to citizens, and the cost reduction of public operations and transactions demand that the government organizations must be ready to provide an adequate interface to their users. This paper presents basic concepts of Enterprise Interoperability, some assessment models and eGovernment practices, models, definitions and concepts, providing an initial analysis of their basic properties and similarities, verifying some possible gaps that may exist.

Keywords: interoperability, assessment, eGovernment, maturity models.

1 Introduction

Nowadays, companies experience an economic and social period characterized by the need for integration and cooperation. Within this scenario, systems interoperability and networking stand for technologies that enable companies to communicate, cooperate and be aligned with their partners in an efficient and effective way. In this regard, the interoperability assessment plays an important role in diagnosing and positioning the enterprise according to its collaborative environment and goals. There are many methods related to interoperability assessment in literature [3].

A domain with current evidence is the public administration sector commonly referred to in literature as eGovernment. The term eGovernment (or its equivalents) is defined in [13] as the use of information and communication technologies to support the government business, such as providing or enhancing public services or managing internal government operations. The eGovernment interoperability refers to the ability of constituencies or public agencies to work together attempting to meet interoperability requirements. Such definitions infer the proximity to the Enterprise Interoperability (EI) concerns and barriers, aspects explored in [2].

In the recent scenario related to eGovernment interoperability, system designers have recognized that the entire interoperability problem consists of more than technical aspects [15]. The complexity presented in the eGovernment context requires

Y.T. Demey and H. Panetto (Eds.): OTM 2013 Workshops, LNCS 8186, pp. 78–85, 2013.

additional effort regarding legal, political and policy, and sociocultural issues. This scenario is particularly prominent in some emergent countries as Brazil, providing a broad field for research in the eGovernment interoperability domain.

The objective of this paper is to present, in addition to the basic concepts of Enterprise Interoperability and Enterprise Interoperability Assessment, some assessment models and an overview of the interoperability government models. Also, the paper aims to analyze their basic similarities and verify some possible gaps that may exist regarding specifically the government related models.

2 Enterprise Interoperability Concepts and Assessment Models

One of the most common definitions of interoperability is the ability of two or more systems or components to exchange information and to use the information that has been exchanged [11], being a mean to achieve integration [4].Enterprise Interoperability has basically three main dimensions: barriers, concerns and approaches. There are three categories of barriers [10]: (1) conceptual, related to the syntactic and semantic differences of information to be exchanged; (2) technological, related to the possible incompatibility of information technologies; (3) organizational, related to definition of responsibility, authority and other "human factors". Regarding the interoperability concerns, there are four areas [3]: (1) data; (2) services; (3) process and (4) business interoperability. The last interoperability dimension is related to the approach method, that is, how to put entities together in order to establish interoperations. According to [14], there are three basic ways: (1) integrated approach; (2) unified approach and (3) federated approach.

Interoperability involves two (or more) enterprises and, usually, these enterprises are different; with different systems, models or organizational structure. Enterprise Interoperability Assessment (EIA) provides a company with the opportunity to know its strengths, weaknesses and prioritize actions to improve its performance and maturity level assessment. Assessing interoperability implies the establishment of measures to evaluate the degree of interoperability between enterprises. One of the measures that can be used and defined is the maturity level that is (intended to be) achieved. There are several interoperability maturity models (IMMs) presented in the literature which describes and graduates the degree of interoperation potentiality [14].

The Levels of Information Systems Interoperability (LISI) [7] provides a reference frame for discussing system-to-system interoperability issues, focusing mainly on technical interoperability. The Organizational Interoperability Maturity Model (OIMM) [5] does not address technical, semantic or syntactical issues, but focuses on the business and organizational areas of concern. Just like OIMM, the Levels of Conceptual Interoperability Model (LCIM), proposed in [22], explores the idea that interoperability goes beyond technical implementations. Proposed by [1], Enterprise Interoperability Maturity Model (EIMM) focuses on the enterprise. Described in [10], Maturity Model for Enterprise Interoperability (MMEI) integrates aspects (such as the four concerns and the three barriers) which are usually dealt in a fragmented way by separated maturity models. All models mentioned have basically five maturity levels, as shown in Table 1.

Table 1. Examples of models, maturity levels and basic comments

Model	Level 1	Level 2	Level 3	Level 4	Level 5
LISI	Isolated. Manual gateway (CD, DVD, flash drives).	Connected. Homogeneous product exchange (e-mails, files).	Functional. Minimal functions. Heterogeneous product exchange.	Domain. Shared databases. Sophisticated collaboration.	Enterprise. Distributed information. Simultaneous interactions.
OIMM	Independent. Communication via personal contacts. Limited shared purpose.	Ad hoc. General guidelines. Basic electronic shared information.	Collaborative. General frameworks. Shared some knowledge.	Combined. Shared communications. Shared culture influenced by home organization.	Unified. Organization interoperating on a daily basis.
LCIM	System Specific Data. Isolated systems. Black box.	Documented Data. Black box with a documented interface.	Aligned Static Data. Black box with a standard interface.	Aligned Dynamic Data. White box. Common Ontology.	Harmonized Data. Common conceptual model. Beyond a white box.
EIMM	Performed. Some collaboration. Ad hoc.	Modeled. Defined collaboration. Repetition occurs.	Integrated. Process is formal and frequently used.	Interoperable. Dynamic. Adaptation to changes and evolution.	Optimizing. Integrating systems, models and technologies.
MMEI	Unprepared. No capability for interoperation.	Defined. Very limited. Simple electronic data exchange.	Aligned. Able to adhere to common formats or standards.	Organized. Interoperate with multiple heterogeneous partners.	Adapted. Dynamically adjustments. Shared domain ontologies.
GIMM	Independent. Interaction between independent organizations.	Ad hoc. Limited frameworks available. Ad hoc arrangements.	Collaborative. Frameworks in place. Shared goals.	Integrated. Shared systems and goals. Preparedness to interoperate with others.	Unified. Goals, value systems, structure and bases shared among organizations.
ISIMM	Manual. Systems not connected. Shared manually.	Ad hoc. Basic data sharing. Separated applications and databases.	Collaborative. Connections facilitated. Separated applications and bases.	Integrated. Data shared. Collaboration at an advanced domain level.	Unified. Data and application fully shared and distributed.

3   Government Interoperability Models

Although the models already presented can be used in various types of organizations, in an abstract way, there are few models regarding specifically government issues. Such models have a strong connection to eGovernment issues, considering it as a key strategy for improving the effectiveness of public policies and programs [16]. Governments should address interoperability issues at least for four reasons [26]:

(1): leads to better decision-making, (2) allows better coordination of government agency services, (3) foundation of a citizen-centric delivery of services and (4) leads to cost savings and/or avoidance. In other words, eGovernment interoperability contributes to good governance.

Basically, eGovernment is the application of information technology to government processes in order to improve services to constituents, considering that various government organizations can share and integrate information between each other [16]. Other complementary and representative definitions for eGovernment are the use of information and communication technologies (ICTs) to: (1) improve public organizations activities [8]; (2) overcome the physical bounds of traditional paper and physically based systems for free movement of information [17] and (3) support the government business, providing or enhancing public services or managing internal government operations [13].

Proposed by [19], the Government Interoperability Maturity Matrix (GIMM) provides an easy, comprehensive and complete way for administrations to evaluate their current status on eGovernment issues. The structure is very similar to other models (presented in this paper), with maturity levels defining the characteristics of the formalism degree and the way of exchanging data and information. The GIMM works with interoperability attributes, such as connectivity with central government gateways, single sign-on facilities for user authentication, existence of web-service interfaces, interoperability with external enterprise systems, and existence of common XML-based data schemas.

In [12], the authors present important issues related to government interoperability, taking into account that eGovernment actions may, also, decrease bureaucracy. The need of a more service providing public service requires a well-defined ICT infrastructure of support. The paper has a main focus regarding technical aspects of information exchange, especially considering the necessity of a single and common language to be adopted, which, in this case, is the XML.

The model for interoperability evaluation in eGovernment services, proposed by [23], identifies some aspects in order to guarantee information and knowledge interoperability in eGovernment services. The paper proposes three basic approaches that must be taken into account: information and knowledge management (e.g. markup languages, open software and formats, and electronic document processing), metadata for knowledge representation in electronic resources, and web accessibility to improve access for all users. In [20], two government e-services in Norway are presented as a case study. The paper proposes a four-staged framework (aligning work processes, knowledge sharing, joining value creation and aligning strategies) crossing with organizational, semantic and technical interoperability issues.

In [16], the authors present a framework that structures eGovernment interoperability in terms of dynamic and interactive policy, management, and technology dimensions. The framework proposes a structure formed by basic categories and dimensions. The Interoperability Practical Implementation Support (IPIS), proposed in [18], presents a practical approach for implementing electronic government interoperability. The approach consists of three main components: support tools, interoperability repositories, and a knowledge-based system. The paper shows a methodology to tie all three components together. The information Systems Interoperability Maturity Model (ISIMM), proposed in [21], also defines levels and degrees of interoperability evolution, focusing on technical aspects regarding data exchange and sharing. The authors present an application case of the ISIMM regarding the Government of Namibia in order to establish its interoperability level considering, mostly, technical issues. Although the ISIMM was not built to deal with government issues specifically, it is mentioned in this section, given that, in this case, it was applied for government assessment. The GIMM and ISIMM are also shown in the comparative Table 1.

The e-PING [9] framework is a Brazilian Government effort that defines a minimum set of premises, policies and technical specifications to regulate the use of ICT in the interoperability of services regarding the eGovernment. E-PING stands, in Portuguese, for "Padrões de Interoperabilidade de Governo Eletrônico", which can be freely translated into English as "eGovernment Interoperability Patterns". This reference model establishes conditions and interactions with other government agencies and the society, covering aspects such as interconnection, security, access, and organization and data interchange. The Brazilian e-PING (and other countries Government Interoperability Frameworks) addresses technical interoperability [25], defines protocols that must be used, hypertext interchange format, databases, image extensions, BPMN notations and other issues. The idea began in 2003 with a visit to the British government to study the UK eGovernment Interoperability Framework (e-GIF). The Brazilian government organized a committee to initiate the first efforts to build the architecture and specifications. In July 2005, this initial committee was nominated as "e-PING Coordination". The areas covered by e-PING are interconnection, security, ways of access, organization and information exchange and electronic government integration areas. The framework does not recommend tools or defines presentations patterns for information, and considers that there are technical, semantic and organizational elements that must be covered in the interoperability.

4   Interoperability Models Analysis and Discussion

All presented models, either related to government or not, have a strong relationship with data communication and information exchange, i.e. they strongly emphasize technical and operational issues. Such view may derive from the most adopted interoperability definition: "the ability of two or more systems or components to exchange information and to use the information that has been exchanged" [11].

The OIMM and EIMM may contain some background aspects of management and organization, whilst LISI and LCIM may refer to computer science. Another main characteristic is that all models have a strong relation with the use of standards and inter systems interoperability, whilst, on the other hand, they are not so strong when dealing with agility in reaction and adaptation. The OIMM is almost the only model that deals with issues directly related to a command style, culture and other organization values besides the technical issues. The GIMM identifies interoperability attributes that must be taken into consideration in order to evaluate the organization in the eGovernment interoperability. These attributes have a correlation with the factors that influence (positively or negatively) the eGovernment interoperability, proposed in [2].It is known, and for the government aspects this is not different, that interoperability is a complex problem, which deals with many conceptual definitions, multiple proposed models and domain areas [13]. Although there are basically three primary goals associated with achieving interoperability in any system (data exchange, meaning exchange and process agreement),when it comes to government, the context can be even more complex because of the necessity of dealing with some influencing factors such as legal, political and sociocultural issues. Which means, in government related interoperability, the context is very important, once some major differences must also be addressed (e.g. poor infrastructures, dictatorial or developed countries).In spite of that, the majority of government related models deal with issues concerning eGovernment, whose objectives are generally to improve efficiency and effectiveness, offering (if pertinent) online services and information that can increase democratic participation, accountability, transparency, and the quality and speed of services [13]. The approach of such eGovernment models is similar to that of the "non eGovernment" models, that is, the main focus is still basically the exchange of information, considering the availability of public services, the integration of the agencies, and other operations involving an interface layer of information exchange.

Figure 1 represents the exchange of information, considering that the dotted line represents a basic division of views related to the goals and types of information exchanged. The "A" arrow is associated to the technical aspects of interoperability, and the operational and tangible issues are well defined and treated through consolidated models. The "B" arrow represents the relationship regarding more intangible items, such as culture and market information exchange. These issues can be considered part of the influencing factors related to the interoperability government context. The "B" arrow is not so well represented in terms of models and practices such as the "A".

As interoperability problems consist of more than technical aspects, the European Commission's European Interoperability Framework (EIF) redefined the concept of interoperability in a more general way: "interoperability is the ability of disparate and diverse organizations to interact towards mutually beneficial and agreed common goals, involving the sharing of information and knowledge between the organizations via the business processes they support, by means of the exchange of data between their respective information and communication technology (ICT) systems" [13].

Considering this overview, and according to the models presented in this paper, there is a certain lack of definitions and models that report organizational barriers and business interoperability more fully. In addition, for the government models, specifically, there could be more issues focusing on cultural, political, intelligence and relationship aspects, i.e. the "B" arrow in Figure 1 could be reinforced.

Taking into account the characteristics of some eGovernment models presented in this paper, and also considering some Brazilian influencing factors (federal, state and municipal), such as the World Cup 2014, Olympics 2016 and the fact that the city of Curitiba was placed first in the Brazilian Index of Digital Cities, 2012 [6], there is a need of ongoing and future works that must address issues as: (1) bibliography review regarding the Brazilian context related to eGovernment aspects; (2) review the barriers, concerns and approaches related to the Brazilian characteristics for eGovernment; (3) review the influencing factors, attributes and barriers (not only considering technical aspects) that influence the eGovernment interoperability in Brazil, such as those proposed in [2], [19] and [24]; (4) propose (and/or adapt) methods to evaluate the eGovernment interoperability in Brazil, also considering some intangible aspects.

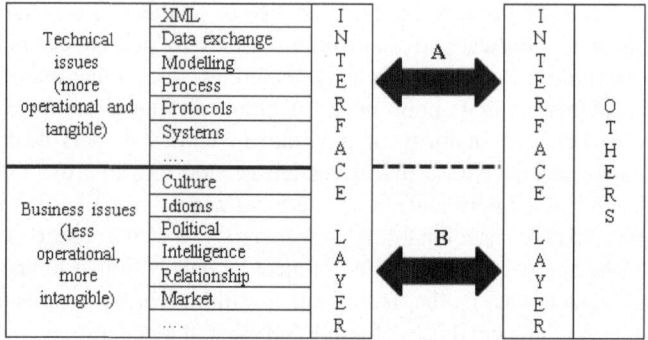

Fig. 1. Data exchange according to the views

References

1. ATHENA. Advanced Technologies for Interoperability of Heterogeneous Enterprise Networks and their Applications (2003)
2. Charalabidis, Y., Panetto, H., Loukis, E., Mertins, K.: Interoperability for Enterprises and Administrations Worldwide. eJETA Special Issue (2008)
3. Chen, D., Vallespir, B., Daclin, N.: An Approach for Enterprise Interoperability Measurement. In: Proceeding of MoDISE-EUS 2008, France (2008)
4. Chen, D., Vernadat, F.B.: Enterprise Interoperability: A Standardization View. In: Proceedings of the IFIP International Conference on Enterprise Integration and Modelling Technology (ICEIMT 2002), April 24-26, Kluwer Academics Publisher, Valencia (2002)
5. Clark, T., Jones, R.: Organizational interoperability maturity model for c2. In: Proc. of the Command and Control Research and Technology Symposium, Washington (1999)
6. CPqD., Wireless Mundi.: Índice Brasil de Cidades Digitais (2012), http://www.wirelessmundi.inf.br/indice-edicao-n-9/903-capa
7. DoD (US Department of Defense), Interoperability Working Group.: Levels of information systems interoperability (LISI), Washington, DC (1998)
8. eGovernment for Development Information Exchange.: What Is eGovernment? University of Manchester's Institute for Development Policy and Management (2008), http://www.egov4dev.org/success/definitions.shtml
9. Governo Brasileiro.: e-PING: Padrões de Interoperabilidade de Governo Eletrônico - Documento de Referência (2013), http://www.governoeletronico.gov.br/biblioteca/arquivos/documento-da-e-ping-versao-2013
10. Guédria, W., Chen, D., Naudet, Y.: A Maturity Model for Enterprise Interoperability. In: Meersman, R., Herrero, P., Dillon, T. (eds.) OTM 2009 Workshops. LNCS, vol. 5872, pp. 216–225. Springer, Heidelberg (2009)

11. IEEE.: A compilation of IEEE standard computer glossaries, standard computer dictionary (1990)
12. Laskaridis, G., Markellos, K., Markellou, P., Panayiotaki, A., Sakkopoulos, E., Tsakalidis, A.: E-government and Interoperability Issues. IJCSNS International Journal of Computer Science and Network Security 7(9) (2007)
13. Novakouski, M., Lewis, G.: Interoperability in the e-Government Context. TECHNICAL NOTE, CMU/SEI-2011-TN-014 (2012)
14. Panetto, H.: Towards a Classification Framework for Interoperability of Enterprise Applications. International Journal of CIM (2007), http://www.tandf.co.uk/journals
15. Pardo, T., Nam, T., Burke, B.: Improving Government Interoperability: A Capability Framework for Government Managers. Center for Technology in Government, SUNY Albany (2008)
16. Pardo, T., Nam, T., Burke, B.: E-Government Interoperability: Interaction of Policy, Management, and Technology Dimensions. Social Science Computer Review 2012 (2011) (originally published online 12 January)
17. Pascual, P.J.: e-Government. eAsean Task Force, UNDP-APDIP (2003), http://www.apdip.net/publications/iespprimers/eprimer-egov.pdf
18. Saekow, A., Boonmee, C.: A Pragmatic Approach to Interoperability Practical Implementation Support (IPIS) for e-Government Interoperability. Electronic Journal of e-Government 7(4), 403–414 (2009)
19. Sarantis, D., Charalabidis, Y., Psarras, J.: Towards standardising interoperability levels forinformation systems of public administrations. The Electronic Journal for e-Commerce Tools & Applications, eJETA (2008)
20. Solli-Sæther, H.: A framework for analysing interoperability in electronic government. Int. J. Electronic Finance 5(1), 32–48 (2011)
21. Staden, S.V., Mbale, J.: The information Systems Interoperability Maturity Model (ISIMM): Towards Standardizing Technical Interoperability and Assessment within Government. I. J. Information Engineering and Electronic Business 5, 36–41 (2012)
22. Tolk, A., Muguira, J.A.: The levels of conceptual interoperability model. In: 2003 Fall Simulation Interoperability Workshop, Orlando, Florida (2003)
23. Usero, J.A., Orenes, P.B., Comeche, J.A., Segundo, R.S.: Model for Interoperability Evaluation in e-Government Services, FORMATEX (2006)
24. Whitman, L.E.: The missing link: culture and language barriers to interoperability. In: IFAC Annual Reviews in Control. 30/2, 233-241, Extended Version from 9th IFAC Symposium on Automated Systems Based on Human Skill And Knowledge, May 22-24. Elsevier, Nancy (2006)
25. United Nations Development Programme.: e-Government Interoperability (2008)
26. United Nations Development Programme.: e-Government Interoperability: Guide (2007)

Supporting Interoperability for Chaotic and Complex Adaptive Enterprise Systems

Georg Weichhart

Metasonic AG, München Straße 29 – Hettenshausen, 85276 Pfaffenhofen, Germany
georg.weichhart@metasonic.de
Department of Business Information Systems – Communications Engineering,
Johannes Kepler University Linz, Altenbergerstr. 69, 4040 Linz, Austria
georg.weichhart@jku.at

Abstract. Living systems like enterprises and enterprise networks not only want to survive but also want to grow and prosper. These organisational systems adapt to changing environments and proactively change the system itself. Continuous evolution (of parts) of these enterprise systems requires diversity, but this heterogeneity is a source of non interoperability. In this article, interoperability and enterprise systems are analysed through the lenses of chaos theory and complex adaptive systems theory and requirements for continuous adaptation and organisational learning to maintain interoperability are identified.

Keywords: organizational learning, interoperability, complex adaptive systems, chaos theory.

1 Introduction

Thrivability is a concept developed to discuss systems that aim at organic growth [1]. The future is not knowable, and growth, in this view, is not a linear process. The system needs to be adaptive and able to learn when reacting to unforeseen situations [2]. Independent and diverse subsystems provide a basis for adoption [3], in particular in contrast to single large integrated enterprise systems with optimised organisational structures [4]. For organisational systems the most fundamental sub-system are human agents. Since heterogeneity is a source of interoperability problems [5], these agents need support for continuous developing and sustaining interoperability.

General Systems Theory (GST) aims at bridging the gap between different fields of science through abstraction [6]. Due to the dynamics of the environment, recognising organisations and organisational networks as "static" systems is not sufficient [7]. In the following two theories are used to characterise enterprise systems. Chaos theory and complex adaptive systems theory are theories which have their roots in GST and put emphasis on dynamic aspects.

We describe complex and chaotic systems theories, their properties, and aspects of these types of system models. These aspects and properties are linked to required support for organisational systems in order to reach and sustain interoperability.

Y.T. Demey and H. Panetto (Eds.): OTM 2013 Workshops, LNCS 8186, pp. 86–92, 2013.

2   Chaos and Complex Adaptive Systems

A system is chaotic if it contains nonlinear relationships between its parts. Its global state is to a large extent unpredictable. It must be a continuously dynamical system, with its future state not being predicable but evolving over time [8]. For this type of system, it is sufficient that simple, but nonlinear relationships between a few variables (parts) exist.

A Complex Adaptive System (CAS) has active elements, called agents, which interact. The overall system state may not be determined by the sum of these individual agents' behaviours, as non-linear relationships exist. The agents are capable of adapting to the environment and other agents, exhibiting self-organised behaviour.

The literature discusses complex adaptive systems and chaos theory from different points of view (as intended by GST), and has not identified a set of properties for these systems. The properties of chaotic systems and Complex Adaptive Systems are briefly discussed and then used for structuring the discussion of enterprise systems and derive requirements for a supportive environment.

2.1   Dependence on Initial Conditions

Depending on small changes somewhere in the overall system this system's state evolves unpredictable over time. This property is exemplified by the often quoted butterfly effect coined by Lorenz [2,8], where a small change at one part of the system results in significant differences in the behaviour of some distant other part of the system over time. In that particular example, a butterfly causes changes in the airflow in Europe which amplifies over time and causes a thunderstorm in North America months later.

2.2   Self-similarity across Scales

Self-similarity is a property of a system that is similar to a part of itself. Self-similarity may occur along different aspects. For example, coastlines are statistical self-similar, where the same statistical properties exist at different scales.

2.3   Strange Attractors

In a dynamic system, a (strange) attractor is a point, towards which, or around which, particles (parts) of a system are moving. The particles remain independent, however are attracted by the attractor, where the force of attraction is dependent on the distance of an attractor to a particle. Particles getting close to the attractor remain close. The ways along which parts are moving are not fixed or predetermined.

2.4   Bifurcation

A bifurcation point marks a moment in time where a system's part comes under the influence of another attractor. This part will (depending on the strength of the attractor) change "direction" and a qualitative leap may happen at this point [9].

The concept of bifurcation implies that multiple local small changes may lead to unpredictable outcomes in the overall system as the system develops over time. This is due to the assumed nonlinear relationship between the individual system parts.

2.5   Active Agents

In a complex adaptive system, "great many independent agents are interacting with each other in a great many ways" [10, p.11]. The agents themselves follow their individual rules how to interact with other agents. This interaction between agents is a local event. Additionally agents may interact with their (also local) environment. Yet it is important to understand, that there is no global control flow, but there are only local interactions. The overall systems state is not planned and even not predicable due to "nonlinear relationships".

2.6   Self-organisation, Co-evolution and Emergent Behaviour

The lack of global control enables the agents to act self-controlled and self-organized. As mentioned above, interactions are locally controlled by the agents that take part in a particular interaction. Local interaction with or without taking the higher system level state into account, facilitates emergent behaviour on the higher system level. The global organisation of the system "naturally emerges out of the interaction of individual agents without any top-down control" [11, p.41].

This can be observed on multiple levels, where for example the interaction of brain-cells influences the behaviour of human agents, and interaction between agents influences the behaviour of the department [3].

3   Enterprise Systems

In the following we discuss enterprise systems from the complex adaptive systems and chaos theory point of view. This discussion assumes a structure, where an organisational network's agents are organisations, and an organisation's agents are humans. On all levels these enterprise systems are complex and adaptive systems which exhibit some chaotic behaviour (see for example [12] with respect to Organisations, and [7] with respect to Supply Networks).

3.1   Dependence on Initial Conditions

Enterprise systems depend on their environment, for example market conditions, or other participants in the supply chain like customers and suppliers. From an enterprise network point of view, the bull-whip effect is used as example where small changes to demand lead to a globally observable phenomenon impacting the overall supply network (from a CAS point of view see [13]). In this particular case, communication delays cause amplifying product orders, which lead to a massive oversupply of products in the overall supply network.

3.2   Self-similarity across Scales

Here organisational systems are seen as collaborations of independent, cooperative organisational units, which are composed of sub-systems, which themselves are composed of sub-systems. Depending on the scale, organisational networks consist of organisations, which consist of departments which consist of agents.

3.3   Strange Attractors and Bifurcation

Qualitative leaps on micro level lead to small gradual changes on the macro level. "We call this "scale invariance" or the fractal dimension of growth: gradual change on a macro-level may be interpreted as a series of small qualitative leaps on a micro-level." [9, p 433]. With respect to enterprise systems, such decisions might be a change of the production technology used by a company. This change allows the company to grow over time. This rather "dramatic" change on lower levels of aggregation is visible at higher levels only as gradual growth.

3.4   Active Agents

The agents in supply networks are the firms and suppliers taking part in these organisational networks [7]. Within organisations these agents are organisational units, which themselves consist of human agents [12] However, all agents (independent on the observed system scale) act independent and interact with other agents.

3.5   Self-organisation, Co-evolution, and Emergent Behaviour

In a social system, an agent's behaviour influences the environment and vice versa, the environment influences the agent [14]. Over time, the agents learn from each other, through copying successful behaviour. However, individual and group learning paths and learning results are not predictable. The performance of a group does not only depend on individuals, but also on the interaction between individuals. Emergent learning takes place, and through multiple qualitative leaps on lower levels the overall system develops [9,7]. Learning and improvement are results of self-organisation of individual agents and of groups of agents. Depending on the level observed an agent may be a learning organisation, which is member of several supply networks [7], or a human agent working in an organisation [12].

4   Supporting Interoperability

So far we have discussed properties of chaos theory and complex adaptive systems theory. We have conceptually established a mapping between enterprise systems and these theories. From a chaotic and complex adaptive systems point of view, in the following implications for a system to support interoperability is discussed.

4.1   Dependence on Initial Conditions

The butterfly effect is often used to explain, why models don't work (see above). A model is intentionally a reduction of the complexity of the reality and there are too many influences which a model would need to integrate in order to deliver a picture close to reality. This has consequences for Enterprise Modelling for integration approaches. Enterprise modelling projects face the challenge that the enterprise system permanently changes, requiring to continuously adapt the model [7]. Models consisting of independent, but interoperable parts have the advantage to provide more stability as not all systems are influencing each other and changes may be limited to sub-parts. A support environment would allow continuous contributions to the model.

4.2   Self-organisation, Co-evolution, and Emergent Behaviour

To maintain a continuous evolution of an enterprise model, a distributed and decentralised approach to enterprise modelling is needed. Taking a CAS point of view, management (being responsible for organisation of the enterprise system) should "[i]nstead of acting as a central authority and exerting top-down control, the manager's role should be facilitating and geared towards creating an open environment, where people are allowed to question rules and procedures" [15, p 345]. Management should encourage self-organisation and emergent behaviour. Enterprise models should provide support for self-organising agents, who contribute to a single enterprise model in a decentralised and distributed fashion. A support environment needs to support these dynamic changes.

4.3   Active Agents

The price for the above described freedom of and for agents is responsibility. It is the responsibility of the agents to maintain interoperability, if there is no centralised top-down management. The environment is needed which allows responsible agents to communicate, coordinate and adapt to emerging interoperability problems.

4.4   Self-similarity across Scales

An "interoperability support environment" supporting responsible agents to collaboratively adapt to changing circumstances requires to support agents on different scales. An interoperability environment needs to support modelling of self-similar systems to support agents to conceptualise and understand the model on different levels of abstractions and scales. This allows agents to receive feedback on local and global level by other agents. A learning environment needs to support both, the local interaction between agents, as well as an overall enterprise model to support making interfaces interoperable. Agents should be enabled to interactively contribute to the enterprise system model with respect to different aspects, depending on the situation at hand.

4.5   Strange Attractors and Bifurcation

As discussed above strange attractors might emerge and provide opportunities for bifurcation points. Both is needed, support for a-priority and a-posteriori interoperability support. "A priori solution consists in negotiation and homogenisation actions before the beginning of an interoperation. A posteriori solution takes place after collaboration starts. It consists in a domination, an adjustment or an exclusion." [5, p 848]. In both cases an environment is needed which allows participating agents to collaboratively "jump" to the next attractor or not. This might be planned a-priory or the need for adjustments might be learned a-posteriori.

5   Conclusions

Due to the dynamic and evolving environment, agents need a learning environment which supports them in understanding the changing requirements for maintaining interoperability. Using chaos theory and complex adaptive systems theory as lenses for discussion, we have identified a few requirements for a learning environment that supports active and responsible agents:

— modelling enterprise systems on different scales
— support for self-organisation and negotiation of interoperability solutions
— collaborative learning about new attractors and possible bifurcation points

Existing interoperability approaches like Enterprise Modelling provide building blocks on which an overall learning environment may be build. Enterprise Models for example may serve as attractors for discussions.

However, in addition to the existing work, the proposed learning environment supports a continual process where learning and work related activities are no longer separate [16]. It aims at enabling adaptation, organic growth, and thrivability of the enterprise system.

This article is only a first attempt to identify learning support features and requirements for interoperability from a dynamic process point of view. It provides a conceptualisation of interoperability from complex adaptive systems and chaos theory point of view. Similar to the learning theory of connectivism [16], which acknowledges the dynamics and technology enhancements in today's learning environments; the conceptual work presented here is an attempt to bring together technology and organisational learning. In this context, interoperability is a key issue for learning.

References

1. Russell, J.: Thrivability - A Collaborative Sketch (2010), http://thrivable.org/ (accessed May 30, 2012)
2. Hite, J.A.: Learning in Chaos - Improving Human Performance in Today's Fast-Changing, Volatile Organizations, p. 300. Gulf Publishing Company, Houston (1999)
3. Holland, J.H.: Hidden Order – How Adaptation Builds Complexity. Basic Books (1996)
4. Weichhart, G., Fessl, K.: Organisational network models and the implications for decision support systems. In: Piztek, P. (ed.) Proceedings of the IFAC World Congress, Praha (2005)
5. Ducq, Y., Chen, D., Doumeingts, G.: A contribution of system theory to sustainable enterprise interoperability science base. Computers in Industry 63(8), 844–857 (2012)
6. von Bertalanffy, L.: General System Theory - Foundations, Development, Applications. George Braziller, New York (1969)
7. Choi, T.Y., Dooley, K.J., Rungtusanatham, M.: Supply networks and complex adaptive systems: control versus emergence. Journal of Operations Management 19, 351–366 (2001)
8. Gleick, J.: Chaos: Making a new science. Penguin, New York (1987)
9. van Eijnatten, F.M.: Chaordic systems thinking - Some suggestions for a complexity framework to inform a learning organization. The Learning Organization 11, 430–449 (2004)
10. Waldrop, M.: Complexity: The emerging science at the edge of order and chaos. Simon and Schuster (1992)
11. Englehardt, C.S., Simmons, R.R.: Creating an organizational space for learning. The Learning Organization 9, 39–47 (2002)
12. Anderson, P.: Perspective: Complexity Theory and Organization Science. Organization Science 10, 216–232 (1999)
13. Pathak, S.D., Day, J., Nair, A., Sawaya, W.J., Kristal, M.M.: Complexity and Adaptivity in Supply Networks: Building Supply Network Theory Using a Complex Adaptive Systems Perspective. Decision Sciences 38(4), 547–580 (2007)
14. Bandura, A.: Social cognitive theory. In: Vasta, R. (ed.) Annals of Child Development. Six theories of child development, vol. 6, pp. 1–60. JAI Press, Greenwich, CT (1989)
15. Harkema, S.: A complex adaptive perspective on learning within innovation projects. The Learning Organisation 10(6), 340–346 (2003)
16. Siemens, G.: Connectivism: a learning theory for the digital age. International Journal of Instructional Technology and Distance Learning 2 (2005)

System Integration for Intelligent Systems

Ryo Saegusa

Toyohashi University of Technology, Japan
ryos@ieee.org
http://www.ryolab.com

Abstract. The paper describes a model of system integration for designing intelligent systems. Systems for services and industries are expected to be coordinated internally and harmonized with the external environment and users. However, integration of the systems is difficult in general since the systems contain a number of processes with multiple tasks in different priority and timing. In this paper, we propose a model of system integration base on process categorization. We then validate the model based on dimension, hierarchy and symbolization comparing with case studies in the field of system intelligence. Discussion of the proposal framework will give us insight for designing interoperable infrastructures.

1 Introduction

System integration is a key issue for coordinating bunch of information in different levels of business scenes where the systems are expected to offer concentrated knowledge for workers in collaboration [12][4][5][2][10]. In a current stream of system intelligence, the system integration has been referred to as a main subject, since systems in the state of the art are required to realize continuous and smooth processing for integration, decision and implementation in task execution. However, the number of elements in recent systems is obviously increasing and the systems are getting more complex. Advanced methods of system integration are therefore desired for optimizing work flows and procedures in services and industries.

Problems in system integration include various issues such as efficient data handling and task priority control that should take care of human factors. In this paper, we focus on complexity in system integration. First, we will introduce categorization of processes in intelligent systems. We will then propose a model that integrates systems by coordinating different types of processes. We will compare the model with actually implemented systems in case studies and validate the proposed framework. The idea of the system integration is surely applicable for designing general structures of work flows and procedures in services and industries. Finally we will summarize the proposed framework and conclude an effective way to integrate systems.

Y.T. Demey and H. Panetto (Eds.): OTM 2013 Workshops, LNCS 8186, pp. 93–100, 2013.

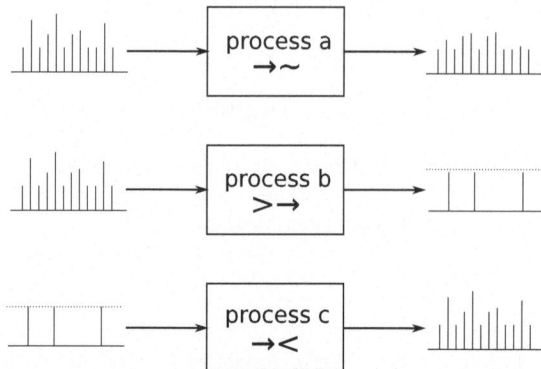

Fig. 1. Computation processes with different signal transformation. Process a, b and c show equivalent, simplificaiton and complication processes in signal transformation.

2   System Integration

We introduce types of computation process. Figure 1 shows three computation processes with different transformation between input and output signals. Process a, b and c in Fig.1 show signal transformation for equivalent, simplification and complication processes. These signal processes typically correspond to continuous modulation, pattern detection and pattern generation, respectively, in the field of system intelligence.

The following equations are respective examples of the process a, b and c in Fig.1:

$$y(t) = \sum_{\tau} x(t - \tau)h(\tau), \tag{1}$$

$$y(t) = \text{step}(\sum_{\tau} x(t - \tau)h(-\tau) - \delta), \tag{2}$$

$$y(t) = \sum_{\tau} x(t - \tau)h_i(\tau), i = \text{step}(\sin(2\pi t/T)), \tag{3}$$

where x, y and t denote input signal, output signal and time. h denote a function. Step function returns 1 or 0 if its argument is positive or anything else, respectively. These processes actually realize convolution-based impulse response, correlation-based pattern detection and switching pattern generation.

These signal processes can be integrated into more complex systems. Figure 2 shows a model of system architectures that allows integration, decision and implementation of signals coordinating with the external environment. Note that input-output transformation in the same level in Fig.2 corresponds to the equivalent process a, and input-output transformation to come up and down layers correspond to the simplification process and complication process in Fig.1, respectively.

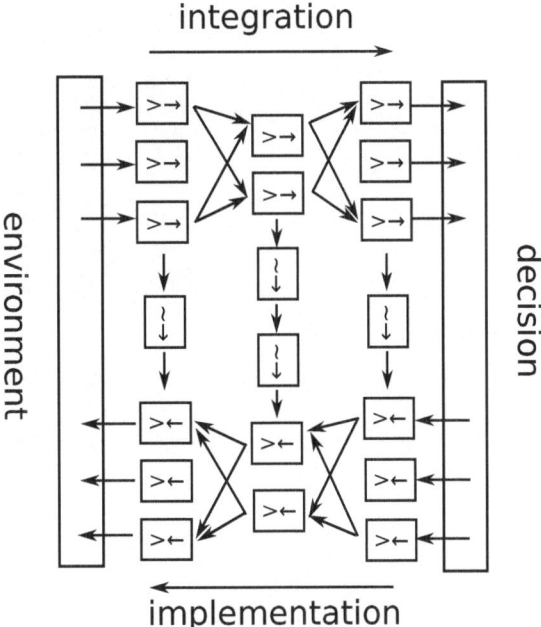

Fig. 2. A model of integrated systems. The model allows integration, decision and realization of signals coordinating with the external enviornment.

In order to handle huge information, a complex system should modulate quality of signals. In the environment side, signals are given from the environment where several events can occur independently. Signals from these events should be transformed into symbol patterns to concentrate information. In the decision side, signals can be sparse and tolerant for time and amplitude, while the number of patterns can increase because of the combinations. The symbol patterns can be evaluated for making decision. The decision is then implemented as continuous signal sequences that can actually affect for the environment. The signal flows through equivalent levels can function as shortcut pathways. The pathways allow prompt signal responses without waiting the results of higher level processes.

3   Case Studies

We will discuss system integration with three case studies in the field of system intelligence. Here we specially focus on the concepts of dimension, hierarchy and symbolization that appear in system architectures of the case studies. These concepts are surely important for designing complex intelligent systems. We will explain each concept in the following subsections.

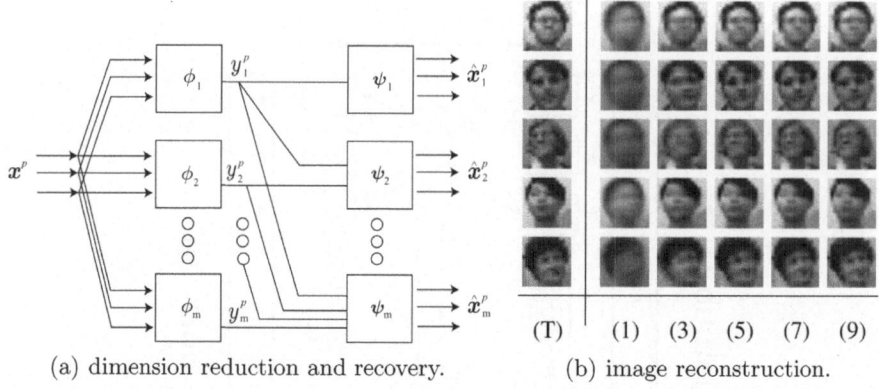

(a) dimension reduction and recovery.   (b) image reconstruction.

Fig. 3. Dimension reduction and recovery in nonlinear principal component analysis [9]. (a) a diagram of nonlinear pca. (b) reconstuction of 256 dimensional images from 1 to 9 dimensional data.

3.1   Dimension

Dimension gives a measure of data complexity. When data is represented as a vector, mathematical dimension of the data is defined as the number of the components of the vector. The data can be compressed by decreasing dimension, while the compressed data can be decompressed by recovering dimension.

In the field of data analysis, principal component analysis (pca) is known as a standard method of linear data compression/decompression [3], while we developed a nonlinearized pca [9] that generalizes the conventional pca to allow nonlinear transformation as follows:

$$y_i = \phi_i(\boldsymbol{x}), \boldsymbol{z}_i = \psi_i(y_1, \cdots, y_i), \tag{4}$$

where $\boldsymbol{x} \in R^n$, $y_i \in R$ and $\boldsymbol{z}_i \in R^n$ are the input vector, ith nonlinear principal component and ith reconstruction vector. The set of functions $\{\phi_i, \psi_i\}_{i=1,\cdots,n}$ are given by minimizing the mean square error $\sum_j ||\boldsymbol{z}_i(\boldsymbol{x}_j) - \boldsymbol{x}_j||^2$. The data in n dimension can be represented in any lower dimension of $m \leq n$ by using the set of m nonlinear principal components $(y_1, \cdots, y_m)$.

Figure 3 shows dimension reduction and recovery with the nonlinear pca. Figure 3(a) depicts a diagram of the nonlinear pca that compresses and decompresses the data vector. Figure 3(b) shows image reconstruction by the nonlinear pca. The face images arranged in column T are 256 dimensional data. As shown in the figure, the 256 dimensional image data were represented in high fidelity with the principal components in 9 dimension.

In summary, dimension of data can be reduced and recovered by functions that are optimized to represent statistical features of the data set. Function ϕ_i and ψ_i

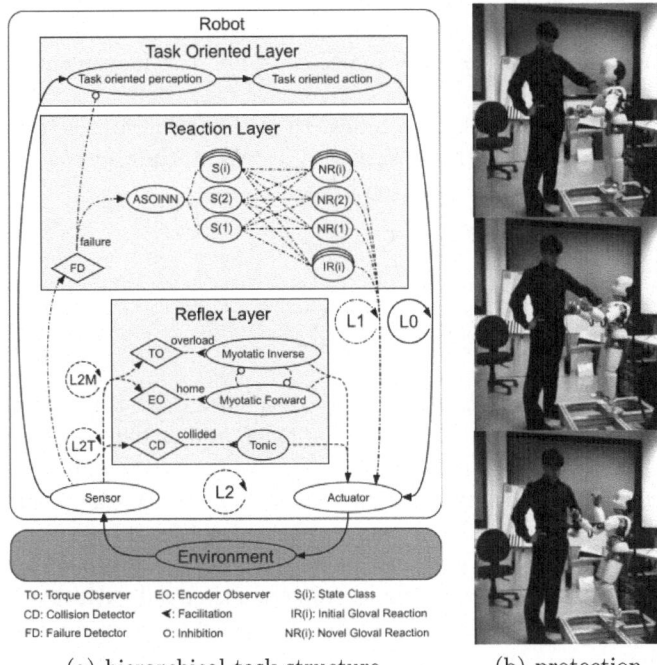

(a) hierarchical task structure.   (b) protection

Fig. 4. A hierarchical task structure for whole body motor leaning of antrhopomorphic robots [11]. (a) a hierarchical task structure. (b) local force reflex that protects a joint from impact.

in the nonlinear pca actually work as the simplification and complication processes in Fig. 1 respectively in terms of dimension control. This summary supports that process organization is important for systems to form signals in appropriate dimension.

3.2   Hierarchy

Hierarchy rules priority of system computation. In order to deal with important processes in high priority, the processes should be positioned in high layers of task hierarchy where the tasks are allowed to overcome the tasks in lower layers [1]. In the filed of system intelligence, self protection is an important task for agents working in the physical environment, since the agents need to be patient for physical damages in learning activity. The agents therefore should be able to protect the self in higher priority than other tasks.

Figure 4 shows a hierarchical task structures for whole body motor learning of anthropomorphic robots [11]. Figure 4(a) shows a hierarchical task structure that allows the robot to protect the self in higher priority during task leaning. Figure 4(b) shows force reflex that inhibits a whole body movement. During the movement, a joint in an arm limb detects unexpected force given by the experimenter and then triggered local reflex that loosed the joint in high priority to protect the joint from impact. Only the movement of the arm colliding with the experimenter was successfully inhibited, while the movements in the other limbs were kept on.

Independently from local force reflex, the robot generates self-protective reactions in high priority as shown in Fig. 4(a). We optimized the reactions base on head momentum M and joint load E as follows:

$$M = \sum_t |\omega(t)|, \tag{5}$$

$$E = \frac{1}{T} \sum_t \sum_i \dot{\theta}_i \tau_i(t) \delta t \tag{6}$$

where ω and t denote the angular velocity of the head and time. θ_i and τ_i denote the angle and torque of the ith joint in limbs. T and δt denote time duration of force impact and time step for sampling. The robot detects danger based on the head momentum and optimized the reactions to minimize the mean joint load.

In summary, the hierarchical task structure in Fig. 4 organizes local force reflex (L2 loop) and whole body reactions (L1 loop) to overcome general tasks (L0 loop). This task hierarchy actually implements signal pathways presented as vertical flows in Fig 2. These shortcut loops enabled the system to drive prompt actions (reflex and reaction in this case study) without passing time-consuming decision. The hierarchy of the system benefits also for temporal aspects.

3.3 Symbolization

Symbolization makes a bridge between raw signals and semantic signals in biological systems [6]. Bio-inspired cognitive systems should also symbolize raw signals in sensor and actuator levels in order to realize efficient pattern recognition and decision making in higher levels.

Figure 5 shows a model of multi-modal signal symbolization and generation [7][8]. Figure 5(a) shows a model of developmental action perception system. The system firstly symbolizes features of an event perceived in multi-modal sensing. The system then decides a suitable behavior in motor repertory. The system finally realizes physical actions of the behavior by combining motor primitives that the robot learned in advance. Figure 5(b) and 5(c) show observation and reproduction of human actions, respectively, where reach, grasp, hold and drop actions were sequentially observed and reproduced by the robot. The time courses of the scenes are from top to bottom.

In decision levels after signal symbolization, the system associates an action symbol with a set of sensory symbols. After this learning, the system is able to estimate an action from observation based on the Bayesian estimation as follows:

$$\hat{a}(E = (\cdots, e_i, \cdots))$$
$$= \arg\max_a p(A = a) \prod_{i=1}^{n} p(E_i = e_i | A = a), \tag{7}$$

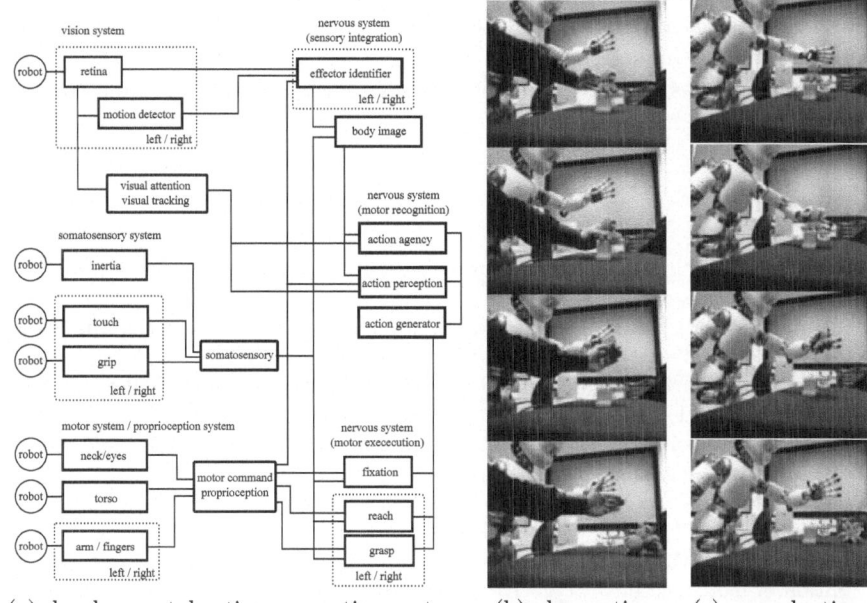

(a) developmental action perception system.   (b) observation.   (c) reproduction.

Fig. 5. A multi-modal signal symbolization and generation. (a) a developmental action perception system [7][8]. (b) observatoin of human actions. (c) reproduction of human actions.

where a, $\hat{a}$ and e_i denote the action symbol, estimated action symbol and sensory symbol of the ith sensory modality (vision, touch or proprioception), respectively. A and E are the corresponding probability variables. This estimation is done by the process of action perception presented in the right side (decision side) of Fig. 5(a). The estimated action symbol is embodied in the processes in sensor and motor layers.

In summary, the developmental action perception system in Fig. 5 symbolizes sensory signals, associates the sensory symbols with action symbols, and generates actual behaviors from the action symbols. These symbolization, association and generation correspond to integration, decision and implementation of the proposed system integration model in Fig. 2, respectively.

4   Conclusion

We discussed system integration for designing intelligent systems. We first categorized computation processes into three types of processes that correspond to equivalent, simplification and complication processes. We then proposed a general model of integrated system by combining the above-mentioned processes. The integrated system coordinates multiple processes by integration, decision and implementation of signals. We validated the proposed integrated system based on dimension, hierarchy and symbolization comparing with actually implemented systems in the field of system intelligence. In conclusion, we confirmed that the proposed model of process categorization and system integration generalizes case studies and gives insight in designing interoperable infrastructures for services and industries.

References

[1] Brooks, R.: Intelligence without representation. Artificial Intelligence 47(1-3), 139–159

[2] Cummins, F.A.: Enterprise integration: an architecture for enterprise application and systems integration. John Wiley & Sons, Inc. (2002)

[3] Duda, R.O., Hart, P.E., Stork, D.G.: Pattern Classification. John Wiley and Sons, New York (2001)

[4] Hohpe, G., Woolf, B.A.: Enterprise integration patterns: Designing, building, and deploying messaging solutions. Addison-Wesley Professional (2004)

[5] Lee, J., Siau, K., Hong, S.: Enterprise integration with erp and eai. Communications of the ACM 46(2), 54–60 (2003)

[6] Rizzolatti, G., Fadiga, L., Gallese, V., Fogassi, L.: Premotor cortex and the recognition of motor actions. Cognitive Brain Research 3(2), 131–141 (1996)

[7] Saegusa, R., Metta, G., Sandini, G.: Body definition based on visuomotor correlation. IEEE Transaction on Industrial Electronics 59(8), 3199–3210 (2012)

[8] Saegusa, R., Metta, G., Sandini, G., Natale, L.: Developmental perception of the self and action. IEEE Transaction on Neural Networks and Learning Systems (in press, 2013)

[9] Saegusa, R., Sakano, H., Hashimoto, S.: Nonlinear principal component analysis to preserve the order of principal components. Neurocomputing 61, 57–70 (2004)

[10] Sandoe, K., Saharia, A.: Enterprise integration. John Wiley & Sons, Inc. (1999)

[11] Shimizu, T., Saegusa, R., Ikemoto, S., Ishiguro, H., Metta, G.: Self-protective whole body motion for humanoid robots based on synergy of global reaction and local reflex. Neural Networks 32, 109–118 (2012)

[12] Vernadat, F.B.: Enterprise modelling and integration. Springer (2003)

ACM 2013 PC Co-Chairs Message

The sign of our time is the amazing speed with which changes in the business world happen. This requires from the enterprises of today, and even more of the future to become *agile*, e.g. capable of adjusting themselves to changes in the surrounding world. Agility requires focus being moved from *optimization* to *collaboration and creativity*. At the same time, current process thinking is continuing to be preoccupied with the issue of optimizing performance through standardization, specialization, and automation. A focus on optimization has resulted in the workflow view (in which a process is considered as a flow of operations) emerging as predominant in the field of Business Process Management (BPM). Besides requiring a long time to develop, predefined sequence of events in a workflow can reduce the creativity of people participating in the process and thereby result in poor performance.

Moving focus to collaboration and creativity requires a paradigm shift in BPM that is already happening in practice. This, for example, can be seen in appearing a strong practical movement called Adaptive Case Management (ACM) which ".. is information technology that exposes structured and unstructured business information (business data and content) and allows structured (business) and unstructured (social) organizations to execute work (routine and emergent processes) in a secure but transparent manner."

While practitioners are trying to overcome the restrictions of workflow thinking, the research on the topic is somewhat lagging. The goal of this workshop is to bring together researchers and practitioners to discuss theoretical and practical problems and solutions in the area of non-workflow based approaches to BPM in general, and Adaptive Case Management (ACM), as a leading movement, in particular. This second edition of the workshop is aimed to promote new, non-traditional ways of modeling and controlling business processes, the ones that promote and facilitate *collaboration* and *creativity* in the frame of business processes.

For the second edition of AdaptiveCM workshop we have chosen six long papers and two short ones. The long papers represent a fare combination of theory and practice, three papers discuses theoretical issues, while three other papers are related to practice. The same is true for the short papers . one is theoretical, the other one is related to practice. Such combination promises interesting discussions on collaboration between research and practice in the area, the topic to which the brainstorming session at the end of the workshop will be devoted.

We thank the Program Committee members for their time and effort in ensuring the quality during the review process, as well as all the authors for the original ideas and for making AdaptiveCM 2013 possible. Also, we thank the OTM 2013 Organizing Committee members for their continuous support.

July 2013

Irina Rychkova
Ilia Bider
Keith Swenson

Y.T. Demey and H. Panetto (Eds.): OTM 2013 Workshops, LNCS 8186, p. 101, 2013.
© Springer-Verlag Berlin Heidelberg 2013

Patterns Boosting Adaptivity in ACM

Helle Frisak Sem, Thomas Bech Pettersen, Steinar Carlsen, and Gunnar John Coll

Computas AS, Lysaker torg 45, N-1327 Lysaker, Norway
{Helle.Frisak.Sem,Thomas.Bech.Pettersen,Steinar.Carlsen,
Gunnar.John.Coll}@computas.com

Abstract. Adaptivity is the ability to adjust behavior to changes in context. In enterprise ACM, the need for control, uniformity, and analysis meet end-user's needs to adapt to situations at hand. The interplay of different layers of declaratively defined templates can meet these needs in a flexible and sustainable manner. A data centric architecture with a library of process snippets building on standard activities and actions and a model of the organization with roles, provides an operational quality system. By combining this with a standardized declarative modeling of the case objects with codes and soft typing, we achieve a flexible platform for domain specific enterprise ACM systems. The result is a case- and goal-driven approach to adaptivity in ACM, taking into account knowledge workers' autonomy and the information context of the work. This paper discusses means of achieving adaptivity in ACM solutions and presents examples of practical realization by these means.

Keywords: Adaptive Case Management (ACM), Domain Specific ACM, Templates, Declarative Knowledge Representation, Task support.

1   Background

This paper is based on three real-world projects that have delivered award-winning operational ACM solutions - the Norwegian Food Safety Authority's MATS application [1, 2, 3], the freight train transporter CargoNet's GTS system [4, 5] and Norwegian Courts Administration's LOVISA solution [6]. All these are developed on the FrameSolutions ACM application framework.

This approach focuses on tasks and task support instead of end-to-end processes. Knowledge workers execute tasks specified as a set of steps where each step represents collaboration between the system and the user. The knowledge worker is always in charge. He may initiate new tasks in a goal-driven manner, with a high degree of freedom regarding sequencing of steps and tasks. Essentially, there is no process model or process model templates. Instead, there are goals and tasks with their steps. These steps may have several conditions associated, specifying the relevant and applicable constraints. The process starts with the selection of a goal and the following flow of work between tasks emerges. Prescriptive process models reflecting all possible paths from start to end is replaced by a set of flexible tasks selected and executed by the knowledge worker, composing a valid and unique "process" – on the fly.

Y.T. Demey and H. Panetto (Eds.): OTM 2013 Workshops, LNCS 8186, pp. 102–111, 2013.
© Springer-Verlag Berlin Heidelberg 2013

We use a *declarative representation* of task logic without a predefined, strict control flow [11]. The use of declarative definitions, separated from programming code, provides flexibility and opens for design-time configuration by the knowledge workers or their experts. Declaratively modeled tasks, libraries, rules, code sets and code relations are all explicitly represented as important business logic. In our approach, these definitions are stored in xml format, separated from the application code, in the form of definition base files. By deploying a new version of the relevant definition files and hot-deploying them, the new definitions are made operational on the fly.

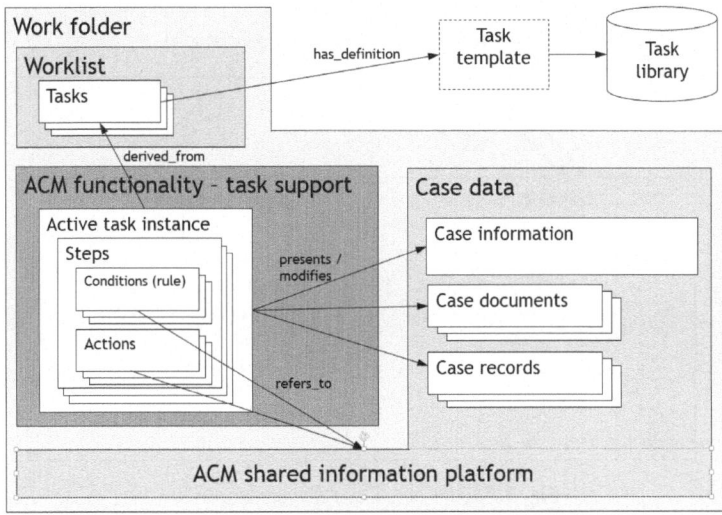

Fig. 1. Work folders providing task support

2   Motivation – ACM and Patterns

The "holy grail" of BPM has been to control behavior by means of process models, providing adaptability through changing these process models. Such changes may ideally come from end-user configuration activity, and the requirements of ACM typically include the possibility for the knowledge worker to perform configurations on the fly without support from professional system developers (as a developer configuration activity). Although important, we think this kind of model-driven change is overrated. In practice, the complexity of current model-based approaches requires implementation by developers understanding both programming languages and the detailed semantics of process modeling notations like BPMN. Consequently, BPMN models often end up as models of IT system behavior, instead of organizational or business behavior.

Contrasting the model-driven approach, we are in search of a *case- and goal-driven* approach, where the result is a dynamic combination of *process snippets*, all contributing to an emergent behavior and workflow. This provides more direct means for achieving adaptivity, than allowing users to change process models. There simply is no (large) process model available to change, instead there are (small) tasks associated with task definitions which can be puzzled and combined in any manner the knowledge worker sees as appropriate – subject to the prevailing constraints, such as deadlines, sequence, state and milestone dependencies. Instead of explicitly representing valid process paths, any path is allowed as long as constraints are adhered to. These constraints reflect means for necessary work performance control.

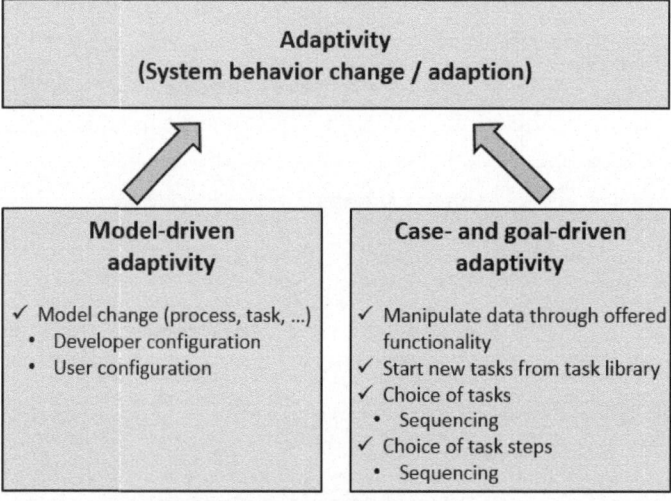

Fig. 2. Model- and Case-driven adaptivity

We are trying to establish a case-driven approach to adaptivity in ACM, taking into account the information context of the work, to provide adaptivity related to case data as well as user behavior. This strongly complements the traditional process model-driven approach.

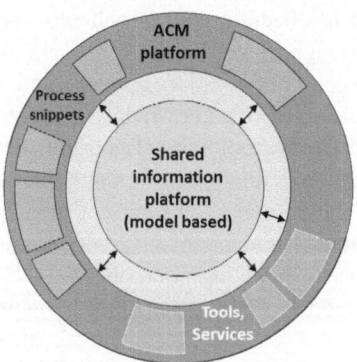

Fig. 3. Data-centric ACM [4]

In this paper, we are concerned with ACM systems with a built-in representation of their domain. The representation of the domain itself provides context - a domain specific ACM may be considered a subclass of a data-centric BPM, where there is a bundle of processes (process snippets in our case) all referring to the same domain model. In most of the BPM literature, this important property of the system is ignored. We think this is a consequence of traditional BPM putting the processes in the center, with data as an afterthought, whereas ACM is inherently data-centric with a shared information model as the core.

The tasks performed by knowledge workers in any organization are often variations of task themes or patterns. Patterns are a well-established metaphor for describing a family of similar phenomena. Patterns are defined by templates, and each individual instance can be described as a specification of the template. The template / pattern concept had a breakthrough in the world of computer programming following the "Hillside Group" in the mid-nineties [8], heavily inspired from Christopher Alexander's work in the field of building architecture in the seventies [7]. In the field of artificial intelligence the same concept was the key result from the European Union Research Project 5146 KADS in the eighties [9], where a catalog of generic reasoning patterns for problem solving is brought forward in order to facilitate the process of knowledge acquisition in complex problem solving scenarios.

Templates in the same tradition can increase the benefit of case management systems in general, and adaptive CM systems in particular, through techniques described below. The use of templates has proven to ease the initial formulation of the content of ACM applications, and more importantly – significantly decreases the cost and complexity of the long-term maintenance of applications and business logic.

3   Providing Adaptivity

For the knowledge worker, the need to be adaptive results from different sources, requiring different coping strategies. Unexpected events may occur in the case, new knowledge may turn up, other agendas may enter into the picture, or the case may have particular properties. A generic ACM approach must therefore include a range of adaptivity-enhancing features. This experience paper looks into the capability to create adaptivity, and outlines generic solution elements that can put the "A" into practical ACM solutions, in a broad sense:

- **Context-sensitive task patterns:** Templates for the functionality supporting the performance of tasks capable of adapting to data in its context; to case data, to system properties and to case state.
- **User-sensitive task patterns:** Templates that open for the user to choose as freely as possible under only required restrictions in order to execute the task in a regular way.
- **Goal-oriented task pattern libraries:** The possibility for the knowledge worker to select freely between goals – starting points of task sequences – in accordance to what he judges fit.

- **Domain model patterns:** A mechanism to set up parts of the case data structure in a declarative way separated from application programming code.
- **User-driven combination of process snippets:** The possibility for the user to build the work connected to the case dynamically without being predetermined. The case is what binds the different work tasks together, not a predefined process.
- **Real time composition of process snippet sequences:** Instead of full processes with all possibilities and choices predefined, the process emerges in a non-predictable way.
- **Business rule base:** business rules separated from application programming code and executed by a rule engine covering situations where the business logic frequently changes.

4   Elements of a Practical Approach

In this chapter, we provide more detail about the various knowledge representations utilized in our approach – task templates, task libraries, business objects and business rules.

The variety of knowledge representations described below has been very stable over the years, while underlying technologies have gone through many changes and shifts. We use knowledge engineering techniques for creating such representations. This can also be combined with other more traditional techniques. We have successfully deployed solutions combining this with Cockburn use case descriptions [10], BPMN, user stories, user story grouping, etc. We consider all these valuable process discovery techniques from the architect's toolbox.

4.1   Task Templates

Instead of trying to support linear and static "end-to-end" processes, ACM solutions can be based on dynamically combinable process snippets of task support functionality. Each such snippet covers a task pattern that can typically be performed by one person within the scope of one day.

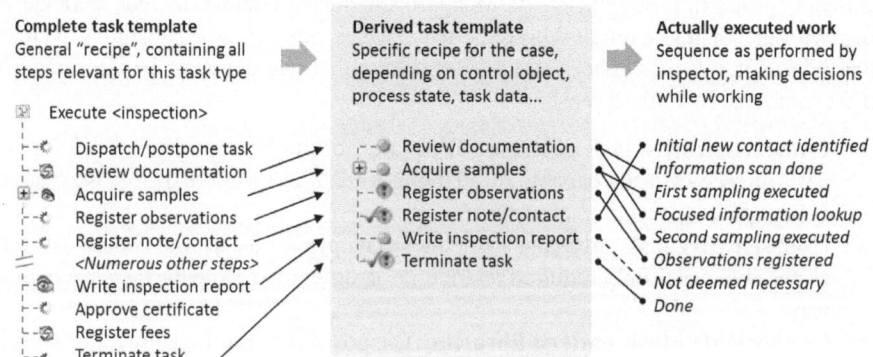

Fig. 4. Task template providing active task support in a particular context [3]

A task pattern is defined by means of a *task template*, which contains a set of *steps* as a general "recipe" for performing the task. These steps are subject to several *conditions*, defined using predicates and rules, which make it possible to derive a task template for the specific context as a unique recipe for a particular instance, always reflecting its state and data. This contextualized derived task template is the basis for offering active task support to the knowledge worker, who then selects and executes permitted steps, based on personal, professional judgment. Step conditions specify pre- and post-conditions in addition to repeat-conditions (step can be repeated), include-condition (step is made available dependent on context) and mandatory-conditions (step must be performed). The interplay between these conditions produces an appropriate set of steps for the user. Each such step will offer relevant functionality, information or tools, often including a user interface component for operating on relevant case data.

All available system services can be invoked from a step. Conditions and actions in the step definitions also have access to all available system functionality. By allowing a step to create new tasks, adaptive workflow can be accomplished.

Thus, a two-way flexibility is obtained. The task template is flexible with regard to the case and the system context – it is context-sensitive. The template also provides flexibility for the knowledge worker – it is user-sensitive. A main goal is to ensure correct practice, provide the right information and functionality, with full freedom to apply the knowledge worker's judgments and expertise. The task support functions as an operational quality system.

4.2   Goals and Goal-Oriented Task Libraries

In order to achieve a particular goal, the knowledge worker can select to create a new task instance. All the task types that the user may opt to start are organized in a runtime task library. Access to the tasks types is controlled by permissions linked to actively managed user roles. The knowledge worker may start any task available to him in the runtime task library, whenever he wants.

Goals may also be identified by the system, triggered by events. Such events may be the arrival of a new document in the document archive system, the submission of an application, the execution of a step in a task, or an event pattern. A typical event pattern is an expected reply from an external source not having arrived in time, giving rise to the need for some other action. When the system identifies the need for action, it can create and dispatch human knowledge worker tasks. Such automatically started tasks are being set up with available context information. Tasks that are created automatically may or may not be accessible from the runtime task library.

4.3   Domain Model Patterns

The diversity of domain object types is one of the main challenges of making a system to help the different functions of an enterprise knowledge organization become unified, uniform, and flexible in its behavior.

Our solution has been to apply modeling in different ways. First, we applied classic Java and database modeling. This is used for those parts of the case types that are common or require special types of functionality, such as identity handling. Second, we have extensively used *soft typing*, applying code sets defined in xml, instead of object typing. Third, we have combined code sets by means of code relations defined in xml, in order to define which acts and regulations are relevant for which types of cases. We have found *codes and code relations* very useful for implementing *interrelated controlled vocabularies*.

A cost driver when creating enterprise applications is the design, development and testing of domain objects and functionality. We have used a pattern that we call *business object definitions* for defining parts of case types that are mainly informational and vary between otherwise equal case types. Soft-typed business objects are defined as xml structures, handling storage and display with generic methods. We have found *soft-typed business objects* useful for realizing generalized solutions that are easy to specialize for future system enhancements.

4.4   Business Rules

Rules can be used to define:

- pre-, post-, and other conditions in connection with task definitions
- permitted logical relationships between data in the system
- calculation rules for various types of complex calculations

For ACM user organizations, declaratively defined business rules provide a particularly useful format for implementing regulations that are subject to frequent change, such that changes can be achieved without modifying the application.

By separating out business rules driving calculations in a rule base, several advantages are achieved:

- The calculations are easy to maintain, they are represented by rules in text form and can be edited in a user friendly way.
- The rules are stored separately from application code and can be changed without having to create and deploy a new version of the application.
- Calculation rules allow for multiple versions of regulations to co-exist in the system, to ensure that every case is evaluated in accordance with the correct set of rules valid when the relevant events of the case occurred.

5   Putting the Elements to Use

In an ACM project, an important part of developing a flexible environment is to develop a common language, toolbox and organizational model. These correspond to the atomic or molecular operations and organizational functions that the system will support, spanning out the room of possibility for realizing the ACM solution. This flexible environment supports establishing local patterns for both the development and the use of the system.

5.1   Subject Matter Experts

In several of our practical ACM applications, subject matter experts (SMEs) from the customer have been engaged in describing a shared data model as well as growing their own vocabulary related to their processes, tasks, business rules and organization roles. The approach enables the combination of snippets, turning them into assets both for discussing and for implementing future system functionality. This helps maintain focus on the customer's knowledge assets in terms of value creation, not only on best practice use of IT technologies for performing "requirements engineering". Working in this way rapidly provides handles for the SMEs and business analysts to identify the key ingredients of a knowledge organization – *value-driven system development*: What are the different user groups? What tasks do they solve on a daily basis? What are their frustrations? How are the tasks related? Who is allowed to initiate which tasks? Who collaborates on the problem solving needed to perform these tasks? Which task components are reusable? Which tasks, steps and conditions are meaningful as standard elements referring to known vocabularies? What added task-support to my application will have the greatest business benefits? How can we benefit from web-based self-service in improving data quality?

Our experience is that growing an adapted vocabulary of standard template fragments makes collaboration between system developers and subject matter experts (SMEs) easier and places the SMEs closer to the driver's seat.

SMEs can theoretically make and maintain the declarative definitions themselves, at least for the more straightforward situations. This amounts to design-time adaptivity without the need for professional system developers. However, creating and changing these definitions does require specialist training. It does after all define the business logic for tasks and domain data for the enterprise in question. It may be wise to let SMEs concentrate on specifications, and let developers perform the actual changes in the configuration controlled declarations and subject the changes to normal test procedures before deploying the new definitions.

5.2   Organizational Roles

We have found the use of a flexible organizational model very useful in ACM systems. This model allows for the representation of several (possibly multi-root) organizational trees spanned out using named relations (like "belongs-to", "reports-to" etc.) where any kind of organizational matrices can be represented. As a declarative structure, it can also be maintained separately from program code. The ability to describe a richer set of functional roles in the organization than the average "directory" solution enables enhanced flexibility in role-based collaboration patterns and provision of task templates for different purposes/roles.

5.3   The Art of Templating - Recognizing Patterns

As the first definitions of tasks and steps emerge from the collaboration between SMEs and knowledge engineers, there will be little repeatability or familiarity between the definitions. As the project team gains speed, a common vocabulary grows in the form of patterns of processes, tasks and steps. The FrameSolutions approach represents these building blocks as *standard elements* – standard steps, conditions, actions, subtasks and tasks.

These standard elements can be connected as *sources of inheritance* to other definition elements, making it easy to maintain a uniform and consistent definition set for an enterprise case management platform. These standard elements are easy to reuse through the inheritance scheme, and the elements that represent the reuse can have their properties and behavior defined as overrides to the standard element properties and behavior.

The ultimate success is obtained when the SMEs start reasoning and communicating using these standard elements as a living meta-language, gradually established through a domain oriented bottom-up approach, well founded in the enterprise's knowledge worker community. By focusing on process snippets the users can "put puzzle pieces together" without the traditional end-to-end processes. The organization can start small and achieve benefits early. Consolidated and suitable end-to-end processes – or even longer process fragments – are often unrealistic in today's dynamic and unpredictable enterprise environments.

5.4   Templating at Higher Levels of Abstraction

While our ACM framework offers various built in template types as described above, a particular ACM system may offer additional higher-level templates that form a package of the basic templates. In such a package, task templates typically are bundled (loosely coupled) with some of their relevant context, such as encoded legislation. This kind of packaging tends to be domain-specific, and may ultimately result in re-usable ACM solutions that can be put to use in similar knowledge organizations. We have successfully "exported" task templates for immigration administration including visa applications from an ACM solution made for UDI (The Norwegian Directorate of Immigration) to other countries also bound by the Schengen Agreement (Denmark, Greece, Macedonia, Kosovo).

6   Conclusion: Towards Case-and Goal-Driven Adaptivity

We have discussed how adaptivity can be achieved in a work context, using active task support, user-decided sequencing of task steps, and goal-driven task libraries [2, 3, 4, 5, 6]. The result is a dynamic combination of process snippets, all contributing to emergent behavior and workflow. This provides more direct means for achieving adaptivity, than allowing users to change models, replacing the traditional model-based policy of "what is allowed is only what is prescribed" with the knowledge worker policy of "anything not forbidden is allowed". Case-driven adaptivity takes the information context of tasks into account – adaptivity is related to case data. Goal-driven adaptivity is the result of putting the knowledge worker in charge, allowing dynamic sequencing of tasks and their steps.

Being *built-to-change*, through the ability to adapt to changes in business logic and the business environment, is a key to delivering successful ACM applications. This can be achieved by combining traditional systems development with a declarative approach to business logic representation, avoiding buried logic in the source code and enabling runtime changes to knowledge representations (task definitions, rules, codes, etc.) by simply reloading xml files.

Declarative business logic representations are essential for building adaptive operational case management solutions. Instead of describing complete and predefined end-to-end processes, the focus is on identifying activities of the organizational actors involved and how to support them in a best possible way. Goal-driven task libraries give access to process snippets as combinable resources for action. The knowledge workers themselves are empowered to combine these process snippets into emerging processes.

References

1. 2012 Winners Announced in Global Awards for Excellence in Adaptive Case Management, http://adaptivecasemanagement.org/awards_2012_winners.html
2. Sem, H.F., Carlsen, S., Coll, G.J.: Norwegian Food Safety Authority, Nominated by Computas AS, Norway. In: Fischer, L. (ed.) How Knowledge Workers Get Things Done - Real-world Adaptive Case Management. Future Strategies Inc., Florida (2012)
3. Sem, H.F., Carlsen, S., Coll, G.J.: On Two Approaches to ACM. In: La Rosa, M., Soffer, P. (eds.) BPM Workshops 2012. LNBIP, vol. 132, pp. 12–23. Springer, Heidelberg (2013)
4. Sem, H.F., Carlsen, S., Coll, G.J., Pettersen, T.B.: ACM for railway freight operations. In: Intelligent BPMS. BPM and Workflow Handbook series. Future Strategies Inc., Florida (2013)
5. Sem, H.F., Carlsen, S., Coll, G.J., Holje, H., Landro, E., Mork, H., Pettersen, T.B.: GTS - Cargonet AS Norway, http://adaptivecasemanagement.org/awards_2013_winners.html
6. Pettersen, T.B., Carlsen, S., Coll, G.J., Matras, M., Moen, T.G., Sem, H.F.: LOVISA - Norwegian Courts Administration (NCA), http://adaptivecasemanagement.org/awards_2013_winners.html
7. Alexander, C.: The timeless way of building. Oxford University Press (1979)
8. Gamma, E., Helm, R., Johnson, R., Vlissides, J.: Design Patterns: Elements of Reusable Object-Oriented Software. Addison-Wesley Professional (1994)
9. Schreiber, G., Wielinga, B., Breuker, J.: KADS: A Principled Approach to Knowledge-Based System Development (Knowledge-Based Systems). Academic Press (1993)
10. Cockburn, A.: Writing effective use cases. Addison-Wesley Professional (2000)
11. Rychkova, I., Regev, G., Wegman, A.: Using declarative specifications in business process design. International Journal of Computer Science and Applications 5(3b) (2008)

CMMN Implementation in Executable Model of Business Process at Order-Based Manufacturing Enterprise

Vadim Kuzin and Galina Kuzina

Mosflowline, Russian Federation, 125599, Moscow, Izhorskaya str., 6
zilbernstein@gmail.com, kuzina@mosflowline.ru

Abstract. Agility - capability of an enterprise to function in the highly competitive and dynamic business environment. To survive and successfully develop companies should have flexible, adaptive business processes and management system that enforces the strategy and ensures achievement of target (commercial) goals. Case management is a paradigm for supporting flexible and knowledge intensive business processes. It is strongly based on data as the typical product of these processes. This paper presents implementation of this paradigm at the manufacturing enterprise based upon principles of CMMN emerging standard, declarative approach to business process modeling and the systems theory. The implementation uses first order logic (Prolog) and elements of lambda calculus. It has been in operation for more than 3 years.

1 Introduction

Modern business environment is highly competitive and dynamic. To survive and successfully develop companies should be not only agility – focused and have flexible, adaptive business processes but also the business management system that enforces implementation of the business strategy and ensures achievement of target (commercial) goals. The operation of business management system includes the online monitoring current state of the business, comparing it to the planned one, analyzing causes of deviation and generating the corrective responses by updating the plan, launching, pausing/stopping the relevant business processes. Therefore for businessmen to have the tool ensuring the achievement of business goals by managing business processes these processes should be closely linked to the state of the business and its management system.

This paper presents the experience obtained in development and operation of flexible and adaptive business process management system at ZAO "Mosflowline" (www.mosflowline.ru) - the manufacturing enterprise with order-based engineering and production processes. It produces polyurethane-insulated components for oil and district heating pipelines. The enterprise operates in highly competitive environment imposing strict requirements on prices, delivery times, payment adjourning periods. The business processes in the enterprise of this type have the following distinctive features: (a) a customer can make changes to the list of the ordered products, their

Y.T. Demey and H. Panetto (Eds.): OTM 2013 Workshops, LNCS 8186, pp. 112–123, 2013.

configurations, scope and time of delivery "on the run" while the order is being executed; (b) a contract manager can pick different ways to execute the contract: production, resale, outsourcing of certain operations depending on the book of orders, availability of production capacity and other factors determining the state of the company; (c) large number of customers resulting in large number of simultaneously executed orders; (d) the size of nomenclature is more than several thousand items due to various combinations of product parameters affecting manufacturing processes. Features (a) and (b) indicate the high level of agility of these processes: they can be implemented in a number of ways depending on specific case and personal preferences of the client and the contract manager while each of the ways is limited to a set of template implementations. The order size can vary from several to several hundred different items. The number of orders in work varies from several dozens to several hundreds. Product data is also continuously changed (both in terms of structure and content) due to requests from the customers and R&D efforts aimed at improving quality and characteristics of the product line.

The main goal of the project was development and introduction of the adaptive and flexible business process management system that should ensure achievement of the enterprise commercial goals. The project required resolving two large problems. The first one – development of the agile enterprise model that in addition to business process definitions should include the definitions of:

— goals represented as integrated metrics identifying the planned state of the business at different levels of management;
— management system ensuring the monitoring of business process execution and achievement of the identified goals;
— resources (material, human, information) used in business processes;
— organization structure identifying subordination of business process participant and responsibility for goal achievement.

The enterprise model should allow for computer-aided verification at the stage of initial development as well as at the stage of modification due to process improvement or adaptation.

The second problem – is development of the system supporting the execution of flexible and adaptive business processes. The system should:

— ensure integration of definitions of goals, resources, organization structure, planned and actual business states into the single information model of the business;
— provide selection of the specific business process implementation depending on the current state of the business and user preferences;
— enable modification of business processes in the course of their execution;
— enable direct execution of declarative definitions of the business processes without the need to translate them into software code.

Solution to the first problem rests upon the mathematical systems theory that deals with the dynamical systems/processes in the physical world [1]. The advanced approach to development of the agile enterprise model and non-workflow theory of business processes based upon the systems theory is described in [2, 3, 4]. According to this approach an enterprise is represented as three-layered model consisting of assets, sensors and business process instances (BPI). Enterprise is defined as multidimensional state space. A BPI is then defined as a trajectory in the space-time, and business process model - as a set of formal rules describing all "valid" trajectories. Business processes support system should assists BPI participants to follow one of the valid trajectories and provide them with a common interactive "map" where they can together try to find their path towards the BPI's goal despite the "roadblocks" appearing where they are not expected.

Development of the system supporting the execution of flexible and adaptive business processes where the information context has the dominating influence (the second problem) is based upon data-centric approach to BPM. It draws on several influences [5, 6, 7, 8, 9, 10, 11, 12, 13, 14, 15, 16, 17, 18, 20].

The work has brought the following results:

- the model of a case has been developed based upon SADT [25] declarative modeling of the semantics of business processes as hierarchical network of business-activities transforming input resources into output resources using mechanisms and guided by control signals;
- the process information model has been developed as a semantic network complemented with the first order logic constructs (Prolog) and the elements of lambda-calculus (Lisp) to define calculated (derived) properties of classes (e. g. aggregated indicators of the business's condition);
- the model of a case has been complemented with process information model (its information context) containing the knowledge of the application domain represented using the basic elements of semantic networks (triplets, relationships, classes), the combined model enables automatic verification of model's consistency (since a model is represented as composition of logical statements);
- the case model interpreter has been developed for direct execution of cases implementing the basic concepts of CMMN standard: (a) rich planning during execution of case instance; (b) declarative/rules – based behavior specifications; (c) tasks, (hierarchical) stages and milestones;
- the information model interpreter has been developed in the form of self-adapting user interface to input and display the data needed to perform specific business activity.

The section 2 contains a real life example of modeling the part of the business-system that implements the process of preparing the price proposals for engineering, production and shipment of oil pipeline components with evaluation of economic efficiency considering the current financial and operational condition of the company. The section 3 contains the fragment of the information model of the process and short description of the business-system information metamodel. The section 4 briefly describes the basic elements of business-system behavior model. The section 6 describes related work. The section 7 contains brief conclusions.

2   Example of Developing Business Process Model

The paper considers an enterprise as a complex adaptive business system that achieves the target goals through execution of business processes. It can be described as the composition:

$$BS = <S, \{G\}, \{F\}, SF, \{R\}>$$

where: S – state space of the system, {G} – set of goals organized in a tree, {A} – set of the activities implemented by the business processes to achieve the goals (e. g. order-based manufacturing of products, making changes to the order, etc.), SF – structure of the system that ensures implementation of the activities and achievement of the goals, {R} – set of resources utilized and consumed in the business processes (materials, equipment, staff, information). The state of a business system is defined through the states of its resources, departments and finished, ongoing and scheduled business processes. The papers considers a business process as transition between states of the business system resulting from coordinated interaction of business system departments that produce and exchange material and information resources.

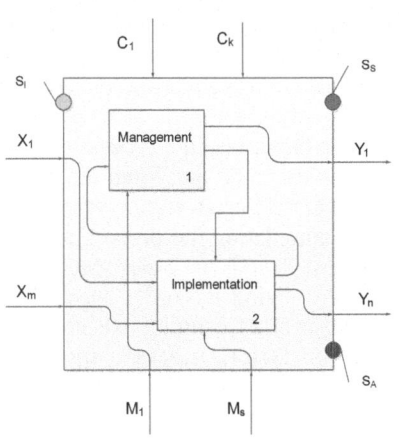

Fig. 1. Business Activity metamodel

The processes causing transitions of the business system and its components between states are defined using the concept of business- activity. The definition of a business - activity (BA) includes (fig. 1): input resources {X1 ... Xm} (materials, parts, documents), output resources {Y1 ... Yn} (products, documents), control signals {C1 ... Ck} (planned indexes), supporting resources {M1 ... Ms} (staff, equipment, instrument), a start state (SI) (a guard counterpart), a successful completion state (SS) (a milestone counterpart), an abort state (SA). The BA execution is represented as two interacting processes:

an implementation process and a control process. The BA's implementation process ensures transformation of the BA's input resources into output resources using the supporting resources. The BA's control process ensures that parameters of implementation process tend to the control signals and is a combination of standard functions: planning, accounting, analysis, monitoring/adaptation implemented for the specific BA.

Business system operation can be represented as hierarchical framework of BAs interacting with each other. The top level BAs implement the company's strategy, the terminal level BAs correspond to activities performed by ultimate performers. Consider the business function of preparation of orders to deliver oil pipeline components from some intermediate level of BAs hierarchy (fig. 2). The BA ensures the transition of the business system from its current state to the state where it has achieved the total value of open orders specified in the sales plan. The BA is implemented by a cross-functional business process involving several departments: commercial (CD), product engineering (ED), procurement (PD) and process engineering (PED). The implementation business process (iBP) starts with search for order resulting in a request for price proposal from customer. The request contains technical description of the products needed by the customer. The ED employee (design engineer) uses the request to create the order specification containing a list of items identifying type and parameters of the products to be delivered. If while creating the order specification the ED employee fails to select the appropriate product from the company's catalog of products then he starts the BA of product development based upon the customer's requirements specified in the received request. The business process implementing the product development BA starts with creating a request for new product development. The request is used in development of product drawings and process maps. The oil pipeline components have complicated configuration. Consequently the description of an oil pipeline component includes parametric geometrical model, the required amount and list of materials required to fabricate the product. In developing the process map the process engineer selects materials and parts from the company's catalogue of materials. If the engineer fails to find some material in the catalogue he queries the procurement department if it is possible to deliver the material with specified parameters within required time period (specified by customer in the request for proposal). The PD employee searches for vendors that could deliver the material/part requesting the price and delivery times. If the PD employee succeeds then the material is input into the company's catalogue of materials. Otherwise the process engineer should change the process map and the requirements to materials. When the process map is finished the notification is generated and sent to the design engineer. When the order specification is finished (and notifications of completing the process maps for all non-standard products are received) the ED employee sends the order specification to CD for commercial proposal preparation. Upon receiving the order specification the CD employee is to choose between various scenarios of contract execution. For example if the business system lacks free production facilities in the period when certain specification item is to be delivered then the CD employee should indicate that the item is to be resold rather than produced. Also if the business system has got products available on stock with parameters close to the parameters of certain specification items then the CD employee starts the BA of agreeing new parameters of the items with the customer. Other parameters of order execution include: payment adjourning period, usage of customer's materials, outsourcing of certain production operations. Therefore the CD employee is to choose the scenario of the order execution considering the current financial condition of the company, forecast of revenue, liabilities, assets, production facilities available in the period when the order is to be executed. After the scenario has been chosen the CD employee specifies the profitability of each specification item, calculates its sell price and the overall order budget. Then the budget is sent to the head of CD department for approval. The head of CD department can return the price proposal to the CD employee for modification if its parameters do not satisfy the control signals of the proposal preparation BA. While the price proposal is being prepared the customer usually makes a number of changes to the contents of order specification as well as technical parameters of its items. Any change to the order specification results in the need to agree the change with the departments involved in the order execution: PD, warehouse and the shop in order to ensure that it is possible to fabricate and deliver the products according to the order specification within the required time period.

The formalized model of the business system has been developed on the basis of IDEF0 notation [24] that has been substantially extended to capture the semantics of the notation constructs. The notation has been selected because: (a) it ensures

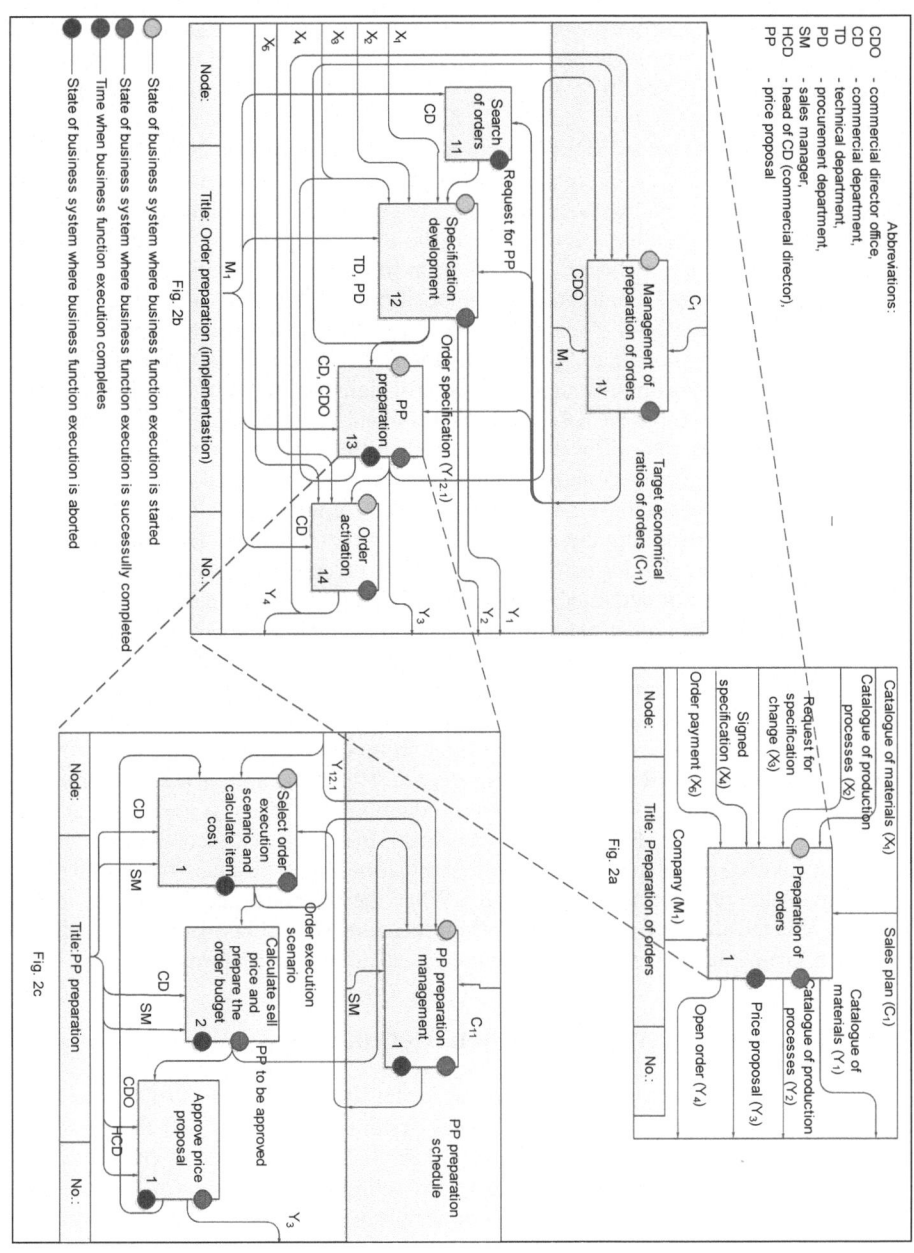

Fig. 2. The fragment of "Preparation of orders to deliver oil pipeline components" case model

top-down consistent design enabling "completeness" of the model; (b) provides most of the constructs to define business system behavior and organization; (c) can be represented using semantic networks; (d) SADT methodology [25] treats processes as transitions between states. It is necessary to note that IDEF0 arrows stand for not sequence of execution but for cause-and-effect relationships between business activities (boxes). Using extended IDEF0 notation the above example can be formalized in the following way (Fig.2). "Preparation of orders" BA (Fig. 2a) ensures transition of the business system from S0 state where it has received the sales plan C1 to the one of the states: S1 where C1 has been fulfilled (the total of open orders in the period T exceeds or equal C1), S2 where C1 has not been fulfilled but the period has finished.

The Fig. 2b presents hierarchical decomposition of "Preparation or order" BA. It includes the following BAs: "Search of orders", "Specification development", "Price proposal (PP) preparation" and "Order activation". Each "child" BA is provided with necessary input, supporting resources and control signals. Output of each BA's serves either as output of the parent BA or the input of one of its "siblings". Also pre- and post-conditions of execution for each BA are identified. "Management of preparation of orders" BA generates the control signals correcting the target economical ratios of the orders such as: profitability, adjourning period, shipment period, etc. The signals are generated upon receiving the feedback from "implementation" BAs that includes: the number of the prepared specifications, the total revenue of prepared price proposals, the total revenue of activated orders. The "Price proposal preparation" BA is decomposed into: "Select order execution scenario and calculate item cost" BA, "Calculate sell price and prepare the order budget" BA, "Approve price proposal" BA, "Management of price proposal preparation" BA. The most interesting BA in the decomposition is "Select order execution scenario...". Depending on the condition of the business system the execution of the BA can involve taking various decisions on whether produce or resell certain items of the order specification, use customer's materials or own materials, outsource certain production operations or perform it at own production facilities, etc. So the list of decisions to be taken and their sequence is not known in advance and depend on the current situation in the business system (book of orders, available production facilities, etc.). When the BA starts and the current condition is evaluated then it becomes clear what decisions should be made. When all necessary decisions have been made the final cost calculation is performed.

3   Business System Information Metamodel

To develop the business system information model first order logic (Prolog) has been used. The following features of the business system have determined the choice of Prolog: (a) need to use the single method to describe complex systems (business systems); (b) need to make automatic formal verification of consistency of the resulting models; (c) easy modification of the model at runtime; (d) easy integration with relational databases of corporate information systems. To use Prolog the entire contextual information about the business process should be represented as a semantic network describing the knowledge about the application domain with use of triplets (object-attribute-value) as well as various relationships and classes. The information metamodel graph can be viewed at: http://en.acm-systems.ru/business-system-information-metamodel. The basic concepts of the information metamodel are: term (concept), entity, relationship, class, lambda-expression, predicate. The term is the abstract supertype of entity and class. Class – is the counterpart of a mathematical set. Class consists of the elements of certain type that is specified by ItemType relationship. Class can be defined by enumeration, operation over sets (union, intersection, subtraction) or with use of predicate. Each class definition method is encapsulated in a certain subclass (Enumeration, Union, Intersection, Subtraction, DefinedByPredicate). Class members are identified by SetInstances relationship. Properties of a class are defined by relationships. Relationship is a subset of Cartesian product of classes (RElement0 x RElement1 x … x RElementn, где 0, 1, .. n – domainindex attribute values). The metamodel includes directed relationships only. Depending on the "direction" of the underlying relationship class properties can be "direct" (where class occupies first position in the relevant Cartesian product (domainIndex attribute = 0)) and "reverse" (in all other cases when domainIndex attribute > 0). The above example demonstrated that business system state can be represented using integrated indexes like the total workload of the equipment, expected profit margin of the book of orders, total revenue of order, etc.

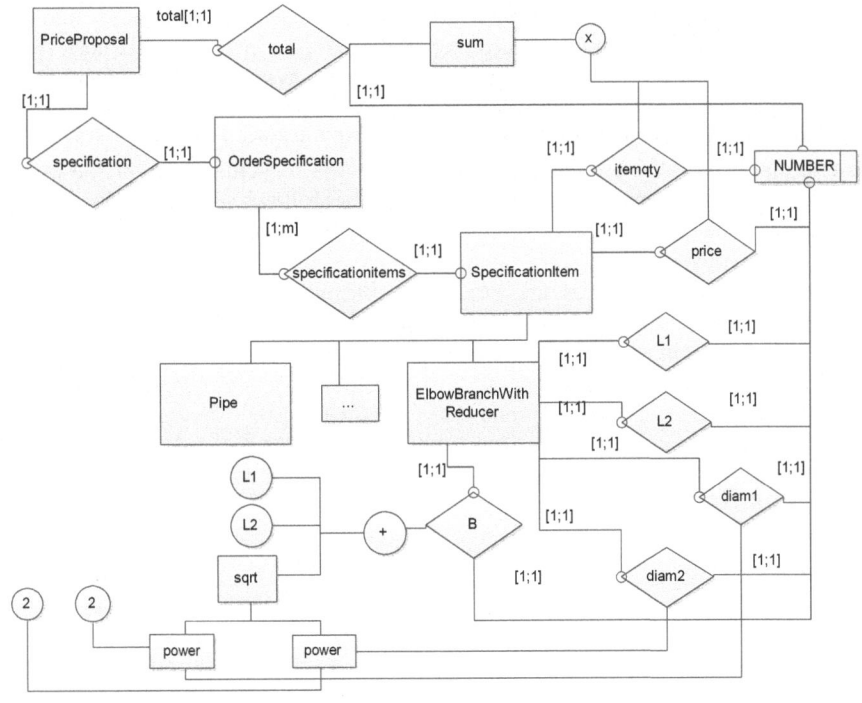

Fig. 3. Fragment of "Preparation of order" information model

To enable definition of such indexes the business system metamodel includes the construct of "derived" property using lambda expressions. Lambda expressions use standard functions like sum, sqrt, power, etc and properties of classes represented as function calls. Consider the fragment of the information model of "Preparation of orders" business process presented in Fig. 3. The model includes the classes: PriceProposal, OrderSpecification, SpecificationItem, Pipe, ElbowBranchWithReducer (subclasses of SpecificationItem with the relationships: specification, specificationitems, total, itemqty, price, L1, L2, diam1, diam2, B. The PriceProposal class has the derived property "total" that can be represented as lambda-expression: (sum (* price(specificationitems(specification(P))) itemqty(specificationitems(specification(P)))), where P is the instance of PriceProposal. In the expression specification, specificationitems, itemqty, price properties are represented as "functions": specification(P) – gives instance of OrderSpecification for the instance P of PriceProposal, specificationitems(specification(P)) gives instances of SpecificationItem. Another example of derived property is geometrical parameter B of ElbowBranchWithReducer class. The lambda-expression of the parameter: (+ (L1(I) L2(I) sqrt (+ power(diam1(I) 2) power(diam2(I) 2))), where I – the instance of SpecificationItem.

4   Executable Model of Business System Represented in Prolog

To execute business processes implementing business activities case model interpreter (CMI) and information model interpreter (IMI) have been built. CMI performs the following main tasks: (a) initial planning of business system track in its state space; (b) creating, starting, pausing, resuming, completing and aborting execution of business activities based upon dynamic evaluation of business system state as well as definitions of the business activities; (c) registration of actual track of the business system in its state space. The IMI performs the following main tasks: (a) auto-generation of data input forms; (b) auto-generation of reports; (c) information model-based creation of instances. CMI operation is based upon the business system operation metamodel developed on the basis of the business system information metamodel. The graphical representation of the business system operation metamodel can be viewed at: http://en.acm-systems.ru/business-system-operation-metamodel. The description of CMI and IMI operation is available at: http://en.acm-systems.ru/description-of-acm-and-im-interpreters/.

5   The Related Work

In the introduction we mentioned the approach proposed in [2, 3, 4]. It is based upon system-related view of business process and consider business process instance (BPI) as a point moving in multi-dimensional state – space. A BPI is then defined as trajectory in space – time, business process model – as a set of formal rules describing all valid trajectories, goal - as a point or surface in the state space, enterprise - as a complex multilevel adaptive system. We have used the same concepts and our approach to agile enterprise modeling (first problem) is very similar to this one. Differences of our model are driven by the practical goal: to develop and introduce the working system at the real-life enterprise which operation is aimed at achieving commercial goals. The differences include: a) introduction of organization structure as the backbone of goal-based management system; b) classification of resources (materials, equipment, staff, information) as predicate-defined sets of objects used in state space definitions; c) application of lambda-calculus and first order logic in calculation of complex information properties needed to evaluate the current business state. Interestingly that the need in flexible "navigator" that can suggest a path from any given position to the goal indicated in [2] has evidently arisen in the course of the operation of our system. Currently we have already developed such a navigator and are testing it.

In our development of the agile and flexible business process support system we have used the basic concepts of CMMN draft standard [19, 20]: guard - pre-condition, milestone - post-condition, stage – business activity with decomposition. As in GSM approach [15, 17] our agile and flexible business process support system uses precise mathematical definition for operation semantics. This aspect enables verification of the executable models. In contrast to GSM approach our model is Prolog-based and is executed directly by the interpreter we have developed. Another difference of our implementation from GSM approach is using the semantic network to represent the enterprise information model. The semantic network allows a) describe complex information context b) provide easy modification of the information model c) definition of calculated properties using first order logic and lambda calculus.

ConDec [21] is fully declarative business process language in which the possible sequencings of activities are governed entirely by constraints expressed in temporal logic. The main problem of using this approach at the real-life manufacturing enterprise is integration of business process definitions and constraints in its information space so that the definitions are described using the enterprise information objects.

Existing commercial products [16, 22, 23] provide support for flexible business processes but their data representation is document-oriented and not suitable for the manufacturing enterprise with parametric product data models, complex integrated indicators of the business state.

6   Conclusions

Designing the flexible business process management systems needs the theory of business processes to be developed using the system-based approach to the modeling of the business processes. The business processes at a manufacturing company are executed in complicated information context. Semantic networks have been chosen to build the formal representation of the context that in business process execution models got naturally mapped on first order logic (Prolog constructs). The declarative definition of the business process models using first order logic has enabled automatic verification of the consistency of the definition. To execute business processes we have built the interpreters of business process models and information models. In introducing the system we have discovered that business process participants are interested in: a) simulation of different cases/situations; b) flexible "navigator" that can suggest the most appropriate way to handle particular case by choosing specific implementation of the corresponding business process; c) more advanced tools to design the case information models; d) further development of reporting tools.

The implementation of basic concepts of CMMN standard in practice has demonstrated that they cover all of the major aspects of designing the adaptive business process management systems: declarative approach to definition of business process semantics; logic-based evaluation of the activities to be run depending on the state of the business; definitions of business process instances can be modified during execution.

We have started to introduce the system more than three years ago by gradually replacing the old ERP system. Currently the system has about 100 online users (each of them can have several dozens of processes running). Scalability of the system is limited to the hardware capacity only (now it runs on 4 x Intel Xeons with 16 GB of RAM). Users have accepted it well in owing to its functional capabilities: a) timely notification about encountered problems (arrears of payments, arrears of receiving originals of the documents, shortage of materials on stock, availability of finished goods to be shipped, etc) and advising on how to handle them by launching specific business processes; b) fast adaptation of the system to the new processes, new conditions of process execution, new information objects and new properties of existing information objects.

The system has been integrated with the accounting system, PDM system, production scheduling system and other applications using ESB (ApacheMQ). The system generates and consumes information objects in XML format that are transferred through the bus. The structure of the objects is native to the applications they go to or they come from. The system generates objects to be exchanged as "reports" obeying the format of the consumer system. When the system receives an object from the external application it parses the object into a fragment of the semantic network in accordance with the enterprise information model.

Acknowledgments. The authors would like to thank the anonymous reviewers for their comments on initial draft of this work that helped to make this paper more readable.

References

1. Kalman, R.E., Falb, P.L., Arbib, M.A.: Topics in Mathematical System Theory. McGraw-Hill (1969)
2. Bider, I.: Towards a Non-workflow Theory of Business Processes. In: Proc. ACM 2012 Workshop (2012)
3. Bider, I., Bellinger, G., Perjons, E.: Modeling an Agile Enterprise: Reconciling Systems and Process Thinking. In: Johannesson, P., Krogstie, J., Opdahl, A.L. (eds.) PoEM 2011. LNBIP, vol. 92, pp. 238–252. Springer, Heidelberg (2011)
4. Bider, I., Perjons, E., Elias, M.: Untangling the Dynamic Structure of an Enterprise by Applying a Fractal Approach to Business Processes. In: Sandkuhl, K., Seigerroth, U., Stirna, J. (eds.) PoEM 2012. LNBIP, vol. 134, pp. 61–75. Springer, Heidelberg (2012)
5. Nigam, A., Caswell, N.S.: Business artifacts: An approach to operational specification. IBM Systems Journal 42(3), 428–445 (2003)
6. Bhattacharya, K., Caswell, N.S., Kumaran, S., Nigam, A., Wu, F.Y.: Artifact-centered operational modeling: Lessons from customer engagements. IBM Systems Journal 46(4), 703–721 (2007)
7. Bhattacharya, K., Gerede, C.E., Hull, R., Liu, R., Su, J.: Towards formal analysis of artifact-centric business process models. In: Alonso, G., Dadam, P., Rosemann, M. (eds.) BPM 2007. LNCS, vol. 4714, pp. 288–304. Springer, Heidelberg (2007)

8. Gerede, C.E., Bhattacharya, K., Su, J.: Static analysis of business artifact-centric operational models. In: IEEE International Conference on Service-Oriented Computing and Applications (2007)
9. Gerede, C.E., Su, J.: Specification and verification of artifact behaviors in business process models. In: Krämer, B.J., Lin, K.-J., Narasimhan, P. (eds.) ICSOC 2007. LNCS, vol. 4749, pp. 181–192. Springer, Heidelberg (2007)
10. Liu, R., Bhattacharya, K., Wu, F.Y.: Modeling business contexture and behavior using business artifacts. In: Krogstie, J., Opdahl, A.L., Sindre, G. (eds.) CAiSE 2007. LNCS, vol. 4495, pp. 324–339. Springer, Heidelberg (2007)
11. Kumaran, S., Liu, R., Wu, F.Y.: On the duality of information-centric and activity-centric models of business processes. In: Bellahsène, Z., Léonard, M. (eds.) CAiSE 2008. LNCS, vol. 5074, pp. 32–47. Springer, Heidelberg (2008)
12. Küster, J.M., Ryndina, K., Gall, H.C.: Generation of BPM for object lifecycle compliance. In: Alonso, G., Dadam, P., Rosemann, M. (eds.) BPM 2007. LNCS, vol. 4714, pp. 165–181. Springer, Heidelberg (2007)
13. Damaggio, E., Deutsch, A., Vianu, V.: Artifact systems with data dependencies and arithmetic. In: ICDT 2011, pp. 66–77 (2011)
14. Marin, M., Hull, R., Vaculín, R.: Data Centric BPM and the Emerging Case Management Standard: A Short Survey. In: La Rosa, M., Soffer, P. (eds.) BPM Workshops 2012. LNBIP, vol. 132, pp. 24–30. Springer, Heidelberg (2013)
15. Damaggio, E., Hull, R., Vaculín, R.: On the equivalence of incremental and fixpoint semantics for business artifacts with guard-stage-milestone lifecycles. In: Rinderle-Ma, S., Toumani, F., Wolf, K. (eds.) BPM 2011. LNCS, vol. 6896, pp. 396–412. Springer, Heidelberg (2011)
16. van der Aalst, W.M.P., Weske, M.: Case Handling: a new paradigm for business process support. Data & Knowledge Engineering 53(2), 129–162 (2005)
17. Hull, R., Damaggio, E., De Masellis, R., Fournier, F., Gupta, M., Heath, T., Hobson, S., Linehan, M., Maradugu, S., Nigam, A., Sukaviriya, P., Vaculín, R.: Business Artifacts with Guard-Stage-Milestone Lifecycles: Managing Artifact Interactions with Conditions and Events. In: Proc. ACM Intl. Conf. Distributed Event-Based Systems (DEBS) (2011)
18. de Man, H.: Case Management: A Review of Modeling Approaches. BPTrends (January 2009)
19. Object Management Group. Case Management Process Modeling (CMPM) Request for Proposal. Document bmi/2009-09-23 (October 2009)
20. BizAgi, Cordys, IBM, Oracle, SAP AG, Singularity (OMG Submitters), Agile Enterprise Design, Stiftelsen SINTEF, TIBCO, Trisotech (Co-Authors). Proposal for: Case Management Modeling and Notation (CMMN) Specification 1.0. (OMG Document bmi/2012-07-10). In response to: Case Management Process Modeling (CMPM) RFP (OMG Document bmi/2009-09-04). Object Management Group (July 2012)
21. van der Aalst, W.M.P., Pesic, M.: Decserflow: Towards a truly declarative service flow language. In: Bravetti, M., Núñez, M., Zavattaro, G. (eds.) WS-FM 2006. LNCS, vol. 4184, pp. 1–23. Springer, Heidelberg (2006)
22. Zhu, W., Becker, B., Boudreaux, J., Braman, S., Do, T., Gomez, D., Marin, M., Vaughan, A.: Advanced Case Management with IBM Case Manager. IBM Redbooks, New York (2011)
23. de Man, H.: Case Management: Cordys Approach. BPTrends (February 2009)
24. ICAM Architecture Part II-Volume IV - Function Modeling Manual (IDEF0)
25. AFWAL-TR-81-4023, Materials Laboratory, Air Force Wright Aeronautical Laboratories, Air Force Systems Command, Wright-Patterson Air Force Base, Ohio 45433 (June 1981)

Process Analysis and Collective Behavior in Organizations: A Practitioner Experience

Paola Mauri

Senior consultant in System Management
Star s.r.l – Via Don Minzoni 15 22060 Cabiate- Italy
paola.mauri@alice.it

Abstract. The analysis of organizational processes could support complexity and heterogeneity of companies if it is able to capture and organize the social behavior of enterprises. The phases - Orienteering, Modeling and Mapping – and the key characteristics of an analysis approach are described, focusing on results and returns. Results are the expected and committed outputs of the analysis process, such as the modeling of workflow processes. Returns are the impacts of the process analysis on individual and social behavior, such as awareness and motivation. Returns support the definition of the key assets of an organization, influence the modeling of workflow processes and are useful to capture the non-workflow components of organizational processes. This approach has been applied through a long-term activity in public and private enterprises. An experience is described presenting strong and weak points of the approach, differences and similarities, in particular between workflow and non-workflow processes.

Keywords: Business Process Analysis, Workflow and Non-workflow Processes, Social Behavior.

1   Introduction

The process approach is a key feature in the development, implementation and improvement of quality management systems [1].

The standard ISO (International Standard Organization) 9001:2008 "Quality Management Systems. Requirements" is based on process approach and the same approach could be applied in the development of other international standards, for instance BS (British Standard) 18001:2007 "Occupational Health and Safety Management Systems. Requirements" and ISO 14001:2004 "Environmental Management Systems. Requirements with guidance for use".

Recently, researches in Management and Organization Science suggest that organizational processes in the current business scenario may be the strategy of firms in unpredictable markets. Processes such as internationalization, product development, acquisitions and alliances enable firms to acquire, shed and recombine resources [8]. Most of these processes are in fact non-workflow processes.

Y.T. Demey and H. Panetto (Eds.): OTM 2013 Workshops, LNCS 8186, pp. 124–133, 2013.
© Springer-Verlag Berlin Heidelberg 2013

These studies propose a new beginning to the behavioral approach that explains psychological and social mechanisms by which mental processes affect organizations. Behavioral strategy merges cognitive and social psychology with strategic management theory and practice [6].As pointed out, also in Business Process Management (BPM), the perspective of a user on a business process corresponds to his/her way of looking at the process [4].

This paper describes the analysis method from two main points of view.

The first assumption is that Business Process Analysis (BPA) can be used to deal with heterogeneous and complex scenarios, where workflow and non-workflow processes are present.

The second one is that, beyond the results in the implementation of management systems, the analysis could help in understanding social behaviors of managers, employee and worker and in finalizing them to define a collective company identity.

In fact, process analysis is a two-way interaction between processes and behaviors: practitioners need to take into account social behavior in developing the analysis while analysis and modeling can influence and modify social behavior.

The analysis processes are presented in section 2, underlining results that is the concrete outputs of the analysis process and returns that are the impacts on individual bias, influence of group, ideologies, political realities, consensus building, etc. Returns could be useful to define a shared frame of collective behavior in the organizations. This frame supports the management of social behaviors such as involvement, participation, acceptance and transversal versus hierarchical relationships.

The method has been tested and validated through long-term activity in different economic contexts: large and small and public and private companies.

Section 3 reports one of these experiences, developed in a large energy company with the objective of an integrated Health and Safety, and Environment Management System.

The conclusion (Section 4) proposes a synthesis and an outlook on future research to promote the synergy between practitioner and researchers of different scientific areas, such as BPM, Adaptive Case Management (ACM) and Strategic Management.

2   The Method

The BPA is part of a project developed to respond to company commitments and requirements. The result of the project is a "new management system".

Management and the project team usually share the project objectives in terms of operating results, such as the implementation of software applications, definition of common procedures, improvement of organization performances, compliance to regulatory requirements and measuring process effectiveness.

For instance, Sales Managers could require to clearly and quickly grasp activity flows to understand employee habits or detect bottlenecks in customer order management; Quality System Managers want to improve operating procedures and integrate them with Health, Safety and Environment requirements.

While the final result of a process analysis could be beneficial, the project team should ensure that the main set of numerous factors and components of the organization that influence process and how they interact are taken into consideration. The analysis method ought to capture these key factors.

During analysis, the practitioner usually stresses topics related to the effectiveness of operating tools and tangible and measurable results. However, improvement can also come from interaction with behavioral characteristics of the organization.

These points are not easily measurable (intangible) but, in fact, they could deeply influence process performances acting as a catalyst of process management.

The presented method is divided into these main phases: Orienteering, Modeling and Mapping, which are described below.

It is emphasized that each of these phases produces short-term results, i.e. direct outputs of process analysis and short or long-term returns, i.e. identification and changes in manager and employee behaviors and awareness.

The method proposes a gradual formalization of the analysis results. This approach could be useful to find out the diversity of company assets.

2.1   Orienteering

In project development, the start-up of a process analysis is linked to a specific management commitment in which not all requirements are clearly stated. Therefore, the first step of the project is perfecting objectives and constraints. For this reason, the term "Orienteering" is used instead of orientation because it produces the result of getting people together to explore "new countries".

The key factor of Orienteering is to understand the heterogeneity, strategies and structures of the organization, including workflow and non-workflow processes, which is supported by tools useful for collecting information, habits, individual and social behaviour, vision, energies and resources.

In order to obtain it, the method is based on "meeting people and sketching on a blackboard". Sketches must easily name company activities and the related assets (e.g. a policy, document and/or database). This activity requires that the project team involved in identifying and describing the processes have competence, experience and sensitivity. Since people often describe the same activity differently, a good description requires the person doing the analysis to involve the process owners. For useful results, the analyst should calibrate and perfect subjective interpretations; several interpretations and interests can often be present in the same area. A working group can help the practitioner in averaging the different evaluations and reducing the bias.

Supporting evaluations with information related to process metrics and results can reduce the subjective bias. Even the point of view of the practitioner doing the analysis could orient the project. If the analysis is driven by the goals of a management system, interviews with process owners may be conditioned by these requirements.

Out from their everyday routine, managers, employees and workers can discover unknown corners of their own company and several requirements of internal supplier-customer relationships.

The tangible **results** of Orienteering is a first taxonomy of assets, habits and praxis, useful to implement the "new system" while the actual **returns** of this phase are sharing expertise and points of view and identifying multiple perspectives in and outside the team.

2.2   Modeling

The translation of visions and feelings (sketches and meeting minutes) produced during Orienteering into effective management tools requires the definition of the company models, finalized to project objectives.

In the Modeling phase, several factors could lead analyst "eyes" and several coordinates could describe the conceptual space. The coordinates define the frame to transform fuzzy assets into more structured models and, therefore, into the "new system".

Some of the most effective factors are presented below based on experienced projects.

Stakeholders and Points of View

The concept of organization stakeholders is a characteristic of Management System Models described in ISO and BSI standards.

Let's consider a well-defined activity, say a manufacturing process producing a semi-finished or finished product. For the same manufacturing step, the description tools (input/output, risks, metrics) are different based on the stakeholder's (client/user) point of view. The quality and product information are key factors in a customer-focused analysis, while the shareholders are interested in prices, costs, profit and loss. In terms of the environmental approach, the same activities could be described focusing on pollution outputs and, finally if the worker safety is the target, the analysis could stress behaviour and consciousness related to potential accidents.

Tangible and Intangible Inputs/Output

The process inputs/outputs could be tangible or intangible and depend on the points of view. A product could be described by several characteristics that can be concrete and perceived by a customer (flavour of a product), or measured and recorded on different media (for instance, the report of a control plan). Some outputs can be easily described through measurable and evident characteristics (e.g., a mechanical part); others require a deep evaluation of customer relationships.

Boundaries and Granularity

Boundaries and granularity are complex components of the process analysis. The practitioner should define system boundaries, and what is inside and outside of the analysis scope. Even the boundaries are strictly related to points of view. In a quality management system, the description of the product workflow is mandatory while for an environmental management system the key points are the factory sites and the related risk analysis.

Once the boundaries have been defined, the granularity is influenced by many variables: organization characteristics, key events and risks and is also related to the commitment and to the objectives of the project.

Time

A subset of company activities is 'flows of works', performed in a serial or parallel way. However, a main part of activities and assets do not depend from time: behaviours, awareness, motivation and capacity to adapt to changes. The system usually encompasses several of them.

The **results** of this phase are the "model of the new system" that would respond to the project commitment. The assets are identified, and the structure of the taxonomy is defined and related to the coordinates, such as workflow drafts, data structure, documents, and control.

The **return** is the awareness in the project team of the interaction of these coordinates, for instance of the different stakeholders of the organization.

2.3   Mapping

Mapping closes the project describing the results (flow, data, and procedures) and transfers them from the project team to the whole company.

The choice of a useful notation is the key factor for an effective Mapping of the modelled system.

The available standard notations are conceived to describe the main workflow processes and the related assets. However, these notations are not useful to describe all coordinates that could characterize the model, such as the assets related to main management commitments.

Furthermore, the choice of the notation depends from the objective of the project. For instance, in software design and implementation the granularity and the symbol types are unambiguous links with codes while sharing management approaches could be meaningful the contemporary description of several outputs, accepting some degree of ambiguity.

The notation to capture non-workflow assets has to deal with quite different entities: data (structure and analysis), individual behaviors (motivations, habits, responses and emotions) and social behaviors (team management). The available notations use naïve symbols: colour, graph, box and text. The challenge is to define an effective set of tools that freely map the system.

A key part of the project **results** are the maps.

Whatever the map, structured or naïve, the **return** of the mapping phase is to orient managers and employees by identifying the roles of everyone within the system. Having a map could improve the perception of their own position and help in managing company activities, giving managers a common and shared frame to view the "company environment".

3   Experience Report

3.1   The Scenario and the Project Objective

In the context of one of the main Italian Energy Company (Business Unit on Green Energy), the management commitment was the implementation of a Health and Safety and Environmental Management System. The main objectives of the management were:

- The improvement on Health and Safety performance through all divisional processes with reduction of incidents, injuries, ill health and risk for contractors and visitors as well as production capacity and quality, respecting time and costs, due to compliance of processes to required standards;
- The improvement in process efficiency by means of a deep analysis of activities and hence the reduction of safety costs (for instance loss of working days for incident).

Starting from these constraints, the project goals were the integration of a Health and Safety (H&S) Management System with investment processes in wind turbine ground farm and the broadening of H&S culture beyond conformity to legal requirements.

In particular, the project was finalized to include the requirements related to Safety in the investment processes, supported by the requirements of Standard BS 18001 "Occupational Health and Safety Management System Requirements".

3.2   The Project Phases

The first step of the **Orienteering** phase was choosing the project team, jointly performed by practitioners and company managers. The first team was composed by the manager of the Health and Safety area. In a concurrent approach, a key point is the choice of the managers: they should be involved in the commitment and have consolidated experience in the company activities.

During the first meetings, a brainstorming approach was used, supported by the requirements of BS 18001, to translate ideas into a first "map of the new country". During this phase, other functional areas, such as Investment and Finance, R&D and Purchasing, were progressively involved in the project.

Questions such as "Do Preliminary Investment reports include health and safety requirements?" or "Who manages safety in the feasibility study?" allows the financial managers to discover unknown fields, for instance regulatory requirements that could dramatically influence the investment costs.

Orienteering produced a better definition of points of view among people and was useful to adjust the project, in particular in defining the required competences. At the end of this phase, the project team was composed of members coming from R&D, Engineering, H&S, Operation, and Purchasing Areas. Practitioners were expert in

Process Analysis, H&S management system and technicalities (for instance equipment safety).

All the involved functions shared the awareness of merging Health and Safety requirements in their processes, in particular in investment management, purchases and engineering activities.

The result of this phase was a first set of meaningful assets such as a list of existing process models, operating procedures and experienced safety criticalities on the equipment and in the creation of the wind farm.

During the **Modeling** phase, with a better definition of coordinates, the rough set of asset was refined and exploited to build the model of the new system.

The identified stakeholders were the shareholders, the employees and workers. For the shareholder, the key characteristics of the model could be related to investment risk, and for workers this could be the safety risk. The line among these risks is not sharp, for instance the business continuity could be interrupted by a serious incident on the wind farm, and the cost of the investment could increase because of the need of dedicated safety structures.

The final results of the investment are tangible. For safety, there are many concrete points such as the shape of fall protection, emergency stairs and safety devices required for maintenance. However, many inputs/outputs were intangible, for instance feasibility and design reports as well as risk assessment documentation. Both tangible and intangible aspects should be taken into account.

The boundaries of the model were extremely large, encompassing several business units, wind farm site and also including supplier facilities. For this reason, the granularity (detail level) was not too stressed because the aim was not to produce software tools but to influence a broad set of company rules and procedures.

The modeling phase was developed by means of frequent team meetings and a broad consultation of data and documents, in particular the existing design and investment process maps that described the workflow activities from the shareholder point of view. During the meeting, the environmental requirements were also established, for instance considering the impact of noise that the equipment has on people and wild animals.

Analysing the health and safety (and environmental) impacts together with the operations gives an idea on the fact that plants generate money as well as personal safety risks as well as environmental pollution risks. These have to be controlled by increasing everyone's attention to these aspects.

The final result of the modeling phase was the updating of the scenario, for instance defining a link with process mapping and workflow management already exploited and the re-definition of processes with attention to H&S points, mainly in wind farm design and building.

The return of this phase was the shared awareness that the project team had on health, safety and environmental impacts on investment and an improved "thinking by processes" skill.

Fig. 1 describes how the Safety (and Environmental) requirements could "contaminate" the existing workflow models, this deployment started with a new awareness in the project team. The **Mapping process** was exploited using the IDEF 0 (Icam

Definition for Function Modelling) notation with the aim of translating the prototype into the company standard process maps based on BPMN (Business Process Modelling Notation). The maps were tracked on the blackboard during project meetings while the team assessed company documents and activities.

For every activity, the mapping allows to define links with company operating documents (such as procedures, instructions and risk assessment) and registration (such as equipment certificate, tender and purchase orders).

This phase was also useful in defining a new relationship among managers and updating operating procedures and registration tools, with particular attention to legal requirements. For instance, the closeout report, usually issued at the end of plant construction, was recognized as a key input during the evaluation of new purchasing contracts and supplier offers were checked in terms of safety and environmental requirements using a specific questionnaire.

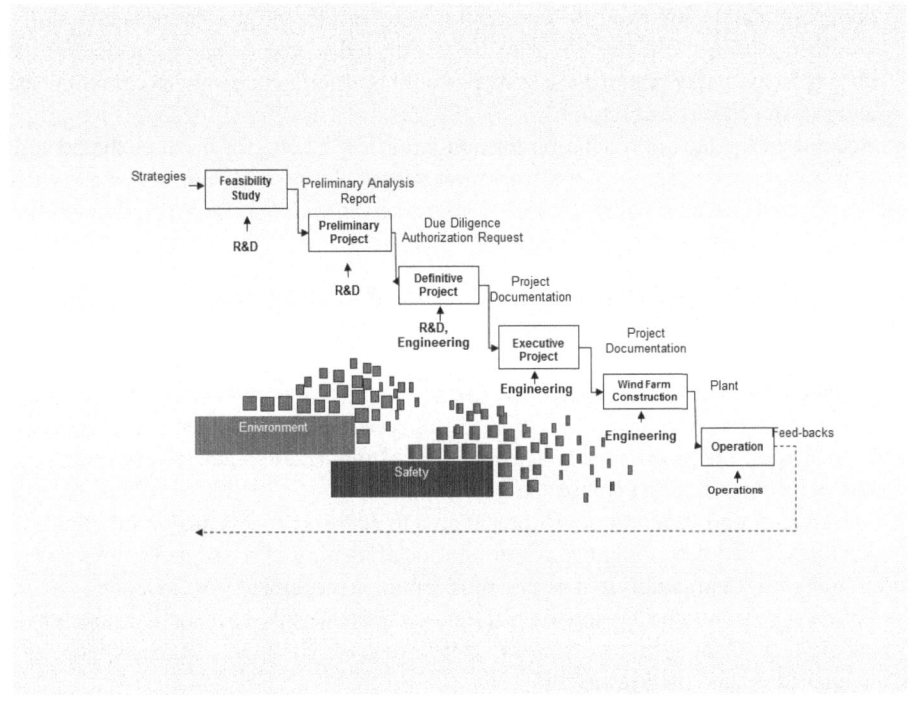

Fig. 1. Environment and Safety Deployment in Investment Processes

The mapping process better defined when and how to take into account safety and environment requirements and what are the rules (forms, procedures) and which are the actual operations (for instance logistic management with attention on personal and environmental safety). The existing process flow (from the shareholder point of view) was integrated with safety and environment requirements. For instance, when evaluating supplier offers, questions regarding compliance with safety requirements and the recyclability of material could be asked.

The results of mapping were the updating of internal workflows, documented procedures and internal software management tools.

In term of returns, the project enriched the Company Identity of shared values on Environment and Health and Safety while their translation into operating tools (e.g. internal procedures) supported the transfer of the new awareness in everyday practice.

The company management appreciated the project results as they find the response to commitment and a driver for change in company perspective.

3.3   Project Discussion

In this section some weak points of the project are proposed for discussion.

- There was the risk that returns and results were restricted only to the part of the company mainly involved in the commitment. In fact, new awareness and skills, confined within the team, ought to be transferred to the company to deploy the change in everyday practices. The maps could be an effective way to communicate and transfer results and returns.
- Because of the lack of a notation for non-workflow assets (for instance the perception of a safety risk), only the workflow part of the new system was clearly described and the new points of view constrained in the workflow notation. Hence the use of the maps was not completely effective.

4   Conclusions

The paper presented a process analysis method exploited to design new management systems. Experience suggests that, beside the concrete results documented in maps and procedures, the process analysis could be useful to capture and modify social and collective behaviour of the companies.

The paper proposes a new development area to address process analysis methods in understanding and describing behaviour and social identity of the organizations and in developing useful notations to describe most of the management system assets.

For these reasons a bridge among different competences that acts on the same environment (e.g. Management System Development, Strategic Management and Computer Science) could be useful.

References

1. Dee Carri Integrated Compliance, Quality and Process Management System. In: BPTrends Column (March 2011)
2. J. Recker Class Notes: BPM Research and Education. In: BPTrends Column (December 2011)

3. Hervizadeh, M., Mendling, J., Rosemann, M.: Dimension of Business Process Quality (QoBP). In: BPM 2008 Workshops. LNBIP, pp. 80–91. Springer, Heidelberg (2009)
4. Koschmider, A., Habryn, F., Gottschalk, F.: Real Support for Perspective-Compliant Business Process Design. In: BPM 2008 Workshops. LNBIP, pp. 32–43. Springer, Heidelberg (2009)
5. Stoitsev, T., Scheidl, S., Flentge, F., Muhlhauser, M.: From Personal Task Management to End-User Driven Business Process Modeling. In: BPM 2008 Workshops. LNBIP, pp. 32–43. Springer, Heidelberg (2009)
6. Powell, T.C., Lovallo, D., Fox, C.R.: Behavioral Strategy. Strategic Management Journal 32, 1369–1386 (2011)
7. Huy, Q.N.: How Middle Managers Group-Focus Emotions and Social Identities Influence Strategy Implementation. Strategic Management Journal 32, 1387–1410 (2011)
8. Bingham, C.B., Eisenhart, K.M.: Rational Heuristics: the 'Simple Rules' that Strategists Learn from Process Experience. Strategic Management Journal 32, 1387–1410 (2011)
9. Levinthal, D.A.: A Behavioral Approach to Strategy. What's the Alternative? Strategic Management Journal 32, 1517–1523 (2011)

Supervision of Constraint-Based Processes: A Declarative Perspective

Sauro Schaidt, Eduardo de Freitas Rocha Loures,
Agnelo Denis Vieira, and Eduardo Alves Portela Santos

Pontificia Universidade Catolica do Parana, Industrial Engineering,
Imaculada Conceicao 1155, 80215 901 Curitiba, Brazil
{sauro.schaidt,agnelo.vieira,eduardo.loures,
eduardo.portela}@pucpr.br
http://www.pucpr.br/

Abstract. Constraint-based processes require a set of rules that limit their behavior to certain boundaries. Declarative languages are better suited to modeling these processes precisely because they facilitate the declaration of little or no business rules.These languages define the activities that must be performed to produce the expected results but not define exactly how these activities should be performed. The present paper proposes a new approach to deal with constraint-based processes. The proposed approach is based on supervisory control theory, a formal foundation for building controllers for discrete-event systems.The controller proposed in this paper monitors and restricts execution sequences of tasks such that constraints are always obeyed. We demonstrate that our approach can be used as a declarative language for constraint-based processes.

Keywords: constraint-based processes, declarative languages.

1 Introduction

Constraint-based processes require a set of rules that limit their behavior to certain boundaries. Declarative languages are better suited to modeling these processes precisely because they facilitate the formal declaration of such business rules [1] [2] [3]. These languages define the tasks that must be performed to produce the expected results but not define exactly how these activities should be performed. Thus, any execution order of tasks is possible provided that the constraints (imposed by the rules) are not violated. On the other hand, there are processes that require a strong imposition of rules for their implementation. These processes are called rigid or highly structured processes. Imperative languages are better suited for modeling these processes because, unlike declarative languages, they define exactly how a set of tasks should be performed. Thus, we need a model that explicitly defines the ordering and execution of activities.

An imperative model focuses on specifying exactly how to execute the process, i.e., all possibilities have to enter into the model by specifying its control-flow. Procedural (or imperative) models (e.g. BPMN, EPC, YAWL, WF-Nets or

Y.T. Demey and H. Panetto (Eds.): OTM 2013 Workshops, LNCS 8186, pp. 134–143, 2013.

Petri Nets), provide constructs such as AND/OR-splits, AND/OR-Joins, etc. A declarative model specifies a set of constraints, i.e., rules that should be followed during the execution. In this way, the declarative model implicitly defines the control-flow as all possibilities that do not violate any of the given constraints.

Many approaches has proposed to add control to the business processes and to avoid incorrect or undesirable executions of the tasks. A stream of research proposes using rule-based or constraint-based modeling languages [11] [12] [13]. DECLARE is developed as a constraint-based system and uses a declarative language grounded in Linear Temporal Logic (LTL) [4] for the development and execution of process models[2] [3]. With DECLARE, constraints determine activity order, and thus, any order of execution sequence is possible as long as constraints go un-violated.

In the present paper we propose a new approach to deal with constraint-based processes founded on the Supervisory Control Theory [5]. The new approach proposes a control system based on modular supervisors [6] which restrain the process to not violate the constraints. This action is accomplished through dynamic disabling of some events in order to restrain the state space of process. We consider that there may contain substrings that are not allowed. These substrings may violate a desired ordering of events and they need to be avoided. Thus, a modular supervisor is built in order to ensure that the whole set of constraints is not violated. This approach is declarative because it does not limit the user by imposing rigid control-flow structures. In fact, the basis of this approach is to inform users of which tasks are not allowed after an observed trace of events at run-time, and users operate with some freedom because they choose execution sequences allowed under supervision.

According to [7], constraints or business rules include the following aspects: ordering-based (i.e., execution order of tasks in cases), agent-based (i.e., involvement of a role or agent in cases and processes), and value-based (i.e., forms belonging to a task). In the present paper we consider only the ordering-based constraints.

2   Supervisory Control

Supervisory control theory (SCT) [5] has been developed in recent decades as an expressive framework for the synthesis of control for Discrete-Event systems (DES). The SCT is based on automata theory, or dually formal language theory, depending on whether one prefers an internal structural or external behavioral description at the start. In SCT, the behavior of a DES is modeled by an automaton. The restrictions to be imposed on the DES can be expressed in terms of a language representing the admissible behavior and it is named specification [5]. The SCT provides computational algorithms for the synthesis of a minimally restrictive supervisor that constrains the behavior of the DES by disabling some events in such a way that it respects the admissible language and that it ensures nonblocking, i.e., there is always an event sequence available to complete a task (or to reach a marked state in terms of automata theory).

Let a Constraint-based Process (CP), modeled at the untimed (or logical) level of abstraction, and whose behavior must be restrained by supervisory control in order to not violate a given set of constraints. Let us assume that the given CP is modeled by automaton G, where the state space of G need not be finite. Let Σ be the event set of G. Automaton G models the uncontrolled behavior of the CP. The premise is that this behavior is not satisfactory and must be modified by control; modifying the behavior is to be understood as restricting the behavior to a subset of $L(G)$. In order to restrain the behavior of G we introduce a supervisor; supervisor will be denoted by S. The language $L(G)$ contains strings that are not acceptable because they violate some constraint or nonblocking condition that we wish to impose on the CP. It could be that certain states of G are undesirable and should be avoided. These could be states where G blocks, via deadlock or livelock; or they could be states that are inadmissible. Moreover, it could be that some strings in $L(G)$ contain substrings that are not allowed because they may violate a desired ordering of certain events. Thus, we will be considering sublanguages of $L(G)$ that represent the legal or admissible behavior for the CP.

SCT consider a very general control paradigm for how S interacts with G. In this paradigm, S sees (or observes) some, possibly all, of the events that G executes. Then, S tells G which events in the current active event set of G are allowed next. More precisely, S has the capability of disabling some, but not necessarily all, feasible events of G. The decision about which events to disable will be allowed to change whenever S observes the execution of a new event by G. In this manner, S exerts dynamic feedback control on G. The two key considerations here are that S is limited in terms of observing the events executed by G and that S is limited in terms of disabling feasible events of G. Thus, it is considered the presence of observable events in Σ - those that S can observe - and the controllable events in Σ - those that S can disable.

In SCT, the event set of G is partitioned into two disjoint sets, being the set of controllable events Σ_c, and the set of uncontrollable events $\Sigma_u c$. An event is classified as controllable if its occurrence can be disabled by supervisor. It is classified as uncontrollable in the opposite case. An event might be modeled as uncontrollable because it is inherently unpreventable. Formally, a supervisor $S : L(G) \rightarrow 2^{\Sigma}$ is a function that maps from the sequence of generated events to a subset of controllable events to be enabled or disabled. The optimal behavior of the process G under supervision of supervisor S is represented by the language marked by the automaton S/G.

3   Modeling of Constraint-Based Processes

In order to apply the SCT for controlling constraint-based process, it is necessary to obtain two models: (1) the model of the system under control and (2) the model of constraints. We consider that a constraint-based process is constituted of a set of tasks. In our approach each task is assigned to an automaton representing its behavior. This automaton represents the states through which a work item passes during execution of such process. This automaton models relevant aspects that will be considered for supervisory control: the beginning, ending and the cancelation of a task. We assume each task t_i (i = 1, 2,,n) is modeled as an automaton with two states: (1) an initial state means the task is not being executed (a case has not entered) and (2) another state means a case is being processed. With event start (t_{is}), the task is initiated (state 1 is reached). When it finishes, signaled by the occurrence of event complete (t_{ic}) or cancel (t_{ix}), it returns to initial state. According to this model, a task may be executed repeatedly over the same instance. We consider that only the beginning of a task is a controllable event. It means the control action is only possible before a task has been initiated. After a task begins, the supervisor can not avoid its ending or canceling. Fig. 1 shows the generic automaton that represents a task t_i.

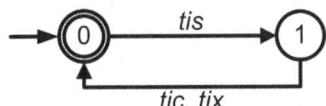

Fig. 1. Automaton representing a task t_i

The tasks involved in a constraint-based process will be considered the system under control. To represent the behaviour of such system, the synchronous composition between automata is the solution. In this case, we obtain the uncontrolled behaviour of the constraint-based process. To calculate the supervisor that avoids undesired sequences (which violate constraints), it is necessary to express constraints in terms of automata. The set of constraints presented in [9] is considered as a start point for building our set of automata.

In the previous work [8] we propose four groups of constraints and each constraint is modeled by a formal model as in [9]: (1) existence, (2) relation, (3) negation and (4) choice. Existence models specify how many times or when one activity can be executed. Relation models define some relation between two (or more) activities. Negation models define a negative relation between activities. Choice models can be used to specify that one must choose between activities. Considering the application of SCT, we use automata to represent the whole set of constraints. Instead of modeling in LTL as in [9], these four groups are modeled by automata. Fig. 2 shows two examples of constraints over the execution of two tasks t_1 and t_2 (the reader may check the whole set of constraints in [8]). The precedence model requires that task t_2 is preceded by task t_1, i.e., it specifies that task t_2 can be executed only after task t_1 is executed. In this case, other tasks can be executed between tasks t_1 and t_2. The $1of2$ model specifies that at least one of the two tasks t_1 and t_2 has to be executed, but both can be executed and each of them can be executed an arbitrary number of times.

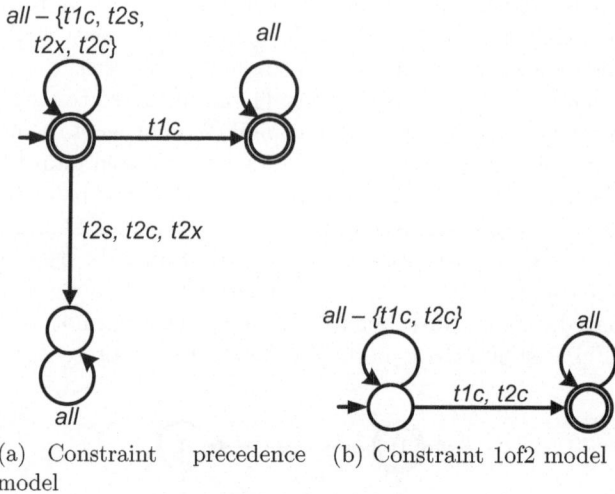

(a) Constraint precedence model   (b) Constraint 1of2 model

Fig. 2. Examples of constraints

4   Example of Application

As an example to illustrate our approach, we use the same process treated in [3]. It is a process for handling a patient at the first aid department in a hospital with a suspicion of a fracture. Fig. 3 shows the activities of such process depicted as boxes. There are four constraints to be imposed to this process. Constraint init $C1$ specifies that task examination must be the first executed task in an instance. A specialist may ask for a X-ray to additional diagnosis. Depending on the absence, presence and type of fracture, there are several types of treatment available, such as sling, fixation, surgery and cast. Except for cast and fixation, which are mutually exclusive (constraint not co-existence $C4$), the treatments can be given in any combination and each patient receives at least one treatment (1of4 constraint $C3$). Additional diagnosis (X-ray) is not necessary when the specialist diagnoses the absence of a fracture during examination. Without this additional diagnosis, the patient can only receive the sling treatment. All other treatments require X-ray to rule out the presence of a fracture, or to decide how to treat the fracture (constraint precedence $C2$). Simple fractures can be treated just by cast. Moreover, the specialist can provide medication at any stage of the treatment. Also additional examinations and X-rays can be done during the treatment.

We assume each task t_i (i=1,,7) of the process for handling patient is modeled by an automaton as shown in Fig. 3. Fig. 4 shows the constraints $C1$, $C2$, $C3$ and $C4$ modeled by automata. Considering that we use a modular approach of SCT [6], one supervisor is synthesized in order to satisfy each constraint. The first step to synthesizing modular supervisors is to obtain the local plant for each constraint. Local plants for $C1$, $C2$, $C3$ and $C4$ are given by

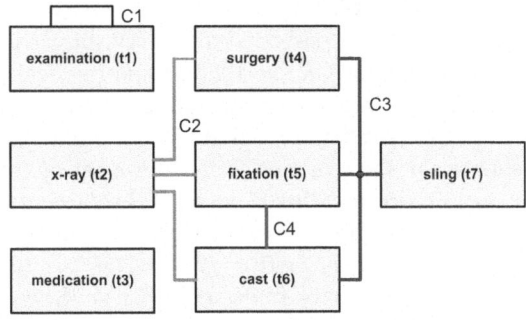

Fig. 3. Process for handling a patient at the first aid

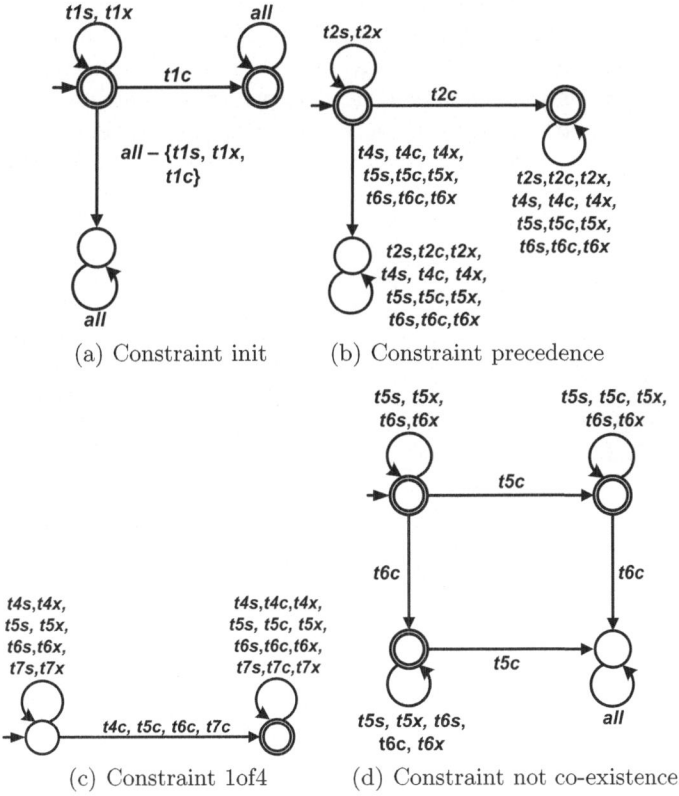

Fig. 4. Examples of constraints

$Gl_{C1} = t1||t2||t3||t4||t5||t6||t7$, $Gl_{C2} = t2||t4||t5||t6$, $Gl_{C3} = t4||t5||t6||t7$, and $Gl_{C4} = t5||t6$, respectively. Synthesis of local supervisor Sj is performed considering corresponding constraint Ck (k=1,2,3,4) and its local plant Gl_k. Using algorithms proposed by [5] and [10], the four modular supervisors are obtained, each one guaranteeing that constraints will not be violated.

Each modular supervisor show in Fig. 5 disables a set of controllable events according to its states. A corresponding pair (Sj, Φ_j) represents each supervisor, where Φ_j represents the output map. Considering local supervisors Sj shown in Fig. 5, their output maps are: S_1 is $\Phi_1(0) = t2s, t3s, t4s, t5s, t6s, t7s$, $\Phi_1(1) = \emptyset$; S_2 is $\Phi_2(0) = t4s, t5s, t6s$, $\Phi_2(1) = \emptyset$; S_3 is $\Phi_3(0) = \emptyset$, $\Phi_3(1) = \emptyset$; and S_4 is $\Phi_4(0) = \emptyset$, $\Phi_4(1) = t5s, t6s$, $\Phi_4(2) = t6s$, $\Phi_4(3) = t5s$. The aim of each modular supervisor is to restrain a set of tasks to a limited state space (defined by each constraint). Thus, the related constraint is not violated. In Fig. 5, the box attached to each state represents the set of disabled events (the output map of each modular supervisor).

Fig. 6 shows the interplay between tasks $t5$ and $t6$ and the modular supervisor $S4$. In the initial state $S4$, there is no controllable event being disabled ($\Phi_4(0) = \emptyset$). Thus, both tasks $t5$ and $t6$ may be initiated (as shown in Fig. 6(a)). It means users are able to choose one of them to initiate. In the case $t5$ has been chosen, the state 1 of $S4$ is reached and a new output map is established. Fig. 6(b) illustrated this situation. In state 1 of $S4$, the controllable events $t5s$ and $t6s$ are disabled ($\Phi_4(1) = t5s, t6s$). It means users can not initiate task $t6$ unless task

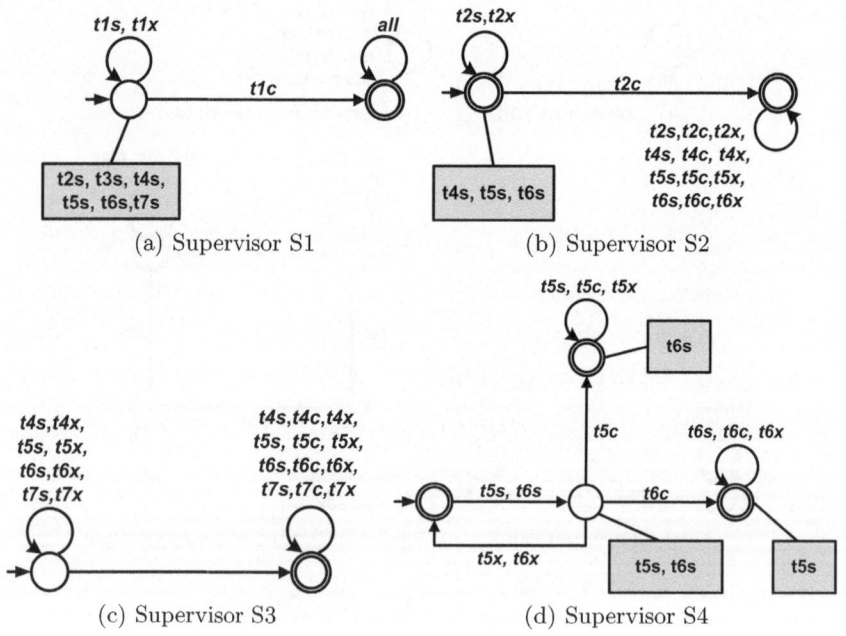

(a) Supervisor S1   (b) Supervisor S2

(c) Supervisor S3   (d) Supervisor S4

Fig. 5. Models of supervisors

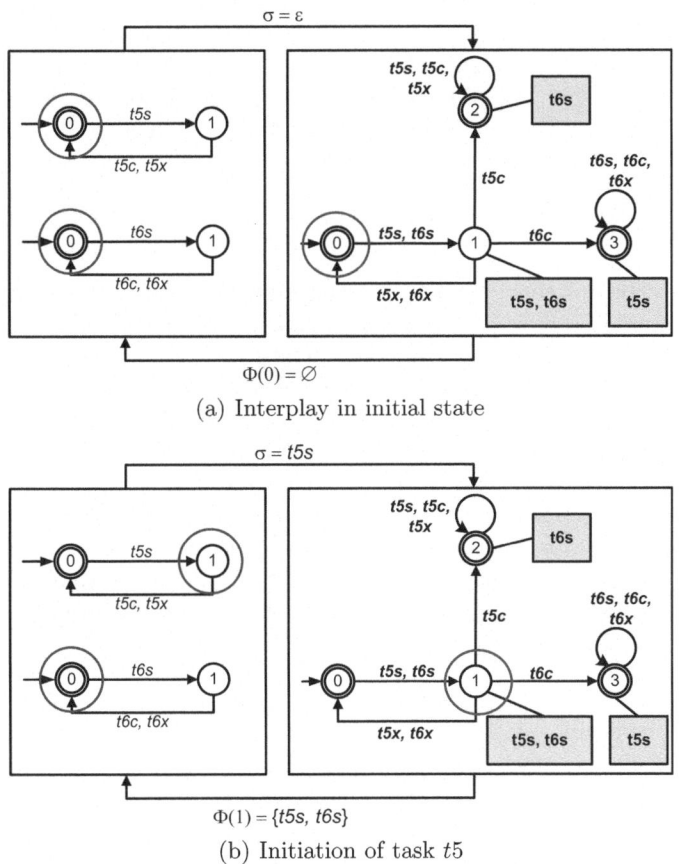

(a) Interplay in initial state

(b) Initiation of task $t5$

Fig. 6. Interplay between tasks $t5$ and $t6$, and supervisor $S4$

$t5$ be canceled. By completing the execution sequence based on output map of supervisor $S4$, users are guaranteed no violation of constraint not co-existence between tasks $t5$ and $t6$.

The control action imposed by modular supervisors allows for many execution paths. Using this approach it is not necessary to include or represent these paths explicitly. For example, the not co-existence constraint between tasks cast ($t5$) and fixation ($t6$) is difficult to express in imperative languages, considering that the choice between these two treatments is not fixed. In an imperative language one would need to decide on the moment of choice, specify the loop behavior, and determine the people making these choices. In the proposed approach, the modular supervisor $S4$ only tells which tasks are allowed to beginning (in some active set of enabled tasks). It does not force which task has to initiate. Instead, the choice is made by users. Also, the behaviour imposed by $1of4$ constraint allows for multiple execution paths. In this case it is necessary a high flexibility of execution of tasks surgery ($t4$), fixation ($t5$), cast ($t6$) and sling ($t7$). The aim is that a patient may receive any of these treatments in any combination and at least one of them. The modular supervisor $S3$ just tell us that any sequence is possible but a marked state is only reached after the ending of one of the treatments. It means while one of these tasks does not finish, the constraint remains violated. Moreover, after the ending of one of the treatments, any combination of the available treatments is possible.

5   Conclusion

Supervisory control theory allows an automatic synthesis of supervisors that the constraints are not violated in a minimally restrictive way and ensures that this behavior is non-blocking (i.e., there is always an event sequence available to complete an activity). Thus, new control actions may be rapidly and automatically designed when modifications, such as redefinition of constraints or tasks arrangements, are necessary. The constraint-based processes can be made to behave optimally with respect to a variety of criteria, where optimal means in minimally restrictive way. Among the criteria are safety specifications like the avoidance of prohibited regions of state space, or the observation of services priorities; and liveness specifications, as least in the weak sense that distinguished target states always remain reachable. Thus, the obtained solution using SCT is correct by construction.

The control approach presented in this paper aims to monitor and restrict execution sequences of tasks such that constraints are not violated. Despite the control logic is built based on constraints, it does not limit the user by imposing rigid control-flow structures. In fact, the basis of our approach is to inform users of which tasks are not allowed after an observed trace of events at run-time, and users operate with some freedom because they choose execution sequences allowed under supervision. Users can adopt this service as a guide to execute tasks with a guarantee that constraints are followed and goals are met. The control approach presented here also offers flexibility to users to choose execution sequences, and it is even possible for users to execute tasks simultaneously with no rules violations.

In constraint-based process is difficult to envision all possible paths and the process are driven by user decisions rather than system decision. Here processes are less repetitive and the emphasis is on flexibility and user empowerment. On the other hand it is difficult to model more abstract relations between tasks when the user has many choices in each state. So, a formal foundation to deal with constraint-based processes is very welcome. Despite the many theoretical results and innovative prototypes, few of the research ideas have been adopted in commercial systems. In fact this is a limitation of the use of the SCT so far.

References

1. Pesic, M., van der Aalst, W.M.P.: A declarative approach for flexible business processes management. In: Eder, J., Dustdar, S. (eds.) BPM Workshops 2006. LNCS, vol. 4103, pp. 169–180. Springer, Heidelberg (2006)

2. Pesic, M., Schonenberg, M.H., Sidorova, N., van der Aalst, W.M.P.: Constraint-based workflow models: Change made easy. In: Meersman, R., Tari, Z. (eds.) OTM 2007, Part I. LNCS, vol. 4803, pp. 77–94. Springer, Heidelberg (2007)

3. Aalst, W., Pesic, M., Schonenberg, H.: Declarative workflows: Balancing between flexibility and support. Computer Science-Research and Development 23(2), 99–113 (2009)

4. Clarke Jr., A., Grumberg, O., Peled, D.A.: Model Checking. The MIT Press, Cambridge (1999)

5. Ramadge, P., Wonham, W.: The control of discrete event systems. Proceedings of the IEEE 77(1), 81–98 (1989)

6. Queiroz, M.H., Cury, J.E.R.: Modular supervisory control of large scale discrete event systems. In: Boel, R., Stremersch, G. (eds.) WODES 2000. Discrete Event Systems: Analysis and Control, pp. 103–110. Kluwer Academic Publishers (2000)

7. Aalst, W., Hee, K., Werf, J., Kumar, A., Verdonk, M.: Conceptual model for on line auditing. Decision Support Systems 50(3), 636–647 (2011)

8. Schaidt, S., Vieira, A.D., Loures, E.F.R., Santos, E.A.P.: Dealing with Constraint-Based Processes: Declare and Supervisory Control Theory. In: Rocha, Á., Correia, A.M., Wilson, T., Stroetmann, K.A. (eds.) Advances in Information Systems and Technologies. AISC, vol. 206, pp. 227–236. Springer, Heidelberg (2013)

9. Pesic, M.: Constraint-based workflow management systems: Shifting control to users. Phd thesis, Eindhoven University of Technology, Eindhoven (2008)

10. Su, R., Wonham, W.M.: Supervisor reduction for discrete-event systems. Discrete Event Dynamic Systems 14, 31–53 (2004)

11. Rychkova, I., Nurcan, S.: Towards Adaptability and Control for Knowledge-Intensive Business Processes: Declarative Configurable Process Specifications. In: 44th Annual Hawaii International Conference on System Sciences, pp. 1–10. IEEE (2011)

12. Rychkova, I., Regev, G., Wegmann, A.: High-Level Design and Analysis of Business Processes the Advantages of Declarative Specifications. In: 2th IEEE International Conference on Research Challenges in Information Science, pp. 3–6. Marrakech (2008)

13. Sadiq, S.W., Orlowska, M.E., Sadiq, W.: Specification and validation of process constraints for flexible workflows. Information Systems 30(5), 349–378 (2005)

Dynamic Context Modeling for Agile Case Management

Manuele Kirsch-Pinheiro and Irina Rychkova

Centre de Recherche en Informatique, Université Paris 1,
Panthéon-Sorbonne 90, rue Tolbiac, 75013, Paris, France
{Manuele.Kirsch-Pinheiro,Irina.Rychkova}@univ-paris1.fr

Abstract. Case Management processes are characterized by their high unpredictability and, thus, cannot be handled following traditional process- or activity-centered approaches. Adaptive Case Management paradigm proposes an alternative data-centered approach for management such processes. In this paper, we elaborate on this approach and explore the role of context data in Case Management. We use the state-oriented representation of the process that allows us to incorporate the contextual information in a systematic and transparent way, leading towards agile case management.

Keywords: business process agility, context awareness, declarative process modeling.

1   Introduction

Davenport [5] [6] defines case management process as a process that is not predefined or repeatable, but instead, depends on its evolving circumstances and decisions regarding a particular situation, a *case*. Case management processes scenarios form dynamically, at run time, and cannot be modeled, managed or analyzed following the traditional BPM approaches [22].

This idea paper builds up on our recent work [19], where we define two forms of agility, leading to more dynamic context-aware business process. The 1st form of process agility is defined as a capacity to handle unpredictable sequences of system events, which results in a dynamically defined order for process activity invocations. The 2nd form of process agility consists in *selecting a right action at the right moment, and with respect to the current situation*. We define it as the ability to monitor and manage *the process context* and to dynamically select and/or alter the execution scenario accordingly. We argue that the second form of process agility is essential for efficient case management. This agility depends heavily on the capability of supporting systems to deal systematically with dynamic process context. Unfortunately, current approaches lack appropriate formalism and mechanisms for context management.

In this paper, we explore the role of context information in the agile case management and propose an extensible meta-model and architecture for representing, capturing and exploring this information in a dynamic and systematic way. We illustrate our findings on the example of crisis management process as defined by the Emergency Plan Specialized on Floods (EPSF) of Hauts-de-Seine [15].

Y.T. Demey and H. Panetto (Eds.): OTM 2013 Workshops, LNCS 8186, pp. 144–154, 2013.

This paper is organized as follows: in Section 2 we discuss the Adaptive Case Management paradigm as opposed to traditional BPM and introduce our example. In Section 3, we define the dynamic context model and illustrate how this model can be instantiated for the crisis management process for process agility. In particular, we focus on the dynamic aspect of the context modeling and discuss the added value of the context model to the case management. In Section 4, we compare our proposals with related works before concluding in Section 5.

2   Case Management Process and Adaptive Case Management

The Case Management Process Modeling (CMPM) Request For Proposal released by OMG [12] expresses the practitioners' demand in the case management solutions. OMG defines case management as "*A coordinative and goal-oriented discipline, to handle cases from opening to closure, interactively between persons involved with the subject of the case and a case manager or case team*". Case management processes (CMP) have multiple applications, including "*...licensing and permitting in government, insurance application and claim processing in insurance, patient care and medical diagnosis in health care...*" [12]. The main resource of a CMP is knowledge obtained as a result of communication between multiple actors/users. This knowledge is used for making decisions during the case handling.

Business Process Management (BPM) and Adaptive Case Management (ACM) demonstrate conceptually different views on the system design. Process-centered view adapted by BPM implies that the data emerges and evolves within a process according to a predefined control flow (Fig. 1-a), similarly to a product evolving on a conveyor belt.

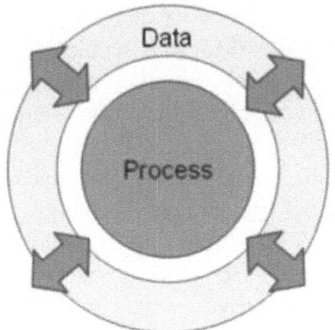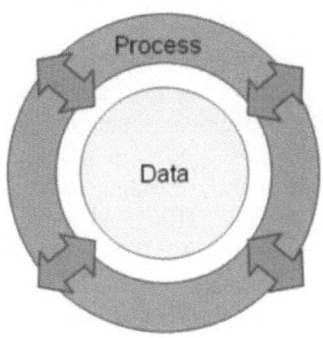

a) BPM – activity centered view on processes

b) ACM – data – centered view on processes

Fig. 1. BPM vs. ACM systems, from [22]

One of the major challenges identified by both practitioners and researchers in the ACM field is the attempts to deal with case management process in the industry the same way as with regular business process - i.e. by applying a process-centered view. In this work, we implement the data-centered view (Fig. 1-b) that is proposed by the

Adaptive Case Management (ACM) practitioners [22]. This view implies that the process shall be adapted at run time, according to evolution of case circumstances and case-related data. This view suits to nondeterministic, knowledge-intensive processes like case management processes [16].

2.1   Case Management Process Example: Crisis Management in Case of Floods

Crisis management process is a typical example of case management: it demands interaction between multiple otherwise independent actors (e.g. government, fire brigades, police, public transport, healthcare, electricity and water supplying services, road maintenance etc.). This process is driven by evolved information about the case rather then predefined sequence of activities and, it is thus, suitable for the data-centered paradigm (Fig. 1-b).

In the example below, we consider a crisis management process triggered in case of flood, in the Hauts-de-Seine department of France [15]. A *flood* is an overflow of water that submerges land that is normally dry. It is happening, for example, due to an increase in the flow of a river provoked by significant rainfalls. The risk of a "major flood" is the main natural risk in the Ile-de-France region, particularly during the winter period from November to March. Cities like Paris[1] are confronted to this risk, and, in case of flood, important damages can be expected, affecting thousand of people. In the Hauts-de-Seine department [15], the risk of flood is considered as particularly important since 1910.

The EPSF (Emergency Plan Specialized on Floods) is triggered immediately when the water level rises until 5.5m at the Austerlitz Bridge and will keep rising according to forecasts. Due to its high dynamic nature, this process cannot be handled by a workflow-based approach. Indeed, activities during crisis management are not necessarily predictable and depend on numerous factors that can dynamically change. We list just a few of these factors: watercourse levels, weather conditions and forecasts, electrical outages, traffic conditions, actors' location, equipment availability, etc.

For example, depending on the water level, the crisis management process may require specific traffic control and deviation, partial or complete disabling of public transport lines (SNCF Paris Rive Gauche, RER C, RATP), blocking the highways and principal roads (A86, A14, N14, etc.). The towns affected by the flood may require regular external drinking water supply, in more severe cases - evacuation and temporary accommodation for people, healthcare and childcare facilities. Moreover, the crisis management shall be assured under condition of possible overload or instabilities in telecommunication network, inaccessible or blocked due to heavy traffic roads etc. For example, a traffic jam can put at risk the evacuation of people or deployment of other emergency services. These situations require alternative scenarios such as traffic deviation or preparation of evacuation by air etc. Such (dynamically changing) information defines the crisis management process *context*.

---

[1] See http://cartorisque.prim.net/dpt/75/75_ip.html

More formally, context can be defined as any information that can be used to characterize the situation of an entity (a person, place or object) that is considered relevant to the interaction between a user and an application [7].

We claim that the capacity to timely observe and measure the context information in a systematic way, in order to select and assemble process activities at run time is indispensible for adaptive case management and for our example of crisis management in particular. Thus, we adapt the data-centered paradigm from Fig. 1-b by including into its core the *contextual data*. In the next section, we introduce the concept of dynamic context modeling and illustrate this concept on the example of crisis management process presented above.

3   Dynamic Context Modeling

3.1   Context Meta-model

The way context information can be exploited for business process flexibility depends on what information is observed and how it is represented. According to Najar et al. [11], the formalism chosen for representing context model determines the reasoning methods that can be used to perform system adaptation to the observed context. A context model (i) ensures the definition of independent adaptation processes and (ii) isolates this process from context acquiring techniques. The same applies to context-aware business process or case management. We claim that the process context information should be acquired, modeled and formally analyzed at run time in order to adapt process execution and to ensure its flexibility.

Several context models have been proposed in the literature [11] [1]. Even if they vary in the adopted formalism (key-values, object-oriented, ontologies, etc.) and in the represented elements, we can generalize some common terms. First of all, most of context models consider a given subject that is observed, typically the user. For instance, Reichle *et al.* [17] and Najar *et al.* [11] consider both that a given "entity" (the user, a device, etc.) is observed. In other models, such as [7], the subject is implicit, since the user is considered as the main observed thing. This subject plays a central role on context modeling, as pointed out by [3] [4], since it is precisely the context of this subject that is currently been observed. Everything we observe is related to this subject. Around it, several elements can be considered. Reichle *et al.* [17] call these observed elements "scope", while Kirsch-Pinheiro *et al.* [9] call these "*context elements*". In both cases, it corresponds to what we really observe from the subject: its location (for a user), the available memory (for a device), etc. When observing such context elements, we obtain *values* corresponding to their status on given moment and that will probably evolve over the time. For instance, by observing the *context element* 'location' for a *subject* 'user', we may obtain *values* for latitude and longitude, corresponding to the current user's location. Besides, some models associate meta-data describing these values. For instance, Reichle *et al.* [17] propose to describe which representation is used for an observed value (*e.g.* a location can be described using latitude and longitude pair or through a postal address). Vanrompay *et al.* [23] consider representing as meta-data a "certainty measure" indicating the reliability of the observed values.

Based on these common terms we identified in the literature, we define a common meta-model presented in Fig. 3. In this meta-model, we consider context as a set of *context elements* that are observed for a given *subject* (e.g. an actor, a device, a resource, etc.). Each subject can be associated with multiple context elements (location, status, etc.); for each context element, we observe *values* that can dynamically change and that can be described by meta-data.

The proposed meta-model must be instantiated in an appropriate model, according to its application domain. This means to transpose and to affine elements from the meta-model in a precise model. Such model can use different formalisms, but ontologies appear as the most interesting to represent context elements [11]. They provide ways to semantically describe these elements and their relationships, as well powerful reasoning mechanisms, notably inference rules. According to Bettini *et al.* [1], *"ontological reasoning can be executed for inferring new context information based on the defined classes and properties, and on the individual objects retrieved from sensors and other context sources"*. The meta-model and an ontology model form a complementary approach, allowing a better understanding of the context modeling.

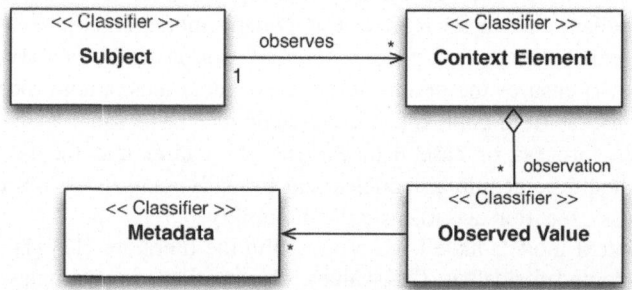

Fig. 2. Context meta-model considering context as a set of context elements

Thus, subject and context elements can be semantically described using ontologies. Choosing what elements will be represent depends on the application domain, in our case, the activity domain related to our case management. For instance, a context ontology for the crisis management process will describe subjects such as the different teams and actors' roles, and context elements such as the location, the availability of a given equipment, etc. Based on such context ontology, we propose to represent *events* as logical constraints over context concepts and observed values. We formalize the context of a subject s in a time t as follows:

$$Context(s,t) = \{ Element(s, ce) \},$$

where *Element(s,ce)* represents the observed value of the context element *ce* for the subject *s*.

For the crisis management, we can monitor different actors (subjects) involved into the process (e.g. police brigades, fire brigades, evacuation teams, etc.). The main parameters (context elements) to observe are location and resources available.

Context (team1, t) = {Element (team1, #location), Element (team1, #vehicle), Element (team1, #agent), Element (team1, #firstAidKit)}

Along those lines, we can observe weather conditions (subject), with temperature, humidity or rainfall prevision (context elements); general traffic conditions (subject) with the current deviations, traffic jams (context elements); main healthcare and childcare facilities (subjects) with their heating, water, electricity supply, accessibility by the roads (contextual elements indicating the need of evacuation), etc.

3.2 Marrying the Dynamic Context Model with the Agile Process Model

Defining and managing an exhaustive context model along with the process model seem to be a challenging task that would potentially raise the complexity and compromise the usability of the overall model. With an appropriate modeling formalism, however, this complexity can be substantially reduced.

In [19], we model a business process as a finite state machine (FSM) [14], where each state represents a process situation at a given time and state transitions define the possible process scenarios. The triggering events specify the underlying process semantics, i.e. conditions for state transitions.

Fig. 3 illustrates the FSM for our example: here process states may evolve from Flood Vigilance (that corresponds to 2.5m water level at the Austerlitz Bridge) to Flood Alert (3.2m) and to Execution of Emergency plan (5.5m). We assume (although this is not documented in [15]) that Federal Alert state can be triggered in case the emergency plan execution is insufficient. Also, at any time, the system can get back to normal state. This FSM is an abstract representation of the process that can be further detailed by refining states and/or adding component state machines showing how separate case-related elements will be handled (road blocks, evacuation process, etc) as described in [20].

According to EPSF [15], at each process state, various activities must/can be executed in order to protect people and goods and to reduce the consequences before, during and after a flood (e.g. the public transport suppression, preparation and executing the evacuation, road blocking, provisioning water, electricity etc.). Due to natural evolution of the crisis situation (e.g. the water level keeps rising) or other conditions (e.g. not enough people/equipment, electricity outage, no road access etc.) execution of some of these activities becomes impossible and alternative sets of actions need to be executed in order to fulfill the crisis management objectives.

Each process state in Fig. 3 can be defined with a (set of) *subject* and its *contextual elements* to observe. Emergent conditions can be modeled as *context events* and expressed using logical conditions on observed values of contextual elements. For example the following condition triggers a hospital evacuation:

Element(#hospital, #heating) = "out of order" OR Element(#hospital, #electricity)="out of order" OR Element(#hospital, #access)="not available"

Thus, context events are expressed referring elements from context ontology. This way, event definition can take advantage of reasoning capabilities offered by ontologies. Besides, a context query language, such as [17], allows the expression of rich context conditions. This is particularly important since context information is naturally imprecise and often incomplete. Process states or events can then be defined in terms of context elements and acceptable interval or sets of values.

Therefore, context information plays the following roles: (i) it is a trigger for process state transitions; (ii) it is a part of process state definition; and (iii) it is a boundary condition for execution one or another process activity.

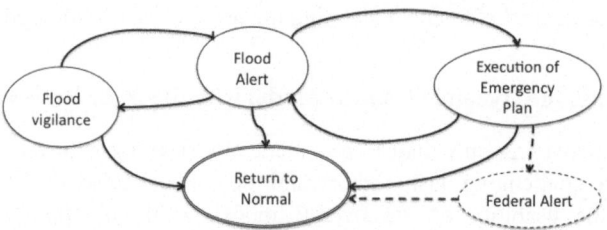

Fig. 3. FSM for Crisis management process in case of Flood

3.3   Towards Context-Aware Case Management

In [19], we present architecture for CAPE – Context-aware Agile business Process Engine – that defines the following elements for agile process management (Fig. 4):

- Dynamic context monitor
- Activity repository (Process specification)
- Navigation manager.

Here the Activity repository provides a set of activities that can (but not necessarily will) be executed during the process; the Navigation manager provides a context-based guidance, offering an appropriate activity (or a list of alternative activities) to execute from the repository; and the Context monitor is in charge of observing context elements during process execution, in order to enable this context-based guiding. Similar to [13], it recognizes context elements using *plugins*, which feed the monitor with dynamic information about a given context element from a subject. Each plugin observes a given context element. It keeps Context Monitor updated concerning changes in observed context values. Such values dynamically observed by context plugins define the current position of the process in its state space.

To support agility on process definition, we consider that context elements observed for a given process might vary during the process executions. As a result, new context elements to be observed and new respective contextual events are dynamically added to the model.

In practice, the Context monitor can be dynamically extended by adding new plugins or sensors for observing new context elements and subjects. Fig. 4 shows the CAPE model for the crisis management process and illustrates the dynamic context management: a new sensor measuring rainfall level is added through a new context plugin (on the left side of the figure), extending the process definition with new events and, possibly, states and triggering conditions.

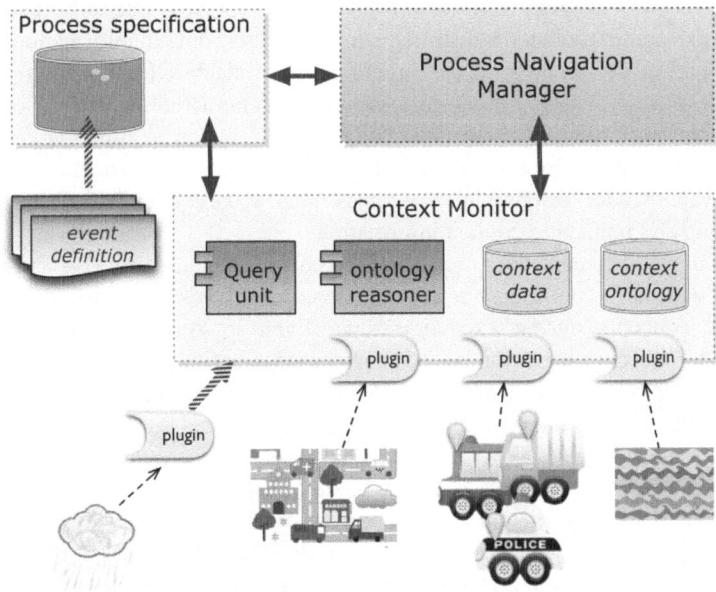

Fig. 4. Context Monitor organization in CAPE architecture

4   Related Work

The notion of context is not totally new on the BPM field. Other researches [18] [10] [21] have already pointed out the use of context information on process definition. Roseman et al. [18], for instance, consider that external context elements may influence business process (e.g. weather influencing a call center process in an insurance company). They propose to incorporate such elements into business process modeling. Saidini et al. [21] also consider context on business process definition, particularly on the roles played by each actor. They assume that role affectation can be influenced by context information.

Unfortunately, in BPM field, context information is not always modeled appropriately. Quite often works lack of formalisms in representing context concepts and properly managing them. Besides, context models, when they are present, are not general enough, consider only a limited set of context information and focus manly on workflow based process needs. Indeed, the way context information can be exploited for business process flexibility depends on what information is observed and how it is represented. The meta-model we proposed here allows dynamic modeling of context information, supplying the high level formalization necessary for process flexibility.

Identifying context information that can affect a business process execution remains problematic. Similar to [18] [11], we consider context information on concentric levels, from internal context directly related to process actors and activities till external environment context. In this sense, context can be seen as a recursive notion, a 'local' context referencing a more global one [3]. Such concentric and recursive vision of context information leads us to represent internal process events and external context events indistinctly. In this way, context information becomes naturally part of the process definition and can be considered under multiple levels. Nevertheless, it is worth noting that we cannot enumerate which aspects of all situations are important, as these will change from situation to situation [7]. In other terms, it is impossible to exhaustively describe all context information needed in a general way. Model extensibility becomes then a key element for successfully representing and managing context information.

Such extensibility depends not only on the context model and its capabilities to be extended with new concepts, but also in the capability of observing and acquiring such new concepts during execution time. Even if some works [18][21] have considered context information on business process definition, at design time, they rarely consider context information at run time, during process execution. Often no architecture is proposed in order to dynamically acquire and take into account context information during process execution. CAPE architecture proposes to overcome this issue by adopting an extensible plugin approach, in which new context elements can be easily observed by connecting the appropriate context plugin.

Finally, a context-aware business process does not necessarily means an agile business process. Although context information may bring an interesting contribution for process flexibility, it does not guarantee that the process will be able to react to unexpected situations. Indeed, works such as [18] still describes process as a predefined and explicit sequence of activities, making it difficult to respond to unpredictable situations. We argue that, in order to support process agility, it is necessary to think business process differently, in terms of events and states instead of in terms of activities.

5   Conclusion

Crisis management process is an example of a case management process, with unpredictable scenarios. Activities are chosen according to actors' expertise, previous experiences and to multiple input events moving the situation from a state to another. It is a typical example of process that cannot be handled in a satisfactory way using traditional workflow-based approaches. A more dynamic approach is necessary.

For better efficiency, especially in the situation where the time matters and complicated decision making may cost even lives, any automated guidance becomes important. Our approach represents the process as FSM, defined by its multiple states and transition events. This representation allows integrating the contextual events and contextual parameters into process definition: both process events and contextual events are handled uniformly in order to provide an automated guidance and to prescribe/suggest an activity that suits best with respect to the process objectives.

In this paper, we went one step forward in modeling context information for business process. We proposed a context meta-model allowing a high level formalization of the context information, which can be combined with powerful query and ontology based reasoning mechanisms, for more process flexibility. We are currently specifying a first implementation for CAPE architecture, including Context Monitor elements. A first prototype is expected soon.

The next step of this research is definition and implementation of techniques for automated user guidance. Formal Concept Analysis (FCA) and Galois lattices [2] [8] is one of the techniques we consider. In [19], we illustrate how Galois lattices can be used to classify/organize the case-related information providing a user with suggestions about which activity to execute at a particular situation. Along those lines, the use of Galois lattices for context analysis provides flexible guidance to end-users at run time and supports them with an expertise required for the process handling.

References

1. Bettini, C., Brdiczka, O., Henricksen, K., Indulska, J., Nicklas, D., Ranganathan, A., Riboni, D.: A survey of context modelling and reasoning techniques. Pervasive and Mobile Computing 6(2), 161–180 (2010)
2. Birkhoff, G.: Lattice Theory, 1st edn. Amer. Math. Soc. Pub. 25, Providence (1940)
3. Brézillon, P.: Expliciter le contexte dans les objets communicants. In: Kintzig, C., Poulain, G., Privat, G., Favennec, P.-N. (eds.) Objets Communicants, Hermes Science Publications, Paris, pp. 293–303 (2002)
4. Coutaz, J., Crowley, J., Dobson, S., Garlan, D.: Context is the key. Communication of the ACM 48(3), 49–53 (2005)
5. Davenport, T.H., Nohria, N.: Case management and the integration of labor. Sloan Management Review 35, 11–11 (1994)
6. Davenport, T.H.: Thinking for a living: how to get better performances and results from knowledge workers. Harvard Business Press (2005)
7. Dey, A.: Understanding and Using Context. Personal and Ubiquitous Computing 5, 4–7 (2001)
8. Egho, E., Jay, N., Raissi, C., Napoli, A.: A FCA-based analysis of sequential care trajectories. In: 8th Int. Conf. on Concept Lattices and their Applications (2011)
9. Kirsch-Pinheiro, M., Gensel, J., Martin, H.: Representing Context for an Adaptive Awareness Mechanism. In: de Vreede, G.-J., Guerrero, L.A., Marín Raventós, G. (eds.) CRIWG 2004. LNCS, vol. 3198, pp. 339–348. Springer, Heidelberg (2004)
10. Mounira, Z., Mahmoud, B.: Context-aware process mining framework for Business Process flexibility. In: iiWAS 2010, Paris (2010)
11. Najar, S., Saidani, O., Kirsch-Pinheiro, M., Souveyet, C., Nurcan, S.: Semantic representation of context models: a framework for analyzing and understanding. In: Information and Ontologies, CIAO 2009, European Semantic Web Conference, ESWC 2009, pp. 1–10 (2009)
12. Object Management Group (OMG): Case Management Process Modeling (CMPM) Request For Proposal (September 23, 2009)
13. Paspallis, N.: Middleware-based development of context-aware applications with reusable components, PhD Thesis, University of Cyprus (2009)
14. Plotkin, G.D.: A structural approach to operational semantics (1981)
15. Préfecture des Hauts-de-Seine: Plan de secours spécialisé sur les inondations Hauts-de-Seine, SIDPC (November 21, 2005), http://www.ville-neuillysurseine.fr/files/neuilly/mairie/services_techniques/plan-secours-inondation.pdf

16. Pucher, M.J.: The Elements of Adaptive Case Management. Mastering the Unpredictable. How Adaptive Case Management Will Revolutionize The Way That Knowledge Workers Get Things Done, pp. 89–134 (2010)
17. Reichle, R., Wagner, M., Khan, M.U., Geihs, K., Valla, M., Fra, C., Paspallis, N., Papadopoulos, G.A.: A Context Query Language for Pervasive Computing Environments. In: 6th IEEE International Conference on Pervasive Computing and Communications, PerCom 2008, pp. 434–440 (2008)
18. Rosemann, M., Recker, J., Flender, C.: Contextualization of Business Processes. Int. J. Business Process Integration and Management 1(1), 46–60 (2007)
19. Rychkova, I., Kirsch-Pinheiro, M., Le Grand, B.: Context-Aware Agile Business Process Engine: Foundations and Architecture. To appear in 14th Working Conference on Business Process Modeling, Development, and Support (2013)
20. Rychkova, I.: Exploring the Alloy Operational Semantics for Case Management Process Modeling. In: Proceedings of 7th IEEE International Conference on Research Challenges in Information Science, RCIS 2013 (2013)
21. Saidani, O., Nurcan, S.: Towards Context Aware Business Process Modeling. In: 8th Workshop on Business Process Modeling, Development, and Support, BPMDS 2007, CAiSE 2007 (2007)
22. Swenson, K.D.: Mastering The Unpredictable: How Adaptive Case Management Will Revolutionize The Way That Knowledge Workers Get Things Do, 354 (2010)
23. Vanrompay, Y., Mehlhase, S., Berbers, Y.: An effective quality measure for prediction of context information. In: 8th IEEE International Conference on Pervasive Computing and Communications Workshops (PERCOM Workshops), pp. 13–17. IEEE Computer Society (2010)

Adaptive Case Management as a Process of Construction of and Movement in a State Space

Ilia Bider[1,2], Amin Jalali[1], and Jens Ohlsson[1]

[1] DSV, Stockholm University, Stockholm, Forum 100, SE-16440 Kista, Sweden
[2] 2IbisSoft AB, Stockholm, Box 19567, SE-10432 Stockholm, Sweden
ilia@{dsv.su,ibissoft}.se, {aj,jeoh}@dsv.su.se

Abstract. Despite having a number of years of experience, adaptive case management (ACM) still does not have a theory that would differentiate it from other paradigms of business process management and support. The known attempts to formalize Case Management do not seem to help much in creating an approach that could be useful in practice. This paper suggests an approach to building such a theory based on generalization of what is used in practice on one hand and the state-oriented view on business processes on the other. In practice, ACM systems use a number of ready-made templates that are picked up and filled as necessary for the case. State-oriented view considers a process instance/case as a point moving in a specially constructed state space. This paper suggests considering a case template as a definition of a sub-space and piking different template on the fly as constructing the state space along with moving in it when filling the template. The result is similar to what in control-flow based theories are considered as a state space with variable numbers of dimensions. Beside suggestions to building a theory, the paper demonstrates the usage of the theory on an example.

Keywords: Adaptive Case Management, State Space, Business Process.

1 Motivation

Adaptive case management (ACM) as a practical discipline has emerged for some years ago [9]. However, it still lacks a theory or a model that could explain what an ACM system is that could be used for analysis, comparison and development of such systems. Moreover, in our view, there is no commonly accepted theory of case management (CM) or case handling systems, even non-adaptive ones. The goal of this idea paper is to suggest an approach to building a theory/model of ACM systems.

As both CM and ACM systems are aimed at supporting workers (so called knowledge workers in case of ACM systems) in driving their working/business processes, naturally, both CM and ACM systems falls in the category of Business Process Support (BPS) systems, and thus belong to the wider domain of Business Process Management (BPM). In contemporary BPM, the predominant view on business processes is the activity or task oriented one. More exactly, a business process instance or case is considered as a set of activities aimed at reaching

Y.T. Demey and H. Panetto (Eds.): OTM 2013 Workshops, LNCS 8186, pp. 155–165, 2013.

some goal. Business process type or model is considered as a set of rules that determine which activities to be executed when running a process instance that belong to the particular type. This view is considered the as a cornerstone when developing BPS systems.

Traditionally, BPS systems are built based on a workflow model of business processes they aim to support. A workflow model is a kind of a graph that connects activities between themselves and thus determines what activities should/could be executed after finishing a particular one. From the point of view of the activity-oriented paradigm, the natural way of developing a theory/model of CM systems is to continue using activities as a primary concept of the theory/model, but drop the idea of being able to represent the connections between them with the help of a graph. The initiative of picking up the next activity to execute is left in the hands of humans, while the system assists the execution of an activity after it has been picked up. An attempt of formalizing this approach has been suggested in [1]. To the best of our knowledge, there were no comprehensive attempts to build a theory for CM and/or ACM systems since van der Aalst et al, [1] work has been published.

The assumption of the concept of activity/task being primary and even mandatory in a theory/model of ACM systems contradicts our experience of business analysis and design of case handling/management systems. Our experience started with analysis of case handling in Swedish municipalities that included general case handling in the Municipality of Motala [3], and case handling in the social welfare office of municipality of Jönköping, e.g. handling applications for child adoption, and later handling cases of suspected child abuse. Case handling that we observed in municipalities were rather template/form driven, than activity driven. There were templates, often of the type of structured forms, for an application, investigation, and decision making.

Templates/forms driven case handling cannot easily be translated into the activities driven one, as the same template/form can be used for several different activities, e.g., for both application and decision making. Activities can be represented in such case handling in different ways. For example, an activity of decision making can be represented in the form by three fields: (a) decision, (b) name of decision maker and (c) date when the decision has been taken. Another example, a set of activities can be represented as a checklist on the form that requires putting a cross beside each activity on the list before the form can be considered as properly filled.

In addition, there are often no strict rules on when starting to work with a certain template. For example, the main result of an adoption case is a report that follows a certain template. The report is based on a series of meetings with the applicant(s), but there is no regulation when to start writing the report, directly after the first meeting or, after the whole series has been completed. The choice is left to individual case managers. The standardization of case handling in municipalities is also done not by specifying activities, but by producing a package of templates/forms mandatory to be used during handling cases. This type of standardization was, for example, used by Swedish National Board of

Health and Welfare for handling cases of suspected child abuse. This process was used as a pilot process when we created our tool for building case-oriented BPS systems iPB [4].

Summarizing our experience, a theory/model of CM systems, including ACM systems does not need to be based on the notion of activity/task as a primary concept. In a simplified form, it does not need to have it at all. It would be enough if the theory can explain the concept of templates/forms, and filling them during the lifespan of each case. The latter can be done using the state-oriented view on business processes [8]. In the state oriented view, a process instance is considered to be a trajectory in a specially constructed state-space, while a process type/model is considered as a set of restrictions on the trajectories of instances that belong to the given type. From this point of view, templates/forms are used to represent the structure of the chosen state space to the end users of a CM system, while filling them represents movement of the instance in the state space. Restrictions on the movement can be defined, for example, by demanding finishing filling one form before starting with another one [4].

The state-oriented view suggested in [4,8] serves well as a basis for the theory of CM, but it does not naturally fit the reality of ACM. The works cited above assume that the state-space is the same for all cases which corresponds well to CM with few pre-defined templates/forms. An ACM system may include many different templates/forms from which the workers pick some for a particular case dependent on the needs. This makes it artificial to consider each instance/case of a given process type having the same state-space. The state-oriented view needs to be extended to consider a possibility of state-space being constructed while a case is in progress. The goal of this paper is to outline the idea of using an evolving state space for creating a theory/model that can be used for analysis, comparison and development of ACM systems.

The discussion of the idea is done through analysis of an example a process for preparing and giving a course in a university borrowed from [6]. The rest of the paper is structured in the following way. In Section 2, we give a short overview of the state oriented view on business processes from [8]. In Section 3, we describe an example of an ACM type of business processes. In Section 4, based on this example, we discuss how the example can be interpreted from the viewpoint of the evolving state space. Section 5 contains concluding remarks and plans for the future work.

2 State Oriented View of Business Processes

We suggest using the state-oriented view on business processes as a foundation for building a theory of ACM. As this is not a standard view, in this section, we give a brief overview of its underlying concepts and principles as suggested in [8]. The origin of the state-oriented view on business processes lies outside the business process domain. The idea comes from the Mathematical System Theory and especially the theory of hybrid dynamical systems [10]. Another source used for developing this theory was an objects-connectors model of human-computer interaction developed in [5]. In essence, the state-oriented view on business processes is an application of the ideas worked out for modeling and controlling physical processes to the domain of business processes. The main concept of the state-oriented view is a state of the process instance that can be defined as a position in some state space. A state space is considered multidimensional, where each dimension represents some important parameter (and its possible values) of the business process. Each point in the state space represents a possible result of the execution of a process instance. If we add the time axis to the state space, then a trajectory (curve) in the space-time will represent a possible execution of a process instance in time. A process type is defined as a subset of allowed trajectories in space-time. As an example, consider an order process from Fig. 1. Its state space can be presented as a set of numeric dimensions from Fig. 2 defined in the following way:

- In the first place there are a number of pairs of product-related dimensions <ordered, delivered>, one pair for each product being sold. The first dimension represents the number of ordered items of a particular product. The second one represents the number of already delivered items of this product. The number of such pairs of dimensions can be considered as equal to the size of the companys product assortment.
- In addition, there are two numeric dimensions concerning payment: invoiced (amount of money invoiced) and paid (amount of money already received from the customer).
- Each process instance of the given type has a goal that can be defined as a set of conditions that have to be fulfilled before a process instance can be considered as finished (i.e. end of the process instance trajectory in the space state). A state that satisfies these conditions is called a final state of the process. The set of final states for the process in Fig. 2 can be defined as follows: (a) for each ordered item Ordered = Delivered; (b) To pay = Total + Freight + Tax; (c) Invoiced = To pay; (d) Paid = Invoiced. These conditions define a surface in the state space of this process type.

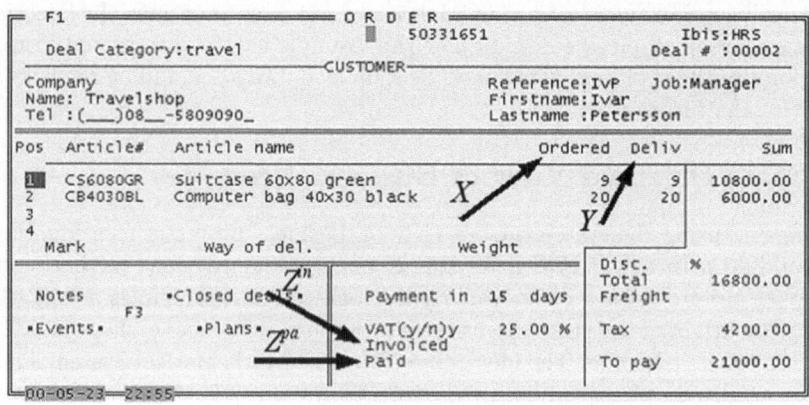

Fig. 1. Example of a process state as a mockup screen

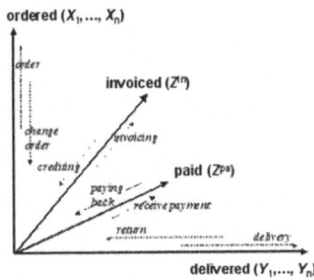

Fig. 2. State space dimensions as axes

The process instance is driven forward through activities executed either automatically or with human assistance. Activities can be planned first and executed later. A planned activity records such information as type of action (goods shipment, compiling a program, sending a letter), planned date and time, deadline, name of a person responsible for an action, etc. All activities planned and executed in the frame of the process should be aimed at diminishing the distance between the current position in the state space and the nearest final state. The meaning of the term distance depends on the business process in question. Here, we use the term informally. For example, activities to plan for the process in Fig. 1 can be defined in the following manner:

- If for some item Ordered > Delivered, shipment should be performed, or
- If To pay > Invoiced, an invoice should be sent, etc.

All activities currently planned for a process instance make up the process plan. The plan together with the current position in the state space constitutes a so-called generalized state of the process, the plan being an active part of it (engine). The plan plays the same role as the derivatives in the formalisms used for modeling and controlling physical processes in Mathematical systems theory. The plan shows the direction (type of action) and speed of movement (deadlines), just as first derivatives do in a continuous state space. Using the concept of process plan, the control over the process instance can be defined in the following manner. First, an activity from the plan is executed and the position of the process instance in the state space is changed. Then, depending on the new position, the plan is corrected, i.e., new actions are added to the plan and some existing ones are modified or removed from it. Correction of the plan can be done manually by the process participants, automatically by a system that supports the process, or in a mixed fashion [1]. The iterations continue until the instance reaches its goal.

---

[1] The mixed fashion of planning can be used for regulating the level of flexibility/rigidity allowed for a process type. Automatic rules gives rigidity, freedom for manual planning gives flexibility. A method of regulating the level of flexibility of planning based on deontic logic is discussed in [7].

3   An Example a Course Process at a University

An example that we will explore when discussing our idea is concerned preparing and giving a course occasion at a university, as presented in [6] [2]. Such an occasion can be the first one of a newly developed course, or the next occasion of an already existing course. So far, only a prototype of a system that supports this process has been built. Nevertheless, we decided to consider this process in our paper and not the one for which a real system is already in operation due to the following reasons:

- The domain is familiar to both academics, who gives courses (though they may not agree with how it is done in our department), and to practitioners who were students at some time in the past. This gives an opportunity to describe the process in a concise manner in the paper of a limited size. Using a process for which a real system is in operation would require becoming familiar with the business of social offices in Swedish municipalities.
- The process has all elements we need for presenting our approach to building a theory of CM/ACM systems.

The templates/forms to be used in instances/cases of the course preparation process are presented in Fig. 3, an example of a template, Lecture/Lesson, is shown in Fig. 4. As follows from Fig. 3, the templates are grouped in two categories templates for preparing a course and templates for gathering feedback from the course. The first group consists of templates: Course general description, Course book, Course compendium, Article compendium, Lecture/Lesson, Seminar, Lab and Exam. The second group consists of the rest of the templates. While preparing a course occasion, the teacher(s) decides on which teaching/learning activities, and which material will be used in the course occasion, picks up a form for each activity or material and fills it in. Naturally, some forms can be employed only once, e.g., Course general description, or Exam, others can be employed several times, or none at all. Though the templates are presented in Fig. 3 in a certain order, this order does not enforce the usage of templates. For example, on one occasion all preparation can be finished before the actual course starts. In another occasion, only the first introductory lecture is prepared before the start, all other teaching/learning activities are prepared and completed while the course is running based on the feedback both from the teachers and the students. The teachers can freely choose the templates for preparation and change information in them at any moment before the actual teaching/learning activity takes place, including deleting some of them. However this is not true for the templates aimed at gathering feedback. These templates should be synchronized with the ones already chosen for teaching/learning activities. For example, if two lectures have been chosen for the course, four feedback forms should be automatically selected for the course occasion: two of the type Lecture/Lesson teacher

---

[2] Bider et al. [6] is an experience report that describes the project of building a model of a course preparation process. It does not discuss any theoretical aspects presented in this paper.

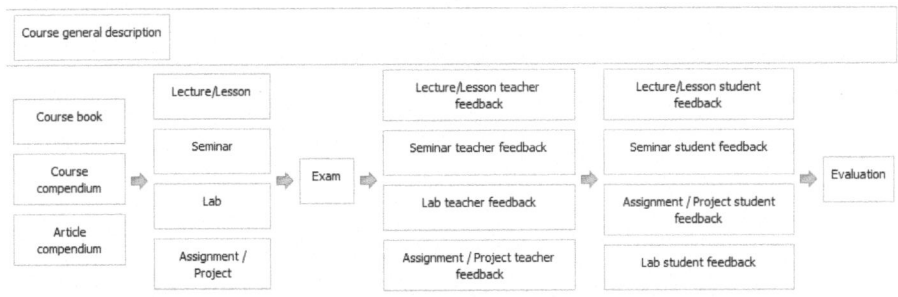

Fig. 3. Templates for course process

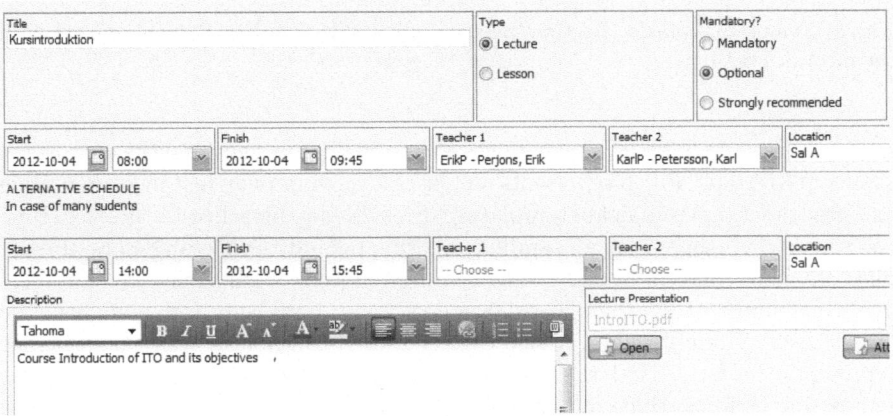

Fig. 4. Template/form for Lecture/Lesson box in Fig. 3

feedback and two of the type Lecture/Lesson student feedback, see Fig. 3. An example for a Lecture/Lesson teacher feedback form is presented in Fig. 5; the figure represents a form synchronized with the one shown in Fig. 4. As we see from Fig. 5, part of the fields in this form (the upper part of the form) are inherited from the form with which the current form is synchronized.

Summarizing the example presented, a template/form driven ACM system to support a course process needs to provide the following basic functionality:

- Repository of templates/forms that can be chosen for attaching to an instance/case
- Navigation through the forms already attached to the instance/case
- Manipulating the templates/forms already attached to the instance/case fill with new data, update the content, delete, marked as finished/closed
- Automatically adding synchronized forms when they are needed
- Providing restrictions on possibility to attach a given template/form to a case based on what other templates/forms have already been attached and their status (e.g. finished).

Title		Type
Kursintroduktion		⦿ Lecture
		○ Lesson

Start		Finish	
2012-10-04 08:00		2012-10-04 09:45	

Lecture Presentation

Intro170.pdf

Open   Attach

Comments on completeion ＋ Add   ✎ Edit   📋 Copy   ⟩ Delete   🖶 Print

Date ▲	By	Comment	No problems, some interesting questions, does not need changing for the next year.
2012-10-04 23:15	Ilia - Bider (Admin), ilia	No problems, some	*By Ilia - Bider (Admin), ilia 2013-06-24 07:37*

Fig. 5. Template/form for Lecture/Lesson feedback box in Fig. 3 synchronized with the form in Fig. 4

An example of how the above functionality can be presented to the end user is shown in Fig. 6 [4]. Fig. 6 represents an upper level view of an instance/case. Blue and green rectangles indicate templates/forms already attached to the case. Blue color is used to show that all templates/forms behind the rectangle are already filled with information considered to be required and/or sufficient. The numbers below the name of the template shows how many templates/forms of this type have already been attached to the case (number 1 is not showen) White color represents the forms that the end user is free to attach to the case, grey color represents the forms that cannot be attached to the case due to some restrictions.

A diagram in Fig. 6 is used for navigation between the forms. By clicking on a rectangle the user goes to a place where he can manipulate the templates/forms of the type the rectangle represents, e.g., create a new form, add information,

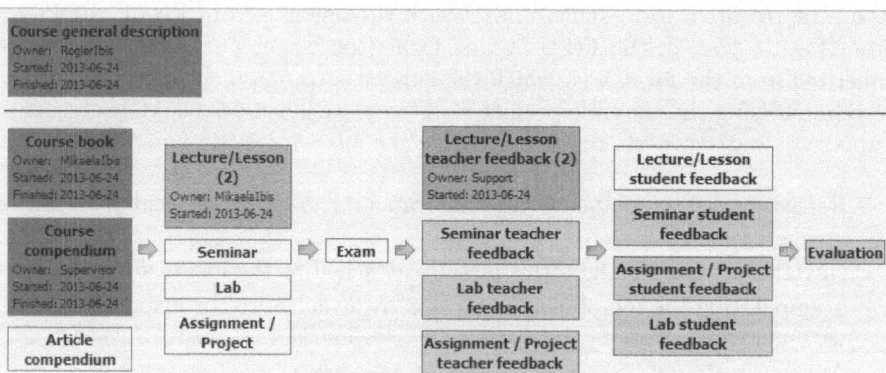

Fig. 6. A course case in iPB

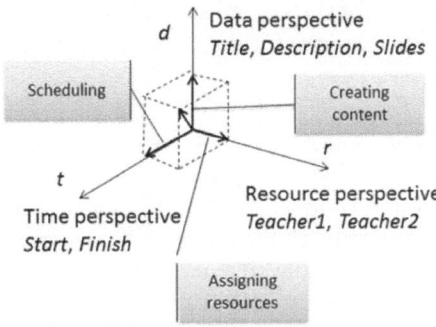

Fig. 7. A subspace that corresponds the form in Fig. 4

change information already entered, delete a form or read what has been entered by others.

4 Interpreting the Example from the State-Oriented Perspective

From the state-oriented view, the idea of case handling discussed in Section 3 can be interpreted in the following way:

- Attaching a new template/form to or deleting the existing template from a case can be considered as an operation of constructing a state-space for a given case. A template here represents a standard subspace that can be added to or subtracted from the case state space. For example, the template in Fig. 4 defines a subspace with the three groups of dimensions expressing different perspectives of case handling, data perspective, time perspective and resource perspective as represented in Fig. 7 [3].
- Filling a template/form corresponds to movement in the subspace defined by this template. For example assigning teachers to a lecture represents movement along r-dimensions in Fig. 7. Creating the lecture content corresponds to movement along d-dimensions in Fig. 7. Deciding on time represents movement along the t-dimensions in Fig. 7. The order in which the movement occurs can be different. In one case, a teacher is assigned first and he/she then creates the content, in another case, the content is borrowed from the previous course occasion, and then a new teacher is assigned to mediate it to the students.
- Restrictions on adding forms to a particular case represent (1) constraints on overall structure of the constructed state space, and (2) the order in which the movement is allowed to occur. The first type of restrictions corresponds to the synchronized forms; they cannot be added without first adding the

---

[3] Actually there are more perspectives that the three ones represented in Fig. 7, for example, space dimension (Location).

basic ones. An example of the second type of restrictions can be to not allow adding lectures before choosing the course book, which will determine the content of the lectures.

5   Concluding Remarks

In this paper, by use of an example, we showed that it is possible to build a CM and ACM system without explicitly introducing the notion of activity/task. This exercise was not aimed at excluding this notion from the world of CM and ACM altogether, as this notion can be useful in making CM and ACM systems more helpful when supporting people in running their process instances/cases. Our main position is not to reject the notion of activity, but show that this notion is secondary to other notions. We also suggested a theoretical underpinning of the template/form driven CM and ACM systems in the form of the state-oriented view suggested in [8]. For ACM system, this view has been extended to include possibility of the state-space being constructed while a process/instance develops in time. This construction is completed by adding new sub-spaces based on the needs arising in the particular process instance/case.

Based on our suggestions it is possible to analyze the functionality of a CM or ACM system to see whether it allows all operations listed in Section 3 and interpreted in Section 4. An immediate result of applying this analysis to our own tool iPB (Bider et al. 2010) showed that while this tool is quite suitable for building CM systems, it becomes cumbersome when applied to ACM systems. One of the main reasons to it is the decision to have all possible templates/forms presented in the case navigation panel of Fig. 6, independently of whether these forms can be used in the given instance/case or not. A better decision would be to have the not used forms outside the panel until they are selected by a user.

Our future plans in regards to this work lie in two directions. One of these directions is full formalization of the ideas presented in the paper; the other one is creating a practical methodology for analysis of CM and ACM systems. One way of approaching the second task could be via defining patterns from which a practically useful state space can be created, and rules for combining them. This would be analogous to the workflow patterns suggested for the standard BPM systems. An approach for defining patterns for the state-oriented view from [2] could be used for this end.

References

1. van der Aalst, W.M.P., Weske, M., Grünbauer, D.: Case handling: a new paradigm for business process support. Data & Knowledge Engineering 53(2), 129–162 (2005)
2. Andersson, B., Bider, I., Johannesson, P., Perjons, E.: Towards a formal definition of goal-oriented business process patterns. Business Process Management Journal 11(6), 650–662 (2005)
3. Andersson, T., Andersson-Ceder, A., Bider, I.: State flow as a way of analyzing business processes–case studies. Logistics Information Management 15(1), 34–45 (2002)

4. Bider, I., Johannesson, P., Perjons, E.: In search of the holy grail: Integrating social software with bpm experience report. In: Bider, I., Halpin, T., Krogstie, J., Nurcan, S., Proper, E., Schmidt, R., Ukor, R. (eds.) BPMDS 2010 and EMMSAD 2010. LNBIP, vol. 50, pp. 1–13. Springer, Heidelberg (2010)

5. Bider, I., Khomyakov, M., Pushchinsky, E.: Logic of change: Semantics of object systems with active relations. Automated Software Engineering 7(1), 9–37 (2000)

6. Bider, I., Perjons, E., Dar, Z.R.: Using data-centric business process modeling for discovering requirements for business process support systems: Experience report. In: Nurcan, S., Proper, H.A., Soffer, P., Krogstie, J., Schmidt, R., Halpin, T., Bider, I. (eds.) BPMDS 2013 and EMMSAD 2013. LNBIP, vol. 147, pp. 63–77. Springer, Heidelberg (2013)

7. Bider, I., Striy, A.: Controlling business process instance flexibility via rules of planning. International Journal of Business Process Integration and Management 3(1), 15–25 (2008)

8. Khomyakov, M., Bider, I.: Achieving workflow flexibility through taming the chaos. In: OOIS 2000, pp. 85–92. Springer (2001)

9. Swenson, K.: Mastering the unpredictable: How adaptive case management will revolutionize the way that knowledge workers get things done, meghan (2010)

10. van der Schaft, A.J., Schumacher, J.M.: An introduction to hybrid dynamical systems, vol. 251. Springer, London (2000)

Dynamic Condition Response Graphs
for Trustworthy Adaptive Case Management

Thomas Hildebrandt[1], Morten Marquard[2],
Raghava Rao Mukkamala[1], and Tijs Slaats[1,2,*]

[1] IT University of Copenhagen, Rued Langgaardsvej 7, 2300 Copenhagen, Denmark
{hilde,rao,tslaats}@itu.dk
http://www.itu.dk
[2] Exformatics A/S, Lautrupsgade 13, 2100 Copenhagen, Denmark
{mmq,ts}@exformatics.com
http://www.exformatics.com

Abstract. By trustworthy adaptive case management we mean that it should be possible to adapt processes and goals at runtime while guaranteeing that no deadlocks and livelocks are introduced. We propose to support this by applying a formal declarative process model, DCR Graphs, and exemplify its operational semantics that supports both run time changes and formal verification. We show how these techniques are being implemented in industry as a component of the Exformatics case management tools. Finally we discuss the planned future work, which will aim to allow changes to be tested for conformance wrt policies specified either as linear time logic (LTL) or DCR Graphs, extend the language with time and data and offer extended support for cross-organizational case management systems.

Introduction

Adaptive case management (ACM) processes are characterized as *unpredictable*, *emergent* and *individual* in nature and typically being carried out by knowledge workers [8,11]. At the same time, many case management processes (e.g. in healthcare or the financial sector) are of a critical nature and subject to regulations, demands for visibility and efficiency.

Consequently, *trustworthy* adaptive case management should allow the case workers to iteratively adapt/model the process during its execution, possibly by combining and adapting process fragments [9] obtained from repositories, and verify if the current process description can indeed fulfill the (currently identified) goals, without violating any of the (current) regulations or rules.

In the present paper we show how Dynamic Condition Response Graphs (DCR Graphs) [1–3] can be used for the specification and trustworthy, adaptive execution of case management processes. DCR Graphs is a formal, *declarative* process modeling notation introduced in the Trustworthy Pervasive Healthcare Services (www.TrustCare.dk) research project as described in the third author's PhD thesis [6], and currently being

---

* Authors listed alphabetically. This research is supported by the Danish Research Agency through an industrial PhD Grant.

Y.T. Demey and H. Panetto (Eds.): OTM 2013 Workshops, LNCS 8186, pp. 166–171, 2013.

embedded in the Exformatics case management tools [10] as part of the industrial PhD project carried out by the last author.

Declarative process notations, such as Declare [12] (based on templates formalized as LTL formulae) and the *Guard-Stage-Milestone* model [5] (based on ECA-like rules) have been put forward as offering flexibility in execution and modelling. By declarative it is usually meant that the notation is aimed at describing *what* is to be achieved, i.e. goals and regulations. This is opposed to *imperative* process notations aiming at describing *how* the goal is to be achieved.

Similar to other declarative models any DCR Graph can be mapped to a (Büchi) automaton describing the possible executions and which executions fulfill the goal of the process. This mapping makes it possible to formally verify the process using standard model-checking tools such as the SPIN model checker.

However, if the process is to be adapted/changed *during* its execution, the compilation of a declarative description into a lower level, imperative description (*before* execution) constitutes a problem. In case the change is applied to the original declarative description, it also affects the process as it was before its execution. On the other hand, if the change is applied to the imperative description of the process being executed, the change must be expressed in terms of the operational model, which requires a non-trivial translation of the meaning of the change between the declarative and the operational model.

A key feature of the DCR Graph notation is that it allows a formal operational semantics in which the intermediate states of running processes are described by a simple marking of the graph, that can also be understood by the case worker. This allows for changes to the declarative description to be applied and take effect in intermediate states of the execution as we will exemplify below.

State of the Art

DCR Graphs by Example. Fig. 1(a) shows an example of a DCR Graph model designed in the DCR Graph editor developed at Exformatics. It represents an invoice workflow with just three events: Enter Invoice Data, Approve and Pay Invoice. The events are represented as boxes with their assigned roles given in small ears at the top. The example process declares two roles: Administration (Adm), representing the administration office of a company and Responsible (Res) the person responsible for the invoice. The administration office has access to the tasks Enter Invoice Data and Pay Invoice and the responsible has access to the task Approve.

Unconstrained events in a DCR Graph can be executed any number of times and in any order. In order to eliminate undesirable behavior in the process, a DCR Graph contains a set of constraints defined using five different kinds of relations between the events, named the condition ($\rightarrow\bullet$), response ($\bullet\rightarrow$), milestone ($\rightarrow\diamond$), inclusion ($\rightarrow+$) and exclusion ($\rightarrow\%$) respectively. The use of the condition, response and milestone relations is illustrated i Fig. 1(a), where we have declared three constraints on the workflow. The first constraint is that we can not pay an invoice before data has been entered. This is declared by the condition relation (an arrow with a bullet at its tip) from Enter Invoice Data to Pay Invoice. But note that we can enter data twice before paying the invoice, and that Pay Invoice is not required to happen when it gets enabled.

The second constraint is that an approval must eventually follow when invoice data has been entered, which is declared by the response relation (an arrow with a bullet at its start) from **Enter invoice Data** to **Approve**. Note that this constraint is also fulfilled if several **Enter Invoice Data** events are followed by a single **Approve** event. Finally, the third constraint is that if an approval is pending, i.e. required but not yet done, then it is not allowed to pay the invoice. This constraint is declared by the milestone relation (an arrow with a diamond at its tip) from **Approve** to **Pay Invoice**. The *stop sign* at the **Pay Invoice** event is not part of the graph, but indicates that the event is not enabled in the current marking (where no events have been executed and thus the condition constraint is not satisfied).

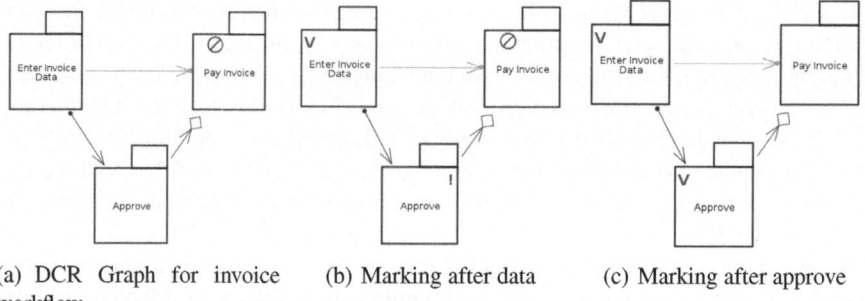

(a) DCR Graph for invoice workflow   (b) Marking after data   (c) Marking after approve

Fig. 1. Examples of DCR Graphs with markings

If **Enter Invoice Data** is executed, the marking of the graph changes to the one in Fig. 1(b). The checkmark inside **Enter Invoice Data** shows that it has been executed, the exclamation mark inside **Approve** shows that it is required to be executed before the workflow has reached its goal. Now, **Enter Invoice Data** can be executed again without changing the marking, since it does not record how many times an event has been executed. **Pay Invoice** is still not enabled, even though the condition constraint that **Enter Invoice Data** should be executed first is fulfilled, the milestone relation disables **Pay Invoice** since **Approve** is required to happen. Now, if **Approve** is executed, the marking changes to the one in Fig 1(c) where all events are enabled, but no events are required.

The final two constraints are the dynamic exclude ($\rightarrow$%) and its dual the dynamic include ($\rightarrow$+). The dynamic exclude relation is used to remove an event dynamically from the workflow when another event happens, and the include relation to add an event (back) to the workflow. Excluded events can never be executed, but neither are they considered when evaluating enabledness or when evaluating whether the workflow is completed.

Fig. 2(a) shows an adaptation of the invoice process that makes use of the dynamic inclusion and exclusion relations. The **Approve** event is adapted to contain three *sub events*: **Responsible Approve**, **Manager Approve** and **CEO Approve**. The meaning of the relations to and from **Approve** is simply that they relate to all sub events of **Approve**. The sub events also inherited the response marking and are thus all required.

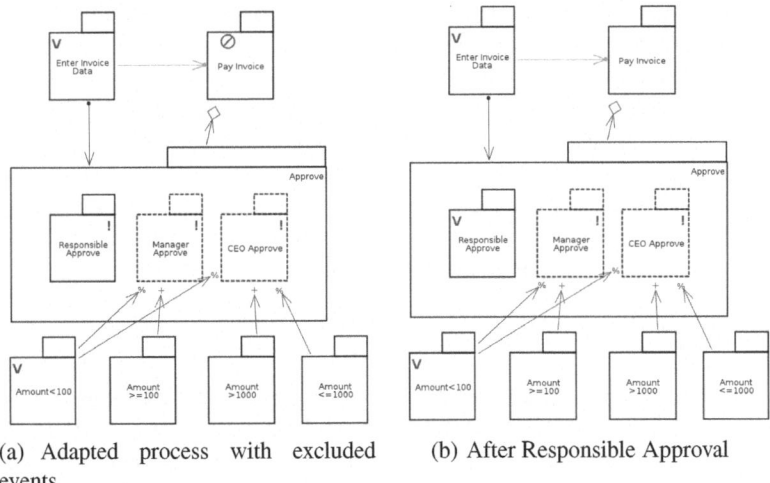

(a) Adapted process with excluded events

(b) After Responsible Approval

Fig. 2. Example of nested events and dynamically included and excluded events

However, three other events have also been added to represent the decision logic behind the detailed approval process: **Amount** < 100, **Amount** $>= 100$ and **Amount** $>= 1000$. These events are to be executed by the system when the amount (entered as part of the **Enter Invoice Data** event) changes and the constraint is satisfied. For the sake of the example, we assume the amount entered was less than 100, so the **Amount** < 100 event has been executed. This resulted in **Manager Approve** and **CEO Approve** to be excluded, as represented by the dashed boxes. Fig. 2(b) shows the resulting marking if **Responsible Approve** is executed. **Pay Invoice** is enabled since the required responses on the excluded events **Manager Approve** and **CEO Approve** are not considered when the milestone relation is evaluated.

Adaptive DCR Graphs. As shown in the previous examples, when using DCR Graphs we maintain information on the original events and relations of the model at runtime. Executing a DCR Graph simply results in a new DCR Graph with a (optionally) changed marking. This makes it easy to adapt the model at runtime: one can add or remove relations and events and continue executing afterwards. In recent work [7], we investigated this in more detail and formalized a number of operations for adding/removing events and relations to DCR Graphs and composing process fragments. In the same paper we presented techniques for checking DCR Graphs for dead- and live-lock, and showed how these techniques can be used for safely adapting DCR Graphs at runtime.

DCR Graphs at Exformatics. DCR Graphs have been adopted by our industrial partner Exformatics A/S as the underlying formal model for workflows in their state-of-the-art Electronic Case Management (ECM) system, which is used by various Danish and international clients, both in the private and public sector, for case- and project-management.

Exformatics has developed a number of tools to support the modeling and execution of DCR Graphs. These tools are stand-alone and can be used without requiring installation of their Electronic Case Management product. The tools include several webservices for execution, verification, storage and visualization of DCR Graphs based workflows and a graphical editor for modelling, simulation and visualization of DCR Graphs. All diagrams in this paper have been produced by the editor, which also supports adaptation during a simulation. However, assignment of data values as part of events and the automatic execution of events based on changes in data values is not supported yet, i.e. it must so far be manually simulated by the designer.

Future Work

Currently we are extending the verification techniques for DCR Graphs to allow for checking any arbitrary property, defined as either a LTL formula or a DCR Graph. This technique will allow us to verify that run-time adaptations of a process model continue to adhere to a set of given policies. We are also exploring different ways of handling data within DCR Graphs, inspired by different application domains that have different requirements to the processes being modelled. The first proposal [6, 10] has been described in the examples. The second proposal is aimed at cross-organizational workflows where there is no central location of the data that all parties have access too. In this approach events are parameterized by variables, for example an employee ID, and occurrences of the same event with different parameters are considered distinct. Relations in this approach are relative to the parameters on the events, ie if Enter Invoice Data[employeeId] requires Approve[employeeId] as a response, then an occurrence of Enter Invoice Data for a specific employee requires approval by that same employee. The third approach is based on a hybrid model that combines DCR Graphs with Coloured Petri nets. [13] The motivation for the hybrid model was an attempt to combine declarative and imperative workflow languages, but it also allows for data constraints to be added to DCR Graphs by using a language that is already popular as a formal foundation for workflows. In future work we will select the approach that best fits to adaptive processes and extend the adaptation operators and verification techniques to also cover this data variant. In addition we will extend the aforementioned techniques to work on timed DCR Graphs [4]. Finally an algorithm for safely distributing the execution of a process has been developed [3]. This can be used to provide a global description of a collaborative process, which can then be distributed on different participants. In future work we plan to extend the theory of distributed DCR Graphs with a behavioral type system, which will allow us to more efficiently verify cross-organizational adaptive processes.

Conclusion

We have outlined by an example the declarative primitives and operational semantics for DCR Graphs and how the model could be used as the foundation for trustworthy adaptive case management. The declarative nature of the model provides flexibility in execution, i.e. it avoids the usual overspecification of flow graphs, as well as flexibility with respect to adaptations: Process fragments can be composed and events and constraints can be added and removed through three basic adaptation operations, without breaking the syntactic validity of the graph, and correspond to the identification of new activities and rules in an emergent process. The representation of the state of a process in terms of a marking that can be understood by the case worker means that adaptations can be made to partially executed processes. The formal semantics and mapping to Büchi-automata (also of intermediate process states), makes it possible to formally verify if it is still possible to achieve the goal of the process after adaptation. We also showed how the work is being implemented by our industrial partner in their ECM system. Finally we discussed planned future work that will make DCR Graphs even more suitable for supporting trustworthy adaptive case management processes.

References

1. Hildebrandt, T., Mukkamala, R.R.: Declarative event-based workflow as distributed dynamic condition response graphs. In: PLACES. EPTCS, vol. 69, pp. 59–73 (2011)
2. Hildebrandt, T., Mukkamala, R.R., Slaats, T.: Nested dynamic condition response graphs. In: Arbab, F., Sirjani, M. (eds.) FSEN 2011. LNCS, vol. 7141, pp. 343–350. Springer, Heidelberg (2012)
3. Hildebrandt, T., Mukkamala, R.R., Slaats, T.: Safe distribution of declarative processes. In: Barthe, G., Pardo, A., Schneider, G. (eds.) SEFM 2011. LNCS, vol. 7041, pp. 237–252. Springer, Heidelberg (2011)
4. Hildebrandt, T., Mukkamala, R.R., Slaats, T., Zanitti, F.: Contracts for cross-organizational workflows as timed dynamic condition response graphs. Journal of Logic and Algebraic Programming (JLAP) (May 2013),
   `http://dx.doi.org/10.1016/j.jlap.2013.05.005`
5. Hull, R.: Formal study of business entities with lifecycles: Use cases, abstract models, and results. In: Bravetti, T., Bultan, M. (eds.) 7th International Workshop on Web Services and Formal Methods. LNCS, vol. 6551 (2010)
6. Mukkamala, R.R.: A Formal Model For Declarative Workflows: Dynamic Condition Response Graphs. PhD thesis, IT University of Copenhagen (June 2012),
   `http://www.itu.dk/people/rao/phd-thesis/`
   `DCRGraphs-rao-PhD-thesis.pdf`
7. Mukkamala, R.R., Hildebrandt, T., Slaats, T.: Towards trustworthy adaptive case management with dynamic condition response graphs. In: Proceedings of the 17th IEEE International EDOC Conference, EDOC (2013)
8. Mundbrod, N., Kolb, J., Reichert, M.: Towards a system support of collaborative knowledge work. In: La Rosa, M., Soffer, P. (eds.) BPM Workshops 2012. LNBIP, vol. 132, pp. 31–42. Springer, Heidelberg (2013)
9. Sirbu, A., Marconi, A., Pistore, M., Eberle, H., Leymann, F., Unger, T.: Dynamic composition of pervasive process fragments. In: Proceedings of the 2011 IEEE International Conference on Web Services, ICWS 2011, pp. 73–80. IEEE Computer Society, Washington, DC (2011)
10. Slaats, T., Mukkamala, R.R., Hildebrandt, T., Marquard, M.: Exformatics declarative case management workflows as dcr graphs. In: Daniel, F., Wang, J., Weber, B. (eds.) BPM 2013. LNCS, vol. 8094, pp. 339–354. Springer, Heidelberg (2013)
11. Swenson, K.D.: Mastering the Unpredictable: How Adaptive Case Management Will Revolutionize the Way That Knowledge Workers Get Things Done. Meghan-Kiffer Press (2010)
12. van der Aalst, W.M.P., Pesic, M., Schonenberg, H.: Declarative workflows: Balancing between flexibility and support. Computer Science - R&D 23(2), 99–113 (2009)
13. Westergaard, M., Slaats, T.: Mixing paradigms for more comprehensible models. In: Daniel, F., Wang, J., Weber, B. (eds.) BPM 2013. LNCS, vol. 8094, pp. 283–290. Springer, Heidelberg (2013)

Setup and Maintenance Factors of ACM Systems

Thanh Tran Thi Kim[1], Max J. Pucher[1], Jan Mendling[2], and Christoph Ruhsam[1]

[1] ISIS Papyrus Europe AG
{thanh.tran,max.pucher,christoph.ruhsam}@isis-papyrus.com
[2] Wirtschaftsuniversität Wien, Institute for Information Business
jan.mendling@wu.ac.at

Abstract. Adaptive Case Management (ACM) is information technology for the secure and transparent management of structured and unstructured business processes, consisting of data, content, related work tasks and rules executed towards well-defined process goals. Thus, it goes beyond combining benefits of workflow diagrams with ad-hoc task mechanisms. One of the notorious weaknesses of classical workflow technology is the experts' effort for getting a sufficiently complete specification of the process to create an executable which typically takes several months. In contrast, ACM provides goal-oriented mechanisms to enable performers to define and execute work tasks ad-hoc. In this paper, based on the definition of the ACM concepts, we analyze which setup steps have to be conducted for an ACM system in a typical scenario from the service industry. Our contribution is an identification of major factors that influence the setup initiated by experts and the maintenance performed by business users.

Keywords: Adaptive Case Management, Business Process Management, ISIS Papyrus ACM.

1 Introduction

Adaptive Case Management (ACM) is information technology for the secure and transparent management of structured and unstructured business processes representing work tasks linked to process goals with data and content [1, 2]. ACM provides mechanisms to enable performers to define and execute work tasks ad-hoc without preliminary process analysis and design. The tasks are always linked to at least one goal with completion rules or need to achieve a customer outcome and are monitored through operational targets. In this way, it embraces flexibility requirements such as variability, adaptation and evolution [3] which classical workflow systems often do not support to the full extent [4].

One of the weaknesses of classical workflow technology is the considerable effort of analyzing a process for creating a workflow implementation. For instance, Herbst and Karagiannis observe that the acquisition of workflow knowledge typically consumes three times more than the actual implementation [5]. While there are notable benefits reported of implementing a process [6, 7], the setup costs often become a roadblock for supporting a process with a dedicated workflow implementation.

Y.T. Demey and H. Panetto (Eds.): OTM 2013 Workshops, LNCS 8186, pp. 172–177, 2013.
© Springer-Verlag Berlin Heidelberg 2013

In this paper, we aim to conceptually investigate how the presumed benefits of ACM in terms of reduced setup effort can be substantiated. The remainder of this paper is structured as follows. First, we analyze the setup and maintenance factors of an ACM system (ACMS). Then, we illustrate the implementation of these factors and point out the adaptability of ACMS in the context of service contract management. Our contribution is an identification of major factors that influence the setup initiated by experts and maintenance performed by knowledge workers (KWs).

2   ACM Setup and Maintenance Factors

ACM methodology takes advantages of the process definition features of BPM to cover specific process fragments, which must be executed in a specific way. This enables ACM to utilize predefined process models like in BPM as a guideline for users but not necessary force them to follow the existing steps from the models unless this is required. However, to deal with unpredictable events happening while working with a predefined process, ACM allows users to create and modify process models at runtime (based on access rights) or create their own step by step performance. Once the well-defined goals are reached the process instance can be converted to an abstract (without the instance data) goal template. Therefore, it eliminates the need for fully sketching out all details of the process beforehand.

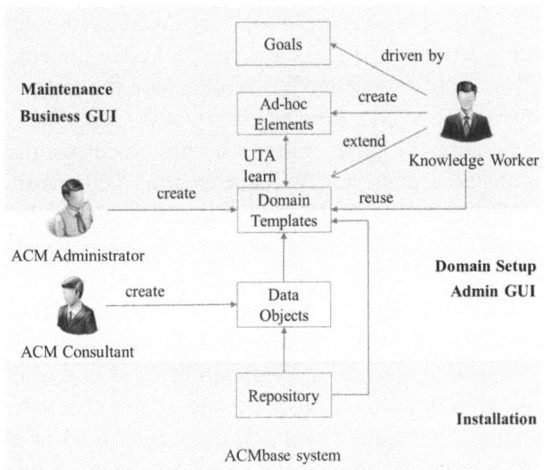

Fig. 1. The ACM environment

Figure 1 depicts the overview of the setup and maintenance of ACM. A process implemented by ACM requires a set of explicitly defined goals. The definition needs access to data for the rule definitions. The rules are performed in natural language and supported with interactive syntax guidance and data attribute validation. Goals can be linked within a case or more importantly also across cases. There are several types of goals: process goals, operational targets, and customer outcomes on the case level and statistically calculated key performance indicators. Process goals are rule definitions using process data or checklists. Operational targets can be financial or service level targets that are monitored at the case/process level and not just at the department or capability level. That allows a drill down analysis when targets are missed. The factors relating to an adaptive process are goals (business view), outcomes (customer view), skill or resources (capability view), work (task types, dependencies, checklists), data (forms and silo interface view), rules (for data and content, resources, work), and content (inbound, outbound, social, email, rules).

In implementation, the ACMbase system is installed by IT people and can be applied in many business domains. Depending on each business domain, specific data objects and templates are created by ACM consultants and Administrators (Admins in short) in the setup phase. The maintenance is operated by KWs who handle instances and ad hoc events in a particular business case. The performance of KWs is driven by goals which are expected when a case closes. The setup and maintenance factors of ACM are investigated with the ISIS Papyrus ACM system (ACMS). The ACMS is illustrated in the context of service contract management in which the rigidity of BPM and the flexibility of ACM are both applied simultaneously.

The setup an ACM is operated in the GUI for Admins. Admins are assumed to have the knowledge of business operation in service contract management and is able to administrate the ACMS. This is similar to other management systems where administrators need to have the knowledge of the system applied in a specific business domain, e.g. database management systems.

The setup deals with the preparation of the base ACM system for use in a specific business application in terms of the five elements of ACM: content, goals, cases, data entities and GUIs. The setup is operated by Admins with the support from consultants who have knowledge about ACM. Admins construct the templates from classes: data entity, document (i.e., content), goals, rules, reusable processes, participants, and the case itself holding all these elements. Without creating code, Admins configure the setup with Admin GUIs based on the existing foundation classes in the ACMS. Thus, comparing with a BPM setup, the ACM setup needs no technical support from IT experts.

Figure 2 is a mash-up screenshot illustrating the implementation of the setup and maintenance factors of the Papyrus ACMS. Within the limit of a short paper, we represent the main interfaces illustrating the flexibility and ease of the ACMS in setup and maintenance. As seen in Figure 2, Part 1 is the tree of objects which are setup by Admins without coding. The Admins work on the Admin GUI to create business objects or templates. Depending on the business application domain, in this case service contract management, the Admins create the suitable templates for KWs to operate their daily business.

Data entities are the essential elements in a data centric system like ACMS. Customer and contract data objects are created by Admins and ACM consultants. Another key element of ACMS is goals comprised of rules as conditions to decide whether the goals are achieved. Rules are defined in Papyrus Natural Language Rule [9] within the Papyrus ACMS. In service contract management, there are several goals such as Service Contract Acquisition, Service Execution, Contract Audition, etc. (see Part 1).

Each main goal can have sub-goals, for instance, the Service Contract Acquisition has sub-goals which are Contract Composition, Contract Negotiation, and Contract Approval.

Each sub-goal can refer to pre-defined processes (i.e. sub-processes) which are executed to achieve the goal. This element enables ACM to operate the BPM-like processes. Although sub-processes are pre-defined to provide work support for the KWs, they can be edited on the execution level (instances) by KWs. However, it is necessary to follow rigid steps in the approval contract process. In this case, the pre-defined sub-process called Approval Contract is operated rigidly.

Case templates contain all the necessary elements to achieve their goals. However, a case in the ACM is driven by goals. Therefore, Admins only define the data objects containing the goals of the case. Based on the templates created by Admins, the KW performs their daily works in business GUI. However using the templates is not obligate for KWs. KWs are assumed to have capability to handle the unpredictable event in their daily business by their own way. The templates created by Admins are used as guidelines for KWs and they can choose or create by themselves the instances based on the current situation they are working on.

When the setup is accomplished, KWs are able to use the system with the business GUI of the ACM system as seen partly in the right parts of Figure 2. We demonstrate how the system supports KWs with the flexibility under the influence of content and goal orientation.

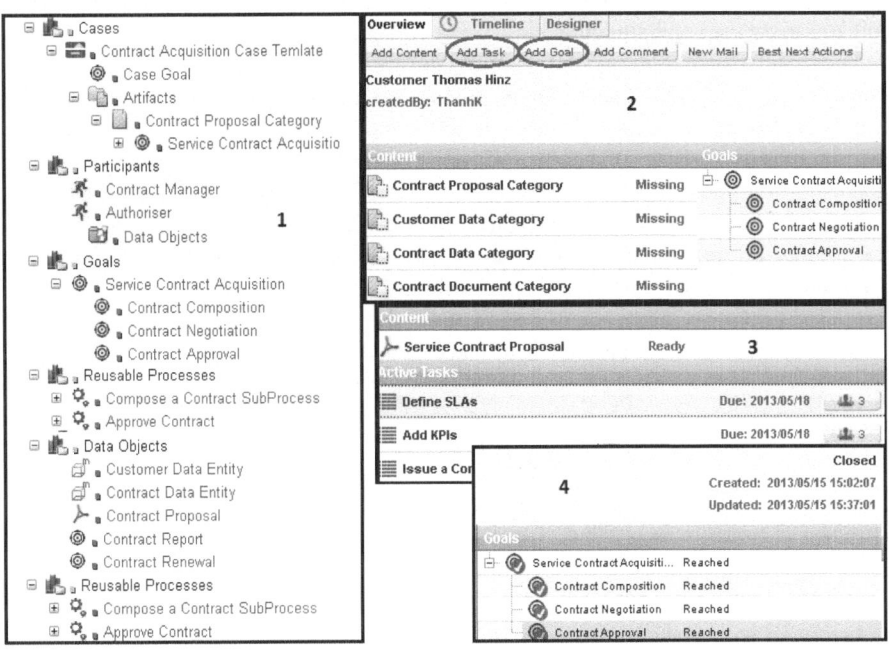

Fig. 2. The implementation of ACM setup and maintenance factors

Part 2 of Figure 2 shows the overview of a case for customer Thomas Hinz GmbH based on the case templates defined by Admins. The case is started with the main goal Service Contract Acquisition. The content related to the case is still missing and needs to be uploaded as Contract Proposal to start the case. In other words, the goal is triggered by the uploading data Contract Proposal. Note that the buttons Add Task and Add Goal enable KWs to add new instances on the fly without the use of templates.

Part 3 depicts the uploaded Contract Proposal and three associated tasks become available for KWs. The KWs choose the task Define SLAs to start compose the service contract definition and the condition contained in the contract document. Since the SLAs and KPIs are completed, the contract is issued. Thus the goal Contract Composition is reached as seen in Part 4. The goal Contract Negotiation does initially not contain any tasks defined by Admins. The KW can add Tasks depending on the current business situation by using the function Add Task as shown in Part 2. Although ACM supports the KW by adding tasks on the fly, the KW cannot edit the pre-defined processes which are important to meet compliance regulations. The goal Contract Approval contains the sub-process Approve Contract which is essential in service contract management. Therefore, the KW must operate this sub-process in the way defined by Admins. This represents the rigidity of BPM applied in ACM.

When all the goals are reached, the main goal Service Contract Acquisition is reached and the case is closed as seen in Part 4. The demonstration of ACMS GUI shows that the system supports the flexibility for KWs to handle the unpredictable tasks in the practical situation. Moreover, with the goal orientation, the system is reliable to satisfy the legal situation.

The maintenance of the system happens during its operating time and proclaims the adaptability of ACMS. The reusable processes category contains the sub-processes templates. When a process is created by KWs and used frequently, it can be added to the reusable processes category by Admins. Moreover, the system supports KWs by suggesting the most proper next step. This is performed by the User Trained Agent (UTA) which examines the data pattern in a certain KW context to suggest future steps based on pattern matching. Thus, the system improves itself by learning from KWs and their activities which lead to successful closing of goals.

Table 1. Setup and maintenance factors

Factors	Setup	Maintenance	Learning
Goals	Template (Tmp)	Instance (Ins)	Tmp derived from Ins
Data objects	Data structure	Data value	
Reusable Processes	Tmp	Ins	Tmp derived from Ins
Cases	Tmp	Ins	Tmp derived from Ins
GUI	Admin GUI	Business GUI	
Participants	Admin	KW	Admin

Table 1 contains the summary of setup and maintenance factors. The minimum effort for setting up a process in an ACM system requires the definition of goals and essential data objects. This is in contrast the factors that drive the effort of a classical workflow implementation. The work by Aysolmaz et al. investigates workflow setup effort and finds that control flow complexity and number of different outputs of the activities in the process model are the significant factors in this context [10]. This means that processes with high control flow complexity and a high variation in outputs might potentially be much easier set up using ACM systems. This hypothesis requires an empirical approach in future research.

3   Conclusion

In this paper we discuss the effort of setting up, maintaining and learning a process using an ACM system. Based on a typical case of service contract management we investigate the steps of setting up the system and compare it to the effort of setting up a classical workflow. Our contribution is an identification of major factors that influence the process creation and reuse. We aim to investigate setup effort further in future research.

References

1. Pucher, M.: The Strategic Business Benefits of Adaptive Case Management. In: Fischer, L. (ed.) How Knowledge Workers Get Things Done - Real-World Adaptive Case Management. Future Strategies Inc. (2012)
2. Pucher, M.: Adaptive Case Management - ISIS Papyrus and ACM. ISIS Papyrus, http://acmisis.wordpress.com/what-is-adaptive-case-management-acm/
3. Reichert, M., Weber, B.: Enabling Flexibility in Process-Aware Information Systems - Challenges, Methods, Technologies, pp. I-XVIII, 1–515. Springer (2012) ISBN 978-3-642-30408-8
4. Reijers, H.A.: Workflow Flexibility: The Forlorn Promise. In: 15th IEEE International Workshops on Enabling Technologies: Infrastructures for Collaborative Enterprises (WETICE 2006), pp. 271–272 (2006) ISBN 0-7695-2623-3
5. Herbst, J., Karagiannis, D.: Integrating machine learning and workflow management to support acquisition and adaptation of workflow models. In: Proceedings of the 9th International Workshop on Database and Expert Systems Applications, p. 745 (1998) 0-8186-8353-8
6. Reijers, H.A., Van Der Aalst, W.M.P.: The effectiveness of workflow management systems. Predictions and lessons learned. Int. J. Inf. Manag. 25(0268-4012), 458–472 (2005)
7. Gruber, H., Huemer, C.: Profitability Analysis of Workflow Management Systems. In: Proceedings of the 2009 IEEE Conference on Commerce and Enterprise Computing, pp. 233–238 (2009) 978-0-7695-3755-9
8. Pucher, M.: The Elements of Adaptive Case Management. In: Mastering the Unpredictable, pp. 89–135. Meghan-Kiffer Press, Florida (2010)
9. ISIS Papyrus: WebRepository Adaptive Case Management Framework - Developer and Administrator Guide. In: ISIS Papyrus Technical Documentation (2013)
10. Aysolmaz, B., İren, D., Demirörs, O.: An Effort Prediction Model based on BPM Measures for Process Automation. In: Nurcan, S., Proper, H.A., Soffer, P., Krogstie, J., Schmidt, R., Halpin, T., Bider, I. (eds.) BPMDS 2013 and EMMSAD 2013. LNBIP, vol. 147, pp. 154–167. Springer, Heidelberg (2013)

EI2N 2013 PC Co-Chairs Message

After the successful seventh edition in 2012, the eight edition of the Enterprise Integration, Interoperability and Networking workshop (EI2N'2013) has been organized as part of the OTM'2013 Federated Conferences in Graz, Austria. The workshop is co-sponsored by the IFAC Technical Committee 5.3 "Enterprise Integration and Networking" (main sponsor) and IFAC TC 3.1, 3.2, 3.3, 5.2, 5.4 and 9.5, the IFIP TC 8 WG 8.1 "Design and Evaluation of Information Systems", the SIG INTEROP Grande-Région on "Enterprise Systems Interoperability", and the French CNRS National Research Group GDR MACS.

Today's rapidly evolving global economy has reiterated the urgent industrial need to achieve dynamic, efficient and effective cooperation of partner organizations within networks of larger enterprises. This requires innovations, which serve as the foundation for more productive and effective collaborative global partnerships, and in turn become the primary drivers for more sustainable businesses. In this information centric context, Enterprise Modelling Techniques, Next Generation Computing Architectures and Platforms along with Semantic Interoperability principles support the achievement of sustainable enterprise integration, interoperability and networking. Our 2013 EI2N workshop has been organized around these important themes.

We were impressed at the overall high quality papers received this year. After rigorous reviews by the international program committee, 8 papers have been accepted out of a total of 18 submissions to this workshop (which is an acceptance rate of 44%). Each of the submitted papers were evaluated by three members of our international program committee.

We have divided the workshop into four sessions. The first three sessions contain selected papers related to the following topics:

- Architectures and Platforms for Interoperability
- Engineering and Modelling
- Sustainable interoperability and interoperability for sustainability

The fourth session involves interactive discussions, which are an integral part of the workshop, focusing on the topic of "The Sensing Enterprise: the Future for the Collaborative Digital enterprise". The outcomes of these discussions are reported during a plenary session jointly organized with the CoopIS'2013 and the OTM Industry Case Studies Program 2013.

We would like to thank the authors, reviewers, sponsors and other colleagues who have together contributed to the success of this workshop.

July 2013

Alexis Aubry
J. Cecil
Kasuhiko Terashima
Georg Weichhart

Y.T. Demey and H. Panetto (Eds.): OTM 2013 Workshops, LNCS 8186, p. 178, 2013.

Towards a Framework for Inter-Enterprise Architecture to Boost Collaborative Networks

Alix Vargas, Andrés Boza, Llanos Cuenca, and Angel Ortiz

Research Centre on Production Management and Engineering (CIGIP),
Universitat Politècnica de València, Camino de Vera s/n Ed 8G -1° y 4° planta Acc D
alvarlo@posgrado.upv.es, {aboza,llcuenca,aortiz}@cigip.upv.es

Abstract. A complete Inter-Enterprise Architecture should be conformed to a framework, a methodology and a modelling language. In this sense, this paper proposes an initial Framework for Inter-Enterprise Architecture (FIEA), which organizes, stores, classifies and communicates in a conceptual level the elements of the Inter-Enterprise Architecture (IEA) and their relationships, ensuring their consistency and integrity. This FIEA provides a clear picture about the elements and perspectives that make up the collaborative network and their inter-relationships, supported for technology base on the Internet for its inter-operation.

Keywords: Inter-Enterprise Architecture, Framework, Supply Chain, Collaborative Networks, Future Internet.

1 Introduction

The current environment of globalization and competition directs the flow of business through the supply chain (SC) or, more recently, collaborative networks (CN), since companies cannot compete individually. Therefore, it is necessary that the companies that comprise these SCs or CNs are integrated and coordinating their processes to become more competitive and efficient, thus enabling the fulfilment of the overall objectives of the CN and its own objectives. On the other hand, organizations are more complex now and require flexible business processes that are supported by an efficient information technology (IT) infrastructure. It is undisputed that IT and information systems (IS) have become strategic functional entities within organizations, and these functions have an increasing impact on business strategy, because IS/IT currently constitute a competitive advantage for organizations to be sustainable over time. In this sense, companies should be managing the increasing technological complexities accrued while they generate added value to business processes, and at the same time achieve integration and coordinate their processes with their partners in the CN in the pursuit of efficiency and competitiveness to ensure survival in the global market. Achieving these goals may be possible using Enterprise Engineering (EE) with an Enterprise Architecture (EA) approach [1].

The concept of Inter-Enterprise Architecture (IEA) has been proposed using the tools and methodologies of EA for individual enterprises, but adapting them in a

Y.T. Demey and H. Panetto (Eds.): OTM 2013 Workshops, LNCS 8186, pp. 179–188, 2013.

collaboratively networked environment between several enterprises that make up SCs and CNs. This will facilitate the collaborative processes of integration between enterprises with their information systems and technology systems, supporting joint processes, reducing risks and redundancies, increasing customer service and responsiveness, reducing technology costs and allowing for alignment on multiple levels [2]. CNs can allow small and medium enterprises (SMEs) to share information through the use of IT in support of their business processes. If a CN is accurately created and managed, this allows SMEs to make being part of the CN more competitive, creating added value in their own business, enabling innovation and boosting learning and knowledge. In the context of CNs, two important approaches will be taken into account in the development of the proposal framework: Virtual Breeding Environments [3] and Digital Business Ecosystems [4]. The Internet has become a necessity in business environments, but many SMEs cannot afford to use it as a management and operational tool due to cost, availability and trust. In order for the Internet to become useful as a real universal business system used by a CN, it is necessary to branch joint efforts among society, government, research and industry. Following the ideas of the FInES Cluster [5], the Framework for Inter-Enterprise Architecture (FIEA) is based on the use of Internet as technology that enables the interoperation between enterprises that form a CN.

Taking into account the blueprint of the newly networked enterprise environment, the paper is structured as follows: Section 2 describes the related work in these fields; Section 3 presents a proposal of FIEA; Section 4 presents the main conclusions and future steps.

2   Research Topics

2.1   Strategic Alignment

According to [6], strategic alignment is: "A dynamic and continuous process that enables integration, adjustment, consistency, understanding, synchronization and support between business and Information Systems/Information Technology (IS/IT), in order to contribute and maintain the correct performance of the organization, creating a competitive advantage that is sustained over time". It is clear that SCs and CNs have to be able to manage the technological complexities of their IS, while ensuring that these generate added value to business processes. This can only be achieved if there is an alignment between business and IS / IT, and this concept became stronger in the 1990s thanks to the Strategic Alignment Model (SAM) proposed by [7]. Although the theory suggests that there should be a strategic fit and functional integration between business and IT, in reality, the implementation of the alignment is quite complicated to carry out, because the studies, models and/or frameworks developed for this purpose are scarce and their utility is often not validated in the real world. However, this strategic alignment can be achieved through the use of enterprise architectures (EA) [8].

2.2   Enterprise Engineering and Enterprise Architecture

Enterprise Engineering (EE) is the discipline applied to carrying out any efforts to establish, modify, or reorganize any enterprise [8]. This discipline is responsible for defining, structuring, designing and implementing enterprise operations as communication networks of business processes, which comprise all their related business knowledge, operational information, resources and organization relationships [9]. The field of EE is concerned with understanding, defining, designing and redesigning business entities, which includes all knowledge and organizational relationships, as well as life cycles [10]. Therefore, EE facilitates the integration of all elements of the enterprise. Enterprise Integration (EI) deals with facilitating information flows, systems interoperability and knowledge sharing among any kind of organization [11]. Achieving EI through the EE is possible thanks to the use of (EA). In [12], taking into account ancient definitions, EA is defined as: "A discipline that provides a set of principles, methods, models and tools used for analysis, design and redesign of a company, thus allowing to represent and document the elements that form the company (such as organizational structure, business processes, systems information and technology infrastructure) and the relations, organization and joints between these elements, allowing the company to be represented in a holistic and integrated perspective, in order to achieve the business objectives and facilitate decision-making processes". The main elements of EA are: methodology, framework and modelling language [12]. These elements must be provided by EA for successful implementation within the enterprise. The methodology defines how the EA will be implemented and how it will develop, use and archive the documentation. The framework allows for structuring of the elements of the EA and their relationships in a graphical and simple way, taking into account different views or perspectives and the life cycle phases. Finally, the identification of a modelling language allows modelling and understanding the relationship between the views that make the company, in a structured way.

2.3   Enterprise Collaboration

Enterprises today do not compete individually, and now the SCs and/or CNs compete with each other in search of increased profits and generating more customer value. Therefore, the necessity of a high degree of integration between partners that make up these SCs or networks is imminent [13], and this degree of integration may be achieved through collaborative mechanisms to ensure the alignment of. individual plans in the search for achieving a goal of a joint plan. Thus, enterprise collaboration emerges as a tool that allows members of the SC and CN to be making decisions together, based on shared information and the exchange of a bilateral form, which allows them to coordinate and synchronize activities with the objective of satisfying the market and increasing joint profits [12]. Base on the main elements provided for several authors we propose the definition of enterprise collaboration process in [12], as: "A joint process between members of the SC, where the decisions are made jointly, based on the information shared and exchanged on a bilateral form, achieving coordinate and synchronize joint activities to meet customer requirements and achieve process efficiency sets to generate a mutually beneficial"

2.4   Collaborative Networks

In the new market environment, enterprises have to deal with the complexity of contemporary products, new customer requirements, geographically distributed partners, and a constantly changing technological environment. This is a big challenge that must be approached delicately, especially by SMEs that do not have the resources (both monetary and skilled workforce) and simply-used and affordable IT solutions to face this challenge by themselves. Therefore, SMEs have to make up CNs in order to be competitive and survive this turbulent environment. According to [14] "CN is a network consisting of a variety of entities (e.g. organizations, people, machines) that are largely autonomous, geographically distributed, and heterogeneous in terms of their operating environment, culture, social capital and goals, but that collaborate to better achieve common or compatible goals, thus jointly generating value, and whose interactions are supported by computer networks". When CNs (industry), Researcher Institutions, Universities and Governmental Organizations join efforts in order to create a community that looks for increasing industrial competitiveness, they are creating traditional "Clusters". A cluster represents an association or pool of enterprises and related supporting institutions that have both the potential and the motivation to cooperate with each other through the establishment of a long-term cooperation agreement [3]. The conceptual foundation of Clusters has given origin to two new fields: Virtual Breeding Environments (VBE) [3] and Digital Business Ecosystems (DBE) [4].

2.5   Future Internet

In the new economic environment, IT and specifically Internet are ubiquitous [15]. The rapid growth of the Internet has enhanced computing, sharing and communication capabilities, but also introduced uncertainties regarding the future of existing traditional business models. In order to sustain and increase business competitively, enterprises should embrace these new technologies taking into account different vital aspects: security, agility, accuracy, interoperability, affordability and reliability. On the other hand, there are some important requirements for the implementation of IT solutions into SMEs in a context of collaboration according to [16] are: cost, time, flexibility, privacy and trust. In this sense, [5] affirms that the next decade is expected to see a thorough change in the way enterprises operate, mainly due to the advent of the Future Internet and the maturity achieved by enterprises in adopting new socio-technical solutions based on the former.

2.6   Emergent Concept of Inter-Enterprise Architecture (IEA)

After a thorough analysis of the current literature in the fields summarized above, we have identified trends, studied models that have strongly related concepts and associated issues, analysed main ideas and common points, and identified a large gap in the literature, due to the fact that there is not currently any documentation tying these fields of research together. As a result of this gap, the concept of Inter-Enterprise Architecture (IEA) is proposed, searching for applications of the tools and methodologies of enterprise architecture, which have been developed for the individual enterprise, but adapting them in a collaborative environment between several enterprises that make up CNs [2]. This will facilitate the collaboration process of integration between enterprises with there IS/IT based on Internet, supporting joint processes, reducing risks and redundancies, increasing customer service and responsiveness, reducing technology costs and allowing for alignment on multiple levels. In Fig. 1, currently completed work is summarized, and the field of intended study is represented in the spotlight.

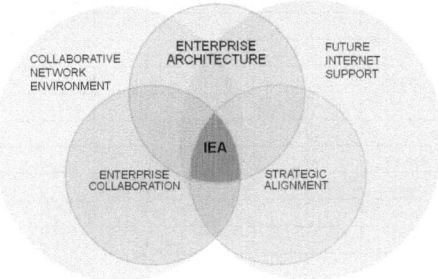

Fig. 1. Origin of IEA concept into a CN environment with supporting of future Internet

The implementation of an IEA is part of establishing a set of architectural guidelines that ensure comprehensive development between models and inter-enterprise needs, with joint business processes and IT. These guidelines will also be responsible for spawning the necessary information for the joint operation of organizations and technologies required to support joint operations and new technology implementation processes in response to ever-changing needs and jointly involved organizations. In this IEA, technology plays a definitive role, according to the concepts of DBE that consider that technology must be the medium that facilitates the formalization and distribution of the knowledge from which the same technology emerged. Essentially, technology becomes a catalyst for development of enterprises, SCs, CNs and DCs. Therefore; technology accelerates the growth and harmony of the DBE.

3   Proposal of the Framework for IEA

Three elements are necessary in any EA: Framework, Methodology and Modelling Language. In this section, we propose a framework for modelling CNs in the context of IEA (FIEA). The FIEA is defined as: "A logical structure for classifying, organizing, storing and communicating conceptual level elements or components of the IEA and their relationships, ensuring consistency and integrity. This structure defines the scope of IEA and provides a basis for assembly and development". The following surveys have been taking into account in our analysis: 1) Total Enterprise Architecture as: CIMOSA [17], GIM-GRAI [18], GERAM [19], IE-GIP [20,21], TOGAF-ADM [22]. 2) In the context of CNs: ARCON [3], VERA [23] and ARDIN-EVEI [24]. Table 1 shows a comparative analysis of the views and life cycle phases for these surveys and in the last column are defined the modelling views and life cycle phases for FIEA.

Table 1. Comparative analysis between framework modelling perspectives of EA and CNEA

FRAMEWORK MODELLING PERSPECTIVES			ENTERPRISE ARCHITECTURES (EA)					COLLABORATIVE NETWORKS EA (CNEA)			FIEA
			CIMOSA	GIM-GRAI	GERAM	IE-GIP	TOGAF-ADM	ARCON	VERA	ARDIN-EVEI	
Modelling views	Modelling views defined in ISO 19439 (2006)	Function	=	±	=	±	±	=	=	=	*Business Process
		Information	=	=	=	=	=		=	=	*Knowledge
		Resources	=		=	=		±	=	=	=
		Organization	=		=	=		±	=		=
	Other views provided by the different architectures	Decision		■						■	
		Data				■					
		Applications				■					*IS/IT base on Internet
		Technology				■					Internet
		Behavioural			■						
		Market						■			
		Support						■ (Exogenous interactions)			
		Societal						■			
		Constituency						■			
Modelling life cycle phases	Life cycle phases defined in ISO 19439 (2006)	Domain identification			=	=			=	=	2 Conceptualization*
		Concept definition		=	=	=		=			
		Requirements definition	=		=				=	=	3 Definition*
		Design specification	=	=	=				=	=	
		Implementation description	=		=	±			=	=	4 Operation*
		Domain operation		=	=			=	=	=	
		Decommission definition			=			±	=	=	6 Dissolution*
	Other phases provided by the different architectures	Definition business				■					
		Creation						■			1 =
		Evolution						■			5 =
		Metamorphosis						■			

Convention	
	It is not included into the framework
=	It is included into the framework with the same o similar name
±	It is not included in an explicit form but it can be deduced from the context
■	Other views provided by different architectures
*	Evolution of the view or phase
1 - 6	Sequence of the life cycle phases

Seeking to propose a useful reference framework for modelling an IEA, we propose the FIEA, of which the structure and elements are shown in the Fig. 2. Following the guidelines of previous work on enterprise architecture frameworks, we must take into account the following perspectives: modelling views, life cycle phases and modelling detail level.

Modelling Views: Six modelling views have been proposed. The function view has been split into two different views: business and process, in order to facilitate the modelling, due to the fact that the business view is focused on strategic issues and the process view is focused on tactical and operational aspects. The knowledge view is an evolution of information view. Here is a brief description of each view: **Business**: This view represents the strategic aspects that must be taken into account in the CN. **Organization**: This view allows the representation and modification of the organizational structure and the teams involved into the CN and decision-making of the CN. **Resources**: This view represents the capabilities and resources necessary to complete business processes and the roles and responsibilities of individuals and organizational units within the CN. **Process**: This view represents CN processes, functionality, performance, inputs and outputs. **Knowledge**: In the continuous learning process where organizations are involved, the information that they handle becomes knowledge which itself and its generation are elements that approaches as VBE and DBE have into account. **IT base on Internet**: This view includes technology and applications views base on the Internet that enables the interoperation among enterprises.

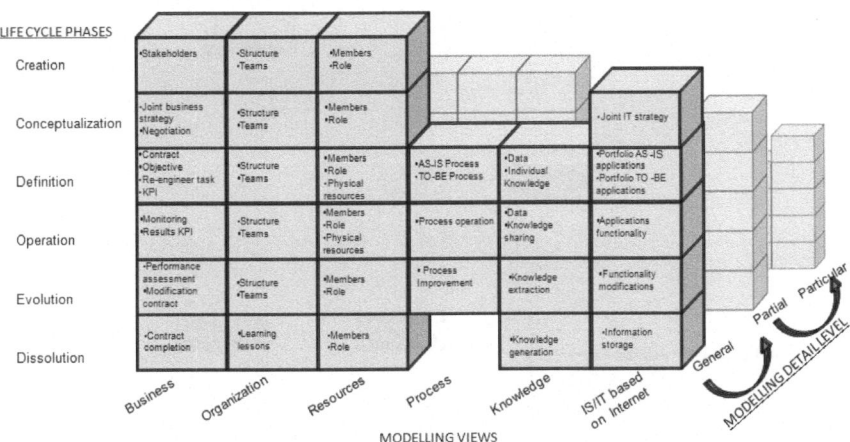

Fig. 2. Framework of Inter-Enterprise Architecture (FIEA)

Life Cycle Phases: The life cycle phases are states of development in the life cycle of the CN. FIEA considers the proposals of ARCON and GERAM in this aspect of its design, due to the fact that these two architectures complement each other. A brief description of each phase: **Creation**: This phase represents the motivation of collaboration from stakeholders into the CN and its incubation. **Conceptualization**: This phase represents the strategic definition of the CN and its implicit negotiation. **Definition**: This phase represents the definition of the elements in the CN. **Operation**: This phase is surely the most important, occuring when the CN operates directly towards achieving its goals. **Evolution**: During the operation of a CN, it may be necessary to make some changes to its membership, process, contract, structural relationships, and roles of its members. **Dissolution**: A CN will typically dissolve after accomplishing its goal.

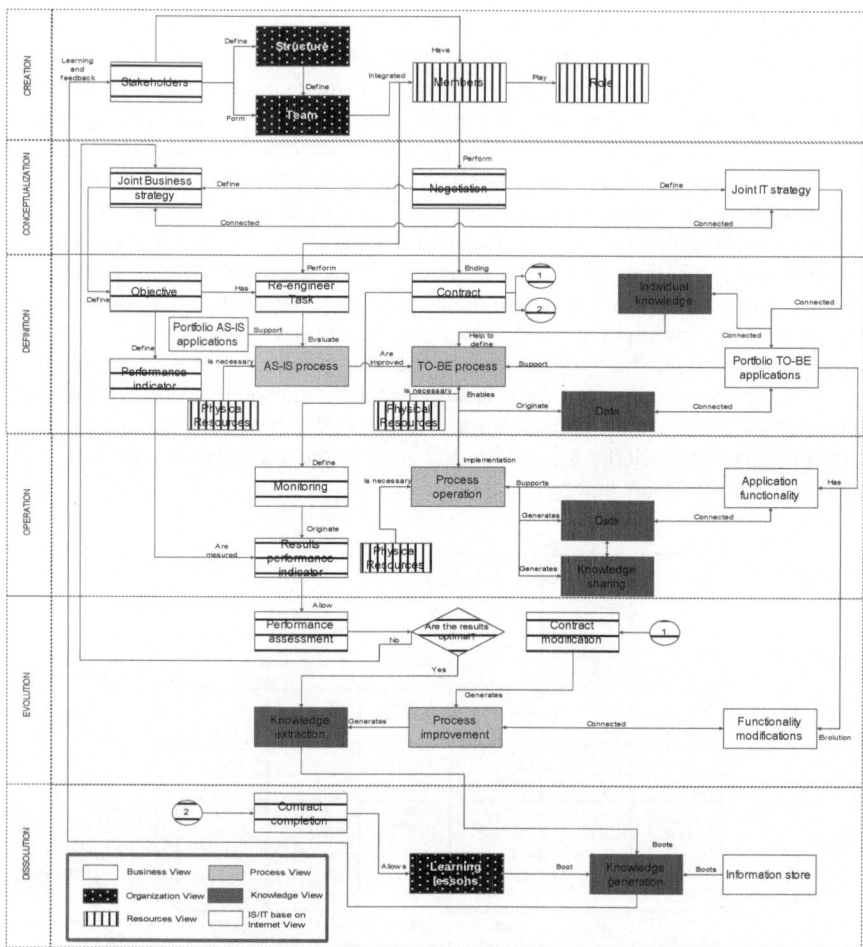

Fig. 3. Relationship Meta Model between elements views and phases of FIEA

***Modelling Detail Level*:** This perspective has to do with the detail level into the modelling, being the general modelling the most neutral that could be used for any kind of CN, partial modelling occurs when the model is developed for a specific cluster and the particular modelling is developed for a specific CN. Each cell in the FIEA represents the intersection of a particular life cycle phase with one modelling view.

In order to validate the correct gear of the FIEA, Fig. 3 shows a Meta-Model of relationship between elements of each view in each life cycle phase, which is according to the definition of ISO 15704 [9]. This Meta-Model has helped to corroborate the right definition from the elements in each view and phase. Due to the complexity of the Meta Model and the proposal of an easy understanding of it, some elements of organization and resources views have been omitted from the model (structure, teams, members, roles), but their participation is crucial to the life cycle phases of the CN.

The main advantage of using FIEA is that it meet the necessary elements of a IEA for modelling enterprises in collaboration context, including elements that VEE and DBE have contributed to build collaborative environments. On the other hand, these elements have associate building blocks and the content definition of them will allow modelling these systems. In addition, the proposed meta-model ensures consistency and integrity of its elements.

4   Conclusions

An IEA should be formed for a framework, a methodology and a modelling language. In this paper, we propose the FIEA. This framework allows for having a visual model that shows the components of CN architecture with the support of Internet, covering the life cycle phases and modelling views. This paper emphasizes the need for a consistent framework for IEA in a context of collaboration, supported for the use of the Internet as a tool that enables interoperability among enterprises. The relationship Meta-Model between elements views and phases of FIEA allows validate the correct definition of the elements for each view and life cycle phase and their connection with each other. These elements and their associate building blocks will define the necessary information to modelling this kind of system. It is really important to prove the FIEA in a real-life scenario, in order to demonstrate the capability of it to support engineering projects. In future papers, we are going to continue working in this line of research in order to propose a more complete IEA supported by future internet, defining the IEA Methodology (IEAM) and choosing the modelling language to use it. Also, it is important to validate different CNs in order to propose specific and particular Architecture Models.

Acknowledge. This research has been carried out for the project "Sistema de ayuda a la toma de decisiones ante decisiones no programadas en la planificación jerárquica de la producción (ADENPRO-PJP)" Ref. SP20120703 Universitat Politècnica de València.

References

1. Cuenca, L., Boza, A., Ortiz, A.: Enterprise Architecture Framework with Early Business/ICT Alignment for Extended Enterprises. In: Ortiz, Á., Franco, R.D., Gasquet, P.G. (eds.) BASYS 2010. IFIP AICT, vol. 322, pp. 11–18. Springer, Heidelberg (2010a)
2. Vargas, A., Boza, A., Cuenca, L., Sacala, I.: Inter-Enterprise Architecture and Internet of the Future. In: Camarinha-Matos, L.M., Tomic, S., Graça, P. (eds.) DoCEIS 2013. IFIP AICT, vol. 394, pp. 25–32. Springer, Heidelberg (2013)
3. Camarinha-Matos, L., Afsarmanesh, H.: Collaborative networks: Reference Modeling. Media, Springer Science + Business (2008)
4. European Commission European Society and Media: Dygital Business Ecosystems. Office for Official Publications of the European Communities, Luxembourg (2007)
5. Future Internet Enterprise Systems (FInES) Cluster: FInES Research Roadmap 2025, http://cordis.europa.eu/
6. Vargas, A., Boza, A., Cuenca, L., Ortiz, A.: The importance of strategic alignment in enterprise collaboration. In: Prado-Prado, J.C. (ed.) Annals of Industrial Engineering 2012, pp. 1–8. Springer, London (2013)

7. Henderson, J., Venkatraman, N.: Strategic alignment: Leveraging information technology for transforming organizations. IBM Systems Journal 32(1), 472–484 (1993)
8. Vargas, A., Boza, A., Cuenca, L.: Lograr la alineación estratégica de negocio y las tecnologías de la información a través de Arquitecturas Empresariales: Revisión de la Literatura. In: XV Congreso de Ingeniería de Organización, Cartagena-España, pp. 1061–1070 (2011a)
9. ISO 15704: Industrial automation systems - Requirements for enterprise-reference architectures and methodologies (2000)
10. Kosanke, K.: CIMOSA Primer on key concepts, purpose and business value. CIMOSA Association, http://cimosa.cnt.pl/
11. Cuenca, L., Boza, A., Ortiz, A.: An enterprise engineering approach for the alignment of business and information technology strategy. International Journal of Computer Integrated Manufacturing 24(11), 974–992 (2011)
12. Vernadat, F.: Enterprise modelling and integration: From fact modelling to Enterprise Interoperability (2003)
13. Vargas, A., Boza, A., Cuenca, L.: Towards Interoperability Through Inter-Enterprise Collaboration Architectures. In: Meersman, R., Dillon, T., Herrero, P. (eds.) OTM-WS 2011. LNCS, vol. 7046, pp. 102–111. Springer, Heidelberg (2011)
14. Plaza, J., Burgos, J., Carmona, E.: Measuring Stakeholder Integration: Knowledge, Interaction and Adaptational Behavior Dimensions. Journal of Business Ethics 93, 419–442 (2010)
15. Camarinha-Matos, L.M., Afsarmanesh, H.: Collaborative networks: A new scientific discipline, pp. 439–452 (2005)
16. Afsarmanesh, H., Msanjila, S.: Inter-organizational trust in VBEs. In: Camarinha-Matos, L.M., Afsarmanesh, H., Ollus, M. (eds.) Methods and Tools for Collaborative Networked Organizations. Springer (2008)
17. Mehandjiev, N., Grefen, P.: Dynamic business process formation for instant virtual enterprises, London (2010)
18. Kosanke, K., Vernadat, F., Zelm, M.: CIMOSA: enterprise engineering and integration. Computers in Industry 40, 83–97 (1999)
19. Chen, D., Vallespir, B., Doumeingts, G.: GRAI integrated methodology and its mapping onto generic enterprise reference architecture and methodology. Computers in Industry 33, 387–394 (1997)
20. IFIP: GERAM: Generalised Enterprise Reference Architecture and Methodology. In: International Federation for Information Processing, http://dl.ifip.org/index.php/index/index
21. Ortiz, A., Lario, F., Ros, L.: Enterprise Integration—Business Processes Integrated Management: a proposal for a methodology to develop Enterprise Integration Programs. Computers in Industry 40, 155–171 (1999)
22. Cuenca, L., Ortiz, A., Boza, A.: Business and IS/IT strategic alignment framework. In: Camarinha-Matos, L.M., Pereira, P., Ribeiro, L. (eds.) DoCEIS 2010. IFIP AICT, vol. 314, pp. 24–31. Springer, Heidelberg (2010b)
23. THE OPEN GROUP: TOGAF, http://www.opengroup.org/togaf/
24. Vesterager, J., T{\o}lle, M., Bernus, P.: VERA: Virtual Enterprise Reference Architecture. In: GMNBook, GLOBEMEN Final Plenary (2002)
25. Chalmeta, R., Grangel, R.: ARDIN extension for virtual enterprise integration. The Journal of Systems and Software 67 (2003)

A Modelling Approach to Support Enterprise Architecture Interoperability

Wided Guédria[1], Khaled Gaaloul[1], Yannick Naudet[1],
and Henderik A. Proper[1,2]

[1] Centre de Recherche Public Henri Tudor, Luxembourg
[2] Radboud University Nijmegen, Nijmegen, Netherlands
{wided.guedria,khaled.gaaloul,erik.proper,yannick.naudet}@tudor.lu

Abstract. In this paper, we elaborate on the Enterprise Architecture
(EA) and how it can be improved by using Enterprise Interoperability
(EI) requirements. We describe how enterprise interoperability is related
to EA concepts by especially analysing the definition and the foundation of interoperability, highlighting the relationships with EA. We then
propose a conceptual model that defines the enterprise architecture interoperability domain. In doing so, conceptual descriptions of systems, interoperability problems and solutions are identified. The designed model
can be inferred for decision-aid related to interoperability. Finally, we
illustrate our approach by means of a case in the automotive industry.

1   Introduction

As technology becomes more far-reaching and interconnected, the need of interoperability is becoming increasingly important. To interact with another system
or to add new components, a system has to be sufficiently flexible to operate
and adapt to other systems. Three main research domains addressing Enterprise
Interoperability (EI) issues were identified in [1]: 1) Enterprise modelling dealing
with the representation of the inter-networked organisation to establish interoperability requirements 2) Architecture & Platform defining the implementation
solution to achieve interoperability 3) Ontologies addressing the semantics necessary to assure interoperability.

In this paper, we focus on the modelling of networked organisation interoperability that need to be taken into account when dealing with Enterprise Architecture (EA). We rely for this on the ArchiMate modelling standard for EA
[2]. Amongst other architecture modelling languages, ArchiMate can be used to
model an organisation's products and services, how these products and services
are realized/delivered by business processes, and how in turn these processes are
supported by information systems and their underlying IT infrastructure [3].
However, such techniques and languages do not address interoperability issues
and its aspects in a satisfactory way [4,5]. In this paper, we put our effort in
the improvement of an architecture language by addressing interoperability core
aspects. We restrict ourselves mainly to modelling concepts that are related to

Y.T. Demey and H. Panetto (Eds.): OTM 2013 Workshops, LNCS 8186, pp. 189–198, 2013.
© Springer-Verlag Berlin Heidelberg 2013

EI concerns (i.e. operational concerns) in enterprise networking context, as discussed in [6]. The use of an EA helps to chart the complexity of an organisation [2]. Many organisations have recognized the value of architectures and use them during the development and evolution of their products, processes, and systems [2]. In light of these, the main research questions addressed in this paper can be summarised as follows: How to integrate interoperability concepts into EA models? In particular, how to integrate EI concepts into ArchiMate meta-model and how this can leverage EA principles to deal with interoperability problems? The structure of the paper will be as follows: Section 2 reviews the EI domain and its core concepts. Section 3 reviews EA modelling languages and presents the motivations of choosing ArchiMate. Section 4 presents the integrated meta-model, which includes the main concepts of interoperability into the ArchiMate meta-model. In section 5 a case study is presented to illustrate this integration. Finally section 6 concludes and presents future work.

2   Enterprise Interoperability

Interoperability is ubiquitous but not easy to understand due to its numerous definitions and interpretations. In [7], the authors point out that thirty-four definitions of interoperability were proposed since 1977. The most commonly acknowledged definition is the one provided by IEEE, considering interoperability as *the ability of two or more systems or components to exchange information and to use the information that has been exchanged* [8]. In order to understand the EI domain, we need to study the core concepts and elements of the EI and the operational entities where interoperations take place within an enterprise. These are mainly defined through the Ontology of Enterprise Interoperability (OoEI) and the Framework of Enterprise Interoperability (FEI), that are reviewed in the following sections.

2.1   The Ontology of Enterprise Interoperability (OoEI)

The first attempt to define the interoperability domain was made by [9], where a model for defining interoperability as a heterogeneous problem induced by a communication problem was proposed. On the basis of these research efforts, the Ontology of Enterprise Interoperability (OoEI) [5] as an extension of the Ontology of Interoperability (OoI) [10] was developed using the Ontology Web Language (OWL). This OoEI aims at formally defining Enterprise Interoperability (EI) while providing a framework to describe problems and related solutions pertaining to the interoperability domain. Interoperability exists because there are at least two *Systems* and a *Relation* between them. The *relation* is of primary importance and is the source of interoperability problems [11]. A *System* is defined as a set of interconnected parts, having a *Structure*, a *Function*, an *Objective* and a *Behaviour* [12]. These concepts are necessary to understand a system. The OoEI was defined based on an analysis on the EI frameworks and models [5]. It describes systems as interrelated subsystems: A *System* is composed of *SystemElements*, which are systems themselves, and *Relations*. The

Relation concept formalizes the existing relationships inside a system, which is the source of the occurrence of interoperability problems. The OoEI makes the distinction between *Structural relation* and *Behavioural relation*. A *structural relation* refers to relations between each couple of sub-systems of the system. It relates to the structure of the related systems and concerns their interfaces, their models or the representation of their models. A *behavioural relation* is a non structural relation. It has a direct influence on systems without being related to a particular subsystem. This kind of relation does not concern the system's structure itself but any relation that influences the system's behaviour without being related to an element of the system's structure.

An enterprise is considered as a complex system in the sense that it has both a large number of parts and the parts are related in ways that make it difficult to understand how the enterprise operates and to predict its behaviour [12].

Dealing with EI requires considering the enterprise from a general perspective, taking into account not only its different components and their interactions but also the environment in which it evolves and the interface through which it communicates with its environment. The *Interface* is a *SystemElement* through which a connection between the *System* and its *Environment* can be established. It also represents the systems boundaries.

The establishment or diagnosis of EI has led to identify the different operational levels that are concerned: *Business*, *Process*, *Service* and *Data* interoperabilies (i.e. the EI concerns as defined by FEI). Interoperability is implemented as a subclass of the *Problem* concept. Problems of interoperability exist when there is a relation, of any kind, between incompatible systems in a super- system they belong to or system they will form. An exhaustive description of the OoEI model can be found in [5].

2.2   Framework for Enterprise Interoperability

The main purpose of an interoperability framework is to provide an organising mechanism so that concepts, problems and knowledge on enterprise interoperability can be represented in a more structured way [13]. The Framework for Enterprise Interoperability (FEI) was developed within the frame of INTEROP Network of Excellence [13] and is published as an international standard (ISO 11354 - 1). It defines a classification scheme for interoperability knowledge according to three dimensions: Interoperability barriers, EI concerns and interoperability approaches. According to FEI, the establishment of interoperability consists in removing all the identified barriers. Three kinds of barriers are identified: *Conceptual* (syntactic and semantic differences of information to be ex-changed), *Technological* (incompatibility of information technologies: architecture & platforms, infrastructure, etc.), and *Organisational* (definition of responsibilities and authorities). *Interoperability Concerns* represent the areas concerned by interoperability in an enterprise. Four concerns are defined, namely *business interoperability* (work in a harmonized way to share and develop business between companies despite the difference of methods, decision making, culture of enterprises, etc.), *process interoperability* (make various processes work together.

In the interworked enterprise, the aim is to connect internal processes of two companies to create a common process), *service interoperability* (making work together various services or applications by solving the syntactic and semantic differences) and *data interoperability* (make work together different data models with different query languages to share information coming from heterogeneous systems). Finally, three *interoperability approaches*, or ways to establish working interoperations, are considered: *The integrated approach* (characterized by the existence of a common format for all the constituents systems); the *unified approach*, characterized by the existence of a common format but at a meta-level; the *federated approach*, in which no common format is defined. This approach maintains the identity of interoperating systems, nothing is imposed by one party or another and interoperability is managed in an ad-hoc manner.

3   Enterprise Architecture

An architecture is the fundamental organisation of a system embodied in its components, their relationships to each other and to the environment,and the principle guiding its design and evolution [14]. The unambiguous specification and description of components and especially their relationships in architecture require a coherent architecture modelling language [15]. Current languages for modelling in the area of organisations, business processes, applications, and technology share a number of aspects on which they score low [16]. The relations between domains (views) are poorly defined, and the models created in different views are not further integrated. Most languages have a weak formal basis and lack a clearly defined semantics. Moreover, these miss the overall architectural vision and are confined to either the business or the application and technology subdomains.

In [15], the authors have compared a selection of standards and languages (e.g. RM-ODP, UML and the UML EDOC profil, BPMN and ARIS) to ArchiMate [17], using three criteria for comparison: frameworks, architectural viewpoints and domains that are covered by each language. According to their comparison, ArchiMate distinguishes itself from most other languages by its well defined meta-model, concepts and, most importantly, its relations. The abstraction level of ArchiMate simplifies the construction of integrated models, where most languages appear to persuade architects to detailed modelling. Detailed modelling of most aspects also can be performed in ArchiMate, used as an "umbrella language" [15]. ArchiMate defines three main layers [16]: 1) *The Business Layer* offers products and services to external customers, which are realized in the organisation by business processes (performed by business actors or roles); 2) *The Application Layer* supports the business layer with application services which are realized by (software) application components; 3) *The Technology Layer* offers infrastructure services (e.g., processing, storage, and communication services) needed to run applications, realized by computer and communication devices and system software.

The core concepts that are found in each layer of the language are depicted in Fig 1. A distinction between structural aspect and behavioural one is made [16].

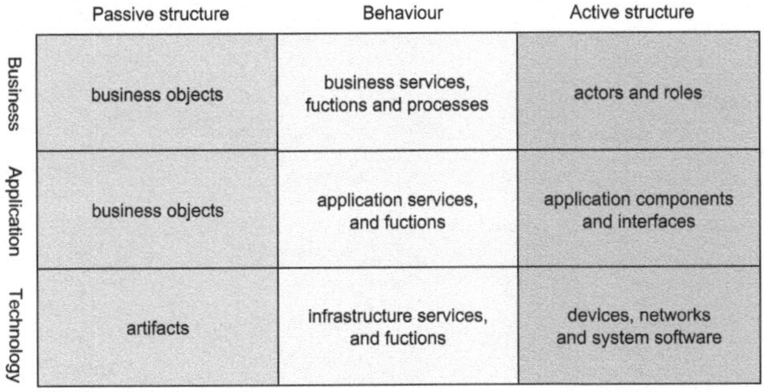

	Passive structure	Behaviour	Active structure
Business	business objects	business services, fuctions and processes	actors and roles
Application	business objects	application services, and fuctions	application components and interfaces
Technology	artifacts	infrastructure services, and fuctions	devices, networks and system software

Fig. 1. The Core Concepts of ArchiMate [16]

4 ArchiMate and Enterprise Interoperability

Besides the core concepts shown in Fig 1, which are mainly operational in nature, there are a number of other important aspects, some of which may cross several (or all) conceptual domains; e.g. Interoperability. In this section we integrate the core concepts of OoEI into the ArchiMate meta-models. In doing so, we propose syntactic and semantic mapping between both meta-models which has been facilitated by applying existing approaches for ontology mapping approaches [18].

4.1 Business Layer and Interoperability

Fig 2 gives an overview of the ArchiMate business layer integrating interoperability aspects. The added concepts, from the OoEI, are presented in dark gray. The structural aspects at the business layer refers to the organisation structure, in terms of the actors that make up the organisation and their relationships. The central concept is the *Business actor* [16]. On the side of EI, the core concepts are the *System* and *Relation*. The whole enterprise, where organisational entities are performing behaviour, is a system. Given that, the *Business actor* is considered as a *SystemElement* within the organisation. The work that an actor performs within an organisation is based on a defined role. In some cases, the work results in a collective effort of more than one business role: this is called Business collaboration. From a behavioural point of view, this is assigned to the concept *Business interaction*. Business interaction is defined as a behaviour element that describes the behaviour of a business collaboration [16]. The ability of an enterprise to interoperate allows business interaction through the collaboration of its business roles. Given that, we define *Business collaboration* as a specialisation of *Structural relation* and *Business interaction* as *Behavioural relation*.

4.2 Application Layer and Interoperability

Fig 3 gives an overview of the ArchiMate application layer integrating main concepts and relations of the EI domain. The main structural concept of the

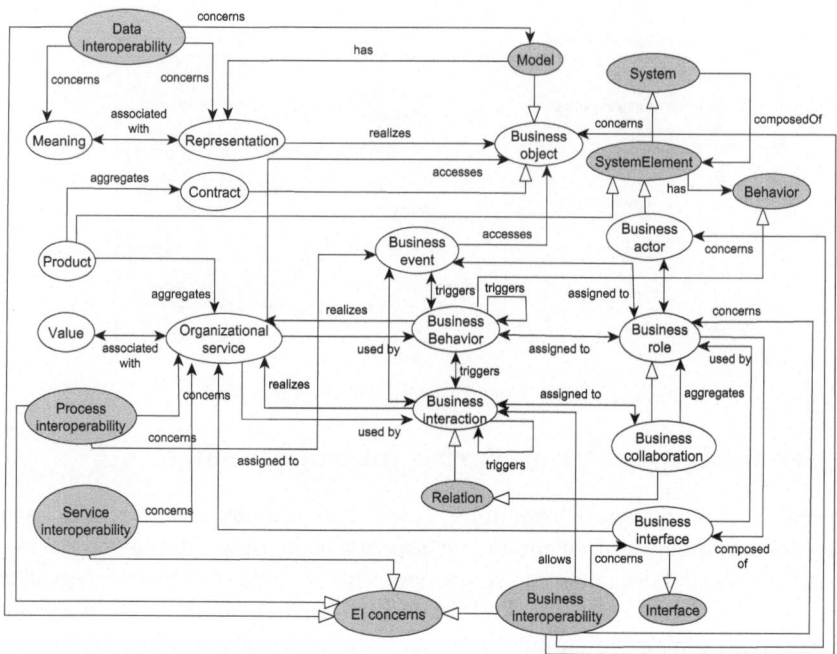

Fig. 2. Business layer meta-model with interoperability concepts

application layer is the *Application component* concept. It is a modular, deployable, and replaceable part of a system that encapsulates its contents and exposes its functionality through a set of interfaces. We define an *Application component* as a specialisation of a *SystemElement*. The interrelationships between components are an essential ingredient in the application of EA techniques. Subsequently we find that the *Application collaboration* concept is assigned to the *Application interaction*. The *application collaboration* is defined as an aggregation of two or more application components that work together to perform collective behaviour [16]. The compatibility and subsequently interoperability between the application components allows application collaboration and application interaction. Given that, we define *Application Collaboration* as a specialisation of *Structural Relation* and *Application Interaction* as a specialisation of *Behavioural Relation*.

4.3   Technology Layer and Interoperability

Fig 4 gives an overview of the ArchiMate technology layer and the main relationships with the integrated interoperability concepts. The main structural concept for the technology layer is the *Node*. It is a computational resource upon which artifacts may be stored or deployed for execution [15]. We define a *Node* as a specialisation of a *SystemElement*. Artifacts are used to model the representation, in the form of, e.g. a file of a data object or an application component,

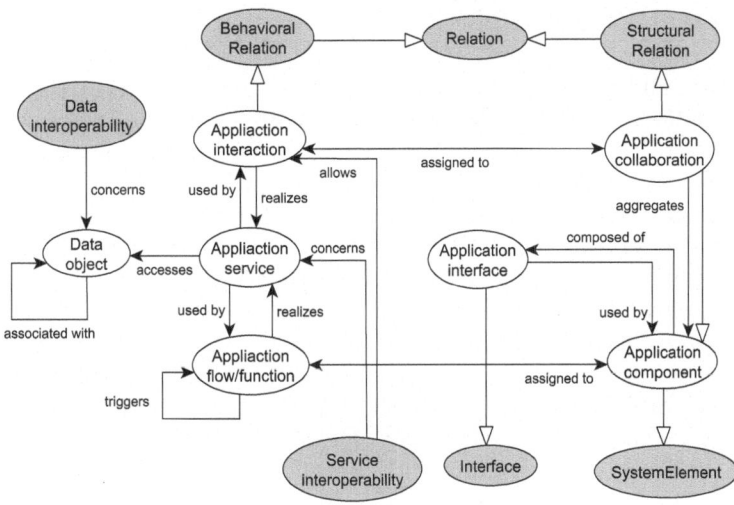

Fig. 3. Application layer meta-model with interoperability concepts

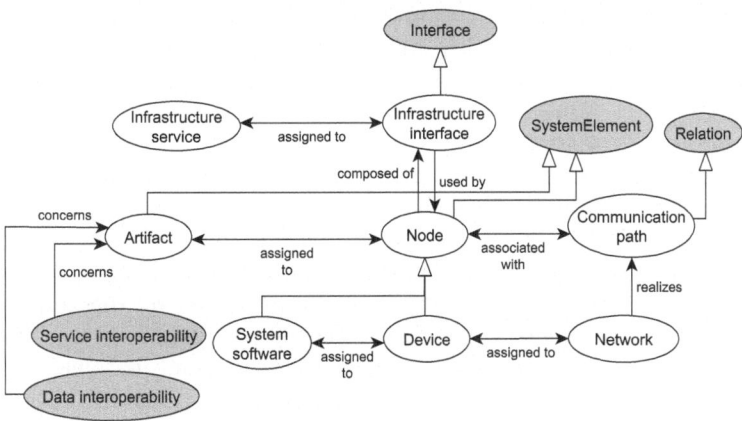

Fig. 4. Technology layer meta-model with interoperability concepts

and can be assigned to (i.e., deployed on) a *node*. Given that, artifacts can be source of interoperability problems at data level as well as service level. The technology layer provides *Infrastructure services* to be used by applications [15]. In this sense, service interoperability concerns *Infrastructure services*, as it can be source of interoperability problems between applications. An *Infrastructure interface* is a specialisation of the concept *Interface*. It specifies how the infrastructure services of a node can be accessed by other nodes (provided interface), or which functionality the node requires from the environment.

5   Illustrative Example

To illustrate and validate the proposed meta-model, we present a case study of a multinational company. Some information are intentionally skipped or not detailed due to the enterprise privacy policies. The company is part of a German group, which is specialized in automobile manufactures with modern wiring harness systems, exclusive interiors and electrical components. The company is 100% export oriented. The entire production is directed to the headquarters in Germany, which are then responsible for the distribution to the clients or other production sites. The "normal business process" starts when the company receives an order of production from the headquarters in Germany. If the order concerns a new product, then a prototyping is needed and a sample is produced. After a decision is reached, the production process can be launched. There are five main stakeholders for the company: 1) The headquarters in Germany, from where the company receives orders; 2) The production site in Poland to whom the company exports the semi-final products; 3) The production sites, from where the company receives semi-final products to finalize; 4) The suppliers of the raw materials and accessories; 5) Customs for the export.

As analyzing relations are the first requirement for identifying interoperability problems, a formal representation of the Company and the main relations that may be source of incompatibility are provided, using the model presented in previous sections. The instantiated concepts are represented by rectangles as shown in Fig 5.

The company is represented by the *Enterprise_GR* concept. As an instance of the *System* concept, it inherits all its properties and constituents. Hence it has its own structure and behaviour, represented respectively by *Structure_GR* and *Behaviour_GR*. The company produces wire harnesses for the cars and has two main objectives: continuous reduction of the costs of its production and to be the leader within its market. This is represented by the concept *Harness_production*, instance of the *Function* concept and two instances of the *objective* concept: *Market leader* and *Reduce costs*. As any multinational enterprise, the company evolves in its environment and has many partners. This is represented by *GR_env* concept, instance of *Environment*. Within this environment, the customs, the supplier of the accessories, the transporter, the headquarters, the supplier of raw material and the provider of all other services are found. This is respectively represented by the concepts: *Customs*, *Ac_supplier*, *Transporter*, *GR_group*, *Rm_supplier*, *Service_provider*. As business event we have added the specific concept *Order receipt* which influences the production of the enterprise. The instantiation of the integrated model provides an overview of the enterprise structure and the main relations that exist.

Based on that model, we can have a clear idea about the actual situation of the enterprise. Moreover, a more complete model integrating interoperability problems will allow us to point out exactly the element that is responsible of a potential problem (be it active or passive) and to fix it by proposing adequate solutions.

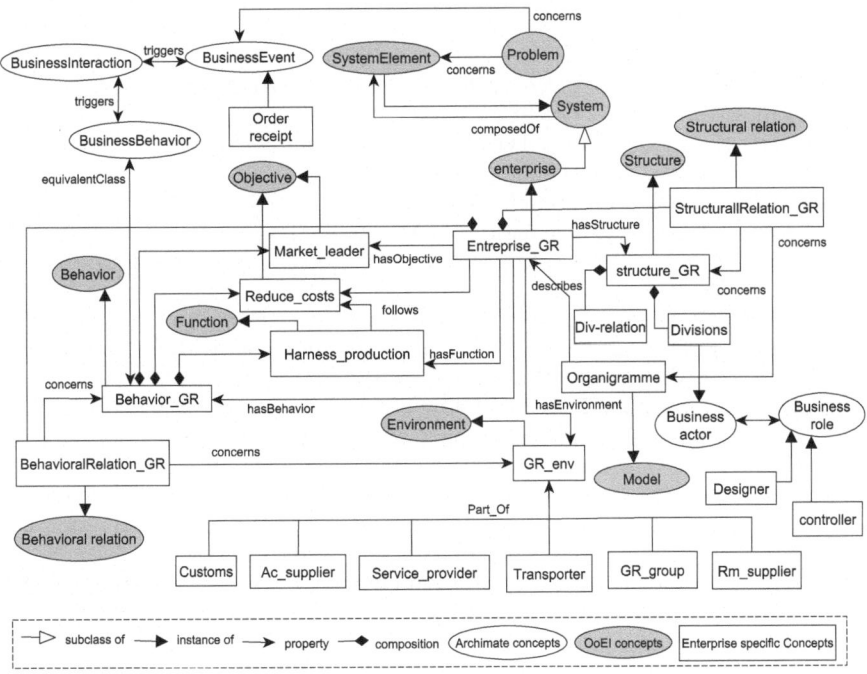

Fig. 5. Main concepts of the integrated model applied to the use case

6   Conclusion and Future work

In this paper, we have proposed an integrated model integrating interoperability and enterprise architecture concepts. At a first stage, the core concepts of the two domains were identified; The main relations between concepts were analysed in order to construct the integrated conceptual model. The evaluation stage was done through a case study in the automative industrial context. The resulting integrated model is based on the OoEI and the ArchiMate model at the three layers which are respectively Business layer, Application layer and Technology layer.

Future work is planned to assess the integration of interoperability concepts within ArchiMate. The idea is to assess the maturity of the meta-model and its future extension, as a generic model, to different modelling techniques and languages. We envisage also the deployment of the meta-model within EA frameworks such as TOGAF (the framework for ArchiMate) [2]. The idea is to support the dynamic definition of the enterprise principles including interoperability as part of the readiness factors for enterprise innovation capacities.

References

1. Chen, D., Doumeingts, G.: European initiatives to develop interoperability of enterprise applications-basic concepts, framework and roadmap. Annual Reviews in Control 27(2), 153–162 (2003)
2. Jonkers, H., Proper, H.A.: TOGAF and ArchiMate: A Future Together. White Paper W192. The Open Group (November 2009)
3. Lankhorst, M.M., Proper, H.A., Jonkers, H.: The Architecture of the ArchiMate Language. In: Halpin, T., Krogstie, J., Nurcan, S., Proper, E., Schmidt, R., Soffer, P., Ukor, R. (eds.) BPMDS 2009 and EMMSAD 2009. LNBIP, vol. 29, pp. 367–380. Springer, Heidelberg (2009)
4. Lankhorst, M., et al.: ArchiMate Language Primer. Telematica institute (2004)
5. Guedria, W.: A Contribution to Enterprise Interoperability Maturity Assessment. Ph.D. thesis, University of Bordeaux1, Bordeaux, France (2012)
6. Chen, D.: Enterprise Interoperability Framework. In: Workshop on Enterprise Modelling and Ontologies for Interoperability (EMOI-INTEROP) (January 2006)
7. Ford, T., et al.: Measuring System Interoperability: An i-Score Improvement. In: Proceedings of the 6th Annual Conference on Systems Engineering Research (2008)
8. Institute of Electrical and Electronics Engineers. IEEE standard computer dictionary: A compilation of ieee standard computer glossaries (1990)
9. Rosener, V., Latour, T.: A model-based ontology of the software interoperability problems: preliminary results. In: CAiSE 1998, vol. 3, pp. 241–252 (2004)
10. Naudet, Y., Latour, T., Haussmann, K., Abels, S., Hahn, A., Johannesonn, P.: Describing Interoperability: the OoI Ontology. In: Workshop on Enterprise Modelling and Ontologies for Interoperability (EMOI-INTEROP) (January 2006)
11. Rosener, V., Naudet, Y.: Latour. T. A model proposal of the interoperability problem. In: EMOI-INTEROP (2005)
12. Giachetti, R.E.: Design of Enterprise Systems: Theory, Architecture, and Methods, 1st edn. CRC Press, Inc., Boca Raton (2010)
13. Chen, D., Dassisti, M., Elvester, B.: Interop noe deliverable di.3: Enterprise interoperability framework and knowledge corpus - final report. Technical report, Interoperability Research for Networked Enterprises Applications and Software (INTEROP Network of Excellence), IST - Contract no.: IST-508 011 (2007)
14. IEEE Computer Society. IEEE Std 1471-2000: IEEE Recommended Practice for Architectural Description of Software- Intensive Systems (2000)
15. Jonkers, H., Lankhorst, M., Van Buuren, R., Bonsangue, M., Van Der Torre, L.: Concepts for modeling enterprise architectures. International Journal of Cooperative Information Systems 13, 257–287 (2004)
16. Lankhorst, M.M.: Enterprise Architecture at Work - Modelling, Communication and Analysis, 4th edn. The Enterprise Engineering Series. Springer (2013)
17. Engelsman, W., Jonkers, H.: Quartel. D. ArchiMate Extention for Modeling and Managing Motivation, Principles and Requirements in TOGAF. White paper. The Open Group (August. 2010)
18. Noy, N.F., Musen, M.A.: The prompt suite: interactive tools for ontology merging and mapping. International Journal of Human-Computer Studies 59(6), 983–1024 (2003)

OptiVE: An Interactive Platform for the Design and Analysis of Virtual Enterprises

Yun Guo, Alexander Brodsky, and Amihai Motro

Computer Science Department, George Mason University
Fairfax, VA, USA
{yguo7,brodsky,ami}@gmu.edu

Abstract. OptiVE is a platform for designing and analyzing virtual enterprises. OptiVE has two modes of operations. In *composition* mode, business entrepreneurs can define elementary enterprises as well as create complex virtual enterprises from enterprises already registered in the system. In *analysis* mode, business analysts can explore the structure and properties of registered enterprises and ask the system to optimize them: Find a particular combination of participants and a specific production path that will deliver the best outcome (produce the target product at the lowest overall cost). OptiVE is founded on a formal model with rigorous syntax and semantics and uses mixed integer linear programming (MILP) to find its optimal solutions. A prototype implementation of OptiVE is also described. The system insulates its users from technical details, offering an intuitive graphical user interface for operating in either mode.

Keywords: Virtual enterprise, design, analysis, optimization.

1 Introduction and Background

One of the attractive properties of virtual enterprises is their *agility*: The ability to respond quickly to changes in the business environment either by creating new enterprises or by adapting existing ones. Arguably, this particular property has the potential to not only reorient individual enterprises, but to invigorate entire areas of business and industry. An important necessity in this regard are flexible and intuitive tools with which business entrepreneurs and analysts can design and analyze virtual enterprises.

In this paper we describe OptiVE: An interactive platform for the design and analysis of virtual enterprises. OptiVE allows business entrepreneurs and analysts who have a target product they wish to manufacture to conveniently browse a directory of business entities that are available for networked collaborations, look up their supply or manufacturing capabilities, as well as their prices and costs. Once the business entities that can assist in the manufacturing of the target product have been selected, OptiVE automatically interconnects them according to the items they consume and produce. The network thus created is then optimized to find a particular combination of the participants and a specific production path that will deliver the best results (e.g., produce the target product at the lowest overall cost). The resulting enterprise may then be registered

Y.T. Demey and H. Panetto (Eds.): OTM 2013 Workshops, LNCS 8186, pp. 199–207, 2013.

in the system to be incorporated in future enterprises. A prototype system of OptiVE was implemented to allow experimentation and gain additional insights.

Several additional contributions of this work are worth mentioning. First, OptiVE is solidly founded on a formal model for which rigorous syntax and semantics have been provided. The model is generic (i.e., domain-independent) and includes only a small number of definitions, yet it can be extended easily to incorporate additional features. Second, OptiVE's focus is to help analysts make optimal decisions. Whereas most design choices are based on intuition and experience, OptiVE models each enterprise design as a mixed integer linear programming (MILP) optimization problem, and suggests an optimal decision. Finally, although the model is mathematically rigorous, the system insulates its users from overly technical details, providing them with an intuitive graphical interface with which their design and analysis tasks may be achieved.

These contributions are described in two sections. Section 2 describes the formal OptiVE model. It includes definitions for three different types of enterprises — manufacturers, suppliers and virtual enterprises — and allows for recursive embedding of virtual enterprises in more complex enterprises. Each enterprise is described by properties such as the items it produces, its production capacity, the items it consumes, its prices and costs, as well as a small set of constraints that govern these parameters. Finally, the semantics of this model are described by defining queries on an enterprise and how they are answered. Section 3 describes a prototype implementation of OptiVE, its software architecture and its functionalities. Essentially, OptiVE operates in two modes: a *composition* mode, in which new enterprises may be defined, and an *analysis* mode, in which existing enterprises may be inspected and optimized.

Before we begin, we provide a brief review of relevant work on the design and formation of new virtual enterprises. The formation of new enterprises is a critical and involved phase in which decisions taken have long-term impact on the eventual success of the enterprise. As proposed in [4], most of the approaches to this phase can be classified in three major categories: manual, agent-based, and service-based. The formation of new virtual enterprises requires a process of partner search and selection. Typically this process is based on traditional "competency" matching rules, and is mostly *manual*, though there have been attempts to take advantage of computer assistance [3]. In a *multi-agent based* approach, initial negotiations among business entities to achieve a common business goal are performed by representative agents [2], [9], [8]. These works often deal with negotiation protocols, auction mechanisms, and distributed matching. In a *service-oriented* approach, the collaborators are published services and enterprise creation involves the selection of services from service directory [10], [5], [7]. Service selection is often based on available quality-of-service (QoS) parameters. Yet there are other contributions that elude this classification. For example, [6] describes a formal process of repetitive refinement that virtual enterprises undergo until they acquire stability.

The work described in this paper can be classified as *computer-assisted enterprise design*. It provides designers with an interactive, graphical tool with which they can select participants (based on their published properties) and configure them in an optimal supply chain. It is unique in that it supports business decisions that are guided by formal utility functions. The work on collaborating business entities was explored in [1], where entities were represented by an "adaptive trade specification", a specification that can capture the models of suppliers and manufacturers described in this paper. However, [1] did not consider issues such as building a tool for defining virtual enterprises, or constructing new enterprises from a library of previously defined components.

2   The OptiVE Model

OptiVE defines three kinds of enterprises: *manufacturer, supplier*, and *virtual*. Manufacturers and suppliers are elementary enterprises; that is, they do not embed other enterprises in their operations; whereas virtual enterprises may embed manufacturers, suppliers, and, recursively, other virtual enterprises.

Items and Enterprises. Each virtual enterprise is associated with a set of *input items* that it consumes and a set of *output items* that it produces. Manufacturers and suppliers are also associated with output items, but whereas a manufacturer consumes input items, a supplier does not.

All input and output items are unique; that is, each item, whether input or output, is assigned a unique identifier id (it never appears in more than one item set). Each item is assigned a *type*, and items of the same type are completely interchangeable. Thus, an item can be viewed as an instantiation of a type. Each item is also associated with a variable that indicates a quantity of the item. Altogether, an item is a triple: $item=<id,\ type,\ quantity>$. The notation $type(id)$ and $quantity(id)$ will denote the type and quantity of a particular item. Note that $type(id)$ is a constant (typically, a string of characters), whereas $quantity(id)$ is a numeric variable (typically, an integer).

Each enterprise is described with a quadruple: $ent\ =\ <eid,\ kind,\ in,\ out>$, where eid is a unique enterprise identifier, $kind$ is either "manufacturer", "supplier" or "virtual", and in and out are sets of item id's. The notation $kind(eid)$, $in(eid)$ and $out(eid)$ will denote the kind and the input and output sets of a particular enterprise. We now define the three different kinds of enterprises.

Manufacturer. A manufacturer is an elementary enterprise. It is defined with a quadruple $<ent,\ bill\text{-}of\text{-}materials,\ catalog,\ constraints>$, where $kind(ent)=$ "manufacturer".[1] *bill-of-materials* is a three-column table that describes the composition of each output item produced by this manufacturer. In this table, each output item $o \in out$ is represented with a set of triples, where each triple describes a single input item i that is required to manufacture o, and the corresponding quantity: $<o,i,quantity>$. The notation $quantity(o,i)$ will denote the quantity of input item i required to manufacture one output item o. *catalog* is a two-column table that associates with each output item $i \in out$ a

---

[1] Recall that ent is a quadruple, so a manufacturer is described altogether by 7 parameters.

price-per-unit $price(i)$. Finally, two constraints are associated with each manufacturer. The first (Equation 1) defines the cost of a manufacturer in terms of the quantities and the price-per-unit, for all the items that it manufactures. The second (Equation 2) guarantees that each input item has the quantity necessary to manufacture the output items that require it.

Supplier. A supplier is an elementary enterprise that requires no input items. It is defined with a triple $<ent, catalog, constraints>$, where $kind(ent)=$ "supplier" and $in(ent) = \emptyset$. $catalog$ is a three-column table that, for every output item $i \in out$ lists the price-per-unit $price(i)$ and the maximal quantity that can be supplied $capacity(i)$. Finally, two constraints are associated with each supplier. The first (Equation 3) defines the cost of a supplier in terms of the quantities and their price-per-unit, for all the items that it supplies. The second (Equation 4) limits quantities to their corresponding capacities.

Virtual Enterprise. A virtual enterprise is defined with a triple $<ent, participants, constraints>$, where $kind(ent)=$ "virtual", and $participants$ is a set of $eids$ of the embedded enterprises.[2] Again, two constraints are associated with each virtual enterprise. The first (Equation 5) defines the cost of an enterprise in terms of the costs of its participants. The second (Equation 6) governs the quantity of input items and output items. In this equation, T_{eid} is the set of all item types in the virtual enterprise eid. For each type $t \in T_{eid}$, $in(t)$ is the set of item ids of all the input items of type t for all the embedded enterprises, plus the item ids of the $outputs$ of type t of the virtual enterprise; $out(t)$ is the set of item ids of all the output items of type t of all the embedded enterprises, plus the item ids of the $inputs$ of type t of the virtual enterprise. Note that $in(t)$ combines the inputs of the enterprise eid with the outputs of its embedded enterprises; this is because both describe commodities that are available to satisfy the inputs of embedded enterprises. Similarly, $out(t)$ combines the outputs of eid with the inputs of its embedded enterprises, because both describe commodities that must be satisfied by the outputs of the embedded enterprises.

$$cost(eid) = \sum_{i \in out(eid)} quantity(i) \cdot price(i) \qquad (1)$$

$$(\forall i \in in(eid)) \; quantity(i) = \sum_{o \in out(eid)} quantity(o) \cdot quantity(o, i) \qquad (2)$$

$$cost(eid) = \sum_{i \in out(eid)} quantity(i) \cdot price(i) \qquad (3)$$

$$(\forall i \in out) \; quantity(i) \leq capacity(i) \qquad (4)$$

---

[2] The participants embedded in a virtual enterprise must not be involved in cycles. That is, when each participant with output type t is connected to each participant with input type t, the resulting graph should be acyclic.

$$cost(eid) = \sum_{e \in participants} cost(e) \tag{5}$$

$$(\forall t \in T_{eid}) \sum_{i \in in(t)} quantity(i) = \sum_{i \in out(t)} quantity(i) \tag{6}$$

Observe that equations (1), (3) and (5) define enterprise costs, whereas equations (2), (4) and (6) express quantity constraints. Although, the overall cost of manufacturers (Equation 1) and suppliers (Equation 3) are defined similarly, the associated item *price* is slightly different. For a supplier (who does not require input items), it is the overall charge for an item, whereas for a manufacturer, it is a manufacturing cost (on top of the cost of its input items). Note that in each case *enterprise cost* refers to the cost of production, which assumes to incorporate all other enterprise costs.

Semantics. So far we have described the *syntax* of the OptiVE model. To express its *semantics*, we define queries against enterprises and their answers. Recall that each enterprise (whether manufacturer, supplier or virtual) is associated with a definition. The set of definitions for all the enterprises that are embedded in a given enterprise is called the enterprise *library* (it includes the definition of the given enterprise itself). Recall also that each enterprise has *quantity* variables for each of its inputs or outputs.[3] We denote with $var(eid)$ the set of all the quantity variables in all the enterprises in the library of eid. Similarly, each enterprise is associated with six constraints. We denote with $con(eid)$ the set of all the constraints in all the enterprises in the library of eid. In addition to the constraints in this set, we allow users who present queries to include additional (optional) constraints (for example, to set a limit on a particular quantity).

We now define an OptiVE query on an enterprise eid as a pair $< I, C >$. The first argument I is a partial instantiation of the variables in $var(eid)$; that is, I assigns constant values to some (possibly none) of the quantity variables. The constraints that express this instantiation will be denoted C_I. The second argument C is a set of user-defined constraints (it could be empty).

The answer to this query is an instantiation of the variables in $var(eid)$ that minimizes $cost(eid)$ subject to the constraints in $con(eid)$, C and C_I. That is, the free quantity variables are assigned values that will minimize the overall cost of the enterprise, while satisfying all three types of constrains. Formally,

$$\textbf{argmin}_{var(eid)} \; cost(eid)$$
$$\textbf{subject to} \quad con(eid) \wedge C \wedge C_I$$

3   Development Platform for Virtual Enterprises

A prototype of the OptiVE development framework for virtual enterprises was implemented and tested. The system works in two modes : *composition* mode and

---

[3] Note that $quantity(o, i)$ used by manufacturers is not a variable, but a constant describing the quantity of items of input item i required to manufacture one output item o.

analysis mode. The system uses Microsoft .NET Framework 4 as the main software platform. SAXON-HE 9.4 edition XQuery processor and Microsoft GLEE (Automatic Graphic Layout) library are the core components in composition mode, and IBM CPLEX Mixed Integer Linear Programming solver is used in analysis mode. The overall architecture of the system is illustrated in Figure 1.

In composition mode, enterprise entrepreneurs manage enterprise configurations. Commands are issued through the graphical user interface; the business logic layer parses each command and stores or retrieves data from a dedicated XML database; and the graphical layout module renders the resulting configuration. In analysis mode, business analysts explore existing enterprises. Commands are issued through the graphical user interface; the business logic layer generates an optimization model and related data are retrieved from XML database; both model and data are then are fed into the solver, which solves the optimization problem and sends its result back to user through the business logic layer.

Details of the two modes are explained in the following two subsections with a simple example.

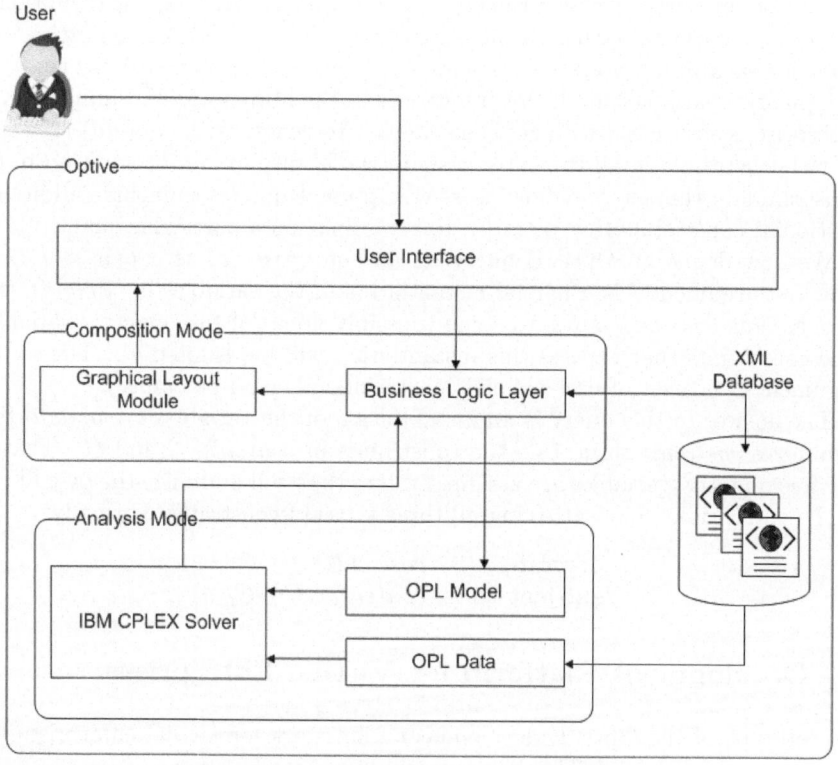

Fig. 1. System architecture of OptiVE

3.1   Composition Mode

In composition mode enterprise entrepreneurs may define elementary enterprises (manufacturers and suppliers) and configure virtual enterprises. Figure 2 illustrates the user interface to OptiVE.[4] Defining elementary enterprises is straightforward: Developers are prompted for the *eid*, *kind*, *in* items, *out* items, and *catalog*, and for manufactures, the *bill-of-materials* (note that constraints need not be specified). Once an elementary enterprise has been defined, it is added to the enterprise library (left frame) making it available for participation in virtual enterprises.

The use of composition mode to design virtual enterprises is demonstrated with the example in Figure 2. After providing the enterprise description consisting of an *eid* (MyFurniture), its *kind* (virtual), its *in* items ({Wood, Leather}) and its *out* items ({Manager Chair}), the developer drags possible participants from the enterprise library in the left frame to the canvas in the middle. To assist the developer in this task, clicking a participant in the library in the left frame, displays its description in the right frame. In the example, the candidate participants are the manufactures M1, M2, and M3, the supplier S2, and the virtual enterprise VE1. Each participant is displayed in different color and shape to reflect its kind.

The system then analyzes the supplier-customer relationships among the participants by matching input and output items according to their types. To assist in the visualization of the flow of items, a pentagon shape, named *aggregator*, is created for each item type. Participants providing a certain type of item as an *out* item are linked to that aggregator with in-coming arrows, and participants requesting that type of item as an *in* item are linked to that aggregator with out-going arrows. Note that the description of M2 shows three input item types (Chair Leg, Chair Back and Chair Seat), and one output item type (Manager Chair), so the graph shows three arrows from the aggregators of the input types to M2, and one arrow from M2 to the aggregator of the output type. Once defined, the new virtual enterprise is added to the library.

It is important to note that the graph (and the virtual enterprise that it models) incorporates all the possible item routings; as such it is an "infrastructure" on which the actual flow will eventually take place. The choice of an actual routing is discussed next.

3.2   Analysis Mode

In analysis mode business analysts can explore existing virtual enterprises. Analysts could present to OptiVE either *data queries* or *optimization queries*. Examples of data queries are "Which participants in a particular enterprise provide items of type chair?" or "What are the output items of manufacturer M2?" Such queries are answered with data extracted from the system databases. All information storage and retrieval is done using XQuery.

---

[4] While all the essential functionalities have been implemented, some of the features shown in this user interface are not yet available.

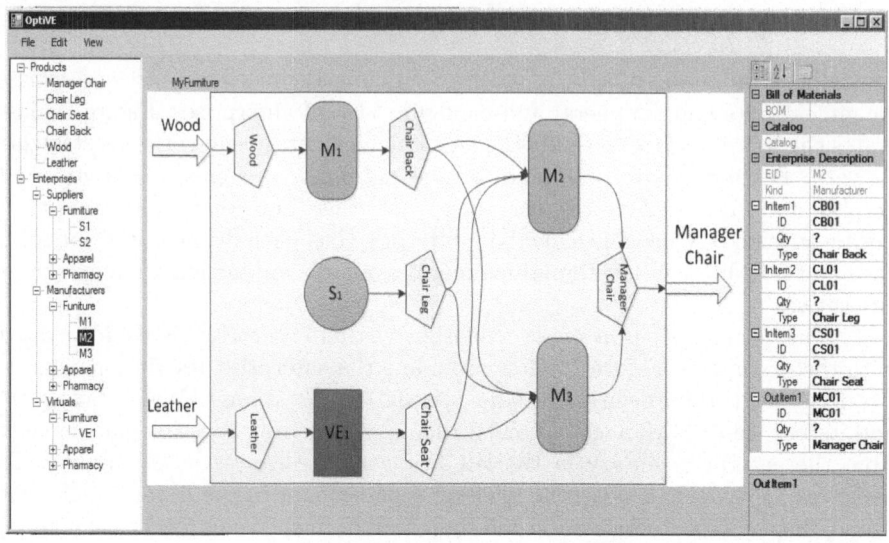

Fig. 2. User interface of OptiVE

Optimization queries are more challenging and are arguably the strongest feature of OptiVE. A typical query might be: "How can I maximize the profit in producing 100 manager chairs?" To answer such questions, OptiVE formulates a query as described at the end of the previous section. This query instantiates the variable *quantity*(Manager Chair) to 100, and sets the optimization target to *cost*(MyFurniture). OptiVE then expresses this query as an optimization problem, solves it, and displays the answer to the analyst. The answer to this query is an instantiation of the unspecified quantity variables, and hence a specification of an actual routing of items among the participants of the virtual enterprise. The description of M2 shown in Figure 2 is prior to the optimization and the quantity variables are given as "?"; when the optimization query concludes these are replaced by specific values. This particular instantiation of the virtual enterprise (the query and its answer) may then be saved as a possible "scenario".

4   Conclusion

We described OptiVE, an interactive system that assists business entrepreneurs and analysts in the creation, evolution, analysis and optimization of virtual enterprises. Both the model and the system are undergoing further research and we mention here two of our directions. First, the OptiVE model described in section 2 is being extended to incorporate (1) additional elementary enterprise types (other than manufacturers or suppliers); for example, *transporters* for moving products from one location to another; (2) additional system variables (other than quantities or prices); for example, time of delivery, reliability, past performance, or risk of failure; and (3) additional optimization targets (other than overall cost); for example, least risk, shortest delivery time, or shortest supply chain. In addition, the user interface of OptiVE described in Section 3 is being improved to provide features that correspond to the new model, and to complete the implementation of a few features that were illustrated in Figure 2, though not yet fully available.

References

1. Brodsky, A., Zelivinski, S., Katz, M., Gozhansky, A., Karpishpan, S.: System and Method for Adaptive Trade Specification and Match-making Optimization. US patent no. US 6751597 B1
2. Camarinha-Matos, L.M., Afsarmanesh, H.: Virtual Enterprise Modeling and Support Infrastructures: Applying Multi-Agent System Approaches. In: Luck, M., Mařík, V., Štěpánková, O., Trappl, R. (eds.) ACAI 2001 and EASSS 2001. LNCS (LNAI), vol. 2086, pp. 335–364. Springer, Heidelberg (2001)
3. Camarinha-Matos, L.M., Afsarmanesh, H., Osorio, A.L.: Flexibility and Safety in a Web-based Infrastructure for Virtual Enterprises. International Journal of Computer Integrated Manufacturing 14(1), 66–82 (2001)
4. Camarinha-Matos, L.M., Silveri, I., Afsarmanesh, H., Oliveira, H.A.I.: Towards a Framework for Creation of Dynamic Virtual Organizations. In: Proceedings of PRO-VE 2005, 6th IFIP Working Conference on Virtual Enterprises (Collaborative Networks and Their Breeding Environments). IFIP AICT, vol. 186, pp. 69–80. Springer, Heidelberg (2005)
5. Danesh, M.H., Raahemi, B., Kamali, M.A.: A Framework for Process Management in Service Oriented Virtual Organizations. In: Proceedings of NWeSP 2011, 7th International Conference on Next Generation Web Services Practices, pp. 12–17. IEEE Press, New York (2011)
6. D'Atri, A., Motro, A.: Evolving VirtuE. In: Proceedings of PRO-VE 2007, 8th IFIP Working Conference on Virtual Enterprises (Establishing the Foundation of Collaborative Networks). IFIP AICT, vol. 243, pp. 317–326. Springer, Heidelberg (2007)
7. Motro, A., Guo, Y.: The SOAVE Platform: A Service Oriented Architecture for Virtual Enterprises. In: Proceedings of PRO-VE 2012, 13th IFIP Working Conference on Virtual Enterprises (Collaborative Networks in the Internet of Services). IFIP AICT, vol. 380, pp. 216–224. Springer, Heidelberg (2012)
8. Patel, J., Teacy, W.T.L., Jennings, N.R., Luck, M., Chalmers, S., Oren, N., Norman, T.J., Preece, A.D., Gray, P.M.D., Shercliff, G., Stockreisser, P.J., Shao, J., Gray, W.A., Fiddian, N.J., Thompson, S.: Agent-based Virtual Organisations for the Grid. International Journal of Multiagent and Grid Systems 1(4), 237–249 (2005)
9. Petersen, S.A., Divitini, M.: Using Agents to Support the Selection of Virtual Enterprise Teams. In: Proceedings of AOIS 2002 @ AAMAS 2002, 4th International Bi-Conference Workshop on Agent-Oriented Information Systems. CEUR-WS.org, vol. 59 (2002)
10. Zhou, B., Zhi-Jun, H., Tang, J.-F.: An adaptive model of virtual enterprise based on dynamic web service composition. In: Proceedings of CIT 2005, 5th International Conference on Computer and Information Technology, pp. 284–289. IEEE Press, New York (2005)

Dynamic Generation of Personalized Product Bundles in Enterprise Networks

Anthony Karageorgos[1] and Elli Rapti[2]

[1] Manchester Business School
University of Manchester, UK
anthony.karageorgos@mbs.ac.uk
[2] Department of Computer and Communication Engineering
University of Thessaly, Greece
rapti@uth.gr

Abstract. Product bundling is a marketing strategy that concerns offering several products for sale as one combined product. Current technology mainly focuses on the creation of static bundles, which involves pre-computing product bundles and associated discounts. However, due to the inherent dynamism and constant change of current and potential customer information, as is particularly the case in enterprise networks, static product bundles prove to be inefficient. In this paper an approach for dynamic generation of personalized product bundles using agents is proposed. Our approach involves creating bundles based on substitution and complementarity associations between product items, and subsequently ranking the produced bundles according to individual preferences and history of each customer. The proposed approach has been implemented in e-Furniture, an agent-based system supporting networking of furniture and wood product manufacturing enterprises.

Keywords: Product Bundling, Personalization, Agent-Based Systems, Enterprise Networks.

1 Introduction

Retailers often encounter situations where a customer has expressed interest in a product or service but wants to negotiate a lower price, for example, a price that is more "market competitive". Such negotiations require sellers to quickly decide on how to lower the price for the product without taking a loss and offer attractive alternatives to the customer [1]. Moreover, the Internet has emerged as a new channel for distribution of information concerning actual and digital products reaching a vast customer base. However, providers of online product information have difficulties as to how to price, package and market them and struggle with a variety of revenue models [2]. Finally, it is quite common to combine products from different suppliers whose availability and price varies dynamically as is often the case in enterprise networks [3]. For example, it is common for shippers in logistics networks to collaborate and combine their shipment requests in order to negotiate better rates and in the food

Y.T. Demey and H. Panetto (Eds.): OTM 2013 Workshops, LNCS 8186, pp. 208–217, 2013.

industry for businesses to combine products, such as organic cold meat and wines, in order to increase their sales.

A common approach to address the above issues is *"bundling"*, which involves combining additional products or services that may be of interest to a customer in lieu of lowering the price for the initial item of interest [1]. For instance, sporting and cultural organizations offer season tickets, restaurants provide complete dinners, and retail stores offer discounts to a customer buying more than one product [4]. Generally, a bundle represents a package that contains at least two elements and presents a value-add on to potential consumers. The creation of such bundles with superior characteristics over individual item offers has long been recognized as an opportunity for companies to increase their competitive advantages in the market [5].

The objective of this paper is to introduce an approach for dynamic generation of personalized product bundles in enterprise networks. The proposed bundles include a primary product item determined from user preferences and additional complementary items that are estimated to offer more utility to the user [6]. Personalization is achieved by ranking the proposed bundles according to user preferences and usage history. The remainder of this paper is structured as follows. In section 2 we provide an overview of the e-Furniture project, while in Section 3 we describe our dynamic product bundling approach. A discussion about preliminary evaluation results is provided in Section 4. Finally, we discuss conclusions and further work in Section 5.

2   The e-Furniture Project

Aiming to support 'smart' collaboration in furniture and wood product enterprise networks the e-Furniture system [7] involves an agent-based infrastructure capable of bundling products and services taking into account individual requirements of both manufacturers and customers. e-Furniture covers both B2B transactions and B2C transactions, targeting economies of scale and profit increase for providers, and increased satisfaction for customers.

A main objective of e-Furniture is to provide assistance in typical purchasing decisions involving product bundles. Bundling products of different providers is a key technique for SME's to increase their range of offered products and hence increase customer satisfaction. In the case of smart business networks in particular, product bundles can be created dynamically according to customer requirements and the solutions offered by the partners in the business network.

The e-Furniture infrastructure is an open system viewed as a grid of distributed interconnecting partner nodes, as shown in Fig. 1. A designated node acts as main coordinator for all other nodes by storing network wide customer and product information, by intermediating to establish communication for new partner nodes joining the network, and by resolving conflicts that may arise.

We have adopted an agent-oriented view in designing the e-Furniture software architecture and all main operations and interfaces are driven by software agents. Upon registration and joining the network, participating companies provide product catalog

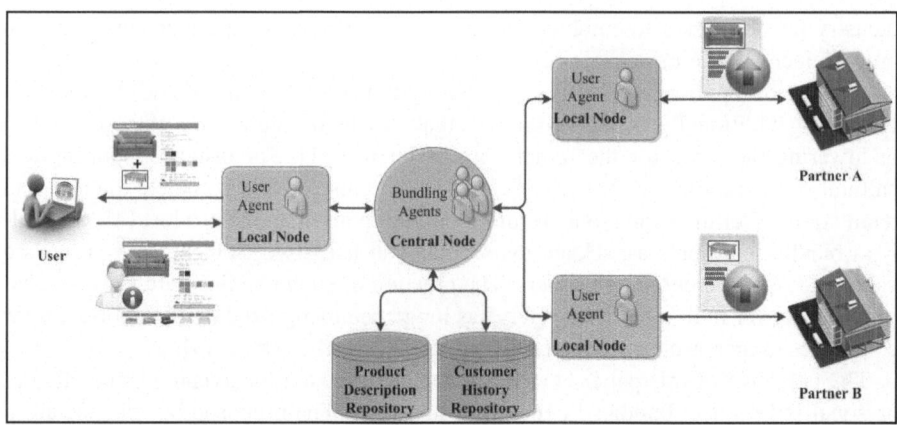

Fig. 1. High-level architecture of the e-Furniture system

descriptions which are uploaded automatically to the main e-Furniture node server. Both business and retail customers connect to the server storing their profile and preferences and navigate searching for products of their interest. In response, a number of e-Furniture agents interact dynamically and the system finally returns a number of product bundle recommendations targeting the particular user characteristics.

3   Dynamic Product Bundling

3.1   Overview

The research area of networked enterprises represents a complex, large scale and multidisciplinary domain, involving distributed, heterogeneous, and autonomous entities [8, 9]. Agent technology provides a natural way to design and implement such enterprise-wide manufacturing environments for distributed manufacturing enterprises. In particular, the multi-agent system (MAS) approach is ideally suited to represent problems that have multiple problem-solving methods, multiple perspectives and/or multiple problem-solving entities [10]. Therefore, we propose an agent-based architecture for integrating information in this highly distributed environment in order to dynamically generate personalized product bundles.

The main features of our approach include extraction of substitution and complementarity associations between products and use them to generate bundles, and ranking the produced bundles based on individual customer historical data. Substitution associations reflect the degree to which two products are similar and can substitute each other. Complementarity associations reflect the degree to which an item enhances the purchasing possibility of another when offered together in a bundle. A more detailed description of the proposed approach is provided in the following sections.

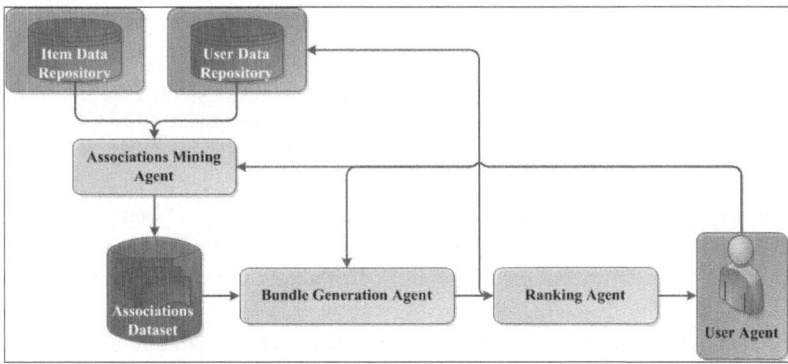

Fig. 2. Agent interactions for dynamic generation of product bundles

3.2   Bundling Multi-Agent System Architecture

The proposed agent system architecture comprises of four basic types of agents, which interact in order to generate and customize personalized product bundles (Fig. 2). Specifically, the proposed architecture includes the following agent types:

- **Associations Mining Agent** (AMA), which is responsible for the generation of associations and relationships between products. It accepts as input the users' historical data and product information, and extracts the substitution and complementarity associations between the products by executing the Associations Mining Algorithm (cf. Sec. 3.3). Subsequently, the collection of associations is stored in tabular form in a structure termed 'associations dataset'.
- **Bundle Generation Agent** (BGA), which accepts as input the associations dataset created by AMA and generates a list of product bundles using the Bundle Generation Algorithm (cf. Sec. 3.4).
- **Ranking Agent** (RA), which accepts as input the list of proposed bundles and based on the user purchase history stored in e-Furniture repository, it executes the Ranking Algorithm (cf. Sec. 3.5) and creates a personalized list of bundles for the respective user.
- **User Agent** (UA), which implements the user interface.

3.3   Associations Mining Agent

AMA detects substitution and complementarity associations between product items in the system repository. Substitution associations are measured by the substitution score which takes values in the range [0,1] and reflects the degree to which two items are similar and can substitute each other. An example of substitutable items could be two different wireless handheld devices that have similar features but are offered by different broadband providers. On the other hand, complementarity associations reflect the degree to which an item enhances the purchasing possibility of another when offered together in a bundle. For example, complementary items for a wireless handheld device might be a wireless plan, a subscription to some broadband provider or a carrying case.

Initially, AMA identifies the primary product items drawn from the product repository either based on a user request or automatically according to predefined settings, such as identifying items with highest sales at regular time intervals or during off-peak processing times. Primary product items can also be identified by users by selecting items from particular product categories. For example, if bundles having as a primary item a sofa are to be generated, the bundle mining system can select the primary product items from the sofa category of products. Furthermore, primary items can also be identified by using one or more keywords in a search, such as 'sofa' or 'three seated', or they can be a product item that the user has explicitly selected.

Subsequently, AMA generates the substitution associations between the primary items by performing an analysis of their attributes, for example by using the cosine similarity measure [11] or a semantic similarity comparison method such as the one proposed in [12]. Items that have more attributes in common have stronger substitution associations and they are given higher association scores, while items that have fewer attributes in common receive lower scores or an association may not be created for them at all. For example, two wireless handheld devices with touchscreen and Wi-Fi connectivity have higher substitution score than two wireless handheld devices with touchscreen but where only one of them has Wi-Fi connectivity. In the proposed approach, we use the cosine similarity metric to compare products considering that each item's attributes are defined in free textual descriptions.

After having determined the substitution associations between primary items, AMA generates the complementarity associations between each primary item and one or more complementary items. Complementarity associations are measured by the complementarity score which takes values in the range $[0, n]$, where n is the total number of customer usage history recordings in the system repository.

Algorithm 1. Mining product associations

Require: ItemsNumber, ItemtoSearch
Ensure: SubstDataset, CompleDataset
for i=0 **to** ItemNumber **do**
PrimaryItems ← search_primary_items(ItemtoSearch)
end for
for i=0 **to** ItemNumber **do**
    for j=0 **to** ItemNumber **do** //calculate using cosine similarity
    SubstDataset ← calculate_substitution_associations(PrimaryItems)
    end for
end for
for i=0 **to** ItemNumber **do**
    while next in purchase history **do** //calculate using Apriori algorithm
    CompleDataset ← calculate_complementarity_associations(PrimaryItems)
    end while
end for

Complementarity associations can be created between items that were purchased together, a method known as Market Basket Analysis [13]. For example, users who purchase a certain type of a wireless handheld device tend to purchase certain accessories and service options in a single transaction. Moreover, complementary items may also be limited to certain categories, such as 'headsets' and 'car kits'. Such associations can be commonly identified using association rule mining algorithms, such as Apriori [14], AprioriTid [15] and Eclat [16]. In our approach, we currently employ the Apriori algorithm because it has wide popularity and it is easy to implement.

Finally, AMA stores both substitution and complementarity associations in an associations dataset. The association mining steps are presented in Algorithm 1.

3.4   Bundle Generation Agent

BGA dynamically creates product bundles corresponding to product items selected by users by considering the substitution and complementarity product information stored in the associations datasets created by AMA.

Firstly, BGA identifies the primary product item selected by a user, and retrieves additional product items from the substitution dataset that have a substitution association with the identified primary item. A subset of these substitutable items is then retained in a substitutable product dataset by selecting a specific number of items with highest substitution association scores.

The next step for BGA is to search in the complementarity associations dataset for product items that have complementarity associations with the selected primary item and the selected substitutable items. A subset of these complementary items is then retained in a complementary product dataset, by retaining a specific number of items with highest complementarity association scores. For example, a user can select a wireless handheld device A and based on the substitution dataset BGA can identify as substitutable item a wireless handheld device B. Based on these two devices, BGA will then search in the complementarity dataset to find complementary products, for example those having complementarity score to either device A or device B above a given threshold, and can identify a headset and a carrying case for instance.

As a next step BGA creates product item bundles by combining the selected complementary items with the primary item and a number of substitutable items, considering all possible combinations. For example, two complementary items and a

---

Algorithm 2. Bundle generation

Require: ItemNumber, SelectedItem, SubstDataset, CompleDataset
Ensure: BundleList
for i=0 **to** ItemNumber **do**
        Substitute ← find_substitutes(SelectedItem, SubstDataset)
        Complementary ← find_ complementary(SelectedItem, CompleDataset)
end for
for i=0 **to** ItemNumber **do**
        BundleList ← bundle_items(SelectedItem, Substitute, Complementary)
    end for

Algorithm 3. Ranking selected bundles

   Require: BundleList, BundleNumber, CustomerHistory
   Ensure: RankedList
   for i=0 **to** BundleNumber **do**
      Affinity ← affinity(CustomerHistory, BundleList)
   end for
   for i=0 **to** BundleNumber **do**
      RankedList ← rank_items(Affinity, BundleList)
   end for

---

substitutable item can form a bundle. In the aforementioned wireless handheld devices example the substitutable item is the wireless device B, and hence a bundle generated by BGA could include wireless device B together with the headset and carrying case.

Finally, the proposed bundles are forwarded to RA to be ranked according to user profile. The bundle generation steps are described in Algorithm 2.

3.5   Ranking Agent

RA is responsible for the personalization of the proposed bundles created by BGA, and ranks them according to each user's browsing and purchase history. Ranking is based on the concept of affinity of a customer C for purchasing a pair of products $\{P_i, P_j\}$, which has been introduced by Batra et al. in [1]. The Affinity index is a measure of the degree of a customer C preferring a particular product tion $\{P_i, P_j\}$, and can be calculated using the following formula:

$$Affinity\big(C, \{P_i, P_j\}\big)$$

$$= Compatibility(\{P_i, P_j\}, R_c) * \max(Affinity(C, \{P_i\}), Affinity(C, \{P_j\}))$$

where R_c is a subset of R containing only the transactions and browsing data of customer C and $Compatibility(\{P_i, P_j\}, R_c)$ is a measure of preference of customer C for the particular pair $\{P_i, P_j\}$. The value of compatibility between a customer C and a pair of items $\{P_i, P_j\}$ can be estimated as the times customer C has viewed or inquired information online or purchased both P_i and P_j.

For a single product, $Affinity(C, \{P_i\})$ can be calculated using the following formula:

$$Affinity(C, \{P_i\}) = \frac{Support(P_i)}{\max(Support(P_m))}$$

where P_m refers to all products selected or purchased by customer C, $Support(P_i)$ expresses the number of times customer C has selected or purchased product P_i and $max(Support(P_m))$ expresses the maximum number of the times customer C has selected or purchased a particular product.

The produced product bundles list is then sorted in decreasing order of the calculated Affinity index. Finally, a subset of the ranked bundle list, for example a predefined

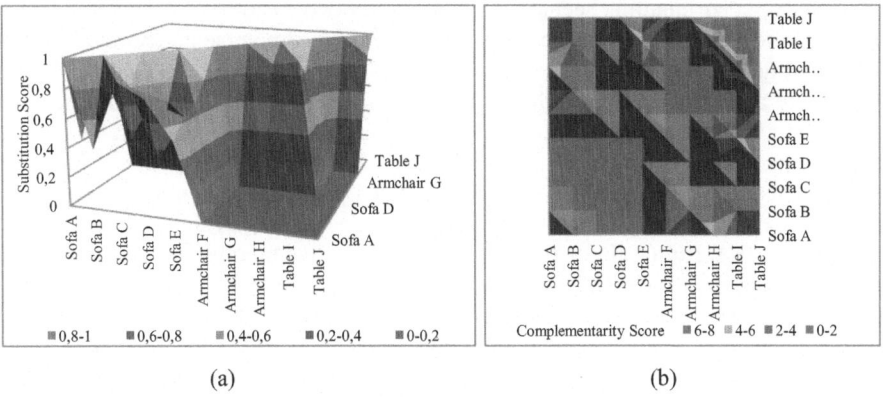

Fig. 3. Substitution (a) and complementarity (b) pairwise association indices (10 products)

number of highest rank bundles, is selected and presented to the user. The steps for ranking product bundles are described in Algorithm 3.

4 Discussion

The proposed approach has been implemented in the e-Furniture system and we are currently experimenting with customer transaction data obtained from the partner individual web sites and ERP systems. For an indicative sample of 10 representative furniture products the viewing and transaction behavior of 5 representative registered customers resulted in the substitution and complementarity associations shown in Fig. 3. We only considered substitution associations between items in the same category, only between sofas for instance, and we used the cosine similarity measure to generate the substitution associations.

Table 1. List of the proposed and personalized product bundles for customers A and B

Bundle	Non-personalized Bundle List	Total Score	Ranked for Customer A	Affinity for Customer A	Ranked for Customer B	Affinity for Customer B
1	Sofa D Armchair H	4	Sofa E Armchair H	3	Sofa A Armchair H	4
2	Sofa D Table J	4	Sofa A Armchair H	1,33	Sofa A Table J	1
3	Sofa E Armchair H	3,8	Sofa E Table J	1	Sofa D Armchair H	0,57
4	Sofa E Table J	3,8	Sofa D Armchair H	0,67	Sofa E Armchair H	0,57
5	Sofa A Armchair H	3,77	Sofa D Table J	0,67	Sofa D Table J	0,29
6	Sofa A Table J	3,77	Sofa A Table J	0	Sofa E Table J	0

As an exemplar bundling scenario we considered two customers, A and B, both selecting to view sofa D. Based on the substitution and complementarity relations depicted in Fig. 3 a non-personalized product bundle list was created (Table 1) where bundles are ranked according to their total score as proposed in [6]. The total score is the algebraic sum of the substitution and complementarity scores and takes values in the range [0, n+1]. Finally, the Affinity index of each bundle was calculated based on customer historical data and the final personalized product bundles for customers A and B were created as shown in the third and fourth columns of Table 1 respectively.

As can be seen from Table 1 the ranking of the product bundles generated with our approach is different for each customer. This is because the preferences of customers A and B for the respective bundles, expressed in terms of the respective affinities, differ considerably. For example, sofa D and armchair H would be the first proposal according to [6] where no personalization takes place. However, according to each customer's historical data, reflected in the values of the respective affinity indices, customers A and B seem to have higher preferences for sofas E and A respectively. Our proposed approach takes this into account by ranking first the bundles comprising sofa E and sofa A for customers A and B respectively. Consequently, since our ranking is based on the affinity of each individual customer the ranked bundle lists produced with our proposed method are more likely to match customer preferences.

5   Conclusions

In this paper we introduced an approach for dynamic generation of personalized product bundles in enterprise networks using agents. The created bundles include a primary item, obtained either by explicit user input or from a generated substitution list, and a number of complementary items selected from a generated complementarity list. The produced bundles are then personalized by ranking them for each user based on individual user data.

The initial results look promising and we now plan to carry out extensive evaluation of our approach by comparing the results with other approaches and test its acceptance through the users' feedback. An issue that needs to be addressed is the complexity incurred when product numbers and features increase. We plan to address this by employing approximation methods for similarity matching and complementarity identification. Furthermore, an issue of concern is the lack of actual transaction data for new customers and partners in the network. Therefore, we plan to explore methods to personalize the generated bundles for customers lacking historical data, for example by using data from customers with similar profiles. Finally, in our current work bundling is based only on product information stored in a central repository. Additional research issues arise when considering obtaining product information directly from partner distributed repositories, including semantic compatibility of product representations and performance of distributed product searches.

Acknowledgements. This research is supported by the Greek "National Strategic Reference Framework 2007-13", Act: "Support for SMEs Groups for Research and Technological Development", Project title: "e-Furniture: Dynamic Networking of Furniture and Wood Product Manufacturing Enterprises".

References

1. Batra, V.S., et al.: Dynamic Product and Service Bundling, p. 10. U.S.P.A. Publication, Editor 2012, International Business and Machines Corporation, USA (2012)
2. Bakos, Y., Brynjolfsson, E.: Bundling and Competition on the Internet. Marketing Science 19(1), 20 (2000)
3. Azevedo, A.L., et al.: An Advanced Agent-Based Order Planning System for Dynamic Networked Enterprises. Production Planning and Control 15(2), 12 (2004)
4. Yang, T.-C., Lai, H.: Comparison of Product Bundling Strategies on Different Online Shopping Behaviors. Electronic Commerce Research and Applications 5, 10 (2006)
5. Lawless, M.W.: Commodity Bundling for Competitive Advantage: Strategic Implications. Journal of Management Studies 28, 14 (1991)
6. Yi, J., Levitan, A.A.: System for Reccomending Item Bundles, p. 23. U.S. Patent, Editor 2012, Amazon Technologies Inc., USA (2012)
7. The e-Furniture Project, http://inflab.kard.teilar.gr/e-Furniture
8. Camarinha-Matos, L.M., Afsarmanesh, H.: Collaborative Networks: a New Scientific Discipline. Journal of Intelligent Manufacturing 16, 14 (2005)
9. Jardim-Goncalves, R., et al.: Reference Framework for Enhanced Interoperable Collaborative Networks in Industrial Organisations. International Journal of Computer Integrated Manufacturing 26(1-2), 17 (2013)
10. Nahm, Y.-E., Ishikawa, H.: A Hybrid Multi-Agent System Architecture for Enterprise Integration Using Computer Networks. Robotics and Computer-Integrated Manufacturing 21, 18 (2005)
11. Lee, M.D., Pincombe, B., Welsh, M.: An Empirical Evaluation of Models of Text Document Similarity. In: Proceedings of the 27th Annual Conference of the Cognitive Science Society, p. 6 (2005)
12. Colucci, S., et al.: Concept Abduction and Contraction for Semantic-based Discovery of Matches and Negotiation Spaces in an E-Marketplace. Electronic Commerce Research and Applications, 10 (2005)
13. Giudici, P., Figini, S.: Market Basket Analysis. In: Applied Data Mining for Business and Industry (2009)
14. Bramer, M.: Association Rule Mining II. In: Principles of Data Mining, p. 17. Springer, Heidelberg (2013)
15. Agrawal, R., et al.: Fast Discovery of Association Rules, p. 22. Advances in Knowledge Discovery and Data Mining A.A.f.A. Intelligence, Editor, Manlo Park, CA, USA (1996)
16. Zaki, M.J., et al.: New Algorithms for Fast Discovery of Association Rules. In: Proceedings of the 3rd International Conference on KDD and Data Mining. Newport Beach, California (1997)

An Information Model for Designing Virtual Environments for Orthopedic Surgery

J. Cecil[1] and Miguel Pirela-Cruz[2]

[1] School of Industrial Engineering & Management, Center for Information
Centric Engineering (CICE), Oklahoma State University,
Stillwater, OK, USA
[2] Department of Orthopedic Surgery, Texas Tech Health Sciences Center,
El Paso, TX, USA

Abstract. In this paper, the role of an information model in the design of virtual environments for orthopedic surgery is discussed. The engineering Enterprise Modeling Language (eEML) is used to model the relationships and precedence constraints in a specific set of orthopedic surgery activities. Our model focuses on a process referred to as LISS plating surgery (LISS- Less Invasive Stabilization System). This information model serves as a basis to develop two orthopedic surgical environments: a non-immersive virtual reality based environment and a haptic interface equipped virtual environment. These virtual environments can be used for training medical residents in specific orthopedic surgical processes.

1 Introduction

The training of medical residents in a given surgical field is an important aspect of their educational process. Before recent decades, the medical training system used to employ the traditional methods for training purposes. These methods of surgical training include the use of cadavers, animals, or synthetic mockups [1]. These traditional methods have some major drawbacks. Animal right activists have criticized the use of animals for surgical training. Use of cadavers creates the possibility of risk of infections. Synthetic mockups for training (for instance, synthetic bones) are expensive and are not patient/human specific. As a result, the interest toward training the surgeons with alternative methods such as Virtual Reality based environments has been increasing over the recent decades [2-6]. The benefits of such environments can vary from providing a long-term low cost training method to enabling a collaborative training system accessible from different geographical locations in the world.

In the literature, there have been few research efforts dealing with creating information models as a basis to develop virtual environments especially in biomedical domains. Cecil and Cruz [7] have presented their work on developing an information model of the micro surgical process. In their work, the detailed information model about this surgical process has been presented. Hirschman et al. [8] has presented their research on developing of a tactile and haptic enabled open

Y.T. Demey and H. Panetto (Eds.): OTM 2013 Workshops, LNCS 8186, pp. 218–227, 2013.

surgery simulator. The objective of their work is to develop a simulator that can effectively simulate the feel for open surgery. Dargar et al. [9] has developed a haptic interface for virtual translumenal endoscopic surgical trainer. Their simulator is a virtual reality haptic interface for training and evaluating new techniques and procedures. Jalote-Parmar et al [10] have elaborated on use of a Work flow integration matrix (WIM) in the design of surgical information systems. WIM uses theories of human behavior in problem solving and investigates the role of evidence-based decision-making for the development of new surgical technologies.

In [13], Jannin highlighted the need for process models in computer assisted surgery. A global methodology is presented which includes the definition of a surgical ontology, the software developed based on this ontology as well as the development of methods for automatic recognition of a surgeon' activities. This discussion of this methodology is in the context of neurosurgery processes. One of the other methods used in surgical task modeling is Hierarchical Task Analysis (HTA), which can be used to analyze and evaluate a surgeon's capabilities for various procedures. A HTA task tree usually contains the primary surgical steps, which are decomposed or divided into various tasks, subtasks and motion level actions [14]. Using this HTA approach, a task analysis of an endoscopic surgical process is discussed in [14]; the surgery process is Hybrid Rigid Scope Natural Orifice Translumenal Endoscopic Surgery (NOTES). Further, motion analysis was also conducted as part of this study. The modeling approach in HTA is very rudimentary as it focuses primarily on the "identification of steps"; a process is divided into a collection of tasks and their children (or sub-tasks). when a time analysis is conducted, the tool used in a specific step (eg: suture needle, etc.) is identified along with the beginning and end of a specific sub-task. However, the HTA approach does not model or capture key attributes such as information or physical inputs, and constraints; modeling such attributes is necessary to obtain a better understanding of functional and process relationships which in turns enables a stronger foundation that is necessary to build a virtual environment.

In general, there is also a lack of emphasis on creation and use of information models in the creation of virtual environments especially for medical process domains (including orthopedic surgery). The information modeling approach discussed in this paper encompasses the major elements of process modeling including capturing the information inputs, constraints, performing mechanisms as well as the intermediate decision outcomes of the various sub-tasks; by modeling such relationships as well as explicitly capturing temporal precedence constraints, it provides a more fundamental basis to understand and analyze a given surgical process.

The objective of this paper is to discuss an information model created to support the design of a VSE for orthopedic surgery. Using this information model, virtual environments for training surgery residents in LISS plating orthopedic processes are being developed. The creation of an information model provides a structure basis not only for understanding and analyzing a given surgical process but also provides a useful   communication   vehicle   between   the   expert   surgical   team   and   the

IT/engineering team (which is building such an environment). As the literature review indicates, there has been a lack of comprehensive approaches for modeling surgical processes including orthopedic surgery. In our research, by adopting such an approach, the interaction and transfer of detailed information between the two teams was also facilitated. The creation of such an information model for orthopedic surgery also provides a structured basis for reasoning and understanding the complex relationships between the various inputs, constraints and performing agents; such an understanding enables a better design of the virtual environment which will be used to train medical residents in orthopedic surgery.

The information modeling language used in this work is called (engineering) Enterprise Modeling Language (eEML), which can be utilized to model the LISS plating surgery at various levels of abstraction [11]. eEML in general can be used as a modeling language to plan activities, design software systems for a given domain, analyze the integration and information exchange needs in a distributed virtual enterprise (VE), and enable understanding of existing, new or changing processes and product development practices [7].

At the highest level, the core activity to be modeled is the Focus Unit (FU) which appears as a verb representing the activity of interest. The Focus Unit (FU) corresponds to the E-0 level which can be decomposed into other levels of abstraction. In an eEML model there are four categories of information attributes: the Influencing Criteria (IC), the Associated Performing Agents (APA), the Decision Objects (DO) and the Task Effectors (TE). Using these attributes, a target set of activities can be modeled, studied and analyzed at various levels of abstraction. Influencing Criteria can be categorized as information inputs (II) and constraints (CO), which directly impact the accomplishment of the target activity (being modeled). The information inputs are the information attributes which are required to accomplish the target process being modeled. The Associated Performing Agents (APAs) refer to the software, personnel and/ or machines/tools agents, which perform the identified tasks. Decision Objects (DO) can be grouped under information and physical objects, which refer to the information or physical outcomes (respectively) of activities performed. The end effectors indicate flow of task accomplishment in either a synchronous or asynchronous manner. Logical AND and OR relationships can also be represented. Consider the eEML diagram in figure 4. This diagram, which represents the highest level of abstraction, illustrates the general layout and use of attributes in eEML (for the LISS plating process context). A modeled (target) activity E-0 (or E0) can be decomposed into a set of related activities E-1, E-2, etc. At various levels, the temporal relationships among these activities can also be captured using appropriate junctions. Subsequently, the tasks that comprise the parent activity can be represented in the decomposition and the process is repeated. This information model discussed in this paper was developed after closely interacting with a orthopedic surgeon (Dr. Pirela-Cruz), which has been lacking in other virtual surgical research initiatives. This developed model is being used as a basis to create a new virtual environment for orthopedic surgery. The outline of this paper is as follows. In section 3, detailed information regarding eEML models of LISS plating surgery is presented. Then in section 4, a brief overview of virtual LISS plating surgery environment is discussed. Finally, section 5 concludes this paper.

2   The Information Model Developed

Less Invasive Stabilization System (LISS) surgery is a specific orthopedic surgery process which is used to deal with fractures on the human femur bone (figure 1). The information model discussed in this paper is restricted to the domain of LISS surgery, which is one of many orthopedic surgical processes. Figure 1 is a view of the LISS plating instruments after completion of such a surgical process.

The main steps in a LISS plate process (or procedure) are shown in Figure 1. After performing the preoperative steps and choosing the proper implants for the observed crack, the surgeon needs to reduce the fracture and put different parts of the cracked bone back to their proper positions. This procedure usually is performed by specific reduction methods [12]. The next step in the surgery is the insertion of the LISS plate into its proper position under the skin and in the constant touch of the femur. The surgeon does this using the insertion guide which is assembled to the LISS plate before this step (figure 1). The next and most important step is to screw the LISS plate to the bone using different types of surgical screws. When the LISS plate is placed properly over the femur, the insertion guide can be detached from the LISS plate (figure 1).

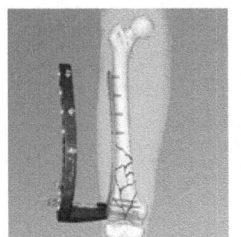 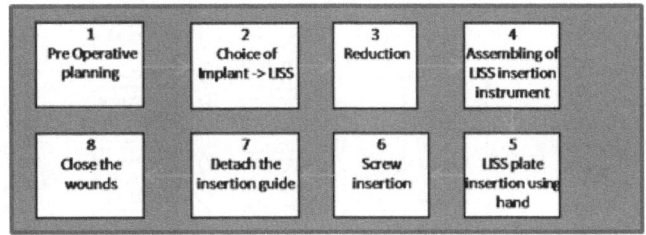

Fig. 1. View of an inserted LISS plate [12] and steps of LISS surgery

We used the eEML modeling language. The tree diagram depicted in Figure 2 shows the whole LISS plating surgery with the decompositions (appearing as child activities in the tree diagram shown). The top level, *E0*, of the process is shown in Figure 3 (using eEML). The elided views are a feature of eEML; it allows a user to obtain a view of the main steps with the main activities and outcomes (figure 4).

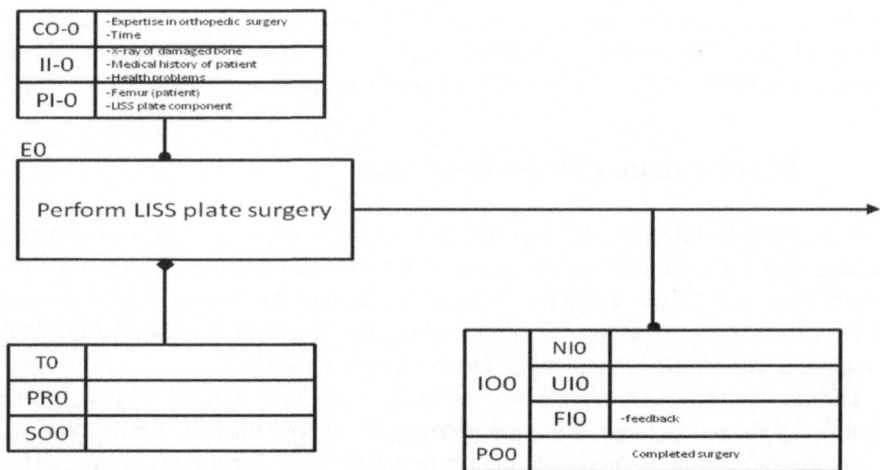

Fig. 2. Top level of LISS plating surgery (*E0*)

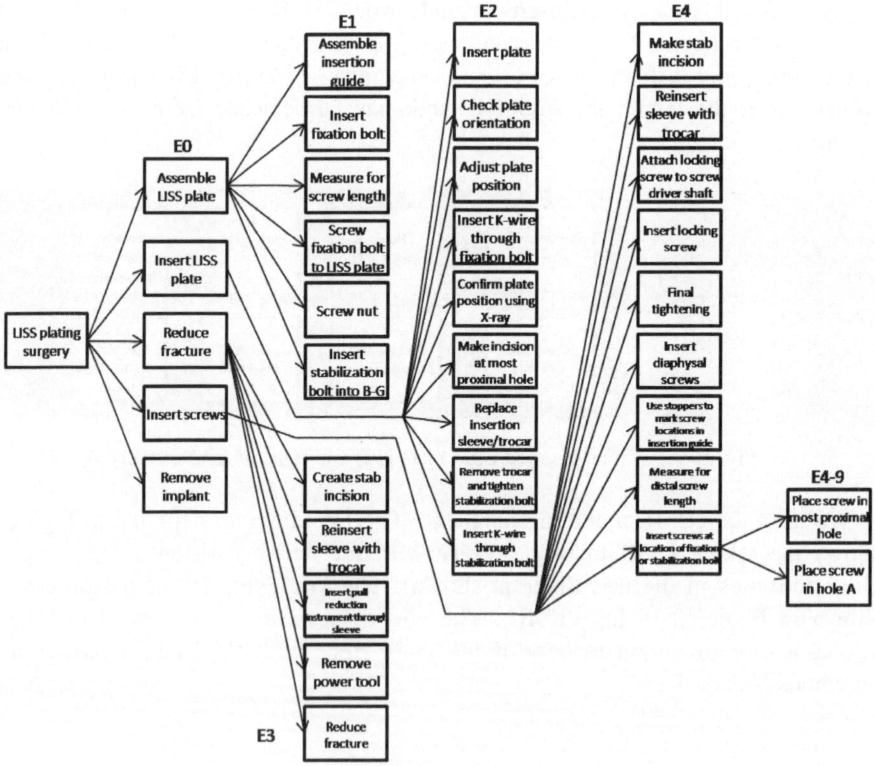

Fig. 3. Tree diagram of LISS plating decompositions

Figures 5 through 8 show the decompositions of the *E0* level diagram.

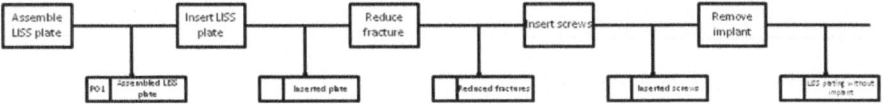

Fig. 4. Elided view of *E0* decomposition

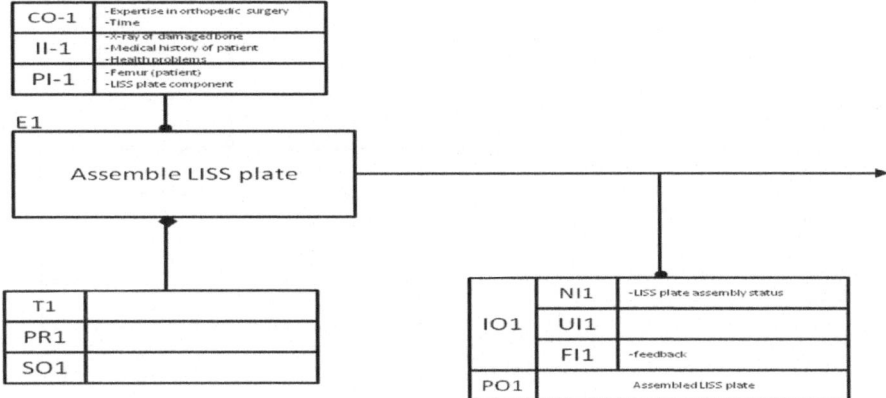

Fig. 5. *E1* decomposition

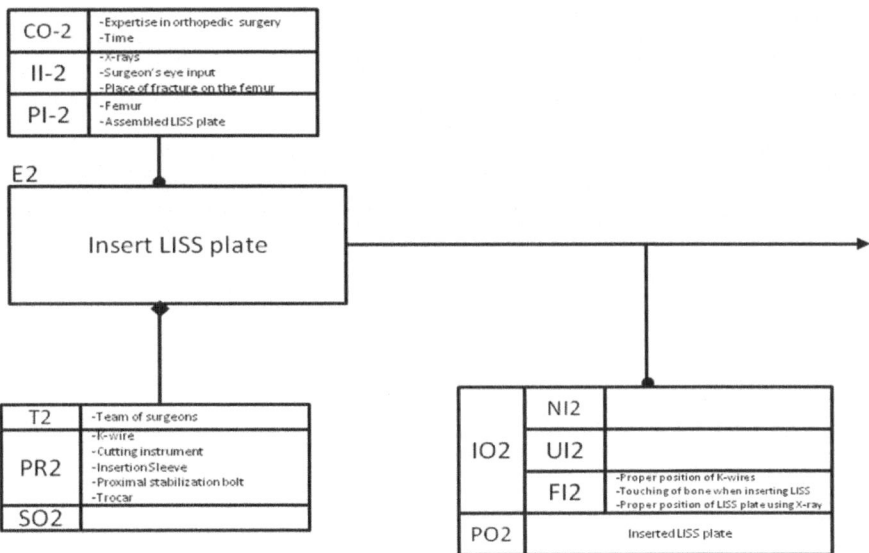

Fig. 6. *E2* decomposition

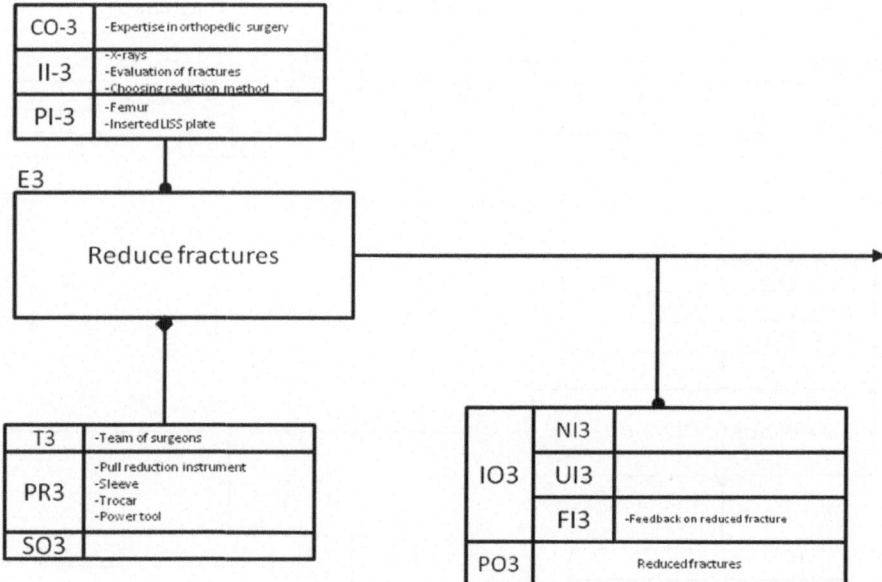

Fig. 7. *E3* decomposition

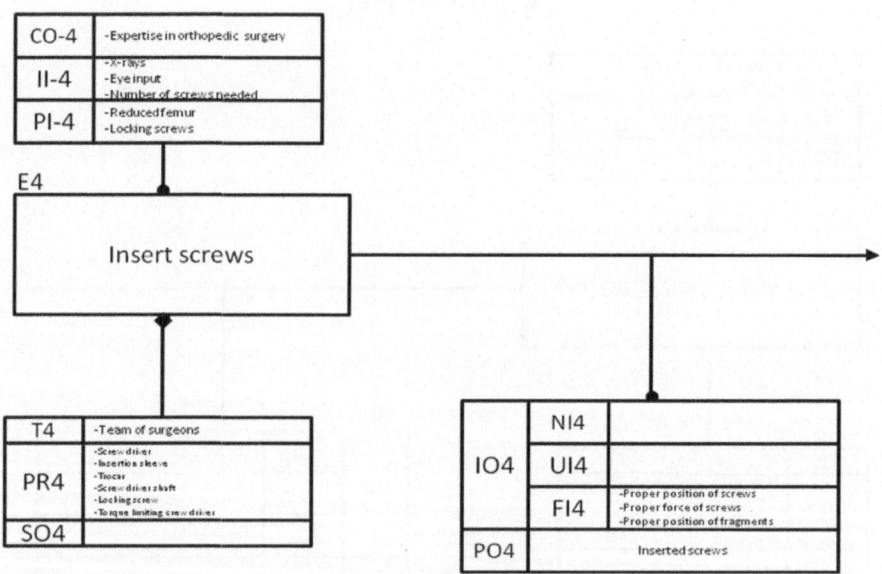

Fig. 8. *E4* decomposition

In *E1* decomposition of the surgery, the surgeon assembles different components of insertion guide and LISS plate together. The key constraints in this stage are time and availability of expertise in orthopedic surgery. The information inputs for this process are X-ray of damaged bone, medical history of patient, and health problems. The performing agents are a team of surgeons and the physical resources needed Distal femur LISS insertion guide, radiolucent extension, main component of insertion guide, fixation bolt, 4.5 mm pin wrench, insertion sleeve, and stabilization bolt. The decision objects include the feedback based on proper positioning of assembly components, screw lengths, and proper screwing of the fixation and stabilization bolts. After the plate is assembled and inserted in contact with fractured bone (shown in *E1* and *E2)*, the fracture is then 'reduced' in *E3*. When the fractured pieces are positioned with care by the surgeon back into their normal positions, locking screws are inserted into the bone in different locations of the insertion guide (*E4*). Then, the injury site (in the leg) is 'closed' by the surgeon which completes the LISS plating process. Later, the final step which is removing the implant, can be performed (*E5*). For purposes of brevity, the other decompositions (of E2 through E5) have not been included in this paper.

3   Virtual Environments for Orthopedic Surgery

The information models described in the earlier sections are being used as the basis to develop a virtual environment for LISS plating orthopedic surgery process. These virtual environments can be used in different modules such as training or evaluating the performance of surgery students. These implementations (both on PC platforms) are in progress. The first environment is a haptic based environment; C++ and Chai3D open source libraries have been used to build this virtual surgery environment. Figure 9 (a) shows Dr. Cruz interacting with this virtual environment using the haptic device. An initial implementation demonstrated linking multiple environments with haptic devices using a next generation GENI network; users were in Oklahoma and Wisconsin and were able to interact with each other (taking on the role of the expert surgeon and a medical resident); control was able to be transferred between both the environments using these next generation networks.

A second environment is also being developed to simulate the virtual LISS surgery environment using Unity software (Figure 9 b). In this environment, the simulation is non immersive and has no haptic device interface. Using this lower cost non-haptic environment, the surgeon can provide a basic introduction to the LISS plating processes; later, using the surgical simulation, he or she can pause the simulation and ask questions about a specific step in the process. The teaching module of the simulator can use the surgeon's voice or popup text for describing the on-going procedure or as an indicator of the level of accuracy achieved by the user when performing the requested task.

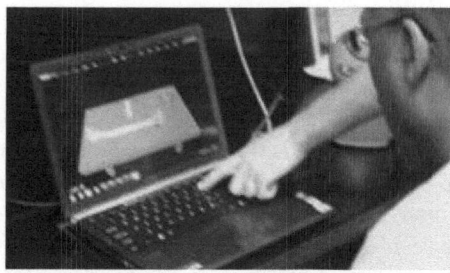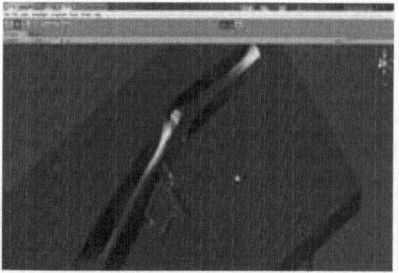

Fig. 9. (a) and (b) The two virtual environments for LISS plating under development

The development of both these virtual environments is continuing. The orthopedic surgeon is also interacting with both these preliminary environments and has provided initial feedback including suggested modifications; modifications to the virtual environments has started as part of the next phase of implementation.

4   Conclusion

In this paper, an information model of the LISS plating orthopedic surgery was discussed. The engineering Enterprise Modeling Language (eEML) was used to model the relationships and precedence constraints in a specific set of orthopedic surgery activities. This information model is being used to create a virtual reality simulator for the LISS plating surgery process in both haptic and non-haptic based environments. Using the presented eEML model for the LISS plating orthopedic surgery simulator, a better understanding of the overall process and the important relationships between information inputs (or information needed by the surgeon), the constraints (availability of equipment, knowledge of patient medical history, etc) was obtained.

Acknowledgements. Funding for this research activity was obtained through grants from the National Science Foundation (grant CNS 1257803) and Oklahoma State University (as part of the Interdisciplinary Planning Grants program, the Office of the Provost). Their assistance is gratefully acknowledged.

References

[1] Sourina, O., Sourin, A.: Virtual Orthopedic Surgery Training on Personal Computer. International Journal of Information Technology 6(1), 16–29 (2000)
[2] Tsai, M.-D., et al.: Bone drilling haptic interaction for orthopedic surgical simulator. Computers in Biology and Medicine 37, 1709–1718 (2007)
[3] Qin, J., Pang, W.-M., Chui, Y.-P., Wong, T.-T., Heng, P.-A.: A Novel Modeling Framework for Multilayered Soft Tissue Deformation in Virtual Orthopedic Surgery. J. Med. Syst. 34, 261–271 (2010)

[4] Delp, S.L., Peter Loan, J.: A Graphics-Based Software System To Develop And Analyze Models Of Musculoskeletal Structures. Comput. Biol. Med. 25(1), 21–34 (1995)

[5] Vankipuram, M., Kahol, K., McLaren, A., Panchanathan, S.: A virtual reality simulator for orthopedic basic skills: A design and validation study. J. Biomed. Inform. 43(5), 661–668 (2010)

[6] Blyth, P., Anderson, I.A., Stott, N.S.: Virtual Reality Simulators in Orthopedic Surgery: What Do the Surgeons Think? Journal of Surgical Research 131, 133–139 (2006)

[7] Cecil, J., Pirela-Cruz, M.: Development of an Information Model for a Virtual Surgical Environment. In: Proceedings of the TMCE 2010, Ancona, Italy, April 12-16 (2010)

[8] Hirschman, G.B., LeRoy, K., Galea, A.M., LaBrecque, B., De, S., Sankaranarayanan, G., Wen, J., Saunders, G., Halic, T., Birkett, D., Nepomnayshy, D.: THEO: Tactile and Haptic enabled open surgery simulator. Poster presentation at 2013 Medicine Meets Virtual Reality Conference NEXTMED/ MMVR20, San Diego, CA, February 20-23 (2013)

[9] Dargar, S., Solley, T., Nemani, A., Brino, C., Sankaranarayanan, G., De, S.: The Development of a haptic interface for the virtual translumenal endoscopic surgical trainer (VTEST). In: Poster presentation at the 2013 Medicine Meets Virtual Reality Conference (NEXTMED/ MMVR20), San Diego, CA, February 20-23 (2013)

[10] Jalote-Parmar, A., Badke-Schaub, P.: Workflow Integration Matrix: A Framework to Support the Development of Surgical Information Systems. Design Studies 29(4), 338–368 (2008)

[11] Cecil, J., Xavier, B.: Design of an engineering Enterprise Modeling Language (eEML). Technical Report (version 2). Virtual Enterprise Technologies, Inc. (VETI), Las Cruces (2001)

[12] Less Invasive Stabilization System (LISS). Allows percutaneous plate insertion and targeting of screws in the distal femur. SYNTHES, West Chester (2000), http://www.synthes.com

[13] Jannin, P.: Surgical Process Modeling: Methods and Applications. Presentation at the 2013 Medicine Meets Virtual Reality Conference (NEXTMED/ MMVR20), San Diego, CA, February 20-23 (2013)

[14] Nemani, A., Sankaranarayan, G., Roberts, K., Panait, L.M., Cao, C., De, S.: Hierarchical Task Analysis of Hybrid Rigid Scope Natural Orifice Translumenal Endoscopic Surgery (NOTES) Cholecystectomy Procedures. In: Proceedings of the 2013 Medicine Meets Virtual Reality Conference (NEXTMED/ MMVR20), San Diego, CA, February 20-23, pp. 293–297 (2013)

Process Integration and Design Optimization Ontologies for Next Generation Engineering

Massimo D'Auria and Roberto D'Ippolito

Noesis Solutions N.V., Gaston Geenslaan 11, B4 – B3001 Leuven, Belgium
{massimo.dauria,roberto.dippolito}@noesissolutions.com

Abstract. The recent years have seen a significant increase in ontology research in the field of engineering due to the needs of domain knowledge capturing, reusing and sharing between software agents and/or engineers.

The increasingly available enhancements of computing resources have considerably increased the role of Computer-aided engineering applications in the product development process by saving time and costs. In this context a key role is played by the Process Integration and Design Optimization tools that facilitate and automate the integration and interoperability of all different Enterprise Applications involved in the simulation of engineering tasks. However, all these tools inherit a severe limitation about the semantic meaning of the tools they automate.

This paper proposes a platform independent Process Integration and Design Optimization (PIDO) ontology that aims at providing an extensive mapping of the PIDO domain, with a special attention to its adoption in software applications. A comparison with existing similar ontologies and an explanation of the reasons that lay behind the classes and relations introduced is provided. Finally, a real application case is illustrated along with the related main benefits.

Keywords: ontologies, optimization, process integration.

1 Introduction

In the recent years a lot of research has been carried out on ontology definition and development due to the growing interests and needs in sharing and reusing the knowledge between different artificial intelligent systems. A clear definition of what is an ontology has been proposed by A. Gruber [1, 2] where he says: *"An ontology is a description (like a formal specification of a program) of the concepts and relationships that can formally exist for an agent or a community of agents."*

In the context of computer science the ontologies are the means by which the knowledge of a specific domain can be formalized in a set of concepts and relationships between couples of concepts. The ontologies in this sense provide a model representation of the domain knowledge that they aim to describe and support the reasoning about the concepts and relations defined for the domain considered. As it is stated in [4] the ontologies enable the machines to discover, combine and compare knowledge between different databases. Noy and Mc Guinnes in [6] identified the main advantages of building an ontology that can be summarized as follows:

Y.T. Demey and H. Panetto (Eds.): OTM 2013 Workshops, LNCS 8186, pp. 228–237, 2013.
© Springer-Verlag Berlin Heidelberg 2013

- Share common understanding of the structure of information among people or software agents
- Enable reuse of domain knowledge
- Make domain assumptions explicit
- Separate domain knowledge from the operational knowledge
- Analyze domain knowledge.

Hence by developing and using ontologies in computer science knowledge and information can be more easily found, shared and combined by users and software agents. Navigli et al. [3] declared that ontologies, i.e. semantic structures encoding concepts, are the backbone of the Semantic Web [4]. Similarly the PIDO ontology aims to build the foundations for a true semantic workflow for engineering that can enable a workflow engine to dynamically create simulation workflows by autonomously discovering and selecting annotated available services without requiring human intervention.

1.1   PIDO Challenges and Benefits

Thanks to the great performance enhancements of available computing resources, the applications of Computer-aided engineering and virtual prototyping are becoming more and more relevant in the product development process (PDP). In many markets (automotive, aerospace, consumer electronics, etc.) computer-based simulations are used to study and analyze the behaviour of complex physical systems. Many tools support engineers in performing different design engineering tasks such as computer-aided design (CAD), finite element analysis (FEA\FEM), multibody analysis and multidisciplinary design optimization [7, 8, 9]. This trend is indeed justified by the considerable reduction of time and costs that is achieved with virtual prototyping. Currently available CAE tools indeed have reached a so relevant maturity such that within innovative companies most of the design verification tests during product development process are now done via computer simulations on virtual prototypes rather than building and testing expensive physical prototypes. Stress, vibration, thermal, are just few examples of analysis that companies perform routinely. However, analysis answers only part of the Product Design question: *"How does the system I have designed behave under the given working conditions?"* Simulation often lags behind the actual design process. Furthermore, design requirements are shifting and becoming more demanding and interrelated between each other. There is a multitude of Design Performance characteristics spanning many different engineering disciplines. Some of these characteristics are conflicting and must be optimized concurrently. Solving such complex problems lies outside the scope of what the current CAE technology can provide. In this context a key role is played by the Process Integration and Design Optimization tools (PIDO) that facilitate and automate the integration and interoperability of all different enterprise CAE applications involved in the simulation engineering tasks by means of the creation of Simulation Workflows. In this way design engineer can focus more on the design aspects of the problem they are addressing rather than wasting time in repetitive, tedious and error-prone tasks like solving interoperability issues with several enterprise applications, platforms, services or implementing best practices explicitly. PIDO tools provide a number of key enabling technologies where the design space can be automatically explored and visualized, gaining the critical insights into the dynamics of the problem. These tools provide also sets of built-in optimization algorithms that enable the engineers to easily find the optimum solution for the design problem addressed.

1.2   Motivations for a PIDO Ontology

However, one severe limitation that both CAE and PIDO tools share is related to the 'meaning' of what they simulate or automate. CAE and PIDO tools do not provide yet means for the design engineer to explicitly express more knowledge about what is simulated or automated, i.e. if a specific design task is a fluidodynamic or a static analysis or what disciplines are involved in a specific problem. This knowledge is currently implicitly captured but not exploited for the benefits of solving the design problems. As such, the natural evolution of these tools is in implementing an ontological layer that allows capturing, managing and reusing the design knowledge already captured and of the new knowledge that can be explicitly expressed by the design engineers. This knowledge, once captured, can be shared between people and software agents of different enterprises and in the context of virtual prototyping.

In this paper a PIDO ontology is proposed in order to leverage the benefits coming from the use of ontologies for the benefit of product design engineering. By developing and using this ontology a first step is taken towards the concepts of a semantic simulation workflow. The PIDO ontology has been developed within the iProd FP7 EC joint research project [5] where the advantages of having a semantic description of this domain in an ontology are fully exploited.

In the following sections 2 and 3 of this paper firstly an overview of the existing typologies of workflows and workflow management systems is provided, then candidate ontologies for simulation workflow and optimization process that have been investigated are presented. In section 4 the PIDO ontology developed is described in terms of main concepts and relationships introduced in order to capture the domain. Section 5 presents one of the case studies addressed in iProd where this ontology has been used to store and retrieve from the knowledge base the necessary information to execute the simulation workflow related to a typical virtual test performed in the automotive PDP. Section 6 in the end summarizes the conclusions of the results achieved by the research work reported in this paper.

2   Workflow Domain

The concept of workflow from the most general point of view can be defined as a sequence of subsequent work activities where each of them follows the previous one without delay or gap in order to perform a specified target job [19]. Workflow can be seen as an abstraction of or a view on any real work. Workflow management systems allow the users to define, modify, control and share workflows, i.e. the activities associated to a business process, simulation process or generic process [19]. Workflow management systems automate redundant tasks allowing a better, cheaper and faster management of the processes. Most of the workflow systems are useful in order to integrate other different systems used by an organization (document management systems, databases, production applications etc.) or software tools (as in case of simulation workflows).

Nowadays there exist plenty of workflow management systems that serve different purposes, provided with various features and based on several workflow languages. An instance of a workflow may involve a series of human tasks rather than tasks that can be executed by tools, machines or software codes. These tasks often need to be repetitively performed.

When considering the context of engineering disciplines, mainly two different workflow categories can be identified: Business Process Workflows and Simulation or Computational Workflows. Within the context of Computational workflows the most important features adopted to evaluate the soundness of a workflow system are: existence of a neutral representation of the computational workflow; distributed computation capability; possibility to implement a set of control flow patterns like those described in [20]. Especially for Simulation Workflows, a big effort has been put in place in order to enable the interoperability and reusability of automated computational design workflows between different tools and enterprises. In this view, the decoupling (or at least loose coupling) of the logic of the computational workflows from their implementation has become fundamental. Hence it is important to have a neutral description of the computational workflows that, in most cases, is achieved by adopting a commonly standardized XML document representation of the workflow like partially done in the EU FP7 project Crescendo [10, 11, 12], where an XML computer readable representation has been drafted in order to allow the interoperability between different computational workflows that can be executed on different platforms and exchanged across different organizations. With this approach no semantic annotation are involved and a thorough conversion of the standardized XML representation to the specific workflow management system is always required and it may lead to mismatching or incompatibility problems between the several platforms and data objects. As a consequence, not all the systems support all the features or patterns and if the conversion is not done consistently by keeping into account all the interoperating systems then a workflow composed in a specific tool may be translated in a completely different one when used in another environment. However, this first tentative tries to respond to the need to formalize knowledge in a neutral format and to share this knowledge across different applications.

This severe issue can be overcome by introducing an ontology neutral standard description of a simulation workflow as the PIDO ontology proposed in this paper. The ontologies allow the definition of the simulation workflow from a higher level, providing a more general representation of the domain that can be easily extended and specified to support completely the different simulation workflow management systems available. The ontological standard representation of a simulation workflow enables the federation of the existing tools rather than their integration (where conversions between the different representations may lead to inconsistencies of the data).

In this context cross-organization simulation collaboration, plug-and-play interoperability between heterogeneous and independent-developed simulation workflow assets and execution time reduction are the major benefits that such approach based on the semantic description provided by the ontology and proposed in this paper can deliver.

3   Simulation Workflow and Optimization Ontologies

In this section a brief literature overview of existing ontologies that aim to capture the knowledge of process integration and design optimization domain is provided. An ontology that covers the simulation workflow and design optimization domains in an exhaustive way does not exist yet. Few attempts have been made in this direction but all have limitations to the scope of the specific application for which they have been developed. These limitations are justified by the fact that the ontologies should not include all the possible information about the domain, but only all those that are relevant and necessary for the specific application for which the ontology itself has been developed. The Workflow Ontology [15, 16] for instance has been created with the objective to capture both sequential and state-based workflows [14]. The ontology captures the different aspects of collaboration workflows and therefore contains concepts more related to a business workflow rather than a simulation workflow. Furthermore the coverage and flexibility of this ontology have been evaluated taking into account only two different collaborative workflows described in the literature like DILIGENT and BiomedGT and so from our point of view is also not general enough to cover any type of collaborative workflow. The ontology for simulation optimization (SoPT) has also been investigated and it includes concepts from both conventional optimization/mathematical programming and simulation optimization. SoPT aims at describing simulation optimization methods and help to detect the correct tool for each specific case and to facilitate component reuse, especially in systems where simulators and optimizers are loosely-coupled. The top-level abstract classes of SoPT are Optimization Component, Optimization Problem and Optimization Method. The relationships among them are shown in Fig. 1. As it is clear from the figure this ontology doesn't contain any concept or relationship related to simulation workflows. Nevertheless, the basic ideas and concepts were taken into account into our PIDO ontology in order to describe the optimization domain. ONTOP, or the Ontology for Optimization, was developed at the University of Massachusetts Amherst with the object to facilitate Engineering Design Optimization (EDO), allowing the instantiation of multiple design optimization models under a single optimization type as well as the creation of multiple model revisions using a single method. The preliminary work with ontologies began with the development of a Finite Element Model (FEM) knowledge-capturing tool, ON-TEAM. ON-TEAM, or the Ontology for Engineering Analysis Models, provides engineers with an ontological framework designed to capture engineering analysis model knowledge [17, 18]. This prototype knowledge framework was founded on the "concept that engineering analysis models are knowledge-based abstractions of physical systems, and therefore knowledge sharing is the key to exchanging, adapting, and interoperating Engineering Analysis Models, or EAMs, within or across organizations,". ONTOP was developed as a knowledge framework tool to incorporate standardized optimization terminology, formal method definitions, and higher-level EDO knowledge. ONTOP's structure affords engineers the ability to approach design optimization problems within an established optimization knowledge base, providing a means to quickly identify feasible optimization techniques for a given design optimization problem.

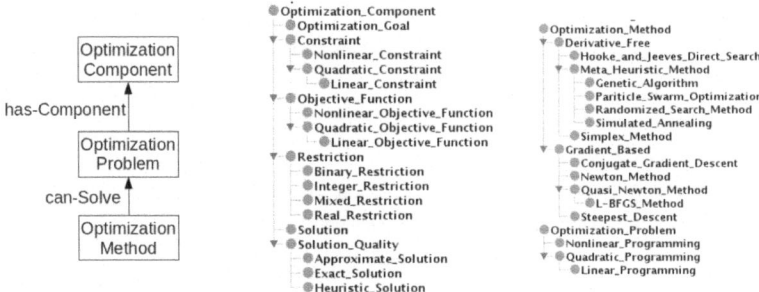

Fig. 1. Main classes of SoPT ontology

4   PIDO Ontology

In this section the Process Integration and Design Optimization ontology is introduced. This ontology aims at formalizing and capturing all the knowledge related to simulation process and design optimization domains. The goal of this ontology is therefore to gather all the necessary information needed to perform a generic simulation task, e.g. virtual test or simulation design optimization. It also provides a formalization of a generic design improvement cycle so that the iterative nature of the design process can be effectively captured. This ontology therefore includes the definition of typical design optimization problems along with a description of the methods and algorithms exploited to solve the considered iterative cycles.

Fig. 2 and Fig. 3 show the fundamental concepts and relationships contained in the PIDO ontology. In most of simulation workflow tools there is the possibility to link to a simulation project one or more simulation workflows representing various simulation tasks. A generic simulation workflow is composed by a sequence of items that are connected each other in order to create the workflow. Depending on the workflow management system adopted, there can be several different items that are put in a user defined sequences so to allow formalization of a specific simulation task. On top of the captured simulation process numerous types of methods can be applied. Also the set of methods available is dependent from the workflow management system used, but some basic methods like the one for performing an optimization process or a design of experiment (DOE) [13] are supported by most of existing systems and have therefore been included in this ontology. For the sake of simplicity and readability only few methods are here reported, but other already exists or can be very easily added as subclass of WorkflowMethod class. An optimization method, for example, is a possible specialization of the more general concept WorkflowMethod, it has constraints and objectives and uses an optimization algorithm in order to solve an optimization problem. (See [5] for more details on the ontology)

However, due to the complexity of the process examined, an iteration of the simulation workflow is computationally expensive and may take hours or even days for the evaluation. In this case surrogate models that mimic the behaviour of the process defined by the simulation workflow turn to be very helpful to find a solution to the optimization problem and are therefore massively used in most real application cases. Surrogate models are built on the base of datasets that are provided by workflow method and obtained by running a number of times the simulation workflow.

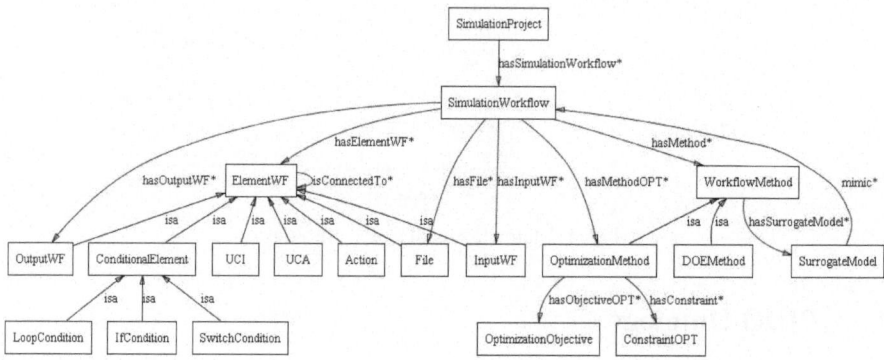

Fig. 2. Main concepts and relationships that formalize a generic simulation workflow in PIDO ontology

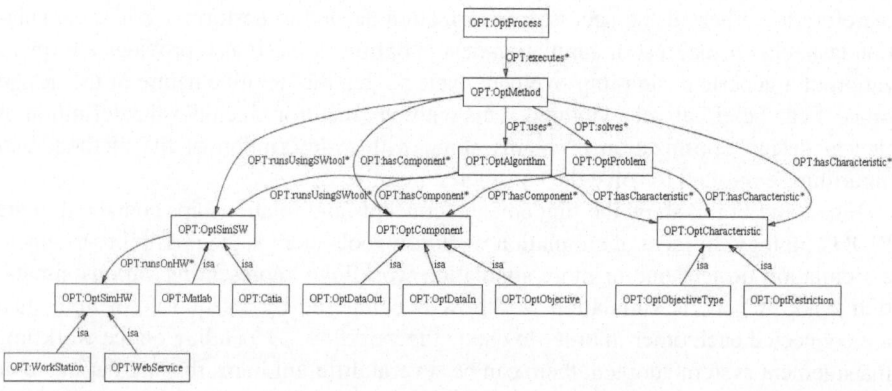

Fig. 3. Main concepts and relationships that formalize the design optimization process in PIDO ontology

The concepts and relationships represented in Fig. 3 are focused on the formalization of a generic design optimization process trying to cover all the entities that occur in an optimization task. As it is shown in the figure an optimization problem is solved by an optimization method by applying one or more optimization algorithms in order to provide the solution. All three entities have some characteristics (that categorize them) and are accompanied by several components (data, objectives, etc.) in order to be performed. The above mentioned workflow problems are implemented by executing some processes that call specific software (SW) tools running on supporting hardware (HW). There is no limit to expanding the problem, method and algorithm entities contained in the ontology, as there are hundreds variations of them. Equally expandable are the SW & HW subclasses that currently focus on the Simulation Workflow applications and are dependent on the product under design/development.

5   Case Study

The PIDO ontology can be used to support the storage and retrieval of the necessary information to execute virtual tests and product design optimizations. These tasks represent the typical simulation processes performed in the PDP of automotive, aerospace and home appliance industries. In this section, an automotive case study is presented where the PIDO ontology have been used to support the execution of a virtual test for a new car door designed by Pininfarina. The virtual design process of a new car door in Pininfarina involves four main simulation tasks: CAD model creation; meshing of the created CAD model; finite element analysis preparation and virtual test execution. These simulation tasks are performed by different tools and are integrated in a seamless way in a simulation workflow that allows automating the execution of this process. The entire simulation process is illustrated in Fig. 4. The objective of the virtual design process here presented is to design a new car door of the NIDO vehicle designed by Pininfarina. In this specific process different versions of hinges have been designed and need to be tested on the virtual prototype of the door. Once the full process is set up the virtual test execution is automated and results delivered for each hinge version. In this case the virtual test consists of verifying the door sag in order to guarantee that the door doesn't fall when opened.

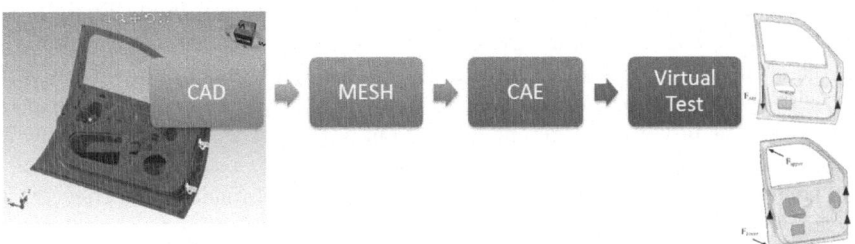

Fig. 4. Virtual design process of a new car door in Pininfarina

This virtual test is captured by the simulation workflow shown in Fig. 5 (created with Noesis Optimus software tool) that is composed of the following elements: input parameters "Config" and "Design Input"; output parameter MaxDisplacement; input file "pininfarina_use_case.dat"; output file "pininfarina_use_case.f06" and an action "NASTRAN" that executes the FEA tool NASTRAN for the stress analysis. All the elements present in this simulation workflow are covered by the concepts present in the above mentioned PIDO ontology. The proposed example has been implemented in iProd in order to validate the PIDO ontology and to proof that this ontology can be easily used in a real application context.

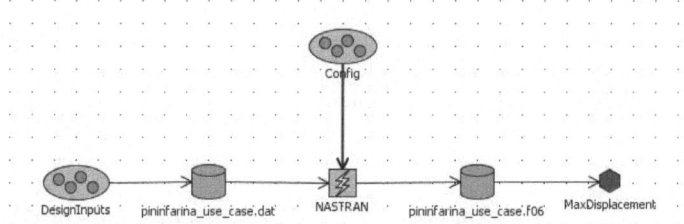

Fig. 5. Simulation workflow that performs the virtual door sag test in Pininfarina case study

The main benefits achieved with this current approach relate to the capability to store and re-use knowledge related to the simulation workflow, to the optimization method used for the solution of the specific problem and of the different elements that lead to a design solution (e.g. constraints, boundary conditions, etc). In this way the design engineer can actually query the knowledge and re-use it for new or similar simulation workflows as well as gather knowledge about the best optimization approaches that have been used in the past for similar problems. This helps the efficient reuse of knowledge by reducing manual steps, by reducing the number of possible mistakes and by avoiding solving two times the same problem. As such, the PIDO ontology constitutes an effective foundation to build semantic workflows where simulation and design improvement knowledge can be captured, re-used and operationalized.

6   Conclusions and Future Works

This paper presented the Process Integration and Design Optimization ontologies developed within the EC 7th Framework joint research project iProd. Firstly a brief introduction on what is an ontology, why develop an ontology and the importance of the role of the PIDO tools in the context of the CAE and virtual prototyping is given. Next an overview of the existing typologies of workflows and workflows management systems is provided. Different existing ontologies for simulation workflow and optimization process have been described highlighting the respective limitations. A PIDO ontology is then introduces and explained in terms of fundamental concepts and objectives. Finally an application case study in the automotive industry implemented in iProd has been used to validate the developed ontology and to proof its usability in a real application context. The proposed ontology is the basis for the future development of a semantic workflow that dynamically creates simulation workflows on the base of the discovered and selected available computing resources without the necessity of the human intervention.

Acknowledgement. The research leading to these results has been supported by the iProd collaborative research project, which has received funding from the European Community's Seventh Framework Programme (FP7/2007-2013) under grant agreement number 257657. The authors are solely responsible for its content. It does not represent the opinion of the European Community and the Community is not responsible for any use that might be made of the information contained therein.

References

1. Gruber, T.R.: A Translation Approach to Portable Ontology Specifications. Knowledge Acquisition 5(2), 199–220 (1993)
2. Gruber, T.: Toward Principles for the Design of Ontologies Used for Knowledge Sharing. International Journal Human-Computer Studies 43(5-6) (1995)
3. Navigli, R., Velardi, P.: Learning Domain Ontologies from Document Warehouses and Dedicated Web Sites. Computational Linguistics (MIT Press) 30(2) (2004)
4. Berners-Lee, T., Hendler, J., Lassila, O.: The Semantic Web. Scientific American Magazine (May 17, 2001)
5. http://www.iprod-project.eu/
6. Noy, N.F., McGuinness, D.L.: Ontology Development 101: A Guide to Creating Your First Ontology. Stanford Knowledge Systems Laboratory Technical Report KSL-01-05 and Stanford Medical Informatics Technical Report SMI-2001-0880 (March 2001)
7. Laplante, P.A.: Comprehensive dictionary of electrical engineering, 2nd edn. CRC Press (2005)
8. Meguid, S.A.: Integrated computer-aided design of mechanical systems. Springer (1987)
9. Matthews, C.: Aeronautical engineer's data book, 2nd edn. Butterworth-Heinemann (2005)
10. http://www.crescendo-fp7.eu/
11. Wenzel, H., Gondhalekar, A., Balachandran, L., Guenov, M., Nunez, M.: Automated generation of Isight-Models through a neutral workflow description. In: 2011 SIMULIA Customer Conference, Barcelona, May 17-19 (2011)
12. Gondhalekar, A.C., Guenov, M.D., Wenzel, H., Balachandran, L.K., Nunez, M.: Neutral Description and Exchange of Design Computational Workflows. In: 18th International Conference on Engineering Design (ICED 2011), Technical University of Denmark, August 15-18 (2011)
13. http://en.wikipedia.org/wiki/Design_of_experiments
14. http://protegewiki.stanford.edu/wiki/Workflow_ontology
15. Sebastian, A., Noy, N.F., Tudorache, T., Musen, M.A.: 16th International Conference on Knowledge Engineering and Knowledge Management (EKAW 2008), Catania, Italy. Springer (published in 2008)
16. Sebastian, A., Tudorache, T., Noy, N.F., Musen, M.A.: 4th International Workshop on Semantic Web Enabled Software Engineering (SWESE) at ISWC 2008, Karlsruhe, Germany (published in 2008)
17. Witherell, P., Krishnamurty, S., Grosse, I.R.: Ontologies for Supporting Engineering Design Optimization, J. Comput. Inf. Sci. Eng. 7 (2007)
18. http://www.scribd.com/doc/59675031/19/Review-of-ONTOP
19. http://en.wikipedia.org/wiki/Workflow
20. Russell, N., ter Hofstede, A.H.M., van der Aalst, W.M.P., Mulyar, N.: Workflow Control-Flow Patterns: A Revised View. BPM Center Report BPM-06-22, BPMcenter.org (2006)

Modelling a Sustainable Cooperative Healthcare: An Interoperability-Driven Approach

Ovidiu Noran[1] and Hervé Panetto[2,3]

[1] School of ICT, Griffith University, Australia
[2] CNRS, CRAN UMR 7039, France
[3] University of Lorraine, CRAN UMR 7039, France
o.noran@griffith.edu.au, herve.panetto@univ-lorraine.fr

Abstract. Modern healthcare is confronted with serious issues that are threatening its viability and sustainability. Increasing costs and complexity, global population ageing and pandemics are major culprits of the healthcare quandary. In this context, effective interoperability of the participants in the healthcare effort becomes paramount. However, this is also a major challenge as unfortunately, healthcare institutions typically feature strong hierarchy and heterogeneity. As the pressure on healthcare resources and management cost is constantly increasing, governments can no longer rely on outdated 'silo' paradigms for managing population wellbeing. New cooperative and integrated models and procedures taking into account all essential cooperation aspects, elements, participants and their life cycle are necessary to drive cooperative healthcare sustainability. Based on previous research and applications, this paper argues that the necessary artefacts can be built using a life cycle-based, holistic paradigm enabled by advances in Interoperability, Enterprise Architecture and Collaborative Networks research and practice. The proposed modelling approach aims to provide a solid base for sustainable solutions to long and short-term challenges to population health and well-being.

Keywords: Healthcare, Sustainability, Interoperability, Enterprise Architecture, Collaborative Networks.

1 Introduction

Worldwide, healthcare is under escalating pressure from population ageing, drug-resistant pandemics, increasing complexity and rising costs. In this context, silo-type legacy governance models have lost relevance as interoperability and cooperation are *sine qua non* requirements for survival and progress in a global environment.

Unfortunately, there are significant challenges in managing the internal and external collaboration of the typically heterogeneous set of participants involved in the healthcare endeavour. New integrated models, methods and tools are required in order to enable proper inter-professional and inter-organisational cooperation, so as to meet these serious long and short term healthcare challenges.

In addition, sustainability (seen in manufacturing as the creation of products using processes that minimize environmental impact, conserve energy and natural

Y.T. Demey and H. Panetto (Eds.): OTM 2013 Workshops, LNCS 8186, pp. 238–249, 2013.

resources, are safe for employees, communities and consumers while also being economically sound [1]) can be extrapolated to the healthcare domain in order to assess its capacity to *endure* in an ever-changing, increasingly complex environment.

Previous research has investigated specific interoperability aspects [2, 3] and the role of Collaborative Networks (CN) [4] and Enterprise Architecture (EA) [5] concepts and methodologies in supporting generic collaboration efforts between heterogeneous organisations [6, 7]. This paper aims to build on the previous results by focusing on the healthcare area in a multifaceted and integrated manner.

2   Challenges in Healthcare Management Collaboration

Healthcare has made significant advances in the last century, such as the development of vaccines, eradication of serious diseases and large reductions in communicable disease epidemics and chronic diseases [8, 9]. While solving some very important problems, some of these advances have unfortunately also contributed to a new set of challenges faced by the public and private healthcare infrastructure and organisations. For example, population growth and ageing triggered by increased longevity [9] reflects mankind progress and provides benefits [10] but also brings significant social security and healthcare challenges [11]. Another major concern are the increasingly complex health incidents (e.g. pandemics) owing to new strains of diseases [12], climate change [13] and population displacements fuelled by regional conflicts.

Whereas healthcare as a system has become somewhat more organised, it has also become more expensive, complex and difficult to manage. The intricate nature of the organisations involved presents significant impediments to technology transfer and diffusion [14] that includes interactional user resistance to the new systems [15]. Research in the field confirms however that the main barriers to healthcare cooperation are of semantic, pragmatic and organisational nature [16-19]. Thus, collaboration between healthcare effort participants does not automatically occur. It must be "constructed, learned, and once established, protected" [16].

The divergent perceptions and expectations of the parties involved [18], owing to a traditionally strong hierarchy and marked difference in status between partners [19], can be best dealt with by the higher ranking participants. They can promote collaboration and trust by employing a participatory and inclusive approach [20] which will also build a beneficial sense of security [21].

Inter-professional and inter-organisational collaborative healthcare is encouraged in various medical and emergency response reports, conferences and journals (e.g. [22-26]) as well as in international projects. For example, the BRAID project [27] advocates the necessity for *collaborative healthcare ecosystems* [28] supported by integrated assistive services and infrastructure [26]. Unfortunately however, the extent of *actual* cooperation in healthcare is still limited as efficient long-term healthcare collaboration requires that organisational cultures, processes and resources of the participants acquire suitable preparedness [22, 29, 30], with ethics playing a prominent role [31, 32]. This requires access to a plethora of multidisciplinary information and knowledge; as such, participatory analysis and design [33] represent important collaborative healthcare enablers that help integrate all necessary scientific, administrative, social and political aspects into a whole-system approach [23, 29, 34].

In a typical health incident scenario, often there is a tendency of the higher ranking and more powerful organisation(s) to override or exclude some participants, adopting a 'central command' approach rather than a cooperative one [35]. This is not desirable as successful disaster management relies on a wide range of community, economic, social-psychological, and political resources.

3   Interoperability for Sustainable Cooperative Healthcare

The concept of interoperability is often used as a measure of cooperation capability assigned to systems [36] and to contrast mere information exchange between those systems, including in the healthcare domain [37, 38]; inter- and intra-organisational interoperability enable companies healthcare effort participants to cope with and sustain in the modern networked, dynamic and challenging environment [39]. Healthcare systems interoperability analysis must include some important aspects, such as extent, approach and aspects covered. For example, as shown in previous research [2, 7], an interoperability degree close to total integration would imply a loss of autonomy, which is undesirable (e.g. in crisis situations where response teams may get isolated). On the other extreme, minimal interoperability (compatibility) of the healthcare or health crisis management effort participants is unsuitable and can only serve as a good starting point. The *desirable* degree of interoperability lies between these depending on the specific healthcare or health crisis management endeavour (**Fig. 1** right). Importantly, a*gile* organisations are able to maintain a high degree of interoperability while adapting to changes in the environment (see **Fig. 1** left).

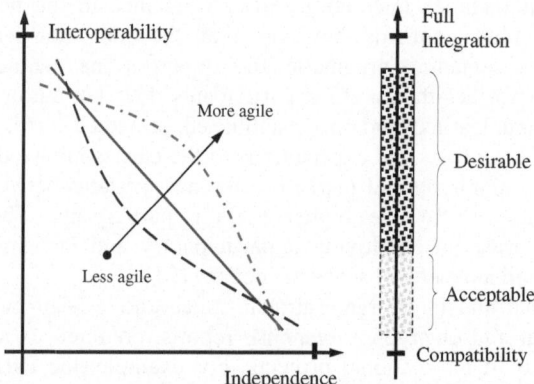

Fig. 1. Interoperability issues and approach in disaster management (based on [2, 7])

The 'full integration' and 'federalisation' interoperability options specified in ISO14258 [40] do not appear to achieve the desired results in healthcare due to pronounced organisational heterogeneity and the impracticality to negotiate in the limited time available during a disaster event. The unified approach [ibid.] appears to be more suitable to this domain as it assumes that ontology is negotiated in advance so as to achieve semantic interoperability; notwithstanding advances in negotiations and ontology research [41, 42], in our opinion the most efficient method to achieve unification is for the organisations to 'spend time together' in order to agree on the meanings associated with the concepts used to exchange knowledge.

Interoperability aspects are provided by various standards [40] and frameworks (e.g. European Interoperability Framework (EIF)[43], IDEAS project [44], ATHENA Interoperability Framework (AIF)[45] and the INTEROP Network of Excellence (NoE) Interoperability Framework [46]). All these frameworks have overlapping and complementary areas; in addition, it is important that *combinations of aspects* are also considered. Therefore, a combined model has been constructed and applied for identifying the most relevant aspects for healthcare interoperability (see **Fig. 2**).

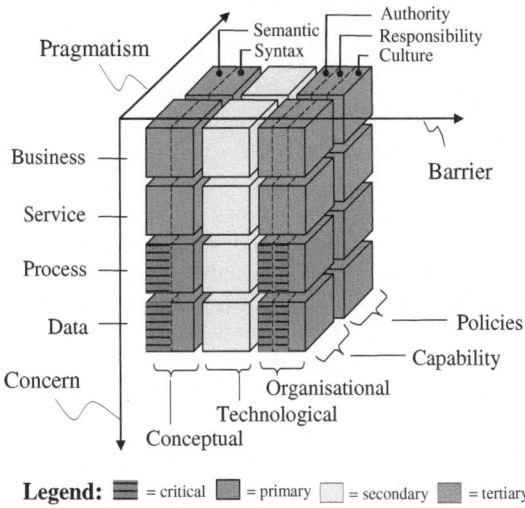

Fig. 2. An interpretation of the INTEROP NoE Interoperability Framework [46] enriched with concepts from ISO14258, EIF, IDEAS, ATHENA AIF, [2] and [7]

The pragmatic interoperability aspect [3, 47] relates to the *willingness* of the participants to interoperate; the two main components, capability and policies (see **Fig. 2**) suggest that the healthcare organisations need to gain appropriate cooperation *preparedness* that must be endorsed and supported by the executive.

The *semantic* aspect of the data and process areas has a typically high priority: in a disaster event, the capability to extract and interpret data from heterogeneous sources is essential for situational awareness preventing life-threatening situations. Therefore, prior agreements on data format and especially on data *meaning* are essential. This is also applicable to long term collaborative healthcare problems as illustrated by current Electronic Health Records (EHR) semantic interoperability problems [48, 49].

The organisational interoperability aspect is an essential aspect in healthcare, where participants exhibit significant structure diversity; thus, the responsibility and authority interoperability aspects [43, 46] are another critical area identified in **Fig. 2**. The roles and hierarchy in long and short term healthcare cooperative structures must be commonly understood and *accepted* if appropriate synergy and focus is to be achieved. The third organisational interoperability component, i.e. cultural [3], is notoriously hard to tackle. Regular immersion of the participant organisations in each other's cultures ('co-habitation') may assist in this direction.

4   Collaborative Networks for Sustainable Semantic, Pragmatic and Organisational Interoperability

The concept of networks in disaster management and recovery has been advocated, studied and applied to some extent for a number of years with mixed results (e.g. [35, 50, 51]). Unfortunately, these attempts appear to have two main shortcomings. Firstly, they use untested models focusing on specific aspects, rather than employing a proven set of integrated models in a whole-system approach. Secondly, they seem to pay less attention to the life cycle aspect of the participant organisations, networks and other relevant entities, including the disaster event/s.

In researching the healthcare-specific interoperability issues, it has been observed that the challenges identified describe a situation similar to that of commercial enterprises who, owing to a global business environment, find themselves compelled to tackle projects requiring resources beyond their own. The usual solution to this problem is to set up (or join) so-called 'Collaborative Networks' (CNs) that act as breeding environments for Virtual Organisations (VOs) who are promptly created in order to bid for and complete projects requiring combined resources and know-how. The view of CNs as commitment-based social systems that absorb uncertainty and reduce complexity [52] supports their use in the typically elaborate long and short term healthcare projects.

The CNs and VOs set up for the healthcare domain would have specific features. Thus, the competitive motivations of commercial CN participants guiding their decisions to create / join / remain / leave the network would transform into the need to cope with increasingly complex health challenges and healthcare systems. Here, a 'Health Management' CN (HMCN) would create 'Health Management' VOs (HMVOs) for long term projects (e.g. as described in [53]), or task forces (HMTFs) for shorter term and more intense events (e.g. pandemics). The use of reference models, customary in commercial CNs, may be limited here due to diversity [54].

For a HMCN to function, scientific, faith and community representatives and all relevant non-governmental and volunteer organisations must also be included in the setup and operation of the HMCN, in addition to the typical participants such as hospitals, allied healthcare [55], fire and rescue services, etc.

Adopting a CN approach for health disaster management provides benefits going beyond mere technical and syntactic-type interoperability. Thus, the participants in a HMCN have the time and suitable environment to overcome the previously described semantic, pragmatic and organisational interoperability barriers and achieve the required preparedness. This is essential in the prompt and successful setup of HMTFs for disasters and in the creation and operation of continuing HMVOs for long term healthcare challenges such as population ageing.

5   The Enterprise Architecture Role in a Holistic and Integrated Approach towards Sustainable Interoperability

Healthcare collaboration requirements are multi-faceted and inherently linked to the life cycle phase(s) of the organisations; it is therefore essential that the proposed networked collaboration analysis is performed in an aspect-integrated manner and in a life cycle context so that the interoperability is achieved, but in a *sustainable* manner.

It is hereby argued that an optimal way to integrate the life cycle aspect in a sustainable collaborative healthcare scenario is by using an EA perspective.

EA is seen in this context as a holistic change management paradigm that bridges management and engineering best-practice, providing the "[…] key requirements, principles and models that describe the enterprise's future state. […] EA comprises people, processes, information and technology of the enterprise, and their relationships to one another and to the external environment" [5]. This EA definition reinforces the view of CNs as social systems composed of commitments [52] and healthcare as socio-technical systems with voluntaristic people [56] in a complex organisational, political and behavioural context [15, 57, 58]. As such, EA is capable of providing a framework integrating all necessary aspects in a life cycle-based set of models ensuring the consistency and sustainability of complex projects.

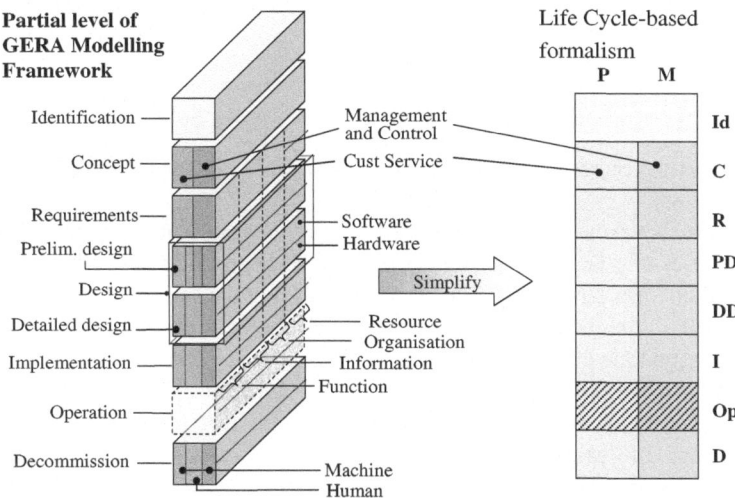

Fig. 3. Using Enterprise Architecture Modelling Framework elements

In this example, we have selected the modelling framework (MF) provided by 'GERAM' (Generalised Enterprise Reference Architecture and Methodology), described in ISO 15704:2005 [59]. This MF provides a large set of aspects, importantly including life cycle, management, organisation and human. Aspect-based subsets of the GERA MF can be turned into life cycle-based constructs used to produce business models requiring a life cycle-based analysis. For example, aspects previously identified as significant in improving cooperation in disaster management (e.g. function, information, resources, organisation) but also additional supporting viewpoints like management vs. operations, automation boundary / human extent, etc) can be represented as shown in **Fig. 3**, left. Aspects can also be separated to promote clarity; for example, the 2-dimensional structure shown in **Fig. 3** right is used to focus on the product/service and management viewpoints in a life cycle context.

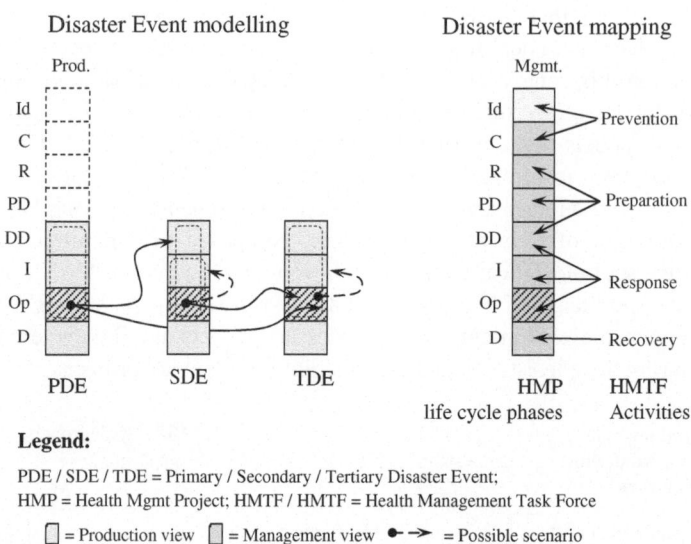

Fig. 4. Disaster event mapping and modelling using a life cycle-based modelling construct

Figure 4 right shows the use of GERA's MF life cycle viewpoint to define and map the life cycle phases of a health management project (HMP) dealing with a health incident on typical health disaster management activities [60]. For the sake of clarity, **Fig. 4** does not consider the time dimension (life *history*); this can be represented orthogonally to illustrate the actual life cycle sequence (i.e, the life cycle *stages*).

The left hand side of **Fig. 4** shows the use of the above-described formalism to represent a disaster event, focusing only on the relevant life cycle phases and relations to other events' life cycles. Thus, **Fig. 4** left shows how a Primary Disaster Event (PDE) can trigger or influence secondary/tertiary etc events (SDE, TDE). For example, an earthquake event (PDE) can trigger a tsunami (SDE) that can in turn trigger a partial nuclear meltdown or a pandemic (TDE). This modelling approach can also show PDEs influencing TDEs directly and 'chain reaction'-type events (arrows from Operation to Implementation within same entity).

6   Life Cycle Integrated Modelling of Collaborative Healthcare Interoperability Requirements

Successful integration modelling of collaborative healthcare depends on an inclusive approach involving all the network participants [34]. The proposed modelling method supports this audience variety with graphical models and complexity management. For example, **Fig. 5** uses the modelling construct shown in **Fig. 3** right to depict data interoperability requirements of HMCN and HMTF / HMVO creation and operation.

The arrows in **Fig. 5** show data-specific influences and contributions requiring interoperability among the entities involved in the long and short term healthcare endeavour. Thus, healthcare organisations HO (e.g. hospitals), allied health professionals (AHP) and scientific, faith, etc and other communities representatives (CSFR) all contribute to the design and operation of a HMCN in its various life cycle phases and thus require proper data interoperability, as detailed in the figure.

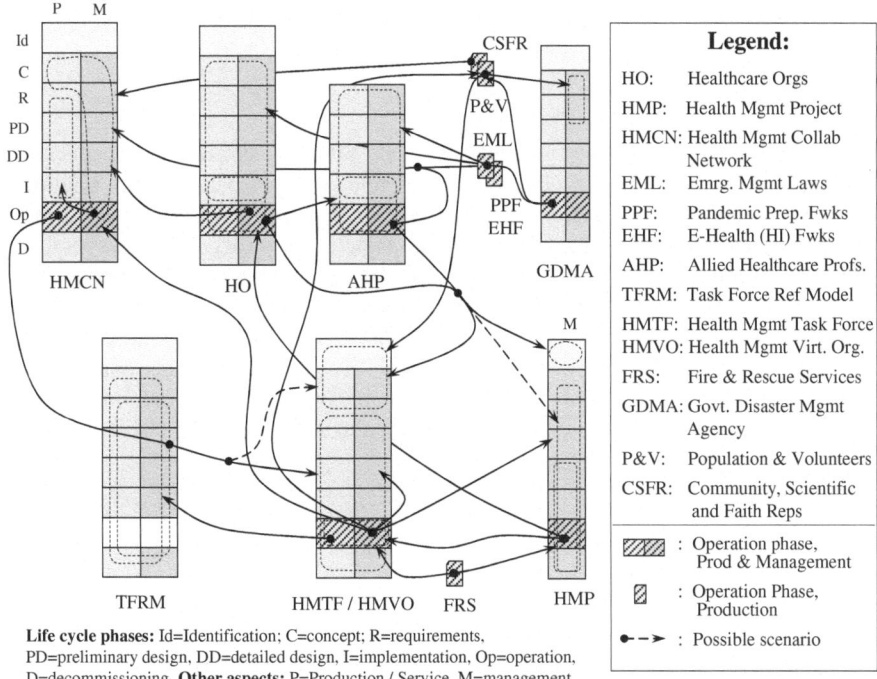

Fig. 5. Data interoperability requirements in a possible HMCN and HMVO / HMTF scenario

These requirements may also extend directly to the design and operation of the HMTFs / HMVOs created by the HMCN, and to the health management projects (HMPs) created by the HTMF/ HMVOs to deal with long and short term healthcare incidents and challenges. Influences and contributions requiring interoperability also come from 'non-physical' artefacts such as emergency management laws (EML), pandemic preparedness (PPF), or e-health strategies / frameworks (EHF) [61, 62]. Properly aggregated and understandable information *must* be provided by HTMFs / HMVOs to population and volunteers (P&V). This is paramount as in an emergency it will directly decide the amount of lost property and casualties; past experience has shown that P&V must receive but also *understand, believes and act on* HMTF warnings and directives. The arrow from HMTF / HMVO's Management side of the Operation life cycle phase to some of its upper phases represents a 'limited agility' requirement allowing the HMTF to remain interoperable in the face of changing conditions on the ground typical to disaster-type events. However, any major HMTF / HMVO interoperability reconfiguration (e.g. involving Requirements or Architectural Design life cycles) must involve the HMCN participants' and other entities' input.

Note that high-level models such as depicted in **Fig.5** do not aim to provide all the details necessary for actual implementation. Their purpose is rather to provide a 'checklist' of the interoperability requirements of the specific collaborative healthcare endeavour and highlight relevant interactions, all in a life cycle context. Such models can represent various autonomy and agility *scenarios* for the collaborative healthcare participants. Once stakeholder consensus on present and future states has been achieved, these models can be evolved into design and implementation blueprints.

7   Conclusions

Politics, hierarchy, diverging perceptions, lack of trust, dissimilar organisational structures and cultures and limited life cycle perspective of the healthcare participants' roles and interactions all inhibit collaboration. This paper has proposed a multidisciplinary solution that draws upon a rich repository of Interoperability, Enterprise Architecture and Collaborative Networks research and practice results.

The paper makes a theoretical contribution by highlighting the synergy between several research areas to advance collaborative healthcare and a practical contribution by providing an example of how interoperability aspects can be analysed and improved using CN concepts from an EA perspective in order to model a collaborative healthcare solution to the current health and well-being challenges.

References

1. International Trade Administration. How does Commerce define Sustainable Manufacturing? (2010),
   http://www.trade.gov/competitiveness/how_doc_defines_SM.asp
2. Panetto, H.: Towards a classification framework for interoperability of enterprise applications. Int. J. of Comp. Integrated Manufacturing 20, 727–740 (2007)
3. Whitman, L., Panetto, H.: The Missing Link: Culture and Language Barriers to Interoperability. Annual Reviews in Control 30(2), 233–241 (2006)
4. Camarinha-Matos, L., Afsarmanesh, H.: Collaborative Networks: A new scientific discipline. Journal of Intelligent Manufacturing 16, 439–452 (2005)
5. Gartner Research. IT Glossary 2012 (2012),
   http://www.gartner.com/technology/it-glossary/
   enterprise-architecture.jsp
6. Noran, O.: Towards a Collaborative Network Paradigm for Emergency Services. In: Camarinha-Matos, L.M., Pereira-Klen, A., Afsarmanesh, H. (eds.) PRO-VE 2011. IFIP AICT, vol. 362, pp. 477–485. Springer, Heidelberg (2011)
7. Noran, O., Bernus, P.: Effective Disaster Management: An Interoperability Perspective. In: Meersman, R., Dillon, T., Herrero, P. (eds.) OTM-WS 2011. LNCS, vol. 7046, pp. 112–121. Springer, Heidelberg (2011)
8. Fielding, J.E.: Public Health in the Twentieth Century: Advances and Challenges. Annual Reviews in Public Health 20, xiii-xxx (1999)
9. World Health Organization. The world health report 1998—life in the 21st century: a vision for all (1998),
   http://www.who.int/whr/1998/en/whr98_en.pdf (cited April 2013)
10. Healy, J.: The Benefits of an Ageing Population - Discussion Paper 63. The Australia Institute (2004),
    http://www.tai.org.au/documents/dp_fulltext/DP63.pdf
    (cited April 2013)

11. International Labour Organisation. Ageing societies: The benefits, and the costs, of living longer (2009),
    http://www.ilo.org/global/WCM_041965/lang-en/index.htm (2013)
12. Kilbourne, E.D.: Influenza Pandemics of the 20th Century. Emerg. Inf. Dis. 12(1) (2006)
13. Donohoe, M.: Causes and health consequences of environmental degradation and social injustice. Social Science and Medicine 56(3), 573–587 (2003)
14. Southon, F.C., Sauer, C., Grant, C.N.: Information technology in complex health services: organizational impediments to successful technology transfer and diffusion. J. Am. Med. Inform. Assoc. 4(2), 112–124 (1997)
15. Markus, M.L.: Power, politics & MIS implementation. Comm. ACM 26, 430–444 (1983)
16. Wilson, K., et al.: Nurse Practitioners' Experience of Working Collaboratively with General Practitioners and Allied Health Professionals in NSW, Australia. Australian Journal of Advanced Nursing 23(2), 22–27 (2005)
17. Braude, R.M.: People and Organizational Issues in Health Informatics. J. Am. Med. Inform. Assoc. 4(2), 150–151 (1997)
18. Krogstad, U., Hofoss, D., Hjortdal, P.: Doctor and nurse perception of interprofessional co-operation in hospitals. Int. J. for Quality Health Care 16(6), 491–497 (2004)
19. Ramanujam, R., Rousseau, D.M.: The Challenges Are Organizational, Not Just Clinical. Journal of Organizational Behavior 27(7), 811–827 (2006)
20. Baker, D., Day, R., Salas, E.: Teamwork as an essential component of high reliability organizations. Health Services Research 41(4), 1577–1598 (2006)
21. Nembhard, I.M., Edmondson, A.C.: Making It Safe: The Effects of Leader Inclusiveness and Professional Status on Psychological Safety and Improvement Efforts in Health Care Teams. Journal of Organizational Behavior 27(7), 941–966 (2006)
22. Kapucu, N., Arslan, T., Demiroz, F.: Collaborative emergency management and national emergency management network. Disaster Prev. and Management 19(4), 452–468 (2010)
23. Utah Department of Health. Governor's Task Force for Pandemic Influenza Preparedness - Final report to Governor (2007),
    http://pandemicflu.utah.gov/docs/
    PandInfluTaskforceFinalReport.pdf (cited April 2013)
24. Waugh, W.L., Streib, G.: Collaboration and Leadership for Effective Emergency Management. Public Administration Review 66(s1), 131–140 (2006)
25. Hughes, R.G.: Chapter 33: Professional Communication and Team Collaboration. In: Patient Safety and Quality: An Evidence-Based Handbook for Nurses, Agency for Healthcare Research and Quality, Rockville (2008)
26. Sansoni, J., et al.: An Assessment Framework for Aged Care (April 2012), Available from: Centre for Health Service Development, University of Woolongong (cited April 2013)
27. BRAID. Bridging Research in Ageing and ICT Development - Consolidated Vision of ICT and Ageing (2011),
    http://auseaccess.cis.utas.edu.au/sites/default/
    files/D4.2Final.pdf (2013)
28. Holzman, T.G.: Computer-human interface solutions for emergency medical care. Interactions 6(3), 13–24 (1999)
29. World Health Organisation. Pandemic Influenza preparedness Framework (2011),
    http://whqlibdoc.who.int/publications/2011/
    9789241503082_eng.pdf (2013)
30. U.S. Dept of Health and Human Services. HHS Pandemic Influenza Plan (2005),
    http://www.flu.gov/planning-preparedness/
    federal/hhspandemicinfluenzaplan.pdf (2013)

31. Thompson, A.K., et al.: Pandemic influenza preparedness: an ethical framework to guide decision-making. BMC Medical Ethics 7(12) (2006)
32. NZ Ethics Advisory Committee. Ethical Values for Planning for and Responding to a Pandemic in New Zealand (2006),
    http://neac.health.govt.nz/sites/neac.health.govt.nz/pandemic-planning-andresponse.pdf (2013)
33. Kristensen, M., Kyng, M., Palen, L.: Participatory Design in Emergency Medical Service: Designing for Future Practice. In: CHI 2006, Montréal, Québec / Canada (2006)
34. Moghadas, S.M., et al.: Managing public health crises: the role of models in pandemic preparedness. Influenza Other Respi Viruses 3(2), 75–79 (2008)
35. Waugh, W.L.: Coordination or Control: Organizational Design and the Emergency Management Function. Int J. of Disaster Prevention and Management 2(4), 17–31 (1993)
36. DoD Architecture Framework Working Group. DoD Arch Fwk Ver 1.0 (2004) (cited 2007)
37. Ray, P., Vargas, B.: Interoperability of hospital IS. In: Proc. of the 5th Int. Workshop on Enterprise Networking and Computing in Healthcare Industry, Santa Monica, CA (2003)
38. Fridsma, D.: Interoperability vs Health Information Exchange: Setting the Record Straight (2013),
    http://www.healthit.gov/buzz-blog/meaningful-use/interoperability-health-information-exchange-setting-record-straight/ (cited May 2013)
39. Molina, A., et al.: Enterprise Integration and Networking: Challenges and Trends. Studies in Informatics and Control 16(4) (2007)
40. ISO, ISO14258 Industrial Automation Sys Concepts and Rules for Enterprise Models (2005)
41. Farquhar, A., et al.: Collaborative Ontology Construction for Information Integration. Technical Report KSL-95-63, Stanford University: Knowledge Systems Laboratory (1995)
42. Pinto, H., Prez, A., Martins, J.: Some Issues on Ontology Integration In: Proceedings of IJCAI 1999, Stockholm, Sweden (1999)
43. EIF, European interoperability framework for pan-European eGovernment services. Luxembourg: Interoperable Delivery of European eGovernment Services to public Administrations, Businesses and Citizens (IDABC) (2004)
44. IDEAS,Project Deliverables (WP1-WP7) Public repts (2003),
    http://www.ideas-roadmap.net (2011)
45. ATHENA State of the art of Enterprise Modelling Techniques and Technologies to Support Enterprise Interoperability. Deliv D.A1.1.1 (2004),
    http://www.athena-ip.org (cited 2012)
46. Chen, D.: Practices, principles and patterns for interop. INTEROP-NOE, Interoperability Research for Networked Enterprises Network of Excellence, n° IST 508-011 (2005)
47. Tsagkani, C.: Inter-Organizational Collaboration on the Process Layer. In: Proc. of the IFIP/ACM SIGAPP INTEROP-ESA Conference, Geneva, Switzerland (2005)
48. Beale, T., Heard, S.: An Ontology-based Model of Clinical Information. S. Stud. Health Technol. Inform. 129 (pt.1), 760–764 (2007)
49. Rector, A., Qamar, R., Marley, T.: Binding Ontologies & Coding systems to Electronic Health Records and Messages. Applied Ontology 4(1) (2009)
50. Australian Psychological Society. Disaster Response Network (DRN) (2013),
    http://www.psychology.org.au/medicare/drn/ (cited 2013)

51. Cooper, S., et al.: Collaborative practices in unscheduled emergency care: role and impact of the emergency care practitioner – qualitative, quantitative and summative fndings. Emergency Medicine Journal (24), 625–633 (2007)
52. Neumann, D., de Santa-Eulalia, L.A., Zahn, E.: Towards a Theory of Collaborative Systems. In: Camarinha-Matos, L.M., Pereira-Klen, A., Afsarmanesh, H. (eds.) PRO-VE 2011. IFIP AICT, vol. 362, pp. 306–313. Springer, Heidelberg (2011)
53. Noran, O.: Collaborative networks in the tertiary education industry sector: a case study. International Journal of Computer Integrated Manufacturing 1-2, 29–40 (2013)
54. Tierney, K., Quarantelli, E.L.: Needed Innovation in the Delivery of Emergency Medical Services in Disasters: Present and Future. Disaster Management 2(2), 70–76 (1989)
55. Queensland Health. Allied health career structure (2012),
    http://www.health.qld.gov.au/allied/career-structure.asp
    (cited 2013)
56. McGregor, D.: The Human Side of Enterprise. McGraw-Hill, New York (1960)
57. Keen, P.G.W., Scott Morton, M.: Decision Support Systems: An Organisational Perspective. Addison-Wesley, Reading (1978)
58. Iivari, J.: A Paradigmatic Analysis of Contemporary Schools of IS Development. Eur. J. Information Systems 1(4), 249–272 (1991)
59. ISO/IEC, Annex C: GERAM, in ISO/IS 15704:2000/Amd1:2005: Industrial automation systems - Requirements for enterprise-reference architectures and methodologies (2005)
60. Australian Government. Attorney's General's Office - Emergency Management in Australia (2011), http://www.ema.gov.au/
61. Council of Australian Governments. National E-health Strategy (2008),
    http://www.ahmac.gov.au/cms_documents/
    national%20e-health%20strategy.pdf (cited April 2013)
62. eHealth Task Force Report - European Commission. Redesigning health in Europe for 2020 (2012),
    http://www.president.ee/images/stories/pdf/
    ehtf-report2012.pdf (cited May 2013)

Sustainability and Interoperability:
Two Facets of the Same *Gold Medal*

Michele Dassisti[1], Ricardo Jardim-Goncalves[2], Arturo Molina[3], Ovidiu Noran[4],
Hervé Panetto[5,6], and Milan M. Zdravković[7]

[1] DIMEG, Politecnico di Bari, Italy
[2] FCT, UNINOVA, Portugal
[3] Tecnológico de Monterrey, Mexico
[4] School of ICT, Griffith University, Australia
[5] University of Lorraine, CRAN UMR 7039, France
[6] CNRS, CRAN UMR 7039, France
[7] LIPS, Faculty of Mechanical Engineering, University of Niš, Serbia
m.dassisti@poliba.it, rg@uninova.pt, armolina@itesm.mx,
o.noran@griffith.edu.au, herve.panetto@univ-lorraine.fr,
milan.zdravkovic@masfak.ni.ac.rs

Abstract. 'To sustain is to endure' - that is, to be able to survive and continue to function in the face of significant changes. The commonly accepted concept of 'sustainability' currently encompasses three main pillars: environmental, social/ethical and economic. In a metaphor of survival, they can be seen as water, food and air; one needs all three, only with varying degrees of urgency. In today's globally networked environment, it is becoming obvious that one cannot achieve environmental, social or economic sustainability of any artefact (be it physical or virtual, e.g. enterprise, project, information system, policy, etc) without achieving ubiquitous ability of the artefact and its creators and users to exchange and understand shared information and if necessary perform processes on behalf of each other - capabilities that are usually defined as 'interoperability'. Thus, sustainability relies on interoperability, while, conversely, interoperability as an ongoing concern relies for its existence on all three main pillars of sustainability. This paper aims to test the hypothesis that interoperability and sustainability are two inseparable and inherently linked aspects of any universe of discourse. To achieve this, it applies the dualistic sustainability / interoperability viewpoint to a variety of areas (manufacturing, healthcare, information and communication technology and standardisation), analyses the results and synthesizes conclusions and guidelines for future work.

Keywords: Sustainability, Interoperability, Manufacturing, Information and Communication Technology, Health Informatics, Standardisation.

1 Introduction

History has shown that the continued existence of businesses depends not only on their economic sustainability but also on their impact on the natural environment and the way they treat their workers. This basic truth was emphasized by Elkington's [1]

Y.T. Demey and H. Panetto (Eds.): OTM 2013 Workshops, LNCS 8186, pp. 250–261, 2013.

Triple Bottom Line (TBL) approach to business sustainability: one must achieve not only economic bottom-line performance but also environmental and social accomplishment. In Blackburn's [2] vision, we can compare economic sustainability to air and environmental and social sustainability to water and food: the first is more urgent but not more important than the others - hence, any successful enterprise must take a whole-system approach to *sustainable development* [3]. In today's globally networked environment, one cannot achieve environmental, social / ethical or economic sustainability of any artefact (be it physical or virtual, e.g. enterprise, project, information system (IS), policy, etc) without achieving ubiquitous ability of the artefact and its creators and users to exchange and *understand* shared information and if necessary perform processes on behalf of each other – in other words, *interoperate*. Thus, sustainability relies on interoperability, while, conversely, interoperability as an ongoing concern relies on all three main pillars of sustainability.

This paper aims to test the hypothesis that interoperability and sustainability are two inseparable, balanced and inherently linked aspects of any universe of discourse (see **Fig. 1**) by applying the proposed dualistic viewpoint to a variety of areas, analysing the results and synthesizing conclusions and guidelines for future work.

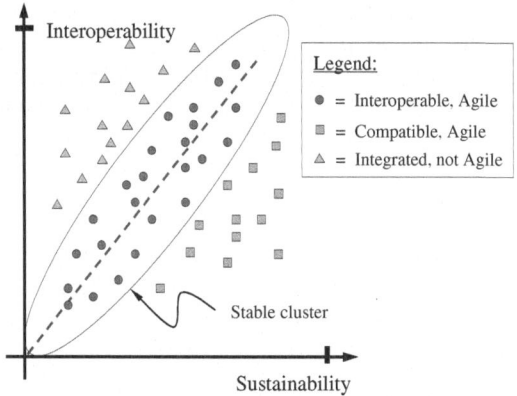

Fig. 1. The Sustainability – Interoperability continuum

2   Sustainability and Interoperability

Interoperability is typically defined as the ability of systems or components to exchange and use information [4]. ISO 16100 [5] defines manufacturing software interoperability as "the ability to share and exchange information using common syntax and semantics to meet an application-specific functional relationship [..]". Thus, generally speaking, interoperability is the ability to work together effectively and to exchange information in a useful and meaningful way [6].

While the term 'sustainability' is nowadays encompassing ecological, economical and ethical concerns, the focus in on the results, rather than on the means to achieve them. Thus, the main question is: *Can one improve the sustainability of a given system by enhancing its capability to interoperate with its environment?* The difference between integration and interoperability has been explained in ISO 14258 [7], who describes three ways in which models could be related: (1) integration, with a standard or pivotal format to represent these models; (2) unification, with a common meta-level structure for semantic equivalence between these models; and (3) federation, when each model exists *per se*, with the mapping between concepts done at an ontology level to formalise interoperability semantics.

Integration is generally considered to involve a degree of functional dependence and hence less flexibility. Integration also deals with organisational issues, albeit in a less formal manner owing to the human factor. Compatibility is something less than interoperability, where systems/units do not interfere with each other's functioning but are not able to exchange services. To conclude, interoperability lies in the middle of an 'Integration Continuum' between compatibility and full integration [6]. It is important to distinguish between compatibility, interoperability and integration in order to have a meaningful debate on how to achieve them.

The question is: is one able to make a similar analysis and demonstration relating to the three main facets of sustainability, i.e. Economic, Ecologic, Ethical / Social?

From an **Economical** perspective, interoperability is an a priori property for the so-called 'Network effect' [8]. For larger networks, interoperability is a *competitive weapon*; they have nothing to gain by interoperating and thus their best strategy is to drive organic growth while waiting for smaller networks to 'wither on the vine'. However, the mid-sized networks can gain market leadership by interoperating with each other; so the risk of this happening has to be weighed by the market leaders. In order for a market leader to establish an insurmountable lead, they would have to create interoperability with a smaller network (ideally the number 2 network) such that the combined value of all remaining competing networks would not be a threat. In this way, interoperability is contributing to the sustainability of the systems that need a capacity to interoperate by improving their economic competitiveness.

From an **Ecological** perspective, interoperability is contributing to the so-called 'Green Information Technology (IT) ', which is a complex and still 'fuzzy' concept, partly due to the complexity and diversity of the IT applications and development. The goal of the IT-related economic development is differs regionally; for example, the European Union countries have devised a plan of 'Green Knowledge Society' [9] to help promoting the application of the Green IT, since knowledge is the dominant element in the economic structure of EU. Green IT is especially useful for the improvement of the green production mode and the supervisory control in traditional industries, the reduction of the pollution emissions and the energy utilization. Recent research results suggest that when ICT is applied in other industries the amount of the energy saving is five times that of its own. Reducing the heterogeneity, improving the quality of data stored by IS and assessing the risks of poor interoperability [10] can help ecological sustainability of those interoperable systems.

From an **Ethical** perspective, interoperability is concerned with data privacy, information protection, trust and access control. Policy makers recognize the need for robust, protected data flows if the benefits of an information economy are to be realized. While the global flow of data is essential for innovation and economic growth, companies face significant challenges when attempting to comply with often conflicting requirements of diverse national and regional data protection laws and regulations. Emerging policies stress the need to create a streamlined system which allows for the smooth movement of data across regimes, in a manner that ensures that individuals and enterprises enjoy the protection afforded by local laws and regulations [10]. That is the *conundrum of sharing information*: the information is essential to improve collaboration towards an economical benefit; however, on the other hand, sharing it presents the risk of possible loss, knowledge theft and protection rights.

3   A Sustainable Interoperability of Standards

Continuous change processes enable enterprises to endure in today's competitive and highly dynamic business ecosystem; however, they also bring about new challenges, such as the potential weakening of internal and external interoperability displayed by the enterprise. Data, application and business process [11] at technical, syntactic, semantic and pragmatic levels [12] may all be affected by change. This problem can occur within enterprises but also between members of collaborative networks (CNs) [13]. The conceptual syntactic aspects of interoperability are typically addressed by agreeing on and upholding standardised formats to overcome barriers [14, 15]. Unfortunately however, the *standards describing such formats are themselves plagued by interoperability problems* and are in fact just another facet of the interoperability challenge inherently posed by mandated continuous change processes.

Currently, it appears that many Technical Committees (TCs) and Sub-Committees (SCs) do not have a holistic, birds-eye view of the standards they administer and develop, mainly due to the lack of a proper central standards repository. In addition, the visibility between the custodian Work Groups (WGs) within TCs and SCs is poor, which leads to potential gaps, overlaps and inconsistencies in standards development. As the mandatory review process occurs in an asynchronous way for each standard, all stakeholder WGs (not just the custodian) should be aware of and have input in the proposed changes. However, in reality the involvement of other potential stakeholders in the development or maintenance of a standard occurs on an irregular and anecdotal basis, relying on the goodwill and knowledge owned by the WG conveners, librarians etc. Hence, changes to a standard (glossary, procedures, etc) do not automatically notify or propagate to other relevant WGs and standards they administer.

Typically, the setup and operation of any project requires a *set* of standards. Currently, it is quite difficult for the typical user to readily find out what standards are required for a particular type of project as the user guides do not explain how to use standards *together*. Furthermore, the terminology inconsistency, gaps and overlaps of the standards selected for a project confuse the users and end up affecting the sustainability and interoperability of the enterprise(s) attempting to use the standards. Thus, current interoperability of standards is itself *low* and *unsustainable*.

Based on the previous results and ongoing research work [16, 17], we propose a structured and widely applicable approach to achieve sustainable interoperability, consistence and redundancy elimination. Thus, a common workspace based on a Structured Repository (SR) would be a good start to address the problems identified.

Interoperability-relevant SR elements (aspects, barriers etc) can be sourced by mapping and decomposing the mainstream interoperability frameworks and relevant standards in respect to a reference framework (e.g. GERA, in [18]).

Rules can then be added to enable querying the SR and thus transforming it into a knowledge base (see Fig. 2 and [17] for details), as part of an expert system guiding standards creation and review in an integrated, collaborative and synergistic manner.

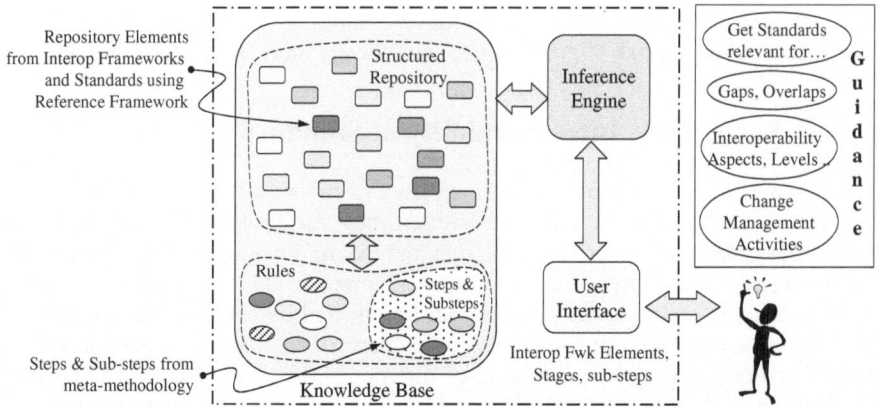

Fig. 2. Proposed expert system supporting a sustainable interoperability of standards

The user employs the inference engine to elicit knowledge such as: what standards cover a specific area; is there a need for a new standard, to retire or to change a standard (any overlaps?); what are the ripple effects of a standard's revision; what are the activities to create / review / retire standards, etc. The expert system responds with ranked solutions on views, aspects, levels, development activities, tools, etc.

Standards interoperability is essential in promoting user acceptance, usability and efficient administration and maintenance; however, it is also a complex undertaking involving a multitude of aspects and levels, from infrastructure to politics and organisational culture of the custodian work groups. The proposed system provides a foundation towards a *sustainable* interoperability of standards – a benefit that will propagate to the enterprises and collaborative networks using the standards.

4   Sustaining Interoperability of Electronic Healthcare Records

The current fragmentation of health science along traditional boundaries is considered as inefficient, particularly when considered in the contemporary patient management context. The Virtual Physiological Human (VPH) is intended to address this issue by providing a framework that enables the integration of data and observations about human's biology. Today, VPH can be specialized to a subset of data, which is manageable in current healthcare settings. This subset of VPH data is an Electronic Health Record (EHR), defined as a longitudinal electronic record of patient health information generated by one or more encounters in any care delivery setting.

Sustainability of EHR is directly related to sustaining their interoperability, namely towards exhibiting the robustness to a change of environment in which EHR is used. That is, EHR is sustainable as long as different clinical IS can operate in the same way (or draw the identical conclusions) based on a single EHR; or, EHR is sustainable as long as the same clinical IS can operate in the same way on basis of the different representations of same EHR data.

One of the related problems is that terminologies are not bound to EHR standards. Rector et al [19] used ontology to bind HL7 messages to SNOMED-CT (Systematized Nomenclature of Medicine - Clinical Terms) codes; however, the *semantic interoperability* between the systems using the above standards is still an issue. The diversity of medical ontologies based on various conceptualization approaches makes mapping difficult. Two development approaches are 1) bottom-up formalization of the vocabularies and 2) semantic analysis of the clinical care and development of facilitating ontologies. Although the first approach is dominant in the research community, Beale and Heard [20] argue that the starting point for a successful model is an ontological analysis of the healthcare delivery process.

In fact, the diversity of conceptualization choices is not necessarily an issue. Bottom-up approaches and narrow scopes are characterized by decreased development time and thus, they contribute to the commoditization of the semantic technologies in a medical sector. The difficulties of integrating such ontologies (caused by implicitness) can be resolved by using *upper* ontologies. Schulz et al [21] addressed logical and ontological issues of SNOMED; the well-known Ontology of Biomedical reality [22] was developed as a result of the process of vertical integration of upper ontology (Basic Formal Ontology - BFO) and domain ontology. Although this approach introduces new artefacts into the context, the sustainability of an integrated knowledge is actually being increased. Due to its general approach in describing the world, one of the key features of the upper ontologies is the resilience to change. When formal models are considered, this resilience decreases with the used level of abstraction in their development. Similar conclusion can be drawn for the increase of the implicitness level, which is notable for more specialized ontologies. When upper ontologies are used in correlating different standards, the total number of mappings decreases. Hence, the effort needed for their maintenance is reduced.

Partitioning can also help the maintainability of the ontological framework. Besides the computational performance benefits, this decoupling allows developers to compensate for these failings without compromising the underlying models.

Clearly, one approach to achieve sustainability would be to identify and maintain the mappings between the concepts of the different EHR standards in their native forms. However, this approach itself would not be sustainable because of decreased scalability of such mappings and high maintenance effort required. Another approach is related to defining and associating the formally defined meanings to the EHR concepts. Hence, the robustness of EHR would be drawn from the capability of systems to interpret the semantic similarities or differences of the EHR concepts, based on their formal representations. The inference capability of these systems would allow the logical correspondences between two representations to be computed on the basis of the relationships between the concepts of the respective representations and the concepts of formal ontologies.

5   Virtualisation: Addressing Interoperability and Sustainability in Distributed Manufacturing

Manufacturing can be defined as a process composed of activities performed using various resources and aimed at transforming a form of matter into another for a given scope (typically responding to a set of customer requirements). There is significant scientific interest in making manufacturing sustainable, as unfortunately it is currently one of the most important causes of global resource depletion. This challenge is compounded by the current distribution of activities and processes; this requires *interoperability* of the activities along the distributed manufacturing chain.

As a reaction to this challenge, the new paradigm of Virtual Manufacturing (VM) has emerged in the last decades as an improved capability of sharing and managing knowledge and synchronizing cooperation activities in a form useful to the human decision factors. The improvements in sensor technologies (hardware) as well as in simulation facilities (software) have been the key driver of this 'soft revolution', making the use of IT and computer simulation more effective in modelling real world manufacturing processes for the purpose of understanding and controlling them [23].

The origins of virtual reality can be traced as far back at least as 'the ultimate display' [24], allowing a user to 'step through' the computer screen into a three-dimensional (3D) world. Thus, with the advance of computer technology, VM turned into a way to reduce the time and cost involved in decision making and simulation (and thus covering the entire product lifecycle, from conceptualization to production). The user can look at, move around, and interact with the virtual world as if they were real. An essential question is *how and to what extent could VM* (as a breakthrough technology to support interoperability in manufacturing) *contribute towards achieving sustainability along the manufacturing chain?*

Given the scarcity of bibliographical references, a possible viewpoint to address this new question is to refer to the very nature of VM, which is in fact synonymous to simulation of the manufacturing processes. Simulation is defined as experimentation (using some model) on a system of interest, whether existing or not [25]. Simulation helps reduce uncertainty in the decision making process by allowing to explore several alternatives with relatively low costs and by presenting knowledge about projected artefacts on various levels of abstraction. In other words, when dealing with VM one adopts a computer system to generate information about the structure, status, and behaviour of a manufacturing system (whether existing or not) as if it was in a real setting, i.e. to provide a capability to 'manufacture in the computer' [24]. In this context, the VM connection to sustainability becomes obvious; VM has the potential to provide a modelling and simulation environment allowing the sustainability of fabrication/assembly of any product, including the related manufacturing processes, to be assessed by computer simulation. For example, one can in measure the energy required to manufacture, or can estimate the amount of material and its footprint from well-known databases (e.g. [26, 27]), or even foresee potential improvements by adopting different materials. Furthermore, it can be shared with other suppliers along the distributed manufacturing chain, even in absence of a predetermined standard.

In this context, a new concept can be introduced, Virtual Sustainability (VS) that can be defined as feature of a product/process obtained by the grace of the above-said virtual paradigm. Provided adequate tools are available, one can assess the sustainability of processes or products before any concrete action is taken, in a pre-conceptual stage and independently of the manufacturing chain stage. It is only a matter of the quality and power of modelling and simulation tools, techniques and applications to offer new opportunities to evaluate the impact on resource consumption and environment because of these features. Virtual sustainability then reflects into 'real sustainability' as products or processes implemented in the real world can be improved to address economical, environmental or even social pillars, since VM application can encompass the entire life cycle of a product or process.

In order to clarify the VS concept, one can refer to three stages of representation of knowledge and information of an entity according to [28]: digital, virtual and real. A digital entity is the representation of the digital information, such as a knowledge model of the entity. The virtual representation of an entity is its representation within a domain for validation purposes, where the link between digital and virtual can be a reference architecture. Finally, the real entity is the implemented actual test scenario and thus reflects the former stages. Whatever the entity we are reasoning about (be a manufacturing system, a process, a product) or its features related to sustainability, it is quite clear that virtualisation is simply a indissoluble part of the same continuum formed by interoperability and sustainability before recalled in **Fig. 1**.

6   Control Systems for Sustainability, Sustainable Control Systems

In the context of the fundamental changes to environmental, social and lifecycle requirements we currently have to deal with, the legacy isolated control system concepts have to be overlapped in order to create better systems where the concept of boundaries disappear [29]. The following shows the control techniques basic laws that are used in Control Systems for Sustainability and Sustainable Control Systems.

Thus, **Intelligent control** uses various Artificial Intelligence computing approaches; **Optimal control** is a particular control technique in which the control signal optimizes a certain cost index; **Robust control** deals with uncertainty in its approach to controller design; **Adaptive control** uses on-line identification of the process parameters, or modification of controller gains; **Hierarchical control** arranges a set of devices and governing software in a hierarchical tree; **Stochastic control** deals with control design with uncertainty in the model and **Energy-shaping control** views the plant and the controller as energy-transformation devices.

The basic considerations for defining Control Systems for Sustainability and Sustainable Control Systems are presented in a new control system concept named Sustainable Control System for Sustainability (SCSFS). This design has to include the primary and secondary factors that are presented below [30, 31]:

1. Defining the control systems limits by the carrying capacity of the environment.
2. Taking account the effect o the social necessities
3. Respecting life forms and supports biodiversity in the design; accidents leading to environmental concerns are key focus areas for governments and public alike;
4. Employing ecological decision-making systems inside the control laws;
5. Creating balanced, open and flexible control laws that incorporate the social, economic and environmental factors as a unique solution;
6. Using global control efforts and natural resources;
7. Appling renewable and reliable sources of energy in the control system;
8. Eliminating harm to the environment from the controller;
9. Designing control systems that use long lifetime cycles;
10. Guarantee the sustainability of the controller during a long period of time for future control systems developments;

11. Employing economical decision-making systems inside the control system;
12. Developing a self-categorization control system, including methodologies for lifetime cycle stages;
13. Utilizing the lifetime cycle stages as a dependent variable in the controller;
14. Generating a positive impact on the life cycle during early control design stage;
15. Developing an integrated control system that includes a cost management function. This is because non-common operating point and maintenance controller strategies are rarely planned at the design phase, so those could affect the lifetime.
16. Adopting new controller technologies to maintain competitive advantage.

The concept of life cycle is a key factor for designing Control Systems for Sustainability and Sustainable Control Systems. It is important to include all the aspects of life cycle: economical, environmental, social, and society, but also controller performance, scalability, reconfiguration and integration. The intention of controls systems for sustainability is to eliminate negative environmental impact completely through skilful, sensitive and sustainable control design and minimum impact on the environment during system operation. The control system concepts are included in the process design for improving the overall performance of the system.

It is expected that the proposed SCSFS based on the above-mentioned principles and concepts will provide suitable solutions for the challenges posed by the next generation of control systems.

7   Sustainability and Interoperability of Negotiation Processes

In a globalised and networked market, businesses face the struggle to perform better and faster, using new approaches and techniques and optimising their way in order to stay in business. In the light of this highly competitive and demanding environment, the establishment of strategic partnerships and outsourcing are common practices that frequently compete with in-house development. To reach a sustainable operation, companies need to continuously negotiate to create and maintain interoperability supported by an appropriate knowledge management framework [32, 33].

Negotiation of tasks and jobs implementation is therefore a task that plays a crucial part on its business evolution. Negotiations often involve several heterogeneous parties, external and internal, using different tools, languages, platforms and Information and Communication Technologies (ICT); hence, several internal company areas compete or collaborate with external parties for the development of a project, or outsource parts of it. Best practices specify that decision analysis must convey a thorough documentation, evaluation and analysis of the alternative solutions in order to reach the best solution and learn from it. On the other hand, the various parties involved in the negotiation need to be interoperable, sharing business, technical data and information seamlessly.

This requires a framework for sustainable interoperability of negotiation processes, using formal description (modelling) to support the coordination of multiple parallel negotiations occurring in business-to-business interactions and offering mechanisms to support negotiations in a distributed environment. This includes a set of hierarchically layered and distributed components that implement the rules of the modelled negotiation and also handle the interoperability aspects of the negotiation.

A sustainable, flexible and generic approach towards the implementation of the underlying infrastructure can be provided by a Cloud web-service-based platform (e.g. Software as a Service, SaaS). Such infrastructures and service provider platforms allow subscribing to processing that matches the negotiation environment needs.

The framework's top layer (Negotiation Manager) is targeted to the Manager of each negotiation party. It handles all business decisions [34] that need to be taken (e.g. proposal, acceptance of proposal, rejection of proposal, invite of another party to take part in the negotiation) and analyses and manages the negotiated parameters, communicating with the lower layers using web-services [35].

A second layer is dedicated to the Coordination Services (CS) which assist the negotiations at a global level (negotiations with different participants on different jobs) and at a specific level (negotiation on the same job with different participants) handling all issues regarding communication at this layer level. The CS shall also handle the on-going transactions and manage the persistence for the status of the negotiation sequences. To improve the interoperability, data shall be exchanged using the standard protocol ISO10303 STEP [35]. This layer is also responsible for handling semantic discrepancies between the negotiating parties via the use of one or more ontologies and may include an agent-based architecture to support the complexities of the negotiation operations through the Middleware layer.

These middleware services shall provide support for performing all aspects related with basic infrastructure, and handling the heterogeneity related with multiple negotiation players; it may also include publication of the job requirements and characteristics, in order to allow potential companies interested in participating to 'subscribe' to it and be able to enter the negotiation.

Each negotiation is organised in three main steps: initialisation; refinement of the job under negotiation; and closure. The initialisation step allows to define what has to be negotiated (Negotiation Object) and how (Negotiation Framework) [36]. In the refinement step, participants exchange proposals on the negotiation object trying to satisfy their constraints. Closure concludes the negotiation.

To manage all issues regarding semantics between the negotiating parties, an ontology can handle generic negotiation terms not bound to any specific business, as well as using dedicated ontologies to handle semantics related to negotiated items. To foster a higher independence of external factors, the services and infrastructure are modelled in a Model-Driven Architecture (MDA) Platform-Independent Model (PIM) [37] defining the basic foundations of the framework, which is then transformed into the final Platform-Specific Model (PSM) set of services [38].

8   Conclusions

This paper has attempted to demonstrate that sustainability and interoperability are intertwined aspects of any universe of discourse. After clarifying and structuring the relevant concepts and areas of these two aspects, we have described several areas of research and practice where the connection between sustainability and interoperation is manifest and we have proposed solutions to existing or emergent problems.

Thus, in the Standardisation area we have analysed the current issues and proposed a system towards improving standards and custodian Work Groups' interoperability in a sustainable manner. In the Health Informatics domain we have analysed existing problems and proposed some improvements to Electronic Health Records sustainability related to their formal representations. In Manufacturing we have explained the virtualisation concept, proposed the Virtual Sustainability model and argued its benefits on the interoperability and sustainability of global manufacturing. In Control Systems we have defined the laws and considerations for sustainable control systems and have explained the merging of control systems, interoperability and sustainability concepts in a Sustainable Control Systems for Sustainability paradigm. In Negotiations we have explored the need for interoperability in the global negotiations required to sustain a business and we have proposed a cloud-based, agent-driven multi-layered negotiation framework providing flexible semantic interoperability.

To sum up, in a global networked environment deeply affected by financial crises, climate change and pandemics, the necessary economic, environmental and social / ethical sustainability cannot be achieved without *sustainable* interoperability.

References

1. Elkington, J.: Cannibals with Forks: The Triple Bottom Line of 21st Century Business (1998)
2. Blackburn, W.R.: The Sustainability Handbook. EarthScan Publish., Cornwall (2007)
3. UN World Commission on Environment and Development, Our Common Future (Brundtland Report). Oxford University Press, Oxford (1987)
4. IEEE, IEEE Std 610.: Standard Glossary of Software Eng. Terminology, pp. 1–84 (1990)
5. ISO, ISO1 16100-1:2009 Ed.2: Industrial automation systems and integration - Manufacturing software capability profiling for interoperability - P 1: Framework (2009)
6. Panetto, H.: Towards a classification framework for interoperability of enterprise applications. Int. J. of Comp. Integrated Manufacturing 20, 727–740 (2007)
7. ISO, ISO14258 Industrial Automation Systems Concepts & Rules Enterprise Models (2005)
8. Robinson, C.K.: Network Effects in Telecommunications Mergers-MCI WorldCom Merger: Protecting the Future of the Internet, in allocution devant le Practicing Law Institute (1999)
9. Forge, S., et al.: A Green Knowledge Society-An ICT policy agenda to 2015 for Europe's future knowledge society, Ministry of Enterprise, Government Offices of Sweden (2009)
10. Yahia, E., Aubry, A., Panetto, H.: Formal measures for semantic interoperability assessment in cooperative enterprise information systems. Comp. Ind. 63, 443–457 (2012)
11. IDEAS. IDEAS Project Deliverables (WP1-WP7), Public reports (2003), http://www.ideas-roadmap.net (cited July 2011)
12. Whitman, L., Panetto, H.: The Missing Link: Culture and Language Barriers to Interoperability. Annual Reviews in Control 30(2), 233–241 (2006)
13. Noran, O.: Collaborative networks in the tertiary education industry sector: a case study. International Journal of Computer Integrated Manufacturing 26(1-2), 29–40 (2012)
14. Chen, D.: Framework for Enterprise Interoperability (2006), http://www.fines-cluster.eu/fines/jm/Download/53-Framework-for-Enterprise-Interoperability-Chen.html (cited 2011)
15. Noran, O., Bernus, P.: Effective Disaster Management: An Interoperability Perspective. In: Meersman, R., Dillon, T., Herrero, P. (eds.) OTM-WS 2011. LNCS, vol. 7046, pp. 112–121. Springer, Heidelberg (2011)

16. Noran, O.: A Meta-methodology for Collaborative Networked Organisations: Creating Directly Applicable Methods for Enterprise Eng Projects. VDM Verlag, Saarbrücken (2008)
17. Noran, O.: Achieving A Sustainable Interoperability of Standards. IFAC Annual Reviews in Control 36, 327–337 (2012)
18. ISO/IEC, Annex C: GERAM, in ISO/IS 15704:2000/Amd1:2005: Industrial automation systems - Requirements for enterprise-reference architectures and methodologies (2005)
19. Rector, A., Qamar, R., Marley, T.: Binding Ontologies & Coding systems to Electronic Health Records and Messages. Applied Ontology 4(1) (2009)
20. Beale, T., Heard, S.: An Ontology-based Model of Clinical Information. S. Stud. Health Technol. Inform. 129(pt.1), 760–764 (2007)
21. Schulz, S., et al.: SNOMED reaching its adolescence: Ontologists' and logicians' health check. Int. J. Med. Inform. 78(1), 86–94 (2009)
22. Rosse, C., Mejino, J.V.L.: A reference ontology for biomedical informatics: the Foundational Model of Anatomy. J. Biomed. Inform. 36, 478–500 (2003)
23. Offodile, O.F., Abdel-Malek, L.L.: The virtual manufacturing paradigm: The impact of IT/IS outsourcing on manufacturing strategy. Int. J. Prod. Econ. 75(1-2), 147–159 (2002)
24. Mujber, T.S., Szecsi, T., Hashmi, M.S.J.: Virtual reality applications in manufacturing process simulation. J. Mater. Process. Technol. 155-156, 1834–1838 (2004)
25. De Vin, L.J., Holm, M., Ng, A.: The Information Fusion JDL-U model as a reference model for Virtual Manufacturing. Robot. Comput.-Integr. Manuf. 26(6), 629–638 (2010)
26. Goedkoop, M., et al.: Introduction to LCA with SimaPro 7. Pré Consult, Netherlands (2008)
27. Goedkoop, M., Oele, M., Effting, S.: SimaPro database manual methods library. Pré Consult, Netherlands (2004)
28. Lanz, M., Tuokko, R.: Generic reference architecture for digital, virtual, and real representations of manufacturing systems. In: Indo-US Workshop, Designing Sustainable Products, Services and Manufacturing Systems. Indian Inst. of Sci., Bangalore (2011)
29. Ponce, P., Molina, A.: Fundamentos de LabVIEW. Alfaomega (2011)
30. Ponce, P., Molina, A., Mendoza, R., Ruiz, M.A., Monnard, D.G., Fernández del Campo, L.D.: Intelligent Wheelchair and Virtual Training by LabVIEW. In: Sidorov, G., Hernández Aguirre, A., Reyes García, C.A. (eds.) MICAI 2010, Part I. LNCS, vol. 6437, pp. 422–435. Springer, Heidelberg (2010)
31. Ponce, P., Molina, A.: LabVIEW for Intelligent Control Research and Education. In: Proceedings of the 4th IEEE Int'l Conference on E-Learning in Industrial Electronics (ICELIE), Arizona, USA, pp. 47–54 (2010)
32. Sarraipa, J., Jardim-Goncalves, R., Steiger-Garcao, A.: MENTOR: an enabler for interoperable intelligent systems. Int. J. of General Systems 39(5), 557–573 (2010)
33. Jardim-Goncalves, R., et al.: Knowledge Framework for Intelligent Manufacturing Systems. Journal of Intelligent Manufacturing 22(5), 725–735 (2009)
34. Cretan, A., et al.: NEGOSEIO: A Framework for Negotiations toward Sustainable Enterprise Interoperability. IFAC Ann. Rev. Ctrl. 36(2), 291–299 (2012)
35. Jardim-Goncalves, R., et al.: Systematisation of Interoperability Body of Knowledge: the foundation for Enterprise Interoperability as a science. EIS 6(3), 1–26 (2012)
36. Duan, L., et al.: A negotiation framework for linked combinatorial optimization problems. Autonomous Agents and Multi-Agent Systems 25(1), 158–182 (2012)
37. Grilo, A., Jardim-Goncalves, R.: Challenging electronic procurement in the AEC sector: A BIM-based integrated perspective. Automation in Construction 20(2), 107–114 (2011)
38. Jardim-Goncalves, R., Popplewell, K., Grilo, A.: Sustainable interoperability: The future of Internet based industrial enterprises. Comp. Ind. 63(8), 731–738 (2012)

ISDE 2013 PC Co-Chairs Message

Information System in Distributed Environment (ISDE) is swiftly becoming a prominent standard in this globalization generation due to advancement in information and communication technologies. In distributed environments, business units collaborate across time zones, organizational boundaries, work cultures and geographical distances, to an increasing diversification and growing complexity of cooperation among units. The main expected benefits from Distributed Software Development (DSD) are improvements in development time efficiency, being close to the customers and having flexible access to greater and less costly resources. Despite the fact that DSD is widely being used, the project managers and professional face many challenges due to increased complexity, cultural as well as various technological issues. Therefore, it is crucial to understand current research and practices in these areas.

Following selected papers of ISDE 2013 international workshop in conjunction with OTM conferences present recent advances and novel proposals in this direction.

Javier Criado, Luis Iribarne, and Nicolas Padilla presented an approach for the runtime generation of Platform Specific Models (PSMs) from abstract definitions contained in their corresponding Platform Independent Models (PIMs). Marta Cimitile, Pasquale Ardimento and Giuseppe Visaggio, presented an experiment in an industrial context in which authors have compared the software development supported by Knowledge Experience Package (KEP) with the development achieved without it. Alok Mishra and Deepti Mishra discussed the role of software architecture and distributed software development.

Amit Raj, Stephen Barrett, Siobhan Clarke discussed the problem of deriving causal relationships of faults in adaptive distributed systems in their paper titled "Run-time Root Cause Analysis in Adaptive Distributed Systems". Deepti Mishra, Alok Mishra, Ricardo Colomo-Palacios, and Cristina Casado-Lumbreras presented a systematic literature review of global software development and quality management.

Jukka Kääriäinen, Susanna Teppola, Antti Välimäki provided a concept solution of upgrade planning for automation systems based on real life case study. In their paper on Inconsistency-tolerant Business Rules in Distributed Information Systems, Hendrik Decker, and Francesc D. Muñoz-Escoí outlined a measure-based inconsistency-tolerant approach to business rules maintenance for distributed applications. Adel Taweel, Emilia Garcia, Simon Miles, Michael Luck in their study "Agent-Oriented Software Engineering (AOSE) of Distributed eHealth Systems" discussed the use of AOSE to develop a particular distributed ehealth system, IDEA, and evaluates its suitability to develop such systems in general.

July 2013

Alok Mishra
Jürgen Münch
Deepti Mishra

Y.T. Demey and H. Panetto (Eds.): OTM 2013 Workshops, LNCS 8186, p. 262, 2013.
© Springer-Verlag Berlin Heidelberg 2013

Distributed Software Development with Knowledge Experience Packages

Pasquale Ardimento[1], Marta Cimitile[2], and Giuseppe Visaggio[1]

[1] University of Bari, Italy
{pasquale.ardimento,giuseppe.visaggio}@di.uniba.it
[2] Unitelma Sapienza University, Italy
marta.cimitile@unitelma.it

Abstract. In software production process, a lot of knowledge is created and remain silent. Therefore, it cannot be reused to improve the effectiveness and the efficiency of these processes. This problem is amplified in the case of a distributed production. In fact, distributed software development requires complex context specific knowledge regarding the particularities of different technologies, the potential of existing software, the needs and expectations of the users. This knowledge, which is gained during the project execution, is usually tacit and is completely lost by the company when the production is completed. Moreover, each time a new production unit is hired, despite the diversity of culture and capacity of people, it is necessary to standardize the working skills and methods of the different teams if the company wants to keep the quality level of processes and products. In this context, we used the concept of Knowledge Experience Package (KEP), already specified in previous works and the tool realized to support KEP approach. In this work, we have carried out an experiment in an industrial context in which we compared the software development supported by KEPs with the development achieved without it.

Keywords: Knowledge packaging, empirical investigation, distributed software development.

1 Introduction

Software development (production and maintenance) is a knowledge-intensive business involving many people working in different phases and activities [7]. The available resources are not increasing at the same pace as the needs; therefore, software organizations expect an increment in productivity [17]. However, the reality is that development teams do not benefit from existing experience and they repeat mistakes even though some individuals in the organization know how to avoid them. Considering that project team members acquire valuable individual experience with each project, the organization and individuals could gain much more if they were able to share this knowledge. Knowledge, therefore, is a critical factor and affects many different aspects of software development such as:

Y.T. Demey and H. Panetto (Eds.): OTM 2013 Workshops, LNCS 8186, pp. 263–273, 2013.

Accessing domain knowledge. Software development requires access to knowledge, not only about its domain and new technologies but also about the domain for which software is being developed. An organization must acquire new domain knowledge either by training or by hiring knowledgeable employees and spreading it throughout the team.

Acquiring knowledge about new technologies. It is difficult for developers to become proficient with a new technology and managers to understand its impact and estimate a projects cost when using it. When developers or project managers use a technology that a projects team members are unfamiliar with, engineers often resort to the learning by doing approach, which can result in serious delays. So, organizations must quickly acquire knowledge about new technologies and master them. Research produces knowledge that should be transferred to production processes as innovation in order to be valuable. Consequently, domain knowledge must be enriched by technical and economical knowledge that allows identifying the best approach for introducing new knowledge in processes together with the resources, risks and mitigation actions [16].

Sharing knowledge about local policies and practices. Every organization has its own policies, practices, and culture, which are not only technical but also managerial and administrative. New developers in an organization need knowledge about the existing software assets and local programming conventions. Experienced developers often disseminate it to inexperienced developers through ad hoc informal meetings; consequently, not everyone has access to the knowledge they need. Passing knowledge informally is an important aspect of a knowledge-sharing culture that should be encouraged. Nonetheless, formal knowledge capturing and sharing ensures that all employees can access it. So, organizations must formalize knowledge sharing while continuing informal knowledge sharing.

Capturing knowledge and knowing who knows what. Software organizations depend heavily on knowledgeable employees because they are key to the projects success [11]. However, access to these people can be difficult. Software developers apply just as much effort and attention determining whom to contact in an organization as they do getting the job done. These knowledgeable people are also very mobile. When a person with critical knowledge suddenly leaves an organization, it creates severe knowledge gaps. Knowing what employees know is necessary for organizations to create a strategy for preventing valuable knowledge from disappearing. Knowing who has what knowledge is also a requirement for efficiently staffing projects, identifying training needs, and matching employees with training offers. So, until knowledge is transferable or reusable, it cannot be considered as part of an organizations assets [11].

All these needs require both formalizing knowledge so that it is comprehensible and reusable by others that are not the author of the knowledge and experience packaging able to guide the user in applying the knowledge in a context. Given these premises, this paper describes an approach for Knowledge Packaging and Representation and reports results of an experimentation of the approach in an industrial context. In our proposed approach we have formalized a KEP and we have defined some packages that are stored in a Knowledge Experience Base

(KEB) [18,14,5,19]. The KEPs have a predefined structure in order to facilitate stakeholders in the comprehension and the acquisition of the knowledge that they contain. We have conducted a validation through a controlled experiment with the aim to answer to the following Research Question (RQ):

Does the proposed knowledge description approach increase the productivity of software development compared to the more traditional ones?

In order to answer this question we use the concept of *Productivity* considered as the effort spent to develop software. Due to the different size of applications considered, we normalized the *Productivity* using the *Function Point* factor. The rest of the paper is organized as follows: related works are described in Section 2; Section 3 illustrates, briefly, the proposed approach for knowledge representation, Section 4 illustrates the experiment planning and measurement model used; results of the study and lessons learned are presented in Section 5; finally in Section 6 conclusions are drawn.

2   Related Work

The topic of knowledge acquisition and collection is being studied by several research and industrial organizations [9,7,12,2,18]. This shows how the concept of KEB is quite mature, and several implementations [12,14,19] are performed. However, the knowledge structure in a KEB is not clear and common rules supporting knowledge sharing and acquisition are missed [15]. For example there are several KEB having a wider scope respect the generality of the collected knowledge [13]. This topic is particularly critical in distributed software development domain [6], were the experience transferring became an important value. In [10], authors focus on product design and development based on design KEB as a new attempt on the organic integration of knowledge management and product development. Moreover, [20] presents a notion of knowledge flow and the related management mechanism for realizing an ordered knowledge sharing and cognitive cooperation in a geographically distributed team software development process. Our approach aims to introduce the concept of KEP as software development KEB content structure. It makes it easier to achieve knowledge transfer among different stakeholders involved during software development and encourage the interested communities to develop around it and exchange knowledge.

3   Proposed Approach

3.1   Knowledge Experience Package Structure

Authors use the term KEP to refer to an organized set of knowledge contents and training units on the use of the demonstration prototypes or tools and all other information that may strengthen the packages ability to achieve the proposed goal. The KEP can be made up of all the elements shown in figure 1. The main component is the *Art&Practices* (*AP*). It describes the kind of knowledge contained in the package. *Evidence* component shows some empirical validation of

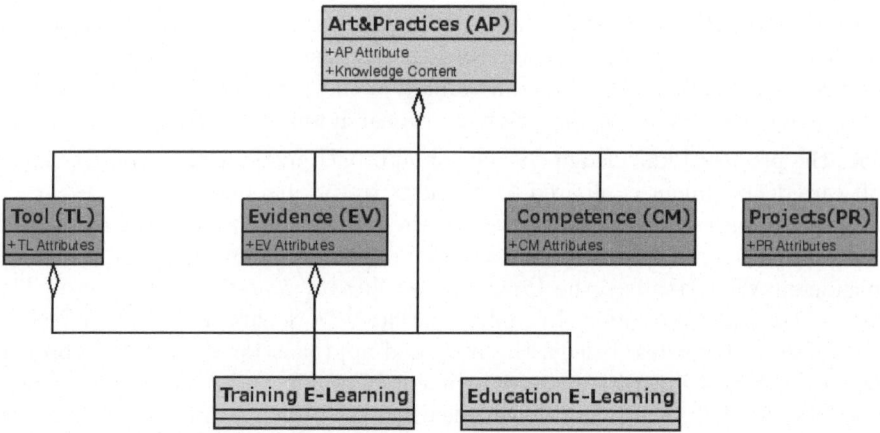

Fig. 1. Diagram of a Knowledge/Experience Package

the knowledge contained in AP. Similarly, the *Tool*, *Project* and *Competence* respectively describe the software tool, the project and all the competences useful to develop and use the described knowledge. A user can access one of the package components and then navigate along all the components of the same package according to her/his needs. The knowledge package must be usable independently of its authors and for this purpose the content must have a particular structure: distance education and training must be available through an e-learning system. In short, the proposed knowledge package contains knowledge content integrated with an *E-learning* function. Search inside the package starting from any of its components is facilitated by the component's *Attributes* and a more extended description of the knowledge is proposed in the *Content* part.

To facilitate the search, a set of selection classifiers and a set of descriptors summarizing the contents are used in *Attributes* component. The *Attributes* component contains the keywords and the problems the package is intended to solve, a brief description of the content and a history of the essential events occurring during the life cycle of the package, giving the reader an idea of how it has been applied, improved, and how mature it is. Also provides the following indicators: necessary competence to acquire it, prerequisite conditions for a correct execution of the package, adoption plan describing how to acquire the package and estimating the resources required for each activity. To assess the benefits of acquisition, they contain a list of: the economic impact generated by application of the package; the value for the stakeholders in the company that might be interested in acquiring the innovation. There are also indicators estimating the costs and risks. It is important to note that each kind of package has other specific attributes. Moreover, in the *Knowledge Content (KC)* a further description of the package is available. The *AP Knowledge Content* is the central one. It contains the knowledge package expressed in a hypermedia form in order to include figures, graphs, formulas and whatever else may help to understand the content. The *KC* is organized as a tree. Starting from the root (level 0) descent to the lower levels (level 1, level 2, . . .) is through pointers. At the increasing of the level of a node, the abstraction of the content decreases focusing more and more on operative elements. The root node is made up of a *Thoughtful Index* and one or more problems. The nodes are the answers to the problems, the solutions proposed for each of the announced problems. Each answer consists of the following: analysis of how far the results on which the innovation should be built can be integrated into the system; analysis of the methods for transferring them into the business processes; details on the indicators listed in the metadata of the *KC* inherent to the specific package, analyzing and generalizing the experimental data evinced from the evidence and associated projects; analysis of the results of any applications of the package in one or more projects, demonstrating the success of the application or any improvements required, made or in course; details on how to acquire the package. The research results integrated by a package may be contained within the same knowledge base or derive from other knowledge bases or other laboratories. The proposed KEP approach is supported by a tool called Prometheus. Prometheus [4,3] also allows to captures, share and retain content to ensure that one or more software processes are automated and managed. To achieve these results PROMETHEUS was interfaced with Drupal (https://drupal.org/). Drupal is a well known open source content management platform, supporting content capture, sharing and retention. The interested reader can find the tool and some package example at the following link [8] and further details are available in [1].

4 Experiment Planning

In the way to answer to the Research Goal (RG) introduced in the first paragraph, we propose an experiment consisting to compare the Prometheus based approach with a traditional one. The experimentation was conduct in collaboration with an PugliaIT Enterprise. We selected a set of projects and developers adopted Prometheus for their development or maintenance. We compared the obtained results with the results obtained by other developers in similar projects without Prometheus support. According to this we can better define our RQ in the following way: Analyze software production following the Prometheus approach with the aim of evaluating it with respect to *Productivity* following without use Prometheus from the view point of the software engineer in the context of company-projects.

4.1 Variables Selection

The dependent variable of the study is *Productivity*. *Productivity* indicates effort spent in man hours to develop a software application normalized on *Function Points*. The independent variables are the two treatments: the applications developed (only production) without Prometheus approach, software development (both production and maintenance) using Prometheus approach. Nine projects were considered, four already developed, and therefore without using Prometheus, and five developed using Prometheus. The projects refer to different application domains with different characteristics such as number of developers, development software methodology and so on. Empirical investigation concerns both development of new applications and maintenance of already existing applications.

4.2   Selection of Experimental Subjects

The experimental subjects involved in the experimentation are developers all belonging to the same company. The developers of the four projects already developed did not know anything about Prometheus approach. All the developers of the five projects developed or maintained using Prometheus attended a training course on using Prometheus before to work on projects.

4.3   Experiment Operation

The experiment was organized in the following five experimental runs:

RUN_1 : retrospective analysis of four projects (P_1, P_2, P_3 and P_4) already developed (legacy projects) for each of one was available documentation;
RUN_2 : five projects (P_5, P_6, P_7, P_8 and P_9) developed from scratch;
RUN_3 : maintenance on P_5, P_6, P_7, P_8 and P_9;
RUN_4 : maintenance on P_5, P_6, P_7, P_8 and P_9;
RUN_5 : maintenance on P_5, P_6, P_7, P_8 and P_9.

RUN_2, RUN3, RUN_4 and RUN_5 refer to the same projects. All runs from the third to the fifth only refer to adaptive maintenance. Four data collections were carried out every fifteen days for each experimental run from second to the fifth.

At the beginning of each run from 2 to 5, each experimental subject received username and password to login Prometheus platform in order to try, access and possibly evolve KEPs stored in it. Researchers measured Function Points for all nine projects using theory of *Function Points analysis* promoted and defined by The International Function Point Users Group (IFPUG) (http://www.ifpug.org/). During RUN_1, data have been collected from both available documentation and through interviews to the project managers. Collected data of all runs were stored on spreadsheets and, finally, the tool Statistica 7.0 developed by StatSoft (http://www.statsoft.com/) was used to execute all the analyses.

4.4   Projects Characterization

All nine industrial projects analyzed in our research present the features of enterprise applications, such as: an extended purpose; a high number of users, a required performance adequate to the application usage. Table 1 shows information about the all the projects. Several project were developed using a *Water-Fall (WF)* software development methodology. It is important to note that number of developers is always different from one project to other one.

It is important to note that the software methodologies used are only those ones known by the company involved in experimentation.

Table 2 shows how each development team was assigned to each experimental run. Assignment was made so that each team worked with a project, and as consequence for each methodology, not more than once.

The turnover of the developers involved in projects from P_5 to P_9 was continuous and occurred at the end of each experimental session through the reallocation of each team on a project different from the previous year. This turn-over was performed to assess the transferability of the use of the knowledge base regardless of the specific project for which you use. Finally, different development methodologies were used to assess the transferability of the use of the knowledge base regardless of the specific development methodology used. Finally, the various dimensions of the development team, as well as the different dimensions of software development, have been normalized using Function Points as explained in the following paragraph.

4.5   Measurement Model

Productivity is defined as:

$$Productivity = \frac{Size}{ManEff} \tag{1}$$

Size is the total number of Function Points (FP_A) added to the application to satisfy requirements of production or maintenance:

$$FP_A = FPd_A + FPr_A \tag{2}$$

FP_A is obtained summing FPd_A, that is the number of the Function Points developed ex-novo, and FPr_A, that is the number of Function Points already developed and reused thanks to Prometheus. ManEffort is the time, expressed

Table 1. Projects description

Id. Brief Description	Software methodology	Developers
P_1 Registration and testing of autovehicle data history	WF	3
P_2 Electronic management of currency exchanges	WF	6
P_3 Management of bank stocks online	WF	5
P_4 Automation of human resources management	WF	2
P_5 Management of utilities energetic	WF	5
P_6 Management of Curriculum Vitae of a company	POD	5
P_7 Sharing of tacit and non structured knowledge present in an industrial	eXtreme Programming	5
P_8 Support the migration to a new SAP version or maintenance of a SAP installation	Light Weight Rational Unified Process	5
P_9 Upgrading of a SAP preconfigured system	LASAP	5

Table 2. Assignment of a development team to Project

Id.	RUN_2	RUN_3	RUN_4	RUN_5
T1	P_5	P_6	P_7	P_8
T2	P_6	P_7	P_8	P_9
T3	P_7	P_8	P_9	P_5
T4	P_8	P_9	P_5	P_6
T5	P_9	P_5	P_6	P_7

in man days (1 man day = 8 hours), spent for the development of a new functionality of an application. It is:

$$ManEff_A = ManEffd_A + ManEffr_A \tag{3}$$

where $ManEff_A$ is the total time for developing all Function Points added to application. It is obtained summing $ManEffd_A$, that is the time spent for developing ex-novo Function Points, and FPr_A, that is the time spent to integrate Function Points already developed and reused thanks to Prometheus.

5   Experimental Results

5.1   Productivity: RUN1 against RUN2

A first evaluation of the obtained result was made comparing the *Productivity* evaluated in RUN_1 with *Productivity* of RUN_2. In RUN_1, without Prometheus, the *Productivity* range is wider than in RUN_2 where developers, were supported by Prometheus. The results are shown in figure 2(a), where the box plots of *Productivity* evaluated during RUN_1 and RUN_2 are reported. From the figure we can observe that in RUN_1 *Productivity* range goes from 0,11 FP per day to

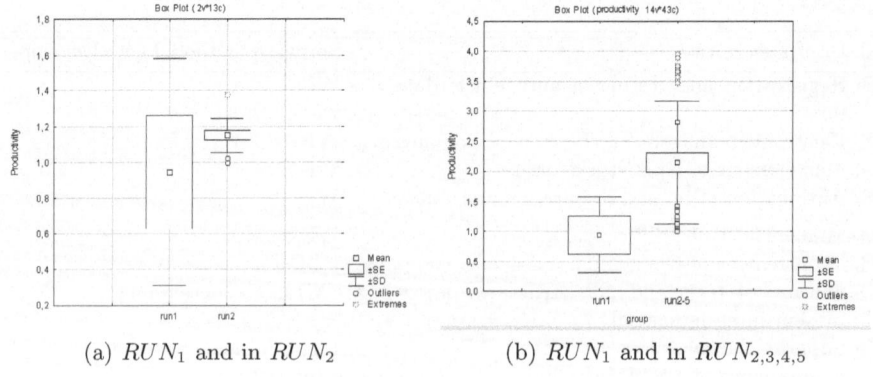

(a) RUN_1 and in RUN_2 (b) RUN_1 and in $RUN_{2,3,4,5}$

Fig. 2. Productivity with Prometheus and without Prometheus

1,58 FP per day with a mean value that is 0,94. In RUN_2, instead, *Productivity* range goes, except for outliers values, from 1,00 FP to 1,37 FP per day, and the mean value is 1,15 FP per day. Also, the dispersion of the results is very high for RUN_1 differently from RUN_2. Consequently interesting questions could be the following ones: Why is the range of FP much higher in RUN_1 than in RUN_2? Why is the mean value higher in RUN_2 than in RUN_1? In our opinion usage of Prometheus has made more predictable number of FP developed per day probably because of the systematic and process automation obtained by the use of CMS interfaced with Prometheus. It seems as if the performances are independent from the used technique.

5.2   Productivity: RUN_1 against $RUN_{2,3,4,5}$

Successively we compare *Productivity* results of RUN_1 with *Productivity* deriving from $RUN_{2,3,4,5}$. *Productivity* goes from mean value of 0,94 FP per day in RUN_1 to the mean value of 2,14 FP per day using Prometheus in the other four experimental runs. In each experimental run Prometheus is always better than the traditional approach and this confirms our hypothesis that Prometheus can increase Productivity of FP per day. Always observing figure 2(b) it is possible to note that the value mean of *Productivity* predictability for RUN_3, RUN_4 and RUN_5 is lower that value mean of RUN_2 probably because of increasing reuse of package.

5.3   Reuse: RUN_3, RUN_4, RUN_5

Figure 3 shows the trend of reuse of packages during $RUN_{3,4,5}$. Reuse grows with the populating of Prometheus. It is important to specify that this is not always true because it depends on matching between requirements to be developed to KEPs present in Prometheus. In other terms reuse grows or could grow with the populating of Prometheus.

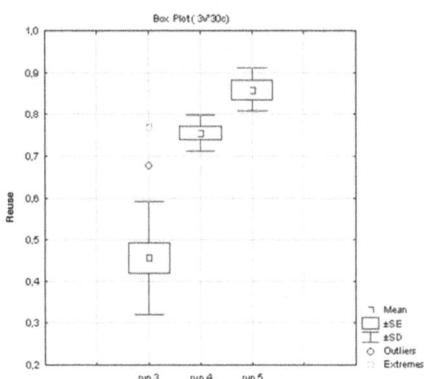

Fig. 3. Reuse in in $RUN_{3,4,5}$ (with Prometheus)

6   Conclusions

This paper proposes an approach based on the concept of KEP for knowledge transferring as further support for the software development. The proposed approach had previously been implemented through a KEB called Prometheus. To validate the approach, an empirical investigation was conducted. The experiment was carried out in an industrial context and consisted of a comparison between proposed approach and the traditional approaches used in the company in terms of *Productivity*. The collected results provide some lessons learned about Prometheus. Indeed Prometheus with respect to the traditional ones systematically formalizes and automates knowledge capturing, sharing and retention. Moreover it promotes reuse of developed functionalities reducing in this way the time necessary to produce them. It is clear that, in order to generalize the validity of the lessons learned proposed in this work, many replications, statistical validation and further studies, extended to other contexts, are needed. It is important to note that the selected set of experimental subjects, even if variegate, is not completely representative of the population of all software developers. As consequence, at this first stage, it is not possible to generalize the results of the empirical investigation. Rather, results represent a first important step towards this direction.

References

1. Ardimento, P., Baldassarre, M., Cimitile, M., Visaggio, G.: Empirical experimentation for validating the usability of knowledge packages in transferring innovations. In: Filipe, J., Shishkov, B., Helfert, M., Maciaszek, L. (eds.) ICSOFT/ENASE 2007. CCIS, vol. 22, pp. 357–370. Springer, Heidelberg (2009)
2. Ardimento, P., Boffoli, N., Cimitile, M., Persico, A., Tammaro, A.: Knowledge packaging supporting risk management in software processes. In: Proceedings of IASTED International Conference on Software Engineering SEA, Dallas, pp. 30–36 (2006)
3. Ardimento, P., Caivano, D., Cimitile, M., Visaggio, G.: Empirical investigation of the efficacy and efficiency of tools for transferring software engineering knowledge. Journal of Information & Knowledge Management 7(03), 197–207 (2008)
4. Ardimento, P., Cimitile, M.: An empirical study on software engineering knowledge/Experience packages. In: Jedlitschka, A., Salo, O. (eds.) PROFES 2008. LNCS, vol. 5089, pp. 289–303. Springer, Heidelberg (2008)
5. Basili, V., Caldiera, G., McGarry, F., Pajerski, R., Page, G., Waligora, S.: The software engineering laboratory: an operational software experience factory. In: Proceedings of the 14th International Conference on Software Engineering, ICSE 1992, pp. 370–381. ACM, New York (1992)
6. Boden, A., Avram, G., Bannon, L., Wulf, V.: Knowledge management in distributed software development teams - does culture matter? In: Fourth IEEE International Conference on Global Software Engineering, ICGSE 2009, pp. 18–27 (2009)

7. Gendreau, O., Robillard, P.N.: Knowledge acquisition activity in software development. In: Rocha, Á., Correia, A.M., Wilson, T., Stroetmann, K.A. (eds.) Advances in Information Systems and Technologies. AISC, vol. 206, pp. 1–10. Springer, Heidelberg (2013)

8. http://prometheus.serandp.com/en/content/
   iterative-reengineering-method-based-gradual-evolution-legacysystem

9. Jedlitschka, A.: An empirical model of software managers' information needs for software engineering technology selection: a framework to support experimentally-based software engineering technology selection. PhD thesis (2009)

10. Jin, H., Peng, W.: Study on product design and development based on design knowledge base. In: Proceedings of the 2009 Second International Symposium on Computational Intelligence and Design, ISCID 2009, vol. 1, pp. 463–466. IEEE Computer Society, Washington, DC (2009)

11. Foray, D., Kahin, B.: Advancing Knowledge and The Knowledge Economy. In: Advances in Intelligent Systems and Computing, vol. 206. MIT Press (2006)

12. Klein, A., Altuntas, O., Husser, T., Kessler, W.: Extracting investor sentiment from weblog texts: A knowledge-based approach. In: CEC, pp. 1–9 (2011)

13. Klein, M.: Combining and relating ontologies: An analysis of problems and solutions (2001)

14. Malone, T.W., Crowston, K., Herman, G.A.: Organizing Business Knowledge: The MIT Process Handbook. MIT Press, Cambridge (2003)

15. Qian, Y., Liang, J., Dang, C.: Knowledge structure, knowledge granulation and knowledge distance in a knowledge base. Int. J. Approx. Reasoning 50(1), 174–188 (2009)

16. Reifer, D.J.: Is the software engineering state of the practice getting closer to the state of the art? IEEE Softw. 20(6), 78–83 (2003)

17. Rus, I., Lindvall, M.: Knowledge management in software engineering. IEEE Software 19(3), 26–38 (2002)

18. Schneider, K., Schwinn, T.: Maturing experience base concepts at daimlerchrysler. In: Software Process: Improvement and Practice, pp. 85–96 (2001)

19. Schneider, K., von Hunnius, J.-P.: Effective experience repositories for software engineering. In: Proceedings of the 25th International Conference on Software Engineering, pp. 534–539 (2003)

20. Zhuge, H.: Knowledge flow management for distributed team software development. Knowledge-Based Systems 15(8), 465–471 (2002)

Resolving Platform Specific Models at Runtime Using an MDE-Based Trading Approach

Javier Criado, Luis Iribarne, and Nicolás Padilla

Applied Computing Group, University of Almería, Spain
{javi.criado,luis.iribarne,npadilla}@ual.es

Abstract. Dynamic service composition provides versatility and flexibility features for those component-based software systems which need to self-adapt themselves at runtime. For this purpose, services must be located in repositories from which they will be selected to compose the final software architecture. Modern component-based software engineering and model-driven engineering techniques are being used in this field to design the repositories and the other elements (such as component specifications), and to implement the processes which manage them at runtime. In this article, we present an approach for the runtime generation of Platform Specific Models (PSMs) from abstract definitions contained in their corresponding Platform Independent Models (PIMs). The process of generating the PSM models is inspired by the selection processes of Commercial Off-The-Shelf (COTS) components, but incorporating a heuristic for ranking the architectural configurations. This trading process has been applied in the domain of component-based graphical user interfaces that need to be reconfigured at runtime.

Keywords: MDE, Trading, Components, Adaptation, Web Services.

1 Introduction

One of the traditional goals of software engineering (SE) has been the need to develop systems by assembling independent modules. The *Component-Based Software Development* (CBSD) is one of the traditional disciplines of SE that is characterized by describing, developing and using components based on techniques for building open, distributed systems such as distributed information systems. This approach makes software engineering faces to new challenges and problems, since this kind of systems requires a "bottom-up" development instead to a traditional "top-down" development. The CBSD process begins with the definition of the architecture, which sets out the specifications of the components at an *abstract* level. In the "bottom-up" perspective, most of the architectural requirements may be covered by other components stored in repositories. These repositories contain "concrete" specifications of components which are required by automated searching processes trying to locate those exact component specifications that meet with those abstract restrictions of the software architecture.

In addition, it is also important to take into account some automated processes which consider dependencies between the components of the architecture, and

Y.T. Demey and H. Panetto (Eds.): OTM 2013 Workshops, LNCS 8186, pp. 274–283, 2013.

generate possible combinations of the components. These combinations could provide a partial or complete solution of the architecture to be rebuilt at runtime. In this paper we propose a solution for systems that use a component-based architecture that can change at runtime, and therefore requiring an automatic reconfiguration. Examples of systems with this type of architecture may be seen for instance in smart home applications [1], robotics [2], communication network infrastructures [3], user interfaces [4], etc.

On the other hand, *Model-Driven Engineering* (MDE) has provided many solutions for software development. In the particular domain of *component-based software systems*, the use of MDE techniques can facilitate design and development of architectures, for example, for defining their structure, the behavior of their components and their relationships, their interaction or functional and non-functional properties [5].

Our research work intends to find a solution to the problem of adapting software systems at runtime, but focuses only on component-based systems. In our methodology, the life cycle for developing component-based architectures is structured on *abstract architectural model*, which corresponds to a PIM (*Platform Independent Model*) level of MDE and represents the architecture in terms of what sort of components it contains and their relationships; and *concrete architectural model*, which corresponds to the PSM (*Platform Specific Model*) level and describes what concrete components comply with the abstract definition of the architecture. The proposal presented in this paper concerns the adaptation process of concrete architectural models that solves a platform specific model fulfilling the component architectural requirements of the system at runtime. Given an starting abstract architecture, the concrete architectural models are realized by a semantical trading process [6], calculating the configurations of concrete components that meet the abstract definitions best, which provides the possibility of generating different software architectures based on the same abstract definition, for example, so it can be executed on different platforms.

The rest of the paper is organized as follows: Section 2 presents the domain for resolving our PSM models. Then, Section 3 explains the trading process. Section 4 shows a case study and describes validation performed. Section 5 reviews the related work and finally, conclusions and future works are given in Section 6.

2   Resolving Platform Specific Models

As outlined in the introduction, our research work focuses on the adaptation of component-based systems. We have chosen the domain of graphical user interfaces as part of research projects of the Spanish Ministry and the Andalusian Government that require adaptation of user interfaces at runtime. Our interest in this domain is due to the trend toward *Social Semantic Web* or *Web 3.0*.

In this context, we understand that it could be useful to have component-based user interfaces that can adapt their functionality depending on the circumstances. Under this scenario, the user interfaces have to be defined as architectural models in which each component represents a user interface component. We therefore assume that there is a repository containing such user interface components that could be fed by components developed by third-parties, as long as they comply with our specifications.

These components are represented in two levels of abstraction: (1) *abstract level*, corresponding to the PIM level of MDE, and (2) *concrete level*, which corresponds to the PSM level of MDE. Both types of component models will be constructed conform to the same metamodel, which is shown in Figure 1. This metamodel represents the main parts of a COTS component. Each component has a Functional part, and optionally, a NonFunctional part. The first contains the functional component properties, which are distinguished between provided and required. Provided properties are related with the services offered by the component, and Required properties represent the services necessary for the component to work properly.

The NonFunctional part contains non-functional properties of the component. For each non-functional property, it is possible to define the name, the value, the priority, if is observable (which means the component has mechanisms to offer its value) and if is editable (indicating the component has mechanisms to edit its value). The difference between abstract and concrete models lies in the latter have the property uri which indicates the location of the final component, while the property_priority attribute is only defined in the first. The fulfillment of this condition as well as verification that the model is correctly defined, is checked using OCL rules [7].

Moreover, for the remainder of the article, we will also use $\mathcal{R}$ to refer to the provided interfaces of a component and $\overline{\mathcal{R}}$ to represent its required interfaces. Similary, $\{MapInfo\}$ denotes an interface providing the $MapInfo$ service, and $\{\overline{UserInfo}\}$ represents an interface requiring the $UserInfo$ service.

From these component specifications, we build our abstract and concrete architectural models. They will be used in an adaptation process that is executed on both levels of abstraction. On the abstract level, M2M transformation processes are executed to adapt the abstract architectural models to the changes in

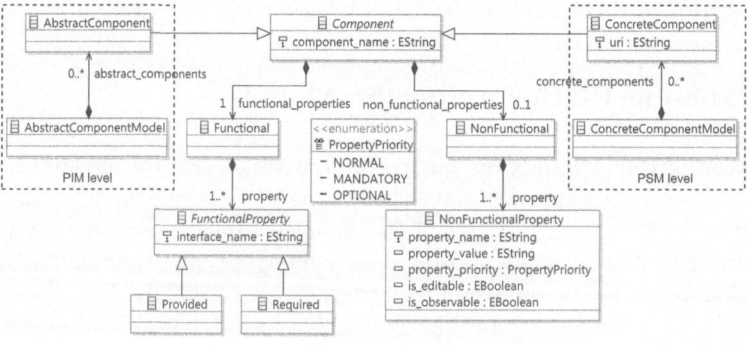

Fig. 1. Component Metamodel

the context [8]. Furthermore, the concrete architectural models are realized by a trading process, which is the goal of this paper, calculating the configurations of concrete components that best fulfill the abstract definitions (Figure 2).

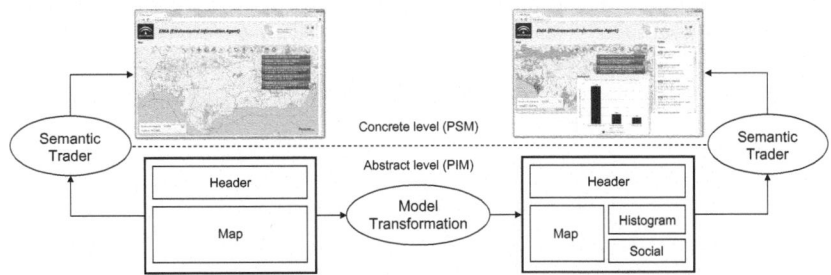

Fig. 2. Adaptation process within our GUI domain

Our trading process uses the information about the meaning given by combining the functional and non-functional properties of the components. Therefore, this mediation service, responsible for managing and selecting the best configuration of COTS-type concrete components, has been named *Semantic Trader service* and will be explained in detail in the next section.

3   Defining the Trading Process

Although there is a lot of work on the selection and evaluation of COTS components [9], our process for the selection of components is based on the proposal of [6]. In this approach, and also in the work presented in this paper, a trading service is developed for the management of the components and the configurations of the system architectures.

The main purpose of this service is to calculate the best possible configurations of available concrete components from the abstract definition of an architecture. These configurations are searched in order to fulfill the requirements described by the abstract definition. From the resolved configurations, the service generates a concrete architectural model as output. The steps of the trading process are shown in Figure 3 that will be explained above.

#1. Selection of candidates: As stated in the article from which this work arises [10], the selection of candidate components (CC) consists of filtering from the repository of concrete component specifications (CCR) those ones that could be part of the architecture. For this purpose, the process checks which are the concrete components of the repository that have at least one common provided interface with the definition given in the abstract architectural model. The filtering does not take into account the required interfaces of each concrete component, and their suitability to be part or not of the resulting configuration will be checked in the following steps.

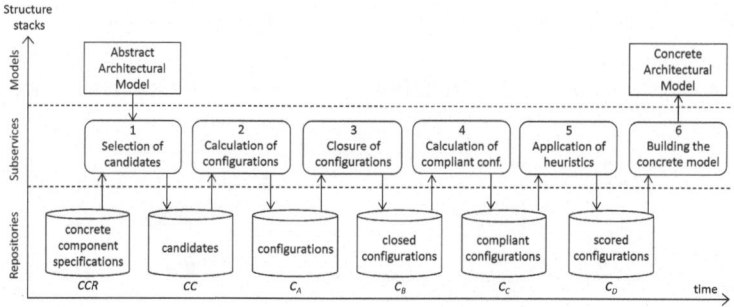

Fig. 3. Semantic Trader service

#2. Calculation of configurations: The next step is to perform the calculation of all the possible configurations of concrete components that could be constructed from the candidates. This process is inspired in the *backtracking* algorithm described in [10]. The aforementioned algorithm was developed for searching and matching components at design time. However, in our case, the adaptation of architectural models should be carried out at runtime, and the time it takes to run the *backtracking* algorithm does not meet our requirements. Furthermore, in our proposal, the configurations must satisfy a one-to-one matching between the components of the abstract architecture and the components of the concrete architecture. In this regard, the *backtracking* algorithm explores and generates a large number of configurations that will not be taken into account for the resulting concrete architecture. Consequently, and based on this premise, the algorithm for the calculation of the configurations has been implemented using a recursive algorithm whose stop condition is that a concrete component had been found for each abstract component existing in the input abstract architectural model. The pseudocode of the algorithm is shown in Table 1.

#3. Closure of configurations: The third step executed in our *Semantic Trader service* is the closure of all the possible configurations previously calculated. This phase is necessary because some of the configurations could generate solutions that are not complete, in the case that any of the concrete components requires some additional component so that the abstract definition runs correctly. The pseudocode of the algorithm is shown in Table 1. In this algorithm, all the candidates that are found for each configuration are checked. If any of these candidates has any additional required interface to the abstract architectural model, that configuration will be considered as unclosed. In contrast, if none of the candidates meet this condition, the configuration will be added to the repository of closed configurations C_B.

#4. Calculation of compliant configurations: As has been described in our approach the configurations must satisfy an one-to-one matching between the components of the abstract architectural model and the components of the concrete architectural model. This matching is pursued in order to facilitate adaptation and synchronization operations of our system, so that the actions

Table 1. Calculation and closure of the configurations

function configurations(i, sol, C_A)
if $i \geq$ card(AAM) **then**
$CC(i) =$ getCandidates(AAM_i)
for $j = 1 \rightarrow$ card$(CC(i))$
$sol := sol \cup \{CC(i)_j.\mathcal{R} \cap AAM_i.\mathcal{R}\}$
configurations$(i + 1, sol, C_A)$
$sol := sol - \{CC(i)_j.\mathcal{R} \cap AAM_i.\mathcal{R}\}$
endfor
else
$C_A := C_A \cup \{sol\}$
endif
endfunction

function closeConfigurations(C_A, C_B)
for $i = 1 \rightarrow$ card(C_A)
$closed :=$ **true**, $conf := (C_A)_i$
for $j = 1 \rightarrow$ card$(conf)$
$candidate := conf_j$
if $(candidate.\overline{\mathcal{R}} \cap AAM.\overline{\mathcal{R}}) <> \emptyset$ **then**
$closed :=$ **false**
endif endfor
endfor
if $closed ==$ **true then** $C_B := C_B \cup \{conf\}$
endif
endfunction

performed on the components of concrete and abstract levels have a direct correspondence with the components of the other level. Therefore, the behavior of this subservice is to discard those configurations that do not comply with the internal structure of the abstract architecture, *i.e.*, those configurations that have divisions or groupings of services that differ from those established in the abstract architectural model. Thus, it is generated the repository of compliant configurations C_C.

#5. Application of heuristics: Once the configurations have been filtered by choosing only those that match with the internal structure of the architecture, it is necessary to define a process that evaluates each configuration to establish a criteria for the selection of the best one. With this aim, a ranking process based on heuristics has been defined. This heuristics process checks the matching between each of the abstract components and their corresponding concrete components that resolve them. The total score of the configuration will be the sum of the partial scores for each component. The heuristics rules could be separated in two categories, each one referring to the main parts of the component definition that has been described in Figure 1. The scores are shown in Table 2. The defined heuristics is based on the analysis performed in which we study what are the most important criteria for the configurations to meet the system requirements. It is also based on a "backwards" analysis from the configurations of concrete components that we know that are better (that resolve an abstract definition

Table 2. Scoring the configurations

Functional Properties	Score
Direct matching between the $\mathcal{R}$ of the abstract component and the $\mathcal{R}$ of the concrete component	+0.5
Direct matching between the $\overline{\mathcal{R}}$ (if the condition of direct matching between provided is met)	+0.3
Each additional provided interface regarding those defined in the abstract component	−0.1
Each additional required interface regarding those defined in the abstract component	−0.2
Each additional binding needed in the architecture	−0.3
Non-Functional Properties	**Score**
Each 'mandatory' property that matches the abstract definition	+0.1
Each 'normal' property that matches the abstract definition	+0.05
Each 'optional' property that matches the abstract definition	+0.02
Each property defined as 'observable'	+0.01
Each property defined as 'editable'	+0.01
Each additional property regarding those defined in the abstract component'	+0.01

better) for our purpose. As a result of applying this process, the repository of scored configurations, C_D, is generated.

#6. Building the concrete model: Once the repository of scored configurations, C_D, has been calculated, the Semantic Trader service builds the concrete architectural model offering it as its output. This model is constructed from the configuration that has a higher score, that is, it is the configuration that best fulfills the abstract definition.

4   Case Study: Implementation and Validation

With the aim of illustrate the presented approach, a case study is shown below. Let us suppose that the current software architecture managed by the system has an abstract definition at the PIM level (*i.e.*, an abstract architectural model) containing the following four abstract components: *Map, Histogram, Header* and *Social*. This architecture could represent the right GUI of the Figure 2. From this abstract architectural model, the *Semantic Trader service* will be called at runtime for resolving the PSM model (*i.e.*, the concrete architectural model). Looking into the repository of concrete component specifications CCR, the concrete candidates components CC shown in Table 3 are selected. Due to space reasons, the table only shows information related to the functional properties, since they are involved in the most of trader subservices.

Once the candidates have been selected, the remaining subservices are called. First, all the possible configurations are calculated. Second, these configurations are filtered with the described closure process. Then, the closed configurations that comply with the architecture are selected. These configurations are scored by applying the defined heuristics and, therefore, the ordered set of configurations shown in the Table 3 is generated.

Table 3. Abstract components, concrete candidates, and resulting configurations

Abstract components														
$Map = \{MapInfo\}, Histogram = \{HistInfo, MapInfo\},$														
$Header = \{UserInfo\}, Social = \{SocialInfo, \overline{UserInfo}\}$														

Concrete candidate components (CC)														
$(1)MapCom1 = \{MapInfo\}$							$(7)HistCom2 = \{HistInfo, MapInfo\}$							
$(2)MapCom2 = \{MapInfo, Feedback\}$							$(8)HeaderCom1 = \{UserInfo, Language, \overline{Logout}\}$							
$(3)MapCom3 = \{MapInfo, \overline{OGCServices}\}$							$(9)HeaderCom2 = \{UserInfo, Logout, \overline{Weather}\}$							
$(4)MapCom4 = \{MapInfo, HistIfo\}$							$(10)HeaderCom3 = \{UserInfo, Logout\}$							
$(5)MapCom5 = \{MapInfo, \overline{UserInfo}\}$							$(11)SocialCom1 = \{SocialInfo\}$							
$(6)HistCom1 = \{HistInfo, Palette, \overline{MapInfo}\}$							$(12)SocialCom2 = \{SocialInfo, \overline{UserInfo}\}$							

#	1	2	3	4	5	6	7	8	9	10	11	12	Score	Configuration
1	M	-	-	-	-	-	H	-	-	U	-	S	2.41	$CC_1, CC_7, CC_{10} - \{L\}, CC_{12}$
2	M	-	-	-	-	-	H	U	-	-	-	S	2.31	$CC_1, CC_7, CC_8 - \{L, I\}, CC_{12}$
3	M	-	-	-	-	-	H	-	-	U	S	-	2.11	$CC_1, CC_7, CC_{10} - \{L\}, CC_{11}$
4	M	-	-	-	-	-	H	U	-	-	S	-	2.01	$CC_1, CC_7, CC_8 - \{L, I\}, CC_{11}$
5	M	-	-	-	-	H	-	-	-	U	-	S	1.51	$CC_1, CC_6 - \{P\}, CC_{10} - \{L\}, CC_{12}$
6	-	-	-	-	M	-	H	-	-	U	-	S	1.5	$CC_5, CC_7, CC_{10} - \{L\}, CC_{12}$
7	-	-	-	-	M	-	H	U	-	-	-	S	1.4	$CC_5, CC_7, CC_8 - \{L, I\}, CC_{12}$
...													...	...
43	-	M	-	-	-	H	-	U	-	-	S	-	0.1	$CC_2 - \{F\}, CC_6 - \{P\}, CC_8 - \{L, I\}, CC_{11}$
44	-	-	-	M	-	H	-	U	-	-	S	-	0.1	$CC_4 - \{M\}, CC_6 - \{P\}, CC_8 - \{L, I\}, CC_{11}$
Key $\rightarrow$ CC_i: i-th candidate, M: $MapInfo$, H: $HistInfo$, U: $UserInfo$, S: $SocialInfo$, L: $Logout$, I: $Language$, P: $Palette$, F: $Feedback$, P: $Palette$														

As a result, the best scored configuration is the one containing the candidates components CC_1, CC_7, CC_{10} and CC_{12}. The concrete component CC_{10} has an additional provided interface (*Logout*) to the abstract definition, so it is necessary to perform a hiding operation of such interface. The given score is due to: (a) the direct matching between provided and required interfaces of CC_1, CC_7 and CC_{12} components $((0.5+0.3)*3 = 2.4)$, (b) the additional provided interface of CC_{10} component (-0.1) and (c) a 'mandatory' non-functional property that matches the abstract definition and which is also 'observable' $(0.1 + 0.01 = 0.11)$, making a total of 2.41. This configuration is used to build the concrete architectural model that will be generated as output of the process.

For the **validation** of our proposal, each of the subservices which are part of the Semantic Web service (see Figure 3) have been implemented and deployed on a web server. These services are described through the corresponding WSDL (*Web Service Description Language*) file to be used in combination with SOAP. Regarding execution times for the case study, total process time is about 54 *ms* which is an acceptable time for resolving the platform specific model at runtime.

5   Related Work

Even though our proposal covers different aspects on adaptation of component-based software systems, this paper is focused on resolving platform specific models of this kind of systems by using a trading service. Therefore, the reviewed papers describe approaches related to the selection and evaluation of COTS components [9]. There are many works dealing with the issue of COTS evaluation. In [11] authors proposed the *Off-The-Shelf Option* (OTSO) method that relies on *Analytic Hierarchy Process* (AHP) [12] with the aim of stablish an evaluation criteria for the components based on their features and the system requirements. In addition, the AHP method is used in a wide variety of COTS evaluation and selection approaches [13–15]. The problem is that this methodology only analyses unidirectional relationships among the different levels that are involved in the evaluation process. However, components are not always independent from each other [16], but often require other components or interact in a way that should be taken into account.

The authors in [17] present a model for the evaluation of the COTS combining TOPSIS (*Technique for Order Performance by Similarity to Idea Solutuion*) and ANP (*Analytic Network Process*) techniques. The describe framework is practical for ranking COTS in terms of their performance regarding multiple criteria. Otherwise, the work in [18] proposed a methodology of six steps based on a quality model that decompose the component characteristics for their evaluation, and it describes a selection process with the DesCOTS system. In contrast, our component evaluation proposal is more simple and only takes into account the component specification in terms of functional and non-functional properties.

In [6] the COTStrader approach which inspired this paper is presented. It describes a trading service for the management of COTS components and how it can be used for build component-based systems at design time. However, our trading service is intended to generate at runtime PSM models from their PIM specification, due to which, the algorithms have been modified. An approach for the selection of COTS based on cots and system requirements is described in [19]. In this paper, the authors present DEER, a framework for COTS selection in the requirement phase of a component-based development process.

None of the processes described in these papers occur during the execution of the system, nor aim to adapt the structure of the component-based architecture at runtime. Instead, our proposal resolves at runtime the configurations of concrete components to achieve the adaptation of architectural models.

6 Conclusions and Future Work

In this paper we have presented an approach for resolving Platform Specific Models at runtime. These PSM models fulfill the specifications of an abstract architectural model, which represents the software architecture at the PIM level. Our architectures are made up of COTS-type components, so we were inspired by the proposals of selection and search for these components to generate our processes and our models. As a consequence, a MDE-based Trading service has been developed for realizing the concrete architectural models from the abstract architectures, calculating the configurations of concrete components that best meet the abstract definitions.

Our trading process provides the possibility of generating different software architectures based on the same abstract definition, for example, so it can be executed on different platforms. It uses the information about the meaning given by combining the functional and non-functional properties of the components for the calculation and the ranking of the configurations, so our trading process has been named *Semantic Trader*. It involves six stages to accomplish the requirements of the abstract model: selection of candidate components, calculation of configurations, closure of configurations, calculation of compliant configurations, application of heuristics, and calculation of the resulting concrete model. Each process has been implemented as a web service to be called from the main Semantic Trader service. This main service has been tested and validated on a case study in which acceptable execution times have been generated for resolving the platform specific models at runtime.

The developed trading service assumes that at least one configuration of concrete components that meets the abstract definition will be resolved. This limitation is intended to be improved in future work from the resolution of mismatches [20], and we want to provide some alternative resolution mechanism if there is a situation that can not calculate a valid configuration. Moreover, we also intend to implement searching algorithms (for calculating the configurations) that will be based on this heuristics to perform tree pruning for not explore possible configurations that do not lead to the optimal solution.

Acknowledgments. This work is supported by the Spanish MINECO under grant of the project TIN2010-15588, and the Spanish MECP under a FPU grant (AP2010-3259), and also by the Junta Andalucía under grant of the project P10-TIC-6114.

References

1. Cetina, C., Giner, P., Fons, J., Pelechano, V.: Autonomic Computing through Reuse of Variability Models at Runtime: The Case of Smart Homes. Computer (IEEE Computer Society) 42(10), 37–43 (2009)
2. Edwards, G., Garcia, J., Tajalli, H., Popescu, D., Medvidovic, N., Sukhatme, G., Petrus, B.: Architecture-driven self-adaptation and self-management in robotics systems. In: SEAMS 2009, pp. 142–151 (2009)
3. Garlan, D., Cheng, S.W., Huang, A.C., Schmerl, B., Steenkiste, P.: Rainbow: Architecture-based self-adaptation with reusable infrastructure. Computer (IEEE Computer Society) 37(10), 46–54 (2004)
4. Grundy, J., Hosking, J.: Developing adaptable user interfaces for component-based systems. Interacting with Computers 14(3), 175–194 (2002)
5. Crnkovic, I., Sentilles, S., Vulgarakis, A., Chaudron, M.R.: A Classification Framework for Software Component Models. IEEE Transactions on Software Engineering 37(5), 593–615 (2011)
6. Iribarne, L., Troya, J.M., Vallecillo, A.: A Trading Service for COTS Components. The Computer Journal 47(3), 342–357 (2004)
7. Cabot, J., Gogolla, M.: Object Constraint Language (OCL): A Definitive Guide. In: Bernardo, M., Cortellessa, V., Pierantonio, A. (eds.) SFM 2012. LNCS, vol. 7320, pp. 58–90. Springer, Heidelberg (2012)
8. Rodríguez-Gracia, D., Criado, J., Iribarne, L., Padilla, N., Vicente-Chicote, C.: Runtime Adaptation of Architectural Models: An Approach for Adapting User Interfaces. In: Abelló, A., Bellatreche, L., Benatallah, B. (eds.) MEDI 2012. LNCS, vol. 7602, pp. 16–30. Springer, Heidelberg (2012)
9. Mohamed, A., Ruhe, G., Eberlein, A.: COTS selection: past, present, and future. In: Engineering of Computer-Based Systems (ECBS 2007), pp. 103–114 (2007)
10. Iribarne, L., Troya, J.M., Vallecillo, A.: Selecting Software Components with Multiple Interfaces. In: IEEE 28th Euromicro Conf., pp. 26–32 (2002)
11. Kontio, J., Caldiera, G., Basili, V.R.: Defining factors, goals and criteria for reusable component evaluation. In: CASCON 1996, p. 21 (1996)
12. Saaty, T.L.: How to make a decision: the analytic hierarchy process. European Journal of Operational Research 48(1), 9–26 (1990)
13. Morera, D.: COTS evaluation using desmet methodology & analytic hierarchy process (AHP). In: Oivo, M., Komi-Sirviö, S. (eds.) PROFES 2002. LNCS, vol. 2559, pp. 485–493. Springer, Heidelberg (2002)
14. Finnie, G.R., Wittig, G.E., Petkov, D.I.: Prioritizing software development productivity factors using the analytic hierarchy process. Journal of Systems and Software 22(2), 129–139 (1993)
15. Min, H.: Selection of software: the analytic hierarchy process. International Journal of Physical Distribution & Logistics Management 22(1), 42–52 (1992)
16. Carney, D.J., Wallnau, K.C.: A basis for evaluation of commercial software. Information and Software Technology 40(14), 851–860 (1998)
17. Shyur, H.J.: COTS evaluation using modified TOPSIS and ANP. Applied Mathematics and Computation 177(1), 251–259 (2006)
18. Grau, G., Carvallo, J.P., Franch, X., Quer, C.: DesCOTS: A Software System for Selecting COTS Components. In: IEEE 30th Euromicro Conf., pp. 118–126 (2004)
19. Cortellessa, V., Crnkovic, I., Marinelli, F., Potena, P.: Experimenting the Automated Selection of COTS Components Based on Cost and System Requirements. J. UCS 14(8), 1228–1255 (2008)
20. Mohamed, A., Ruhe, G., Eberlein, A.: Mismatch handling for COTS selection: a case study. J. Softw. Maint. Evol.-Res. Pract. 23(3), 145–178 (2011)

Software Architecture in Distributed Software Development: A Review

Alok Mishra[1] and Deepti Mishra[2]

[1] Department of Software Engineering, Atilim University, Ankara, Turkey
alok@atilim.edu.tr
[2] Department of Computer Engineering, Atilim University, Ankara, Turkey
deepti@atilim.edu.tr

Abstract. This paper presents a literature review of distributed software development (DSD) or global software development (GSD) and software architecture. The main focus is to highlight the current researches, observations, as well as practice directions in these areas. The results have been limited to peer-reviewed conference papers and journal articles, and analysis reports that major studies have been performed in software architecture and global software development, while the empirical studies of interfacing distributed/global software development and software architecture has only received very little attention among researchers up to now. This indicates the need for future research in these areas.

Keywords: Software Architecture, Global Software Development, Distributed Software Development, Knowledge Management.

1 Introduction

Global software development is becoming a widely accepted practice in software industry [35]. The advent of the Internet has supported Global Software Development (GSD) by introducing new concepts and opportunities, resulting in benefits such as scalability, flexibility, interdependence, reduced cost, resource pools, and usage tracking. GSD brings challenges to distributed software development activities due to geographic, cultural, linguistic, and temporal distance among project development teams [18]. The number of organizations distributing their software development processes worldwide to attain increased profit and productivity as well as cost reduction and quality improvement is growing [24]. Ensuring quality issues in distributed software development projects is a significant issue [23, 26].

The popularity of GSD is expected to continue growing for many reasons, such as reducing cost, improving quality, shortage of skilled people, and improving time-to-market [5]. Ali et al. [2] further argue that software development companies are discovering new ways of leveraging software development resources that are geographically dispersed and, therefore, there is an increasing need to identify and understand mechanisms for scaling the processes and practices of traditional software development to meet the requirements of GSD.

Y.T. Demey and H. Panetto (Eds.): OTM 2013 Workshops, LNCS 8186, pp. 284–291, 2013.

Software Architecture is a recognized and indispensable part of system development defined in terms of components, connectors, and is usually represented in different views, where each view shows certain concerns to stakeholders [33]. Architecture serves as a blueprint for developers, and it constitutes an abstract description of the application which serves as a basis for verifiable architecture rules. Architecture-based development, thus, facilitates communication by improving comprehension through one common object of work that all participants use and understand [21]. Software architecture can be used to reduce the need for communication in a multi-site development project as the gross structure of the system, the software architecture, can be used to divide work amongst sites [33].

According to Yildiz et al. [34] notably, architecting in GSD has not been widely addressed and key research focus in the GSD seems to have been in specific related to tackling the problems related to communication, coordination and control concerns.

A review of the literature in distributed or global software development shows that little deliberation has been paid on the software architecting process and software architecture as an artifact in the context of distributed software development. Therefore, the motivation of this paper is to provide summary of literature encompassing software architecture in distributed software development.

The paper is organized as follows. The next section presents major research studies in software architecture related with GSD/DSD areas. Finally, section 3 concludes with observations and limitations of the study.

2 Major Studies in Software Architecture in DSD

Distributed software development usually consists of several sites, on which different teams are working to develop a component of a software project. Distributed software development projects have to manage different challenges in different domains including software architecture, eliciting and communicating requirements, setting up suitable environments and tools, and composition of the information system project.

2.1 Software Architecture and DSD

A software architecture design includes components and interfaces [28], which connect different components [2]. A software architecture drives the structure of an organization [4, 15, 16, 20, 31] and is used as a means for coordinating projects [4, 20]. It is used as a coordination mechanism in distributed organizations to allocate tasks and coordinate the distributed teams [16, 19].

An extremely important kind of knowledge that needs to be shared is that concerning the software architecture, where, the global structure of the system to be built is decided upon. This structure, among others, should capture the major architectural decisions that led to it [10]. Capturing these architectural decisions facilitates a better decision-making process in a shorter time, reducing rework and improving the quality of the architecture [7]. In the context of GSD, sound management of architectural knowledge can help overcome the challenges innate to

GSD. Architectural knowledge management can be implemented by performing a series of well-defined practices [14].

Software architecting is a knowledge-intensive process, involving many different stakeholders and, as the size and complexity of system increases, more people get involved, and architecting turns into collaboration [33]. Sharing architectural knowledge is crucial, in particular for reusing best practices, obtaining a more transparent decision-making process, providing traceability between design artifacts, and recalling past decisions and their rationale [33]. All the challenges that face GSD have to do with different forms of distance: temporal distance, geographical distance, and socio-cultural distance [33]. These challenges have to do with [1]:

- Communication and collaboration among team members
- Tasks coordination, and
- Work supervision

Table 1 shows major studies performed in various areas of DSD software architecture during the last decade according to the review performed.

Table 1. Major Relevant papers in various areas of software architecture and GSD/DSD

Software Architecture and GSD	Major Relevant Studies
Knowledge Management	[2], [7], [13], [14], [17], [33]
Process and Quality	[2], [8], [12], [13], [17], [22], [30], [31], [32]
Framework and Tool Support	[5], [6], [27]

2.2   Software Architecture Knowledge Management and Rules

Clerc et al. [15] reported on the use of the so-called architectural rules to handle GSD concerns. Architectural rules are defined as "principles and statements about the software architecture that must be complied with throughout the organization". They have defined four challenges in GSD: time difference and geographical distance, culture, team communication and collaboration, and work distribution.

Part of overcoming these challenges has to do with adequate knowledge management, including the management of architectural knowledge [33]. Important information regarding architecture can be shared among sites in a GSD project, and also the architecture itself may serve as a kind of a proxy for communication, coordination, and control tasks. For instance, less informal meetings are required when all is clearly documented in the architecture documentation, making the coordination of work a lot easier [33].

Nour Ali et al. [2] presented a review of architectural knowledge management in GSD, and suggested that architectural styles and design decisions are important inputs for defining coordination strategies in an organization, while they have to be carefully selected when developing interfaces of components. However, their review is limited to practices associated in a global software environment by identifying the various constructs and their relationships by summarizing these relationships in a meta model and showing constructs inter-relations. Clerc et al. [14] concluded that architectural knowledge management practices that promote decentralization get much more attention that those promoting centralization at the agile GSD organization.

Rocha de Faria and Adler [30] showed that architecture-centric strategies can soften the impacts of physical distances. They argued that despite cultural barriers, GSD can bring advantages to the business, as long as an organization knows how to coordinate its distributed processes, requiring every person involved to be engaged in the effort - just like any conventional process improvement program - with an established architecture supporting and orienting all the activities. However, the benefits of gaining architectural knowledge that focuses on architecting as a decision-making process (i.e, assumptions, alternatives, and rationale) have not yet been widely accepted in GSD [13]. For example, performance is an important quality criterion, which demands to be addressed by architectural knowledge (according to the auditors, and acknowledged by Bachmann and Bass [8]).

In this respect, Hashmi et al. [18] have proposed cloud paradigm to meet the different challenges posed by GSD. This will result in GSD benefitting from the cloud's infrastructure, platform, and provision of software as a service feature, in which information and data on the cloud is transmitted and shared by means of web services which, in turn work on the underlying Service Oriented Architecture (SOA) principle. They further suggested that cloud can facilitate GSD both as a process and a product. The former could have implications for the GSD business model, in which service providers are organizations, and their services are parts of a GSD process; for instance, requirements, design, coding, and testing. SOA as a product is developed, run, and distributed globally [18].

2.3   Process and Quality

A global software process, based on a well-defined architecture, grants all team members a common language to define tasks and activities, allowing a better understanding of the business domain terms and project milestones in spite of their differences in terms of cultural and organizational settings [32].

Nord et al. [29] proposed a structured approach for reviewing architecture documentation (AD) which also builds on the stakeholders of the artifact and aims to engage and guide them to assure that the architecture documentation meets their quality concerns.

Non-functional requirements (quality issues) have to be satisfied in a software architecture and, once a high-level architecture is designed, the non-functional requirements should become stable [13, 30, 31]. An architect has to collaborate in the requirements elicitation phase to understand and model the non-functional requirements [2].

The distributed nature of software development and the related communication problem make tools and analysis that address these issues necessary to improve software quality and evolution. Del Rosso [17] has studied Social Network Analysis (SNA) by using the Apache web server, and found that metrics such as affiliation networks, centrality, betweenness, density, cohesion, communities, and brokerage roles allow a software architect to understand cohesion, communities, and communication in large and distributed software development teams [17].

Clerc [13] investigate the relationship between the number of distributed teams and the usefulness of architecture knowledge coordination strategies and practices. They further suggested that a high-level architecture design should be defined through architects from different sites meeting at collocated face-to-face meetings. A practice used for improving coordination is that each distributed team can include an architect. One of the architects from the distributed teams can be selected to be the leading architect from the site close to the customer [12] or at the headquarters of the organization [22].

2.4   Framework and Tool Support

Babar [5] has presented a framework for a groupware-supported software architecture evaluation process, which does not require the simultaneous participation of all the stakeholders; nor do stakeholders need to be physically collocated. This framework can be helpful in software assessment in distributed software development.

Avritzer et al. [3, 4] presented their experience report of the assessment of the coordination implications of software architecture in a global software development project. They observed that in GSD projects, it is especially important to minimize the need for communication among teams that are not collocated, and to maximize such communication within a local team instead.

According to Babar [6] software architecture evaluation is usually performed in a face to face meeting. Collocating large numbers of stakeholders is difficult and expensive to organize, particularly in the context of GSD projects and he proposed a groupware-supported software architecture evaluation process. Ovaska et al. [27] found in their studies that architecture could be used to coordinate distributed development, requiring that the chief architect be capable of maintaining the integrity of the architecture and of communication for all stakeholders.

3   Conclusions

This paper has presented brief summary of the current research themes related with software architecture in the global/distributed software development. There are still very few studies, including empirical ones, which focus in detail on software architecture and distributed or global development issues. The analysis revealed that most research has been done in software process and quality, knowledge management and framework and tool support areas while empirical industrial case studies, designing and modeling of software architecture for global/distributed software development, comparative case studies of different organizations, visualization, security, trust, standards and deployment issues could get too little attention in global/distributed information system development [25].

In near future, the authors intend to extend this literature review to include further dimensions and studies related with architecture and global software development.

Various case and industrial experience report may be included to enrich architecture issues related with GSD. As future work systematic review in this issue with available databases can also be carried out in this area.

References

1. Agerfalk, P., Fitzgerald, B.: Flexible and Distributed Software Processes: Old Petunias in New Bowls? Commun. ACM 49(10), 27–34 (2006)
2. Ali, N., Beecham, S., Mistrik, I.: Architectural Knowledge Management in Global Software Development: A Review. In: 2010 5th IEEE International Conference on Global Software Engineering (ICGSE), pp. 347–352 (2010)
3. Avritzer, A., Paulish, D., Cai, Y., Sethi, K.: Coordination implications of software architecture in a global software development project. J. Syst. Softw. 83(10), 1881–1895 (2010)
4. Avritzer, A., Paulish, D., Yuanfang, C.: Coordination implications of software architecture in a global software development project. In: Seventh Working IEEE/IFIP Conference on Software Architecture (WICSA 2008), pp. 107–116 (2008)
5. Babar, M.A.: A framework for groupware-supported software architecture evaluation process in global software development. J. Softw. Evol. and Proc. 24, 207–229 (2012)
6. Babar, M.A.: A Framework for Supporting the Software Architecture Evaluation Process in Global Software Development. In: Proceedings of the 2009 Fourth IEEE International Conference on Global Software Engineering (ICGSE 2009), pp. 93–102. IEEE Computer Society, Washington, DC (2009)
7. Babar, M.A., de Boer, R.C., Dingsøyr, T., Farenhorst, R.: Architectural Knowledge Management Strategies: Approaches in Research and Industry. In: Second ICSE Workshop on SHAring and Reusing Architectural Knowledge - Architecture, Rationale, and Design Intent 2007 (SHARK ADI 2007). IEEE Computer Society, Minneapolis (2007)
8. Bachmann, F., Bass, L.: Introduction to the Attribute Driven Design Method. In: 23rd International Conference on Software Engineering (ICSE 2001), pp. 745–746. IEEE Computer Society, Toronto (2001)
9. Baldonado, M., Chang, C.-C.K., Gravano, L., Paepcke, A.: The Stanford Digital Library Metadata Architecture. Int. J. Digit. Libr. 1, 108–121 (1997)
10. Bass, L., Clements, P., Kazman, R.: Software Architecture in Practice, 2nd edn. SEI Series in Software Engineering. Addison-Wesley Pearson Education, Boston (2003)
11. Bruce, K.B., Cardelli, L., Pierce, B.C.: Comparing Object Encodings. In: Ito, T., Abadi, M. (eds.) TACS 1997. LNCS, vol. 1281, pp. 415–438. Springer, Heidelberg (1997)
12. Caprihan, G.: Managing software performance in the globally distributed software paradigm in global software engineering. In: International Conference on Global Software Engineering (ICGSE 2006), pp. 83–91 (2006)
13. Clerc, V.: Do Architectural Knowledge Product Measures Make a Difference in GSD? In: 2009 Fourth IEEE International Conference on Global Software Engineering (ICGSE), pp. 382–387. IEEE Computer Society (2009)
14. Clerc, V., Lago, P., van Vliet, H.: Architectural Knowledge Management Practices in Agile Global Software Development. In: Proceedings of the 2011 IEEE Sixth International Conference on Global Software Engineering Workshop (ICGSE-W 2011), pp. 1–8. IEEE Computer Society, Washington, DC (2011)

15. Clerc, V., Lago, P., Van Vliet, H.: Global Software Development: Are Architectural Rules the Answer? In: Second IEEE International Conference on Global Software Engineering (ICGSE 2007), August 27-30, pp. 225–234 (2007)
16. Clerc, V., Lago, P., Van Vliet, P.: Assessing a Multi-Site Development Organization for Architectural Compliance. In: Sixth Working IEEE/IFIP Conference on Software Architecture. IEEE Computer Society (2007)
17. Del Rosso, C.: Comprehend and analyze knowledge networks to improve software evolution. J. Softw. Maint. Evol.: Res. Pract. 21, 189–215 (2009)
18. Hashmi, S.I., Clerc, V., Razavian, M., Manteli, C., Tamburri, D.A., Lago, P., Di Nitto, E., Richardson, I.: Using the Cloud to Facilitate Global Software Development Challenges. In: Proceedings of the 2011 IEEE Sixth International Conference on Global Software Engineering Workshop (ICGSE-W 2011), pp. 70–77. IEEE Computer Society, Washington, DC (2011)
19. Herbsleb, J.D., Grinter, R.E.: Architectures, Coordination, and Distance: Conway's Law and Beyond. IEEE Software 16(5), 63–70 (1999)
20. Herbsleb, J.D.: Global software engineering: the future of socio- technical coordination. In: Future of Software Engineering (FOSE 2007), pp. 188–198 (2007)
21. Kornstadt, A., Sauer, J.: Tackling Offshore Communication Challenges with Agile Architecture-Centric Development. In: The Working IEEE/IFIP Conference on Software Architecture (WICSA 2007), January 6-9, p. 28 (2007)
22. Laredo, J.A., Ranjan, R.: Continuous improvement through iterative development in a multi-geography. In: Third IEEE International Conference on Global Software Engineering 2008, pp. 232–236 (2008)
23. Mishra, D., Mishra, A.: A Global Software Inspection Process for Distributed Software Development. J. UCS 18(19), 2731–2746 (2012)
24. Mishra, D., Mishra, A.: A review of non-technical issues in global software development. International Journal of Computer Applications in Technology 40(3), 216–224 (2011)
25. Mishra, D., Mishra, A.: Research Trends in Management Issues of Global Software Development: Evaluating the Past to Envision the Future. Journal of Global Information Technology Management 14(4), 48–69 (2011)
26. Mishra, D., Mishra, A.: A software inspection process for globally distributed teams. In: Meersman, R., Dillon, T., Herrero, P. (eds.) OTM 2010. LNCS, vol. 6428, pp. 289–296. Springer, Heidelberg (2010)
27. Ovaska, P., Rossi, M., Marttiin, P.: Architecture as a coordination tool in multi-site software development. Software Process: Improvement and Practice 8(4), 233–247 (2003)
28. Perry, D.E., Wolf, A.L.: Foundations for the study of software architecture. SIGSOFT Software Engineering Notes 17(4), 40–52 (1992)
29. Nord, R., Clements, P., Emery, D., Hilliard, R.: A Structured Approach for Reviewing Architecture Documentation. Technical Note, CMU/SEI-2009-TN-0302009, SEI-CMU (2009)
30. Rocha de Faria, H., Adler, G.: Architecture-Centric Global Software Processes. In: International Conference on Global Software Engineering (ICGSE 2006), pp. 241–242 (2006)
31. Salger, F.: Software architecture evaluation in global software development projects. In: Meersman, R., Herrero, P., Dillon, T. (eds.) OTM 2009 Workshops. LNCS, vol. 5872, pp. 391–400. Springer, Heidelberg (2009)

32. Vanzin, M., Ribeiro, M.B., Prikladnicki, R., Ceccato, I., Antunes, D.: Global Software Processes Definition in a Distributed Environment. In: 29th Annual IEEE/NASA Software Engineering Workshop, April 7, pp. 57–65 (2005)
33. van Vliet, H.: Software Architecture Knowledge Management. In: van Vliet, H. (ed.) 19th Australian Conference on Software Engineering (ASWEC 2008), pp. 24–31 (2008)
34. Yildiz, B.M., Tekinerdogan, B., Cetin, S.: A Tool Framework for Deriving the Application Architecture for Global Software Development Projects. In: IEEE Seventh International Conference on Global Software Engineering (ICGSE 2012), pp. 94–103 (2012)
35. Yu, L., Mishra, A.: Risk Analysis of Global Software Development and Proposed Solutions. Automatika 51(1), 89–98 (2010)

Run-Time Root Cause Analysis in Adaptive Distributed Systems

Amit Raj, Stephen Barrett, and Siobhan Clarke

School of Computer Science and Statistics
Trinity College of Dublin, Ireland
{araj,Stephen.Barrett,Siobhan.Clarke}@scss.tcd.ie

Abstract. In a distributed environment, several components collaborate with each other to cater a complex functionality. Adaptation in distributed systems is one of the emerging trends that re-configures itself through components addition/removal/update, to cope up with faults. Components are generally inter-dependent, thus a fault propagates from one component to another. Existing root cause analysis techniques generally create a static faults' dependencies graph to identify the root fault. However, these dependencies keep on changing with adaptations that makes design-time fault dependencies invalid at run-time. This paper describes the problem of deriving causal relationships of faults in adaptive distributed systems. Then, presents a statechart-based solution that statically identifies the sequence of methods execution to derive the causal relationships of faults at run-time. The approach is evaluated, and found that it is highly scalable and time efficient that can be used to reduce the Mean Time To Recover (MTTR) of a distributed system.

Keywords: Distributed Systems, Root cause analysis, Fault causal relationship, adaptive system, component-based system.

1 Introduction

In pervasive computing, the adaptive distributed systems (ADS) adapt (add/remove/update components) themselves to meet the changing functional and non-functional requirements both (say location, bandwidth, QoS, SLA, etc.,). Such a system is fault prone as it may assemble large number of un-foreseen components at run-time that may cause a number of run-time faults such as interface mismatch, component failed, service failed, etc. As components are generally interdependent, a fault in one component may propagate and cause another fault in another component. Thus, the original fault becomes manifest as a different fault [1]. The symptoms or evidence of such a fault may not contain the sufficient information to discover the root cause fault.

Existing root cause analysis (RCA) techniques generally use a graph to analyze the faults causal relationships. When a fault causes another fault, such faults are referred as causally connected faults and represented in a faults' causal-connection graph (FCG). We define FCG as a directed graph $G = (V, E)$, where

Y.T. Demey and H. Panetto (Eds.): OTM 2013 Workshops, LNCS 8186, pp. 292–301, 2013.

V is a set of faults that will be represented as nodes and E is the set of causal relationships among faults that will be represented as edges. Our FCG mainly aims to represent inter-component faults causal relationships. In an ADS, the construction of such an FCG is non-trivial primarily due to two reasons. Firstly, FCG constructed at design-time becomes invalid at run-time due to components adaptation. Thus, a run-time FCG construction mechanism is required. Secondly, in an ADS that is constituted dynamically through plug-in/out of components at run-time, there is no opportunity to apply existing FCG construction techniques such as simulations, testing, fault injections, statical analysis, etc. A few run-time techniques exist such as failure path analysis, execution path analysis, log analysis [2] [3] [4] [2], but they drastically increase the MTTR.

2   State of the Art

RCA approaches can be categorized into two categories: non-dependency based and dependency-based approaches. In ADS, RCA techniques generally require dependency-based approaches [3] [5] [2], thus we focus our review on this category, which are further subdivided into design-time and run-time techniques.

2.1   Dependency-Based RCA Approaches

Dependency-based approaches generally use the topology of components or dependency relationship between faults. These approaches include codebook approach, fault propagation/causal graphs and active probing. The dependency-based approaches generally use a graph, for example, codebook approach uses a directed graph that has faults and evidence events as the nodes, fault propagation/causal graph approaches use a directed graph having faults as nodes, and active probing uses more specific graphs such Bayesian network.

Design-time FCG Construction for RCA. The design time techniques perform simulations and tests on design-time available components to analyze the causal relationships between faults to construct an FCG. Candea et al. [4] and Le et al. [6] illustrate an automatic failure-path generation technique. They declare two faults that lie on a same execution path as causally connected. Candea et al. [4] technique takes no prior information, but takes hours to run and require several reboots that is not feasible for a highly available ADS.

Andrews et al. [7] describe the use of directed graph of component's variables to construct the fault tree where faults are linked with logical operators. This approach assumes a static set of components, whereas the set is likely to change after an adaptation at run-time. Prescott et al. [8] describe the fault propagation analysis using petri-net representation of a system, where fault propagation is observed through relevant tokens that propagate across the petri-net model. It constructs an FCG only when a symptom is identified that will do a reactive RCA and increases the MTTR. Liu et al. [5] describe a fault diagnosis mechanism that uses a fault dependency relationship matrix. However, the derivation of matrix was not described in the paper. Moreover, in a dynamic system, such matrices are required to be re-generated after each adaptation that becomes a bottleneck in the performance. Most design-time techniques carry out fault correlation through simulations, test cases, deployment information or static analysis. However, the limitation to foresee the run-time situations, limits the use of design-time generated FCG.

Run-time FCG Construction for RCA. The run-time fault causal relationship detection techniques either tag the request to analyze the visited components [2], analyze the logs [3], or analyze the execution paths identified after each request response cycle and incrementally create the graph [4]. For example, Bellur et al. [3] discover the call traces and aggregate them to generate the topology graph of components and construct a Bayesian network of faults. However, it does not explain how to derive a causal relationship between two faults. Similarly, Lo et al. [9] create a Bayesian network where nodes are the components and edges represent the causal connection between components. When a fault evidence is detected, the Bayesian network is analyzed to locate the faulty component. However, the mechanism does not identify the specific fault in the faulty component.

Huang et al. [10] describe a passive event correlation technique that correlates the symptoms with faults. However, until the symptoms occur, faults cannot be analyzed. Similarly, Yemini et al. [11] describe an event correlation technique in real-time. They consider a set of symptoms as a code that is decoded to analyze the problem. The technique uses the topology of the system to create a bipartite graph that is required to generate the code. In an ADS, the topology of the system changes, thus bipartite graph changes and hence the code is required to be regenerated that may become bottleneck in performance. Ensel [12] describes an approach for automatically creating service dependency in a service-based system. Chen et al. [2] identify a fault propagation path by tagging a request and tracking it while traversing through components. It identifies the failed and successful component for a specific request id. Based on the success and failure status of a component for a specific request, it identifies a component that has the closest proximity for the existence of a fault. It helps in identifying the faulty component, however further analysis will be required to find out the exact root cause of a fault in the faulty component.

The discussed techniques cannot derive faults causal relationships to construct/update an FCG at run-time. This is because (1) Non-dependency based approaches do not construct an FCG, and (2) Dependency-based approaches cannot work because:

3 Problem

The research problem is illustrated through our case study that is an extended version of a smart office scenario described by Morin et al. [13]. The smart office uses an ADS that is a Message Transmission System (MTS, see Figure 1), to facilitate the communication between office employees. When a boss wants to send meeting details to one of his employees, the message is transmitted through MTS. The MTS adapts itself according to the context change and delivers a message at a suitable endpoint. For example, a voice message is delivered to employee's smart phone when he is driving, whereas an email message is delivered when he is at the office desk, assuming that the office does not allow the use of smart phones in their premises. The adaptations in MTS occur according to changes in the context variables. An environment may have several context variables, however, for brevity, only two context variables have been chosen: (1) employee location, and (2) internet bandwidth.

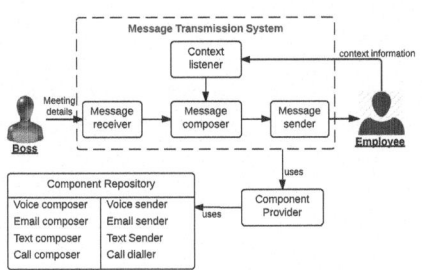

Fig. 1. Message Transmission System

Table 1. Adaptation Matrix

Scenario	Employee location	Internet Bandwidth	Message composer	Message sender
1	Driving	High	Voice composer	Voice sender
2	Office Desk	High	Email composer	Email sender
3	Cafeteria	High	Call composer	Call dialer
4	*	Low	Text composer	Text sender

When the context variables' values changes, the MTS imports the required components from Component Repository (CR) and deploys into the system at run-time to provide the required functionality. The MTS requests the Component Provider (CP) to provide the requested component. The CP connects to the CR, take out the required component that will be deployed into the MTS. Similar practices have been seen in dynamic discovery of services using UDDI registry [14]. A possible set of adaptation scenarios is described in Table 1.

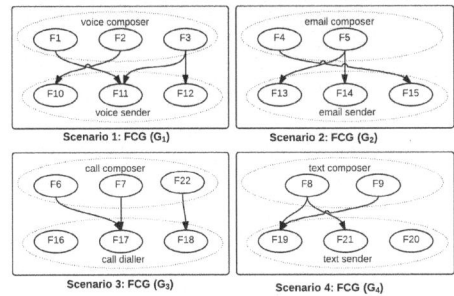

Fig. 2. Varying FCG for different scenarios

The MTS dynamically deploys and un-deploys several components at run-time. An analysis of faults in such components was carried out. Due to space constraint, detailed faults were not described, but they are labeled as f_1, f_2 ... f_{22}. The required FCGs for different scenarios are described in Figure 2. Assuming these scenarios will occur in a sequence ($1\rightarrow2\rightarrow3\rightarrow4$), an existing FCG will become invalid for the current scenario. In scenario 1, a fresh FCG (G_1) was created, but in scenario 2, the FCG (G_1) becomes invalid and a new FCG (G_2) is required. Similarly, in scenario 3, G_2 becomes invalid requiring G_3, and in scenario 4, G_3 becomes invalid and needs G_4.

The first step in constructing an FCG is to detect the causal relationship between faults. The causal relationship in an FCG can be broadly categorized into two categories: (1) Intra-component, and (2) Inter-component. Intra-component fault causal relationship detection does not require information about run-time coworker components. Thus, such relationships in a component can be analyzed in isolation from rest of the system at design-time using existing techniques [4] [6] [8].

However, the inter-component faults causal relationship detection is a challenging task primarily because it requires information about run-time coworker components. The key problem is to proactively derive faults causal relationships, in a dynamically constituted ADS, among faults of different components to construct/update an FCG after an adaptation.

4   Approach

The paper illustrates a state-based approach to determine the causal relationship between two faults. Our approach is based on the following hypothesis.

4.1   Hypothesis

Several fault correlation techniques (discussed in section 2) illustrate that two faults are causally connected if they fall in same execution path [6]. An execution path is a sequence of methods execution. When two methods lie on an execution path, the faults of these methods will be inter-dependent. Given this information, our hypothesis states that if two methods are in a sequence of execution, then the faults of preceded method are causally connected with the faults of succeeded method.

4.2   Part-Whole Statechart

The Part-Whole Statechart (PWS) [15] [16] describes the notion of a system-wide statechart (Whole) and components statecharts (Part or PC or PSC). In the Whole statechart, a transition from one state to another happens when an activity occurs whose statechart is described by a Part statechart. The PWS mechanism is described in Figure 3. The state transition in Whole statechart is carried out through an event whose functionality is implemented by a component. When the component statechart is executed and reached its final state, the component functionality is completed, and at that instant, the Whole statechart makes a transition to a next state.

In order to derive the fault causal relationships, the Part statecharts are further analyzed. We are using voicemail sending scenario of MTS, but the following

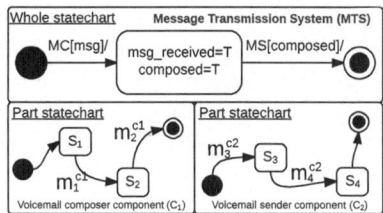

Fig. 3. A detailed PWS of MTS for voicemail sending scenario

Algorithm 1. State-based fault correlation Algorithm

Input: Whole statechart (W), the set of Part statecharts (P= $\{P_1...P_n\}$) where n is the number of components, and FCG.

Output: FCG

  $state \leftarrow$ start state of W
  $Q \leftarrow$ Breadth First Search Queue for W
  $Q.enqueue(state)$
  while $Q \neq empty$ **do**
    $state \leftarrow Q.dequeue()$
    $\{E\} \leftarrow$ set of all outgoing transition events from $state$
    for each e in E **do**
      $P_e \leftarrow$ Part statechart for e
      $\{M^{ce}\} \leftarrow$ set of methods making transition to <u>final state</u> in P_e
      $\{F^{ce}\} \leftarrow$ set of faults for all method $m \in M^{ce}$
      $nextstate \leftarrow$ getDestination_State_Of_Event(e)
      $Q.enqueue(nextstate)$
      $\{E_{next}\} \leftarrow$ set of all outgoing transition events from $nextstate$
      for each e_{next} in $\{E_{next}\}$ **do**
        $P_{e_{next}} \leftarrow$ Part statechart for e_{next}
        $\{M^{ce_{next}}\} \leftarrow$ set of methods making transition from <u>start state</u> in $P_{e_{next}}$
        $\{F^{ce_{next}}\} \leftarrow$ set of faults for all method $m \in M^{ce_{next}}$
        Node $n_{src} \leftarrow$ FCG.createNodeIfNotExist(F^{ce})
        Node $n_{dest} \leftarrow$ FCG.createNodeIfNotExist$(F^{ce_{next}})$
        FCG.makeEdgeBetween(n_{src}, n_{dest})
      end for
    end for
  end while

---

mechanism is generic and can be applied to any scenario of an ADS. In the Whole statechart, the first event is the message compose 'MC' event. This event will be carried out by voicemail composer component. In a Java based component, a task is carried out by executing a set of Java class methods. Therefore, the state transitions in a Java based component will happen through its class methods. In Figure 3, the method m_2^{c1} finishes the voicemail composition functionality and makes a transition to the final state of its Part statechart, and then, the Whole statechart reaches the next state. When the voicemail is composed, the Whole statechart executes the message sending event 'MS'. In the voicemail sender component, the method m_3^{c2} makes a transition from start state to S_3 state. Following the sequence of events, it is clear that the methods m_2^{c1} and m_3^{c2} are in a sequence where later one executes next to the former one. According to the hypothesis (section 4.1), it can be established that the faults of method m_2^{c1} are causally connected with the faults of m_3^{c2} using Algorithm 1. Now, the fault correlation will have two cases:

- **Case 1:** When a method has only one fault, say m_2^{c1} has f_{21}^{c1} and m_3^{c2} has f_{31}^{c2}, it can be derived that the faults f_{21}^{c1} is causally connected with f_{31}^{c2}.
- **Case 2:** When methods have more than one fault, say m_2^{c1} has f_{21}^{c1}, f_{22}^{c1} and m_3^{c2} has f_{31}^{c2}, f_{32}^{c2}, the causal connection between specific faults cannot be derived. The causal connection can be derived between fault sets such as the fault set $\{f_{21}^{c1}, f_{22}^{c1}\}$ is casually connected with the fault set $\{f_{31}^{c2}, f_{32}^{c2}\}$. Thus, a further investigation will be required to derive fault correlations between specific faults.

4.3 Results

As we are the partners of EU project "TRANSFoRm" [17], we applied this approach in the project. It is a distributed system that is composed of several components situated across different geographical locations. In order to collaborate with different partner's components, we implemented the system-wide workflow in Apache Camel. The components, developed by the partners, may add/delete/update dynamically in the workflow. This property is similar to that mentioned in section 3. Thus, we choose "TRANSFoRm" project as a good use-case.

In the "TRANSFoRm" project, different components provide their functionality through web-services. We build components as OSGi bundles that are running on OSGi platform to support adaptation. The owner of each component supplied the component's Part Statechart, and Whole statechart was built from the workflow written in Apache Camel. We applied our approach and found inter-component faults correlation graph as shown in Figure 4.

4.4 Limitations

Our approach is limited to find the correlation between faults arise due to functional requirements violations. However, in highly critical domains, our analysis is likely to be not sufficient for the faults occur due to violations of non-functional requirements.

5 Evaluation

5.1 Scalability

Scalability is one of the important factor to assess the applicability of a mechanism in todays distributed systems. Here, scalability mean efficiency of our algorithm against the number of components in a system. In order to assess

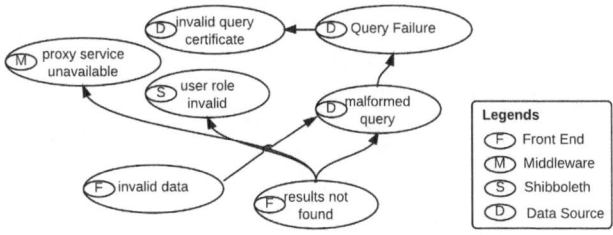

Fig. 4. A correlation between faults

the scalability of our mechanism, we ran several experiments on Java Virtual Machine having a heap memory of 1024 MB. As our mechanism requires only Whole and Part state charts as input (Algorithm 1), we developed a Java-based agent that automatically creates a Whole statechart and several Part statecharts based on a given domain theory [18]. An extremely large-scale system may have thousands or millions of components, thus, our experiments ran over a system having 100 to 1000,000 PSCs. The results are described in Figure 5. The time taken in case of 1000,000 PSCs was high, thus we ran our algorithm on 2 and 3 Java threads separately. We found a tremendous downfall in the time taken as shown in Figure 6. It is worth noting that the time taken was extremely low because we managed to keep a list of pointers in a statechart that directly points to the states that have direct transition to final states. Thus, our statecharts can be defined as a quintuple $< E, S, s_0, \delta, F, \phi >$ where E is a set of input alphabet, S is the set of states, s_0 is the initial state, $\delta : S \times E \times S$ is the state transition function and F is the set of final states, ϕ is the set of states that have direct transitions to final states F. It avoids the traversal time to find out the required states and increases time efficiency. It reduces the time for root cause analysis that reduces MTTR.

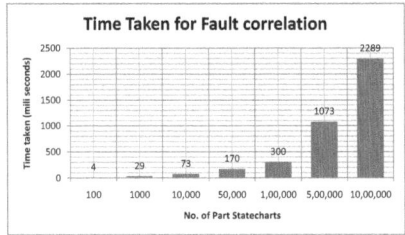

Fig. 5. Scalability Analysis for fault correlation time taken in an ADS

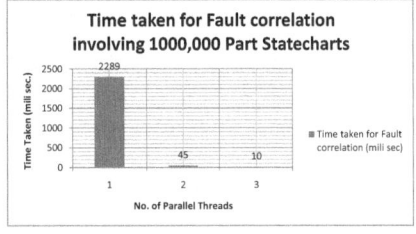

Fig. 6. Scalability Analysis for fault correlation time taken in an ADS having 1000,000 PWCs

5.2   Parallelism

A fault correlation between three faults, i.e., $f_1 \rightarrow f_2 \rightarrow f_3$ can be divided into two pairs of faults relationship, i.e., $f_1 \rightarrow f_2$ and $f_2 \rightarrow f_3$ (assuming transitive relationship between faults). In order to detect such pairs of faults, only two PSCs are required: one corresponding to preceding transition of a state in Whole statechart (preceding PSC), and second corresponding to succeeding transition of the same state in the Whole statechart (succeeding PSC). A pair of preceding and succeeding PSCs can be analyzed independently to detect fault correlation between two faults (as described in Algorithm 1). It is the property of our mechanism that makes our algorithm parallel. Thus, it can be scaled for an extremely large-scale system.

6   Conclusion

The paper describes the problem of fault correlation in adaptive distributed systems and presents a statechart-based solution. In an adaptive distributed system, a component is likely to dynamically install/update/remove in a system. In such cases, fault correlations are changed with every adaptation that makes an existing fault correlation graph invalid after an adaptation.

The paper illustrates that current techniques for fault correlation are not suitable as (1) either they work at design-time and cannot foresee run-time situations, or (2) they work at run-time that increases the MTTR. We presented a state-chart based run-time technique to analyze the fault correlations to support the root cause analysis in adaptive distributed systems. The paper presents the results of our experiment and evaluated our approach for scalability. We found that our approach is highly scalable and can be utilized in large-scale system involving thousands of components.

Acknowledgments. This work was supported, in part, by Science Foundation Ireland grant 10/CE/I1855 to Lero - the Irish Software Engineering Research Centre (www.lero.ie).

References

1. Abdelmoez, W., Nassar, D., Shereshevsky, M., Gradetsky, N., Gunnalan, R., Ammar, H., Yu, B., Mili, A.: Error propagation in software architectures. In: Software Metrics. In: Proceedings of 10th International Symposium on Software Metrics, pp. 384–393 (September 2004)
2. Chen, M.Y., Kiciman, E., Fratkin, E., Fox, A., Brewer, E.: Pinpoint: Problem determination in large, dynamic internet services. In: Proceedings of the 2002 International Conference on Dependable Systems and Networks, DSN 2002, pp. 595–604. IEEE Computer Society, Washington, DC (2002)
3. Bellur, U., Agrawal, A.: Root cause isolation for self healing in j2ee environments. In: Proceedings of the First International Conference on Self-Adaptive and Self-Organizing Systems, SASO 2007, pp. 324–327. IEEE Computer Society, Washington, DC (2007)

4. Candea, G., Delgado, M., Chen, M., Fox, A.: Automatic failure-path inference: A generic introspection technique for internet applications. In: Proceedings of the The Third IEEE Workshop on Internet Applications, WIAPP 2003, p. 132. IEEE Computer Society, Washington, DC (2003)
5. Liu, Y., Ma, L., Huang, S.: Construct fault diagnosis model based on fault dependency relationship matrix. In: Proceedings of the 2009 Pacific-Asia Conference on Circuits, Communications and Systems, PACCS 2009, pp. 318–321. IEEE Computer Society, Washington, DC (2009)
6. Le, W., Soffa, M.L.: Path-based fault correlations. In: Proceedings of the Eighteenth ACM SIGSOFT International Symposium on Foundations of Software Engineering, FSE 2010, pp. 307–316. ACM, New York (2010)
7. Andrews, J., Brennan, G.: Application of the digraph method of fault tree construction to a complex control configuration. Reliability Engineering and System Safety 28(3), 357–384 (1990)
8. Remenyte-Prescott, R., Andrews, J.: Modeling fault propagation in phased mission systems using petri nets. In: 2011 Proceedings - Annual Reliability and Maintainability Symposium (RAMS), pp. 1–6 (January 2011)
9. Lo, C.H., Wong, Y.K., Rad, A.B.: Bond graph based bayesian network for fault diagnosis. Appl. Soft Comput. 11(1), 1208–1212 (2011)
10. Huang, X., Zou, S., Wang, W., Cheng, S.: Fault management for internet services: Modeling and algorithms. In: IEEE International Conference on Communications, ICC 2006, vol. 2, pp. 854–859 (June 2006)
11. Yemini, S., Kliger, S., Mozes, E., Yemini, Y., Ohsie, D.: High speed and robust event correlation. IEEE Communications Magazine 34(5), 82–90 (1996)
12. Ensel, C.: Automated generation of dependency models for service management. In: Workshop of the OpenView University Association, OVUA 1999 (1999)
13. Morin, B., Barais, O., Jezequel, J.M., Fleurey, F., Solberg, A.: Models@ run.time to support dynamic adaptation. Computer 42, 44–51 (2009)
14. Walsh, A.E. (ed.): Uddi, Soap, and Wsdl: The Web Services Specification Reference Book. Prentice Hall Professional Technical Reference (2002)
15. Pazzi, L.: Part-whole statecharts for the explicit representation of compound behaviours. In: Evans, A., Caskurlu, B., Selic, B. (eds.) UML 2000. LNCS, vol. 1939, pp. 541–555. Springer, Heidelberg (2000)
16. Harel, D.: Statecharts: A visual formalism for complex systems. Sci. Comput. Program. 8(3), 231–274 (1987)
17. 7th Framework Programme European Commision: Transform project (April 2013), http://www.transformproject.eu/
18. Whittle, J., Schumann, J.: Generating statechart designs from scenarios. In: Proceedings of the 22nd International Conference on Software Engineering, ICSE 2000, pp. 314–323. ACM, New York (2000)

Global Software Development and Quality Management: A Systematic Review

Deepti Mishra[1], Alok Mishra[2], Ricardo Colomo-Palacios[3], and Cristina Casado-Lumbreras[4]

[1] Department of Computer Engineering, Atilim University, Ankara, Turkey
deepti@atilim.edu.tr
[2] Department of Software Engineering, Atilim University, Ankara, Turkey
alok@atilim.edu.tr
[3] Computer Science Department, Universidad Carlos III de Madrid, Madrid, Spain
ricardo.colomo@uc3m.es
[4] Universidad Internacional de La Rioja, Madrid, Spain
cristina.casado@unir.net

Abstract. This paper presents a systematic literature review of global software development (GSD) and quality management aspects. The main focus is to highlight the current research and practice direction in these areas. The results have been limited to peer-reviewed conference papers and journal articles, published between 2000 and 2011. The analysis reports that major studies have been performed in quality and process management, while verification and validation issues of GSD can only get limited attention among researchers. This indicates the need for future research (quantitative and qualitative) in these areas.

Keywords: Global software development, Quality, Process, Verification, Validation.

1   Introduction

Globalization has produced a new way to develop software: Global Software Development (GSD). GSD is a particular kind of Distributed Software Development (DSD) in which the teams are distributed beyond the limits of a nation [1]. Thus, software development is evolving from a single site development to multiple localization team environments [2] and projects are being contracted out in whole or in part [3]. GSD provides several outstanding benefits. In these terms of benefits, the accounts about cheaper work and "follow the sun" approaches are fading, while factors like proximity to the markets, access to specific expertise, productive friction and innovation capability tend to take the lead in driving the trend toward global software development [4]. In spite of its newness, GSD has been analysed in depth in scientific literature [5, 6, 7, 8].

The importance of GSD management has led to a huge effort in the art and science of organizing and managing globally distributed software development, but there is

Y.T. Demey and H. Panetto (Eds.): OTM 2013 Workshops, LNCS 8186, pp. 302–311, 2013.
© Springer-Verlag Berlin Heidelberg 2013

still a significant understanding to be achieved, methods and techniques to be developed, and practices to be evolved before it becomes a mature discipline [9]. Given that quality management is an important competitive advantage in organizations with geographically distributed software development centres [10], this paper aims at finding out what the main efforts and issues discovered are in the literature on the interaction between software quality management and GSD.

The paper is organized as follows. The next section presents research methodology. Section 3 reports the current status of research in software quality, software process, verification and validation related with GSD. Finally, section 4 concludes with results, discussions and limitations of the study.

2   Research Methodology

2.1   Motivation and Objectives

GSD has recently become an active research area and there is still a lack of quantitative studies in GSD. The effect of using best practices, models, and tools in DSD projects is still scarce in the literature [11]. Smite et al. [12] concluded in her systematic review that the amount of empirical studies in GSD/DSD areas are small, hence the field is still immature. So, this reflects that research in this theme is still in its early stages and requires maturation. On The other hand, quality is a significant component in software engineering and as a result of this for GSD. One of the challenges for GSD is quality and its management [13]. Although quality usually is not directly affected by its geographical location [14], some papers describe the indirect effects of distributed collaboration on quality [15, 16]. It was reported that regular quality problems exist in the products developed offshore [17] and "follow the sun" model is essentially a quick-and-dirty strategy that converts a schedule problem into a quality disaster [18]. Therefore, the aim of this paper is to perform a systematic review that includes software quality and GSD. This study will provide a comprehensive examination on the current status of research of quality, process, verification/ validation in GSD.

2.2   Research Method and Conduct

The research was initially designed to be a systematic literature review following the guidelines provided by Kitchenham and Charters [19]. This section presents all the steps taken in designing and performing the systematic review according to these authors. Regarding the need for conducting a systematic literature review in the area the following research questions are formed:

RQ1: What is the current status of quality practices (quality, process, verification & validation) in GSD?
RQ2: What are the software quality areas in which there is a gap regarding their application in GSD?

2.3   Data Retrieval and Data Sources/Resource Searched

Search strings were formulated by combining different quality practices and different types of distribution. It can be summarized as: (X1 OR X2........OR Xn) AND (Y1 OR Y2..........OR Yn), where X covers quality practices (quality, process, testing, inspection, review, verification, validation ...) and Y includes different alternatives of GSD and DSD as following:

X: {quality, process, testing, inspection, review, verification, validation}

Y: {global software development, distributed software development, global software engineering, GSD}

Furthermore, some limitations were applied on the searches. 1) The search was only performed in the following databases: Science@Direct, IEEE Explore, ACM Digital Library, SpringerLink. 2) The search items were journal articles, workshop papers and conference papers. In this study only peer-reviewed publications were taken into consideration and grey literature (like Google Scholar) has not been explored. 3) The publication period was set to be between 2000 and 2011. 4) The written language was set to be English. 5) Search was applied to full text to avoid exclusion of the papers that do not include our keywords in titles or abstracts, but which are still relevant to the review.

2.4   Results of Literature Review

The outcome of a search generally resulted in a rather high proportion of papers, some of which were later considered as being out of scope. Therefore, it was insufficient to use the search strings as the sole criteria for deciding whether to include or exclude a specific paper. The criteria for including a specific paper in this systematic review was that the paper should have sufficient focus on GSD as well as one of the quality practices (quality, process, testing, inspection, review, verification, validation,.......). More formally, the authors read through all abstracts with the following exclusion criterion:

- Exclude if the focus of the paper is clearly not on GSD.
- Exclude if the focus of the paper is clearly not on software quality.
- Exclude if the method, tool or theory described is not tested.

This process reduced the number of articles to 144. Table 1 presents the results of this process with respect to its source. Table 2 shows major studies performed in various areas of GSD quality practices during the last decade according to the review performed.

Table 1. Results of Literature Review

Source → Issue ↓	Science Direct	IEEE	ACM	Springer	TOTAL
Quality	1	15	10	31	57
Process	3	19	7	19	48
Verification & Validation	0	18	5	16	39
				Total	144

Table 2. Major Relevant papers in various areas of GSD Quality Practices

Quality Practices	Major Relevant Studies
Quality	[20], [21], [22], [23], [24], [25], [26], [27], [28], [29]
Process	[30], [31], [32], [33], [34], [35], [36], [37], [38], [39], [40]
Verification & Validation	[41], [42], [43], [44], [45], [46], [47]

3   Quality Management in GSD

This section reviews the main studies related with GSD and quality management.

3.1   Quality

Agarwal et al. [24] proposed a new model that modifies the core quality assurance facilitators' structure by entrusting the quality facilitation activity within business groups. According to this model, each business group has a quality manager supported by a group of Virtual Quality Assurance Facilitators. Annous, Livadas, and Miles [25] presented OffshoreQA, a framework that can be deployed and used in an offshore software development outsourcing organization aiming to implement an ISO 9001:2008 compliant quality management system. Caprihan [26] proposed an experience-based methodology on how to manage the performance of an application that is developed under this radically new development paradigm. Kuni and Bhushan [27] described Wipro Offshore Outsourcing Methodology (WOOM) that focus to include quality metrics in the outsourcing process and provided guidelines to practitioners and decision makers to estimate the cost of IT Application Offshore Outsourcing. Laredo and Ranjan [28] identified challenges faced by global teams working in a very dynamic environment. According to them, challenges for such engagements are mainly two. The first challenge is to understand the team dynamics and project variables and the second one is to adjust the performance in an iterative feedback mechanism to evolve efficiency over time. They further suggested that more structure and innovation can be introduced in the process if a new suite of tools is designed specifically for GSD arrives in the industry. Cusick and Prasad [29] presented a model for offshore development and insights into their management and engineering techniques, which can be replicated in other environments. The proposed model provides a structural framework and the guidelines necessary to maintain the quality of offshore engagements. More specifically, they recommend specifying coding standards in detail and enforcing them.

3.2   Process

The software development process is considered one of the most important success factors for distributed projects [48]. Unclear requirements and new technologies make the waterfall model unsuitable for offshore developing strategic systems [30]. Although the use of a spiral model is uncommon in the development of business information systems, the strategic importance of a system warrants detailed planning, experimentation, verification, validation and risk management provided by the spiral model [30]. As a result of this, the literature has produced a handful of remarkable contributions to GSD process.

Ramasubbu et al. [32] proposed a process-maturity model that features 24 new key process areas (KPA) mapped into four theoretical concepts for distributed work: mutual knowledge, technology readiness, collaboration readiness, and coupling in work. These KPAs address the wide-ranging capabilities needed for managing such development and arrange them in an evolutionary order similar to the CMM framework. Cusumano et al. [33] investigated offshore software development firms and observed that key CMM process areas can be used to create a platform for learning, thus making offshore development process improvement more effective.

Recently, Prikladnicki and Audy [40] reported systematic review of process models in the practice of distributed software development. Jalali, and Wohlin [34] presented a systematic review of agile practices in global software engineering (GSE) while Dullemond et al. [35] discussed advantages and challenges of combining GSE with agile development. Nisar and Hameed [38] and Xiaohu et al. [31] reported their experiences in using XP in offshore teams collaborating with onshore customers. Both papers discuss projects where the development work is done in offshore teams, whereas the onshore customer is tightly involved in project communication. They concluded that the reported projects have been very successful, and that the XP principles they have followed have proven to work. Karlsson et al. [39] found the XP practices useful but hard to implement in distributed projects. There is still scope towards defining the process framework and maturity level standards like CMMI, SPICE etc. for distributed software development towards quality.

3.3   Verification and Validation

Sangwan and LaPlante [41] reported that geographically distributed development teams in large projects can realize Test Driven Development's (TDD) considerable advantages. With good communication and judicious use of automated testing, they can overcome many problems. The transition from unit to system level testing is challenging for TDD, as in general TDD is not intended to address system and integration testing – certainly not for globally distributed development teams at any rate. Still, developers can realize the advantages of TDD through increased informal and formal communication, facilitated by appropriate change management and notification tools [41]. Recently, SoftFab tool infrastructure which enables projects to automate the building and test process and which manages all the tasks remotely by a control center was given by Spanjers et al. [43]. Tervonen and Mustonen [46] considered challenges of test automation in a company which has been involved in offshoring before. The challenges were studied with three test automation offshoring cases. Successful offshore subcontractors are willing to provide better know-how and quality all the time to keep their current customers, as competition is tightening. Salger, Engels and Hofmann [47] presented a systematic yet flexible assessment framework which addresses four challenges: Appropriateness of a software requirements specification (SRS), viability of software architectures and SRS, wholeness of work packages, and compliance of results with predefined quality objectives. Mishra and Mishra [45] presented a software inspection process in the distributed software development towards quality assurance and management. Salger et al. [47] found that the issue of assessing the correctness and completeness of SRS (Software Requirements Specification) is compounded in GSD inspections due to impeded communication. Heinonen and Tanner [44] introduced a potential solution for selecting and utilizing the proper validation practices in distributed environments from the requirement engineers' point of view.

4   Results of the Study and Discussion

4.1   Summary

Out of total 144 studies, according to figure 1, a majority of studies are limited to quality (40%) and process (33%). Verification and validation (27%) in GSD is the least explored area among the three significant issues of software quality management.

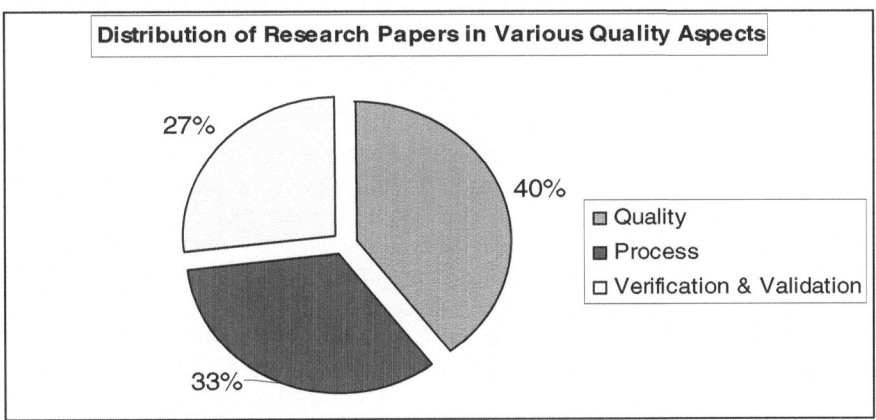

Fig. 1. Distribution of research papers in various quality issues

After an extensive systematic literature survey, it has been observed (According to figure 2) that global software development research started in early 2000 and most of the work related with quality, process and testing issues in GSD was published in 2006. Later on, the trend is downward in all these three with few papers published in these areas. It is also interesting to note that a good number of works got published related with process and quality while studies on various verification and validation issues associated with GSD are still limited. As globally distributed teams become prevalent, top management needs a framework to assess its performance and to initiate activities for continuous improvement in the management of such teams [32].

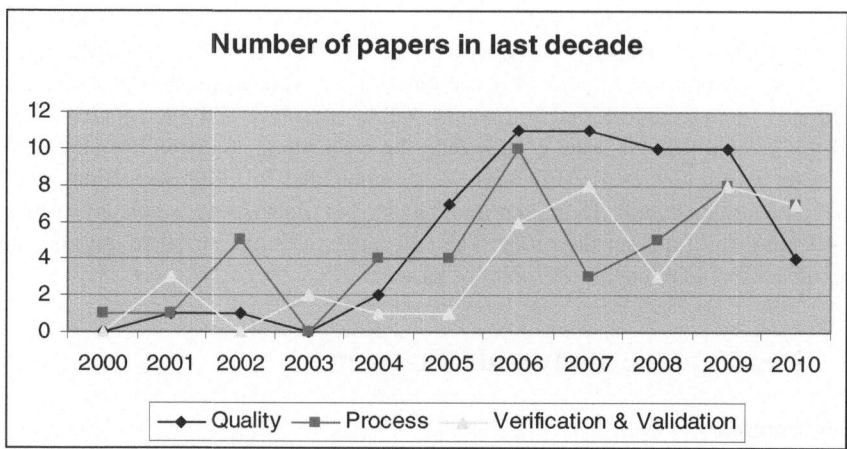

Fig. 2. Number of papers in last decade in various quality issues

4.2   Limitations of the Study

A major concern with any type of research is reliability. Therefore, four researchers were involved in this systematic review study, discussing the reliability threats early in the design phase. Moreover, the review procedure was discussed and agreed upon considering the activities to mitigate the effect of one researcher's bias.

In order to address the conclusion validity, we collected as many papers as possible from a variety of sources including, ACM, IEEE, Science Direct, SpringerLink. We included as many alternatives as possible for the keywords when formulating the search strings. Furthermore, the period was set to be from 2000 to 2011, which was wide enough to capture most of the relevant publications due to the fact that global/distributed software development is not older than one decade. It was possible to observe the trends in the area over the past decade.

Some papers may have been missed due to application of constraints on the search strings in order to reduce the number of irrelevant papers found in the searches. Further, there are some papers in the list which are related with teaching issues of GSD/DSD in an academic environment with teams of students and may not represent the real software industry environment and IT professionals working in this context.

Further due to time and budget constraints, the search did not consider some databases that are suggested by [19]: Wiley InterScience, InspectDirect, etc. This may represent a limitation and a threat to validity. However, main journals and conference outlets related to the area have been included in this study.

5   Conclusions

In this paper, we have reviewed significant quality issues in GSD like process, verification and validation and quality assurance. However, studies selected for this systematic review are from significantly different contexts and backgrounds. Therefore, results presented in these studies may not be applicable as a general standard in all settings. Consequently, there is a need to build the body of knowledge on how to manage the quality in GSD projects which will classify experiences and practices in order to understand circumstances and contexts that will help to achieve positive results.

As a future work, we would like to extend this review on various other attributes, dimensions and comparisons. Further, we would like to include that area which could get only scant attention in GSD, for instance verification and validation. Various case/industrial experience report may be included to enrich these issues related with GSD. As future work other databases can also be included and review rules can be modified towards inclusion of further studies. It would be interesting to interview (using online tools) the authors of significant studies to know their views about these assessments.

References

1. Herbsleb, J.D., Moitra, D.: Global software development. IEEE Software 18(2), 16–20 (2001)
2. Hernández-López, A., Colomo-Palacios, R., García-Crespo, A., Soto-Acosta, P.: Trust Building Process for Global Software Development Teams A review from the Literature. International Journal of Knowledge Society Research 1(1), 66–83 (2010)
3. Madachy, R.J.: Cost Modeling of Distributed Team Processes for Global Development and Software-Intensive Systems of Systems. Software Process: Improvement and Practice 13(1), 51–61 (2008)
4. Avram, G.: Of Deadlocks and Peopleware - Collaborative Work Practices in Global Software Development. In: Proceedings of the International Conference on Global Software Engineering, August 27-30, pp. 91–102. ICGSE (2007)
5. Yu, L., Mishra, A.: Risk Analysis of Global Software Development and Proposed Solutions. Automatika 51(1), 89–98 (2010)
6. Mishra, D., Mishra, A.: A Global Software Inspection Process for Distributed Software Development. Journal of Universal Computer Science 18(19), 2731–2746 (2012)
7. García-Crespo, A., Colomo-Palacios, R., Soto-Acosta, P., Ruano-Mayoral, M.: A Qualitative Study of Hard Decision Making in Managing Global Software Development Teams. Information Systems Management 27(3), 247–252 (2010)
8. Colomo-Palacios, R., Soto-Acosta, P., García-Peñalvo, F.J., García-Crespo, A.: A study of the impact of global software development in packaged software release planning. Journal of Universal Computer Science 18(19), 2646–2668 (2012)
9. Damian, D., Moitra, D.: Global software development: How far have we come? IEEE Software 23(5), 17–19 (2006)
10. Sa, L., Marczak, S., Antunes, D., Audy, J.L.N.: Quality Management as a Competitive Strategy in a Distributed Software Development Environment. In: Proceedings of the Americas Conference on Information Systems Paper 208 (2003)
11. da Silva, F.Q.B., Costa, C., Franca, A., Cesar, C., Prikladinicki, R.: Challenges and Solutions in Distributed Software Development Project Management: A Systematic Literature Review. In: 5th IEEE International Conference on Global Software Engineering 2010, pp. 87–96 (2010)
12. Smite, D., Wohlin, C., Gorschek, T., Feldt, R.: Empirical Evidence in Global Software Engineering: A Systematic Review. Journal of Empirical Software Engineering 15(1), 91–118 (2010)
13. Jiménez, M., Piattini, M., Vizcaíno, A.: Challenges and Improvements in Distributed Software Development: A Systematic Review. Advances in Software Engineering, Article ID 710971 (2009)

14. Lamersdorf, A., Münch, J.: Studying the Impact of Global Software Development Characteristics on Project Goals: A Causal Model. The Open Software Engineering Journal 4, 2–13 (2010)
15. Sakthivel, S.: Managing Risks in Offshore Systems Development. Commun. ACM 50(4), 69–75 (2007)
16. DeLone, W., Espinosa, J.A., Lee, G., Carmel, E.: Bridging global boundaries for IS project success. In: Proceedings of the 38th Hawaii International Conference on System Sciences (2005)
17. Jaakkola, H.: Towards a Globalized Software Industry. Acta Polytechnica Hungarica 6(5), 69–84 (2009)
18. Seshagiri, G.: GSD: not a business necessity but a of folly. IEEE Software 23(5), 63–64 (2006)
19. Kitchenham, B., Charters, S.: Guidelines for Performing Systematic Literature Reviews in Software Engineering Technical Report EBSE- 2007-01 School of Computer Science and Mathematics Keele University (2007)
20. Sangwan, R., Neill, C., Bass, M., El Houda, Z.: Integrating a software architecture-centric method into object-oriented analysis and design. Journal of Systems and Software 81(5), 727–746 (2008)
21. Cataldo, M., Nambiar, S.: On the relationship between process maturity and geographic distribution: an empirical analysis of their impact on software quality. In: Proceedings of the the the 7th Joint Meeting of the European Software Engineering Conference and the ACM SIGSOFT Symposium on The Foundations of Software Engineering (ESEC/FSE 2009), pp. 101–110. ACM, New York (2009)
22. Fukui, S.: Introduction of the Software Configuration Management Team and Defect Tracking System for Global Distributed Development. In: Kontio, J., Conradi, R. (eds.) ECSQ 2002. LNCS, vol. 2349, pp. 217–225. Springer, Heidelberg (2002)
23. Münch, J., Pfahl, D., Rus, I.: Virtual Software Engineering Laboratories in Support of Trade-off Analyses. Software Quality Control 13(4), 407–428 (2005)
24. Agarwal, R., Nayak, P., Malarvizhi, M., Suresh, P., Modi, N.: Virtual Quality Assurance Facilitation Model. In: Proceedings of the International Conference on Global Software Engineering (ICGSE 2007), pp. 51–59. IEEE Computer Society, Washington, DC (2007)
25. Annous, H., Livadas, L., Miles, G.: OffshoreQA: A Framework for Helping Software Development Outsourcing Companies Comply with ISO 9001:2008. In: 5th IEEE International Conference on Global Software Engineering, pp. 313–315 (2010)
26. Caprihan, G.: Managing Software Performance in the Globally Distributed Software Development Paradigm. In: Proceedings of the IEEE International Conference on Global Software Engineering (ICGSE 2006), pp. 83–91 (2006)
27. Kuni, R., Bhushan, N.: IT Application Assessment Model for Global Software Development. In: Proceedings of the IEEE International Conference on Global Software Engineering (ICGSE 2006), pp. 92–100. IEEE Computer Society, Washington, DC (2006)
28. Laredo, J.A., Ranjan, R.: Continuous Improvement through Iterative Development in a Multi-Geography. In: Proceedings of the 2008 IEEE International Conference on Global Software Engineering (ICGSE 2008), pp. 232–236 (2008)
29. Cusick, J., Prasad, A.: A Practical Management and Engineering Approach to Offshore Collaboration. IEEE Software 23(5), 20–29 (2006)
30. Sakthivel, S.: Virtual workgroups in offshore systems development. Information and Software Technology 47(5), 305–318 (2005)
31. Xiaohu, Y., Bin, X., Zhijun, H., Maddineni, S.: Extreme programming in global software development. In: Canadian Conference on Electrical and Computer Engineering 2004, vol. 4, pp. 1845–1848 (2004)

32. Ramasubbu, N., Krishnan, M.S., Kompalli, P.: Leveraging Global Resources: A Process Maturity Framework for Managing Distributed Development. IEEE Software 22(3), 80–86 (2005)
33. Cusumano, M.A., MacCormack, A., Kemerer, C.F., Crandall, W.: Critical Decisions in Software Development: Updating the State of the Practice. IEEE Software 26(5), 84–87 (2009)
34. Jalali, S., Wohlin, C.: Agile Practices in Global Software Engineering-A Systematic Map. In: 5th IEEE International Conference on Global Software Engineering, pp. 45–54 (2010)
35. Dullemond, K., Gameren, B., Van Solingen, R.: How Technological Support Can Enable Advantages of Agile Software Development in a GSE Setting. In: ICGSE Fourth IEEE International Conference on Global Software Engineering, pp. 143–152 (2009)
36. Bendjenna, H., Zarour, N., Charrel, P.-J.: Enhancing elicitation technique selection process in a cooperative distributed environment. In: Rolland, C. (ed.) REFSQ 2008. LNCS, vol. 5025, pp. 23–36. Springer, Heidelberg (2008)
37. Oliveira, S.B., Valle, R., Mahler, C.F.: A comparative analysis of CMMI software project management by Brazilian Indian and Chinese companies. Software Quality Control 18(2), 177–194 (2010)
38. Nisar, M.F., Hameed, T.: Agile methods handling offshore software development issues. In: Proceedings of INMIC 2004 8th International Multitopic Conference, pp. 417–422 (2004)
39. Karlsson, E., Andersson, L., Leion, P.: Daily build and feature development in large distributed projects. In: Proceedings of the 22nd International Conference on Software Engineering, ICSE 2000, pp. 649–658 (2000)
40. Prikladnicki, R., Audy, J.L.N.: Process models in the practice of distributed software development: A systematic review of the literature. Information and Software Technology 52(8), 779–791 (2010)
41. Sangwan, R.S., LaPlante, P.A.: Test-Driven Development in Large Projects. IT Professional 8(5), 25–29 (2006)
42. Avram, G., Bannon, L., Bowers, J., Sheehan, A., Sullivan, D.K.: Bridging Patching and Keeping the Work Flowing: Defect Resolution in Distributed Software Development. Computer Supported Cooperative Work 18(5-6), 477–507 (2009)
43. Spanjers, H., Huurne, M.T., Graaf, B., Lormans, M., Bendas, D., Solingen, R.V.: Tool Support for Distributed Software Engineering. In: Proceedings of the IEEE International Conference on Global Software Engineering (ICGSE 2006), pp. 187–198 (2006)
44. Heinonen, S., Tanner, H.: Early Validation of Requirements in Distributed Product Development - An Industrial Case Study. In: Meersman, R., Dillon, T., Herrero, P. (eds.) OTM 2010. LNCS, vol. 6428, pp. 279–288. Springer, Heidelberg (2010)
45. Mishra, D., Mishra, A.: A software inspection process for globally distributed teams. In: Meersman, R., Dillon, T., Herrero, P. (eds.) OTM 2010 Workshops. LNCS, vol. 6428, pp. 289–296. Springer, Heidelberg (2010)
46. Tervonen, I., Mustonen, T.: Offshoring Test Automation: Observations and Lessons Learned. In: Proceedings of the 2009 Fourth IEEE International Conference on Global Software Engineering (ICGSE 2009), pp. 226–235 (2009)
47. Salger, F., Engels, G., Hofmann, A.: Assessments in global software development: a tailorable framework for industrial projects. In: Proceedings of the 32nd ACM/IEEE International Conference on Software Engineering, vol. 2, pp. 29–38 (2010)
48. Prikladnicki, R., Audy, J.L.N., Evaristo, R.: A Reference Model for Global Software Development: Findings from a Case Study. In: Proceedings of the IEEE International Conference on Global Software Engineering (ICGSE 2006), pp. 18–25 (2006)

Building a Concept Solution for Upgrade Planning in the Automation Industry

Jukka Kääriäinen[1], Susanna Teppola[1], and Antti Välimäki[2]

[1] VTT, Oulu, Finland
{jukka.kaariainen,susanna.teppola}@vtt.fi
[2] Metso Automation Inc., Tampere, Finland
antti.valimaki@metso.com

Abstract. Industrial automation systems are long living systems controlling industrial processes such as power stations or pulp and paper production. These systems have strict requirements on the system's availability since all downtime is costly for factories. In such circumstances, all upgrades require special concern and planning, in a context of collaboration between the automation system's provider and user, to minimize downtimes in the user's critical processes. This paper discusses the problem of upgrade planning for such automation systems. It presents a concept solution based on a case study. The research is a part of broader research aiming at a better understanding of system upgrades in the case study company's service sales. The aim is also to enhance solutions for handling the identification and analysis of upgrades in collaboration between the case study company's internal teams and customers.

Keywords: Automation system, Upgrade, Transparency.

1   Introduction

Long-living automation systems need to operate for periods in excess of 15 years. They are used to control industrial processes such as water management and pulp and paper production [1]. The systems are firstly installed, then operated and maintained, and finally replaced when they reach their end-of-life.

Automation systems have strict requirements regarding the system's availability and consequently all upgrades need special concern and planning to minimize downtimes in the critical processes they control. However, long-living systems need to be upgraded every once in a while in order to meet environmental changes (standards, technologies, devices) or in response to requests from users (bugs, new features)[2]. Automation system vendors seek to prevent a situation arising in which an automation installation at their customer's place of business reaches the point where a major investment is the only way of ensuring their survival. This could open the door to rival system providers. Therefore, it is advantageous for system providers to provide a more cost-effective path for their customer's automation system, one which evolves through a series of small and manageable steps in order to meet any changing needs. It is also easier for customers to justify and schedule the upgrade of discrete elements of the system than a "big-bang" change that would require long downtimes.

Y.T. Demey and H. Panetto (Eds.): OTM 2013 Workshops, LNCS 8186, pp. 312–321, 2013.
© Springer-Verlag Berlin Heidelberg 2013

Automation system vendors have upgrade or evolution programs that aim at the systematic and controllable evolution of an installed system. Customer offerings have their own special characteristics but in essence all offerings comprise similar activities, such as understanding the customer's business needs, analysing the current installation and creating and presenting a life cycle plan/analysis for the customer's tailored installation. With these analyses the customer gains an insight into their system from the life-cycle management point of view and also the timing for future upgrades of their system, thus assisting the customer in their budgeting process.

The purpose of this paper is to present a concept solution based on a case study conducted in an automation company. The concept presents stakeholders, information systems and data flows related to the automation systems upgrade process. The first version of the concept, presented in this paper, was constructed in cooperation with the case study company. The concept is generic and does not discuss the tools or technologies used by the case study company in detail. This initial concept solution will be developed further and refined iteratively. At the same time, the case study company will build and pilot tools and guidelines reflecting the solution. In this way, iterative concept definition, practical solution development and pilots gradually accumulate and validate the concept.

This research and its resultant concept should be of interest to companies that are seeking solutions for the upgrade planning process. The concept also aims to discuss the problem area of upgrade planning, and reports on practical cooperation between the research organisation and the industrial company. Therefore, this research should also be of interest to research organisations.

The paper is organized as follows: Chapter 2 presents the background to industrial automation systems, their upgrading and the role of transparency in this context. The research process is discussed in Chapter 3. Chapter 4 introduces the draft concept for an upgrade planning solution. Chapter 5 draws conclusions.

2   Background

Industrial automation systems are used to control industrial processes such as water management and pulp and paper production [1]. Such systems are "long-living" comprising life-cycle steps from installation, operation and maintenance to their end-of-life (shut-down) [2]. Furthermore, the systems work in conjunction with the other systems and devices in the place of business in which they have been installed, such as the user company's information systems (e.g. ERP, Enterprise Resource Planning), process equipment and electrical system [3] (Fig. 1).

It has been estimates that the value of the worldwide installed base of automation systems reaching the end of their useful lives is approximately 65 billion dollars [4]. This can be seen as a big opportunity for both end users and system providers [4]. End users have an opportunity to consider new system providers and system providers have an opportunity to offer system migration paths in order to gain new customers.

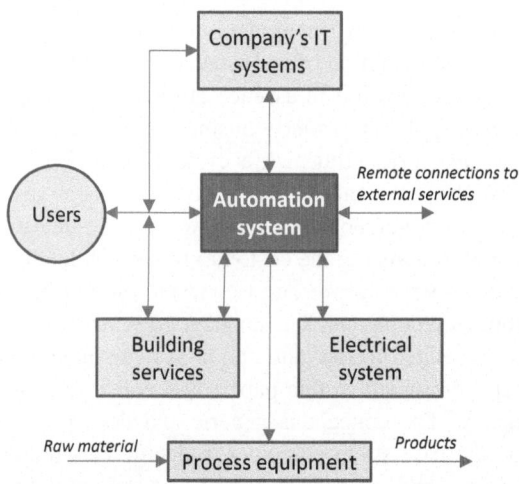

Fig. 1. Automation system as part of external systems [3]

Automation system vendors have upgrade or evolution programs that aim at the systematic and controllable evolution of an installed system. They seek to protect their customer base and prevent a situation in which the system installed at their customer's place of business reaches a point where a major investment in their automation plant is the only way to ensure their survival. Instead, automation system vendors provide a cost-effective path for a customer's automation system to evolve through a series of small and manageable steps in order to meet changing needs. Vendor-specific evolution/upgrade programs have their own special characteristics but in essence they all comprise the same logic, containing steps including understanding the customer's business needs, analysing the current installation and creating and presenting a life cycle plan/analysis for the customer's tailored installation. Within these analyses the customer gains an insight into the system from the life-cycle management point of view and understands the timings for future upgrades, thus assisting their budgeting process. However, the cost-efficient maintenance of automation system is complex challenge since they are subject to new requirements, new standards, failures, and technology changes during their operation time [1]. Therefore, automation system vendors are interested to build sustainable long-living systems [1]. They also try to provide evidence for customers about the value of the continuous maintenance of existing equipment [5].

Transparency, both inside and outside of a company, has become an important precondition for successful operations in today's technology industry. With better transparency, companies are targeting at improved control mechanisms and decision making in order to react quickly to market changes and opportunities. Transparency is defined in different ways in the literature [6, 7, 8], but in general, each of these slightly varying definitions highlights the importance of transparency in supporting informed decision-making in companies.

For an automation system vendor offering aftermarket services to B2B customers, transparency becomes critical. With the practices and tools supporting transparency, information important for decision making can be provided in a useful way for decision-makers. From the sales team's (automation system vendor's) point of view a great deal of information is needed in order to make informed decisions in sales negotiations and in preparing profitable offers for potential customers. For the vendor's service organization it is important to get up-to-date information from its R&D department, for instance relating to the content of hardware (HW) and software (SW) releases and their compatibility. Furthermore, complex industrial systems have dependencies to third party components [9] and it is important to understand the dependencies between the system and third party components and their evolution roadmaps. Customer data, offers and contracts are also important information for the sales team. The sales team is also interested in the current system in use by a potential customer. It is also highly beneficial to be aware of the business targets and requirements that the customer has in regard to the system's further evolution. Customer requirements in general are a vital input for the sales team and in fact the customer's whole business needs to be taken into account when considering any innovation and roadmapping processes. Therefore, transparency around the relevant information is very much needed by the sales team for creating successful offers to potential customers.

3   Research Process

This work was carried out within the international research project Varies (Variability In Safety-Critical Embedded Systems) [10]. The research was undertaken in cooperation with a company that operates in the automation systems industry. The company offers automation and information management application networks and systems, intelligent field control solutions, and support and maintenance services. This research focuses on the automation system product sector. Automation systems are multi-technological systems comprising HW and SW. The role of SW is increasing in automation systems – as it is across all engineering domains. Typically, the customer-specific, tailored installation of the system is based on a generic product platform and a new version of this product platform is released annually. The (generic) main sub-systems in an automation system include: Control Room, Engineering Tools, Information Management and Process Controllers.

Engineering tools are used to configure the automation system to fit the customer's context. This includes, for instance, the development of process applications and related views. The customer-specific configurations of automation systems are long-living and need to be maintained and updated, if necessary. Case company highlighted that the importance of upgrade services has increased. An increasing proportion of revenue comes from the service business. Each update will be analysed individually to find the optimal solution for the customer based on the customer's business needs. Because of the demands of customer-specific tailoring there are many customer-specific configurations in the field containing sub-systems from different platform releases (versions). Therefore, the service organisation (the system provider) needs to track each customer configuration of an automation system and detect what upgrades are possible for each customer. Upgrade requirements may mean that an upgrade escalates across several sub-systems for compatibility reasons. This needs to be detected and analysed in order to produce accurate information for upgrade sales negotiations. Since the prominence of service business (offered by the system provider) has increased, it is important to fine-tune the upgrade service sales process to enable focused and accurate upgrade service offerings.

This research is part of broader research aiming at a better understanding of system upgrades in the case study company's service sales team and at enhancing the solutions for handling upgrade identification and analysis in the case study company. The aim of the paper is to present the first version ("Iteration 1", Fig. 2) of the concept. This illustrates the stakeholders, information systems and data flows related to the automation system's upgrade planning process. This concept will be refined iteratively in future (Fig. 2). At the same time, the case study company is enhancing its existing tools, developing new tools and piloting them in relation to upgrade planning. Therefore, iterative concept definition, practical solution development and prototypes/pilots gradually accumulate and validate the concept.

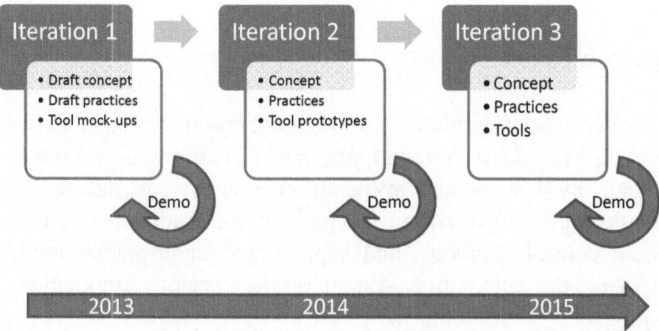

Fig. 2. Iterative plan for the development of concept, practices and tools in collaboration with a case study company

The concept presented here is based on the case study data that was collected using interviews and workshops. Firstly, five people from the case study company's service team were selected for interview. All interviewees had in-depth experience of working within the company's service function. Secondly, participants were selected for workshops, drawn from both the service and R&D teams. These workshops were held *in situ* at the case study company, during which additional case study data was uncovered, then fed back and discussed. The case study data revealed what solutions for upgrade planning are currently in use by the case study company and what existing or desired features the service team finds most useful. Furthermore, two to three people from the case study company participated in a number of workshops where the focus of the work was refined and the practices and concept were drafted, presented and reviewed. Concept-building was supported by a collaborative environment tool providing concurrent access for the case study company representatives and researchers whilst describing the concept solution (Fig. 3). (The research team was located in Oulu, northern Finland, and the case study company is located in Tampere, southern Finland.) The intention was to collect all concept-related discussions and material in a shared space where both the researchers and company representatives could easily share the material and ideas related to concept-building. The collaborative environment implemented was a SharePoint extranet site.

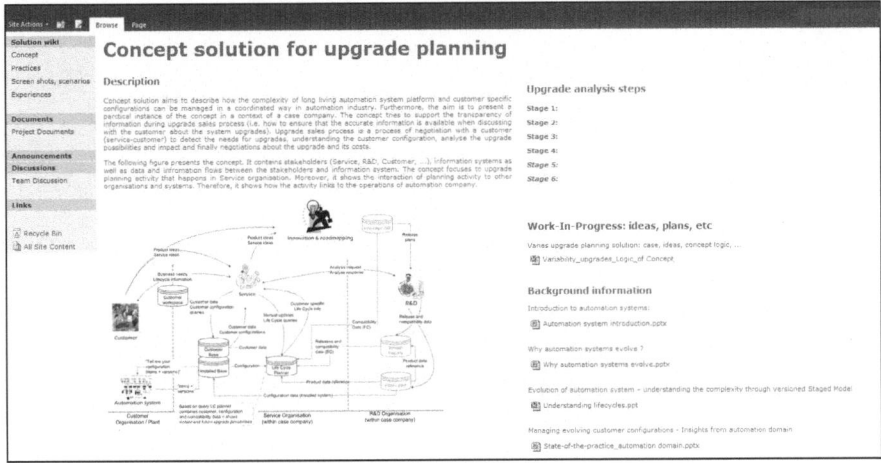

Fig. 3. Collaborative environment for concept development

4   Concept Solution

The concept solution aims to describe how the complexity of long-living automation system platforms and customer specific configurations can be managed in a coordinated way from an automation system provider perspective. The concept highlights the transparency of information during the upgrade sales process, such as how to ensure that accurate information is available when discussing system upgrades with the customer. The upgrade sales process lies within the remit of the service team and is about: negotiating with the customer to detect the requirements for upgrades; understanding the customer's tailored configuration; analysing the upgrade opportunities and impacts; and finally negotiating over the upgrade and its costs. In this context, collaboration and transparency across the organizational boundaries internally at the provider company and with the customer company is vital.

Fig. 4 illustrates the first version of the concept defined during the first iteration. It contains stakeholders/organizational functions (Service, R&D, Customer, Innovation/Roadmapping) and information systems as well as the data and information flows across organizational boundaries and their information systems. The concept solution focuses on upgrade planning activity that lies within the remit of the service team.

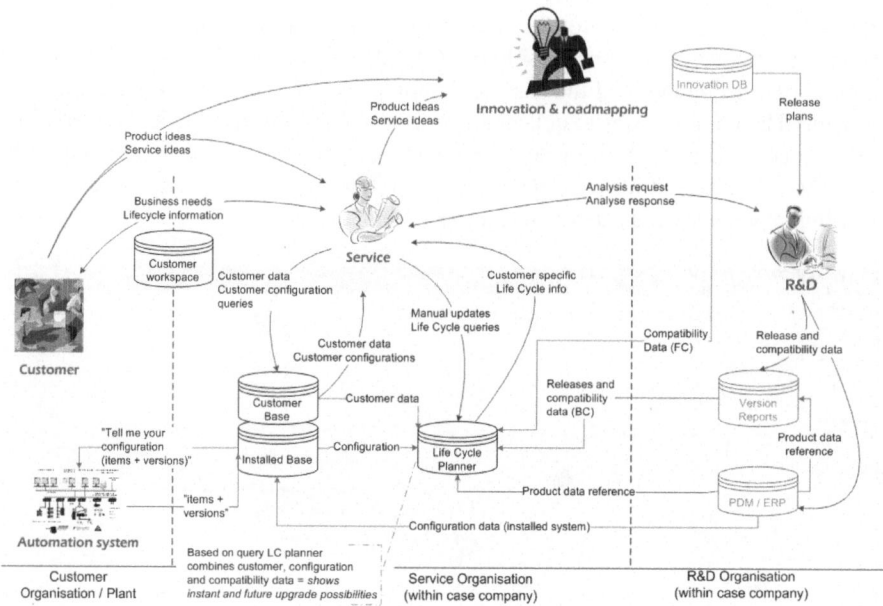

Fig. 4. First version of the upgrade planning concept solution

The concept identifies the information systems that are needed internally for managing customer-specific configurations, dependencies and customer information. Furthermore, it incorporates an information system for communication and collaboration externally with customers. The primary information systems that relate to the upgrade planning process are: Customer Workspace, Customer Base, Installed Base and Life Cycle Planner. These are described as follows:

- *Customer Workspace*: a collaborative tool where the service organization and customer can discuss, share material and comments regarding the installed automation system.
- *Customer Base*: a database containing information about customers and customer sites.
- *Installed Base*: a database containing information about customers' installed systems, including: SW versions, applications, HW, third-party SW and HW versions, licence information, etc. Some of this information is collected automatically via a network connection with the customer's automation system.
- *Life Cycle Planner (LCP)*: a tool that combines the platform's forward (FC) and backward (BC) compatibility information together with the installed base information. Based on this information, the LCP describes the dependencies existing in a single customer configuration taking into account the needs of that customer (remembering that small changes may escalate into other sub-systems). Furthermore, it describes the future upgrade requirements for the sub-systems in a timeline (for instance, the upgrade requirements for each sub-system during the next five years).

The process of upgrade sales begins with the identification of the customer's requirements for upgrades. Here the understanding of the customer's business logic is extremely important in identifying any bottlenecks in the customer's industrial processes, and proposing remedies for them. Service engineers work closely with customers, typically at the customer's place of business, which puts them in a good position to understand the customer's issues and requirements. Close cooperation with the customer allows the identification and collection of product and service ideas for the innovation and roadmapping function that contributes to future product and service offerings. The impetus for an upgrade may originate from the customer side (e.g. a requirement for a new functionality) or from the automation system provider side (e.g. a component or third party SW end-of-life notification from a component supplier).

Identifying the customer's configuration reveals the exact configuration for that customer's automation system. The information is stored in an Installed Base database. The system comprises information such as SW and HW versions, applications, third-party SW/HW, etc. Accurate information is needed to minimize errors in the update planning process since the existing configuration is needed as a baseline for upgrade analysis.

In the analysis phase, the service team - in cooperation with the R&D team - analyses what needs to be updated in the customer's configuration in order to meet the requirements of the customer whilst maintaining the customer's automation system in good condition. Here, the information about system dependencies is crucial. Dependency information shows how far updating one sub-system may escalate to other sub-systems in a customer's configuration. This information is important for the service team in order for them to compose an accurate upgrade offer for a customer. In this concept, the Life Cycle Planner tool combines dependency information with the information on the customer configuration and upgrade requirements. Based on this information it produces life cycle plans. The life cycle plan presents the life cycle of each part of the system, illustrating for a single customer what needs to be upgraded and when, and at what point in time a bigger migration might be needed. The plan supports the customer in preparing themselves for the updates, e.g. by predicting costs, schedules for downtimes, rationale for management, etc. For the service team, this tool gives an understanding of upgrade needs from which they can propose and justify updates for a customer in a timely manner that maintains the customer's automation system in good condition.

5   Conclusions and Future Work

This paper presents a concept solution based on a case study conducted in an automation systems company. The concept presents stakeholders, information systems and data flows related to the automation systems upgrade planning process. The concept highlights the importance of transparency of information between the provider company's own internal organizational units and their customer during the upgrade sales process. The main question is how to ensure that accurate information is readily available when discussing system upgrades with the customer.

The first version of the concept was constructed in cooperation with the case study company. The concept is generic and does not discuss in detail the names of the tools or technologies that are used in the company. This concept will be refined iteratively. At the same time the company will enhance, build and pilot tools and guidelines reflecting the solution. Therefore, iterative concept definition, practical solution development and pilots gradually accumulate and validate the concept. The limitations of the study relate to the nature of the case study method. The concept will be iteratively constructed and demonstrated in cooperation with a case company operating in automation industry. Therefore, first the concept will be limited to that context. However, there is an intention to harvest more experiences about the use of concept also in other domains (e.g. telecommunication domain).

This paper also reports on practical cooperation between a research institute and an automation company. The paper explains how researchers and company representatives have cooperated to contribute to both research and practice.

This research and its resultant concept should be of interest to companies that are seeking solutions for the upgrade planning process. The concept also addresses the problem area of upgrade planning in general and reports on research cooperation between a research organisation and an industrial company. Therefore, this research should also be of interest to research organisations.

References

1. Koziolek, H., Weiss, R., Durdik, Z., Stammel, J., Krogmann, K.: Towards Software Sustainability Guidelines for Long-living Industrial Systems. In: Proceedings of Software Engineering 2011 (SE 2011), 3rd Workshop Long-living Software Systems (L2S2), pp. 47–58 (2011)
2. Stammel, J., Durdik, Z., Krogmann, K., Weiss, R., Koziolek, H.: Software Evolution for Industrial Automation Systems: Literature Overview. In: Karlsruhe Reports in Informatics 2011-2. Karlsruhe Institute of Technology. Faculty of Informatics (2011) ISSN 2190-4782
3. Finnish Society of Automation (Suomen Automaatioseura ry): Automaatiosuunnittelun Prosessimalli - Yhteiset käsitteet verkottuneen suunnittelun perustana. Helsinki (2007) (in Finnish)
4. O'Brien, L., Woll, D.: The Control Systems Migration Survival Manual. ARC Strategies, ARC Advisory Group (2010)
5. Töytäri, P., Alejandro, T.B., Parvinen, P., Ollila, I., Rosendahl, N.: Bridging the theory to application gap in value-based selling. Journal of Business & Industrial Marketing 26(7), 493–502 (2011)
6. Klotz, L., Horman, M., Bi, H., Bechtel, J.: The impact of process mapping on transparency. International Journal of Productivity and Performance Management 57(8), 623–636 (2008)
7. Womack, J.P., Jones, D.T.: Lean Thinking: Banish Waste and Create Wealth in Your Corporation. Free Press (2003)

8. Okland, A., Lillebo, B., Amdahl, E., Seim, A.: A Framework for Transparency. In: POMS 21st Annual Conference, Vancouver, Canada (2010)
9. Klatt, B., Durdik, Z., Koziolek, H., Krogmann, K., Stammel, J., Weiss, R.: Identify Impacts of Evolving Third Party Components on Long-Living Software Systems. In: 16th European Conference on Software Maintenance and Reengineering (CSMR), pp. 461–464 (2012)
10. Varies -project web-site: (Variability In Safety-Critical Embedded Systems), http://www.varies.eu (accessed June 14, 2013)

Inconsistency-Tolerant Business Rules
in Distributed Information Systems

Hendrik Decker* and Francesc D. Muñoz-Escoí*

Instituto Tecnológico de Informática, UPV, 46022 Valencia, Spain

Abstract. Business rules enhance the integrity of information systems. However, their maintenance does not scale up easily to distributed systems with concurrent transactions. To a large extent, that is due to two problematic exigencies: the postulates of *total* and *isolated* business rule satisfaction. For overcoming these problems, we outline a measure-based inconsistency-tolerant approach to business rules maintenance.

1 Introduction

Business rules, a.k.a. integrity constraints, are an approved means to support the consistency of the modeling [26], the design [21], the development [4], the operation [18], the quality maintenance [22] and the evolution [9] of information systems, in particular if these activities are encased in distributed environments.

Although business rules are meant to avoid inconsistency, they also must work well in the presence of data that violate some of the rules. This requirement of inconsistency tolerance imposes itself even stronger in distributed systems, since the risk of inconsistency is higher there than in centralized systems. The problem addressed in this paper is to enable inconsistency-tolerant business rules not only for individual updates of single-user databases, but also for concurrent database transactions. Concurrency is the norm for distributed systems.

Many methods for checking declarative business rules have been proposed in the literature [17]. Concurrent transactions also have been broadly covered [12] [3] [28]. This paper deals with two common postulates that impede a combination of controlling data consistency by checking business rules, on one hand, and guaranteeing consistency preservation by concurrent transactions, on the other. The first postulate is that an update can be efficiently checked for integrity only if the state before the update totally satisfies all constraints, without exception. We call that *the total integrity postulate*. The second is that, for guaranteeing integrity preservation by serializable concurrent transactions, each transaction is supposed to preserve integrity when executed in isolation. We call this requirement *the isolated integrity postulate*. It will turn out that both postulates are unrealistic and indeed not necessary to their full extent in practice.

We point out that the isolated integrity postulate must not be confused with the well-known requirement of an isolated execution of transactions [3], i.e., that

* Supported by ERDF/FEDER and MEC grants TIN2009-14460-C03, TIN2010-17139, TIN2012-37719-C03-01.

Y.T. Demey and H. Panetto (Eds.): OTM 2013 Workshops, LNCS 8186, pp. 322–331, 2013.

concurrent transactions should not step into each other's sphere of control [5], so that anomalies such as phantom updates, dirty or non-repeatable reads are avoided. That requirement usually is complied with by ensuring the serializability of schedules, or some relaxation thereof [28,27]. However, serializability is independent of the isolated integrity postulate, requiring that integrity be preserved in isolation: while serializability can be guaranteed automatically by the scheduler of the DBMS, the isolated integrity postulate is usually expected to be complied with by the designers, programmers and users of transactions.

The dispensability of the total integrity postulate has been unveiled in [10]. The isolated integrity postulate has been discussed and relaxed in [11]. More precisely, total integrity has been shown to be a superfluous, and the isolated integrity postulate has been significantly relaxed, both by a concept of inconsistency-tolerant integrity checking. That concept was based on 'cases', i.e., instances of integrity constraints. Their violation can be tolerated as long as integrity checking can guarantee that the amount of violated cases does not grow. In [7], a significant generalization has been presented, based on inconsistency measures. The latter permit the tolerance of integrity violation as long as integrity checking can guarantee that the amount of measured inconsistency is not increased by updates. In this paper, we show that measure-based integrity checking also enables a significant weakening of the isolated integrity postulate.

In section 2, we characterize the postulates of total and isolated integrity. In section 3, we recapitulate measure-based integrity checking. We are going to see that it serves to get rid of the total integrity postulate as well as to relax the isolated integrity postulate. In section 4, we address related work, with an emphasis on integrity checking for concurrent transactions. If not specified otherwise, we use conventional terminology and notations for logic databases [1], as well as some basic notions of transaction concurrency [3].

2   Two Unnecessary Postulates

The total integrity postulate is going to be explained in 2.1, the isolated integrity postulate in 2.2. Both postulates are unnecessary and actually bad, since they invalidate predictions of the traditional theories of transaction processing [3] and integrity maintenance [17] if databases contain inconsistent data.

2.1   The Total Integrity Postulate

Integrity checking can be exceedingly costly, unless some simplification method is used [20]. That can be illustrated as follows. (As usual, lower-case letters x, y, z denote variables, in the example below.)

Example 1.   Let *emp* be a relation about employees, whose first column is a unique name and the second a project assigned to the employee. The formula I = $\leftarrow proj(x,y), proj(x,z), y \neq z$ is a primary key constraint on the first column of *proj*, a relation about projects, with unique identifiers in the first column. The foreign key constraint $I' = \forall x, y \exists z \, (emp(x,y) \rightarrow proj(y,z))$ on the y of *emp* references the primary key of *proj*. Now, assume a transaction T that inserts $emp(Jack, p)$. Most integrity checking methods $\mathcal{M}$ ignore I for checking T, since I does not constrain *emp*. They only evaluate $\exists z\,(emp(Jack, p) \rightarrow proj(p, z))$, or rather its simplification $\exists z\, proj(p, z)$, since $emp(Jack, p)$ becomes *true* by the transaction. If, e.g., (p, e) is a row in *proj*, $\mathcal{M}$ accepts the insertion. If no tuple in *proj* matches (p, z), then $\mathcal{M}$ signals a violation of integrity.

Proofs of the correctness of methods for simplified constraints checking in the literature all rely on the total integrity postulate, i.e., that integrity always be totally satisfied, before updates are checked for preserving consistency. In practice, however, it is rather the exception than the rule that this postulate is complied with. In particular for applications such as business intelligence, distributed and replicated databases, legacy data maintenance, data warehousing, data federation, etc, a certain amount of inconsistent data that violate constraints in committed states has to be lived with, at least temporarily.

Suppose that, for instance, the constraint I' in Example 1 is violated due to the element $emp(Jack, Illustra)$ in D, after a deletion of the *Illustra* project. Thus, by definition, no traditional method that imposes the total integrity postulate may check T, since not all constraints are satisfied. However, if the project that *Jack* is assigned to is stored in the *proj* relation, T is rightfully sanctioned by all common implementations of integrity checking, as already indicated in Example 1. Example 2, in 3.1, will illustrate essentially the same point.

Hence, the total integrity postulate, which conventionally has always been imposed, does not approve the correctness of integrity checking in practice, since the latter often is performed in the presence of consistency violations. Fortunately, however, that postulate can be abolished without incurring any cost and without losing its essential guarantees, as shown in 3.1.

2.2   The Isolated Integrity Postulate

Integrity preservation has been a pronounced concern already in the early literature on transaction processing. We cite from [12]: "*it is assumed that each transaction, when executed alone, transforms a consistent state into a consistent state; that is, transactions preserve consistency*". This is what we have called the isolated integrity postulate. (The execution of a transaction T is *isolated* when it is not concurrent with other transactions, or when the state transition effected by T is as if having been executed alone.) Thus, the isolated integrity postulate effectively presupposes the total integrity postulate. From the isolated integrity premise, most authors in the field infer that then, also all sequentializable schedules of concurrent transactions preserve 'consistency', i.e., integrity.

In general, not only the requirement of total integrity, but also the isolated integrity postulate seems to be illusionary, particularly for distributed multi-user databases, let alone for transactions in the cloud. In fact, it is hard to believe than any client who authors a transaction T would ever bet on a consistency-preserving outcome of T by blindly trusting that all other clients have taken the same care as herself for making sure that their transactions preserve integrity in isolation. Yet, in practice, most clients are confident about the integrity preservation of their transactions, although there is no theory to justify their optimism, in the presence of inconsistency. Such a justification is given in Section 3.

3   Inconsistency Tolerance

Business rules state and enforce the integrity of business data. However, inconsistencies due to violations of business rules are unavoidable in practice. Hence, rather than insisting that all business rules must be totally satisfied at all times, it is necessary to tolerate constraint violations. Attempts to reduce or repair such manifestations of inconsistency often are not affordable at update time. Thus, updates should be checkable for consistency preservation even if some constraints are violated. That idea is revisited in 3.1. In 3.2–3.4, we outline a generalization of the results in 3.1 to concurrent transactions.

Throughout the rest of the paper, let the symbols D, I, IC, T, $\mathcal{M}$ stand for a database, an integrity constraint, a set of integrity constraints, a transaction and, resp., an integrity checking method. By $D(IC) = true$ and $D(IC) = false$, we denote that IC is satisfied or, resp., violated in D. We suppose that all constraints are represented in prenex form, i.e., all quantifiers of variables appear leftmost. That includes the two most common forms of representing integrity constraints: as denials or in prenex normal form. Moreover, let D^T denote the database state obtained by applying the write set of T to D.

In general, each method $\mathcal{M}$ is a mapping which takes triples (D, IC, T) as input and returns either OK, which means that $\mathcal{M}$ sanctions T as integrity-preserving, or KO, which indicates that T would violate some constraint.

3.1   Getting Rid of Total Integrity

In [10], we have shown that, contrary to common belief, it is possible to get rid of the total integrity postulate for most approaches to integrity checking without any trade-off. Methods which continue to function well when this postulate is renounced are called inconsistency-tolerant. The basic idea is illustrated below.

Example 2. Let I and I' be as in Example 1. Most integrity checking methods $\mathcal{M}$ accept the update *insert* $(Jack, p)$ if, e.g., (p, e) is a row in *proj*. Now, the positive outcome of this integrity check is not disturbed if, e.g., also the tuple (p, f) is a row in *proj*. That may be somewhat irritating, since the case $\leftarrow \text{proj}(p, e), \ \text{proj}(p, f), \ e \neq f$ of I then is violated. However, this violation has not been caused by the insertion just checked. It has been there before, and the assignment of *Jack* to p should not be rejected just because the data about p are not consistent. After all, it may be part of *Jack*'s new job to cleanse potentially inconsistent project data. In general, a transaction T that preserves the integrity of all consistent data without increasing the amount of extant inconsistency should not be rejected. And that is exactly what $\mathcal{M}$'s output indicates: no case of any constraint that is satisfied in the state before T is committed is violated after T has been committed.

3.2   Inconsistency Measures

Example 2 conveys that each update which does not increase inconsistency can and should be accepted. The following definitions serves to make precise what it means to have an increase or decrease of inconsistency.

Definition 1. $(\mu, \preceq)$ is called an *inconsistency measure* (in short, *measure*) if μ maps tuples (D, IC) to a metric space that is partially ordered by $\preceq$. We may identify a measure $(\mu, \preceq)$ with μ if $\preceq$ is understood.

Example 3. A simple border-case measure β is given by $\beta(D, IC) = D(IC)$, with the ordering *true* $\prec$ *false*, i.e., constraint satisfaction ($D(IC) = true$) means lower inconsistency than constraint violation ($D(IC) = false$). In fact, β is used by all conventional integrity checking methods, for deciding whether a given transaction T on a database D that satisfies its constraints IC should be accepted (if $D^T(IC) = true$) or rejected (if $D^T(IC) = false$).

A less trivial inconsistency measure, for example, as defined in [8], is the function that maps (D, IC) to the cardinality of the set of cases of violated constraints. Inconsistency can also be measured by taking such sets themselves, as elements of the powerset of all cases of IC, together with the subset ordering.

3.3   Generalizing Inconsistency-Tolerant Integrity Checking

Inconsistency-tolerant integrity checking can now be defined as follows.

Definition 2. *(measure-based inconsistency tolerance)*
Let $\mathcal{M}$ be a mapping from triples (D, IC, T) to $\{OK, KO\}$, so that T is either accepted or, resp. rejected, and $(\mu, \preceq)$ an inconsistency measure. $\mathcal{M}$ is called a *sound*, resp., *complete* method for integrity checking if, for each triple (D, IC, T), (1) or, resp., (2) holds.

$$\mathcal{M}(D, IC, T) = OK \;\Rightarrow\; \mu(D^T, IC) \preceq \mu(D, IC). \tag{1}$$

$$\mu(D^T, IC) \preceq \mu(D, IC) \;\Rightarrow\; \mathcal{M}(D, IC, T) = OK. \tag{2}$$

If (1) holds, then $\mathcal{M}$ is also called *measure-based*, and, in particular, *μ-based*.

Definition 2 generalizes the traditional definition of integrity checking significantly, in two ways. Firstly, the traditional measure used for sizing constraint violations is binary, and thus very coarse: IC is either *violated* or *satisfied* in D, i.e., there is no distinction with regard to different amounts of (in)consistency. As opposed to that, the range of an inconsistency measure μ may be arbitrarily fine-grained. Secondly, the total integrity postulate is imposed traditionally, i.e., $D(IC) = true$ is required. As opposed to that, this postulate is absent in Definition 2, i.e., $\mathcal{M}$ does not need to worry about extant constraint violations.

Definition 2 formalizes that a method $\mathcal{M}$ is inconsistency-tolerant if its output OK for a transaction T guarantees that the amount of inconsistency in (D, IC) as measured by μ is not increased by executing T on D. Moreover, each T that, on purpose or by chance, repairs some inconsistency without introducing any new violation will be OK-ed too by $\mathcal{M}$. Thus, inconsistency-tolerant integrity checking will decrease the amount of integrity violations over time.

Note that it follows by the definition above that each inconsistency-tolerant $\mathcal{M}$ returns KO for any transaction the commitment of which would violate a hitherto satisfied case of some constraint. It is then up to the agent who has called $\mathcal{M}$ for checking integrity to react appropriately to the output KO

A defensive reaction is to simply cancel and reject the transaction. A more offensive reaction could be to modify ('repair') the database, the constraints or the transaction, so that an increase of the amount of integrity violations is undone. Such measure-based database repairs are dealt with in [6].

3.4   Relaxing Isolated Integrity

To say, as the isolated integrity postulate does, that a transaction T "preserves integrity in isolation", means: For a given set IC of integrity constraints and each state D, each $I \in IC$ is satisfied in D^T if I is satisfied in D.

Now, let us apply the concept of inconsistency-tolerant business rules checking in 3.1 not only to transactions executed in isolation, but also to concurrent transactions. Thus, we abandon the premise "if I is satisfied in D" and weaken the consequence "each $I \in IC$ is satisfied in D^T", as in Definition 2.

In [11], we could show that this is possible for integrity checking methods that preserve all satisfied cases of integrity constraints, while tolerating those that are violated in the state before a given transaction is executed. By an analogous abstraction, the isolated integrity postulate can be weakened as follows.

For each tuple (D, IC), each measure $(\mu, \preceq)$ and each transaction T,

$$\mu(D^T, IC) \preceq \mu(D, IC) \quad (*)$$

must hold whenever T is executed in isolation.

Clearly, (*) relaxes the traditional isolated integrity postulate, since neither D nor D^T are required to satisfy all business rules in IC. Rather, T only is required to not increase the measured amount of inconsistency. Thus, by analogy to the proof of Theorem 3 in [11], we arrive at the following generalization.

Theorem 1.   Let H be the execution of a serializable history of transactions, T be a transaction in H such that (*) holds whenever T is executed in isolation, D_i be the input state of T in H and D^o be the output state of T in H. Then, $\mu(D_o^T, IC) \preceq \mu(D^i, IC)$ holds.

We point out that this result does not endorse that the inconsistency of all of D and D^T must be measured. On the contrary: measure-based inconsistency-tolerant integrity checking can proceed as for distributed systems without concurrency. In other words, T is committed only if it does not increase the amount of inconsistency, which usually is checked incrementally, without actually assessing the total amount of inconsistency in any state.

Note that the relaxation of the isolated integrity postulate outlined above still asks for the serializability, i.e., a highly demanding isolation level, of all concurrent transactions. Thus, we cannot expect that integrity guarantees of the form (*) would continue to hold in general if the isolation level is lowered. (For a general critique of lowering isolation levels, see [2].) Future work of ours is intended to investigate possible relaxations of the isolation level of concurrent transactions such that sufficient integrity guarantees can still be given.

4   Related Work

Most papers about integrity maintenance do not deal with transaction concurrency. Also the work in [14], which proposes realizations of declarative integrity checking in distributed databases, largely passes by transaction concurrency. On the other hand, most papers that do address concurrency take it for granted that transactions are programmed such that their isolated execution never causes any integrity violation, i.e., they don't care how integrity is ensured.

As an exception, the work documented in [15], addresses both problem areas. However, the proposed solutions are application-specific (flight reservation) and seem to be quite ad-hoc. Also the author of [23] is aware of the problem, and argues convincingly to not be careless about consistency issues. However, with regard to semantic integrity violations in concurrent scenarios, he only exhibits a negative result (the CAP theorem [13]), but does not investigate inconsistency-tolerant solutions. There do exists solutions for reconciling consistency, availability and partition tolerance in distributed systems, e.g., [29] [24]. However, the consistency they are concerned with is either transaction consistency (i.e., the avoidance of dirty reads, unrepeatable reads and phantom updates) or replication consistency (i.e., that all replicas consist of identical copies, so that there are no stale data), not the semantic consistency as expressed by business rules.

A proposal to rewrite concurrent transactions such that conflicts at commit time are avoided is proposed in [16]. The authors outline how to augment transactions with read actions for simplified constraint checking and with locks, so that their serializable execution guarantees integrity preservation. However, ad-hoc transactions are not considered.

For replicated database systems, the interplay of built-in integrity checking, concurrency and replication consistency has been studied in [19]. In that paper, solutions are provided for enabling integrity checking even in systems where the isolation level of transactions is lowered to *snapshot isolation* [2]. However, inconsistency tolerance in the sense of coping with extant integrity violations has not been considered in [19]. Thus, for the snapshot-isolation-based replication of databases, more research is necessary in order to clarify which consistency guarantees can be given when inconsistency-tolerant integrity checking methods are used in the presence of inconsistent cases of constraints.

5   Conclusion

Since the beginnings of the field of computational databases, the obligation of maintaining the integrity of business rules in multi-user systems, and thus the avoidance of inconsistency, has rested on the shoulders of designers, implementers, administrators and end users of transaction processing. More precisely, integrity maintenance for concurrent transactions, particularly in distributed systems, is delegated to a multitude of individual human actors who, on one hand, have to trust on each other's unfailing compliance with the integrity requirements, but, on the other hand, usually do not know each other.

The long-term objective toward which this paper has made some steps is that this unreliable distribution of responsibilities for integrity preservation should give way to declarative specifications of integrity constraints that are supported by the DBMS, just like some fairly simple kinds of constraints are supported for sequential transactions in non-distributed database systems.

With this goal in vision, we propose the following. For each transaction T, the DBMS should determine autonomously whether the state transition effected by T preserves integrity or not, and react accordingly. In this paper, we have removed two major obstacles that hitherto may have turned away researchers and developers from striving for such solutions: the postulates of total and isolated integrity preservation.

For overcoming the total integrity postulate, i.e., the traditional misbelief that integrity can be checked efficiently for a transaction T only if the state before T totally satisfies all constraints, we have revisited the work in [10]. There, it has been shown that the total integrity postulate can be waived without further ado, for most (though not all) integrity checking methods.

We have reaffirmed that the advantages of dumping the total integrity postulate even extend to relaxing the isolated integrity postulate. More precisely, the use of an inconsistency-tolerant integrity checking method to enforce business rules for concurrent sequentializable transactions guarantees that no transaction can violate any case of any constraint that has been satisfied in the state before committing if all transactions preserve the integrity of the same cases in isolation. Conversely stated, our result guarantees that, if any violation happens, then no transaction that has been correctly and successfully checked for integrity preservation by an inconsistency-tolerant method can be held responsible for that. The most interesting aspect of this result is that it even holds in the presence of inconsistent data that violate some business rule.

We have seen that more research is needed for systems in which the isolation level of concurrent transactions is compromised. In particular, for non-sequentializable histories of concurrent transactions, it should be interesting to elaborate a precise theory of different kinds of database states. Such a theory should allow to differentiate between states that are committed locally, states that are committed globally, states that are "seen" by a transaction and states that are "seen" by (human or programmed) agents or clients that have issued the transaction. It should also be able to predict which consistency guarantees can be made by which methods for transitions between those states.

This area of research is important because most commercial database management systems compromise the isolation level of transactions in favor of a higher transaction throughput, while leaving the problem of integrity preservation to the application programmers. First steps in this direction had been proposed in [11].

Another important, possibly even more difficult area of upcoming research is that of providing inconsistency-tolerant transactions not only in distributed and replicated systems with remote clients and servers, but also for databases in the cloud, for big volumes of data and for No-SQL data stores. These are intended to be the objectives of future projects. So far, some special-purpose solutions exist (e.g., [30]). Their generalizability is doubtful, or at least less than obvious. In fact, the lack of genericity may be a weakness or a strength. After all, a move away from the universality-oriented attitude toward solutions to problems in the field of databases, which was common in the past, seems to be the way of the future, as argued in [25].

References

1. Abiteboul, S., Hull, R., Vianu, V.: Foundations of Databases. Addison-Wesley (1995)
2. Berenson, H., Bernstein, P., Gray, J., Melton, J., O'Neil, E., O'Neil, P.: A critique of ANSI SQL isolation levels. In: Proc. SIGMOD 1995, pp. 1–10. ACM Press (1995)
3. Bernstein, P., Hadzilacos, V., Goodman, N.: Concurrency Control and Recovery in Database Systems. Addison-Wesley (1987)
4. Butleris, R., Kapocius, K.: The Business Rules Repository for Information Systems Design. In: Proc. 6th ADBIS, vol. 2, pp. 64–77. Slovak Univ. of Technology, Bratislava (2002)
5. Davis, C.T.: Data Processing sphere of control. IBM Systems Journal 17(2), 179–198 (1978)
6. Decker, H.: Partial Repairs that Tolerante Inconsistency. In: Eder, J., Bielikova, M., Tjoa, A.M. (eds.) ADBIS 2011. LNCS, vol. 6909, pp. 389–400. Springer, Heidelberg (2011)
7. Decker, H.: Causes of the violation of integrity constraints for supporting the quality of databases. In: Murgante, B., Gervasi, O., Iglesias, A., Taniar, D., Apduhan, B.O. (eds.) ICCSA 2011, Part V. LNCS, vol. 6786, pp. 283–292. Springer, Heidelberg (2011)
8. Decker, H.: New measures for maintaining the quality of databases. In: Murgante, B., Gervasi, O., Misra, S., Nedjah, N., Rocha, A.M.A.C., Taniar, D., Apduhan, B.O. (eds.) ICCSA 2012, Part IV. LNCS, vol. 7336, pp. 170–185. Springer, Heidelberg (2012)
9. Decker, H.: Controlling the Consistency of the Evolution of Database Systems. In: Proc. 24th ICSSEA, Paris (2012)
10. Decker, H., Martinenghi, D.: Inconsistency-tolerant Integrity Checking. IEEE Transactions on Knowledge and Data Engineering 23(2), 218–234 (2011)
11. Decker, H., Muñoz-Escoí, F.D.: Revisiting and Improving a Result on Integrity Preservation by Concurrent Transactions. In: Meersman, R., Dillon, T., Herrero, P. (eds.) OTM 2010 Workshops. LNCS, vol. 6428, pp. 297–306. Springer, Heidelberg (2010)
12. Eswaran, K., Gray, J., Lorie, R., Traiger, I.: The Notions of Consistency and Predicate Locks in a Database System. CACM 19(11), 624–633 (1976)
13. Gilbert, S., Lynch, N.: Brewer's Conjecture and the feasibility of Consistent, Available, Partition-tolerant Web Services. ACM SIGACT News 33(2), 51–59 (2002)

14. Ibrahim, H.: Checking Integrity Constraints - How it Differs in Centralized, Distributed and Parallel Databases. In: Proc. 17th DEXA Workshops, pp. 563–568. IEEE (2006)
15. Lynch, N., Blaustein, B., Siegel, M.: Correctness Conditions for Highly Available Replicated Databases. In: Proc. 5th PODC, pp. 11–28. ACM Press (1986)
16. Martinenghi, D., Christiansen, H.: Transaction Management with Integrity Checking. In: Andersen, K.V., Debenham, J., Wagner, R. (eds.) DEXA 2005. LNCS, vol. 3588, pp. 606–615. Springer, Heidelberg (2005)
17. Christiansen, H., Decker, H.: Integrity checking and maintenance in relational and deductive databases and beyond. In: Ma, Z. (ed.) Intelligent Databases: Technologies and Applications, pp. 238–285. Idea Group (2006)
18. Morgan, T.: Business Rules and Information Systems - Aligning IT with Business Goals. Addison-Wesley (2002)
19. Muñoz-Escoí, F.D., Ruiz-Fuertes, M.I., Decker, H., Armendáriz-Íñigo, J.E., de Mendívil, J.R.G.: Extending Middleware Protocols for Database Replication with Integrity Support. In: Meersman, R., Tari, Z. (eds.) OTM 2008, Part I. LNCS, vol. 5331, pp. 607–624. Springer, Heidelberg (2008)
20. Nicolas, J.-M.: Logic for improving integrity checking in relational data bases. Acta Informatica 18, 227–253 (1982)
21. Novakovic, I., Deletic, V.: Structuring of Business Rules in Information System Design and Architecture. Facta Universitatis Nis, Ser. Elec. Energ. 22(3), 305–312 (2009)
22. Pipino, L., Lee, Y., Yang, R.: Data Quality Assessment. CACM 45(4), 211–218 (2002)
23. Stonebraker, M.: Errors in Database Systems, Eventual Consistency, and the CAP Theorem (2010),
http://cacm.acm.org/blog/blog-cacm/83396-errors-in-database-systems-eventual-consistency-and-the-cap-theorem
24. Stonebraker, M.: In search of database consistency. CACM 53(10), 8–9 (2010)
25. Stonebraker, M.: Technical perspective - One size fits all: an idea whose time has come and gone. Commun. ACM 51(12), 76 (2008)
26. Taveter, K.: Business Rules' Approach to the Modelling, Design and Implementation of Agent-Oriented Information Systems. In: Proc. CAiSE workshop AOIS, Heidelberg (1999)
27. Vidyasankar, K.: Serializability. In: Liu, L., Özu, T. (eds.) Encyclopedia of Database Systems, pp. 2626–2632. Springer (2009)
28. Weikum, G., Vossen, G.: Transactional Information Systems. Morgan Kaufmann (2002)
29. Vogels, W.: Eventually Consistent. ACM Queue 6(6), 14–19 (2008)
30. Pereira Ziwich, P., Procpio Duarte, E., Pessoa Albini, L.: Distributed Integrity Checking for Systems with Replicated Data. In: Proc. ICPADS, vol. 1, pp. 363–369. IEEE CSP (2005)

Agent-Oriented Software Engineering of Distributed eHealth Systems

Adel Taweel[1], Emilia Garcia[2], Simon Miles[1], and Michael Luck[1]

[1] King's College London, UK
{adel.taweel,simon.miles,Michael.luck}@kcl.ac.uk
[2] Universitat Politecnica de Valencia, Spain
mgarcia@dsic.upv.es

Abstract. Development of distributed ehealth systems is increasingly becoming a common necessity to work across organisations to provide efficient services. This requires healthcare information to be accessible, under appropriate safeguards, for research or healthcare. However, the progress relies on the interoperability of local healthcare software, and is often hampered by ad hoc development methods leading to closed systems with a multitude of protocols, terminologies, and design approaches. The ehealth domain, by requirements, includes autonomous organisations and individuals, e.g. patients and doctors, which would make AOSE a good approach to developing systems that are potentially more open yet retain more local control and autonomy. The paper presents the use of AOSE to develop a particular distributed ehealth system, IDEA, and evaluates its suitability to develop such systems in general.

Keywords: eHealth, Agent Architectures, Contracts, System of Systems.

1 Introduction

Scalable and autonomous distributed systems are increasingly in more demand to fulfil the emerging requirements of complex domains. *eHealth* is a typical example, which is rapidly becoming more and more dependent on large-scale integrated distributed software systems. These systems are increasingly required to provide new and innovative ways to improve patient care across dispersed organisations and interoperate with various types of other demanding systems, such as those for clinical research. The health domain presents a number of challenges and puts greater demands on a number of aspects that invite new methods and techniques to rethink the way its systems are developed. The continual expansion of need to provide services at the point of care, led to the spread and distribution of healthcare organisations and systems. Each functions autonomously, falls under its own sphere of control, and utilises its own domain techniques and speciality, yet they are all required collectively to provide an integrated and improved healthcare. A typical example is the UK National Health Service, which is, also, beyond its normal function is required to integrate with and provide the data and knowledge to drive clinical research. In this context, interactions are required to take place between components, systems, people and

Y.T. Demey and H. Panetto (Eds.): OTM 2013 Workshops, LNCS 8186, pp. 332–341, 2013.

organisations managed by parties with different goals, possibly conflicting policies, incompatible data representations, and different needs and work methods. Not surprisingly, this can lead to serious challenges when they are required to work as a unit raising the need for integrating different systems in a trustworthy and consistent manner. This leads to the emergence of strict regulatory controls to manage not only the internal behaviour, but also the interactions that may take place between them.

Multi-agent technology has emerged over the last decade as a new software engineering paradigm for building complex, adaptive systems in distributed, heterogeneous environments. Although not mainstream, but it is provides a promising development approach. It fits well with several of the above concepts that often well addressed in the multi-agent systems, such as organisational autonomy, inherent regulatory frameworks, local control, regulated interactions and so forth. Indeed, there have been several agent-based e-health systems developed over a period of many years [1], [16], but they do not explicitly employ agent-oriented software engineering (AOSE) methodologies and, as such, do not directly evaluate the suitability of AOSE to this domain in general.

In this paper, we apply AOSE to develop a distributed ehealth system and investigate, more generally, the suitability of using AOSE for the development of distributed e-health systems. In doing so, we use a specific methodology, ROMAS (Regulated Open Multi-agent Systems) [10], [12]. ROMAS is an AOSE methodology that guides developers all the way from the requirements analysis phase to the actual implementation, taking into account the notions of agents, organizations, services and contracts. We apply the ROMAS methodology to a particular (real) e-health system: IDEA [20], [21], as an example, to allow exemplifying, more generally, the features of such systems, and to assess the suitability of AOSE in addressing them.

Section 2 describes the IDEA distributed ehealth system and summarizes the main challenges of the development of ehealth systems; Section 3 describes the design of the IDEA ehealth system using ROMAS; section 4 analyses the benefits that the IDEA system has obtained by means of using AOSE techniques; Section 5 discusses the suitability and general benefits of using agent methodologies in the analysis and design of e-health systems. We identify a number of strengths and weaknesses of AOSE for such systems, as well as suggesting improvements to better support the needs of the domain; finally, Section 6 presents some conclusions and future work.

2   IDEA eHealth System: Requirements and Challenges

Clinical trials are used to study various aspects of medical science, using evidence-based medicine [20], [21]. Currently, however, such trials are frequently unsuccessful at recruiting sufficient patients. This is because discovering and contacting eligible potential recruits is both logistically and legally challenging. IDEA is a new system, currently under deployment in the UK healthcare system, for recruiting patients for clinical trials in real-time. Fig. 1 illustrates the overall conceptual architecture of IDEA. It notifies practitioners in real-time whenever an eligible patient is in consultation. When a patient visits a practice, IDEA compares their details against a registry of trials; if the patient is found eligible for one or more, the practitioner is prompted to help recruit the patient if they are interested. The IDEA project is discussed more fully here [20].

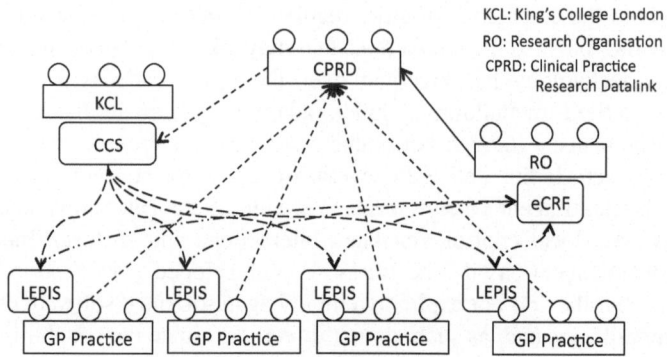

Fig. 1. IDEA Conceptual Architecture

However, to reach a more open system a more flexible development methodology needs to be used. To do so and to be able to identify, assess and use an effective methodology for the development of the IDEA system [21], its core challenges need to be considered. Below are the most important of these identified challenges to gain a better understanding of how AOSE might be more generally used effectively in the development process of such systems, which are typically of those in the medical domain.

Integration of Independent Systems. In order to recruit eligible patients, it is necessary for researchers, practitioners, patients, databases and practices to interact. This means that several independent institutions, which are completely autonomous and have their own independent goals, must cooperate to achieve a common objective. However, the integration of multiple heterogeneous and autonomous systems can be a complicated and resource-consuming task. Some of the issues that must be solved include [18], [19]: (i) *Distributed Data* (ii) *Technical Interoperability* (iii) *Process Interoperability* (iv) *Semantic Interoperability* (v) *Trustworthiness*. For an open and flexible healthcare system that involves multiple organizations, it must take all these aspects into account to ensure successful operation.

Regulation of Independent Systems. Healthcare systems must fulfil strict clinical and governmental regulations concerning the privacy and security of personal patient data. Moreover, each research institute and practice has its own regulations, specific goals, priorities and restrictions to regulate the behaviour of each of its members. Healthcare systems must therefore often take into account several regulatory environments.

Scalability of the System. Healthcare systems, by their nature, present scalability problems. For example, the effectiveness of the recruitment system is measured in the number of eligible patients that it is able to detect. In order to detect an adequate number of eligible patients for a specialized trial, the system must be able to get the information from as many practices as possible (more than 10000 GP practices in the UK) and manage a huge number of clinical trials requirements. However, due to the number of potential active trials (potentially several hundreds) with the size of each trial description and eligibility criteria makes it impossible for GPs to know all active trials to assess patient eligibility during, the often short, consultation.

System Evolution. Medical institutions are constantly adapting their systems to reflect new legislation, software and medical techniques. As these autonomous organisations often operate with a range of aims and priorities, it is possible that changes may take place without necessarily propagating to all other parts of the system. In this respect, a change within one sub-system could result in violations of responsibilities in another sub-system (e.g. changes in data formats). Healthcare systems that consist of multiple organizations must therefore ensure some formal procedure by which all parties understand and adhere to their responsibilities. Thus, to achieve, Institutions must also be contractually obliged to adhere to a standard interaction mechanism and data format, although their internal process or storage technology may differ [15].

3 Designing IDEA Recruitment System with ROMAS

This section details the design of the IDEA system using the ROMAS methodology [10], [12]. Fig. 2 depicts the main structure of the system in terms of agent-oriented software engineering key concepts including organisations, roles, norms and contracts. These are described below in more details.

Organizations and Processes. Several organizations are involved in the key processes performed in IDEA, as follows. When a research body wishes to create a new clinical trial, they can register it through a service called the Central Control Service (CCS), which is hosted at *King's College London* (KCL). The CCS stores trials within a large database in a pre-defined format that all researchers must adhere to. Each trial includes eligibility criteria of potentially eligible patients, which are managed by the *Clinical Practice Research Datalink* (CPRD), which operates a large data warehouse containing over 12 million up-to-date patient records. A software agent (named LEPIS) located on practitioners' computers communicates with CCS to obtain respective trials and their eligibility criteria for its own participating *practice* and general practitioner (GP). LEPIS agents continually listen to the interactions between the practitioner and their local Electronic Health Record (EHR), which manages patients' clinical information (e.g. diagnoses, treatments, drugs, etc.). During consultations, LEPIS agents check the eligibility of the patient to any of the registered trials. If the patient is found to be eligible for a trial, the practitioner is notified, and if the patient agrees to participate, LEPIS loads the appropriate electronic case report forms (eCRF) from a website provided by the *research organisation* responsible for the trial, allowing the patient's recruitment to be completed. Thus, the following organizations are involved: KCL, CPRD, GP practices and the research organisations.

Roles. The system is composed of six different roles presented below. The *CPRD Manager Role* is responsible for updating and controlling access to the CPRD database. It offers a service to pre-compute potential eligible patients for individual trials with complex search criteria (*CreateEligibilityList* service). The role must also offer a service to decide when a GP (and their own practice) is authorized to perform recruitment for each trial (*AuthorizeGP* service), while adhering to local and good clinical practice regulations.

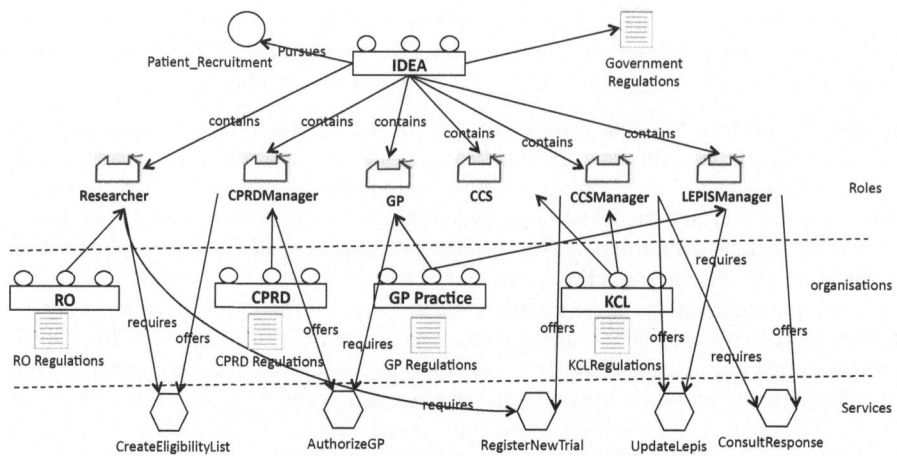

Fig. 2. IDEA Services and Organisations

The *Researcher Role* is responsible for defining the specific features of each trial under its jurisdiction. Researchers are also responsible for inserting these trials into the CCS database by means of the service offered by the CCS role (described below). They are not allowed to directly contact patients unless they have agreed and consented to participate in one of their own clinical trial. For obvious reasons, each researcher should be part of a specific research institution and follow its specific normative restrictions.

The *CCS Role* is a software application responsible for controlling the CCS database, which stores data about active clinical trials. It offers three services to the other members of the system: (i) a *Register New Trial* service that allows researchers to inject new clinical trials in CCS; whenever a Researcher tries to inject a new trial into the CSS database, the CSS role must verify that this trial follows the specified standards and regulations; (ii) an *Update LEPIS Database* service that ensures consistency with LEPIS agents to update their information about active clinical trials; and (iii) a *Consult Patients Response* service that, in communication with LEPIS Agents, records the response of each consulted patient (and/or their GP) to be registered (whether they have agreed or refused to participate in a trial). In the current implementation, the CCS role is performed by an agent located at the KCL organization. Clearly, this agent must comply with established norms concerning replication of information and privacy.

The *CCS Manager Role* is responsible for controlling the information in the CCS (i.e. it has control over the CCS Role). Due to the specific requirements described by the domain expert, there must be a human responsible for this. A member of KCL undertakes this role, who complies with KCL's restrictions and rules.

The *LEPIS Manager Role* is played by a software application that resides in each practice and investigates the eligibility of patients. LEPIS agent plays this role for each practitioner in each GP practice participating in the recruitment system. LEPIS agents continually communicate with the CCS service to acquire information about trials related to the type of patients and speciality of GPs and practices. LEPIS agents also provide the GP with a simple interface to notify them of a patient's eligibility, as well as the option to launch the appropriate eCRF website if the patient has agreed to participate.

The *GP Role* represents a practitioner working in a practice. GPs must be previously authorized by the *CPRD Manager* before they can recruit patients into trials. This authorization involves the acceptance of some norms related to good clinical practice, privacy, and specific restrictions described for each clinical trial. Clearly, each GP must also comply with the rules of their own clinic. Finally, patients are considered external entities for the IDEA system because their interaction with the system is always executed through their GP. Each role description is associated to a graphical diagram that allows a fast general overview. They have been omitted due to space restrictions.

Norms and Contracts. *The Governmental regulations* related to the privacy of patient data and clinical trials are described at a system-wide level; i.e., every agent playing a role inside IDEA system should comply with these regulations. At the same time, each institution and practice defines its own regulations, so the entities of the system should meet the general governmental regulations and the restrictions established by the institution to which they pertain. For instance, each LEPIS agent should follow both global and practice-specific regulations. The rights and duties that any specific agent implementation must fulfil to play a role in IDEA are formalized by means of a *Social Contract*. Even though contracts are dynamic entities that cannot be completely defined at the design stage, designers can specify the predefined restrictions that all final contracts of a specific type should follow.

These restrictions are defined in a *Contract Template*, where *Hard Clauses* indicates mandatory clauses that any contract of this type must contain and *Soft Clauses* indicate more flexible recommendations. Due to space constraints, a comprehensive set of norms and contracts in IDEA cannot be listed; thus, we briefly cover a small number of examples.

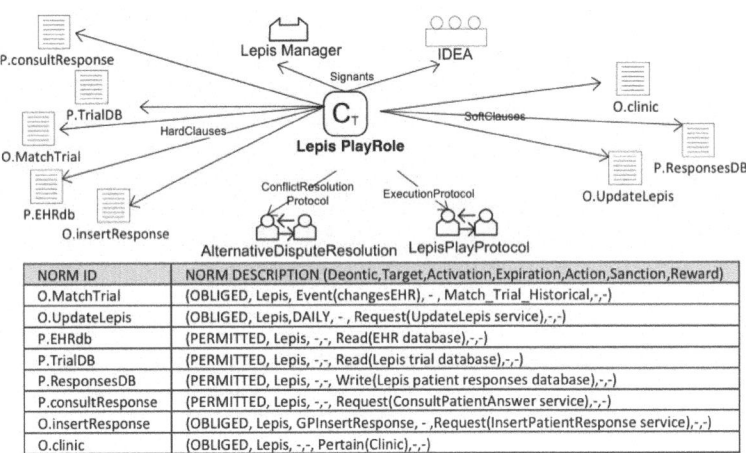

NORM ID	NORM DESCRIPTION (Deontic,Target,Activation,Expiration,Action,Sanction,Reward)
O.MatchTrial	(OBLIGED, Lepis, Event(changesEHR), - , Match_Trial_Historical,-,-)
O.UpdateLepis	(OBLIGED, Lepis,DAILY, - , Request(UpdateLepis service),-,-)
P.EHRdb	(PERMITTED, Lepis, -,-, Read(EHR database),-,-)
P.TrialDB	(PERMITTED, Lepis, -,-, Read(Lepis trial database),-,-)
P.ResponsesDB	(PERMITTED, Lepis, -,-, Write(Lepis patient responses database),-,-)
P.consultResponse	(PERMITTED, Lepis, -,-, Request(ConsultPatientAnswer service),-,-)
O.insertResponse	(OBLIGED, Lepis, GPInsertResponse, - ,Request(InsertPatientResponse service),-,-)
O.clinic	(OBLIGED, Lepis, -,-, Pertain(Clinic),-,-)

Fig. 3. LEPIS PlayRole Contracts

Fig. 3 describes the *LEPIS PlayRole* contract template. It specifies that any agent playing the LEPIS Manager role must detect changes in the EHR system and then it must check the eligibility of the patient for any of the registered trials (*Norm O.MatchTrial*). The contract template also recommends that the final contract includes a norm specifying that the local LEPIS database must be updated with new clinical trials every day (*Norm O.UpdateLepis*). This clause is merely a recommendation so that at runtime, LEPIS agents are able to negotiate with the IDEA organization exactly how often they should update their local registry. The remaining clauses relate to the use of the local registry and the service dependencies that LEPIS requires.

In this design, each practice can implement its own LEPIS agent (if it complies with the required contracts and norms), allowing each practice to adapt the behaviour of LEPIS in line with its own priorities. For example, a practice could decide that its LEPIS agent should not increase patient queues; e.g. GPs should not be notified during busy periods. Similarly, each entity that plays any role in IDEA can be adapted to the different requirements and restrictions of its own institution. Each institution would thus maintain its own technology, with different implementations of each role interacting independently of the technological differences.

4   Benefits of AOSE Design for Distributed eHealth Systems

To reflect on the above AOSE design and the effectiveness of ROMAS for distributed ehealth systems, we revisit the design challenges listed above in Section 2.

Integration of Independent Systems. ROMAS found to offer an effective design platform for modelling and integrating the different IDEA systems by enforcing a high level of abstraction, to real-world concepts (e.g. organizations). First, it helped domain experts, who are typically not familiar with the relevant technology, to gain a better understanding of the system. Beyond this, it also provided well-defined boundaries between different agents and organizations, allowing individual objectives and regulations to be specified, as well as to maintain the privacy of each institution's data and processes. More importantly, technical and semantic interoperability challenges are also addressed by means of standardized web service interfaces.

Regulation of Independent Systems. The regulatory requirements of IDEA were found to fit well into the ROMAS principles. Specifically, it allowed different normative environments for each GP practice and research institution to be explicitly described and combined with global governmental norms. This allowed the behaviour of the different entities to be formally constrained --- an extremely important feature for some domains, e.g. the medical domain. Furthermore, different technologies can be used to implement the agents that play each role. For instance, each practice could specify and implement its own LEPIS agents according to its aims, restrictions and priorities, while maintaining the stability of the system through global governmental regulations. This is particularly important when potentially deploying agents across multiple research institutions and practices from different countries.

System Evolution. More generally, ROMAS offers an effective paradigm for assisting in system evolution in IDEA. Through norm and contract regulation, each sub-system can evolve while ensuring that it does not compromise its responsibilities to other parties. Common examples include adaptation to new internal regulations or to the use of a new software technology. Moreover, global system evolution can also take place by publishing new contracts and norms, thereby forcing sub-systems to adapt.

5   Evaluation and Discussion

In the above sections, we have considered the use of an agent methodology to design an ehealth system, and the benefits achieved in doing so. We now consider the more general hypothesis that AOSE is more generally appropriate for the development of ehealth systems. For the evaluation, we can draw more widely, not just on the experience from the IDEA system, but also on other multi-agent systems in ehealth. In general, AI technology including agent-based systems have been used in healthcare to tackle endemic issues such as distributed information and expertise, unpredictable dynamics, uncertainty in reasoning and simulation of systems [17], [23] [13].

We present the argument in terms of AOSE's features that make it well suited to the characteristics of distributed ehealth systems; and those that are not well addressed by AOSE. On the one hand, AOSE methodologies commonly include analysis and design based on a few key ideas: *agents* as autonomous, pro-active, flexible and social entities; *interactions* of a flexible and well-defined nature between those agents; and *organizations* in which agents operate, modelled either implicitly or explicitly [5], [2], [14]. The functionality that agents enact in such designs is sometimes modelled as *services* [8]. Other features present in some methodologies, including ROMAS, are the assumptions of *openness* in the system, and of *regulation* to be followed by agents (e.g. norms, responsibilities, rights, contracts, etc. [3], [7], [16]). Through the lessons learned during the development of IDEA, we now present some features of AOSE that indicate its suitability for general ehealth applications.

Autonomy. A critical aspect of ehealth systems is that they are comprised of subsystems that have their own regulations, privacy issues, localised authority, localised flexibility, and so on. For instance, in IDEA, different policies are applied in different GP practices, hospitals and regions in the UK. In this context, it is clear that ehealth systems must also take into account this diversity. The autonomy of agents and organisations assumed at the analysis stages in AOSE means that this is a particularly well-suited approach.

Openness. There are can be thousands of independent sites involved in healthcare. A common feature of large-scale ehealth systems, such as IDEA, is the expectation that more sites will join the system as they develop the technical capability to do so (e.g. new GP practices, research institutes etc.). In practice, openness is enabled by a design specifying exactly what a new party must adhere to in order to join the system, such as through contracts (as in ROMAS) or roles, as well as lower level concerns such as interfaces and interaction protocols.

Explicit Norms. Due to the confidentiality issues mentioned above, healthcare is highly regulated at all levels, and these regulations must be considered as a primary influence on any ehealth system. Regulations apply both to individual GP practices and researchers, and across the whole system due to national or potentially international laws. The advantage of a norm-based design approach is that there is a ready way for developers to specify these regulations explicitly in the development process, such that they become part of the design.

On the other hand, two weaknesses were found in applying ROMAS to IDEA. Although they are weaknesses of ROMAS, we believe they apply more generally to current AOSE methodologies.

First, while conceptualizing the system in terms of agents, organizations and norms was found to be intuitive by domain experts, the language itself was not. For example, `patient' is a critical concept in the healthcare domain, modelling it as abstract as `agent' only obfuscates the intention.

Second, while there are explicit regulations in the domain, there are also many implicit good practices for medicine and healthcare. Capturing these as part of the engineering process is possible but prone to accidental exclusion. One approach to address this issue could be to have domain constraints as an embedded part of the methodology.

6   Conclusions and Future Work

The paper presents the application of AOSE methodology for the development of complex distributed ehealth systems and assesses its suitability for the development of such systems more generally in the medical domain. To investigate this domain, we have applied the ROMAS methodology to the design of a real ehealth system for the identification of eligible patients for clinical trials in real-time. The results obtained show that the use of AOSE concepts, such as organizations, roles, norms and contracts, apply to the analysis and design of ehealth systems.

Although, it has been shown that the use of AOSE techniques offers several advantages to produce a flexible system design that can deal with the dynamics of the normative and technological environment in the healthcare domain; however, it has also shown that the current AOSE techniques and languages are not easily accessible by the domain experts and require further research to achieve greater domain-driven usability and adaption.

Acknowledgment. The authors would like to thank all colleagues from the IDEA project who contributed to this work, through discussions or providing insights.

References

1. Bajo, J., Fraile, J.A., Pérez-Lancho, B., Corchado, J.M.: The thomasarchi- tecture in home care scenarios: A case study. Expert Syst. Appl. 37(5), 3986–3999 (2010)
2. Bordini, R.H., Dastani, M., Winikoff, M.: Current issues in multi-agent systems development. In: O'Hare, G.M.P., Ricci, A., O'Grady, M.J., Dikenelli, O. (eds.) ESAW 2006. LNCS (LNAI), vol. 4457, pp. 38–61. Springer, Heidelberg (2007)
3. DeLoach, S.: Omacs a framework for adaptive, complex systems. In: Handbook of Research on Multi-AGent Systems: Semantics and Dynamics of Organizational Models, pp. 76–104. IGI Global (2009)
4. DeLoach, S.A.: Developing a multiagent conference management system using the O-maSE process framework. In: Luck, M., Padgham, L. (eds.) AOSE 2008. LNCS, vol. 4951, pp. 168–181. Springer, Heidelberg (2008)
5. DeLoach, S.A., Padgham, L., Perini, A., Susi, A., Thangarajah, J.: Using threeAOSE toolkits to develop a sample design. International Journal Agent-Oriented Software Engineering 3, 416–476 (2009)
6. Dignum, F., Dignum, V., Padget, J., Vázquez-Salceda, J.: Organizing web services to develop dynamic, flexible, distributed systems. In: iiWAS 2009, pp. 225–234 (2009)
7. Dignum, V.: A model for organizational interaction:based on agents, founded inlogic. PhD thesis, Utrecht University (2003)

8. Fernández, R.F., Magarinõ, I.G., Gómez-Sanz, J.J., Pavoń, J.: Integration of web services in an agent oriented methodology. Journal International Transactions on Systems Science and Applications 3, 145–161 (2007)
9. Fernandez, R.F., Magarinyo, I.G., Gomez-Sanz, J.J., Pavon, J.: Integration of web services in an agent oriented methodology. Journal International Transactions on Systems Science and Applications 3, 145–161 (2007)
10. Garcia, E., Giret, A., Botti, V.: Developing Regulated Open Multi-agent Systems
11. Garcia, E., Giret, A., Botti, V.: Software engineering for service-oriented MAS. In: Klusch, M., Pěchouček, M., Polleres, A. (eds.) CIA 2008. LNCS (LNAI), vol. 5180, pp. 86–100. Springer, Heidelberg (2008)
12. Garcia, E., Giret, A., Botti, V.: Regulated open multi-agent systems based on contracts. In: Information Systems Development, pp. 243–255 (2011)
13. Gonzalez-Velez, H., Mier, M., Julia-Sape, M., Arvanitis, T., Garcia-Gomez, M.R.J., Lewis, P., Dasmahapatra, S., Dupplaw, D., Peet, A., Arus, C., Celda, B., Huel, S.V., Lluch-Ariet, M.: Healthagents: distributed multi-agent brain tumor diagnosis and prognosis. Applied Intelligence 30 (2009)
14. Lin, C.-E., Kavi, K.M., Sheldon, F.T., Daley, K.M., Abercrombie, R.K.: A methodology to evaluate agent oriented software engineering techniques. In: HICSS 2007, p. 60 (2007)
15. Oren, N., Panagiotidi, S., Vázquez-Salceda, J., Modgil, S., Luck, M., Miles, S.: Towards a formalisation of electronic contracting environments. In: Hübner, J.F., Matson, E., Boissier, O., Dignum, V. (eds.) COIN@AAMAS 2008. LNCS, vol. 5428, pp. 156–171. Springer, Heidelberg (2009)
16. Paranjape, R., Sadanand, A., Paranjape, R., Sadanand, A.: Multi-Agent Systems for Healthcare Simulation and Modeling: Applications for System Improvement, 1st edn. Information Science Reference - Imprint of: IGI Publishing, Hershey (2009)
17. Rammal, A., Trouilhet, S., Singer, N., Pecatte, J.-M.: An adaptive system for home monitoring using a multiagent classification of patterns. In: International Conference on Business Process Management, pp. 3:1–3:8 (2008)
18. Taweel, A., Delaney, B., Speedie, S.: Towards achieving semantic interoperabil- ity in ehealth services. In: Watfa, M. (ed.) E-Healthcare Systems and Wireless Communications: Current and Future Challenges, pp. 388–401. IGI (2012)
19. Taweel, A., Speedie, S., Tyson, G., Tawil, A.R., Peterson, K., Delaney, B.: Service and model-driven dynamic integration of health data. In: Proceedings of the First International Workshop on Managing Interoperability and Complexity in Health Systems, MIXHS 2011, pp. 11–17. ACM (2011)
20. Tyson, G., Taweel, A., Miles, S., Luck, M., Staa, T.V., Delaney, B.: An agent- based approach to real-time patient identification for clinical trials. In: Kostkova, P., Szomszor, M., Fowler, D. (eds.) eHealth 2011. LNICST, vol. 91, pp. 138–145. Springer, Heidelberg (2012)
21. Tyson, G., Taweel, A., Zschaler, S., Staa, T.V., Delaney, B.: A model-driven approach to interoperability and integration in systems of systems. In: Modelling Foundations and Applications: MBSDI Workshop (2011)
22. Vecht, B., Dignum, F., Meyer, J.-J., Dignum, M.: Handbook of research on multi- agent systems: Semantics and dynamics of organizational models. In: Autonomous Agents Adopting Organizational Rules, pp. 314–333. IGI Global (2009)
23. Zhang, X., Xu, H., Shrestha, B.: Building a health care multi-agent simulation system with role-based modeling. In: MAS for Health Care Simulation and Modeling: Applications for System Improvement, ch. VI. IGI Global (2009)

Meta4eS 2013 PC Co-Chairs Message

The future eSociety - renamed "OnTheMoveSociety" in the context of Meta4eS - is an e-inclusive society based on the extensive use of digital technologies at all levels of interaction between its members. It is a society that evolves based on knowledge and that empowers individuals by creating virtual communities that benefit from social inclusion, access to information, enhanced interaction, participation and freedom of expression, among other.

In this context, the role of the World Wide Web in the way people and organizations exchange information and interact in the social cyberspace is crucial. Large amounts of structured data are being published and shared on the Web and a growing number of services and applications emerge from it. The applications must be designed in such a way to help people use their knowledge at best and generate new knowledge in return, while keeping intact their privacy and confidentiality. A current popular initiative adopted by a growing number of actors from transversal domains (e.g. governments, city municipalities, etc.) encourage publishing structured data (e.g. RDF) on the Web of Data. Managing such data in order to produce services and applications for end-user consumption is presently a big challenge. The final goal is to lower the barrier between end-users and information and communication technologies via a number of techniques stemming from the fields of multilingual information, information visualization, privacy and trust, rich multimedia retrieval, etc.

To discuss, demonstrate and share best practices, ideas and results, the 2nd International IFIP Workshop on Methods, Evaluation, Tools and Applications for the Creation and Consumption of Structured Data for the e-Society (Meta4eS 2013), an event supported by IFIP TC 12 WG 12.7 and the Open Semantic Cloud for Brussels project, brings together researchers, professionals and experts interested to present original research results in this area.

We are happy to announce that, for its second edition, the workshop raised interest and good participation in the research community. After a thorough review process, with each submission refereed by at least three members of the workshop Program Committee, we accepted 7 full papers and 6 poster and demo abstracts covering topics such as ontology engineering, multimedia annotation, natural language modeling, spatiotemporal linked open data, business process management, knowledge creation, extraction and sharing, social semantics, services, user profiling and usability testing, and applied to the fields of linked cities, cultural events, e-Health, building design and simulation.

We thank the PC members for their time and effort in ensuring the quality during the review process, as well as the authors and the workshop attendees for the original ideas and the inspiring discussions. We also thank the OTM 2013 Organizing Committee members for their support. We are confident that Meta4eS will bring an important contribution towards the future eSociety.

July 2013

Ioana Ciuciu
Anna Fensel

Y.T. Demey and H. Panetto (Eds.): OTM 2013 Workshops, LNCS 8186, p. 342, 2013.

Towards the Integration of Ontologies with Service Choreographies

Mario Cortes-Cornax, Ioana Ciuciu, Sophie Dupuy-Chessa, Dominique Rieu, and Agnès Front

Laboratoire Informatique de Grenoble – Univ. Grenoble-Alpes
{Mario.Cortes-Cornax,Ioana.Ciuciu,Sophie.Dupuy,Dominique.Rieu,
Agnes.Front}@imag.fr

Abstract. This paper discusses the integration of ontologies with service choreographies in view of recommending interest points to the modeler for model improvement. The concept is based on an ontology of recommendations (evaluated by metrics) attached to the elements of the model. The ontology and an associated knowledge base are used in order to extract correct recommendations (specified as textual annotations attached to the model) and present them to the modeler. Recommendations may result in model improvements. The recommendations rely on similarity measures between the captured modeler design intention and the knowledge stored in the ontology and knowledge bases.

Keywords: business process, service choreography, ontology, knowledge base, annotation, recommender system.

1 Context and Motivation

Today, organizations are moving towards inter-organizational communications. Therefore, their business processes depend on services provided by external organizations. Modular solutions relying on service oriented approaches (Service Oriented Computing - SOC) [1] are becoming popular in the implementation of business processes where business activities are conceived as services. One way to realize processes involving services is by means of **service choreography** [2], which gives an overall view of interactions between organizations. The global view provided by choreographies is necessary to better understand, build, analyze and optimize inter-organizational processes. This interest is illustrated within the CHOREOS project [3]. One of the applications of this project is to achieve a "passenger-friendly airport" that coordinates the different airport services in a decentralized way.

However, **analyzing and optimizing is not a one shot process**. They need to be integrated into a continuous improvement cycle [4]. In our vision, business processes are modeled in languages such as BPMN [5]. Then, they are annotated by quality recommendations such as average latency or the number of messages sent and received. For that purpose, we plan to use ontologies.

Ontologies are used in this paper in order to model the domain knowledge related to the recommendation annotations attached to the choreography elements. Ontology

Y.T. Demey and H. Panetto (Eds.): OTM 2013 Workshops, LNCS 8186, pp. 343–352, 2013.

is a formal way to represent a common, explicit, agreed-upon conceptualization of a domain in view of interoperability [6]. Choreographies are highly-collaborative models, which imply the need for (semantic) interoperability due to heterogeneity of the background knowledge of each participant. Our main motivation for coupling ontologies with the choreography model is in order to enable reasoning in view of information extraction. The objective of this study is to enrich the choreography model proposed with semantics by means of ontologies in view of their evaluation and improvement. This paper presents the methodology and an integrated tool to help modelers understand, better exploit and iteratively improve their models. The proposed tool is a recommender system extending an existing tool [7], which captures the process modeler design intention via an intuitive interface. This system relies on ontologies in order to extract recommendations, resulting in well structured semantic annotations. The annotations represent interest points in the model that will guide the extraction of the information concerning execution properties but also model-specific properties.

The structure of the paper is as follows. A motivating scenario inspired from one of the CHOREOS use-cases is presented in Section 2. Section 3 illustrates the overview of the approach. Section 4 and 5 briefly introduce the choreography model and the ontology concepts respectively, in the context of this study. Section 6 relies on the motivating scenario in order to demonstrate the application of our approach. Section 7 discusses related work of the paper. Finally, Section 8 concludes the paper and situates the results within a broader perspective.

2   Motivating Scenario – Unexpected Airplane Arrival

Throughout this paper, we use a case study that we describe hereafter. The chosen case study deals with the management of an unexpected arrival of passengers to an alternative airport because of bad weather conditions at destination. The scenario illustrated in Fig. 1 is inspired from one of the case studies discussed in the CHOREOS project.

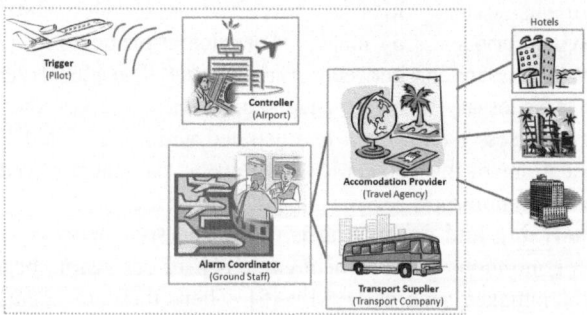

Fig. 1. Illustration of a choreography use case – Unexpected arrival of a plane at an airport

The roles required to implement this choreography are: a *Trigger* which will be played by the pilot, a *Controller* played by the airport, an *Alarm Coordinator* played by the company ground staff, an *Accommodation Provider*, played by a travel agency and a *Transport Provider* which is played by a transport company. In this scenario, we observe that several roles are involved. None of them has the capacity to make the overall decisions as a central control point. Moreover, it would be very risky to have a single point of failure. The solution to this problem is naturally provided by the **choreography** paradigm, which has a distributed nature.

When choreography is modeled, some information, e.g., the load between roles, may be critical. We observe that the load between roles could be measured using different metrics such as the number of relations, the average latency, the number of messages sent and received, etc. This information could be extracted when the choreography is enacted, but also the structure of the model could give some insights about the balance (e.g., the number of relations). Also, a modeler might be interested in particular parts of the model because they are considered critical (e.g., the relationship between *Controller* and *Alarm Coordinator*) whereas other parts might be considered to be less important. The different nature of the information and the need of personalization motivate the inclusion of structured annotations as survey points in the model. The annotations will help extracting valuable information in order to better understand and improve the choreography model. An example of annotation that a modeler may be interested to insert in a choreography model is given in section 5.1.

3   Approach Overview

This section presents the global overview of the approach. We followed a continuous improvement process to describe the integration between ontologies and service choreographies. The steps in the methodology are derived from Deming's PDCA cycle (*Plan Do Check Act*) [4] (See Fig. 2). This process is modeled using the BPMN 2.0 process notation [5]. In addition to the methodology phase, this model also represents the different states in which the choreography model will evolve as well as the information bases related to the ontology.

The phases concerning the methodology are the following: (i) **Model**: this phase refers to the construction of the requirements elicitation and the construction of the choreography model. (ii) **Annotate**: this phase refers to the enrichment of the choreography model with the recommendation annotations. The modeler indicates here what the interest points within the model are. The modeler relies on a knowledge-based (recommendation) system as an annotation helper, on recommendation ontology and on a knowledge base that stores correct recommendations. (iii) **Survey**: in this phase, the choreography is enacted and then studied. The numerical values corresponding to the recommendation annotations will be extracted. (iv) **Improvement Analysis**: in this phase the analysis of the evaluated model is realized. The modeler might decide what corrective actions may be necessary to perform. If the modeler decides that there are no more improvements to do, the process stops. However, if after the analysis, the modeler considers that the choreography model has to be improved, then she returns to the Model phase. If the modeler considers that the annotations are not appropriate to her intentions, she returns to the Annotate phase. (v) **Update**: In this phase, the ontology engineer updates the knowledge base and/or the recommendation ontology with the newly identified recommendations. The annotation system therefore will be limited by the information stored in the knowledge base. This information will be enriched as the system is used and new recommendations are proposed by the modeler and the ontology expert.

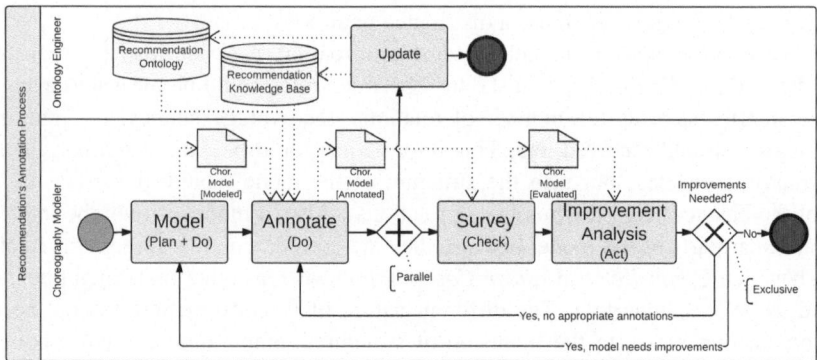

Fig. 2. Overview of the approach

Note that *Choreography Modeler* may represent several organizational roles such as analyst, architect or developer but we did not represent them for simplicity reasons. We focus on the distinction between the parts of the process concerning the choreography model and the ones concerning the ontology. The two parts are explained in the following two sections.

4   Service Choreographies

In this section we introduce the concept of service choreographies through a simplification of choreographies in BPMN 2.0.

4.1   Choreography Model

Choreography generally refers to a description of **coordinated interactions between two or more parties**. Messages exchanged between the different services are tracked from a global viewpoint. There is no central coordinator so all parties are distributed [2]. Decker et al. [8] give a critical overview of different choreography languages such as *Let's Dance*, *BPEL4Chor* and *WS-CDL*. These different proposals seem to converge in the latest version of the Business Process Model and Notation (BPMN 2.0) [5], which is the de-facto standard for business process models. In the latest version of BPMN, choreography has been adopted as a first-class citizen.

In this paper we will only focus on an abstract level of choreographies where the fundamental elements of choreography are presented. This level, illustrated in Fig. 3, might be considered as **a simplification of choreographies in BPMN 2.0**. The small differences in this level from BPMN 2.0 are justified by several issues detected when evaluating the support of choreographies in BPMN 2.0 [9].

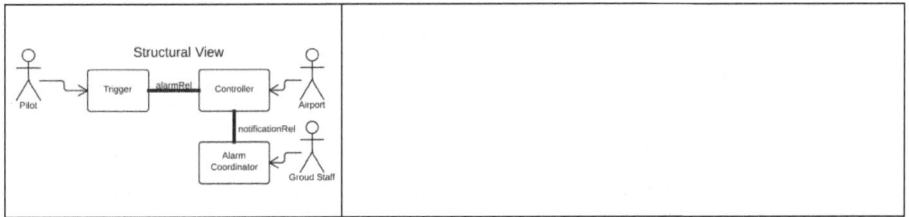

Fig. 3. BPMN 2.0 simplification described by a Structural View and a Behavioral View

The choreography model in Fig. 3 is divided in two views: (1) the structural view ; and (2) the behavioral view. In the **structural view**, let us consider a set of **roles** (*Role*) as for example *Trigger* and *Controller* linked in two by two **relationships** (*RoleRelationship*). The relationship represents the existence of a previous knowledge between both roles. A role is an abstract entity played by an **actor** (*Actor*). For example, the *Pilot* plays the *Trigger* role. In the **behavioral view,** we represent the flow of interactions between roles.

After explaining the choreography concept, let's look in more detail at the kind of information that we are interested to extract and how this is represented in the model.

4.2   Choreography Recommendations

Our approach is somehow similar to monitoring approaches [10]. However, process monitoring mainly focus on execution. In our study, we also want to extract useful information from the model construction. For example, if a modeler wants to look at the roles load, some useful information could be directly extracted from the model without execution. Just considering the number of relations defined for a role, or the number of interactions the role is involved in, a modeler may conclude that the model should be improved. This information could be complemented by additional information extracted at run time. In this study, we focus on information retrieved from the model as a first step of the application of our approach.

We called these interest points **recommendations**. In order to identify them, we looked at cross organizational monitoring and QoS requirements [10]. We also looked at choreography modeling requirements [9]. The classification of these requirements is out of the scope of this paper, therefore we do not go into details. Hence, the goal is to provide to modelers a mean to annotate a choreography model so that this markers result in information extraction that will be used to improve the model. The following section explains how these recommendations are defined and structured by means of ontologies. In Section 6 we explain in more detail the extraction of information though an application scenario.

5   Ontologies for Service Choreographies

This section illustrates how the choreography model presented in the previous section is enriched with semantics. It describes 1) the recommendation ontology and knowledge base used to annotate the choreography model; 2) the structure of the recommendations; and 3) the supporting annotation tool proposed.

5.1   Recommendation Ontology and Knowledge Base

In this study, the recommendations attached to the model elements are represented by an OWL ontology designed under Protégé[1].

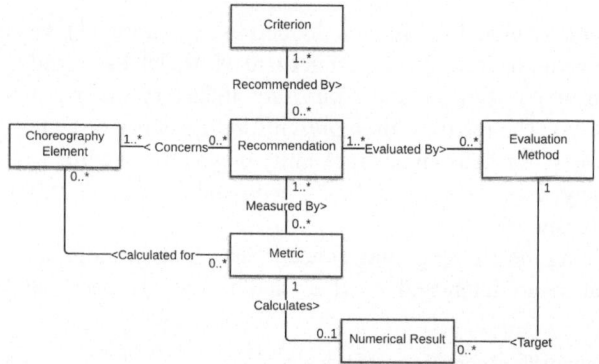

Fig. 4. Overview of the Recommendation Model

The **recommendation ontology** consists of facts and application-specific constraints applied to these facts. An example of a fact is: "a recommendation is measured by a metric / a metric measures a recommendation". A constraint imposed on this fact could be "There is at least one recommendation associated to a metric".

The **knowledge base** stores a set of correctly defined instances of recommendations. The recommendations in the knowledge base represent a collaborative (community) and continuous effort. The recommendations need to be approved by an expert (ontology engineer) before entering the knowledge base. An example of syntactically and semantically correctly defined recommendation that marks a point of interest on a "role" element regarding the number of relationships in order to analyze the choreography load balance among roles is:

```
@RoleLinkability  [criterium="Load"  choreography  element
="Role" metric="RoleRelationshipNb"].
```

The recommendation ontology and knowledge base are used to annotate the following elements of the choreography model: *Role, Actor, RoleRelationship, Gateway, Choreography Activity, Event* and *Choreography*. Fig. 4 gives an overview of the recommendation ontology structure that we propose. This model is inspired from the

---

[1] http://protege.stanford.edu/

QUIMERA quality meta-model proposed by Frey et al.[11]. A recommendation applies to at least one choreography element (1..*). A recommendation is in relation to a criterion which it recommends (1..*), it is measured by zero or more metrics (0..*) and is evaluated by an evaluation method, according to numerical results returned by the metric(s). The structure of a recommendation annotation within the ontology is described in the following sub-section.

5.2   Recommendation Annotation

A recommendation annotation is a text annotation attached to a choreography element in order to mark a point of interest in the model. The syntax of a recommendation annotation is specified by a recommendation term, followed by a parameter-value list, as follows: `@RecommendationTerm [parameter = value]`.

The parameters are: the criterion, the choreography element being annotated and one or more metrics representing numerical information about the recommendation.

It could be argued that the insertion of many annotations into the choreography model could result in a visually overloaded model. Therefore, we will propose graphical markers to visually represent annotations while managing the complexity of the annotated model.

5.3   Extraction of Recommendations

The specification of the recommendations is not a straightforward task, especially when dealing with tens or hundreds of recommendations, with their intrinsic properties. In order to overcome the difficulties the process modeler might encounter when defining a recommendation annotation, we propose a knowledge-based recommender system as a supporting tool for our methodology. The recommender system is able to: 1) **capture** the process modeler intention thanks to a user-friendly interface; 2) **compare** it with the knowledge expressed in the ontology and in the knowledge base; and 3) **propose** a valid set of recommendations.

The tool is based on a previously proposed solution [7]. The proposed architecture contains several modules encapsulating the main functions of the system. In this study, we focus on the annotator and the retriever components adapted to choreographies: 1) the **annotator** is the module that assists the user with concepts from the ontology base, in order to define syntactically correct annotations. It is used either as an auto-completion operation while the user is typing in the desired elements or as an ontology browser; 2) the **retriever** component extracts objects from the knowledge base that are similar to the input object provided by the user. This component is based on graph-based retrieval (e.g., SPARQL queries) and on various similarity measures. For example, the user only wants to retrieve those objects with a particular value for "criterion". The result of the retrieval operation is a set of recommendations.

The retriever performs similarity check in order to compare and classify the user request with the set of recommendations available in the knowledge base. The **matching** can be performed at a **string**, a **lexical**, or a **graph** (**ontology**) level depending on the user input. For example, when a user performs a typing error, the system could perform a string matching operation in order to find the correct term. In other cases, when several organizations participate in the design of a choreography model, the differences between their vocabularies must be taken into account. The system handles this by performing lexical matching according to predefined organization-specific dictionaries.

The following section shows how the annotation approach was applied in order to define correct recommendation annotations within the *unexpected plane arrival* scenario presented in Section 2.

6   Example of the Application of the Methodology

In this section, we present the application scenario relying on the motivating scenario of Section 2. Fig. 5 shows a simplified choreography model in its three possible states. At the end of the *Model* phase, we get a **Modeled** choreography model. In the *Annotate* phase, the recommendations will be introduced relying on the Recommendation System to produce an **Annotated** model. The structured annotations are extracted relying on user's keywords as explained in Section 5.3.

Fig. 5 shows that we might have several *RoleLinkability* recommendation instances linked to different elements of the model. The example also illustrates how the same recommendation may be linked to different metrics (i.e., different ways to calculate the numerical values). In the *Survey* phase, the annotations may extract some numerical values and some interpretation help so that the modeler can proceed to the analysis. The way these values are calculated has to be defined in the evaluation method (see Fig. 4) attached to a recommendation. For the moment, we focus on

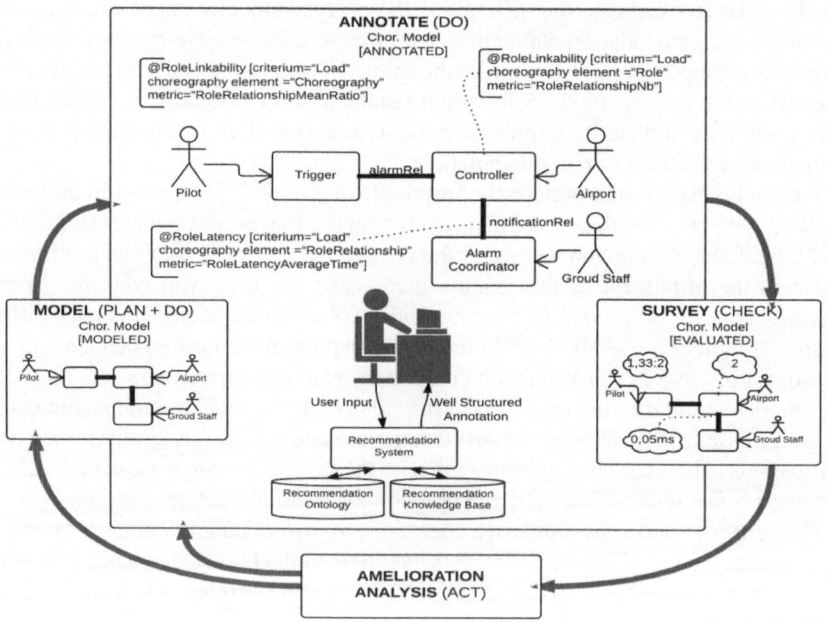

Fig. 5. Overview of the Application Scenario

model properties that can be easily extracted from the model serialization (e.g., the number of relationships). Note that the numerical values given in the figure are just an example and that the extraction of the execution properties is not yet implemented. The resulting model in this phase is **Evaluated**. The latter model is the entry point for the *Improvement Analysis* phase where the modeler decides if the model should be improved and if the defined annotations are appropriate or there may be changed.

This scenario shows the interest of the approach giving an application example that implements the methodology explained before. It also illustrates how ontologies, via the recommender system, are integrated with choreographies.

7   Related Work

The importance of adding semantics to business process models has been recognized within the business process community for several years now [12]. Currently, Semantic Web technologies are applied in order to enrich the business processes. The common instrument for specifying the semantics are the semantic annotations, used in order to either model the process dynamics [13] or the process structure, as demonstrated within the SUPER project [14]. Other approaches focus on the semantic interoperability of the business process knowledge [15]. Moreover, semantic annotations have been added to business processes in order to provide user support during the model design process, as described in [16]. This paper is mostly in-line with the last two mentioned approaches, aiming at capturing the user design intentions and providing appropriate recommendations to the process modeler and in the same time enforce the semantic interoperability.

Regarding the recommender systems, they have been extensively used applications such as, for example, e-commerce [17]. Semantic recommender systems are the next-generation recommender systems [7]. This study goes beyond the state of the art, focusing on personalized recommendations, by capturing the user design intentions and their similarity to an evolving knowledge base and ontology.

We extend our previous work by proposing a user-friendly recommender system which is intended to support the modeler during the evaluation and improvement of a choreography model.

8   Conclusion and Future Work

This paper presents an ongoing study for the retrieval of choreography recommendations in view of model analysis and improvement. The paper presents a methodology that brings together choreography models and ontologies. The paper suggests relying on a continuous improvement process based on these recommendations to help modeler(s) in the design of choreographies.

Future work concerns the extension of the current study with an intuitive interface with respect to capturing the process modeler design intentions and the presentation of the results. We are planning to integrate an existing prototype of a graphical editor for choreographies with the aforementioned ontology-based tool Protégé, so that we can query the ontology from the editor to extract the annotations. Another interesting approach could be to use the annotated criteria for feeding a simulation model.

The extension of the retriever component with new similarity metrics is work in progress. The enrichment of the knowledge base with expert knowledge and the study of automatizing its evolution is also ongoing work.

Another interest point to be studied is the possibility to link the recommendations and the corresponding numerical value to the three levels of the choreography meta-model that we defined in our previous work in view of adapting the extracted information to the desired level of detail. We consider validating the approach by an empirical experiment to observe if recommendations help modelers to improve their models without adding extra-complexity.

References

1. Papazoglou, M.P., Georgakopoulos, D.: Service-Oriented Computing. Comm. of the ACM 46(10), 24–28 (2003)
2. Peltz, C.: WS orchestration and choreography. Computer 36(10), 46–52 (2003)
3. CHOREOS project: http://www.choreos.eu/bin/view/Main/
4. Deming, W.E.: Out of the crisis, vol. 4(1). MIT Press (2000)
5. OMG, Business Process Model and Notation, Business (2011)
6. Gruber, T.R.: Toward Principles for the Design of Ontologies used for Knowledge Sharing. In: Formal Ontology in Conceptual Analysis and Knowledge Representation. Kluwer Academic Publishers (1993)
7. Ciuciu, I., Zhao, G., Mülle, J., von Stackelberg, S., Vasquez, C., Haberecht, T., Meersman, R., Böhm, K.: Semantic support for security-annotated business process models. In: Halpin, T., Nurcan, S., Krogstie, J., Soffer, P., Proper, E., Schmidt, R., Bider, I. (eds.) BPMDS 2011 and EMMSAD 2011. LNBIP, vol. 81, pp. 284–298. Springer, Heidelberg (2011)
8. Decker, G., Kopp, O., Leymann, F., Weske, M.: BPEL4Chor: Extending BPEL for Modeling Choreographies. In: IEEE Int. Conf. on Web Services, pp. 296–303 (2007)
9. Cortes-Cornax, M., Dupuy-Chessa, S., Rieu, D., Dumas, M.: Evaluating choreographies in BPMN 2.0 using an extended quality framework. In: Dijkman, R., Hofstetter, J., Koehler, J. (eds.) BPMN 2011. LNBIP, vol. 95, pp. 103–117. Springer, Heidelberg (2011)
10. Wetzstein, B., Karastoyanova, D., Kopp, O., Leymann, F., Zwink, F.: Cross-organizational process monitoring based on service choreographies. In: Proc. of ACM Symp. on Appl. Computing (2010)
11. García Frey, A., Céret, E., Dupuy-Chessa, S., Calvary, G.: QUIMERA. In: Proc. of 3rd ACM SIGCHI Symp. on Engineering Interactive Computing Systems, pp. 265–270 (2011)
12. Hepp, M., Leymann, F., Domingue, J., Wahler, A., Fensel, D.: Semantic business process management: a vision towards using semantic Web services for business process management. In: IEEE Int. Conf. on e-Business Engineering, pp. 535–540 (2005)
13. Wetzstein, B., Ma, Z., Filipowska, A., Kaczmarek, M., Bhiri, S., Losada, S., Lopez-Cobo, J.M., Cicurel, L.: Semantic business process management: A lifecycle based requirements analysis. In: Proc. of Semantic Business Process and Product Lifecycle Mgt. (2007)
14. SUPER Project: http://www.ip-super.org/
15. Lin, Y.: Semantic annotation for process models: Facilitating process knowledge management via semantic interoperability, Norwegian University of Technology (2008)
16. Betz, S., Klink, S., Koschmider, A., Oberwiseis, A.: Automatic user support for business process modeling. In: Proc. of Semantics for Business Process Mgt., pp. 1–12 (2006)
17. Schafer, J., Konstan, J., Riedl, J.: E-commerce recommendation applications. In: Data Mining and Knowledge Discovery, vol. 5(1-2), pp. 1–24 (2001)

Compliance Check in Semantic Business Process Management

András Gábor[1], Andrea Kő[2], Ildikó Szabó[2], Katalin Ternai[2], and Krisztián Varga[2]

[1] Corvinno Technology Transfer Center Ltd
Közraktár utca 12/a, Budapest, Hungary, 1093
agabor@corvinno.hu
[2] Department of Information Systems,
Corvinus University of Budapest
Fővám tér 13-15. Budapest, Hungary, 1093
{ko,iszabo,ternai,kvarga}@informatika.uni-corvinus.hu

Abstract. With a steady increase of requirements against business processes, support of compliance checking is a field having increased attention in information systems research and practice. Compliance check is vital for organizations to identify gaps, inconsistency and incompleteness in processes and sometimes it is mandatory because of legal, audit requirements. The paper gives an overview about our research and development activities in the field of compliance checking with the help of semantic business process management (SBPM). We propose a compliance checking approach and solution, illustrated with a use case from higher education domain.

Keywords: compliance checking, semantic business process management, ontology matching.

1 Introduction

The paper discusses a semantic technology-based approach for checking the compliance of business processes. Business process management (BPM) means modeling and managing processes which are interpreted as know-how platforms of the organization. BPM helps to maintain and manage the organizational processes and process attributes like input/output information, technology used and human resources needed to perform each activity. However current BPM approaches are not able to reflect to the fast changes in complex economic, social, and regulatory environment. Traditional and widely used BPM life cycles covers business process strategy formulation, process documentation, analysis and design, implementation and change management, operation, monitoring and controlling. A business process is seen as a sequence of activities, including the definition from the resource management perspective, which is responsible for the execution of each activity in terms of authority, responsibility (accountability) and competences (knowledge, skill, and attitude). Typically this information is stored in the RACI matrix (Responsible, Accountable, Consulted, Informed), which connects the organizational model to the process model. One of the

Y.T. Demey and H. Panetto (Eds.): OTM 2013 Workshops, LNCS 8186, pp. 353–362, 2013.
© Springer-Verlag Berlin Heidelberg 2013

overall objectives of BPM is the articulation of the hidden knowledge in the organizational, production and service dimensions. An obstacle in achieving this objective is the contradiction between the static business process model and the dynamically changing organizational knowledge, that is aimed to be solved using agile BPM, interaction centric BPM or event-driven BPM. With a steady increase of requirements for business processes, automation support of compliance management is a field having growing attention in information systems research and practice. Several approaches have been developed to support compliance checking of process models [9] [15] [21] [23]. One major challenge in such approaches is their ability to handle different modeling techniques and compliance rules in order to enable widespread adoption and application in the organization. Compliance check is vital for organizations, because of the following reasons:

- to assess of processes by checking compliance with standards, regulation, benchmarks and reference models.
- to identify gaps, inconsistency and incompleteness of processes using open data as source
- to improve processes via recommendations and the collaboration mechanisms.

Compliance check of the processes and the embedded knowledge has to be proactive. Decision makers need to be supported via smart, semi-automated or automated compliance checks in their day-to-day work, which are currently not applied in practice, meanwhile open data; linked open data has the proper capacity to provide knowledge for the business process assessment. Becker, Defman, Hervig and Lis [2] draw attention to consider domain semantics in business process compliance-checking approaches, opening another important research field. Their review revealed the lack of real-world evaluation is a common problem in the field of business process compliance checking. The paper is structured as follows: A theoretical overview on semantic process management, ontology learning and ontology matching is presented along with its implications to the research approach. A short overview is given about compliance checking solution, illustrated by a use case from higher education domain. Finally, conclusion is drawn and future research directions are set.

2   Related Work

2.1   Semantic Process Management

Business processes have to perform well within dynamically changing organizational environments. The main challenge in BPM is the continuous translation between business requirements view on the process space and the actual process space. It can be expected that BPM will only come closer to its promises if it allows for a better automation of the two-way translation. SBPM is a new approach of increasing the level of automation in the translation between these two levels, and is currently driven by major players from BPM, and Semantic Web Services domain. The core paradigm of SBPM is to represent the two spheres using ontology languages and to employ machine reasoning for automated or semi-automated translation.

A competitive enterprise has to adapt core value-added processes with unprecedented speed, to act appropriately regardless of the situation. The focus of process designers is to make more sophisticated use of process architectures and continuous improvement of processes. Conceptual model captures the semantics of an application through the use of a formal notation, but the descriptions resulting from conceptual model are intended to be used by humans and not machines. The basic idea of SBPM is to combine Semantic Web Services frameworks, ontology representation, and BPM methodologies and tools, and to develop a consolidated technology [10] [23]. The SUPER project elaborated a semantic framework for compliance management. They presented five perspectives on compliance checking: design-time/run-time; forward/backward; active/passive; task checking/process checking or engine-based/query-based perspective [6].

2.2   Ontology Learning

Web 2.0 solutions, social media applications are characterized by the huge amount of content created, shared and consumed by the users. In most of the cases information exchange and knowledge sharing require semantic interoperability. Ontologies play a decisive role in supporting the interoperability, because they provide the necessary structure and framework. Manual ontology building is expensive, time consuming, error-prone, biased towards their developer, inflexible and specific to the purpose of construction [8][19]. Ontology learning is a research area, which deals with the challenges to turn facts and patterns from content into shareable high-level constructs or ontologies [21]. One of the first ontology learning surveys was published by the OntoWeb Consortium in 2003 [8]. They investigated 36 approaches of ontology learning from text. Shamsfard & Barforoush introduced a framework for comparing ontology learning approaches [20]. Buitelaar and his colleagues introduced the "ontology learning layer cake" phrase to describe the different subtasks of ontology learning process [3]. Zhou concluded that human involvement into ontology learning still remains necessary and desirable [24]. He highlighted the need for common benchmarks for evaluating ontologies. Discovery of fine-grained associations are open problem, too. Existing techniques should be customized for cross-domain text on a Web-scale, because expert-curate domain knowledge is no longer adequate. Researchers agreed that ontology learning requires more work in the following areas: 1) discovery of fine-grained relations between concepts; 2) developing common evaluation platforms for ontologies, and 3) knowledge acquisition should focus on Web - to make ontology learning operational on a Web-scale. It was also revealed from the surveys that fully automatic learning of ontologies may not be possible [22] [24].

2.3   Ontology Matching

Alasoud et al. [1] define ontology matching problem as follows: "given ontologies O1 and O2, each describing a collection of discrete entities such as classes, properties, individuals, etc., we want to identify semantic correspondences between the components of these entities."

The general ontology mapping tools investigated by Noy [17] and Choi et al. [4], or the one developed by Protégé community use different kind of methods to identify the semantic correspondences between two ontologies. The most well-known methods are axiomatic correspondences (e.g. OWLDIFF [18], Compare Ontologies function in Protégé 4.X) or calculating similarity values. The latter takes probability distributions (e.g. Glue [5], OMEN [16]) or text similarity functions (e.g. LOM [14]) as a basis. Jung discussed the process specific methods [11] and used logical assertions and similarity measures to facilitate the interoperability among processes. Koschmider and Oberweis [12] used Petri nets „to obey an operational semantics that facilitates composition, simulation, and validation of business processes".

3   Compliance Checking Solution Overview

The logic of the solution is summarized in the Figure 1:

1. Knowledge extraction and representation from open data (guidelines, standards, etc.) – Components populates the *reference ontology*.
2. Knowledge extracted from the business processes populates the *process ontology*.
3. Compliance check will be done with the reference and process ontology resulting the gap identification.
4. The identified gaps are interpreted and fed back to the process owner.

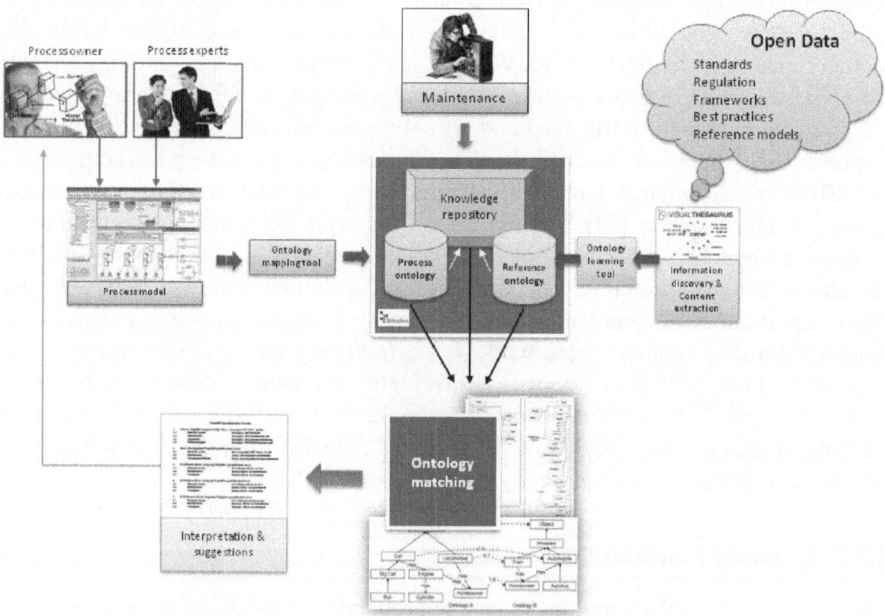

Fig. 1. Overview of compliance checking solution

The detailed description of the components will be given in the appropriate parts of the next section.

4   Use Case: Compliance Checking of the 'Quality Assurance' Process in a Higher Education Institution

Quality assurance is vital part of university governance, under the frame of Bologna process several directives give framework of quality assessment. One of the most accepted is the ESG [7].

4.1   Process Ontology

Adonis process modeling tool was applied as a business process modeling environment, in which "quality assurance" process was created. For the sake of extension and mapping the conceptual model to ontology model, XML export of the Adonis process was generated. In the export all objects of the business process model is an 'instance' in the XML structure, the attributes have the tag 'attribute', while the connected objects (such as the performer, the input/output data, etc.) have the tag 'interref'. The next step is to establish links between model elements and ontology concepts. [13]. The *„conceptual models - ontology models" converter* maps the Adonis business process modeling elements to the appropriate ontology elements in meta-level. The model transformation aims at preserving the semantics of the business model. The general rule is to express each model element as a class in the ontology and its corresponding attributes as attributes of the class. This transformation is done by the means of XSLT script which performs the conversion. The converted OWL ontology in the structure of Protege/OWL XML format is imported into the editor of Protege 4.2.

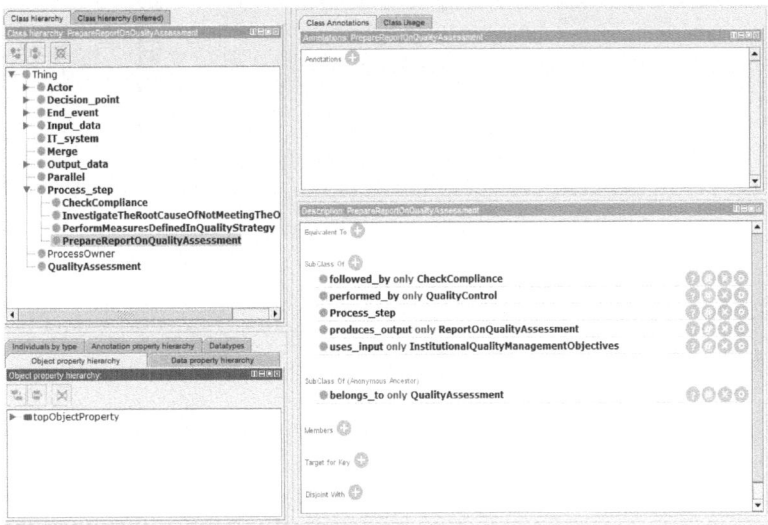

Fig. 2. The process ontology in Protege 4.2

The business model first must be represented within the ontology in order to specify the semantics of ADONIS model elements through relations to ontology concepts. In regard to the representation of the business model in the ontology, one can differentiate between a representation of ADONIS model language constructs and a representation of ADONIS model elements. ADONIS model language constructs such as "activity", as well as the control flow are created in the ontology as classes and properties. Subsequently, the ADONIS model elements can be represented through the instantiation of these classes and properties in the ontology. The linkage of the ontology and the ADONIS model element instances is accomplished by the usage of properties. These properties specify the semantics of an ADONIS model element through a relation to an ontology instance with formal semantics defined by the ontology (Figure 2).

4.2   Reference Ontology

The name "reference" comes from the fact that the main sources of reference ontology development are standards, best practices, policies and laws. Several guidelines, standards, best practices, benchmarks in quality assurance are available; we don't discuss the specific issues on discovery and collection of that. ESG as a source document was processed. The first step in text mining process executed by SPSS Modeler was to split the document into sentences. 1287 words were found, possessives, attributive structures in 1026 sentences. Based on these sentence elements 125 categories were defined (see in Figure 3).

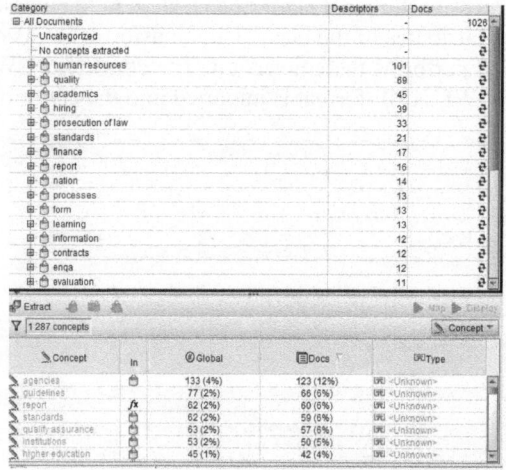

Fig. 3. Categories extracted by SPSS Text Mining

The categories did not follow the meta-structure given by the process model. In order to identify the main objects of the process model (Process step, Document, Actor) the restructuring of the existing categories were needed, new categories were inserted. The rationale behind of the text mining was to reveal sentences of the ESG document that relate to the process models. In above another text mining model was built in

RapidMiner in which ESG document was analyzed and resulted n-grams (4706 2-grams of tokens) and their occurrences. In the course of reference ontology the 2-grams of tokens provided by RapidMiner were taken into consideration. We dispensed the elements of these concomitances into the appropriate categories (see in Figure 4.).

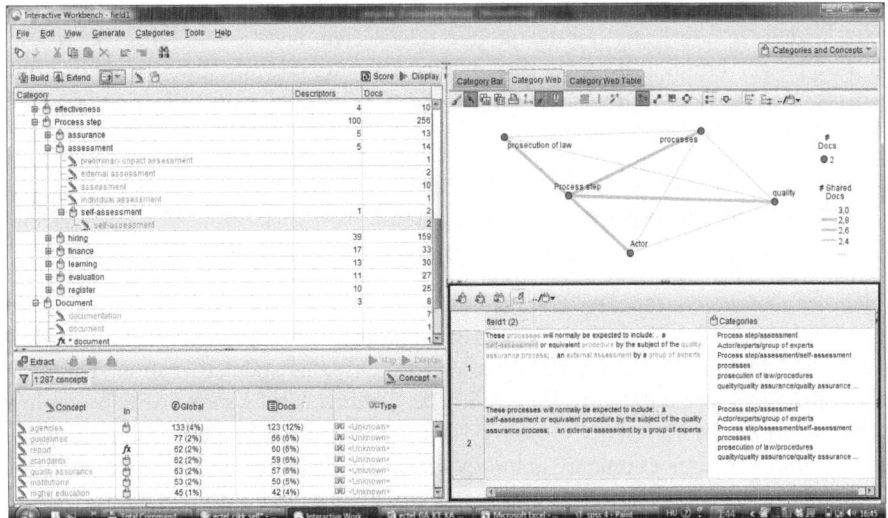

Fig. 4. The concomitances of categories

The next step of the text mining was to find the concomitances of these categories in sentences. Figure 4 shows the results for *self-assessment* category.

An algorithm written in Java searched the categories named by process model objects. The process model objects served as meta-classes in the process ontology, hence the sub-categories became sub-classes (Fig. 5).

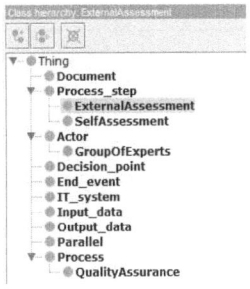

Fig. 5. Reference Ontology in Protégé

4.3   Ontology Matching

Protégé 4.2 and OWL DIFF [18] Protégé plugin was used as an ontology matching environment. *Compare Ontologies* is a built-in function in Protégé 4.X. It is capable of comparing ontologies with different name space while OWL DIFF isn't. The report created by *Compare Ontologies* is transparent; appropriate for ontology matching.

In the current stage of research it deals with building taxonomy from unstructured texts, without creating any non-taxonomic relationship between the classes; we used the matching solution to discover discrepancies among the subclasses of a given meta-class (Process step, Actor etc.). Using *Compare Ontologies* the following questions are answered:

- Q1: Are the same actors responsible for the execution of the processes?
- Q2: Do the processes consist of the same steps?
- Q3: Are the same documents used or created in the processes?

Compare Ontologies function compares two versions of the same ontology. In our case the Process Ontology was considered to be the original model, and, in order to assess the matching, the Reference Ontology was used as updated version. The result of the matching is exhibited in Figure 6. The *Created blocks* shows which ontology elements are in the Reference Ontology and are not in the Process Ontology. *Compare Ontologies* cannot compare ontology elements semantically. There are two possible outputs: 1) elements exist in Process Ontology, but with different names that are semantically similar; 2) elements do not exist in Process Ontology, therefore we have to insert them into the actual process. The *Deleted blocks* present which ontology elements are in the Process Ontology and are not in the Reference Ontology. There are two possible conclusions: 1) they are not identified in the text yet. In the future work, we have to elaborate a method to evaluate the efficiency of our ontology learning method, 2) they do not exist in the Reference Ontology, we have to eliminate them from Process Ontology. The ontology elements in the *Renamed and Modified block* are common and exist in the same taxonomic or non-taxonomic – axiomatic – relationship, but paired with a different element.

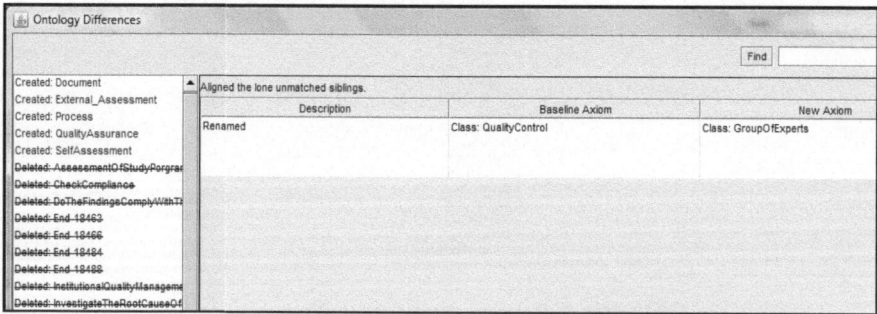

Fig. 6. Part of the output of the Compare Ontologies ontology matching tool

In summary, the Created block can discover the new elements, the Deleted block can show the out-of-dated elements, and the Renamed and Modified block can reveal the structurally discrepancies between the process models. The first two blocks answer questions Q1 and Q3, the last blocks replies for Q2 question. The result of matching is the following: *Document process model* object appears in Process Ontology as *Input data* and *Output data*. In the course of ontology learning, we have to elaborate a rule to identify the role of a document in the process, based on its context. Decision maker should decide about the creation of a separate process for self-assessment and an external assessment, too. The tool discovered that a 'group of experts' is interested in the quality assurance process, instead of the 'Quality Control actor'. The *interpretation component* gives a verbose explanation of the findings summarized in the above paragraph.

5   Conclusion and Future Research

This paper provided an overview about a compliance checking solution in SBPM. The main goal of our approach to demonstrate a way to assess business processes by checking compliance with standards, regulation, benchmarks and reference models. Higher education "quality assurance" process was detailed in our use case. Through the use case the suggested solution was justified as a proof of concept in terms of the potential to identify gaps, inconsistencies and incompleteness of processes. The solution heavily builds on open data as input. Our solution provides a semi-automatic support for compliance checking. The XSLT-transformation and the ontology matching can be executed automatically by using a Java API. The building of the Reference Ontology requires human intervention due to the interpretation of the ontology learning results. Future work includes the extension of the compliance checking solution with web mining, crawlers to support identification and collection the relevant sources and to continue testing the solution in other processes and domains. Another development direction is associated with the disadvantage of *Compare Ontologies* ontology matching tool. The tool does not compare semantically the name of ontology elements and as a consequence, the generated report may be less transparent in the case of complex process ontologies. Since it is open source software, we are going to improve it with a new algorithm working with similarity measure.

References

1. Alasoud, A., Haarslev, V., Shiri, N.: An Effective Ontology Matching Technique. In: An, A., Matwin, S., Raś, Z.W., Ślęzak, D., et al. (eds.) ISMIS 2008. LNCS (LNAI), vol. 4994, pp. 585–590. Springer, Heidelberg (2008)
2. Becker, J., et al.: Generalizability and Applicability of Model-Based Business Process Compliance-Checking Approaches – A State-of-the-Art Analysis and Research Roadmap, vol. 5(2), pp. 221–247. German Academic Association for Business Research, VHB (November 2012)
3. Buitelaar, P., et al.: Ontology Learning from Text: An Overview. IOS Press (2003)
4. Choi, N., et al.: A survey on ontology mapping. SIGMOD Rec. 35, 34–41 (2006)

5. Doan, A.H., et al.: Ontology matching: A machine learning approach. In: Staab, S., Studer, R. (eds.) Handbook on Ontologies, pp. 385–516 (2004)
6. El Kharbili, M., et al.: Towards a framework for semantic business process compliance management. In: Proceedings of the Workshop on Governance, Risk and Compliance for Information Systems, pp. 1–15 (2008)
7. ESGStand: European Standards and Guidelines, http://www.eqar.eu/application/requirements/european-standards-and-guidelines.htm (accessed April 9, 2013)
8. Haller, A.: Ontologies and semantic Business Process Management 2007 Digital Enterprise Research Institute (2007), http://www.soberit.hut.fi/T-86/T-86.5161/2007/Ontologies%20and%20semantic%20BPM.pdf
9. Hepp, M., Cardoso, J., Lytras, M.D.: The Semantic Web: Real-World Applications from Industry. Springer (2007) ISBN: 0387485309
10. Gómez-Pérez, A., Manzano-Macho, D.: A survey of ontology learning methods and techniques. In: OntoWeb Consortium (2003)
11. Jung, J.J.: Semantic business process integration based on ontology alignment. Expert Systems with Applications 36(8), 11013–11020 (2009)
12. Koschmider, A., Oberweis, A.: Ontology based business process description. In: Proceedings of the CAiSE, pp. 321–333 (2005)
13. Kramler, G., Murzek, M.: Business Process Model Transformation Issues (2006)
14. Li, J.: LOM: a lexicon-based ontology mapping tool. In: Information Interpretation and Integration Conference, I3CON (2004)
15. Liu, A.Y., Müller, S., Xu, K.: A Static Compliance-Checking Framework for Business Process Models. IBM Systems Journal 46(2), 335–361 (2007)
16. Mitra, P., Noy, N., Jaiswal, A.R.: OMEN: A Probabilistic Ontology Mapping Tool. In: Gil, Y., Motta, E., Benjamins, V.R., Musen, M.A. (eds.) ISWC 2005. LNCS, vol. 3729, pp. 537–547. Springer, Heidelberg (2005)
17. Noy, N.F.: Semantic integration: a survey of ontology-based approaches. SIGMOD Rec. 33, 65–70 (2004)
18. OWLDiff: OWL Diff Documentation (2008), http://krizik.felk.cvut.cz/km/owldiff/documentation.html
19. Sabou, M., et al.: Learning domain ontologies for Web service descriptions: an experiment in bioinformatics. In: Proceedings of the 14th International Conference on World Wide Web, pp. 190–198. ACM, New York (2005)
20. Shamsfard, M., Barforoush, A.: The state of the art in ontology learning: a framework for comparison. The Knowledge Engineering Review 18(4), 293–316 (2003)
21. Schmidt, R., Bartsch, C., Oberhauser, R.: Ontology-based representation of compliance requirements for service processes. In: Proceedings of the Workshop on Semantic Business Process and Product Lifecycle Management, SBPM 2007 (2007)
22. Wong, W., et al.: Ontology learning from text: A look back and into the future. ACM Comput. Surv. 44(4), 20:1–20:36 (2012)
23. Wetzstein, B.: Zhilei Ma; Filipowska, A.; Kaczmarek,M.; Bhiri, S.; Losada, S.; Lopez-Cobo, H.M.; Cicurel L.: Semantic Business Process Management: A Lifecycle Based Requirements Analysis. In: Proceedings of the Workshop SBPM (2007), http://ceur-ws.org/Vol-251/paper1.pdf
24. Zhou, L.: Ontology learning: state of the art and open issues. Information Technology and Management 8(3), 241–252 (2007)

Dynamic, Behavior-Based User Profiling Using Semantic Web Technologies in a Big Data Context

Anett Hoppe, Ana Roxin, and Christophe Nicolle

CheckSem Group,
Laboratoire Electronique, Informatique et Image,
Université de Bourgogne
Dijon, France
http://www.checksem.fr

Abstract. The success of shaping the e-society is crucially dependent on how well technology adapts to the needs of each single user. A thorough understanding of one's personality, interests, and social connections facilitate the integration of ICT solutions into one's everyday life. The MindMinings project aims to build an advanced user profile, based on the automatic processing of a user's navigation traces on the Web. Given the various needs underpinned by our goal (e.g. integration of heterogeneous sources and automatic content extraction), we have selected Semantic Web technologies for their capacity to deliver machine-processable information. Indeed, we have to deal with web-based information known to be highly heterogeneous. Using descriptive languages such as OWL for managing the information contained in Web documents, we allow an automatic analysis, processing and exploitation of the related knowledge. Moreover, we use semantic technology in addition to machine learning techniques, in order to build a very expressive user profile model, including not only isolated "drops" of information, but inter-connected and machine-interpretable information. All developed methods are applied to a concrete industrial need: the analysis of user navigation on the Web to deduct patterns for content recommendation.

1 Introduction

The emergence of the World Wide Web has shaped our lives like hardly any invention of the last century. The way humans perceive and process information has been altered and is still evolving based on new technologies each day. The last decade has been marked by a evolution of the paradigm underlying web development. There is a new vision of Web facilities as ubiquitous, human-centered technologies, designed to assist individual information needs in every life situation. For the first time, in online applications, we have the opportunity to target an individual user, not only to a rough group of consumers.

This vision has to be supported by a thorough understanding of the forces that drive a user, by the means of data that are perceived from him and not

Y.T. Demey and H. Panetto (Eds.): OTM 2013 Workshops, LNCS 8186, pp. 363–372, 2013.
© Springer-Verlag Berlin Heidelberg 2013

intervening with his normal course of action – and thereby treating his privacy with responsibility. The research work presented in this paper describes a novel approach for user profiling based on his behavior observed by a server-side application.

This complex application associates numerous research domains – e.g. natural language processing and semantic annotation for the analysis of the related web sites; knowledge bases for the integration of the multi-shaped information sources along with their organization and exploitation. Following the scope of this workshop, we limit the focus here to the envisioned insertion points for Linked Open Data to our system.

2   Project Context

The MindMinings project is set up in the context of a collaboration between the Ezakus Labs HQ (based in Bordeaux, France) and the CheckSem research group from the University of Burgundy, Dijon, France. The following paragraphs aim to provide an overall vision on the project, its context and the arising challenges. The industrial partner is a two years-old enterprise that settles in the online advertising sector. Specialising the offer to the needs of the digital advertisement ecosystem, it provides analysis solutions for enhanced customer targeting.

Our profiling approach will be integrated to the company current structures. For such, it is essential to capture the implicit knowledge of the professionals within the enterprise in an explicit, ontological representation, and to offer the possibility to integrate already existing, well-established procedures and their results. Apart from that, the main focus will be the realisation of a new module of semantic analysis that shall complement the currently used techniques.

The company offers its services to all actors within the digital advertisement ecosystem. Among its clients, it counts some of the mayor French online publishers. In consequence, the amount of data that has to be processed on a continuous basis is immense and growing. Each user event registered on a partner site is submitted in real-time, summing up to about 2.4 billion user events per month. These events, collected in navigation logs, contain all facts that are known from a user as they can be retrieved by his activity and that are contained in cookies.

At the current state, Ezakus uses enhanced machine learning and data analysis techniques to predict user interests relevant to the targeting purpose. Our ontology-based approach aims to complement this approach, (a) by integrating existing results and methods, (b) by extending them with the help of semantic-based analysis, (c) ontological-inference for the deduction of the user's final profile.

All these analysis' have to be realized within the constraints of the real-world application. That is, be able to scale up to immense and variously-shaped amounts of data and deduct information in reasonable time. Given the orientation to give suggestions of advertisements within the user session, this demands real time-like performance. The extraction of knowledge from textual resources is a complex task, therefore, a semantic analysis on huge amounts of data might exceed the time available. Hence, we split the necessary tasks into online and offline components. The websites that have to run through semantic analysis are a huge set of data – but limited to the client domains of Ezakus. Thus, we will be able to run the analysis those textual data in an offline process and store the results in the ontology – leaving only the combination of the contained information and the deduction of the user profile to the online process. Figure 2 shows a schematic overview of the information sources that are used to populate the ontology and their splitting into online and offline processes.

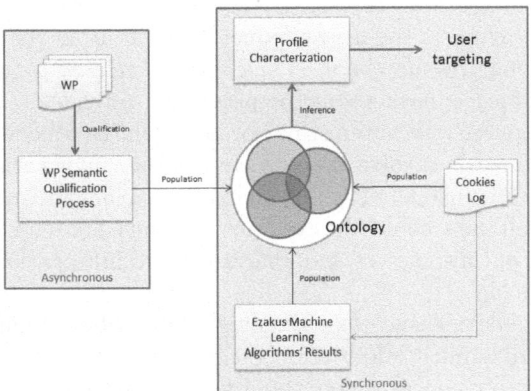

Fig. 1. Overview of the information that will be used to populate the ontology

It is notable that in the current developments, we work in a mostly French environment. Even though the client profiles to deduct are very similar for Western countries, the main language of the sources that we analyze leads to additional issues. The most available frameworks for the treatment of natural language are focused on the analysis of English resources and offer only limited functionalities for other. The toolkit OpenCalais[1] for example offers the discovery of more than 120 named entities and events from English text, but only a set limited to 15 named entities for French language. The adaptation of techniques for their usage on French resources will thus constitute one important branch of the development work.

3   Related Work

As shown in the section describing the context of the project (Section 2), various working steps have to be accomplished. Naturally, research works directly concerned with user profiling will form the starting point of the analysis. However, given the dynamic environment, various other steps will have to be executed automatically and without supervision. We focus here on the tasks concerning information integration and external data sources querying to emphasize the role

---

[1] www.opencalais.com

of linked open data for the integration of a multitude of heterogeneous information sources.Current systems mainly differ in their combinations of techniques
for the different stages of the profiling process, (a) information gathering, (b)
data representation, (c) exploitation, and (d) updating.

3.1   Information Gathering

The most popular classification of information gathering methods was introduced
by Gauch et al. [3]. They propose a categorization based on the degree of active
involvement demanded from the user. On the one end of the scale, explicit information gathering refers to the direct request of facts from the user. Therefore,
surveys or questionnaires may be used and directly related to a unique user ID,
one may also ask for feedback about the previously provided resources (indicating if a certain resource was "interesting" or not). On the other extreme, implicit
methods do not directly involve the user, but gather information based on observation of behavior. Instead of asking an explicit opinion about a resource, one
may accumulate all data about the resources displayed (content, time stamp of
the request etc.), but also access and analyze stored information such as emails
or calender events [5].

The usage log analysis, such as envisioned in the MindMinings project, falls
into the category of implicit information gathering. As we will only access server-
side data, the privacy concerns connected to the analysis of personal data are
omitted. Similar approaches were proposed in personalized information retrieval
[5], adapting search results by an analysis of the click-through behavior and
queries [15,10].

3.2   Information Representation

Representations for user profiles can be classified in three main groups according to [3]: keyword-based, semantic network-based and concept-based techniques.
Each of the techniques employs a different basic unit for knowledge representation that affect the amount of information that is exploitable later on [1].
Keyword-based approaches use a set of terms (often weighted) to summarize the
user interest. The main advantage of these techniques is their simplicity; however, they tend to reach the limits of their expressiveness when coming across
certain particularities of natural language, such as homonyms and synonyms.

Semantic networks were designed to tackle this issue: Concepts are represented
by nodes, whereas the arcs in between are established based on the analysis of the
user information. Entering information enriches the profile with new keywords
that get interconnected with existing nodes [4]. As the developed algorithms did
not come up to the expectations [8,12], concept-based approaches are on the
rise. By relating the discovered terms with predefined semantic resources, one is
able to make their sense machine-processable.

In recent works, several approaches have been presented, using different semantic resources for the identification of concepts. Several approaches use Word-
Net to adapt their features spaces [2]. Other use light-weight ontologies such as
the Yahoo Web Directory [6] or the Open Directory Project [14]. Methods vary

in their usage of the ontological reference – from using the high-level concepts to map the resources to a clearly defined category [7,13] to the extraction of ontology parts and their integration into the profile ontology [1]. In contrast to former approaches, the latter uses YAGO as reference, criticizing former approaches for their adaptation of light-weight frameworks such as WordNet and ODP [9].

4   Project Tasks

As noted in the Introduction section, the overall vision of the project relies on the following elements: a comprehensive model of the user, including estimations of his mayor interests and deductions on his customer behavior. The goal is ambitious as the only input information the analysis relies on are the navigation logs captured while a user browses a publisher's website.

4.1   Web Page Analysis

The server-side information, the log file, will be parsed for the information that are relevant to our analysis: time stamps, the URLs of the requested pages, the browser configuration of the user. Given the URLs in the user's usage log, one is able to recover the content of the web page. A parser has been developed that retrieves the textual information of the page which then is fed to the actual analysis, featuring pre-processing steps (removal of stop words, stemming etc.), the discovery of the core concepts contained (keyword extraction and disambiguation) and the restructuring of this information to fit the profile ontology representation.

4.2   Information Integration and Exploitation

All information gathered has to be integrated in one single data structure to enable thorough and easy exploitation. This includes on the one hand the results form the above-named evaluation and, on the other hand, information obtained from the analysis' that are already effectuated in-house at Ezakus. The data model has to fulfill a number of crucial demands defined by the commercial setting of its final usage.Based on the demands of their commercial partners, Ezakus has to classify users as belonging to certain market segments. The definition of those segments may differ from one partner to another and over time, the rendering of new segment specifications has to be intuitively. Also, the adaptation of the knowledge structure has to be made automatic.

Other necessities have already been evoked in the description of the project context (Section 2) – the evaluation of user behavior, based on the linkage of the viewed resources has to happen in real time, parallel to his/her actions, even when encountering vast amounts of data.

4.3   Summary

In the above sections, we provided a short summary of the project context and the tasks to be realized by our system in development. Given the ambitious goal of the project and the constraints imposed by the context of the commercial partner, we need to adopt a highly flexible, structured and intuitive data model that, additionally is able to answer complex requests in real-time. In consequence, we took the choice to adopt an ontological structure for the representation of information throughout the complete profiling process.

Ontologies and their formal languages allow the expressive description of the informational content within all processing steps. Not only do they provide the means to connect the concepts to clearly defined external knowledge sources, but also to specify customized relations between them. Those may extend the commonly adopted taxonomic relations by rich descriptions adapted to the specific context. Therefore, Semantic Web resources are integrated in the analysis process as pre-existing, community-based knowledge resources. They provide the evidence to disambiguate terms and background knowledge to help the deduction of concept's relations. These resources are mainly obtained through the integration of Linked Open Data sets, such as DBPedia[2], Freebase[3]. By using state-of-the-art storage technology for the management of semantic data, we will still come up to the demands concerning real-time and big data processing.

5   The Ontology

Building an ontology is an incremental process of transforming implicit domain knowledge to its explicit representation. Thus, as a first step, we aimed to gain a thorough understanding of Ezakus' working context, the concepts involved and their relations. The result is a customized application ontology, comprising the specification of entities in the ecosystem, such as Ezakus' partners and their affiliated domains and websites, but also abstract concepts such as the user profile itself, the keywords used in the analysis process and so on.

All analysis centers around a BID ("Browser ID"), identifying a user when surfing on a partner website. Attributed to this BID are "hits", the minimal entities of user behavior, each one carrying a time stamp, the URL of the website visited and basic information about the user's browser. Consecutive hits can be assembled to a "session", a set of hits that has been effectuated in no larger temporal distance than thirty minutes. Figure 2 shows a visualization of the upper-level classes of the ontology.

From the context of Ezakus, we include supplemental information about the web pages. These information build the base for our system's analysis. The contents of the web page are extracted and processed. The resulting keywords and, if need be, means to their disambiguation, are fed to the ontology. Known keywords can be directly related to the defined categories. For unknown instances, the associated topics relations and their weighting has to be computed. Combined with the results of Ezakus' internal application of enhanced statistical analysis and machine learning, this gives the final user interest profile.

---

[2] http://dbpedia.org/
[3] http://www.freebase.com/

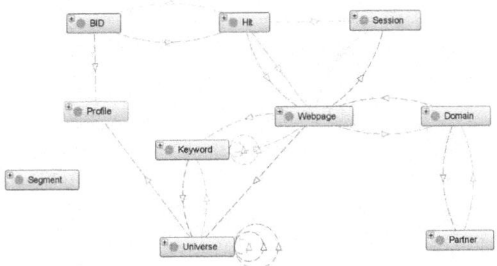

Fig. 2. The high-level concepts of the customised ontology (visualised using the OntoGraf-plugin for Protégé)

The ontology has been modeled in Protégé and then published on a OWL Triple store for its automatic population. Figure 3 shows the an example of the usage of the inference engine for customer segmentation. The segment "Sporty-Mom" has been defined as a user that (a) is female, (b) belongs to a certain age group, (c) lives in a household with children (all the latter summed up by using a pre-defined segment "Mother") and (d) being interested in articles treating sports-related topics. Statements added by the inference engine are marked with a yellow overlay – thus, the affiliation of the instance "user1" to the segment class has been computed automatically.

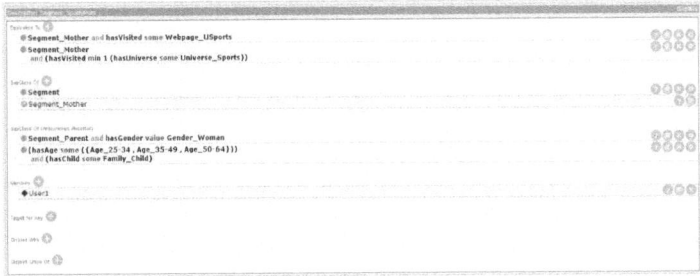

Fig. 3. Example of automatic inference for the segment "SportyMom" (signifying a person that was identified female, with children and interested in topic "Sport")

Ezakus objective of targeting web users for commercial usage leads us to add another abstraction layer. Marketing segments are a classification of customers, specified by a set of rules applied to their profile attributes. Those rules are included in the ontology to enable the inference engine to automatically deduct a user profiles affiliation to a defined segment.

6   Prototype

A prototype of the system has been developed during the recent months. It provides a proof of concept for our approach and validates the proposed workflow.

The core element of the prototype is the above described enterprise ontology that has been in close collaboration. Even though ontology engineering is an iterative process, it is a first exact representation of the knowledge generated and processed in the context of Ezakus. Web pages are automatically parsed and textual elements extracted. After pre-processing using a stemming algorithm and a part-of-speech tagger [11], a basic tf/idf-implementation is used to discover pertinent keywords to represent the core topics covered.

Ezakus already employs a topic-oriented categorization in their internal processes, and it seems reasonable to stay as close to this existing taxonomy as possible in all stages of the implementation. For the moment, all categories are attributed with a list of keywords that suggest a close relation between a resource and the category in question. These word clouds have been used to compute the similarity between a textual resource and the category, employing a word vector-based approach. To use the information available in already existing external knowledge sources, we provide a mapping between those customized categories and a community-accepted classification scheme, such as the Open Directory Project[4]. Apart from enabling the exploitation of those structured external resources, this will also facilitate evaluation of our approach by the scientific community. Based on this computation, every entering web resource is classified to one of the pre-defined categories. Using the distance value that results from the vector comparison, the membership can be quantified to a certain degree.

All information available about the resource, such as its URL, keywords, assigned categories is entered to the ontology. Additionally, information from Ezakus' internal working processes are integrated, comprising results of machine learning approaches and basic values calculated directly from the user log files. As a matter of fact, the currently used market segments have been defined in a rule-like fashion so far. The known definitions are included in the ontology as classes to enable inference on a class- and instance-level.

For the exploitation of the integrated information, a server has been set up using OWLIM and allowing queries using Sesame. Benchmark tests gave response times of about 5ms for the insertion of a new triplet to the knowledge base and of about 40ms to answer a posed query. Those values conform with the constraints posed by Ezakus at this day.

7   Scientific Contribution

The ontological base structure allows to not only measure the similarity of two sets of words, but to consider additional features of evaluation, especially features of semantic nature. Those enhanced distance evaluations will confront us with a number of issues to solve in our research work:

Text analysis. As the analysis of textual resources has been a key issue to numerous research domains (e.g. information retrieval, cross-language applications),

---

[4] http://www.dmoz.org/

there is a rich body of research contributing to the resolution of problem tasks. However, most tools have been developed for English language while the support for French is still limited. The platform GATE[5] offers utilities and frameworks for the development of customized language processing solutions – and may thus offer a good starting point to enhance existing solutions for French language.

Different Degrees of Structure: The integration of heterogeneous knowledge sources involves not only to handle different semantics, but also varying degrees of specificity of those semantics. A certain analyzed document is represented by a few connected concepts, whereas a carefully constructed word cloud associated to a category may comprise several hundred, highly connected concepts.

Interpretation of Relation Types: In the internal storage as well as in the external sources, relations connecting the concepts can have different types. There is comparably few research work on how to deal with the interpretation of those types for distance computation. Some approaches do already use the synonym-sets from WordNet to extend keyword sets – but how to proceed, for example, when coming across a link that states a certain degree of similarity or, in contrary, the fact that two terms are antonyms? Depending on the application context, those connection types may bear rich information. We will examine their influence on performance in the upcoming stages of the project.

8   Conclusion and Future Work

We describe a novel architecture for user profiling from implicit data. Using navigational data of web users, we adopt natural language processing methods for the analysis of the underlying web resources. If need be, we use external knowledge sources for disambiguation and relation discovery. One important research issue is the adaptation of all algorithms and background resources to French language. All process steps have to be realised respecting the constraints of the industrial partner, in particular concerning the issues of working in real-time and on large-scale data.

After the correct construction of the profile, its maintenance becomes the next issue to tackle. Updates have to be incremental, as it is not possible to store and re-analyze every information when a user re-enters the vision of the system. We adopted a weighting scheme within the ontology to model the degree of affiliation of a customer to a certain segment. To capture the evolution related to short- and long-term interests, an appropriate update mechanism has to be developed. Promising results come from approaches using Spreading Activation for that objective (e.g. [16]).

Acknowledgements. The research work presented in this paper is supported by Ezakus Labs HQ (www.ezakus.com).

---

[5] http://gate.ac.uk/biz/usps.html

References

1. Calegari, S., Pasi, G.: Personal ontologies: Generation of user profiles based on the {YAGO} ontology. Information Processing & Management 49(3), 640–658 (2013)
2. Degemmis, M., Lops, P., Semeraro, G.: A content-collaborative recommender that exploits wordnet-based user profiles for neighborhood formation. User Modeling and User-Adapted Interaction 17(3), 217–255 (2007)
3. Gauch, S., Speretta, M., Chandramouli, A., Micarelli, A.: User profiles for personalized information access. In: Brusilovsky, P., Kobsa, A., Nejdl, W. (eds.) Adaptive Web 2007. LNCS, vol. 4321, pp. 54–89. Springer, Heidelberg (2007)
4. Gentili, G., Micarelli, A., Sciarrone, F.: Infoweb: An adaptive information filtering system for the cultural heritage domain. Applied Artificial Intelligence 17(8-9), 715–744 (2003)
5. Ghorab, M.R., Zhou, D., O'Connor, A., Wade, V.: Personalised information retrieval: survey and classification. In: User Modeling and User-Adapted Interaction, pp. 1–63 (2012)
6. Labrou, Y., Finin, T.: Yahoo! as an ontology: using yahoo! categories to describe documents. In: Proceedings of the Eighth International Conference on Information and Knowledge Management, pp. 180–187. ACM (1999)
7. Ma, Z., Pant, G., Sheng, O.R.L.: Interest-based personalized search. ACM Transactions on Information Systems (TOIS) 25(1), 5 (2007)
8. Magnini, B., Strapparava, C.: Improving user modelling with content-based techniques. In: Bauer, M., Gmytrasiewicz, P.J., Vassileva, J. (eds.) UM 2001. LNCS (LNAI), vol. 2109, pp. 74–83. Springer, Heidelberg (2001)
9. Mizoguchi, R.: Part 3: Advanced course of ontological engineering. New Generation Computing 22(2), 193–220 (2004)
10. Qiu, F., Cho, J.: Automatic identification of user interest for personalized search. In: Proceedings of the 15th International Conference on World Wide Web, pp. 727–736. ACM (2006)
11. Schmid, H.: Probabilistic part-of-speech tagging using decision trees. In: Proceedings of International Conference on New Methods in Language Processing, Manchester, UK, vol. 12, pp. 44–49 (1994)
12. Semeraro, G., Lops, P., Degemmis, M.: Wordnet-based user profiles for neighborhood formation in hybrid recommender systems. In: Fifth International Conference on Hybrid Intelligent Systems, HIS 2005, p. 6. IEEE (2005)
13. Shen, X., Tan, B., Zhai, C.: Implicit user modeling for personalized search. In: Proceedings of the 14th ACM International Conference on Information and Knowledge Management, pp. 824–831. ACM (2005)
14. Sieg, A., Mobasher, B., Burke, R.: Ontological user profiles for representing context in web search. In: 2007 IEEE/WIC/ACM International Conferences on Web Intelligence and Intelligent Agent Technology Workshops, pp. 91–94. IEEE (2007)
15. Stamou, S., Ntoulas, A.: Search personalization through query and page topical analysis. User Modeling and User-Adapted Interaction 19(1-2), 5–33 (2009)
16. Su, Z., Yan, J., Ling, H., Chen, H.: Research on personalized recommendation algorithm based on ontological user interest model. Journal of Computational Information Systems 8(1), 169–181 (2012)

A Virtual Organization Modeling Approach for Home Care Services

Luz-Maria Priego-Roche*, Christine Verdier, Agnès Front, and Dominique Rieu

Université de Grenoble, LIG-SIGMA
FirstName.LastName@imag.fr

Abstract. We follow a Virtual Organization (VO) approach for Requirements Engineering (RE) to define and describe the collaborative models needed in a French home care scenario. We use the Intentional level of abstraction for building the models to define the alliance, collaboration and objectives. In this level we identify the intra, inter and extra relationships between the organizations. The approach is illustrated in the context of a French regional project looking for innovative ideas for the care of fragile people within legal, medical, technical and volunteering concerns. Our goal is to facilitate iterative modeling taking into account all organizations' points of view and manage complexity with a top-down refinement.

Keywords: virtual organizations, collaboration modeling, eCare.

1 Introduction

In most countries there is a concern to satisfy not only the health of their population but also their social needs as part of an integral heal. This trend is related to the improvement of health, life expectancy and the change of people's traditional patterns (e.g., demographic, social, epidemiological, science and technology innovation, attitudes and expectations among other political priorities) [9]. Health care Information Systems (IS) in general and home care for the frail in particular involve a myriad of actors to facilitate an autonomous life at home. On the one hand, the collaboration between these actors (sometimes competing between them) is a complex task that requires the integration and coordination of skills and resources. On the other hand, designing the IS supporting collaboration is a challenge. Therefore, modeling was chosen as a reliable RE elicitation technique to "facilitate communication, uncover missing information, organize information gathered from other elicitation techniques, and uncover inconsistencies"[2].

Well known RE modeling approaches have evolved, matured and are source of many publications such as i*, KAOS, Map, scenarios and e³value [4]. Some works use business process to express changes during the business process life cycle (i* [3]), to determine goal satisfaction (KAOS [1]), to capture goal achievement variability (Map [8]) and to identify value objects (e³value [10]). Although they explore actor's relationships and allow refinement, must of them were originally conceived for one organization and offer partial models and analysis.

---

* Work supported by the InnoServ project and the French National Research Agency
https://anrinnoserv.wordpress.com/

Y.T. Demey and H. Panetto (Eds.): OTM 2013 Workshops, LNCS 8186, pp. 373–377, 2013.

Frail people's home care can be addressed throughout a Virtual Organization (VO) approach as defined in [6]: "an alliance for integrating competences and resources from several independent real companies, that are geographically dispersed. This integration is possible throughout the layout of an information system infrastructure to satisfy customer's requirements, or to seize a business opportunity without having to form a new legal entity".

In this paper, we present the development of Intentional models based on the 360° VisiOn [6] for VOs a comparative analysis of model based approaches can be found in [7]. This proposal aims to define the VO requirements taking into account each organization with different specialties and competences and the set of organizations committed to work together by sharing a common objective. It consists in exploring, assembling and visualizing the information that defines requirements of different people. The analysis of the Intentional models is useful to set a common language to the different participants and backgrounds.

We instantiate the 360° VisiOn models using a case study of the InnoServ project to guide frail people's home care service modeling. The ongoing project involves private, public and volunteer health care service providers and researchers from the French Rhône-Alpes region. The team is concerned about legal, medical, technical and social matters. The objective of the project is to offer innovative services for frail people to allow the person to stay as long as possible at home in a secure environment, avoid unnecessary hospitalizations or specialized home services after hospitalization, and break people's isolation and improve their quality of life and care.

The paper is structured accordingly. Section 2 gives an overview of the 360° VisiOn framework. Section 3 illustrates the approach with the InnoServ project and Section 4 summarizes our proposal, discusses our findings and prospects for future study.

2   Overview of the 360° VisiOn

The 360° VisiOn proposes a framework for eliciting VO's requirements from a horizontal and a vertical view. The former analyzes the *Intentional* (actors in a service, common and individual goals and collaboration), *Organizational* (the BP to be performed by each actor according to the objectives) and *Operational* (the IS's implementation based on the BP) levels. The latter analyzes three dimensions: *intra-organizational* (participant organizations internals), *inter-organizational* (participant organizations relationships) and *extra-organizational* (external environment relationships). The horizontal and vertical characterization is composed of a set of aspects formalized in UML diagrams [5]:

- *Alliance Identification* of the agreement (e.g., the duration based on time or a project), the actors involved (e.g., stakeholders, users, organizations) and the services offered (the general output expected from these actors and their role in the service).
- *Collaboration Willingness* characterizes actor's compromises in terms of the availability to the relationship (priority, time), the investments willing to be made (financial and material assets, organizational, human and relational capital), the elements to be coordinated (people, process) and the regulation (the expected behavior to assure actors' good performance).

- *Common Objective* characterizes the shared goal and the directions to be followed for achieving it. The latter could answer customer's needs (e.g., integral services), satisfy companies' objectives (to share costs, benefits, to create more effective processes), make new business (new markets, new products or services) or confront difficulties (absence of knowledge).

3   The 360° VisiOn Intentional Models in InnoServ

To guide the collaboration modeling process in the team (with varied actors and concerns), we use the 360° VisiOn models for visualizing, analyzing and exploring the diverse stakeholders scattered in the French health care service. In this section we describe some of the models used so far.

The *Alliance Identification* is implemented in a software tool prototype [5]. The Inter view starts at a macro level with the *Groups of Organizations* providing the health care service *Take Care of Fragile People* described as "organization and implementation of the services required by a fragile person in order to ease his/her everyday life". Guided by the 360° VisiOn the groups, relationships and group decomposition were identified in three participative sessions and four iterations with all project members:

- *Fragile People* are chronic or occasional patients, elderly, disable and momentary prevented people needing help to continue living at home.
- *Non-professional Caregivers* are unpaid neighbors, family, friends and volunteer associations engaged to help fragile people.
- *Health Professionals* are individuals and certified institutions working in physical or mental health with knowledge and specialized expertise to maintain or improve the health care of individuals.
- *Health Care Service Providers* are private or public organizations (offering devices and equipments to overcome physical barriers and limitations) and laboratories (performing medical analysis or imaging to diagnose and treat disease).
- *Non Health Care Service Providers* are organizations offering services that help simplify fragile people's daily lives while providing tax benefits, like personal assistance (e.g., food), home maintenance (e.g., housework).
- *Social Professionals* are nonprofit institutions helping patients to cope with financial difficulties, state health suppliers agreements, encourage prevention.
- *Indirect Service Providers* facilitate the work of the various actors in the health care field with materials (e.g., medical and ambulatory equipment) and services (e.g., mobile health).
- *State & Local Authorities* are tutorships and regulators of health legislations which gradually delegate government actions to the regions.

The relationships in the French health care system are defined by: *regulation* (representing organizational behavior control through laws and regulations), *coordination* (synchronizing, monitoring, planning and implementing processes), *execution* (carrying out the planned tasks defined in the processes) and *prescription* (giving medical prescriptions or non-medical recommendations).

Each *Group of Organizations* was decomposed giving a total of 45 organizations, e.g., *Indirect Service Providers* are Support Equipment Suppliers, Support Service Providers and Research and Development Labs; *Non-professional Caregivers* are Neighbors, Family, Friends and Volunteer Associations.

Four scenarios glimpsed during the first year of the project (homecoming, toilet, Alzheimer's and diabetes disease) we first illustrate our proposal with the former. The homecoming scenario is described as follows: "Mrs. Dubois is a widow woman in her late 80's. She lives alone in a small village in the mountains, she had being autonomous and independent so far. She was taken to the hospital emergency services due to a fall while at home. After several examinations she was diagnosed with distal femur fracture and had to stay in the hospital for three days. Since the accident she had considerable lost autonomy. In addition, she has always faced economic difficulties and does not have relatives to take care of her. Returning home becomes complicated". Based on the general decomposed model, 35 organizations were considered to participate in this scenario with an average of 2 relationships (one organization has four relationships) representing the service in an *Alliance Identification* decomposed model.

From this model, *Collaboration Willingness* representations were developed for defining: first the *engagement* to allocate investments (e.g., *State & Local Authorities* provide 80% of the money needed in the service). Second, the *coordination* of processes (e.g., hospital discharge, treatment proposal, refunding), describing where, when and how the communication is done (e.g., hospital discharge starts locally, is event-triggered by the hospital doctor, requires mobile access and data is transmitted to the medical record). And third, establishing *trust* with process regulations (e.g., private medical information exchange) and penalization in case of nonfulfillment (e.g., violation of access consent to private information).

One of the *Common Objectives* is to provide a "quality homecoming service". Regarding the intra objectives we can cite "optimize homecoming costs"(from the *State & Local Authorities*); "encourage social participation"(from the General Council). The expected *benefit* of an objective represents the foreseen goal yield (e.g., "maximize caregivers visits"). In turn, goals can emerge from *opportunities* (conjectural circumstance that facilitates objective achievement like "increment of social volunteers") or *problems* (a difficulty that can justify the objective like "rise of isolated people in the region").

4   Conclusions and Future Work

In this paper we reported on an approach for VOs modeling in the French health care domain which provides information about the problem space and handles the complexity linked to the numerous organizations involved in the service. The main contribution of the 360° VisiOn is to delimit the analysis at an intra, inter and extra dimensions to explore and analyze more alternatives, while other RE modeling approaches offer at best, two dimensions. It is important to consider these dimensions when exploring collaboration due to the different needs of organization's internals, organizations providing a service and environmental organizations.

We also described some of the models for the identification of actors, collaboration and objectives. Models have helped to establish a common language and facilitate communication among project members helping to organize information from a top-down approach in a iterative way. Some innovative ideas have started to emerge from the alliance identification models which are currently validated, full validation for collaboration willingness and common objectives models is left as future works. A bottom-up approach based on business processes is being developed with other InnoServ partners, we are planning to analyze the impact of both approaches in the project.

Acknowledgements. We thank all partners of the InnoServ project for their useful comments and discussions during the work sessions.

References

1. Ghose, A.K., Koliadis, G.: Relating business process models to goal-oriented requirements models in kaos. In: Faculty of Informatics-Papers, p. 573 (2007)
2. Hickey, A.M., Davis, A.M.: Elicitation technique selection: How do experts do it. In: Proceedings of the 11th IEEE International Conference on Requirements Engineering, p. 169. IEEE Computer Society (2003)
3. Koliadis, G., Vranesevic, A., Bhuiyan, M.A., Krishna, A., Ghose, A.K.: Combining i* and BPMN for business process model lifecycle management. In: Eder, J., Dustdar, S. (eds.) BPM Workshops 2006. LNCS, vol. 4103, pp. 416–427. Springer, Heidelberg (2006)
4. Nuseibeh, B., Easterbrook, S.: Requirements engineering: a roadmap. In: ICSE 2000: Proceedings of the Conference on The Future of Software Engineering, pp. 35–46. ACM, New York (2000)
5. Priego-Roche, L.M., Thom, L.H., Front, A., Rieu, D., Mendling, J.: Business process design from virtual organization intentional models. In: Ralyté, J., Franch, X., Brinkkemper, S., Wrycza, S. (eds.) CAiSE 2012. LNCS, vol. 7328, pp. 549–564. Springer, Heidelberg (2012)
6. Priego-Roche, L.-M., Rieu, D., Front, A.: A 360° vision for virtual organizations characterization and modelling: Two intentional level aspects. In: Godart, C., Gronau, N., Sharma, S., Canals, G. (eds.) I3E 2009. IFIP AICT, vol. 305, pp. 427–442. Springer, Heidelberg (2009)
7. Priego-Roche, L.M., Rieu, D., Front, A.: Vers une caractérisation intentionnelle des organisations virtuelles: Towards an intentional characterization of virtual organizations. Ingénierie des systèmes d'information 15(3), 61–86 (2010)
8. Rolland, C., Prakash, N.: On the adequate modeling of business process families. In: 8th Workshop on Business Process Modeling, Development, and Support (BPMDS 2007), Electronic Ressource (2007)
9. Tarricone, R., Tsouros, A.D.: Home care in Europe: The solid facts. World Health Organization (2009)
10. Weigand, H., Johannesson, P., Andersson, B., Bergholtz, M., Edirisuriya, A., Ilayperuma, T.: Value object analysis and the transformation from value model to process model. In: Enterprise Interoperability, pp. 55–65 (2007)

Querying Brussels Spatiotemporal Linked Open Data

Kevin Chentout and Alejandro Vaisman

Université Libre de Bruxelles
{kchentou,avaisman}@ulb.ac.be

Abstract. The "Open Semantic Cloud for Brussels" (OSCB) project aims at building a platform for linked open data for the Brussels region in Belgium, such that participants can easily publish their data, which can in turn be queried by end users using a web browser to access a SPARQL endpoint. If data are spatial and we want to show them on a map, we need to support this endpoint with an engine that can manage spatial data. For this we chose Strabon, an open source geospatial database management system that stores linked geospatial data expressed in the stRDF format (spatiotemporal RDF) and queries them using stSPARQL (spatiotemporal SPARQL), an extension to SPARQL 1.1. In this paper we show how the SPARQL endpoint is built and the kinds of queries it supports, also providing a wide variety of examples.

1 Introduction

"Open Data" aims at making public sector data easily available and encouraging researchers and application developers to analyze and build applications around that data in order to stimulate innovation, business and public interests. "Linked Data"[1] is a global initiative to interlink resources on the Web using Uniform Resource Identifiers (URI) for accessing the resources, and the Resource Description Framework (RDF) [2] for representing knowledge and annotating those resources. The conjunction of both concepts originated the notion of "Linked Open Data" (LOD). The goal of the "Open Semantic Cloud for Brussels" (OSCB) project[2] is to pave the way for building a platform for LOD for the region of Brussels. The objective is that participants benefit from the OSCB, linked data-based architecture to publish their data. To facilitate this, data will be published in RDF format. The final users should be able to query data in an ubiquitous, intuitive and simple way. In this paper we show how these data can be queried by OSCB users.

Background. RDF is a data model for expressing assertions over resources identified by a URI. Assertions are expressed as *subject-predicate-object* triples, where *subject* is always a resource, and *predicate* and *object* could be a resource

---

[1] http://www.linkeddata.org
[2] http://www.oscb.be

Y.T. Demey and H. Panetto (Eds.): OTM 2013 Workshops, LNCS 8186, pp. 378–387, 2013.

or a string. *Blank nodes* are used to represent anonymous resources or resources without a URI, typically with a structural function, e.g., to group a set of statements. Data values in RDF are called *literals* and can only be *objects*. Many formats for RDF serialization exist. In this paper we use Turtle[3], and assume that the reader is familiar with this notation.

SPARQL is the W3C standard query language for RDF [4]. The query evaluation mechanism of SPARQL is based on subgraph matching: RDF triples are interpreted as nodes and edges of directed graphs, and the query graph is matched to the data graph, instantiating the variables in the query graph definition. The selection criteria is expressed as a graph pattern in the WHERE clause, consisting basically in a set of triple patterns connected by the '.' operator.

Contributions and Paper Organization. In OSCB, data providers deliver their data in relational tables or XML documents. To be accessed and linked, these data are mapped to RDF triples using the R2RML[4] standard. These data are used to populate a SPARQL endpoint, which can be accessed using a browser. Since OSCB data are essentially spatiotemporal, we do not only need to extend the R2RML mapping (which we explain in [1]), we also need to empower the endpoint with a spatial-enabled engine. For this, we have chosen Strabon [3], an open-source semantic geospatial database management system (DBMS) that stores linked geospatial data expressed in the stRDF format (spatiotemporal RDF) and queries these data using stSPARQL (spatiotemporal SPARQL). In this paper we describe the data, and how it can be queried using stSPARQL. In Section 2 we introduce Strabon. Then, in Section 3 we describe how we process the data that populates the endpoint. In Section 4 we present a comprehensive set of example queries. We conclude in Section 5.

2   Strabon, stRDF and stSPARQL

The availability of geospatial data in the linked data cloud has motivated research on geospatial extensions of SPARQL. These works have formed the basis for GeoSPARQL, a proposal for an Open Geospatial Consortium (OGC)[5] standard, currently at the "candidate standard stage". *Strabon* [3] is an open-source semantic geospatial database management system that extends the RDF store *Sesame*, allowing it to manage both thematic and spatial RDF data stored in the PostGIS[6] spatial DBMS. In this way, Strabon provides features similar to those offered by geospatial DBMS that make it one of the richest RDF stores with geospatial support available today. These features made us chose Strabon as the spatial RDF data engine for the OSCB project, and the backend for our spatial data-enabled endpoint. In this way, Strabon allows us to support spatial queries and display their result on a map.

---

[3] http://www.w3.org/TeamSubmission/turtle/

[4] http://www.w3.org/TR/r2rml/

[5] http://opengeospatial.org

[6] http:postgis.org

Strabon works over stRDF, a spatiotemporal extension of RDF. In stRDF, the data types `strdf:WKT` and `strdf:GML` represent geometries serialized using the OGC standards WKT and GML. WKT is a widely accepted OGC standard and can be used for representing geometries, coordinate reference systems and transformations between coordinate reference systems. Since our contribution is built on Strabon, we next explain the latter's main features in order to make the paper self-contained.

The stSPARQL language extends SPARQL 1.1 with functions that take as arguments spatial terms and can be used in the SELECT, FILTER, and HAVING clause of a SPARQL query. A spatial term is either a spatial literal (i.e., a typed literal with data type `strdf:geometry` or its subtypes), a query variable that can be bound to a spatial literal, the result of a set operation on spatial literals (e.g., union), or the result of a geometric operation on spatial terms (e.g., buffer). Also, stSPARQL can express spatial selections, i.e., queries with a FILTER function with arguments a variable and a constant, and spatial joins, i.e., queries with a FILTER function like `strdf:contains(?geoA, ?geoB)`.

The stSPARQL extension functions can also be used in the SELECT clause of a SPARQL query. As a result, new spatial literals can be generated on the fly during query time based on pre-existing spatial literals. For example, to obtain the buffer of a spatial literal that is bound to the variable ?geo, we would use the expression SELECT (`strdf:buffer(?geo,0.01)` AS ?geobuffer). We show examples of how we exploit these features in Section 4.

In stSPARQL aggregate functions over geospatial data are supported, like: (1) `strdf:geometry strdf:union(set of strdf:geometry a)`, returns a geometry that is the union of the set of input geometries. (2) `strdf:geometry strdf:intersection (set of strdf:geometry a)`, returns the intersection of the set of input geometries. (3) `strdf:geometry strdf:extent(set of strdf:geometry a)`, returns the minimum bounding box of the set of input geometries.

3   Building the SPARQL Endpoint

In previous work [1] we showed how we can map spatial data to the stRDF format extending the R2RML[7]. standard. The Strabon-powered stSPARQL endpoint which we analyze in this paper contains three datasets from Belgian organizations: Agenda.be, Bozar, and STIB. These datasets are complemented by external data sources, which provide the context for analysis. These data was obtained from other data publishers. We next present these datasets.

Organizational Data. The **Agenda.be** data reports cultural events in Brussels and the institutions where they take place. It is delivered in two XML documents: events.xml, containing events and institutions.xml. The size of the XML files is approximately 6MB. Applying the spatial R2RML mapping we obtain triples like the following one, containing the spatial coordinates of the

---

[7] http://www.w3.org/TR/r2rml/

institution where the event takes place. Note that we use the WGS84 standard coordinate system for the geographic data reference.

```
...
<http://www.agenda.be/db/Address_of_Institution/3>
    ...
    <http://www.w3.org/2003/01/geo/wgs84_pos#geometry>
        "POINT(4.357527 50.854287);http://www.opengis.
        net/def/crs/EPSG/0/4326"^^<http://strdf.di.
        uoa.gr/ontology#WKT> .
```

The **BOZAR database** contains approximately 130MB of data. Addresses are stored in a table denoted location_lng. This table contains information about name, address, zip and city. Its schema has the form (id, lng, field, content). The address information is represented as values of the attribute field. We preprocessed this table to obtain a new one with schema (fullAddress,id). As an example, applying the mapping over the following tuple in this table: < *ABC Factory* 175 *rue Bara* 1070 *Bruxelles Belgique* >, results in the triple (corresponding to a location with id=110):

```
<http://bozar.be/db/Locations/110>
    a       <http://starpc18.vub.ac.be:8080/gospl/ontology
        /2#Location> ;
    <http://www.w3.org/2003/01/geo/wgs84_pos#geometry>
        "POINT(4.292185 50.82917);http://www.opengis.
        net/def/crs/EPSG/0/4326"^^<http://strdf.di.
        uoa.gr/ontology#WKT> .
```

The **STIB**, *Société des Transports Intercommunaux de Bruxelles* is the main company of public transport in Brussels. Spatiotemporal data from STIB are stored in an SQL database in four tables: Block, Stop, Trip and Tripstop. A Block can be seen as the time elapsed between the moment in which a vehicle leaves the warehouse and returns to it. The Stop table corresponds to a stop (bus, tram or metro) with its description, in French and Dutch, and its location, in x and y coordinates as well as in GPS coordinates (longitude / latitude). A Trip is a part of a block and it is defined as the path between the starting point and the ending point for a route. Finally, the Tripstop describes the stop and the time during a trip when the vehicle reaches the stop. The spatial mapping here is straightforward because we already have the longitude and latitude of a stop. For example, the instance of in Table 1 produces the following triple representing the location of stop 8042.

```
<http://www.stib.be/location/8042>
    a    <http://starpc18.vub.ac.be:8080/gospl/ontology/60#
        Location> ;
    <http://starpc18.vub.ac.be:8080/gospl/ontology/60#
        Location_of_Stop>
        <http://www.stib.be/stop/8042> ;
    ...
    <http://www.w3.org/2003/01/geo/wgs84_pos#geometry>
```

Table 1. Sample of Stop table

stp_identifier	stp_description	ud_stp_desc_flam	stp_longitude	stp_latitude
8042	ARTS-LOI	KUNST-WET	4.36963	50.8453
8032	PARC	PARK	4.36293	50.8458

```
"POINT(4.36963 50.8453);http://www.opengis.net/def/
    crs/EPSG/0/4326"^^<http://strdf.di.uoa.gr/
    ontology#WKT> .
...
```

External Datasets. To provide context to the analysis we added places of interest in Brussels, e.g., cafes, restaurants, banks, schools, etc. To obtain these data we queried three datasets from the linked open data web: DBPedia, Geonames and LinkedGeoData. **DBPedia** is a dataset containing structured information extracted from Wikipedia. This dataset is available on the Web and can be queried via a SPARQL endpoint[8]. For data extraction, we built a tool in Java, which queries the DBPedia service and returns RDF triples in a file. For example, a portion of a triple representing the Royal Palace looks like:

```
<http://dbpedia.org/resource/Royal_Palace_of_Brussels>
    <http://www.w3.org/2000/01/rdf-schema#label>
        "Royal Palace of Brussels@en" ;
    <http://www.w3.org/2003/01/geo/wgs84_pos#geometry>
        "POINT(4.36222 50.8417);http://www.opengis.net/
            def/crs/EPSG/0/4326"^^<http://strdf.di.uoa.
            gr/ontology#WKT> ;
        ...
    <http://xmlns.com/foaf/0.1/isPrimaryTopicOf>
        "http://en.wikipedia.org/wiki/
            Royal_Palace_of_Brussels" .
```

We got 50 different places in Brussels for which we know the location. The second source we used was **Geonames**[9], a geographical database containing information from over 8 million place. A geonames Java library allows us to access the geonames web services. This added 114 different places for Brussels. Finally, we search data in **LinkedGeoData**, a spatial database derived from OpenStreetMaps, a project aimed at building a free world map database. These data can be accessed and queried via a SPARQL endpoint[10]. Similar to what we did for the DBPedia dataset, we queried a service and build RDF triples from the results. In total, we collected 2355 places from the external sources, which we aded to our basic dataset.

---

[8] http://dbpedia.org/sparql
[9] http://geonames.org
[10] http://live.linkedgeodata.org/sparql

4   Querying the SPARQL Endpoint

We next give examples of queries that the endpoint supports[11], classifying them according their type. We remark that this classification is just aimed at organizing the presentation and does not pretend to be a query taxonomy. In the queries that follow, we omit the prefixes for the sake of space.

Queries over a Single Dataset. These queries are posed over just one dataset. That means that there is a unique "FROM" clause in the SPARQL query, which is mandatory.
The following query asks for STIB route data. The result is given in Figure 1a.
Query 1. *"Give me all STIB stops corresponding to route 25"*

```
SELECT DISTINCT ?stop_loc ?geo ?description
FROM <http://stib.be>
WHERE {
  ?name stib:Route_with_Name "25" .
  ?route_name stib:Route_with_Route_Name ?name.
  ?trip stib:Trip_with_Route ?route_name .
  ?trip stib:Trip_with_Trip_Stop ?trip_stop .
  ?trip_stop stib:Trip_Stop_with_Stop ?stop_loc .
  ?stop_loc stib:Stop_with_Description ?description.
  ?node stib:Location_of_Stop ?stop_loc.
  ?node geo:geometry ?geo.
}
```

In this query, in variable ?stop_loc we return a link to the triple corresponding to the stop location. In variable ?geo we return the geometry (the point coordinates, which allows us to display the result in a map), and in ?description the name of the stop. The rest of the query is self-descriptive.

Queries Including Aggregate Functions. These queries include a GROUP BY clause. The following query computes the twenty stops closest to the Brussels central square, displaying the result in a map (Figure 1b).
Query 2. *"Twenty stops closest to the Grand Place"*

```
SELECT distinct ?stop (GROUP_CONCAT(distinct ?line) AS ?
    someLine) (SAMPLE(?description) AS ?someDescription) ?geo
    (strdf:distance(?geo, "POINT (4.3525 50.8467);http://www
    .opengis.net/def/crs/EPSG/0/4326", <http://www.opengis.
    net/def/uom/OGC/1.0/metre>)as ?dist )
FROM <http://stib.be>
WHERE {
  ?stop_loc a stib:Location .
  ?stop_loc geo:geometry ?geo.
  filter(strdf:distance(?geo, "POINT (4.3525 50.8467);http://
    www.opengis.net/def/crs/EPSG/0/4326", <http://www.
    opengis.net/def/uom/OGC/1.0/metre>) < 1000)
```

---

[11] The complete list of example queries can be found at the endpoint in the address http://eao4.ulb.ac.be:8080/strabonendpoint/

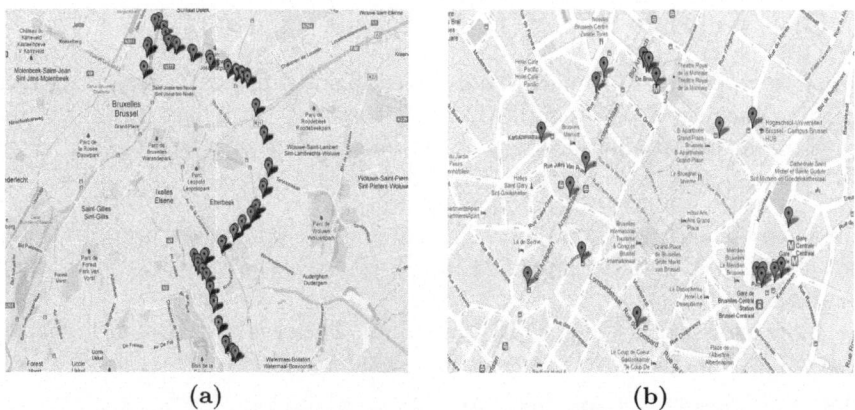

(a)   **(b)**

Fig. 1. (a) Stops of Tram 25; (b) Twenty stops closest to Brussels central square

```
?stop_loc stib:Location_of_Stop ?stop .
?stop stib:Stop_with_Description ?description .

?trip_stop stib:Trip_Stop_with_Stop ?stop .
?trip_stop stib:Trip_Stop_of_Trip ?trip .

?trip stib:Trip_with_Route ?route_name .
?route_name stib:Route_with_Route_Name ?name.
?name stib:Route_with_Name ?line .
}
GROUP BY ?stop ?geo ?dist
ORDER BY ?dist
LIMIT 20
```

Note that in the SELECT clause we compute the distance between a stop (variable ?geo) and the position of the Grand Place, which we assume the user (or an application querying the endpoint) knows. It is returned in variable ?dist.

Statistical Queries. This class includes queries returning statistical data obtained from the datasets. These queries are normally also aggregate queries.
Query 3. *"Number of stops per route"*

```
SELECT (str(?res) as ?line) (count(*) as ?total)
FROM <http://stib.be>
WHERE {
  ?name stib:Route_with_Name ?line .
  ?route stib:Route_with_Route_Name ?name.
  ?route stib:Route_with_Stop ?stop .
  BIND( xsd:integer(?line) as ?res)
}
GROUP BY ?res
ORDER BY ?res
```

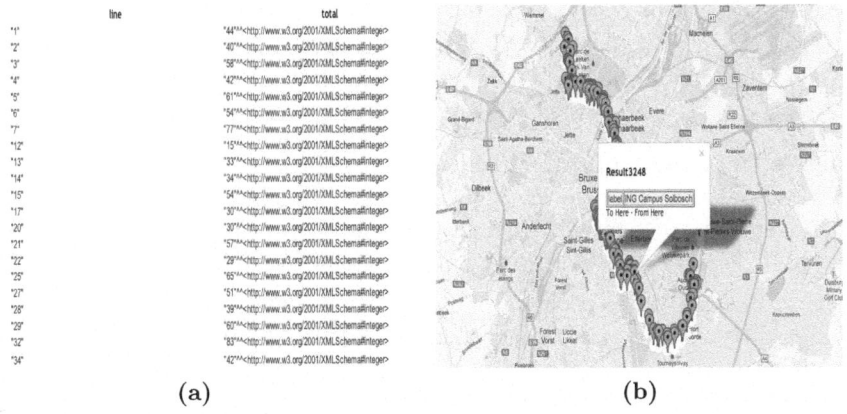

Fig. 2. (a) Number of stops per route; (b) Places of interest within 200m of a stop of tram 94

The result is displayed in Figure 2a, and it is in textual format. Note that the BIND function allows to display the result ordered by route number.

Queries Involving Several Datasets. This class includes queries over many different datasets, that means, there is more than one FROM clause in the query. The query below retrieves data from Agenda.be and Bozar, as we can see in the two FROM clauses. This is also an aggregate query. Note that we do not distinguish from which dataset the information is retrieved, since the data from Bozar and Agenda.be are organizational, and were mapped using the common vocabulary given by the GOSPL ontology (prefix gospl).

Query 4. *"Places which host at least 10 events"*

```
SELECT ?nameInstit ?geo1 ?street ?zip ?city (GROUP_CONCAT(?
    title; separator = ' - / - ') as ?events)
FROM <http://bozar.be>
FROM <http://agenda.be>
WHERE {
  ?event gospl:Event_taking_place_at_Institution ?instit .
  ?instit gospl:Institution_with_Address ?addr .
  ?addr geo:geometry ?geo1 .

  ?event gospl:Event_has_Title ?title .
  FILTER(langMatches(lang(?title), "FR"))
  ?instit gospl:Institution_with_Name ?nameInstit .
  FILTER(langMatches(lang(?nameInstit), "FR"))

  ?addr gospl:Address_with_Street ?street .
  FILTER(langMatches(lang(?street), "FR"))
  ?addr gospl:Address_with_Postal_Code ?zip .
  ?addr gospl:Address_with_City ?city.
  FILTER(langMatches(lang(?city), "FR"))
```

```
}
GROUP BY ?nameInstit ?geo1 ?street ?zip ?city
Having (count(*) > 9)
```

Queries Drawing Buffers and Lines on a Map. This class includes queries
whose output includes drawing a line between two points on a map, or a buffer
around a geometric figure. The result of the next query is depicted in Figure 2b.
Query 5. *"Places of interest in a radius of 200m from a stop of line 94"*

```
SELECT (strdf:buffer(?geo1, 200, <http://www.opengis.net/def/
    uom/OGC/1.0/metre>) as ?buf) ?geo ?label
WHERE {
  ?name stib:Route_with_Name "94" .
  ?route stib:Route_with_Route_Name ?name.
  ?route stib:Route_with_Stop ?stop .

  ?stop stib:Stop_with_Description ?description.
  ?stop stib:Stop_with_Location ?loc .
  ?loc geo:geometry ?geo1.

  ?node a ?type .
  ?node geo:geometry ?geo .
  filter(strdf:distance(?geo, ?geo1, <http://www.opengis.net/
      def/uom/OGC/1.0/metre>) < 200)
  ?node rdfs:label ?label .
}
```

Queries Including Spatial and Temporal Conditions. Note that this query
also uses a buffer, which is returned in the SELECT clause.
Query 6. *"Places hosting events on May 23rd, 2013 in a radius of 200m of a
stop of line 3"*

```
SELECT ?geo ?node ?title (GROUP_CONCAT(?description ;
    separator=", ") AS ?someDescription) ?start ?end (strdf:
    buffer(?geo, 200, <http://www.opengis.net/def/uom/OGC
    /1.0/metre>) as ?buf)
FROM <http://agenda.be>
FROM <http://bozar.be>
FROM <http://stib.be>
WHERE {
  ?node gospl:DateTimeSpecification_valid_from_Date ?start .
  ?node gospl:DateTimeSpecification_valid_until_Date ?end .
  FILTER(?start <= "2013-05-23"^^xsd:date && "2013-05-23"^^
      xsd:date <= ?end)
  ?node gospl:Event_has_Title ?title .
  FILTER(langMatches(lang(?title), "FR"))
  ?node gospl:Event_with_Description ?description .
  FILTER(langMatches(lang(?description), "FR"))
```

```
?node gospl:Event_taking_place_at_Institution ?inst .
?inst gospl:Institution_with_Address ?addr .
?addr geo:geometry ?geo .

?name stib:Route_with_Name ?line .
FILTER (?line = "3")
?route stib:Route_with_Route_Name ?name.
?route stib:Route_with_Stop ?stop .
?stop stib:Stop_with_Location ?loc .
?loc geo:geometry ?geo1.

FILTER (strdf:distance(?geo, ?geo1, <http://www.opengis.net
    /def/uom/OGC/1.0/metre>) < 200)
}
GROUP BY ?geo ?node ?title ?start ?end ?buf
```

5   Conclusion

In this paper we have described how a spatial data-enabled SPARQL endpoint
has been built in the framework of the OSCB project. The endpoint is powered
by the Strabon open-source semantic geospatial DBMS. Data are stored in the
stRDF format, and are queried using an spatiotemporal extension to SPARQL,
called stSPARQL. We have focused on illustrating the interesting kinds of queries
that our solution supports, to give an idea of how external applications could
make use of our platform.

Acknowledgement. Alejandro Vaisman has been partially funded by the
"Open Semantic Cloud for Brussels (OSCB)" project, funded by Innoviris.

References

1. Chentout, K., Vaisman, A.: Mapping Spatial Data using R2RML (submitted, 2013)
2. Klyne, G., Carroll, J.J., McBride, B.: Resource Description Framework (RDF): Concepts and Abstract Syntax (2004), http://www.w3.org/TR/rdf-concepts/
3. Kyzirakos, K., Karpathiotakis, M., Koubarakis, M.: Strabon: A Semantic Geospatial
   DBMS. In: Cudré-Mauroux, P., Heflin, J., Sirin, E., Tudorache, T., Euzenat, J.,
   Hauswirth, M., Parreira, J.X., Hendler, J., Schreiber, G., Bernstein, A., Blomqvist,
   E. (eds.) ISWC 2012, Part I. LNCS, vol. 7649, pp. 295–311. Springer, Heidelberg
   (2012)
4. Prud'hommeaux, E., Seaborne, A.: SPARQL Query Language for RDF (2008),
   http://www.w3.org/TR/rdf-sparql-query/

Towards Standardized Integration of Images in the Cloud of Linked Data

Ruben Tous[1], Jaime Delgado[1], Frederik Temmermans[2,3], Bart Jansen[2,3], and Peter Schelkens[2,3]

[1] Universitat Politècnica de Catalunya - BarcelonaTech (UPC), Barcelona, Spain
{rtous,jaime.delgado}@ac.upc.edu
[2] Department of Electronics and Informatics - ETRO, Vrije Universiteit Brussel, Brussels, Belgium
[3] iMinds, Dept. of Future Media and Imaging (FMI), Ghent, Belgium
ftemmerm@etro.vub.ac.be

Abstract. Currently, there are several ways of describing and referring to images in RDF. This ambiguity results in a proliferation of vocabularies for image descriptions, complicating the cross-community data integration of information related to digital images. In addition, there are no standardized guidelines on how to integrate RDF data into the image metadata. Therefore, the JPEG standardization committee has recently initiated some activities to streamline the integration of images in the cloud of Linked Data. One effort is the standardization of an ontology for describing digital images. JPEG aims at providing a technology that enables the uniform description of photos and videos with technical, administrative and semantic metadata compliant with the RDF specification and the principles of Linked Data. Secondly, specifications to integrate RDF data into JPEG images are elaborated. Finally, since descriptions often only apply to a certain part of an image, a last effort is to formalize the specification of regions of interest. In this paper, members of the JPEG committee provide a detailed overview of these ongoing activities.

Keywords: Ontology, JPEG, JPSearch, image, photo, video, controlled vocabulary, semantic description, RDF (Resource Description Framework), linked data, computer vision.

1   Introduction

Semantic image annotation is nowadays a hot topic and hundreds of different metadata vocabularies are being developed in an ad-hoc way [10,3,2]. A metadata vocabulary is a specification of what terms to use in the metadata for a certain domain, and how these terms are defined. Modern metadata vocabularies have transitioned from shared natural-language definitions to shared machine-processable representations [4]. Commonly, adopting the shared formal model provided by the W3C's RDF, which is used to support Linked Data. Linked Data is a method of publishing metadata, where every single item is a resource.

Y.T. Demey and H. Panetto (Eds.): OTM 2013 Workshops, LNCS 8186, pp. 388–397, 2013.

Every resource can be linked to other resources, public Linked Data databases (e.g. DBpedia) or to formal vocabularies, i.e. ontologies. Since anyone can define ontologies, the development of new ontologies is unlimited. However, for the sake of interoperability and to prevent proliferation, someone should select, refine, harmonize, catalogue, register and disseminate those vocabularies. Therefore, the Joint Photographic Experts Group (JPEG, formally ISO/IEC JTC1/SC29/WG1) has recently initiated some new activities on next generation image metadata. The main goal of this activity is to provide a simple and uniform way of annotating JPEG images with metadata compliant to the Linked Data principles. To accomplish this objective, a first task is the specification of a JPEG Ontology for Still Image Description (JPOnto). JPOnto provides a set of classes, properties, and restrictions that can be used to represent and interchange information about still and moving images generated in different systems and under different contexts. It can also be specialized to create new classes and properties to model image information for different applications and domains. A second task is designing a mechanism which allows embedding RDF metadata annotations within JPEG (ISO/IEC 10918) or JPEG 2000 (ISO/IEC 15444) files. Finally, since descriptions often only apply to a certain part of an image, a last effort is to formalize the specification of regions of interest.

Section 2 describes the context of this work while Sections 3, 4 and 5 explain the new activities in more detail. It should be noted that the described work is work in progress and has to go to several revisions and procedures before becoming an International Standard. During the process some specifics might change. The authors of this article are members of the JPEG committee and participated in launching and elaborating this work.

2   Contextualization

2.1   The JPEG Committee

JPEG is a joint working group of the Joint Technical Committee 1 (JTC 1) of the International Standardization Organization (ISO) and the International Electrotechnical Commission (IEC). More specifically, the JPEG committee is Working Group 1 (WG1), Coding of Still Pictures, of JTC 1's subcommittee 29 (SC29), Coding of Audio, Picture, Multimedia and Hypermedia Information. The word "Joint" in JPEG does not refer to the joint efforts of ISO and IEC, but to the fact that the JPEG activities are the result of an additional collaboration with the International Telecommunication Union ITU [5]. The JPEG committee is well known for its image coding standards, including JPEG and JPEG2000. In addition, JPEG produced standards related to image security (JPSEC), transfer protocols (JPIP) and image metadata and search (JPSearch). The work described in this article is part of the activities of the JPSearch group.

2.2   JPSearch

JPSearch is an activity within JPEG that aims to address interoperability in image search and retrieval systems [6,7,1]. For this purpose, JPSearch puts forward an abstract image search and retrieval framework. Interfaces and protocols for data exchange between the components of this architecture are standardized, with minimal restrictions on how these components perform their respective tasks. The use and reuse of metadata and associated metadata schemas is thus facilitated. A common query language enables search over distributed repositories. Finally, an interchange format allows users to easily import and export their data and metadata among different applications and devices. In the JPSearch framework, interoperability can be defined in different ways: between self-contained vertical image search systems providing federated search, between layers of an image search and retrieval system so that different modules can be supplied by distinct vendors, or at the metadata level such that different systems may add, update, or query metadata [6]. JPSearch currently consists of five Parts, all of them recently reached the state of International Standard:

Part 1. System framework and components
Part 2. Registration, identification and management of schema and ontology
Part 3. JPSearch Query Format
Part 4. File format for metadata embedded in image data
Part 5. Data interchange format between image repositories
Part 6. Reference Software

2.3   JPSearch RA

JPSearch compliant systems can manage multiple proprietary or community-specific metadata vocabularies formalized as XML schemas or RDF ontologies. The multiplicity of vocabularies is solved by allowing the publication of machine-readable translations between metadata terms belonging to proprietary vocabularies and metadata terms in the core metadata vocabulary provided by JPSearch. This core vocabulary is formalized as an XML Schema, but all its terms have equivalent counterparts within the JPOnto ontology, thus facilitating the linkage to them from Linked Data.

In order to rationalize the usage of vocabularies and translation rules across different JPSearch systems, a global authority for schemas and their translation rules has been established. JPSearch RA is the official body designated by ISO to serve as a registration authority for Part 2 of ISO/IEC 24800 (JPSearch). Via the authority, all JPSearch compliant applications can obtain the information they need. The JPSearch RA was assigned to the Distributed Multimedia Applications Group (DMAG) of the Universitat Politècnica de Catalunya - BarcelonaTech (UPC). The JPSearch RA entered into full operation early 2013 at http://dmag.ac.upc.edu/jpsearch-ra. It provides a registration procedure for the publication of metadata vocabularies and translation rules. The information is directly stored in the RA's internal server. Furthermore, it provides a registry look up service in which the RA displays a list of registered metadata vocabularies and translation rules on the website. The displayed vocabulary information includes links to the schema or ontology and also to its related ISO/IEC 24800-2 translation rules. Registration forms are available and any person or organization is eligible to apply.

2.4   Workplan

The work items discussed in this article will initially be amendments to the current Parts of JPSearch and as such, become part of International Standards. More specifically, ontologies will extend Part 2, while image integration will extend Part 4. The region of interest specification is shared with a new REST API activity that will amend Part 3. In order to officially complement a standard, amendments go trough the following stages:

- Proposed Draft Amendment (PDAM)
- Final Proposed Draft Amendment (FPDAM)
- Final Draft Amendment (FDAM)
- Amendment (ADM)

The committee meets three times a year, at each meeting cycle, a document can move from one stage to the next stage. At the time of writing, the work is in the first stage, i.e. initial drafts have been produced. As a consequence, it will take at least one year before this work can promote to International Standard. At that point, a new version of a particular Part can be created that integrates the amendment(s).

3   JPEG Ontology for Image Description (JPOnto)

The JPEG work on the JPSearch Ontology for Still Image Description (JPOnto) started in February 2012 [9] and the first working draft was released in April 2013 [8]. JPOnto provides a set of classes, properties, and restrictions that can be used to represent and interchange information about still images generated in different systems and under different contexts. It can also be specialized to create new classes and properties to model still image information for different applications and domains. JPOnto users may only need to use parts of the entire ontology, depending on their needs and according to how much detail they want to include in their still image information. For this, the JPOnto terms (classes and properties) are grouped into two sub-vocabularies to provide an incremental introduction to the ontology, **JPOnto-core** and **JPOnto-visual**.

On the one hand, a core vocabulary named JPOnto-core is the basic set of entities and properties which serves as a central component to interconnect all the other sub-vocabularies of JPOnto. Three classes provide a basis for the remaining part of the JPOnto-core:

- **jponto:Image** : Represents a digital still image.
- **jponto:RegionOfInterest** : A class specialized in representing a certain region within a still image.
- **jponto:Agent** : An agent (eg. person, group, software or physical artifact).

In addition to these primary classes JPOnto provides classes and properties for describing organizations (*jponto:Organization*) and people (*jponto:Person*). Figure 2 outlines the relationships among the JPOnto-core classes but also includes some relevant relationships with some classes from JPOnto-visual (*jponto:PersonGroup* and *jponto:People*). JPOnto provides also many other datatype properties (that link individuals to data values) that are not depicted in the figure (e.g. *jponto:creationDate, jponto:boundingPolygon*, etc.).

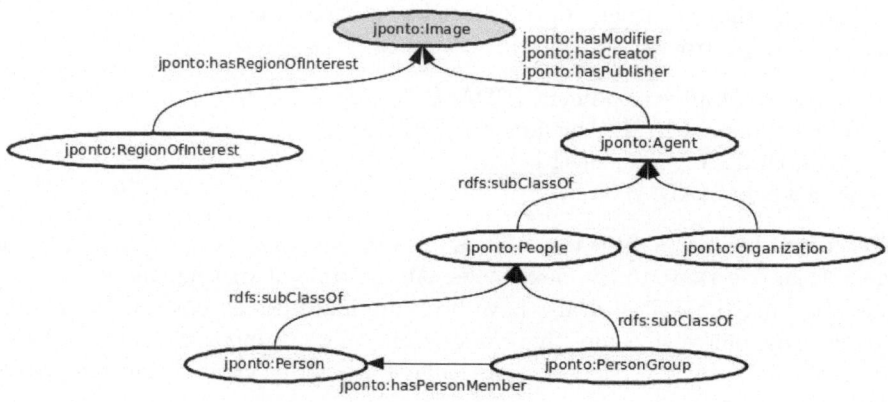

Fig. 1. Outline of JPOnto-core

JPOnto partially overlaps with well known vocabularies including, but not limited to, Dublin Core, the W3C Ontology for Media Resources and Friend of a Friend (FOAF). JPEG aims at releasing a self-included specification in order to ease the development of compliant tools. For this reason, terms in JPOnto with equivalent counterparts in external vocabularies have been redefined within the JPOnto namespace instead of directly reusing or subtyping the external terms. The proper links between related terms (e.g. *owl:equivalentClass, owl:sameAs, etc.* will be included in the final specification.

On the other hand, **JPOnto-visual** provides a rich set of constructs for semantic visual content description, including, but not limited to, a uniform description of identities, features, aspect, relationships, actions and emotional information of people appearing in the images, as well as description of events, locations and objects. JPOnto-visual will enable the description of the semantics of digital images in a simple, structured and uniform way. The resulting speci-fication will have multiple applications, such as serving as a unified annotation format for evaluation forums about the annotation and retrieval of digital im-ages (e.g. ImageCLEF), for improving Web accessibility for visually impaired Web users, and many others.

The **jponto:depicts** property is the core component of JPOnto-visual. The *jponto:depicts* property allows binding an image with the real world objects and events that it represents. Defining the *jponto:RegionOfInterest* as a subclass of *jponto:Image*, allows to also use the *jponto:depicts* predicate to bind ROIs with real world objects and events.

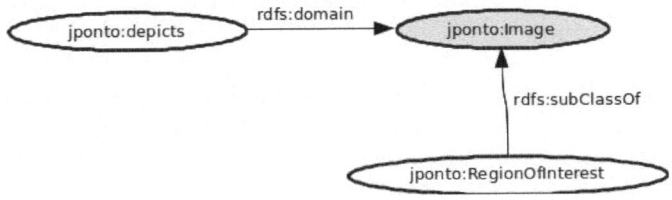

Fig. 2. The *jponto:depicts* property allows binding an image with the real world objects and events that it represents

The example in Code 1 shows the usage of the *jponto:depicts* predicate for the semantic description of the contents of an imaginary image.

Code 1. Semantic description of the contents of an imaginary image

```
@prefix jponto: <http://www.jpeg.org/ns/jponto#> .
@prefix rdf: <http://www.w3.org/1999/02/22-rdf-syntax-ns#> .
@prefix : <http://example.com/> .
:image1
  rdf:type jponto:Image;
  jponto:depicts [
      rdf:type   jponto::Person;
      jponto:givenName "Ruben Tous";
      jponto:mbox <mailto:rtous@ac.upc.edu> ];
  jponto:depicts [
    rdf:type   jponto::Building;
    jponto:givenName "Namdaemun gate";
    jponto:wikipedia <https://en.wikipedia.org/wiki/Sungnyemun> ].
```

To describe people appearing in an image, JPOnto-visual allows for describing their:

- identities and relationships
- actions and emotions
- type (gender, age, race, profession, etc.).
- aspects (make up, clothes, etc.)

In addition to the class *jponto:Person* defined in JPOnto-core, JPOnto-visual provides an alternative class for referring to persons appearing in the photo in an unspecific way (class *jponto:People*) and a class to refer to specific groups of 2 or more persons (class *jponto:PersonGroup*). Other classes related to the description of people are *jponto:Feeling* and *jponto:Action*.

JPOnto-visual provides also classes and properties for the description of events, locations, objects, atmospheric conditions, lighting and combustion effects, image views, etc.

4 Embedding JPOnto Instances within JPEG and JPEG 2000 Images

JPEG is currently specifying a compact and uniform way to embed JPOnto instances within JPEG (ISO/IEC 10918) or JPEG 2000 (ISO/IEC 15444) files. The work is focused on providing a canonical serialization syntax for the metadata statements. The location and signaling of the resulting metadata UTF-8 stream within the image file is specified by the JPSearch Part 4 standard (ISO/IEC 24800-4).

An embedded JPOnto instance, which is basically an RDF graph, must follow the following rules to be compliant with the standard:

- It makes use of character encoding UTF-8.
- It is serialized using the W3C's Terse RDF Triple Language (a.k.a. Turtle) and the canonical serialization syntax style defined by JPEG.

As the Turtle syntax is very flexible, JPEG wants to constraint its usage to a canonical serialization syntax style to facilitate the development of of conformant readers. The canonical serialization syntax specifies that the serialized metadata must include one predicate list referring to a single instance of the Class jponto-core:Image. Any triple with a subject different to IMAGE_INSTANCE_RELATIVE_IRI will be represented using nested unlabeled blank nodes as shown in the example of Code 2.

Code 2. Embedded JPOnto instance basic structure (Turtle syntax)

```
@base <IMAGE_INSTANCE_BASE_IRI>.
@prefix jponto: <http://www.jpeg.org/ns/jponto#> .
@prefix rdf: <http://www.w3.org/1999/02/22-rdf-syntax-ns#> .
:IMAGE_INSTANCE_RELATIVE_IRI
    rdf:type jponto:Image;
    jponto:hasCreator [
        jponto:givenName "Ruben Tous";
        jponto:mbox <mailto:rtous@ac.upc.edu> ].
```

More compact serializations are also enabled under certain circumstances. When the instance only makes use of namespaces endorsed by the standard (e.g. the JPOnto and RDF namespaces) it is possible to omit the namespaces declaration if the standard prefixes are used (e.g. jponto, rdf, etc.). It is also valid to omit the jponto prefix. The example in Code 3 shows a very compact serialization.

5 Region of Interest Specification

Often, descriptions only apply to a certain part of an image rather than to the whole image. Therefore, a proper Region Of Interest (ROI) specification is an

Code 3. Embedded JPOnto instance using a compact serialization style

```
:hasView   :Outdoor;
:hasQuality :MotionBlur;
:depicts [
    a   :Building;
    :givenName "Namdaemun gate";
    :wikipedia <https://en.wikipedia.org/wiki/Sungnyemun> ].
:depicts [
    a   :Vehicle;
    :color    :Green  ];
:depicts [
    a   :Person;
    :givenName "Ruben Tous";
    :mbox <mailto:rtous@ac.upc.edu> ].
:depicts :Rainy.
```

important part of the description framework. Currently, some ad-hoc methods of specifying ROI's in RDF have been proposed. The W3C Wiki[1] provides an example that adopts the SVG (Scalable Vector Graphics) Path specification to specify a polygonal ROI, analogously to the example given in Code 4.

Code 4. ROI specification using the SVG representation

```
@prefix foaf: <http://xmlns.com/foaf/0.1#> .
@prefix rdf: <http://www.w3.org/1999/02/22-rdf-syntax-ns#> .
<http://www.site.com/image.jpg>
    img:hasPart [
    a   img:Polygon;
    img:polypath "M20 160 L80 160 L80 20 L20 20 Z";
    foaf:regionDepicts [
      a   foaf:Person;
      foaf:name "Ruben Tous";
    ].
    ].
```

The path specification is a sequence of points, specified by the two coordinates of the point preceded by M or L. M stands for "move to" and is in this case used to move to the start position. L stands for "line to" and connects the current position with the associated point. The path specification ends with a Z, which is the "close path" command. The SVG path specification provides additional commands allowing to describe more complex shapes. Moreover, SVG specifies alternative representations for common shapes include rectangles, circles, ellipses and polygons. These could be used analogously. This representation is often used

---

[1] http://www.w3.org/wiki

because its SVG compatibility might allow specific applications to render the region. However, it is not at all guaranteed that clients can interpret the syntax.

Another approach is specifying a region with a specific resource identifier, allowing a much shorter and readable notation. One option is to adopt W3C's Media Fragments recommendation[2]. A fragment is the part of a URL preceded with a "#". The current specification only supports rectangular selections using the *xywh* parameter. The value is a comma separated sequence of four integers denoting respectively the upper left corner's x and y coordinates, width and height. The example in Code 5 describes a person in an area of 128 by 68 starting at x=66 and y=89.

Code 5. ROI specification using a custom resource identifier

```
@prefix foaf: <http://xmlns.com/foaf/0.1#> .
@prefix rdf: <http://www.w3.org/1999/02/22-rdf-syntax-ns#> .
<http://www.site.com/image.jpg#xywh=66,89,128,64>
    foaf:depicts [
    a   foaf:Person;
    foaf:name "Ruben Tous";
    ].
```

Currently, another ongoing activity within JPSearch is the definition of a standardized REST API for image search and retrieval. ROI specification is also part of it. Rather than fragments, the region is specified by some specific arguments in the query string of a URL. The query string of a URL is the part consisting of key value pair arguments and preceded by a "?". The query syntax implies that the specific region could be requested by a client application. For compatibility reasons, the preferred syntax in this context is taken over from JPIP (ISO/IEC 15444-9). JPIP allows specifying many types of regions, including rectangles, ellipses, quadrilaterals, oriented ellipses or arbitrary polygons. For example, a rectangle is specified by its width and height ($rsiz$) and coordinates of the upper left corner ($roff$). The following resource identifier specifies a rectangle region of 128 by 64 pixels with the upper left corner at position 66, 89: http://www.site.com/image.jpg?rsiz=128,64&roff=66,89.

Since the JPSearch API is still under development, it has not yet been decided which specification will be recommended for usage in RDF image descriptions. A main predicament is finding a good balance between flexibility and complexity.

6   Conclusions

Image metadata descriptions are evolving from natural-language definitions to shared machine-processable representations. In the open world of Linked Data anyone can define his own ontologies, leading to a proliferation of vocabularies.

---

[2] http://www.w3.org/TR/media-frags/

To obtain interoperability, someone should select, refine, harmonize, catalogue, register and disseminate those vocabularies. In addition, seamless integration of images in the cloud of Linked Data requires standardized guidelines on how to embed these descriptions into images. Finally, a formal region of interest specification allows more precise and interoperable descriptions. The Joint Photographic Experts Group aims to provide an answer to these predicaments with the initiatives described in this article.

Acknowledgments. This work has been partly supported by the Spanish government (TEC2011-22989) and iMinds. Bart Jansen is currently funded by Innoviris.

References

1. Doeller, M., Tous, R., Temmermans, F., Yoon, K., Park, J.-H., Kim, Y., Stegmaier, F., Delgado, J.: Jpeg's jpsearch standard: Harmonizing image management and search. IEEE Multimedia 99 (PrePrints), 1 (2012)
2. Hollink, L., Worring, M.: Building a visual ontology for video retrieval. In: Proceedings of the 13th Annual ACM International Conference on Multimedia, MULTIMEDIA 2005, pp. 479–482. ACM, New York (2005)
3. Hollink, L., Schreiber, G., Wielemaker, J., Wielinga, B.: Semantic annotation of image collections. Knowledge Capture, 41–48 (2003)
4. Miller, Y., Zhitomirsky-Geffet, M., Bar-Ilan, J.: Exploring the effectiveness of ontology based tagging versus free text tagging (2012)
5. Schelkens, P., Bruylants, T., Temmermans, F., Barbarien, J., Dooms, A., Munteanu, A.: The jpeg 2000 family of standards, 724802–724802-9 (2009)
6. Temmermans, F., Dufaux, F., Schelkens, P.: Jpsearch: Metadata interoperability during image exchange [standards in a nutshell]. IEEE Signal Processing Magazine 29(5), 134–139 (2012)
7. Temmermans, F., Doeller, M., Vanhamel, I., Jansen, B., Munteanu, A., Schelkens, P.: Jpsearch: An answer to the lack of standardization in mobile image retrieval. Signal Processing: Image Communication 28(4), 386–401 (2013)
8. Tous, R., Bailer, W., Delgado, J., Temmermans, F.: ISO/IEC JTC1/SC29/WG1/N6369 JPEG Ontology for Image Description (JPOnto) WD 1.0. Output Document of the 61st JPEG Meeting, Incheon, Korea (April 2013)
9. Tous, R., Delgado, J.: ISO/IEC JTC1/SC29/WG1/N5995 Proposal for Innovations in Metadata Management in JPEG. Input Document of the 57th JPEG Meeting, San Jose, US (February 2012)
10. Tousch, A.-M., Herbin, S., Audibert, J.-Y.: Semantic hierarchies for image annotation: A survey. Pattern Recognition 45(1), 333–345 (2012)

Adding Spatial Support to R2RML Mappings

Kevin Chentout and Alejandro Vaisman

Université Libre de Bruxelles
{kchentou,avaisman}@ulb.ac.be

Abstract. The "Open Semantic Cloud for Brussels" (OSCB) project aims at building a platform for linked open data for the Brussels region in Belgium, such that participants can easily publish their data. In OSCB, data providers deliver their data in the form of relational tables or XML documents. These data are mapped to RDF triples using the R2RML mapping language. Since OSCB data are spatiotemporal in nature, we needed to adapt R2RML to be able to produce spatiotemporal linked open data in order to build to a spatial data-enabled SPARQL endpoint where the result of spatiotemporal SPARQL queries can be shown on a map. In this paper we show how we achieved this goal.

1 Introduction

"Open Data" aims at making public sector data easily available and encouraging researchers and application developers to analyze and build applications around that data in order to stimulate innovation, business and public interests. "Linked Data"[1] is a global initiative to interlink resources on the Web using Uniform Resource Identifiers (URI) for accessing the resources, and the Resource Description Framework (RDF) [5] for representing knowledge and annotating those resources. The conjunction of both concepts originated the notion of "Linked Open Data" (LOD). The goal of the "Open Semantic Cloud for Brussels" (OSCB) project[2] is to pave the way for building a platform for LOD for the region of Brussels. The objective is that participants benefit from the OSCB, linked data-based architecture to publish their data. To facilitate this, data will be published in RDF format, so final users and application developers would be able to query data in an ubiquitous, intuitive and simple way.

Background. RDF is a data model for expressing assertions over resources identified by an URI. Assertions are expressed as *subject-predicate-object* triples, where *subject* are always resources, and *predicate* and *object* could be resources or strings. *Blank nodes* are used to represent anonymous resources, typically with a structural function, e.g., to group a set of statements. Data values in RDF are called *literals*. Many formats for RDF serialization exist. In this paper we use Turtle [1], and assume that the reader is familiar with this notation.

---

[1] http://www.linkeddata.org
[2] http://www.oscb.be

Y.T. Demey and H. Panetto (Eds.): OTM 2013 Workshops, LNCS 8186, pp. 398–407, 2013.

SPARQL is the W3C standard query language for RDF [6]. The query evaluation mechanism of SPARQL is based on subgraph matching: RDF triples are interpreted as nodes and edges of directed graphs, and the query graph is matched to the data graph, instantiating the variables in the query graph definition. The selection criteria is expressed as a graph pattern in the WHERE clause, consisting basically in a set of triple patterns connected by the '.' operator.

Strabon[3] is an open-source semantic geospatial DBMS that can be used to store linked geospatial data expressed in the *stRDF format* (spatiotemporal RDF) and query them using stSPARQL (spatiotemporal SPARQL). Strabon extends the RDF store *Sesame* [2], allowing it to manage both thematic and spatial RDF data stored in the PostGIS spatial DBMS. In this way, Strabon provides features similar to those offered by geospatial DBMS that make it one of the richest RDF stores with geospatial support available today, and the main reason to adopt it as the spatial RDF data engine for the OSCB project. The data types strdf:WKT and strdf:GML allow representing geometries serialized using the OGC standards WKT and GML. The stSPARQL language extends SPARQL with functions that take as arguments spatial terms and can be used in the SELECT, FILTER, and HAVING clause of a query. Since in this paper we focus on the spatial mappings, we do not extend in the description of Strabon.

Paper Contributions. In OSCB, data providers deliver their data in relational tables or XML documents. To be openly accessed, these data are mapped to RDF triples using the R2RML mapping[4]. OSCB data are essentially spatiotemporal, therefore the mapping has to be adapted to produce spatiotemporal linked open data. Some of the datasets do not include spatial coordinates of the locations, so we had to: (a) compute the coordinates from addresses; and (b) account for this conversion in the mapping. Finally, we added data from external sources to provide context for query and analysis. In this paper we describe how we performed the above tasks in order to build a spatial data-enabled SPARQL endpoint, powered by the *Strabon* engine. In Section 2 we explain how we map spatial organizational data from OSCB contributors to stRDF triples. Section 3 describes how we obtain data and produce stRDF triples from public data providers. We also give an example of the queries that the spatial endpoint can support (Section 4). We conclude in Section 5.

2   Mapping Spatial Data Using R2RML

The W3C standard for mapping relational to RDF data, denoted R2RML, is a customized mapping whose result is a collection of RDF triples in Turtle syntax that represents all or a portion of a relational database. The main object of an R2RML mapping is the "triples map". Each triples map yields a collection of triples, composed of a "logical table", a "subject map", and zero or more "predicate object maps". A logical table is either a table name (using the predicate

---

[3] http://www.strabon.di.uoa.gr/
[4] http://www.w3.org/TR/r2rml/

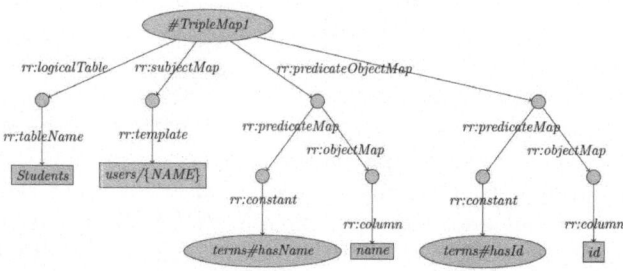

Fig. 1. R2RML mapping example

rr:tableName) or an SQL query (using the predicate rr:sqlQuery). A predicate object map is composed of a predicate map and an object map. Subject maps, predicate maps and predicate object maps are constants (rr:constant), column-based maps (rr:column) or template-based maps (rr:template). As an example, Figure 1 shows how a table Students, with attributes id and name, is mapped to RDF using the R2RML specification. This mapping can be then applied to any instance of the table, to produce the triples.

In summary, given a relational or an XML database, we produce a mapping file containing the specification for translating relational data into RDF triples (using R2RML). The mappings are generated using a common vocabulary defined in the *Gospel* ontology[5]. Finally, a mapping engine takes the database instance and the mapping file to produce the RDF document.

Adding Spatial Support to R2RML. In what follows we use three datasets provided as input by three Belgian companies: *Agenda.be, Bozar,* and *STIB.* To geolocate places we need their longitude and latitude. However, sometimes datasets contain just the address of a place (street, number, city, and postal code), thus we need to convert a full address into coordinates. This is called geocoding. From the many geocoding providers, we used Yahoo! PlaceFinder[6], a RESTful Web service which can be accessed through a web browser to get the result in JSON format. We then parse the result and retrieve the longitude and latitude, which we use in our spatial mapping.

The **Agenda.be** data reports cultural events in Brussels and the institutions where they take place. It is delivered in two XML documents: events.xml, containing events, and institutions.xml. The size of the XML files is approximately 6MB. The place and organizer in events.xml correspond to an institution in institutions.xml. For example, the (non-spatial) mapping of the event #190989 in the XML file events.xml will produce the RDF triples in Listing 1.

```
<Event_Instance>
        <EventID>190989</EventID>
```

---

[5] http://starpc18.vub.ac.be:8080/gospl/ontology/60
[6] http://developer.yahoo.com/boss/geo/docs/index.html

```
        ...
        <Event_Place>
            <Event_Place_InstitutionID >246340</
                Event_Place_InstitutionID >
            ...
        </Event_Place>
        <Event_Organisator>
            <Event_Organisator_InstitutionID >246340</
                Event_Organisator_InstitutionID >
            ...
        </Event_Organisator>
        ...
</Event_Instance>
```

```
...
<http://www.agenda.be/db/Institution/246340>
        <http://starpc18.vub.ac.be:8080/gospl/ontology/2#
            Institution_organizer_of_Event >
                <http://www.agenda.be/db/Event/190989> ;
        <http://starpc18.vub.ac.be:8080/gospl/ontology/2#
            Institution_place_of_Event >
                <http://www.agenda.be/db/Event/190989> .
```

Listing 1. Result of non-spatial mapping of events and institutions

Once we have linked events and institutions to each other, we must transform the institutions' addresses into points. The *PlaceFinder* API must receive a string with the full address, thus we need to concatenate information to produce these data. Although we can browse the XML file with XPath, this language does not allow us to create new node containing the full address. Thus, we use XSLT which allows this. The code is shown in Listing 2. When the program reaches an "Institution_Street_FR" node (we use French to find the coordinates), it looks for the zip code and city and concatenates them in a new node "Institution_Full_Address". The temporary file is then used as the original file on which the mapping is performed. Below we show how addresses are represented.

```
<Institution_Street_FR >pl. Sainte-Croix 1</
    Institution_Street_FR >
<Institution_Street_NL >Heilig-Kruisplein 1</
    Institution_Street_NL >
<Institution_HouseNumber >1</Institution_HouseNumber >
<Institution_ZipCode >1050</Institution_ZipCode >
<Institution_City_FR >Ixelles </Institution_City_FR >
<Institution_City_NL >Elsene </Institution_City_NL >
```

```
<?xml version="1.0" encoding="UTF-8" ?>
<xsl:stylesheet xmlns:xsl="http://www.w3.org/1999/XSL/
    Transform" version="2.0" >
  <xsl:template match="/">
    <xsl:apply-templates select="*"/>
```

```
  </xsl:template>
  <xsl:template match="node()">
    <xsl:copy><xsl:apply-templates select="node()"/></xsl:
        copy>
  </xsl:template>
  <xsl:template match="Institution_Street_FR">
      <xsl:copy><xsl:apply-templates select="node()"/></xsl:
          copy>
      <Institution_Full_Address>
      <xsl:apply-templates select="node()"/>
      <xsl:text> </xsl:text>
      <xsl:value-of select="../Institution_ZipCode"/>
      <xsl:text>, </xsl:text>
      <xsl:value-of select="../Institution_City_FR"/>
      </Institution_Full_Address>
  </xsl:template>
</xsl:stylesheet>
```

Listing 2. XSL file

Then, we apply the mapping in Listing 3 over the new file (we show the part relevant to the spatial mapping). Listing 4 shows the result of a concrete mapping. Note that the geographic triples are already generated in stRDF format.

```
...
    rr:logicalTable [
    rr:xpathQuery """//Institution_Instance~
      ./InstitutionID~
      ./Institution_Street_FR~
      ...
      ./Institution_City_FR~
      ./Institution_Full_Address """; ];

  rr:subjectMap [
    rr:class gospl:Address;
    rr:template "http://www.agenda.be/db/
        Address_of_Institution/{InstitutionID}";];
  ...
   rr:predicateObjectMap [
    rr:predicate geo:geometry;
    rr:objectMap [
      rr:column "Institution_Full_Address" ;
      rr:termType rr:Literal;
      rr:datatype virtrdf:Geometry;  ]; ];.
```

Listing 3. (Spatial) Mapping file for an institution

```
....
<http://www.agenda.be/db/Address_of_Institution/3>
      a    <http://starpc18.vub.ac.be:8080/gospl/ontology/2#
          Address> ;
```

```
<http :// starpc18 . vub . ac . be :8080/ gospl/ ontology /2#
    Address_of_Institution >
        <http :// www . agenda . be/ db/ Institution /3> ;
    <http :// www . w3 . org /2003/01/ geo/ wgs84_pos# geometry >
        "POINT (4.35752750.854287) ; http :// www . opengis . net/
            def/ crs/ EPSG /0/4326"^^< http :// strdf . di . uoa . gr
            / ontology# WKT > .
```

Listing 4. Portion of the result of the mapping

The **BOZAR database** stores approximately 130MB of data. The logical table in the Bozar mapping file is an aggregation of several tables dealing with activities. Addresses are stored in a table denoted location_lng, which contains information about name, address, zip and city. Its schema has the form (id, lng, field, content). The address information is represented as values of the attribute field. The concatenation is performed with a simple SQL query. For example, from the set: $\{< 110, fr, zip, 1070 >, < 110, fr, name, ABC\ Factory >$ $, < 110, fr, address, 175\ rue\ Bara >, < 110,\ fr,\ country, Belgique >, < 110, fr, city, Bruxelles >\}$, we obtain the tuple with schema (fullAddress,id): $< ABC\ Factory\ 175\ rue\ Bara\ 1070\ Bruxelles\ Belgique >$. The mapping file and resulting triple are depicted in Listings 5 and 6.

```
rr : subjectMap [
    rr : template "http :// bozar . be/ db/ Locations /{ id}";
    rr : class gospl : Location; ];

rr : predicateObjectMap [
rr : predicate geo : geometry ;
rr : objectMap [
    rr : column "fullAddress ";
    rr : termType rr : Literal ;
    rr : datatype virtrdf : Geometry ;];];
```

Listing 5. Mapping file for locations from Bozar

```
<http :// bozar . be/ db/ Locations /110>
    a       <http :// starpc18 . vub . ac . be :8080/ gospl/ ontology
        /2# Location > ;
    <http :// www . w3 . org /2003/01/ geo/ wgs84_pos# geometry >
        "POINT (4.292185 50.82917) ; http :// www . opengis .
            net/ def/ crs/ EPSG /0/4326"^^< http :// strdf . di .
            uoa . gr/ ontology# WKT > .
```

Listing 6. Triples for location id

The third component of our use case adds the *spatiotemporal* dimension. The **STIB**, *Société des Transports Intercommunaux de Bruxelles*, is the main company of public transport in Brussels. Data from STIB are stored in an SQL database that consists of four tables: **Block**, **Stop**, **Trip** and **Tripstop**. A **Block** can be seen as the time elapsed between the moment in which a vehicle leaves the warehouse and returns to it. The **Stop** table corresponds to a stop (bus, tram or

Table 1. Sample of Stop table

stp_identifier	stp_description	ud_stp_desc_flam	stp_longitude	stp_latitude
8042	ARTS-LOI	KUNST-WET	4.36963	50.8453
8032	PARC	PARK	4.36293	50.8458

metro) with its description, in French and Dutch, and its location, in x and y coordinates as well as in GPS coordinates (longitude / latitude). A Trip is a part of a block and is defined as the path between the starting point and the ending point carried on a particular route. Finally, Tripstop describes the stop and the time during a trip when the vehicle reaches the stop. The spatial mapping here is straightforward because we already have the longitude and latitude of a stop, so we can compute the point as an SQL query. Listing 7 shows the mapping file for stop locations. Listing 8 shows the resulting triple for location of stop 8042 in Table 1. Note that although the mapping produces the latitude and longitude coordinates, as well as the POINT geometry in the WKT reference system, for the sake of space we only show the latter which is what we use in the endpoint.

```
<#TM_location>
    a rr:TriplesMap ;
    rr:logicalTable [
      rr:sqlQuery """
        SELECT stp_identifier, stp_longitude, stp_latitude,
           CONCAT('POINT(',stp_longitude,' ',stp_latitude,')
           ;http://www.opengis.net/def/crs/EPSG/0/4326') as
           point
        FROM stop      """; ];

    rr:subjectMap [
      rr:template "http://www.stib.be/location/{
         stp_identifier}";
      rr:class gospl:Location;    ];
    ...
      rr:predicateObjectMap [
      rr:predicate gospl:Location_with_Latitude;
      rr:objectMap [
        rr:column "stp_latitude";
        rr:termType rr:Literal;
        rr:datatype xsd:double;    ];];

    rr:predicateObjectMap [
      rr:predicate geo:geometry;
      rr:objectMap [
        rr:column "point";
        rr:termType rr:Literal;
        rr:datatype virtrdf:Geometry; ];]; .
```

Listing 7. Mapping for a STIB location

```
<http://www.stib.be/location/8042>
    a    <http://starpc18.vub.ac.be:8080/gospl/ontology/60#
        Location> ;
    <http://starpc18.vub.ac.be:8080/gospl/ontology/60#
        Location_of_Stop>
            <http://www.stib.be/stop/8042> ;
    ...
    <http://www.w3.org/2003/01/geo/wgs84_pos#geometry>
        "POINT(4.36963 50.8453);http://www.opengis.net/def/
            crs/EPSG/0/4326"^^<http://strdf.di.uoa.gr/
            ontology#WKT> .
    ...
```

Listing 8. An RDF triple for location of stop 8042

3   Adding External Datasets

To give context to the queries over organizational data, we added places of interest in Brussels, e.g., restaurants, banks, etc. To obtain these data we queried three datasets from the linked open data web: DBPedia, GeoNames and Linked-GeoData. *DBPedia* contains structured information extracted from Wikipedia, which can be queried via a SPARQL endpoint[7]. For data extraction we built a tool in Java which queries a DBPedia service and returns RDF triples. To find places in Brussels, we used the property "is dbpedia-owl:location of". We obtained 50 different places in Brussels for which we know the location.

Our second source, *GeoNames*[8], is a geographical database covering all countries and containing information of over 8 million places. A geonames Java library allows us to access the geonames web services. We obtained 114 different places for Brussels. For example, for the Brussels central square (note that after obtaining the data we must convert spatial data into the stRDF format):

```
<http://geonames.org/6930484>
        <http://www.w3.org/2000/01/rdf-schema#label>
            "Grand Place Brussels" ;
        ...
        <http://www.w3.org/2003/01/geo/wgs84_pos#geometry>
            "POINT(4.35189 50.84681);http://www.opengis.net
                /def/crs/EPSG/0/4326"^^<http://strdf.di.uoa
                .gr/ontology#WKT> ;
```

Listing 9. A triple from GeoNames

The third data source was *LinkedGeoData*[9], a spatial database derived from OpenStreetMaps, a project that aims at building a free world map database. It consists of more than 1 billion nodes and 100 million ways (geometric constructs in which the data are based). Data can be accessed and queried via a SPARQL

---

[7] http://dbpedia.org/sparql
[8] http://geonames.org
[9] http://live.linkedgeodata.org/sparql

endpoint. As it was done for DBPedia, we queried a service and constructed RDF triples transforming the results. Since LinkedGeoData does not provide information about the city, we checked if the places are really in Brussels, adding a FILTER clause which verifies if the place is in a radius of 8 km from the center of Brussels. We obtained 2191 new places. Thus, in total we collected 2355 places from the three sources external sources, and added these data to our use case dataset, to build the spatial-enabled SPARQL endpoint.

4   Querying the SPARQL Endpoint

With all data in place we can now pose queries over the Strabon-powered endpoint[10]. Queries can return textual data or spatial data on a map. We give full details of this in [3]. As an example of a spatiotemporal query, we can ask for the *"places of events occurring on the 23 May 2013 in a radius of 200m of a stop of tram line 3"*. The following stSPARQL query computes the answer.

```
SELECT ?geo ?node ?title (GROUP_CONCAT(?description ;
    separator=",") AS ?someDescription) ?start ?end (strdf:
    buffer(?geo, 200, <http://www.opengis.net/def/uom/OGC
    /1.0/metre>) as ?buf)
FROM <http://agenda.be>
FROM <http://bozar.be>
FROM <http://stib.be>
WHERE {
  ?node gospl:DateTimeSpecification_valid_from_Date ?start .
  ?node gospl:DateTimeSpecification_valid_until_Date ?end .
  FILTER(?start <= "2013-05-23"^^xsd:date && "2013-05-23"^^
      xsd:date <= ?end)
  ?node gospl:Event_has_Title ?title .
  FILTER(langMatches(lang(?title), "FR"))
  ?node gospl:Event_with_Description ?description .
  FILTER(langMatches(lang(?description), "FR"))
  ?node gospl:Event_taking_place_at_Institution ?inst .
  ?inst gospl:Institution_with_Address ?addr .
  ?addr geo:geometry ?geo .

  ?name stib:Route_with_Name ?line .
  FILTER (?line = "3")
  ?route stib:Route_with_Route_Name ?name.
  ?route stib:Route_with_Stop ?stop .
  ?stop stib:Stop_with_Location ?loc .
  ?loc geo:geometry ?geo1.

  FILTER (strdf:distance(?geo, ?geo1, <http://www.opengis.net
      /def/uom/OGC/1.0/metre>) < 200)}
group by ?geo ?node ?title ?start ?end ?buf
```

---

[10] The endpoint can be accessed at http://eao4.ulb.ac.be:8080/strabonendpoint/

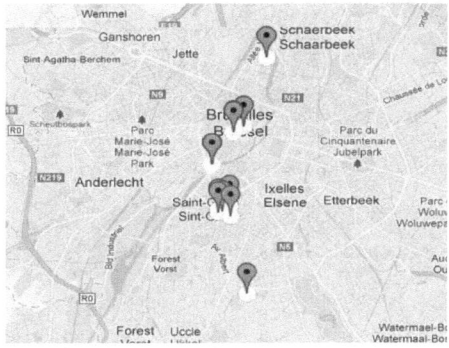

Fig. 2. Result of a query submitted to the endpoint

Figure 2 shows the result over a map. Note that in spite of the complexity of the query, it is expressed relatively easily. The query operates over the graphs in the FROM clause, then performs typical joins though the variables, and finally filters by route and distance. Other kinds of queries can be found at the endpoint.

5   Conclusion

In this paper we have described how relational to RDF mapping using the R2RML standard can be extended to support spatial data. We explain the method we used, and show the use cases employed in the OSCB project, which expose three different kinds of data: relational (Bozar), XML (Agenda.be), and spatiotemporal relational data (STIB). We show how we imported Brussels data from external sources in order to build a spatially-enabled SPARQL endpoint.

Acknowledgement. Alejandro Vaisman has been partially funded by the "Open Semantic Cloud for Brussels (OSCB)" project, funded by Innoviris.

References

1. Beckett, D., Berners-Lee, T.: Turtle - Terse RDF Triple Language (2011), http://www.w3.org/TeamSubmission/turtle/
2. Broekstra, J., Kampman, A., van Harmelen, F.: Sesame: An Architecture for Storing and Querying RDF Data and Schema Information. In: Spinning the Semantic Web Dagstuhl Seminar, pp. 197–222 (2003)
3. Chentout, K., Vaisman, A.: Mapping Spatial Data using R2RML (submitted, 2013)
4. Harris, S., Seaborne, A.: SPARQL 1.1 Query Language (2010), http://www.w3.org/TR/sparql11-query/
5. Klyne, G., Carroll, J.J., McBride, B.: Resource Description Framework (RDF): Concepts and Abstract Syntax (2004), http://www.w3.org/TR/rdf-concepts/
6. Prud'hommeaux, E., Seaborne, A.: SPARQL Query Language for RDF (2008), http://www.w3.org/TR/rdf-sparql-query/

FRAGOLA: Fabulous RAnking of GastrOnomy LocAtions

Ana Alvarado, Oriana Baldizán, Marlene Goncalves, and María-Esther Vidal

Universidad Simón Bolívar, Venezuela
{aalvarado,obaldizan,mgoncalves,mvidal}@ldc.usb.ve

Abstract. Nowadays, large open datasets are frequently accessed to select, for example, restaurants that best meet gastronomy criteria and are
closer to their current geo-spatial locations. We have developed a skyline-
based ranking approach named FOPA, which is able to efficiently rank
resources that fullfil this type of multi-objective queries. As a proof of
concept, we developed FRAGOLA (Fabulous RAnking of GastrOnomy
LocAtions), a tool that implements FOPA and ranks gastronomy locations based on multi-objective criteria. We will demonstrate FRAGOLA,
and attendees will observe scenarios where FOPA overcomes performance
of existing skyline-based approaches by up to two orders of magnitude.

1 Introduction

Under the umbrella of the Semantic Web and the Open Data initiatives, large
datasets have been published and can be publicly accessed from any node of the
Internet. Although the democratization of the information provides the basis to
manage large volumes of data, there are still applications where it is important
to efficiently identify only the best tuples that satisfy a user requirement. Particularly, large datasets of government and private recreational data are available,
and these data can be accessed to identify the places that best meet users' cuisine
requirements and are closer to her current geo-spatial location. Based on related
work, we devised a solution to this ranking problem and developed techniques
able to identify the gastronomy locations that best meet these multi-objective
queries, i.e., the gastronomy locations are not better than other gastronomy locations in terms of the multi-objective criteria. The set of non-dominated points is
known as *skyline*, i.e., set of points such that, none of them is better than the rest
[2,3]. We developed an algorithm that combines ideas from the approaches described by Balke et al. [2] and Chen et al. [3] to compute the skyline points that
best meet a multi-objective query; the algorithm implements different pruning
criteria and avoids traversing the whole space of data to compute the skyline.
Thus, the execution time as well as the number of probes required to output
the answer is minimized. We illustrate the performance of our approach on a
dataset of gastronomy locations downloaded from Zagat,[1] where restaurants are

---

[1] http://www.zagat.com/paris

Y.T. Demey and H. Panetto (Eds.): OTM 2013 Workshops, LNCS 8186, pp. 408–413, 2013.

characterized by six parameters, and queries required to rank the best restaurants expressed in terms of these parameters as well as with respect to different geo-spatial locations. The demo is published at http://fragola.ldc.usb.ve/.

2   The FRAGOLA System

An RDF document is comprised of triples that describe resources in terms of several properties; formally, this can be seen as a set of multi-dimensional points that describe each resource in terms of their properties. A multi-objective *query* is comprised of: *i*) a *condition* or list of RDF properties, and the **MIN** or **MAX** directives indicating if the values of the corresponding property must be minimized or maximized, and *ii*) the user current location. The *answer of a query q* corresponds to the points or resources in the multi-dimensional dataset D that are incomparable, i.e., the *skyline* that is composed of all the points p, such that: *i*) there is not other point p' in D with values better or equal than p in all the attributes of p, and *ii*) other points in the skyline are better than p in at least one attribute. The problem of computing the skyline is polynomial on the size of the dataset, and the goal of state-of-the-art skyline algorithms is to compute the set of incomparable points without having to perform a polynomial number of comparisons [4,5]. The FRAGOLA System seeks to illustrate how our Final Object Prunning Algorithm (FOPA) [1] achieves this goal by using some data properties, and extending features of the algorithms RSJFH [3] and IDSA [2].

These three algorithms assume that the data is stored following a vertically partitioned table representation, i.e., for each dimension or RDF property a, there exists a relation aR composed of two attributes, *Subject* and *Value*; tuples are ordered according to the attribute *Value*. Further, indices are kept on top of these tables to provide direct and sequential access, and a data structure is used to track the last values of the objects seen in each dimension. The algorithms work on iterations, where the best entry(ries) in each of the vertical tables is(are) considered in one iteration. The goal of the three algorithms is to minimize the number of comparisons between data dimensions to compute the skyline. First, the RDFSkyJoinWithFullHeader (RSJFH) algorithm proposed by Chen et al. [3], uses the data structure named header point, to record the worst values of the tuples explored in previous iterations; this information is used to guide the pruning of tuples seen in future iterations. Second, the Improved Distributed Skyline Algorithm (IDSA) proposed by Balke et al. [2] guides the search into the space of the final object, i.e., an object that has been considered in all the vertical tables; once the final object is found IDSA can ensure that a super-set of the skyline has been found, and a post-processing step is fired to discard the tuples in the super-set that are not incomparable. Although experimental studies reported in the literature [2,3] suggest that RSJFH and IDSA are efficient, both may suffer of the following drawbacks:

i) RSJFH produces incomplete results for multi-objective criteria of three or more dimensions, and *ii*) IDSA performs poorly when the final object is comprised of the worst value of at least one dimension. To overcome these limitations, we propose the skyline algorithm FOPA that assumes the following: *i*) tuples in a dataset are characterized by multi-dimensions and *ii*) tuples are stored following the vertical partition approach ordered and indexed by two indices.

Additionally, FOPA maintains information about the last values seen so far, and uses this information to guide the search of the final object. The algorithm also uses a correct pruning strategy in order to discard within the group of objects read in a given iteration, the ones that will not be part of the skyline. This allows FOPA to compute the skyline set as soon as it finds the final object or a dimension has been completely scanned, not incurring in any further comparisons. Thus, FOPA can ensure completeness while the number of comparisons and data accesses is reduced. As a proof of concept, we implemented FOPA, RSJFH and IDSA in the FRAGOLA system on top of the multi-dimensional dataset of restaurants in Paris that is provided by Zagat. Our goal is to illustrate the performance and behavior of these three algorithms.

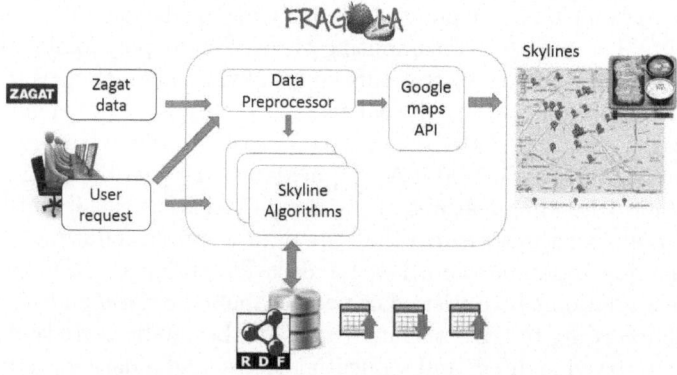

Fig. 1. The FRAGOLA Architecture

The *restaurant ontology*[2] is used to describe each restaurant, while Geonames[3] is used to describe restaurants' geo-spatial locations. FRAGOLA receives multi-objective queries that express conditions over characteristics (RDF properties) of the restaurants and users' current geo-spatial locations. The answer to a multi-objective query is the set of incomparable restaurants that comprises the skyline with respect to the attributes and directives considered in the query. FRAGOLA is comprised of the following components: a data preprocessor, the skyline engine, and Google maps' API.

The data preprocessor transforms the data provided by Zagat into a [0,1] scale and calculates the distance between the users' current geo-spatial location and that of each restaurant. The user's request allows the selection of the dimensions (RDF properties) of interest for the ranking algorithms. The processed data is then stored in vertically partitioned tables and the triples are ordered in terms of

---

[2] http://schema.org/Restaurant
[3] http://www.geonames.org/

the property values. A skyline engine implements the three skyline algorithms: IDSA, developed by Balke et al. [2], RSJFH, developed by Chen et al. [3], and FOPA. The Google map API is then used to visualize the resulting restaurant skyline set in the map. Additionally, FRAGOLA reports on the algorithms' performance in terms of the number of readings, vertically partitioned table joins, comparisons, prunnings, and the size of the skyline.

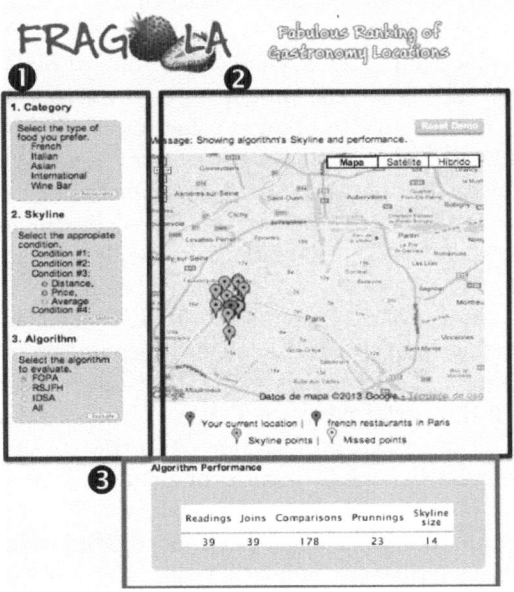

Fig. 2. The FRAGOLA GUI for the ZAGAT dataset. 1-Query Area (Three Steps: 1. Category; 2. Skyline; 3. Algorithm. These steps need to be executed in order); 2-Google Map that reports the Skyline Restaurants; 3-Metrics on the Algorithms' Performance.

Figure 2 shows the FRAGOLA interface for the ZAGAT dataset of restaurants in Paris. The area enclosed inside the rectangle number 1 shows the query interface; where the user can select restaurants of different categories, select four multi-objective queries, and compare three algorithms. Since FRAGOLA is a demo and the data used has been previously calculated the user must make each of his selections effective by clicking the "Get Restaurants", "Get Skyline" and "Evaluate" buttons after each selection, in this order. Results are reported in the Google map window in the area enclosed by the rectangle number 2; where the user's current location (fixed in Paris) is highlighted in blue, the skyline restaurants in green, and the restaurants in the skyline that cannot be found by the RSJFH algorithm are reported in yellow as missed skyline points. The user can reset the demo at all times using the "Reset Demo" button enclosed in the blue rectangle. Finally, performance is reported in the area enclosed by the rectangle 3.

3   Demonstration of Use Cases

As of February 2013, ZAGAT for Paris contains 481 restaurants, described in terms of: address, geo-spacial location[4], food category and quality, decoration, service quality, average price, overall average, and popularity index; the corresponding RDF document is comprised of 7,696 triples. We will show the impact of the dataset and skyline size on the performance and completeness of the three algorithms. First, attendees will be able to select different categories of restaurants, then, different multi-objective queries, and finally, the different algorithms. We will illustrate the location of the skyline restaurants with respect to the user current location, and the rest of the properties of these restaurants; additionally, the attendees could be able to observe values of the different metrics that measure the performance and behavior of the selected algorithms.

We will show that for the non-selective restaurant food category criterium, i.e., the french, the multi-objective query represented by *Condition 1*[5], FOPA produces the complete skyline, i.e., 13 restaurants, while the number of readings and joins is reduced by one order of magnitude and the number of comparisons is decreased by almost three orders of magnitude. RSJFH overcomes IDSA, but is only able to produce the complete answer when the skyline is small, e.g., skyline of 2 points in *Condition 2*. Otherwise, RSJFH produces incomplete answers and never overcomes the performance of FOPA. This poor performance with respect to FOPA is because RSJFH always needs to traverse at least one of the partitioned tables completely, and the number of readings, joins and comparisons increase with the size of the database. On the contrary, FOPA resembles IDSA and stops when a resource is seen in all the partitioned tables; additionally, it uses information about the resources seen in previous iterations to avoid accessing the same resource multiple times. Thus FOPA performs less number of comparisons and is able to build the skyline before traversing one of the tables completely; outperforming both RSJFH and IDSA while it generates the whole skyline.

4   Conclusions

We have stated the problem of identifying the nearest locations that best meet a set of characteristics as a skyline-based ranking problem, and proposed an algorithm that provides an efficient solution to this problem. As a proof of concept, we have developed FRAGOLA and implemented the proposed skyline algorithm on top of a dataset of restaurants annotated with geo-spacial information. We demonstrate the capabilities of the ranking techniques as well as the performance of our solution with respect to state-of-the-art solutions. Results suggest that FOPA overcomes other approaches by up to two orders of magnitude.

---

[4] Geo-spacial annotations were done manually.

[5] Condition 1 represents the restaurants that are incomparable with respect to minimal distance to the current location, minimal price and maximal popularity.

References

1. Alvarado, A., Baldizan, O., Goncalves, M., Vidal, M.-E.: Fopa: A final object pruning algorithm to efficiently produce skyline points. In: Accepted at DEXA (2013)
2. Balke, W.-T., Güntzer, U., Zheng, J.X.: Efficient distributed skylining for web information systems. In: Bertino, E., Christodoulakis, S., Plexousakis, D., Christophides, V., Koubarakis, M., Böhm, K. (eds.) EDBT 2004. LNCS, vol. 2992, pp. 256–273. Springer, Heidelberg (2004)
3. Chen, L., Gao, S., Anyanwu, K.: Efficiently Evaluating Skyline Queries on RDF Databases. In: Antoniou, G., Grobelnik, M., Simperl, E., Parsia, B., Plexousakis, D., De Leenheer, P., Pan, J. (eds.) ESWC 2011, Part II. LNCS, vol. 6644, pp. 123–138. Springer, Heidelberg (2011)
4. Fuhry, D., Jin, R., Zhang, D.: Efficient skyline computation in metric space. In: EDBT, pp. 1042–1051 (2009)
5. Skopal, T., Lokoc, J.: Answering metric skyline queries by pm-tree. In: DATESO, pp. 22–37 (2010)

User Satisfaction of a Hybrid Ontology-Engineering Tool

Christophe Debruyne[1] and Ioana Ciuciu[1,2]

[1] Vrije Universiteit Brussel – STARLab
chrdebru@vub.ac.be
[2] Joseph Fourier University – SIGMA / LIG
ioana-georgiana.ciuciu@imag.fr

Abstract. In an effort to continuously improve a research prototype for collaborative ontology engineering, we report on the reapplication of a usability test within an ontology-engineering experiment involving 36 users. The tool offers additional functionalities and measures were taken to address the problems identified in a previous study. The evaluation criteria proposed in the study were developed by taking into account the people involved, the processes and their outcomes, focusing on the user experience, in an approach that goes beyond usability; users were asked if the tool helped them in achieving their goals. We identify the problems the users encountered while using the system and also investigate whether the measures did tackle the problems observed in the first study. A set of recommendations is proposed in order to overcome these new problems and to improve the user experience with the system.

Keywords: Usability testing, user satisfaction, socio-technical systems theory, ontology engineering, social dynamics, community, HCI.

1 Introduction

We present the result of an ongoing study on the usability and user satisfaction of a collaborative ontology-engineering tool developed in the context of the Open Semantic Cloud for Brussels project[1]. The tool – which we will describe later in this paper – offers additional functionalities and measures were taken to address the problems identified in a previous study, reported in [2]. This tool was then used in an experiment similar in size and complexity as the experiment mentioned in [2], of which the user satisfaction will be presented in this paper. Next to identifying the main (usability) problems to draw conclusions and recommendations for future improvement, we also examine whether the problems reported in the previous study were properly addressed.

The rest of the paper is organized as follows: Section 2 provides the background of the paper. The usability test design is described in Section 3 and Section 4 reports on the results and presents some recommendations for improvement. Section 5 concludes and presents the future work of this research.

---

[1] http://www.oscb.be/

Y.T. Demey and H. Panetto (Eds.): OTM 2013 Workshops, LNCS 8186, pp. 414–423, 2013.

2   Background

Usability is defined by the ISO-9241 standard [7] as *the effectiveness, efficiency and satisfaction with which specified users can achieve specified goals in particular environments.* Usability is a key factor in making the systems easy to learn and to use. Usability testing has been extensively studied and applied by Lewis [10] at IBM Software Group. Classically, usability tests gather both subjective and objective data coming from realistic use case scenarios, as well as descriptions of the most common problems encountered by the test participants [8]. Subjective data reflect the participants' opinions regarding the evaluated system, while objective data reflect the participants' observed performance when using the system.

The focus of this study is the *user satisfaction* of an ontology-engineering system based on dynamic social processes. A classic way to measure the user satisfaction is via questionnaires (e.g., After-Scenario Questionnaire - ASQ, Computer System Usability Questionnaire - CSUQ [8], System Usability Scale - SUS [1]). However, a common mistake is to rely on questionnaires only while evaluating the user satisfaction. There are alternatives to measuring satisfaction with a questionnaire, e.g., the Microsoft "Desirability Toolkit". However, while the questionnaires are often biased towards positive responding, this tool helps elicit negative comments from participants [13].

A proven standard and effective instrument to assess the user satisfaction is the Post-Study System Usability Questionnaire (PSSUQ). PSSUQ was developed for scenario-based usability evaluation at IBM [8]. The environment used was an enterprise-wide and networked office application suite. A follow up study by IBM [9] was performed in the domain of speech recognition [9] using data from five years of usability studies. The follow up produced similar psychometric properties as the original survey. Fruhling and Lee [6] validate these results of the PSSUQ instrument and assess its adaptability to other domains, such as telemedicine. The reason for choosing PSSUQ for this study is mainly the richness of the provided information, with little effort from the user, and the extensive IBM documentation and experience for the statistics it can provide.

2.1   The Post-Study System Usability Questionnaire (PSSUQ)

In this study, the user satisfaction was measured using a standard instrument, namely the Post-Study System Usability Questionnaire (PSSUQ) [8,9] developed by IBM. PSSUQ originally consisted of 19 questions, each question being a statement about the usability of the system. Participants need to answer each statement using a Likert scale of 7 points, where 1 indicates that the user "strongly agrees" with the statement whilst 7 indicates that the user "strongly disagrees" with it. PSSUQ is based on a comprehensive psychometric analysis, providing scales for three sub-factors, namely: (1) system usefulness; (2) information quality; and (3) interface quality. The short version of PSSUQ (and the most recent one, see Table 1) was used with the purpose of saving study time.

PSSUQ is used in order to measure the user satisfaction when dealing with GOSPL (the collaborative ontology-engineering method and tool described in

Table 1. PSSUQ - short version [10] . The questions correspond with the three sub-factors as follows: (1) System usefulness: the avg. of items 1 through 6; (2) Information quality: the avg. of items 7 through 12; (3) Interface quality: the avg. of items 13 through 15; (4) Overall: the avg. of items 1 through 16.

Item	Item Text
Q01	Overall, I am satisfied with how easy it is to use this system.
Q02	It was simple to use this system.
Q03	I was able to complete the tasks and scenarios quickly using this system.
Q04	I felt comfortable using this system.
Q05	It was easy to learn to use this system.
Q06	I believe I could become productive quickly using this system.
Q07	The system gave error messages that clearly told me how to fix problems.
Q08	Whenever I made a mistake using the system, I could recover easily & quickly.
Q09	The information provided with this system was clear.
Q10	It was easy to find the information I needed.
Q11	The information was effective in helping me complete the tasks and scenarios.
Q12	The organization of information on the system screens was clear.
Q13	The interface of this system was pleasant.
Q14	I liked using the interface of this system.
Q15	This system has all the functions and capabilities I expect it to have.
Q16	Overall, I am satisfied with this system.

the next section). An advantage is that besides the 16 items in the test, the test participants can make comments and elaborate on their answers. Based on these comments, conclusions are drawn and recommendations for improving the human-system interaction provided.

2.2 GOSPL

GOSPL [4] is a method and tool for collaborative hybrid ontology engineering. A hybrid ontology is an ontology in which the community is promoted to first-class-citizen and all ontology evolution operators are grounded with the community agreements in which information between human stakeholders are exchanged in natural language [11]. It supports communities of stakeholder in collaboratively achieving an approximation of the domain to support their semantic interoperability requirements. Hybrid ontologies are ontologies where concepts are both described informally in natural language by means of glosses for high level reasoning between the community members and formally suitable for machine reasoning and data annotation.

Starting from co-evolving communities and requirements, the informal descriptions of key terms have to be gathered before formally describing those concepts. Communities define the semantic interoperability requirements, out of which a set of key terms is identified. Those terms need to be informally described before the formal description can be added. Concept are represented formally by means of lexons [12], which depicts a relation between to terms (referring two concepts) that hold in a particular context and in which the two roles of that relation are made explicit. In order for a lexon to be entered, at least one of the terms needs to be articulated. The terms and roles in lexons can be constrained and the community can then commit to the hybrid ontology by annotating an individual application symbols with a constrained subset of the lexons. At the same time, communities can interact to agree on the equivalence of glosses and the synonymy of terms. Synonyms are agreements that two terms refer to the same concept, and gloss-equivalences are agreements that two descriptions refer to the same concept. Committing to the ontology allows for the data to be explored by other agents via that ontology. Commitments also enable the community to re-interpret the ontology with its extension (i.e. the instances in each annotated system). This will trigger new social processes that lead to a better approximation of the domain, as the community is able to explore the increasingly annotated data, e.g., by formulating queries.

Ever since the publication of [4], the following functionalities have been added to the GOSPL prototype:

- Explicit social processes for defining the key terms and goals that constitute the semantic interoperability requirements of a community.
- Social processes for communities to agree that terms and roles in formal descriptions refer to the same concepts as classes and properties in other ontologies stored somewhere on the Web (e.g., OWL ontologies).
- Tool support for collaboratively managing application commitments.
- An RSS feed such that users did not need to check the platform for any new discussions and observe the activity by means of an RSS reader. The RSS feed has for each community commitment a separate channel, allowing one to filter to the community of interest.
- A reputation framework[2]. The reputation framework provides users how well he or she performs with respect to following the method. The reputation framework also took into account an evaluation of other users on a user's action. The users were presented "scores" as to encourage them to do better.

The problems reported in [2] were addressed as follows:

- **"The (error) messages displayed by the system were often not clear to the user. There was in general no online help or documentation available"** While teaching the method to the participants, they were offered a document and slide set (available online) in which the method and tool were explained. A running example for the creation of an application commitment was also provided.
- **"There is no "undo" or "edit" option available"** The problem reported here was not so much to undo an action, but rather to edit mistakes such as typos. Also, the outcome of a discussion sometimes differs from the initial proposition. For some social interactions, the users are now able to conclude with the final outcome.

---

[2] Details on the reputation framework will be reported elsewhere.

- **"No (top menu) link to the current community in the discussion page"** The style of the prototype has been adapted and the link to the community is made more obvious.
- **"It took a while to understand how the system works"** The availability of online documentation should solve that problem.
- **"Sometimes, listing items in the dynamic tables did not go well when after returning to a page it displayed the first item again"** This remark basically boiled down to search parameters being stored in a session such that users did not have to enter the same filter every time they leave the page. This was easily solved by storing the filters in a cookie.
- **"There was no "delete" option for the communities who "died" during the process"** As explained in [2], we did not wish to provide such a feature, as one can never know when a particular community can have an uptake. We therefore did not provide such functionality for the next experiment.
- **"The user name is not clear (just email addresses appear)"** We did not request users to provide an additional username, instead we strongly encouraged the users to use their institution's address or an address containing their names.
- **"Sometimes, more clicking necessary that one would expect (e.g. when browsing through several discussions)"** In communities with many discussions, browsing through the different discussions could have been cumbersome. This has been partly tackled by storing the filters in a cookie.

3   Test Design

The user satisfaction when interacting with the GOSPL prototype was assessed within a larger ontology-engineering experiment with a group of MSc students of a course on ontology engineering. The goal of the test is to evaluate the usability of GOSPL in two dimensions: *formative* and *summative*, from a user satisfaction point of view. The formative usability testing aims at identifying the usability problems of the tool. The summative usability test consists of a series of measurements (e.g., effectiveness, efficiency, satisfaction) which are performed in order to compare the usability results against a set of predefined objectives.

The objective of the experiment is to create a prototype ontology capturing the (shared) concepts and relations of two applications involving cultural events (e.g. concerts, exhibitions). One information system (IS) is developed by the experiment participants and one application whose database schema and data is provided to them. Both applications are portals. The objectives identified in the test are thus: (1) the ontology creation and (2) the annotation (of the IS and the existing database) with the ontology, together with their subsequent subtasks:

- Propose discussion;
- Discuss and vote;
- Conclude (accept/reject discussion);

– Create and manage a community;
– Use the ontology to annotate existing information systems.

The annotation of the existing systems is not a social process across groups of stakeholders and only concerns the users "representing" their own information system. The annotation of these systems, however, can result in new discussions as insights are gained while annotating the systems.

The satisfaction test was undertaken by a group of 23 end-users. The answers on the survey are depicted in Table 2. These end-users were part of a wider experiment involving 36 MSc in Computer Science students. In this experiment, the students were formed groups up to 4 persons to: develop their own information system, create a prototype ontology to enable semantic interoperability between those systems, and annotate their systems with the ontology.

The purpose of this study is to assess the user satisfaction with the system. The results are reported in the following section. The overall usability testing was carried out both implicitly by analyzing the data logs and the user-system interactions and explicitly, by collecting the user feedback via several questionnaires. The outcome of the experiment highlights three aspects of the evaluation: 1) effectiveness; 2) efficiency and 3) satisfaction [10]. Following the recommendations in [5] we have developed the evaluation criteria looking at the people involved, the processes and their outcomes. Some groups were completely represented in the survey (one group of 2 persons, 4 groups of 4 persons). The groups are also found in Table 2. As groups obviously worked together to ensure their own systems were annotated and hence divided the work, we will analyze the results looking at the groups and all the participants as a whole. We will furthermore compare these results with the ones reported in [2].

4 User Satisfaction: Results and Recommendations

The results delivered by the PSSUQ questionnaire are as follows (cfr. Table 3): **SysUse**: the average of all groups remained the same as in the previous study. The overall average, however, had a small decline in satisfaction with 0.1 points. **InfoQual**: compared with the previous study, the system performed better in terms of information quality with 0.3 points for the groups and 0.4 points for the overall average. **IntQual**: for both the group average and the overall average, the interface quality was deemed more satisfying with 0.1 points compared to the previous study. **Overall**: the system performed slightly better in terms of user satisfaction.

4.1 Formative User Satisfaction

Of the 23 respondents, 17 have left comments. These comments were analyzed to pinpoint the problems of the tool. When indicating an occurrence, this corresponds with a respondent making a remark about the issue at least once. Some respondents commented about a certain issue multiple times in different comment sections of the survey. The problems identified by the users in the comments section of each item are as follows:

Table 2. Respondents. On the left the answers of each of the respondents on questions Q01 to Q16. On the right we have the number of communities created (Con), discussions started (Pro), interactions in a discussion (Dis), number of votes (Vot), the number of discussions concluded (Con) and total (Tot) of all aforementioned numbers for each respondent.

User	Q01	Q02	Q03	Q04	Q05	Q06	Q07	Q08	Q09	Q10	Q11	Q12	Q13	Q14	Q15	Q16	Com	Pro	Dis	Vot	Con	Tot	Group Tot.
Group A																							1051
x1	3	2	3	2	3	2	5	3	3	2	3	2	2	2	2	5	0	24	82	156	55	317	
x2	5	5	5	4	2	4	6	5	3	3	3	5	4	4	3	4	0	16	45	106	61	228	
x3	2	2	4	1	3	4	3	3	2	5	2	1	4	3	2	2	1	41	39	151	24	256	
x4	3	2	3	2	2	2	2	4	3	2	3	4	3	4	4	2	1	74	16	132	27	250	
Group B																							1693
x5	3	3	3	2	4	3	2	3	5	3	3	2	2	2	2	2	3	84	81	187	109	464	
x6	2	2	2	3	3	3	2	3	4	4	4	4	3	3	5	3	2	85	90	365	105	647	
x7	3	3	4	3	3	4	2	3	5	3	3	2	3	2	2	2	3	82	76	136	76	373	
x8	2	3	3	3	2	3	6	5	4	4	3	4	3	4	3		2	46	7	103	51	209	
Group C																							701
x9	5	4	2	2	4	6	6	6	5	3	3	3	4	6	6	6	2	71	35	46	38	192	
x10	4	3	5	5	5	5	4	6	4	6	4	3	6	5	5	4	0	12	51	163	75	301	
x11	4	4	5	6	3	5	4	5	4	4	4	4	5	6	4	6	0	1	4	18	2	25	
x12	5	3	3	3	2	4	6	4	3	4	3	5	5	3	5	3	0	2	11	161	9	183	
Group D																							354
x13	5	6	5	4	7	5	5	6	4	4	5	6	3	3	6	5	0	7	12	58	9	86	
x14	3	3	4	3	2	4	2	4	3	4	3	3	4	4	2	3	0	11	11	59	5	86	
x15	3	2	2	2	2	3	4	2	2	2	2	1	3	3	3	3	0	3	12	52	2	69	
x16	3	3	3	2	2	3	5	2	5	2	2	2	2	2	2	2	1	34	24	38	16	113	
Group E																							448
x17	3	3	2	3	2	3	7	5	5	6	5	3	2	2	5	3	1	31	8	83	20	143	
x18	2	2	1	1	4	1	2	1	5	3	1	2	1	1	3	1	0	58	57	152	38	305	
Remainder																							N/A
x19	3	3	2	2	2	3	3	2	3	2	1	1	1	2	2		1	23	13	36	6	79	
x20	4	2	6	5	5	2	3	6	2	6	1	1	2	2	6	3	0	49	23	35	32	139	
x21	3	2	2	4	2	3	3	2	2	1	4	1	5	5	2	3	0	13	5	23	0	41	
x22	3	3	5	4	2	6	4	5	3	5	2	3	2	3	5	4	0	38	8	127	37	210	
x23	5	4	5	3	2	4	5	5	4	4	4	6	3	4	3	4	0	13	29	139	7	188	

- Keeping an overview of the discussions (10 occurrences). Some proposals have been made to tackle this problem: 2 respondents proposed a central notification system, one respondent proposed the ability to follow the actions of a particular user, another proposed an RSS feed per community complementing the overall feed[3]. Other proposals were: identifying the "hottest" discussions, offering the changes after last login and even a search function over the whole system.
- The new version of the prototype offered possibilities for creating and managing application commitments, which are built according to a particular grammar. Users noted that the errors while parsing application commitments were often too obscure to be practical and had to rely too much on our help (5 occurrences).
- Correcting mistakes (5 occurrences). The changes made to the tool to cope with mistakes or changes in a discussion proved inadequate to improve the user's satisfaction. They wished the ability to "undo" or "cancel" an interaction. One respondent also suggested the possibility to alter a comment.

---

[3] Even though one could filter on channel.

Table 3. Summative user satisfaction: results looking at the groups, average of all complete groups, average all respondents and results of the previous study

Metric	A	B	C	D	E	Average groups	Average all users	Average reported in [2]
SysUse $(Q01 \rightarrow Q06)$	2.9	2.9	4.0	3.4	2.3	3.1	3.2	3.1
InfoQual $(Q07 \rightarrow Q12)$	3.2	3.5	4.3	3.3	3.8	3.6	3.5	3.9
IntQual $(Q13 \rightarrow Q15)$	3.1	2.8	5.0	3.1	2.3	3.3	3.3	3.4
Overall $(Q01 \rightarrow Q16)$	3.1	3.1	4.4	3.3	2.8	3.3	3.3	3.4

- Problems creating constraints (4 occurrences). Surprisingly, the functionality of building constraints has not changed and yet 4 people reported that the construction of constraints was confusing. 2 of these 4 respondents also mentioned that the verbalization of these constraints were not clear.
- The voting mechanism (4 occurrences). 3 respondents wished the system would require a justification when one is against a proposal. With an additional respondent stating the voting system to be inadequate for stimulating the discussion.
- Imposing the GOSPL Method (2 occurrences). The tool has been developed for the GOSPL method, yet some freedom is allowed as to offer possibilities to deviate from the method or adopt other methods such as Business Semantics Management [3] that prescribe similar activities in a different order.
- Even though documentation was available as well as a running example in the slide set, participants wished for documentation within the tool next to the material offered (5 occurrences) and more examples (4 occurrences). Three participants merely noted there was not enough documentation without providing further details.
- Availability of concrete (worked out) examples and tutorials next to the documentation (3 occurrences).
- Availability of help functionality within the tool rather than online in separate documents (2 occurrences).
- Lastly, there were 4 complaints of the back button resulting in a warning on a discussion page. This needed to be added as the reputation framework kept track of the discussions visited by a user and one of the popular browsers not capturing the event of clicking the back-button properly. To this end, we asked the users whether they "wished to leave the page", whereupon a click on the button "Yes" called the method for logging.

4.2   Recommendations for Improvement

Taking the satisfaction results obtained from PSSUQ and the user comments, we drive the following conclusions: out of the three sub-factors identified by PSSUQ the system usefulness performed best (3.2). The users of this study seemed to be less satisfied than in the previous study. Information quality had a fairly important improvement in terms of satisfaction with respect to the previous study. Taking into account the complaints on error handling of the commitment

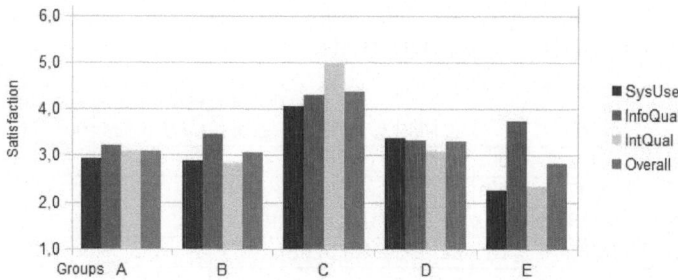

Fig. 1. Bar chart of user satisfaction results per sub-factor, per group

manager (which was added to the prototype), we can conclude this is a very positive evolution. Both the interface quality and overall satisfaction evolved positively. The following steps will be taken to improve the system:

1. Investigating how the overview of all the discussions can be improved.
2. Improving the interface for managing the application commitments.
3. Allowing actions to be undone (i.e., "cancel" or "undo") in case of error.
4. Improving the verbalization and forms for constructing constraints.
5. Participants complained that the voting system did not require users not agreeing to a proposal to justify their opinion. The goal of the voting system was to allow users to participate to discussions in a "lightweight" manner. After the experiment, however, we feel that the voting mechanisms did not contribute to the discussion and sometimes lead to confusion. We therefore will most remove the voting mechanism.
6. Imposing the method. In other words, add pre-conditions to the social interactions such that the tool is completely compliant with the GOSPL method, thereby loosing the possibility to use the tool with other methods.

We observed a need for more worked out examples and the availability of help functionality within the tool rather than online in a separate document.

5   Conclusion and Future Work

In conclusion of this study, we provide a synthesis of the results in Fig. 1 illustrating the 3 sub-factors per group. Compared to the previous iteration of the user satisfaction testing, and as discussed in the previous section, we observe a overall improvement of the user satisfaction. In particular, positive evolutions have been obtained regarding the information quality and the interface quality.

Future work will consider testing the user satisfaction in particular and the usability testing in general from a socio-technical systems theory point of view with users from various domains, different than students.

Acknowledgements. This study was supported by the INNOViris Open Semantic Cloud for Brussels project, financed by the Brussels Capital Region.

References

1. Brooke, J.: Sus-a quick and dirty usability scale. Usability Evaluation in Industry, 189–194 (1996)
2. Ciuciu, I., Debruyne, C.: Assessing the User Satisfaction with an Ontology Engineering Tool Based on Social Processes. In: Herrero, P., Panetto, H., Meersman, R., Dillon, T. (eds.) OTM-WS 2012. LNCS, vol. 7567, pp. 242–251. Springer, Heidelberg (2012)
3. De Leenheer, P., Christiaens, S., Meersman, R.: Business semantics management: A case study for competency-centric HRM. Computers in Industry 61(8), 760–775 (2010)
4. Debruyne, C., Meersman, R.: GOSPL: A Method and Tool for Fact-Oriented Hybrid Ontology Engineering. In: Morzy, T., Härder, T., Wrembel, R. (eds.) ADBIS 2012. LNCS, vol. 7503, pp. 153–166. Springer, Heidelberg (2012)
5. Dillon, A.: Beyond usability: process, outcome and affect in human-computer interactions. Journal of Library and Information Science 26(4) (2008)
6. Fruhling, A.L., Lee, S.M.: Assessing the reliability, validity and adaptability of pssuq. In: Khazanchi, D., Zigurs, I. (eds.) AMCIS, p. 378. Association for Information Systems (2005)
7. ISO: ISO 9241-11: Ergonomic requirements for office work with visual display terminals (vdts) – part 11: Guidance on usability. Technical report, ISO (1998)
8. Lewis, J.R.: IBM computer usability satisfaction questionnaires: Psychometric evaluation and instructions for use (technical report 54.786). Technical report, Human Factors Group, IBM (1993)
9. Lewis, J.R.: Psychometric evaluation of the pssuq using data from five years of usability studies. International Journal of Human-Computer Interaction 14(3-4), 463–488 (2002)
10. Lewis, J.R.: Usability testing. In: Handbook of Human Factors and Ergonomics, 4th edn., pp. 1267–1312. John Wiley (2012)
11. Meersman, R., Debruyne, C.: Hybrid Ontologies and Social Semantics. In: Proceedings of 4th IEEE International Conference on Digital Ecosystems and Technologies (DEST 2010). IEEE Press (2010)
12. Meersman, R.: The Use of Lexicons and Other Computer-Linguistic Tools in Semantics, Design and Cooperation of Database Systems. In: CODAS, pp. 1–14 (1999)
13. Travis, D.: Measuring satisfaction: Beyond the usability questionnaire (2009), http://www.userfocus.co.uk/articles/satisfaction.html

Towards a Hierarchy in Domain Ontologies

Peter Bollen

Department of Organization and Strategy
School of Business and Economics
Maastricht University
P.O. Box 616
6200 MD Maastricht, The Netherlands
p.bollen@maastrichtuniversity.nl

Abstract. This paper defines a language for modeling ontologies in business applications and application services. This language consists of the modeling constructs from Natural Language Modeling (NLM). It will be shown in this article how the application of this modeling language will enable us to model a hierarchy for a domain ontology.

1   Introduction

As the number of information services (e.g. web-services, application service providers and e-commerce applications) continues to grow and the need for interoperability between those services becomes apparent (i.e. the semantic web), the availability of a modeling language that enables analysts to capture the precise semantics of such an application information service will become a necessity. Such a language should not only be able to capture the application semantics for the user-group that is the provider of the information service, but it should also contain modeling provisions that enable comprehension by the potential client groups of such an information service (e.g. autonomous agents). The language; therefore; must be able to establish links with common business ontologies and should be easy to understand by non-expert users. Such a language must be very close to the natural language that is used by people in their daily communications.

We will define ontology in this paper as "the definition of the basic terms and relations comprising the vocabulary of a topic area"[1], or according to Gruber [2]: "an anthology is a description of the concepts and relationships for an agent or a community of agents." We will, therefore, provide modeling constructs in this paper that can be used within the context of a specific universe of discourse in which in principle different users are involved. The information modeling constructs in NLM are based upon the axiom that all verbalizable information (computer screens, reports, note-books, traffic signs and so forth) can be translated into *declarative natural language sentences* [3]. It means that it is *neither* a real *nor* an abstract world that is subject to modeling, but the *communication about* such a real or abstract world. This will constrain the feasible modeling constructs to those constructs that enable analysts to model natural language sentences.

Y.T. Demey and H. Panetto (Eds.): OTM 2013 Workshops, LNCS 8186, pp. 424–431, 2013.

2   The Modeling Constructs in NLM for the Information Structure

A name in human communication is used to refer to a concept or a thing in a real or abstract world [4]. A *name* is a sequence of words in a given language that is agreed upon to refer to *at least* one concept or thing in a real or abstract world, for example, *Jake Jones, 567893AB, General Electric*. We will call the union of all names the *archetype*.

The choice of names used in communication is constrained by the reference requirement for effective communication. For example, the university registration office will use a *student ID* for referring to an individual *student*. The use of names from the name class *last name* in the university registration subject area for referring to individual students, however, will not lead to effective communication because in some cases two or more students may be referenced by *one* name instance from this name class. This is one of the reasons why not all names can be used for referencing entities, things or concepts in a specific part of a real or abstract world.

2.1   The Natural Language Axiom

In every (business) organization examples of communication can be found. These examples can be materialized as a computer screen, a worldwide web page, a computer report or even a formatted telephone conversation. Although the outward appearance of these examples might be of a different nature every time, their content can be expressed using natural language. We will refer to this class of examples of communication as *verbalizable* information [5].

V⊔	Vandover University Enrollment	
Student ID	**Last Name**	**Major**
1234	Thorpe	Science
5678	Jones	Economics
9123	Thorpe	History

Fig. 1. Example Vandover University Enrollment

Now that we have defined the possible application areas for NLM we can start defining modeling constructs that can take natural language sentences as a starting point. In figure 1 an example of a *university enrollment document* is given. In this example the Vandover University wants to record information about the major for each of its students. It is assumed that the *student ID* can be used to identify a *specific* student among the *union* of students that are (and have been) enrolled in the Vandover University, and that a *major name* can be used as identifier for a *specific* major among the *union* of majors that are offered by the Vandover University. The application of the natural language axiom on the example of communication from figure 1 can lead to for eample following sentence instances.

The student 1234 majors in Science..*(sentence 1.1)*
The student 5678 majors in Economics...*(sentence 1.2)*

2.2   Roles

If we analyze example sentences 1.1 an 1.2 that have resulted from verbalizing the university enrollment example in figure 1, we can divide them into two groups according to the type of sentence predicate (..majors..., respectively ..has last name..). If we focus on the first group we can derive two sentence group templates in which we have denoted the predicate as text, and the variable parts as text between brackets: *Student <enrolled student> majors in major <chosen major>* and *Student <enrolled student> has chosen the major <chosen major>*. We will refer to the variable parts as *roles*. Figure 2 shows a graphical representation of the two sentence groups in the University Enrollment example. Each role is represented by a "box", e.g. *enrolled student*. Each sentence group is represented by a combination of role boxes. Sentence group *Sg1* is represented by the combination of role boxes *enrolled student* and *chosen major*. Sentence group *Sg2* is represented by the combination of "role" boxes *registered student* and *last name*. For each sentence group one or more sentence group templates are positioned underneath the combination of role boxes that belong to the sentence group. In the diagram of figure 2, sentence group templates 1 and 2 belong to sentence group *Sg1*. Sentence group template 3 belongs to sentence group *Sg2*.

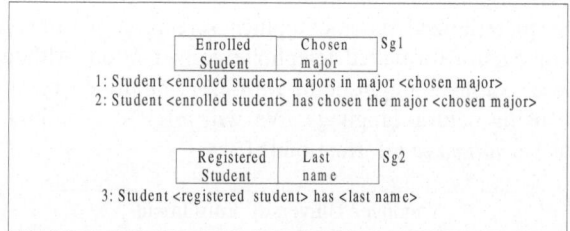

Fig. 2. Roles, sentence group and sentence, group template(s) for university enrollment

If we inspect figure 2 we will see that a sentence group template can reveal additional information about the type of things that can be "inserted" into a *role* variable. For example, the word "student" specifies what type of thing (or concept) is allowed to play the role "enrolled student" but also what type of thing (or concept) is allowed to play the role "registered student". We will call the "student" part in the sentence groups in figure 2 the *intension* of the roles "enrolled student" and "registered student".

To make an application's ontology explicit, we need to incorporate a definition of the concepts in the sentence group templates including the intensions. For example, the defintion of the concept *Student: A student is a person that studies at a University.* The names of things or concept instances to which such a definition of intension applies within a *specific* application subject area at a *specific* point in time is called the *extension*. We can now give an example extension for the intension *Student*: *(1234, 5678, 912)*. In the remainder of this paper we will use the term *intension* to denote the *type* of thing or concept to which a *specific* thing or concept belongs. In the following illustration we have given an example of such a list for the university enrollment UoD.

Concept	Definition
Student	a person that studies at Vandover University
Student ID	a name class
Major	a course program offered to [student]s by Vandover University
Major name	a name class
Last name	a name class

Such a list of concepts and their definitions should contain a definition for *each* intension in the UoD. The definition of an intension should specify how the knowledge forming the intension (*definiendum*) is to be constructed from the knowledge given in the definition itself and in the defining concepts (*definiens*). A defining concept should either be an intension or a different concept that must be previously defined in the list of concepts or it should be defined in a common business ontology.

2.3   Naming Convention Fact Types

In this section we will further formalize the outcome of the process of the selection of a name class for referring to things in a real or abstract world. The outcome of such a naming process will result in the utterance of sentences, for example sentence 2.1

1234 is a name from the   student ID name class that can be used to identify a student within the union of students at Vandover University..(sentence 2.1)

We see that sentences 2.1 express that a certain *name* belongs to a certain *name class* and that instances of the name class *student ID*, can be used to identify an instance of a *student,* and an instance of the name class *major name*, can be used to identify an instance of a *major* within the UoD of Vandover University. We can give, for example, the definition of the concept *Student ID*: *Student ID is a name class.* The 'intension' of the names in sentence 2.1 is a   *name class* and NOT a type of *thing, entity* or *concept* in the real world. We will, therefore, refer to facts 2.1 as a *naming convention facts*. The corresponding fact type will then be called a *naming convention fact type.*

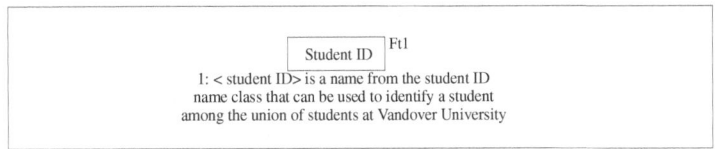

Fig. 3. Naming convention fact type for *student*

The unification of simple reference schemes and the different types of compound reference schemes into one uniform way of referencing, and the capability to capture the precise semantics of naming conventions are improvements in NLM to the predecessor methodologies.

2.4 The Basic Information Model

A *basic information model* (BIM) for a Universe of Discourse *U* is defined by a list of concepts and their definitions applicable to that UoD, a set of roles, a set of fact types, and a set of sentence group templates for every fact type. The *extension* of a BIM is the union of the extensions of the fact types that are contained in that basic information model (see figure 4).

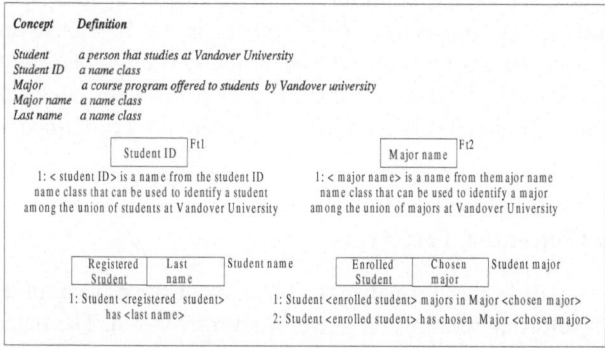

Fig. 4. Basic information model University enrollment

3 Population Constraints

In this section we will introduce the modeling constructs that will make it possible to explicitly show that some extensions of a *basic information model* are **not** allowed to exist. In order to make a distinction between an extension of a basic information model (regardless of the fact whether it is allowed to exist), and an extension of a basic information model that is allowed to exist, we will introduce the concept of *population state*. A *population state* is an extension of a basic information model that is allowed to exist.

We can consider a *population state* as a further reduction of the extensions in the set of *possible* extensions of a basic information model. After the restriction of the names to the name classes that can be used to identify a specific *thing*, *entity* or *concept* in the application UoD, we will further restrict the extensions that are allowed to exist by incorporating specific *domain knowledge* or those *domain rules* (sometimes called *business rules*) that can be expressed as propositions on the basic information model that must be true for **every** population state. We will call such a proposition a *population state constraint*. A *population state constraint p* in a basic information model *BIM* limits the allowed extensions of the basic information model *BIM* to those extensions that comply to the proposition specified in the population state constraint *p*.

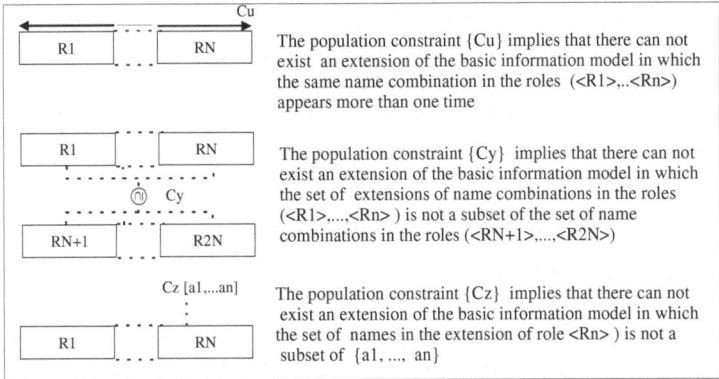

Fig. 5. Legend for uniqueness, subset and value population state constraints

The business rule: a student can be enrolled in at most one major, can be expressed as the following constraint instance from the constraint legend in figure 5: The population constraint c7 implies that there can not exist an extension of the basic information model in which the same name in the role **enrolled student** appears more than one time. If we check this example thoroughly we can conclude that the addition of a population state constraint onto a (basic) information model actually eliminates those extensions from the set of extensions that do **not** comply to the proposition. In this example we can see that the example extension : {student 1234 majors in major science, student 1234 majors in major economics} does **not** comply to the proposition of population state constraint c7.

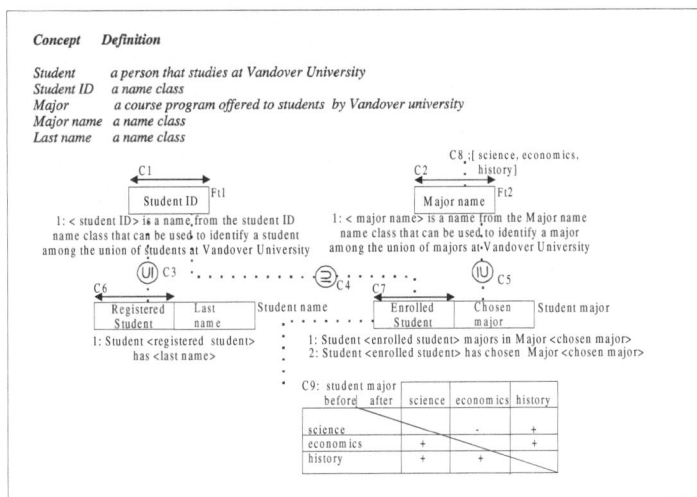

Fig. 6. Information model for university enrollment example

We can now define an information model. An information model referring to a universe of discourse is a *basic information model* for that UoD together with all *population constraints* that reflect the business rules in that UoD and that can be defined on the roles of the basic information model for that UoD. In figure 6 the resulting information model for the student enrollment UoD application area is shown. The legend for the interpretation of the population state constraint symbols that are used in figure 6 is given in figure 5.

4 Integration of the NLM Information Model and the Application Ontology

We can put the concepts of *archetype, name class, naming convention fact type* and *non-naming convention fact type* in a *hierarchy*. In every application subject area (including the analyst's subject area) we can distinguish three segments in an information model.

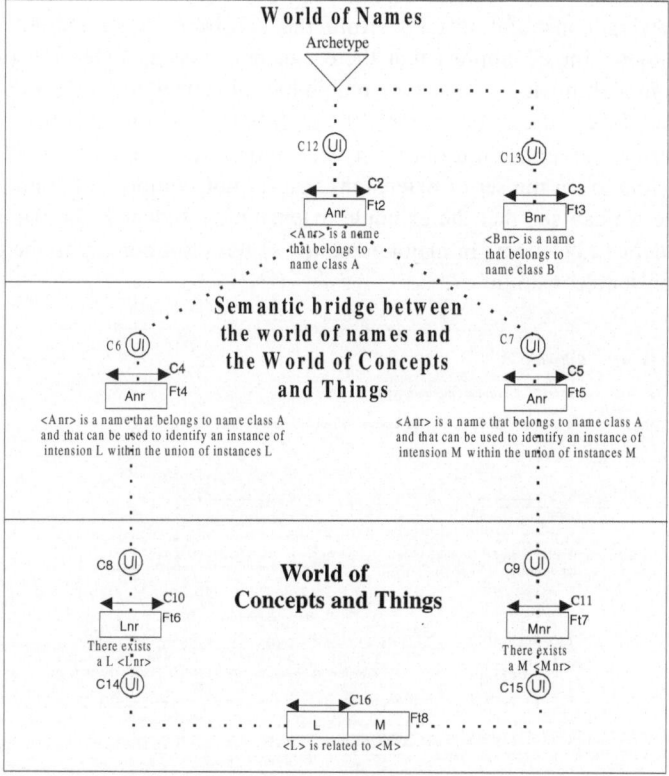

Fig. 7. Hierarchy in information models

The *top* segment consists of the world of names in which the *archetype,* (and, when applicable, the relevant *scale types)* and the *relevant name classes* for the application subject area are defined. In the *middle* segment we find the naming convention fact types for the intensions that are relevant for the application subject area. How this 'semantic bridge' is created should be laid down precisely in an information modeling procedure. The *lowest* segment in the application information grammar consists of the application fact types that can be derived whenever the verbalization axiom is applied to an application subject area.

5   Conclusion

In this paper we have defined the modeling constructs in *natural language modeling*. The defined constructs will enable us to define a hierarchy in every information model. This hierarchy replaces the distinction between *concepts* and *names* by considering names as populations of fact types in the hierarchy. The verbs in the fact types then will explicitly show whether a fact type declares the existence of a concept, the existence of a name that can be used to identify a concept or a semantic relationship among concepts. In case the Universe of Discourse refers to an application service environment in which different (partly unknown) user groups are involved, the list of concept definitions serves as a semantic connection between the provider of the application service and the different user- "agents" that do not necessarily share the same ontological background. NLM enables an application analyst to create multiple lists of concept definitions, if necessary, to share the application's semantics with users having a different ontological background.

References

1. Neches, R., et al.: Enabling technology for knowledge sharing. AI Magazine, 36–56 (Fall 1991)
2. Gruber, T.: A translation approach to portable ontologies. Knowledge Acquisition 5(2), 199–220 (1993)
3. Nijssen, G.: An axiom and architecture for information systems. In: Information systems concepts: an in-depth analysis (1989)
4. Senko, M.: DIAM as a detailed example of the ANSI/SPARC architecture. In: Nijssen, G. (ed.) Modelling in Database Management Systems. North-Holland (1976)
5. Nijssen, G.: On experience with Large-Scale Teaching and Use of fact-based Conceptual Schema's in Industry and University. In: Meersman, R., Steel, J. (eds.) IFIP Conference on Data Semantics (DS-1), pp. 189–204. North-Holland (1986)

Semantic Oriented Data Structuration
for MABS Application to BIM
Short Paper

Thomas Durif[1], Christophe Nicolle[1], Nicolas Gaud[2], and Stéphane Galland[2]

[1] Le2I, Université de Bourgogne, Dijon, France
{thomas.durif,christophe.nicolle}@checksem.fr
http://www.checksem.fr
[2] IRTES-SET, UTBM, Belfort, France
{nicolas.gaud,stephane.galland}@utbm.fr
http://set.utbm.fr

Abstract. This paper presents a multiagent-based simulation approach to qualify the usage of buildings from the design phase. Our approach combines ontology and evolution process based on machine learning algorithms. The ontology relies on semantic data structures for the representation of environment components, agent knowledge and all data generated during the simulation.

Keywords: ontology, modular ontology, Building Information Modeling, MultiAgent-Based Simulation.

1 Introduction

This paper[1] focuses on the application of multiagent-based simulation at the design phase of a civil engineering project. The output of the design phase is a 3D digital mockup that represents the future building. From this digital modeling, each stakeholder, according to their business, adds information to enrich the specification of the building model. All this data represents the Building Information Model (BIM) [2]. Each actor in this lifecycle uses specific norms and tools according to their domain of expertise.

To reduce the risk of heterogeneity the Building smart consortium developed a standard, called Industry Foundation Classes (IFC), that merges structural and geometrical data of a building to reduce heterogeneity. Unfortunatelly even if the structural, syntactic and semantic heterogeneity of data is limited, this standard doesn't deal with the gap between the conception of the building and its final use. To bridge this gap, our idea consists in simulating the behavior of the end users of a building to assess the quality of a building in terms of safety (e.g. security protocols), usability (e.g. the adaptation of capacity building are consistent with its use), comfort (e.g. limitation of movements required for routine tasks), etc.. To reach this goal, we use the field of Multiagent-based simulations (MABS), which are simulations that imply a group of interacting agents. Our approach

---

[1] This work is partially funds by the Burgundy region.

Y.T. Demey and H. Panetto (Eds.): OTM 2013 Workshops, LNCS 8186, pp. 432–436, 2013.

combines a set of ontology (IFC ontology, multiagent ontology, environment ontology), with machine learning algorithms.

From there, we propose a new process for create MABS. It is based on an auto generated phase of different parts of MABS: environment, agents, interactions, simulations (specific features, logs, etc.) [5]. On the one hand, the semantically informed environment of the simulation is auto generated from an industrial file format of building representation IFC. On the other hand, minimal patterns of mobile learning agents are auto generated, based on specific features, from the agent part of the model we create. These elements will be discussed in the section entitled Approach, after introducing works in the field of semantics and MABS in the section entitled Related Works.

2 Related Work

Various proposals includes semantics to improve Multi-Agent Based System (MABS). In [6], authors defined a taxonomy for an agent. Unfortunately, this task is complex because many approaches have different agents' definitions. It is possible to fit a large number of definitions, while limiting to a minimum specific constraints to certain areas. Semantics are the key point of this generic definition, as each expert can bring its own domain knowledge to each of the characteristics of a MABS. [3] focuses on the description of the interactions in an ontology. Goals are modeled as states of the environment. These goals are reached by means of inference based on the related ontology. Nevertheless, the contribution of semantics is limited to interactions including all MABS concepts. In [8], the work involves using an ontology to store the management of the agent's knowledge. Several specific features of ontologies are used (inferences, class hierarchy, queries, etc.). However, only the part affected to the agent's knowledge has been enhanced by the use of semantics. [4] describes a more complete approach. For managing the three basic elements of a multi-agent system : agents, environment and interactions. This approach represents the knowledge to lead a person to manipulate an object in a hazardous environment. It models the interactions of objects, but also the results produced by an interaction. This approach is also focused on training agents in a virtual environment. In this approach, the population process of the ontology is long. Each object required a manual specification for states, interactions, transitions, etc. All these approaches presented models don't consider the ontology as the central point for managing all data inherent to a simulation applied to MABS. Each approach addresses only a specific element of a MABS, that is either the agent, the simulation or the environment. To break these limits, our approach is based on a industrial process (building design) and its standards (IFC). Thus, the population of the ontology is dynamically made from the IFC files generated from CAD softwares.

3 Approach

We propose a new methodology to create a MABS based on: automatic generation of the physical informed environment and self built smart agents. This feature provides the process of creating and managing a MABS. Our approach addresses four elements of a MABS : environment, agents, interactions and simulations. Our approach is based on a set of linked ontologies [10]. Each ontology is a domain ontology dedicated to the modeling of a specific area of expertise. In our context of knowledge managment, we use the term ontology to mean a specification of a conceptualization, as defined by [7]. This mixed of ontologies is depicted in figure 1.

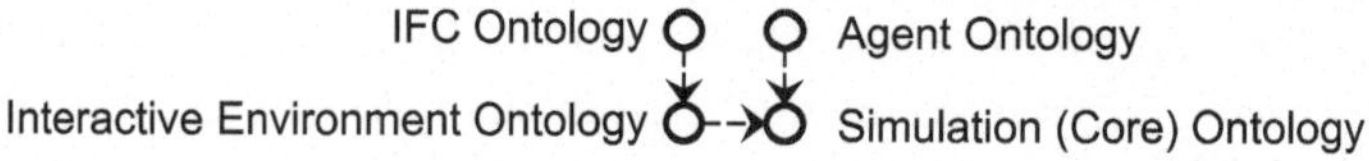

IFC Ontology ○   ○ Agent Ontology
Interactive Environment Ontology ○--→○ Simulation (Core) Ontology

Fig. 1. overview of the general ontology model

The IFC ontology contains the formal modeling of semantic and geometric information which model a building. These information are built during the design phase with CAD softwares. These softwares store the 3D digital mockup into an IFC files that are used to populate the IFC ontology. To populate this ontology we use a home made memory model in Java programming language. This first element allows our approach to be closed from industrial requirements. The 3D digital mockup is directly extract for CAD software not modeled using modeler software as usual in MABS proposals.

We propose a semantically aware environment automatically generated from the IFC standard [11]. The interactive environment ontology is dedicated to the modeling of the dynamical part of the simulation. this ontology uses some entities of the IFC ontology to combined building element (semantic and geometric definition) with smart objects (behavioral definition) [9]. A smart object is an object that can describe its own possible interactions. Thanks to the semantic obtain from the IFC ontology, the binding between smart objects and building objects is easier. A behaviour of a door can be connected with all *IFCDoor* instances defined in the IFC ontology. Thus the modeling time of the simulation is greatly reduced. The population process of this ontology is made by the domain expert, which defined the various states of a building objects and the different processes to move from an original state to a final state. The agent ontology describes the agent elements of the simulation. The agent are made of many concepts describing their ability to move, to interact with environmental objects, to interact with other agents, and to exchange requirements with the system managing the simulation. This definition of agent is derived from the ontology defined in [1] which aims to standardize the various definitions of multiagent-based simulation. The use of this ontology allow our approach to be compatible with different types of multi-agent based systems. The population of this ontology is made by the expert of the simulation.

The top ontology integrates many entities of these various ontology. The simulation results, whatever their forms (3D modeling, knowledge, decisions, etc..) can be (re)used at any time during the simulation or other processing. This ontological foundation helps to provide a consistent basis for heterogeneous information, from both specific concepts related to contributing experts, and to the use of simulations and MABS.

A specific inference engine complete our architecture. It fixes the issues raised by agents that are unable to solve complex situations. The agents are autonomous and they need four basic characteristics: mouvement, perception, interaction and reasoning. To increase their knowledge, we force these agents to face simple situations. This results in an improved agents ability to face more complex behaviors. These agents will face simple situations to progress in knowledge that results in more complex behaviors. Secondly, we place these agents in real life simulation in environments based on real building plans.

In the followoing, we give a short overview of the process to build this simulation (see figure 2)

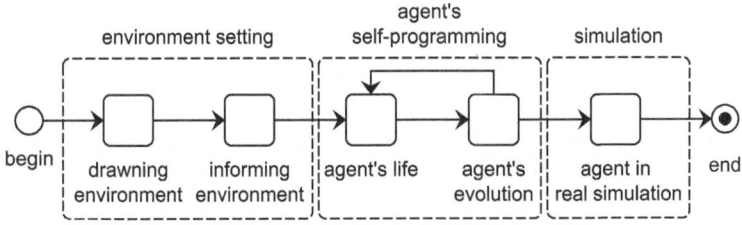

Fig. 2. overview of the process to build the simulation

To build a MABS, the environment and the agents need to be programmed. Firstly, the environment is created. IFC file and its implementation in the IFC ontology sets necessary information for structural and semantic perspectives. The environment needs an additional layer of information: everything related to the description of interactions. In the Interactive Environment Ontology, this information is already available. So as we already have all the information about the environment, this phase (environment setting) can be performed automatically.

Secondly, agents should be incorporated into the simulation. All the tools for defining agents are modeled in the Agent Ontology. From this ontology, the basic characteristics of agents are selected and extracted to create some basic agents. The designer of the simulation will put these agents in simple situations. A simple situation does not require from an agent specific knowledge to achieve the goal. Agents will accumulate knowledge about the behaviors needed on how to use objects. The designer sets a level for which it is considered that the agent has enough evolve in terms of knowledge to be confronted with the simulation in real conditions.

When this level is reached by the agents, they will be placed at different places of the environment with various profiles and they will move freely and test the usage of the building. Observation and treatment of agents' actions in certain contexts and according to their profiles will qualifying the usage of the building.

4   Conclusion

This paper outlined the steps necessary to build our ontology and the need to define semantic knowledge a MABS. Thanks to the ontology, our approach improve simulation process (reducing the definition of the environment, introducing a new way for agent progamming) and insert MABS in civil engineering projects. Future works concerns the development of the full platform combined with real building projects.

References

1. Béhé, F., Durif, T., Nicolle, C., Galland, S., Gaud, N., Koukam, A.: Ontology-based multiagent systems using Inductive Recommendations. In: 12th International Conference on Design & Decision Support Systems in Architecture and Urban Planning, Eindhoven, Pays-Bas (August 2012)
2. Bernstein, P.G., China, F.: Building information modeling. Structural Engineer (Atlanta, Ga) 6(7), 18–21 (2005)
3. Chang, P.H.M., Chien, Y.H., Kao, E.C.C., Soo, V.W.: A knowledge-based scenario framework to support intelligent planning characters. In: Panayiotopoulos, T., Gratch, J., Aylett, R.S., Ballin, D., Olivier, P., Rist, T. (eds.) IVA 2005. LNCS (LNAI), vol. 3661, pp. 134–145. Springer, Heidelberg (2005)
4. Edward, L., Amokrane, K., Lourdeaux, D., Barthes, J.P.: An ontology for managing a virtual environment for risk prevention. In: 2010 First International Conference on Integrated Intelligent Computing (ICIIC), pp. 62–67. IEEE (2010)
5. Ferber, J.: Multi-agent systems: an introduction to distributed artificial intelligence, 1st edn. Addison-Wesley Reading (1999)
6. Franklin, S., Graesser, A.: Is it an agent, or just a program?: A taxonomy for autonomous agents. In: Jennings, N.R., Wooldridge, M.J., Müller, J.P. (eds.) ECAI-WS 1996 and ATAL 1996. LNCS, vol. 1193, pp. 21–35. Springer, Heidelberg (1997)
7. Gruber, T.R.: Toward principles for the design of ontologies used for knowledge sharing. Int. J. Hum.-Comput. Stud. 43(5-6), 907–928 (1995)
8. Holmes, D., Stocking, R.: Augmenting agent knowledge bases with owl ontologies. In: 2009 IEEE Aerospace Conference, pp. 1–15. IEEE (2009)
9. Kallmann, M., Thalmann, D.: Modeling objects for interaction tasks. In: 9th Eurographics Workshop on Animation and Simulation, pp. 73–86 (1998)
10. Stuckenschmidt, H., Parent, C., Spaccapietra, S.: Modular Ontologies: Concepts, Theories and Techniques for Knowledge Modularization, vol. 5445. Springer, Heidelberg (2009)
11. Vanlande, R., Nicolle, C., Cruz, C.: IFC and Buildings Lifecycle Management. Automation in Construction (18), 70–78 (2008)

Towards Bottom Up Semantic Services Definition

Cristian Vasquez

Semantics Technology and Applications Research Lab,
10G731, Vrije Universiteit Brussel, Brussels, Belgium
cvasquez@vub.ac.be

Abstract. This paper explores a bottom up approach to support service interoperability between distinct stakeholders. Bottom up approaches are useful in ecosystems where coming up with semantic agreements is difficult. Key here is the flexibility for the distinct stakeholders to diverge and converge by means of agreement in their service definitions, driven in an emergent dynamic process that eventually may lead to a stable service network using a bottom up approach.

Keywords: Collaborative service construction, Web Blackboards.

1 Introduction

Within this paper, we explore an approach that aims to support a group of stakeholders in their collaborative definition of information services. Although we observe that there is no wide consensus on what the exact meaning of "service" is, we still can categorize them according to their context of use, such as: (i) IT context, which regards to the implementation or specification to build semantic applications and (ii) business context, which can be seen as a theoretical model referring to real-world objects aligned to some process among stakeholders [7].

When a group of stakeholders need to define services collaboratively on decentralized environments such as the WWW, they will face numerous difficulties. To archive an effective service interaction, first they have to benefit of agreed semantics, a task that is usually not trivial. Here, each stakeholder need to express their intended meaning explicitly (i.e. agreeing on the meaning of the terms used by each service), keeping a minimal coherence between conceptual, implementation and their business directives. At the same time they have to keep a sufficient level of implementation independence between their models, methods and business requirements [4]. In order to cope with all these difficulties, we want to make use of representation mechanism called *Web Blackboard*, that will help us to incrementally convey the shared understanding on the concepts used by those services, and therefore underlying agreements about the services behavior.

Through this paper, we will explore how multiple stakeholders can represent and interlink their service descriptions using artifacts in decentralized environments. We want to explore the possible benefits of an environment where multiple stakeholders (i) collaboratively define their information services and (ii) build up a network of semantic mappings, in order to reach configurations that

Y.T. Demey and H. Panetto (Eds.): OTM 2013 Workshops, LNCS 8186, pp. 437–441, 2013.

promote collaborative information sharing, (iii) allowing them to use their own terminology and conceptualizations.

This document is organized as follows: Section 2 presents a brief description of our problem. Section 3 will explore the related work on this subject. Section 4 will explain what is our current approach. Section 5 will describe the dynamics this representation mechanism. Section 6 presents our conclusions and future work.

2 Problem Description

Suppose that we have a group of stakeholders that want to provide information services concerning cultural events in a city. Consider the task of finding relevant events via the composition of multiple services, such as transport schedules services, musical events agendas etc. In this case, the stakeholders may need to compose distinct functionalities in order to provide results that are relevant to the users. Composing these services may imply (i) discovering services with one or more functionalities, (ii) retrieving definitions for these functionalities and (iii) to integrate them into a resulting service. If the stakeholders have well defined semantic interoperability requirements for all these tasks, they can integrate the information sources through the use of global interchange schemas or ontologies, which are usually built by authorities or stakeholder communities. But there will be cases where we cannot count with these central authorities. In these cases to reach agreement about schemas will be difficult. One approach to overcome this situation is to support incremental processes, where the distinct peers interact making agreements with each other within a peer to peer network. In this paper, we make use of shared artifacts used by the distinct peers, used to collaboratively convey into structures to be used by information services. A peer to peer network is characterized by its fast conceptual framework evolutions, which are common in information systems constructed socially. Therefore top-down approaches may not be sufficient to flexibly respond to the dynamic requirements present on those networks.

3 Related Work

Although service decomposition and composition techniques allow us to scale into large service networks, they may become difficult to manage in ecosystems where multiple stakeholders interact, mainly due to misinterpretation issues. These ambiguity and interoperability difficulties can be diminished by the use of semantic web services that make use of shared and explicit semantics to maintain coherence between a net of distinct stakeholders. These services make use of ontologies to facilitate an acceptable "understanding" between agents. In IT related domains, an ontology is understood as a shared, computer stored conceptualization in a formal language agreed upon a group of stakeholders that enables system interoperability [5].

The nature of the ecosystem will determine largely how these ontologies are constructed, depending on the difficulty and scope of the needed semantic agreements. The stakeholders may adopt distinct strategies to identify and determine their relevant concepts, following top-down, bottom up, or a combination of both approaches.

In the case of systems where "global interoperability" is hard to archive, then we can see the agreement processes as emerging from the interactions of autonomous agents [2], where services may profit from a web of mappings between autonomously created ontologies that follow the individual conceptions of the stakeholders. We want to support this behavior using artifacts called *Blackboards* [1] that allow the stakeholders to incrementally construct mappings between their ontological systems, seeking acceptable degrees of agreements. Within this paper we make use of a blackboard variant called *Web Blackboards* [8], that provides us higher degrees of descentralization and flexibility. Blackboards are playgrounds where the stakeholder community describe their conceptualizations, business rules, service definitions etc. Its decentralized architecture aims to support a network where the stakeholder community describe and interlink their descriptions organically and incrementally. One important characteristic of these networks is that their evolution is traced along their stakeholder community in order to support high level interactions such as service composition and orchestration.

4 Approach

Whenever some stakeholders want to share information through services, they will need a clear idea about the intended meaning of these services, meaning ideally externalized by some machine understandable representation formalism. The idea of using shared artifacts such as blackboards is to capture these representations of intended meaning. Theoretically, a blackboard can hold any implementable representation, such as a data model, decision model, a rule or business role. In this paper we will use *Service Definitions* as the studied models, where we use a blackboard to represent a single service, or to represent the dependencies between distinct services. When a stakeholder wants to make use of certain service, he may commit to the blackboard that holds its service definition (B_{sd}). Wherever a stakeholder want to make modifications, it may clone the service definition and perform the modifications in the new variant. Other stakeholders may then change their commitment to the new service definition variant. Another approach is to start a modification agreement dialog with the stakeholders that commit to the same service description blackboard.

Each time that a B_{sd} is cloned, we generate a new derived B_{sd} that will be the result of a change with respect to the previous one via a set of *change operators* applied sequentially by the stakeholders. Which change operators are going to be used to let evolve certain service elicitation is a matter of design and will depend on the nature of the service network. We may use very granular ones such as `update query` or `add new dataset`, while others may be of higher complexity such as binding two services together. The distinct change operators can be constructed via composition of granular ones via a framework of layered operators [6]. Within a blackboard network, the use of defined change operators is convenient since they allow the possibility of binding the operators to automatic verification and validation processes [3].

B_{sd} may represent services that can be grouped into different strands, each one with its own representation needs and distinct levels of formalism. Examples of these representations may be SOA, Semantic WS, SAAS, Service networks etc. The choice of which representation formalism will depend on the semantic inter-operability requirements and the scope of the service integration. For example, we may need a formal and unambiguous grammar to map concepts precisely to the implementation artifacts, or natural language definitions to support general business processes. In this way, the choice of the representation mechanism depends on the distinct modeling processes. In this way, a blackboard can be seen as a design artifact, to build purposeful artifacts that address unsolved problems.

Stakeholders can perform distinct actions within the blackboard network, such as (i) to consume semantically enabled services (ii) perform individual queries (iii) to annotate content (iv) or to modify the underlying ontologies among others. The approach itself does not force specific role assignments or ontology ownership policies since this may differ from one community to another, but as a general rule, when a service is published by a stakeholder in a B_{sd}, we may say that the published commits to its artificial declaration. If another stakeholder commits to the same B_{sd}, then we can assume that he agrees with the conceptualization behind the service.

5   Blackboard for Service Definition Evolution

A B_{sd} will hold service representations contextualized within a particular task, each B_{sd} is triggered by the creation of services and is augmented with machine readable facts and terms that result from the annotations and dialogues between the stakeholders. In this way, each blackboard is divided in multiple meta levels such as agreement layer, discussion layer, service description layer, implementation layer etc.

Whenever a group of stake holders is involved in the incremental an collaborative change of a B_{sd}, the number of mappings of services in the network will increase. The diverging and merging capabilities are supported by a direct an acyclic graph model (DAG) that allow us to represent (i) the branching of a B_{sd} variant (ii) merging two B_{sd} variants and (iii) record full the traceability by means of sequences of change operators used to merge or diverge the variants. This non-linear B_{sd} development is currently used successfully in other fields (e.g., collaborative software development with version control systems such as GIT[1]).

6   Discussion and Future Work

In this paper, we treat each service description as a first-class citizen, a hub that uses each service's metadata and dynamic schemas together in order to provide

---

[1] http://git-scm.com/

semantically enabled services, constructed by their community of use. The stakeholders are free to create new blackboards, seeking peer-to-peer collaboration, via the definition of services and collaborative modeling.

We expect that using these blackboards as a pivot will help to improve the community's local interaction promoting adaptative self oganization for modelling and annotation activities. Full traceability is supported in order to be able of analyzing the evolution of a service network in order to observe how the consumers, mediated by a set of artifacts, are driven in a emergent dynamic process that eventually may lead to a stable service network. Finding out the characteristics of these dynamic service networks may enable us to understand better a service system. Such an approach leaves us space for further questions, such as:

(i) What should be the agreement mechanisms between the stakeholders that commit to a B_{sd}?
(ii) How we can profit from B_{sd} networks to compose and orchestrate semantically enabled services?
(iii) How these networks evolve, and how they can be observed by the stakeholders increasing their awareness?

Acknowledgments. The research described in this paper was partially sponsored by the INNOViris Open Semantic Cloud for Brussels (OSCB) project.

References

1. Corkill, D.D.: Blackboard systems. AI Expert 6, 40–47 (1991)
2. Philippe cudr E-mauroux: Emergent Semantics: Rethinking interoperability for large scale descentralized information systems (2006)
3. Demey, Y., Tran, T.K.: Using SOIQ(D) to Formalize Semantics within a Semantic Decision Table. Rules on the Web: Research and Applications (D), 224–239 (2012)
4. Ferrario, R., Guarino, N., Janiesch, C., Kiemes, T., Oberle, D., Probst, F.: Towards an Ontological Foundation of Services Science: The General Service Model (February 2011)
5. Gruber, T.R.: A Translation Approach to Portable Ontology Specifications, vol. 5, pp. 199–220. Academic Press Ltd., London (1993)
6. Javed, M., Abgaz, Y.M., Pahl, C.: A Layered Framework for Pattern-based Ontology Evolution. Framework (2011)
7. De Leenheer, P., Cardoso, J., Pedrinaci, C.: Ontological Representation and Governance of Business Semantics in Compliant Service Networks (257593), 155–169 (2013)
8. Vasquez, C.: Blackboard Data Spaces for the Elicitation of Community-based Lightweight ontologies. In: Advances in Social Networks Analysis and Mining (2012)

A Structural $\mathcal{SHOIN}(\mathcal{D})$ Ontology Model for Change Modelling

Perrine Pittet, Christophe Cruz, and Christophe Nicolle

LE2I, UMR CNRS 630, University of Burgundy - Dijon, France
{perrine.pittet,christophe.cruz,cnicolle}@u-bourgogne.fr

Abstract. This paper presents a complete structural ontology model suited for change modelling on $\mathcal{SHOIN}(\mathcal{D})$ ontologies. The application of this model is illustrated along the paper through the description of an ontology example inspired by the UOBM ontology benchmark and its evolution.

Keywords: $\mathcal{SHOIN}(\mathcal{D})$ Description Logic; Change Modelling, OWL DL.

1   Introduction

Ontologies make possible to application, enterprise, and community boundaries of any domain to bridge the gap of semantic heterogeneity. Ontologies development, to be correctly achieved, requires a dynamic and incremental process (Djedidi & Aufaure, 2008.). It starts with a rigorous ontological analysis (Guarino, 1995) that provides a conceptualization of the domain to model agreed by the community. The ontology, specified in a formal language, approximates the intended models of the conceptualization: the closer it is the better it is. The ontology needs to be revised and refined until an ontological commitment is found. Ulterior updates of the ontology, addressed by ontology evolution, aim at responding to changes in the domain and/or the conceptualization (Flouris, 2008). Changes are consequently inherent in the ontology life cycle. Modelling changes then implies having an exhaustive and non-ambiguous definition of the ontology model according to its language, so that each element of the ontology impacted by changes can be formally described.

This paper focuses on the $\mathcal{SHOIN}(\mathcal{D})$ level of expressivity, on which the ontological language OWL DL is based (Horrocks I. , 2005). After presenting the structural constraints of a $\mathcal{SHOIN}(\mathcal{D})$ ontology, it describes a list of basic changes, constrained by this structural model to avoid performing structural inconsistent updates on the ontology.

2 $\mathcal{SHOIN}(\mathcal{D})$ Ontology Model

To formalize our framework the Karlsruhe Ontology Model (Ehrig, 2004) is used and extended to cover the whole $\mathcal{SHOIN}(\mathcal{D})$ constructors. From a mathematical point of view, an ontology can be defined as a structure. Formally, a structure is a triple

Y.T. Demey and H. Panetto (Eds.): OTM 2013 Workshops, LNCS 8186, pp. 442–446, 2013.
© Springer-Verlag Berlin Heidelberg 2013

$A=(S, \sigma, F)$ consisting of an underlying set S, a signature σ, and an interpretation function F that indicates how the signature is to be interpreted on S.

Definition 1: $\mathcal{SHOIN}(\mathcal{D})$ Ontology Model

A $\mathcal{SHOIN}(\mathcal{D})$ ontology is a structure $O=(SO, \sigma O, FO)$ consisting of:

- The underlying set SO containing:
  - Six disjoint sets sC, sT, sR, sA, sI, sV, sK_R and sK_A called concepts, datatypes, relations, attributes, instances, data values, relation characteristics (among Symmetric, Functional, Inverse Functional, Transitive) and attribute characteristics (Functional),
  - Four partial orders $\leq_C$, $\leq_T$, $\leq_R$ and $\leq_A$, respectively on sC called concept hierarchy or taxonomy, on sT called type hierarchy, on sR called relation hierarchy and on sA called attribute hierarchy,

  such that $SO :=\{(sC, \leq_C),(sT, \leq_T),(sR, \leq_R),(sA, \leq_A), sI, sV, sK_R, sK_A,\}$,
- The signature σO containing two functions $\sigma_R:sR{\rightarrow}sC^2$ called relation signature and $\sigma_A:sA{\rightarrow}sC \times sT$ called attribute signature, such that $\sigma O :=\{\sigma_R, \sigma_A\}$,
- The interpretation function FO containing:
  - A function $\iota_C:sC{\rightarrow} 2^{sI}$ called concept instantiation,
  - A function $\iota_T:sA{\rightarrow} 2^{sV}$ called data type instantiation,
  - A function $\iota_R:sC{\rightarrow} 2^{sI \times sI}$ called relation instantiation,
  - A function $\iota_A:sC{\rightarrow} 2^{sI \times sV}$ called attribute instantiation,
  - A function $\kappa_R:sR{\rightarrow} 2^{sKR}$ called relation characterization,
  - A function $\kappa_A:sA{\rightarrow} 2^{sKA}$ called attribute characterization,
  - A function $\varepsilon_C:sC{\rightarrow} 2^{sC}$ called concept equivalence,
  - A function $\varepsilon_R:sR{\rightarrow} 2^{sR}$ called relation equivalence,
  - A function $\varepsilon_A:sA{\rightarrow} 2^{sA}$ called attribute equivalence,
  - A function $\varepsilon_I:sI{\rightarrow} 2^{sI}$ called instance equivalence,
  - A function $\delta_C:sC{\rightarrow} 2^{sC}$ called concept disjunction,
  - A function $\delta_I:sI{\rightarrow} 2^{sI}$ called instance differentiation,
  - A function $-_C:sC{\rightarrow} 2^{sC}$ called concept complement specification,
  - A function $-_R:sR{\rightarrow} 2^{sR}$ called relation inverse specification,
  - A function $maxCardR:sR{\rightarrow}N$ called relation maximal cardinality restriction,
  - A function $minCardR:sR{\rightarrow}N$ called relation minimal cardinality restriction,
  - A function $\sqcap_C:sC{\rightarrow}2^{sC}$ called concept intersection,
  - A function $\sqcup_C:sC{\rightarrow}2^{sC}$ called concept union,
  - A function $\sqcup_{iC}:sI{\rightarrow}2^{sC}$ called concept union enumeration,
  - A function $\sqcup_V:sV{\rightarrow}2^{sC}$ called data value union,
  - A function $\sqcap_{iC}:sC{\rightarrow}2^{sI}$ called concept enumeration,
  - A function $\rho_{\exists R}:sR{\rightarrow}2^{sC}$ called relation existential restriction,
  - A function $\rho_{\forall R}:sR{\rightarrow}2^{sC}$ called relation universal restriction,
  - A function $\rho_{R:}:sR{\rightarrow}2^{sI}$ called relation value restriction,
  - A function $\rho_{\exists A}:sA{\rightarrow}2^{sT}$ called attribute existential restriction,
  - A function $\rho_{\forall A}:sA{\rightarrow}2^{sT}$ called attribute universal restriction,
  - A function $\rho_{A:}:sA{\rightarrow}2^{sV}$ called attribute value restriction,

such that $FO:=\{\iota_C, \iota_T, \iota_R, \iota_A, \kappa_R, \kappa_A, \varepsilon_C, \varepsilon_R, \varepsilon_A, \varepsilon_I, \delta_C, \delta_I, -_C, -_R, maxCard_R, minCard_R, \sqcap_C,$ $\sqcup, \sqcup_{iC}, \sqcup_V, \sqcap_{iC}, \rho_{\exists R}, \rho_{\forall R}, \rho_{R:}, \rho_{\exists A}, \rho_{\forall A}, \rho_{A:}).$

2.1 $\mathcal{SHOIN}(\mathcal{D})$ Change Modelling

To model changes, we give the five definitions below.

- **Definition 2: Change.** A change ω is the application of a modification on an ontology O, that potentially affects one or more elements of its structure as defined by the $\mathcal{SHOIN}(\mathcal{D})$ Ontology Model.

- **Definition 3: Log of Changes.** Given an ontology O a log of changes, noted log_i, is defined by an ordered set of changes (simple and complex) $<\omega_1, ..., \omega_n>$ that applied to O results in O.

  Like in (Klein, 2004), 2 change types are distinguished: basic and complex.

- **Definition 4: Basic Change.** A basic change on an ontology O is a function $\omega_B:sK \rightarrow 2^O$ with $sK:=\{sC \cup sI \cup sR \cup sA\}$ that corresponds to an addition, a removal of a modification of one element $\in O$.

- **Definition 5: Complex Change.** A complex change on an ontology O is a disjoint union of basic changes. It is a function $\omega_C:nsK \rightarrow 2^O$ such that $\omega_C:=\omega_{B1} +...+ \omega_{Bn}$.

  The application of a change on an ontology, basic or complex, can be an addition or a deletion. It is traced as such in the log of changes.

- **Definition 6: Addition of a Change.** The addition of a change ω_i traced in the log of changes log_i, noted $log_i +\{\omega_i\}$, is defined by the disjoint union between the two disjoint sets log_i and $\{\omega_i\}$.

- **Definition 7: Deletion of a Change.** The deletion of a change ω_i traced in the log of changes log_i, noted $log_i - \{\omega_i\}$, is defined by the set-theoretic complement such that $log_i - \{\omega_i\}=\{x \in log_i \mid x \notin \{\omega_i\}\}$.

2.2   Basic Changes Modelling

To produce the list of basic change operations on $\mathcal{SHOIN}(\mathcal{D})$ ontologies, the $\mathcal{SHOIN}(\mathcal{D})$ Ontology Model is exploited as described in Table 1. The third column lists the 47 operators representing basic changes, which, if applied on the ontology, affect the corresponding $\mathcal{SHOIN}(\mathcal{D})$ model element. According to our model, every basic change can be declined as an addition or a deletion of an element of the underlying set, the signature or the interpretation function.

Table 1. Correspondence between $\mathcal{SHOIN}(\mathcal{D})$ Description Logic Descriptions, Axioms and Facts, the $\mathcal{SHOIN}(\mathcal{D})$ Ontology Model and the $\mathcal{SHOIN}(\mathcal{D})$-based List of Basic Changes

	DL Syntax	Model	$\mathcal{SHOIN}(\mathcal{D})$-based Changes Abstract Syntax
Descriptions	C	sC	Class(Class)
	$C_1 \sqcap ... \sqcap C_n$	$\sqcap_C$	IntersectionOf(Class$_1$,...,Class$_n$)
	$C_1 \sqcup ... \sqcup C_n$	$\sqcup_C$	**UnionOf(Class$_1$,...,Class$_n$)**
	$\neg C$	$-_C$	**ComplementOf(Class)**
	$\{I_1\} \sqcup ... \sqcup \{I_n\}$	$\sqcup_{IC}$	**OneOf(Class, Instance$_1$,...,Instance$_n$)**
	$\exists R.C$	$\rho_{\exists R}$	SomeValuesFrom(ObjectProperty, Class)
	$\forall R.C$	$\rho_{\forall R}$	AllValuesFrom(ObjectProperty, Class)

Table 1. (*continued*)

$R : I$	$\rho_{R:}$	HasValue(ObjectProperty, Instance)
$\geq n\,R$	$maxCard_R$	MinCardinalityProperty(ObjectProperty, n)
$\leq n\,R$	$minCard_R$	MaxCardinalityProperty(ObjectProperty, n)
$\exists A.T$	$\rho_{\exists A}$	SomeValuesFrom(DatatypeProperty, Datatype)
$\forall A.T$	$\rho_{\forall A}$	AllValuesFrom(DatatypeProperty, Datatype)
$A : V$	$\rho_{A:}$	HasValue(DatatypeProperty, Datavalue)
T	sT	Datatype(Datatype)
$\{V_1\}\sqcup\ldots\sqcup\{V_n\}$	$\sqcup_V$	**OneOf(Datavalue$_1$,...,Datavalue$_n$)**
R	sR	ObjectProperty(ObjectProperty)
A	sA	DatatypeProperty(DatatypeProperty)
I	sI	Instance(Instance)
V	sV	Datavalue(Datavalue)
$C \equiv C_1 \sqcap \ldots \sqcap C_n$	$\sqcap_C$	**IntersectionClass(Class, (Class$_1$,...Class$_n$))**
$C \equiv \{I_1\}\sqcap \ldots \sqcap\{I_n\}$	$\sqcap_{iC}$	**EnumeratedClass(Class, (Instance$_1$,...Instance$_n$))**
$C_1 \sqsubseteq C_2$	$\leq_C$	SubClassOf(Class$_1$, Class$_2$)
$C_1 \equiv \ldots \equiv C_n$	ε_C	**EquivalentClass(Class$_1$,...Class$_n$)**
$\perp \equiv C_1 \sqcap C_2$	δ_C	DisjointClass(Class$_1$, Class$_2$)
$T_1 \sqsubseteq T_2$	$\leq_T$	SubDatatypeOf(Datatype$_1$, Datatype$_2$)
$V \in T_i$	ι_T	InstancesOfDatatype(Datavalue, Datatype)
$\geq 1R \sqsubseteq C_i$	σ_R	DomainProperty(ObjectProperty, Class)
$T \sqsubseteq \forall R.C_i$		RangeProperty(ObjectProperty, Class)
$R \equiv R_0^-$	$-_R$	InverseOf(ObjectProperty$_1$ ObjectProperty$_2$)
$R \equiv R^-$	κ_R	SymmetricProperty(ObjectProperty)
$T \sqsubseteq\, \leq 1R$		FunctionalProperty(ObjectProperty)
$T \sqsubseteq\, \leq 1R^-$		InverseFunctionalProperty(ObjectProperty)
$Tr(R)$		TransitiveProperty(ObjectProperty)
$R_1 \sqsubseteq R_2$	$\leq_R$	InheritanceObjectPropertyLink(ObjectProperty$_1$, ObjectProperty$_2$)
$R_1 \equiv \ldots \equiv R_n$	ε_R	**EquivalentProperty(ObjectProperty$_1$,...,ObjectProperty$_n$)**
$A \sqsubseteq A_i$	A	DatatypeProperty(DatatypeProperty)
$\geq 1A \sqsubseteq C_i$	σ_A	DomainProperty(DatatypeProperty Class)
$T \sqsubseteq A.T_i$		RangeProperty(DatatypeProperty, Datatype)
$T \sqsubseteq\, \leq 1A$	κ_A	FunctionalProperty(DatatypeProperty)
$A_1 \sqsubseteq A_2$	$\leq_A$	InheritanceDatatypePropertyLink(DatatypeProperty$_1$, DatatypeProperty$_2$)
$A_1 \equiv \ldots \equiv A_n$	ε_A	**EquivalentProperty(DatatypeProperty$_1$,...,DatatypeProperty$_n$)**
$I \in C_i$	ι_C	InstancesOf(Instance, Class)
$\{I, I_i\} \in R_i$	ι_R	InstancesOfObjectProperty(Instance, Instance$_1$, ObjectProperty)
$\{I, V_i\} \in A_i$	ι_A	InstanceOfDatatypeProperty(Instance, Datavalue, DatatypeProperty)
$\{I_1\} \equiv \ldots \equiv \{I_n\}$	ε_I	**SameAs(Instance$_1$,...,Instance$_n$)**
$\{I_i\} \sqsubseteq \neg\{I_j\}, i \neq j$	δ_I	**DifferentFrom(Instance$_1$,...,Instance$_n$)**

2.3   Complex Changes Modelling

More generally, an infinite set of complex changes can be generated from the aggregation of basic changes (Plessers, 2005). Their pertinence depends on the need of particular changes implied by particular uses. For example, the renaming of a concept is often used in collaborative development of an ontology to reach a consensus but can be unused in other contexts. For this reason, our model natively provides the limited set of 47 basic changes but, depending on change modelling needs, gives the opportunity to build complex changes from these basic changes.

3   Discussion and Conclusion

Our model aims at facilitating the modelling of basic and complex changes. It aims at contributing to the maintenance of the ontology structural consistency by clearly defining each change impact on the structure of the ontology. This model is the structural basis of a change management methodology called OntoVersionGraph (Pittet, 2012). To ensure a complete consistent evolution of the ontology, it is used in conjunction with a logical inconsistency identification methodology called CLOCk (Gueffaz, 2012), based on ontology design patterns and model-checking.

References

Djedidi, R., Aufaure, M.A.: Change Management Patternsfor Ontology Evolution Process –. IWOD at ISWC 2008, Karlsruhe (2008)

Ehrig, M.H.: Similarity for ontologies-a comprehensive framework. Workshop Enterprise Modelling and Ontology: Ingredients for Interoperability, at PAKM (2004)

Flouris, G.M.: Ontology Change: Classification & Survey. The Knowledge Engineering Review 23(2), 117–152 (2008)

Guarino, N.: Formal ontology, conceptual analysis and knowledge representation. International Journal of Human Computer Studies 43(5), 625–640 (1995)

Gueffaz, M.P.: Inconsistency Identification In Dynamic Ontologies Based On Model Checking, pp. 418–421. INSTICC, ACM SIGMIS (2012)

Horrocks, I.: Owl: A description logic based ontology language. Logic Programming, 1–4 (2005)

Klein, M.C.: Change management for distributed ontologies (2004)

Pittet, P.N.: Guidelines for a Dynamic Ontology-Integrating Tools of Evolution and Versioning in Ontology. arXiv (2012)

Plessers, P., De Troyer, O.: Ontology Change Detection Using a Version Log. In: Gil, Y., Motta, E., Benjamins, V.R., Musen, M.A. (eds.) ISWC 2005. LNCS, vol. 3729, pp. 578–592. Springer, Heidelberg (2005)

ORM 2013 PC Co-Chairs Message

Following successful workshops in Cyprus (2005), France (2006), Portugal (2007), Mexico (2008), Portugal (2009), and Greece (2010 and 2011), and Rome (2012), this is the ninth fact-oriented modeling workshop run in conjunction with the OTM conferences. Fact-oriented modeling is a conceptual approach for modeling and querying the semantics of business domains in terms of the underlying facts of interest, where all facts and rules may be verbalized in language readily understandable by users in those domains.

Unlike Entity-Relationship (ER) modeling and UML class diagrams, fact-oriented modeling treats all facts as relationships (unary, binary, ternary etc.). How facts are grouped into structures (e.g. attribute-based entity types, classes, relation schemes, XML schemas) is considered a design level, implementation issue irrelevant to capturing the essential business semantics. Avoiding attributes in the base model enhances semantic stability, simplifies populatability, and facilitates natural verbalization, thus offering more productive communication with all stakeholders. For information modeling, fact-oriented graphical notations are typically far more expressive than other notations. Fact-oriented modeling includes procedures for mapping to attribute-based structures, so may also be used to front-end those other approaches.

Though less well known than ER and object-oriented approaches, fact-oriented modeling has been used successfully in industry for over 30 years, and is taught in universities around the world. The fact-oriented modeling approach comprises a family of closely related "dialects", including Object-Role Modeling (ORM), Cognition enhanced Natural language Information Analysis Method (CogNIAM) and Fully-Communication Oriented Information Modeling (FCO-IM). Though adopting a different graphical notation, the Object-oriented Systems Model (OSM) is a close relative, with its attribute-free philosophy. The Semantics of Business Vocabulary and Business Rules (SBVR) proposal adopted by the Object Management Group in 2007 is a recent addition to the family of fact-oriented approaches.

Software tools supporting the fact-oriented approach include the ORM tools NORMA (Natural ORM Architect), ActiveFacts, InfoModeler and ORM-Lite, the CogNIAM tool Doctool, and the FCO-IM tool CaseTalk. The Collibra ontology tool suite and DogmaStudio are fact-based tools for specifying ontologies. Richmond is another ORM tool under development. General information about fact-orientation may be found at www.ORMFoundation.org.

This year, submissions were contributed by authors from Australia, Belgium, Canada, Italy, Malaysia, Norway, The Netherlands, and the USA. After an extensive review process by an international program committee, with each paper receiving four reviews, we accepted the 11 papers that appear in these proceedings. Congratulations to the successful authors! We gratefully acknowledge the generous contribution of time and effort by the program committee, the OTM General Chairs (Robert Meersman, Tharam Dillon and Hervé Panetto), the OTM Workshops General Chair (Yan Tang Demey), and the Logistics Team (Jan Demey and Daniel Meersman).

July 2013   Terry Halpin

Y.T. Demey and H. Panetto (Eds.): OTM 2013 Workshops, LNCS 8186, p. 447, 2013.
© Springer-Verlag Berlin Heidelberg 2013

Towards a Core ORM2 Language
(Research Note)

Enrico Franconi and Alessandro Mosca

Free University of Bozen-Bolzano, KRDB Research Centre, Italy
{franconi,mosca}@inf.unibz.it

Abstract. The introduction of a provably correct encoding of a fragment of ORM2 (called ORM2^{zero}) into a decidable fragment of OWL2, opened the doors for the definition of dedicated reasoning technologies supporting the quality of the schemas design. In this paper we discuss how to extend ORM2^{zero} in a maximal way by retaining at the same time the nice computational properties of ORM2^{zero}.

1 ORM2^{zero+}: The Core Fragment of ORM2

In [1,2] we introduced a fragment of ORM2, called ORM2^{zero}, that captures the most frequent usage patterns of the conceptual modelling community. The language has a formal semantics specified in **FOL**, and a provably correct (bidirectional) encoding in the description logic $\mathcal{ALCQI}$ [1]. $\mathcal{ALCQI}$ is a decidable fragment of the OWL2 Web ontology language (a complete introduction of the syntax and semantics of $\mathcal{ALCQI}$ can be found in [3]), for which optimised very efficient tableaux-based reasoning algorithms and tools have been developed. The encoding of ORM2^{zero} in description logics provably preserves satisfiability and entailment, and so the reasoning in the description logic (such as the strong and weak satisfiability of the schema, of the entities and of the predicates, and the entailment of new or stricter constraints) can be transposed back to ORM2^{zero}. In [1,2] we extensively comment on the limits and the incorrectness of alternative similar proposals.

Figure 1 introduces the list of the constraints that are natively present in ORM2^{zero}, together with their graphical notations. The table also reports about the restrictions we need to impose on the applicability of these constraints in order to preserve the decidability of the language and the feasibility of the encoding, so that we can rely on available reasoning tools. In ORM2^{zero} we can express typing constraints, simple mandatory constraints, internal frequency constraints restricted to single roles, arbitrary subtyping constraints, and subset and exclusion constraints restricted to pairs of whole predicates. Note that in ORM2^{zero} the subtyping is not strict (namely, subtyping is interpreted as a subset-or-equal relation between entities), and that root entities (without supertypes) are not mutually disjoint.

Despite the apparent weakness of the ORM2^{zero} language, suitable combinations of the ORM2^{zero} constructs can be used to encode a number of other relevant ORM2 constraints, thus extending the expressive power of ORM2^{zero} to what we call ORM2^{zero+}. The following constraints are in ORM2^{zero+}: unrestricted objectification; reference

Y.T. Demey and H. Panetto (Eds.): OTM 2013 Workshops, LNCS 8186, pp. 448–456, 2013.

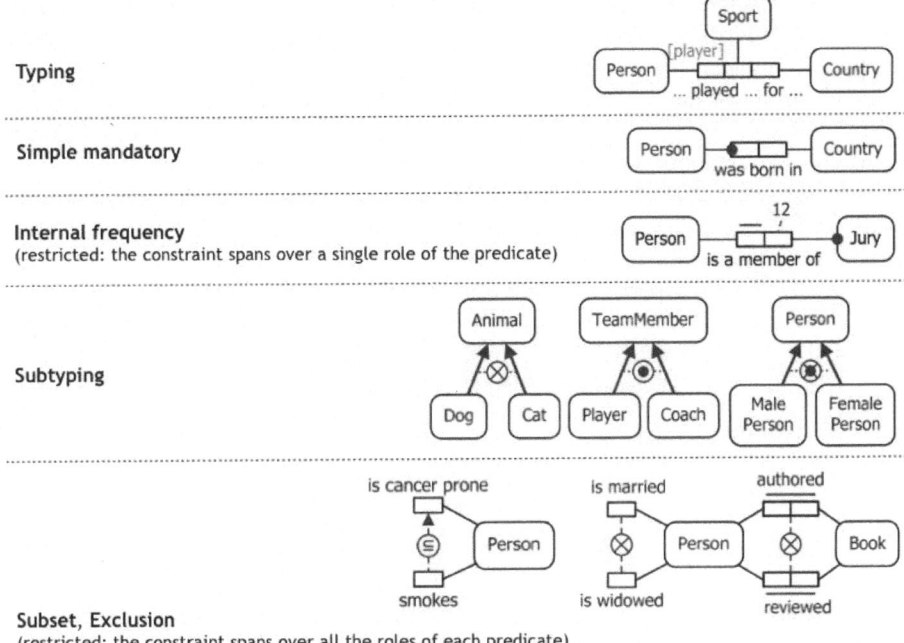

Typing	
Simple mandatory	
Internal frequency (restricted: the constraint spans over a single role of the predicate)	
Subtyping	
Subset, Exclusion (restricted: the constraint spans over all the roles of each predicate)	

Fig. 1. List of primitive ORM2^{zero} constraints by means of examples from [4]

modes; unrestricted internal and external uniqueness and frequency constraints; unrestricted and strict subtyping; subset, exclusion, inclusive-or, exclusive-or and equality constraints restricted to pairs of single roles and to pairs of whole predicates; and the *primitive entity types disjointness* assumption. This paper describes the way how these constraints can be reduced to combinations of the primitive constraints of ORM2^{zero}. Most notably ORM2^{zero+} misses with respect to ORM2: value constraints; cardinality constraints; subset, exclusion, inclusive-or, exclusive-or and equality constraints restricted to pairs of sequences of roles of length different from one and from the arity of the involved same-arity predicates; ring constraints. If present, value, cardinality, and ring constraints would invalidate the correctness of the encoding of objectification, while unrestricted subset, exclusion, inclusive-or, exclusive-or and equality constraints would lead to undecidability of reasoning (due to the undecidability of unrestricted functional and inclusion dependencies). To complete the picture, we are exploring the possibility to add to ORM2^{zero+} derivation rules and deontic constraints.

All the ORM2^{zero+} constraints considered (with the exception of objectification) are logically equivalent to their ORM2^{zero} encodings, namely they constrain the world in the very same way and they identify the same legal databases (i.e., they have the same logical models). The encoding of an objectification constraint is weaker whenever in the schema it is necessary to have *both* the original n-ary predicate *and* the entity representing the objectified predicate *together* with its n binary predicates representing the reified roles of the original n-ary predicate. In this case the encoding is only preserving satisfiability and entailment, but it does not preserve the models. As far as schema reasoning is concerned, this is not a limitation, since schema reasoning is based on satisfiability and entailment.

In what follows, the ORM2^{zero} reductions are introduced by means of examples, the majority of which have been grasped from [4]. Many reductions are already well known in the ORM community, and some have been already presented in [4].

We assume that: a countable number of new fresh entity types TOP, TOP1, ..., TOPn are part of the language, where n is the maximum arity of predicates in the schema; TOP is a supertype of all the entity types in the schema; TOP$_1$ ··· TOP$_i$ are supertypes of all the objectified predicates of arity i, for each $1 \leq i \leq n$; each TOP, TOP1, ..., TOPn is covered by its subtypes. The schemas presented in this paper may not have these assumptions explicitly written.

Reference Mode Constraint

(a)   (b)

The schema (a) on the left making use of a reference mode constraint can be reduced in ORM2^{zero} as shown in the schema (b) on the right. This is well known from standard ORM2.

External Frequency Constraint

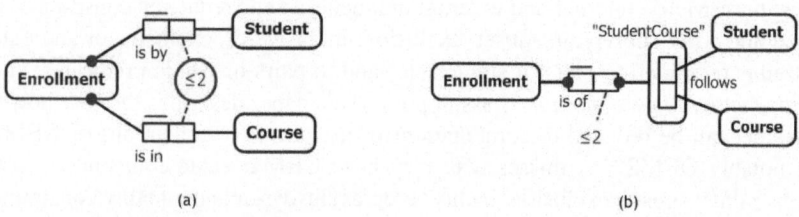

(a)   (b)

The case of the external frequency constraint is of particular interest. The external frequency is a frequency constraint that applies to roles from different predicates and its meaning relies on the implicit join operation. The main idea behind its encoding in ORM2^{zero} is to make use of the objectification in order to represent the functional relationships between the tuples and the identified individuals. In the example above, **Enrollment** is connected with mandatory and uniqueness constraint to a new predicate whose second role is played by identifiers of (**Student, Course**) pairs. It is obvious that, if a model exists for the ORM2 schema, then in this model no enrolment can be repeated, and a student may enrol in the same course at most twice. The very same situation is forced by the internal frequency spanning over the second role of the new introduced predicate **is of**: each identifier of a (**Student, Course**) tuple can play that role twice (remember that the internal frequency spanning over single roles is among the primitive constructs of ORM2^{zero}).

External Uniqueness Constraint

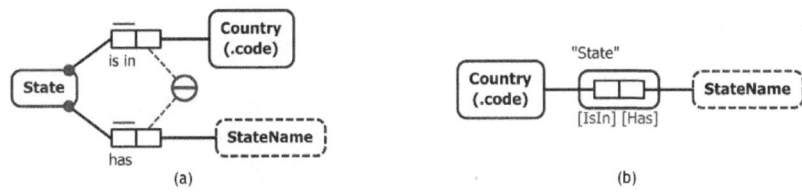

In the example, the external uniqueness constraint says that each State is univocally determined by a pair (Country, StateName). In other terms, the relationship between a pair (Country, StateName) and State is the same holding between a objectified binary tuple and its identifier: it is a bijection, indeed. Therefore, the external uniqueness in ORM2^{zero} reduces to building a new fresh predicate that, once objectified, is used to identify the individuals of State. In figure (b), State is indeed represented as the objectification of IsIn and Has. Alternatively, one can observe that uniqueness (both external and internal) is a special case of the frequency constraint "$= 1$", and therefore one could apply the reductions for frequency constraints.

Internal Uniqueness and Frequency Constraint

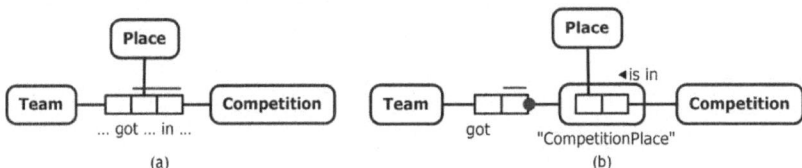

In ORM2, an internal uniqueness says that individuals of a given type can play a role only once. Moreover, for an 'elementary n-ary association' in ORM2, each internal uniqueness constraint must span over n-1 roles. In the figure above, the internal uniqueness forbids to record for ties: two different teams cannot occupy the same place in the same competition. Again, the reduction to ORM2^{zero} of this constraint is based on an objectification: a new predicate is introduced and objectified in order to explicitly identify the pair (Place, Competition), and its objectification is then linked with Team by means of the new predicate symbol got. The fact that a pair (Place, Competition) cannot be related twice with an instance of Team is finally represented by an internal uniqueness spanning over a single role, that is, by a native ORM2^{zero} constraint. Notice that ORM2^{zero} does not introduce internal uniqueness spanning over entire predicates because of its set-based semantics. A very similar reduction can be applied for internal frequency constraints, by replacing in the example the uniqueness constraint with the frequency constraint.

Unary Subset, Exclusion, Inclusive-or, Exclusive-or and Equality Constraints

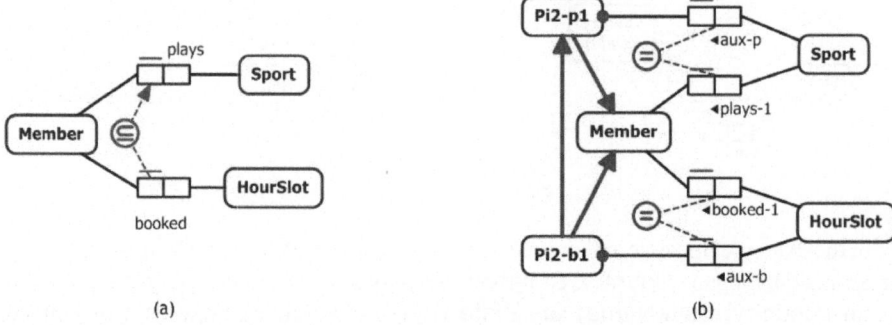

(a)   (b)

Let's first recall that in ORM2^{zero+} unary subset, exclusion, inclusive-or, exclusive-or and equality constraints are allowed in addition to the subset, exclusion and equality constraints involving whole predicates allowed in ORM2^{zero}. The idea of this encoding for the general case is based on generating entities as the projections of the roles involved. In the example above, the entities *Pi2-p1* and *Pi2-b1* are are the projections of the two original binary predicates over the first role. The unary boolean constraints (subset, exclusion, inclusive-or, exclusive-or and equality) over those single roles are then encoded with the corresponding constraint among the two subentities representing the projections – in this example a *subset* between the two roles becomes a subtype between the two subentities. The inability of ORM2 to reuse the same role for multiple typings obliges us to introduce an additional equal copy of each involved predicate; equality among predicates is encoded in ORM2^{zero} as a cycle of *subset* between the predicates.

Strict Subtyping

In ORM2 there is the assumption that for each entity A being a subtype of an entity B there at least a legal database state (i.e., satisfying all the constraints in the conceptual schema) such that the extension of A in that state is different from the extension of B in that state, namely the extension of A is *strictly* a subset of the the extension of B. In other words, it is impossible to have only legal database states in which the extension of A is equal to the extension of B. In ORM2^{zero} this is achieved by checking that no cyclic subtyping among any distinct pair of entities is entailed by the schema. This check is decidable and very efficient in ORM2^{zero}.

Primitive Entity Types Disjointness

According to the ORM2 modelling methodology, in any domain (or 'Universe of Discourse') there is always a top-level partitioning of its entities into exclusive types. These entities without supertypes are called 'primitive entity types', and ORM2 assumes that *primitive entity types never overlap*. We observe that the (default) disjointness between the primitive entity types can be easily represented in ORM2^{zero} by exploiting the introduction of the **TOP** element as the common supertype of all the types in a ORM2^{zero} schema: only top level entities are explicitly set as subentities of **TOP**, and they are also said to be exclusive.

Objectification

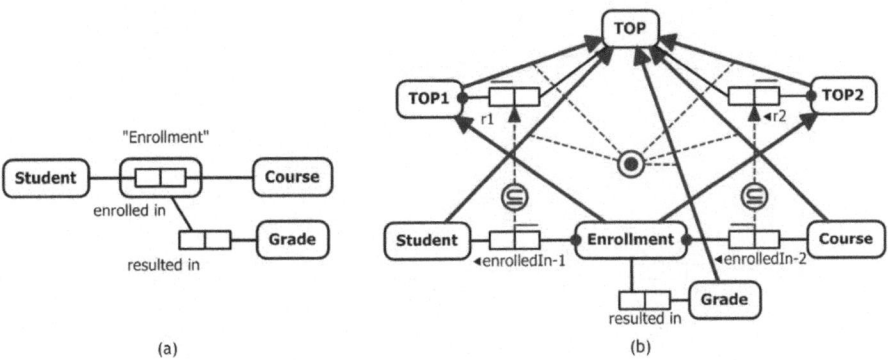

(a)   (b)

The figure (a) above shows an ORM2 schema representing the objectification of a fact type as an entity type whose instances can play the **resulted in** role. The reduction of the schema in ORM2^{zero} is shown on the right side. There is a new entity "Enrolment" representing the objectified predicate, connected with two functional binary predicates objectifying the roles of the original predicate. The objectified predicate is a subtype of both **TOP1** and **TOP2**, representing the set of the identifiers of all tuples having at least one or two roles respectively. The objectified roles in the objectified predicate are subset of the general argumental binary predicates $r1$ and $r2$. In this way, a tuple in a legal database of the schema is always represented by a unique individual (the identifier) having one functional role for each tuple component.

The ORM2^{zero} reduction above fixes the one of theorem **N/CR** (*nest/coreference*) in [4]: according to our encoding a tuple identifier is *global* to the schema, rather than *local* to the context of a predicate, thus satisfying the formal semantics given to objectification. The *local* semantics for tuple identifiers from [4] may lead to wrong conclusions. Let's consider the example schema in Fig. 2. With tuple identifiers local to an objectified predicate, a legal database exists with non-empty binary predicates "... has Spouse ..." and "... is BloodRelative of ..." one including the other and with

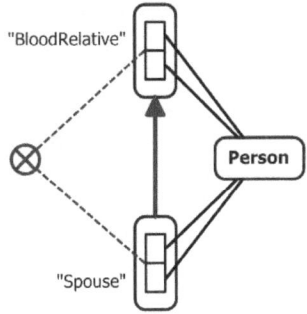

Fig. 2. The entity "Spouse" is not inconsistent with *local* semantics for tuple identifiers

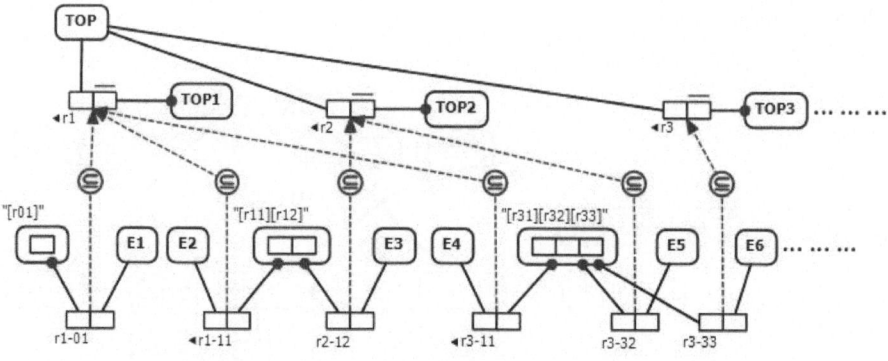

Fig. 3. Encoding of objectified predicates; the subtypes of the general TOP$_i$ entities are not explicitly shown

non-empty disjoint "*Spouse*" and "*BloodRelative*" entities. Such a legal database should not exist, and indeed it does not exist with global tuple identifiers.

The global interpretation comes from the introduction of TOP1, TOP2, ... – each one identifying a component of a tuple by means of the objectified roles $r1, r2, \ldots$ – and by the reuse of the common predefined set of objectified roles. Thus, the identifier of a binary tuple is of type TOP1 and TOP2 (by subtyping), and it is univocally determined by a given tuple of TOP individuals. Now, the fact that the objectified roles linking TOP1 and TOP2 are the same used in the objectification of all the predicates in the schema, does the rest: a tuple (a, b), identified by t in TOP1 and TOP2, is identified in the very same way by all the objectified predicates in the schema. A general pattern for the encoding is shown in figure 3.

For those who are familiar with the 'coreference' interpretation of the objectification presented in [4], it should be evident that in the ORM2^{zero} reduction the external unique-ness constraints (forcing the objectified entity to be coreferenced by the pair of linked types) simply disappeared. Indeed, the external uniqueness can be safely removed in the ORM2^{zero} representation of the objectification because of the semantics the language. The crucial bit to understand the redundancy of this uniqueness in ORM2^{zero} relates to the so-called 'relation-descriptiveness' of the involved models, a model-theoretic prop-erty that have been discussed in, e.g., [5] for formal languages having the 'tree model property' (as, for example, the logic $\mathcal{ALCQI}$). Without entering into the technical de-tails, a model is said to be relation-descriptive if each tuple in an objectified predicate is represented by one and only one individual. Formal results then show that if one is interested in reasoning on schemas represented in languages showing the relation-descriptive property, at least one of such a model is always available. Since ORM2^{zero}, and its logical counterpart, enjoy both the relation-descriptive property, external unique-ness constraints are no longer necessary to enforce a bijection between identifiers and objectified tuples. Because of this, there is a theorem stating that this encoding for objectification does preserve satisfiability and entailment, but does not necessarily pre-serve the structure of the legal databases (the models). As we claimed before, this is not very relevant for our purposes, which are about reasoning over the schema.

Whenever there are additional constraints on the roles of an objectified predicate, we need a strategy for adequately encoding them to the target ORM2^{zero} schema: given an ORM2^{zero} schema with an objectified predicate, (a) copy all the unary frequency and mandatory constraints in some role of the objectified predicate to the corresponding binary predicate representing the objectified role in the target schema, (b) copy the subset and exclusion constraints in the objectified predicate to the corresponding entity, possibly continuing by objectifying also other predicates involved in these constraints.

2   Concluding Remarks

The complete picture thus shows that ORM2^{zero} is an extremely powerful conceptual modelling language. As we have already said, ORM2^{zero+} misses with respect to ORM2: value constraints; cardinality constraints; ring constraints; constraints among roles corresponding to non unary or non-total inclusion dependencies. There are strong computational reasons for not including these constraints. We plan to add to ORM2^{zero} both derivation rules and deontic constraints, in order to support sound, complete, and efficient reasoning for a significant fragment of ORM2.

In an earlier empirical study of conceptual models created at LogicBlox Inc. [6], the authors found that a restricted subset of ORM2, called ORM$^-$, includes the vast majority of constraints used in practice and, moreover, allows scalable test data generation. More recently [7], ORM$^-$ has been extended to include features that resolved to be routinely used by LogicBlox developers. This last version of ORM$^-$ includes: (i) simple mandatory constraints, (ii) frequency constraints (with the restriction that such a constraint spans one or more roles from the same fact type and the sets of roles spanned by different frequency constraints do not overlap), (iii) internal uniqueness constraints, (iv) subtype constraints, (v) value constraints, (vi) objectification, and (vii) external uniqueness constraints (with the restriction that one role in each of the involved fact types is not covered, and the types of the role players of the uncovered roles are 'type compatible'). Although an NP-hard algorithm for consistency checking is provided in [7], the algorithm itself is declared to be *not* complete under the ORM2 semantics (i.e. a full legal instance of an ORM$^-$ schema may exist under the ORM2 semantics, even if the proposed algorithm has no solutions).

On the other hand, our paper introduced a *minimal* conceptual modelling language, called ORM2^{zero}, whose expressive power can be extended so as to cover the majority of the ORM2 constructs, and for which a complete algorithm for reasoning exists. We refer to the maximal expressivity covered by ORM2^{zero} as ORM2^{zero+}. ORM2^{zero+} has a clearly specified formal semantics and provably correct encoding into OWL2 ontology language, and its expressivity is comparable to that of ORM$^-$. Differently from ORM$^-$, our language has no special support for value constraints, since together with objectification falsify relation-descriptiveness. Nonetheless, ORM2^{zero} is able to represent many constraints which are not present in ORM$^-$. As for the frequency occurrences and the uniqueness, the restrictions imposed in ORM$^-$ are similar to those we have in ORM2^{zero}.

Several extensions of ORM2^{zero} are currently under investigation. Among these, the integration of deontic modalities, allowing for the representation of obligation and permission rules, have been already deeply investigated in the context of the SBVR language [8], and the results we got there could be easily transferred in ORM2^{zero}. Nonetheless, the most interesting extension of ORM2^{zero} is about the integration in the language of the so-called 'derivation rules': logical rules that may be used to derive new facts from other facts. Our main goal here is to identify a language for the specification of the rules that is decidable and whose computational properties do not negatively affect the complexity of the current ORM2^{zero}. Similar analyses in the context of conceptual modelling have been recently conducted for the combination of the UML class diagram and the rule language OCL (see, for example, [9]).

We thank two anonymous reviewers who helped us to fix several mistakes of a previous version of this papers.

References

1. Franconi, E., Mosca, A., Solomakhin, D.: ORM2: Formalisation and encoding in OWL2. In: Herrero, P., Panetto, H., Meersman, R., Dillon, T. (eds.) OTM-WS 2012. LNCS, vol. 7567, pp. 368–378. Springer, Heidelberg (2012)
2. Franconi, E., Mosca, A.: The formalisation of ORM2 and its encoding in OWL2. Technical Report KRDB12-2, KRDB Research Centre, Free University of Bozen-Bolzano (2012), http://www.inf.unibz.it/krdb/pub/TR/KRDB12-2.pdf
3. Baader, F., Calvanese, D., McGuinness, D.L., Nardi, D., Patel-Schneider, P.F. (eds.): The description logic handbook: theory, implementation, and applications. Cambridge University Press, New York (2003)
4. Halpin, T., Morgan, T.: Information Modeling and Relational Databases: From Conceptual Analysis to Logical Design, 2nd edn. Morgan Kaufmann (2008)
5. Calvanese, D., Lenzerini, M., Nardi, D.: Unifying class-based representation formalisms. J. Artif. Intell. Res. (JAIR) 11, 199–240 (1999)
6. Smaragdakis, Y., Csallner, C., Subramanian, R.: Scalable satisfiability checking and test data generation from modeling diagrams. Automated Software Engineering 16(1), 73–99 (2009)
7. McGill, M.J., Dillon, L.K., Stirewalt, R.E.K.: Scalable analysis of conceptual data models. In: Proceedings of the 2011 International Symposium on Software Testing and Analysis, ISSTA 2011, pp. 56–66. ACM, New York (2011)
8. Franconi, E., Mosca, A., Solomakhin, D.: Logic-based reasoning support for SBVR. Fundamenta Informaticae 124, 1–18 (2013)
9. Queralt, A., Artale, A., Calvanese, D., Teniente, E.: OCL-lite: Finite reasoning on UML/OCL conceptual schemas. Data Knowl. Eng. 73, 1–22 (2012)

Reference Scheme Reduction on Subtypes in ORM

Andy Carver and Terry Halpin

INTI International University, Malaysia
andy.carver@yahoo.com, t.halpin@live.com

Abstract. Object-Role Modeling (ORM) allows composite reference schemes for object types to be portrayed using either objectification (in the sense of situational nominalization) or coreference (as defined in ORM rather than linguistics). In practical modeling, cases can arise where a subtype of a compositely identified object type has a natural reference scheme that utilizes only some components of the supertype's reference scheme. Using the supertype's reference scheme to verbalize facts for the subtype then leads to redundancy or other irrelevance in the verbalization. Moreover, if such cases are input directly to the ORM's standard relational mapping procedure (Rmap), this can lead to table schemes that are not fully normalized. The paper identifies ways in which such problems can arise, and proposes ways to avoid these problems, partly by extending earlier work on reference scheme reduction, role redirection, and disjunctive reference, illustrating the approach with some practical examples.

1 Introduction

Fact-oriented modeling approaches such as Object-Role Modeling (ORM) [11], Cognition enhanced Natural language Information Analysis Method (CogNIAM) (*http://www.cogniam.eu/*), and Fully Communication Oriented Information Modeling (FCO-IM) [1] capture facts in attribute-free fact types, facilitating validation of conceptual data models with non-technical domain experts by verbalization in natural sentences and use of sample fact populations. Fact-oriented approaches also provide a graphical notation for business constraints that is more expressive than the graphical notation for data modeling in the Unified Modeling Language (UML) or industrial versions of Entity Relationship (ER) modeling. This paper focuses on ORM, discussing recent extensions to its schema transformation and relational mapping procedures.

ORM allows *composite reference schemes* for object types to be portrayed using either *objectification* (in the sense of situational nominalization, where relationships are objectified as states of affairs rather than propositions [7]) or *coreference* (as defined in ORM [11], where two or more relationships combine to provide reference, rather than in linguistics, where coreference involves multiple reference schemes). While this support for composite reference enables ORM to capture many natural identification schemes, it also presents some special challenges if one is to avoid data redundancy. In providing a reference scheme for an entity type, ORM modelers must determine which components are needed to identify entities of that type. But complicating this task is the fact that in ORM there are various ways in which an entity type will by default "inherit", so to speak, a reference scheme (possibly composite).

Y.T. Demey and H. Panetto (Eds.): OTM 2013 Workshops, LNCS 8186, pp. 457–466, 2013.

There are at least three ways in which such "inheritance" occurs. First, an entity type that objectifies a binary or longer fact type "inherits", by default, a composite reference scheme based on the fact type it objectifies. Second, composite reference schemes can include referential relationships with one or more other entity types, each with its own reference scheme, perhaps composite, which is then incorporated into the original reference scheme. A third kind is the inheritance of a supertype's reference scheme by its subtype(s).

Reference-scheme inheritance can generate subtler instances of reference-scheme component irrelevance. For even if it is true that the components, and only those, of some entity type A's composite reference scheme are relevant for identifying A-type objects, it may also be true, due to some contextual rule(s), that not all of those same components are relevant for identification of entities of type B—even if, according to the ORM schema, B inherits the complete reference scheme of entity type A.

The inclusion of components that are actually irrelevant, in a particular object reference, may result in generation of a database schema that allows data redundancy in some object references. In some cases, it could even allow fact redundancy, and hence lead to a table scheme that is not fully normalized. An earlier ORM paper [3] touched upon reference scheme reduction transforms required for correcting reference-component irrelevance generated via the first two kinds of "inheritance" just mentioned. The current paper considers cases of the third kind, viz. a subtype's inheritance of a supertype's reference scheme.

It is important to note that another way to think of that third kind (viz., the irrelevance of a certain referential component for some subtype's instances' identifications) is that there is a constraint or rule that restricts which objects may play a certain role. This situation is similar to the subtype situation: on the one hand, such a textual constraint would commonly be implemented as a subtype definition in ORM; and on the other hand, we normally introduce subtypes in ORM to declare that some specific role(s) are played only by instances of that subtype. In any case, only when subtypes do host—and thus restrict—some role, is there a chance of this subtyping-based referential irrelevance causing data redundancy. Thus, for our purposes, we may consider all such situations as effectively involving subtyping, even if the "subtype" is only one that is implied by a rule restricting which entities can play a particular role(s).

Subtype-specific referential irrelevance may be due to the referential component's data being *redundant* for objects of that subtype. Examples of this are discussed in Section 2. On the other hand, it could be due to the data's being *derivable* from the rest of the object reference. Examples of this are discussed in Section 3. Finally, it could be because some referential component is *inapplicable* to objects of that subtype. Examples of this are discussed in Section 4. Section 5 concludes the paper by summarizing the main contributions, suggesting some related topics for further research, and listing the references cited.

2   Subtype-Specific Referential Irrelevance Due to Redundancy

Mapping a subtype graph from an ORM schema to a relational schema may involve absorption, separation, or partition [11]. A subtype's non-functional roles (those without a simple uniqueness constraint) always map to a table separate from the supertype's table. A subtype's functional roles may be absorbed into the supertable, or placed into a separate table, depending on the designer's choice. Referential redundancy of the kind of interest here can occur when a subtype's role is mapped to a separate table from that of its supertype(s), and the subtype inherits from a supertype a compound reference scheme that has at least one component that is not needed to identify instances of the subtype. As we will see shortly, without special precautions this can result in tables that are not fully normalized.

Subtype-specific referential irrelevance because of data *redundancy* could conceivably be due to a restricted uniqueness constraint, whose restriction-rule specifies exactly the same set of objects as does the subtype's definition, but such cases are unlikely to be met in practice. A much more likely possibility is a subtype definition that itself implies the restricted uniqueness constraint—and thus coordinates with it for free, as it were. We restrict our examples to such cases.

2.1   A Simple Example of Subtype-Specific Referential Redundancy

As a simple example of referential redundancy caused by subtyping, consider the ORM schema on the left side of Fig. 1. The subtyping ensures that a Flower-Containment has an additional Color only if the Bouquet-Pattern involved in the Flower-Containment is a Bouquet-Pattern that contains exactly one Floral Species. The restricted uniqueness constraint implied by this rule is seen more easily in the relational schema to which this Rmaps, shown on the right side of Fig. 1.

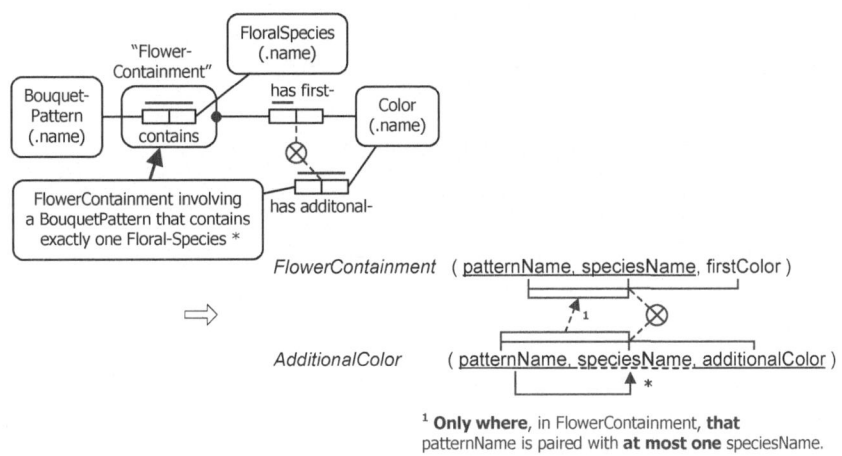

Fig. 1. A simple example that calls for reference-scheme reduction

Here the AdditionalColor table scheme has an extraneous column, speciesName, that is implicitly functionally dependent on just part of the key, so the table scheme is not in second normal form, allowing fact redundancy. This functional dependency (FD) is the restricted uniqueness constraint, implied here by the textual rule to which our subtype's derivation rule Rmaps, qualifying the foreign key constraint between the two tables. Enforcing this textual rule will thus enforce also the functional dependency, controlling the denormalization.

Note that the subtype-defining rule in our ORM schema is of a peculiar sort: the subtype is defined as that subset of the supertype's objects where, *in the current population of any total table for the supertype's objects,* the objects have the same data value populating a particular component of their reference (viz., the Floral Species component). Thus it is the barest rule one could contrive that would imply the restricted uniqueness constraint. We will shortly consider an example with a more-specific subtyping rule. For our current example, we may remove the redundancy by applying a *role-redirection transformation,* to obtain the ORM schema in Fig. 2(b), which Rmaps to the relational schema in Fig. 2(c). The extraneous column is now absent from the AdditionalColor table; and the qualified subset constraint is now single-column, simplifying its enforcement.

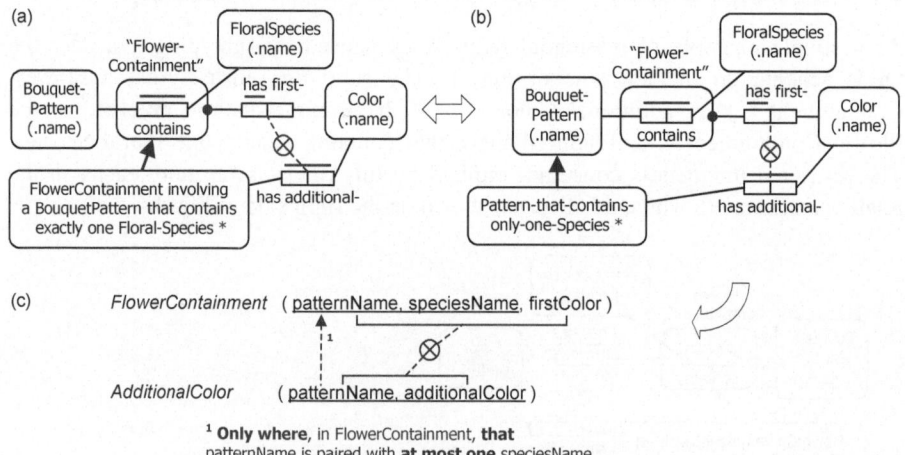

Fig. 2. Using a role-redirection transform to remove the referential redundancy

An abstract pattern for this kind of transformation—which applies only to the case where the nested supertype objectifies a binary, not an *n*-ary—is shown in Fig. 3. The fact type shown with a dashed-line in Fig. 3(a) is a link fact type implied by the objectification. The exact semantics of, and particular constraints shown on, the two right-most fact types in each schema are there for clarity, but not part of the pattern.

In general, a table scheme that is not in 3rd normal form can also result if a fact type (or another entity type) has at least one non-key role hosted by an entity type that has a redundant component in its reference scheme. Such cases may be dealt with in a similar manner. For our earlier work on role redirection and role reduction transforms in ORM, see [3, 9], and for further aspects on ORM and normalization theory see [4].

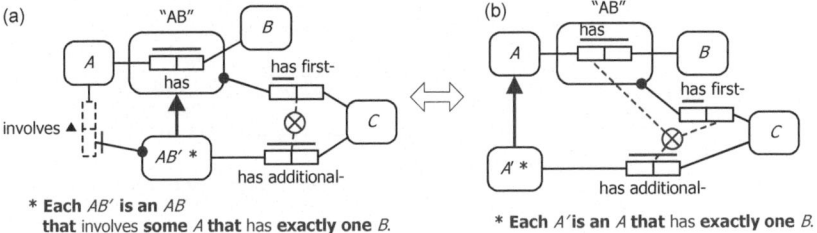

Fig. 3. A role redirection transform pattern

2.2   A Related Case Where the Supertype Is a Nested *n*-ary

A more complicated role redirection transform to remove referential redundancy involving a nested, *n*-ary fact is shown abstractly for the case of *n*= 3 in Fig. 4. The original ORM schema shown in Fig. 4(a) is transformed to the schema in Fig. 4(b). Note the nested binary in the transformed schema, and that its objectifying entity type is non-independent. For convenience, we have added some non-standard ORM graphics on top of the subtype shapes: the ternary fact-type shapes added there depict the restricted uniqueness constraint (spanning only two roles) graphically. Although this illustrates the ternary case, this approach is easily extended for higher arities.

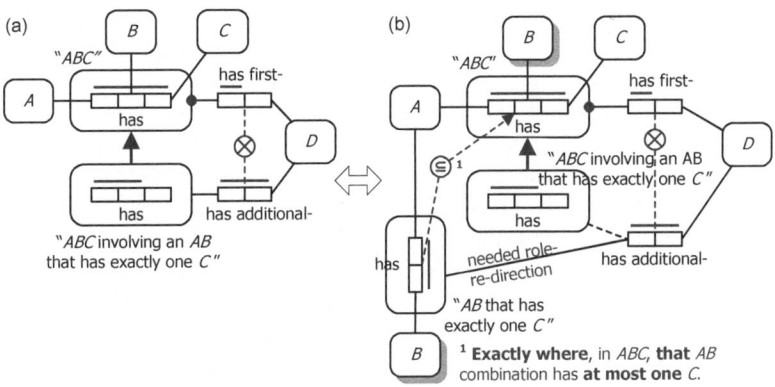

Fig. 4. A role redirection transform involving nesting of an *n*-ary fact type

3   Subtype-Specific Referential Irrelevance Due to Derivability

This section considers cases with a more specific subtyping rule that effectively enables derivation of supertype referential components, which become irrelevant for identifying instances of the subtype. An example containing such a subtyping rule is shown in Fig. 5. In this universe of discourse, we are interested in only three kinds of academy awards: best picture, best actor, and best actress.

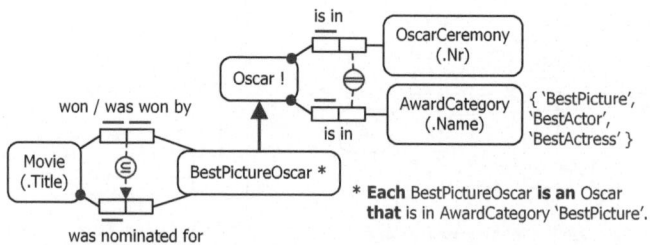

Fig. 5. Another pattern that calls for reference-scheme reduction

Any role hosted by the subtype that Rmaps to a table different from the Oscar table will map to two columns, one for its Oscar ceremony and one for its award category. However the entries in the awardCategory column of this table will all be the same, viz. 'BestPicture'. So, if the subtype's role is non-functional, its award ceremony column is not a key but it functionally determines its award category column, so the table scheme is denormalized. For example, the nomination fact type maps to the table·
Movie(movieTitle, bestPictureNominationOscarCeremony, bestPictureNominationAwardCategory, ...)

This conceptual schema presents a more difficult set of problems than the prior one. If we try verbalizing a sample fact of, say, the fact type BestPictureOscar was won by Movie, we immediately notice some referential irrelevance, even before completing the first object-reference: "The BestPictureOscar that is [an Oscar] in the AwardCategory 'BestPicture' and is in the OscarCeremony ...". Surely a more natural way of verbalizing a sample fact of this type would start out more simply: "The BestPictureOscar that is in the OscarCeremony ...". So while the Fig. 5 scheme might seem a natural way to model this domain, it leads to strange and awkward verbalization.

It is important to realize that there is a second way for referential data to be irrelevant: A referential component is irrelevant also if its value is derivable (by some contextual rule applying to this role) from other information in the entity reference. In the present case, the information from which the entity's AwardCategory ("BestPicture") is derivable is in the object (sub)type stated, "BestPictureOscar". The contextual rule that shows its derivability is the very derivation rule for that subtype. The formal-structural reason for this component's irrelevance is thus that the fact type by which the supertype instance is categorized (by the subtype's derivation rule), Oscar is in AwardCategory, is also a component of the supertype's reference scheme. This is exactly why the fact verbalization sounds like a circumlocution.

What is a solution for this kind of irrelevance? A role-redirection transform could be devised; but it would seem an unnatural way to model, because it would relegate to the predicate text the mention of 'the bestPictureOscar", in every fact type in which that subtype currently hosts a role (by redirecting all its roles to the OscarCeremony entity type). The insistent mentioning of an object of this "BestPictureOscar" type in the fact-verbalizations suggests—especially when there are other types of Oscar in the domain—that a BestPictureOscar entity type should host roles in these facts.

However, as discussed in the next section, there are other ways to model this domain that may offer a way to resolve the problem.

4   Subtype-Specific Referential Irrelevance Due to Inapplicability

If we were to base our initial elementary fact types on natural-sounding verbalizations of the facts of interest about Best Picture Oscars and other sorts of Oscars, the verbalizations would, in fact, not include referential components (for the specific sort of Oscar) that were either "redundant" or "derivable"—precisely because they would be irrelevant for unique identification of the entities.

Imagine that, in doing the Conceptual Schema Design Procedure (CSDP) Steps 1 and 2 upon this Oscar domain, our modeling, based on sample-fact verbalizations, led us to the two kinds of Oscar entity types shown in Fig. 6. Imagine also that we wish to record the same unary predicate ("... was fairly judged") for both of these entity types, and report facts of this type, for both of them, in the same report or query result.

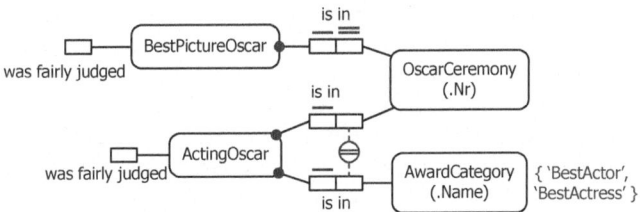

Fig. 6. Distinguishing Oscars with different reference schemes

In this modeling situation, when we came to Step 3 of the CSDP, we might generalize these two "...Oscar" entity types to a common Oscar entity type—even though the two types are mutually exclusive. However, while they have a common referential component, ActingOscar has more such components than does BestPictureOscar. The only way to combine them into one reference scheme would be for the reference scheme for Oscar to be *disjunctive* [12]. We might then end up with a schema at least functionally equivalent to that shown in Fig. 7. Here, the external uniqueness constraint with the small 'o' through its uniqueness bar has outer join semantics [8], so for a given OscarCeremony there is at most one Oscar with no ActingAwardCategory.

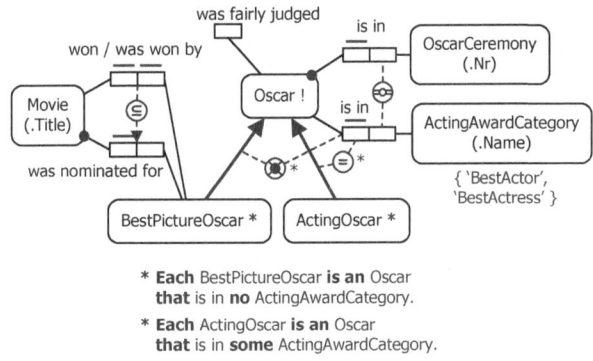

Fig. 7. A disjunctive reference-scheme for Oscar

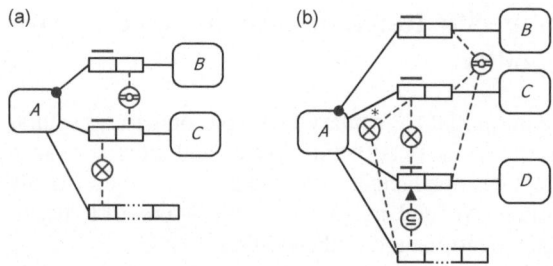

Fig. 8. Two patterns that lead to extraneous, inapplicable relational columns

However, this approach presents us still with a problem of extraneous data—or, to be more precise, extraneous nulls. For we still get an extraneous column—viz. the one for AwardCategory—where any of the BestPictureOscar subtype's roles map to a table different from that to which functional, non-referential (and non-restricted) roles hosted by the supertype map. The only differences will be that such a column will be filled with nulls on every row, instead of the AwardCategory 'BestPicture', and that the column is extraneous not because it is derivable, but because it is *inapplicable*. This is true for any case of disjunctive reference where the restricted role is either explicitly or implicitly spanned by an exclusion constraint spanning also one of the optional referential roles of the entity type. Fig. 8 shows two such schemes.

A role-redirection transform could be devised; but would be unnatural, because the predicate text in every fact type specific to that subtype would include "bestPictureOscar". A better solution for this kind of irrelevance, as well that caused by derivability, is to qualify Step 4 of our Rmap procedure [11] to ensure that when one "unpacks" any surrogate columns produced by Rmapping roles hosted by either explicit or implicit subtypes, where the role maps to a table other than that for any functional, non-referential roles of the supertype, then one unpacks that role only into its *relevant* (i.e. its *applicable, non-derivable, and non-redundant*) referential components.

Another solution is to transform the ORM schema before Rmapping by using one of the strategies for implementing other kinds of disjunctive reference: introduce a simple identifier; concatenate referential components to a simple identifier applying type casting where needed; render the optional referential roles mandatory by using special default values instead of nulls [11, 12]. Of these, introduction of a simple identifier is usually the best option (e.g. OscarId in Fig. 9 removes the problem). The third option (using default values) still leads to derivable irrelevance, unless the Rmap modification suggested above is employed.

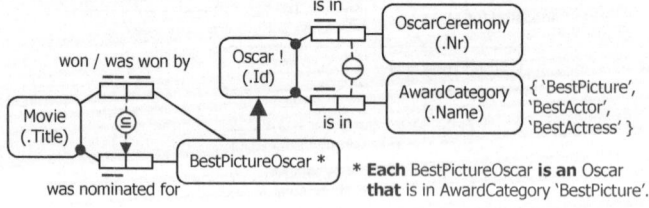

Fig. 9. Introducing a simple identifier

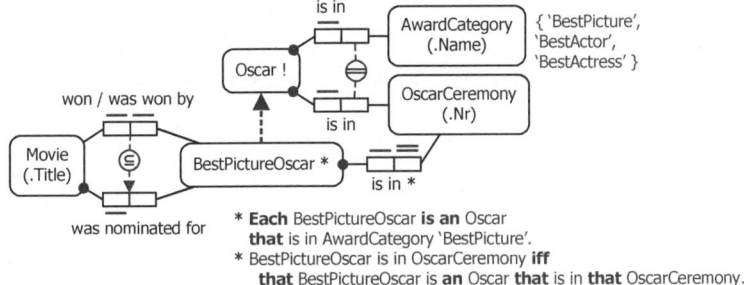

Fig. 10. An alternative approach using a derived reference-scheme

Yet another solution would be to extend ORM to allow preferred reference schemes to be based on derived fact types, as shown in Fig. 10. Here the subtype introduces its own, simpler context-dependent reference scheme which is itself derived using the rule shown. After relational mapping, Oscars in the Oscar supertable are identified compositely, but Oscars in the Movie table are simply identified.

5   Conclusion

This paper examined cases where a subtype of a compositely identified object type has a natural reference scheme that utilizes only some components of the supertype's reference scheme. As well as leading to redundancy in verbalizing some subtype facts at the conceptual level, such cases can map to relational schemas involving table schemes that are not fully normalized unless special precautions are taken.

We identified ways in which such problems can arise, and proposed ways to avoid these problems, partly by extending earlier work on reference scheme reduction, role redirection, and disjunctive reference. We used the term "redundancy" to refer to referential-component irrelevance of a very restricted sort, not based on the component's derivability or inapplicability. In the very broadest sense, of course, the term "redundancy" could include the latter two cases. But they seem different enough conceptually, from this most restricted case, that they deserve their own categories. Also, we found that whereas role-redirection was a feasible and seemingly appropriate solution for this most restricted type of "redundancy", it did not seem appropriate for cases of component derivability or inapplicability. For all three kinds of referential irrelevance for a subtype, however, we found that an extension to RMap Step 4 would be an effective solution for avoiding redundancy in the relational schema. Often, the most natural way of modelling a supertype's reference scheme is disjunctive reference; for which are available also other remedies for any relational-level redundancy.

Future plans in this area of research include implementing an extended version of Rmap in the NORMA tool [5] to deal properly with such cases, including introduction of surrogate identifiers as a mapping choice, and investigating further cases of disjunctive reference in which supertypes that are partitioned into subtypes with different reference schemes are allowed to abstract reference schemes from their subtypes.

References

1. Bakema, G., Zwart, J., van der Lek, H.: Fully Communication Oriented Information Modelling. Ten Hagen Stam (2000)
2. Carver, A.: How To Avoid Redundant Object-References. In: Meersman, R., Tari, Z., Herrero, P. (eds.) OTM-WS 2008. LNCS, vol. 5333, pp. 770–779. Springer, Heidelberg (2008)
3. Carver, A.: Roles in ORM: A Suggested Semantics. In: Meersman, R., Dillon, T., Herrero, P. (eds.) OTM-WS 2011. LNCS, vol. 7046, pp. 360–369. Springer, Heidelberg (2011)
4. Carver, A., Halpin, T.: Atomicity and Semantic Normalization. International Journal of Information System Modeling and Design 1(2), 23–39 (2010)
5. Curland, M., Halpin, T.: The NORMA Software Tool for ORM 2. In: Soffer, P., Proper, E. (eds.) CAiSE Forum 2010. LNBIP, vol. 72, pp. 190–204. Springer, Heidelberg (2011)
6. Halpin, T.: What is an Elementary Fact? In: Nijssen, G.M., Sharp, J. (eds.) Proc. 1st NIAM-ISDM Conf. (1993)
7. Halpin, T.: Objectification of Relationships. In: Siau, K. (ed.) Advanced Topics in Database Research, vol. 5, pp. 106–123. Idea Publishing Group, Hershey (2006)
8. Halpin, T.: Modeling of Reference Schemes. In: Nurcan, S., Proper, H.A., Soffer, P., Krogstie, J., Schmidt, R., Halpin, T., Bider, I. (eds.) BPMDS 2013 and EMMSAD 2013. LNBIP, vol. 147, pp. 308–323. Springer, Heidelberg (2013)
9. Halpin, T., Carver, A., Owen, K.M.: Reduction Transformations in ORM. In: Meersman, R., Tari, Z. (eds.) OTM-WS 2007, Part I. LNCS, vol. 4805, pp. 699–708. Springer, Heidelberg (2007)
10. Halpin, T., Curland, M.: Recent Enhancements to ORM. In: Demey, Y.T., Panetto, H. (eds.) OTM 2013 Workshops. LNCS, vol. 8186, pp. 467–476. Springer, Heidelberg (2013)
11. Halpin, T., Morgan, T.: Information Modeling and Relational Databases, 2nd edn. Morgan Kaufmann Publishers (2008)
12. Halpin, T., Ritson, R.: Fact-Oriented Modelling and Null Values. In: Srinivasan, B., Zeleznikov, J. (eds.) Research and Practical Issues in Databases. World Scientific, Singapore (1992)
13. Levinson, S.C.: Pragmatics. Cambridge University Press, Cambridge (1983)

Recent Enhancements to ORM

Terry Halpin[1] and Matthew Curland[2]

[1] INTI International University, Malaysia
[2] ORM Solutions, USA
{t.halpin,mcurland}@live.com

Abstract. Fact-oriented modeling approaches such as Object-Role Modeling (ORM) employ rich graphical notations for capturing business constraints, and validate their data models with domain experts by verbalizing the models in natural language, and by populating the relevant fact types with concrete examples. This paper discusses several recent enhancements to ORM, including the following: further constraints on supertype link roles and their relevance to restricted mandatory role constraints; inclusive-or constraints on roles hosted by different types; refinements to the concept of independent object types; additional kinds of reference schemes and associated uniqueness constraints; and verbalization of further constraint cases involving subtyping, additional reference scheme patterns, uniqueness and frequency constraints involving unaries, and external uniqueness constraints involving *n*-ary fact types. The paper also includes some discussion of how these enhancements have been supported, or are soon to be supported, in the Natural ORM Architect (NORMA) tool.

1 Introduction

Fact-oriented modeling approaches formulate data models in terms of fact types whose fact instances are expressed in natural sentences easily understood by business users of the information systems for which the data models are designed. A fact type corresponds to a set of typed predicates of arity one (e.g. Person smokes), two (e.g. Person was born on Date), or higher (e.g. Person hired Person on Date). Since all facts are expressed as relationships, this differs from Entity relationship (ER) modeling [2] and class diagramming within the Unified Modeling Language (UML) [18], which encode some facts in attributes (e.g. Person.isSmoker, Person.birthdate). Fact-orientation's attribute-free nature facilitates validation with domain experts by verbalizing the model's fact types, constraints and derivation rules in natural sentences, and populating the fact types with concrete examples. It also promotes semantic stability (e.g. no remodeling is needed to talk about an attribute). Moreover, fact-orientation's graphical constraint notation for data modeling is much richer than that of industrial ER or UML.

The family of fact-oriented modeling approaches include various dialects such as Object-Role Modeling (ORM), Natural-language Information Analysis Method (NIAM) [20], Fully-Communication Oriented Information Modeling (FCO-IM) [1] and the Predicator Set Model (PSM) [16]. This paper focuses on recent enhancements to second generation ORM (ORM 2) [6]. Overviews of ORM may be found in [8, 9],

Y.T. Demey and H. Panetto (Eds.): OTM 2013 Workshops, LNCS 8186, pp. 467–476, 2013.
© Springer-Verlag Berlin Heidelberg 2013

and a detailed coverage in [15]. The rest of this paper is structured as follows. Section 2 considers constraints on supertype link roles and their relevance to restricted mandatory role constraints. Section 3 considers inclusive-or constraints on roles hosted by different types. Section 4 refines the concept of independent object types. Section 5 discusses additional kinds of uniqueness and frequency constraints, and their verbalization support in the Natural ORM Architect (NORMA) tool [3]. Section 6 concludes by summarizing the main contributions, identifying future research areas, and listing the references cited.

2   Constraints on Supertype Link Roles

In Figure 1(a) the role of using a company car is optional for employees, but mandatory for executives. The restricted mandatory role constraint is displayed as a footnoted textual constraint. In ORM, mandatory role and or-constraints over subtyping links are understood to apply to *supertype link roles* (i.e. the supertype roles of the implied, instance-level, identity relationships linking subtype and supertype instances). For example, the exclusive-or constraint in Figure 1(b) applies to the supertype roles of the subtyping identity fact types shown with dashed lines in Figure 1(c). We recently extended ORM and NORMA to allow other kinds of constraint to apply to supertype link roles. Among other things, this enables restricted mandatory role constraints to be expressed graphically, as shown by the subset constraint in Figure1(d), which is interpreted as in Figure 1(e). In NORMA we automatically verbalize this constraint as follows: **If some** Employee is **some** Executive **then that** Employee uses **some** CompanyCar.

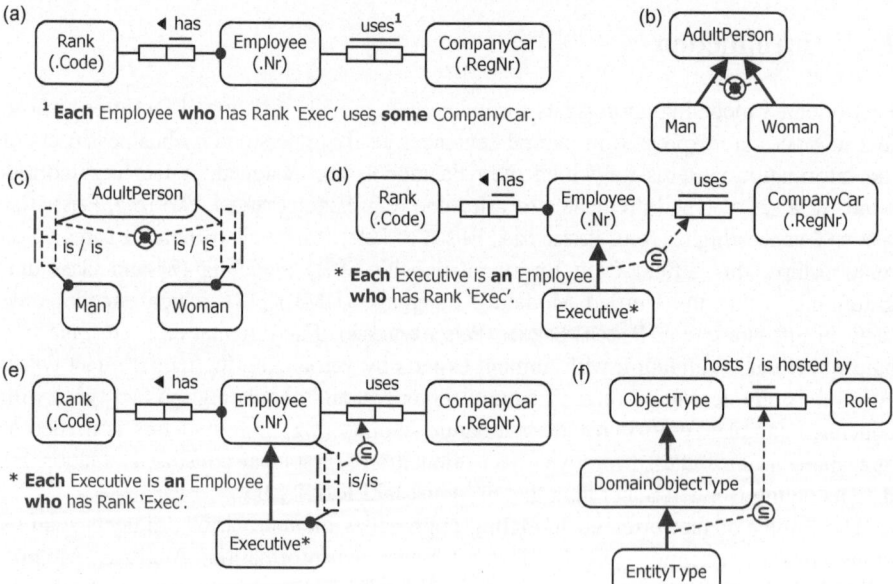

Fig. 1. Using subset constraints on subtyping link roles for restricted mandatory constraints

Another example is provided by Figure 1(f), which is extracted from a recent draft of a common metamodel for fact-based modeling being developed by the fact-based modeling working group. Here the subtypes are asserted rather than being derived, and the subset constraint ensures that each entity type hosts some role.

3   Inclusive-or Constraints on Roles Hosted by Different Types

Typically, an inclusive-or constraint applies to two more roles hosted by the same object type. Recently, we extended ORM to allow such constraints to apply to roles hosted by different types, so long as those types are compatible (and hence may share instances). For such cases, we define the inclusive-or constraint thus: for each state of the model, *each instance in the population of the minimal common supertype of the types hosting the constrained role must play at least one of the constrained roles.* Typically, the minimal common supertype will be the root of the subtype graph.

A simple example is shown in Figure 2(a), where one constrained role is hosted by Employee and the other by Manager. Employee and Manager are compatible since Manager is a subtype of Employee. Here, the inclusive-or constraint means that each employee reports to some manager, or is a manager who manages some employee. For a one-person company, this is satisfiable only if we allow self-management.

Verbalization patterns for inclusive-or constraints are presented in our earlier work [4], and we recently extended these patterns by including the implied link fact type (see Figure 2(b)) as part of the verbalization path. Assuming that Employee is declared personal, our current NORMA verbalization for this constraint is as shown below. In the longer term, we plan to optimize the verbalization simply to: **Each** Employee reports to **some** Manager **or** is **some** Manager **who** manages **some** Employee:

> **For each** Employee
> **that** Employee reports to **some** Manager
> **or some** Manager **who** is **that** Employee manages **some** Employee.

Figure 2(c) includes a reading for the reporting fact type in one direction only. For this case, NORMA currently generates the following verbalization:

> **For each** Employee,
> **some** Manager manages **that** Employee
> **or some** Manager **who** is **that** Employee manages **some** Employee.

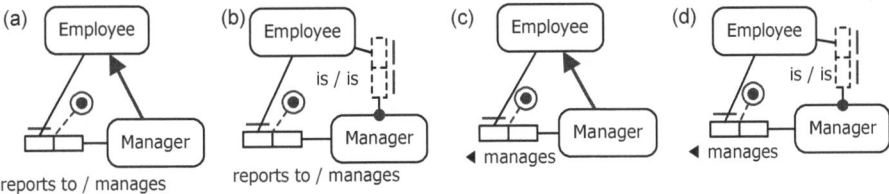

Fig. 2. An inclusive-or constraint on roles hosted by different types

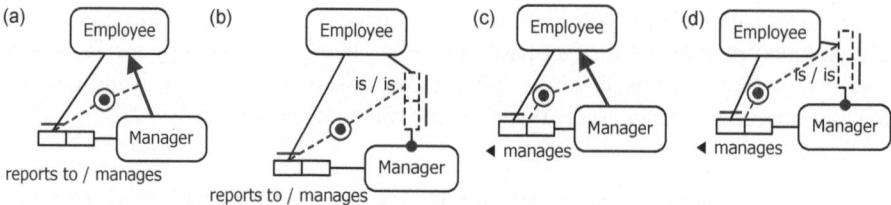

Fig. 3. A multi-type inclusive-or constraint on a supertype link role

Figure 3(a) shows an example of a more realistic inclusive-or constraint involving multiple types. In this case, one of the constrained roles is a supertype link role, as shown explicitly in Figure 3(b). Our previous verbalization patterns may be applied to this situation simply by using the link predicate reading like a normal predicate in the constraint path. Figure 3(a) has forward and inverse predicate readings available, so the inclusive-or constraint may be verbalized thus:

> **Each** Employee reports to **some** Manager **or** is **some** Manager.

Figure 3(c) includes a reading for the reporting fact type in one direction only, so the inclusive-or constraint is verbalized as follows:

> **For each** Employee,
> **some** Manager manages **that** Employee
> **or that** Employee is **some** Manager.

For all cases, if the constraint has deontic rather than alethic modality [7], an appropriate deontic operator is prepended (e.g. "**It is obligatory that**" or "**It is forbidden that**" for positive and negative forms of the verbalization respectively) [4].

4   Independent Object Types Revisited

The notion of independent object types was introduced to ORM in an earlier paper [5], where we originally described them as "lazy object types". Later, we defined an independent object type to be a primitive object type whose fact roles (if any) are collectively optional [15, p. 219]. A primitive object type is an object type that is not a subtype, and "fact role" in this context means a role in an elementary fact type. The basic idea is that an independent type can contain instances that simply exist, independently of playing in any other *elementary* facts. We now use the term "atomic fact" to include elementary facts (which simply apply a predicate to one or more objects), and *existential* facts (which are used to simply assert the existence of, or refer to, an entity instance). Existential fact types are also known as reference types.

Recently, we refined the concept of independent object types to clearly distinguish the kinds of types and roles involved, and to exclude from consideration facts that can be derived. Without the latter exclusion, situations can arise where full software tool support for determining the consistency of independent type settings could require extremely complex computations over derivation paths.

To assist in formulating our new definition for independent object types, some terminology is first provided. Our recent formalization of ORM [10] partitioned ORM object types into entity types (e.g. Employee, Country), semantic value types (e.g. EmployeeNr, CountryCode), and datatypes (e.g. integer, string). Semantic value types are now called *domain value types* (or simply *value types*).

A *referential role* (or existential role) *of an entity type* is a role that it hosts in one of its existential fact types, i.e. a fact type in its preferred reference scheme. Note that implied, objectification link fact types [15, p. 442] that are used in the reference scheme for the objectified entity type are existential fact types for that entity type.

A *non-referential role of an object type* is a role that is hosted by that object type but is not referential for that object type. All roles hosted by a value type are non-referential because value types have no reference scheme. A *non-referential role* is a role that is not a referential role of any object type. For example, Figure 4 displays with gold fill the referential roles for (a) Country, (b) Room, and (c) Enrolment. All roles displayed with white fill are non-referential.

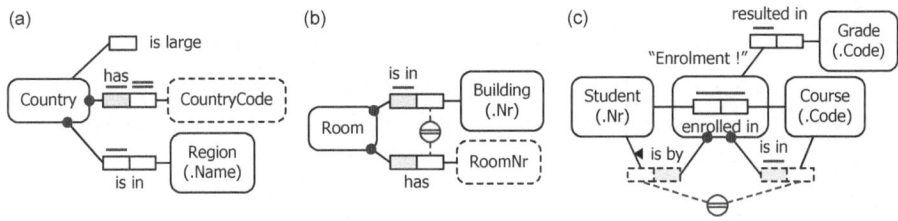

Fig. 4. Referential roles of Country, Room and Enrolment are displayed with gold fill

Implied identity link roles of subtypes are non-referential, even if the subtyping arrow connection is displayed with a solid line (showing an inheritance path to the reference scheme) [15, p. 519].For example, the identity link roles played by the subtypes in the previous figures, such as Figure 1(e), are non-referential.

An *assertable role* is a role in a fact type that is either asserted or semiderived. Hence, if an object type hosts an assertable role, *some* of its instances may be asserted to play that role. If the fact type is asserted, all instances in the object's type's population may be asserted to play the role. Roles in derived fact types are not assertable.

We now refine the definition of independent object type as follows. An *independent object type* is a primitive, domain object type that may include instances that are simply asserted to exist, without playing any assertable, non-referential roles (i.e. instances of it may exist independently of playing any such role). A *non-independent object type* is an object type that is not independent. In this case, the disjunction of its assertable, non-referential roles is non-empty and is implied to be mandatory.

For example, Enrolment in Figure 4(c) is independent (as indicated by the "!" appended to its name), allowing some enrolments to be recorded before the resulting grade of the student in that course is known. The domain object type requirement ensures that no datatype can be an independent object type. Moreover, an object type that hosts no assertable, non-referential role is implicitly independent. For example, if Room in Figure 4(b) hosts no other role in the conceptual schema, then it is implicitly independent.

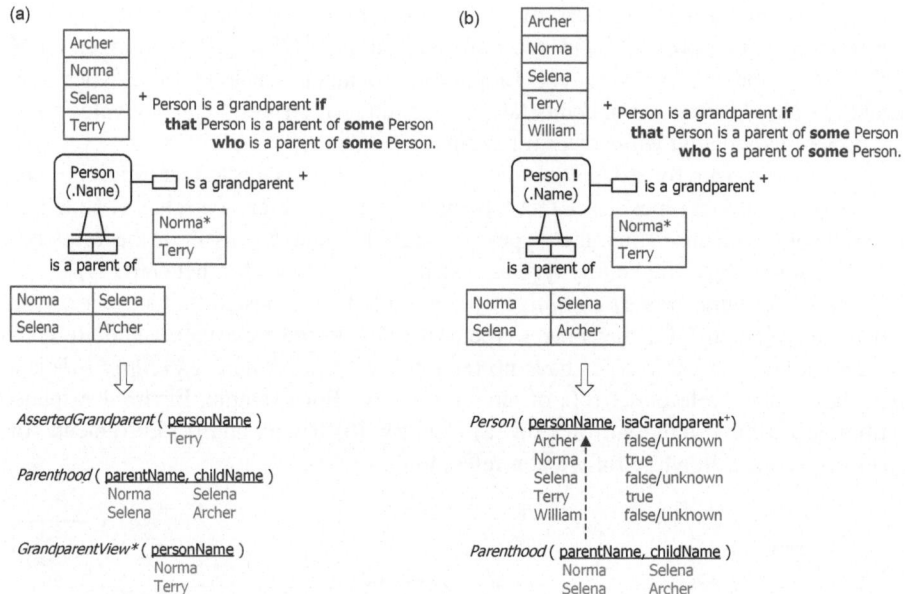

Fig. 5. Influence of independence status on relational mapping of a semiderived fact type

The different semantics for independence status involving semiderived fact types is illustrated by the different relational mapping results in Figure 5 (other mapping choices are possible). In the ORM schema of Figure 5(a), Person is non-independent, so each recorded person must be asserted to play at least one of the assertable, non-referential roles (i.e. the role of being a parent, the role of being a child, or the role of being a grandparent). If desired, one may add a view for Person as the union of the columns in the two base tables.

In the ORM schema of Figure 5(b), Person is independent, so a person may be recorded without being recorded to play any assertable, non-referential role (e.g. as illustrated by William in the sample data). The semiderived isaGrandparent column may be implemented by setting its default to false or unknown depending on whether closed world or open world semantics respectively is assumed for the semiderived fact type, and by using a trigger or stored procedure for derived grandparenthood. Alternatively, one may replace the isaGrandparent column by an asserted isAssertedGrandparent column, and include a derived GrandparentView. The key difference is that for independent types the relational schema must enable recording of instances that play no other roles.

5   Additional Uniqueness and Frequency Constraints

In ORM, an external uniqueness constraint spans two or more roles and is displayed as a circled bar connected to the constrained roles. If the constraint underlies the preferred reference scheme for an entity type at the other end of the relationships, the roles at the other end must be mandatory, and a double bar is used, as in Figure 6(a).

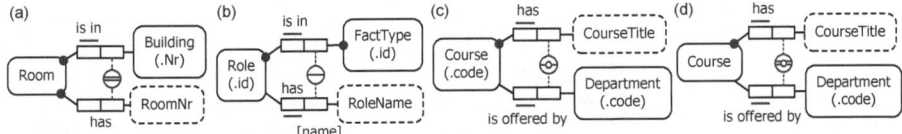

Fig. 6. External uniqueness constraints with (a), (b) inner or (c), (d) outer join semantics

The external uniqueness constraint in the ORM metamodel fragment shown in Figure 6(b) ensures that role names within a given fact type must be distinct. This constraint has *inner join semantics* so is equivalent to an internal uniqueness constraint on the relational inner join of the binary fact types: *Role*(<u>roleId</u>, <u>factType, roleName</u>). So in general a fact type may have many unnamed roles, but any named role can be identified by the combination of its name and its fact type.

External uniqueness constraints with inner join semantics can be used for the primary reference scheme of an entity type only if the coroles hosted by that entity type in the constrained relationships are mandatory, as in Figure 6(a) but not Figure 6(b).

The external uniqueness constraints in Figures 6(c) and 6(d) are depicted with an *inner "o" through the uniqueness bar*. We recently added this graphical notation to indicate that the uniqueness constraint has *outer join semantics, with the added proviso that nulls produced in the outer join are treated as actual values*. Hence each course may be referenced by exactly one of the following patterns: the combination of its course title and its department (where the course is offered by a department); its course title (where the course is offered by no department). External uniqueness constraints of this nature are verbalized in two sentences, one for the inner join semantics and one for the additional semantics of the outer join. The external uniqueness constraint in Figure 6(c) verbalizes thus:

> **For each** CourseTitle **and** Department,
> **at most one** Course has **that** CourseTitle **and** is offered by **that** Department.
> **For each** CourseTitle,
> **at most one** Course has **that** CourseTitle **and** is offered by **no** Department.

External uniqueness constraints with outer join semantics involve at least one optional corole but can be used for primary reference, as shown by the double uniqueness bar in Figure 6(d). If there are multiple optional roles, the order of outer joins is relevant, and is determined by the role selection order of the uniqueness constraint. The schemas in Figures 6(c) and (d) exemplify disjunctive reference, a capability introduced to ORM in [16], using a now outmoded notation. For a comparative review of reference schemes in ORM, Barker ER, UML, the Web Ontology Language (OWL) [19] and relational databases, see [11].

Though exceedingly rare in practice, it is possible to have an external uniqueness constraint over roles projected from a join path involving multiple joins some of which have inner join semantics and some of which have outer join semantics. For such mixed join semantics cases, we use "o" with a dashed line for the uniqueness bar, as in Figure 7(a), which also depicts the weakest constraint pattern allowed for a reference. The join types (inner or outer) for specific roles are not depicted graphically, but in an extended version of the NORMA tool may be specified in its join path editor, and then automatically verbalized.

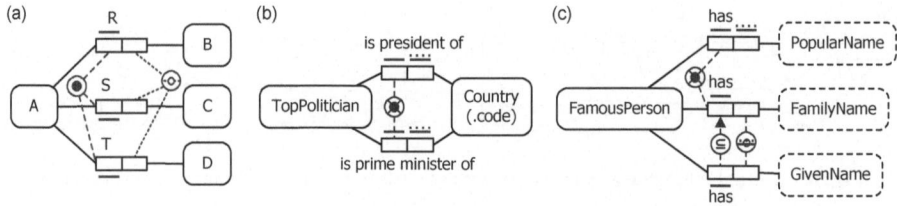

Fig. 7. Further varieties of uniqueness constraints

The schemas in Figures 7(b) and (c) show a graphical notation we recently introduced to deal with other reference cases found in practice. A *uniqueness constraint displayed with both a solid and a dotted bar* may be used to reference just some instances of the relevant entity type. A disjunctive reference scheme for the entity type may then be provided by two or more *partial, preferred reference schemes*. In Figure 7(b), some top politicians may be identified by being the president of a specified country, while other top politicians are identified by being prime ministers of a specified country. For example, the reference scheme in Figure 7(b) verbalizes as follows.

> **For each** Country,
> **at most one** TopPolitician is president of **that** Country, **and**
> **at most one** TopPolitician is prime minister of **that** Country.
> **These associations with** Country **provide the preferred identification scheme for** TopPolitician.

In Figure 7(c), some famous persons may be identified simply by their popular name (e.g. 'Confucius'), some others by their family name (e.g. 'Einstein'), and the rest by combining their family name and a given name (e.g. 'Marie Curie', 'Pierre Curie'). Disjunctive reference may be implemented directly in SQL by a table with no primary key, or indirectly using a simple identifier that is auto-generated. In some cases, a simple character string identifier can be derived by concatenating the reference components with suitable separator characters and recasting types as needed.

Although *external uniqueness and frequency constraints* typically apply to roles in binary fact types, we now support their *use with n-ary and unary fact types*. We have space here to discuss just a few examples. In Figure 8(a) the external uniqueness constraint restricts roles from binary and ternary and ternary fact types. This is equivalent to an internal uniqueness constraint on the corresponding roles in the inner join of the two fact types, and verbalizes as follows: **For each** Performer **and** Date, **there is at most one** Concert **such that that** Concert features **that** Performer **in some** Position **and is on that** Date.

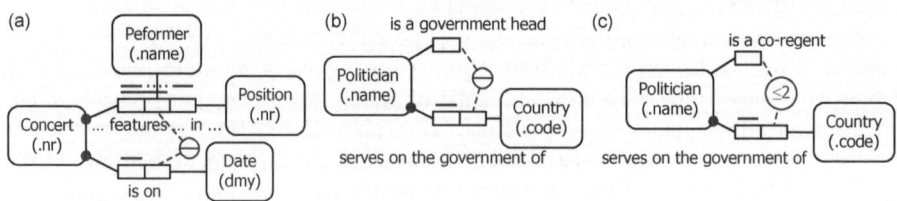

Fig. 8. Further cases of external uniqueness and frequency constraints

The external uniqueness constraint in Figure 8(b) is a *unique-where-true constraint*, where the uniqueness applies only to those politicians who are government heads (i.e. where it is true that they play the unary predicate). This kind of constraint was introduced to ORM in [11], using a now outmoded notation. We now use the usual constraint symbol for external uniqueness, and have improved the automated verbalization. For this example, the unique-where-true constraint verbalizes thus:

> **For each** Country,
>> **at most one** Politician is a government head
>> **and** serves on the government of **that** Country.

Recently, we extended *external frequency constraints* to cater for such *where-true* cases. For example, NORMA verbalizes the frequency constraint in Figure 8(c) as follows:

> **For each** Country,
>> **there are at most** 2 **instances of** Politician **such that**
>>> **that** Politician is a co-regent
>>> **and** serves on the government of **that** Country.

6   Conclusion

This paper has provided a concise treatment of several of our recent enhancements to ORM, including: further constraints on supertype link roles and their relevance to restricted mandatory role constraints; inclusive-or constraints on roles hosted by different types; refinements to the concept of independent object types; additional kinds of reference schemes and associated uniqueness constraints; and verbalization of further constraint cases involving subtyping, additional reference scheme patterns, external uniqueness and frequency constraints involving unaries or *n*-ary fact types. It should be noted that these extensions have been added to enable modeling of practical cases that we have met in industrial modeling. Business domains can be complex, and models that reflect them faithfully need to provide the relevant expressive power.

We have implemented in NORMA all of the work described in this paper, with the sole exception of the additional flavors of external uniqueness constraints relating to disjunctive reference, which we plan to soon support. Other research plans in this area include extending NORMA's relational mapping support for such advanced cases, and refining the constraint verbalization. For example, adding pluralization support would enable more natural rendering of many constraints (e.g. compare "**at most** 2 **instances of** Politican" with "**at most** 2 Politicians". Although some research efforts have been made to provide verbalization of ORM models in languages other than English, much more work needs to be done in this regard.

References

1. Bakema, G., Zwart, J., van der Lek, H.: Fully Communication Oriented Information Modelling. Ten Hagen Stam (2000)
2. Chen, P.P.: The entity-relationship model—towards a unified view of data. ACM Transactions on Database Systems 1(1), 9–36 (1976),
   http://csc.lsu.edu/news/erd.pdf

3. Curland, M., Halpin, T.: The NORMA Software Tool for ORM 2. In: Soffer, P., Proper, E. (eds.) CAiSE Forum 2010. LNBIP, vol. 72, pp. 190–204. Springer, Heidelberg (2011)

4. Curland, M., Halpin, T.: Enhanced Verbalization of ORM Models. In: Herrero, P., Panetto, H., Meersman, R., Dillon, T. (eds.) OTM-WS 2012. LNCS, vol. 7567, pp. 399–408. Springer, Heidelberg (2012)

5. Halpin, T.: What is an elementary fact? In: Nijssen, G.M., Sharp, J. (eds.) Proceedings of First NIAM-ISDM Conference. Utrecht. (1993)

6. Halpin, T.: ORM 2. In: Meersman, R., Tari, Z. (eds.) OTM-WS 2005. LNCS, vol. 3762, pp. 676–687. Springer, Heidelberg (2005)

7. Halpin, T.: Modality of Business Rules. In: Siau, K. (ed.) Research Issues in Systems Analysis and Design, Databases and Software Development, pp. 206–226. IGI Publishing, Hershey (2007)

8. Halpin, T.: Object-Role Modeling: Principles and Benefits. International Journal of Information Systems Modeling and Design 1(1), 32–54 (2010)

9. Halpin, T.: Fact-Orientation and Conceptual Logic. In: Proc. 15th International EDOC Conference, pp. 14–19. IEEE Computer Society, Helsinki (2011)

10. Halpin, T.: Formalization of ORM Revisited. In: Herrero, P., Panetto, H., Meersman, R., Dillon, T. (eds.) OTM-WS 2012. LNCS, vol. 7567, pp. 348–357. Springer, Heidelberg (2012)

11. Halpin, T.: Modeling of Reference Schemes. In: Nurcan, S., Proper, H.A., Soffer, P., Krogstie, J., Schmidt, R., Halpin, T., Bider, I. (eds.) BPMDS 2013 and EMMSAD 2013. LNBIP, vol. 147, pp. 308–323. Springer, Heidelberg (2013)

12. Halpin, T., Carver, A., Owen, K.: Reduction Transformations in ORM. In: Meersman, R., Tari, Z. (eds.) OTM-WS 2007, Part I. LNCS, vol. 4805, pp. 699–708. Springer, Heidelberg (2007)

13. Halpin, T., Curland, M.: Automated Verbalization for ORM 2. In: Meersman, R., Tari, Z., Herrero, P. (eds.) OTM 2006 Workshops. LNCS, vol. 4278, pp. 1181–1190. Springer, Heidelberg (2006)

14. Halpin, T., Curland, M.: Enriched Support for Ring Constraints. In: Meersman, R., Dillon, T., Herrero, P. (eds.) OTM-WS 2011. LNCS, vol. 7046, pp. 309–318. Springer, Heidelberg (2011)

15. Halpin, T., Morgan, T.: Information Modeling and Relational Databases, 2nd edn. Morgan Kaufmann, San Francisco (2008)

16. Halpin, T., Ritson, R.: Fact-Oriented Modelling and Null Values. In: Srinivasan, B., Zeleznikov, J. (eds.) Research and Practical Issues in Databases. World Scientific, Singapore (1992)

17. ter Hofstede, A., Proper, H., van der Weide, T.: Formal definition of a conceptual language for the description and manipulation of information models. Information Systems 18(7), 489–523 (1993)

18. Object Management Group: OMG Unified Modeling Language (OMG UML), version 2.5 FTF Beta 1 (2012), http://www.omg.org/spec/UML/2.5

19. W3C: OWL 2 Web Ontology Language: Direct Semantics, 2nd edn. (2012), http://www.w3.org/TR/owl2-direct-semantics/

20. Wintraecken, J.: The NIAM Information Analysis Method: Theory and Practice. Kluwer, Deventer (1990)

Including Spatial/Temporal Objects in ORM

Gerhard Skagestein[1] and Håvard Tveite[2]

[1] University of Oslo, Department of Informatics
[2] Norwegian University of Life Sciences

Abstract. We suggest to include spatial entities and corresponding spatial values as first class citizens in fact oriented models using ORM. A spatial entity is just a piece of some space. A spatial value is seen as a possibly infinite set of positions in some coordinate system. This makes the conceptual model very independent of the implementation platform. On this basis, we suggest a notation for spatial values. Further, we investigate some rather useful spatial constraints; the no overlap constraint and the no overlap exclusion constraint, which turn out to be spesializations of the uniqueness and the exclusion constraints. Finally, we discuss some possible implementation platforms.

1 Introduction

The idea to be discussed here is to introduce spatial entities and values as first order citizens in ORM, which hopefully will make it easier to model spatial concepts, such as countries, rivers, buildings and mechanical constructions.

Fig. 1a depicts a traditional model for a time period. The reader of this model has to implicitly assume that not only the startday and the endday belong to the time period, but also all the days in between. The same holds for the application program that handles this time period. In Fig. 1b, we rather see the time period as a spatial entity represented by a spatial value consisting of an infinite set of time positions on the time line. The notation for the value will be explained later. What we have done here, is to exploit to its full extent one

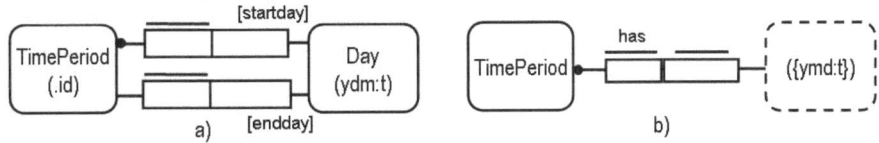

Fig. 1. Introducing a spatial value as a first order citizen

of the fundamental principles of ORM, namely the principle of separating the model from its representation. The model in Fig. 1b may be implemented in many different ways, but the model will stay the same, independent of how we choose to represent the spatial value.

Y.T. Demey and H. Panetto (Eds.): OTM 2013 Workshops, LNCS 8186, pp. 477–486, 2013.
© Springer-Verlag Berlin Heidelberg 2013

This distinction between the conceptual and the implementation level will get even more important for multidimensional spatial values, where a large variety of representations may be found in the literature, see for example [19, Chapter 10] (raster and vector), [16] (time) and [3] (indeterminate boundaries).

The paper is organized as follows: Section 2 gives an overview of related work. Extensions to ORM to cover spatial facts are described in Sect. 3 to 5. In Sect. 6, we look at some of the rather challenging implementation issues. Sect. 7 concludes the paper with a discussion and some suggestions for further work.

2   Related Work

There are many proposals for including spatial values as first class citizens in modeling languages. For example, Tryfona and Hadzilacos [25] have included spatial values in the relational model, whereas Shekhar et al. [23] have proposed an enhanced entity relationship model with spatial values. A rather thorough work along the same lines is the MADS data model, described in the book by Parent, Spaccapietra and Zimnyi [18]. The introduction of Abstract Data Types (ADTs) in relational databases (see for example [9]) and object-oriented models (see [4]) made it possible to define also spatial values. A comprehensive overview of the theoretical foundation of spatial modeling can be found in the book by Molenaar [17]. Halpin has discussed the inclusion of time in fact-oriented models [13,14], but mentions only briefly period seen as an atomic, not decomposable spatial value. To our knowledge, a thorough treatment of extending ORM to also handle spatial entities and values does not yet exist. A taxonomy of spatial data integrity constraints has been published by Cockcroft [5].

Most discussions are based on the point set theory and the point set topology approach [11], where a spatial value is seen as an infinite set of points. Based on the point set theory, it is possible to define topological predicates in a consistent way. Well known is the 9-intersection model [6,7], where the topological relations between two spatial objects A and B are defined in terms of the intersections of A's interior, boundary an exterior with B's interior, boundary and exterior. Schneider and Behr [22] have extended the domain of spatial values from simple points, curves and regions (surfaces) to complex points, curves and regions (surfaces). Complex values are finite sets of the simple ones, and may have holes. Schneider and Behr have further used the 9-intersection model to investigate all possible combinations of complex points, curves and regions. However, their discussions handle only up to two-dimensional spatial values. For the three-dimensional case there are several publications [2,26]. In for example [10], the authors describe a spatial/temporal datatype, the simple abstract model and the more complicated discrete model that is needed for an implementation.

3   Concepts and Notation

In ORM, we make a clear distinction between the entities found in the real world and the representations – i.e. the values. A spatial entity is a real world entity that describes a location in space. Its representation is a spatial value. Now we may establish a fact saying that Something in the real world is occupying that location, see Fig. 2.

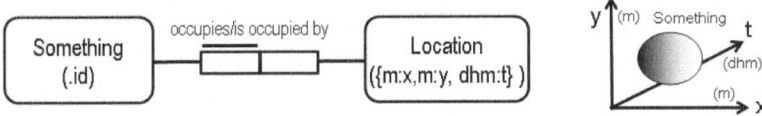

Fig. 2. Notation for spatial entities and values

In the point set theory approach [11], a spatial value is seen as a usually infinite set of points. We adopt this view here, with the modification that we follow the International Standards Organization (ISO) [15] and the Object Management Group (OMG) [12] and instead of points are using so called *direct positions*, each referenced by a coordinate tuple – i.e. a value – within a coordinate system. A direct position, then, is a position in space where something happens to be — like the middle point of a line. Thus we can avoid paradoxes like the question of where the middle point goes when a line is cut in two halves [24].

A coordinate in n-dimensional space is denoted as an n-tuple, for example x_i, y_i, t_i where x, y and t are the axes for a 3-dimensional space. The units along the axes may be included as usual in ORM, for example m:x, m:y, dhm:t where m stands for meter and dhm for day-hour-minute. Then we propose to use set brackets { } to denote the set of coordinates and hence the spatial value type, i.e. {m:x, m:y, dhm:t}.

Note that the number of elements in the coordinate tuple is determined by the dimensionality of the space at hand, i.e. the number of axes in the coordinate system. It does not say anything about the dimensionality of the spatial entity, which may be equal to or smaller than the dimensionality of the space.

4   Topological Relationships

Because we see a spatial value as a mathematical set of direct positions, all the mathematical operators of set theory stand at our disposal, and combined with first order predicate logic, this gives us a rather strong language for handling spatial values. Here, we will concentrate on the interesting topic of topology.

Informally, a topological relationship (like for example being inside or adjacent) is a relationship that does not change even if the space itself is subject to topological transformations like scaling, rotation and translation — see for example [21], page 81. Topology and topological relationships are of great interest, especially to the cartography and the GIS community, and there exists an abundant amount of written material on the matter [2,6,7,17,22]. By using set operators combined with Boolean operators, it is possible to define topological relationships like disjoint, overlap, meet and so on.

The most precise definitions are based on the so called three object part system (see for example [21], page 87), where we distinguish between the *interior* A°, the *boundary* ∂A and the *exterior* A⁻ of a spatial value. In [22], Schneider and Behr give precise definitions of the interior, boundary and exterior of a possibly complex (i.e. non-contiguous) spatial value. Informally, we can say that a zero-dimensional spatial value (a Point swarm) has no boundary, the boundary of a one-dimensional value (a set of lines) is the end points of the lines, the boundary of a two-dimensional value (a set of regions) is the bounding lines — also around any holes, and the boundary of a three-dimensional value (a set of solids) is the bounding surfaces. Schneider an Behr further investigate all possible combinations of the interior, boundary and exterior between two zero-, one- or two-dimensional spatial values A and B. Then, by sensible grouping they arrive at the eight predicates *disjoint, meet, inside, contains, coveredBy, covers, equal* and *overlap*.

Three of those are of special interest to us: A and B are *disjoint* if the parts of one value intersects at most with the exterior of the other, A and B *meet* if their interiors do not intersect, but the interior or the boundary of one value intersects the boundary of the other, and A is *equal* to B if the interiors are the same — another way of saying this is that the interior of one value has no direct positions in common with the exterior of the other, and the boundary of one value has no direct postions in common with the interior or the exterior of the other.

$$disjoint(A, B) \overset{\text{def}}{=} A° \cap B° = \emptyset \wedge A° \cap \partial B = \emptyset \wedge \partial A \cap B° = \emptyset \wedge \partial A \cap \partial B = \emptyset$$

$$meet(A, B) \overset{\text{def}}{=} A° \cap B° = \emptyset \wedge (A° \cap \partial B \neq \emptyset \vee \partial A \cap B° \neq \emptyset \vee \partial A \cap \partial B \neq \emptyset)$$

$$equal(A, B) \overset{\text{def}}{=} A° \cap B^- = \emptyset \wedge A^- \cap B° = \emptyset \wedge A° \cap \partial B = \emptyset \wedge \partial A \cap B° = \emptyset$$
$$\wedge \partial A \cap B^- = \emptyset \wedge A^- \cap \partial B = \emptyset$$

Later, we will have good use of a *noOverlap*-predicate saying that two spatial values either are *disjoint* or *meet*. Using the framework in [22], A *noOverlap* B if the only direct positions they have in common are on a boundary:

$$noOverlap(A, B) \overset{\text{def}}{=} A° \cap B° = \emptyset \wedge A^- \cap B° \neq \emptyset \wedge A° \cap B^- \neq \emptyset$$

In plain language, this states that

1. the interior of one of the spatial values has no direct positions in common with the interior of the other, and
2. the interior of one of the spatial values has at least one direct position in common with the exterior of the other and vice versa. This last condition is included to rule out situations where one of the spatial values is *equal* to or *inside* the boundary of the other.

5   Spatial Constraints

5.1   Topological Constraints

All kinds of spatial topological constraints can be defined by checking the outcome of topological relationships against the empty set $\emptyset$. These constraints may be expressed by extensions to the ORM diagram language or by a textual language like FORML or CQL. Here, we will only discuss some constraints that are of particular interest, namely the ORM uniqueness and set comparison constraints when extended to spatial entities and values.

The uniqueness constraint requires a test on whether two entities or values are different. But what does "different" mean when we come to spatial values? One interpretation is *"not equal"*, i.e. that the two spatial values differ in at least one direct position. The normal uniqueness constraint on spatial values would then be: For the occurences x_i of the spatial entity type X in some fact or reference type, the following should hold:

$$Uniqueness\ constraint:\ \forall i, j(i \neq j \Rightarrow \neg(x_i\ equal\ x_j))$$

This interpretation is needed when referencing a spatial entity by a spatial value, as already used in Fig. 1.

For fact types, however, it turns out that a stronger requirement is far more useful, namely that the spatial values do not overlap at all. Using the predicate noOverlap from Sect. 4, we can now define what we choose to call the *no overlap constraint*: For the occurences x_i of the spatial entity type X in some fact type, the following should hold:

$$No\ overlap\ constraint:\ \forall i, j(i \neq j \Rightarrow x_i\ noOverlap\ x_j)$$

Since the no overlap constraint is stronger than the uniqueness constraint, we suggest drawing it by means of a fatter uniqueness constraint line, as shown in Fig. 3a and b. In Fig. 3a, the no overlap constraint does not only say that a certain region can be the region of only one country, but also that these regions do not overlap. In Fig. 3b, the long uniqueness constraint, of which a part is a no overlap constraint, says that a person can not be busy with more than one task during a certain time period. Observe that for non-spatial values, the no overlap constraint coinsides with a uniqueness constraint. This means that we in Fig. 3b could have used a long, fat line without any change in the meaning. Further, since the no overlap constraint is a specialization of a uniqueness constraint, a long uniqueness/no overlap constraint may be objectified, as shown in Fig. 3b.

Of the set comparison constraints, both the equality constraint and the subset constraint require tests on "equality" between occurences, and when it comes to spatial values, the *equal* predicate as defined in Sect. 4.1 is the obvious choice. Likewise, the usual exclusion constraint can be defined by means of the expression *not equal*.

However, similar to the uniqueness constraint, also the exclusion constraint needs a spatial companion; a no overlap exclusion constraint where the occurences should not only be *not equal*, but also satisfy the *noOverlap*-predicate.

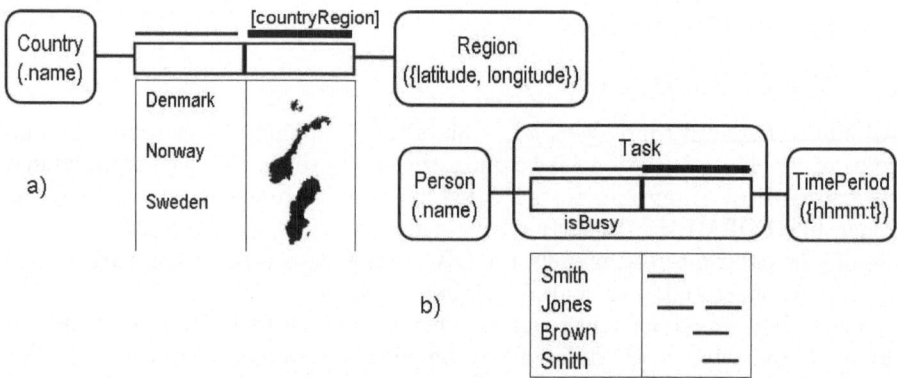

Fig. 3. The no overlap constraint

Since the no overlap exclusion constraint is stronger than the normal exclusion constraint, we suggest drawing it in the ORM-diagrams as a fatter exclusion constraint symbol. Further, since the *noOverlap* predicate coincides with a plain not equal for non-spatial values, there will be no change in meaning by letting the no overlap exclusion constraint symbol involve both roles in the fact types in Fig. 4.

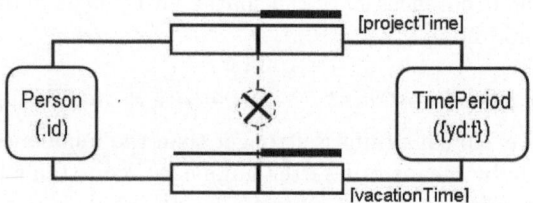

Fig. 4. The no overlap exclusion constraint

5.2   The Pattern "The whole and its Parts"

In the example in Fig. 5, we see Countries that are partitioned into smaller pieces, here called Provinces. Then each countryRegion of a Country should equal the union of the provinceRegions of the Provinces in the same country. This pattern shows up everywhere where something that occupies a space is partitioned into smaller pieces. It is for example very useful for cutting a spatial/temporal entity into slices along the t-axis.

5.3   Value Constraints

If that adds to the clarity of the model (and makes the implementation easier), we may use well known subtypes of the spatial entity, like for example

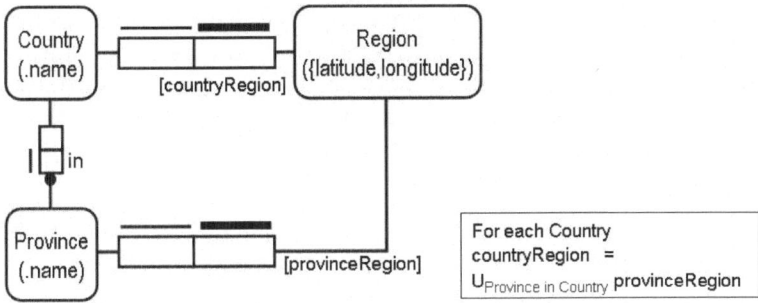

Fig. 5. The whole and its parts

MultiCurve, MultiRegion (MultiSurface), MultiPolygon and MultiPoint (Point swarm) (see [15]). For some subtypes, the set of direct positions may be written as a mathematical expression, like for example $\{x, y \mid x_1 < x < x_2 \wedge y_1 < y < y_2\}$ for a filled Polygon that has the shape of a rectangle. Such subtypes are really the result of value constraints, in that only certain direct positions within the space may be included in the value. Please note that in our approach, a Point swarm with only one element is still a Point swarm.

6   Implementation Issues

Spatial values can usually not be physically represented directly and exactly. In the literature, we find an abundant number of proposals for representations, whose primary objective is to speed up operations and save storage space. We find vector representations of network and spaghetti type, and a variety of raster representations (see for example [21], chapter 2.2). We may even see that different kinds of physical representations are used in the different roles played by the very same spatial entity.

Our modeling approach, characterized by spatial entities and spatial values defined in a very general way on a high level of abstraction, may ease the modeling effort. However, to map those values to efficient physical representations, e.g. in a database, is as challenging as ever. With a traditional ORM-model, automated tools for mapping to a relational database structure are available (like the NORMA mapping tool). An ORM-model including spatial entities and values is considerably more difficult to handle.

The major problem is that a traditional relational database (pre SQL3) simply cannot cope with non-zero dimensional values in multidimensional space[8]. If such a database is our only option, we have to replace the spatial values by a number of non-spatial values and give the application programs the responsibility to "see" the space behind those values. This is exactly what we do when we model a time period by means of the start- and end-day, like in Fig. 1a.

So, if we abandon the traditional relational database, what then? That depends on the nature of the problem at hand and the capabilities of the available implementation platforms. We have one model, but many possibilities for implementation. This makes it challenging to create an automated tool for mapping the model to some kind of database structure. On the other hand, this is a sign of health: We are now able to model the Universe of Discourse without being influenced by concerns for the implementation.

Some possible implementation platforms are:

1. A tessellation based implementation, where the infinite sets of direct positions are replaced by finite sets of tiles. The tiles can be of equal size, as in a raster model (pixles in 2D and voxels in 3D). A Triangulated Irregular Network (TIN) is an example of a tessellation with irregular tiles. The main advantage of a tessellation based representation is that it can represent any spatial entity, although with a precision determined by the size of the tiles. The primary disadvantage is that it is relatively costly in terms of storage space and processing time. This problem may with time be alleviated by cheaper and larger computer storage and quicker processors.

   In a tessellation based implementation, boundaries are not represented explicitly – they will always run along the edges of the tessellation elements. Then it is rather convenient that our definition of the no overlap constraint does not involve the boundary.

2. The relational database language SQL/MM Spatial [1], which has been extended with spatial abstract datatypes (ADTs) for geometry (abstract), 0D (point), 1D (curve with specialisations), 2D (surface with specialisations), 2D tesselations (polyhedral surface with TIN as a specialisation), collections (of geometries, points, curves and surfaces) and topology.

3. A special purpose DBMS, like a Geographic Information System (GIS), which may be an attractive option for the many systems that handle geographic information. Most such systems have at least a built in datatype called polygon, which can be used for representing the boundary, and then inherently also the interior, of a two-dimensional spatial entity in two-dimensional space. However, those systems are not really set up to handle spatial values of the kind encountered outside the GIS-world.

   If the model follows the pattern "The whole and its parts" from Sect. 5.2, as is often the case for maps, we may use the so called network model (see for example [21] paragraph 2.3.2).

4. A Constraint database system, see [20] and [21, chapter 4]. The general idea is to represent an infinite set of direct positions by a set of constraints that cuts the spatial value out of the space, and then to store only the constraints. Constraint databases seem to be a promising technology for databases containing spatial values.

5. An object-oriented system, where all the difficulties of representing the spatial values are hidden inside classes and objects; from the outside we can only see the interface as a collection of methods to set and get the spatial values, to do spatial operations and to check constraints. This means that the implementor has full freedom in choosing the internal representation of a spatial value, as long as the methods are working as expected. Further, all

objects have their own internal object identifier (OID) that may be used to refer to the object from elsewhere.

However, in the object-oriented world there may be no police force that is enforcing the rules defined by the constraints. The philosophy is rather that every object is responsible for behaving according to the rules. So, for example, to enforce the no overlap constraint, a new (or changed) spatial entity has to call some method like checkNoOverlap(anotherObject) for all the other objects. It may be a better option to maintain a spatial object for the unused space (which is the exterior of the union of the already existing spatial entities) and let a new (or changed) object check for being inside that unused space.

7   Discussion and Further Work

In this paper, we have proposed to extend ORM with spatial entities and values on a rather high abstraction level, based on values defined as possibly infinite sets of direct positions. Spatial calculations can then be done in point set algebra. Many other modeling language approaches work on a more implementation oriented level where you see lines and polygons, nodes and edges.

This high level, however, makes the mapping from the model to a database structure rather challenging. Many spatial constraints should not be mapped into constraints on the implementation level, but rather be used to find "smart" representations where the constraints are inherently satisfied. Other constraints may be mapped into a topological structure on top of the geometric one. Much work is needed to establish the mapping rules, and to investigate whether parts of this process can be automated. It may very well be that some intermediate schema-transformations requiring manual intervention will be necessary. Advances in storage- and database technology may in the future make the transition to implementations more straightforward.

More work has to be done on the notation for specifying value-constraints on the spatial entities so that more complicated cases can be covered. And it would probably be of value to work out the constraints that correspond to the primitive geometries and the complexes found in the ISO 19100 series of standards.

Integrating spatial values within different spatial domains has not been addressed in this paper. This must be solved using transformations, such as projections from a higher dimensional space to a lower, or coordinate transformations between different coordinate systems.

Even though the spatial constraints mentioned in this paper cover some of the cases found in the real world, more types of constraints are needed. It would also be nice to have some general applicable modeling patterns, beyond the pattern "the whole and its parts".

References

1. Ashworth, M.: Information Technology, Database Languages, SQL Multimedia, and Application Packages, Part 3: Spatial. ISO/IEC 13249-3 (1999)

2. Borrmann, A., Rank, E.: Topological Operators in a 3D Spatial Query Language for Building Information Models. In: Proc. of the 12th Int. Conf. on Computing in Civil and Building Engineering, ICCCBE-XII (2008)
3. Burrough, P.A., Frank, A.: Geographic Objects with Indeterminate Boundaries. Taylor and Francis (1996)
4. Catell, R.G.G.: Object Databases and Standards. In: Goble, C.A., Keane, J.A. (eds.) BNCOD 1995. LNCS, vol. 940, pp. 1–11. Springer, Heidelberg (1995)
5. Cockcroft, S.: A Taxonomy of Spatial Data Integrity Constraints. Geoinformatica 4(4), 419–433 (2000)
6. Egenhofer, M.J., Franzosa, R.D.: Point-set Topological Spatial Relations. Int. J. Geographical Information Systems 5(2), 161–174 (1991)
7. Egenhofer, M.J., Clementini, E., di Felice, P.: Topological Relations between Regions with Holes. Int. J. Geographical Information Systems 8(2), 128–142 (1994)
8. Egenhofer, M.J., et al.: Progress in Computational Methods for Representing Geographical Concepts. Int. J. of Geographical Information Science 13(8), 775–796 (1999)
9. Elmasri, R., Navathe, S.: Fundamentals of Database Systems. Benjamin Cummings, Redwood City (1994)
10. Erwig, M., et al.: Abstract and Discrete Modeling of Spatio-Temporal Data Types. In: 6th ACM Symp. on Geographic Information Systems, pp. 131–136 (1998)
11. Gaal, S.: Point Set Topology. Academic Press, New York (1964)
12. OGC. OGC Abstract Specification. OpenGIS Consortium (OGC) (1999), http://www.opengis.org/techno/specs.htm
13. Halpin, T., Morgan, T.: Information Modeling and Relational Databases. Morgan Kaufmann, Amsterdam (2008)
14. Halpin, T.: Temporal Modeling and ORM. In: Meersman, R., Tari, Z., Herrero, P. (eds.) OTM-WS 2008. LNCS, vol. 5333, pp. 688–698. Springer, Heidelberg (2008)
15. International Standard ISO 19107. Geographic information – Spatial schema (2003)
16. Langran, G.: Time in Geographic Information Systems. Taylor & Francis (1992)
17. Molenaar, M.: An Introduction to the Theory of Spatial Object Modelling for GIS. Taylor and Francis, London (1998)
18. Parent, C., et al.: Conceptual Modeling for Traditional and Spatio-Temporal Applications: The MADS Approach. Springer, Heidelberg (2006)
19. Peuquet, D.J.: A Conceptual Framework and Comparison of Spatial Data Models. Cartographica 21(4), 66–113 (1984)
20. Revesz, P.: Introduction to Constraint Databases. Springer, Heidelberg (2002)
21. Rigaux, P., Scholl, M., Voisard, A.: Spatial Databases with Application to GIS. Morgan Kaufmann, Academic Press, London (2002)
22. Schneider, M., Behr, T.: Topological Relationships between Complex Spatial Objects. ACM Transactions on Database Systems 31(1), 39–81 (2006)
23. Shekhar, S., Coyle, M., Goyal, B., Liu, D., Sarkar, S.: Data Models in Geographic Information Systems. Communication of the ACM 40(4) (1997)
24. Sowa, J.: Knowledge Representation. Logical, Philosophical, and Computational Foundations. Brooks/Cole Pacific Grove, CA (2000)
25. Tryfona, N., Hadzilacos, T.: Logical Data Modeling of SpatioTemporal Applications: Definitions and a Model. In: Proc. of the 1998 International Symposium on Database Engineering & Applications, IDEAS, p. 14 (1998)
26. van Oosterom, P., et al.: Integrated 3D modelling within a GIS. In: Proc. of the Workshop on Advanced Geographic Data Modelling (1994)

NORMA Multi-page Relational View

Matthew Curland

ORM Solutions, USA
mcurland@live.com

Abstract. The NORMA (Natural Object-Role Modeling Architect) tool has long supported a single-page view of the generated relational model. This view automatically shows one shape per table. Unfortunately, as the number of tables and foreign keys grows, this single-page approach becomes impractical. Therefore, for advanced users wishing to display readable relational models, it is necessary to move beyond this single-page approach. The NORMA *multi-page relational view* was created to address these concerns by allowing multiple relational diagrams in the same model. However, the multi-page environment has inherent issues that do not occur with a single-page approach. This paper discusses how we handle shape creation for tables and foreign keys with no corresponding display shape, how we display foreign keys when the referenced table is not on the diagram, and how column associations are displayed for foreign keys. We also discuss the display options used to balance explicit display of column information and complexity of the connecting lines. The result is a flexible system for rapid population of targeted relational diagrams that scales seamlessly for large models.

1   Introduction

One of the strongest features of Object-Role Modeling (ORM) methodology [1] is the ability to automatically generate a relational model from a conceptual ORM model. The Natural ORM Architect (NORMA) tool [2], which implements a version of ORM2 [3, 4], also has a feature to graphically display this relational model as a diagram. The *relational view* extension enables visualization of the relational form of the model and facilitates communication with database practitioners who might not be familiar with the ORM methodology and notation.

The relational diagram included in the open source version of NORMA automatically creates a shape for each relational table, places these shapes in a single diagram, and then connects these table shapes with directional arrows to indicate foreign key constraints. The user can manually arrange the table shapes on the single diagram to achieve a presentation that is reasonable for a small relational model, but the usability of the diagram rapidly deteriorates for models that produce a significant number of tables and connections. As a model approaches 100 tables the single-page view is overwhelmingly complex.

This paper will discuss the design of a multi-page relational view extension that allows users to spread their complex relational models across multiple pages. Section 2

Y.T. Demey and H. Panetto (Eds.): OTM 2013 Workshops, LNCS 8186, pp. 487–491, 2013.
© Springer-Verlag Berlin Heidelberg 2013

discusses the design approach for helping users manually populate table shapes and section 3 discusses available display options for foreign key connectors.

2　Populating Table Shapes

As with the single-page relational view extension, the multi-page relational view (MPRV) is added to a NORMA model using the *Extension Manager* dialog. When the single-page view is added, a diagram entitled *Relational View* is automatically created and populated with one shape per table in the generated relational model. The MPRV extension also adds a diagram called *RelationalPage1*, but no table shapes are placed on this diagram. Unlike the single *Relational View* diagram, the user is free to rename the relational page diagram, and add additional relational pages using the diagram tab context menu in NORMA. This behavior parallels the mechanism for adding multiple ORM diagrams to a model.

The primary impetus for the MPRV is to distribute table shapes across multiple pages, so automatically adding all table shapes to a newly created relational page is counterproductive. This means the user must manually add a table shape to one or more relational page diagrams for each table in the relational model. The direct way to do this is to drag a table from the *Relational Schema* branch of the *ORM Model Browser* and drop the table on a diagram. While this is a supported approach, there are several areas where the tool can help the user know when the model file contains a diagrammatic representation of all of the tables and foreign keys in their model.

1. The tool can track which tables have no shape on any MPRV diagram.
2. The tool can track foreign keys which are not displayed.
3. The tool can manage a validation error if the state of #1 or #2 changes.
4. The tool can simplify adding shapes for tables that are referenced by an existing table shape, but do not have a table on the same diagram.

The MPRV accomplishes the first three items by introducing a *group type* that automatically populates a *group* with undisplayed tables and foreign keys. A group in NORMA is a collection of references to elements defined in the model. Grouping allows the user to relate elements of the same or different types for arbitrary conceptual reasons. For example, a user may create a group named *Under Discussion* and populate it with references to fact types and constraints that require additional analysis. While this freeform use of groups is valuable, the true power of group comes when a *group type* is associated with that group.

A group type associates behavior with elements in a group, or automates the population of the group. An example of a behavior associated with a group type is shape coloring, whereby user-specified colors can be associated with elements explicitly included in the group by the user, or automatically by a group type. For the MPRV, we create a group type that automatically causes the group to reference tables and foreign keys with missing shapes (see Figure 1). The behavior of the group type is as follows:

1. When the MPRV extension loads for the first time in a model, create a new group called *Schema 'SCHEMANAME' Missing Shapes* and associate the *Relational Shape Missing* group type. Note that a group with this group type could also be manually added or deleted by the user at any time.
2. The group type populates the group by adding a reference to each table with no corresponding shape. The table reference can be dragged from the model browser onto an MPRV diagram to create a shape for that table.
3. The group includes a reference to a foreign key if a shape exists for the referencing table, but the referenced table does not have a shape on any diagram that displays a referencing shape. Dragging a foreign key onto an MPRV diagram creates a shape for either the referencing or referenced table: if a shape already exists for one table, then dropping the foreign key will create a shape for the other table. If neither table is shown on the drop-target diagram, then the referencing table is created and a drag action initiated to create the opposite shape.
4. Add a validation error if a group with a *Relational Shape Missing* group type has any elements in it. To minimize clutter in the *Error List* tool window, we create one error regardless of how many tables are missing shapes. Double-clicking the error opens the *shape missing* group in the model browser tool window and selects the node for the group type.
5. Explicitly deleting a table or foreign key from this group will add an 'x' over the model browser icon for that item and change the text to gray. This is a standard NORMA group feature used to enable the user to override automatically included items. The action can be reversed at any time with the *Include In Group* command, which is available on the model browser context menu for each explicitly excluded item.

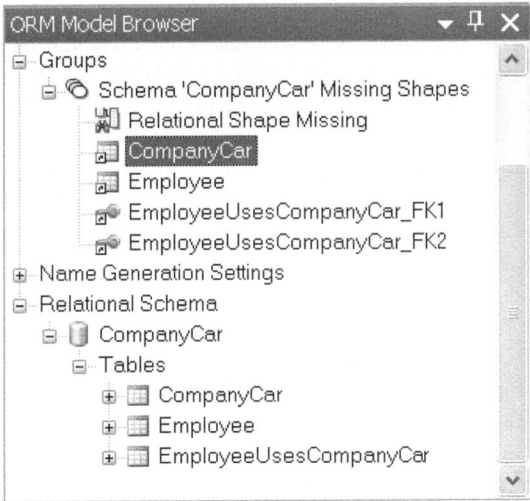

Fig. 1. The ORM Model Browser tool window displaying a *Relational Shape Missing* group for a small model. Comparing all tables and the group content indicates that the *EmployeeUsesCompanyCar* table is on an MPRV diagram with two unconnected foreign keys.

The *Relational Shape Missing* group type allows the user to easily track the remaining work required to diagrammatically represent the full relational model. However, it offers very little help in determining referenced tables that are not on the same diagram as a shape for a referencing table. To find referenced tables, the user would need to locate the table in the model browser, then expand that table and its *Foreign Keys* section, then drag those foreign keys onto the diagram. To fix this problem, the default MPRV display options show a stub foreign key connection arrow pointing away from the shape for each foreign key that references a table that has no shape on the diagram. Dragging these placeholder foreign key arrows has the same behavior as dragging a foreign key from the model browser—dropping creates the referenced table. Once all of the desired shapes are displayed, any remaining unconnected foreign key arrows can be hidden by adjusting the *UnattachedForeignKeyDisplay* option.

3 Foreign Key Connector Options

The single-page view connects tables related by foreign key constraints with lines that automatically route around intervening tables and have arrow heads on the referenced end. These lines can connect at any point on the connected shapes, so there is no graphical feedback to indicate the referencing and referenced columns. The lines also jump over each other when they cross. Jumping may be desired when lines are sparse, but jumps add a lot of graphical distractions when they are large or frequent. The MPRV display options default to no jumps. The per-model defaults for display options on all diagrams can be controlled from the expandable *DefaultDisplaySettings* property shown with each MPRV diagram. There is also a corresponding *LocalDisplaySettings* property that can override the default settings for each diagram.

The feature that has the most effect on the display of an MPRV diagram is the *ForeignKeyColumnDisplay* property, which determines whether the foreign key connection lines on a diagram should begin and/or end at the columns associated with that foreign key. See Figure 2 for connections displayed with different options. Anchoring keys to specific columns conveys significantly more information than a simple shape-to-shape connection, but also causes additional display issues.

1. Only the left and right sides of the table shape can be used for attach points because the top and bottom edges do not correspond to specific columns. The edge is dynamically determined based on relative table location. (The built-in engine provided by Microsoft determines the final routing.)
2. It is common to have multiple foreign key constraints pointing to columns from the same primary uniqueness constraint. This overlap causes multiple connector lines to point to the same location on a referenced shape.
3. It is much harder to get straight lines between shapes when the connectors have fixed attach points on both shapes.
4. It is possible to have the same unique columns be in the referencing table for one foreign key and the referenced table of another. In this case, as well as when where multiple foreign keys share columns, we use multiple vertical connection channels on the side of the shape to minimize overlap.

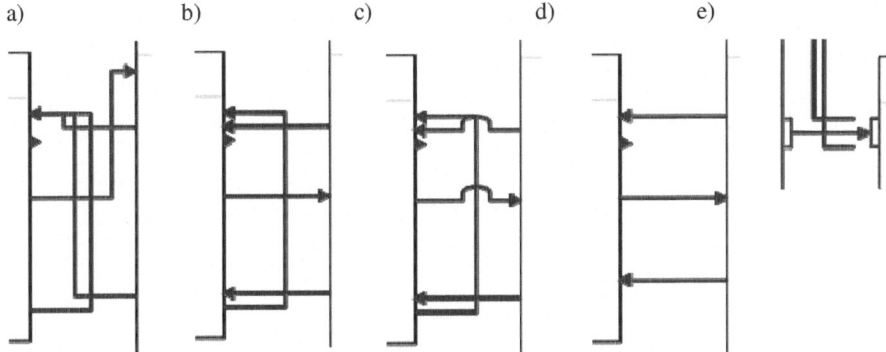

Fig. 2. Foreign key connectors between tables shapes. Items *a* through *d* display the same connections with different display options. The left table has one unconnected foreign key, one self-referential key, two incoming keys from the right table, and one outgoing key to the right table. Item *a* shows the default display (all columns anchored), *b* anchors only the referencing columns, *c* is the same as *b* with line jumps turned on, and *d* attaches with no column affinity. The self-referential constraint is not shown in *d* because it displays on the bottom edge of the left shape, far away from the other keys. Item *e* shows a two-column foreign key connector referencing a uniqueness constraint where both columns reference other uniqueness constraints, resulting in one paired incoming key and two individual outgoing keys for the right table. Note the bracketing used to graphically associate a foreign key with two or more columns. Hovering over any line highlights the entire line and displays a tooltip details of the foreign key.

4   Conclusion

This paper has provided a brief overview of the *Multi-Page Relational View* extension for NORMA. The implementation allows the user to rapidly add table shapes to multiple custom diagrams, track undisplayed tables, and configure the display options for each diagram. While this extension works side-by-side with the single-page relational view, it is expected that modelers in large systems will prefer the relational display and scalability offered by this extension.

The future work in this area includes additional display options for the interior of the table shapes, and possibly color support on the relational diagrams.

References

1. Halpin, T.: Object-Role Modeling: Principles and Benefits. International Journal of Information Systems Modeling and Design 1(1), 32–54 (2010)
2. Curland, M., Halpin, T.: The NORMA Software Tool for ORM 2. In: Soffer, P., Proper, E. (eds.) CAiSE Forum 2010. LNBIP, vol. 72, pp. 190–204. Springer, Heidelberg (2011)
3. Halpin, T.: ORM 2. In: Meersman, R., Tari, Z. (eds.) OTM-WS 2005. LNCS, vol. 3762, pp. 676–687. Springer, Heidelberg (2005)
4. Halpin, T., Morgan, T.: Information Modeling and Relational Databases, 2nd edn. Morgan Kaufmann, San Francisco (2008)

Metis: The SDRule-L Modelling Tool

Yan Tang Demey and Christophe Debruyne

Department of Computer Science,
Vrije Universiteit Brussel, 1050 Brussel, Belgium
{yan.tang,christophe.debruyne}@vub.ac.be

Abstract. Semantic Decision Rule Language (SDRule-L), which is an extension to Object-Role Modelling language (ORM), is designed for modelling semantic decision support rules. An SDRule-L model may contain *static* (e.g., data constraints) and *dynamic* rules (e.g., sequence of events). In this paper, we want to illustrate its supporting tool called Metis, with which we can graphically design SDRule-L models, verbalize and reason them. We can store and publish those models in its markup language called SDRule-ML, which can be partly mapped into OWL2. The embedded reasoning engine from Metis is used to check consistency.

Keywords: fact based modeling, object role modeling, conceptual modeling, semantic decision making, SDRule-L.

1 Introduction

Semantic decision support systems are a means to support group decision making using domain ontologies. Interoperability – the basic characteristic from any ontology-based systems – will enhance the mutual understanding between decision makers within a decision group (or community). Semantic Decision Rule Language (SDRule-L, [1]) is a bridge connecting ontologies and decision making processes. In other words, we can use SDRule-L to model decisions based on domain ontologies.

SDRule-L is an extension to ORM2 [2]. SDRule-L supports both *static* (e.g., data constraints) and *dynamic* rules (e.g., sequence of events). It also supports higher-order modelling. As most first-order static rules can be modelled in ORM2, in this paper, we will focus on the extended constraints and operators, which are recently implemented in a tool called Metis. Metis contains functions of designing SDRule-L models graphically and verbalizing the graphical models. The models are stored and published in the markup language called SDRule-ML, which is a hybrid language of ORM-ML [3] and FOL Rule-ML [4]. SDRule-ML can be partly mapped into Web Ontology Language (OWL2). In addition, it has an embedded SDRule-L reasoner, with which we can validate linked data.

The paper is organized as follows. Sec 2 is the related work. We will discuss specific SDRule-L constraints and operators in Sec. 3. Metis is illustrated in Sec. 3.5. We will discuss in Sec. 4. We will conclude and illustrate our future work in Sec.5.

Y.T. Demey and H. Panetto (Eds.): OTM 2013 Workshops, LNCS 8186, pp. 492–502, 2013.

2   Related Work

Since 1999, the Fact Based Modeling (FBM[1]) methodological principles have been adopted for modeling ontologies. The authors in [5] [3] have illustrated how a particular FBM dialect – ORM [2] – can be used for modeling ontologies and ontology verbalization. Dogma Modeler[2] and Collibra Studio[3] were thus developed. Dogma Modeler supports simple verbalization in English, Dutch, German, French, Spanish, Arabic and Russian. Ontologies, in view of DOGMA Modeler, are made of reusable modules (or patterns). Collibra Studio is a commercialized tool, with which business people can model and share their data semantics.

Later on, ORM/ORM2 has been extended for modeling ontology-based application rules and enabling an application to easily commit to a domain ontology. One extension is called Semantic Decision Rule Language (SDRule-L, [1]), which is used to model semantically rich decision support rules. A markup language – SDRule-ML – has been designed to store and exchange SDRule-L models. The focus of this paper is the supporting tool called Metis[4]. Since the tool is to enhance decision making processes in order to get better and wiser decisions, it is named after Metis, a goddess of wisdom (or wise counsel/wise decision) in Greek mythology.

A related work of the sequence constraint discussed in this paper is UML[5] sequence diagram, which focuses on message interchanges between lifelines. Each lifeline corresponds to exactly one individual participant in the interaction. Another related work is BPMN[6] flow objects for describing sequence flows and message flows. Compared to their work, the sequence constraint in this paper focuses on different types of sequences and the relation between two events. One event may be played by more than one participant when a combination of sequence and cluster is applied.

Other FBM tools, which are more for modeling databases and information in general, are VisioModeler, NORM[7], CogNIAM Studio[8], Richmond[9] and Active Facts[10]. Unlike most of the mentioned FBM tools, which deal with local databases, Metis uses the Resource Description Framework (RDF) to deal with *Linked Data*, which can be considered as a collection of relevant databases or web data. Linked Data is referred to as a Semantic Web initiative to interlink web resources. It uses Uniform Resource Identifiers (URI) for accessing the resources and RDF for representing knowledge and annotating the resources. In addition, Metis contains extended graphical notations, such as cluster, sequence and decisional alternatives (implication), which are specific for modelling decision rules. In the following section, we will discuss the extensions.

---

[1] FBM official website: www.factbasedmodeling.org
[2] DOGMA Modeller can be downloaded from www.jarrar.info/Dogmamodeler
[3] Collibra Studio is now merged into Collibra Data Governance Software
  (www.collibra.com)
[4] Metis can be downloaded from
  sourceforge.net/projects/sdrulel/files/Metis/
[5] http://www.omg.org/spec/UML/2.0/
[6] http://www.bpmn.org/
[7] Both Visio Modeler and NORMA can be downloaded from www.ormfoundation.org
[8] A commercialized tool developed by PNA Group www.pna-group.nl
[9] A tool created by Victor Morgante.
[10] Active Facts can be retrieved from dataconstellation.com

3   SDRule-L Constraints and Operators

The extensions include constraints and operators like annotation (including sample instances), sequence, cluster, implication, necessity, possibility, cross-context subtyping and cross-context equivalence. In this paper, we want to focus on *sequence*, *cluster* and *implication*.

3.1   Sequence

We often use sequences to describe the relations between events. The graphical notation of a sequence is an arrow-tipped bar that connects two event types. Each event type is represented as an object type.

Currently, SDRule-L contains six types of sequence as illustrated in **Table 1**.

Table 1. SDRule-L Sequence (E_1: event on the right of the connector;E_2: event on the left)

ID	Name	Graphical Notation	Verbalization
1	Succession	———》——▶	E_1 is before E_2
2	Continuation	———_ _—▶	E_1 is exactly before E_2
3	Overlap	◀——-_—▶	E_1 and E_2 overlap
4	Trigger	➤——》——▶	E_1 triggers E_2
5	Terminator	———》——○	E_1 is terminated by E_2
6	Coincidence	◀—|=|—▶	E_1 and E_2 are in parallel

Given two events E_1 and E_2, and their begin time stamps ($E_1.T_1$ and $E_2.T_1$) and end time stamps ($E_1.T_2$ and $E_2.T_2$), the semantics of the sequences illustrated in **Table 1** is illustrated as follows.

- **Succession:** $(E_1.T_1 < E_2.T_1) \wedge (\{\exists e | e \in E_2\} \rightarrow \{\exists e | e \in E_1\})$
- **Continuation:** $E_1.T_2 + \alpha = E_2.T_1$ where α is a given time interval
- **Overlap:** $(E_1.T_1 \leq E_2.T_1) \wedge (E_1.T_2 > E_2.T_1) \vee (E_2.T_1 \leq E_1.T_1)$ $\wedge (E_2.T_2 > E_1.T_1)$
- **Trigger:** $(E_1.T_1 < E_2.T_1) \wedge (\{\exists e | e \in E_1\} \leftrightarrow \{\exists e | e \in E_2\})$
- **Terminator:** $(E_1.T_1 \leq E_2.T_2) \wedge (E_1.T_2 = E_2.T_2)$
- **Coincidence:** $(E_1.T_1 = E_2.T_1) \wedge (E_1.T_2 = E_2.T_2)$

Note that, given an event E, it is valid iff $E.T_1 \leq E.T_2$.

An SDRule-L model containing sequences (containing both *dynamic* and *static* rules) can be partly mapped into an OWL[11]-compatible model (containing *static* rules). Suppose we have a succession as illustrated in the left figure from **Fig. 1**. The OWL-compatible model that is *partly* mapped from the succession model is shown on the right in **Fig. 1**.

---

[11] Web Ontology Language: http://www.w3.org/TR/owl2-overview/

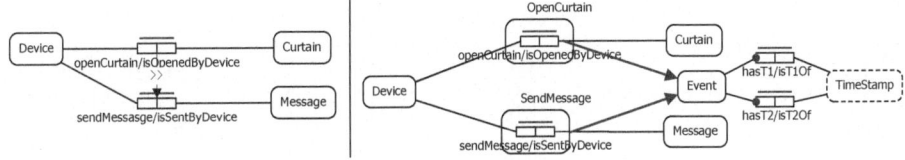

Fig. 1. Left: an example of succession; Right: an OWL-compatible model (partly mapped)

When a set of linked data is claimed to comply with the succession model in **Fig. 1**, we can check the data consistency by embedding the dynamic rule – $E_1.T_1 > E_2.T_1$ – in a query language (in our case, SPARQL[12] is chosen). This idea is adopted from [6]. In particular, sequences are translated into SPARQL ASK queries to check whether counterexamples exist.

For example for a succession – "E_1 is before E_2", it is valid iff $E_2.T_1 < E_1.T_1$. Counterexamples are sought by looking for two facts that violate this condition ($E_2.T_1 \geq E_1.T_1$). It is also invalid if E_2 happens but E_1 did not happen. We give the SPARQL query as illustrated below.

```
ASK {
    {
        ?a <http://…/ont#r1> ?rc1.
        ?a <http://…/ont#r2> ?rc2.
        ?rc1 <http://…/#T1> ?t1.
        ?rc2 <http://…/#T2> ?t2.
        FILTER(?t1 >= ?t2)
    } UNION {
        OPTIONAL{ ?a <http://…/ont#r1> ?rc1. }
        ?a <http://…/ont#lr2> ?rc2.
        FILTER(!BOUND(?rc1))
    }
}
```

3.2 Cluster

A cluster is used to group a set of fact types. We treat such a set as an object, with which we can reify a model. For instance, the concept "helpdesk task", which points to a task, may contain other concepts/tasks, such as "people dial a number" and "people pick up a phone", which are used to explain "helpdesk task".

The graphical notation of a cluster is a round-cornered box indicated with a cluster name. A cluster (also called 'parent cluster') may contain another cluster (also called 'component cluster'), which is attached with a symbol of modality. **Table 2** shows the graphical notions of possible and necessary compositions.

---

[12] Query Language for Resource Description Framework (RDF):
http://www.w3.org/TR/rdf-sparql-query/

Table 2. SDRule-L Cluster

ID	Name	Graphical Notation	Verbalization
1	Possible composition	⟨ParentCluster / ChildCluster⟩ ⟨ParentCluster⟩	… possibly contains …
2	Necessary composition	⟨ParentCluster / ChildCluster⟩ ⟨ParentCluster⟩	… must contain …

A component cluster is either possible or necessary. A *possible* component cluster is a component cluster that may be or may not belong to its parent cluster. The task that corresponds to a parent cluster can be executed with or without the tasks that correspond to its possible component cluster. A component cluster is by default possible. A *necessary* component cluster is a component cluster that must be included in its parent cluster; otherwise, the task that corresponds to the parent cluster cannot be executed without the tasks in the necessary component cluster.

Fig. 2 shows an example of cluster. The cluster "Opening Curtain" is composed of a necessary cluster "Listen and React" and a possible cluster "Sending Msg". The cluster "Listen and React" contains two fact types – Device received Signal and Device open(s) Curtain. The cluster "Sending Msg" contains one fact type – Device send(s) Message. The three clusters are subtypes of "Task".

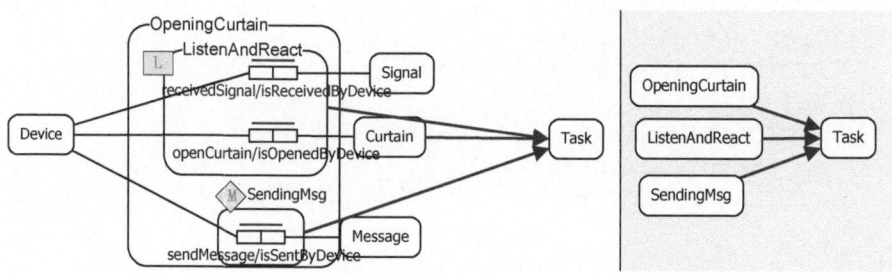

Fig. 2. Left: An example of cluster in SDRule-L; Right: a zoom-out view

When a cluster is populated, its necessary components must be populated while we do not require its optional components to be populated. Suppose that we have a data table containing a set of linked data as illustrated in **Table 3**.

Table 3. A table containing linked data that needs to be complied with **Fig. 2**

ID	Device	Signal	Curtain	Message
1	D1	S1	C1	M1
2	D2	S2	C2	NULL
3	D3	S3	NULL	NULL
4	D4	NULL	NULL	M4
5	D5	NULL	C5	M5
6	D6	NULL	NULL	NULL

When we validate it with the model as illustrated in **Fig. 2**, the data record with ID 4 does not satisfy the model because *SendingMsg* is populated, which implies that *OpenCurtain* must be populated. *OpenCurtain* contains a necessary cluster called "*ListenAndReact*", which consists of the two following optional fact types.

$$l_1 = \langle Device, receivedSignal, isReceivedByDevice, Signal \rangle$$
$$l_2 = \langle Device, openCurtain, isOpenedByDevice, Curtain \rangle$$

Since *Opencurtaion* must be populated, at least one from the above two fact types must be populated. However, in record with ID 4, none of these two fact types are populated. Therefore, it does not satisfy the model.

For the other data records, which are valid facts, we present the analysis as follows.

- 1: all fact types are populated
- 2: the optional component from cluster "*OpeningCurtain*" – *SendingMsg* – is not populated. All the rest are populated.
- 3: the optional component (referred to l_1 , see above) from the cluster " *ListenAndReact* ", which is a necessary component from the cluster "*OpeningCurtain*", is populated. All the rest are not populated.
- 4: invalid (see the earlier discussion)
- 5: the optional component (referred to l_2 , see above) from the cluster " *ListenAndReact* ", which is a necessary component from the cluster "*OpeningCurtain*", is populated. Another optional component (referred to l_1, see above) from the cluster "*ListenAndReact*" is not populated.
- 6: the cluster "*ListenAndReact*" is not populated.

With cluster, a model can easily embrace higher ordered rules. The advantage is that we can simplify the process of model reification. The disadvantage is that it brings complexity to the reasoning engine. We will explore the issues on how to combine cluster with other constraints in the future.

Similar to the constraint of sequence, we first map clusters to OWL-compatible models as illustrated in **Fig. 3**.

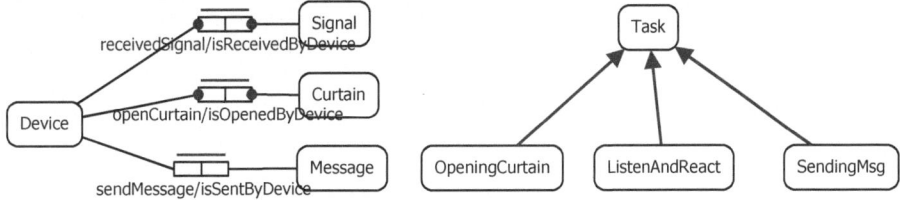

Fig. 3. OWL-compatible models partly transformed from **Fig. 2**

Then, we provide the following SPARQL queries[13] for finding counterexamples.

---

[13] "l2", "l3" and "l1" are the identifiers for respectively the first, second and third binary fact type on the left hand side of the example in Fig.2.

```
ASK {
  ?a a <http://…/ont#Device>.
  OPTIONAL {
    ?a <http://…/ont#l2f> ?x1.
    ?x1 a <http://…/ont#l2>.
  }
  OPTIONAL {
    ?a <http://…/ont#l3f> ?x2.
    ?x2 a <http://…/ont#l3>.
  }
  FILTER(!BOUND(?x1) || !BOUND(?x2))
}
```

```
ASK {
  ?a <http://…/ont#l1f>
?b.
  ?b a
<http://…/ont#l1>.
  OPTIONAL {
    ?a ?z ?c. ?c a
<http://…/ont#l2>.
  }
  FILTER(!BOUND(?c))
}
```

3.3   Other Operators and Constraints

SDRule-L also includes other extensions, such as implication, negation, skipper (exception), cross-context equivalence and cross-context subtyping. Due to the limit of paper length, we refer to [1] for the details.

An important point we want to make in this paper is, all the operators and constraints that we have discussed earlier are supposed to be further used for modeling decisional alternatives (also called non-monotonic decision rules). *Implication* can be used for this purpose.

Fig. 4 shows an example of implication and its verbalization. An arrow tipped bar indicated with ¬ is a negation[14]. Implication can be mapped into a subset constraint when the decision rule is monotonic. When the rules are non-monotonic, we must use implication instead. Sometimes, one fact type may appear more than once within one SDRule-L model (e.g., as shown in **Fig. 4**). Note that in ORM, such duplications are not allowed.

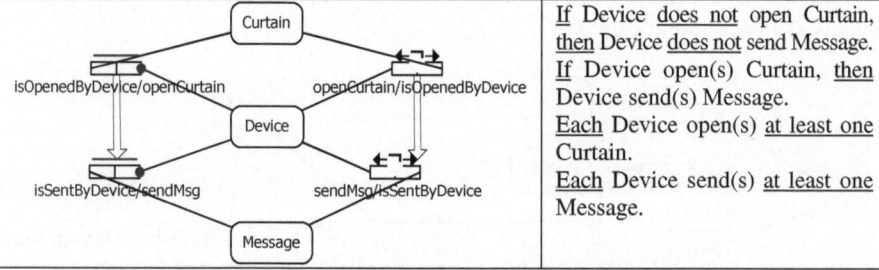

| | If Device does not open Curtain, then Device does not send Message. If Device open(s) Curtain, then Device send(s) Message. Each Device open(s) at least one Curtain. Each Device send(s) at least one Message. |

Fig. 4. An example of implication and its verbalization

When negation is applied on a role of the antecedent of an implication, it is a checksum of empty population. When it is applied on a role of the consequence of an implication, it is a denial of populating this role. For instance in **Fig. 4**, if

---

[14] When negation is used in a conditional statement, it is a constraint. When it is used in a conclusion, it is an operator.

openCurtain/isOpenedByDevice is populated, then *isSentByDevice/sendMsg* must be populated; otherwise, the latter must not be populated. Therefore, if we get an empty set of linked data, then it is valid. If we get a set of data as illustrated in **Table 4**, then the first record is valid and the second one is invalid.

Table 4. A table containing linked data that needs to be complied with **Fig. 4**

ID	Curtain	Device	Message
1	C1	D1	M1
2	C1	D1	NULL

The SPARQL queries are provided as follows.

```
ASK {
    ?a ont:OpenCurtain ?y.
    OPTIONAL{?a ont:sendMsg ?x.}
    FILTER(!BOUND(?x))
}
```

```
ASK {
    OPTIONAL{?a ont:sendMsg ?x.}
    ?a ont:OpenCurtain ?y.
    FILTER(!BOUND(?x))
}
```

Although implication can be used to model decisional alternatives, we want to use a neater and more concise means to model ontology-based decision rules. This particular approach is called semantic decision tables [7] [8]. How to use semantic decision tables for modeling decisional alternatives will be illustrated in the next subsection.

3.4   Using Semantic Decision Tables to Model Decisional Alternatives

A decision table is a table representing an exhaustive set of mutually exclusive conditions. It contains conditions, actions and decision rules. A condition consists of a condition stub represented as a label and a condition entry represented as a value or value range. Similarly, an action is composed of an action stub represented as a label, and an action entry, which is often a Boolean value[15]. A decision rule is a decision column or a decision row, depending on the layout of the decision table. A decision rule consists of a set of conditions and a set of actions.

A semantic decision table (SDT) is a decision table annotated with a domain ontology. With the annotation, we are able to specify the meta-rules and relations between table elements into axioms, which are processable by machines. **Fig. 5** shows an example of SDT that is equivalent to the SDRule-L illustrated in **Fig. 4**.

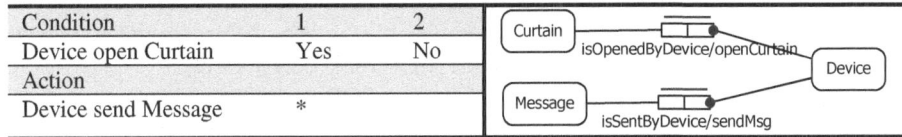

Condition	1	2
Device open Curtain	Yes	No
Action		
Device send Message	*	

Fig. 5. An SDT example that is equivalent to **Fig. 4**

---

[15] If it is not a Boolean value, then we need to map it into a Boolean value.

In the decision table from **Fig. 5**, "*Device open Curtain*" is a condition stub. "*Yes*" and "*No*" are the two condition entries. "*Device send Message*" is an action stub. " * " and the absence of "*" are the two action entries. There are two conditions in the decision table:⟨*Device open Curtain, Yes*⟩ and ⟨*Device open Curtain, No*⟩. There are also two actions:⟨*Device send Message,*⟩ and ⟨*Device send Message,*⟩. The two columns indicated with 1 and 2 are the two decision rules. We annotate this decision table with the fact types (from a domain ontology), which are constrained in the ontology as shown on the right in **Fig. 5**.

When we have complicated decision rules, SDTs are much better than the models containing implications for the following reasons.

- Within an SDT, decisional alternatives are easier to be compared.
- Decision rules in an SDT are an exhaustive set of mutually exclusive conditions. Therefore, the completeness of a rule set is ensured. When there are a lot of conditions, it is difficult to manually check the completeness of an SDRule-L model containing implications.
- It is easier to group rules and detecting irrelevant rule sets using the existing SDT rule engine. For SDRule-L implications, it is a big challenge to group similar rules.

3.5   Metis

As most tools from other fact-based modeling dialects as discussed in Sec. 2, Metis contains functions of graphically design and verbalization of SDRule-L models. The SDRule-L reasoner is also embedded to ensure the consistency of data.

Metis has been developed as a plugin framework. We have used Eclipse[16] Java software development kit (SDK) for the implementation. In particular, the Graphical Editing Framework (GEF) has been adopted for the rich graphical editor and views of Metis user interface. **Fig. 6** and **Fig. 7** show two screenshots of Metis.

Including the function of graphical modeling using drag and drop, Metis also supports importing/exporting SDRule-L models from/into SDRule-ML.

4   Discussion

An SDRule-L model can contain *dynamic* and *static* rules, and, *monotonic* and non-*monotonic* rules. Sequence can be used to create dynamic rules seeing that it contains dynamic aspects like time. Most SDRule-L constraints that are inherited from ORM2 are considered to be static. Implication (and the equivalent SDTs) is the only one constraint that can make a rule non-monotonic. All the rest, if they are not combined with implications, can only be used to model monotonic decision rules.

In this paper, we have illustrated how to use SDRule-L to validate linked data, which complies with an SDRule-L model. Our method of checking data consistency contains three steps: 1) transform into a static, OWL-compatible model; 2) create SPARQL queries that contain dynamic rules; 3) find counterexamples.

---

[16] www.eclipse.org

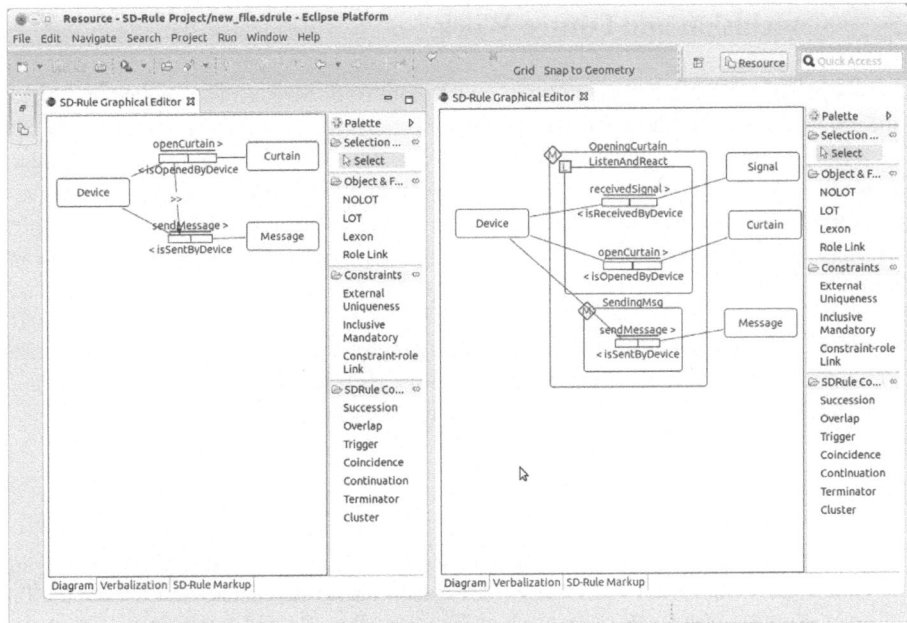

Fig. 6. Screenshots of Metis: graphical models w.r.t. **Fig. 1** and **Fig. 2**

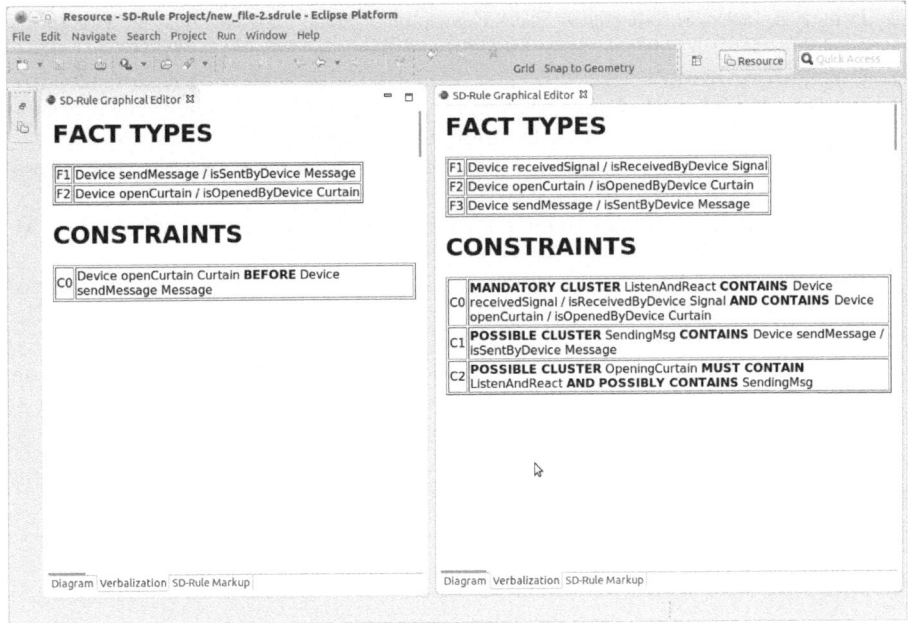

Fig. 7. Metis screenshot: Views of verbalization for the two graphical models in **Fig. 6**

5   Conclusion and Future Work

In this paper, we have discussed three constraints from SDRule-L – sequence, cluster and implication – and how we can use them to validate linked data. Implications can be further mapped into semantic decision tables, with which we can analyse the decision rules. We have also illustrated the first version of SDRule-L tool called Metis.

In the future, we want to add a function of model checksum to Metis. For example, we shall allow two continuation constraints with inverse directions to be used on two events.

Acknowledgements. This study was supported by the INNOViris Open Semantic Cloud for Brussels project, financed by the Brussels Capital Region. Our use case and experimental data in this paper are taken from this project.

References

1. Tang, Y., Meersman, R.: SDRule Markup Language: Towards Modeling and Interchanging Ontological Commitments for Semantic Decision Making. In: Giurca, A., Gasevic, D., Taveter, K. (eds.) Handbook of Research on Emerging Rule-Based Languages and Technologies: Open Solutions and Approaches Sec. I, ch. V. IGI Publishing, USA (2008)
2. Halpin, T., Morgan, T.: Information Modeling and Relational Databases, 2nd edn. Morgan Kaufmann (2008)
3. Demey, J., Jarrar, M., Meersman, R.: A Conceptual Markup Language that Supports Interoperability between Business Rule Modeling Systems. In: Meersman, R., Tari, Z. (eds.) CoopIS/DOA/ODBASE 2002. LNCS, vol. 2519, pp. 19–35. Springer, Heidelberg (2002)
4. Biletskiy, Y., Boley, H., Ranganathan, G.: RuleML-based learning object interoperability on the Semantic Web. Interact. Techn. Smart Edu. 5(1), 39–58 (2008)
5. Jarrar, M.: Towards Methodological Principles for Ontology Engineering. PhD Thesis, Vrije Universiteit Brussel, Brussel (2005)
6. Tao, J., Sirin, E., Bao, J., McGuinness, D.L.: Integrity Constraints in OWL. In: Fox, M., Poole, D. (eds.) AAAI, Atlanta, Georgia, USA (2010)
7. Tang, Y.: On Semantic Decision Tables. PhD Thesis, Department of Computer Science, Vrije Universiteit Brussel, Brussels (2009)
8. Tang, Y.: Semantic Decision Tables - A New, Promising and Practical Way of Organizing Your Business Semantics with Existing Decision Making Tools. LAP LAMBERT Academic Publishing AG & Co., Saarbrücken, Germany (2010)

Mapping BPMN Process Models to Data Models in ORM

Herman Balsters

University of Groningen, Faculty of Economics and Business
P.O. Box 800 9700 AV Groningen, The Netherlands
h.balsters@rug.nl

Abstract. Business processes define workflow dependencies inside an industry and/or organization. Business processes drive machines and people, and use business data to function properly. By systematically integrating data and processes, we can understand and assess complete business processes from beginning to end. Practice, however, often reveals that there is no systematic link between a business process and associated business data. The aim of this paper to tackle some of the problems encountered in deriving business data from process models. We will show how to systematically map basic business process models using Business Process Modeling Notation (BPMN) to data models specified in ORM. From the resulting ORM model, we can generate a complete (corporate) relational database, containing the business data that is tailor-made to support the business process.

Keywords: Process models, data models, mapping process models to data models, fact-based modeling.

Introduction

Object-Role Modeling (ORM) is a fact-oriented approach for modeling information in terms of the underlying facts, where facts and rules may be verbalized in a language easily understandable by non-technical domain experts. In contrast to Entity-Relationship (ER) modeling [2] and Unified Modeling Language (UML) class diagrams [15], ORM models are attribute-free, treating all facts as relationships (unary, binary, ternary etc.). ORM does, however, include procedures (e.g. the RMap [13]) for mapping to attribute-based structures, such as those of ER or UML. For a basic introduction to ORM see [10], for a thorough treatment see [13]. We will use the term Fact-based modelling (FBM [13]) as the general name of several fact-based conceptual data modelling dialects, such as ORM, Natural language Information Analysis Method (NIAM) [11], and Fully-Communication Oriented Information Modeling (FCO-IM) [1].

Business processes define workflow dependencies inside an industry and/or organization. Business Process Model and Notation (BPMN) is a standard for specifying business processes providing a graphical representation based on workflow diagramming. BPMN 1.0 was developed by the Business Process Management Initiative (BPMI) and then was further developed by the Object Management Group

Y.T. Demey and H. Panetto (Eds.): OTM 2013 Workshops, LNCS 8186, pp. 503–512, 2013.
© Springer-Verlag Berlin Heidelberg 2013

(OMG); as of 2011, the current version of BPMN is 2.0 [5]. Business *processes* define the whole work-flow dependency inside an industry and/or organization, whereas   Business *data* is data inside some *database*. Properly designed databases can handle the collecting of data that can guarantee the business data quality. By systematically integrating data and processes, we can –in principle- understand and assess complete business processes from beginning to end. Practice, however, all too often indicates that there is no systematic link between a business process and associated business data. In the case of BPMN, there are hardly any academic papers on the relation between BPMN process models and corresponding data elements (called *artifacts* in BPMN terminology). We note that a *meta-model* description of BPMN (described in ORM) can be found in [14,16]; in [14] it is also discussed, be it not in terms of a systematic mapping, how activities in BPMN could relate to fact types in an information model.

In this paper, we will offer general principles of how to transform a basic BPMN process model to an ORM data model. In section 1, we will describe the elements of a basic BPMN process model, and offer an example of such a BPMN model. Section 2 shows how to derive, step by step, an ORM data model fragment from each element in a BPMN model. Eventually this procedure will result in a tailor-made data model supporting the complete BPMN process model. Section 3 describes a general mapping from a BPMN process model to an ORM data model. Section 4 offers conclusions. This paper uses basic ORM notations, cf. [10,13].

Section 1 Basic BPMN

This section describes some basics of the BPMN notation. We note that in our description of BPMN, we are not striving for completeness. On the contrary, *we wish to focus only on the very basic elements of BPMN notation, in order to explain the fundamentals of our approach to mapping Business Process Diagrams (BPD's) to ORM data models*. We refer the reader interested in more details of BPMN models to [5]. BPMN process models are composed of two basic categories of elements. The first category concerns activity nodes, denoting business events or items of work performed by humans or by software applications. The second category concerns control nodes capturing the flow of control between activities. Activity nodes and control nodes can be (almost arbitrarily) connected by means of a flow relation. Furthermore, activities within a process can be split into so-called pools and swimlanes. We will discuss some basic building blocks of BPD's below.

Events and Activities
An *Event* is represented by a circle and is something that "happens" during the course of a business process. Events affect the flow of the process and usually have a cause (trigger) or an impact (result). We will discern two types of events: the *start event* indicating the start of a flow, and the *end event* indicating the end of the flow. An *Activity* is represented by a rounded-corner rectangle and indicates a piece work or a task to be performed within the process. An Activity can be atomic or non- atomic

(compound). The types of Activities are: *Task* and *Sub-Process*. In this paper we will confine ourselves to simple tasks.

Control
A *Gateway* is represented by a diamond shape and is used to control the divergence and convergence of Sequence Flow. Thus, it will determine decisions, as well as the forking, merging, and joining of paths. Internal Markers indicate the type of behavior control.

Flow Relations
A *Sequence Flow* is represented by a solid line with a solid arrowhead and is used to show the order (the sequence) in which activities are performed in a Process.

An Example: The Thermostat
Our BPMN example concerns the modeling of a Thermostat: an example of a feedback-control based system used to steer a technical process. A thermostat is representative of many typical technical (but also business!) processes. For example, its behavioral characteristics lay the basis for airplane flight control (a Homeostat), or the basis for a quality management control system within an organization.

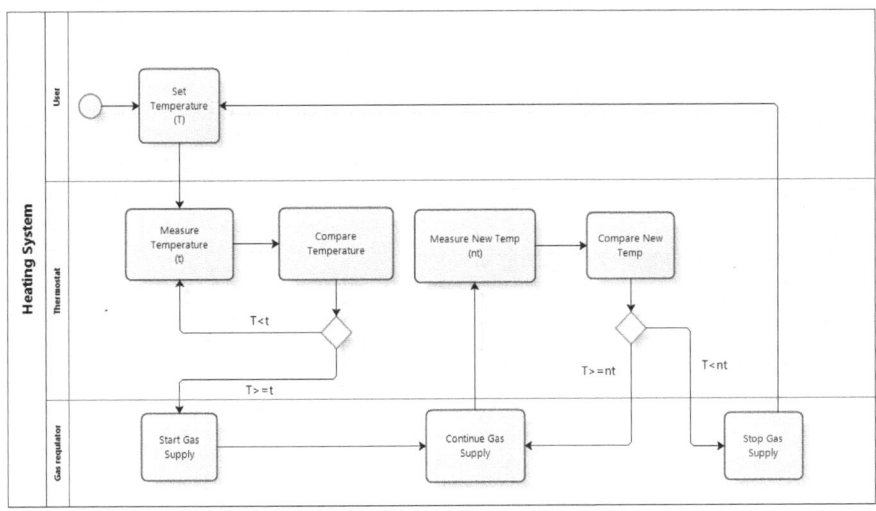

Fig. 1. Heating System with a Thermostat

Here we see a very simple (in some aspects over-simplified) Heating System described as a BPMN process model (designed using the BiZaGi BPMN process modeler tool [4]). The system distinguishes three swimlanes, associated to a user, the thermostat, and the gas regulator, respectively. The system starts by having a user setting a temperature (T), followed by the thermostat measuring the environment temperature (t) and comparing t and T. Should it hold that T<t, then the thermostat measures (at some set time interval, say, e.g. each 30 seconds) the environment again, until the set temperature equals or exceeds that measured temperature. In the latter case, the gas regulator starts the gas supply, and will continue the gas supply as long a newly measured temperature (measured again at some set time interval, say) is indeed higher than the set temperature. In the latter case, the gas supply is stopped, and the system turns back to the start event waiting for a newly set temperature value. We note that this system has no end event: it is a typical example of an embedded system, constantly running and constantly returning to its start event.

Section 2 Transforming Basic BPMN Process Models into ORM Data Models

This section describes, using the example of our Thermostat in figure 1, a transformation of a basic BPMN process model into an ORM data model. Let's have a look at the first task in the process: an activity where a user sets some temperature. We could depict that task textually as follows:

BPMN-task1: <Set: Temperature>

where we employ a general format describing a BPMN task: <Verb-phrase present tense: Noun-phrase>

We could translate each occurrence (at a certain instant in time) of BPMN-task1 into an *event* as follows:

ORM-event1: [Temperature Setting: is logged]

where we employ a general format describing an event: [Noun-phrase Nominalized Verb-phrase: is logged]

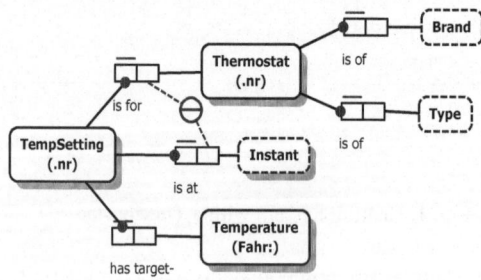

Fig. 2. Temperature setting (ORM-event1)

We will call the change of a verb into a corresponding noun phrase, the *nominalization* of that verb [13].We note that we use the word "event" as it is used in database terminology; i.e., in a CRUD sense. In the event [Temperature Setting: is logged], "is logged" refers to the time stamping of that event. A structure of an event is offered by a data model fragment capturing the occurrence of an activity at a certain instant in time. Using ORM, we could depict **ORM-event1** as follows:

We have arrived at this data model fragment (in this case pertaining to the event TemperatureSetting, written as TempSetting for short) by asking the following (not necessarily complete) set of general *event-identifying questions* against the task in question:

1. How do we *identify* the event?
2. At what *instant* (timestamp) does the event happen?
3. What do we have as *input* for the event?
4. What do we have as *output* of the event?

Of course, answering such a set of questions, will -in general- often need the support of domain expert knowledge. Using our framework of starting from a BPMN model, and posing such event-identifying questions, we can systematically arrive at a data model supporting the business process. Hence, the business process is seen as the *context* in which the business data is offered its place. In the case of our example, a temperature setting is identified by its own local number (a choice we have made), or by a particular thermostat together with an instant indicating the moment that the event occurs. Output of the event is a target temperature. This set of fact types as offered above, is *minimal* in the sense that it is tailor-made to offer exactly that data necessary to get the task of a temperature setting to run properly.

The second task that we investigate is

BPMN-task2 <Measure: Temperature>, resulting in the event

ORM-event2   [TempMeasurement: is logged]

The corresponding minimal ORM model is

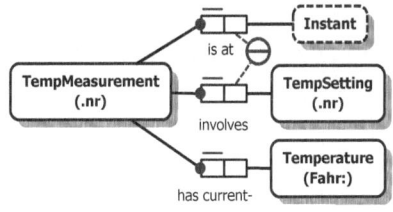

Fig. 3. Temperature measurement (ORM-event 2)

This model fragment was obtained by answering the same event-identifying question list as in the case of the previous TempSetting event. We note that we also need a rule (written here in OLE: ORM-Logic driven English [3]) indicating that a temperature measurement event is preceded (in time) by a temperature setting event

for each TempSetting, TempMeasurement, Instant1, **and** Instant2:
if that TempSetting is at **that** Instant1 **and** TempMeasurement is at **that** Instant2 **then that** Instant1<**that** Instant2.

Capturing dynamic aspects (such as TempSetting is followed by TempMeasurement) is taken care of by explicitly modeling time, and stating (static) rules about instants in time. This approach has been adopted from [2,12]. The subsequent BPMN-task is

BPMN-task3 <Compare: temperature>, and is followed by an exclusive-or fork, resulting in the event

ORM-event3:   [TempComparison: is derived and logged]

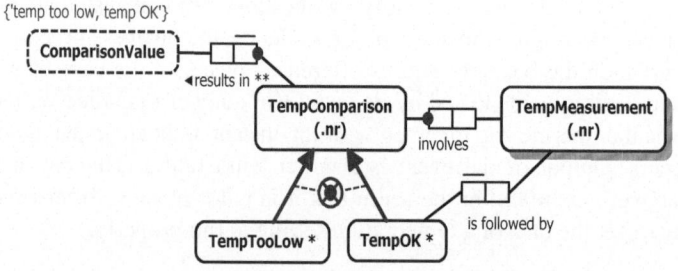

Fig. 4. Temperature comparison (ORM-event 3)

A temperature value will be called 'OK', exactly when the measured temperature is equal to or higher than the temperature value that has been set. Otherwise the temperature value is called 'too low'. In the case that the temperature value is 'OK', the system moves on to the next temperature measurement.
The derivation rule (written in OLE [3]) is offered by

for each TempComparison: **the** comparisonValue of **that** TempComparison **equals** `OK', **exactly when the** temperature **of the** tempMeasurement **of that** TempComparison **is equal to or higher than the** temperature **of (the** tempSetting **of the** tempMeasurement **of that** TempComparison)

Our process of mapping the remainder of the BPMN-model to an ORM model moves along the same path as applied in the steps up till now. In summary, a BPMN-ORM procedure can be formulated as follows:

1. Create a BPMN-task
2. Transform that task into a desired ORM-event
3. Find a minimal model that realizes the desired ORM-event
4. Generate the corresponding relational view of a database
5. Create the next BPMN-task
6. Transform that task into a subsequent ORM-event
7. Find the minimal extension to the previous ORM model that realizes that subsequent ORM-event
8. Generate the next step in the evolution of the underlying database
9. Etc.

At the end of applying this procedure, you will have created a tailor-made corporate data model associated to a given BPMN process model. Subsequently, this model can be used to generate a relational database using NORMA [7,8]: the corporate database tailor-made to support the business process model.

Section 3 General Rules for Transforming BPMN Models to ORM Models

In this section, we offer some general rules for transforming a simple BPMN process model to an associated ORM data model. Bellow, in figure 6, you see a simple BPMN model containing the basic constructions for building a process: a start event, followed by two activities in sequence, followed by a gateway (in this case an exclusive-or fork) resulting in a divergence of two activities, after which the process stops. This very general type of model in BPMN transforms into an ORM data model.

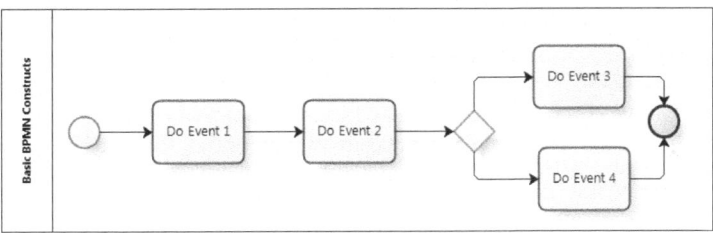

Fig. 5. Basic BPMN process model

Activities will be denoted by employing a general format <Do EventName>, where an event here denotes the (time-stamped) occurrence of an activity in the CRUD sense. For example, the activity <Set: Temperature> (cf. the notation as introduced in section 2), can be reformulated to <Do Temperature Setting> to fit such a format. We will now step by step transform figure 6 into an ORM data model

1.   The Start event is transformed into

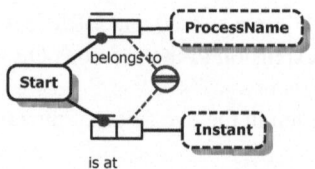

2.   The sequence flow of activity <Do Event1> followed by <Do Event2> is transformed into

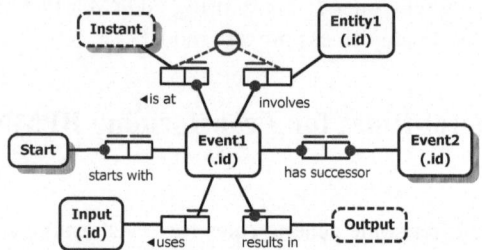

We note that we also need a rule to indicate that Event2 is preceded (in time) by Event1 (written here in OLE)

for each Event1, Event2, Instant1, **and** Instant2:
if that Event1 has successor **that** Event2 **and that** Event1 is at **that** Instant1 **and that** Event2 is at **that** Instant2
then that Instant1<**that** Instant2

3.   Activity <Do Event2> is followed by a gateway (in this case an exclusive-or fork) resulting in a divergence of two activities followed by an exclusive gateway, which is transformed into

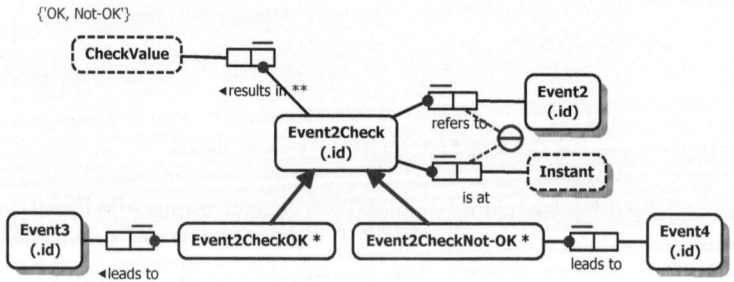

where the two subtypes are defined (in OLE) by

- **an** Event2CheckOK **is an** Event2Check**, exactly when the** checkValue **of that** Event2Check **is** "OK"
- **an** Event2CheckNot-OK **is an** Event2Check**, exactly when the** checkValue **of that** Event2Check **is** "Not-OK"

4. The exclusive-or gateway results in a divergence of two activities <Do Event3> and <Do Event4>, after which the process stops; this results in the following transformation into an ORM model

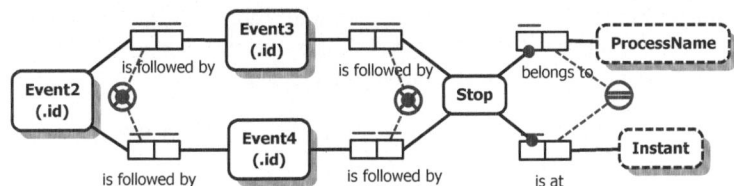

We also need an extra constraint stating that if Event2 is followed by Event3, then Event3 is followed by some Stop event (and an analogous rule in the case that Event2 is followed by Event4). We can state this (in OLE) as follows

for each Event2 **and** Event3:
if that Event2 is followed by **that** Event3 **then that** Event3 is followed by **some** Stop

We note that an inclusive-or gateway in the process model, replacing the exclusive-or gateway, would result in replacing the exclusive-or constraint in the ORM model by a corresponding inclusive-or constraint. Parallel gateways can be treated analogously.

Section 4 Conclusions

This paper is aimed at tackling some of the problems encountered in deriving business data from process models. We have shown how to systematically map basic business process models using Business Process Modeling Notation (BPMN) to data models specified in ORM. From the resulting ORM model, we can generate a complete (corporate) relational database, containing the business data that is tailor-made to support the business process.

References

1. Bakema, G., Zwart, J., van der Lek, H.: Fully Communication Oriented Information Modelling. Ten Hagen Stam (2000)

2. Balsters, H., Halpin, T.: Formal Semantics of Dynamic Rules in ORM. In: Meersman, R., Tari, Z., Herrero, P. (eds.) OTM-WS 2008. LNCS, vol. 5333, pp. 699–708. Springer, Heidelberg (2008)

3. Balsters, H.: ORM Logic-Based English (OLE) and the ORM ReDesigner Tool: Fact-Based Reengineering and Migration of Relational Databases. In: Herrero, P., Panetto, H., Meersman, R., Dillon, T. (eds.) OTM-WS 2012. LNCS, vol. 7567, pp. 358–367. Springer, Heidelberg (2012)

4. BiZaGi Process Modeler, http://www.bizagi.com/

5. BPMN, http://www.omg.org/spec/BPMN/2.0/

6. Chen, P.P.: The entity-relationship model—towards a unified view of data. ACM Transactions on Database Systems 1(1), 9–36 (1976)

7. Curland, M., Halpin, T.: Model Driven Development with NORMA. In: Proc. 40th Int. Conf. on System Sciences (HICSS-40). IEEE Computer Society (January 2007)

8. Curland, M., Halpin, T.: The NORMA Software Tool for ORM 2. In: Soffer, P., Proper, E. (eds.) CAiSE Forum 2010. LNBIP, vol. 72, pp. 190–204. Springer, Heidelberg (2011)

9. FBM working group: Fact-based modeling exchange schema. Version 20111021c (2011), http://www.factbasedmodeling.org/

10. Halpin, T.: ORM 2. In: Meersman, R., Tari, Z. (eds.) OTM-WS 2005. LNCS, vol. 3762, pp. 676–687. Springer, Heidelberg (2005)

11. Halpin, T.: ORM/NIAM Object-Role Modeling. In: Bernus, P., Mertins, K., Schmidt, G. (eds.) Handbook on Information Systems Architectures, 2nd edn., pp. 81–103. Springer, Heidelberg (2006)

12. Halpin, T.: Temporal Modeling and ORM. In: Meersman, R., Tari, Z., Herrero, P. (eds.) OTM-WS 2008. LNCS, vol. 5333, pp. 688–698. Springer, Heidelberg (2008)

13. Halpin, T., Morgan, T.: Information Modeling and Relational Databases, 2nd edn. Morgan Kaufmann, San Francisco (2008)

14. Morgan, T.: Business Process Modeling and ORM. In: Meersman, R., Tari, Z. (eds.) OTM-WS 2007, Part I. LNCS, vol. 4805, pp. 581–590. Springer, Heidelberg (2007)

15. OMG/UML: OMG Unified Modeling Language (OMG UML), Superstructure. Version 2.3 (May 2010)

16. Russel, N., ter Hofstede, A.: Modern Business Process Automation, ch. 2. Springer (2010)

Elementary Transactions

Jan Pieter Zwart and Stijn Hoppenbrouwers

Research Group Model-Based Information Systems
Academy of Communication and Information Technology
HAN University of Applied Sciences
Ruitenberglaan 26, 6826 CC Arnhem, The Netherlands
janpieter.zwart@han.nl, stijn.hoppenbrouwers@han.nl

Abstract. Designing the *data* perspective of an information system has bene-fited greatly from modeling at the conceptual level. From such a model, logical data structures (ERM, Relational, DWH) can be generated automatically. In this paper, we describe how to generate the elementary building blocks of the *process* perspective from the conceptual data level. Our goal is to derive a com-plete set of elementary transactions from the elementary fact types and con-straints at the conceptual level. Definitions of the required concepts and rules for their basic behavior are given.

Keywords: elementary transaction, operator, snapshot, parameter, precondition.

1 Introduction

1.1 Integration of Data and Process Perspective

Data modeling has benefited greatly from considering data structures and constraints at the conceptual level, ignoring all implementation considerations such as table struc-tures (logical level) or access paths (physical level). Especially Fact Oriented Model-ing (FOM) techniques that consider *elementary fact types* (attribute-free modeling: no premature grouping of facts), such as FCO-IM [1, 2] and ORM [3], have been shown to lead to reliable, validatable and verifiable data models. From such data models, different logical levels can be easily generated automatically (relational database schemas [1, ch.4], [3: ch.11], ERM schemas, UML class diagrams, DWH star sche-mas [3, 4, 5] etc.): see figure 1, arrow 1.

Process modeling is often done without a direct connection to a conceptual data model. Nijssen [6] was the first to link fact types from the data model to information flows in the process model at the conceptual level. However, a proper integration between data models and process models remains a problem today.

One of the main topics in our research group Model-Based Information Systems is generating applications from (the metadata of) database structures. Luursema and coworkers have built the engine IMAGine [5] that generates user interfaces from a relational database schema and additional metadata. However, this generator works on the logical level (see figure 1, arrow 2), and it still involves arbitrary choices

Y.T. Demey and H. Panetto (Eds.): OTM 2013 Workshops, LNCS 8186, pp. 513–523, 2013.

between several alternative possibilities. This shows there is still a gap in our under-standing how satisfactory user tasks can be generated from metadata. The approach with elementary transactions (arrow 3 in figure 1) in combination with the results of a task analysis (arrow 4) might help to bridge this gap.

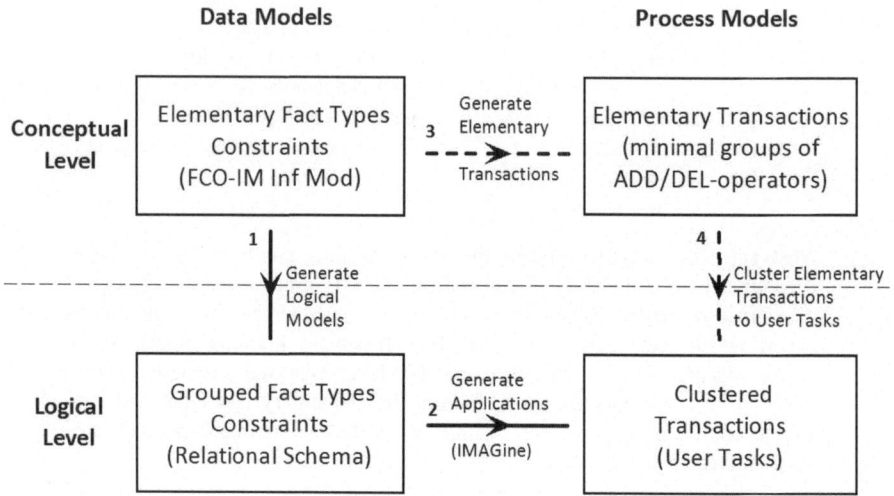

Fig. 1. Data and Process Perspectives

This paper deals only with arrow 3 in figure 1: we will show it is possible at the *conceptual* level to generate the basic building blocks of the process perspective, in the form of elementary transactions, from the metadata in the conceptual information model. These elementary transactions are the basic and indivisible building blocks that must be used for all meaningful processes the information system should provide: all user tasks will consist of clusters of one or more elementary transactions, and all elementary transactions will be a part of at least one user task.

1.2   Transactions

The concept of a transaction has always been a part of relational database systems, and every RDBMS has implemented it: see [7, p.14], [8, p.413], [9, Ch.25.2], [10, p.183], [11, p.137], [12, Ch.7], [13] to name but a few. Dietz uses the word in a broader sense [14]. Bollen [15] uses the term Exchange Rule for a similar concept.

None of these authors however discusses an *elementary* transaction, but in the Fact Oriented Modeling (FOM) world this concept has also been recognized in principle for a long time as well. Nijssen [6, p.533] discusses it briefly. Halpin mentions 'ele-mentary update' and 'compound transaction' [3, p.35]. In an earlier edition of the same book [16, p.685], Halpin briefly discusses elementary transactions, but adds: "this approach is simply too time-consuming for data-intensive systems and is often too unstable, since business processes tend to change far more rapidly than the under-lying data." This passage is absent in his more recent book [3] however.

An approach that resembles our ideas was reported by Pepels and Plasmeijer [17]. They describe a "plan to infer from an ORM [Object Role Model] groups of basic operations associated with objects/fact types [...]. Such a Group we define to be a *logical unit of work* (an *luw*)". They remark "Real life ORM's with a substantial number of fact types result in an enormous amount of *luw's*.". Furthermore they use three basic operations: add, delete and update. So their approach differs from ours in essential ways: their *luw's* are not necessarily elementary, and an update operator is inconsistent with the concept of elementary facts since it operates at a sub-elementary level. To our knowledge their paper has had no follow-up to date.

Bollen [15] does not discuss the elementarity of the exchange rules he defines, though the examples he gives are indeed elementary.

In the present paper we will show in detail how elementary transactions can be defined, and indicate how they can be derived from an FCO-IM information model.

2   Materials and Methods

The concept of an elementary transaction does not depend on the modeling technique used, as long as that technique supports elementary facts. All FOM techniques can serve, and we will use FCO-IM [1, 2] to illustrate and concretize the theory.

We will develop the theory by defining the concepts and prescribing their opera-tional behavior. The following example will be used to illustrate the results.

2.1   Concrete FCO-IM Example

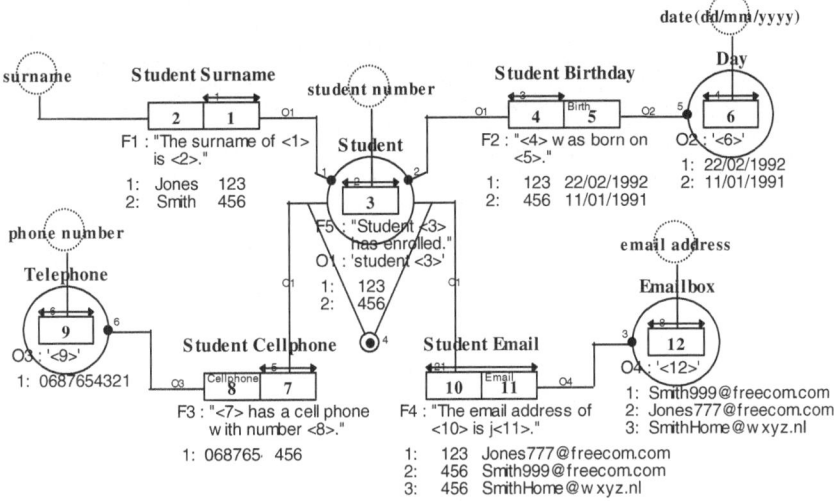

Fig. 2. Example IM

Figure 2 shows a trivially small example FCO-IM information model (see [1] for a detailed explanation of FCO-IM, freely downloadable from www.fco-im.nl). There are eight fact types, shown as named sets of small rectangles, like Student Surname. Each rectangle is called a role. Five fact types have a fact type expression (FTE), numbered F1, F2, ... F5, which can be regarded as sentence types (predicates). Four fact types are nominalized [1, ch.2.4.6], (i.e. nested, enclosed in a solid circle), and can be regarded as object types (although in FCO-IM they are technically just nested fact types). All object types have an object type expression (OTE), which can be regarded as parts of sentence types, to be used in fact types attached to the object type, numbered O1, O2, ... O4.

Each role can be played by a *label type* (dotted circle), which can be regarded as a source of labels, or an object type. In the latter case the name of the OTE to be used in the corresponding blank of the FTE is written next to the line joining the role and the object type.

When one tuple in the population is properly substituted into a FTE, a verbalization of one concrete elementary fact results, called a fact expression (FE). From F1, tuple 2: "The surname of student 456 is Smith.". Note that O1 has been substituted into the blank <1> in F1.

A small arrow above a role indicates a uniqueness constraints (UC): all values in the population of the role(s) under it must be unique. A big dot indicates a Totality Constraint (TC): every tuple in the population of the object type must play this role.

3   Results

3.1   Definitions

Snapshot
Each fact type can in principle have a population of 0, 1 or more tuples, depending on the constraints and the course of fact registrations.

Def1: A valid snapshot is a population of a data model at one point in time that does not violate any constraint in the model. The notation S1, S2, ... will refer to particular snapshots. The population in figure 2 is a valid snapshot.

Def2: The current snapshot is the snapshot that exists just before a transaction is executed.

Operators
The building blocks of transactions are only the operators ADD and DEL. An ADD-operator will add one complete elementary fact, and a DEL-operator will delete one complete elementary fact. Parts of elementary facts cannot be changed, only a whole fact can be added or deleted. An update of a fact is to be seen as a combination of one DEL and one ADD operation, replacing the old fact with a new one.

Def3: ADD(IM, S, FTE, FE) is the operator to add in model IM, with S as the current snapshot, to the fact type with fact type expression FTE the fact expression FE.

Def4: DEL(IM, S, FTE, FE) is the operator to delete in model IM, with S as the current snapshot, from the fact type with fact type expression FTE the fact expres-sion FE.

The parameters IM and S are included to stress that the operators need access to the metadata and to the current snapshot. For brevity, when the context is clear, they can be omitted, so ADD(FTE, FE) etc. will suffice.

Clearly, the action of an operator will depend strongly on the current snapshot: for instance adding FE to FTE might be allowed with S1 as current snapshot, but might violate a constraint (e.g. a uniqueness constraint) with S2 as current snapshot.

Transactions

The reason transactions are needed at all is that the constraints in the IM will in general require combining ADD and/or DEL operators, because the population created by executing only a part of the operators in the transaction will in general yield an invalid snapshot. A common example: if an object type plays two roles (namely R1 in FTx, and R2 in FTy), and both R1 and R2 have a single-role TC and a single-role UC, then any addition of a fact Fx to FTx will also require the addition of a fact Fy to FTy. Note that the two possible sequences of these operations {ADD(FTx, Fx); ADD(FTy, Fy)} and {ADD(FTy, Fy); ADD(FTx, Fx)} both result in an invalid snapshot half-way: after executing just the first operator, the population will violate a totality constraint before the second operation is executed. Therefore it is conceptually essential to consider the transaction as a whole: a single set of operations, without a sequence.

Def5: A transaction is an operation T that transforms a given valid snapshot S1 of an IM into another valid snapshot S2 of the same IM. Notation: T(S1)=S2.

A transaction T is a set of ADD and/or DEL operators. The notation T1, T2 … will refer to particular transactions. Note that all transactions are to be defined in such a way that if T(S1)=S2 and S1 is valid, then S2 must be valid as well.

Since the execution of a single operator can involve constraints that do not apply directly to the FTE concerned, as the example with the two totality constraints above illustrates, operators cannot be executed without being embedded in a transaction, even if such a transaction consists of just this one operator.

Any two transactions T1 and T2 can be combined into a composite transaction T12, by simply performing them both. Particularly interesting therefore are transactions that contain just a minimal set of operators: leaving out at least one of these operators would fail to generate a valid new snapshot.

Def6: An elementary transaction is a transaction that contains a minimal set of ADD and/or DEL operators.

As an example, one of the elementary transactions for the IM in figure 2 would be:

```
TRANSACTION T1
     ADD(F1, FE1)                    ADD(F2, FE2)
     [ADD(F3, FE3) | ADD(F4, FE4)]   ADD(F5, FE5)
END TRANSACTION
```

Here the notation [x|y] means: choose either x or y, but not both.

This transaction would add a new student, identified by a student number (F5), surname (F1 because of TC 1), birthday (F2 because of TC 2) and either an email address or a cellphone number (F3 or F4 because of TC 4 on roles 7 and 10).

3.2   Variables and Input Parameters

In transaction T1, the same student number must be entered into roles 1, 3, 4 and [7|10]. This can be made clear by using variables and input parameters (see [15] for a similar approach, which does not specify recursive structures however):

TRANSACTION T1(V1(O1),V2(surname),V3(O2),V4(O3),V5(O4))
    ADD(F1, {1:V1, 2:V2})   ADD(F2, {4:V1, 5:V3})
    [ADD(F3, {7:V1, 8:V4}) | ADD(F4, {10:V1, 11:V5})]
    ADD(F5, 3:V1[O1<3[student number]>])
END TRANSACTION

Explanation of notation: V1(O1) means: variable V1 must contain an OE of type O1; V2(surname) means: V2 must contain a label of type surname; 5:V3 means: variable V3 must be substituted into role 5; V1[O1<3[student number]>] means: the student number that is in blank <3> that is in OTE O1 that is in variable V1. This way of designating a constituent part of a variable, by recursively going as deeply into the nested structure as needed, is often necessary.

3.3   Preconditions

Every transaction can have one or more preconditions that specify when it can be executed (see [15] for a similar approach). Transaction T1 must concern a new student: the student number entered in the OE that goes into V1 must not yet exist in the population of object type Student. This can be expressed as V1(O1<3[student number]>) NOT IN F5<3[student number]>. We will abbreviate this to NEW(V1) below. Similar preconditions with IN (must already exist in the population, abbreviated as OLD(V1)), COUNT and other functions can be specified as well. T1 now reads:

TRANSACTION T1(V1(O1),V2(surname),V3(O2),V4(O3),V5(O4))
    PRECONDITION NEW(V1)
    ADD(F1, {1:V1, 2:V2})   ADD(F2, {4:V1, 5:V3})
    [ADD(F3, {7:V1, 8:V4}) | ADD(F4, {10:V1, 11:V5})]
    ADD(F5, 3:V1[O1<3[student number]>])
END TRANSACTION

3.4   Working Mechanisms

Transactions

The working of a transaction T1(S1)=S2 can be seen as a simultaneous joint application of all its constituent operators to S1, resulting in S2 appearing without any intermediate stages. Of course, any actual implementation would have to use a particular sequence of operations, even if 4GL techniques are used, but that is not of concern here. A conceptual working mechanism can be formulated in pseudo code as:

START TRANSACTION (T1(S1)=S2)
    Disable all constraints. Perform all operations in T1 (in any order).
    Check S2 against all constraints. IF at least one constraint is violated
    THEN give error message and rollback ELSE re-activate all constraints
END TRANSACTION

DEL Operators

An ADD operator needs input parameters for all the new values. A DEL operator can do with fewer parameters: if all facts about a student are to be deleted, only the student number is required. So we have chosen to minimize the number of parameters for DEL operators.

In addition, to minimize the number of required preconditions, we assume the following general behavior for a DEL operator. Suppose a DEL(FTEx, FEy) operation is to be carried out. If FEy exists in the current population of FTEx, the operator deletes the fact. If FEy does not exist in the population, it does nothing. This choice simplifies the formulation of elementary transactions considerably, because it eliminates the need to check for every DEL operation whether or not FEy exists in the current snapshot. Here is an example transaction with a DEL operator for the IM in figure 2:

TRANSACTION T5(V1(O1))
    PRECONDITION COUNT(F4(10)=V1)>0
    DEL(F3, 10=V1)
END TRANSACTION

The complete set of elementary transactions for the information model in figure 2 is given in the appendix to this paper.

4   Discussion

4.1   Population of Object Types without FTE

ADD and DEL operators only deal with one complete elementary fact at a time. Therefore only fact types with a fact type expression (FTE) have to be considered. We assume that the population of fact types without a FTE, which in FCO-IM can only be nominalized fact types (object types) [1, ch.2.5.2], is handled automatically by any system that implements this theory. Indeed CaseTalk [2], a software tool that supports creating FCO-IM information models, does this. It is a crucial property of FCO-IM that 'real-world objects' are not modeled separately, but are present only in the form of 'object expressions' in verbalizations of elementary facts.

4.2   Arbitrary Choices

We have made a few arbitrary choices, aimed at reducing the number of conditions or transactions, which could also be made differently.

The possibility to choose exactly one item from a list of alternative operators, e.g.:
```
TRANSACTION T1
    ADD(F1, FE1)                    ADD(F2, FE2)
    [ADD(F3, FE3) | ADD(F4, FE4)]  ADD(F5, FE5)
END TRANSACTION
```
The alternative would be to define two separate transactions:
```
TRANSACTION T1a                    TRANSACTION T1b
    ADD(F1, FE1)  ADD(F2, FE2)         ADD(F1, FE1)  ADD(F2, FE2)
    ADD(F3, FE3)  ADD(F5, FE5)         ADD(F4, FE4)  ADD(F5, FE5)
END TRANSACTION                    END TRANSACTION
```
We prefer the single-transaction version, because it complies with the definition of elementary transactions (Def6): since exactly one operator must be chosen in any concrete instance of the transaction, no operator can be left out in this instance. This greatly reduces the number of elementary transactions if several multiple-role TC's are involved (a situation that is fortunately not very common in practice).

We chose to minimize the number of parameters for DEL operators. The alternative would be to define input parameters for all values concerned. This would however be unnecessary and inconvenient (see also section 4.3 below).

4.3   Update Transactions

An update of an elementary fact can be viewed as replacing the old fact with a new one, i.e.: of a DEL operation followed by an ADD operation of a complete elementary fact. Therefore an update operator is not needed. Manipulating a *part* of an elementary fact (replacing part of a fact keeping the rest the same) would mean going below the elementary fact level, and we choose to not consider sub-elementary operations. We can call a transaction that combines exactly one ADD and DEL operation on the same fact type an *update transaction*.

It can be argued that update transactions are not even needed: suppose we have an update transaction UT, which performs an update on snapshot S1: UT(S1)=S2. The same snapshot S2 can be created from S1 by performing several other elementary transactions. In the example in figure 2: to update a surname of a student: either use transaction T7 (see the appendix), or delete everything about this student using transaction T4 followed by adding all facts about this student anew using transactions T1, and possibly T2 and/or T3 as well.

The paragraph above shows that a set of elementary transactions is not necessarily a minimal set of transactions. Strictly theoretically, update transactions are not needed, but would be very convenient in practice. We choose to allow all transactions that comply with definition Def6: they must all be elementary, i.e. if at least one operation is removed, then the resulting snapshot will not be valid. Note that this is the reason that there is no update transaction for F4 in the appendix: it would not be elementary. The same result can be obtained with T3 followed by T6. In practice of course several non-elementary transactions will be defined as combinations of elementary transactions, and then an update transaction for F4 can be added, but here we are concerned only with elementary transactions.

Finally consider the update transaction below:

TRANSACTION T7(V1(O1), V2(surname))
    PRECONDITION OLD(V1)
    DEL(F1, 1=V1)   ADD(F1, {1:V1, 2:V2})
END TRANSACTION

It would seem that here a definite *order* for executing the two operators is called for: if the ADD is performed first and the DEL afterward, the result is that both facts are deleted. The reason is our choice for a minimal set of parameters for DEL operators (see section 4.2 above): if the DEL operator had two parameters, with the second one containing the old surname, there would be no problem. However we can easily preserve the conceptual orderlessness by letting an implementing system find all the 'missing' values for the delete operations in the current snapshot first, and then execute fully parameterized versions of the DEL operators with these values. So this is an implementation matter, not a conceptual one since all the necessary information is specified in the transaction as it is defined above.

4.4   Algorithm

Presently we are working on an algorithm to generate all elementary transactions from any given FCO-IM information model. We have built a proof-of-concept implementation that generates all transactions with only ADD operations for information models with a limited set of types of constraints, and are continuing with transactions with only DEL operations, and will tackle the mixed transactions with both ADD and DEL operations last.

We recognize that such an algorithm cannot be complete, unless it takes all possible (types of) constraints into account, which is impossible. We do however think it can be made complete for a specific subset of all types of constraints. We trust it will be possible that a transaction generator can generate the majority of the elementary transactions correctly, leaving only some handwork to incorporate exotic constraints.

4.5   Number of Transactions

Halpin [16] and Pepels [17] have expressed their concern that the number of elementary transactions will be very large (see the quotes in section 1.2 above). That is not our experience so far. The number of elementary transactions seems to be of the order of the number of fact types (see the small example in this paper, and preliminary results with larger information models give the same indication). Although Bollen [15] does not give all the exchange rules, he too arrives at a number of that order. Elementary transactions cannot change with varying user processes; so their number and composition depend only on the constraints in the information model.

4.6   User Interface

If a list of all elementary transactions can be generated from an information model, it will be relatively easy to generate a user interface for executing these transactions (without grouping them into user tasks yet). This interface could for example show a list of transactions with their purpose (add a new student, update the cellphone number of a student, …). If the user chooses a transaction, the interface could present the facts to be supplied in the form of sentences with blank fields to be filled in. Such an interface would amount to a full DML at the conceptual level.

5   Conclusion

We have shown in this paper how elementary transactions can be defined in terms of sets of operators on elementary facts, with input parameters and preconditions. We have also indicated several behavioral aspects of these operators and transactions. The number of such transactions is of the order of the number of fact types.

We are developing an algorithm for generating all elementary transactions for a given FCO-IM information model, with a limited set of types of constraints. If successful, we will have generated a DML at the conceptual level.

Whether these elementary transactions will help in generating user interfaces (arrow 4 in figure 1) would be an interesting topic for further research.

Appendix: All Elementary Transactions for the Example IM

```
TRANSACTION T1(V1(O1),V2(surname),V3(O2),[V4(O3)|V5(O4)])
   PRECONDITION NEW(V1)   ADD(F1, {1:V1, 2:V2})   ADD(F2, {4:V1, 5:V3})
   [ADD(F3, {7:V1, 8:V4}) | ADD(F4, {10:V1, 11:V5})]
   ADD(F5, 3:V1[O1<3[student number]>])   END TRANSACTION

TRANSACTION T2(V1(O1), V2(O3)   PRECONDITION OLD(V1) AND
   COUNT(F3(7)=V1)=0    ADD(F3, {7:V1, 8:V3})   END TRANSACTION

TRANSACTION T3(V1(O1), V2(O4))
   PRECONDITION OLD(V1) ADD(F4, {10:V1, 11:V2}) END TRANSACTION

TRANSACTION T4(V1(O1))   DEL(F1, 1=V1) DEL(F2, 4=V1)
   DEL(F3, 7=V1) DEL(F4, 10=V1) END TRANSACTION

TRANSACTION T5(V1(O1))
   PRECONDITION COUNT(F4(10)=V1)>0   DEL(F3, 10=V1) END TRANSACTION

TRANSACTION T6(V1(O1), V2(O4))    PRECONDITION COUNT(F4(10)=V1)>1 OR
   COUNT(F3(7)=V1)>0) DEL(F4, 10=V1 AND 11=V2)   END TRANSACTION

TRANSACTION T7(V1(O1), V2(surname)) PRECONDITION OLD(V1)
   DEL(F1, 1=V1) ADD(F1, {1:V1, 2:V2}) END TRANSACTION

TRANSACTION T8(V1(O1), V2(O2)) PRECONDITION OLD(V1)
   DEL(F2, 4=V1) ADD(F2, {4:V1, 5:V2}) END TRANSACTION

TRANSACTION T9(V1(O1), V2(O3)) PRECONDITION OLD(V1)
   DEL(F3, 7=V1) ADD(F3, {7:V1, 8:V2}) END TRANSACTION
```

References

1. Bakema, G.P., Zwart, J.P.C., van der Lek, H.: Fully Communication Oriented Information Modeling, FCO-IM (2002), http://www.fco-im.nl
2. Wobben, M.: CaseTalk, FCO-IM modeling tool, http://www.CaseTalk.com
3. Halpin, T., Morgan, T.: Information Modeling and Relational Databases, 2nd edn. Morgan Kaufmann Publishers (2008) ISBN-13: 978-0-12-373568-3
4. Bakema, G.P., Manoku, E., et al.: FCO-IM Bridgetoolset, a software package for repository based information model transformations
5. Luursema, E.D., van Bers, A.C., Nabben, M.T.J.O.: IMAGine. In: Conference Proceedings of Information Systems, the Next Generation. HAN University (2007)
6. Nijssen, G.M.: Universele Informatiekunde. PNA Publishing bv (1993) ISBN 90-5540-001-7
7. Codd, E.F.: The Relational Model for Database Management, version 2. Addison Wesley Publishing Company (1990) ISBN 0-201-14192-2
8. Date, C.J.: An Introduction to Database Sytems, 4th edn. Addison Wesley Publishing Company (1986) ISBN 0-201-14201-5
9. Van der Lans, R.: Het SQL Leerboek, 6th edn. Academic Service (2006) ISBN 90-395-2302-9
10. De Brock, E.O.: De Grondslagen van Semantische Databases. Academic Service (1989) ISBN 90-6233-333-8
11. Ter Bekke, J.H.: Database Ontwerp. Stenfert Kroese b.v. (1988) ISBN 90-207-1659x
12. Ter Hofstede, A.H.M.: Information Modelling in Data Intensive Domains. PhD-thesis, Radboud University Nijmegen, the Netherlands (1993) ISBN 90-9006263-X
13. Proper, H.A.: A theory for Conceptual Modelling of Evolving Application Domains. PhD Thesis, Radboud University Nijmegen, the Netherlands (1994) ISBN 90-9006849-X
14. Dietz, J.L.G.: Introductie tot DEMO. Samsom Bedrijfsinformatie (1996) ISBN 90-14-05327-4
15. Bollen, P.: Fact-Oriented Modeling in the Data-, Process- and Event Perspectives. In: Meersman, R., Tari, Z. (eds.) OTM-WS 2007, Part I. LNCS, vol. 4805, pp. 591–602. Springer, Heidelberg (2007)
16. Halpin, T.: Information Modeling and Relational Databases. Morgan Kaufmann Publishers (2001) ISBN-13: 978-1-55860-672-2
17. Pepels, B., Plasmeijer, R.: Generating Applications from Object Role Models. In: Meersman, R., Tari, Z. (eds.) OTM-WS 2005. LNCS, vol. 3762, pp. 656–665. Springer, Heidelberg (2005)

Comparative Analysis of SOA and Cloud Computing Architectures Using Fact Based Modeling

Baba Piprani[1], Don Sheppard[2], and Abbie Barbir[3]

[1] MetaGlobal Systems, Canada
[2] ConCon Management Services, Canada
[3] Bank of America, Canada
baba@metaglobal.ca, don@concon.com,
abbie.barbir@bankofamerica.com

Abstract. With the ever-changing dynamic Information and Communications Technology environment and the new shared deployment options for computing, a paradigm shift is occurring that enables ubiquitous and convenient computing on a pay-as-you-go basis. Access on demand is becoming available to networks of scalable, elastic, self-serviceable, configurable physical and virtual resources. On a more narrowly focused IT and business front, there is a parallel shift towards designing information systems in terms of the services available at an interface. The Service Oriented Architecture (SOA) development style is based on the design of services and processes and the realization of interoperability and location transparency in context-specific implementations. This paper analyzes the Cloud Computing and SOA Reference Architectures being developed by ISO ISO/IEC JTC1 SC38 (in collaboration with ITU-T SG13/WP6 for Cloud Computing), and offers a concept comparison using Fact Based Modeling (FBM) methodology. FBM has allowed us to distill the concepts, relationships and business rules - thereby exposing the strengths and weakness of each, and identifying the gaps between the two.

Keywords: Cloud Computing, SOA, Service Oriented Architecture, Reference Architecture, metamodel, ISO, Fact Based Modeling.

1 Introduction and Background

Information and Communications Technology (ICT) is being transformed to a model based on services that are commoditized and delivered in a standardized manner. In a service-based model, users access services based on their requirements without regard to where the services are hosted or how they are delivered.

Several computing paradigms have promised to deliver this computing vision, of which the latest is known as Cloud Computing. The term "Cloud" denotes a computing infrastructure from which businesses and users are able to access applications from anywhere in the world, on-demand. Thus, the ICT world is rapidly evolving to develop software for millions to consume as a service, rather than to run

Y.T. Demey and H. Panetto (Eds.): OTM 2013 Workshops, LNCS 8186, pp. 524–533, 2013.

on individual computers. Cloud computing represents a paradigm shift that will redefine the relationship between buyers and sellers of IT-related products and services [1]. The ISO (International Organization for Standardization) SC38 Study Group on Cloud Computing in their 2011 report [1] identified at least 23 Cloud Computing industry initiatives that had published material, were developing standards or were doing at least some work in this area. One influential organization has been the US NIST [9,10].

With multiple Cloud Computing initiatives on the horizon, ISO decided to initiate standardization work on a Cloud Computing vocabulary and a Cloud Computing reference architecture. On a parallel front, ITU-T was also in the process of developing Recommendations for Cloud Computing terminology and reference architecture. So now, the two groups have successfully initiated collaborative work on developing a common set of standards/recommendations for Cloud Computing vocabulary and reference architecture.

On a more narrowly focused IT and business front, there is also a shift occurring in the design of systems in terms of making services available at an interface and to provide well-specified outcomes. The Service Oriented Architecture (SOA) development style is based on services and processes that realize interoperability and location transparency for context-specific implementations. ISO SC38 is also addressing standardization in the area of SOA terminology and architecture.

Considering that both of these technologies address distributed platforms and services, it is important the Cloud Computing and SOA architectures be compatible, and that there exists a harmonious set of interfaces and common points of overlap. Without this harmonization we would be back at "square one" facing a plethora of incompatible standards.

Recognizing this trend, the ISO Joint Technical Committee (JTC1) formed a Sub-Committee, called SC38 and named Distributed Application Platform and Services, to harmonize the ISO work on standardization for Web Services, Service Oriented Architecture and Cloud Computing. This initiative was largely driven by the IT marketplace having to face multiple incompatible choices of product sets, which essentially creates barriers to interoperability efforts.

This paper examines the basic concepts that have been developed for both Cloud Computing and Service Oriented Architecture, and illustrates how Fact Based Modeling (FBM) provides a useful means to compare and contrast these initiatives, hopefully leading to a more cohesive and consistent direction for the next generation of ICT.

NOTE: The standards for Cloud Computing and SOA are still under development and are subject to change. The contents of this paper are intended to be illustrative and should not be considered as an authoritative description of the emerging ISO standards.

In this paper, we have used the FBM notation and methodology as a description technique to define semantic models abstracted from the current Cloud Computing and SOA documents being progressed for standardization. FBM is a methodology for modeling the semantics of a subject area.

FBM is based on logic and controlled natural language, whereby the resulting fact based model captures the semantics of the domain of interest by means of fact types, together with the associated concept definitions and the integrity rules [8].

The roots of FBM go back to the 1970s. NIAM, a FBM notation style, was one of the candidate methodologies used for developing conceptual schemas as defined in ISO TR9007:1987 Concepts and Terminology for the Conceptual Schema and the Information Base. Subsequently, several developments have taken place in parallel, resulting in several fact based modeling "dialects", including NIAM, ORM2, CogNIAM, DOGMA and FCO-IM. The notation used in this paper is ORM2 notation.

A simplistic description of usage and reading the ORM2 notation follows. The subject area is seen as consisting of semantic objects (representing objects in the real world model) that can be described using natural language sentences---consisting of an object, predicate and possible one or more objects, each connected with a predicate-object pair. A real world object is represented by an object type denoted by a circle, also known as an entity type. Object types may have subtypes denoted by arrows from the subtype to supertype (e.g. object type Role has subtype Sub-role). Object types are involved in fact type sentence descriptions that can be binary, or n-ary (ternary, quaternary etc.), as depicted by rectangle boxes, each box representing a role that the object type plays in that sentence. Integrity rules are then associated with the fact types like mandatory (shown as a dark dot on the object type connector), and also a horizontal bar on top of a role of a fact type denoting a restriction on the occurrence of the set of role populations. The ORM2 notation contains several other rules that can be graphically depicted but are out of scope for our discussions. An example of a fact type reading from Figure 2 is: A Party (in the cloud computing paradigm schema) shall be assigned to one or more Role(s). A Role may be assigned to one or more Parties.

2   Cloud Computing Concepts

Figure 1 depicts the main Cloud Computing concepts using FBM, along with examples, as defined in the ISO draft document [2]. The concepts are defined in terms of the cloud services that are available to cloud service customers and the cloud deployment models that describe how the computing infrastructure that delivers these services can be provided and shared by users.

It is interesting to note that the Cloud Computing vocabulary and concepts were developed prior to an agreed upon architecture. The architecture itself takes its basis from the approach used in the ISO Open Distributed Reference Model [4] by utilizing the user view and functional view.

The cloud paradigm is composed of key characteristics, roles and activities, service capabilities and service categories, deployment models, and cross cutting aspects as shown. The concept relationships generally appear in the cloud computing reference architecture.

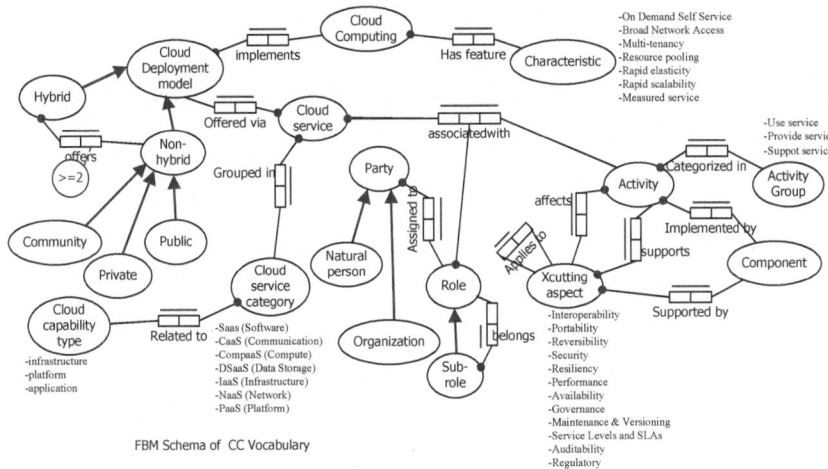

FBM Schema of CC Vocabulary

Fig. 1. Basic Cloud Computing Concepts from CD 17788.2

Tables 1 and 2 are the relevant definitions pertaining to the cloud computing models shown.

Table 1. Definitions of concepts used in Cloud Computing

Concept	Definition	Examples
Party	Entities that play one or more roles (and sub-roles)	natural person, or an organization
Role	Sets of activities	Cloud Service Customer Cloud Service Provider Cloud Service Partner
Subrole	A subset of the activities associated with a role	Sub-roles for a partner role are: service integrator, auditor, and cloud broker
Activity	A logical functional element of a Cloud Service	Using services, providing services, and supporting services
Component	An implementation of an activity.	
Cross-cutting Aspect	Behaviors or capabilities that need to be implemented & coordinated across roles	Interoperability, Portability, Reversibility, Security, Privacy, Governance, etc
Cloud Computing	paradigm for enabling network access to a scalable and elastic pool of shareable physical or virtual resources with on-demand self-service provisioning and administration	
Cloud Characteristic	Basic user-oriented features of a Cloud Computing environment	On-demand self-service, Broad network access, Multi-tenancy, Resource pooling, Rapid elasticity & scalability, Measured service

Table 2. Definitions of concepts used in Cloud Computing-continued

Concept	Definition	Examples
Cloud Service	one or more capabilities offered via cloud computing invoked using a declared interface	natural person, or an organization
Cloud Service Category	group of cloud services that possess some qualities in common with each other	Infrastructure as a Service, Platform as a Service, Software as a Service, Network as a Service, Data Storage as a Service, Compute as a Service, Communication as a Service
Capability	A quality of being able to perform a given activity	
Cloud Capability Type	Classification of the functionality, based on the type of resources used Cloud capability types follow the principle of separation of concerns, i.e. they have minimal functionality overlap between each other.	Infrastructure capabilities, Platform capabilities, Application capabilities
Cloud Deployment Model	The way in which cloud computing can be organized based on control of physical or virtual resources and how those resources are shared	Community cloud, Public cloud, or Private cloud
Hybrid cloud	A cloud deployment model that includes at least two different deployment models	Interoperability, Portability, Reversibility, Security, Privacy, Governance, etc

3   Cloud Computing Reference Architecture

A Fact Based Model for the Cloud Computing Reference Architecture (CCRA) is shown in Figure 2.

As noted earlier, the CCRA takes as its basis the ODP reference model but focuses only on the user and functional views. The CCRA does not address the implementation and deployment views. The user view is the ecosystem (or system context) including the parties, the roles, the sub-roles and the activities. The functional view is the distribution of functions necessary for the support of cloud activities.

The Fact Based Models in this paper represent the distillation and transforms as interpreted from the SOA text [6] [7] and the CCRA text [3]. The purpose of the diagrams is being able to compare them using a formal methodology to represent the involved facts and relationships as opposed to comparing text paragraphs.

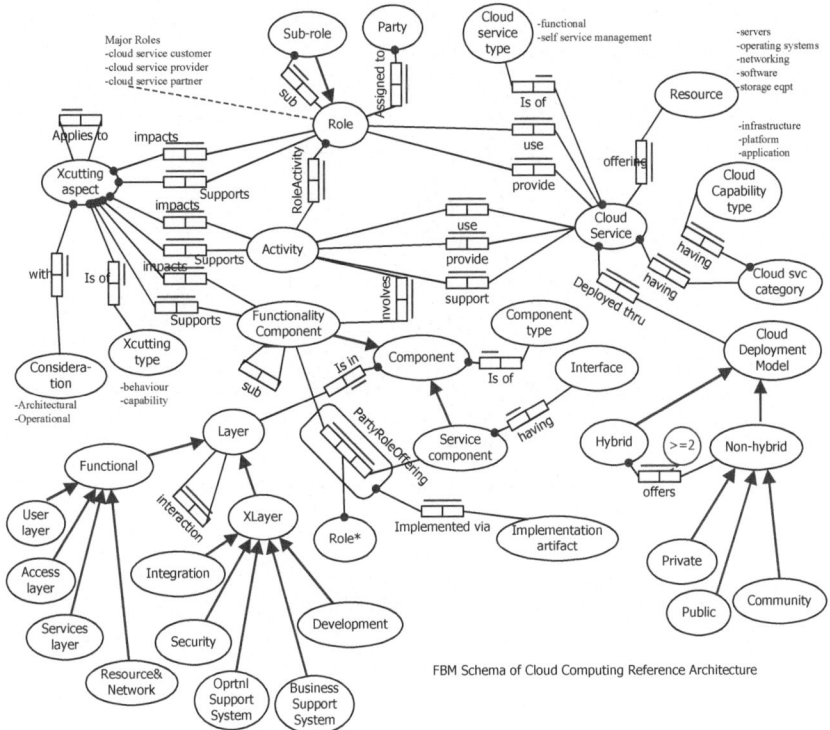

Fig. 2. Cloud Computing Reference Architecture Model from CD 17789.1

4   SOA Concepts

The basic SOA concepts [6] were derived from work already progressing in industry consortia and other standardization bodies. In a similar fashion to the Cloud Computing work, SOA terminology was first established in a Technical Report TR30102 [5]. Figure 3 includes the basic SOA concepts of entity, actors and their roles, and their relationship to a service. Figures 4 and 5 portray the SOA capability model as it relates to the service capability component. Figure 6 relates services with tasks, compositions, and processes.

The use of FBM has highlighted the overloading of the term 'element' in the SOA WD18384-1. The text defines element as 'a unit that is indivisible at a given level of abstraction and has a clearly defined boundary'. It does appear that the document also uses element in a natural English language construct. However, the term "element" is specifically formally portrayed in the figures in order to include a service, human actor, task, system, and that the element orchestrates a composition. The authors can only conclude the term is being over-used. The use of FBM modeling in Figure 4 makes the overloading obvious by the depiction of subtype relationships in the FBM schema. Figure 5 provides a portrayal of the same relationships, but with the element concept removed.

Figure 6 portrays the SOA service capability model depicting how capabilities are related to services, components and architectural blocks.

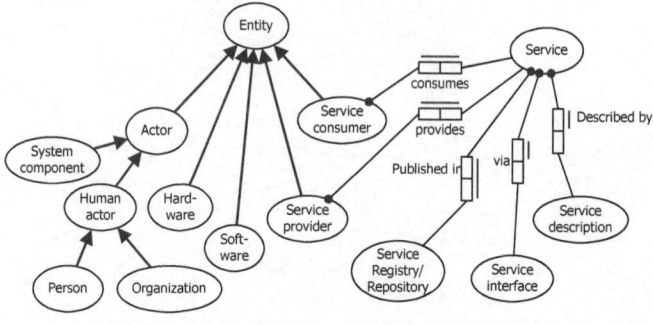

SOA - Basic concepts

Fig. 3. SOA Basic Concepts Model from WD18384-1

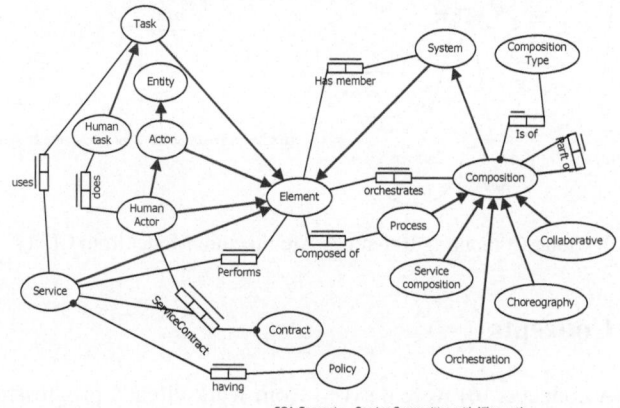

SOA Concepts – Service Composition with 'Element'

Fig. 4. SOA Task Composition Model – with 'Element' from WD18384-1

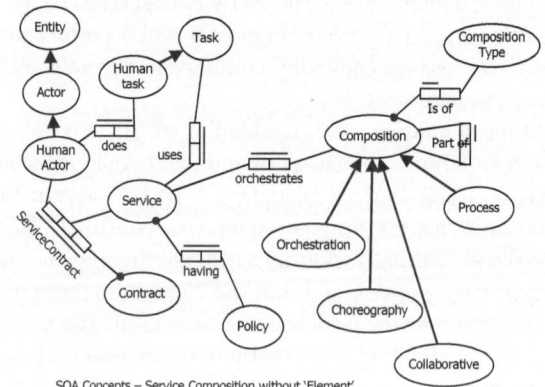

SOA Concepts – Service Composition without 'Element'

Fig. 5. SOA Task Composition Model – without 'Element' from WD18384-1

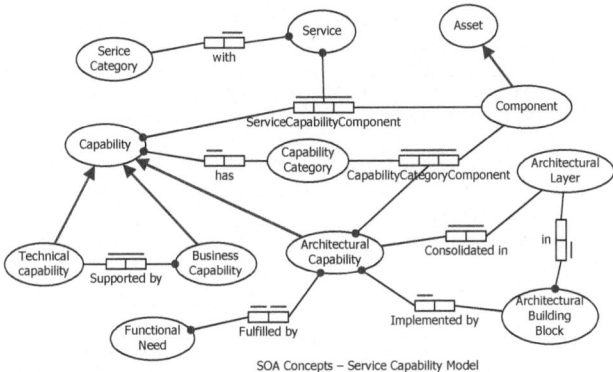

Fig. 6. SOA Service Capability Model from WD 18384-1

5   SOA Reference Architecture

The SOA reference architecture [7], illustrated in Figure 7, describes nine layers of considerations and responsibilities.   For each layer, there are three aspects that should be supported by the SOA Reference Architecture:

- Requirements (exemplified by the capabilities for each layer). The requirements aspect reflects what the layer enables and includes all of its capabilities.
- Logical (exemplified by the architectural building blocks). The logical aspect includes all the architectural building blocks, design decisions, options, KPIs, etc.
- Physical (this aspect will be left to the implementation of the standard by an adaptor of the standard). The physical aspect of each layer includes the realization of each logical aspect using technology, standards and products that are determined by taking into consideration the different architectural decisions that are necessary to be made to realize and construct the architecture.

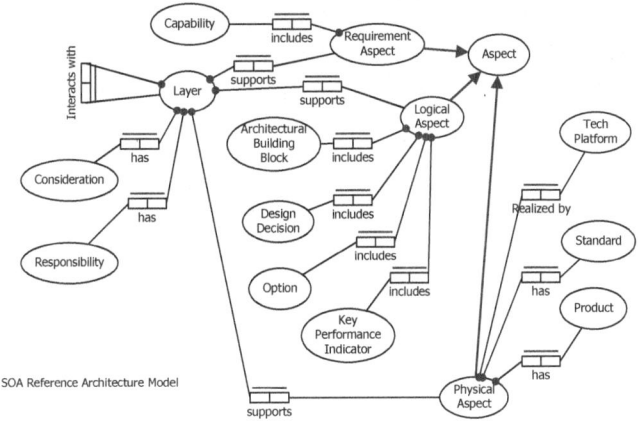

Fig. 7. SOA Reference Architecture from WD18384-2

Table 3. Definitions of concepts used in SOA

Concept	Definition	Examples
Entity	Individual in a service system with an identity which can act as a service provider or consumer.	organizations, enterprises and individuals, software and hardware
Actor	A person or system component who interacts with the system as a whole and who provides stimulus which invoke actions	Human actor
Task	Atomic action which accomplishes a defined result	Human task
Service	Logical representation of a set of repeatable activities that has specified outcomes, is self-contained, may be composed of other services, and is a "black box" to consumers of the service	Note: The word "activity" in the definition is used in the general English language sense of the word.
Composition	Result of assembling a collection of things for a particular purpose	Orchestration Choreography Collaborative
Process	Composition whose elements are composed into a sequence or flow of activities and interactions with the objective of carrying out certain work	
Service Component	Element that implements services	

6   Cloud Computing and SOA Analysis

By transforming each of the SOA and Cloud Computing concepts, terminology and architectures using Fact Based Modeling, we are able to distill the salient object types, relationships and some of the business rules to enable a comparative analysis of the two architectures.

It immediately becomes apparent that, cloud computing uses the term 'cloud service' so as to not be confused with a 'service' in SOA. The two architectures appear to skirt the issue of whether an SOA service is a cloud service or not.

Cloud Computing uses ODP views whereas SOA focuses on compositions and nine layers of considerations and capabilities.

The issue of entity and roles also appears to be not in sync between the two. Cloud Computing has distinctly identified the various roles of the various providers, brokers, auditors and users of the cloud services. SOA includes hardware and software as entities and appears to be using the roles of service consumer and service provider--- and differentiating at times with actors and human actors.

Cloud Computing stays away from the physical implementation and deployment area, whereas SOA includes the physical aspect in each layer.

One question that arises is: Is there a true difference between an SOA service and a cloud service? SOA attempts to partly address the difference between a process and a service, whereas cloud computing distinctly isolates a 'process' as an operational process or business process.

These are only some of the examples of divergence between the cloud computing and SOA concepts and architectures.

It is clear that there needs to be an accord between the Cloud Computing standards group and the SOA standards group - especially since they are part of the same ISO committee.

7   Conclusions

In this paper we have demonstrated the use of Fact Based Modeling to facilitate a comparative analysis of the emerging ISO vocabulary and reference architecture standards for Cloud Computing and Service Oriented Architecture. As a result, we have identified a number of areas where the concepts in the vocabulary and architecture documents are misaligned. We have also identified a number of areas where Cloud Computing and SOA are using similar concepts, typically in ways that are not readily compared.

Fact Based Modeling appears to provide significant assistance both in the development of consistent architectures based on sound concepts and also in the analysis and comparison of different architectures.

Further effort to analyze the models in more detail would provide valuable insight into the complex relationships between Cloud Computing and SOA.

References

1. ISO/IEC JTC1 SC38 N430 JTC1 SC38 Study Group on Cloud Computing Report – Final Version 2011-09-30
2. ISO/IEC JTC1 SC38 N887 CD 17788.2 Information technology — Distributed application platforms and services — Cloud computing — Overview and vocabulary (April 23, 2013)
3. ISO/IEC JTC1 SC38 N893 CD 17789.2 Information technology — Distributed application platforms and services — Cloud computing — Reference Architecture (April 23, 2013)
4. ISO/IEC 10746-1:1998, Information technology – Open distributed processing – Reference Model: Overview
5. ISO/IEC TR 30102, Distributed Application Platforms and Services (DAPS) - General Technical Principles of Service Oriented Architecture (SOA)
6. ISO/IEC WD 18384-1, Distributed Application Platforms and Services (DAPS) - Reference Architecture for Service Oriented Architecture (SOA RA) Part 1
7. ISO/IEC WD 18384-2, Distributed Application Platforms and Services (DAPS) - Reference Architecture for Service Oriented Architecture (SOA RA) Part 2
8. Nijssen, G.M., Halpin, T.A.: Conceptual Schema and Relational Database Design. Prentice Hall, Victoria (1989)
9. NIST Special Publication 500-292, The NIST Cloud Computing reference Architecture (September 2011)
10. NIST special Publication 800-145, The NIST Definition of Cloud Computing (September 2011)

A Simple Metamodel for Fact-Based Queries

Clifford Heath

Data Constellation
http://dataconstellation.com

Abstract. Fact-based models are built by expressing elementary facts using natural verbalizations. By generalizing individual objects to object types, facts to fact types, and adding constraints, a schema for any domain can be constructed.

Fact-based schemas have many advantages, including being highly amenable to construction of natural verbalizations, since they were originally derived from such verbalizations.

However, it is not common practice to consider queries during modeling, so only limited attention has been paid to how to model them. Queries are not only useful for extracting data, but also to express complex business constraints. An effective meta-model for fact-based queries is presented, as an extension of a tiny subset of the meta-model of Object Role Modeling. Examples expressed in the Constellation Query Language show how to populate the query meta-model.

1   Fact Based Models

In a fact-based model, an object type may be either:

- a data type - a set of values (potentially infinite) for which there exists a canonical written (lexical) form;
- a value type - a type relevant to the domain of discourse and which maps to a data type (a meaningful thing you can write down, like a name); or
- an entity type, of which each instance is uniquely identified by the combination of one or more roles played (in so-called existential fact types) by that instance.

Each fact asserts some relationship between objects, or a characteristic or self-relationship of one object, and is an instance of a single fact type. Each fact type allows the assertion of the predicate (which describes the relationship or characteristic) over objects of certain specified object types or their sub-types. Some or all instance facst of a given fact type may be derived using a query. Fact-based models also include various kinds of constraints, but those are not considered further here.

In addition to the object types and fact types, a fact-based model also contains a population of objects and facts, which are the subject of queries.

Y.T. Demey and H. Panetto (Eds.): OTM 2013 Workshops, LNCS 8186, pp. 534–544, 2013.

2   Approaches to Fact-Based Queries

A fact-based model contains a population of object instances and elementary fact assertions. A query over such a model asks whether the population contains certain objects related to one another (or not) by specified facts. Although querying of fact-based information models has been a consideration since the inception of such models, the approaches have seldom been adequately explored, and very little has been published. One of the first fact-based modeling languages, RIDL[2] included a powerful query language, but it is unknown whether an implementation of this query language was ever completed. Instead, papers say "the meaning should be self-evident" and suggests that manual effort is required to write a program to evaluate the query[3]. Many researchers have treated Fact Based Modeling (FBM) as a means to design a conventional relational database, and relegate querying to the existing relational query tools such as SQL, as in CLCE[1], or refer to other work in mapping the query to first-order logic and thence to PROLOG, for example. However, mapping a fact-based query to a relational query is not a well-defined operation unless the original query is well-defined, and neither the mapped query nor the relation which results from processing the query can easily be represented in the terms of the original fact-based model unless the reverse mapping is also well-defined. Halpin[6] et al implemented ConQuer, which has multiple presentation modes including purely textual and tree-structured text with graphical annotations. Examples of ConQuery show its power, and the papers explain that the semantics is based on the domain relational calculus (or alternatively, a first order logic), but this author is unaware of the publication of a complete language specification or its metamodel. Query execution is by translation to SQL, with several good examples provided, but the results are not represented or verbalised using the original fact model, which could cause difficulties in model evolution due to exposing the underlying relational mapping and/or identification schemes. ACE[5] has been the focus of various experiments in synthesising programs and in theorem proving. Kuhn[4] defines his query language by defining its grammar; its semantics is defined only in terms of a parser implementation that maps it to PROLOG, and he does not elaborate further. Within the more limited framework of the semantic web (open-world binary fact types represented as RDF triples) SPARQL[8] provides a query language, and there exist reasoners/inferencers such as RacerPro[9] which execute such queries. Queries are also present as derived fact types within NORMA[10] Pro, but this is not yet publicly available.

   The goal of this paper is to present a metamodel for queries as an extension to the metamodel of ORM, so that a verbal or graphical query can be compiled (conceptualised) into a fact population using the query metamodel. This compiled form is capable of being re-verbalised into equivalent (though not necessarily identical) source text. Both these operations have been implemented (excluding full support for aggregates and alternation) in the English versions of the Constellation Query Language[7] and this implementation is publicly available. A French version currently supports compilation, but not yet re-verbalisation, and work on Mandarin support is underway. Evaluation of such queries is an ongoing subject of work not discussed in this paper.

3   Query Model

The ORM2 diagram in Figure 1 shows the core features of fact-based models (Object Type, Role, Fact Type, omitting their reference schemes) across the top, then it introduces the concept of a Query, that contains Variables which may be satisfied by objects of a specific type, subject to certain conditions. The rest of this paper discusses the conditions under which a query is satisfied. The queries used for the examples are shown using the Constellation Query Language, though other fact-based query languages could also be used.

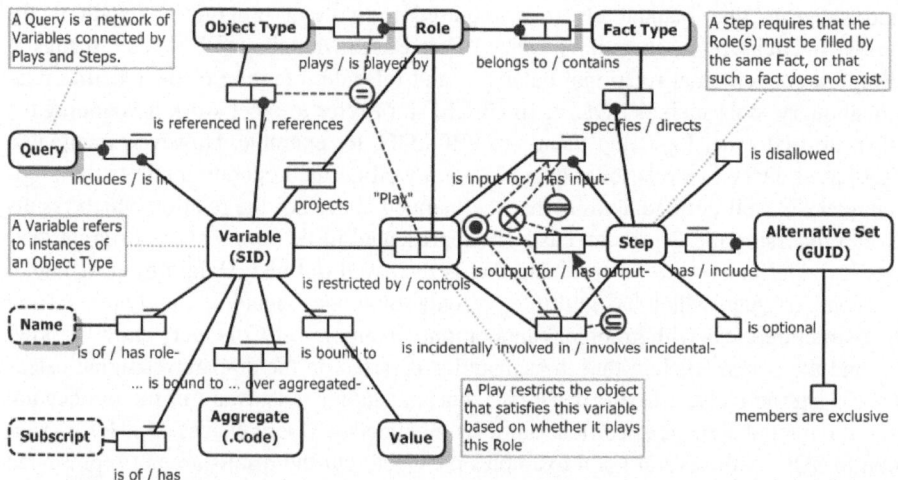

Fig. 1. Query Metamodel

Some of the variables in the query may be bound to particular values (hence are individually satisfied if those values exist), while others are bound only (via Play and Step) to other variables. It is not interesting to consider queries which contain disjoint graphs, since the result is just the cartesian product of the results of the separate subqueries. Although a Variable may involve many connections, we do not use n-ary steps, rather we model the query as a di-graph. The direction of an arc (a Step) only matters in the case of outer joins (optional steps), but we retain the notion of an input Play and an output Play for each Step. Because a step may traverse an n-ary fact type, the extra roles are each assigned to a Play with an associated Variable; these incidental Plays are not conceptually distinct from output Plays, but are a vestige of the current implementation. We now begin the full exposition of the meta-model.

4   Variables

Each query contains at least one variable. Each variable references one object type. When more than one variable in a query references the same object type, either the optional role-Name or Subscript must be populated to prevent ambiguity in the CQL verbalisation.

In satisfying a query, each variable may only be paired with an object (drawn from the model's population) of the respective object type, or in the case of an object type which is a data type, with a value which is included in that data type's value set (regardless of whether that value occurs in the model's population).

The query is satisfied when all variables are correctly paired and all other query conditions (described later) are met. Query results include the values of data- or value-types, and the identifying role values for entity types. Additional values linked to the projected objects may also be returned, but the details are not covered in this paper.

Assuming a data type, a value type, and an entity type called respectively Integer, Name, and Person, the following CQL queries containing one variable will be satisfied by any Integer (an infinite set, or as defined by the data type), any Name that exists in the model's population, and any Person that exists in the model's population:

```
Integer?
Name?
Person?
```

Simple conjunction of multiple variables with no other restriction is satisfied by any combination of the variables:

```
Performer, Venue?
```

is satisfied by any combination (existing in the population) of Performer and Venue. As noted, any such query containing disjoint sub-queries returns the cartesian product.

The remaining features of the query meta-model provide different ways to restrict the combinations of variable values that satisfy a query.

5   Query Conditions

5.1   Bound Variables

A variable may be bound to a specific value if that variable references an object type that maps to a single value. Allowable object types are any data type, any value type, or an entity type having a single identifying role (i.e. played by a bindable object type). A variable which references an entity type that has more than one identifying role, or whose single identifying role is played by such an entity (transitively) may not be bound to a value. Steps over the entity's existential facts must instead be provided to select the compound identifier. However, a proposed short-hand feature for CQL would allow definition (using an extended regular expression with named capture groups) of a syntax for a single literal to be parsed into the required multiplicity of identifying values, allowing (for example) given-name and family-name to be extracted from either "Heath, Clifford" or "Clifford Heath".

A bound variable that references a data type is satisfied only by that value (which must be valid for the data type). A bound variable that references a value type is only satisfied by the instance of that value type (populated in the model) which maps to that value. A bound variable that references an entity type is only satisfied by the instance of that entity type (populated in the model) which is transitively identified by that value.

As an example if Person is identified by the (value type) Name, the following query is satisfied only if the respective Person exists in the model's population:

```
Person 'Daniel'?
```

This query asks the question *"Does there exist a Person named Daniel?"*

5.2   Role Playing (Plays)

Often, each object type that is referenced by a variable will be expected to play one or more roles (or possibly, *not* to play a possible role, but more on that later). Each such possible case of role playing is indicated by a **Play** instance. Each Play instance must be linked via a **Step** instance to the fact type that contains that role. The details surrounding the Step restrict the variable to a subset of the otherwise available objects that might have satisfied the query.

For example, in a model that has the unary fact type *"Person smokes"*, only a Person who smokes satisfies the following CQL query:

```
Person smokes?
```

In this case there is a Play that indicates that it is relevant whether or not the person smokes (a role they can play). The Play instance is linked to a Step that specifies the unary fact type, so that the query can only be satisfied by a Person who smokes.

Fact Conditions (Steps)

The case of a unary step has been covered, but more commonly, two variables may be restricted to objects playing roles of the same fact instance. We say that the two Plays (one input Play, one output Play) are connected by a **Step**. This query model does not directly represent that three or more roles must be in the same fact – that is made possible by adding Steps over a shared Play.

In the case of an n-ary fact type (more than two roles), the fact that satisfies the step will have additional roles, which may be represented as incidental Plays. These are included in the meta-model for the sake of completeness, though it's not required that they play any other part in the query. The variables associated with the incidental Plays provide the instances that complete the facts for the respective steps.

A Step may be one of a set of **alternates**, may be **disallowed** or may be **optional**, as discussed in following sections.

In a model where perhaps *"Person has birth Date"*, then only a Person born on the specified date satisfies the following query:

```
Person was born on birth Date '20/07/1987'?
```

This query contains two variables, two plays (the roles *Person* has a birth-date, *Date* is birth-date of some person) and one step (over *"... was born on birth-..."*).

Any Person who smokes and whose birth-date is known satisfies the following query:

```
Person smokes and was born on birth Date?
```

Here Date has one Play and Person has two (one for possibly being a smoker, and one for possibly having a recorded birth date). The two steps require that the person actually be a smoker (this step has no output play), and to link the person with their birth date.

5.3   Disallowed Steps

Sometimes it's necessary to require that a matching fact does not exist in the population. In this case the unary "Step is disallowed" is asserted. Any instance of a fact disallowed by a Step disqualifies the role players from satisfying those respective Plays in the query.

If we have a model containing *"Person attended Party"* and *"Person was invited to Party"*, we could ask the following:

```
Person attended Party and was not invited to?
```

This verbalization contains two separate contractions (both are optional) and an implicitly-negated fact type reading. It is short for:

```
which Person attended which Party and it is not the case
that that Person was invited to that Party?
```

Again, there are two variables, but here there are four plays and two steps, one of which is negated. The left- and right-contractions above involve the same players as in the previous clause, and each is allowed only when the player is in the same end position in both predicates. In some situations, only one or no contraction is possible.

Implicit negation applies when a reading can only be matched by dropping the word *"not"* from any position in the clause. This allows very non-English expressions, and should only be used where an explicit negative reading has not been provided. The negation prefix *"it is not the case that"* may be used before any reading, and is preferred for unary fact types. Better than either is the new capability to define explicit negative readings for any fact type, such as *"Person doesn't smoke, Person is a non-smoker"* as negative readings for *"Person smokes"*.

Here, the earlier formulations are preferable to the later ones:

```
which Person is a non-smoker?
it is not the case that Person smokes?
which Person smokes not?
```

Explicit negative readings are preferable in most instances, not least because the limited linguistic tools available cannot correctly re-insert implicit negations when re-verbalising a query.

5.4　Optional Steps

Sometimes a step may be optional - taken if a matching fact exists but ignored otherwise. This allows the relational equivalent of an outer join. The step is simply marked optional. For example, any Person who smokes satisfies the following query, and we also learn their birth Date **only** if that is recorded.

```
Person smokes and maybe was born on birth Date?
```

In this case it may happen that a Variable that is only reached by the output side of optional steps (birth Date in this case) is not populated; the query can still be satisfied. In the above query, a smoker may be identified without a birth date. This is the only sense in which a Step is directional (having an input side that is not interchangeable with its output side).

A variable that is not necessarily populated may be projected into a derived fact type, but the incompletely populated results of the projection are omitted, otherwise the derived fact instances would be incomplete.

5.5　Alternate Steps

When there are alternate steps that may be taken, each step is implicitly optional, but at least one step must be taken (or exactly one, if the steps are exclusive). The alternative steps are collected into an Alternative Set. In CQL, exclusive steps are expressed using *"but not both"* key phrase (or *"but only one"* if there are more than two alternatives) after all the alternatives.

```
some Person may attend some Party where
    that Person was invited to that Party or
    that Party is not invitation-only;
```

The syntax of CQL allows mixing conjunction (*and* or *comma*) with alternation (*or*) but only with a fixed precedence and no parentheses (apart from the use of parentheses in aggregates, see below). It does not allow arbitrary combinations of these conjunctions. The *and* operator has highest precedence, followed by *or*, followed by ',' (comma). More complex nesting of Boolean conditions can only be expressed using a derived fact type (which will be represented as a nested query).

6　Special Fact Type Steps

6.1　Subtyping

When an object type is a subtype, there is an implicit identity fact type for the subtyping. In CQL, these identity fact types have the predicate *"is a kind of/is a"*, so they can be explicitly invoked in query steps. However, in the case where a query invokes a predicate with an object type that is a sub-type or super-type of the expected type, an implicit subtyping Step (over the identity fact type) is created in order to complete the query. This subtyping step may be optionally included or omitted from a subsequent re-verbalization, as long as omitting it creates no ambiguity.

6.2   Objectification Steps

For each role of an objectified fact type, there is an implicit binary "link" fact type that relates the role player to the objectifying instance, as exemplified here:

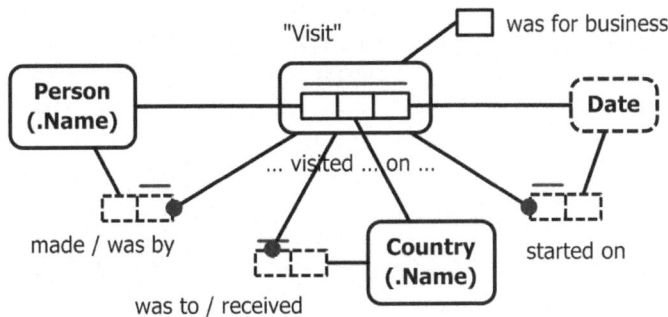

Fig. 2. Example of objectification link fact types

In CQL, these link fact types (for which the readings shown cannot yet be specified) can be traversed in an objectification step using special syntax, as exemplified here:

```
Visit (in which Person 'James' visited Country on Date)
was for business?
```

This syntax creates a step over the respective link fact type, which completes the query asking *"when and where did James travel for business?"* The unbound variables that must be populated to satisfy the query are Visit, Country and Date. Even when the objectifying entity type is not present in the query, a step through the objectified fact type is represented using two such objectification steps and a variable is created for the objectification. The re-verbaliser can elide this extra variable if it plays no other role in the query.

6.3   Arithmetic Steps

Arithmetic facts may also be included in queries. For example, addition is a ternary fact type ($a = b + c$, or alternate readings $b + c = a$, $a - c = b$, etc.) These fact types come from the mathematics of the underlying data types, so the same patterns re-occur for each numeric data type. In CQL, any role that maps to a single value may be used to invoke them. It's perfectly valid to ask:

```
Integer 1 + Integer 1 = Integer 2?
```

As another example, assuming the system value instance *"Now"*, and the date fact type *"Date(1) + Days = Date(2)"* where Days is an Integer defined in units of 1 day, and our model contains *"Person was born on birth- Date"*, we might ask:

```
Person was born on birth Date <= Now - 21 years?
```

Any Person who was born at least 21 years ago satisfies this query. The required approximate conversion from years to days is provided by the *units* subsystem in CQL. This subsystem also provides for exact (rational), accurate (floating point), approximate or ephemeral conversions between 500 different standard units, and has a syntax for user-provided conversions. Conversion functions can be generated between arbitrary values by algebraic manipulation through fundamental units. Ephemeral conversions are provided by an outside source, such as the conversion rate on a specific day from Australian to USA dollars. The details of the units model are yet to be published, but are largely derived from existing work.

6.4   Data Type Conversion Steps

Where incompatible data types are used to populate a step (or roles that map to such data types), appropriate type conversion steps may be automatically provided. These step over data type conversion fact types, which are binary fact types having the two data types as players. The implicit steps should not be verbalized, but whether or not to populate them explicitly is a decision for the implementer.

6.5   Identification or Mapping Steps

When a role that requires a data type is populated with a value type or an entity type having a single identifying value, the required fact type step over the existential fact type is implied, but is not populated into the query model. Similarly when a value type is required but a singly-identified entity type is provided, the step which specifies the identifying fact type(s) is elided from the query model. This is an implementation choice which does not affect the interpretation.

7   Projection and Derived Fact Types

It's not necessarily the case that we're interested in the values that satisfy **all** of the unbound variables of a query. What we want instead is to project the distinct combinations of values for one or more variables, while ignoring the values that satisfy other variables. The other values must exist for the query to be satisfied, but we don't want to know the details. In CQL, this is supported using the *which* and *some* qualifiers in the query:

```
which Person came to some Party and was not invited to?
```

Here we don't care about the actual party, just the fact that the person is a gate-crasher. Note that "some" here refers to the existence of some particular Party as required to satisfy the fact type. CQL never refers to collections, instead it defines rules about individual objects which may be used to derive collections of suitable objects. In the same way, multiple individual people may satisfy the query, but the query refers to each one individually. This avoids the ambiguity of plural verbalisations.

Alternatively, we may wish to use such a query to define a new derived fact type:

```
Person is a gate-crasher where
    that Person came to some Party and was not invited to;
```

Person is projected from the query to define a role in a new unary fact type. If the same person has gate-crashed more than one party, the single fact remains that he or she is a gate-crasher – the individual instances are lost. A variable is projected into a derived fact type by populating the query meta-model with the fact *"Variable provides projected- Role"*. A query may only project variables into a single derived fact type. To construct a query that requires multiple levels of projection requires the use of derived fact types, since projection only occurs on the result of each sub-query.

8   Aggregates

An aggregate summarizes a single variable projected from a sub-query. Each aggregating function is identified by a code-name, such as "sum", "count", "average", "stdev", etc. Here's an example of the use of an aggregate in a derived fact type:

```
Company pays SalaryBill where
    Company employs Person and
    SalaryBill = sum of Salary in (Person receives Salary);
```

Note that the sub-query may include variables that occur only in the sub-query, as well as variables that occur also in the enclosing query, but not variables that occur in other queries. The CQL parser allows any aggregate function name to be used, which allows custom implementations to easily be added.

9   Conclusion

A simple yet powerful meta-model has been presented which covers a large class of queries of interest across a wide range of domains. The model is straightforward to correctly populate and to verify the validity of query results, and supports effective re-verbalisation of the compiled query into equivalent source text. Furthermore, the results that satisfy such a query can also be verbalised into complete or relative answer sentences, though this has not yet been implemented in CQL.

References

1. Sowa, J.: Common Logic Controlled English,
   http://www.jfsowa.com/clce/specs.htm
   (February 24, 2004, downloaded May 2013)
2. Meersman, R.: The RIDL conceptual language. In: Research Report, Int. Centre for Information Analysis Services, Control Data Belgium, Brussels, Belgium (1982)
3. Meersman, R., Van Assche, F.: Modeling and manipulating production data bases in terms of semantic nets. In: Proceedings IJCAI 1983 Proceedings of the Eighth International Joint Conference on Artificial Intelligence (1983)
4. Kuhn, T.: Controlled English for Knowledge Representation. PhD thesis, Faculty of Economics, Business Administration and Information Technology of the University of Zurich (2009)
5. Fuchs, N.E., Schwertel, U., Schwitter, R.: Attempto Controlled English (ACE) Language Manual Version 3.0. Technical Report, University of Zurich (1999)
6. Halpin, T.A., Bloesch, A.C.: Conceptual Queries Using ConQuer-II. In: Embley, D.W. (ed.) ER 1997. LNCS, vol. 1331, pp. 113–126. Springer, Heidelberg (1997)
7. Heath, C.: The Constellation Query Language. In: Meersman, R., Herrero, P., Dillon, T. (eds.) OTM 2009 Workshops. LNCS, vol. 5872, pp. 682–691. Springer, Heidelberg (2009)
8. The World Wide Web Consortium, SPARQL Query Language, W3C Recommendtion,
   http://www.w3.org/TR/sparql11-query/
9. Racer Systems, downloaded, Racer Pro 2.0: A system overview (May 2013),
   http://www.racer-systems.com/
   products/racerpro/preview/overview.phtml
10. Halpin, T., Curland, M.: NORMA, ORM Solutions Limited,
    http://www.ormfoundation.org/files/folders/norma_the
    _software/default.aspx

Verbalizing ORM Models in Malay and Mandarin

Shin Huei Lim and Terry Halpin

INTI International University, Malaysia
shinhuei.lim@i.edu.my, t.halpin@live.com

Abstract. The rich graphical notations provided by fact-oriented modeling approaches such as Object-Role Modeling (ORM) for capturing business constraints assist modelers to visualize fine details of their data models. However, the data models themselves are best validated with domain experts by verbalizing the models in a controlled natural language, and by populating the relevant fact types with concrete examples. While a number of fact-based modeling tools provide extensive verbalization support in English, comparatively little work exists to provide fact-based model verbalization support for other languages, especially Asian languages. This paper describes our initial work on verbalizing ORM models in Bahasa Malaysia (Malay) and Mandarin. We discuss aspects of these languages that are not found in English, which require special treatment in order to render natural verbalization (e.g. noun classifiers, and the order in which sentence elements are placed), and describe our current implementation efforts, which involved creating both a prototype and an extension to the NORMA (Natural ORM Architect) tool.

1   Introduction

A conceptual data model includes a conceptual schema and a population of instances. The fact structures and business rules (constraints or derivation rules) are best validated with subject matter experts, who best understand the business domain. Since such domain experts often lack technical expertise in the graphical languages used by modelers to capture the model, model validation is best performed by verbalizing the model to the domain experts in a controlled natural language (an unambiguous subset of natural language with restricted grammar and vocabulary) and by populating the relevant fact types with concrete examples.

This process of validation by verbalization and population is central to, and facilitated by, fact-oriented modeling approaches, such as Object-Role Modeling (ORM) [11, 12, 16], Cognition enhanced Natural Information Analysis Method (CogNIAM) [23], and Fully Communication Oriented Information Modeling (FCO-IM) [2], which use fact types as their sole data structure, unlike attribute-based approaches such as Entity Relationship (ER) [4] modeling and the class diagramming technique in the Unified Modeling Language (UML) [24].

While some fact-based modeling tools provide extensive verbalization support in English, comparatively little work exists to provide fact-based model verbalization support for other languages, especially Asian languages. As far as we know, no work

Y.T. Demey and H. Panetto (Eds.): OTM 2013 Workshops, LNCS 8186, pp. 545–554, 2013.
© Springer-Verlag Berlin Heidelberg 2013

has yet been published on verbalizing conceptual data models in Bahasa Malaysia (Malay) or Mandarin. This paper describes our initial work on verbalizing ORM models in Malay and Mandarin (more specifically, the Simplified Chinese version of Mandarin, as adopted in mainland China, Singapore and Malaysia). We discuss aspects of these languages that require special treatment in order to render natural verbalization (e.g. noun classifiers, and the order in which sentence elements are placed), and describe our current implementation efforts, which involved creating both a prototype and an extension to the NORMA (Natural ORM Architect) tool.

The rest of this paper is structured as follows. Section 2 briefly overviews related work on high level textual languages for data modeling, both within and outside the fact-oriented community. Section 3 provides a brief summary of how various logical constructs relevant to verbalization are mapped to Malay and Mandarin, and discusses our overall strategy for dealing with noun classifiers. Section 4 illustrates our prototype implementation for verbalizing ORM constraints in Malay and Mandarin. Section 5 summarizes the main contributions and outlines future research directions.

2   Related Research

To our knowledge, the first controlled natural language for conceptual data modeling was Reference and Idea Language (RIDL) [22], which was developed in the 1980s based on a binary relationship version of NIAM; the model declaration part was implemented in the RIDL* tool, but the query part was never implemented. Afterwards, other fact-oriented languages were developed. In the late 1980s and the 1990s, one of us specified the first version of Formal ORM Language (FORML) to capture ORM constraints in textual form, and provided patterns to automatically generate verbalizations of constraints in some early ORM tools (InfoDesigner, InfoModeler, VisioModeler, Microsoft Visio for Enterprise Architects). The Language for Information Structure and Access Descriptions (LISA-D), based on Predicator Set Model (PSM), was specified [19] by researchers at Radboud University, but was not fully implemented. ConQuer, an ORM-based language for conceptual queries, was implemented in the ActiveQuery tool, which generated SQL code from ConQuer queries [3].

More recently, FORML version 2 (FORML 2) was implemented in the NORMA tool [5], providing enhanced, automated verbalization of constraints and derivation rules in second generation ORM (ORM 2) [9] in English [6, 14, 15]. Preliminary work has also been made to extend FORML 2 for full model input and queries [17].The Constellation Query Language (CQL) [18] is under development in the Active Facts tool to provide modeling and conceptual query functionality for ORM. The DogmaModeler tool has been extended to verbalize basic ORM constraints in ten languages (English, Dutch, German, Italian, Spanish, Catalan, French, Lithuanian, Russian and Arabic) [20], but while the range of languages addressed is impressive the verbalizations generated are not always grammatically correct (e.g. Each Person must Has at least one Name. Each Person WorksFora Company must AffiliatedWith that Company.).

Outside the fact-oriented modeling community, several high level textual modeling and/or query languages have been developed. The Object Constraint Language (OCL) [29] is used to augment UML class models with rules that cannot be expressed graphically in UML. However, OCL's attribute-based nature leads to semantic instability, its rule contexts are restricted to classes, and OCL expressions are often too technical for business users to understand and hence validate. Some textual languages for ER have been proposed (e.g. see section 16.3 of [16]), but these are limited in scope, and are prone to semantic instability caused by an underlying attribute-based model.

Controlled natural languages are often linguistics-based, employing a formal, executable subset of natural language (typically English). Attempto Controlled English (ACE) [1] supports a wide range of natural statements and queries, relying on interpretation rules (e.g. **and** has priority over **or**) to enable its text to be unambiguously translated into discourse representation structures, a syntactic variant of first-order logic (FOL). John Sowa's Common Logic Controlled English (CLCE) [28] has the full expressibility of FOL, but its use of untyped variables tends to make its expressions look more mathematical than natural. Processable ENGlish (PENG) [25] uses a controlled lexicon of predefined function words as well as domain-specific content words that can be defined by the author on the fly. For further details on controlled natural languages, see [21, 25, 27].

3   Logical Elements and Noun Classifiers

To automate verbalization of ORM constraints, we utilize patterns based on an intermediate, logical form, which is transformed to a linguistic form suitable to the target natural language. A mapping of basic ORM constraints to unsorted first order logic is provided in [7]. ORM 2 extended ORM with several constraint types, and is best formalized in terms of sorted first order logic supplemented by modal operators to indicate the constraint modality. For our most recent formalization of ORM 2, see [13].

The logic form patterns include slots for various logical elements such as quantifiers and operators which have corresponding textual representations in natural languages. Table 1 lists the correspondences for all the *modal operators* relevant to our verbalizations. We use Kripke semantics and define a possible world as a state of the information model (not necessarily a possible state of the real world being modeled). Alethic constraints restrict the possible states or state transitions of fact populations, e.g. each person was born on at most one date. Deontic constraints are obligations that restrict the permitted states or state transitions of fact populations. For example, in a model that reflects a monogamous culture it is obligatory that each person has at most one wife (a deontic constraint that may be violated in practice) [10].

Table 1. Modal operators and their verbalizations in three natural languages

Modality	Symbol	English	Malay	Mandarin
Alethic	□	it is necessary that	Ia adalah perlu bagi	是必要的
	◊	it is possible that	Ia adalah mungkin bagi	是可能的
	~◊	it is impossible that	Ia adalah mustahil bagi	是不可能的
deontic	*O*	it is obligatory that	Iaa dalah wajib bagi	是强制性的
	P	it is permitted that	Ia adalah dibenarkan bagi	是允许的
	F	it is forbidden that	Ia adalah dilarang bagi	是被禁止的

Table 2. Basic quantifiers and their verbalizations (here, $\triangle$ denotes a noun classifier)

Symbol	quantifier kind	English	Malay	Mandarin
$\forall$	universal	each, for each	setiap, bagi setiap	每$\triangle$
$\exists$	existential	some,	sese$\triangle$,	某一$\triangle$,
		at least one	sekurang-kurangnya satu$\triangle$	至少一$\triangle$
$\exists^{0..1}$	at most 1	at most one	paling banyak satu$\triangle$	最多一$\triangle$
$\exists^1$	exactly 1	exactly one	hanya satu$\triangle$	只有一$\triangle$
$\exists^{2..}$	more than 1	more than one,	lebih daripada satu$\triangle$	多过一$\triangle$,
		at least two		至少两$\triangle$

Table 2 lists the most common quantifiers and their verbalizations in three languages. Here, the symbol "$\triangle$" denotes any appropriate *noun classifier* for the term being quantified. Unlike English, when quantifiers are used Malay and Mandarin typically require additional words to classify the kind of thing being counted. Table 3 provides a few examples in Malay and Mandarin. Note that Mandarin often has many choices of classifier for the same usage category. In Malay, 'orang' can be a noun phrase or a classifier; if an entity type is named 'Orang' (meaning Person), no noun classifier is used for it. In Malay, for value type names such as 'Nama' ('Name'), 'Nombor Akaun Bank' ('Bank Account Number') etc., no noun classifier is used.

A detailed list of noun classifiers for Malay may be accessed online from *http://mbsskl.edu.my/panitia_bm/files/2009/02/mengenal-kata.pdf*. For a list of noun classifiers for Mandarin, see *http://xh.5156edu.com/page/z7949m2560j18586.html*.

Mappings for other logical or linguistic elements such as Boolean operators (**and, or, not**respectively render as "**dan**", "**atau**" and "**bukan**" in Malay, and as "和" and "或" and "不" in Mandarin.) and pronouns are also needed (e.g. "**that**" and "**the same**" render as "**itu**" and "**yang sama**" in Malay, and as "那$\triangle$" and "一样的" in Mandarin).

Quantifiers are used in verbalizing many kinds of ORM constraints, including internal and external uniqueness and frequency constraints. We have space here to discuss only internal uniqueness constraints on binary fact types, but this will suffice to convey our general approach to enable incorporation of noun classifiers into the verbalization process. For discussing logical forms, we focus on the $n{:}1$ cases shown in Figure 1, but the forms for $1{:}n$, $1{:}1$ and $m{:}n$ cases may be dealt with similarly.

Table 3. A small sample of noun classifiers in Malay and Mandarin

Noun classifier	Usage	Examples
batang	For long and thin things	pencils, rivers, teeth
buah	For large or box-shaped objects	cars, houses, books
ekor	For all kinds of animal	ants, horses, elephants
orang	For humans	teachers, nurses, doctors
根、条、只、瓶、...	For long and thin things	pencils, bottles, trees
只、尾、条、头 ...	For animals	fish, cats, dogs, cows
本、册	For book-like objects	books, diaries, albums
个、位、名、...	For humans	teachers, nurses, doctors

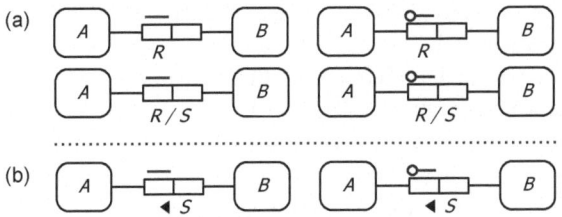

Fig. 1. Some uniqueness constraint cases for binary fact types

An ORM predicate may have many readings, each of which may be composed of various parts, such as front text and text parts (prebound, postbound, and trailing). The structure of a predicate reading is irrelevant to the logical form, which denotes a predicate by a single predicate symbol (e.g. *R* or *S*). Verbalizations may be displayed in positive form (e.g. **Each** Person was born on **at most one** Date.) or negative form (e.g. **It is impossible that some** Person was born on **more than one**Date.).

Table 4 shows the logical forms of the verbalizations for the cases in Figure 1, with positive (+ve) verbalizations shown first. For each case, the alethic constraint is shown before the deontic constraint. The Malay and Mandarin forms include a noun classifier (denoted here by Δ) to categorize the kind of thing being counted. In Malay, the modal operator appears first (as in English), but in Mandarin it appears last. For positive verbalizations, the modal operator may be omitted (this is a user choice).

The absence of a simple, alethic uniqueness constraint on a role of an *n*:1 binary is also explicitly verbalized for the fact type (e.g. **It is possible that more than one** Person was born in **the same** Country). Such verbalizations translate in a similar way. For example the English logical form of the above verbalization is $\lozenge\exists y:B\exists^{2\cdots}x:AxRy$. In Malay this becomes $\lozenge\exists y:B\exists^{2\cdots}\Delta x:AxRy$; in Mandarin we get $\exists y:B\exists^{2\cdots}\Delta x:AxRy\lozenge$.

Table 4. Logical forms of the constraint verbalizations for the cases in Figure 1

Case	English	Malay (omit Δ if type is a value type or is Orang)	Mandarin
+ve (a)	$\Box\forall x:A\exists^{0..1}y:B\ xRy$ $O\forall x:A\exists^{0..1}y:B\ xRy$	$\Box\forall x:A\exists^{0..1}\Delta y:B\ xRy$ $O\forall x:A\exists^{0..1}\Delta y:B\ xRy$	$\forall\Delta x:A\exists^{0..1}\Delta y:B\ xRy\Box$ $\forall\Delta x:A\exists^{0..1}\Delta y:B\ xRyO$
+ve (b)	$\Box\forall x:A\exists^{0..1}y:B\ ySx$ $O\forall x:A\exists^{0..1}y:B\ ySx$	$\Box\forall x:A\exists^{0..1}\Delta y:B\ ySx$ $O\forall x:A\exists^{0..1}\Delta y:B\ ySx$	$\forall\Delta x:A\exists^{0..1}\Delta y:B\ ySx\Box$ $\forall\Delta x:A\exists^{0..1}\Delta y:B\ ySxO$
-ve (a)	$\sim\lozenge\exists x:A\exists^{2\cdots}y:B\ xRy$ $F\exists x:A\exists^{2\cdots}y:B\ xRy$	$\sim\lozenge\exists\Delta x:A\exists^{2\cdots}\Delta y:B\ xRy$ $F\exists\Delta x:A\exists^{2\cdots}\Delta y:B\ xRy$	$\exists\Delta x:A\exists^{2\cdots}\Delta y:B\ xRy\sim\lozenge$ $\exists\Delta x:A\exists^{2\cdots}\Delta y:B\ xRyF$
-ve (b)	$\sim\lozenge\exists x:A\exists^{2\cdots}y:B\ ySx$ $F\exists x:A\exists^{2\cdots}y:B\ ySx$	$\sim\lozenge\exists\Delta x:A\exists^{2\cdots}\Delta y:B\ ySx$ $F\exists\Delta x:A\exists^{2\cdots}\Delta y:B\ ySx$	$\exists\Delta x:A\exists^{2\cdots}\Delta y:B\ ySx\sim\lozenge$ $\exists\Delta x:A\exists^{2\cdots}\Delta y:B\ ySxF$

4 Implementing ORM Verbalization in Malay and Mandarin

As indicated in Table 3, Mandarin differs from Malay in allowing more than one choice of noun classifier for the same usage category, or noun type. For example, the combination of mandatory role and ≥ 2 frequency constraints on Fishmonger's role in the fact type Fishmonger sells FishKind, may be verbalized in English as "**Each** Fishmonger sells **more than one**FishKind.". In Malay, the classifier for FishKind is "jenis". Showing logical words in **bold** and classifiers in red, this verbalizes in Malay as: "**Setiap** Penjua-llkan menjual **lebih daripada satu** jenis SpesiesIkan.". In Mandarin however, one might choose any of the classifiers shown for humans in Table 3, so anyof these verbaliza-tions could be used: 每**个**鱼贩卖**多过**一种鱼类; 每**位**鱼贩卖**多过**一种鱼类; 每**名** 鱼贩卖**多过**一种鱼类. Which one is best, is decided by the user.

In a given ORM model, each object type has a distinct name. This name may be a simple noun but in general is a noun phrase (e.g. "Student", "Postgraduate Student", "Doctor or Dentist"). Using "NounType" for usage category, and "Classifier" for noun classifier, the situation for Mandarin may be modeled as shown in Figure 2(a). The fact type NounType has Classifier may be prepopulated with known data. However, in general the fact type NounPhrase is of NounType needs to be populated by the user. One reason for this to avoid massive databases (e.g. consider the number of noun phrases allowed for a give language). Another pragmatic reason is that the modelers often invent their own noun phrases to name various object types in their model, even though the terms they choose are not recognized in a standard language dictionary (e.g. "PostgradStudent", "PGstudent", or "Postgrad").

So the user interface for Malay or Mandarin needs to accept the noun type choice for a given object type from the user. Using the data in the prepopulated fact type for NounType has Classifier, the system can derive the allowed classifer(s), using the deriva-tion rule shown in Figure 2. For Malay, where the NounType has Classifier is n:1, that derived classifier will be the only possibility. For Mandarin however, it will often be the case that more than one classifier is derived, so the user needs to be presented with the list of possible classifiers from which to choose his/her preferred one. As we illu-strate later in this section, these requirements are met by our prototype tool.

The metamodel fragment in Figure 2(b) provides one way to view the situation if, instead of using a separate model for each language, one wishes to use a single model with multiple display options based on the language choice.

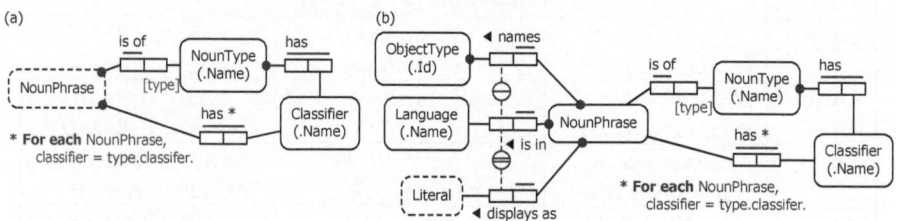

Fig. 2. Metamodel fragment for noun classifiers in (a) one language, (b) multiple languages

When implementing verbalization support for Malay, we initially utilized the ver-balization framework built-in to the NORMA tool. NORMA's fact editor readily accepts fact types entered in any language using Roman characters, so this was no problem for entering Malay. Moreover, it was an easy task to provide modified snip-pets to choose corresponding logical elements such as quantifiers, and place them in different positions. However, dealing with noun classifiers requires extending NORMA's property sheets (e.g. adding properties for noun type and noun classifier in the properties window for object types). Moreover, extra work is required to modify the fact editor for input of Mandarin. With that in mind, before making these extensions to NORMA, we prototyped verbalization support for noun classifiers by building our own tool in C# for this purpose. We now briefly illustrate this implementation.

Figure 3 is a screenshot from our prototype tool for entering and verbalizing binary fact types in ORM using Bahasa Malaysia (shown here as the option BM) or Mandarin. In this example, Mandarin is selected, and the user is entering the fact type Country is the birth country of Politicianin Pinyin, the official phonetic script for translating Mandarin into Roman characters. In the upper screenshot shown, the user has just entered the word "shi". The system displays a list of Mandarin characters with this sound, for the user to choose the one with the intended meaning (in this case "是" meaning "is").

The noun phrases that name object types are entered in square brackets, facilitating parsing of the fact type text which in general may use mixfix predicate readings. The object type names are colored red, with the predicate text in blue. The lower screenshot in Figure 3 shows the complete entry for the fact type: 国家是政治家的出生地. Notice that the predicate text which is infix in English becomes mixfix in Mandarin with the second object type name embedded within the predicate text.

Pressing Ctrl+Enter causes the tool to draw a diagram for the fact type in the upper left window. As usual, each object placeholder in the predicate text is denoted by an ellipsis ("…"). The user now double-clicks each object type shape to invoke the dialog window for choosing the relevant noun classifier for that object type.

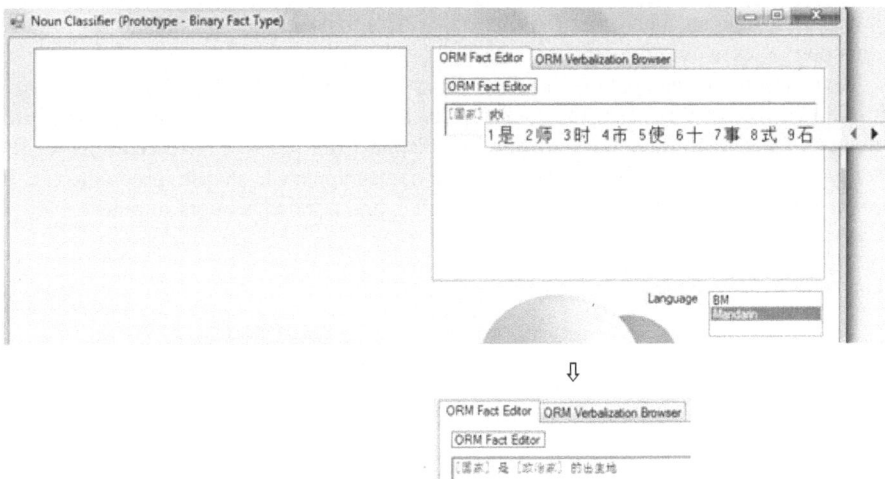

Fig. 3. Entering a fact type in Mandarin

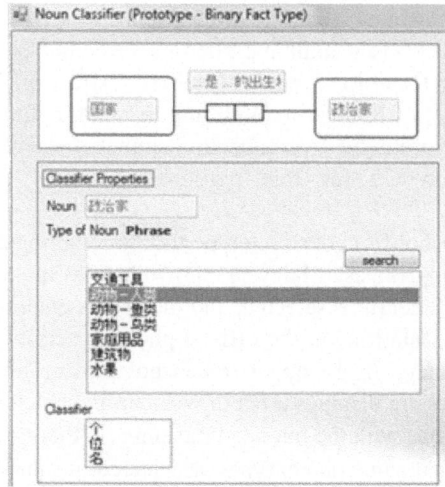

Fig. 4. Choosing the NounType and Noun Classifier

The name of the selected object type '国家'appears in the Noun box, and a list of noun types is displayed for the user to select the right one. As this list can be quite long, a search button enables the user to quickly find the correct type by entering its sound in Pinyin (this aspect is not shown here). In this case, the user selects the second item shown on the displayed list of noun types, and the relevant classifiers for this are displayed in the Classifier window. The user selects his/her preferred choice (in this case '个'). Similarly, for the other object type name, '政治家' the user chooses the relevant classifier (in this case '名'). The classifiers appear as tooltips when one mouses over the object type names.

Next the uniqueness pattern for the binary ($n{:}1$, $m{:}n$, 1:1, 1:n) is selected from a drop-down list. In this case, the user selects 1:n (the same country may be the birth country of many politicians), and the tool displays the positive verbalization for the fact type, as shown in Figure 5. Object type names appear in purple, predicate text in green, logical elements (e.g. quantifiers) in blue, and noun classifiers in red.

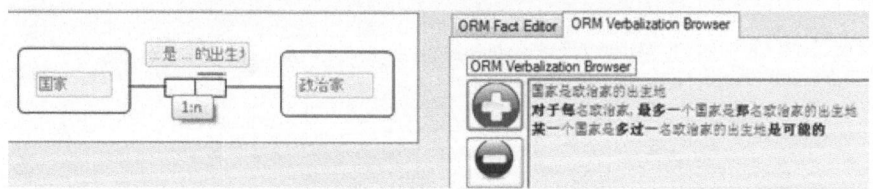

Fig. 5. Positive verbalization of a 1:n fact type.

Table 5 shows the corresponding positive verbalizations in English and Mandarin. The negative form of the verbalizations may be displayed by selecting the negative (-) button. Verbalizations in Malay are performed in a similar manner. Figure 6 shows the final screen for the $n{:}1$ fact type Politician was born in Country.

Table 5. English and Mandarin verbalizations for fact type in Figure 5.

English	*Mandarin*
Country is the birthcountry of Politician.	国家是政治家的出生地
For each Politician, at most one Country is the birthcountryof that Politician.	对于每名政治家，最多一个国家是那名政治家的出生地
It is possible that some Country is the birthcountry of more than one Politician.	某一个国家是多过一名政治家的出生地是可能的

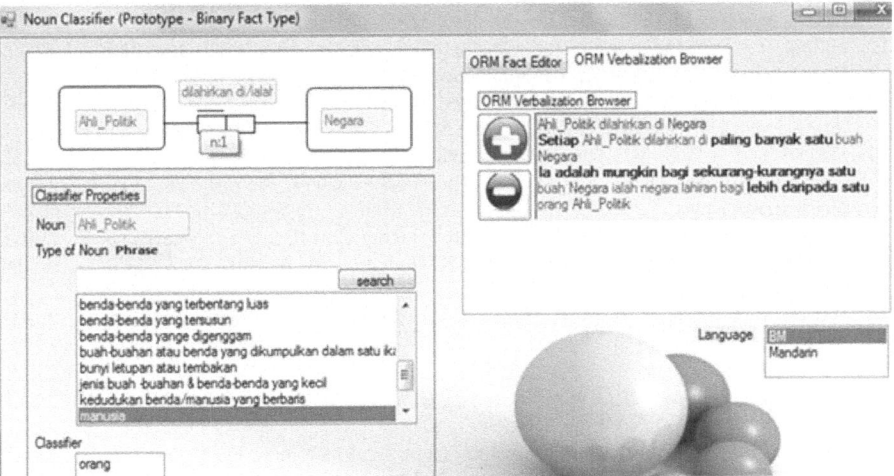

Fig. 6. Verbalization of an *n:*1 fact type in Malay

5   Conclusion

This paper described our initial work in verbalizing ORM models in Malay and Mandarin, with special attention to verbalizing noun classifiers. Future plans include implementing our approach via language extensions to the NORMA tool, and fully covering all of the many ORM graphical constraint varieties in these Asian languages.

References

1. Attempto project (Attempto Controlled English),
   http://attempto.ifi.uzh.ch/site/
2. Bakema, G., Zwart, J., van der Lek, H.: Fully Communication Oriented Information Modelling. Ten Hagen Stam (2000)
3. Bloesch, A., Halpin, T.: Conceptual queries using ConQuer-II. In: Embley, D.W. (ed.) ER 1997. LNCS, vol. 1331, pp. 113–126. Springer, Heidelberg (1997)
4. Chen, P.P.: The entity-relationship model—towards a unified view of data. ACM Transactions on Database Systems 1(1), 9–36 (1976),
   http://csc.lsu.edu/news/erd.pdf
5. Curland, M., Halpin, T.: The NORMA Software Tool for ORM 2. In: Soffer, P., Proper, E. (eds.) CAiSE Forum 2010. LNBIP, vol. 72, pp. 190–204. Springer, Heidelberg (2011)

6. Curland, M., Halpin, T.: Enhanced Verbalization of ORM Models. In: Herrero, P., Panetto, H., Meersman, R., Dillon, T. (eds.) OTM-WS 2012. LNCS, vol. 7567, pp. 399–408. Springer, Heidelberg (2012)
7. Halpin, T.: A Logical Analysis of Information Systems: static aspects of the data-oriented perspective. Doctoral dissertation, University of Queensland (1989)
8. Halpin, T.: Business Rule Verbalization. In: Doroshenko, A., et al. (eds.) Proc. ISTA 2004. Lec. Notes in Informatics, vol. P-48, pp. 39–52 (2004)
9. Halpin, T.: ORM 2. In: Meersman, R., Tari, Z. (eds.) OTM-WS 2005. LNCS, vol. 3762, pp. 676–687. Springer, Heidelberg (2005)
10. Halpin, T.: Modality of Business Rules. In: Siau, K. (ed.) Research Issues in Sys. Analysis and Design, Databases and Software Dev., pp. 206–226. IGI Publishing, Hershey (2007)
11. Halpin, T.: Object-Role Modeling: Principles and Benefits. International Journal of Information Systems Modeling and Design 1(1), 32–54 (2010)
12. Halpin, T.: Fact-Orientation and Conceptual Logic. In: Proc. 15th International EDOC Conference, pp. 14–19. IEEE Computer Society, Helsinki (2011)
13. Halpin, T.: Formalization of ORM Revisited. In: Herrero, P., Panetto, H., Meersman, R., Dillon, T. (eds.) OTM-WS 2012. LNCS, vol. 7567, pp. 348–357. Springer, Heidelberg (2012)
14. Halpin, T., Curland, M.: Automated Verbalization for ORM 2. In: Meersman, R., Tari, Z., Herrero, P. (eds.) OTM 2006 Workshops. LNCS, vol. 4278, pp. 1181–1190. Springer, Heidelberg (2006)
15. Halpin, T., Curland, M.: Enriched Support for Ring Constraints. In: Meersman, R., Dillon, T., Herrero, P. (eds.) OTM-WS 2011. LNCS, vol. 7046, pp. 309–318. Springer, Heidelberg (2011)
16. Halpin, T., Morgan, T.: Information Modeling and Relational Databases, 2nd edn. Morgan Kaufmann, San Francisco (2008)
17. Halpin, T., Wijbenga, J.P.: FORML 2. In: Bider, I., Halpin, T., Krogstie, J., Nurcan, S., Proper, E., Schmidt, R., Ukor, R. (eds.) BPMDS 2010 and EMMSAD 2010. LNBIP, vol. 50, pp. 247–260. Springer, Heidelberg (2010)
18. Heath, C.: The Constellation Query Language. In: Meersman, R., Herrero, P., Dillon, T. (eds.) OTM 2009 Workshops. LNCS, vol. 5872, pp. 682–691. Springer, Heidelberg (2009)
19. ter Hofstede, A., Proper, H., van der Weide, T.: Formal definition of a conceptual language for the description and manipulation of information models. Information Systems 18(7), 489–523 (1993)
20. Jarrar, M., Keet, C.M., Dogilli, P.: Multilingual verbalization of ORM conceptual models and axiomatized ontologies. Technical Report, Vrije Universiteit Brussel, Brussels (2006)
21. Kuhn, T.: A Survey and Classification of Controlled Natural Languages, Computational Linguistics. MIT Press (to appear)
22. Meersman, R.: The RIDL Conceptual Language. Int. Centre for Information Analysis Services, Control Data Belgium (1982)
23. Nijssen, M., Lemmens, I.M.C.: Verbalization for Business Rules and Two Flavors of Verbalization for Fact Examples. In: Meersman, R., Tari, Z., Herrero, P. (eds.) OTM-WS 2008. LNCS, vol. 5333, pp. 760–769. Springer, Heidelberg (2008)
24. Object Management Group: OMG Unified Modeling Language (OMG UML), version 2.5 FTF Beta 1 (2012), http://www.omg.org/spec/UML/2.5
25. Pool, J.: Can Controlled Languages Scale to the Web? In: Proc. CLAW 2006 (2006), http://utilika.org/pubs/etc/ambigcl/clweb.html
26. Schwitter, R.: PENG (Processable English) (2007), http://web.science.mq.edu.au/~rolfs/peng/
27. Schwitter, R.: http://sites.google.com/site/controllednaturallanguage/
28. Sowa, J.: Common Logic Controlled English (2004), http://www.jfsowa.com/clce/specs.htm
29. Warmer, J., Kleppe, A.: The Object Constraint Language, 2nd edn. Addison-Wesley (2003)

SeDeS 2013 PC Co-Chairs Message

Decision support has gradually evolved in both the fields of theoretical decision support studies and practical assisting tools for decision makers since the 1960's. Ontology Engineering (OE) brings new synergy to decision support. On the one hand, it will change (and actually now is changing) the decision support landscape, as it will enable new breeds of decision models, decision support systems (DSS) to be developed. On the other hand, DSS can bring theories and applications that support OE, such as ontology integration, ontology matching and ontology integration.

The theme of the fourth international workshop on Semantics & Decision Support (SeDeS'13) is to study the integration of DSS with some of the most practical domains of information systems: such as business process management, risk management, and computer aided design systems.

After a thorough and extensive review process, this year we accepted 4 papers for presentation at SeDeS'13. Each of these submissions was rigorously peer reviewed by at least three experts. The papers were judged according to their originality, significance to theory and practice, readability, and relevance to workshop topics.

Papers selected for publication and presentation at the workshop were organized into a number of tracks, namely:

- Decision support and Ontology Engineering
- Decision support and Risk Management
- Decision support for Business Process Management

We would like to express our deepest appreciation to the Program Committee members and external reviewers for their generous contribution of time and effort in maintaining the quality during the review process. We would also like to thank the authors of the submitted papers and all the workshop attendees for their discussions and ideas and for turning the SeDeS'13 workshop into a success. Lastly, we would like to thank the members of the OTM Organizing Committee, who played an important role in the smooth running of the workshop. We feel that the papers and discussions in the various tracks of SeDeS'13 will further inspire research in the DSS, OE and BPM - especially in the areas of ontology development, semantic interoperability, decision support for human-computer interactions and decision support for business process management.

July 2013

Avi Wasser
Jan Vanthienen

Y.T. Demey and H. Panetto (Eds.): OTM 2013 Workshops, LNCS 8186, p. 555, 2013.
© Springer-Verlag Berlin Heidelberg 2013

Minimizing Risks of Decision Making
by Inconsistency-Tolerant Integrity Management

Hendrik Decker*

Instituto Tecnológico de Informática UPV,
Ciudad Politécnica de la Innovación, 46022 Valencia, Spain

Abstract. In practice, knowledge-based reasoning for decision making must be inconsistency-tolerant since, for decision making, contradictory data are unavoidable. We present a measure-based concept of inconsistency-tolerant knowledge engineering for decision support. It enables the preservation of consistency across updates, as well as the computation of sound answers to queries in knowledge bases with violated integrity. Hence, our framework supports the consistency of decision making in the presence of contradictory data. By an extended example, we show how inconsistency-tolerant integrity maintenance can minimize risks in decision making that result from inconsistent knowledge.

1 Introduction

In computational knowledge engineering, inconsistency tolerance is the capacity of sound information processing in the presence of inconsistent data [3]. Its main applications are query answering [7], database integration [13] and integrity maintenance [10]. The application of inconsistency tolerance proposed in this paper is knowledge engineering for decision support, which involves integrity checking, inconsistency repairing and query answering. The main contribution of this paper is to provide evidence of the feasibility of a measure-based concept of inconsistency-tolerant knowledge engineering for consistent decision support including the minimizations of risks resulting from contradictory data.

Nowadays, decision making in enterprises is supported by knowledge-based computing systems that provide for a rational analysis of large amounts of stored business data. The backbone of such knowledge-based systems are databases. They support the evaluation of complex queries, which is essential for proper decision making. Answers on which far-reaching decisions depend should be as consistent as possible, since otherwise, fatally wrong decisions could be taken.

Decision support systems should be able to work in the presence of inconsistent data, since they are unavoidable and may even be useful, e.g., for finding optimal tradeoffs between contradictory goals. Thus, query answering should provide reasonable answers even if integrity is violated. Similarly, integrity checking should make reasonable decisions to accept or reject updates in the presence of inconsistencies. In fact, sound reasoning with unsound data is a big challenge for

---

* Supported by ERDF/FEDER and MECgrants TIN2009-14460-C03, TIN2010-17139, TIN2012-37719-C03-01.

Y.T. Demey and H. Panetto (Eds.): OTM 2013 Workshops, LNCS 8186, pp. 556–565, 2013.

database logic, which is based on classical predicate logic. The latter does not survive contradictions [18], predicting that everything, thus nothing valuable, can be inferred as an answer to a query in an inconsistent database.

Section 2 illustrates how semantic consistency as well as properties of potential risks can be captured in the syntax of integrity constraints. In Section 3, inconsistency-tolerant integrity checking (abbr. *ITIC*) is shown to prevent a deterioration of decision making. In Section 4, *ITIC* is used also for repairing damaged data, without insisting on a total elimination of all violations. In Section 5, we sketch how valid answers to queries for decision making can be obtained from knowledge bases that contain risky or inconsistent data. In Section 6, we feature an example of managing risky data, with comparisons to several alternative approaches. In Section 7, we address related work. In Section 8, we conclude.

Terminology and notations in this paper come from deductive databases [1]. Throughout, symbols like D, I, IC, U always stand for a database, an integrity constraint, a finite set of constraints (also called *integrity theory*) and, resp., an update. The result of updating D by U is denoted by D^U, and $D(S)$ is the result of evaluating a set of sentences S in D.

2   Modeling Risk as Constraints

Integrity constraints (in short: constraints) in databases are asserted as logical sentences and often as *denials*, i.e., clauses of the form $\leftarrow B$, where the body B states what *should not* be true. Thus, each instance of B that is true in the database indicates an integrity violation. We begin with two examples of classical integrity constraints, and then argue by further examples that properties for capturing risky data can be modeled in the same syntax.

In a database for decision making by medical staff,

$$\forall x \forall y \forall z (myoglobin(x, y, z) \rightarrow person(x) \wedge \mu mol\text{-}per\text{-}l(y) \wedge time(z))$$

stipulates that the first attribute of the *myoglobin* table always is a person, the second a micromoles/liter value and the third of type *date*. Similarly, the denial

$$\leftarrow myoglobin(x, y1, z), \ myoglobin(x, y2, z), \ y1 \neq y2$$

declares a primary key constraint on the first and third columns, preventing multiple entries for a person with different myoglobin values at the same time.

Likewise, conditions for characterizing data as risky can be modeled in the syntax of integrity constraints. For instance, consider $\leftarrow risk(x, z)$, where *risk* is defined by $risk(x, z) \leftarrow person(x), \ myoglobin(x, y, z), \ above\text{-}threshold(y)$, and $above\text{-}threshold(y)$ be a predicate that compares the value of y with a suitable constant boundary. Thus, the health of a person x at time z is considered to be at risk if the myoglobin level y exceeds some critical threshold.

The denial $\leftarrow dubious(x,y)$ states doubts (i.e., a risk of incorrectness) about the data in a municipal database for decision making by the mayor, where the predicate *dubious* is defined by $dubious(x, y) \leftarrow birth\text{-}date(x, y), \ y < 1900$. Thus, each entry of a person x with birth date z prior to the 20th century is considered dubious, i.e., it is risky to trust such data.

The following clause serves to define the constraint $\leftarrow risky(x)$, by disqualifying the trustworthiness of rows x in database tables y whose confidence value z is below some threshold th: $risky(x) \leftarrow confidence(row(x,y),z) \land z < th$.

The denial $\leftarrow suspect(x)$ models suspect and thus risky email, where $suspect$ is defined by $suspect(x) \leftarrow email(x, from(y)), \sim authenticated(y)$, which warns that an email x sent by y is suspect or risky because it may contain malicious elements if y cannot be authenticated. Note that emails x that qualify as suspect may well be acceptable despite the risks caused by senders y.

Conventionally, updates that would violate any constraint are rejected. As opposed to that, the preceding examples illustrate that violations of constraints describing risks may be tolerable; some more, some less. In the remainder, we show that not only conventional integrity constraints, but also risk constraints can be maintained by inconsistency-tolerant methods of integrity management for checking the preservation of integrity by updates, for repairing violations, and for providing answers that have integrity in knowledge bases that don't.

3   Inconsistency-Tolerant Constraint Checking

Constraints are meant to be checked upon each update, which is committed only if it does not violate any constraint. The same can be done for risk constraints. However, a total absence of risks is hard to be maintained, and constraint violations may at times be acceptable anyway, as we have seen in Section 2. Thus, methods for checking constraints that can tolerate extant violations are needed.

In [11], we have shown that most (but not all) known integrity checking methods are inconsistency-tolerant, even though they have been designed to work only if integrity is totally satisfied before any update is checked. In [10], we have seen that most integrity checking methods can be described by *violation measures*. Each such measure maps pairs (D, IC) to some partially ordered space, for sizing the violated constraints in (D, IC). Thus, an update can be accepted if it does not increase the measured amount of constraint violations.

Definition 1 characterizes each constraint checking method $\mathcal{M}$ (in short, method) as an I/O function that maps input triples (D, IC, U) to $\{ok, ko\}$. The output ok means that the checked update is acceptable, and ko that it may not be acceptable. For deciding to ok or ko an update U, $\mathcal{M}$ uses a violation measure μ, the range of which is structured by some partial order $\preccurlyeq$, for determining if U increases the amount of measured violations or not.

Definition 1. (*Measure-based ITIC*)
An integrity checking method maps triples (D, IC, U) to $\{ok, ko\}$. For a violation measure $(\mu, \preccurlyeq)$, a method $\mathcal{M}$ is *sound* (resp., *complete*) for μ-based integrity checking if, for each (D, IC, U), (1) (resp., (2)) holds.

$$\mathcal{M}(D, IC, U) = ok \;\Rightarrow\; \mu(D^U, IC) \preccurlyeq \mu(D, IC) \tag{1}$$

$$\mu(D^U, IC) \preccurlyeq \mu(D, IC) \;\Rightarrow\; \mathcal{M}(D, IC, U) = ok \tag{2}$$

The only real difference between conventional methods and integrity checking as defined above is that the former additionally requires total integrity before the update, i.e., that $D(IC) = true$ in the premise of Definition 1. The measure μ used by conventional methods is binary: $\mu(D, IC) = true$ means that IC is satisfied in D, and $\mu(D, IC) = false$ that it is violated.

As seen in [11], many conventional methods can be turned into sound (though not necessarily complete) inconsistency-tolerant ones, simply by waiving the premise $D(IC) = true$ and comparing violations in (D, IC) and (D^U, IC). If there are more or new violations in (D^U, IC) that are not in (D, IC), then they output ko; otherwise, they may output ok.

4   Inconsistency-Tolerant Repairs

Essentially, repairs are updates of databases that eliminate their constraint violations. However, the user or the application may not be aware of each violation, so that some of then may be missed when trying to repair a database.

Below, we recapitulate the definition of repairs in [11] which is inconsistency-tolerant since it permits that some violations may persist after a partial repair.

Definition 2. (*Repair*)
For a triple (D, IC, U), let S be a subset of IC such that $D(S) = false$. An update U is called a *repair* of S in D if $D^U(S) = true$. If $D^U(IC) = false$, U is also called a *partial repair* of IC in D. Otherwise, if $D^U(IC) = true$, U is called a *total repair* of IC in D.

Unfortunately, partial repairs may inadvertently cause the violation of some constraint that is not in the repaired subset.

Example 1. Let $D = \{p(1,2,3), p(2,2,3), p(3,2,3), q(1,3), q(3,2), q(3,3)\}$ and $IC = \{\leftarrow p(x,y,z) \wedge \sim q(x,z), \leftarrow q(x,x)\}$. Clearly, both constraints are violated. $U = \{delete\ q(3,3)\}$ is a repair of $\{\leftarrow q(3,3)\}$ in D and hence a partial repair of IC. It tolerates the persistence of the violation $\leftarrow p(2,2,3) \wedge \sim q(2,3)$ in D^U. However, U also causes the violation $\leftarrow p(3,2,3) \wedge \sim q(3,3)$ of the first constraint of IC in D^U. That instance is not violated in D. Thus, the non-minimal partial repair $U' = \{delete\ q(3,3),\ delete\ p(3,2,3)\}$ is needed to eliminate the violation of $\leftarrow q(3,3)$ in D without causing a violation that did not yet exist.

Although U' does not cause any unpleasant side effect as U does, such repair iterations may in general continue indefinitely, as known from repairing by triggers [5]. However, that can be alleviated by checking if a given repair is an update that *preserves integrity*, i.e., does not increase the amount of violations, with any measure-based method that prevents inconsistency from increasing while tolerating extant constraint violations. Hence, we have the following result.

Theorem [10] Let μ be a violation measure, $\mathcal{M}$ a μ-based integrity checking method and U a partial repair of IC in D. For a tuple (D, IC), U preserves integrity wrt. μ if $\mathcal{M}(D, IC, U) = ok$.

For computing partial repairs, any off-the-shelve view update method can be used, as follows. Let $S = \{\leftarrow B_1, \ldots, \leftarrow B_n\}$ be a subset of constraints to be repaired in the database D of an information system. Candidate updates for satisfying the view update request can be obtained by running the view update request *delete violated* in $D \cup \{violated \leftarrow B_i \mid 0 \leq i \leq n\}$. For deciding if a candidate update U is a valid repair, U can be checked for integrity preservation by some measure-based method, according to the preceding theorem. More details about the computation of partial and total repairs can be found in [10].

5   Answers That Tolerate Violations of Constraints

Violated risk constraints may impair the validity of query answering, since the data that provide the answers are precarious. Thus, an approach to provide answers with integrity in knowledge bases with violated constraints is needed.

Consistent query answering (abbr. *CQA*) [2] provides answers that are true in each minimal total repair of IC in D. CQA uses semantic query optimization [6] which in turn uses integrity constraints for query answering. A similar approach is to abduce consistent hypothetical answers, together with a set of hypothetical updates that can be interpreted as integrity-preserving repairs [12].

A new approach to provide answers that have integrity (abbr. AHI), and a comparison to CQA, is presented in [9]. AHI determines two sets of data: those by which an answer is deduced, i.e., the causes of the answer, and those that cause constraint violations. Each cause is a set of ground instances of if- and only-if halves of predicate completions in $comp(D)$ [8]. An answer θ has integrity if the intersection of one of the causes of the answer with the causes of constraint violations is empty, since θ is deducible from data that are independent of those that violate constraints.

AHI is closely related to measure-based *ITIC*, since some convenient violation measures are defined by causes: cause-based methods accept an update U only if U does not increase the number or the set of causes of constraint violations [10]. Similar to *ITIC*, AHI is inconsistency-tolerant since it provides correct results in the presence of constraint violations. However, AHI is not as inconsistency-tolerant as measure-based *ITIC*, since each answer accepted by AHI is independent of inconsistent parts of the database, while measure-based *ITIC* may admit updates that violate constraints. For instance, U in Example 1 causes the violation of a constraint while eliminating some other violation. Now, if U is checked by a method based on a measure that assigns a greater weight to the eliminated violation than to the newly caused one, U will be *ok*-ed, because it decreases the measured amount of inconsistency.

In fact, it should be possible to provide answers that, despite some tolerable degree of contamination with inconsistency, are appreciable. The idea is to provide answers that tolerate a certain amount of violations of constraints that may be involved in the derivation of answers. To quantify that amount, some application-specific tolerance measure is needed. In ongoing research, we elaborate a theory based on that idea.

6   Risk Management – An Example

Risky data often cannot be totally avoided. Hence the desire to contain or reduce risky data, so that their amount does not grow and won't compromise the
validity of answers too much. In this section, we illustrate how to meet that
desideratum by inconsistency-tolerant integrity management, and discuss some
more conventional alternatives. In particular, we compare inconsistency-tolerant
integrity management with brute-force constraint evaluation, conventional integrity checking that is not inconsistency-tolerant, total repairing, and CQA, in
6.1–6.6.

The example below is open to interpretation. By assigning convenient meanings to predicates, it can be interpreted as a model of risky data in a decision
support systems for, e.g., stock trading, or controlling operational hazards in a
complex system.

Let D be a database with the following definitions of view predicates rl, rm,
rh that model risks of low, medium and, respectively, high degree:

$rl(x) \leftarrow p(x, x)$

$rm(y) \leftarrow q(x, y), \sim p(y, x)$; $rm(y) \leftarrow p(x, y), q(y, z), \sim p(y, z), \sim q(z, x)$

$rh(z) \leftarrow p(0, y), q(y, z), z > th$

where th be a threshold value that always is greater or equal 0. Now, let risk
be denied by the following integrity theory:

$IC = \{\leftarrow rl(x), \quad \leftarrow rm(x), \quad \leftarrow rh(x)\}$.

Note that IC is satisfiable, e.g., by $D = \{p(1, 2), p(2, 1), q(2, 1)\}$. Now, let the
extensions of p and q in D be populated as follows.

$p(0, 0), p(0, 1), p(0, 2), p(0, 3), \ldots, p(0, 1000000)$,

$p(1, 2), p(2, 4), p(3, 6), p(4, 8), \ldots, p(500000, 1000000)$

$q(0, 0), q(1, 0), q(3, 0), q(5, 0), q(7, 0), \ldots, q(999999, 0)$

It is easy to verify that the low-risk denial $\leftarrow p(x, x)$ is the only constraint
that is violated in D, and that this violation is caused by $p(0, 0)$.

Now, let us consider the update $U = insert\ q(0, 999999)$.

6.1   Brute-force Risk Management

For later comparison, let us first analyze the general cost of brute-force evaluation
of IC in D^U. Evaluating $\leftarrow rl(x)$ involves a full scan of p. Evaluating $\leftarrow rm(x)$
involves access to the whole extension of q, a join of p with q, and possibly many
lookups in p and q for testing the negative literals. Evaluating $\leftarrow rh(x)$ involves a
join of p with q plus the evaluation of possibly many ground instances of $z > th$.

For large extensions of p and q, brute-force evaluation of IC clearly may last
too long, in particular for safety-critical risk monitoring in real time. In 6.2, we
are going to see that it is far less costly to use an ITIC method that simplifies
the evaluation of constraints by confining its focus on the data that are relevant
for the update.

6.2 Inconsistency-Tolerant Risk Management

First of all, note that the use of conventional simplification methods that require the satisfaction of IC in D is not allowed in our example, since $D(IC) = false$. Thus, conventional integrity checking has to resort on brute-force constraint evaluation. We are going to see that inconsistency-tolerant integrity checking of U is much less expensive than brute-force evaluation.

At update time, the following three simplifications of medium and high risk constraints are obtained from U. (No low risk can be caused by U since $q(0, 999999)$ does not match $p(x, x)$.) These simplifications are obtained at hardly any cost, by simple pattern matching of U with pre-simplified constraints that can be compiled at constraint specification time.

$$\leftarrow \sim p(999999,0); \quad \leftarrow p(x,0), \sim p(0,999999), \sim q(999999,x); \quad \leftarrow p(0,0), 999999 > th$$

By a simple lookup of $p(999999, 0)$ for evaluating the first of the three denials, it is inferred that $\leftarrow rm(x)$ is violated.

Now that a medium risk has been spotted, there is no need to check the other two simplifications. Yet, let us do that, for later comparison in 6.3.

Left-to-right evaluation of the second simplification essentially equals the cost of computing the answer $x = 0$ to the query $\leftarrow p(x, 0)$ and successfully looking up $q(999999, 0)$. Hence, the second denial is $true$, which means that there is no further medium risk. Clearly, the third simplification is violated if $999999 > th$ is true, since $p(0, 0)$ is true, i.e., there possibly is a high risk.

Now, let us summarize this subsection. Inconsistency-tolerant integrity checking of U essentially costs a simple access to the p relation. Only one more lookup is needed for evaluating all constraints. And, apart from a significant cost reduction, ITIC prevents medium and high risk constraint violations that would be caused by U if it were not rejected.

6.3 Inconsistency-Intolerant Risk Management

ITIC is logically correct, but, in general, methods that are not inconsistency-tolerant (e.g., those in [14,16]) are incorrect, as shown by the example below.

Clearly, p is not affected by U. Thus, $D(\leftarrow rl(x)) = D^U(\leftarrow rl(x))$. Recall that each method that is not inconsistency-tolerant assumes $D(IC) = true$. Thus, such methods would wrongly conclude that the unfolding $\leftarrow p(x, x)$ of $\leftarrow rl(x)$ is satisfied in D and D^U, although $p(0, 0) \in D$. That conclusion is then applied to $\leftarrow p(0, 0), 999999 > th$, (the third of the simplifications in 6.2), which thus is taken to be satisfied in D^U. That, however, is wrong if $999999 > th$ is true. Thus, non-inconsistency-tolerant integrity checking may wrongly infer that the high risk constraint $\leftarrow rh(z)$ cannot be violated in D^U.

6.4 Risk Management by Repairing (D, IC)

Conventional integrity checking requires $D(IC) = true$. To comply with that, all violations in (D, IC) must be repaired before each update. However, such repairs can be exceedingly costly, as argued below.

In fact, already the identification of all violations in (D, IC) at update time may be prohibitively costly. But there is only a single low risk constraint violation in our example: $p(0, 0)$ is the only cause of the violation $\leftarrow rl(0)$ in D. Thus, to begin with repairing D means to request $U = delete\ p(0, 0)$, and to execute U if it preserves all constraints, according to the theorem in Section 4.

To check U for integrity preservation means to evaluate the simplifications

$$\leftarrow q(0, 0) \quad \text{and} \quad \leftarrow p(x, 0),\ q(0, 0),\ \sim q(0, x)$$

i.e., the two resolvents of $\sim p(0, 0)$ and the clauses defining rm, since U affects no other constraints. The second one is satisfied in D^U, since there is no fact matching $p(x, 0)$ in D^U. However, the first one is violated, since $D^U(q(0, 0)) = true$. Hence, also $q(0, 0)$ must be deleted. That deletion affects the constraint

$$rm(y) \leftarrow p(x, y),\ q(y, z),\ \sim p(y, z),\ \sim q(z, x)$$

and yields the simplification

$$\leftarrow p(0, y),\ q(y, 0),\ \sim p(y, 0).$$

As is easily seen, this simplification is violated by each pair of facts of the form $p(0, o)$, $q(o, 0)$ in D, where o is an odd number in $[1, 999999]$. Thus, deleting $q(0, 0)$ for repairing the violation caused by deleting $p(0, 0)$ causes the violation of each instance of the form $\leftarrow rm(o)$, for each odd number o in $[1, 999999]$.

Hence, repairing each of these instances would mean to request the deletion of many rows of p or q. We shall not further track those deletions, since it should be clear already that repairing D is complex and tends to be significantly more costly than ITIC. Another advantage of ITIC: since inconsistency can be temporarily tolerated, ITIC-based repairs do not have to be done at update time. Rather, they can be done off-line, at any convenient point of time.

6.5 Risk Management by Repairing (D^U, IC)

Similar to repairing (D, IC), repairing (D^U, IC) also is more expensive than to tolerate extant constraint violations until they can be repaired at some more convenient time. That can be illustrated by the three violations in D^U, as identified in 6.1 and 6.2: the low risk that already exists in D, and the medium and high risks caused by U and detected by ITIC. To repair them obviously is even more intricate than to only repair the first of them as tracked in 6.4.

Moreover, for risk management in safety-critical applications, it is no good idea to simply accept an update without checking for potential violations of constraints, and to attempt repairs only after the update is committed, since repairing takes time, during which an updated but unchecked state may contain possibly very dangerous risks of any order.

6.6 Reliable Constraint Evaluation in Risky Databases

As already mentioned in Section 5, CQA is an approach to cope with constraint violations for query evaluation. There is a clear kinship of ITIC and CQA, since checking and repairing risk constraints involves their evaluation. However, the evaluation of constraints by CQA is unprofitable, since consistent answers are defined to be those that are true in each minimally repaired database. Thus, by definition, CQA returns the empty answer for each queried denial constraint I, indicating the satisfaction of I. Thus, answers to queried constraints computed by CQA have no meaningful interpretation.

For example, CQA computes the empty answer to the query $\leftarrow rl(x)$ and to $\leftarrow rh(z)$, for any extension of p and q. However, the only reasonable answers to $\leftarrow rl(x)$ and $\leftarrow rh(z)$ in D are $x = 0$ and, resp., $x = 999999$, if $999999 > th$. These answers correctly indicate low and high risks in D and, resp., D^U.

For computing correct answers to queries (rather than to denials representing constraints), AHI is a viable alternative to CQA. A comparison, which turned out to be advantageous for AHI, has been presented in [9].

7   Related Work

Although integrity, i.e., conditions of semantic consistency, and properties that capture risks of some sort are obviously related, it seems that they never have been approached in a uniform way, as in this paper, neither in theory nor in practice. However, similarities and differences between the integrity of data and data that capture properties such as risks are identified in a collection of work on modeling and managing uncertain data [17]. In that book, largely diverse proposals to handle data that lack quality, and hence may involve some risk, are discussed. In particular, approaches such as probabilistic and fuzzy set modeling, exception handling, repairing and paraconsistent reasoning are dealt with. However, no particular approach to integrity checking is considered.

Several paraconsistent logics that tolerate inconsistency of data have been proposed, e.g., in [3,4]. Each of them departs from classical first-order logic, by adopting some annotated, probabilistic, modal or multivalued logic, or by replacing standard axioms and inference rules with non-standard axiomatizations. As opposed to that, inconsistency-tolerant integrity checking fully conforms with standard datalog and does not need any extension of classical logic.

Work on semantic inconsistencies in databases is also done in the field of measuring logical inconsistency [15]. Our violation measures also work in databases with non-monotonic negation, whereas inconsistency measures in [15]. do not deal with non-monotonicity, as argued in [10].

8   Conclusion

We have presented a non-standard approach to risk management. We have shown that risk can be modeled by integrity constraints. It can be contained and reduced by conventional integrity maintenance methods that are inconsistency-tolerant. From [10], we have adopted a generic description of inconsistency-tolerant methods on the basis of violation measures. Such measures also enable an evaluation of queries in knowledge bases for decision making such that the computed answers are not contaminated by risk-inflicted data. As illustrated in

Section 6, the use of inconsistency-tolerant approaches is essential, since wrong, possibly fatal decisions can be inferred from deficient data by methods that are not inconsistency-tolerant.

Apart from the investigations mentioned in Section 5, ongoing work is dedicated to scale up the results of this paper to maintaining constraints across concurrent transactions in distributed and replicated databases.

References

1. Abiteboul, S., Hull, R., Vianu, V.: Foundations of Databases. Addison-Wesley (1995)
2. Arenas, M., Bertossi, L., Chomicki, J.: Consistent query answers in inconsistent databases. In: Proc. 18th PODS, pp. 68–79. ACM Press (1999)
3. Bertossi, L., Hunter, A., Schaub, T. (eds.): Inconsistency Tolerance. LNCS, vol. 3300. Springer, Heidelberg (2005)
4. Carnielli, W., Coniglio, M., D'Ottaviano, I. (eds.): The Many Sides of Logic. Studies in Logic, vol. 21. College Publications, London (2009)
5. Ceri, S., Cochrane, R., Widom, J.: Practical Applications of Triggers and Constraints: Success and Lingering Issues. In: 26th VLDB, pp. 254–262. Morgan Kaufmann (2000)
6. Chakravarthy, U., Grant, J., Minker, J.: Logic-based approach to semantic query optimization. Transactions on Database Systems 15(2), 162–207 (1990)
7. Chomicki, J.: Consistent query answering: Five easy pieces. In: Schwentick, T., Suciu, D. (eds.) ICDT 2007. LNCS, vol. 4353, pp. 1–17. Springer, Heidelberg (2006)
8. Clark, K.: Negation as Failure. In: Gallaire, H., Minker, J. (eds.) Logic and Data Bases, pp. 293–322. Plenum Press (1978)
9. Decker, H.: Answers That Have Integrity. In: Schewe, K.-D. (ed.) SDKB 2010. LNCS, vol. 6834, pp. 54–72. Springer, Heidelberg (2011)
10. Decker, H.: Measure-Based Inconsistency-Tolerant Maintenance of Database Integrity. In: Schewe, K.-D., Thalheim, B. (eds.) SDKB 2013. LNCS, vol. 7693, pp. 149–173. Springer, Heidelberg (2013)
11. Decker, H., Martinenghi, D.: Inconsistency-tolerant Integrity Checking. TKDE 23(2), 218–234 (2011)
12. Fung, T.H., Kowalski, R.: The IFF proof procedure for abductive logic programming. J. Logic Programming 33(2), 151–165 (1997)
13. Fuxmann, A., Miller, R.: Towards Inconsistency Management in Data Integration Systems. In: Proc. IJCAI 2003 Workshop IIWEB, pp. 143–148 (2003)
14. Gupta, A., Sagiv, Y., Ullman, J., Widom, J.: Constraint checking with partial information. In: Proc. 13th PODS, pp. 45–55. ACM Press (1994)
15. Hunter, A., Konieczny, S.: Approaches to measuring inconsistent information. In: Bertossi, L., Hunter, A., Schaub, T. (eds.) Inconsistency Tolerance. LNCS, vol. 3300, pp. 191–236. Springer, Heidelberg (2005)
16. Lee, S.Y., Ling, T.W.: Further improvements on integrity constraint checking for stratifiable deductive databases. In: 22th International Conference on Very Large Data Bases, pp. 495–505. Morgan Kaufmann (1996)
17. Motro, A., Smets, P.: Uncertainty Management in Information Systems: From Needs to Solutions. Kluwer (1996)
18. Restall, G.: Laws of Non-contradiction, Laws of Excluded Middle and Logics. In: Priest, G., et al. (eds.) The Law of Non-Contradiction - New Philosophical Essays, pp. 73–85. Oxford University Press (2004)

Modelling Ontology-Based Decision Rules for Computer-Aided Design

Ioana Ciuciu[1,2] and Yan Tang Demey[2]

[1] Laboratoire Informatique de Grenoble - University Joseph Fourier, France
[2] STARLab - Vrije Universiteit Brussel, Belgium
{iciuciu,yan.tang}@vub.ac.be

Abstract. A challenge in computer-aided design is how to parameterize shape functions in order to model a desired shape. Such design phases often include both systematic design and user-oriented design. In the paper, we want to focus on the latter case by bringing ontology-based decision rules to a computer-aided design system. Domain specific constraints and operative rules will be modelled in an artefact called semantic decision table.

Keywords: ontology, semantic decision table, decision table, computer-aided design.

1 Introduction

Computer-aided Design (CAD) is one of the fields where decision-making is intensively used in processes involving computer-human interactions. In this context, a challenge is how to create intuitive modeling tools in order to support and guide the modeler during the design phase, to ensure that the best design decisions are taken starting early in the design process. Therefore, a major aspect to be taken into account is how to integrate decision-making with computer-aided design tools.

This paper discusses the extension of an existing intuitive Computer-Aided Design system by integrating semantic decision tables with the purpose of enhancing the human-computer interaction. In our previous work [1], we have introduced a representation of the user-specific knowledge by means of ontologies and its major contribution to the computer-human interaction. Ontologies are used to store the semantics of the CAD model at five architectural levels, from business-level (non-expert level) to technical geometric level (expert level). We use Semantic Decision Table (SDT), which is a decision table enhanced with ontology technologies, to assist the user in specifying domain-specific design rules in a user-friendly approach. The proposed concept is illustrated on a case study related to the insertion of dies in a car parcel shelf while respecting the volumetric constraint, among others.

2 Background

A Semantic Decision Table (SDT [2]) is a decision table containing well specified meta-data and meta-rules. Its decisional environment and settings are studied in the

Y.T. Demey and H. Panetto (Eds.): OTM 2013 Workshops, LNCS 8186, pp. 566–572, 2013.

specifications. It allows decision makers, rule modelers, knowledge engineers or eva-luators to analyze a decision table using domain ontologies. It is also possible to assist a group of experts or stakeholders to draw a group decision.

An SDT consists of a set of formal agreements called commitments, grounded on domain ontology, and specified by a community of business stakeholders (domain experts). A commitment specifies how to use a binary fact types defined in the ontol-ogy. It can be 1) instantiation of a concept or a binary fact type, 2) a constraint, 3) selecting/grouping binary fact types from one or several contexts, 4) instantiation of a value for a concept if its value range is defined in a constraint, 5) articulation, which is a mapping between a concept and the glosses defined in a glossary, dictionary and thesaurus, 6) interpretation and implementation of role pairs, and 7) alignment of concepts within/across contexts.

3   Use Case Scenario

Our decision-based approach is demonstrated on a use case scenario from the automo-tive industry around the computer-aided design of a car parcel shelf. In this scenario, the user virtually interacts with the surface of the car parcel shelf in order to arrive to the desired shape, by applying dies onto the surface at various abstraction levels, according to his expertize [1] (see Fig. 1).

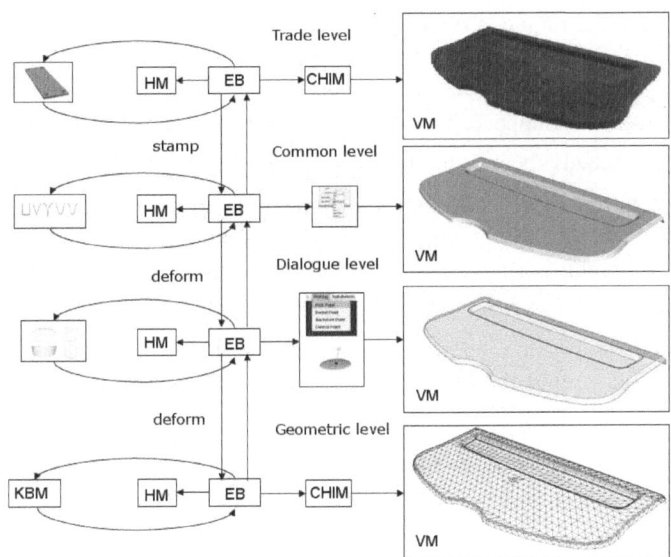

Fig. 1. Scenario: Die insertion on a car parcel shelf

This operation is done according to a specific parameterization, which integrates application-specific constraints related to spatial limitations and material resistance (e.g., the minimum distance between two dies is 2 cm when the dies diameter is less than 10 cm). These operations require intensive decision-making and reasoning, since for every user-system interaction multiple constraints must be verified and enforced, according to the user design intent.

For the concrete example in this study, the user interactively applies dies on the surface of the parcel shelf, using the virtual tools available in the system and an intuitive visualization technique. However, the dies must not exceed a certain number and their dimensions must respect the parameters specified at the beginning of the deformation, according to well-established business rules. The specific parameters are illustrated in Table 1.

Table 1. Parameters for the insertion of dies on the surface of a car parcel shelf

Parameter	
maximum number of dies allowed	N_{max}
distance between 2 dies	d_{max}
maximum volume of a die	V_{max}
maximum height (depth) of a die	h_{max}

In case the user does not respect the above-mentioned constraints (parameters) while inserting a die on the surface, the system will propagate the deformation either upwards, or on the die's neighboring surface (if possible).

Let us describe the case when the user makes a deformation which does not respect the height constraint. Suppose, in the first case, that the user selects a height h for the die which exceeds the maximum allowed height, h_{max} (i.e., $h > h_{max}$). In this case, the system must make several pre-computations in order to decide what action to take. Therefore, the system first computes the volume (i.e., v) of the die corresponding to the height indicated by the user. If the volume is inferior to the maximum volume allowed for a die (i.e., $v \leq v_{max}$), then this volume is imposed (fixed) by the system and the deformation iteratively propagates on the non-deformable neighboring zone on the surface until the height converges towards the maximum allowed value (i.e., $h \rightarrow h_{max}$).

If on the contrary, for the second case, the volume computed for the selected height exceeds the maximum volume allowed (i.e., $v > v_{max}$), then the system imposes (fixes) the maximal height h_{max} and the deformation propagates on the neighboring zone on the surface until the volume converges towards the maximal volume allowed (i.e., $v \leq v_{max}$).

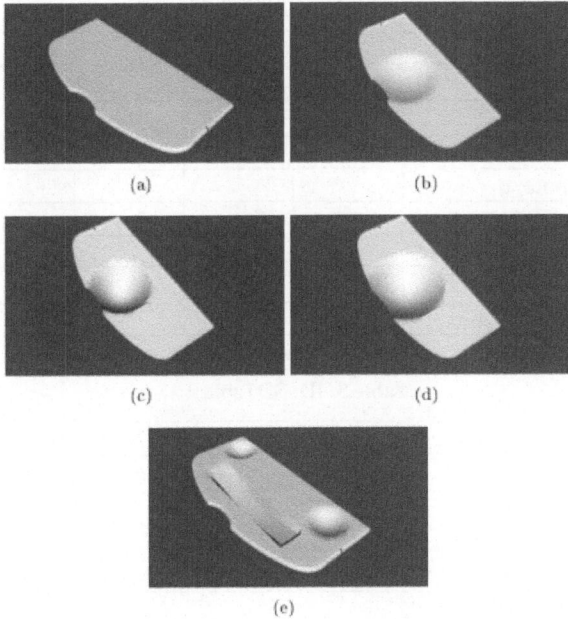

Fig. 2. Design of a car parcel shelf obtained by applying dies on the initial surface; (a) initial parcel shelf (courtesy of FAURECIA Acoustics and Soft Product Line Mouzon R&D Center, France); (b) die style when $h \leq h_{max}$; (c) die when $h = h_{max}$; (d) die style "bombed" when $h > h_{max}$; (e) example of parcel shelf obtained by insertion of three dies with different contours while respecting the specified constraints

The two cases are illustrated in Fig. 2. In the following section, we will discuss how semantic decision tables can be used in this scenario.

4   An SDT Approach for CAD

An SDT contains a decision table, a set of lexons and a set of commitments [3,4]. The decision tables of the corresponding SDTs that are designed for the deformation function are illustrated in the following tables, namely SDTable 1, SDTable 2 and SDTable 3. Table 5 contains an extract of the binary fact types (lexons) that are used to understand the decision tables (see [1,3,4] for more details on the ontology engineering formalism). More precisely, it provides the formal representation of the deformation tools at different architectural levels of the CAD system.

Based on the above fact types, we present in Table 6 the rules that compose the Commitment layer. These rules represent application axiomatizations, where the application is the insertion of a parcel shelf using a "Thermoforming" deformation tool.

Table 2. ID: SDTable 1

Condition	1	2	3	4
h	$> h_{m_{ax}}$		$\le h_{m_{ax}}$	
v	$> v_{m_{ax}}$	$\le v_{m_{ax}}$	$> v_{m_{ax}}$	$\le v_{m_{ax}}$
Action	*	*		
Compute v		*		
Impose v		*		
CALL SDTable 2				
Impose $h_{m_{ax}}$	*			
CALL SDTable 3	*			

Table 3. ID: SDTable 2

Condition	1	2
$h > h_{m_{ax}}$	Yes	No
Action		
Propagate deformation	*	
Call SDTable 2	*	

Table 4. ID: Table 3

Condition	1	2
$v > v_{m_{ax}}$	Yes	No
Action		
Propagate deformation	*	
Call SDTable 3	*	

Table 5. Lexons representing the 3D surface deformation tools [1]

Context (architect. level)	Head Term	role	co-role	Tail Term
Trade	Thermoforming	deforms	is deformed by	Surface
Trade	Thermoforming	has	characterizes	Height
Trade	Thermoforming	produces	is produced by	Loading Zone
Common	Die Stamp	deforms	is deformed by	Surface
Common	Die Stamp	has	characterizes	Shape
Common	Die Stamp	has	characterizes	Height
Common	Die Stamp	has	characterizes	Volume
Dialogue	Deformation	affects	affected by	Surface
Dialogue	Deformation	has	characterizes	Contour
Dialogue	Deformation	has	characterizes	Initial Point
Dialogue	Deformation	has	characterizes	Target Point
Dialogue	Deformation	has	characterizes	Height
Dialogue	Deformation	has	characterizes	Volume

Table 6. Commitments based on the binary facts (in *Italic*) from Table 1

Abstraction Level	Rule
Trade level	Every *thermoforming* has exactly one maximal *height*.
Common level	Every *die stamp* has exactly one maximal *height*.
Common level	Every *die stamp* has exactly one maximal *volume*.
Dialogue level	The *contour* of the *deformation* lies on the *surface*.
Dialogue level	The *initial point* lies on the *surface*.
Dialogue level	The *initial point* lies inside the *contour*.

5   Related Work

One advantage of using SDTs is that we can easily validate and verify (V&V) decision rules using domain semantics. There are a few existing V&V approaches for decision tables. Shwayder [5] proposes combining decision columns in a decision table in order to reduce redundancies. Pooch [6] illustrates a survey on decomposition and conversion algorithms of translating decision tables in order to check for its redundancy, contradiction and completeness.

Vanthienen et al. [7] illustrate using PROLOGA5 (a decision table tool) to discover the intra-tabular anomaly, which is caused by a cyclic dependence between a condition and an action, and inter-tabular anomaly, which is caused by redundancy, ambivalence and deficiency. Qian et al. [8] use the approach of approximation reduction to managing incomplete and inconsistent decision tables. Incomplete and inconsistent decision tables are reduced into complete and consistent sub tables.

Compared to their work, our approach is focused on using ontological axioms as the meta-rules for validating a decision table. As the ontology is shareable and community based, the SDT validation process thus supports group activities in a natural way. Decision modelers and rule auditors share their common view through this process. By doing so, misunderstanding is minimized and the cost is consequently reduced.

6   Conclusion

In this paper, we demonstrate how an SDT can be used to unambiguously model and parameterize decision rules for a computer-aided design system. The advantages of using an SDT-based approach are multiple: 1) it is community-grounded and therefore enables knowledge (decision rules) sharing in highly collaborative contexts (e.g., for CAD); 2) it closes the gap between domain knowledge (ontologies) and end users (rule modelers); and 3) it ensures consistency and completeness of the decision rules.

Future work includes the integration of an existing SDT-based visualization client with the CAD system for setting the user's design preferences (parameters). Usability tests are also envisaged in order to evaluate the usability of SDTs. This implies extending the real-world industrial scenario presented here to be tested with groups of end users.

References

1. Ciuciu, I., Meersman, R., Perrin, E., Danesi, F.: Semantic Support for Computer-Human Interaction: Intuitive 3DVirtual Tools for Surface Deformation in CAD. In: Meersman, R., Dillon, T., Herrero, P. (eds.) OTM 2010. LNCS, vol. 6428, pp. 645–654. Springer, Heidelberg (2010)
2. Tang, Y., Meersman, R.: Towards directly applied ontological constraints in a semantic decision table. In: Olken, F., Palmirani, M., Sottara, D. (eds.) RuleML - America 2011. LNCS, vol. 7018, pp. 193–207. Springer, Heidelberg (2011)
3. Meersman, R.: Ontologies and databases: More than a Fleeting Ressemblance. In: Raś, Z.W., Skowron, A. (eds.) ISMIS 1999. LNCS, vol. 1609, pp. 30–45. Springer, Heidelberg (1999)
4. Spyns, P., Tang, Y., Meersman, R.: An ontology engineering methodology for DOGMA. Journal of Applied Ontology 3(1-2), 13–39 (2008)
5. Shwayder, K.: Combining decision rules in a decision table. Commun. ACM 18(8), 476–480 (1975)
6. Pooch, U.W.: Translation of decision tables. ACM Comput. Surv. 6(2), 125–151 (1974)
7. Vanthienen, J., Mues, C., Aerts, C.: An illustration of verification and validation in the modelling phase of kbs development. Data Knowl. Eng. 27(3), 337–352 (1998)
8. Qian, Y., Liang, J., Li, D., Wang, F., Ma, N.: Approximation reduction in inconsistent incomplete decision tables. Knowl. -Based Syst. 23(5), 427–433 (2010)

Decision Support for Operational and Financial Risk Management - The ProcessGene Case Study

Maya Lincoln and Avi Wasser

University of Haifa, Israel
{mlincoln,awasser}@haifa.ac.il

Abstract. This work suggests a generic framework for risk related decision making from a business process management viewpoint. The framework is based on the methodology embedded in the ProcessGene Risk Management software suite. The suggested method aims to assist risk managers in making risk related decisions along the entire lifecycles of risk management, governance and compliance. This decision making is based on knowledge that is encapsulated within existing business process repositories. The method is demonstrated using a real-life process repository from a manufacturing industry.

Keywords: Business process decisions, Operational risk management, Financial risk management, Business process management, ProcessGene.

1 Introduction

With the increase of regulatory requirements on one hand, and the attempts to optimize business outcomes on the other, organizations are required to invest more efforts in identifying and managing risks. Executive officers are specifically required to demonstrate effective risk management practices, and to ensure corporate transparency and visibility into the business. The risk management process is continuous, and needs to be closely monitored. As management is personally responsible for monitoring risk levels, this responsibility requires significant management attention and allocation of time and effort.

As risk management is an ongoing organizational task, several decision making processes are required during its lifecycle. For example: deciding regarding likelihood and impact of the risk for the organization, deciding how to mitigate risks, and determining the organization's tolerance level regarding its risks.

Research in this field has focused mainly on specific business cases and business types, for example, on real-time decision making (e.g. [2,3]), on specific industries (e.g. [4,10]), or on specific risk types (e.g. [7,11]).

This work aims to suggest a complete framework for risk related decision making from a business process management viewpoint. The framework is based on the risk management methodology embedded in the ProcessGene Risk Management software suite [8]. The suggested method aims to assist risk managers in making risk related decisions along the entire lifecycle of risk management. The paper contributes to the state of the art literature in the following way: it presents

Y.T. Demey and H. Panetto (Eds.): OTM 2013 Workshops, LNCS 8186, pp. 573–578, 2013.
© Springer-Verlag Berlin Heidelberg 2013

a complete framework for risk decision making related to risk management that takes into account changes during the organization's lifecycle. Examples in this paper are taken from a real-life paper manufacturing process repository.

The paper is organized as follows: we present related work in Section 2, positioning our work with respect to previous research. In Section 3 we present the ProcessGene business process model structure and terminology as background to this work. We describe the method for risk related decision making in Section 4. We conclude in Section 5.

2   Related Work

The content layer of business process models can be utilized for supporting business users in performing several types of business tasks [15,16]. One of these utilizations is the support of process related decisions [14].

Research on decision making related to risk management focuses on several aspects. Some researches focus on real-time decision making. For example, the work in [2] suggests a framework for decision making support during unexpected events in the operation of large-scale systems. The authors of [3] suggest a decision support framework for situations in which a number of interconnected decisions are required at the same time.

Other works focus on a specific industry or risk category. The work in [12], for example, focuses on flood risk mapping, and provides support for forecasting of floods and inundation phenomena and evaluating the effects of decisions aimed at reducing social, economical and environmental related damages. Similarly, a generalized decision-support system for water-resources planning and operational management is suggested in [1]. The work in [9] analyzes how numeracy influences risk comprehension and medical decision making; and a framework for managing decisions in a child protective services is suggested in [4]. A specific analysis of risk related decision making in banks is presented in [10].

In addition, another stream of research focuses on decision making related to specific risk types, for example, on ethical [6,7], operational [2], or financial [11] risks.

Each of the above described frameworks focuses on a specific niche of risk related decision making. In doing so, these works assist in making risk related decisions related to a specific industry, risk type, or business situation. Nevertheless, an end-to-end, more generic framework is also required - to support the entire lifecycle of risk related decisions in any organization. Therefore, in this work we present a generic risk related decision support system.

3   Background: The ProcessGene Business Process Model Structure

This section describes the ProcessGene business process model structure. We first introduce the activity flow structure, and then we introduce the process artifacts notion. To illustrate the process model and related GRC artifacts we make use of the paper manufacturing repository (see Section 1).

The Workflow Management Coalition (WFMC) [5] defines business process as a "set of one or more linked procedures or activities which collectively realize a business objective or policy goal." An example of such business process model is the "Pack paper" process model, presented in Fig. 1. This figure is based on YAWL [13] with two slight visual representation modifications, convenient for our needs: (a) roles were added at the top of each activity; and (b) predecessor and successor processes are presented as nested activities at the beginning and at the end of the workflow.

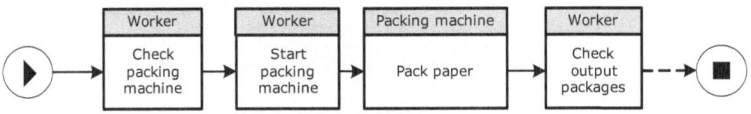

Fig. 1. An example: the "Pack paper" process model

In the ProcessGene process model each activity is related to several process artifacts (e.g. risks, controls, change requests), as illustrated in Fig. 2, using UML relationship symbols. Process artifacts provide an additional data to the activities. In particular, GRC artifacts (risks and controls) provide data regarding risks that are related to the activity, and controls-aimed at mitigating these risks.

For example, in Fig. 1, the activity "Check output packages" is related to the risk "Worker didn't pay attention to damaged packages" and to the mitigating control: "Sample packages for additional QA," that is executed by the QA team.

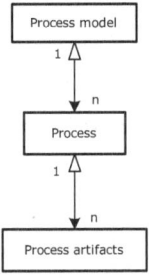

Fig. 2. The ProcessGene process model

4   Framework for Risk Related Decision Making

In this section we present a framework for supporting decisions related to the management of risks and mitigating controls during an organization's lifecycle.

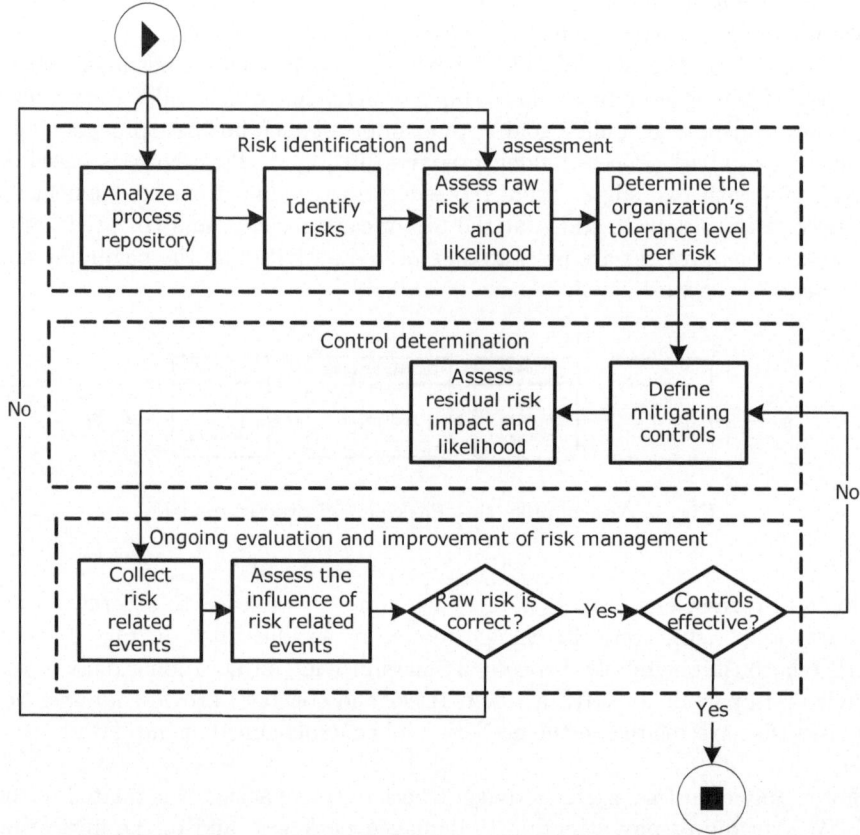

Fig. 3. ProcessGene's framework for risk related decision making

The framework receives a process repository as input and describes how to manage decisions related to risk identification, evaluation, mitigation and updates.

ProcessGene proposes a ten-step framework to support risk related decision making for organizations, as illustrated in Fig. 3 (using "Yet Another Workflow Language" (YAWL) [13]). According to this framework, we first analyze a process repository, and understand the organization's operations. Second, based on the process repository, we search for activities that may induce operational or financial risks. For example, in the paper manufacturing repository, the activity "Check packing machine" is related to the operational risk: "Worker injury," and the activity "Review financial quarterly report" is related to the financial risk: "Wrong financial data."

At the third step, we analyze each identified risk and assess its raw likelihood (the chance it will occur), and its raw impact (the magnitude of damage it may cause the organization, once the risk happens). As a fourth step we determine the organization's tolerance regarding each risk, meaning: the level of risk it would consider as acceptable. this threshold is calculated as the tolerated impact multiplied by the tolerated likelihood. The above first four steps are conducted on a given process model repository based on the risk manager's assessment, and are considered as "preparation" phases - since they are conducted only once (or after each time the repository changes). The data determined in these first phases will be modified according to real risk events on an ongoing basis.

As a fifth step, the risk manager lists all risks in which the multiplication of raw impact and likelihood is above the organizational tolerance level. For each such "non-tolerated" risk, the risk manager defines mitigating controls - aiming at reducing the raw risk level. For example, in order to reduce the risk level of "Worker injury," the mitigating control: "Worker wears a helmet during machine checkups" is defined. After defining the mitigating controls, in the sixth step we re-assess the risk likelihood and impact levels while taking into account the execution of the related controls. The reduced impact and likelihood are referred to as "residual." The above two additional steps are also conducted based on the risk manager's assessment, and are also considered as "preparation" phases.

The next four steps aim at maintaining and updating the risks and controls in the process repository according to real risk events, as follows. The seventh step is an ongoing phase in which the organization collects risk related events. For example, a "Worker hand injury" event will be related to the "Worker injury" risk, and financial costs will be documented (e.g. costs related to treatments, law suits, loss of work hours, etc.). After each such risk event, the risk manager re-evaluates the risk and whether it was assessed correctly (see step #8). For example, if the "Worker injury" risk likelihood was defined as "unlikely" and there were ten injury events in 6 months-the risk manager should find a gap between the definition and actual risk likelihood level. As a result of this re-assessment, in the ninth step the risk manager checks if the raw risk was defined correctly (meaning-if the control was not carried out-are the raw risk levels compatible with the actual risk events?). If the answer is "yes"-the risk manager returns to step 3 and corrects the risk's raw impact and likelihood levels. He then continues to steps four-six and corrects their output data. If the answer is "no" (the raw data was defined correctly), we continue to the tenth step in which the risk manager determines whether the control is effective or not. This is the most important step-because it makes sure that risks are mitigated correctly with regard to the organization's risk tolerance. If no - the control needs to be redefined (step 5) and residual risk levels should be reassessed accordingly (step 6). If yes (the control was effective) - the risk manager completes the handling procedure of the specific risk event.

5   Conclusions

We presented the ProcessGene framework for supporting risk related decision making from a process management viewpoint. The proposed framework is already applied in real-life scenarios, yet several research issues remain open. We mention two such extensions here. First, analyzing the framework's strengths and searching for possible improvements. Second, adding a case study and experiments to measure the efficiency of the presented framework.

References

1. Andreu, J., Capilla, J., Sanchís, E.: Aquatool, a generalized decisionsupport system for water-resources planning and operational management. Journal of Hydrology 177(3), 269–291 (1996)
2. Beroggi, G.E.G., Wallace, W.A.: Operational risk management: A new paradigm for decision making. IEEE Transactions on Systems, Man and Cybernetics 24(10), 1450–1457 (1994)
3. Brehmer, B.: Strategies in real-time, dynamic decision making. Insights in Decision Making, 262–279 (1990)
4. Camasso, M.J., Jagannathan, R.: Decision making in child protective services: a risky business? Risk Analysis (2012)
5. Coalition, W.M.: The workflow management coalition specification - terminology & glossary. Technical report, Technical Report WFMC-TC-1011, Workflow Management Coalition (1999)
6. Ferrell, O.C., Fraedrich, J., Ferrell, L., et al.: Business Ethics: Ethical Decision Making & Cases. South-Western Pub. (2012)
7. Loe, T.W., Ferrell, L., Mansfield, P.: A review of empirical studies assessing ethical decision making in business. In: Citation Classics from the Journal of Business Ethics, pp. 279–301. Springer (2013)
8. ProcessGene. Processgene website (2013), http://www.processgene.com
9. Reyna, V.F., Nelson, W.L., Han, P.K., Dieckmann, N.F.: How numeracy influences risk comprehension and medical decision making. Psychological Bulletin 135(6), 943 (2009)
10. Saita, F.: Value at Risk and Bank Capital Management: Risk Adjusted Per- formances, Capital Management and Capital Allocation Decision Making. Academic Press (2010)
11. Schubert, R., Brown, M., Gysler, M., Brachinger, H.W.: Financial decision-making: are women really more risk-averse? The American Economic Review 89(2), 381–385 (1999)
12. Todini, E.: An operational decision support system for flood risk mapping, forecasting and management. Urban Water 1(2), 131–143 (1999)
13. van der Aalst, W.M.P., Ter Hofstede, A.H.M.: YAWL: yet another workflow language. Information Systems 30(4), 245–275 (2005)
14. Wasser, A., Lincoln, M.: Ontology based method for supporting business process modeling decisions. In: Herrero, P., Panetto, H., Meersman, R., Dillon, T. (eds.) OTM-WS 2012. LNCS, vol. 7567, pp. 505–514. Springer, Heidelberg (2012)
15. Wasser, A., Lincoln, M.: Semantic machine learning for business process content generation. In: Meersman, R., Panetto, H., Dillon, T., Rinderle-Ma, S., Dadam, P., Zhou, X., Pearson, S., Ferscha, A., Bergamaschi, S., Cruz, I.F. (eds.) OTM 2012, Part I. LNCS, vol. 7565, pp. 74–91. Springer, Heidelberg (2012)
16. Wasser, A., Lincoln, M., Karni, R.: Processgene query–a tool for querying the content layer of business process models. In: Demo Session of the 4th International Conference on Business Process Management, pp. 1–8 (2006)

Selection of Business Process Alternatives Based on Operational Similarity for Multi-subsidiary Organizations

Avi Wasser and Maya Lincoln

University of Haifa, Israel
{awasser,mlincoln}@haifa.ac.il

Abstract. This work suggests a method for machine-assisted support for multi-subsidiary organizations in selecting business process alternatives, based on operational similarity. Operational similarity between processes can be derived from process repositories using a linguistic analysis of process descriptors. The suggested method aims to assist operation managers in multi-subsidiary organizations in identifying similar processes, that can substitute processes that cannot be carried out within a certain subsidiary. This decision making is based on knowledge that is encapsulated within existing business process repositories. The method is demonstrated using a real-life process repository from the paper manufacturing industry.

Keywords: Business process decisions, Process similarity, Multi-subsidiary organizations, Business process repositories, Semantic analysis, Process ontologies, Natural language processing.

1 Introduction

In many cases multi-subsidiary organizations perform similar processes in different geographical locations. For example, an insurance company may operate in several branches, each delivers a similar product (insurance) by conducting different processes for achieving a common goal. In some cases, such "parallel" processes can even be very different. For example, pharmaceuticals companies may manufacture different medicines in different factories- using a totally different process.

Due to various reasons, there are situations in which an organizational subsidiary cannot carry out a process. For example, due to a problem in one of its machines, a pharmaceuticals factory may not be able to proceed with its manufacturing process. In these cases the enterprise may need to perform the process in one of its other subsidiaries. Since each such subsidiary has a different modus-operandi, it is required to compare between the subsidiaries' processes and select the subsidiary that operates in the most similar way to the "blocked" process.

Research in this field has focused mainly on semantic (textual) similarity analysis (e.g. [3,4]) or structural similarity (e.g. [15]) between processes. Despite

Y.T. Demey and H. Panetto (Eds.): OTM 2013 Workshops, LNCS 8186, pp. 579–586, 2013.

the efficiency of these methods, they are not always relevant for the problem in hand: in some cases minor semantic differences may indicate major operational differences. For example, two manufacturing processes can be highly similar in textual terms, except one difference in one of their activities' tag: instead of "ink cleaning" in one process - the other process involves "ink injection." In this case it is possible that another process that contains more non-common activities, but involves the activity "ink injection," may be more similar to the blocked process n operational terms, and therefore may be more adequate to replace it.

This work aims to take state-of-the-art process similarity comparison methods a step forward by: (1) proposing a machine assisted mechanism that will take into account the operational characteristics of process models and suggest a ranked list of similar processes in operational terms; and (2) applying the suggested framework on real-life processes.

The suggested method aims to assist operation managers in identifying similar processes in case the original processes cannot be carried out. The extended framework is illustrated throughout the paper using an example based on real-life processes from the manufacturing industry.

The paper is organized as follows: we present related work in Section 2, positioning our work with respect to previous research. In Section 3 we present models and a method for evaluating process model similarity as background to this work. We describe the method for analyzing operational similarity between process models in Section 4. We conclude in Section 5.

2   Related Work

Research on standardization and analysis of the content layer of business process models mainly focuses on the analysis of linguistic components - actions and objects that describe business activities. Most existing languages for business process modeling and implementation are activity-centric, representing processes as a set of activities connected by control-flow elements indicating the order of activity execution [15]. In recent years, an alternative approach has been proposed, which is based on objects (or artifacts/entities/documents) as a central component for business process modeling and implementation. This relatively new approach focuses on the central objects along with their life-cycles. Such object-centric approaches include artifact-centric modeling [10,1], data-driven modeling [9] and proclets [11].

Although most works in the above domain are either object or activity centric, only a few works combine the two approaches in order to exploit an extended knowledge scope of the business process. The work in [5] presents an algorithm that generates an information-centric process model from an activity-centric model. The works in [8,7,6] present the concept of business process descriptor that decomposes process names into objects, actions and qualifiers, and suggest several taxonomies to express the operational knowledge encapsulated in business process repositories. In this work we take this model forward by: (a) testing it on real-life processes from the high-tech domain; (b) showing how the suggested taxonomies can assist in common usages of business process management.

Research on process similarity mainly focuses on three metrics for measuring the similarity between business process models. The label-based metric tries to match the nodes in process models by comparing their labels. Based on this matching, a similarity score is calculated taking into account the overall size of the models [3,4]. The structure based metric compares between graphs based on graph-edit distance [2]. This metric takes into account both the node labels and the topology of the process models. The third metric - the behavioral one - takes into account the causal relations between activities in a process model. These causal relations are represented as a causal footprint [14,13].

Despite the efficiency of the above described methods, they are all based on the *semantics* of the business process model. Nevertheless, a *semantic*-based similarity does not necessarily indicate an *operational* similarity. Minor semantic differences may indicate major operational gaps.

In this work we combine the notions of state-of-the-art similarity analysis methods with the operational analysis model of business process content as proposed in [7] and extended in [16]. We also use the concepts presented in [17] for segmenting the operations of enterprises based on operational characteristics. The proposed framework takes state-of-the-art similarity comparison methods forward by: (a) comparing between process models based on *operational* (and not *textual*) similarity; and (b) testing the proposed method on real-life processes.

3   Background: Models and Methods for Evaluating Process Model Similarity

3.1   The Descriptor Model

This section describes a formal model of business process decomposition and analysis as presented in [8] and further developed in [7]. We first introduce the descriptor model, and then, based on the descriptor model, we introduce four taxonomies of objects and actions. Finally, we describe the descriptor space model, which will be used in the next section. To illustrate the taxonomies we make use of the paper manufacturing repository (see Section 1).

The Activity Decomposition Model. In the Process Descriptor Catalog model ("PDC") [8] each activity is composed of one action, one object that the action acts upon, and possibly one or more action and object qualifiers. Qualifiers provide an additional description to actions and objects. In particular, a qualifier of an object is roughly related to an object state. State-of the art Natural Language Processing (NLP) systems. For example, the activity "Manually clean assembly machine" generates an activity descriptor containing the action "clean," the action qualifier "manually," the object "machine" and the object qualifier "assembly."

The Action and Object Taxonomies. The descriptor model has two basic elements, namely objects and actions, and it serves as a basis for four taxonomies, namely: the *action hierarchy model*, the *object hierarchy model*, the *action sequence model*, and the *object lifecycle model* (see [7]).

The action and object hierarchy models organize a set of activity descriptors according to the hierarchical relationships among business actions and objects, respectively. This hierarchical dimension of actions and objects is determined by their qualifiers: an addition of a qualifier to an action or an object makes them more specific, since the qualifier limits their meaning to a specific range. In the action hierarchy model, for example, the action "Manually clean" is a subclass (a more specific form) of "Clean," since the qualifier "Manually" limits the action of "Clean" to reduced action range.

The action sequence model organizes a set of activity descriptors according to the relationships among business actions and objects in terms of execution order. In this model, each object holds a graph of ordered actions that are applied to that object. For example, the object "Assembly machine"is related to the following action sequence: "Clean" followed by "Reset," "Start," and finally "Monitor."

The object lifecycle taxonomy model organizes a set of activity descriptors according to the relationships among business actions and objects in terms of execution order. In this model, each object holds a graph of ordered objects that expresses the object's lifecycle, meaning - the possible ordering of the object's states. For example, the object "Assembly machine" is part of the following object lifecycle: "Uncleaned assembly machine"–> "Cleaned assembly machine"–>"Working assembly machine"–> "Stopped assembly machine."

The Quad-Dimensional Descriptor Space. The Quad-Dimensional Descriptor Space is described in [7] as follows. Based on the activity decomposition model, it is possible to visualize the operational range of a business process model as a descriptor space comprised of related objects and actions. The descriptor space is a quad-dimensional space describing a range of activities that can be carried out within a process execution flow. The coordinates represent the object dimension, the action dimension, and their qualifiers. Therefore, each space coordinate represents an activity as a quadruple $AC = \langle O, OQ, A, AQ \rangle$, where O is an object, OQ is a set of object qualifiers, A is an action, and AQ is a set of action qualifiers.

For every two coordinates in the descriptor space a *distance function* is defined, representing a linear combination of changes within each of its dimensions. This distance is used in this work for calculating the operational similarity between labels in process models. For more details on how this function is calculated - see [7].

3.2   Structure based Similarity between Graphs

The work in [2] presents a graph distance measure that is based on the structure similarity between graphs, and more specifically, on the maximal common subgraph of two graphs. In that work each graph comprises labeled nodes and edges. Labels are matched only when they contain identical texts.

We will use the above graph distance measure to calculate the similarity between process models, with one main difference: labels on vertices will be compared based on their operational distance (see Section 3.1).

4   Method for Evaluating Operational Similarity of Process Models

In this section we present a framework for supporting decisions related to the selection of alternative processes when the original process is blocked. The framework receives the name of a blocked process as input and outputs a sorted list of alternative process models - available at the process repository of a multi-subsidiary organization.

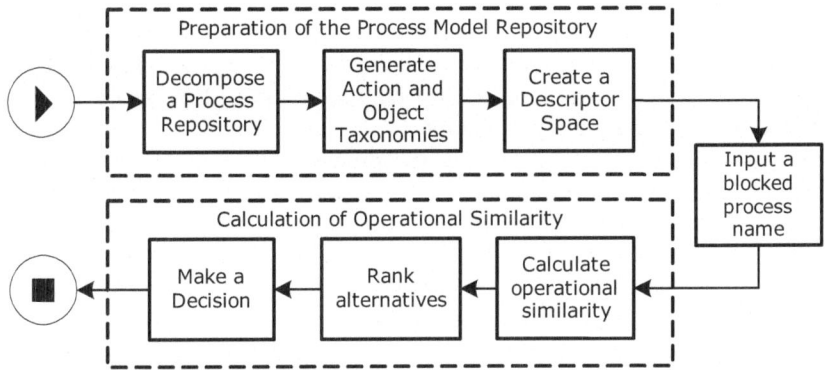

Fig. 1. A framework for evaluating operational similarity of process models

We propose a seven-step framework to support the selection of business process alternatives in multi-subsidiary organizations, as illustrated in Fig. 1 (using "Yet Another Workflow Language" (YAWL) [12]). First, we create an operationally meaningful decomposition of a process repository. We use state-of-the-art Natural Language Processing (NLP) techniques to automatically decompose the content layer (text) of the repositories into its structured linguistic components (objects and actions and their qualifiers). As part of this decomposition, each business activity is encoded automatically as a *descriptor*, using the Process Descriptor Catalog ("PDC") notation (see Section 3.1).

Second, we analyze the generated decomposition and create four action and object models, that represent operational aspects of the process repository (Section 3.1). As a third step we build a descriptor space using the four action and object taxonomies (see Section 3.1). The above first three steps are conducted automatically on a given process model repository of a multi-subsidiary organization, and are considered as "preparation" phases - since they are conducted only once (or after each time the repository changes).

As a fourth step, an operations manager inputs a blocked process name. This name can be given either as a descriptor or in natural language. If the second option is being used- the name is automatically decomposed into a descriptor format. The next three steps aim at producing a list of alternative process models that can replace the original, blocked process, as follows.

In the fifth step the blocked process model is compared to each process in the repository-in all subsidiaries, including the subsidiary of the blocked process itself (since maybe an alternative process from this repository will be found useful as well). The comparison between each process model pairs is performed using the method suggested in [2] with the following modification: labels on vertices are compared based on their operational distance in the descriptor space. In case the distance is different than "no distance" (see [7]), it means that there is some level of similarity between the nodes' functionality, and therefore the comparison algorithm proceeds until it reaches a "no distance" node. As a result, this step outputs for each process model in the repository: (1) its maximal common subgraph comparing to the blocked process model, and (2) a set of distances - calculated for each matched node pairs.

The sixth step is aimed at ranking the process models in the repository according to their operational similarity to the blocked process model. In general, we aim at a maximal size of the common subgraph, with higher similarity scores of its vertices. The second consideration is more important for our goal: in case of a trade-off, we prefer fewer matched nodes with higher similarity than the opposite - since the first case allows the subsidiary to perform its process partially, while the second only allows it to perform a larger part of its process - but differently. Due to the above considerations, the total grade for each process model is calculated as follows: (1) eliminate all options where the maximal common subgraph contains less than x% of the blocked process size (x is a parameter that should be determined according to the operations manager preferences); (2) For each of the remaining process models: sort the set of the nodes' similarity scores - where the highest score is at the top of the list; and (3) Sort the remaining process models - so that a process model is ranked higher in the list if its node score list starts with higher scores. As a result, a list of alternative process models is generated and ranked according to the user's input, so that higher ranked suggestions are believed to be closer to the user needs. Finally, at the seventh step the operations manager receives suggestions and supporting information (the common subgraph) and makes his decision accordingly.

5   Conclusions

We proposed a framework for machine-assisted support for multi-subsidiary organizations in selecting process alternatives, based on operational similarity. The proposed framework provides a starting point that can already be applied in real-life scenarios, yet several research issues remain open. We mention two such extensions here. First, extending the comparison method by referring also to labels on edges, not only on vertices. Second, adding a case study and experiments to measure the efficiency of the proposed framework that will perform actual validation in a multi-subsidiary organizational environment.

References

1. Bhattacharya, K., Gerede, C.E., Hull, R., Liu, R., Su, J.: Towards formal analysis of artifact-centric business process models. In: Alonso, G., Dadam, P., Rosemann, M. (eds.) BPM 2007. LNCS, vol. 4714, pp. 288–304. Springer, Heidelberg (2007)
2. Bunke, H., Shearer, K.: A graph distance metric based on the maximal common subgraph. Pattern Recognition Letters 19(3), 255–259 (1998)
3. Dijkman, R., Dumas, M., Dongen, B.V., Käärik, R., Mendling, J.: Similarity of business process models: Metrics and evaluation. Information Systems 36(2), 498–516 (2011)
4. Ehrig, M., Koschmider, A., Oberweis, A.: Measuring similarity between semantic business process models. In: Proceedings of the Fourth Asia-Pacific Conference on Comceptual Modelling, vol. 67, pp. 71–80. Australian Computer Society, Inc. (2007)
5. Kumaran, S., Liu, R., Wu, F.Y.: On the duality of information-centric and activity-centric models of business processes. In: Bellahsène, Z., Léonard, M. (eds.) CAiSE 2008. LNCS, vol. 5074, pp. 32–47. Springer, Heidelberg (2008)
6. Lincoln, M., Gal, A.: Searching business process repositories using operational similarity. In: Meersman, R., Dillon, T., Herrero, P., Kumar, A., Reichert, M., Qing, L., Ooi, B.-C., Damiani, E., Schmidt, D.C., White, J., Hauswirth, M., Hitzler, P., Mohania, M. (eds.) OTM 2011, Part I. LNCS, vol. 7044, pp. 2–19. Springer, Heidelberg (2011)
7. Lincoln, M., Golani, M., Gal, A.: Machine-assisted design of business process models using descriptor space analysis. In: Hull, R., Mendling, J., Tai, S. (eds.) BPM 2010. LNCS, vol. 6336, pp. 128–144. Springer, Heidelberg (2010)
8. Lincoln, M., Karni, R., Wasser, A.: A Framework for Ontological Standardization of Business Process Content. In: International Conference on Enterprise Information Systems, pp. 257–263 (2007)
9. Müller, D., Reichert, M., Herbst, J.: Data-driven modeling and coordination of large process structures. In: Meersman, R., Tari, Z. (eds.) OTM 2007, Part I. LNCS, vol. 4803, pp. 131–149. Springer, Heidelberg (2007)
10. Nigam, A., Caswell, N.S.: Business artifacts: An approach to operational specification. IBM Systems Journal 42(3), 428–445 (2003)
11. Van der Aalst, W.M.P., Barthelmess, P., Eliis, C.A., Wainer, J.: Proclets: A framework for lightweight interacting workflow processes. International Journal of Cooperative Information Systems 10(4), 443–482 (2001)
12. van der Aalst, W.M.P., Ter Hofstede, A.H.M.: YAWL: yet another workflow language. Information Systems 30(4), 245–275 (2005)
13. van Dongen, B.F., Dijkman, R., Mendling, J.: Measuring similarity between business process models. In: Bellahsène, Z., Léonard, M. (eds.) CAiSE 2008. LNCS, vol. 5074, pp. 450–464. Springer, Heidelberg (2008)
14. van Dongen, B.F., Mendling, J., van der Aalst, W.M.P.: Structural patterns for soundness of business process models. In: 10th IEEE International Enterprise Distributed Object Computing Conference, EDOC 2006, pp. 116–128. IEEE (2006)

15. Wahler, K., Kuster, J.M.: Predicting Coupling of Object-Centric Business Process Implementations. In: Dumas, M., Reichert, M., Shan, M.-C. (eds.) BPM 2008. LNCS, vol. 5240, pp. 148–163. Springer, Heidelberg (2008)
16. Wasser, A., Lincoln, M.: Semantic machine learning for business process content generation. In: Meersman, R., Panetto, H., Dillon, T., Rinderle-Ma, S., Dadam, P., Zhou, X., Pearson, S., Ferscha, A., Bergamaschi, S., Cruz, I.F. (eds.) OTM 2012, Part I. LNCS, vol. 7565, pp. 74–91. Springer, Heidelberg (2012)
17. Wasser, A., Lincoln, M., Karni, R.: Accelerated enterprise process modeling through a formalized functional typology. In: van der Aalst, W.M.P., Benatallah, B., Casati, F., Curbera, F. (eds.) BPM 2005. LNCS, vol. 3649, pp. 446–451. Springer, Heidelberg (2005)

SMS 2013 PC Co-Chairs Message

The SMS workshop 2013 on Social Media Semantics was held this year in the context of the OTM ("OnTheMove") federated conferences, covering different aspects of distributed information systems in September 2013 in Graz.

The topic of the workshop is about semantics in Social Media. The Social Web has become the first and main medium to get and spread information. Everyday news is reported instantly, and social media has become a major source for broadcasters, news reporters and political analysts as well as a place of interaction for everyday people. For a full utilization of this medium, information must be gathered, analyzed and semantically understood. In this workshop we ask the question: how can Semantic Web technologies be used to provide the means for interested people to draw conclusions, assess situations and to preserve their findings for future use?

The program committee selected four papers for presentation that address the areas of emotional properties of verbs, the coverage of Twitter collection campaigns, the structuring of the Blogosphere, and the specification of a semantic wiki ontology through a collaborative process.

We are very grateful to the reviewers who worked hard to meet the tight deadline. We also like to thank the OTM organizers, especially the workshop chair Yan Tang for her constant support in all phases of the workshop preparation. We would also like to thank the IEEE Special Technical Community on Social Networking (STCSN) for their support and endorsement.

We hope that this edition of Social Media Semantics will be a founding stone to a means of targeted research in the area of Social Media Semantics.

July 2013   Dimitris Spiliotopoulos
                                                                      Thomas Risse
                                                                    Nina Tahmasebi

Y.T. Demey and H. Panetto (Eds.): OTM 2013 Workshops, LNCS 8186, p. 587, 2013.
© Springer-Verlag Berlin Heidelberg 2013

On the Identification and Annotation of Emotional Properties of Verbs

Nikolaos Papatheodorou[1], Pepi Stavropoulou[1], Dimitrios Tsonos[1],
Georgios Kouroupetroglou[1], Dimitris Spiliotopoulos[1],
and Charalambos Papageorgiou[2]

[1] Department of Informatics and Telecommunications,
National and Kapodistrian University of Athens, Greece
koupe@di.uoa.gr
[2] Department of Psychiatry, Eginition Hospital,
National and Kapodistrian University of Athens, Greece

Abstract. Adequate and reliable lexical resources are essential for effective sentiment analysis and opinion mining. This paper proposes a methodology for the emotional assessment and annotation of words. The process is based on the Self Assessment Manikin test, and is coupled with two psychometric measurements for identifying possible bias due to the annotator's psychological condition and personality: the EPQ scale and the SCL-90-R scale. A web based tool was developed to support the process. The methodology was validated through a pilot study in which 10 participants were asked to assess the emotional state elicited by each of 75 verbs that were used as stimuli. Results are compared with SentiWordNet's emotional scoring on respective verbs, and primarily show logical continuity and consistency.

Keywords: Verbs, Emotional State, SentiWordNet.

1   Introduction

Sentiment analysis and opinion mining [1] have become an important area of research pertaining to a range of applications such as socially aware conversation agents, affective Text to Speech engines, speech analytics solutions and other data mining applications that allow for quality monitoring of people's views on products, services and processes. The majority of machine learning techniques and algorithms for opinion mining depend upon the presence of negative and positive words, which are typically defined in resources such as sentiment lexicons. Accordingly, development of such adequate and reliable resources is crucial for effective sentiment analysis. SentiWordNet [2, 3, 4], for example, is an attempt to extend WordNet [5] with sentiment scores for each sense in the semantic network, in order to aid tasks such as affective reasoning, subject engagement in e-learning, polarity analysis and computational humor.

While the SentiWordNet labeling handles polarity identification, a richer sentiment analysis on the emotional level is often needed for affective computing tasks. This paper presents a novel methodology for the effective classification and annotation of

Y.T. Demey and H. Panetto (Eds.): OTM 2013 Workshops, LNCS 8186, pp. 588–597, 2013.

the emotional properties of words and phrases. The methodology supports an emotional assessment procedure based on the Self Assessment Manikin (SAM) Test [6, 7, 8], measuring emotions elicited by words on three dimensions: pleasure, arousal and dominance. This approach is evaluated through a dedicated web-based environment, developed for this task, so that it can be easily and immediately accessible to the public, potentially ultimately serving as a crowdsourcing technique for fast and cost effective creation of lexical resources [9]. The process is coupled with psychometric questionnaires (EPQ and SCL-90-R scale), in order to verify the reliability of the annotation and prevent any bias due to the psychological condition of the annotator. In addition, the results of this process can provide insight into how people respond emotionally to the words they use, listen and/or read, as well as the affective meaning of the verb they perceive.

We further review existing resources, SentiWordNet in particular, and present the results of a pilot experiment run to evaluate the validity of the proposed emotional assessment methodology by comparing the annotation outcome of the procedure to SentiWordNet sentiment scores. For evaluation, this work focuses on Greek verbs. However, the methodology is also applicable to other languages, such as English, which can provide even more data that can lead to a more comprehensive survey with many ramifications. The techniques presented and evaluated in this paper would be useful for all natural language processing research where emotion-level sentiment analysis is required such as emotion prediction [10]. The main contribution of this work is a psychology-based method for identification of emotional properties of verbs based on pleasure, arousal, dominance parameters and comparative evaluation of the SentiWordNet polarity values.

In the following sections, we first present SentiWordNet and other lexical resources that were utilized for the collection of materials used in the pilot study. In section 3 we present the emotional assessment process. Finally, the results of the study are presented and discussed.

2   Lexical Resources for Sentiment Analysis

2.1   SentiWordNet

SentiWordNet constitutes an extension to the original WordNet developed to support "sentiment classification and opinion mining applications" [4]. In SentiWordNet each synset of WordNet (i.e. each set of (near-) synonyms corresponding to the same sense) is assigned a numerical score corresponding to the polarity of the synset, i.e. how objective, positive or negative the sense is (and consequently how objective, positive or negative each word within the synset is). More specifically, each synset of WordNet is associated to three numerical scores Obj(s), Pos(s) and Neg(s), describing the degree of Objectivity, Positivity and Negativity of each term contained in the synset. Each of the three scores ranges from 0.0 to 1.0, and their sum adds up to 1.0 (Figure 1). Essentially, this means that a synset may have nonzero scores for all three polarity axes, which would indicate that the corresponding terms have each of the three opinion-related properties only to a certain degree.

A semi-supervised algorithm was used for the annotation of the complete set of WordNet synsets with polarity (objective, positive and negative) scores. Initially, a small set of "seed" synsets was used derived from sentiment lexicons. The set was then expanded based on the semantic relations (antonymy, hyponymy etc.) between synsets to be used as a training corpus for the polarity classifiers. The final classification algorithm was based on the presence or/and absence of negative, objective and positive senses within each synset's gloss. Due to the fact that scores are automatically assigned, and contextual information is not taken into account, mistakes may sometimes occur in the classification. For example, protect#1 (gloss: "shield from danger, injury, destruction, or damage") assigns a 0.75 score on the negative axis and a 0.25 score on the objective axis, arguably because of the presence of many negative terms in the synset's gloss. Not taking context into account, the classification algorithm fails to acknowledge the full impact of the term "shield". To minimize the possibility of mistakes in the classification of SentiWordNet verbs used for the experimental evaluation at hand, we only used verbs that scored over 0.8 on one of the three axes.

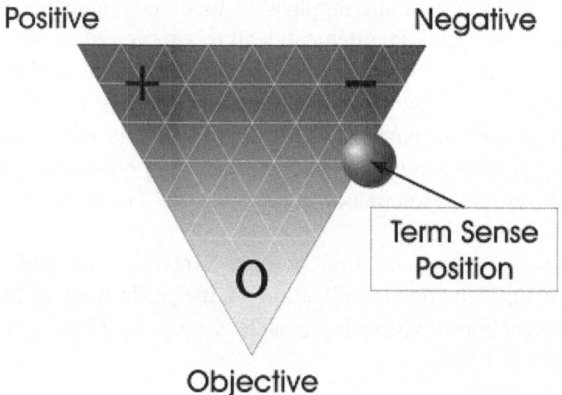

Fig. 1. Graphical model representation of the three scores for each synset

2.2   Corpus of Contemporary American English / Stimuli Selection

In order to reduce the large number of verbs available for the experimental evaluation, we referred to the lexical database of the Corpus of Contemporary American English [11], which is claimed to contain some of the most accurate lemma frequency lists. We first identified the 1000 most frequently used verbs within the list of the 5000 most frequently used lemmas. Next we extracted the polarity scoring of these verbs in SentiWordNet. However, a significant percentage of these verbs rated similarly on more than one axis (<0.6 per axis), which practically made it impossible to unambiguously determine their polarity. Therefore, in order to have a clearer assessment of the emotional value of verbs, we only used the verbs that scored high (>0.8) on the positive, negative or neutral axis, and were thus assigned with an unambiguous emotional value. As a result, we ended up with a total of 75 verbs, 25 in each category (positive, negative, and neutral). These verbs were then translated to Greek. The translation was done in accordance with the widely known online dictionary Babylon English - Greek [12]. Table 1 shows the 75 verbs classified according to their basic emotional value (Positive, Negative, Neutral).

Table 1. The 75 verbs classified according to their SentiWordNet scoring

| Verb ID | Positive | | Neutral | | Negative | |
	Word	Greek Translation	Word	Greek Translation	Word	Greek Translation
1	prefer	προτιμώ	do	κάνω	deny	αρνούμαι
2	fit	ταιριάζω	say	λέγω	protect	προστατεύω
3	question	ερωτώ	go	πηγαίνω	hate	μισώ
4	deserve	αξίζω	can	μπορώ	complain	παραπονούμαι
5	suit	αρμόζω	make	κατασκευάζω	damage	ζημιώνω
6	accommodate	διευκολύνω	know	γνωρίζω	abuse	καταχρώμαι
7	qualify	δικαιούμαι	will	διαθέτω	fear	φοβούμαι
8	admire	θαυμάζω	think	σκέφτομαι	murder	δολοφονώ
9	please	ευχαριστώ	take	λαμβάνω	average	υπολογίζω
10	donate	δωρίζω	see	βλέπω	apologize	απολογούμαι
11	love	αγαπώ	come	έρχομαι	spare	εξοικονομώ
12	teach	διδάσκω	look	κοιτάζω	lose	χάνω
13	save	σώζω	use	χρησιμοποιώ	face	αντικρίζω
14	check	ελέγχω	find	βρίσκω	imagine	φαντάζομαι
15	tend	τείνω	tell	διηγούμαι	worry	ανησυχώ
16	define	ορίζω	work	εργάζομαι	replace	αντικαθιστώ
17	contribute	συνεισφέρω	try	προσπαθώ	ignore	αγνοώ
18	respect	σέβομαι	ask	ζητώ	disappear	χάνομαι
19	possess	κατέχω	become	γίνομαι	warn	προειδοποιώ
20	satisfy	ικανοποιώ	leave	φεύγω	steal	κλέβω
21	rid	απαλλάσω	put	θέτω	mind	νοιάζομαι
22	lend	δανείζω	mean	εννοώ	confront	αντιμετωπίζω
23	rescue	διασώζω	keep	κρατώ	endure	αντέχω
24	diagnose	διαγιγνώσκω	let	αφήνω	injure	τραυματίζω
25	instruct	Καθοδηγώ	begin	αρχίζω	vanish	Εξαφανίζομαι

Analysis of the final set of verbs indicates the following: most positive and negative verbs do not directly refer to emotional states (e.g. "fear"), but rather refer to contexts that elicit positive or negative emotional responses (e.g. "murder" or "rescue"). Accordingly, a lot of emotion state denoting verbs that have been typically used in psychological research on emotions [13] did not end up in this set due to their low frequency of occurrence (e.g. "resent") or their ambiguous scoring in Senti-WordNet (e.g., "satisfy", "encourage"). Finally, analysis of subcategorization and thematic roles associated with each verb showed that "experiencer" is a more frequent role for positive and negative terms compared to neutral (36%, 32% and 20% respectively), while more positive and negative verbs impose a [+human] selectional restriction on their subject/object compared to neutral ones (40% and 16% respectively).

Both observations are in line with long identified characteristics of emotion verbs and verbs of psychological state [14, 15]. Overall, the most frequent role in the thematic grid was that of "agent/actor".

3   Emotional Assessment Tool and Experimental Process

The tool developed for the estimation of the emotions elicited by each verb is based on the Self Assessment Manikin (SAM) Test [6, 7, 8] and the "Pleasure", "Arousal" and "Dominance" (PAD) three-dimensional model for measuring the effect [16]. The SAM method measures the emotional response, based on the dimensional model of emotions, allowing the users to self-assess and express their emotional response visually rather than verbally. The latter makes it fast and easy to use in the application at hand and further enables a more coherent, consistent, independent of cultural and linguistic characteristics assessment, suitable for use in different countries and cultural groups [7, 8].

SAM Test measures emotion scales on the PAD dimensions:

- "Pleasure" (also referred to as "evaluation", "valence"). It measures how pleasant, positive, negative or neutral, an emotion is. This dimension is primarily depicted on SentiWordNet's scoring.
- "Arousal" (also referred to as "activation", "activity"). It measures the intensity, strength of the emotion (e.g. frighten vs. terrify).
- "Dominance" (also referred to as "power", "potency"). It measures how controlling/dominant or submissive the emotion is (e.g. fear vs. anger).

Participants in the experimental procedure can choose one from at least five figures. In the present study we used a 5-point scale (Figure 2). To assess the emotional state of "Pleasure", the extreme values are a smiling and a sad figure. In case of "Arousal" one pole is represented by a figure of great vigor and the opposite by a calm manikin, with eyes closed. Similarly, in the "Dominance" dimension, submissiveness is represented as controlled by a small manikin and dominance by a large one. When evaluating the results, users' answers can be easily converted from scale points to a group of values which ranges in the interval [-1, 1] or [-100%, 100%]. The value "0" represents the neutral state in each of the three dimensions.

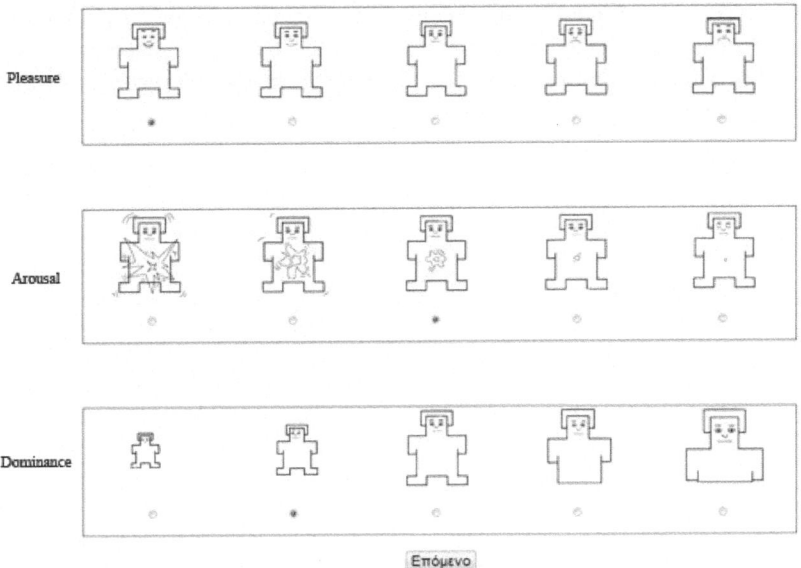

Fig. 2. The manikins of the 5-point scale SAM Test as presented during the test. The verbal expressions of "Pleasure", "Arousal" and "Dominance" do not appear during the test.

The implementation of the tool is based on PHP [17] and MySQL [18] in order to give the participants the possibility to automatically submit their answers from their own computer. Also, it gives researchers the functionality to easily and quickly retrieve and process the data. In addition, technologies like HTML [19], JavaScript [20] and CSS [21] were used in order to enhance the usability, administration and visual characteristics of the interface (e.g. to accurately control the projection time of the verb).

The second part of the experiment involved the completion of two questionnaires that evaluate the mental condition of the participant, specifically Scale EPQ and Scale SCL-90-R [22, 23]. The EPQ scale defines the personality in Eysenck's model and the SCL-90-R scale shows the actual self assessment psychological condition.

4   Results

Ten native Greek speakers participated in the experiment, 5 men and 5 women (mean age = 37,5 years, SD = 13,7 years). The stimuli were 75 Greek verbs, 25 positively, 25 negatively and 25 objectively classified (Table 1). Each participant was asked to fill in her/his demographic information and complete a consent form that she/he agrees to participate in the experiment. Then, they were familiarized with the annotation tool through a demo of the SAM test (three stimuli). After the completion of the experiment, they filled in the EPQ and SCL-90-R questionnaires. The mean duration of the total experimental procedure (introduction and familiarization with the tool, SAM test and psychometric tests) was 48.4 minutes.

Figures 3, 4 and 5 present the average values of participants' responses for each verb, on each scale, namely "Pleasure", "Arousal" and "Dominance" respectively. Each verb is represented by an integer ID number in the interval [1, 25] (Table 1 shows the matching ID number-verb).

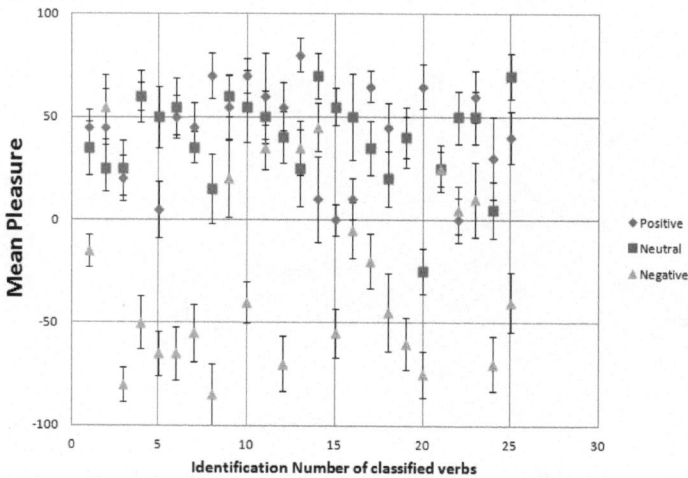

Fig. 3. The graphical representation of the average rating (with the corresponding standard error) of the 75 classified verbs on "Pleasure" dimension in percentage scale. Positive values correspond to positively assessed emotions, while negative values correspond to negatively assessed emotions.

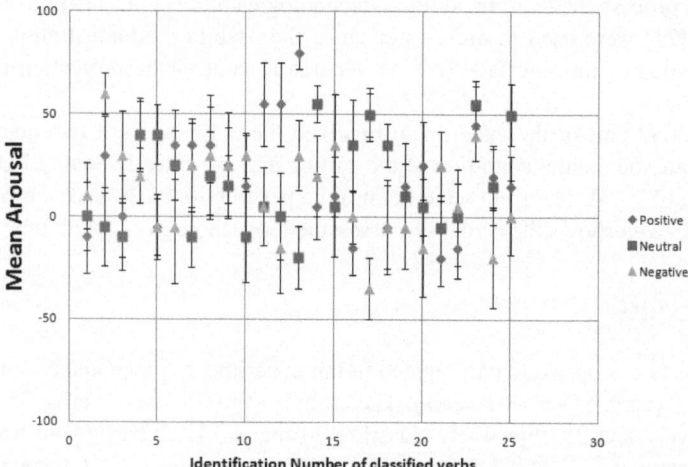

Fig. 4. The graphical representation of the average rating (with the corresponding standard error) of the 75 classified verbs on "Arousal" dimension in percentage scale. Positive values indicate higher intensity.

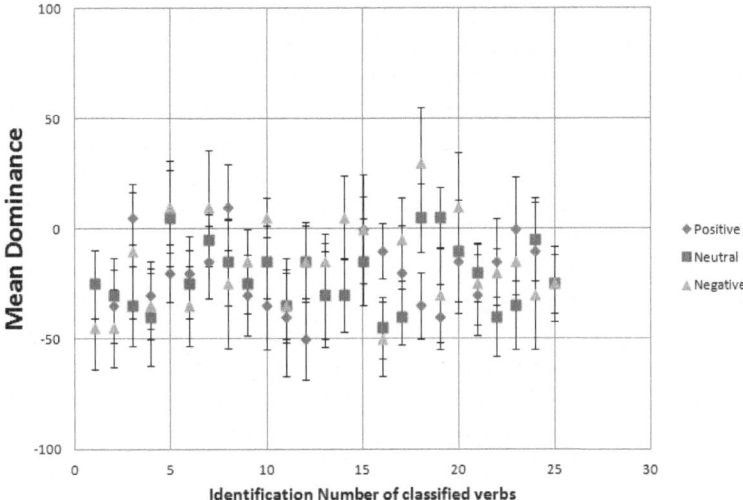

Fig. 5. The graphical representation of the average rating (with the corresponding standard error) of the 75 classified verbs on "Dominance" dimension in percentage scale. Positive values correspond to submissive emotions, while negative values correspond to dominant emotions.

Overall, positive verbs display a mean pleasure value of +42, contrary to negative verbs that have a mean value of -26.6. Neutral verbs also scored relatively high (mean 39), due to the positive connotations of verbs such as "can" (id 4), "know" (id 6), "find" (id 14) etc. There were no major differences across verb categories in the case of the other two axes, where mean arousal was 20.8, 16 and 11.4 for positive, neutral and negative verbs respectively, while mean dominance was -21.8, -21.8 and -16.2 respectively.

5   Discussion

The results of the pilot study indicate coherence and consistency in the evaluation. All positively classified verbs in SentiWordNet were assigned positive values with only two verbs ("tend" and "lend") scoring a zero, thus neutral value. Similarly, the majority of negative verbs is concentrated below the middle of the Pleasure axis. It should be noted that 8 out of the 25 negatively classified verbs recorded a positive score. We argue that this is mainly due to the inconsistencies in SentiWordNet's classification algorithm (e.g. "protect" (id 2)).

With regards to arousal, there is a high concentration of verbs around the middle of the y axis. Pairwise comparisons indicate that the evaluation was in the right direction. The verb "love" for example scored +51, while "prefer" scored merely -10. Similarly, in the case of dominance "fear", for example, which is submissive, scored +10, while "murder" and "save" scored -25 and -50 respectively. Brandley and Lang [24] present the results of the emotional rating, based on SAM test, called Affective Norms for English Words (ANEW). Our study extends ANEW in order to: a) implement a methodology that can be accessed by a large statistical sample of participants and applied in different languages and cultures (web based experiment implementation), b) potentially ultimately serve as a crowdsourcing technique for fast and cost effective creation of lexical resources, c) provide insight into how people respond emotionally to the words they use, listen and/or read, as well as the affective meaning of the verb they perceive, d) include psychometric questionnaires (EPQ and SCL-90-R) and e) verify the validity of SentiWordNet respective results as a comparison to the ones of our own study.

The verbs are annotated using "Pleasure", "Arousal" and "Dominance" dimensions providing additional information than those in SentiWordNet. The addition of "Arousal" and "Dominance" dimensions overcomes this issue by offering enhanced information and showing the different influences (e.g. intensity, activation, potency).

Regarding the issues faced during the development of the whole experimental process, some users showed lack of concentration after the first half of the experiment, which suggests that the large number of verbs could be potentially decreased. Finally, we plan to add support of touch sensitive controls in order to make the experimental process easier and more straightforward, as well as support for blind users.

Acknowledgements. This research has been co-financed by the European Union (European Social Fund – ESF) and Greek national funds through the Operational Program "Education and Lifelong Learning" of the National Strategic Reference Framework (NSRF) under the Research Funding Project: "THALIS-University of Macedonia- KAIKOS: Audio and Tactile Access to Knowledge for Individuals with Visual Impairments", MIS 380442.

References

1. Pang, B., Lee, L.: Opinion Mining and Sentiment Analysis. Foundations and Trends, Information Retrieval 2, 1–135 (2008)
2. SentiWordNet, http://sentiwordnet.isti.cnr.it/
3. Esuli, A., Sebastiani, F.: SENTIWORDNET: A Publicly Available Lexical Resource for Opinion Mining. In: 5th Conference on Language Resources and Evaluation (LREC 2006), Genoa, Italy, pp. 417–422 (2006)
4. Esuli, A., Baccianella, S., Sebastiani, F.: SentiWordNet 3.0: An Enhanced Lexical Resource for Sentiment Analysis and Opinion Mining. In: 7th Conference on International Language Resources and Evaluation (LREC 2010), Malta (2010)
5. WordNet, Lexical database of English, http://wordnet.princeton.edu/
6. Lang, P.J., Bradley, M.M., Cuthbert, B.N.: International Affective Picture System (IAPS): Affective retings of pictures and instruction manual. Technical report A-8, University of Florida, Gainesville, FL (2005)
7. Bradley, M.M., Lang, P.J.: Measuring emotion: The self-assessment manikin and the semantic differential. Journal of Behavior Therapy and Experimental Psychiatry 25(1), 49–59 (1994)
8. Morris, J.D.: Observations SAM: The Self-Assessment Manikin - An Efficient Cross-Cultural Measurement of Emotional Response. Journal of Advertising Research 35(8), 63–68 (1995)

9. Kouroupetroglou, G., Papatheodorou, N., Tsonos, D.: Design and Development Methodology for the Emotional State Estimation of Verbs. In: Holzinger, A., Ziefle, M., Hitz, M., Debevc, M. (eds.) SouthCHI 2013. LNCS, vol. 7946, pp. 1–15. Springer, Heidelberg (2013)
10. Alm, C.O., Roth, D., Sproat, R.: Emotions from text: Machine learning for text-based emotion prediction. In: Conference on Human Language Technology and Empirical Methods in Natural Language Processing (HLT/EMNLP 2005), Vancouver, pp. 579–586 (2005)
11. Word frequency lists and dictionary from the Corpus of Contemporary American English, http://www.wordfrequency.info/intro.asp
12. Babylon 9 translation Software and Dictionary Tool, http://www.babylon.com
13. Scherer, K.R.: What are emotions? And how can they be measured? Social Science Information 44(4), 695–729 (2005)
14. Giouli, V., Fotopoulou, A.: Emotion verbs in Greek. From Lexicon-Grammar tables to multi-purpose syntactic and semantic lexica. In: 15th Euralex International Congress (EURALEX 2012), Oslo (2012)
15. Belletti, A., Rizzi, L.: Psych-Verbs and θ–theory. Natural Language and Linguistic Theory 6, 291–352 (1988)
16. Russell, J.A., Mehrabian, A.: Evidence for a three-factor theory of emotions. Journal of Research in Personality 11(3), 273–294 (1977)
17. PHP Hypertext Preprocessor, http://www.php.net/
18. Welling, L., Thomson, L.: PHP and MySQL Web Development, 4th edn. Addison-Wesley Professional, USA (2008)
19. HTML Tutorial, http://www.w3schools.com/html/default.asp
20. JavaScript Tutorial, http://www.w3schools.com/js/default.asp
21. CSS Reference, http://www.w3schools.com/cssref/default.asp
22. Sybil, B.G., Eysenck, H., Eysenck, J.: Paul Barrett: A revised version of the psychoticism scale. Personality and Individual Differences 6(1), 21–29 (1985)
23. Derogatis, L.R.: SCL-90-R: Administration, Scoring and Procedures Manual-II. Clinical Psychometric Research, Inc., Towson (1977)
24. Bradley, M.M., Lang, P.J.: Affective norms for English words (ANEW): Instruction manual and affective ratings. Technical Report C-1, The Center for Research in Psychophysiology, University of Florida (1999)

Assessing the Coverage of Data Collection Campaigns on Twitter: A Case Study

Vassilis Plachouras[*], Yannis Stavrakas[**], and Athanasios Andreou

Institute for the Management of Information Systems (IMIS)
ATHENA Research Center
Artemidos 6 & Epidavrou, Maroussi 15125, Athens, Greece
{vplachouras,yannis}@imis.athena-innovation.gr,
athan.andreou@gmail.com

Abstract. Online social networks provide a unique opportunity to access and analyze the reactions of people as real-world events unfold. The quality of any analysis task, however, depends on the appropriateness and quality of the collected data. Hence, given the spontaneous nature of user-generated content, as well as the high speed and large volume of data, it is important to carefully define a data-collection campaign about a topic or an event, in order to maximize its coverage (recall). Motivated by the development of a social-network data management platform, in this work we evaluate the coverage of data collection campaigns on Twitter. Using an adaptive language model, we estimate the coverage of a campaign with respect to the total number of relevant tweets. Our findings support the development of adaptive methods to account for unexpected real-world developments, and hence, to increase the recall of the data collection processes.

Keywords: Social networks, data management, event tracking.

1 Introduction

There is a growing number of applications that analyze data from online social networks and microblogging platforms, in order to detect breaking news as they happen, or to monitor the interests of users with respect to ongoing events. The quality of the analysis results depends to a great extent on the availability of exactly those data that are relevant to the task at hand. Microblogging platforms such as Twitter, however, limit the access to the full stream of data, and applications typically employ one of the following alternatives for collecting thematically focused tweets: (a) tracking a number of terms or users over a small random sample of the full stream, or (b) executing repetitive queries of limited expressiveness that usually include a number of terms or users against which the full stream of tweets is matched.

---

[*] Supported by the European Commission under ARCOMEM (ICT 270239).
[**] Supported by the EU/Greece funded KRIPIS: MEDA project.

Y.T. Demey and H. Panetto (Eds.): OTM 2013 Workshops, LNCS 8186, pp. 598–607, 2013.
© Springer-Verlag Berlin Heidelberg 2013

While the first alternative may provide a balanced distribution of terms and users with respect to the full stream, allowing therefore the discovery of trending topics, it only returns a small percentage of the relevant content. On the other hand, the second alternative returns all the content matching the query conditions, but suffers when a topic evolves over time and the query conditions become gradually irrelevant. Consider the case of unexpected developments in an event, for example the terrorist attack during the Boston Marathon on April 15, 2013. Querying with an immutable set of hashtags (such as *#bostonmarathon*) would result in a significantly lower coverage of the relevant data, as the focus shifted from the marathon itself to the attack and the events that followed. The ideal approach would be to use the second alternative, but with varying query conditions that reflect the evolution of the topic in question.

In this work, (a) we describe a methodology to evaluate the coverage of data collection campaigns from Twitter on a given topic, based on the work by Lin *et al.* [1], and (b) we use this methodology to demonstrate the impact of unexpected developments during an event on the quality of the collected data. Specifically, we employ our evaluation framework to assess the coverage of four data collection campaigns about the 2012 and 2013 Boston marathons and the 2012 and 2013 London marathons. Our results show that the coverage of a data collection campaign achieved by querying with a topic specific hashtag is relatively high in case an event develops as expected. On the other hand, a data collection campaign based on a predefined immutable hashtag achieves a low coverage when the relevant event develops in unexpected ways, because users are more likely to spontaneously start using new hashtags reflecting the current developments. In the case of 2013 Boston marathon, where a terrorist attack took place, a data collection campaign based only on the hashtag *#bostonmarathon* would retrieve approximately 45% of the relevant tweets. Notice that adapting the search to the unexpected developments within a topic is of paramount importance in many applications, like for example in data-driven journalism. Consequently, in such cases, it is important to consider methods for the automatic adaptive updating of the query used to guide the data collection campaign.

The remainder of this paper is organized as follows. In Section 2, we describe a platform for the management of social network data we are developing and outline the motivation for this work. In Section 3, we present the methodology for evaluating the coverage of a data collection campaign. In Section 4 we describe the experimental setting and present the results. We discuss related works in Section 5 and we close with some concluding remarks in Section 6.

2   Collecting Tweets with TwitHoard

Our need to assess the coverage of a data collection campaign from Twitter arises in the context of developing TwitHoard, a platform for collecting data from Twitter [3], and modeling the dynamics of terms and term associations [2].

The aim of TwitHoard is to aid users in defining and managing data collection campaigns on Twitter. The platform allows the concurrent running of multiple campaigns. A user defines a campaign by providing its duration, a set of terms or hashtags, a set of Twitter usernames, and possibly specifying other filters on language or geographic locations. A campaign can be paused, restarted, and refined, by updating its definition at any time instance. The user can also enable the crawling of Web pages linked from tweets to archive them for future reference. Figure 1 shows a screenshot of TwitHoard's filtering screen, where a user can create a selection of tweets coming from a specific user, or containing a given hashtag.

TwitHoard will also integrate a model of the temporal evolution of entities and a set of query operators to enable users to create views of the collected datasets according to complex temporal conditions. For example, a journalist may be interested in finding the tweets during the period in which the association strength between the hashtags *#boston* and *#marathon* is increasing. The model and the query operators allow the expression of such queries with varying time granularities.

An important feature that will be integrated in TwitHoard, is the capability of the system to automatically adapt the campaign definition so as to reflect the evolution in the topic at hand. The study in this paper is a first step towards this direction.

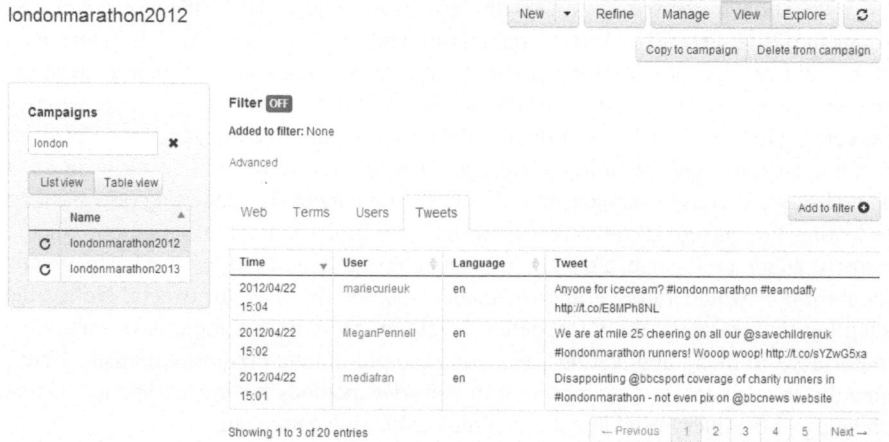

Fig. 1. Screenshot of TwitHoard campaign management platform from the 2012 London marathon dataset

3 Methodology

In this section, we describe a framework for assessing the coverage of a data collection campaign. The framework is based on the work of Lin *et al.* [1], but our objective is different, as we explain in Section 5.

We assume that a data collection campaign is defined by a set of hashtags $H = \{h_1, h_2, ..., h_n\}$. Given a stream of tweets T, if the current tweet tw contains at least one hashtag from H, we add it to the ground-truth set G_w, where w is the maximum cardinality of the set. If adding a tweet in the ground-truth set increases its cardinality over w we remove the oldest tweet to maintain the maximum cardinality equal to w. If the tweet tw does not contain any hashtag from H, then we classify it as *missed-relevant* or *non-relevant* to the campaign. Our objective is to estimate the number of tweets that are relevant to a campaign, but do not match any of the hashtags in H. We expect few such tweets for a campaign that is well characterized by the hashtags in H. However, for a campaign defined by a set of hashtags that do not capture well the topic or event of interest, or for a campaign about an event where there are unexpected developments, we expect that the number of relevant tweets that do not contain hashtags in H will be higher.

The relevance of a tweet to the campaign defined by H is determined by its similarity to the set G_w. More specifically, a tweet is relevant to the campaign if its perplexity with respect to the language model of the tweets in G_w is lower than a threshold k. In the remainder of this section, we describe the language model built from tweets in G_w and the perplexity classifier.

3.1   Adaptive Language Model for Topic Tracking

Given the set G_w of the w most recent tweets that match the campaign definition, we build a foreground language model, which is combined with a background model using Jelinek-Mercer smoothing [1]. In preliminary experiments, we have also used smoothing techniques based on absolute discounting, Dirichlet priors and stupid back-off, but Jelinek-Mercer smoothing resulted in models with lower average perplexity. The probability of a word x is given by the following equation:

$$P(x) = \lambda \frac{c(x, G_w)}{\sum_x c(x, G_w)} + (1 - \lambda) P_B(x) \tag{1}$$

where λ is a hyper-parameter, $c(x, G_w)$ is the frequency of word x in the ground-truth set G_w, and $P_B(x)$ is the probability of x in the background model. As described in [1], the background model is also smoothed using absolute discounting with $\delta=0.5$. We set the value of λ for Jelinek-Mercer smoothing such that we minimize the average perplexity of tweets containing at least one hashtag from H with respect to the set G_w. In other words, the value of λ is set such that we optimize the prediction of the next tweet by the language model $P(x)$.

3.2   Perplexity Classifier

We use a simple perplexity classifier to decide whether a tweet, which does not contain any of the hashtags in H, is relevant to the data collection campaign defined by H, and thus, it would have been beneficial to also collect it. The perplexity of a tweet with respect to language model $P(x)$ is defined as follows:

$$pow\left(2, -\frac{1}{N} \sum_{i=1}^{N} \log_2 P(x_i)\right) \tag{2}$$

where N is the number of words in the considered tweet and x_i is the i-th word of the tweet. Perplexity expresses the surprise of seeing a sample of size N given the distribution $P(x)$. Hence, a lower perplexity value means that the considered tweet is more similar to the distribution $P(x)$. In our experiments, we mark a tweet as relevant if the computed perplexity is lower than a threshold k.

3.3   Assessing the Coverage of a Campaign

We evaluate the coverage of a data collection campaign in terms of the collected tweets that contain at least one of the hashtags from the campaign definition and the missed-relevant tweets, which are relevant but do not contain any of the specified hashtags. We use recall at time t, denoted by $R(t)$, which is defined as follows:

$$R(t) = \frac{G_{\infty}(t)}{G_{\infty}(t) + Missed(t)} \tag{3}$$

where $G_{\infty}(t)$ is the total number of tweets that belonged to G_w at some point in the past up to time t, and $Missed(t)$ is the number of missed-relevant tweets, i.e. the tweets encountered up to time t that are on topic but do not contain any hashtag from set H. A high value of recall $R(t)$ means that the definition of the data collection campaign captures well the topic or event of interest, and Twitter users writing relevant tweets are very likely to use at least one hashtag from H. On the other hand, a low value of recall means that there are many tweets, which are similar to the ones containing a hashtag from the campaign definition but which do not themselves contain any such hashtag. This may be either due to an incomplete definition of the campaign, or unexpected developments in the topic or event of interest, resulting in a change of the vocabulary present in relevant tweets.

4   Evaluation

We employ the methodology described in Section 3 to evaluate the coverage of four data collection campaigns about marathon events in Boston and London for 2012 and 2013. While there were no major incidents during either versions of the marathon in London and the 2012 Boston marathon, the 2013 Boston marathon was marked by the explosion of two bombs near the finish line, followed by the identification and the hunt of the terrorists. For each of the four events, we simulate a data collection campaign. The simulation targets a corpus of tweets that we have collected during the relevant time periods, by archiving a random sample of the Twitter stream. Our goal is to evaluate the coverage of each campaign, expecting that the coverage for the 2013 Boston marathon will be significantly lower than that of the rest of the campaigns.

4.1   Datasets

We have used Twitter's Streaming API to collect a set of tweets for each of the 2012 and 2013 Boston and London marathons. More specifically, we have collected tweets containing at least one English stop-word. Given the high volume of tweets matching this condition and the limitations of the Streaming API, we have collected 50 tweets per second, and hence, more than four million tweets per day. We filter out tweets that do not contain any hashtag, after tokenizing the text of each tweet and removing stop-words; we further filter out those tweets that have fewer than 5 distinct words or fewer than 10 words in total. We run the simulated campaigns on these datasets using the hashtags shown in Table 1.

Table 1 shows the start and end times of each dataset, the number of tweets contained in each dataset after the filtering described above, and the set of hashtags H used to define the corresponding data collection campaigns. For the datasets covering the 2012 and 2013 London marathons and the 2012 Boston marathon, the data covers three days, starting the day before the event and ending the day after. The dataset for the 2013 Boston marathon covers 8 days in order to include tweets about the events that took place during and after the marathon.

Table 1. Description of datasets for the 2012 and 2013 London and Boston marathons. Start and end times are given in UTC.

Dataset	Start date	End date	# tweets	Hashtags H
London12	2012/4/21 00:00	2012/4/24 00:00	445,137	#londonmarathon, #vlm, #vlm2012, #bbcmarathon
London13	2013/4/20 00:00	2013/4/23 00:00	485,701	#londonmarathon, #vlm, #vlm2013, #bbcmarathon
Boston12	2012/4/15 00:00	2012/4/18 00:00	457,373	#bostonmarathon
Boston13	2013/4/14 00:00	2013/4/22 00:00	1,344,471	#bostonmarathon

4.2   Estimating Coverage

We estimate the coverage of a data collection campaign as follows. For each tweet in the stream of tweets we have collected, we check whether it contains a hashtag from the set H. If this is true, then we add it to the set G_w and we update the language model $P(x)$. Otherwise we compute its perplexity with respect to the set G_w. If the computed perplexity is lower than the threshold k we mark the tweet as missed-relevant, because the data collection campaign would not download it.

We set the value of the λ hyper-parameter in Jelinek-Mercer smoothing from Eq. (1) as follows. For each dataset, we compute the average perplexity of tweets containing a hashtag in H with respect to G_w of the w most recently seen tweets containing a hashtag in H. We have used several values for w ranging from 100 to 10000. According to the results, $\lambda = 0.1$ was the value that most often resulted in the minimum average perplexity. For this reason, we fix $\lambda = 0.1$ for the remaining of the experiments. The background model $P_B(x)$ is built from a set of tweets collected during a period of one week from 2012/3/25 to 2012/3/31. The perplexity of the unigram language model built from tweets in the ground-truth for Boston2013 is 252.84. The average perplexity of tweets in ground-truth for Boston2013 is significantly higher, because it is computed as new tweets are added to the ground-truth, and hence, the probabilities for previously unseen words are low.

We set the perplexity threshold $k = 5000$ for the classifier, meaning that a tweet is marked as relevant if it does not contain a hashtag in H and its perplexity with respect to the language model $P(x)$ is lower than 5000. The value of threshold k controls the trade-off between precision and recall. For example, a higher value of k will increase the number of missed-relevant tweets but they may not be on the same topic as tweets in G_w. The magnitude of the threshold k depends on the specific dataset we use. We have selected the value 5000 after performing preliminary experiments, where we observed a high number of relevant tweets. More specifically, for the Boston2013 dataset, we have manually inspected a random sample of 200 missed-relevant tweets and found that 87% were about the Boston marathon and subsequent events.

Table 2. Recall achieved for the data collection campaigns regarding the 2012 and 2013 London and Boston marathons

Dataset	G_∞	Missed	Recall
London12	873	92	0.9047
London13	1105	99	0.9178
Boston12	245	10	0.9608
Boston13	6726	8255	**0.4490**

4.3 Results

Table 2 shows the achieved recall for the employed datasets after processing all available tweets. We set the parameter w to a high enough number so that practically G_∞ in Table 2 denotes the number of tweets containing any hashtag in H for each simulated campaign. The results in the table show that collecting tweets containing hashtags in H for the 2012 and 2013 London marathons and the 2012 Boston marathon retrieves the majority of the relevant tweets. For example, both campaigns about the London marathon would have gathered more than 90% of the relevant tweets. We attribute the high recall value to the fact that most of the tweets that are about the 2012 and 2013 London marathons do have one of the hashtags in the set H. Moreover, there was no unexpected development during either of the marathons in order to lead people to change the vocabulary used in their tweets. We obtain similar results for the 2012 Boston marathon. On the other hand, the recall for the 2013 Boston marathon is significantly lower, reaching only 0.4490. The low recall value is due to the terrorist attacks that took place at the 2013 Boston marathon and the following events. These unexpected developments have led users to employ other hashtags, such as *#prayforboston*, *#watertown*, *#boston*, in addition to or in place of *#bostonmarathon*. Next, we focus on the analysis of the results for the 2013 Boston marathon.

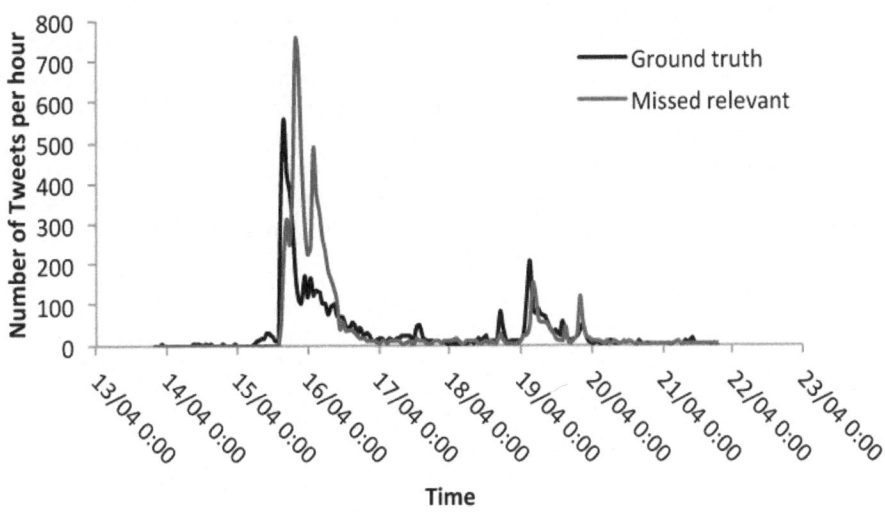

Fig. 2. Hourly frequency of ground-truth and missed-relevant tweets

Figure 2 illustrates the temporal evolution of the hourly frequency of tweets in the ground-truth (containing the hashtag *#bostonmarathon*), and the missed-relevant ones, which are marked as relevant by the perplexity classifier but do not contain *#bostonmarathon* (times are shown in EDT). We observe that there is a significant spike in the use of *#bostonmarathon* at 15/04 15:00, just after the bomb explosions near the finish line of the Boston marathon. This spike is followed by a higher spike in the number of relevant tweets that do not contain *#bostonmarathon*. Similarly, we observe smaller spikes at 18/04 17:00 when images of the suspects are released, 19/04 2:00 when police hunts the suspects, and 19/04 20:00 when the second suspect is arrested. Each spike in the number of ground-truth tweets is followed by the number of relevant tweets that do not contain *#bostonmarathon*. Overall, we observe that a campaign that collects tweets relevant to the Boston marathon would need to adapt very quickly in order to increase the number of collected relevant tweets.

Table 3. Top-5 frequent hashtags in ground-truth and missed-relevant tweets

Ground-truth		Missed relevant	
Hashtag	**Freq**	**Hashtag**	**Freq**
#prayforboston	701	*#prayforboston*	5564
#boston	342	*#boston*	1055
#watertown	152	*#watertown*	254
#fbi	121	*#breaking*	125
#breaking	78	*#marathon*	103

Next, we examine the frequency distribution of hashtags in the ground-truth and in the set of missed tweets. Table 3 shows the top-5 most frequent hashtags in the ground-truth set (excluding *#bostonmarathon*) and in the set of missed relevant tweets, respectively. We observe that four hashtags are common in both sets. Hence, we expect that by automatically updating the campaign definition to include some of the frequently co-occurring hashtags, we could collect more relevant tweets. Figure 3 shows the temporal evolution of the frequency of #*prayforboston* (top) and #*watertown* (bottom) when they occur in the ground-truth and in the missed-relevant tweets, respectively. We observe that for #*prayforboston* the start of the peak in missed-relevant tweets coincides with a smaller peak in the number of ground-truth tweets containing #*prayforboston*. For the hashtag #watertown, a peak in missed-relevant tweets is preceded by a smaller peak for the same hashtag in the ground-truth.

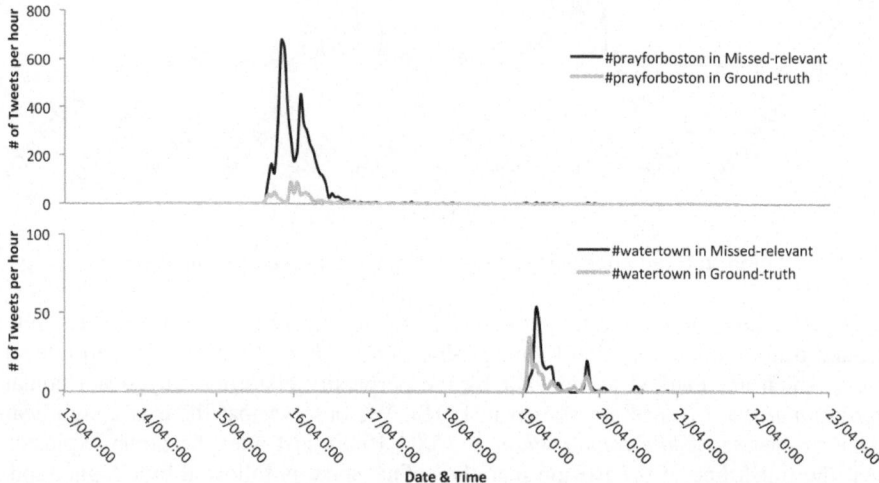

Fig. 3. Hourly frequency of tweets containing the hashtags #prayforboston and #watertown in the ground-truth and missed-relevant tweets, respectively

5   Related Works

Our work is broadly related to Topic Detection and Tracking (TDT) [4]. However, there are important differences. For example, we need to track the evolution of a topic or event by actively querying a social network API to obtain data. Hence, the query affects the data that is available for further processing.

The framework we have described is based on the work of Lin *et al.* [1], which studies various smoothing and history retention methods for adaptive language models built from tweets containing a given hashtag. They evaluate the adaptive language models in terms of perplexity and precision/recall, where the relevance of each tweet is based on the output of a perplexity classifier. Our work, however, is different, because we consider all tweets that contain a given hashtag as relevant, and we estimate the number of tweets which would be relevant but do not contain the given hashtag.

Ward [6] presents an automatic query expansion method to collect tweets about TV programs. We do not make any assumption about the events or topics and, hence, we cannot use domain-specific knowledge as in [6] or other works for Social TV [5].

There is a number of works aiming to predict the popularity of hashtags in the future. Ma et al. [7] develop classifiers using content and contextual features to predict the popularity of a hashtag on a daily basis. Tsur and Rappoport [8] investigate content and temporal features to predict the popularity of hashtags with linear regression.

6   Conclusions

In this work, we have described a framework based on language models to assess the coverage of a data collection campaign on Twitter. We have employed this framework to evaluate the coverage of four simulated data-collection campaigns. Our results show that we can achieve high coverage of relevant data if the focus of the topic does not change significantly over time. However, if there are unexpected developments and users modify the vocabulary of their status updates, the coverage is harmed considerably. In our use case of marathon races, this finding is observed for the 2013 Boston marathon, which was marked by the explosion of two bombs. Overall, our findings support the need to automatically adapt the campaign definition, to maximize the relevant data collected.

References

1. Lin, J., Snow, R., Morgan, W.: Smoothing techniques for adaptive online language models: topic tracking in tweet streams. In: Procs. of the 17th ACM SIGKDD Intl. Conf. on Knowledge Discovery and Data Mining, pp. 422–429 (2011)
2. Plachouras, V., Stavrakas, Y.: Querying Term Associations and their Temporal Evolution in Social Data. In: Procs. of the 1st Intl. Workshop on Online Social Systems (2012)
3. Stavrakas, Y., Plachouras, V.: A Platform for Supporting Data Analytics on Twitter: Challenges and Objectives. In: Procs. of the 1st Intl. Workshop on Knowledge Extraction & Consolidation from Social Media (2012)
4. Allan, J. (ed.): Introduction to Topic Detection and Tracking: Event-based Information Organization. Kluwer Academic Publishers (2002)
5. Dan, O., Feng, J., Davison, B.: Filtering microblogging messages for social tv. In: Procs. of the 20th Intl. Conf. Companion on World Wide Web, pp. 197–200 (2011)
6. Ward, E.: Tweet Collect: short text message collection using automatic query expansion and classification. MSc thesis, University of Upsala (2013)
7. Ma, Z., Sun, A., Cong, G.: On Predicting the Popularity of Newly Emerging Hashtags in Twitter. J. Am. Soc. Inf. Sci., doi:10.1002/asi.22844
8. Tsur, O., Rappoport, A.: What's in a Hashtag? Content based Prediction of the Spread of Ideas in Microblogging Communities. In: Procs. of the 5th ACM Intl. Conf. on Web Search and Data Mining (2012)

Structuring the Blogosphere on News from Traditional Media

Georgios Petasis

Software and Knowledge Engineering Laboratory
Institute of Informatics and Telecommunications
National Centre for Scientific Research (N.C.S.R.) "Demokritos"
GR-153 10, P.O. BOX 60228, Aghia Paraskevi, Athens, Greece
petasis@iit.demokritos.gr

Abstract. News and social media are emerging as a dominant source of information for numerous applications. However, their vast unstructured content present challenges to efficient extraction of such information. In this paper, we present the SYNC3 system that aims to intelligently structure content from both traditional news media and the blogosphere. To achieve this goal, SYNC3 incorporates innovative algorithms that first model news media content statistically, based on fine clustering of articles into so-called "news events". Such models are then adapted and applied to the blogosphere domain, allowing its content to map to the traditional news domain. In this paper an unsupervised approach to do-main adaptation is presented, which exploits external knowledge sources in order to port a classification model into a new thematic domain. Our approach extracts a new feature set from documents of the target domain, and tries to align the new features to the original ones, by exploiting text relatedness from external knowledge sources, such as WordNet. The approach has been evaluated on the task of document classification, involving the classification of newsgroup postings into 20 news groups.

1 Introduction

News content in the internet, available through both traditional news media portals and the blogosphere, constitutes valuable information to both professionals and casual internet users, who however can be inundated by its vast amount. Clearly, such information could be much more useful if presented and delivered in a well-structured way. Many attempts, taking the form of either research projects or commercial solutions, have been made to provide centralised repositories of such content [1–3]. However, to date, there exists no integrated system that structures blog post content across these two broad sources of news information in parallel, capable to meet the requirements of a broad range of end users, such as professional journalists, communication experts, and citizen bloggers. The SYNC3 system [18] aims to fill this gap, efficiently structuring content from both domains, rendering it accessible, manageable, and re-usable.

The SYNC3 system is a solution for aggregating news from both traditional news media (i.e. news portals, etc.) and the blogosphere, providing the end users

Y.T. Demey and H. Panetto (Eds.): OTM 2013 Workshops, LNCS 8186, pp. 608–617, 2013.
© Springer-Verlag Berlin Heidelberg 2013

with sophisticated capabilities with respect to content structuring, management, and delivery. The methodology adopted applies the news domain structure derived from well-organised news portals to the less structured blogosphere. More specifically, SYNC3 automatically builds a news thematology, based on a statistical modelling approach that derives fine clusters of news articles, the so-called "news events". Subsequently, the system *adapts* the statistical news event models to the blogosphere domain, allowing the system to automatically find blog posts that comment on these events. Classifying blog posts into events extracted from news items can be easy, if the domain of both blog posts and news items are relatively similar. This can be the case for professional journalists who are also bloggers, as their writing style roughly remains the same when they write news items or blog posts. However, the vast majority of bloggers do not fall into this category, as they typically are individuals expressing personal thoughts, while their writing style may vary significantly from what is observed in the news. In order to associate blog posts from the latter category to the news, an adaptation of the classification model is required, in order to accommodate any possibly new writing styles. This process, known as domain adaptation, must extent a model for handling documents from a different domain (i.e., blog posts), without losing the ability to classify documents from the original domain (i.e., news items replicated in blog posts, or blog posts from journalists).

The portability of natural language processing (NLP) systems to new thematic domains is still a research area that attracts a significant research interest. During the last two decades, the use of machine learning has greatly improved the adaptability to new domains, or even languages. However, the vast majority of machine learning algorithms operate under a basic assumption: both the training and test data should use the same feature space, and follow the same distribution, suggesting that both should originate from the same thematic domain. When the distribution changes, the models must be re-generated from newly collected data. The adaptation can be separated into three large categories, according to the available data from the new domain. In supervised approaches, there is an adequate number of labelled data to train the model from scratch, on the new domain. When a limited number of labelled data are available, usually too few to train a model with satisfactory performance, along with unlabeled ones, the adaptation process is characterised as semi-supervised. Finally, unsupervised approaches must adapt their model to a new domain by learning solely from unlabelled examples.

Transfer learning or knowledge transfer is a research area, which tries to extract knowledge from previous experience and apply it on new learning tasks. Based on the idea that prior knowledge (i.e. identifying oranges) can be used on new tasks (i.e. identifying lemons), transfer learning researches three main central problems [22]: 1) how to extract the prior knowledge that is related, 2) how to represent the knowledge, and 3) how to apply the knowledge in the new learning task. Domain adaptation is a sub-category of transfer learning, where [17]:

- The source and target domains are different, but related.
- The source and target tasks are the same (i.e. classification or regression).
- Labelled examples are available for the source domain.
- Only unlabeled examples are available for the target domain.

In this paper, we propose a novel approach for the task of domain adaptation, in the context of document classification: we will try to classify (unlabelled) newsgroup posts from a target thematic domain D_T by performing model adaptation on a model acquired from labeled newsgroup posts belonging to a similar source domain D_S. Our method concentrates on the *feature space*, by trying to expand the features of the source domain with features that appear only in the target domain. Features that originate from the two different domains are aligned or linked to each other, through text relatedness. Text relatedness can take many forms, but we have opted for a simple relatedness measure, based on WordNet [15] synonymity. The rest of the paper is organized as follows: in section 2 related work is presented, where our method is compared to existing approaches. In section 3 our approach to model adaptation based on text relatedness is presented, while section 4 presents evaluation on the 20-newsgroup corpus [13]. Finally, section 5 concludes this paper and presents some future directions.

2   Related Work

The task of transfer learning can be defined as follows: given a source domain D_S, a source task T_S, a target domain $D_T \neq D_S$, and a target task T_T, transfer learning aims to learn a function f_T that accomplishes task T_T, by exploiting knowledge derived from D_S and T_S. A fairly recent overview of the area of transfer learning is given in the survey of [17], including the definition of transfer learning, its relation to traditional machine learning, a categorisation of transfer learning approaches, and practical applications of transfer learning. More recent approaches that target the task of domain adaptation can be found on the ACL 2010 Workshop on Domain Adaptation for Natural Language Processing (DANLP 2010) [8].

A lot of approaches exist that perform model adaptation in a fully supervised way (i.e. requiring labelled examples for both the source and target domains). For example, EASYADAPT [9] augments the source domain feature space using features extracted from labelled data in target domain. Prior work on semi-supervised approaches to domain adaptation also exists in literature. Recent work in domain adaptation has focused on approaches such as *self-training* and *structural correspondence learning* (SCL). The former approach involves adding self-labelled data from the target domain produced by a model trained in-domain [14]. The latter approach focuses on ways of generating shared source-target representations based on good pivot features [4, 5, 9]. However, the approach presented in this paper follows an *unsupervised approach*, thus requiring no labelled examples from the target domain. Unsupervised approaches try to exploit knowledge either from external knowledge sources, like our approach and [11], or from the distribution followed by the target domain [7, 20]. The work presented in this paper can be categorised as an "unsupervised feature construction" approach, according to [17]. Thus, approaches that try to extend a feature set through the unsupervised extraction of new features share some common ground with our approach. In [11] an approach that extracts new features by exploiting world knowledge is presented. World knowledge is represented through publically available ontologies, such as the Open Directory Project (ODP), where features from the source domain are mapped to appropriate ontology concepts, and "is-a" relations are exploited in order to acquire new features that augment the original feature set. Finally, the most appropriate features are selected through a feature selection phase. The work presented in [22] is also closely related to our approach: *feature correlation* is used in order to group features into *correlated groups*. For example, words like "orange", "lemon", "apple" and "pear" may often appear together in documents: aggregating them into a new correlated group "fruits", creates a new feature. If enough evidence exists in a document from the target domain (i.e. some of the features of the correlated group appear in the document), the feature that corresponds to the correlated group may help the task T_T in the target domain. In a sense, both approaches exploit information that can be characterised as "text relatedness" (or "feature relatedness"), as both "is-a" relations and correlation can be viewed as a relatedness measure between features.

However, our method has also some important differences with these two methods. Our text relatedness measure is based on synonymity, as provided by an electronic dictionary such as WordNet. An electronic dictionary may be an easier resource to find than an ontology or hierarchy, thus our approach may have a small advantage in initial requirements when compared to [12]. On the other hand, the calculation of feature correlation has no initial requirements in resources, but requires a corpus of adequate size, in order to extract the correlated groups. In addition, mining correlated groups may be computationally intensive if the feature set from the source domain is large enough (a problem tackled by limiting the source domain feature set to 2000 features, selected through mutual information, as reported in [22]). Finally, synonymity is a slightly more restricted text relatedness measure, compared to "is-a" relations (that can have many levels in the concept hierarchy) or correlation (which can relate possible unrelated features). Being a slightly more accurate text relatedness metric, it constitutes the need for feature selection, after the expansion of the source feature set, less important. In fact, our approach does not have a feature selection phase at all, in contrary to the two related approaches.

3   Domain Adaptation Based on Text Relatedness

The proposed methodology assumes a source domain D_S, a target domain $D_T \neq D_S$, a task T common for both domains, a feature space for the source domain $\mathcal{X}_S$, a label space $\mathcal{L}$ common for both domains, and a set of labelled examples originating from the source domain $L_S = \{X_1, \cdots, X_n\}$, where $X_i = \{x_1, \cdots, x_n, l_i\}$, $x_i \in \mathcal{X}_S$, $l_i \in \mathcal{L}$. In addition, our approach assumes a function $r(x_\alpha, x_\beta) \in \mathbb{R} : 0 \leq r \leq 1.0$, $x_\alpha, x_\beta \in \mathcal{X}_S$, $\mathcal{X}_T$, which decides if two features are related, according to a text relatedness metric. Finally, a function $f_{\mathcal{X}_T}$ is assumed, that can extract a feature space $\mathcal{X}_T$ from the target domain D_T. The function $f_{\mathcal{X}_T}$ can be even a naive one, i.e. a function that returns all words in a corpus from the target domain D_T.

3.1   Text Relatedness Based on Synonymity

Our approach assumes a relatedness function $r\,(x_\alpha,\ x_\beta)$, that can compare two features (either from the source or from the target feature spaces), and return whether the two features are related or not. Although many relatedness metrics can be devised and used, we have opted for a simple one, based on synonymity. Assuming an electronic dictionary, which contains synonyms, text relatedness that is based on synonymity can be described with the following algorithm:

1. If x_α and x_β are the same, return 1.
2. Let S_α be the set of synonyms of x_α, and S_β the set of synonyms of x_β, according to the dictionary.
3. If $x_\beta \in S_\alpha$ or $x_\alpha \in S_\beta$, return 1.
4. If $S_\alpha \cap S_\beta \neq \emptyset$, return 1.
5. Else, return 0.

In simple words, our synonymity relatedness metric returns true, if the two features are synonyms, or when they have at least one common synonym. The electronic dictionary that has been chosen is WordNet [15], as has already been mentioned. It should be noted that all synonyms for all senses are treated equally, without performing any kind of word sense disambiguation [16], as is performed for example in the approach described in [12].

3.2   Extracting Features from the Target Domain

Our approach assumes that there is a function $f_{\mathcal{X}_T}$, which can extract features from the target domain D_T. Since no further requirements are assumed about this function, the function can be as naive or complex as the task T requires. We have considered a feature extraction procedure, which examines all documents of a corpus from the target domain D_T, and calculates the TF-IDF score for every word of the document. "Stop words" are rejected, and the rest of the remaining words are sorted according to their TF-IDF score, in a descending list. Then, an amount of the best scoring words, specified through a parameter θ (interpreted as a percent of the total words in a document), is extracted from each document, and added to the feature space that will be returned as the result.

3.3   Extracting New Features

Once we have a method for extracting possible new features from the target domain D_T, through the function $f_{\mathcal{X}_T}$, and a text relatedness metric $r\,(x_\alpha,\ x_\beta)$, we can apply these two functions in order to acquire a feature set from the target domain:

1. Let $\mathcal{X}_T^{Initial}$ be the feature space, as extracted from the target domain D_T by the function $f_{\mathcal{X}_T}$.
2. Each feature $x_s \in \mathcal{X}_S$ from the source feature set is compared to each feature $x_T \in \mathcal{X}_T^{Initial}$ in the extracted from the target domain feature set. The function $r(x_\alpha, x_\beta)$ is used for comparing the pair of features.
3. Features from the $\mathcal{X}_T^{Initial}$ that are not related to any feature in $\mathcal{X}_S$, are eliminated from $\mathcal{X}_T^{Initial}$, leading to a new feature space $\mathcal{X}_T^{Related}$.
4. As a final step, all features $x_T \in \mathcal{X}_T^{Related}$ are examined: every feature x_T that is related to more than one features in $\mathcal{X}_S$, is removed from $\mathcal{X}_T^{Related}$, leading to the final feature space that relates to the target domain $\mathcal{X}_T^{Final}$.

The result of this procedure, the final feature space that should be used for performing task T on the target domain D_T is the union of the two feature spaces: $\mathcal{X} = \mathcal{X}_S \cup \mathcal{X}_T^{Final}$.

3.4   Representing the Extracted Knowledge

The augmented feature space $\mathcal{X}$ that has been extracted as described in the previous subsection, contains all features of the source domain D_S, and new features from the target domain D_T, each of which is unambiguously related to a single feature from D_S. The only unsolved issue is how this augmented feature space is going to be represented as vectors, which can be used with a machine learning algorithm. Although this decision may rely on the particular machine learning algorithm that will be used, empirical evaluation suggested that the best alternative is to form "groups of features", where each old feature is replaced by a set of "related" features: the original one, plus the related ones from the target feature space, if they exist. This representation has been proved beneficial, at least for the task we have chosen to evaluate our approach (document classification), the chosen representation (bag-of-words) and the chosen classifier (kNN with $k = 1$ and cosine similarity as its distance metric).

4   Empirical Evaluation

In order to evaluate the algorithms proposed in the previous sections, we performed experiments on the 20-newsgroup dataset [13]: the 20-newsgroup dataset is a collection of approximately 20000 newsgroup documents, partitioned (nearly) evenly across 20 different newsgroups, and is a standard evaluation corpus in many works related to domain adaptation or transfer learning. The task chosen for our empirical evaluation is document classification.

4.1   The 20-newsgroup Corpus

The 20-newsgroup corpus is preconfigured in training and testing material. Despite the fact that it is a popular evaluation corpus for domain adaptation approaches, it is unclear to us if all works that report results on the corpus use the same train/test partitioning, as different results are reported even for the base cases, as in [17] for example. In order to ease comparison with other approaches

Table 1. Corpus characteristics of the 20-newsgroup corpus

Pair	Posts for Domain	
	Source	Target
rec vs sci	4762	3169
rec vs talk	4341	2891
sci vs talk	4325	2880

we opted in using the predefined train/test segmentation of the corpus, as it is distributed. Regarding the task, we will limit evaluation to the three more popular evaluation pairs: "rec vs talk", "rec vs sci", "sci vs talk". The main idea behind the separation of these pairs, is that newsgroup posts from relevant but different newsgroups are put in the source/target domains. The "rec vs talk" class for example, may contain posts from the newsgroups "talk.politics.misc", "talk.politics.guns", "rec. motorcycles", and "rec.sport.hockey" as training material representing the source domain, while the test data (representing the target domain) may comprise from posts of the following newsgroups: "talk.politics.mideast", "talk.religion.misc", "rec.autos" and "rec.sport.baseball".

4.2   Experiment Setting

All posts in the three pairs of interest were pre-processed, in order for words to be recognised. A feature space from the posts constituting the training material was extracted, using the approach described in subsection 3.2, which extracts the top scoring words according to their TF-IDF weights, the number of which is controlled through a percentage of the total words of each post. This parameter was set to 0.003%, as it was found to roughly correspond to about one word from each post, leading for example to 4564 features for "rec vs sci", whose training material contains 4762 newsgroup posts. The reason behind this choice was to avoid possible over-fitting in the presence of too many features, and to provide our domain adaptation approach a chance to discover a large number of features from the target domain. As a measure of comparison, in [22] an initial feature space of 2000 features was selected.

Another point of interest is the choice of the machine learning algorithm, which will be used in order to learn a classification model. Support Vector Machines (SVMs) [6] are quite popular as a base case in model adaptation problems, since prior studies found SVMs to offer the best performance, at least for document classification using a bag-of-words representation [10,21]. However, since our approach expands the feature space, we wanted to evaluate the effect of the augmented feature space with the least possible intervention from the chosen machine learning algorithm. Thus, we selected one of the simplest machine learning algorithms available, the k-nearest neighbour algorithm (kNN). kNN does not have a training phase, as it just classifies test instances using a similarity metric to measure distances from the training instances. In all experiments reported in this work, a kNN implementation was used with $k = 1$, and cosine similarity as the distance metric.

The bag-of-words representation was used for all experiments in this paper. Under this representation, each document (newsgroup post) is represented with a single vector, which has the same dimension as the feature space in use. The value for each feature is a real number, the TF-IDF weight of the feature in the document. The characteristics of the 20-newsgroup corpus, as well as evaluation results for the base classifier are shown in Tables 1 and 2 respectively.

4.3   Evaluation Results

The evaluation results of our approach are shown in Table 2. The upper part of Table 2 contains the evaluation results of our approach. The rows correspond to the examined pairs of newsgroups, while columns include information about the performance of the kNN classifier for the feature-space expansion phase. Evaluation results are presented in terms of precision, recall and F-measure (F_1). In table columns concerning recall, the improvement from the corresponding base case is also displayed, as difference between percentages. The lower part of Table 2 contains evaluation results from [19], where two model adaptation approaches were evaluated and compared with SVMs, used as a base case. As

Table 2. Evaluation results on domain adaptation for the 20-newsgroup corpus. Results from [19] are also shown for comparison purposes.

Feature space expansion based on text relatedness		
Pair	kNN ($k = 1$, cosine similarity)	
	Accuracy (base)	Accuracy (model adaptation)
rec vs sci	40.07%	55.35% (+15.28)
rec vs talk	51.78%	68.52% (+16.74)
sci vs talk	41.67%	58.44% (+16.77)
(Shi, Fan and Ren, 2008) [19]		
Pair	Accuracy (base/SVM)	Accuracy (TrAdaBoost)	Accuracy (AcTraK)
rec vs sci	59.1%	67.4% (+8.3)	70.6% (+11.5)
rec vs talk	60.2%	72.3% (+12.1)	75.4% (+15.2)
sci vs talk	57.6%	71.3% (+13.7)	75.1% (+17.5)

we can see from Table 2, the increase in performance achieved by our approach ranges from 15% (for "rec vs sci") to 19% (for "rec vs talk"). In comparison, the algorithm TrAdaBoost [7] achieved an increase ranging from 8% to 14%. The algorithm TrAdaBoost employs boosting in a semi-supervised approach, which exploits a small set of labelled data from the target domain, in addition to a large labelled data set from the source domain, in order to minimise the importance of labelled data from source domain (through weighting) whose distribution does not match the one of the target domain. AcTraK [19] achieves an additional improved of about 4% compared to TrAdaBoost, with the help of active learning in a semi-supervised approach, where labelled data may be asked when necessary. Our approach outperforms both approaches that represent the state of the art in the field, when applied on the task of document classification.

In addition, another interesting aspect of feature space expansion should be noted: the classifiers are able to provide an answer for a much larger number of newsgroup posts, even if the answer is not correct. For example, only 1571 (out of 3169) posts of the target domain contained features from the feature space of the source domain, in the case of the "rec vs sci" pair. After our approach has expanded the feature space with features from the target domain, 2309 posts of the target domain contained at least one feature from the augmented feature space, offering the possibility for classifying a larger number of posts.

5   Conclusions

In this paper, a domain adaptation approach was presented, that exploits text relatedness in the form of WordNet synonymity, in order to augment an initial feature space, derived from the source domain, with new features from the target domain. The proposed approached was empirically evaluated with the help of a manually annotated corpus. Evaluation results suggest that our approach can achieve an improvement comparable to other approaches that can be found in the bibliography, despite the fact that it employs kNN as its classifier to the task of document classification.

Acknowledgments. The author would like to acknowledge partial support of this work from the European Community Seventh Framework Programme, as part of the FP7 – 231854 SYNC3 project.

References

1. Europe Media Monitor (EMM) News Explorer, http://emm.newsexplorer.eu
2. Silobreaker Premium, http://info.silobreaker.com
3. Thoora Service, http://thoora.com
4. Ando, R.K.: Exploiting unannotated corpora for tagging and chunking. In: Proceedings of the ACL 2004 on Interactive poster and demonstration sessions, ACLdemo 2004. Association for Computational Linguistics, Stroudsburg (2004)
5. Blitzer, J., McDonald, R., Pereira, F.: Domain adaptation with structural correspondence learning. In: Proceedings of the 2006 Conference on Empirical Methods in Natural Language Processing, EMNLP 2006 (2006)
6. Cortes, C., Vapnik, V.: Support-vector networks. Machine Learning 20(3), 273–297 (1995), http://dx.doi.org/10.1007/BF00994018
7. Dai, W., Yang, Q., Xue, G., Yu, Y.: Boosting for transfer learning. In: Proceedings of the 24th International Conference on Machine Learning, ICML 2007 (2007)
8. Daumé III, H., Deoskar, T., McClosky, D., Plank, B., Tiedemann, J. (eds.): Proceedings of the 2010 Workshop on Domain Adaptation for Natural Language Processing. Association for Computational Linguistics, Uppsala (2010)
9. Daumé III, H., Kumar, A., Saha, A.: Frustratingly easy semi-supervised domain adaptation. In: Proceedings of the 2010 Workshop on Domain Adaptation for Natural Language Processing (2010)

10. Dumais, S., Platt, J., Heckerman, D., Sahami, M.: Inductive learning algorithms and representations for text categorization. In: Proceedings of the Seventh International Conference on Information and Knowledge Management, CIKM 1998, pp. 148–155. ACM, New York (1998), http://doi.acm.org/10.1145/288627.288651

11. Gabrilovich, E., Markovitch, S.: Feature generation for text categorization using world knowledge. In: Proceedings of the 19th International Joint Conference on Artificial Intelligence, IJCAI 2005, pp. 1048–1053. Morgan Kaufmann Publishers Inc., San Francisco (2005)

12. Gabrilovich, E., Markovitch, S.: Feature generation for text categorization using world knowledge. In: IJCAI 2005, pp. 1048–1053 (2005)

13. Lang, K.: 12th International Conference on Machine Learning (ICML 1995) (1995)

14. McClosky, D., Charniak, E., Johnson, M.: Reranking and self-training for parser adaptation. In: Proceedings of the 21st International Conference on Computational Linguistics and the 44th Annual Meeting of the Association for Computational Linguistics, ACL-44, pp. 337–344. Association for Computational Linguistics, Stroudsburg (2006)

15. Miller, G.A.: Wordnet: a lexical database for english. Commun. ACM 38(11), 39–41 (1995)

16. Navigli, R.: Word sense disambiguation: A survey. ACM Comput. Surv. 41(2), 10:1–10:69 (2009)

17. Pan, S.J., Yang, Q.: A survey on transfer learning. IEEE Transactions on Knowledge and Data Engineering 22(10), 1345–1359 (2010)

18. Sarris, N., Potamianos, G., Renders, J.M., Grover, C., Karstens, E., Kallipolitis, L., Tountopoulos, V., Petasis, G., Krithara, A., Gallé, M., Jacquet, G., Alex, B., Tobin, R., Bounegru, L.: A System for Synergistically Structuring News Content from Traditional Media and the Blogosphere. In: Cunningham, P., Cunningham, M. (eds.) eChallenges e-2011 Conference Proceedings. IIMC International Information Management Corporation, Florence, Italy, October 26-28 (2011)

19. Shi, X., Fan, W., Ren, J.: Actively transfer domain knowledge. In: Daelemans, W., Goethals, B., Morik, K. (eds.) ECML PKDD 2008, Part II. LNCS (LNAI), vol. 5212, pp. 342–357. Springer, Heidelberg (2008), http://dx.doi.org/10.1007/978-3-540-87481-2_23

20. Thrun, S., Pratt, L.Y.: Learning to Learn. Kluwer Academic Publishers (1998)

21. Yang, Y., Liu, X.: A re-examination of text categorization methods. In: Proceedings of the 22nd Annual International ACM SIGIR Conference on Research and Development in Information Retrieval, SIGIR 1999, pp. 42–49. ACM, New York (1999), http://doi.acm.org/10.1145/312624.312647

22. Zhang, J., Shakya, S.S.: Knowledge transfer for feature generation in document classification. In: Proceedings of the 2009 International Conference on Machine Learning and Applications, ICMLA 2009, pp. 255–260. IEEE Computer Society, Washington, DC (2009)

Specifying a Semantic Wiki Ontology through a Collaborative Reconceptualisation Process

António Lucas Soares[1,2], Cristovão Sousa[1,3], and Carla Pereira[1,3]

[1] INESC Porto, Campus da FEUP, Rua Dr. Roberto Frias, 378, 4200-465 Porto, Portugal
[2] DEI, FEUP, University of Porto, Rua Dr. Roberto Frias, sn 4200-465 Porto, Portugal
[3] CIICESI-ESTGF-IPP, Rua do Curral, 4610 – 156 Margaride, Felgueiras, Portugal
{asoares,cpsousa,csp}@inescporto.pt

Abstract. This paper describes an action-research approach to the specification of an ontology to be applied in the information organisation of a community of forest planning experts. Like many others, a community of forest planning experts does not see their technical domains in unison, rather it voices several points of view that need to be shared and understood. This research started by addressing the practical problem of achieving an effective information structure and organisation for a semantic wiki platform. This was supported by a method and platform for the collaborative specification of ontologies: conceptME. Simultaneously, an empirical study was carried out aiming at understanding better how a technical community pragmatically develops conceptual representations of a domain. The results of this research show the benefits of collaboration in the development of conceptual models for knowledge organisation and information retrieval.

Keywords: conceptualisation process, knowledge organisation, action-research.

1 Introduction

Knowledge management, in the context of a technical community, can be supported by several types of content management systems, semantic wikis being one of them. A semantic wiki provides the tools to describe and organise a community generated information (content) [1] in a way that is meaningful and conceptually related with the scientific and technical domains of work. Nevertheless, to fulfill this potential, the knowledge organisation principles, models and techniques, as well as the governance of the collaborative activities should be shared and agreed by the community. As argued in [2], a common conceptualisation of the domains involved in a project is the cornerstone for an effective and efficient management the project's (i) information organisation, classification and retrieval, (ii) knowledge sharing and (iii) collaboration governance and support. Setting up an information/knowledge organisation system implies that all partners share (even if implicitly) a set of conceptual structures (concepts, their descriptions and their relationships) with which the domain and processes of work are to be understood. This view is in line with a more interpretive view of knowledge organisation in information science: classification work involves some sort of "interpretive flexibility" in which the distance between what is classified (the object) and those who classify (the subject) is not kept at an artificial distance [3, 4].

Y.T. Demey and H. Panetto (Eds.): OTM 2013 Workshops, LNCS 8186, pp. 618–627, 2013.

The more aligned, with the users conceptual vision, the semantic artifacts (classifications, taxonomies, ontologies) are, the easier will be for them to classify (annotate) a piece of content.

Following a socio-semantic vision of the creation of semantic artifacts, in particular ontologies [5], we have been developing a collaborative platform to support the early phases of an ontology specification. We call it the conceptualisation phase. The conceptME collaborative platform [6], is a "conceptual Modelling Environment" where groups of specialists can find tools and resources to collaboratively develop conceptual representations, organise them in libraries, share them with other colleagues and reuse them when needed. Currently, conceptME supports concept maps as representational notation. For several applications, these conceptual representations can assume the role of ontology specifications (in some ways also known as informal, lightweight ontology representations). The platform is functionally organised as follows: i) a set of functionalities to manage collaborative modelling projects; ii) a collaborative modelling environment, allowing users to build their models individually or editing them collaboratively (either on their own or through available templates), while discussing concepts, relationships and models; iii) a set of terminological services, supported by a domain specific textual corpus, allowing users to associate relevant resources to their projects, performing extraction operations to retrieve candidate terms that can be used in their collaborative process; and iv) a negotiation baseline model to ensure simple negotiation mechanisms, leading to agreements for a shared model [2].

This paper reports and discusses the findings resulting from an action-research project aimed at improving the information organisation of a community's knowledge management system implemented in a semantic wiki platform. This was done through a process of collective reconceptualisation of the meta-data schema (ontology) used to annotate the wiki pages and define its structure.

2   Problem Description

The FORSYS[1] knowledge management system is a semantic wiki-based platform for information management and knowledge sharing within a community of practice dedicated to study decision support systems (DSS) for forest management. The main idea of the FORSYS wiki site is to provide a repository on Decision Support in Forest Management continuously evolving over time and serving as a reference for future DSS projects. In spite of the proven usefulness of the platform, the FORSYS community representatives (developers and final users) identified hindrances to the effective achievement of the knowledge management goals. The initial development of the platform's knowledge organisation structure resulted in a logical structure addressing the established goals. However, two main problems affecting the efficiency of information retrieval were identified.

The first conceptual model implemented was composed by a small number of classes, each with a long list of properties. Although usable, this model had evident drawbacks for the users: long wiki pages made difficult to locate the needed information, need to repeat the same information in several pages, and the need to scroll up

---

[1] COST Action FP0804 - Forest Management Decision Support Systems.

and down instead of navigating between pages through hyperlinking. Another conse-quence of the implemented conceptual model was the rather simplistic way the do-main was apprehended by the users. A domain modelled by few classes characterised by long property lists only enables a superficial understanding as it is difficult to grasp the details from the property lists. A more detailed conceptual account of a domain increases the user's capabilities for undertaking successfully domain related tasks such as searching, retrieving and organising information.

The community managers decided to improve the platform's knowledge organisa-tion structure involving as much as possible the community members. This called for an approach effectively supportive of building a shared understanding of the domain, resulting in a specification of a conceptualisation socially accepted by the community [2]. An approach focused on content, context and addressing social factors in the construction of basic structures of knowledge that would inform the problem solving process, whereas, semantic theories should underlie the development of artefacts to share the information [7].

3   Research Methodology

The redesign of the community knowledge management platform was taken as an op-portunity to research the practices of knowledge organisation and representation of a specific scientific and technical community. Therefore, given the dual objective of the project - (i) to improve the knowledge organisation of the platform (problem solving) and (ii) to know more about about the practices of knowledge organisation and repre-sentation in technical communities (creation of scientific knowledge) - the principles of Action Research (AR) were applied. AR consists in a holistic approach of problem-solving where knowledge is learned by working in a context of action and where people try to work together to address key problems in their organisations. Typically an AR based project involves more or less systematic cycles of action and reflection: in action phases co-researchers test practices and gather evidence; in reflection stages they make sense together and plan further actions [8]. Often, research approaches in this category are also referred as participatory AR [9]. What separates this type of research from gen-eral professional practices is the emphasis on the scientific study, which is to say the researcher studies the problem systematically and ensures the intervention is informed by theoretical considerations. Therefore, much of the researcher's time is spent on refin-ing the methodological tools to suit the exigencies of the situation, and on collecting, analysing, and presenting data on an ongoing, cyclical basis [10].

The problem characterised in the previous section fostered the following research question: "does the collaborative development of conceptual domain models, by rep-resentatives of a technical community, lead to better quality specifications of a knowledge organisation system?". This question addresses two dimensions: the se-mantic process and the semantic artefact. The later is the result of a set of related activities (process) undertaken in collaboration and represents a (semantic) agreement within the technical community. The former includes the collaborative activities structured by the method and mediated by the conceptME platform. These were characterised in the previous section.

The research method adopted was qualitative. Questionnaires and interviews were used to collect preliminary data while the main data collection technique was participatory observation [11]. Content analysis was made by text interpretation (from interviews transcriptions, observation notes), without codification. The findings were collectively interpreted regarding the suitability of the results according to the users expectations. The validity of the results depends on (1) the degree to which the developed artefacts provide a common understanding about the context in which the research was conducted; and (2) to which extent it provides the essential rational not only about how semantic categories are related, but how the achieved models provide the gateways for the semantic wiki structure.

Two expert groups were formed, and a third group of non-domain experts participated with the role of observer and facilitator. The planned actions were developed based on the principles and assumptions of the ColBlend method [2]. Basically, this method proposes three steps: (i) the development of the individual proposals, (ii) publishing of the proposals and (iii) discussion/negotiation/merging of the proposals.

4   Results

From the analysis of the answers of the first questionnaire we become aware that, unsurprisingly, the participants were comfortable with the forest management DSS concept, but not so much with the current conceptualisation of it. Additionally, we verified that all participants had information and knowledge management concerns in their daily activities and they revealed their preferences for graphical knowledge representations, despite of being aware of the difficulties of building such representations. The boundaries of the domain being conceptualised were specified by formulating a set of focus questions to which the models should provide answers. Meetings took place at the end of each step where the results were discussed, based on the data collected from interviews and observation, as well as from the conceptME platform. The first iteration of the AR cycle happened in two moments.

In the moment a) a group composed of FORSYS representatives and KR specialists paved the way for the rest of the project and produced a first conceptual representation of the Decision Support System domain area. Recommendations on how to address the optimisation of conceptual models aimed at specifying a knowledge organisation system were outlined. The moment b) involved two independent FORSYS expert groups debating the two other main domain areas: Lessons Learned and Case Study. It resulted in two models that were the inputs for creating a merged, agreed model in the second iteration. At the end of this moment, we were able to know more about the implicit conceptual relations structures used by the domain experts. The second iteration corresponds to the negotiation and agreement regarding the conceptual models developed by the several groups in the first iteration.

The main result was a complete conceptual model of the FORSYS domain, agreed by the stakeholders and optimised for implementing the knowledge organisation system of the wiki platform. At the end of this iteration, the recommendation process for conceptual relations elicitation in conceptual modelling was completed. Table 1 details the goals and expected results of each AR iteration.

Table 1. Action and research goals and expected results

	action goals	action results	research goals	research results
1st iteration moment a)	• to define the requirements for the metamodel improvement • to elaborate a "proof of concept" for the DSS conceptual model	• a strategy for the improvement of the metamodel • a DSS conceptual model • the DSS metamodel part and the wiki template structure	• to characterise a process of re-conceptualisation by the domain experts in knowledge representation oriented to information organisation and retrieval	• recommendations on how to address the optimisation of conceptual models aimed at specifying knowledge organisation systems
1st iteration moment b)	• to debate and learn, individually, about the *lessons learned* and *case study* conceptualisation	• conceptual representations of the *lessons learned* and *case study* areas of FORSYS (one for each group) • a better and shared understanding of the domain (partial)	• to characterise the use of conceptual relations by the domain experts • to assess the value of using *focus questions* to assist the collaborative development of the models	• knowledge of the implicit conceptual relations structures used by the domain experts
2nd iteration	• to debate, learn and agree about the conceptualisation of the main areas of FORSYS: *DSS, lessons learned* and *case study* • to complete the conceptual specification of the knowledge organisation system for the wiki platform • to specify the semi-automated linking between conceptME and the FORSYS wiki	• a complete conceptual model of the domain, agreed by the stakeholders and optimised for implementing the knowledge organisation system of the wiki platform • validated specification of the semi-automated linking between conceptME and the wiki	• to further characterise the use of conceptual relations by the domain experts • to improve the conceptual negotiation process centred around the discussion of conceptual structures	• optimisation of the recommendation process for conceptual relations elicitation in conceptual modelling

Semantic Wiki Structure

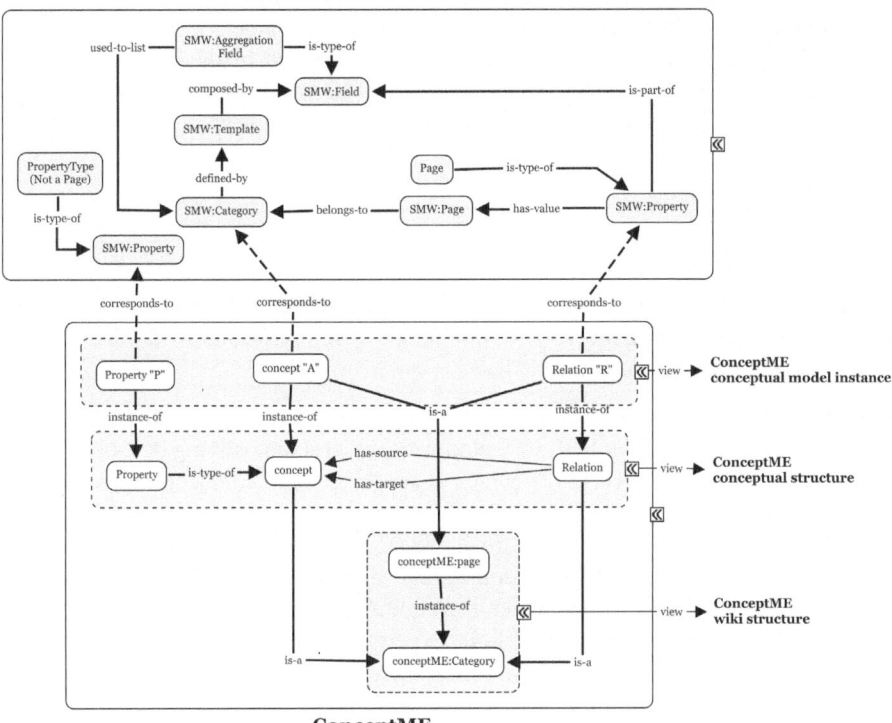

ConceptME

Fig. 1. ConceptME to SMW meta-model mapping

One of the action goals of this project was to determine to what extent conceptME could serve as a modelling front-end to specify the meta-model of the FORSYS wikiplatform, replacing the spreadsheet currently specifying the FORSYS properties model. Figure 1 depicts the meta-model which matches the structure of concepts developed in conceptME with Semantic MediaWiki (SMW).

ConceptME runs itself on top of an instance of SMW which means that every content such as a specific instance of concept, relation or property, added to the platform, is a wiki page belonging to a specific category, namely, a concept, a relation or property. The mapping between the developed models in conceptME and the SMW follow a simple set of basic rules: r1) a concept within a conceptME model (represented as Concept "A" in the above picture), corresponds to a specific category in SMW; r2) a relation connecting two concepts within a conceptME model (represented as Relation "R" in the above picture), corresponds to a specific property in SMW; r2.1) a property (in SMW) resulting from a relation between two concepts (from conceptME) must be of the Page type and its value should be a wiki page. r3) a concept within a conceptME property model (represented as Property "P" in the above picture), corresponds to a specific property in SMW; r3.1) a property (in SMW) resulting from a concept in a property model (from conceptME) can be of any type but Page; r4) a template to define new categories in SMW should be defined to cope with these rules and its member fields types should correspond to the properties translated from conceptME model. r4.1) special fields, such as aggregated fields, should be used in the definition of SMW categories that correspond to the target concept in a typical conceptME conceptual structure. That means, the direction of the link among concepts must be taken into account. The aggregated fields will list all the "source pages" where a specific "target page" is used by means of a property page.

5   Discussion

The results were analysed according to the followed process and the developed models. Given the AR approach, this discussion is based on the data collected by the researchers through participatory observation and joint reflection with the domain experts (acting as co-researchers) [10].

The Process. As described above, the process designed to improve the knowledge organisation structure of the FORSYS platform (the problem solving part of the AR) followed the method devised in [2], which is supported by the conceptME modelling environment. Two groups of specialists addressed the same focus questions and independently developed a concept map for it. Then, the groups debated the similarities and differences of the respective outcomes and, supported by the model merging facilities of conceptME, negotiated a common model (concept map). From our observation, and from the reflection made with the experts, it was evident there was an initial difficulty in understanding entirely the concept maps produced by the other group due to the lack of textual definitions for the concepts. This was overcome by the debate and discussion between the two groups, albeit at the expense of more time to reach an agreement [12]. In fact, an extra effort to sustain and argue in favour of the proposed conceptual structures was observed. The definition of focus questions was very useful as a pragmatic way to define the domain boundaries as well as to assist in the validation of the completeness of the developed concept maps. The roles and composition of the teams developing the models revealed to be important both for the process and the quality of the results. The expert role was fulfilled with people with different backgrounds, differences that contributed positively for debating the different points of view when merging the concept maps. The facilitator role also revealed a major importance. As in every social process involving collaboration, facilitation and leadership are fundamental for the efficiency and effectiveness of the results. From the observations during the project, we conclude that it was beneficial that facilitation encompassed both the knowledge representation and the technical domains.

The Developed Models. Several aspects of the resulting conceptual models were analysed: the set of elicited concepts, the differences between those and the set of concepts (categories and properties) extracted from the existing meta-model, the differences between the elicited concept sets from the two groups, the set of elicited relationships, the meaning of the basic conceptual structures (a concept and directly related concepts). Due to limited space in this paper, we will look at the aspects related to relationships. Conceptual relationships elicitation is difficult in practice leading to oversimplified and imprecise conceptual models. In fact, one of the most difficult problems in a conceptualisation process is the elicitation of conceptual relations [13,14]. While the elicitation of concepts is close to the basic cognitive process of categorisation the same is not true for the relationships as, for their elicitation, additional ontological knowledge is necessary. In the particular case of the FORSYS project the relationships elicitation was of great importance because of the need to transform part of the relatively big sets of concept properties into conceptual structures. As explained before, this would lead to a better organised, less monolithic content organisation in the wiki platform. A great part of the conceptual structures represented in the models were not precise enough due to the use of the "has" relationship. In fact, this relationship had already been amply used in the starting conceptual models proposed to the groups after the 1st iteration (moment a). Although the participants have been invited to use a catalog of predefined types of relations provided by conceptME, and despite of reporting its usefulness, in most cases the groups tended to accept the proposed conceptual structures as final and stable. Observing in detail those structures reveals that the intention of their creators seem to have been to represent: i) a chain of entities and their member fields; ii) a compound structure, in which an entity is composed or made up of other entities; iii) a containment structure, in which an entity belongs to another entity. These results were expected as [15] concludes that the "has" relation is a too generic conceptual relation and most of the times is used to represent a physical relation between entities. In the same line, [16] concludes that "has" is used generally as meaning some kind of contiguity engagement.

During the analysis of the shared model (2nd iteration) a new proposal, derived from the merged one, was developed trying to focus on the mentioned gap. The intention was, on the one hand, to clarify the use of the "has" conceptual relation and, on other hand to re-build the conceptual structures considering a set of primitive relation types [17]. The facilitators helped the groups to debate the meaning of "has" by posing simple questions. Table 2 presents examples of the results.

Table 2. Examples of the transformation of "has" conceptual relations

Conceptual structure (CS)	Posed question	New CS according to the answer
*"Lesson learned **has** DSS"*	**has** Lesson learned a DSS as Scope?	*Lesson learned **has-scope** DSS*
*"Lesson learned **has** Source"* and *"Case study **is-type-of** Source"*	**has** Lesson learned, a Case study as Source?	*Lesson learned **has-source** Case study*

At the beginning, the experts showed themselves some reluctance regarding the new proposal. This is explained due to the fact that they were already committed to a monolithic view of the DSS concept structure, regarding the construction of the FORSYS wiki. Moreover, we found that maintaining the concepts but changing the relations could result in a substantially different perspective over the subject. The relationships are, indeed, the dynamic part of the structures of knowledge. It is important to point out that this kind of conceptual modelling will work the better, the earlier it starts. It is a good practice not to start from what we want to achieve but from what we want to know. Finally, the developed conceptual models were subjected to an assessment against the competency questions. The conclusion was that the models already answered all the questions except one: How lessons learned should be applied? This implies to define the processes on how to apply a lesson, which was out of the scope of FORSYS project.

6   Conclusions and Further Work

The research described in this paper makes a contribution to the scarce literature on domain conceptualisation processes in the context of communities of experts. First, it helped a community of forest planning experts to create a shared conceptualisation of the decision support systems for forest management domain by debating and learning from the joint construction of conceptual models. At the end of this process, the participants acknowledged, both individually and in group, the achievement of an higher level of ontological understanding of the domain. Second, the empirical findings achieved during the action-research cycles will shed more light on the characterisation of socio-semantic processes involved in knowledge representation. This knowledge will be also valuable for improving the conceptME platform in a way that supports more effectively the collaborative conceptualisation processes. In particular, the conclusions about the identification and use of conceptual relations by the experts were of utmost importance. These findings will be reflected in future releases of the conceptME platform. Similar action-research projects need to be done in different expert communities to enable cross-case analysis, enabling more sound generalisation of the research results.

Acknowledgements. This work was partially financed by the ERDF – European Regional Development Fund through the COMPETE Programme (operational programme for competitiveness), by National Funds through the FCT – Fundação para a Ciência e a Tecnologia (Portuguese Foundation for Science and Technology) within project «FCOMP - 01-0124-FEDER-022701»" and by the North Portugal Regional Operational Programme (ON.2 – O Novo Norte), under the National Strategic Reference Framework (NSRF), through the European Regional Development Fund (ERDF).

References

1. Schaffert, S., Bry, F., Baumeister, J., Kiesel, M.: Semantic Wikis. IEEE Software 25(4), 8–11 (2008)
2. Pereira, C., Sousa, C., Soares, A.: Supporting conceptualisation processes in collaborative networks: a case study on an R&D project. International Journal of Computer Integrated Manufacturing, 1–21 (2012)
3. Hjørland, B.: Is classification necessary after Google? Journal of Documentation 68, 299–317 (2012)
4. Mai, J.-E.: The Modernity of Classification. Journal of Documentation 67(4), 710–730 (2011)
5. Pereira, C., Sousa, C., Lucas Soares, A.: A socio-semantic approach to collaborative domain conceptualisation. In: Meersman, R., Herrero, P., Dillon, T. (eds.) OTM 2009 Workshops. LNCS, vol. 5872, pp. 524–533. Springer, Heidelberg (2009)

6. Sá, C., Pereira, C., Soares, A.L.: Supporting collaborative conceptualisation tasks through a semantic wiki based platform. In: Meersman, R., Dillon, T., Herrero, P. (eds.) OTM 2010. LNCS, vol. 6428, pp. 394–403. Springer, Heidelberg (2010)
7. Hjørland, B.: Semantics and knowledge organization. Annual Review of Information Science and Technology 41, 367–405 (2008)
8. Reason, P., Hilary, B.: Handbook of Action Research - Participative Inquiry and Practice. SAGE Publications, London (2008)
9. Baskerville, R., Myers, M.D.: Special issue on action research in information systems: making is research relevant to practice-foreword. Mis Quarterly 28(3) (2004)
10. O'Brien, R.: An Overview of the Methodological Approach of Action Research. In: Richardson, R. (ed.) Theory and Practice of Action Research, Universidade Federal da Paraíba, João Pessoa (2001) (English version),
    http://www.web.ca/~robrien/papers/arfinal.html
    (accessed May 20, 2013)
11. Rahaman, M.A.: Some Trends in the Praxis of Participatory Action Research. In: Handbook of Action Research - Participative Inquiry and Practice, pp. 49–63. SAGE Publications, London (2008)
12. Stock, W.G.: Concepts and Semantic Relations in Information Science. Journal of the American Society for Information Science and Technology 61(10), 1951–1969 (2010)
13. Auger, A., Barrière, C.: Probing Semantic Relations. Probing Semantic Relations: Exploration and Identification in Specialized Texts 23(1) (2010)
14. Elsayed, A.: Relations for Graphical Conceptual Representations. In: 2009 Ninth IEEE International Conference on Advanced Learning Technologies, Riga, Latvia (2009)
15. Shams, R., Elsayed, A.: Development of a conceptual structure for a domain-specific corpus. In: 3rd International Conference on Concept Maps CMC, Estonia, Finland (2008)
16. Nuopponen, A.: Concept Relations: An Update of a Concept Relation Classification. In: Madsen, B.N., Erdman, H. (eds.) Copenhagen 7th International Conference on Terminology and Knowledge Engineering, TKE 2005 (2005)
17. Sousa, C., Soares, A., Pereira, C., Costa, R.: Supporting the identification of conceptual relations in semi-formal ontology development. In: ColabTKR 2012 - Terminology and Knowledge Representation Workshop at International Conference on Language Resources and Evaluation, Istanbul, Turkey (2012)

SOMOCO 2013 PC Co-Chairs Message

Social Computing considers relationships between the evolution of Information and Communication Technologies (ICTs) and the pervasiveness of new devices and embedded sensors, which enable a wide access by people and an effective use of new services.

Social networking is one of the most important topics of social computing and its connection with the use of mobile devices represents one of the most relevant recent phenomena with its challenging problems, such as robustness, privacy, security access, content management in large scale collections, context awareness, multimedia search and retrieval, etc.

Mobile computing plays an important role in many social and collaborative activities involving personal, group and ubiquitous issues, supporting interpersonal connections and involving human technology interaction in different, and dispersed, contexts.

To discuss such research activities, challenges and solutions, the International Workshop on SOcial and MObile COmputing for collaborative environments (SOMOCO'13) was organized in conjunction with the OTM Federated Conferences. This year, six papers were accepted after a peer review process according to originality, significance to theory and practice, readability, and relevance to the workshop topics. The selected papers investigated how relationships among members of a social network can be used to explicitly specify the relevant features of a friend sourcing recommendation algorithm, and provided a multimodal framework for gaming environments, which allows increasing people engagement in a participatory and collaborative way. Moreover, they proposed a new measure of betweenness centrality suitable for Social Internetworking Scenarios, and an efficient solution to the problem of measuring the structural balance of large social networks. Finally, the papers proposed a framework that involves different Social Media in order to promote and develop a sustainable tourism in a shared and participatory approach, and rubric for assessing quality of open educational resources and open courseware based on a socio-constructivist quality model.

SOMOCO 2013 will have a special track from the 9th IFIP workshop on Semantic Web and Web Semantics (SWWS 2013).

The success of the SOMOCO 2013 workshop would not have been possible without the contribution of the OTM 2013 organizers, PC members and authors of papers, all of whom we would like to sincerely thank.

July 2013

Fernando Ferri
Patrizia Grifoni
Arianna D'Ulizia
Maria Chiara Caschera
Irina Kondratova

Y.T. Demey and H. Panetto (Eds.): OTM 2013 Workshops, LNCS 8186, p. 628, 2013.
© Springer-Verlag Berlin Heidelberg 2013

Analyzing Linked Data Quality with LiQuate

Edna Ruckhaus, Oriana Baldizán, and María-Esther Vidal

Universidad Simón Bolívar, Venezuela
{eruckhaus,obaldizan,mvidal}@ldc.usb.ve

Abstract. In the last years, the number of datasets in the Linking Open Data (LOD) cloud and the applications that rely on links between these datasets to discover patterns or potential new associations, have exploded. However, because of data source heterogeneity, published data may suffer of redundancy, inconsistencies or may be incomplete; thus, results generated by linked data based applications may be imprecise or unreliable. We illustrate LiQuate (Linked Data Quality Assessment), a tool that combines Bayesian Networks and rule-based systems to analyze the quality of data and links in the LOD cloud.

1 Introduction

Linking Open Data initiatives have made a diversity of collections available, and facilitate scientists the mining of linked datasets to discover patterns or suggest potential new associations. To ensure trustworthy results, linked data must meet high quality standards; however, data in the LOD cloud has not been necessarily curated, and tools are required to detect possible ambiguities and quality problems. To achieve this goal, we developed LiQuate, a semi-automatic tool able to identify ambiguities among the linked data, and suggest possible inconsistencies and incompleteness. LiQuate implements a two-fold approach that combines Bayesian Networks and rule-based systems to analyze the quality of data and propose new links to resolve the identified ambiguities. First, a Bayesian Network models dependencies among resources in a set of linked datasets [4]; conditional probability tables annotate the nodes of the network and represent joint probability distributions of relationships among resources. Queries against the Bayesian Network represent the probability that different resources have redundant labels or that a link between two resources is missing; thus, the returned probabilities can suggest ambiguities or possible incompleteness in the data or links. Second, a probabilistic rule-based system is used to infer new links that associate equivalent resources, and allows to resolve the ambiguities and incompleteness identified during the exploration of the Bayesian Network.

We demonstrate the data quality validation capabilities of LiQuate and the benefits of the approach on the Life Science datasets: *LinkedCT*[1], *Diseasome*[2], *Drugbank*[3], and *DBPedia*[4] datasets. We show the following key issues:

---

[1] http://www.cs.toronto.edu/~oktie/linkedct/ downloaded Sept 2011.
[2] http://datahub.io/dataset/fu-berlin-diseasome downloaded Sept 2011.
[3] http://datahub.io/dataset/fu-berlin-drugbank downloaded Sept 2011.
[4] http://wiki.dbpedia.org/Downloads32 downloaded Sept 2012.

Y.T. Demey and H. Panetto (Eds.): OTM 2013 Workshops, LNCS 8186, pp. 629–638, 2013.

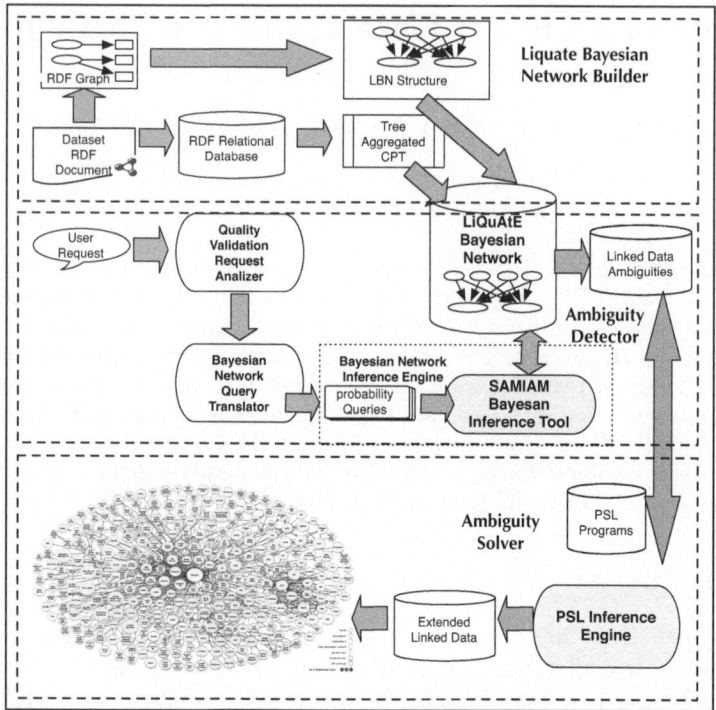

Fig. 1. The LiQuiate System Architecture

redundancy of labels that correspond to drugs in *LinkedCT* and *Drugbank*, and to diseases in *LinkedCT* and *Diseasome*, and incompleteness and inconsistencies of links between these Life Science datasets. The demo is published at http://liquate.ldc.usb.ve.

The structure of this paper is as follows: In Section 2 we present the LiQuate System Architecture and components. Following this section we present the formalization of our approach, the Linked Bayesian Network (LBN). Next we present the related work and our experimental study, and finally, section 6 concludes and outlines interesting future directions.

2   The LiQuate System

LiQuate implements a two-fold approach where first, ambiguities are detected and then, links to solve these ambiguities are inferred and suggested to the user for resolving the identified quality problems; Figure 1 illustrates the LiQuate architecture. Currently, three types of quality validation requests can be expressed: *i*) probability that labels or names of a given (type of) resource are redundant, *ii*) probability of incomplete links among a given set of resources, and *iii*) probability of inconsistent links. LiQuate is comprised of three components: the LiQuate Bayesian Network Builder, the Ambiguity Detector and the Ambiguity Solver. The LiQuate Bayesian Network Builder is a semi-automatic off-line process; it relies on an expert's knowledge about the properties in the RDF linked datasets that are going to be represented in the Bayesian Network. Relevant data is retrieved from SPARQL endpoints, and stored in a relational database to compute the histograms that implement the conditional probability tables (CPTs) associated with the nodes of the network. The `Ambiguity Detector` is a probabilistic model that supports the analysis of the above mentioned linked data quality problems. The `Ambiguity Detector` is in turn comprised of three components: *1)* the `Quality Validation Request Analyzer`, *2)* the `Bayesian Network, Query Translator`, and *3)* the `Bayesian Network Inference Engine`. The `Quality Validation Request Analyzer` receives a user request and decides if it can be satisfied with the existing Bayesian Network. The `Bayesian Network Query Translator` considers the user request and generates the set of queries that must be posted against the Bayesian Network. It also gathers the answers of these queries and answers the user request. Finally, the `Bayesian Network Inference Engine` is responsible of performing the inference process required to answer each of the queries posted against the Bayesian Network; this engine is implemented by the *SamIam* Bayesian Inference Tool[5].

The `Ambiguity Solver` is a rule-based system that infers new links that solve the ambiguity and incompleteness problems identified by the `Ambiguity Detector`. The rule-based system is implemented as a set of probabilistic rules [9] that reason about similarity to generate additional links with a certain degree of uncertainty. These new links may associate resources to control resource redundancy, or to control link inconsistency. The Ambiguity Solver has been implemented on top of the Probabilistic Soft Logic tool (PSL)[6]. The PSL Inference Engine receives a set of weighted rules, and infers with a certain degree of uncertainty when two terms are duplicates, incomplete or incorrect. PSL similarity metrics are implemented to decide when two labels are similar. Inferred data quality problems between two terms are used to suggest RDF intra- and inter-links. The output of this component is an RDF document comprised of `owl:sameAs` links that relate redundant resources; the quality of the new generated links can be determined by experts or against a given ground truth.

To conclude, the conditional probabilistic approach is used to suggest possible ambiguities in linked datasets, while the PSL approach is just used to suggest new links for ambiguity resolution. PSL allows to infer with a certain degree of uncertainty if a given new link can be included to resolve an ambiguity identified by the `Ambiguity Detector`, and this degree can be configured. Thus users can decide the appropriate level of uncertainty for a given domain and assign different ground truths to analyze the quality of the new links. Additionally, in the current version of LiQuate, the `Ambiguity Solver` does not perform any prediction task; it just uses information inferred from the Bayesian network to suggest with a certain degree of uncertainty, a link between two possible redundant concepts. However, it is important to highlight that PSL features can be also exploited to implement prediction techniques that rely on graph analysis algorithms, to

---

[5] http://reasoning.cs.ucla.edu/samiam/help/recursiveconditioning.html

[6] http://psl.umiacs.umd.edu/

determine the density of the linked datasets and based on this, suggest potential missing links. This problem is out of the scope of this paper, and we mainly focus on the `Ambiguity Detector` component.

Finally, Figure 2 presents the workflow that is followed for the construction of the LBN CPTs. The steps are the following:

1. RDF datasets are loaded as vertically partitioned relational tables [1] (one table per property with subject and object columns).
2. A CPT for root nodes `s-<property>` and `o-<property>` is created in O_B through queries to the property tables which count and group the different object or subject values.
3. A CPT for link nodes, `b-<linkprop>-<typeres1>-<typeres2>` is created through queries to the link property tables which count and group the different linked resources.
4. A CPT for join nodes, `s-s-<property1>-<property2>` and other join nodes is created through join queries to the property tables and their parent property tables which count and group the parent object/subject values.
5. All CPT tables are ordered by their probability value, and the frequency histogram is generated. Some auxiliary data structures have been created in order to speed-up the lookup of the CPT histogram values: (1) the *Corr* structure that registers the correspondence of each CPT value with a sequential number, and (2) the *CptIndex* structure for non-root nodes, where for each sequential number representing a parent CPT value, there is a reference to the corresponding entry in the parent's aggregated histogram.

3   The Liquate Bayesian Network

A Liquate Bayesian Network (LBN) is a probabilistic model of a network of linked RDF datasets. It represents all the conditional dependencies among property subjects and objects in single RDF datasets and in linked datasets. The analysis of these dependencies is used to detect linked data quality problems.

The LBN model is based on the Bayesian network model developed for relational domains in [4], the Probabilistic Relational Model (PRM). Although an LBN resembles a PRM, its nodes and arcs have a particular semantics based on the linked RDF graph semantics. Nodes represent property objects and subjects, and intra- and inter-links. Figure 3 presents the LBN for RDF datasets **LinkedCT**, **Diseasome**, **Drugbank** *circa* September 2010.

Definition 1 (LiQuate Bayesian network). *Given an RDF directed graph* $O_R = (V_R, E_R)$ *where* V_R, *and* E_R *are the nodes and arcs in the RDF graph. A* **LiQuate Bayesian network** R_B *for* O_R, *is a pair* $R_B = \langle O_B, CPT_B \rangle$, *where* $O_B = (V_B, E_B)$ *is a DAG.* V_B *are the nodes in* O_B, *and* E_B *are the arcs in* O_B, *and an homomorphism* $f : \mathbb{P}(E_R) \Rightarrow \mathbb{P}(V_B)$ *establishes a mapping between the power set of sets of graph edges (sets of triples) in* O_R *and sets of nodes in* O_B. CPT_B *are the Conditional Probability Tables for each node.*

There are three types of nodes:

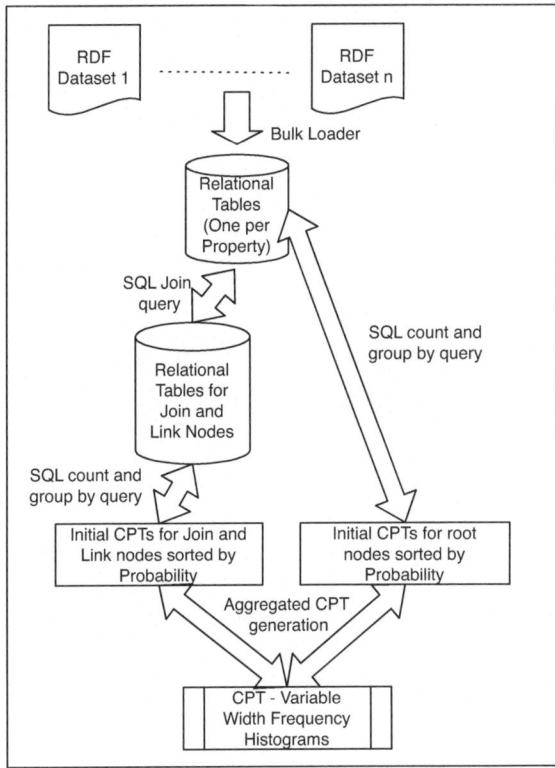

Fig. 2. A Workflow to Build an LBN Given Several RDF Datasets

1. **Value** nodes: `s-<property>` and `o-<property>` represent property subjects or objects in a single dataset. For example, node `o-hasintervention` represents the object values of interventions in clinical trials.
2. **Join** nodes: `s-s-<pro₁>-<pro₂>`, `o-s-<pro₁>-<pro₂>` and `o-o-<pro₁>-<pro₂>` correspond to boolean variables, and represent the matching of subjects or objects in related properties in a single dataset.
   For example, node `s-s-hascondition-hasintervention` represents the "join" over a trial, that is, a condition and an intervention are part of a trial.
3. **Link** nodes: `b-<linkprop>-<typeres₁>-<typeres₂>` corresponds to a boolean variable, and represents the existence of links among related resources. For example, node `b-sameas-condition-disease` represents the existence of *owl:sameAs* links among conditions in Clinical Trials (LinkedCT) and diseases in Diseasome.

The first two types of nodes represent data items and intra-dataset links [12], respectively, while the third type of nodes corresponds to inter-dataset links. Arcs represent dependencies between nodes. The event represented by node `s-s-hascondition-hasintervention` is conditioned by the values of condition, intervention (nodes `o-hascondition` and `o-hasintervention`), by the existence of

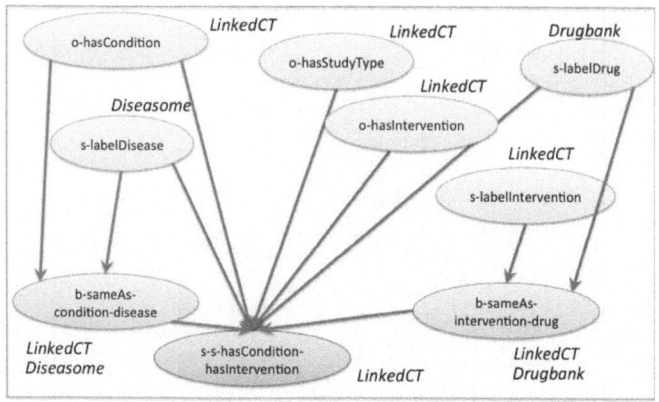

Fig. 3. LiQuate Bayesian network for the Life Sciences Domain

an *owl:sameAs* link among the condition and a disease, and among the intervention and a drug (nodes `b-sameAs-condition-disease` and `b-sameAs-intervention-drug`). For each modeled dataset, there is a set of nodes annotated with the URI of the dataset. The basic LBN inference task is a marginal posterior probability query *prob(X|e)*, where the marginal variable X is represented by a **Join** or **Link** node, and where the evidence E is set up according to the particular query. LiQuate uses an exact inference algorithm: *Shenoy-Shafer*. For example, a query will check if given - the evidence - that the drug *Paclitaxel* has as possible disease target *Leukemia*, there is a clinical trial that backs this relationship with an equivalent - *owl:sameAs* - condition and intervention:

*prob(*s-s-hascondition-hasIntervention|
        b-possibleDisease-drug-disease ∧ s-labelDrug='Paclitaxel' ∧
        s-labelDisease='Leukemia' ∧ b-sameAs-condition-disease ∧
        b-sameAs-intervention-drug)

The answer to this probability query is 1.0; this result indicates that this relationship is backed by a clinical trial.

The homomorphism $f : \mathbb{P}(E_R) \to \mathbb{P}(V_B)$ establishes a mapping between O_R and O_B. f defines the set of nodes V_B. The CPT_B are multidimensional histograms ordered by value. If a node v is a source node, the histogram will be one-dimensional, because in this case the CPT_B only represents the distribution of values taken up by the variable represented by the node. The size of a CPT for one node depends on the number of predecessors, and on the number of possible values for the node and its predecessors. In our case the structure of the Bayesian network is related to the number of properties in the RDF datasets; in general, the RDF datasets are not complex in terms of their classes and properties. As to the set of possible values, these were aggregated in an indexed histogram that represents the CPT values.

4 Related Work

The publication of clinical trials as linked RDF data is described in [6]. In this work, the authors emphasize the challenges of linking resources in the trials data, and linking different datasets. The authors demonstrated how state-of-the-art approximate string matching and ontology-based semantic matching can be used for discovery of such semantic links between several data sources. Differently from our work, the emphasis is on link discovery while LiQuate's focus is on the detection of linked data quality problems and the enrichment of data links.

The framework xCurator proposed by Hassas et al [7] aims to produce high quality linked RDF data from semi-structured sources where unique URIs are generated, duplicates are merged, resources are linked to vocabularies using entity type extraction techniques, and links are established to external RDF sources. The framework was applied to clinical trial and to bibliographic data, and the quality of the data was improved with respect to previous transformations that were done manually. This work is focused on the entity extraction component as the means to improve linked data quality; Contrary, LiQuate exploits semantics encoded in the Bayesian network during a statistical inference process, and is able to suggest possible ambiguities and inconsistencies not only by considering the names of the entities, but also by looking at the different entities that are related to the studied entities.

In [8], the applicability and benefits of using linked data in the Life Sciences domain is studied, specifically for clinical trials, drugs, and related sources. The authors present several challenges and among them, the need of progress in finding links between data items where no commonly used identifiers exist, and the need to develop techniques for record linkage and duplicate detection with methods from the database and knowledge representation communities. The challenges presented summarize some of the data quality problems that we detected in our experimental study.

Demartini et. al. [2] develop a probabilistic framework in combination with crowdsourcing techniques, in order to improve the quality of links in the LOD cloud. The system, *ZenCrowd* combines algorithmic and manual matching techniques to link entities. It exploits probabilistic models using factor-graphs to represent probabilistic variables. This approach is based on evaluating several alternative links, whereas our system proposes evaluating the quality of the current links in some specific domain.

Network approximate measures are used to analyze the quality of linked data in [5] using the LINK-QA framework. An original local network and extended networks are constructed around resources to be evaluated by querying the Web of Data. Five metrics are used. degree, clustering coefficient, number of *owl:sameAs* chains, centrality and richness of description. Fürber et. al. [3] propose a conceptual model for data quality management that allows to formulate a set of data quality and data cleaning rules, classification of data quality problems, and the computation of quality scores for Semantic Web data sources. The authors present several use cases and competency questions, but these are all related to the quality of the classes, properties and instances on the datasets, but not in the consistency or quality of the links. A set of quality and cleaning rules is established, but none of these refer to links among datasets.

Memory et. al. [11] present a work on summarization of annotation graphs where PSL is the framework used. The work integrates the multiple types of evidence from the annotation links, the various similarity metrics, and two graph summarization heuristics: a similarity heuristic and a summarization heuristic within a probabilistic model, using PSL. This approach uses PSL to model the summarization graph whereas in our work, a PSL system is used to propose additional links with a certain degree of uncertainty.

5   Experimental Study

As of September 2011, LinkedCT contains 106,308 trials, 2.7 million entities and over 25 million RDF triples. Additionally, we consider the following datasets that are linked to LinkedCT: *i*) Drugbank (over 765,936 triples), *ii*) Diseasome (around 91,182 triples), and *iii*) DBPedia (links from LinkedCT 25,476). We built local RDF storage with LinkedCT triples and the triples from these three datasets that are related to LinkedCT. The Bayesian network and its corresponding CPT's were computed and stored in the *SamIam* Bayesian Inference Tool. The generated network is comprised of 17 nodes and the aggregated CPTs are of up to 167, 616 entries; for the cases to be shown, the average response time of LiQuate is 4, 715 ms.

For each dataset, we partition the entities according to their label, e.g., diseases are partitioned according to their name. The metrics that are considered in the experimental study are % of partitions with size > 1, % partitions with at least one *owl:sameAs* (resp. *rdfs:seeAlso*) link, and % partitions with all labels with *owl:sameAs*(resp. *rdfs:seeAlso*) links. We conducted the following studies:

Ambiguities between labels of Interventions or Drugs: starting with Alemtuzumab as an exemplar, we retrieve the intersection of Monoclonal antibodies and Antineoplastic agents. This creates a dataset of 12 drugs: Alemtuzumab, Bevacizumab, Brentuximab vedotin, Cetuximab, Catumaxomab, Edrecolomab, Gemtuzumab, Ipilimumab, Ofatumumab, Panitumumab, Rituximab, and Trastuzumab. These drugs are frequently tested in clinical trials, and there are up to 723 clinical trials for a given drug or intervention, e.g., the intervention that corresponds to the drug Alemtuzumab is associated with 112 different clinical trials. We can observe that 15.74% of partitions have a size > 1, i.e., are redundant.

Incompleteness of links between LinkedCT, Drugbank, Diseasome and DBPedia: We will consider the family of the 12 drugs and for each of the partitions induced by duplicated labels, we consider the owl:sameAs and rdfs:seeAlso links. Some cases are: a percentage of redundant labels is not linked through owl:sameAs to neither Drugbank or DBPedia, but 100% of the labels are linked through rdfs:seeAlso, e.g., Bevacizumab; none of the redundant labels is linked to Drugbank or DBPedia, e.g., Brentuximab vedotin; in this case, the drug is not present in Drugbank; all of the redundant labels are linked to DBPedia and none to Drugbank, e.g., Catumaxomab; a percentage of redundant labels is linked to DBPedia through `owl:sameAs`, all of them are linked to DBPedia through `rdfs:seeAlso` and none to Drugbank, e.g., Ipilimumab.

Inconsistencies of links between LinkedCT, Drugbank, Diseasome and DBPedia: We will analyze if the relationships that represent that a disease is a possible target of a drug and if a drug can target a disease, are supported by a clinical trial, i.e., diseases targeted by a drug with a link *possibleDiseaseTarget*, are supported by at least one clinical trial with a condition and drug intervention, and vice versa. Approximately 10, 000 probability queries were generated for each drug and disease and all the combinations of linked (through `owl:sameAs`) conditions and interventions. The marginal node is `s-s-hascondition-hasintervention` (violet node in Figure 3), and the evidence is a disease, drug, condition, intervention and the existence of `owl:sameAs` links among them. The result is that only 13,5% of the drugs and targeted diseases are supported by clinical trials that can be found through `owl:sameAs` links. Similarly, another hypothesis is that drugs that can possibly treat diseases (*possibleDrug* links) are supported by the same number of clinical trials. The result is 13, 5% and this number suggests that both links *possibleDiseaseTarget* and *possibleDrug* are the inverse of each other. Particularly, for the dataset of 12 drugs we can observe the following: the drugs Brentuximab vedotin, Ipilimumab and Ofatumumab do not appear in Drugbank while these drugs have been studied in a large number of clinical trials. The rest of these 12 drugs do appear in Drugbank, but are associated with much less diseases through the property *possibleDiseaseTarget* in Drugbank, than to conditions through a clinical trial in LinkedCT; e.g., the drug Cetuximab can possibly target eighteen diseases while this drug has been tested in completed clinical trials for 82 conditions; only four of the eighteen diseases in the property *possibleDiseaseTarget* in Drugbank, are included in the list of 82 conditions in LinkedCT. This ambiguity can be also observed in the rest of the drugs.

6   Conclusions and Future Work

We present LiQuate, a data and link validation tool that relies on a Bayesian Network to identify redundancies, incompleteness and inconsistencies, and makes use of a probabilistic rule-based system to infer the links that solve the identified quality problems with a certain degree of uncertainty. We demonstrate the main quality validation capabilities of LiQuate, and illustrate different quality problems that may currently occur in the LOD cloud. Particularly, we can observe some ambiguities that suggest the experts to check for uncontrolled redundancy, incompleteness or inconsistency: *i*) the same label or name of intervention is assigned to different resources, *ii*) incomplete `owl:sameAs` and `rdfs:seeAlso` links between datasets, and *iii*) associations between drugs and diseases in Drugbank may be not supported by trials in LinkedCT. Provenance information of the datasets will be taken into account in order to not only enrich the datasets with the solution to the quality problems, but to be able to modify them.

Furthermore, the generation of the CPT tables for the LBN can be developed using the RDFStats[10] statistics generator, or use their API for accessing statistics including several estimation functions that also support SPARQL filter-like expressions. Finally, experimental studies will be developed for other domains in order to do a thorough evaluation of the system and validate the proposed links. Particularly, we plan to validate links to terms of Geonames[7].

References

1. Abadi, D.J., Marcus, A., Madden, S.R., Hollenbach, K.: Scalable semantic web data management using vertical partitioning. In: Proceedings of VLDB 2007 (2007)
2. Demartini, G., Difallah, D.E., Cudré-Mauroux, P.: Zencrowd: leveraging probabilistic reasoning and crowdsourcing techniques for large-scale entity linking. In: WWW (2012)
3. Fürber, C., Hepp, M.: Towards a vocabulary for data quality management in semantic web architectures. In: EDBT/ICDT Workshop on Linked Web Data Management (2011)
4. Getoor, L., Taskar, B., Koller, D.: Selectivity estimation using probabilistic models. SIGMOD Record 30(2), 461–472 (2001)
5. Guret, C., Groth, P., Stadler, C., Lehmann, J.: Linked data quality assessment through network analysis. In: ISWC 2011 Posters and Demos (2011)
6. Hassanzadeh, O., Kementsietsidis, A., Lim, L., Miller, R.J., Wang, M.: Linkedct: A linked data space for clinical trials. CoRR, abs/0908.0567 (2009)
7. Hassanzadeh, O., Yeganeh, S.H., Miller, R.J.: Linking semistructured data on the web. In: WebDB (2011)
8. Jentzsch, A., Andersson, B., Hassanzadeh, O., Stephens, S., Bizer, C.: Enabling Tailored Therapeutics with Linked Data. In: Proceedings of the WWW 2009 Workshop on Linked Data on the Web (LDOW 2009) (2009)
9. Kimmig, A., Bach, S.H., Broecheler, M., Huang, B., Getoor, L.: A short introduction to probabilistic soft logic. In: NIPS Workshop on Probabilistic Programming: Foundations and Applications (2012)
10. Langegger, A., Wöß, W.: Rdfstats - an extensible rdf statistics generator and library. In: DEXA Workshops (2009)
11. Memory, A., Kimmig, A., Bach, S.H., Raschid, L., Getoor, L.: Graph summarization in annotated data using probabilistic soft logic. In: URSW (2012)
12. Ruckhaus, E., Vidal, M.-E.: The BAY-HIST Prediction Model for RDF Documents. In: Proceedings of the 2nd ESWC Workshop on Inductive Reasoning and Machine Learning on the Semantic Web-CEUR, vol. 611, pp. 30–41 (2010)

---

[7] http://www.geonames.org/

A Prufer Sequence Based Approach to Measure Structural Similarity of XML Documents

Ramanathan Periakaruppan and Rethinaswamy Nadarajan

PSG College of Technology, Coimbatore, India
rm_pk@yahoo.com

Abstract. XML is a W3C standard for exchange of semi-structured data. For many applications it is necessary to extract information from semi-structured data which is a complex task. In this paper we address the problem of computing structural similarity of XML documents which play a crucial role in clustering process. Previous works on path based approach fail to capture the sibling relationship among the nodes and also ignore the similarity when the nodes in the paths to be matched, are not in the same order but still convey same semantics. Another weakness of this approach is in the case of the partial path match, is that the level information is not taken into account when the nodes to be compared appear in different hierarchical level. To address these issues, we describe a method based on Prufer Sequence for measuring the structural similarity of XML documents, in this paper. Benefit of Prufer sequence based representation is that, it stores the ancestor-descendant and sibling relation. XML trees are encoded based on Prufer sequence which establishes a one-to-one mapping between XML tree and sequence. Instead of extracting all paths only common nodes are extracted based on Prufer sequence code. We have devised an algorithm to compute similarity by exploring all relations among the common nodes namely parent-child, ancestor-descendant and sibling. The experimental results show that the proposed approach is effective.

Keywords: XML, Structural Similarity, Prufer Sequence.

1 Introduction

Due to the increasing usage of XML documents, efficient techniques are needed to manage high volume of XML data, so that it can be used in many web based applications. Semantic Web technologies RDF, RDF Schema and OWL are based on XML and study of the structural similarity of XML documents are easily extensible to ontology matching. Two important ontology matching methods are Linguistic Similarity Matching (LSM) and Structure Similarity Matching (SSM). Wang et al. [18] stress the importance of structural information of ontology in case of ontology mapping. In this paper, our focus is on matching similar XML documents based on structural semantic relations. Main objective of this study is to integrate heterogeneous XML documents so that the information is more relevant to the user. Our proposed algorithm is capable of finding structural relations among XML elements and hence we can use it

Y.T. Demey and H. Panetto (Eds.): OTM 2013 Workshops, LNCS 8186, pp. 639–648, 2013.
© Springer-Verlag Berlin Heidelberg 2013

to find the structural relations among concepts in ontology mapping. Grouping similar XML document gains much attention in research communities [1]. Since XML documents are hierarchical in nature grouping /clustering of similar XML documents is a challenging task [2]. Challenges are mainly due to the heterogeneous nature of XML documents (i.e.) XML documents are from different sources and they do not follow a common DTD/Schema. The key factor is to find an efficient technique for computing similarity between XML documents.

XML document similarity, in general, can be classified as structure, content and semantic. The term semantic is applicable to content, element name and structure. In this paper our focus is on computing structural similarity by considering semantics. By structural similarity we mean that the nodes of XML documents to be compared have same hierarchical order. However, we observe that sometimes even though the nodes of the paths to be compared are in different hierarchical order and still the semantics are not affected. For example the paths *actor→movie →title* and *movie →title → actor* are semantically the same. Also two nodes that have parent-child relationship in one document may have ancestor-descendant or sibling relationship in another document and still they are semantically similar.

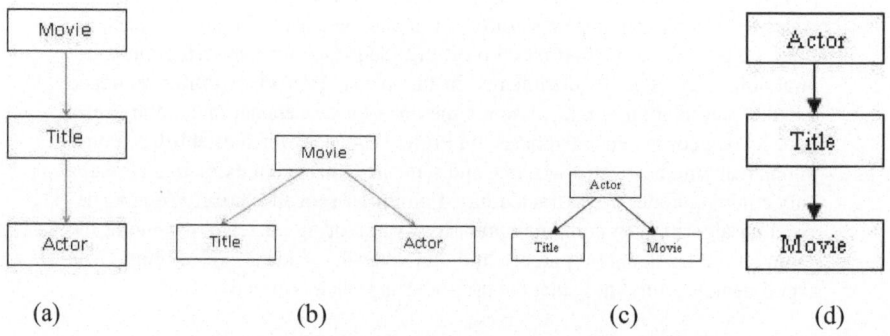

Fig. 1. XML document Structural Similarity example

For example in Fig 1, the elements *title* and *actor* have parent-child relation in document (a), sibling relation in document (b) and inverse parent-child relation in both document (c) and document (d) (i.e. when compared with document (a)) and in all the cases they have similarity based on semantics.

Another issue in structural similarity is the partial match. For example in Fig 2 the path *Book →title →id* in document (b) is partially mapped with the path *Book →id* in document (a). Here the *id* element occurs at different levels in both documents and to compute the similarity accurately, level weight should be considered.

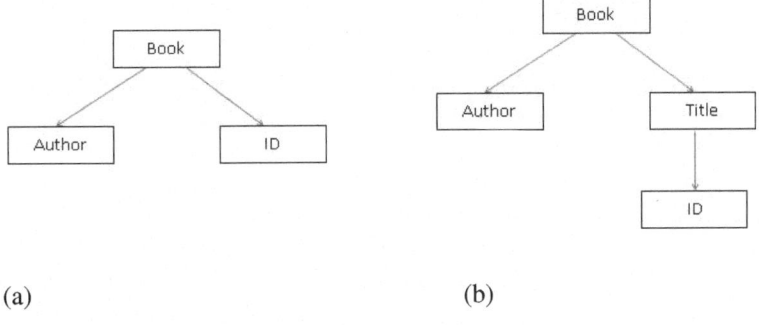

(a)   (b)

Fig. 2. Partial Match example

From the above examples we observe that the following factors are to be considered to compute XML document structural similarity using path based approach.

1. Sibling relation.
2. Ancestor–descendant relation.
3. Nodes in two paths are the same but in different hierarchical order.
4. Level weights should be given to nodes in case of partial match.
5. Extraction of common paths.
6. To capture all relations between nodes an efficient XML representation is needed.

Existing path based approaches handle some of the above issues but not all. A comparison is provided in Table 1.

Table 1. Comparison of various path based approaches

Approach	Extraction of paths	Sibling Match	Ancestor-Descendant Match with Level weight	Nodes in different hierarchical order	XML Representation
Rafiei et al. [3]	All paths including subpaths	No	No	No	Path Set
Buttler et al. [4]	Reduction of paths based on Shingle	No	No	No	Reduced path sets in terms of hash values
Joshi et al.[5]	All Xpaths	Partial	No	No	Xpath Set
Zhang et al.[6]	Paths as closed frequent association tag sequence	Yes	Yes, without level weight	No	Frequent Association tag sequence (FATS) set

2   Related Work

Earlier approaches for finding structural similarity between XML documents are based on tree edit distances. In this approach XML documents are represented as ordered labeled trees and they aim to compute cheapest edit sequence operations that can transform one tree to another. Tai [7] was first to introduce non exponential algorithm for finding minimum edit distance between trees. Shasha et al. [8] provides an edit distance algorithm in which they allow insertion, deletion and relabeling of single nodes anywhere in the tree, however insertion and deletion of entire sub trees were not considered. Later Chawathe [9] framed an algorithm with time complexity $O(n^2)$ which considers the edit operations, insertion and deletion at the leaf node level and allows replacement of node anywhere in the tree but disallows the move operation. Identification of sub tree similarities was considered by Nierman et al. [10], however the overall complexity of the algorithm is $O(n^2)$. Combined methods of tree edit distance and semantic similarity based on information retrieval was proposed by Tekli et al. [11]. In general XML document similarity based on tree edit distance needs to compute pair wise similarity and hence there is huge computational complexity and has scalability issue.

Various algorithms were proposed to measure XML document based on path [3,4,5]. Buttler [4] shows that the similarity comparison can be reduced to constant time complexity by using path Shingle technique. Rafiei et al. [3] shows that two XML documents are similar if they have more common paths in their path sets and they have a linear time complexity. Joshi et. al [5] uses XPaths which captures the sibling information and the experimental results shows improved clustering results when compared with normal path based approaches. However in all these approaches semantic structural similarity is not considered. Vinson et. al [12] developed an algorithm PathSim which uses edit distance algorithm to compute similarity and does not consider the structural similarity with semantics. Choi et. al [13] proposed a clustering method called PSim based on path similarities of XML data. The clustering process was more efficient and scalable than the previous approaches, however the structural similarity with semantics is not considered. Zhang et. al [6] proposed a method for clustering XML documents by computing similarity measure based on mining frequent association tags. Here, all types of relation among the nodes are considered, the process, however fails to detect when the hierarchical order of node changes and also the similarity measure doesn't consider level weight of nodes.

3   XML Document Representation Based on Prufer Sequence

In this section we introduce some basic definitions and concepts to model XML document tree as Prufer Sequence, benefits of Prufer Sequence based representation and the method of generating prufer sequence.

3.1   Basic Definitions

Definition 3.1 [XML Document Tree]

An XML document is an rooted ordered labeled directed Tree $T=(R_T, N_T, E_T, L_T)$ where R_T is the root node of the tree T, N_T is finite set of nodes, $E_T \subseteq [N_T]^2$ is set of edges and each node $n \in N_T$ has a label from L_T.

Definition 3.2 [Parent – Child]

Let $n_i, n_j \in N_T$. Then ni ,nj have Parent-Child relation if $(n_i,n_j) \in E_T$.

Definition 3.3 [Path]

A Path from node n_1 to n_k is a sequence of nodes $<n_1,n_2,...n_k>$ such that n_i is the Parent of n_{i+1} for $1 \le i < k$.

Definition 3.4 [Ancestor-Descendant]

If there is a Path from the node n_i to n_j then the node pair (n_i, n_j) is said to have Ancestor-Descendant relation.

Definition 3.5 [Sibling]

Let $n_1, n_2 \in N_T$. Then n_1 and n_2 are said to have Sibling Relation if $(n_1,n_p) \in E_T$ and $(n_2,n_p) \in E_T$ where n_p is parent of both n1 and n2. If n_2 has greater order number than n_1, then n_2 is said to be Right-Sibling of n_1.

Definition 3.6 [Inverse Parent-Child]

Let T_1 and T_2 be two trees. Two nodes ni and nj are said to have Inverse Parent-Child relation if $(n_i,n_j) \in E_{T1}$ and $(n_j,n_i) \in E_{T2}$.

3.2   Benefits of Prufer Sequence Based Representation

Many techniques are available to represent structural information of XML documents and some of them are Level Structure, Level Edge and Path Set. The main drawback of these techniques is all structural relations cannot be represented. Level Structure method fails to capture parent/child or sibling relations, Level Edge fails to capture partial relations and Path set method fails to capture sibling relations. But prufer sequence based representation overcome these limitations by capturing all structural relations namely parent-child, ancestor-descendant and sibling.

3.3   Construction of Prufer Sequence

In order to capture structural relation among nodes, XML documents are represented based on Prufer Sequence code. Prufer [14] proposed an algorithm that describes the one-to-one mapping between tree and sequence by deleting one node from the tree at a time until two nodes is left. To construct Prufer sequence, traversal methods like pre-order, post-order can be used such that every node is assigned a unique number between 1 and n where n is the total number of nodes. A modified Prufer sequence was proposed by Rao et al. [15] in which a XML document tree T_1 is modified by adding a dummy node as the child for every leaf in T_1. Using Post Order traversal, nodes in T_1 are numbered from 1 to n called Post Order Traversal number (POTN). Then T_1's Prufer sequence is constructed by deleting leaf node with the smallest number in T_1 in the increasing order of post-order number and the number of its parent is recorded. In the resulting tree this process is repeated until only the root node is left. The resulting sequence is called Numbered Prufer Sequence (NPS) and the associated node label is called Labeled Prufer Sequence(LPS). Thus an XML document is represented using NPS and LPS. Ontology matching based on prufer sequence was described by Algergawy et al. [19], which construct prufer sequence of ontologies as explained above and the structural similarity was computed by considering three types of node contexts.

3.4   Example for Prufer Sequence

Consider the XML document tree T_1 describing actor information which is shown in Fig 3. Post order traversal is done and each node is associated with Post Order Traversal Number (POTN) which is shown as circle. Dummy nodes are inserted for all leaf nodes which are shown as dashed lines. Prufer sequence is generated as explained above and the corresponding LPS and NPS are shown in Table 2.

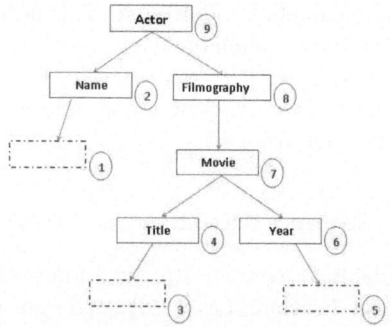

Fig. 3. XML Document Tree T_1 with POTN

Table 2. Prufer Sequence of XML document Tree T_1 with LPS and NPS

LPS	Name	Actor	Title	Movie	Year	Movie	Filmogra-phy	Actor
NPS	2	9	4	7	6	7	8	9

3.5   Algorithm for XML Document Structural Similarity

Given two XML document trees T_1 and T_2, based on section 3.3 prufer sequence is generated. Then the algorithm for computing structural similarity between T_1 and T_2 is given below.

Algorithm   StructSim(T_1,T_2)
Input: T_1,T_2 // T_1,T_2 are XML Document Trees $T_1$and T_2
Output: Structural Similarity between T_1 and T_2
1     $LPS_1[1..m]$ ← Labeled Prufer Sequence of T_1 with 'm' nodes
2     $NPS_1[1..m]$ ← Numbered Prufer Sequence of T_1
3     $LPS_2[1..n]$ ← Labeled Prufer Sequence of T2 with 'n' nodes

4     $NPS_2[1..n]$ $\leftarrow$ Numbered Prufer Sequence of T_2

5     $CN[1..k]\leftarrow$ $LPS_1 \cap LPS_2$ /* CN – Common nodes between T_1 and T_2, k is the
                                                      number of common nodes*/

6   **if** k>1 then go to step 7
      else
              $Sim(T_1, T_2)\leftarrow 0$
              go to step 17
      end if

7     $CN_1[1..k] \leftarrow Sort(CN)$ /*Sort Common nodes of Tree T_1 based on NPS_1 */

8     $CN_2[1..k] \leftarrow Sort(CN)$ /* Sort Common nodes of Tree T_2 based on NPS_2 */

9   **for** index i varying from 1 to k-1 do
      begin
      Form the Relation Set $\mathfrak{R}_1$ from the set of common nodes CN_1 as follows
      $\mathfrak{R}_1=\{(CN_1[i], CN_1[j]) / CN_1[i]\mathfrak{R}CN_1[j], 1<j<=k$ and $j > i)$
                  Where $\mathfrak{R}$ is Parent-Child Relation
      If Parent-Child Relation is not found then find immediate Ancestor-Child
      Relation and   all Right-Sibling Relation   based on   NPS1
      end for

10   Similarly form the Relationt $\mathfrak{R}_2$ from the set CN_2 based on NPS_2 as follows
      $\mathfrak{R}_2=\{(CN_2[i], CN_2[j]) / CN_2[i]\mathfrak{R}CN_2[j], 1<j<=k$ and $j > i)$

11    $\forall(CN_2[i],CN_2[j])\in \mathfrak{R}_1$ find exact match relations in $\mathfrak{R}_2$.
      $\mathbf{E_{sim}} \leftarrow$ number of exact matches

12   Eliminate all exact match relations in both $\mathfrak{R}_1$ **and** $\mathfrak{R}_2$

13    $\forall$ $(CN[i],CN[j])\in \mathfrak{R}_1$ **and** $\mathfrak{R}_2$,
          find the weighted similarity using the formula
      $$\mathbf{W_{Sim}} = \sum_{n=1}^{p} W_n \text{ , where p is the number of remaining}$$
      pair of relations in $\mathfrak{R}_1$ **and** $\mathfrak{R}_2$ and W_n is given by

      $$Wn = \frac{LT_1(CN[i]).LT_2(CN[i]) + LT_1(CN[j]).LT_2(CN[j])}{[max(LT_1(CN[i], LT_2(CN[i])]^2 + [max(LT_1(CN[j], LT_2(CN[j])]^2}$$
      Where
              $LT_i(CN[i])$ -   Level weight of CN[i] in tree T_i
      Level weight of a node n in a tree T_i is found as $LT_i(n) \leftarrow level(n)/ height(T_i)$

14   Root similarity is computed as
      $\mathbf{R_{Sim}}$ = RSim1 + RSim2, where RSim1 and RSim2 is 0 if root is not
                                        matched and 1 if root is matched

15   Common node similarity is computed by the formula
      $$\mathbf{C_{Sim}} = \frac{E_{Sim} + W_{Sim} + R_{Sim}}{E_n + P_n + 2}$$
      E_n number of exact match, P_n number of partial match and 2 is added for
      root similarity match

16   Overall similarity is computed by the formula

$$\text{Sim}(\mathbf{T_1}, \mathbf{T_2}) = C_{Sim} \cdot \frac{|LPS_1 \cap LPS_2|}{|LPS_1 \cup LPS_2|}$$

17   End

4   Experimental Results and Analysis

Experiments were performed to prove the effectiveness of our algorithm. Evaluation metrics namely Precision, Recall and F measures are used to compare our algorithm with other competitive algorithms. We have used two real time datasets. The first dataset is from Niagara project experimental data set namely movies and actors which we have downloaded from the web site **http://www.cs.wisc.edu/niagara/data**. The second data set is from ACM SIGMOD Record and DBLP. The dataset information is provided in Table 3.

Table 3. Real time XML Document datasets

Data Sets	Number of XML Documents
Movie Database #1	490
Actor Database #1	477
DBLP #2	3104
ACM SIGMOD #2	6150

Clustering is done by agglomerative hierarchical clustering with complete linkage which groups clusters at different levels. The principle behind agglomerative hierarchical clustering is that, it begins with as many clusters as objects and clusters are successively merged until one cluster remains. The clustering results were evaluated based on average precision, average recall and average F measure. First experiment is based on Movie and Actor Database. We have chosen this dataset because the movie and actor XML documents have semantic structural relationship. The comparison is done with XCLUST [17] and XEDGE [16] and the results are depicted in Fig 4.

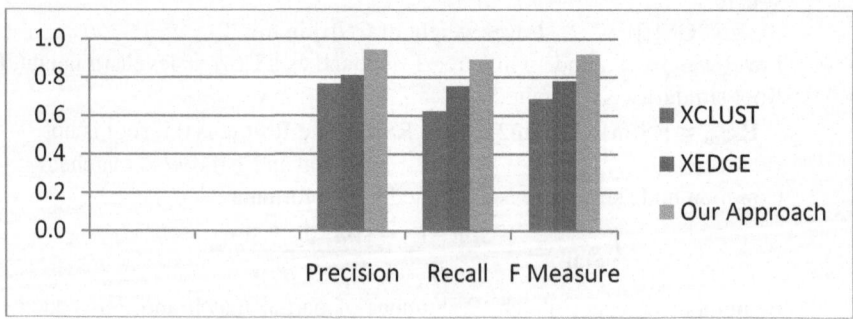

Fig. 4. Precision, Recall and F measure comparison for Actor and Movie dataset

From Fig.4 we observe that our approach reports better precision and recall when compared with XCLUST and XEDGE clustering techniques. We achieved 94% average precision, 89% average recall and 91% and average F measure when compared with XEDGE which reports 80% average precision, 75% average recall and 77% average F measure. The XCLUST algorithm reports still reduced values than XEDGE. This is mainly because XCLUST does not consider hierarchical relations. The drawback of XEDGE is that it does not consider the paths in different hierarchical order. Hence our algorithm outperforms both XEDGE and XCLUST.

Our next set of experiment is based on second dataset namely DBLP and ACM SIGMOD record as mentioned earlier. We compared our algorithm with XCLUST [17], XEDGE [16] and FATS [6]. As in previous experiment we clustered the documents based on agglomerative hierarchical clustering and the results are depicted in Fig 5.

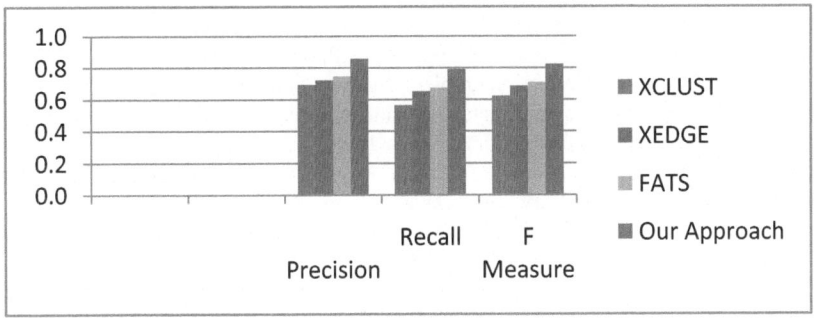

Fig. 5. Precision, Recall and F measure comparison for DBLP and Sigmod Dataset

From Fig 5 we observe that our approach outperforms three algorithms namely XCLUST, XEDGE and FATS. We further observe that the precision and recall are much less in XCLUST and XEDGE when compared with our algorithm. This is because sibling relations are not considered in both algorithms. FATS algorithm reports 74% precision and 67% recall, which is less than our algorithm. This is due to the fact that FATS algorithm doesn't consider the hierarchical weight in case of partial match.

5   Conclusion

In this paper we have proposed an effective algorithm for computing structural similarity of XML documents using Prufer Sequence. Main advantage of our algorithm is computing similarity by considering all structural relationships including structural semantics. Through experiments we have demonstrated that our algorithm is more effective than some of the previous works. In future we have planned to extend our work by computing both structural and content semantic similarity.

References

1. Tekli, J., Chbeir, R., Yetongnon, K.: An overview on XML similarity: background, current trends and future directions. Computer Science Review 3(3), 151–173 (2009)
2. Aggarwal, C.C., Ta, N., Wang, J., Feng, J., Zaki, M.: Xproj: a framework for projected structural clustering of xml documents. In: Proceedings of the 13th ACM SIGKDD International Conference on Knowledge Discovery and Data Mining, pp. 46–55. ACM (2007)
3. Rafiei, D., Moise, D.L., Sun, D.: Finding syntactic similarities between xml documents. In: 17th International Workshop on Database and Expert Systems Applications, DEXA 2006, pp. 512–516. IEEE (2006)
4. Buttler, D.: A short survey of document structure similarity algorithms. United States. Department of Energy (2004)
5. Joshi, S., Agrawal, N., Krishnapuram, R., Negi, S.: A Bag of Paths Model for Measuring Structural Similarity in Web Documents. In: Proceedings of the ACM SIGKKD Conference on Knowledge Discovery and Data Mining, USA, pp. 577–582 (2003)
6. Zhang, L., Li, Z., Chen, Q., Li, X., Li, N., Lou, Y.: Mining frequent association tag sequences for clustering XML documents. In: Sheng, Q.Z., Wang, G., Jensen, C.S., Xu, G. (eds.) APWeb 2012. LNCS, vol. 7235, pp. 85–96. Springer, Heidelberg (2012)
7. Tai, K.: The tree-to-tree correction problem. Journal of the ACM, JACM (1979)
8. Shasha, D., Zhang, K.: Approximate tree pattern matching, Pattern Matching in Strings, Trees and Arrays, ch. 14. Oxford Univ. Press (1995)
9. Chawathe, S.: Comparing hierarchical data in external memory. In: Proceedings of the International Conference on Very Large Databases, pp. 90–101 (1999)
10. Nierman, A., Jagadish, H.V.: Evaluating structural similarity in XML documents. In: Proc. of ACM SIGMOD WebDB, pp. 61–66 (2002)
11. Tekli, J., Chbeir, R.: A novel XML document structure comparison framework based-on sub-tree commonalities and label semantics. J. Web Sem. 11, 14–40 (2012)
12. Vinson, A.R., Heuser, C.A., da Silva, A.S., De Moura, S.: An Approach to XML Path Matching. In: The 9th Annual ACM International Workshop on Web Information and Data Management, pp. 17–24 (2007)
13. Choi, I., Moon, B., Kim, H.-J.: A clustering method based on path similarities of XML data. Data & Knowledge Engineering 60(2) (2007)
14. Prufer, H.: Neuer beweis eines satzes uber permutationen. Archiv für Mathematik und Physik 27, 142–144 (1918)
15. Rao, P., Moon, B.: PRIX:Indexing and querying XML using Prufer Sequences. In: Proceedings of ICDE (2004)
16. Antonellis, P., Makris, C., Tsirakis, N.: XEdge: clustering homogeneous and heterogeneous XML documents using edge summaries. In: Proceedings of the 2008 ACM Symposium on Applied Computing, pp. 1081–1088. ACM (2008)
17. Nayak, R.: Fast and effective clustering of XML data using structural information. Knowledge and Information Systems 14(2), 197–215 (2008)
18. Wang, Y., Liu, W., Bell, D.A.: A structure-based similarity spreading approach for ontology matching. In: Deshpande, A., Hunter, A. (eds.) SUM 2010. LNCS, vol. 6379, pp. 361–374. Springer, Heidelberg (2010)
19. Algergawy, A., Schallehn, E., Saake, G.: A sequence-based ontology matching approach. In: Proceedings of 18th European Conference on Artificial Intelligence Workshops (2008)

Recommendations Given from Socially-Connected People

Daniel González, Regina Motz, and Libertad Tansini

Facultad de Ingeniería, Universidad de la República, Montevideo, Uruguay
danielgonzalezbernal@gmail.com, {rmotz,libertad}@fing.edu.uy

Abstract. This paper presents how relationships among members of a social network can be used to explicitly specify the relevant features of a friendsourcing recommendation algorithm. One important contribution is to show how to conceptualize previous evaluations of items made by socially-connected users and the different features involved in this kind of algorithms, in a set of criteria for similarity between users in a social network. The paper presents how these specified criteria are used by the proposed friendsourcing recommendation algorithm and shows how the recommendation algorithm is integrated into a real recommender system to be used in a healthcare social network for the medical service of a university. Moreover, the work shows preliminary results which indicate that the information contained in social networks, processed with the proposed algorithm, is relevant for the generation of personalized recommendations.

Keywords: Friendsourcing, Recommendation Algorithm, Recommender Systems.

1 Introduction

According to the *Association for Computing Machinery* (ACM), recommender systems are computer applications which guide users in their decision-making during the time they interact with large amounts of information. Considering the explicit or implicit preferences expressed by users, recommender systems produce personalized recommendations of items [1]. There are various fields of application for these systems. For instance, they have a main role in electronic commerce (e-commerce), helping buyers to choose products and as a consequence, they substantially improve the sales [2]. Thus, the main goal of recommender systems is to find and retrieve information that satisfies the interests and needs of web users. The quality level of a recommender system is measured by the accurate and precise results it produces regarding the search intentions of the users [3]. When the context of recommendations is the web, the large amounts of available information as well as the massive usage of social networking websites imply big challenges for recommender systems, such as the ability to provide relevant results [3]. Considering the social networking, *Collaborative Filtering* (CF) is a well-known technique which improves recommender systems with a social feature [4, 5, 6]. In CF, items are recommended to new users based on the preferences of similar users [7]. CF, which falls in the category of

Y.T. Demey and H. Panetto (Eds.): OTM 2013 Workshops, LNCS 8186, pp. 649–655, 2013.

crowdsourcing techniques, uses the wisdom of crowd's theory [8]. In traditional *crowdsourcing*, problems are broadcast to an unknown group of people in a sort of an open call for solutions [3], whereas *friendsourcing* is a type of crowdsourcing aimed at collecting accurate information available only to a small, socially-connected group of people [9]. In line with this approach, there are several techniques to generate personalized recommendations. In this paper, we present mechanisms that collect accurate information available only from a trusted and eventually reduced, socially-connected group of people taking into account their friendship relations. This work also proposes what kind of information should be extracted from social networks and shows how the recommendation algorithm processes this information to achieve desirable results.

The remaining part of this paper is organized as follows: In Section 2, the friendsourcing-based recommendation algorithm is described. Section 3 discusses the integration of the algorithm into a real recommender system such as the one developed for the *Quality Health Information Retrieval* (QHIR) LACCIR project[1]. In Section 4, test cases and their preliminary results are described. Section 5 presents some conclusions and discusses improvements that could be made to the recommendation algorithm.

2   A Friendsourcing Recommendation Algorithm

The main contribution of this work is the proposal of a friendsourcing recommendation algorithm, which is thought to be used in a social network context, this implies that users are members of a social network and have relationships defined amongst them. Currently, there are many social networks with particular features or objectives, such as professional networks, celebrity news networks, for sharing videos and so on. In this way, it is desirable that the recommendation algorithm can be used independently of the kind of social network. In some cases, social networks bring the users the opportunity to choose the sort of relationship they share. For simplicity, the algorithm considers only one type of relationship between users in a social network, which is the *friendship*. Different types of relationships could be considered in future versions of the algorithm, but as first approach all the relationships are considered to be of the same sort. However, the opinion about an item given by a direct friend may not weight the same as the opinion about the same item given by a friend of a friend. Thus, the information contained in a social network can be modeled as an undirected graph, where the nodes are the users and the links are the relationships between them.

One input of the recommendation algorithm is the information contained in the social network, which is information about the users and their relationships. The algorithm takes the evaluations of items made by users as other input. Each user has the opportunity to rate the different quality attributes of the items. In this work, an item may be any object that can be identified and recommended to the users such as web pages, images, videos, and so on. Other input is the importance of each quality attribute. In this manner, the criteria of the recommendations are specified on the

---

[1] URL http://www.laccir.org/web/#/Projects/HealthCare/
InformationRetrieval/

social network. Each user must have an identifier in order to produce personalized recommendations, so the algorithm takes the identifier of the user who will receive the recommendations, called *current user*, as other input of the algorithm. Additionally, a value which represents the maximum number of desired recommended items should be considered as another input. The algorithm returns a list of identifiers of recommended items ordered by the suggested importance for the current user.

Crowdsourcing is not used in this algorithm since it does not take into account the information available from the entire crowd to make recommendations. On the contrary, our algorithm takes the information available only from a trusted and eventually reduced, socially-connected group of people. One of the critical points of the algorithm is the selection of that group of people that will be used to make personalized recommendations. As previously mentioned, a social network can be modeled as an undirected graph, so we begin obtaining the users of the first level of the graph that has the current user as the root. In other words, the direct friends of the current user are obtained. Then, we order them based on similarity to the current user. The similarity between two users in a social network is defined as a normalized value between 0 and 1, which represents how similar they are, and is composed of three different components of similarity that will be described further on: the component of *similarity in the friendship relations*, the component of *similarity in the evaluations of items*, and the component of *similarity in the activity of rating items*. The first component to be taken into account, in order to find the similarity between users, is the similarity in the friendship relations. The more friends in common with the current user, the more similar they are. Let x be the current user and let y be a friend of x. Let *simFriend(x, y)* be the component which represents the similarity in the friendship relations between two individuals x and y. We calculate its normalized value between 0 and 1, as shown in formula (1), where $nf(y)$ is the number of friends of the individual y, and $nfic(x, y)$ is the number of friends in common between the individuals x and y.

$$simFriend(x, y) = nfic(x, y) / (nf(y) - 1) \text{ if } nf(y) > 1, \text{ otherwise } simFriend(x, y) = 0 \quad (1)$$

Another component is the similarity in the evaluations of items, which captures to what extent two different users rate items in the same way. If both users rate the same items similarly in a positive or negative way, then they probably rate other items in a similar manner, that is, they have similar taste. Let *simEval(x, y)* be the component which represents the similarity in the evaluations of items between the individuals x and y, we calculate its normalized value between 0 and 1, as shown in formula (2), where $qAttrEval(x, i, j)$ is the evaluation of item i produced by the individual x for the quality attribute j used in the recommendation criteria. The evaluations of the quality attributes of an item are normalized values between 0 and 1. In this work, the set of quality attributes $qAttr$ is composed of the following attributes: *trustworthy*, *objective*, *complete* and *well-written*. Let $niric(x, y)$ be the number of items rated in common between the individuals x and y, and let n be the number of quality attributes of the set $qAttr$.

$$simEval(x, y) = (\sum_{i=1}^{niric(x,y)}((\sum_{j \text{ in } qAttr}(1 - |qAttrEval(x, i, j) - qAttrEval(y, i, j)|)) / n))$$
$$/ niric(x, y) \text{ if } niric(x, y) > 0 \text{ and } n > 0, \text{ otherwise } simEval(x, y) = 0 \quad (2)$$

The last component is the similarity in the activity of rating items. It is important that members of the social network have an active attitude regarding the activity of rating items. A friend that has previously rated a large set of items is more trustworthy because his behaviour is better described by his ratings than other friends with less activity. Active friends have probably seen more items and hence give more trustworthy evaluations so it is important to consider this feature in the algorithm. If both users rate the same number of items, they probably have the same attitude considering the activity of rating items. Let *simActiv(x, y)* be the component which represents the similarity in the activity of rating items. We calculate its normalized value between 0 and 1, as expressed in formula (3) where *nir(x)* is the number of items rated by the individual *x*.

$$simActiv(x, y) = nir(y) / nir(x) \text{ if } nir(x) \geq nir(y) \text{ and } nir(x) > 0, simActiv(x, y) = nir(x) / nir(y) \text{ if } nir(y) > nir(x) \text{ and } nir(y) > 0, \text{ otherwise } simActiv(x, y) = 0 \tag{3}$$

A pondered value or weight, between 0 and 1, is defined for each of the three components of similarity. The main advantage of using weights is the possibility of making any component disappears by assigning zero to its weight, allowing more flexibility at the time of testing the algorithm and analysing the accuracy of the results. Let *sim(x, y)* be the similarity between the individuals *x* and *y*, and let α, β, γ be the respective weights for the three components. The sum of the three components is less or equal to 1. We calculate its normalized value between 0 and 1, as shown in formula (4).

$$sim(x, y) = \alpha * simFriend(x, y) + \beta * simEval(x, y) + \gamma * simActiv(x, y) \tag{4}$$

After the group of friends is ordered by similarity, the algorithm obtains the best rated items for each friend starting with the most similar friend of the current user. The rating for each item is a calculated value based on the evaluations of the quality attributes. Weights, which are values between 0 and 1, are also defined for each quality attribute so it is possible to set the importance for each one. The sum of the weights is less or equal to 1. We define a *value of acceptance* in order to require a minimum level of quality of the recommended items. Let *wqAttr(j)* be the weight defined for the quality attribute *j* of the set *qAttr*. Let *rating(f, i)* be the rating of the item *i* made by the individual *f*, friend of the current user. We calculate its value as shown in formula (5).

$$rating(f, i) = \sum_{j \text{ in } qAttr}(wqAttr(j) * qAttrEval(f, i, j)) \tag{5}$$

By ordering the items by its ratings, a preliminary list of recommendations is produced. After that, each item is reevaluated with the following process: if the rating is greater or equal to the value of acceptance, then the identifier of the item is added to the final ordered list of identifiers of recommended items. This process is repeated until the maximum number of recommended items is reached.

3   Integration of the Algorithm

In the QHIR LACCIR project, a healthcare social network for the Medical Service of the University of Cauca in Colombia and a recommender system, have been developed. The Medical Service provides care services and activities of disease pre-ventions [10]. In order to integrate the recommendation algorithm into the recom-mender system we developed a set of classes in Java which implements the proposed algorithm, together with a main method and a web service which invokes that method. We represent the social network, the evaluations of items and the weights of the quali-ty attributes by xml files.

Sample xml files can be accessed from the following website: http://www.fing.edu.uy/inco/grupos/sis/www/index.php?content=./m iembros/dgonzalez.

To obtain the personalized recommendations, the main class *Friendsourcing* must be instantiated and the main method *friendsourcingalgorithm* must be invoked as shown in the following code:

```
Friendsourcing f = new Friendsourcing();
ArrayList<String> recommendations =
f.friendsourcingalgorithm(id, maxitems, pathsocialnet,
pathevaluations, pathweightsattr);
```

Where *id* is the identifier of the current user, *maxitems* is the maximum number of recommended items, *pathsocialnet* is the path of the social-network xml file, *pathe-valuations* is the path of the evaluations-of-items xml file, *pathweightsattr* is the path of the weights-of-quality-attributes xml file, and *recommendations* is the list of iden-tifiers of recommended items.

4   Test Cases and Preliminary Results

This section describes the test cases generated in order to test the recommendation algorithm. This section also explains the goal for each test case and analyzes the pre-liminary results. To evaluate the efficiency of the results obtained by the algorithm, we use two measures commonly used in the information retrieval, which are *precision* and *recall* [11]. Since the recommendation algorithm has three different components of similarity, we define three test cases to individually test each component. Four users of the social network are randomly chosen and recommendations of items are generated for each user using the algorithm. The selected users have a number of friends close to the average, which is considered a suitable selection criterion, as the tests aim to analyze the algorithm in general cases. Then, standard deviations for the measures of efficiency are also calculated. The tests are made in a social network with fifty users and ten items. The weights of the quality attributes have the same value (0.25), and the value of acceptance is set to 0.5.

The first test case aims to test the component of similarity in the friendship rela-tions, so we set the weight for that component to the maximum value and eliminate the other two components, setting their value to zero. The results depicted in Table 1, shows that the evaluations of items made by friends that have a common circle of friends with the current user, should be considered when recommending items.

Table 1. Results of testing the component of similarity in the friendship relations

	Mean	Std. Deviation
Precision	0.650	0.167
Recall	0.718	0.282

The second test case aims to test the component of similarity in the evaluations of items, so we set its weight to the maximum value and eliminate the other two components in order to test individually that component. The results depicted in Table 2, shows that the similarity in the evaluations of items made by similar users is also useful in order to select items of interest to the current user.

Table 2. Results of testing the component of similarity in the evaluations of items

	Mean	Std. Deviation
Precision	0.700	0.224
Recall	0.719	0.180

The third test case aims to test the component of similarity in the activity of rating items, as in the other test cases, we set the weight for that component to the maximum value and eliminate the other two components. The results depicted in Table 3 shows that the similarity in the activity of rating items may be relevant for the generation of recommended items.

Table 3. Results of testing the component of similarity in the activity of rating items

	Mean	Std. Deviation
Precision	0.750	0.219
Recall	0.782	0.219

5   Conclusions and Future Work

In most cases, the recommendation algorithms used in websites are not made public due to the impact they have on certain activities on the web, such as e-commerce. Therefore, the knowledge of such algorithms is very valuable. Despite that fact, we designed a recommendation algorithm to be used in recommender systems which uses the information contained in the social network as well as evaluations of items made by socially-connected users. The recommendation algorithm was integrated into a real recommender system, specifically the one developed for the QHIR LACCIR project. Regarding the results of the performed tests, we may conclude that the similarity in the friendship relations should be considered when selecting similar users. The similarity in the evaluations of items made by similar users is also useful in order to select items of interest to the current user. Considering the similarity in the activity of rating items may be relevant to recommender systems, at the time of generating personalized recommendations. Extensions of the recommendation algorithm can be made as future work. For instance, the information contained in the profile of the members of the social network, such as demographic and academic information, may be incorporated to find similarity between users. Other future work includes generating larger test cases to further analyse the performance of the algorithm. Another interesting line of future work is evaluating its use in a real scenario such as the recommender system developed for the QHIR LACCIR project which is currently starting to be used by healthcare workers and needs to be in production for some time before it is possible to apply our algorithm, since there has to be at least a minimum number of users and evaluations of items.

Acknowledgements. This work was partially funded by: the LACCIR R1210LAC007 Project and PEDECIBA. We would especially like to thank the members of the QHIR LACCIR project for their collaboration in this work.

References

1. The ACM Conference Series on Recommender Systems, http://recsys.acm.org
2. Schafer, J.B., Konstan, J., Riedl, J.: Recommender Systems in E-Commerce. In: EC 1999: Proceedings of the 1st ACM Conference on Electronic Commerce, pp. 158–166. ACM, New York (1999)
3. Díaz, A., Motz, R., Fernández, A., Valdeni de Lima, J., López, D.: Quality Web Information Retrieval: Towards Improving Semantic Recommender Systems with Friendsourcing. VI Congreso Ibero-Americano de Telemática (2011)
4. Sarwar, B., Karypis, G., Konstan, J., Reidl, J.: Item-based Collaborative Filtering Recommendation Algorithms. In: WWW 2001: Proceedings of the 10th International Conference on World Wide Web, pp. 285–295. ACM, New York (2001)
5. Bergman, L., Tuzhilin, A., Burke, R., Felfernig, A., Schmidt-Thieme, L. (eds.): RecSys 2009: Proceedings of the Third ACM Conference on Recommender Systems. ACM, New York (2009)
6. Jannach, D., Geyer, W., Dugan, C., Freyne, J., Singh Anand, S., Mobasher, B., Kobsa, A.: Workshop on Recommender Systems and the Social Web. In: RecSys 2009: Proceedings of the Third ACM Conference on Recommender Systems and the Social Web, pp. 421–422. ACM, New York (2009)
7. Good, N., Schafer, J.B., Konstan, J.A., Borchers, A., Sarwar, B., Herlocker, J., Riedl, J.: Combining Collaborative Filtering with Personal Agents for Better Recommendations. In: Proceedings of the Sixteenth National Conference on Artificial Intelligence, pp. 439–446 (1999)
8. Surowiecki, J.: The Wisdom of Crowds: Why the Many Are Smarter Than the Few and How Collective Wisdom Shapes Business, Economies, Societies and Nations. Doubleday (2004)
9. Bernstein, M., Tan, D., Smith, G., Czerwinski, M., Horvitz, E.: Personalization via Friendsourcing. ACM Transactions on Computer-Human Interaction (2010)
10. López, D., Blobel, B., González, C.: Architectural Approach for Quality and Safety Aware HealthCare Social Networks (2012)
11. Manning, C., Raghavan, P., Schütze, H.: Introduction to Information Retrieval. Cambridge University Press (2008)

A Framework to Promote and Develop a Sustainable Tourism by Using Social Media

Tiziana Guzzo, Alessia D'Andrea, Fernando Ferri, and Patrizia Grifoni

Institute of Research on Population and Social Policies (IRPPS-CNR)
00185, Rome (Italy)
{tiziana.guzzo,alessia.dandrea,fernando.ferri,
patrizia.grifoni}@irpps.cnr.it

Abstract. The paper provides a framework which involves different Social Media (such as Social networks, Wiki, Podcasting, Blogs and Really Simple Syndication) able to promote and develop a sustainable tourism in a shared and participatory approach. More in detail, the paper starts from an analysis of the tools used in the old and the new economy, by highlighting the technological tourism trend . Then the paper illustrates how Social Media can develop a sustainable tourism involving both tourists and local communities. Finally, future scenarios of virtual tourism are given.

Keywords: Social Media, Virtual Tourism, Sustainable Tourism, Social Networks.

1 Introduction

Tourism is one of the world's largest economic fields, which continues to grow very rapidly. It represents an opportunity of development for many countries, but it can also have very negative impacts on social structures, socio-cultural authenticity of host communities and natural and cultural heritage.

Sustainable tourism, according to sustainable development, aims at minimising the cons of tourism and maximize the pros [1]. Sustainable development is "the development that meets the needs of the present without compromising the ability of future generations to meet their own needs" (World Commission on Environment and Development 1987). It empathizes the use of environmental resources to minimise the ecological impacts. Moreover it allows respecting the socio-cultural authenticity of host communities and improving the economy of local communities reducing poverty [1].

In this context, the new tourism trends are represented by the tourists' search for sustainable tourism using the Internet and mobile technologies [2]

Every year, millions of tourists use the Internet to find tourism information about vacations, flights, guides, last minute proposals, cruises, destinations, routes etc. The Web affirms itself as a relevant reference and a necessary resource in all professional fields, also in the field of tourism for both customers and companies. It allows the speed for information exchange, the development of interaction among people that are located in different places, the sharing of information, knowledge and services among

Y.T. Demey and H. Panetto (Eds.): OTM 2013 Workshops, LNCS 8186, pp. 656–665, 2013.

all users, the competitiveness of prices and the possibility for companies to widely differentiate the offer and reach the market niches, real time services every time and everywhere [3]. But how can Internet and the new technologies develop sustainable tourism? A very important role in answering this question can be played by Social Media; in fact, they enable people to interact via communication media such as forums, blogs, virtual communities for exchanging information, experiences and sharing interests. People use Social Media to search new and unique contents, uncontaminated places, a kind of "discovering tourism", not commercials and far from mass-tourism. However in order to develop a sustainable tourism, it is necessary to involve both tourists and local communities to build a useful communication and cooperation. People living in historic centers, near archaeological sites or close to natural protected areas can play a key role in the conservation and promotion of those resources, promoting a sustainable tourism by using Social Media.

Starting from these considerations, the aim of the paper is to provide a framework that involves different Social Media (such as Social networks, Wiki, Podcasting, Blogs and Really Simple Syndication) which will be able to promote and develop a sustainable tourism. The framework involves the needs of both the "consumers" (tourists) who search for information about nature and culture tourism and the "producers" (local communities), which promote the local territory, the cultural traditions and the environment, in accordance with sustainable development.

This paper is organized as follows: Section 2 introduces the technological tourism trends. Section 3 analyses Social Media in the field of tourism. Section 4 describes the Framework proposed to promote and develop sustainable tourism. Section 5 delineates future scenarios for a sustainable tourism. Section 6 concludes the paper.

2   Technological Tourism Trends

The trend of tourism in the last fifteen years has been represented by the transformation from "old economy tools" into "new economy tools". "Old economy tools " such as travel agencies, paper guidebooks, television, promotions in external place and magazines present several limitations for tourism services in terms of: the type of the message they can deliver; the size and quality of audience that they can reach; the measurability of their impacts and costs involved. Moreover, contents in paper guidebooks could be outdated and many hotels and other tourist activities may no longer exist. The development of "new economy tools" represented by Social Media provides distinctive advantages that are more appropriate for tourism services such as the possibility for users and local communities to:

• create creative messages: thanks to the use of multimedia features (pictures, video, 3 dimensional worlds) tourists can test the tourism service before they buy it or travel to it.

• establish synchronous and asynchronous interactive communication to exchange travel information.

• reach international audience.

• easily track and monitor the impacts of tourism on-line services through the number of website visits, click thoughts, amount of time spent on the website, unique visitors, number etc to measure and improve the return of investment.

• create real time and multi-channel distribution of tourism services.

• create more effective marketing segmentation of travellers.

• provide a cost effective customer support 24 hours per day and 365 days per year.

Different studies analyse the evolution from "old economy" to "new economy" tools. In their research Schwabe and Prestipino [4] compare paper guidebooks to on line tourism communities to understand how the information quality and consequently the travel quality are improved.

A very good example of the transformation from paper guidebooks to Social Media is also provided by Stockdale and Borovicka [5]. The authors analysed how an historical brand for travel guidebook as Lonely Planet has also become an important reference site for online tourism community. Even if the site is active since 1994, it gained great consideration after the 2004 tsunami, when it became the principal reference site for missing people in the devastated countries. Now the concept of Lonely Planet as an information and community site for tourists is strong all over the world.

Many Social Media can be used to offer tourism services such as Social networks, Wiki, Podcasting, Blogs and Really Simple Syndication.

Social Networks have the great potential to serve ubiquitous information and communication needs. This applies especially to the tourism field where the need for information, communication and services is deeply felt.

Among worldwide travel social networks the most famous and visited ones are Tripadvisor, Virtualtourist, Gusto and TripIt. They enable tourism organizations and local communities to communicate with tourists to share travel experiences [6]. This can significantly inspire travel and boost one's willingness to visit places. An example is the social networking of Sheraton's website where users can upload their stories, experiences, videos, pictures, and comments and share them with other website visitors. Social networks can also support and enhance the promotion and adoption of sustainable tourism among all tourism stakeholders. An example is www.wayn.com a social network connecting and enabling interactions among local communities, travelers and tourism firms.

Wiki is a Web-based application that allows users to add content supporting collaborative writing, opening discussions, interaction and Web-authoring [7]. Thanks to wiki, anyone can write anything about a place, a city or a country, and can read everything, or improve what is already written. Wiki is the most important example of collaborative online community applied to tourism. It gives every traveler the chance to share their own experience with other members and collaboration, activeness and loyalty to the site is guaranteed. The most famous example is Wikitravel, a project to create a free, complete and updated worldwide guidebook (www.wikitravel.org). Many travel agencies take the opportunity to promote and create links to their websites through wikitravel.com to create and direct drive traffic to their own websites (an example is http://wikitravel.org/en/London).

Another important kind of Social Media, is represented by podcasting that refers to the uploading of video and audio files by users on websites. The most popular website for sharing audio and video contents is youtube.com. Many tourism organizations use podcasting as a customer communication tool. Some examples are the Jumeirah hotel that uploads podcasts on its website to update and deliver to its potential guests information about what is happening in its properties every day and the Orbitz.com a site that provides podcasting of many destinations that travelers can download and use as guides while visiting the destination.

Regarding blogs, they provide a forum for communication, collaboration, knowledge building, information gathering and publishing. In the blog every author talks about her/his own favorite topics, and it is easy to quote other's news or opinions in this way; for example, a list of travel blogs links each other to compose a thematic travel network. Blogs are becoming a useful tool for local communities to get more involved in destination marketing and to communicate with tourists. The participation of local communities can ensure a better blend between locals and travelers thus enable multi-stakeholder communication and understanding in tourism decision-making activities. Several examples of travel blogs exist in the tourism industry, such as travelblog.org, tripadvisor.com, hotelchatter.com, igougo.com.

The Really Simple Syndication (RSS) is a Web feed formats used by users to subscribe to a webpage to receive new content and to allow the creation of links and interactive communication among other Web 2.0 applications and users. Travel organizations use RSS to keep a communication with their consumers and to send them programs of cultural events organised in particular places. An example of RSS is visitdublin.com that include several specialised RSS feeds (for music events, last minute deals, etc.) to which any user can subscribe to receive automatic updates.

3   Social Media in the Tourism Field

Social media are deeply changing the way tourists search, find, use and collaboratively produce information about tourism. In Social Media, people can share reviews of hotels, restaurants and/or attractions and speak about good and bad experiences, provide or receive information and share knowledge and services. An example of Social Media that today are used by consumers are Virtual communities (VCs).

Rheingold (1994) [8] defines VCs as: "…a social aggregation that emerge from the Net when enough people carry on those public discussions long enough, with sufficient human feeling, to form Webs of personal relationship in cyberspace. A VC is a group of people who may or may not meet one another face to face, and who exchange words and ideas through the mediation of computer bulletin boards and networks".

According to Preece [9] members are the first element of a VC and it is fundamental to understand their needs. In fact, the elements of a VC are: people who communicate with each other to satisfy their needs, shared interests and common purpose, rules of communication between the community itself, technological applications and protocols that allow this process.

VCs can represent also a good business opportunity, in particular in the field of tourism. Since 1997, VCs has been considered by Werry [10] as the centre of every business model of commercial Internet. Traditional business models are now turned into community environment. Hagel and Armstrong also see in a business model VCs, because "What starts off as a group drawn together by common interests ends up as group with a critical mass of purchasing power, partly thanks to the fact that communities allow members to exchange information on such things as a product's price and quality" [11].

Timmers considers VCs as a business model in which "the ultimate value ... [comes] from the members (customers or partners) who add their information ... " [12].

Virtual Travel Communities (VTCs) are particularly relevance in the field of tourism.

According to Buhalis & Law [13] VTCs have become popular since they provide potential tourists with up to date, personalized and user-generated content, including trust-worthy reviews and recommendations.

Armstrong and Hagel [14] stated that VTCs provide four different benefits to its members: transaction, interest, fantasy, and relationship. Transaction refers to the action of purchasing airline tickets and making hotel reservations; while the community of interest refers to the opportunity for members to share information and experiences. On considering the community of fantasy this indicates the hedonic features, such as a game or an event, while community of relationship allows members to find their travel companions for a trip.

In their study about VTCs, Wang, Yu and Fesenmaier [15], show that since tourism is traditionally studied referring to geography, location and space, it is noticeable that tourism-marketing organizations are missing skills in how an online community can be used as a marketing tool. People can obtain a lot of benefits by joining the community depending on different nature of community and the various characteristics of community members. Many people want to make efficient business transactions and interact with other people. Many other people want to have fun, meet fellow traveler and express their own opinions. Each one wants to develop a sense of belonging, to express their cultural and economic interests and establish relationships.

Moreover, Wang, Yu and Fesenmaier [15] analysed the needs of VTCs related to tourism organization marketing. They individuated three main classes of needs: the functional, the social and the psychological one, that include transaction, information, entertainment, convenience, value, relationship, interactivity, trust, communication, escape among humans, identification, engagement, sense of belonging, relatedness and creativity.

Wang and Fesenmaier's study [15] only considers the needs of the "consumers" (tourists) that search travel information. However, in order to develop a sustainable tourism it is also important to consider the needs of the "producers" (local communities) that want to promote tourism marketing.

The "producers" can give important information about a particular territory, not because they have visited it as tourists, but because they were born and still live there: many of them provide tourism services. They know the real community and its cultural, social, economic and services perspectives. In the field of tourism "the producers" can play a very important role for the members satisfaction.

In the next section, in order to improve the study of Wang and Fesenmaier's [15], a framework that combines both the "consumers" and the "producers" needs which are important to consider to develop a sustainable tourism, is provided.

4   A Framework to Promote and Develop a Sustainable Tourism

Tourism can contribute to the socio-economic development of a country. People are more and more attracted by an high environmental quality. However, environmental resources are limited. That is why a lot of organizations, companies, administrators and citizens invest in a sustainable tourism. This kind of tourism is based on the safeguard and respect of the environment and local traditional culture. Currently, there is a great interest to promote the territory and safeguard the environment and the culture of the different countries; several websites promote this kind of tourism (e.g.: ecoturism.org, sustainabletourism.net, ecoturism.cc) but many of these websites only consider the needs of "consumers" without paying attention to sustainability; social media allow a more participative action also by involving the local communities living in particular places of interest, which can give important information for positive outcomes.

Brunt and Courtney [16] stated that the attitudes of community towards the impacts of tourism should be an important issue for planning and policy considerations for sustainable tourism projects. The communities' involvement in the tourism process is fundamental to maximise socio-economic benefits of tourism for the community [17] and to improve the awareness of common shared behaviours in order to adopt behaviours in coherence with sustainability goals.

In order to achieve this aim, a framework based on different Social Media (such as Social networks, Wiki, Podcasting, Blogs and Really Simple Syndication) that "consumers" (tourists) and "producers" (local communities) can use to exchange information and knowledge is provided in Figure 1.

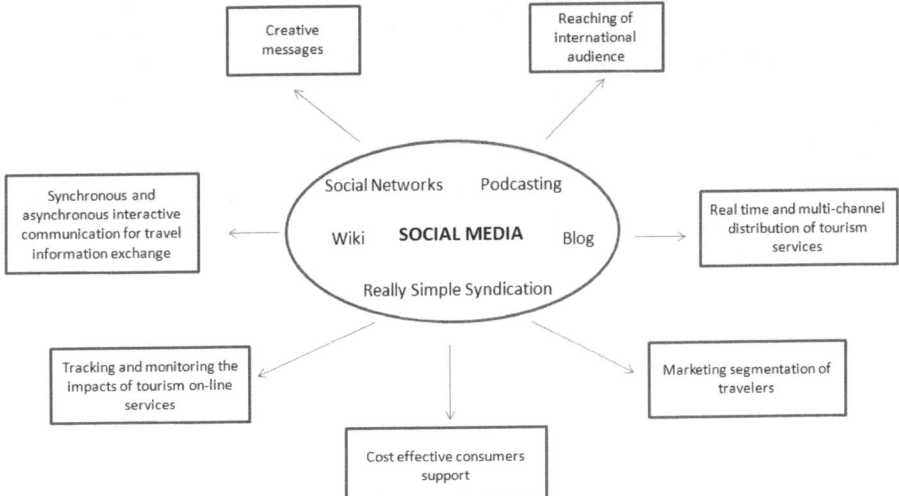

Fig. 1. A framework to promote and develop a sustainable tourism

The framework gives "consumers" the possibility to create creative messages and establish synchronous and asynchronous interactive communication for the exchange of travel information by satisfying their functional, psychological and social needs. As said before travelers are changing the way of doing tourism: while in the past there was a strong question about organized tourism, package deals (all included), today people are searching for a new kind of tourism linked to undiscovered places and cultures. Therefore, the framework represents a chance to create innovative contents that can be integrated and shared.

Moreover the framework involve the "producers" of information who have the opportunity to create creative messages by reaching an international audience. Moreover producers have also the possibility to easily track and monitor the impacts of tourism on-line services and create real time and multi-channel distribution of tourism services and also a more effective marketing segmentation of travelers. Finally they can also provide a cost effective customer support 24 hours per day and 365 days per year.

In the framework, each user can dynamically change her/his role and a producer can become a consumer (and vice-versa). That is, each user lives in a place that can have particular traditions that s/he is interested to promote and to share with other users of other places. The role of users can change so that, for example, a producer can be interested to search or to discover and visit new places, then in turn s/he becomes a consumer. Consumers can use information and promotion that other producers have given and they also in turn can become producers providing information about their own country. The users are interested to promote their culture, their local products and also to acquire culture and products of other people introducing a symmetry in the community.

Exchanging information and knowledge between consumers and producers represents an opportunity to improve the vitality and the economy of a country. According to [18] when people travel they have a chance to see real problems and electronic support may give them an occasion (even after return home) to participate in social help/support or projects developed in places already visited or in locations where the tourists plan to go. This concept applied in the case of sustainable tourism, can enable both tourists and local communities, by using social media, to:

- promote the territory and the sustainable tourism,
- share information aiming to build the wide awareness of sustainable behavior,
- improve the local economies,
- socialize with other distant people,
- reinforce the sense of belonging,
- produce added value to products of a place,
- characterize thematic itineraries, fairs that distinguish a country,
- create new job and new opportunities,
- create and share new services improving the quality of tourism,
- stimulate the development and innovation.

All these elements can remove the risk of cultural marginality or isolation because they represent an opportunity for cultural exchange and a possibility to integrate local knowledge into social, economic and cultural development.

5   Future Scenarios for a Sustainable Tourism

In the next years, a future scenario for tourism is evolving in a tourism which includes both systems to visualize data and information about travel social network and their dynamics considering location, time and classes of interests and virtual services and tours.

The visualization systems for travel social networks will provide a spatial representation of individuals or groups of individuals that share specific interests in order to support people during making travel. Moreover, they will allow exploring information about the changing of interests for typology of tourism of the travellers and the evolution of comparing the sequence of temporal layers, supporting also Tour Operator to plan better services and travels [6].

Another scenario is represented by virtual travel. It can also represent an opportunity, offering entertainment media with the travel experience without a physical journey to a remote destination. It is logistically and financially easier to visit virtual worlds than to make real trips.

Virtual travel can be a preparation to a real visit or an option if time, distance or money prevents people from physically travelling.

These forms of virtual tourism can help people who cannot move because they have problems of disability, or political or financial reasons.

In the future virtual trips may become a very important challenge for sustainable tourism. Virtual tours can help preserve environments that are in danger of losing their natural and cultural identity from an invasive and destructive tourism. In fact, "Virtual Stonehenge" or "virtual Tibet" projects are born with this objective.

There are numerous non-profit websites, such as "The Grand Canyon Explorer," which provides for example virtual tour guides, or educational sites that teach the history, the environment and the culture of a place through a virtual travel.

The digital images are accompanied by texts interpretations that conceptualise the natural environment; the texts also provide an essential characteristic movement of tourism.

The web-cam on the Internet provides digital images in real-time of the Grand Canyon National Park, accessible at anytime and anywhere, reaffirming the ubiquitous "eyes tourism" [19]. Travelers can also make purchase in various digital souvenir shops, to make their virtual experience more real.

Speaking of virtual environment Milgram et al. [20] have coined the term "mixed reality" (MR) environment, where real and virtual are mixed to any degree. Other features are the interactivity in real time and the existence of three dimensions [21]. An example of augmented reality is the virtual guide, for example in the virtual environment Bruges in Second Life, when the avatar looks at a building, real world information and pictures about the real world city are shown in the HUD (Heads-Up Display). Another example of augmented reality in real world are the guides in a real world museum, where visitors can hire a walkman with the description of the paintings or the sculptures when they walk [22].

In the future the development of these virtual technologies could change the tourist experience. Virtual worlds will become increasingly similar to real ones: the 3D dimensions, the smells, the sensations will improve the virtual tourism experience of disable people. Moreover, the virtual tourism experience increases the interest to see the original places. In case the special original sites have to be protected, the virtual trip can be a substitute to see those places, sustaining the sustainable development.

6   Conclusion

This paper analyses the new frontiers of tourism and sustainable tourism using social media. In the first part of the paper the technological tourism trends have been discussed. In particular the paper analysed the transformation from "old economy tools" such as paper guidebooks and travel agencies, into "new economy tools" such as Social networks, Wiki, Podcasting, Blogs and Really Simple Syndication.

The paper then provided a framework that involves different Social Media which are able to promote and develop sustainable tourism. The framework considers the needs of both the "consumers" (tourists) that search information about nature and culture tourism, and the "producers" (local communities) that promote their local territory, cultural traditions and environment, in accordance with sustainable development. The framework, involving the different social media, aims at promoting the differences of the various places as well as their rich historic, environmental and cultural heritage. The framework also helps the sharing of information, knowledge and services, and to build a common feeling on sustainability, attracting tourists out of traditional tourism circuits to respect the environment. The opportunity of business is both for local administration because it can develop the economy of the territory and, local people who will participate to sustainable development of their country and will have many social and economic advantages. The participatory approach promoted by the use of social media according to the described framework allows to obtain an optimization between the needs of the travelers and the local communities in a sustainable development. Finally, future scenarios of virtual tourism have been discussed in the paper.

Future works will provide experiments to validate the proposed framework, according to social, cultural and economic users' needs.

References

[1] World Trade Organization WTO: Annual Report. Switzerland (2004)
[2] Ferri, F., Grifoni, P., Guzzo, T.: Social aspects of mobile technologies on the web tourism trend. In: Handbook of Research on Mobile Business: Technical, Methodological and Social Perspectives, pp. 896–910. IGI Publishing (2008)
[3] Ferri, F., Grifoni, P., Guzzo, T.: New Forms of Social and Professional Digital Relationships: The Case of Facebook. Social Network Analysis and Mining Journal 2(2), 121–137 (2012)
[4] Schwabe, G., Prestipino, M.: How tourism communities can change travel information quality. In: 13th European Conference on Information Systems, ECIS (2005)
[5] Stockadale, R., Borovicka, M.: Developing an Online Business Community: A Travel Industry Case Study (2006)

[6] Caschera, M.C., Ferri, F., Grifoni, P., Guzzo, T.: Multidimensional Visualization System for Travel Social Networks. In: 6th International Conference on Information Technology: New Generations ITNG 2009, April 27-29, pp. 1510–1516. IEEE Computer Society, Las Vegas (2009)

[7] Desilets, A., Paquet, S., Vinson, N.: Are wikis usable? In: WikiSym Conference, San Diego CA USA, October 16-18 (2005)

[8] Rheingold, H.: The Virtual Community: Homesteading on the Electronic Frontier, pp. 57–58. Addison Wesley Pub. Co. (1993)

[9] Preece, J.: Online Communities: Designing Usability, Supporting Sociability. Wiley, John Wiley & Sons, Chichester, New York (2000)

[10] Werry, C.: Imagined electronic community: Representations of virtual community in contemporary business discourse. First Monday 4(9) (1999), http://firstmonday.org/issues/issue49/werry/index.htm

[11] Hagel III, J., Armstrong, A.: Net Gain: Expanding markets through virtual communities (1997)

[12] Timmers, P.: Business Models for Electronic Markets EM - Electronic Markets. The International Journal of Electronic Markets and Business Media 3 (1998)

[13] Buhalis, D., Law, R.: Progress in infor-mation technology and tourism management: 20years on and 10 years after the Internet - the stateof e-tourism research. Tourism Management 29, 609–623 (2008)

[14] Armstrong, A., Hagel, J.: The Real Value of On-line Communities. Harvard Business Review 74(3), 134–141 (1996)

[15] Wang, Y., Yu, Q., Fesenmaier, D.R.: Defining the Virtual Tourist Community: Implications for Tourism Marketing. Tourism Management 23(4), 407–172001 (2008)

[16] Brunt, P., Courtney, P.: Host perceptions of sociocultural impacts. Annals of Tourism Research 26(3), 493–515 (1999)

[17] Inskeep, E.: Tourism Planning: An Integrated and Sustainable Development Approach. Van Nostrand Reinhold, New York (1991)

[18] Wojciechowski, A.: Models of Charity Donations and Project Funding in Social Networks. In: Meersman, R., Herrero, P., Dillon, T. (eds.) OTM 2009 Workshops. LNCS, vol. 5872, pp. 454–463. Springer, Heidelberg (2009)

[19] Urry, J.: The Tourist Gaze, 2nd edn. SAGE Publications Ltd., London (2002)

[20] Milgram, P., Kishino, F.: A taxonomy of mixed reality visual displays. IE-ICE Trans. on Information and Systems (Special Issue on Networked Reality) E77D(12), 1321–1329 (1994)

[21] Azuma, R.T.: A survey of augmented reality. Presence 6(4), 355–385 (1997)

[22] Kerremans, P.: Virtual Tourism in Bruges: The Travel Guide, LouisPlatini.com (2007)

Measuring Betweenness Centrality in Social Internetworking Scenarios

Francesco Buccafurri*, Gianluca Lax, Serena Nicolazzo,
Antonino Nocera, and Domenico Ursino

DIIES, University "Mediterranea" of Reggio Calabria
{bucca,lax,s.nicolazzo,a.nocera,ursino}@unirc.it

Abstract. The importance of the betweenness centrality measure in
(on-line) social networks is well known, as well as its possible applications to various domains. However, the classical notion of betweenness
centrality is not able to capture the centrality of nodes w.r.t. paths crossing different social networks. In other words, it is not able to detect those
nodes of a multi-social-network scenario (called Social Internetworking
Scenario) which play a central role in inter-social-network information
flows. In this paper, we propose a new measure of betweenness centrality suitable for Social Internetworking Scenarios, also applicable to the
case of different communities of the same social network. The new measure has been tested in a number of synthetic networks, highlighting the
significance and effectiveness of our proposal.

1 Introduction

Centrality is one of the most important and widely used measures in Social
Network Analysis [9,7,3]. A large variety of applications can benefit of this measure: for instance, think of information flow and strategic marketing, to name
a few. Among the centrality measures, one of the most known is betweenness
centrality. The betweenness centrality of a node is defined as the fraction of
shortest paths between node pairs that pass through it. It is capable of measuring the influence of a node over the information spread through the network
[1,10]. Due to its relevance in network analysis, this measure has been largely
investigated, and several extensions, tailored to particular contexts, have been
proposed in the past [11,5,6,2]. Unfortunately, the existing notion of betweenness centrality is not able to capture the centrality of nodes w.r.t. paths crossing
different social networks (or different communities in the same social network).
In other words, it is not able to detect those nodes of a multi-social-network
scenario (called Social Internetworking Scenario) which play a central role in
inter-social-network information flows. In this paper, we propose a new measure
of betweenness centrality, called *cross betweenness centrality (CBC)*, suitable for
Social Internetworking Scenarios, also applicable to the case of different communities of the same social network. Intuitively, the CBC of a node works by

---

* Corresponding author.

Y.T. Demey and H. Panetto (Eds.): OTM 2013 Workshops, LNCS 8186, pp. 666–673, 2013.

considering only paths which cross the different social networks about which we want to measure the interconnection capability of this node. We investigate the relationship between the new measure and the classical one also by analyzing some features of CBC. Finally, with the support of some synthetic networks, we substantiate the significance and the effectiveness of our measure also by showing where the classical one fails. The plan of this paper is as follows: in the next section, we formally define cross betweenness centrality. In Section 3, we present our tests. Finally, in Section 5, we draw our conclusions.

2   Cross Betweenness Centrality

Consider a Social Internetworking Scenario, from now on called SIS, consisting of a set $\mathcal{S} = \{S_1, \ldots, S_k\}$ of social networks. It can be represented as a graph $G = \langle N, E \rangle$, where N is the set of its nodes and E is the set of its edges. A node $a \in N$ belongs to exactly one social network of the SIS. We denote by $S(a)$ this social network. E is partitioned into two subsets E_f and E_m. E_f is said the set of *friendship edges* and E_m is the set of me *edges*. A me edge links the accounts of the same user in two different social networks and can be easily declared by the user himself [4]. E_f is such that for each $(a, b) \in E_f$, $S(a) = S(b)$, while E_m is such that for each $(a, b) \in E_m$, $S(a) \neq S(b)$.

An edge $(a, b) \in E_f$ means that the account b is a friend of the account a in the social network $S(a)$. An edge $(c, c') \in E_m$ means that the user of account c in $S(c)$ has declared a me edge between c and the account c' in $S(c')$. In this case, we say that c is a *bridge*. We observe that our definition of bridge does not correspond to the classical one defined in the context of single social networks, even though a strong relationship between the two notions can be argued.

Given a node $u \in N$, the classical definition of betweenness centrality is the following:

$$BC(u) = \sum_{s,t \in N, s \neq u, t \neq u} \frac{\sigma_{st}(u)}{\sigma_{st}}$$

where σ_{st} is the total number of shortest paths from s to t, and $\sigma_{st}(u)$ is the number of those shortest paths passing through u.

This formula involves all the shortest paths. Thus, it is not able to measure how much the node u is central w.r.t. the information flow crossing different social networks. This could be a very important information. For instance, think of a music band and consider a SIS consisting of MySpace and LinkedIn. The capability of disseminating information from nodes of MySpace to nodes of LinkedIn is extremely relevant for the marketing goals of the band, which probably is already known in MySpace but unknown in LinkedIn. A bridge allowing the connection (and the subsequent information flow) between MySpace and LinkedIn can open a lot of new opportunities to the band. Therefore, the importance of this bridge in this SIS is extremely high even in case the paths involving it would be not numerous, which would imply a low value of its betweenness centrality. We thus need to revise the definition of betweenness centrality to our purpose, in order to bring out the importance of nodes w.r.t. the information flow crossing different social networks, as done for weak ties in classical studies on social networks [8].

Our definition of betweenness centrality in a SIS, which we call *cross betweenness centrality (CBC)*, is the following:

$$CBC(u, \Omega) = \sum_{s,t \in N, s \neq u, t \neq u, S(s) \neq S(t), S(t) \in \Omega} \frac{\sigma_{st}(u)}{\sigma_{st}}$$

Here, Ω is any subset of $\mathcal{S}$.

This definition allows the computation of the cross betweenness centrality of a node to be limited (if this is desired) to a subset of the social networks of the SIS. Observe that:

$$BC(u) = CBC(u, \Omega) + CBC(u, \overline{\Omega}) + IBC(u)$$

where:

$$IBC(u) = \sum_{s,t \in N, s \neq u, t \neq u, S(s)=S(u)=S(t)} \frac{\sigma_{st}(u)}{\sigma_{st}}$$

and

$$\overline{\Omega} = \mathcal{S} \setminus \Omega$$

We call $IBC(u)$ the *internal betweenness centrality* of u. Therefore, the betweenness centrality of a node consists of three components: The first two have an inter-social-network nature, whereas the third one is an intra-social-network component. Three important properties can be derived from the above equation:

1. $CBC(u, \Omega) \leq BC(u)$ for each $u \in N$ and for each $\Omega \subseteq \mathcal{S}$;
2. in the trivial case of a single-social-network SIS, $BC(u) = IBC(u)$;
3. if u belongs to a fragment of a social network not connected with the rest of the SIS, then $CBC(u, \Omega) = 0$ for each Ω.

Interestingly, CBC could be identically applied to the case of different communities of a single social network, by considering the social network nodes as partitioned into communities and by substituting the concept of social network in a SIS with the concept of community in a social network.

3   Tests

In this section, with the support of two synthetic networks, we show the significance and the effectiveness of our cross betweenness centrality measure.

The first network is shown in Figure 1. In this case we have a SIS consisting of three social networks whose nodes are colored in black, gray and white, respectively. We compute the betweenness centrality BC and the cross betweenness

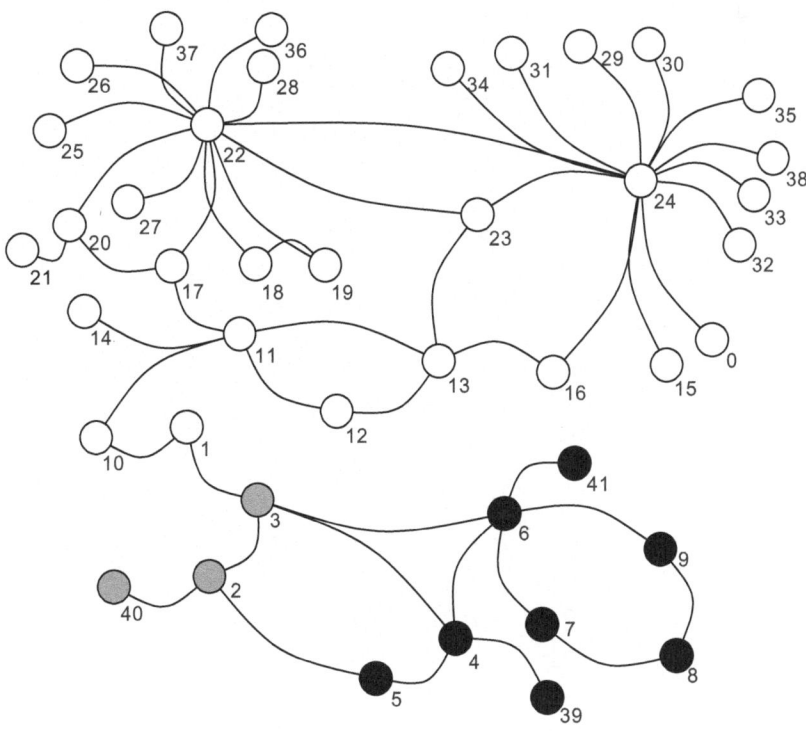

Fig. 1. A first synthetic network

centrality CBC for each node of the SIS. For CBC we choose Ω in such a way as to consider all the social networks of the SIS. In Table 1 we report the values of BC and CBC, along with the corresponding ranks, for the most significant nodes of the SIS.

From the analysis of Figure 1 and Table 1 we can observe that: *(i)* the three most ranked nodes for BC and CBC are totally different; *(ii)* the three most ranked nodes for BC are high-degree nodes and none of them is a bridge or is directly connected with a bridge; *(iii)* the three most ranked nodes for CBC are either bridges (e.g., nodes 1 and 3) or directly connected to bridges (e.g., node 10); *(iv)* none of the most ranked nodes for CBC is a high-degree node.

This example clearly shows how CBC is capable of capturing and representing a phenomenon high relevant for a SIS (since it is strictly connected with information spread), that BC is not able to capture in this scenario.

All these observations are further enforced by examining the second network, shown in Figure 2. In this case we have a SIS consisting of three social networks, where a great fragment of one of them is disconnected from the rest of the SIS. We compute BC and CBC as in the previous case. In Table 2 we report the corresponding values and ranks for the most significant nodes of the SIS.

Table 1. Values and ranks of BC and CBC for the most significant nodes of the SIS of Figure 1

Node	BC	Rank	CBC	Rank
11	802	1	614	4
22	771	2	374	6
24	734	3	220	8
1	660	5	660	1
3	644	6	644	2
10	696	4	636	3

Table 2. Values and ranks of BC and CBC for the most significant nodes of the SIS of Figure 2

Node	BC	Rank	CBC	Rank
3	264	1	0	7
10	120	2	0	7
24	102	3	0	7
21	66	5	50	1
17	48	6	48	2
16	42	7	42	3

All the observations drawn for the previous example are still valid, and further reinforced, in this case. For instance, the three most ranked nodes for BC belongs to the disconnected fragment of a social network of the SIS, and information passing through them has no chance to reach nodes of the other social networks. As a further observation, we evidence that this example confirms the third property of CBC derived at the end of Section 2.

4   Related Work

In this section, we survey the approaches proposed in the literature strictly related to the topic of betweenness centrality.

Betweenness centrality is capable of measuring the influence of a node over the information spread through the network. This concept has been widely investigated in [1,10]. In [1], the analysis of betweenness centrality of nodes in large complex networks. obtaining that it is increasing with connectivity as a power law with an exponent η, which is equal to 2 for trees or networks with a small loop density. In contrast, while a larger density of loops leads to $\eta < 2$. For scale-free networks, characterized by an exponent γ which describes the connectivity distribution decay, betweenness centrality is also distributed according to a power law with a non universal exponent δ.

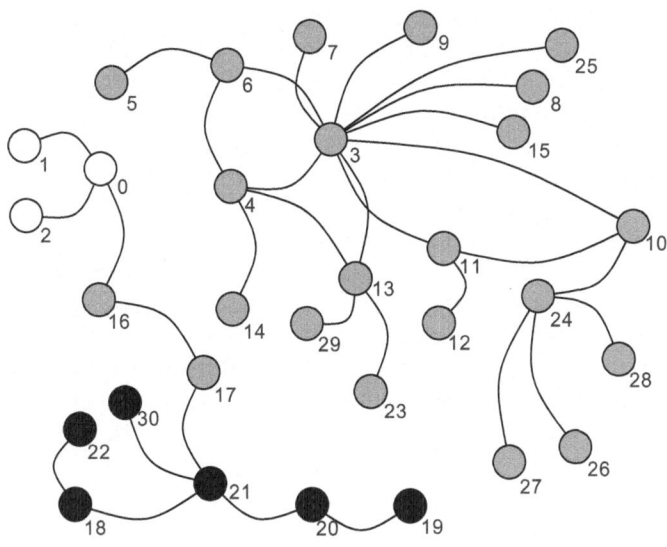

Fig. 2. A second synthetic network

In [10], Newman proposes a new betweenness centrality measure, called Random-Walk betweenness, that essentially counts all the paths between vertices (excluding those that do not actually lead from the designated source to the target), and which makes no assumptions of optimality. This measure is based on random walks between vertex pairs. It asks, in essence, how often a given vertex will fall on a random walk between another pair of vertices. This measure is particularly useful for finding vertices of high centrality that do not happen to lie on geodesic paths or on the paths formed by maximum-flow cut-sets. The author shows that the new betweenness centrality can be calculated using matrix inversion methods in a time that scales as the cube of the number of vertices on a sparse graph, making it computationally tractable for the networks typical of current sociological studies.

Due to its relevance in network analysis, several extensions of betweenness centrality, tailored to particular contexts, have been proposed in the past [11,5,6,2].

In [11], the authors generalize Freeman's geodesic centrality measures for betweenness centrality on undirected graphs to the directed case. This is an important step in the development of scientific propositions concerning social networks.

[5] extends the standard network centrality measures of degree centrality, closeness centrality and betweenness centrality to apply to groups and classes as well as individuals. The group centrality measures enable researchers to answer questions such as "how central is the engineering department in the informal influence network of this company?" or "among middle managers in a given organization, which are more central, the men or the women?" By means of these measures, they can also solve the inverse problem: "given the network of

ties among organization members, how can we form a team that is maximally central?" The authors define different group centralities and formalize a measure of group centrality efficiency, which indicates the extent to which a group's centrality is mainly due to a small subset of its members.

In [6], the authors look at the betweenness centrality of the ego in an ego network. They discuss the issues concerning normalization and develop an algorithm for computing the betweenness centrality score. The computation of all the ego betweenness scores for a whole network would be one order of magnitude faster than the computation of real betweenness centrality scores. The authors examine also the relationship between the betweenness centrality of an actor in her ego network and her betweenness centrality in the whole network. Even if, they show that there is no theoretical link between these two measures, they present a simulation study which indicates that the local ego betweenness centrality is highly correlated with the one of the actor in the complete network. Specifically, Ego betweenness centrality gives a good approximation of betweenness centrality in two situations, i.e. when all the actors have very similar betweenness centrality scores, and when there are highly differentiated scores.

In [2], the authors study the problem of analyzing multidimensional networks. They start from the consideration that complex networks have been receiving an increasing attention by scientific community, thanks also to the increasing availability of real-world network data. The aim of [2] is then to give the basis for multidimensional network analysis. The authors present a repertoire of basic concepts and analytical measures, which take the general structure of multidimensional networks into account. They test the framework on different real-world multidimensional networks, showing that the measures introduced are able to extract important and non-random information about complex phenomena in such networks.

All the notions of centrality described above have been conceived for single social network. Therefore, they are not able to capture the centrality of nodes w.r.t. paths crossing different social networks (or different communities in the same social network). This is the main contribution of our paper, which is the first one proposing a centrality measure specifically conceived for a multi-social-network scenario.

5   Conclusion

In this paper, we have presented cross betweenness centrality, a measure that adapts betweenness centrality to a SIS. In particular, we have defined this measure, we have analyzed its relationship with classical betweenness centrality, we have investigated some of its features, and we have highlighted its significance by means of synthetic networks also showing that the classical measure of betweenness centrality is not able to capture the centrality of nodes w.r.t. paths crossing different social networks. As pointed out in the introduction, this short paper presents our preliminary results about this issue. In the future, we plan to extend our research efforts in several directions. Specifically, we plan to conduct an experimental campaign to better evaluate the new measure in real SIS contexts, instead of in synthetic networks, also considering its application to different communities of a single social network. Finally, we plan to investigate the relationship between our notion of centrality and the concept of weak ties introduced in [8], on the basis of the similarity observed in Section 2.

Acknowledgment. This work has been partially supported by the TENACE PRIN Project (n. 20103P34XC) funded by the Italian Ministry of Education, University and Research.

References

1. Barthelemy, M.: Betweenness centrality in large complex networks. The European Physical Journal B-Condensed Matter and Complex Systems 38(2), 163–168 (2004)
2. Berlingerio, M., Coscia, M., Giannotti, F., Monreale, A., Pedreschi, D.: Multi-dimensional networks: foundations of structural analysis. In: World Wide Web, pp. 1–27 (2012)
3. Bonacich, P.: Factoring and weighting approaches to status scores and clique identification. Journal of Mathematical Sociology 2(1), 113–120 (1972)
4. Buccafurri, F., Foti, V.D., Lax, G., Nocera, A., Ursino, D.: Bridge Analysis in a Social Internetworking Scenario. In: Information Sciences, pp. 224:1–224:18. Elsevier (2013)
5. Everett, M.G., Borgatti, S.P.: The centrality of groups and classes. The Journal of Mathematical Sociology 23(3), 181–201 (1999)
6. Everett, M.G., Borgatti, S.P.: Ego network betweenness. Social Networks 27(1), 31–38 (2005)
7. Freeman, L.C.: Centrality in social networks conceptual clarification. Social Networks 1(3), 215–239 (1979)
8. Granovetter, M.S.: The strength of weak ties. American Journal of Sociology 78(6), 1360–1380 (1973)
9. Katz, L.: A new status index derived from sociometric analysis. Psychometrika 18(1), 39–43 (1953)
10. Newman, M.E.J.: A measure of betweenness centrality based on random walks. Social Networks 27(1), 39–54 (2005)
11. White, D.R., Borgatti, S.P.: Betweenness centrality measures for directed graphs. Social Networks 16(4), 335–346 (1994)

Efficient Solution of the Correlation Clustering Problem: An Application to Structural Balance

Lúcia Drummond[2], Rosa Figueiredo[1], Yuri Frota[2], and Mário Levorato[3]

[1] CIDMA, Department of Mathematics, University of Aveiro
3810-193 Aveiro, Portugal
rosa.figueiredo@ua.pt
[2] Department of Computer Science, Fluminense Federal University
24210-240 Niterói-RJ, Brazil
{lucia,yuri}@ic.uff.br
[3] Petróleo Brasileiro S.A.
levorato@petrobras.com.br

Abstract. One challenge for social network researchers is to evaluate balance in a social network. The degree of balance in a social group can be used as a tool to study whether and how this group evolves to a possible balanced state. The solution of clustering problems defined on signed graphs can be used as a criterion to measure the degree of balance in social networks. By considering the original definition of the structural balance, the optimal solution of the Correlation Clustering (CC) Problem arises as one possible measure. In this work, we contribute to the efficient solution of the CC problem by developing sequential and parallel GRASP metaheuristics. Then, by using our GRASP algorithms, we solve the problem of measuring the structural balance of large social networks.

1 Introduction

Signed graphs were introduced by Heider [1] with the purpose of describing sentiment relations between people pertaining to a same social group and to provide a systematic statement of social balance theory. Cartwright *et al.* [2] formalized Heider's theory stating that a balanced social group could be partitioned into two mutually hostile subgroups each having internal solidarity. In the last decades, signed graphs have shown to be a very attractive discrete structure for social network researchers [3–8]. One challenge in this area is to evaluate balance in a social network. Different criteria and different solution approaches have been used in the literature as an attempt to quantify and evaluate balance in a signed social network [5, 8–10].

Clustering is the action of partitioning individual elements into groups based on their similarity. Clustering problems defined on signed graphs arise in many scientific areas [11–16]. The common element among these applications is the collaborative *vs.* conflicting environment in which they are defined. The solution of clustering problems defined on signed graphs can be used as a criteria to measure the degree of balance in social networks [4, 5, 17]. By considering the original definition [1] of structural balance, the optimal solution of the very known Correlation Clustering (CC) Problem arises as a measure for the degree

Y.T. Demey and H. Panetto (Eds.): OTM 2013 Workshops, LNCS 8186, pp. 674–683, 2013.

of balance in a social network. Alternative measures to the structural balance and the clustering problems associated with them were recently discussed [5, 17].

To the best of our knowledge, the CC problem was addressed for the first time in [4] (not under this name) where its heuristic solution was used as a criteria for analyzing structural balance in social networks. The heuristic approach proposed by the authors is a simple greedy neighborhood search procedure that assumes a prior knowledge of the number of clusters in the solution. This heuristic is implemented in software Pajek [18]. Lately, motivated by the solution of a document clustering problem the unweighted version of the CC problem was formalized in [13]. The weighted version of the problem was addressed in [19]. The CC problem has been largely investigated from the point of view of constant factor approximation algorithms and has been applied in the solution of many applications (see references in [20]). A comparison of several heuristic strategies (greedy and local search methods) for this problem is presented in [20] and applied to document clustering and natural language processing. In [7] the CC problem is called *community mining* and an agent-based heuristic is proposed to its solution. An approach based on genetic algorithm has been proposed in [21] for the CC problem and applied to documents clustering.

From a practical point of view, in solving the clustering problem treated in this paper, heuristic approaches are primarily of interest since large social networks may have to be analyzed [8, 9, 22]. The definition of a measure to represent the balance/imbalance of a social network involves itself a degree of approximation for the task of evaluating balance in a social network. Thus, it is imperative that the clustering problem associated with this measure be solved efficiently. To the best of our knowledge, [21] presents the only metaheuristic approach applied to the CC problem. However, the Greedy Randomized Adaptive Search Procedure (GRASP) [23] has been successfully applied to clustering problems [24–26] and to a related problem [27]. Moreover, numerical experiments described in [20] indicate that combining greedy heuristics with local search procedures is an efficient strategy to the solution of the CC problem.

Our contributions are two-fold. At first, we contribute to the efficient solution of the CC problem by developing sequential and parallel GRASP metaheuristics for this problem. Then, by using our GRASP algorithms we solve the problem of measuring the structural balance of a large social network.

2 Problem Definition and Mathematical Formulation

Let $G = (V, E)$ be an undirected graph where V is the set of n vertices and E is the set of edges. In this text, a graph is assumed to have no loops. For a vertex set $S \subseteq V$, let $E[S] = \{(i,j) \in E \mid i, j \in S\}$ denote the *subset of edges induced by* S. For two vertex sets $S, W \subseteq V$, let $E[S : W] = \{(i,j) \in E \mid i \in S, j \in W\}$. One observes that, by definition, $E[S : S] = E[S]$. Consider a function $s : E \to \{+, -\}$ that assigns a sign to each edge in E. An undirected graph G together with a function s is called a *signed graph*. An edge $e \in E$ is called *negative* if $s(e) = -$ and *positive* if $s(e) = +$. Let E^- and E^+ denote, respectively, the set of negative and positive edges in a signed graph.

A *partition* of V is a division of V into non-overlapping and non-empty subsets. Consider a partition $P = \{S_1, S_2, \ldots, S_l\}$ of V. The *cut edges* and the *uncut edges* related with this partition are defined, respectively, as the edges in sets $\cup_{1 \leq i < j \leq l} E[S_i : S_j]$ and $\cup_{1 \leq i \leq l} E[S_i]$. Let w_e be a nonnegative edge weight associated with edge $e \in E$. Also, for $1 \leq i, j \leq l$, let

$$\Omega^+(S_i, S_j) = \sum_{e \in E^+ \cap E[S_i:S_j]} w_e \text{ and } \Omega^-(S_i, S_j) = \sum_{e \in E^- \cap E[S_i:S_j]} w_e.$$

The *imbalance* $I(P)$ of a partition P is defined as the total weight of negative uncut edges and positive cut edges, i.e.,

$$I(P) = \sum_{1 \leq i \leq l} \Omega^-(S_i, S_i) + \sum_{1 \leq i < j \leq l} \Omega^+(S_i, S_j). \tag{1}$$

Likewise, the *balance* $B(P)$ of a partition P can be defined as the total weight of positive uncut edges and negative cut edges. Clearly, $B(P) + I(P) = \sum_{e \in E} w_e$.

Problem 21 (CC problem). *Let $G = (V, E, s)$ be a signed graph and w_e be a nonnegative edge weight associated with each edge $e \in E$. The correlation clustering problem is the problem of finding a partition P of V such that the imbalance $I(P)$ is minimized or, equivalently, the balance $B(P)$ is maximized.*

The classical formulation for the CC problem is an integer linear programming (ILP) model proposed to uncapacitated clustering problems (see references in [28]). In this formulation a binary decision variable x_{ij} is assigned to each pair of vertices $i, j \in V$, $i \neq j$, and defined as follows: $x_{ij} = 0$ if i and j are in a common set; $x_{ij} = 1$ otherwise. The model minimizes the total imbalance.

$$\text{minimize} \sum_{(i,j) \in E^-} w_{ij}(1 - x_{ij}) + \sum_{(i,j) \in E^+} w_{ij} x_{ij} \tag{2}$$

$$\text{subject to } x_{ip} + x_{pj} \geq x_{ij}, \qquad \forall\, i, p, j \in V, \tag{3}$$

$$x_{ij} = x_{ji}, \qquad \forall\, i, j \in V, \tag{4}$$

$$x_{ij} \in \{0, 1\}, \qquad \forall\, i, j \in V. \tag{5}$$

The triangle inequalities (3) say that if i and p are in a same cluster as well as p and j, then vertices i and j are also in a same cluster. Constraint (4) written to $i, j \in V$ establishes that variables x_{ij} and x_{ji} assume always the same value in this formulation. Constraints (5) impose binary restrictions to the variables while the objective function (2) minimizes the total imbalance defined by equation (1). Notice that, according to constraints (4), half of the variables can be eliminated which reduces both the number of variables and the number of constraints.

A set partitioning formulation [28] is proposed in the literature to uncapacitated clustering problems and could also be used in the solution of the CC problem. As we can expect, these two formulations are not appropriate solution approaches when time limit is a constraint in the solution process. The authors in [17] reports that the classical formulation starts to fail (time limit set to 1h) with random instances of 40 vertices and negative density equal to 0.5.

3   Sequential and Parallel GRASP to CC Problem

Metaheuristics have been used successfully for solving hard combinatorial optimization problems as they can provide sub-optimal solutions in a reasonable time. GRASP is a multi-start metaheuristic in which each iteration consists basically of two phases: construction and local search [29].

In this work, we develop a GRASP method to the solution of the CC problem. The proposed heuristic ($GraspCC$) is based on a GRASP method for the maximum modularity problem [26]. It is composed of a construction phase $coCC$ and a local search phase $lsCC$. In phase $coCC$, a randomized greed function is used to build up an initial feasible solution. Let $P = \{S_1, S_2, ..., S_l\}$ denote a *partial partition* (i.e., a partition of a proper subset of V) and let $M_{n \times n} = (m_{ij})$ be the *modularity signed matrix* [26]. We define below a *function* $f : (V \backslash \bigcup_{1 \leq k \leq l} S_k) \to \mathbb{R}$, which will measure the impact of inserting a vertex i in the partial partition P.

$$f(i) = \max \left(m_{ii}, m_{ii} + \max_{1 \leq k \leq l} \sum_{j \in S_k} 2m_{ij} \right). \tag{6}$$

Our $GraspCC$ is described in Algorithm 1. The parameter *iter* denotes the maximum number of iterations without improvement in the best solution found. The first task in every iteration of $GraspCC$ is to construct a solution in a greedy randomized fashion. This task is performed in phase $coCC$ described in Algorithm 2. In this phase, the ordered set L_f is defined (line 3) as the set of vertices $V \backslash \bigcup_{1 \leq k \leq l} S_k$ ordered in decreasing order of function f. At each iteration, in lines 4-8, we choose a vertex i randomly among the first $\lfloor \alpha . | L_f | \rfloor$ vertices in this set and add it to the partial partition. Note that parameter α defines the degree of randomness the construction phase will have. This process is repeated until a partition of V is obtained.

Algorithm 1. $GraspCC$

---

1 **Input:** $G = (V, E)$ and α
2 **Output:** partition P^*
3 $P^* = \emptyset$; $I(P^*) = \infty$; $i = 0$;
4 **while** $i \leqslant iter$
5     $P = coCC(G, \alpha)$;
6     $P = lsCC(P, G)$;
7   **if** $(I(P) < I(P^*))$
8         $P^* = P$; $i = 0$;
9   **end if**
10    $i = i + 1$
11 **end while**
12 **return** P^*;

There is no guarantee that the construction method returns a locally optimal solution with respect to some neighborhood. Therefore, the solution P obtained in phase $coCC$ may be improved by the local search procedure $lsCC$ described in Algorithm 3. The neighborhood $N_r(P)$ is defined as the family of all partitions obtained by moving r vertices in P from one cluster into another. Note that the neighborhood analyzes partitions with different number of clusters (i.e. a vertex can be moved into a new cluster or can be removed from a single vertex cluster) The $lsCC$ method starts with the partition provided by the construction phase. It iteratively replaces the current partition by that with minimum imbalance cost within its neighborhood (lines 4-8). The local search halts when no better partition is found in the neighborhood of the current solution. In this work we employed a neighborhood with $r \leq 2$.

Although metaheuristics aim to reduce historical difficulties of conventional construction and local search methods (such as premature stops in local optima solutions distant from an optimal solution) in optimization problems, they may require a large amount of time to find good primal bounds as penalty in many cases. This fact has motivated the development of a parallel metaheuristic, taking advantage of the inherent parallelism present in the GRASP method [30].

In this work, the well known independent approach was employed in the parallel program. This scheme limits communication between processors only for problem input, detection of process termination, and determination of best overall solution. When p processors are used, a single process reads the problem data and passes it to the remaining $p - 1$ processes. Each process executes a copy of the GRASP program. Processes send a message to all others when they either stop upon finding a solution at least as good as the target value or complete the maximum number of allotted iterations.

Algorithm 2. $coCC$

---

1 **Input:** $G = (V, E)$ and α
2 **Output:** partition P
3 $P = \emptyset$; $L_f = Order(V)$;
4 **while** $(L_f \neq \emptyset)$
5   Choose vertex i randomly among the first $\lfloor \alpha . \mid L_f \mid \rfloor$ elements of L_f
6   Update $S_k = S_k \cup \{i\}$ where k is the component in P that maximizes f
7     $L_f = L_f - \{i\}$; Re-order(L_f);
8 **end while**
9 **return** P

---

4   CC Solution Applied to Structural Balance and Conclusions

The algorithms described in the previous section were implemented in ANSI C and MPI(MPICH2) for message passing. All experiments were performed (with exclusive access) on a cluster with 42 nodes, each one with two processors Intel Xeon QuadCore 2.66Hz and 16Gb of RAM under Linux (Red Hat) 5.3 operating system. The formulation is coded in Xpress Mosel 3.2.0 with solver Xpress Optimizer 21.01.00. The CPU time limit is set to 1 hour for the ILP formulation.

Algorithm 3. *lsCC*

---

1 **Input:** $G = (V, E)$ and a partition P
2 **Output:** partition P
3 **while** (P improving)
4   **for all** $\overline{P} \in (N_1(P) \cup N_2(P))$
5   **if** ($I(\overline{P}) < I(P)$)
6         $P = \overline{P}$
7   **end if**
8   **end for**
9 **end while**

All heuristic outcomes are average results of 5 independent executions. Computational experiments were carried out on (i) a set of 28 social networks from the literature, (ii) a set of 6 network instances that represent the United Nations General Assembly (UNGA), and (iii) a set of 12 random instances. Next, we describe briefly these instances[1].

(i) This set of instances is composed by 22 small size instances normally used in blockmodeling approaches to structural balance (see [5, 17, 31]) and 6 signed networks extracted from the large scale social network representing the technology-related news website Slashdot (see [8, 9]). The small instances were used to parametrize the GRASP heuristics.

(ii) We generated 6 medium-sized social networks based on UNGA voting records of the separate annual sessions between 2003 and 2008[2]. These instances are weighted versions of UNGA signed graphs described in [27].

(iii) We generated random social networks with 50 vertices ($n = 50$) varying network density $d = 2 \times |E|/(n^2 - n)$ and negative graph density defined here as $d^- = |E^-|/|E|$. We considered a set of 12 random instances having d and d^- ranging, respectively, in sets $\{0.1, 0.2, 0.5, 0.8\}$ and $\{0.2, 0.5, 0.8\}$. These instances were also used in [17].

As reported in the literature [28], the linear relaxation of the ILP formulation described in Section 2 provides a very good representation of the problem which allows to find the optimal solution for many instances by solving this linear relaxation. Experiments reported in [17] confirm this assertion: the 22 small instances in set (i) were solved to optimality in some seconds; the formulation failed to solve the random instances in set (iii) having $d \geq 0.2$ and $d^- = 0.5$. In our experiments, the 6 instances in set (ii) were solved to optimality by the ILP formulation in the root of the branch and bound tree. The results obtained on these instances with the ILP formulation and with the sequential GRASP (*iter* $= 400$, $r \leq 2, \alpha = 0.8$, time limit set to 30 minutes) are reported in Table 1.

---

[1] All instances are available in http://www.ic.uff.br/~yuri/files/CCinst.zip.
[2] United Nations General Assembly Voting Data, by Anton Strezhnev and Erik Voeten, http://hdl.handle.net/1902.1/12379. Accessed in June 2013.

Table 1. Results obtained on UNGA instances with Xpress and the sequential GRASP algorithm (400 iterations without improvement). Number of vertices (n); number of negative $(|E^-|)$ and positive $(|E^+|)$ edges; sum of negative $(w(E^-))$ and positive $(w(E^+))$ weights; number of clusters (k) in the optimal solution $\bar{P}$; percentage imbalance $(\%I = 100 \times IP(\bar{P})/w(E))$; negative percentage imbalance $(\%I^- = 100 \times IP^-(\bar{P})/w(E^-))$ where $IP^-(\bar{P})$ is the sum of weights of negative edges in the optimal solution; positive percentage imbalance $(\%I^+ = 100 \times IP^+(\bar{P})/w(E^+))$ where $IP^+(\bar{P})$ is the sum of weights of positive edges in the optimal solution; and time in seconds spent by the Xpress software to solve the ILP formulation $(T(Xpress))$ and by the sequential GRASP procedure GraspSeq $(T(seq))$.

			Instance				Optimal Solution			Times (s)	
Session	n	$|E^-|$	$|E^+|$	$w(E^-)$	$w(E^+)$	k	$\%I$	$\%I^-$	$\%I^+$	$T(Xpress)$	$T(seq)$
2003	191	1119	16636	247.33	8247.60	2	0.09	0.47	0.08	281	1327
2004	191	945	17121	315.15	8646.75	2	0.23	2.74	0.14	301	1410
2005	192	1120	16566	251.28	8271.56	3	0.47	3.03	0.40	338	1783
2006	192	886	17378	248.60	8873.92	2	0.32	1.59	0.28	223	1739
2007	192	1109	17148	260.26	8646.04	2	0.51	4.18	0.40	262	1468
2008	192	1055	17091	256.66	8854.55	2	0.40	5.05	0.27	178	1342

Table 2. Results obtained on Slashdot signed graphs. BestSol is the value of the best solution found in the time limit.

		Instance			ILP Formulation		GraspSeq		GraspPar 8	
n	$|E^-|$	$|E^+|$	$w(E^-)$	$w(E^+)$	k	BestSol	k	BestSol	k	BestSol
200	62	825	62	825	1	65	12	48.4	12	49.0
300	82	981	82	981	1	85	23	58.8	25	61.8
400	87	1192	87	1192	1	87	23	64.6	23	64.6
600	156	1761	156	1761	–	–	29	121.4	31	121.8
800	371	2965	371	2965	–	–	50	257.4	54	254.5
1000	859	5132	859	5132	–	–	62	647.0	63	650.25

We can conclude that these signed networks are almost perfect balanced with most part of the imbalance given by negative relations.

The drawback of the ILP approach appears when we try to solve the instances based on Slashdot: the ILP formulation turn to be very big and Xpress is not able to solve any of it. To solve these instances with our heuristics, we propose two approaches. First we tackle the problem with the sequential GRASP with $iter = 400$, $r = 1$, $\alpha = 0.4$ and time limit of 1 hour. Then we solve these intances with our parallel GRASP by using 8 processors (GraspPar 8) with the same parameters but $iter = 50$. We discard the costly neighborhood with $r = 2$ and increase the time limit in order to manage the large number of vertices and edges. On the other hand, we drop the randomness of the method to avoid low quality solutions with (probably) a reduced number of iterations. These results are reported in Table 2. The notations in this table are the same as in Table 1 ("–" means no feasible integer solution was reported in the time limit).

Table 3. Results obtained on random instances ($n = 50$) with sequential and parallel GRASP algorithm

File	ILP BestSol	GraspSeq BestSol	$T(seq)$	GraspPar 8 BestSol	$T(8)$	$Su(8)$	$E(8)$
$d = 0.1\ d^- = 0.2$	48	48.00	51.64	48.00	9.24	5.59	0.70
$d = 0.1\ d^- = 0.5$	55	56.43	395.57	56.80	85.84	4.61	0.58
$d = 0.1\ d^- = 0.8$	18	18.43	648.25	18.20	129.46	5.01	0.63
$d = 0.2\ d^- = 0.2$	98	98.00	8.69	98.00	1.69	5.13	0.64
$d = 0.2\ d^- = 0.5$	**159**	149.57	164.24	150.00	35.45	4.63	0.58
$d = 0.2\ d^- = 0.8$	58	58.20	999.26	58.20	209.45	4.77	0.60
$d = 0.5\ d^- = 0.2$	245	245.00	7.52	245.00	1.25	6.03	0.75
$d = 0.5\ d^- = 0.5$	**523**	461.00	205.82	461.80	61.03	3.37	0.42
$d = 0.5\ d^- = 0.8$	196	197.67	1800.61	197.20	519.89	3.46	0.43
$d = 0.8\ d^- = 0.8$	392	392.00	7.52	392.00	1.18	6.36	0.80
$d = 0.8\ d^- = 0.5$	**879**	775.29	228.47	775.60	51.15	4.47	0.56
$d = 0.8\ d^- = 0.8$	334	335.00	1803.40	334.80	809.19	2.23	0.28
Avg	250.42	236.22	526.75	236.30	159.57	4.64	0.58

In [17], computational experiments are reported with Pajek [18] on the 22 small instances in (i) and on the random instances in (iii). We run our GRASP procedures on these instances and they performed equally or better than the greedy heuristic implemented in Pajek: strictly better in (i) 1 instance; and in (iii) 7 instances.

Table 3 compares the results obtained on the set of random instances (iii) by GraspSeq ($iter = 400$, $r \leq 2$ and $\alpha = 0.8$) and GraspPar 8 ($iter = 50$, $r \leq 2$ and $\alpha = 0.8$) with time limit set to 30 minutes. The instances that were not solved to optimality by the ILP formulation are marked with bold values in column (ILP-BestBound); in that case this column exhibits the value of the best integer solution found in the time limit. Clearly the GRASP algorithms achieved strong bounds, reaching an average imbalance of 236.22 (236.30 for the parallel version) while the average imbalance found by the exact method was 250.42. The parallel algorithm presents average speed-up and efficiency of 4.64 and 0.58 for 8 processors (one core per processor): speed-up measures the acceleration observed for the parallel algorithm when compared with its sequential version; efficiency measures the fraction of time along which each process is effectively used. Thus, $Su(8) = T(seq)/T(8)$, such that $T(8)$ is the time required for the parallel algorithm run on 8 processors, and $E(8) = Su(8)/8$. We did not obtain linear speedups due to the different stopping criteria employed in those algorithms. In the sequential version, the program finishes after 400 consecutive iterations without improvement while in the parallel algorithm every task must execute 50 iterations without improvement to finish. The sequential algorithm reached that condition proportionately faster than its parallel counterpart.

The obtained computational results indicate that our GRASP metaheuristic is an efficient approach for the heuristic solution of the CC problem. Additional numerical experiments need to be done with instances from other applications. The numerical experience over larger social networks indicates that, in order to handle the enlarged instances like Epinions (131.828 vertices and 841.372 edges) or Slashdot (82.144 vertices and 549.202 edges) networks, we need to implement better parallelization strategies. As we have mentioned in the introduction, alternative measures have been proposed in the literature to the structural balance [5, 17]. The next steps of this research includes the adaptation of the GRASP heuristic to deal with these different measures.

Acknowledgements. Rosa Figueiredo is supported by FEDER founds through COMPETE-Operational Pro- gramme Factors of Competitiveness and by Portuguese founds through the CIDMA (University of Aveiro) and FCT, within project PEst-C/MAT/UI4106/2011 with COM- PETE number FCOMP-01-0124-FEDER-022690.

References

1. Heider, F.: Attitudes and cognitive organization. Journal of Psychology 21, 107–112 (1946)
2. Cartwright, D., Harary, F.: Structural balance: A generalization of heiders theory. Psychological Review 63, 277–293 (1956)
3. Abell, P., Ludwig, M.: Structural balance: a dynamic perspective. Journal of Mathematical Sociology 33, 129–155 (2009)
4. Doreian, P., Mrvar, A.: A partitioning approach to structural balance. Social Networks 18, 149–168 (1996)
5. Doreian, P., Mrvar, A.: Partitioning signed social networks. Social Networks 31, 1–11 (2009)
6. Inohara, T.: On conditions for a meeting not to reach a deadlock. Applied Mathematics and Computation 90, 1–9 (1998)
7. Yang, B., Cheung, W., Liu, J.: Community mining from signed social networks. IEEE Transactions on Knowledge and Data Engineering 19, 1333–1348 (2007)
8. Facchetti, G., Iacono, G., Altafini, C.: Computing global structural balance in large-scale signed social networks. Proceedings of the National Academy of Sciences of the United States of America 108, 20953–20958 (2011)
9. Leskovec, J., Huttenlocher, D., Kleinberg, J.: Signed networks in social media. In: CHI 2010 Proceedings of the SIGCHI Conference on Human Factors in Computing Systems, pp. 1361–1370 (2010)
10. Srinivasan, A.: Local balancing influences global structure in social networks. Proceedings of the National Academy of Sciences of the United States of America 108, 1751–1752 (2011)
11. Huffner, F., Betzler, N., Niedermeier, R.: Separator-based data reduction for signed graph balancing. Journal of Combinatorial Optimization 20, 335–360 (2010)
12. DasGupta, B., Encisob, G.A., Sontag, E., Zhanga, Y.: Algorithmic and complexity results for decompositions of biological networks into monotone subsystems. BioSystems 90, 161–178 (2007)
13. Bansal, N., Blum, A., Chawla, S.: Correlation clustering. In: Proceedings of the 43rd Annual IEEE Symposium of Foundations of Computer Science, Vancouver, Canada, pp. 238–250 (2002)
14. Gülpinar, N., Gutin, G., Mitra, G., Zverovitch, A.: Extracting pure network submatrices in linear programs using signed graphs. Discrete Applied Mathematics 137, 359–372 (2004)

15. Macon, K., Mucha, P., Porter, M.: Community structure in the united nations general assembly. Physica A: Statistical Mechanics and its Applications 391, 343–361 (2012)
16. Traag, V., Bruggeman, J.: Community detection in networks with positive and negative links. Physical Review E 80, 36115 (2009)
17. Figueiredo, R., Moura, G.: Mixed integer programming formulations for clustering problems related to structural balance (2012) (Paper submitted)
18. Pajek, http://pajek.imfm.si/ (accessed June 2013)
19. Demaine, E.D., Emanuel, D., Fiat, A., Immorlica, N.: Correlation clustering in general weighted graphs. Theoretical Computer Science 361, 172–187 (2006)
20. Elsner, M., Schudy, W.: Bounding and comparing methods for correlation clustering beyond ilp. In: ILP 2009 Proceedings of the Workshop on Integer Linear Programming for Natural Language Processing, pp. 19–27 (2009)
21. Zhang, Z., Cheng, H., Chen, W., Zhang, S., Fang, Q.: Correlation clustering based on genetic algorithm for documents clustering. In: IEEE Congress on Evolutionary Computation, pp. 3193–3198 (2008)
22. Kunegis, J., Lommatzsch, A., Bauckhage, C.: The slashdot zoo: mining a social network with negative edges. In: WWW 2009 Proceedings of the 18th International Conference on World Wide Web, pp. 741–750 (2009)
23. Resende, M., Ribeiro, C.: Search Methodologies, 2nd edn. Springer (2011)
24. Nascimento, M., Toledo, F., de Carvalho, A.: Investigation of a new grasp-based clustering algorithm applied to biological data. Computers Operations Research 37, 1381–1388 (2010)
25. Frinhani, R., Silva, R., Mateus, G., Festa, P., Resende, M.: Grasp with path-relinking for data clustering: A case study for biological data. In: Pardalos, P.M., Rebennack, S. (eds.) SEA 2011. LNCS, vol. 6630, pp. 410–420. Springer, Heidelberg (2011)
26. Nascimento, M.C., Pitsoulis, L.: Community detection by modularity maximization using grasp with path relinking. Computers Operations Research (2013) (available online on March 2013)
27. Figueiredo, R., Frota, Y.: The maximum balanced subgraph of a signed graph: applications and solution approaches (2012) (paper submitted)
28. Mehrotraa, A., Trick, M.: Cliques and clustering: A combinatorial approach. Operations Research Letters 22, 1–12 (1998)
29. Resende, M., Ribeiro, C.: Grasp with path-relinking: Recent advances and applications. In: Ibaraki, T., Nonobe, K., Yagiura, M. (eds.) Metaheuristics: Progress as real problem solvers, pp. 29–63. Springer (2005)
30. Aiex, R.M., Binato, S., Resende, M.G.C.: Parallel grasp with path-relinking for job shop scheduling. Parallel Computing 29, 393–430 (2004)
31. Brusco, M.: An enhanced branch-and-bound algorithm for a partitioning problem. British Journal of Mathematical and Statistical Psychology 56, 83–92 (2003)

Towards Assessment of Open Educational Resources and Open Courseware Based on a Socio-constructivist Quality Model

Monica Vladoiu and Zoran Constantinescu

UPG University of Ploiesti, Romania
monica@unde.ro, zoran@upg-ploiesti.ro

Abstract. In this paper we introduce a rubric for assessing quality of open educational resources and open courseware based on our socio-constructivist quality model (QORE) that includes 70 criteria grouped in four categories related with content, instructional design, technology, and courseware evaluation. Quality is assessed from an educational point of view, i.e. how useful are such resources for various actors involved in educational processes taken into account their goals, objectives, abilities etc. QORE's focus is on the resources' potential to act as true *open educational content available online* that has a genuine educational value in this context. Several challenges of using this rubric for evaluation of such educational resources are discussed as well.

Keywords: open courseware, open educational resources, quality assurance, quality criteria, quality model, quality rubric.

1 Introduction

Quality assurance of educational content is seen conventionally as being the responsibility of subject and instructional experts, but in the context of Open Educational Resources (OERs), OpenCourseWare (OCW), and Web 2.0, guaranteeing quality seems more and more a community endeavor based on the collaboration between experts in education, subject scholars, students, teachers, developers etc. both during and after the teaching and learning process through study groups and practice communities around the world [1]. Consequently, sense of community becomes more and more present in quality models of Web 2.0 applications and special focus has to be on user-centered, participatory nature of these emergent applications. However, such collaborative efforts are very difficult to undertake in absence of appropriate models, frameworks, and tools for evaluating quality of OERs and OCW, yet for the time being, no quality assurance framework that could provide support for various categories of users (learners, instructors, designers, faculty, evaluators etc.) is available.

In this paper we introduce a rubric for assessing OERs and OCW based on our socio-constructivist quality model, called QORE, which includes 70 criteria grouped in four categories related with *content, instructional design, technology and courseware evaluation*. QORE had been introduced in [2], put to work in [3-7], and refined

Y.T. Demey and H. Panetto (Eds.): OTM 2013 Workshops, LNCS 8186, pp. 684–693, 2013.

further for this work according with what we have learned from those use experiences. The paper is structured follows: the next section presents the related work, the third one introduces a detailed rubric for assessing quality of OERs and OCW that is based on our quality model, and the last one includes a discussion on the challenges of using this rubric, along with some conclusions and future work ideas.

2   Related Work

We overview here the related work and, because in terms of rubrics for OERs and OCW there are only very few similar works, we approach it in a larger sense of rubrics for learning objects and online courses as well. Thus, in [8, 9, 10] the authors show that quality of learning objects may be improved by better educating their designers, by incorporative formative assessments and learning testing in design and development models, by taking into account the use context, and by providing summative reviews that should be maintained as metadata, which users can use when searching, sorting, and selecting learning resources. They have developed an instrument for reviewing quality of learning objects (called LORI) that incorporates several aspects as follows: content quality, learning goal alignment, feedback and adaptation, learners' motivation, presentation design, interaction usability, accessibility, reusability, and standards compliance. Furthermore, they use LORI within a suite of tools for collaborative evaluation that small evaluation teams (including subject matter experts, learners, instructional designers) use to produce *an aggregated view of ratings and comments*. Several works have tested LORI in particular cases [9, 11, 12] and have pointed out that it can be used to reliably assess some aspects of learning objects and that using a collaborative assessment process can improve inter-rater reliability. In [13] seven categories for assessing OERs are provided, five of them being adapted from LORI (*content quality, motivation, presentation design, usability, accessibility*), while the other two are new: *educational value* and *overall rating. Educational value* refers to the resource's potential to provide learning, to its accuracy, clarity, and unbiasedness, while the *overall evaluation* captures the perceived usefulness of resources in educational contexts. Several other rubrics have been proposed for evaluating learning objects and/or online courses, neither of them being as visible in the literature as LORI [14-20]. Finally, Achieve, working together with the OER community, has developed a rubric, which provides for establishing both the degree of alignment to the Common Core State Standards and some quality aspects of OERs [21]. Recently, Achieve has jointed up with OER Commons to provide an online evaluation tool based on their rubric [22], and currently, each resource available in OER Commons may be assessed, the resulted evaluation is stored in a pool of metadata, and it may be shared through the Learning Registry with other interested repositories [23]. This rubric includes the next aspects: degree of alignment to standards, quality of explanation of the subject matter, utility of materials designed to support teaching, quality of assessment, quality of technological interactivity, quality of instructional and practice exercises, opportunities for deeper learning, and assurance of accessibility.

3   Quality Rubric for Evaluation of OERs and OCW

We detail here the rubric based on the QORE quality model introduced in [2]. The QORE criteria may be used for quality assessment of either small learning units or entire courseware, and they are grouped in four categories related with *content, instructional design, technology,* and *courseware evaluation.* The majority of these criteria will be explained further on, along with their corresponding scoring scale. However, due to space limitations, some of the criteria will not be rubricated here. Nevertheless, they can be easily scored as it can be seen throughout this rubric. The not applicable N/A rating is used when a particular criterion cannot be evaluated for a specific resource. The fulfillment of each criterion is assessed on a scale between 0 and 5, as follows: 0=absence, 1=inadequate, 2=satisfactory, 3=good, 4=very good and 5=excellent. Quality is assessed from an educational point of view, i.e. how useful are such resources for various actors involved in educational processes taken into account their goals, objectives, knowledge, abilities etc. QORE's focus is on the resources' potential to act as true *open educational content available online* that has a genuine educational value in this context. For the time being, the evaluation is subjective, being based, in our case, on many decades of evaluators' experience in Higher Education. However, this subjective evaluation seems to be the tendency of other works in this area [8, 13, 21-23]. First and foremost, there is necessary to point out that a good *alignment* between learning objectives, learning outcomes, teaching and learning activities, assessment methods, and curriculum standards (where appropriate) is crucial, and further on, when we use the term "align(ment)" we keep in mind all these aspects [12, 15, 16, 18, 19].

Content Related (CR) criteria decide to what degree particular OERs/OCW allows learners to have *engaging multiple learning experiences* that provide *content mastery.*

CR1: Readability and understandability – the text is readable and it has clear writing, spelling and grammar are consistent and accurate, language is friendly and supportive, being easy to understand. The evaluation here is from an educational viewpoint.
N/A to non-textual resources;
0=the text cannot be read due to various problems (for instance, font-related);
1=the text can be read, but is almost impossible to understand (e.g. poor translation);
2=the text is sufficiently readable and understandable;
3=the text can be acceptably read and understood;
4=the text can be read and understood properly;
5=the text is excellently written, being highly readable and understandable.

Uniformity and appropriateness of language, terminology, and notations (CR2) is also important for most educational resources. The criteria *CR3* to *CR8* that are presented further on are not applicable (N/A) for resources that are small instructional units, being applicable only to courseware.

CR3: Availability, easiness of locating and using the course syllabus, and its completeness is crucial, as various users may benefit from the information within it.
0=the syllabus is unavailable;
1=the syllabus is available, but hard to locate and it contains deficient information;
2=the syllabus is given and easy to locate, but it offers only a brief course overview;
3=the syllabus is available, easy to locate, and contains almost complete information about the course (e.g. overview, learning objectives and outcomes);
4=the syllabus is available, easy to locate and use, and contains complete information (prerequisites, overview, learning objectives and outcomes at course level, completion requirements, time advisory/learning unit); easy printable for convenience;
5= in addition to 4, the syllabus includes also learning objectives and outcomes at unit level, completion requirements, time advisory per learning unit, and, when applicable, course schedule, information on instructors, developers, evaluators etc., expectations of availability of and turnaround time for feedback.

The comprehensiveness of the course content (CR4) is also considered, i.e. whether the course content and assignments demonstrate sufficient wideness, deepness, and rigor to reach the educational standards, goals, objectives etc. being addressed. *Modular course components (CR5)* are desirable as they are units of content that may be distributed and accessed independently, giving each user the possibility to *select easily the most suitable learning unit* (CR6) and the opportunity *to choose effortlessly the most appropriate learning path (CR7)* that match her goals, needs, abilities, etc. and a variety of options to approach the resources: *top-down, bottom-up or combined (CR8)*. Modularity may be approached at chapter level, i. e. each chapter is in a .pdf file, or at learning unit level, the latter being preferable.

CR9: Availability of proper assignments is important as well, as they are content items that enhance the main content. We measure here what the resource has to offer in terms of providing for engaging learning experiences that contribute to increased content mastery and learning efficiency (having assignments with solutions and built-in feedback being valuable in this respect). Based on the requirement for alignment, the focus is twofold: (1) establishing to what degree the assignments measure the achievement of the stated course learning objectives and outcomes, and (2) how appropriate they are in each particular case. For example, a composition is a proper assignment for evaluating writing skills, while a multiple choice quiz is suitable to test vocabulary knowledge [16].
N/A to resources that are not supposed to be assessed (for example, a guest lecture);
0=no assignments are available;
1=an inadequate set of assignments that are weakly aligned and fitted is offered;
2=a limited collection of sufficiently aligned and fitted assignments is offered;
3=an average set of acceptably aligned and suitable assignments is provided;
4=a complete set of assignments both strongly aligned and suitable is available;
5=there is an excellent variety of fully aligned and highly appropriate assignments.

When looking at a particular learning resource, other than courseware, which can be a small learning unit, a course module, a lesson etc. the quality model retains various features *related to that small resource* (CR10) that are of interest for users, such as accuracy[1], reasonableness[2], self-containedness[3], context[4], relevance[5], multimedia inserts[6], interactive elements[7], correlation with the entire course[8], re-usability[9], links to related relevant resources[10] (audio, video etc.). To keep things simple we have these features placed on levels of significance: (1) accuracy, reasonableness, and relevance, (2) self-containedness, correlation with the course, (3) multimedia inserts, interactive elements, (4) context, re-usability, and (5) links to related relevant resources.
N/A to entire courseware;
0=the resource is deficient in all the aspects relevant to the quality model;
1=the resource is accurate, reasonable, and relevant;
2=in addition to 1, the resource is self-contained and correlated with the entire course;
3=in addition to 2, the resource contains multimedia inserts and interactive elements;
4=in addition to 3, information about proper context of use and re-usability is given;
5=in addition to 4, links to other related relevant resources are provided.

Instructional Design (ID) related criteria address supporting learning theories, instructional design and strategies, and other pedagogical aspects of teaching and learning of that resource that provide for both increased educational value and high efficiency. *Learning goal and objectives (ID1)* outline the material and they should be aligned and suitably designed for the course level. They need to be: defined clearly both at course-level and unit level, consistent with each other, and explained from users' perspective. They help users focus their efforts and clarify expected quantifia-ble learning outcomes, and, hence instructions on how to achieve them must be stated clearly [14, 16, 18, 20]. *Learning outcomes (ID2)* state the learner's achievements after performing a learning activity, i. e. what learners will know and/or will be able to do as a result of such an activity, in terms of *knowledge, abilities, skills, attitudes, and values.* The course learning objectives describe outcomes that are measura-ble/observable/demonstrable and that are clearly stated and explained to be easily understood by students [14, 18, 19]. Moreover, learning outcomes must be aligned and relevant, i.e. useful and appropriate for the intended users, and, of course, achiev-able, realistic, and appropriate to the rigor and the breadth of the learning objective. Learning outcomes must include, if necessary, the skills required (1) for using the resource, in a manner that is consistent with a stated pedagogical paradigm, (2) for proving achievement of the learning objectives, and (3) for linking new knowledge with existing knowledge and future contexts (element of reflection). Pedagogically, covering a good range of learning outcomes in both Bloom's taxonomy and Fink's taxonomy is welcome [19].

ID1: Learning goal and objectives
N/A to resources that have no explicit learning goal and objectives;
0=no statement about learning goal and objectives;
1=the learning goal and objectives are stated only at course level;
2=in addition to 1, they are stated, partially, at unit level, being sufficiently aligned;

3=in addition to 2, they are almost completely aligned, and match the degree's level;
4=in addition to 3, they are consistent, stated at both levels, and aligned completely;
5=in addition to 4, users are provided with explanations and how-to-reach roadmap.

ID2: Learning outcomes
N/A to resources that have no explicit learning outcomes;
0=no statement about the learning outcomes is available;
1=the learning outcomes are stated only at course level;
2=the learning outcomes are stated and explained clearly at course level and, partly, at unit level, being partially quantifiable and, to some extent, achievable, realistic, and appropriate; they are sufficiently aligned and relevant;
3=the learning outcomes are stated and explained clearly at course level and, partially, at unit level, being suitably quantifiable and, to some extent, achievable, realistic, and appropriate; they are almost completely aligned and have acceptable relevance;
4=the learning outcomes are stated and explained clearly both at course level and at unit level, being completely quantifiable and fully achievable/realistic/appropriate; they are completely aligned and have strong relevance; they cover a proper range in both Bloom's taxonomy and Fink's taxonomy;
5=in addition to 4, they cover most of the outcomes in both Bloom's taxonomy and Fink's taxonomy; moreover, they include extra-skills (e.g. reflection).

The educational resources are ought to provide for multiple opportunities for learners to be actively engaged in efficient learning processes, having meaningful and authentic learning experiences, which address multiple learning styles, during which they undertake various *appropriate instructional activities (ID3)* such as problem- or project-based learning, e-simulations, webcasts, scavenger hunts, guided analysis, guided research, discovery learning, collaborative learning groups, case studies, serious games, portfolios etc. Other users may benefit also: instructors, developers etc. There is likely that these activities promote the achievement of the stated learning objectives and outcomes (with which they are aligned) [14, 16, 17, 19]. As shown before, a good alignment between learning objectives, learning outcomes, teaching and learning activities, and assessment methods is necessary. Consequently, learning objectives must have corresponding appropriate assessments [18, 19]. Ongoing multiple assessment strategies are desirable to measure content knowledge, skills, abilities, attitudes, and values. Students' self-assessments (similar to the final ones) and peer feedback opportunities throughout the course are needed. When possible, options among assignments should be provided to allow learners with different interests, backgrounds, and personal learning styles to demonstrate their proficiency [18]. Learners learn more effectively if they receive frequent, meaningful, and rapid feedback, which may come from the instructor directly (when appropriate) or from assignments and assessments that have built-in feedback [16]. Hence, a*ppropriate assessments and self-assessments means, with or without solutions (ID4)* are highly desirable, as a quality feature, when aiming at mastery of educational content. Users may be also interested in the *supporting learning theory* (behaviorist, cognitivist, constructivist, humanist and motivational etc.) and in the *instructional design model*

(ADDIE, ARCS, ASSURE etc.) that have been used to develop that particular educational resource *(ID5)*. *Effective instructional strategies* (direct, indirect or interactive instruction, independent study, experiential learning etc.) may also impact on the efficiency of instruction *(ID6)*. Moreover, learning experiences that provide for *reflective and deeper learning (ID7)* will always add to the overall quality of educational resources. Under the reflection perspective, the desired outcome of education becomes the construction of coherent functional knowledge structures adaptable to further lifelong learning [2, 5]. *Deeper learning* is expected to prepare learners for mastering of core content, for thinking critically and solving complex problems, for working collaboratively, for communicating effectively, for learning how to learn, and for developing academic mindsets [24].

Technology Related (TR). Both OERs and OCW are expected to benefit from ICT technologies, to have user-friendly interfaces, to comply with standards for *interoperability (TR1)*, and to provide for appropriate access for all learners *(accessibility - TR2)*. *Extensibility (TR3)* of each educational resource, aiming at expanding learning opportunities, from a technological point of view, refers to *easiness of adding content, activities, and assessments* for designers, developers, teachers, learners etc. A high quality *user interface* is based on technical aspects related to the capabilities of the supporting hardware, software, and networking *(TR4: user interface's basic technological aspects)*. A clear specification of the *supporting technology requirements at user's end* (both hardware and software) – *TR5*, along with the *prerequisite skills to use the supporting technology (TR6)* are useful to help users understand how the resource should be used to benefit fully from its content. High quality OERs and OCW are expected to work smoothly on a variety of platforms *(multi-platform capability – TR7)*. Having a true engaged learning relies on multiple learners' opportunities to interact with the content and with other learners, which is not possible without a suite of rich *supporting tools* that provide for adaptation and personalization *(TR8)*.

CourseWare evaluation (CW). Despite of the original claim of just offering high quality educational materials, all major OER/OCW initiatives have recently become more involved with their learners. Hence, regular assessment of effectiveness of open courseware becomes essential, along with using the results for further improvements.

CW1:Courseware overview: content scope[1] and sequence[2], intended audience[3], grade level[4], periodicity[5] of content updating, author's credentials[6], source credibility[7], multiple-languages[8], instructor facilitation[9] or semi-automated support[10], suitableness for self-study[11], classroom-based[12] study, and/or peer collaborative[13] study, time requirements[14], grading policy[15], instructions on using[16] the courseware, reliability[17], links to other[18] educational resources (readings, OCW, OERs etc.), alignment[19]
N/A to small learning units;
0=the courseware is deficient in all its aspects relevant to the quality model;
1=basic information about the content scope[1] and sequence[2], intended audience[3], and grade level[4] is available;

2=in addition to 1, information about the author's credentials[6], source credibility[7], and alignment[19] is provided;

3=in addition to 2, information about the instructional paradigm[9-13] is offered;

4=in addition to 3, information on time advisory[14], grading[15], how-to use the courseware[16], and reliability[17] is given;

5=in addition to 4, information on updating periodicity[5], multiple-languages[8] and links to other related educational resources[18] is offered.

Availability of prerequisite knowledge (CW2) and of *required competencies (CW3)* is useful for users at the beginning of a learning process. *Matching the course schedule, if any, with learner's own pace (CW4)*, may be also needed in some contexts. Another useful criterion regards the *terms of use (service) – CW5, i.e.* availability of repository or institutional policies with respect to copyright and licensing issues, security for primary, secondary and indirect users, anonymity, updating and deleting personally identifiable information, age restrictions, netiquette, etc. OERs and OCW that show *freeness of bias and advertising* and *cultural sensitiveness (CW6)* are also desirable. *Suitable design and presentation of educational content (CW7)* is also wanted, along with *user interface richness (style) - CW8 -* as it is defined by its navigational consistency[1], friendliness[2], multimedia inserts[3], interactivity[4], and adaptability[5] (both to user's needs and context). Another quality criterion is concerned with the option to provide, or aiming to provide, a *formal degree or a certificate of completion (CW9)*. *Participatory culture and Web 2.0 facets (CW10)* are also important and they can be detailed as it can be seen beneath.

CW10: Participatory culture and Web 2.0 facets: contribution to the content[1], collection of users' feedback[2], collaboration with fellows[3], sharing the development[4]/using[5] experience

N/A to resources that do not comply with Web 2.0 paradigm;

0=the courseware do not show any of the important Web 2.0 features;

1=user feedback is collected to be used for further improvements;

2=in addition to 1, (some) collaboration with fellows is possible;

3=in addition to 2, (some) contribution to the content from developers is allowed;

4=in addition to 3, contribution from learners is feasible;

5=in addition to 4, sharing using and development experience is possible.

4   Conclusions, Challenges, and Future Work

Helping lifelong learners to find efficiently and effectively the most relevant OERs and/or OCW according with their goals, needs, knowledge, abilities, etc. is crucial, and communities play a central role in this process, by collaborating distributedly within virtual environments and by socially constructing and sharing knowledge related to this kind of educational content. We introduced here a rubric based on our socio-constructivist quality model for quality assessment of OERs and OCW, as one of our first steps towards the construction of a quality evaluation framework, which may help various users to utilize, modify, re-use, re-mix, design, evaluate, compare, recommend etc. OERs and OCW, while pursuing their educational goals. We are currently focusing our efforts on developing a working prototype of this framework, which aims at classifying and recommending OERs and OCW based on both quality evaluations performed by various users (instructors, learners, instructional experts, designers, developers etc.) using this rubric and collaborative feedback from peers [5, 7]. One huge challenge in this moment is the "contributing problem", i. e. how to have as many reviewers as possible performing quality assessment using our rubric. Thorough quality assessment of educational resources takes time, effort, and expertise, and therefore such quality reviews are not very common, especially when a high number of criteria is considered. To cope with this shortcoming we intend to develop a rubric-applying tool that facilitates human assessment so that potential evaluators will be, hopefully, keener on performing evaluations. This tool could provide them with samples of various similar pieces of educational content that pertain to different quality classes, along with their score and a brief explanation of that score. We also consider automatic evaluation of some of the criteria, which can be achieved by parsing intelligently each resource's website. Human evaluators may keep the results of these automatic assessments or they may change them to reflect their viewpoint. This could help also with incomplete evaluations that have scores only for some of the quality criteria. To obtain assessments from learners' point of view we think to involve, at first, our undergraduate and graduate Computer Science students and to have them assessing OERs and OCW for their semester projects. The first base is having gathered in a common pool of resources and evaluated several OCW and OERs (around 10 resources per subject) that are necessary to graduate majoring in Computer Science. Further on, we consider automating some activities of our framework: the federated retrieval of OERs/OCW based on a retrieving taxonomy, capturing context and knowledge about user, and so on. Another direction to work on is concerned with objective measurements that could be included in the quality model: number of accesses, time spent with a resource, number of bookmarks, number of times a bookmark is followed, number of citations etc. Nevertheless, the semantics of such information has to be modeled properly if it is ought to complement seamlessly the explicit quality ratings. A weighting mechanism between the assessments of various users could be also useful to favor, for instance, a subject-matter expert's or an instructional designer's evaluation when compared with one of an anonymous on-line user. False positive (unfair) evaluations need to be banned somehow and we think about using Bayesian Belief Networks for that. Another idea we would like to pursue refers to refining our quality model towards a hierarchical approach, aiming at categorizing open educational resources for specific contextual goals and needs. The prototype will be used both in formal and informal environments, then evaluated, and, hopefully, the viability of our approach will be validated.

References

1. Piedra, N., Chicaiza, J., Tovar, E., Martinez, O.: Open Educational Practices and Resources Based on Social Software: UTPL Experience. In: 9th ICALT 2009, pp. 497–498 (2009)
2. Vladoiu, M.: Quality Criteria for Open Courseware and Open Educational Resources. In: 11th ICWL 2012 Workshops. LNCS, vol. 7697. Springer, Heidelberg (to appear, 2013)
3. Vladoiu, M., Constantinescu, Z.: Evaluation and Comparison of Three Open Courseware Based on Quality Criteria. In: Grossniklaus, M., Wimmer, M. (eds.) ICWE Workshops 2012. LNCS, vol. 7703, pp. 204–215. Springer, Heidelberg (2012)

4. Vladoiu, M.: Towards Assessing Quality of Open Courseware. In: 11th ICWL 2012 Workshops. LNCS, vol. 7697. Springer, Heidelberg (to appear, 2013)

5. Moise, G., Vladoiu, M., Constantinescu, Z.: Multi-Agent System for Evaluation and Classification of OERs and OCW Based on Quality Criteria (submitted for publication, 2013)

6. Constantinescu, Z., Vladoiu, M.: Evaluation and Comparison of Eight Open Courseware based on a Quality Model. In: 9th Int'l Scientific Conference eLearning and Software for Education, ELSE 2013. Ed. Universitara, Bucharest (2013)

7. Vladoiu, M., Constantinescu, Z., Moise, G.: QORECT – A Case-Based Framework for Quality-Based Recommending Open Courseware and Open Educational Resources. In: Nguyen, N.-T. (ed.) ICCCI 2013. LNCS, vol. 8083, pp. 681–690. Springer, Heidelberg (2013)

8. Nesbit, J.C., Li, J.Z., Leacock, T.L.: Web-Based Tools for Collaborative Evaluation of Learning Resources. Journal of Systemics, Cybernetics and Informatics 3(5) (2005), http://www.iiisci.org/journal/sci/Contents.asp?var= &previous=ISS2829

9. Vargo, J., Nesbit, J.C., Belfer, K., Archambault, A.: Learning Object Evaluation: Computer-Mediated Collaboration and Inter-Rater Reliability. International Journal of Computers and Applications 25(3), 1–8 (2003)

10. Leacock, T.L., Nesbit, J.C.: A Framework for Evaluating the Quality of Multimedia Learning Resources. Educational Technology & Society 10(2), 44–59 (2007)

11. Akpinar, Y.: Validation of a Learning Object Review Instrument: Relationship between Ratings of Learning Objects and Actual Learning Outcomes. Interdisciplinary Journal of E-Learning and Learning Objects 4(1), 291–302 (2008)

12. Krauss, F., Ally, M.: A Study of the Design and Evaluation of a Learning Object and Implications for Content Development. Interdisciplinary Journal of E-Learning and Learning Objects 1(1), 1–22 (2005)

13. Burgos Aguilar, J.V.: Rubrics to evaluate OERs (2011), http://www.temoa.info/sites/default/files/OER_Rubrics_0.pdf

14. Programs, Q.M.: Quality Matters Rubric Standards 2011-2013 edition, http://www.qmprogram.org/rubric

15. Buzzetto-More, N.A., Pinhey, K.: Guidelines and standards for the development of fully online learning objects. Interdisciplinary Journal of Knowledge and Learning Objects 2, 95–104 (2006), http://ijklo.org/Volume2/v2p095-104Buzzetto.pdf

16. Minnesota Assessment Center, Peer Course Review Rubric - Standards with Point Value and Annotations, eassessment.project.mnscu.edu

17. CSU Faculty Development Center, Quality Online Learning and Teaching (QOLT) Rubric Summary, fdc.fullerton.edu/teaching

18. CSU-Chico, Instruction Design Tips for Online Learning and Rubric for online instruction, http://www.csuchico.edu/roi/

19. University of Utah, TLT Grant Hybrid Course Proposal Rubrics, https://eq.utah.edu

20. Central Piedmont Community College, CPCC eLearning: Quality Course Review (QCR), http://www.cpcc.edu/elearningcommunity/quality/ QCR_Rubric.pdf

21. ACHIEVE, http://www.achieve.org

22. OER Commons, http://www.oercommons.org

23. Learning Registry, http://www.learningregistry.org

24. The Hewlett Foundation, Deeper learning competencies (2013), http://www.hewlett.org

Multimodal Interaction in Gaming

Maria Chiara Caschera, Arianna D'Ulizia, Fernando Ferri, and Patrizia Grifoni

Institute of Research on Population and Social Policies (IRPPS) –
National Research Council (CNR)
00185, Rome (Italy)
{mc.caschera,arianna.dulizia,fernando.ferri,
patrizia.grifoni}@irpps.cnr.it

Abstract. Gaming environments are applications that have the great potential to increase people engagement in a participatory and collaborative way. Players interact with games under various situations, where the content, the form, and the modalities will be manipulated to fit the player's behaviours. This paper provides a multimodal environment for gaming by using a grammar-based approach for supporting the interaction process in the application scenario of scope card game, instantiating grammar by the elements and the rules of the game. Moreover, the paper focuses on the correct interpretation of the player's input during the game by the use of a HMM-based approach.

Keywords: Multimodal interaction, Gaming, Multimodal Language, Multimodal Grammar, Multimodal Ambiguity.

1   Introduction

Nowadays, innovations in user interface consist in making computer behaviour closer to human–human communication paradigm. In everyday life, during natural human–human communication, human beings use the five senses of touch, hearing, sight, smell, and taste in order to interact with external world. To create a natural and flexible human-computer communication paradigm, several efforts have been made to evolve traditional interfaces to multimodal interfaces. Therefore, multimodal interfaces have gained increasing importance as they allow a communication by simultaneous or alternative use of several channels of input/output at a time.

The most innovative solutions for user interfaces are usually proposed for gaming environments [1], as these applications generally have the great potential to provide new forms of engagement. The player interacts with games under various conditions where the content, the form, and the modalities will be manipulated to fit the player's behaviours. These considerations imply that multimodal interfaces play a fundamental role for the achievement of a high degree of interactivity during the gaming process.

In line with these considerations, this paper provides a multimodal platform for gaming for the achievement of a high degree of interactivity during the gaming process. In particular, the interaction process, which has been implemented in the application scenario of "scope card game", is based on a linguistic approach that uses the multimodal attribute grammar defined by the elements and the rules of the game, and the interpretation process is trained by examples of multimodal inputs of the players during the game.

Y.T. Demey and H. Panetto (Eds.): OTM 2013 Workshops, LNCS 8186, pp. 694–703, 2013.
© Springer-Verlag Berlin Heidelberg 2013

The remainder of the paper is structured as follows. The state of the art on multimodal interaction systems for gaming is presented in Section 2. Section 3 presents the multimodal interaction gaming environment focusing both on the definition of the multimodal grammar for the game (section 3.1) and on interpretation of the multimodal player's input during the interaction process (section 3.2) in the application scenario of scope card game. Finally, conclusions are presented in Section 4.

2   Multimodal Interaction and Gaming

The application of the multimodal paradigm is increasing in computer interfaces in order to make computer behaviour closer to human communication. Indeed, communication among people is often multimodal as it is obtained combining different modalities, such as speech, gesture, facial expression, sketch, and so on. Similarly, multimodal interfaces allow several modalities of communication to be harmoniously integrated, making the system communication characteristics more and more similar to the human communication approach. The main features of multimodal interaction, such as the different classes of cooperation between different modes, the time relationships among the involved modalities and the relationships between chunks of information connected with these modalities, are described in [2].

Multimodal interaction paradigm are becoming more and more popular also in gaming platforms (e.g. Nintendo Wii) and in mobile games combining speech and graphics [3], using location (i.e., a passive/perceptual modality) as in the pervasive mobile game ARQuake [4], and including sensors such as accelerometers, proximity sensors and tactile screen with two handed interactions as in the recent iPhone [5]. A flexible multimodal interaction framework has been integrated in STARS [6] in order to provide a computer-augmented board games including simple mainstream board games such as Monopoly, and complex tabletop strategy or role-playing games. A multimodal multiplayer gaming environment has been developed in [7] where players interact by speech and gesture in a co-located home gaming complementarily using the speech for specifying abstract or discrete actions and gesture for describing location. In [8] a multimodal speech understanding game, which features incremental understanding, is provided. The work focuses on the relevant role of the incremental understanding with graphical feedback, through the use of highlighting, shading, and flashing. This work underlines the relevance of the use of grammar-based approach to provide incremental recognition results from the speech recognizer, as the user speaks.

In line to this consideration, this work provides a multimodal interaction gaming environment that uses an approach based on context free grammar in order to create an easy and intuitive interaction with the game. This approach utilizes a "by example" paradigm for defining the multimodal grammar through the use of game rules and examples of multimodal inputs in the game environments. The interpretation process is supported by a HMM-based approach that is able to disambiguate ambiguous multimodal inputs.

3   The Multimodal Interaction Gaming Environment

In order to provide a natural interaction between players in a game environment, the multimodal environment for gaming is proposed here. Figure 1 shows the client-server architecture of the gaming environment.

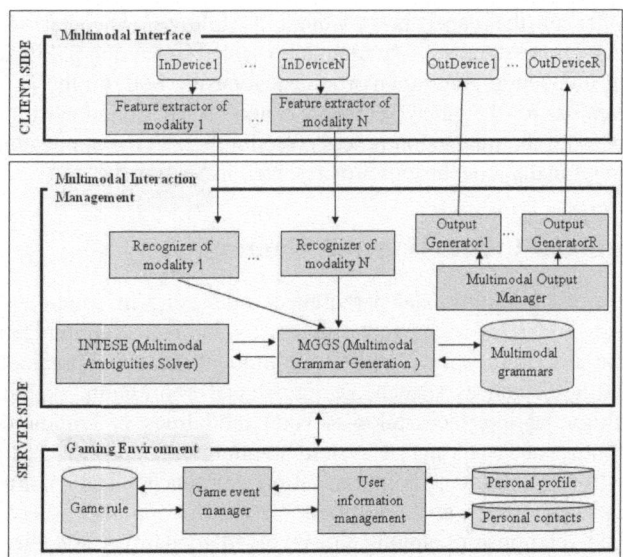

Fig. 1. Architecture of the multimodal gaming environment

The client side includes specific I/O devices (e.g. display, cameras, microphone, and loudspeakers) as well as the components for extracting features from the received signals. The server side consists of the "multimodal interaction management" and the "gaming environment". The multimodal interaction management has the role of recognizing unimodal inputs coming from the features extractors of each modality, correctly interpreting these inputs by the support of module for solving ambiguous input, integrating these different interpretations into a joint semantic interpretation, and understanding, which is the better way to react to the interpreted multimodal request by activating the most appropriate output devices. The game-based environment consists of: the game event manager, which provides the objects and rules definition for the game stored in the Game rule knowledge base, and the user information management, which is devoted to store and manage personal data of players, such as personal profile and personal contacts.

In the design of multimodal interaction environment, the process of combining information from different modalities, in order to have a comprehensive representation of the user's message, is a crucial point. In [9], a more extensive discussion about multimodal input fusion strategies has been provided. The combined information need to be interpreted by the system in order to provide an effective interaction. Therefore, the interpretation process is a further focal step. The interpretation of user input depends on different features, such as available interaction modalities, user's behaviours, conversation focus, and context of interaction. Moreover, an unambiguous interpretation of the user's input can be achieved by simultaneously considering semantic, temporal and contextual constraints. In [10], an overview of methods for interpreting multimodal input is provided. According to these considerations, this paper describes a multimodal interaction environment for gaming focusing on: the definition of the multimodal grammar for addressing the combination of information from different modalities (the MGGS-Multimodal

Grammar Generation in Figure 1) [11]; and addressing an unambiguous interpretation of the user's input by a HMMs-based approach (INTESE-Multimodal Ambiguities Solver in Figure 1) [12]. In detail, it describes the platform functionalities of the multimodal gaming environment used in order to play an Italian card game: scopa.

The following sections will describe how the platform acquires the multimodal grammar for playing "scopa card game", and how the player's input is correctly interpreted during the interaction process with the multimodal gaming environment.

3.1   The Grammar for the Multimodal Interaction Gaming Environment

In the Multimodal interaction gaming environment, a grammar for interacting with the gaming environment has been instantiated. The grammar has been generated by the multimodal attribute grammar generator system described in [11]. The grammar for the "scopa card game" has been inferred providing concrete examples of multimodal inputs of players, and the grammar inference algorithm automatically generated the grammar rules to parse the inputs. The MGGS interface allows the acquisition of the examples of the sentences and the concepts used during the interaction with the game. The MGGS takes the elements of the players' inputs and their semantic properties (i.e., actual value, syntactic role, modality, and kinds of cooperation between modalities), and integrates them opportunely, in order to generate a linear sequence of elements. In detail, the player interacts with the system in order to set for each element (see Figure 2): the actual value of the element; the modality used to express the input element; the syntactic role that the element has inside the unimodal sentence [13]; the kind of cooperation with the other input elements (e.g. redundancy, complementarity...). The linearization process combines the elements and groups them opportunely in order to generate their linear sequence.

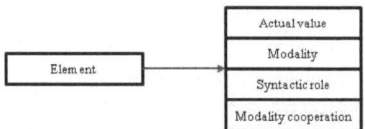

Fig. 2. Attributes of input elements

The linearization process considers: the modality cooperation for determining whether input elements convey information that has some relation with the information conveyed by the other elements; and syntactic roles for determining whether input elements can be considered close together in syntax (syntactic proximity criterion). The multimodal linearized input is sent to the MAG inference component for grammar inference [14]. By the grammatical inference algorithm, the MAG inference generates the set of production rules and the associated semantic functions that are able to parse the sentence. This process has defined the multimodal grammar, which was stored into the multimodal grammars repository (see Figure1).

In order to clarify this process, let us suppose that, in the definition process of the grammar, the player provides the multimodal input composed by the speech input "Select this card" and by the sketch modality for selecting card icon on a touch-screen display "⬚". The sequence of input elements has associated sets of attributes as Figure 3 shows.

According to the modality cooperation (complementarity in this example), the speech elements "this" and "card" and the sketch element " X " have to be close in the linearized sentence. The syntactic proximity criterion, which occurs because input elements with the same syntactic role are close together, reduces the number of acceptable linearized sentences.

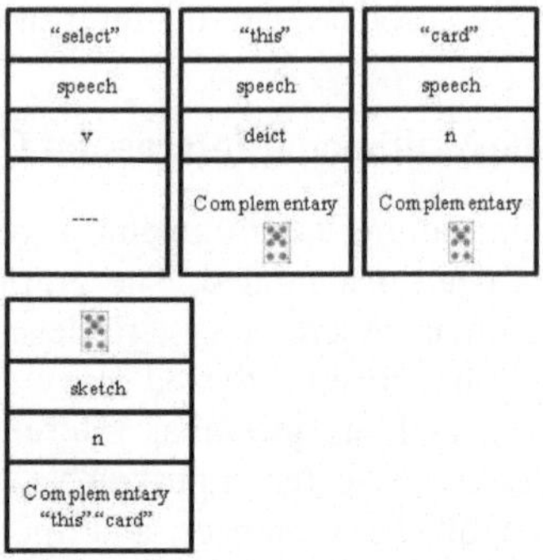

"select"	"this"	"card"
speech	speech	speech
v	deict	n
----	Complementary X	Complementary X

X
sketch
n
Complementary "this" "card"

Fig. 3. Input element representation for the example

Therefore, the speech element "card" and the sketch element associated with " X " are close together in the linearized sentence. The linearization process stops giving the following linear sequence of input elements: "Select" "this" "card" " X ".

In summary, the system enables the user to input the multimodal sentence by using devices corresponding to the inserted modalities (e.g., a microphone for speech modality, a touch screen for sketch modality). Moreover, the system converts the acquired inputs into concepts through the appropriate input recognizers (e.g., speech, sketch recognizers). Once the unimodal inputs are recognized, the language developer defines constraints both on syntactic roles and types of cooperation between modalities. After the specification of the multimodal sentence, the MGGS performs the linearization process, which translates the recognized unimodal inputs into a linear sequence of elements. This sequence is given as input to the revised CYK algorithm [14]. The running of this algorithm generates the set of production rules and the associated semantic functions.

3.2   The Interpretation in the Multimodal Interaction Gaming Environment

During the interaction process, each linearized multimodal sentence defined by the player's input can have: no interpretation, one or more than one; in the last case the multimodal sentence is ambiguous. This section describes how the player's multimodal input is unambiguously interpreted in the gaming environment on the basis of the INTESE method (the Multimodal Ambiguities Solver in Figure 1) proposed in [12]. Starting from the hypothesis that each multimodal sentence is associated to a syntax-graph, defined in [12], elements are combined to express the different interpretations by sentences in Natural Language (NL). When a multimodal sentence is ambiguous there are two or more different sentences in NL that are associated with it, i.e., the candidate interpretations of the multimodal sentence. Resolving ambiguities involves complex information, and methods. This paper uses the InteSe model developed in [12].

This model addresses the complexity of the multimodal input involving layered hidden Markov models (LHMMs) [15] structured by:

- hierarchical hidden Markov models (HHMMs) [16] that give a multilevel syntactic representation of a multimodal sentence and to resolve syntactic ambiguities using a training process [17];
- Hidden Markov models HMM [18] to assign only one meaning to each multimodal sentence, identifying the most probable sense for each element. This model is also influenced by HMMs that model context, where with context we are only considering the gaming domain.

A detailed description on how the model works is provided in [12] by showing the different steps of the multimodal dialog from a multimodal sentence in input, to the ambiguity resolution characterizing multimodal interaction.

In summary, the InteSe consists of three connected levels: the *context level*, the *syntactic sentence level* and the *semantic element level* (see Figure 4). The HHMMs syntactic sentence level enables the identification of the correct path on the syntax-graph for reaching each terminal element. Considering the semantic element level, lexical ambiguities are managed by the InteSe model assigning them the most probable sense. For dealing with issues of univocally assigning the sense tag, the InteSe model uses HMMs. The estimation of the probability is done by using information about the context, and, therefore, it is connected with the context level. The *context* and *semantic element levels* are used for the resolution of the *multimodal semantic ambiguities,* and the *syntactic sentence level* answers the need of resolving classes of *multimodal syntactic ambiguities.*

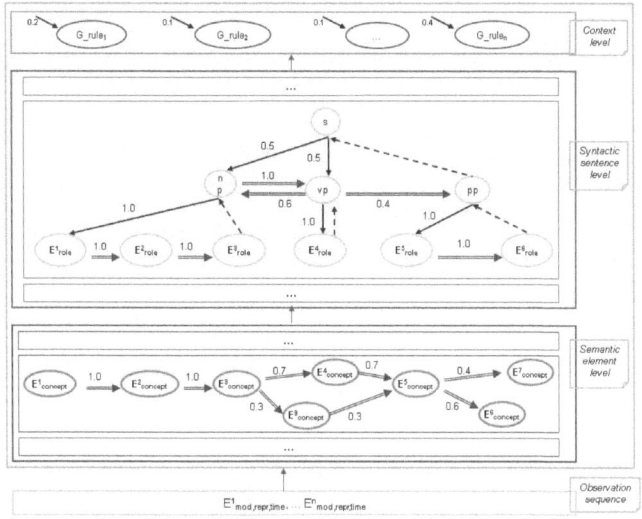

Fig. 4. Schema of the InteSe model for a multimodal sentence

In the gaming environment, it is crucial the *context game level* (see Figure 4 showing the schema of the InteSe model for a multimodal sentence), which consists of an HMM that associates the multimodal sentence to the context of the gaming environment according to the sequence of concepts that the sentence contains.

The context level supports the process of semantic element ambiguity resolution. In fact, the different meanings can be associated with the elements by considering their sequences as well as the gaming contexts in which they occur. The *context HMM* (context level in Figure 4) allows the association of each terminal element of the multimodal language with a semantic tag representing the meaning of the element in that context. The HMM states of the context level represent the rules of the games defined during the construction of the grammar for the game. Those states are linked to the game rules that are referred during the interaction process with the game.

In order to clarify the description of the used method, and example of ambiguous input is provided. In the example, the table card is shown in the Figure 5.

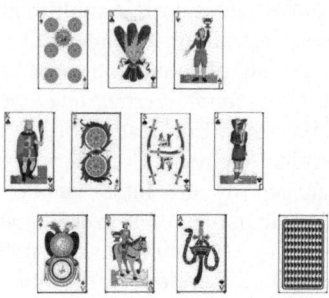

Fig. 5. Example of table cards

Let us suppose the player on the top of the Figure 4 is interacting with the game by sketch and speech.

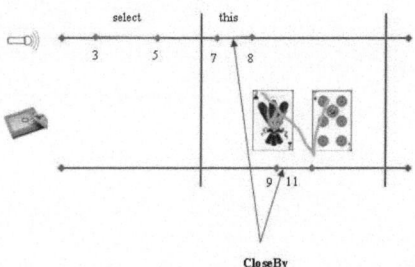

Fig. 6. Player's multimodal input that defines a target ambiguity

Using the speech modality the player says:

⊏◗)) *"select this card"*

and, at the same time, the player selects by sketch two cards: the three of clubs and the seven of coins, as in Figure 6.

After, the player says:

⊏◗)) *"capture the two of coins and the five of swords"*

The last sentence gives the discourse context.

The target ambiguity appears in the first player's multimodal sentence (Figure 6) because the player checks two different elements ("three of clubs" and "seven of coins") using the sketch modality. This player's sentence defines the syntax-graph in Figure 7.

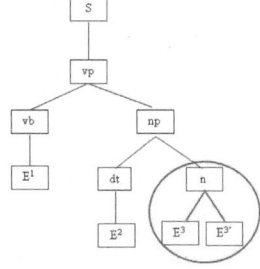

Fig. 7. Syntax-graph of the Multimodal Sentence that defines a target ambiguity

Elements defined by the speech are:

- E^1 is! $(E^1_{mod}=speech)$ $\otimes$! $(E^1_{repr}=$ ◁)) *"select"*)) $\otimes$! $(E^1_{time}=(3,5))$ $\otimes$!
  $(E^1_{concept}=(verb))$ $\otimes$ $!(E^1_{role}=(vb))$

- E^2 is! $(E^3_{mod}=speech)$ $\otimes$! $(E^2_{repr}$ $=$ ◁)) *"this"*)) $\otimes$! $(E^2_{time}=(7,8))$ $\otimes$
  $!(E^2_{concept}=(deictic))$ $\otimes$ $!(E^2_{role}=(dt))$

And using the sketch modality the player checks the following elements:

- E^3 is ! $(E^3_{mod}=sketch)$ $\otimes$! $(E^3_{repr} =$ 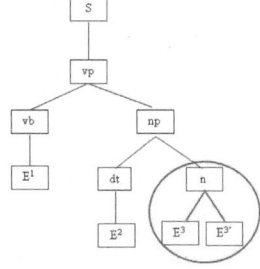)) $\otimes$! $(E^3_{time}=(9,11))$ $\otimes$! $(E^3_{concept}=($
  three of clubs)) $\otimes$ $!(E^3_{role}=(nn))$

- $E^{3'}$ is ! $(E^5{}'_{mod}=sketch)$ $\otimes$! $(E^{3'}_{repr}$ $=$)) $\otimes$! $(E^{3'}_{time}=(9,11))$ $\otimes$!
  $(E^{3'}_{concept}=(seven\ of\ coins))$ $\otimes$ $!(E^{3'}_{role}=(nn))$

The alignment of the element E2 with the elements E3 and E3' detects a target ambiguity due to the fact that using sketch modality two different elements, "three of clubs" (E3) and "seven of coins" (E3'), are identified. Two candidate interpretations are:

    1.   "select this three of clubs";
    2.   "select this seven of coins";

For dealing with this target ambiguity, the HMM of the semantic element level is used. Figure 8 shows the hidden states, the observation sequences and the values of the probabilities of the model for dealing the provided example. The probabilities are computed starting from the information contained by examples of multimodal sentences defined by the players, the rules of the scopa game and the discourse context during the interaction (e.g. the speech sentence "capture the two of coins and the five of swords" in the example). The parameters of the model were estimated by a generalization of the Baum–Welch algorithm [19].

The trained model is able to correctly interpret multimodal sentences by identifying the most probable sequence of the LHMM states by the use of Viterbi algorithm [20].

In detail, the model returns the sequence of syntactic roles and concepts contained in the multimodal sentence having the highest probability value, according to the trained model.

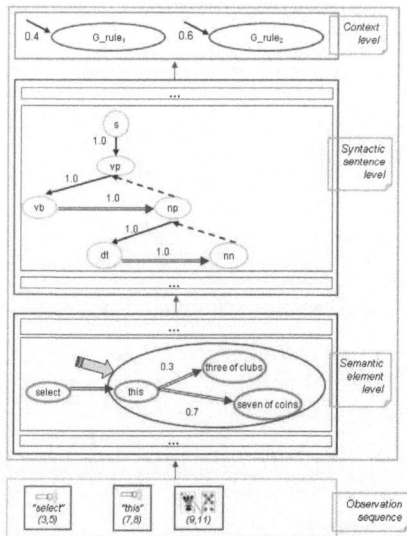

Fig. 8. Trained model for solving the target ambiguity

In this example, according to the model in Figure 8, the system interprets the multimodal player's input as follows:

"Select" "this" "card" "⚅"

4   Conclusion

This paper presented a multimodal interaction gaming environment to provide pervasive game applications on an interactive table and additional devices, such as camera and microphone. The work particularly focused on the grammar-based approach for supporting the interaction process. The definition of the multimodal grammar for the specific game, in the example scopa card game, and the method for correctly interpreting the multimodal user's input during gaming, were provided.

For the scopa card game, the multimodal grammar was inferred by concrete examples of multimodal inputs of players, and the grammar inference algorithm has automatically generated the grammar rules that were used to parse the inputs. The correct interpretation of the player's input was achieved by the use of the HMM-based approach that is able to incrementally learn the peculiar interaction features of each player, and in the specific gaming environment is crucial the training of the context layer of the model by the rules of the game.

In future works, a large-scale test of the environment will be developed for a set of meaningful games, in order to evaluate the level of user satisfaction in the use of multimodal interaction type.

References

1. Crawford, C.: Lessons from Computer Game Design. In: Laurel, B. (ed.) The Art of Human-Computer Interface Design, pp. 103–111. Addison-Wesley Pub. Co., Reading (1990)

2. Caschera, M.C., Ferri, F., Grifoni, P.: Multimodal interaction systems: information and time features. International Journal of Web and Grid Services (IJWGS) 3(1), 82–99 (2007)

3. Zyda, M., et al.: Educating the Next Generation of Mobile Game Developers. IEEE Computer Graphics and Applications 27(2), 96, 92–95 (2007)

4. Piekarski, W., Thomas, B.: ARQuake: The Outdoor Augmented Reality Gaming System. Communications of the ACM 45(1), 36–38 (2002)

5. iPhone, http://www.apple.com/iphone

6. Magerkurth, C., Stenzel, R., Streitz, N., Neuhold, E.: 2003. A multimodal interaction framework for pervasive game applications. Artificial Intelligence in Mobile System (Aims), Fraunhofer Ipsi (2003)

7. Tse, E., Greenberg, S., Shen, C., Forlines, C.: Multimodal multiplayer tabletop gaming. ACM Comput. Entertaint. 5(2), Article 12, 12 pages (2007), http://doi.acm.org/10.1145/1279540.1279552, doi:10.1145/1279540.1279552

8. Gruenstein, A.: Shape game: A multimodal game featuring incremental understanding. Term project, Massachusetts Institute of Technology (May 2007)

9. D'Ulizia, A.: Exploring Multimodal Input Fusion Strategies. In: The Handbook of Research on Multimodal Human Computer Interaction and Pervasive Services: Evolutionary Techniques for Improving Accessibility, pp. 34–57. IGI Publishing (2009)

10. Caschera, M.C.: Interpretation methods and ambiguity management in multimodal systems. In: Grifoni, P. (ed.) Handbook of Research on Multimodal Human Computer Interaction and Pervasive Services: Evolutionary Techniques for Improving Accessibility, pp. 87–102. IGI Global, USA (2009)

11. D'Ulizia, A., Ferri, F., Grifoni, P.: Generating Multimodal Grammars for Multimodal Dialogue Processing. IEEE Transactions on Systems, Man and Cybernetics, Part A: Systems and Humans 40(6), 1130–1145 (2010)

12. Caschera, M.C., Ferri, F., Grifoni, P.: InteSe: An Integrated Model for Resolving Ambiguities in Multimodal Sentences. IEEE Transactions on Systems, Man, and Cybernetics: Systems 43(4), 911–931 (2013)

13. Mitchell, P.M., Santorini, B., Marcinkiewicz, M.A.: Building a large annotated corpus of English: The penn treebank. Comput. Linguistics 19(2), 313–330 (1994)

14. D'Ulizia, A., Ferri, F., Grifoni, P.: A Learning Algorithm for Multimodal Grammar Inference. EEE Transactions on Systems, Man, and Cybernetics, Part B 41(6), 1495–1510 (2011)

15. Oliver, N., Garg, A., Horvitz, E.: Layered representations for learning and inferring office activity from multiple sensory channels. Computer Vision and Image Understanding 96(2), 163–180 (2004)

16. Fine, S., Singer, Y., Tishby, N.: The hierarchical hidden Markov model: Analysis and applications. Machine Learning 32(1), 41–62 (1998)

17. Skounakis, M., Craven, M., Ray, S.: Hierarchical hidden Markov models for information extraction. In: Proc. of the 18th Int. Joint Conference on Artificial Intelligence, Acapulco, Mexico, pp. 427–433. Morgan Kaufmann, San Francisco (2003)

18. Rabiner, L.R.: A tutorial on hidden Markov models and selected applications in speech recognition. Proc. of the IEEE 77, 257–285 (1989)

19. Fine, S., Singer, Y., Tishby, N.: The hierarchical hidden Markov model: Analysis and applications. Machine Learning 32(1), 41–62 (1998)

20. He, J., Hu, S., Tan, J.: Layered hidden Markov models for real-time daily activity monitoring using body sensor networks. In: Int. Workshop Wearable and Implantable Body Sensor Network, Hong Kong, China (2008)

CoopIS 2013 PC Co-Chairs Message

Cooperative Information Systems (CIS) enable, support, and facilitate cooperation between people, organizations, and information systems. CIS provide enterprises and user communities with flexible, scalable and intelligent services to work together in large-scale networking environments. The CIS paradigm integrates several technologies: distributed systems technologies (such as middleware, cloud computing), coordination technologies (such as business process management) and integration technologies (such as service oriented computing, semantic web).

The CoopIS conference series has established itself as a major international forum for exchanging ideas and results on scientific research in all aspects of cooperative information systems such as computer supported cooperative work (CSCW), middleware, Internet & Web data management, electronic commerce, business process management, agent technologies, and software architectures, to name a few.

As in previous years, CoopIS'13 is part of a joint event with other conferences, in the context of the OTM ("OnTheMove") federated conferences, covering different aspects of distributed information systems. The call for papers attracted 65 submissions this year. In a thorough evaluation process where each paper was reviewed by at least 3 reviewers, the program committee selected 15 papers as full papers and 6 as short papers (acceptance rate 23% for full papers and 32% for short papers) which are contained in these proceedings. In addition, 6 submissions accepted as posters are published in the workshop proceedings of OTM 2013.

We extend our dear thanks to all who made CoopIS 2013 possible: Robert Meersman and his team for organizing OTM 2013 with experience and dedication, all the PC members and external reviewers who worked hard to meet the tight deadline and who provided insightful and constructive reviews for sharing their time and expertise. And last but not least to all the authors and presenters who made CoopIS again a thriving scientific event.

July 2013

Johann Eder
Zohra Bellahsene
Rania Y. Khalaf

Y.T. Demey and H. Panetto (Eds.): OTM 2013 Workshops, LNCS 8186, p. 704, 2013.
© Springer-Verlag Berlin Heidelberg 2013

Repairing Event Logs Using Timed Process Models

Andreas Rogge-Solti[1], Ronny S. Mans[2], Wil M.P. van der Aalst[2], and Mathias Weske[1]

[1] Hasso Plattner Institute at the University of Potsdam
Prof.-Dr.-Helmert-Strasse 2-3, 14482 Potsdam
{andreas.rogge-solti,mathias.weske}@hpi.uni-potsdam.de
[2] Department of Information Systems, Eindhoven University of Technology, P.O. Box
513, NL-5600 MB, Eindhoven, The Netherlands
{r.s.mans,w.m.p.v.d.aalst}@tue.nl

Abstract. Process mining aims to infer meaningful insights from process-related data and attracted the attention of practitioners, tool-vendors, and researchers in recent years. Traditionally, event logs are assumed to describe the as-is situation. But this is not necessarily the case in environments where logging may be compromised due to manual logging. For example, hospital staff may need to manually enter information regarding the patient's treatment. As a result, events or timestamps may be missing or incorrect.

In this work, we make use of process knowledge captured in process models, and provide a method to repair missing events in the logs. This way, we facilitate analysis of incomplete logs. We realize the repair by combining stochastic Petri nets, alignments, and Bayesian networks.

Keywords: process mining, missing data, stochastic Petri nets, Bayesian networks.

1 Introduction

Many information systems record detailed information concerning the processes they support. Typically, the start and completion of process activities together with related context data, e.g., actors and resources, are recorded. In business process management, such event data can be gathered into logs. Subsequently, these logs can be analyzed to gain insights into the *performance* of a process. In many cases, information systems do not force the process participants to perform tasks according to rigid paths, as specified by process models. Rather, the process participants are responsible to track their manual work which is sometimes not reflected in the system. In other words, the event logs might be *incomplete* or noisy [1]. These data quality issues affect process mining methods and often lead to unsatisfactory results.

Existing approaches can be used to *repair* the model based on event data. However, if steps are recorded manually this may lead to misleading results as little weight is given to a priori domain knowledge. Therefore, we adopt a stochastic approach to modeling process behavior and introduce a novel approach to *repair event logs* according to a given stochastically enriched process model [2]. To model the as-is process we use Petri nets enhanced with stochastic timing information and path probabilities.

Y.T. Demey and H. Panetto (Eds.): OTM 2013 Workshops, LNCS 8186, pp. 705–708, 2013.

In fact, we use a variant of the well-known Generalized Stochastic Petri nets (GSPNs) defined in [3]. As a first step, using path probabilities, it is determined which are the most likely missing events. Next, Bayesian networks [4] capturing both initial beliefs of the as-is process and real observations are used to compute the most likely timestamp for each inserted entry. The complete procedure is described in more detail and evaluated in the technical report [5].

2 Realization of Repairing Logs

For this realization, we make the following assumptions:

– The supported models, i.e., the SPN models, are *sound*, and *free-choice*, but do not necessarily need to be (block-)structured. This class of models captures a fairly large class of process models and does not impose unnecessary constraints.
– The stochastic Petri net model is normative, i.e., it reflects the as-is processes in structural, behavioral and time dimension.
– Activity durations are independent and have normal probability distributions, containing most of their probability mass in the positive domain.
– The recorded timestamps in the event logs are correct.
– Each trace in the log has at least one event, and all events contain a timestamp.
– The activity durations of a case do not depend on other cases, i.e., we do not look at the resource perspective and there is no queuing.
– We assume that data is *missing at random* (MAR), i.e., that the probability that an event is missing from the log does not depend on the time values of the missing events.

The algorithm is depicted in Fig. 1, and repairs an event log as follows.

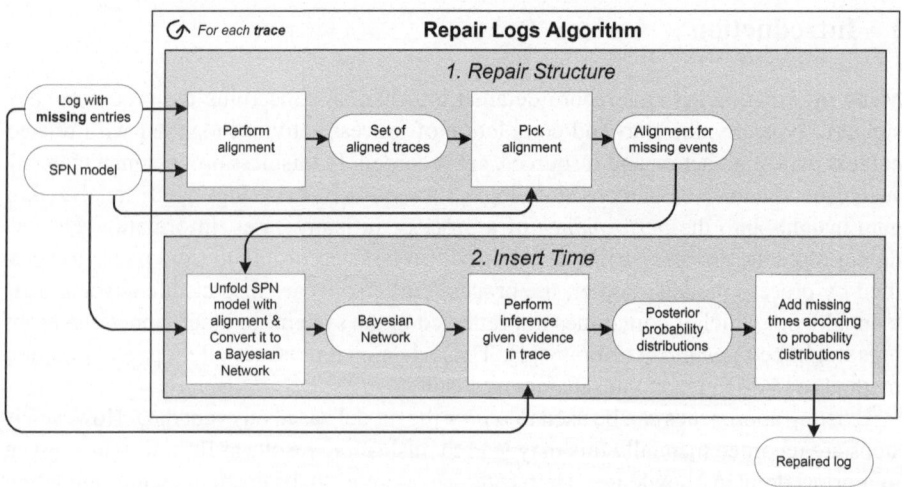

Fig. 1. The repair approach described in more detail

2.1 Repairing the Structure

For each trace, we start by repairing the structure. This becomes trivial, once we identified a path in the model that fits our observations in the trace best. The notion of cost-based alignments [6] is used for this part. We obtain a set of possible alignment candidates that are all cost-minimal in terms of costs for asynchronous moves.

In the next step, cf. box *Pick alignment* in Fig. 1, we decide which of the returned cost-minimal alignments to pick for repair. The algorithm replays the path taken through the model and multiplies the probabilities of the decisions made along the path. This allows us to take some probabilistic information into account, i.e., we can choose from the structural alignments one of the highest probability, or pick randomly according to the probability of such a path. Once we decided on the structure of how our repaired trace will look like, we can continue and insert the times of the missing events in the trace, i.e., the identified *model moves*.

2.2 Inserting Time

In the previous step, we identified the path through the SPN model. With the path given, we can eliminate choices from the model by removing branches in the process that were not taken. We unfold the net from the initial marking along the chosen path. Note that loops are but a special type of choices and will be eliminated from the model for any given trace. We transform the resulted unfolded model into a Bayesian network with a similar structure.

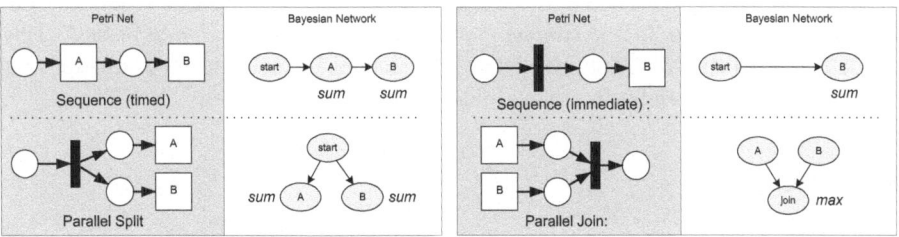

Fig. 2. Transformation of SPN models to Bayesian Networks

Fig. 2 shows the transformation of sequences, parallel splits, and synchronizing joins. These are the only constructs remaining in the unfolded form of the SPN model. In the resulting Bayesian network, we use the *sum* and *max* relations to define the random variables given their parents. More concretely, let t_i be a timed transition with a random variable with duration distribution $D_i(x)$ followed by another timed transition t_j with distribution $D_j(x)$ in a sequence. We can convert this fragment into a Bayesian network with random variables X_i and X_j. Then, the parent variable X_i has the unconditional probability distribution $P(X_i \leq x) = D_i(x)$ and the child variable X_j has the conditional probability distribution $P(X_j \leq x \mid X_i) = P(X_j + X_i \leq x)$. For each possible value of the parent $x_i \in X_i$, the probability is defined as $P(X_j \leq x \mid X_i = x_i) = P(X_j + x_i \leq x) = D_j(x - x_i)$. This means that the distribution of X_j is shifted by its parent's value to the right. A parallel split, cf. lower left part in Fig. 2, is treated as two sequences sharing the same parent node.

The *max* relation that is required for joining branches at synchronization points, cf. lower right in Fig. 2 is defined as follows. Let X_i and X_j be the parents of X_k, such that X_k is the maximum of its parents. Then, $P(X_k \leq x \mid X_i, X_j) = P(max(X_i, X_j) \leq x) = P(X_i \leq x) \cdot P(X_j \leq x) = D_i(x) \cdot D_j(x)$, i.e., the probability distribution functions are multiplied. This proves to be a challenge, as the maximum of two normally distributed random variables is no longer normally distributed. We use a linear approximation, as described in [7]. This means that we express the maximum as a normal distribution, with its parameters depending linearly on the normal distributions of the joined branches. The approximation is good, when the standard deviations of the joined distributions are similar and it degrades when they strongly diverge, cf. [7]. The resulting Bayesian network model is a linear Gaussian model, which is a class of continuous type Bayesian networks, where inference is efficiently possible, i.e., in $O(n^3)$.

Once we determined probable values for the timestamps of all missing events in a trace, we can proceed with the next trace starting another iteration of the algorithm.

3   Conclusion

Here, we presented a method to repair timed event logs in order to make them available for further analysis, e.g., with process mining tools. The formal specification, and evaluation results can be found in [5]. The method works by decomposing the problem into two sub-problems: (i) repairing the structure, and (ii) repairing the time.

This work can be considered as the first step towards eliciting a SPN model from logs with *missing data* in a *maximum likelihood* or *multiple imputation* fashion. This way, allowing to take all the observed data into account and get efficient estimations for the activity durations and path probabilities.

References

1. van der Aalst, W., et al.: Process mining manifesto. In: Daniel, F., Barkaoui, K., Dustdar, S. (eds.) BPM Workshops 2011, Part I. LNBIP, vol. 99, pp. 169–194. Springer, Heidelberg (2012)
2. Rogge-Solti, A., van der Aalst, W., Weske, M.: Discovering Stochastic Petri Nets with Arbitrary Delay Distributions From Event Logs. In: BPM Workshops. Springer (to appear)
3. Marsan, M.A., Conte, G., Balbo, G.: A Class of Generalized Stochastic Petri Nets for the Performance Evaluation of Multiprocessor Systems. ACM TOCS 2(2), 93–122 (1984)
4. Pearl, J.: Probabilistic Reasoning in Intelligent Systems: Networks of Plausible Inference. Morgan Kaufmann (1988)
5. Rogge-Solti, A., Mans, R., van der Aalst, W., Weske, M.: Repairing Event Logs Using Stochastic Process Models. Technical Report 78, Hasso Plattner Institute (2013)
6. Adriansyah, A., van Dongen, B., van der Aalst, W.: Conformance Checking using Cost-Based Fitness Analysis. In: EDOC 2011, pp. 55–64. IEEE (2011)
7. Zhang, L., Chen, W., Hu, Y., Chen, C.: Statistical Static Timing Analysis With Conditional Linear MAX/MIN Approximation and Extended Canonical Timing Model. In: TCAD, vol. 25, pp. 1183–1191. IEEE (2006)

AnonyFacebook - Liking Facebook Posts Anonymously[*]

Pedro Alves[1] and Paulo Ferreira[2]

[1] Opensoft / INESC-ID / IST, Rua Joshua Benoliel, 1 - 3D, Lisboa, Portugal
pedro.h.alves@gmail.com
[2] INESC-ID / IST, Rua Alves Redol 9, Lisboa, Portugal
paulo.ferreira@inesc-id.pt

Abstract. In several countries the simple act of liking (on Facebook) an anti-government article or video can be (and has already been) used to pursue and detain activists. Given such a scenario, it is of great relevance to allow anyone to anonymously "like" any post.

In this paper we present anonyFacebook, a system that allows Facebook users to "like" a post (e.g., news, photo, video) without revealing their identity (even to the social network administrators). Obviously, such anonymous "likes" count to the total number of "likes". Anonymous "likes" are ensured by means of cryptographic techniques such as homomorphic encryption and shared threshold key pairs.

Keywords: social networks, privacy, anonymity, homomorphic encryption.

1 Introduction

Social Networks (SNs) allow users to connect each other at an unprecedented scale. They are primarily being used to share media and keep in touch with friends, family and colleagues; however, they are also used to raise awareness and coordinate large communities around important topics, such as the political status of some countries [4,1,6]. For example, Egyptian activist Wael Ghonim credited Facebook with the success of the Egyptian people's uprising, in particular for its key role in organizing the most important protest on January 25th.[1]

Wael Ghonim was arrested for 12 days, shortly after the protest.[2] Like Wael, many activists suffered from their activities on SNs as Egypt (and several other countries) have been reported to track down activists on SNs to the point where bloggers died while in custody for their anti-government articles.[3]

Thus, we developed AnonyFacebook, a system for Facebook in which users can promote/raise awareness to news, links, photos or videos (which we will refer

---

[*] This work was partially supported by national funds through FCT – Fundação para a Ciência e a Tecnologia, under projects Pest-OE/EEI/LA0021/2013 and PTDC/EIA-EIA/113993/2009.
[1] http://huff.to/14v9xBd
[2] http://huff.to/hWjthA
[3] http://readwrite.com/2011/04/12/bahraini_blogger_dies_in_custody

Y.T. Demey and H. Panetto (Eds.): OTM 2013 Workshops, LNCS 8186, pp. 709–713, 2013.
© Springer-Verlag Berlin Heidelberg 2013

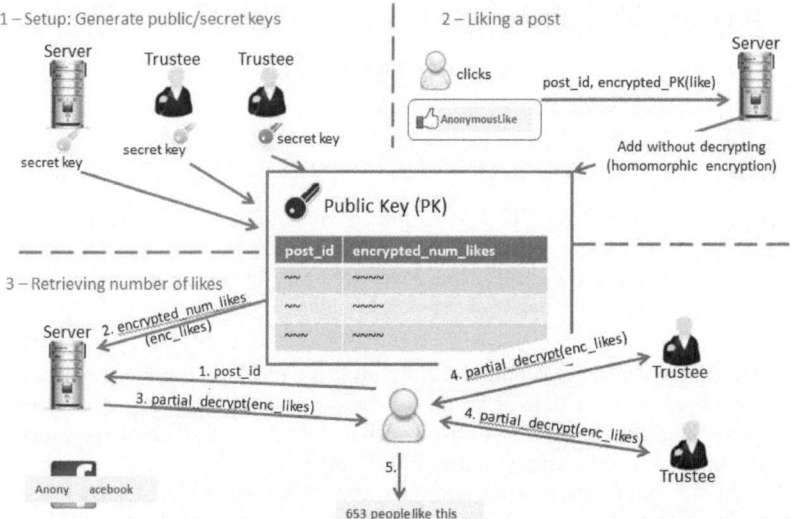

Fig. 1. AnonyFacebook global view

generically as posts) without revealing their identity. Such anonymity is ensured even to Facebook administrators. While implemented as a plug-in for Facebook, AnonyFacebook can be used in other similar SNs.

The interface supported by AnonyFacebook is similar to the one already existent in the original Facebook, and to which users are accustomed - a "like button", which can be embedded into a blog or news site, associated with a given post along with the number of "likes" already submitted by other users.

Despite such interface similarity, AnonyFacebook uses a completely different protocol than the original Facebook, whereby messages exchanged with the SN server are encrypted in such a way that:

– it is not possible to ascertain which post each user "liked";
– it is possible to know how many people "liked" a certain post.

These two aspects are ensured using a combination of homomorphic encryption [5] and shared threshold key pairs [3] as described in the next section.

2   Protocol

The global view of the AnonyFacebook protocol is illustrated in Figure 1: "likes" are encrypted with a key that is shared among the Facebook infrastructure (Facebook server, for short) and a set of independent entities (e.g., NGOs) so that none of these entities alone can decrypt it. By using a special property of the encryption algorithm, the Facebook server is able to sum the number of "likes" of a given post without having to decrypt them (i.e., the sum is also encrypted). When a user wants to know how many "likes" are associated with a given post, he coordinates all the entities to jointly decrypt the sum. We now present the details of the solution.

AnonyFacebook assumes a server S (hosted at facebook.com) and a set of Trustees T_i which can be public national institutes, NGOs, etc. Facebook clients exchange encrypted messages with S, and communicate with T_i to decrypt such messages (in particular, the number of "likes" of a given post).

The protocol has an initial setup process where a shared threshold key pair is generated across S and all T_i. This key will be published and used to encrypt all the "like" messages. Each entity (S and T_i) stores its part of the private key (also called shadow). To decrypt such "like" messages (or, being more precise, the result of operations on those messages), a certain number of T_i (depending on the threshold) must collaborate (i.e., Facebook server S alone is not be able to decrypt them).

After the setup stage, the system is ready to accept anonymous "like" messages. A "like" message in AnonyFacebook is a tuple ($post\_id, like$), where:

- $post\_id$ is a unique identifier of the post, and
- $like$ is an integer indicating if the user "liked" that post (value=1) or not (value=0).

On each one of these "like" messages, the $like$ value is encrypted with the public key (generated in the initial setup phase) and the tuple is then sent to S. It's worthy to note that $post\_id$ has to be sent in cleartext to prevent duplicate "likes", as explained in the next paragraph. Thus, since the $post\_id$ is sent in cleartext, the AnonyFacebook client cannot send only the posts the user effectively "likes"; it has to also send posts the user didn't "like". Consequently, every time a user "likes" a given post, the client sends not only that $post\_id$ but also n random other $post\_ids$, so that S is not able to know which exact post the user "liked". Therefore, S knows that the user "liked" one of those posts but is not sure which one.

Sending multiple $post\_ids$ each time the user "likes" a post is fundamental to prevent duplicate likes. Given that "likes" are encrypted, S can not know if the user already "liked" a given post. However, S knows that the user *potentially* "liked" a given post from those sent: every $post\_id$ sent to the Facebok server ("liked" or not "liked") is a potential "like" with probability $1/n$ (n is the number of $post\_ids$ sent for each "like").

To prevent duplicate "likes", S applies a probabilistic detection of multiple "likes" for the same post: it refuses $post\_ids$ that were already received, because there is a high probability that it is a "like" for a post the user previously "liked" (i.e. it is a duplicated "like"). Clearly, there may be false positives (i.e., S may refuse legitimate "likes") but the probability is low enough to guarantee the usability and usefulness of the system. Our estimates, based on Facebook numbers, show that (even being conservative) this probability is less than one collision per year for Facebook users; i.e., of all the "likes" the user does in Facebook during an year, one of them won't be successful.

The AnonyFacebook protocol allows users to see the number of "likes" of a given post, without knowing who did each individual "like". This functionality relies on the additive homomorphic properties of an ElGamal variant known as exponential ElGamal [2]. Using exponential ElGamal, it is possible to add two encrypted ("like") messages, without having to decrypt them first; in addition, the decryption of the encrypted sum equals the sum of the decrypted values. Thus, S applies this property by adding each encrypted "like" (note that the "like" value is either 1 or 0) with the already existent encrypted sum of that *post_id* (or zero if it is the first). When an AnonyFacebook user retrieves the number of "likes" of a given post, it is actually retrieving the encrypted sum associated with that post. Then, the client coordinates with the necessary number of Trustees (based on a pre-defined threshold) in order to decrypt the previously mentioned sum, for which each Thrustee uses its part of the private key.

3   Conclusion

In this paper, we propose AnonyFacebook, a SNA similar to Facebook that allows users to anonymously "like" any post; in other words, users can provide quantitative feedback without revealing their identity, even to the social network infrastructure itself. AnonyFacebook employs strong cryptographic techniques (homomorphic encryption, shared threshold key pairs) to guarantee users privacy. In particular, the AnonyFacebook server does not store individual "likes"; it does store the count of "likes" on any given post. Moreover, count of "likes" is encrypted in such a way that several entities (trustees) must collaborate to decrypt it (i.e., it is not possible for a single entity to decrypt it).

AnonyFacebook prevents duplicated "likes" using a *probabilistic* approach without breaking user's privacy. This is done by mixing the real "like" with several fake "likes": the client sends several post_ids for which the AnonyFacebook server does not know if they have been "liked" or not. This solution can wrongly prevent a legitimate "like"; however, as we have shown, this happens only once per year on average. So, we believe that our solution effectively prevents duplicated "likes" while achieving an acceptable tradeoff between privacy and usability.

We have implemented AnonyFacebook (within a Facebook replica), using an interaction model very similar to Facebook: developers can easily embed an anonymous "Like" button next to any content (blog post, video, etc.). The same mechanism also displays the current number of "likes" of a post. This implementation is publicly available (https://bitbucket.org/anonymousJoe/anonylikes); it can be used by any developer wishing to support privacy-preserving quantitative feedback in SNAs.

AnonyFacebook performance has been evaluated. We found that even though some encryption operations are computing intensive, the system can be implemented today without breaking user expectations (regarding the response time of client software) and usability for this kind of applications. In addition, since the performance of such encryption operations are mostly tied to CPU speed, it will tend to improve in the upcoming years with advances in processor technology.

References

1. Al-Ani, B., Mark, G., Chung, J., Jones, J.: The Egyptian blogosphere: a counter-narrative of the revolution. In: Proceedings of the ACM 2012 Conference on Computer Supported Cooperative Work (2012)

2. Cramer, R., Gennaro, R., Schoenmakers, B.: A secure and optimally efficient multi-authority election scheme. European Transactions on Telecommunications 8(5), 481–490 (1997)

3. Desmedt, Y.G., Frankel, Y.: Threshold cryptosystems. In: Brassard, G. (ed.) CRYPTO 1989. LNCS, vol. 435, pp. 307–315. Springer, Heidelberg (1990)

4. Lotan, G., Graeff, E., Ananny, M., Gaffney, D., Pearce, I., Boyd, D.: The Revolutions Were Tweeted: Information Flows During the 2011 Tunisian and Egyptian Revolutions. International Journal of Communication 5, 1375–1406 (2011)

5. Rivest, R.: On data banks and privacy homomorphisms. Foundations of Secure Computation 4(11) (1978)

6. Wulf, V., Misaki, K., Atam, M.: On the ground'in Sidi Bouzid: investigating social media use during the tunisian revolution. In: Proceedings of the 2013 ACM Conference on Computer Supported Cooperative Work, pp. 1409–1418 (2013)

E-Contract Enactment Using Meta Execution Workflow

Pabitra Mohapatra[1], Pisipati Radha Krishna[2], and Kamalakar Karlapalem[1]

[1] Center for Data Engg., International Institute of Information Technology, Hyderabad, India
`pabitra.mohapatra@research.iiit.ac.in`, `kamal@iiit.ac.in`
[2] Infosys Labs, Infosys Limited, Hyderabad, India
`radhakrishna_p@infosys.com`

Abstract. E-contract fulfillment has many challenges because enactment is cross organizational and it involves interdependencies among its various elements namely parties, activities, clauses, exceptions, payments and commitments. E-contract needs inter organizational workflow services for monitoring its enactment. In this paper, we introduce the concept of e-contract elements based workflow views in order to bridge the gap between different aspects of e-contract and the services provided by a meta-workflow system. The enactment of e-contract is carried out using the meta execution workflow. It enables coordination among the workflow views and the workflow system for successful fulfillment.

Keywords: E-contract, Workflow Views, Dependencies, Exceptions.

1   Introduction

This paper focuses on e-services driven meta-workflow system for monitoring e-contract enactment. Usually, e-contract enactment and deployment necessitate inter- and intra- organizational workflows. Enterprises implement their own workflows, however, capturing and handling various dependencies that exist among six contract elements (namely *parties*, *activities*, *clauses*, *payments*, *exceptions* and *commitments*) is a challenging task. The interdependencies among elements for e-contract fulfillment include (i) activities carried out by specified parties(at times involves sub-contracts to carry out some of the activities), (ii) satisfaction of a set of clauses associated with activity executions, (iii) handling exceptions, if any clause violation and (iv) ensuring payments before commitments [2][3]. Thus, a workflow management system (WFMS) should support the functions of each contract element, besides the activity/task execution. Our research question is how to monitor the activities' execution from multiple perspectives of e-contracts such as activity commitment, clause violation and payments due. We propose an Execution Workflow based services for effectual monitoring and successful completion of e-contract. For e-contract monitoring, we have associated *workflow views* for each e-contract element.

Y.T. Demey and H. Panetto (Eds.): OTM 2013 Workshops, LNCS 8186, pp. 714–717, 2013.
© Springer-Verlag Berlin Heidelberg 2013

2   E-Contract Enactment System

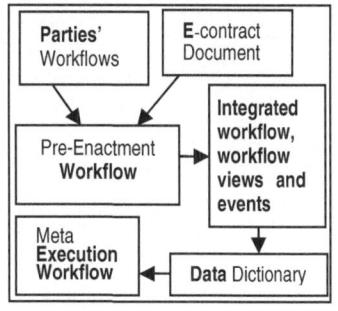

Fig. 1 shows an overview of our system, which consists of two major components: (i) *Pre-enactment workflow* and (ii) *Meta execution workflow* [4]. The *pre-enactment workflow* builds an integrated contract workflow that comprises of parties' workflows. The e-contract *meta execution workflow drives* the e-contract execution and enables workflow views to support the contract elements. We specify individual workflows for parties, each having some tasks, and the tasks have some pre-events and post-events. The

Fig. 1. System Overview

pre-enactment workflow is a *specification component* and the input to this component is the workflows belonging to different parties and the e-contract document. This component maps the contract elements and their dependencies into an *integrated contract workflow*. Further, workflow views are derived from the integrated workflow. All the specifications are stored in the Data Dictionary.

A major problem of having multiple workflows is that incorporation of tasks and events related to clauses, exceptions and payments at appropriate places might get ignored. In e-contract, the tasks are attached to the elements so that it ensures the execution of the tasks for e-contract enactment. Further, clauses are dependent on the execution of the tasks by one or more parties. So, multiple workflows defined for various tasks are difficult to coordinate among various parties as there are dependencies between tasks. The question is how to monitor and control the execution of an e-contract using workflows. The parties need to know the events and the coordination between the parties, and they should be specified explicitly. The parties involved can resolve exceptions by triggering alternate workflows or at times human intervention is required for resolving the exceptions.

We build an *integrated workflow that combines individual workflows (of parties) in the required order and allows the flexibility of augmenting additional tasks and events (with the help of user interaction) as required by the contract specifications.* To construct the integrated contract workflow the steps followed are given below:

- Identification of the six elements in the e-contract document using MTDC approach [1].
- After mining the document, the output will be a set of tasks executed by the parties.
- Determine coordinated set of tasks using the Workflow Specification Model of MTDC.
- Arrange the tasks in the sequence of their execution, the events generated after task completion is received by the intended party's task. It will help understanding the interdependencies among the tasks and orchestration of workflow execution.
- Derive/augment integrated workflow with the coordinated tasks in case these tasks are executed in a sequence, otherwise derive independent workflow and complement it with the integrated contract workflow.
- Represent the workflow using Yet Another Workflow Language (YAWL) [5].

Consider the Seller-carrier-buyer Example. Individual workflow of the parties is shown in Fig. 2 and the integrated workflow is shown in Fig. 3. The three parties involved are *buyer*(P1), *carrier*(P2) *and seller*(P3). Buyer's Activity (BA), Seller's Activity (SA) and Carrier's Activity (CA) are BA1, SA2, SA3, SA4, CA5, SA6, SA7, SA8, CA9, CA10, BA11, BA12, BA13, BA14, BA15, BA16, CA17, BA18.

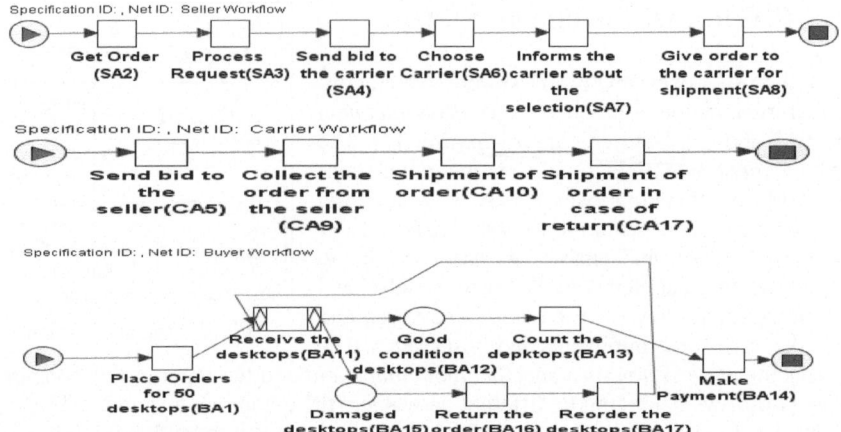

Fig. 2. Individual workflows for seller-buyer-carrier

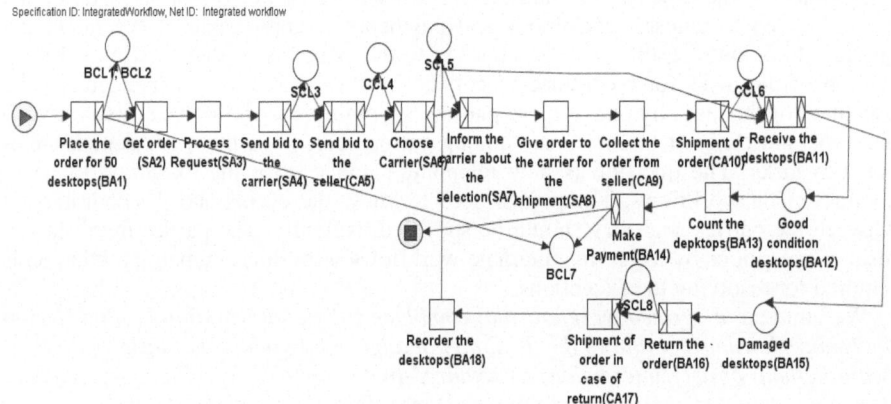

Fig. 3. Integrated workflow for seller-buyer-carrier

The clauses are denoted as BCL (buyer's clause), SCL (Seller's clause), and CCL (carrier's clause) and the exceptions are denoted as BX (buyer's exception), SX (seller's exception) and the CX (carrier's exception). BCL1 says the quantity has to be specified by the buyer while placing the order, if it fails then the BX1 will occur and the seller would not fulfill the order. BCL2 says customer details should be provided, if not done the BX2 will occur and the seller would not give the shipping address to the carrier. SCL3 says the carrier should be chosen by a bidding process. CCL4 says the response to the bid by the carrier to the seller should be done in three working days. SCL5 says the carrier has to be chosen in five working days. CCL6 says the shipment should be done in three working days if it fails to do so then CX3 will occur and the seller will choose another carrier. BCL7 is regarding the mode of payment, it had to be decided at the time of placing order if it fails to do that the BX4 will occur that the seller would not ship the item. SCL8 represents free shipment in case of damaged goods. The payment task is BA14. Once all the tasks are done then commitment of the contract will happen, which is decided by the parties. The results of this approach will help setting up a coherent relationship among the elements.

We developed e-contract elements based views for six elements namely *Activity view, Party view, Clauses view, Exceptions view, Payments view* and *Commitments view* in order to monitor the progress of e-contract execution during its enactment. Mapping of the tasks of integrated workflow is done with the respective views. The views will have information regarding the input and output events for their respective set of tasks. Along with HOW, WHEN, WHERE and WHO of tasks got executed, the views can monitor the workflow execution based on the events captured during e-contract execution. Here, the views (or sub-views) serve as a black box, and focus more on the input and output data, conditions and events.

Activities View: BA1→SA2→SA3→SA4→CA5→SA6→SA7→SA8→CA9→CA10→BA11→BA12→BA13→ BA14→BA15→BA16→CA17→BA18→BA11→BA12→BA13→BA14.

Parties View: P1: BA1→BA11→BA12→BA13→BA14→BA15→BA16; P2: SA2→SA3→SA4→SA6→SA7→ SA8; P3: CA5→ CA9 → CA10 → CA17;

Clauses View: BCL1: BA1→SA2; BCL2: BA1→SA2; SCL3: SA4→CA5; CCL4: CA5→SA6; SCL5: SA6→SA7; CCL6: CA10→ BA11; BCL7: BA1→BA14; SCL8: BA16→CA17

Exceptions View: BX1:BCL1→BA1→SA2; BX2:BCL2→BA1→SA2;CX3:CCL6→CA10→BA11; BX4:BCL7→BA1→BA14

Payments View: In our example, the activity A9 corresponds to payments. PY: BA14

Commitments View: C1: CA10→BA11; C2: BA14

Meta Execution Workflow (EW) defines and executes the integrated workflow. The change in workflow definition occurs when some exception occurs. For instance, if any of the exceptions like BX1, BX2, CX3 or BX4 occurs, then the EW will try for another EW definition. In our approach, the workflow instance and the EW instance are coupled together. Here, the EW helps in keeping track of all the events that in-turn helps in monitoring the e-contract elements successfully.

3   Conclusion

In this paper, we developed pre-enactment workflow to take the individual workflows from parties and generate integrated contract workflow. We also presented an execution workflow component that facilitates execution of integrated workflow and monitors the execution through workflow views specified for various contract elements. We illustrated our methodology by using the seller-carrier-buyer contract.

References

1. Khandekar, A., Krishna, P.R., Karlapalem, K.: A Methodology and Toolkit for Deploying Contract Documents as E-contracts. In: Tutorials, Posters, Panels and Industrial Contributions at ER 2007, vol. 83, pp. 91–96. Australian Computer Society Inc. (2007)
2. Krishna, P.R., Karlapalem, K.: Electronic Contracts. IEEE Internet Computing 12(4), 80–88 (2008)
3. Krishna, P.R., Karlapalem, K., Chiu, D.K.W.: An ER^EC Framework for E-Contract Modeling, Enactment and Monitoring. Data and Knowledge Engineering 51(1), 31–58 (2004)
4. Sharma, S., Karlapalem, K., Krishna, P.R.: A Case for a Workflow Driven Workflow Execution Engine. In: Proc. of Workshop on Info. Tech. and Systems (WITS), Florida (2012)
5. van der Aalst, W., ter Hofstede, A.: YAWL: yet another workflow language. Information Systems 30(4), 245–275 (2005)

Difference-Preserving Process Merge

Kristof Böhmer and Stefanie Rinderle-Ma

University of Vienna, Faculty of Computer Science
a1063026@unet.univie.ac.at, stefanie.rinderle-ma@univie.ac.at

Abstract. Providing merging techniques for business processes fosters the management and maintenance of (large) process model repositories. Contrary to existing approaches that focus on preserving behavior of all participating process models, this paper presents a merging technique that aims at preserving the difference between the participating process models by exploiting the existence of a common parent process, e.g., a reference or standard process model.

Keywords: Process Design, Process Merging.

1 Motivation

Nowadays, many companies face a multitude of different business process models or versions being in use simultaneously. As an example take the SAP reference process catalog containing more than 600 different process definitions [1]. Aside modeling and enacting these processes, their models have to be maintained and often adapted to reflect constantly changing market situations which can be the result of takeovers, acquisitions or amendments [2]. Hence, techniques to support users in keeping track and managing different process models or model versions are of great importance [3]. This has been recognized by literature, particularly resulting in techniques for process (model) merge [4,5]: given a set of process models $\{P_1, \ldots, P_n\}$ existing techniques aim at preserving the behavior of each process model P_i within the merged model P_{merge}. An example for this approach is depicted in Figure 1. On the left side process models *Process 1* and *Process 2* are to be merged. The behavior-preserving merge produces the result depicted in the middle of the figure. Without presenting formal details on the process model due to space restrictions, the number of paths from the original models (1 or 2 respectively) has increased to 8 paths in P_{merge}. In some cases, even some additional executions paths might added which were not present in one of the original process models P_i.

Despite obvious advantages of this kind of merge techniques such as quickly giving an overview about the merged processes, they might create quite complex and hard to understand results [6] with increasing number of execution paths. This high number of execution paths might also necessitate that users have to configure the resulting process model for each use case.

This leads to the following questions:

1. Are there any other ways of merging process models?
2. How can process merging techniques be evaluated?

Y.T. Demey and H. Panetto (Eds.): OTM 2013 Workshops, LNCS 8186, pp. 718–721, 2013.

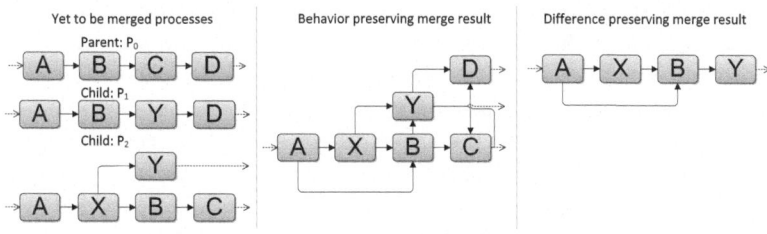

Fig. 1. Comparison of behavior and difference preserving merge

2 Difference-Preserving Merge

Following the above two questions, in this paper, we try to adopt the idea of merging software code (cf. e.g., [7]) in merging process models in a difference-preserving way. One assumption that has to be made is that the process models to be merged (*child processes*) all relate to an initial process (for now on called *parent process*), i.e., a child process has been derived from the parent process by applying a set of change operations, e.g., inserting or deleting nodes. An example is show in Figure 1 where P_1 and P_2 are children of P_0. P_1, for example, was derived from P_0 by deleting node C and inserting node Y. These differences are then to be preserved in the merge result.

Our presumption is that the difference-preserving merge will create much smaller, transparent, understandable and accessible results especially if the results should e.g. be merged again. Take result of difference-preserving merge as shown in Fig. 1 (right side): this model contains 4 instead of 6 elements and 2 instead of 8 paths when compared to the behavior-preserving merge result.

Approach: In the following we consider a set of three basic change operations which can be applied on the edges or nodes of a parent process to create a new child process. So we will tackle operations to add new edges and nodes using insert(edge(from, to)), and insert(node), to delete information by delete(node) or delete(edge) and to modify existing nodes e.g. by changing it's properties by calling modify(node, new data). Other high level operations like replace or move can be constructed using this basic operations. We also assume that all the applied operations will be used to create sound processes so that the later applied conflict resolution techniques only have to tackle merge related process conflicts.

Information gathering. The following steps will be executed sequentially to merge multiple processes. The first step will investigate the parent process in combination with the yet to be merged child processes. The behavior preserving merge ignores the parent process but we propose to use this additional information so that a so called *three way merge* can be applied [3]. It will be used to detect which elements (nodes and edges) have been deleted, added, or modified to create one of the merged child processes. For each change operation an individual set including the affected elements (edges and nodes) will be created. The algorithms start by detecting the elements which have been deleted from the parent process. This information will then be stored at a set R. The set will be filled by comparing each element of the parent process with the child processes. If at least one child process does not contain the element it will be added to R. A similar approach will be used to detect newly generated elements. Therefore each element of the child processes will be compared with the parent process. If an element exists at a child but not at the parent it will be added to the set N. Also a set M containing the modified elements will be generated. For each element at the child processes it's companion at the parent process will be identified and, if any exists, their content will be compared. The element will be added to M if the compared content differs. If the element has been modified differently, at multiple child processes, the user has to decide which version should be taken. The last piece of information contains which elements have been transferred from the parent process to the child process without any modifications. So all the elements available at the parent process which are not present at the set R and M will be stored at a newly generated set O.

Creating the merged process. The second step will be used to merge the various changes\differences gathered from the parent and child processes. So the identified changes from all child process will be combined. Therefore the sets generated during the previouis step will be used. They are combined using the union operation to create $P_{merged} = (N \cup M \cup O)$. The set R will here be ignored because it has already been used to generate O so that all the detected delete operations will be preserved.

Optimizing the results. The third step will be used to enhance the result quality and will be applied onto P_{merge}. The first optimization will detect parts at the merged control flow where the merge created a new, not present at any child process, parallel control flow branch. Such a parallel execution can be problematic because it can cause concurrency issues like incorrect execution states, incomplete data or inappropriate calculations. On the other hand, it is also possible that it just cannot be realizable in day-to-day work. So if such a newly generated execution order (which was not present at the child processes) is detected the merger asks the user if she or he wants to reorder this e.g. to a sequential ordering by choosing between multiple auto generated alternative control flow recommendations.

The second optimization will try to find gaps at the control flow. Therefore each node n at P_{merge} will be checked if it has been correctly integrated, so that incoming and outgoing edges exists for this node. It also has to be taken into account that start and end nodes only need an incoming or outgoing edge. After a gap has been detected it will be closed by adding a newly generated edge. The end\start of the new edge will be n if incoming\outgoing edges are missing. The opposite side of the edge will be detected by analyzing the original control flow path which was used to integrate the node. At first the child processes will be investigated, followed up by the parent process, if necessary. So the predecessors\successors, ordered by their distance to n, will be checked. The nearest node which is also available at P_{merge} will then be used as the start\end of the edge.

3   Evaluation and Conclusion

All algorithms and concepts behind the difference-preserving merge have been implemented as a proof of concept prototype. We experimented with different use cases of different complexity. Overall, we can conclude that the difference-preserving merge tends to excel the behavior-preserving merge in terms of simplicity of the produced merge results. This is advantageous for understandability, maintainability, and possible automation of the resulting process models. In turn, behavior-based approaches provide a complete overview on all participating models and can be produced with lower computational effort.

In future research, we will further investigate means to compare both approaches, preferably based on a real-world case study. Further on, we will work on "proving" that the approach is always difference-preserving. Another goal is to integrate the approach with existing work on calculating difference between process models such as [8].

References

1. Curran, T., Keller, G.: SAP R/3 Business Blueprint: Business-Engineering mit den R/3-Referenzprozessen. Addison-Wesley (1999)
2. Davenport, T.H., Short, J.E.: The New Industrial Engineering: Information Technology and Business Process Redesign. Sloan Mgmt. Review 31(4), 11–27 (1990)
3. Hallerbach, A., Bauer, T., Reichert, M.: Capturing variability in business process models: the Provop approach. Journal of Software Maintenance 22(6-7), 519–546 (2010)
4. Gottschalk, F., van der Aalst, W.M.P., Jansen-Vullers, M.H.: Merging Event-Driven Process Chains. In: Meersman, R., Tari, Z. (eds.) OTM 2008, Part I. LNCS, vol. 5331, pp. 418–426. Springer, Heidelberg (2008)
5. La Rosa, M., Dumas, M., Uba, R., Dijkman, R.: Merging Business Process Models. In: Meersman, R., Dillon, T.S., Herrero, P. (eds.) OTM 2010. LNCS, vol. 6426, pp. 96–113. Springer, Heidelberg (2010)
6. Mendling, J., Reijers, H.A., Cardoso, J.: What Makes Process Models Understandable? In: Alonso, G., Dadam, P., Rosemann, M. (eds.) BPM 2007. LNCS, vol. 4714, pp. 48–63. Springer, Heidelberg (2007)
7. Mens, T., Demeyer, S.: Software Evolution. Springer (2008)
8. Küster, J., Gerth, C., Förster, A., Engels, G.: Detecting and resolving process model differences in the absence of a change log. In: Dumas, M., Reichert, M., Shan, M.-C. (eds.) BPM 2008. LNCS, vol. 5240, pp. 244–260. Springer, Heidelberg (2008)

Towards Personalized Search for Tweets

Akshay Choche and Lakshmish Ramaswamy

Department of Computer Science,
The University of Georgia,
Athens Georgia 30602
{choche,laks}@cs.uga.edu

Abstract. Powerful search capabilities are fundamentally important for micro-blog-based information systems such as Twitter. While recently there has been some works aimed at enhancing the scalability of micro-blog search, very few existing techniques incorporate personalization into their search and ranking processes. This paper argues that since Twitter is a social network (SN)-based micro-blog system, it is essential to personalize search results taking into account the social relationships among various users. In this paper, we outline a scalable and personalized tweet search framework that takes into account the search parameters, the distances of the follower relationships, and the temporal aspects of the tweets when ranking the search results.

Keywords: Micro-blogs, Search, Social Network, Personalization.

1 Introduction

Powerful search techniques are indispensable to micro-blog-based cooperative information systems such as Twitter, as they seek to establish themselves within the highly competitive online social media space [5]. However, searching on SN-based microblog platforms is radically different than searching content on the World Wide Web, and it poses several unique challenges. First and foremost, micro-blogs (henceforth referred to as *tweets*) being very short pieces of text (maximum of 140 characters), heavyweight text analytic techniques are not very effective. Second, as Twitter is most commonly used for sharing updates about current events and issues, freshness and timelines of search results become critically important. Third, since Twitter also incorporates SN features, it is important to take SN-relationships into account during search and ranking processes. Unfortunately, very few existing works comprehensively address the above challenges [1] [2] [4]. To the best of our knowledge, none of the existing works incorporate *personalization* into their search and ranking strategies. Thus, the social network aspect of Twitter is ignored during search.

In this paper, we argue that it is important to personalize search results based on SN relationships. The follower relationship in Twitter is often an indicator of commonality of interests and opinions. Thus, it is natural for a user issuing a query to expect higher rankings to matching tweets from users that she

Y.T. Demey and H. Panetto (Eds.): OTM 2013 Workshops, LNCS 8186, pp. 722–725, 2013.

is transitively following even when those tweets are not the most recent ones. However, personalization also raises new scalability issues not only because it requires additional analytics, but also because it reduces the efficacy of caching. In this paper, we outline a scalable and personalized search technique for tweets. Our technique combines three major tweet relevance factors, namely, degree of syntactic match, distance of the follower relationships, and the temporal recency of tweets into a unique tweet ranking metric.

2   Personalized Tweet Search Scheme

Shortness of tweets (limited to 140 characters), makes it necessary to use additional contextual information during search and ranking. The follower relationships in Twitter often embody commonalities in interests and opinions. When a user U_1 chooses to follow another user U_2, it inherently signifies that U_1 is interested in the updates and opinions being posted by U_2. Applying this logic transitively, we hypothesize that U_1 will be much more satisfied with the search results if matching tweets (tweets containing one or more search query words) from users that she is directly or indirectly following are ranked high. A second benefit of using SN-relationships is in terms of *search query disambiguation*. For example, the search query "Stephen King" can either refer to the famous author or the famous soccer player. It may be possible to discern the querier's intent by checking if she predominantly follows literary personalities or sport commentators.

2.1   Technique Overview

Our search technique operates in two phases. First, we use a simple keyword-based filter to retrieve tweets that are relevant to a given query. This phase is intentionally kept simple so as to filter-out large fractions of obviously-irrelevant tweets. The tweets that are deemed relevant are processed by the second phase which generates personalized search results by using our novel personalized tweet ranking algorithm. Adopting a two phase scheme vastly reduces the overheads of personalization [3].

Personalized Tweet Ranking: One of the main challenges in ranking tweets is that several factors influence the relative importance of tweets. In our work, we have identified three main factors that influence the relative significance of tweets to a given query. The first is the strength of the SN-relationship between the tweet's author and the user issuing the query. We call this the *personalization factor*. The second is the *temporal significance factor*, which capture the temporal relevance of a tweet to the query. The third is the *author influence* factor, which measures social influence of a tweet's author. Each of these factors have very distinct significance, and we combine these factors into a personalized tweet ranking function as follows.

$$CRS(Tw_k) = w_1 * PS(Tw_k) + w_2 * TS(Tw_k) + (1 - w_1 - w_2) * AIS(Tw_k) \ (1)$$

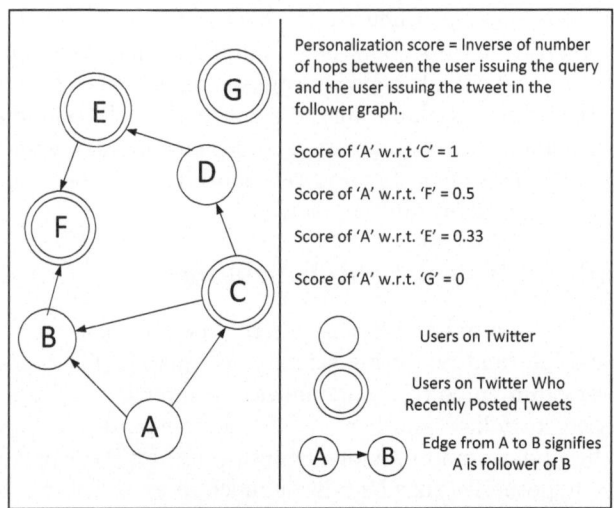

Fig. 1. Personalization using relationship property

In this function, $CRS(Tw_k)$ indicates the cumulative ranking score for tweet TW_k, $PS(Tw_k)$ denotes the tweet's personalization score, $TS(Tw_k)$ denotes its temporal score and $AIS(Tw_k)$ indicates its author influence score. w_1 and w_2 are system-defined weight parameters such that $w_1 \geq 0$, $w_2 \geq 0$ and $w_1 + w_2 \leq 1$. The values of w_1 and w_2 determine the relative importance of the different factors. We now discuss our mechanisms for quantifying each of these factors.

Personalization Score (PS): This score measures the *social affinity* of the user issuing the query to the tweet's author. To compute the social affinity, we model the follower relationship as an unweighted directed graph in which vertices correspond to users and edges correspond to the follower relationship between users. We use the inverse of the length (number of hops) of the shortest path to quantify the personalization score. Our choice is influenced by computational efficiency and stability of the parameter over time. Figure 1 illustrates the personalization score computation on a hypothetical follower graph. Personalization score of A with respect to C is 1 because A is a direct follower of C, whereas the personalization score of A with respect to G is zero because there is A is not a direct or indirect follower of G.

Temporal Score (TS): The temporal score measures the temporal closeness of a tweet to a query. The rationale is to provide higher preference to more recent tweets. Suppose a tweet Tw_i was posted at time T_x. This tweet's temporal score with respect to query Q_j issued at time T_y is quantified as $\frac{1}{T_y - T_x + 1}$.

Author Influence Score (AIS): The author influence score measures the influence of a tweet's author on the Twitter user community. The rationale is to give higher ratings to tweets from more popular Twitter users. The author influence score of a tweet is defined as the ratio of the number of followers of the tweet's author to the total number of currently active Twitter users.

Ranking Algorithm: At a conceptual-level, the ranking algorithm is quite simple – the CRS of each matching tweet is calculated and the tweets are ranked in the decreasing order of their CRS values. However, this naive implementation does not scale well because personalization score computation will quickly become a bottleneck. Thus we need smarter ways to generate the ranking. Our system incorporates an approximation strategy to accelerate the ranking process. Our algorithm proceeds as follows. First, we select only tweets whose temporal score exceeds a certain threshold μ. Computing this list is computationally scalable because we are essentially selecting tweets that are more recent than a certain time-point. We compute the PS and the AIS values only for the tweets whose TS value exceeds μ. Once these values are available, we generate the ranked list. Since PS values (which are the most expensive) are computed only for a limited number of tweets, our algorithm is much more scalable and efficient. Our experiments show that the above approximation strategy is very effective in minimizing personalization overheads [3].

3 Summary

In this paper, we outlined a scalable approach for incorporating personalization into search and ranking of tweets. Our approach is based upon a unique tweet ranking metric for generating personalized search results. This ranking metric takes into consideration three major tweet relevance factors, namely, the syntactical similarities between the tweet and the query, the distance of follower relationships, and the temporal recency of the tweet. We also presented a two-phased approximation strategy for enhancing the efficiency and scalability of personalized search.

References

1. Busch, M., Gade, K., Larson, B., Lok, P., Luckenbill, S., Lin, J.: Earlybird: Real-time search at Twitter. In: ICDE (2012)
2. Chen, C., Li, F., Ooi, B.C., Wu, S.: TI: An Efficient Indexing Mechanism for Real-time Search on Tweets. In: ACM-SIGMOD (2011)
3. Choche, A., Ramaswamy, L.: REPLETE: A Realtime Personalized Search Engine for Tweets. Technical Report, Dept. of Computer Science, The University of Georgia (2013)
4. Dong, A., Zhang, R., Kolari, P., Bai, J., Diaz, F., Chang, Y., Zheng, Z., Zha, H.: Time is of the essence: improving recency ranking using twitter data. In: ACM-WWW 2010 (2010)
5. Teevan, J., Ramage, D., Morris, M.R.: # TwitterSearch: A Comparison of Microblog Search and Web Search. In: ACM-WSDM 2011 (2011)

Linked Data Based Expert Search and Collaboration for Mashup

Devis Bianchini, Valeria De Antonellis, and Michele Melchiori

Dept. of Information Engineering, University of Brescia
Via Branze, 38 - 25123 Brescia (Italy)
{bianchin,deantone,melchior}@ing.unibs.it

Abstract. Web mashup is becoming more and more popular for both general and enterprise purposes in order to implement applications that leverage on third party components. However, developing a mashup requires specialized knowledge about Web APIs, their technologies and the way to combine them in a meaningful way. For this problem, we describe in this paper an approach for searching experts in the context of enterprise mashup development and in particular, we describe how to implement typical expert search patterns. The approach is based on the integration of knowledge both internal and external to the enterprise and represented as a linked data.

1 Approach Overview

In this paper we discuss the LINKSMAN (LINKed data Supported MAshup collaboratioN) framework for expert search finalized to collaboration in enterprise mashup development. Generally speaking, expert search systems aim at identifying candidate experts on a topic of interest and ranking them with respect to their expertise using available sources of evidence, typically content of documents. With respect to the expert search approaches for general purpose, our proposal: (i) is specialized in enterprise mashup development; (ii) exploits in an integrated way both the internal enterprise knowledge and the public external one; (iii) keeps into account social relationships between expert candidates to rank them. Specifically, internal knowledge mainly concerns developers, their organization inside the enterprise, their social connections and software artifacts they have developed, and cane be extracted by Enterprise 2.0 platforms. External knowledge concerns mashups and Web APIs from public repositories and to this purpose we adopt ProgrammableWeb[1]. Modeling social aspects for building web mashups has been discussed in [1]. The approach has been also extended in [2] where we provided a framework based on different Web API features to support Web API search and reuse. Related efforts in literature about Linked Web services or Linked Web APIs for discovery purposes are the ones described in [4]. Traditional expert search approaches and systems use as sources of evidence closed sets of document and databases. On the contrary, the work [3]

---

[1] See http://www.programmableweb.com

Y.T. Demey and H. Panetto (Eds.): OTM 2013 Workshops, LNCS 8186, pp. 726–729, 2013.

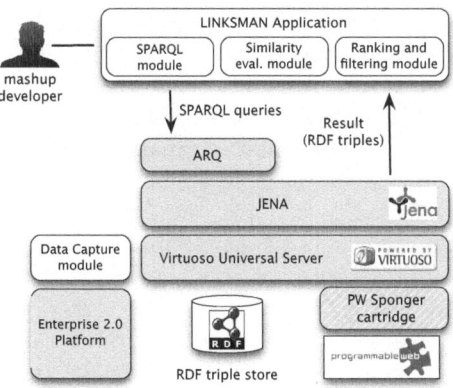

Fig. 1. The LINKSMAN functional architecture

discusses the potential benefits and drawbacks of using Linked Open Data (LOD) for expert search.

In LINKSMAN the external and the internal knowledge are modeled as two Linked Data (LD) vocabularies and data sets. Then, a set of perspectives are identified and associated with the main classes of the LD vocabularies. The perspectives allow for introducing descriptors on the data objects and similarity measures on them. Four different expert search patterns are then identified (see Section 2). The functional architecture of the prototype is illustrated in Figure 1 and uses the Virtuoso RDF data storage system. In the figure, the white blocks are component specifically developed for the LINKSMAN prototype and the grey ones are third party software components. The internal knowledge data set is stored in the is data storage component. A developer in order to submit a request in LINKSMAN specifies: (i) the goal (e.g., searching for competencies on a given Web API); (ii) either one Web API, for the first three patterns $R1$, $R2$ and $R3$, or one/more Web APIs for pattern $R4$. The submitted request is then translated by the *SPARQL module* into a set of SPARQL queries processed by *ARQ*, a SPARQL query engine to translate the query into Jena API calls. The RDF triples returned to the LINKSMAN application are used to build descriptors evaluated by the *Similarity evaluation module*, according to the metrics discussed in the next section. The search results are then filtered and ranked to be presented on the application GUI.

1.1 Perspectives and Descriptors for Expert Search

In the external and the internal knowledge LD vocabularies, we identify a set of classes that are suitable sources of evidence for establishing the expertise of a developer. These classes are: `InternalDeveloper`, `InternalMashup`, `WebAPI` and `Mashup` and a set of perspectives applicable to each of them is identified. A perspective is a set of class attributes describing a given aspect of the knowledge in the vocabularies. The attributes belong to one or more classes of the vocabularies. We consider four perspectives, describing: (i) enterprise-related information about developers (*Organization perspective*) and their social relationships (*Social perspective*); (ii) Web APIs involved in the mashup construction (*Web APIs perspective*); (iii) technologies, such as data formats and protocols, of the involved Web APIs (*Technologies perspective*); (iv) functionalities offered by Web APIs (*Functionality perspective*). For example, the `InternalDeveloper` class has an *Organization perspective* that collects the attributes in the vocabularies that provide organization related information about an internal developer, such as the office and department.

Descriptors are associated with the objects of these four classes based on the perspectives applicable to each class. A descriptor for an object o_i of the class C according to a perspective p is defined as a set of terms that are values of the attributes defined by p on C:

$$des_p(o_i) = \{t_{i1}, t_{i2}, ..., t_{in}\} \tag{1}$$

For example, for an `InternalDeveloper` object, a descriptor according to the *Organization* perspective is build as the union of values of attributes describing the knowledge about the organization of a developer working for the organization (e.g., `city`, `department`, `office`).

Descriptors for other perspectives and classes are defined in a similar way. A measure of similarity between two descriptors on the same perspective is defined according to the classical Dice's formula for similarity over sets:

$$Sim(des_p(o_i), des_p(o_j)) = \frac{2 \cdot |des_p(o_i) \cap des_p(o_j)|}{|des_p(o_i)| + |des_p(o_j)|} \tag{2}$$

The similarity ranges in $[0..1]$.

2   Expert Search Patterns

An expert search pattern specifies a type of expertise request. We define in a general way a request R submitted by a developer D_R as follows: *R1*) search for experts on a specific Web API W_R; *R2*) search for experts on the technologies of a Web API W_R; *R3*) search for experts on the functionalities of a Web API W_R; *R4*) search for experts on a mashup whose component APIs are $\{W_{Ri}\}$. In the case *R4*, the developer D_R is looking for developers that have experience in mashups that are built from a given set of Web APIs (or a not empty subset of it). A metrics for each search pattern is defined in order to measure the matching between a candidate developer and R, using the similarity between descriptors as in Equation (2). Application of an expert search pattern produces a list of developers, possibly empty, matching the request R. The list is ordered according to a ranking function and a threshold is used to filter out the less relevant results. Let us introduce informally the rationale for defining the metrics m for the pattern *R2*. The metrics for *R1*, *R3* and *R4* are defined in a similar way. In the case *R2*, if the developer D_i has used APIs that share technologies with the Web API W_R (that is, $Sim(des_{pT}(D_i), des_{pT}(W_R)) \neq 0$, where pT denotes the *Technologies* perspective), then $m(R, D_i)$ is not equal to zero and is based on a weighted sum of three terms: i) similarity m of D_i and D_R with respect the *Organization* perspective, ii) similarity of D_i and D_R with respect to the *Social* perspective, iii) similarity between the technologies that D_i has used in developer's mashups and technologies featuring W_R.

Considering the aging of experience In order to take into account the obsolescence of the experience of a developer D_i in using a given Web API W_j, its technologies or its functionalities in the context of developing a mashup we extend the definition of descriptor assigning an age to its components. Aging is meaningful when a descriptor of a developer is considered according to the *WebAPIs*, *Functionalities* and *Tecnologies* perspectives. The age associated with an element t_{ij} in the experience of D_i is therefore weighted by introducing an obsolescence factor that reduces accordingly the m value:

$$obs(t_{ij}, D_i) = \frac{1}{K^{age(t_{ij}, D_i)}} \tag{3}$$

where $K > 1$.

3   Conclusions and Future Work

In this paper, we described a Linked Data based framework to support expert search for collaboration in enterprise mashup development. The more relevant features of the framework are: (i) the internal and external knowledge sources are modeled and made suitable as RDF datasources; (ii) four patterns to support different kinds of expert search have been defined; (iii) an architecture and a prototype application have been designed and implemented. Future work includes more extensive experimentation and use of additional data sources (e.g., Mashape, http://www.mashape.com).

References

1. Bianchini, D., De Antonellis, V., Melchiori, M.: A Linked Data Perspective for Effective Exploration of Web APIs Repositories. In: Daniel, F., Dolog, P., Li, Q. (eds.) ICWE 2013. LNCS, vol. 7977, pp. 506–509. Springer, Heidelberg (2013)
2. Bianchini, D., De Antonellis, V., Melchiori, M.: A Multi-perspective Framework for Web API Search in Enterprise Mashup Design. In: Salinesi, C., Norrie, M.C., Pastor, Ó. (eds.) CAiSE 2013. LNCS, vol. 7908, pp. 353–368. Springer, Heidelberg (2013)
3. Stankovic, M., Wagner, C., Jovanovic, J., Laublet, P.: Looking for experts? what can linked data do for you? In: Proc. of Linked Data on the Web (LDOW) at WWW 2010 (2010)
4. Taheriyan, M., Knoblock, C.A., Szekely, P., Ambite, J.L.: Semi-Automatically Modeling Web APIs to Create Linked APIs. In: Proceedings of the ESWC 2012 Workshop on Linked APIs (2012)

ODBASE 2013 PC Co-Chairs Message

We are delighted to present the proceedings of the 12th International Conference on Ontologies, DataBases, and Applications of Semantics (ODBASE) which was held in Graz (Austria) on September 10-12, 2013. The ODBASE Conference series provides a forum for research and practitioners on the use of ontologies and data semantics in novel applications, and continues to draw a highly diverse body of researchers and practitioners. ODBASE is part of On the Move to Meaningful Internet Systems (OnTheMove) that co-locates with two other conferences: DOA-Trusted Cloud (International Conference on Secure Virtual Infrastructures) and CoopIS (International Conference on Cooperative Information Systems).

Of particular interest in the 2013 edition of the ODBASE Conference are the research and practical experience papers that bridge across traditional boundaries between disciplines such as ontologies, databases, knowledge engineering, data mining, information extraction, and computational linguistics.

In this edition, we received 50 paper submissions and had a program committee of 92 dedicated colleagues, including researchers and practitioners from diverse research areas. Special arrangements were made during the review process to ensure that each paper was reviewed by 3-4 members of different research areas. The result of this effort is the selection of high quality papers: fourteen regular papers (28%), eleven short papers (22%), and six posters (12%). Their themes included studies and solutions to a number of modern challenges such as querying and management of linked data and RDF documents, ontology engineering, semantic matching and mapping, application of data mining techniques, semantic discovery, and probabilistic data management.

Enjoy the reading!

July 2013

Pieter De Leenheer
Deijing Dou

Y.T. Demey and H. Panetto (Eds.): OTM 2013 Workshops, LNCS 8186, p. 730, 2013.
© Springer-Verlag Berlin Heidelberg 2013

Imposing a Semantic Schema for the Detection of Potential Mistakes in Knowledge Resources[*]

Vincenzo Maltese

DISI – University of Trento, Trento, Italy

Abstract. Nowadays, there is a pressing need for very accurate, up-to-date and diversity-aware knowledge resources. As their maintenance is very expensive, we argue that the only affordable way to address this is by complementing automatic with manual checks. This paper presents an approach, based on the notion of *semantic schema*, which aims to minimize human intervention as it allows the automatic identification of potentially faulty parts of a knowledge resource which need manual checks. Our evaluation showed promising results.

1 Defining and Enforcing a Semantic Schema

In modern ICT applications, there is a pressing need for very accurate, up-to-date and diversity-aware knowledge resources [1]. Unfortunately, so far the attempts often failed to meet the expectations [10]. While automatically built resources can scale up to millions of entities, they can hardly compete in accuracy w.r.t. manually built resources. For this reason, we argue that the only affordable way to address this is by complementing automatic with manual checks. State of the art tools focus on the automatic detection and fixing of mistakes, especially for consistency checks. Notable examples include ontology development toolkits [6] and diagnostic tools [5]. Some authors concentrate on OWL ontologies [4]; some others on RDF ontologies [7].

This paper presents an approach to the automatic detection of potential mistakes in knowledge resources, based on the notion of *semantic schema* which takes into account the meaning of the terms in the resources and enforces additional constraints on their content. As combination of machine and human processing, violations to the schema are automatically detected and directed to manual checks. We evaluated the approach on the YAGO *ontology* [2] which was selected mainly because it does not have a fixed schema, and whose 2009 version has been never evaluated before. A similar experiment, performed on the GeoNames *database*, is described in [11].

The quality of a knowledge resource can heavily depend on the strategy employed for the data representation [9]. Databases ensure certain levels of quality by enforcing integrity constraints, but they do not support the explicit encoding of domain knowledge. For instance, it is not possible to specify that what applies to generic locations also applies to lakes and mountains. Instead, the constraints that ontologies can specify depend on the expressiveness of the language used. While OWL is very expressive, RDF(S) has well-known limitations: even if it distinguishes between

---

[*] A detailed longer description of this work is available as DISI technical report with same title.

Y.T. Demey and H. Panetto (Eds.): OTM 2013 Workshops, LNCS 8186, pp. 731–734, 2013.

classes and instances, a class can be potentially treated as an instance; it is not possible to explicitly represent disjointness between classes; transitivity cannot be enforced at the level of instances. We compensate for the limitations of databases and RDF(S) ontologies by defining additional constraints that constitute what we call a *semantic schema*. The semantic schema is built on the data model described in [8] that provides the *formal language* for the schema in the following sets:

- C is a set of *classes*;
- E is a set of *entities* that instantiate the classes in C;
- R is a set of binary *relations* relating entities and classes, including *is-a* (between classes in C), *instance-of* (associating instances in E to classes in C) and *part-of* (between classes in C or between entities in E) relations. We assume *is-a* and *part-of* to be transitive and asymmetric;
- A is a set of *attributes* associating entities to the data type values.

The semantic schema is defined as a set of constraints:

- on the domain and range of the attributes in A, such that the domain is always constituted by the entities in E which are instances of one or more classes in C and the range is a standard data type (e.g. Float, String);
- on the domain and range of the relations in R, such that both the domain and range are always constituted by the entities in E which are instances of one or more classes in C;
- about known disjoint classes.

We call *types* those classes in C which are explicitly mentioned as the domain or range of a relation in R or an attribute in A. Entities in E and facts about them is what in [8] is called the *knowledge level*. It can be easily observed that the above addresses all the limitations we described for databases and RDF(S). Once the semantic schema is defined, the content of the knowledge resource is processed by enforcing the schema in two steps. With the first step each entity in the resource is assigned exactly one type X from the schema. The selection of X is performed by checking that:

1. ALL the classes associated to the entity have at least a candidate sense (a possible disambiguation) which is more specific or more general than X
2. ALL the attributes of the entity are allowed for the type X
3. X is the only type exhibiting properties 1 and 2

Entities failing this assignment are considered to violate the semantic schema and are spotted as potential mistakes. With the second step, and for those entities passing the test, corresponding classes, attributes and relations are disambiguated accordingly.

2   The YAGO Use-Case

The YAGO Ontology. YAGO is automatically built by using WordNet noun synsets and the hypernym\hyponym relations between them as backbone and by extending it with additional classes, entities and facts about them extracted from Wikipedia. The YAGO model is compliant with RDF(S). For instance, for *Elvis Presley* it includes:

Elvis_Presley	isMarriedTo	Priscilla_Presley
Elvis_Presley	bornOnDate	1935-01-08
Elvis_Presley	type	wordnet_musician_110340312
Elvis_Presley	type	wikicategory_Musicians_from_Tennessee

isMarriedTo corresponds to a relation between entities, *bornOnDate* is an attribute, and *type* connects an entity to a class, which can be a WordNet class (taken from WordNet) or a Wikipedia class (taken from Wikipedia and linked to WordNet).

Definition of the Semantic Schema. For demonstrative purposes, we focused on locations, organizations and persons. The language was defined as follows:

- C includes *location, person, organization*, their more specific subclasses and their more general super-classes taken from WordNet.
- E is initially empty and is later populated with entities from YAGO.
- R contains *is-a, instance-of, part-of* relations and the subset of *YAGO* relations whose domain and range intersects with the classes in C.
- A contains the subset of *YAGO* relations whose domain intersects with the classes in C and the range is a standard data type.

In order to resolve their ambiguity, the names of attributes and relations were refined, disambiguated and renamed in order to identify corresponding synsets for them in WordNet. We then defined a semantic schema where, for instance:

- **Persons, locations and organizations** can all have the following relations: {hasWebsite, hasWonPrice, hasMotto, hasPredecessor, hasSuccessor}
- **Organizations** can also have the following relations: {hasNumberOfPeople, isAffiliatedTo, hasBudget, hasRevenue, hasProduct, establishedOnDate, createdOnDate, isLeaderOf, influences, dealsWith, participatedIn, isOfGenre, musicalRole, produced, created}
- Locations, persons and organizations are pairwise disjoint.

Enforcing the Semantic Schema. Facts about locations, organizations and persons were extracted from YAGO and imported into a database. The selection of relevant knowledge was performed by using *ontology modularization* techniques [3]. Overall, we identified 1,568,080 entities that correspond to around 56% of YAGO. The classes are limited to those in C and were extracted via specifically designed NLP tools. We unambiguously assigned a type to 1,389,505 entities corresponding to around 89% of the entities extracted (case I). 20,135 entities were categorized as ambiguous because more than one type X is consistent with the classes and the attributes of the entity (case II). 158,441 entities were not categorized because of lack of information - e.g., the entity has only one class and no attributes - or conflicting information - i.e., with classes or attributes of different types (case III). Attributes and relations were mapped to attributes in A or relations in R according to the type X. Values were considered to be correct only if they were consistent with the corresponding range constraints.

Evaluation. We manually evaluated the accuracy of our class disambiguation (performed only for case I) w.r.t. YAGO on randomly selected entities. For case I, over 100 randomly selected entities our type assignment is always correct, while our disambiguation of their 250 classes is **98%** correct, which is comparable to what we found in YAGO for the same entities (**97.2%**). The mistakes tend to be the same. For case II, over 50 entities we found that the accuracy of their 65 YAGO classes is **72.3%**. Mistakes include for instance bank as river slope instead of institution.

However, **7** of those are not even entities (they include articles about events). For case III, over 50 entities we found that the accuracy of their 101 classes in YAGO is **86.14%**. Mistakes include for instance unit as unit of measurement instead of military unit. However, **72%** of the candidates present some form of wrong information or they are not even entities. They include entities which are both animals and persons; entities which are both organizations and persons; sex and political positions as locations. Thus, the evaluation confirms the need to manually inspect entities falling in cases II and III, as their quality is significantly lower than those in case I.

3   Conclusions

We presented an automatic semantic schema-based approach for the identification of those parts of a knowledge resource which are particularly noisy and therefore would benefit from manual checks. The evaluation conducted on YAGO provided promising results. The future work will include (a) an extended schema for a higher coverage on YAGO and (b) the design of crowdsourcing tasks necessary to refine noisy parts.

Acknowledgements. This research has received funding from the CUbRIK EU Project, Grant agreement no. 287704. Thanks to Fausto Giunchiglia, Biswanath Dutta, Aliaksandr Autayeu, Feroz Farazi, Mario Passamani and the other members of the KnowDive group for their help.

References

1. Giunchiglia, F., Maltese, V., Dutta, B.: Domains and context: first steps towards managing diversity in knowledge. Journal of Web Semantics 12-13, 53–63 (2012)
2. Suchanek, F.M., Kasneci, G., Weikum, G.: YAGO: A Large Ontology from Wikipedia and WordNet. Journal of Web Semantics 6(3), 203–217 (2008)
3. Doran, P., Tamma, V., Iannone, L.: Ontology module extraction for ontology reuse: an ontology engineering perspective. In: 16th ACM CIKM Conference, pp. 61–70 (2007)
4. Parsia, B., Sirin, E., Kalyanpur, A.: Debugging OWL ontologies. In: WWW, pp. 633–640 (2005)
5. McGuinness, D.L., Fikes, R., Rice, J., Wilder, S.: An environment for merging and testing large ontologies. In: 7th International Conference on Principles of Knowledge Representation and Reasoning (KR 2000), pp. 483–493 (2000)
6. Noy, N., Sintek, M., Decker, S., Crubezy, M., Fergerson, R., Musen, M.: Creating semantic web contents with Protégé-2000. In: IEEE Intelligent Systems (2000)
7. Ding, L., Finin, T.W.: Characterizing the Semantic Web on the Web. In: Cruz, I., Decker, S., Allemang, D., Preist, C., Schwabe, D., Mika, P., Uschold, M., Aroyo, L.M. (eds.) ISWC 2006. LNCS, vol. 4273, pp. 242–257. Springer, Heidelberg (2006)
8. Giunchiglia, F., Dutta, B., Maltese, V., Farazi, F.: A facet-based methodology for the construction of a large-scale geospatial ontology. Journal of Data Semantics 1(1), 57–73 (2012)
9. Martinez-Cruz, C., Blanco, I., Vila, M.: Ontologies versus relational databases: are they so different? A comparison. Artificial Intelligence Review, 1–20 (2011)
10. Jain, P., Hitzler, P., Yeh, P.Z., Verma, K., Sheth, A.P.: Linked data is merely more data. In: Linked Data Meets Artificial Intelligence, pp. 82–86 (2010)
11. Maltese, V., Farazi, F.: A semantic schema for GeoNames. In: INSPIRE Conference (2013)

Towards Efficient Stream Reasoning

Debnath Mukherjee, Snehasis Banerjee, and Prateep Misra

TCS Innovation Labs, Tata Consultancy Services
Kolkata, India
{debnath.mukherjee,snehasis.banerjee,prateep.misra}@tcs.com

Abstract. We present a stream reasoning system, QUARKS, which has features like knowledge packets, application managed window and incremental query. Combination of rules and continuous queries along with application optimization has been used to address high performance requirements. Experimental results show that our proposed methodology is effective.

Keywords: stream reasoning, continuous query, rule, SPARQL, RDF.

1 Introduction

With the high volume of data being generated in real time from many sensors, there arises a need for reasoning on the data in real time [6]. Stream reasoning performs reasoning on a combination of real time streams of facts (usually represented as RDF triples) and static or slowly changing facts (known as background knowledge). A triple is of the form <subject, predicate, object>. For example, a fact could be <John, locatedAt, North Street>. Here "John" is the subject, "locatedAt" is the predicate and "North Street" is the object. In the context of stream reasoning, the real time streams of facts are synonymous with event streams.

In this paper, we describe a stream reasoner QUARKS (QUerying And Reasoning over Knowledge Streams) which uses registered continuous SPARQL queries and rule based reasoners. The contribution of this work is a stream processing layer on top of an existing Rete reasoner [4] and SPARQL processor to achieve good performance. QUARKS has three novel features: application managed windows, knowledge packets and incremental queries described in Section 2.

An early work in stream reasoning is C-SPARQL [1], a language for continuous queries over streams of facts combined with background knowledge. It extends the SPARQL language, adding features for RDF streams, windows etc. QUARKS uses continuous queries augmented by rules. CQELS [3] is another prototype which takes a native approach (without using existing data stream management systems or existing SPARQL processors). [2] has presented extensive experimental evaluation of the engine presented in [3]. QUARKS uses existing reasoners and SPARQL processors. [5] had briefly introduced the features of the stream reasoner QUARKS and had presented the results of using incremental queries for ad-hoc ride sharing scenario. In this paper, we show how a combination of rules and queries along with some application optimization can give good performance.

Y.T. Demey and H. Panetto (Eds.): OTM 2013 Workshops, LNCS 8186, pp. 735–738, 2013.
© Springer-Verlag Berlin Heidelberg 2013

2   Features of QUARKS

In this section, we present some of the salient features of QUARKS.

Knowledge Packets: QUARKS supports processing of multiple triples at a time. A set of triples describing an event is called a knowledge packet (KP). The KP's triples are processed all at once to avoid processing partial knowledge. A KP has a "type" which could be "add" or "delete" depending on whether the KP is being added or removed. A KP has a timestamp, and a name referred to as the "class" of the KP.

Application Managed Window: Consider that a fire has broken out in a building – this leads to a "fire event". Here only the event sender knows when to delete the fire event. Thus a new type of window, called Application Managed Window (AMW) is required where the client application is allowed to control the deletion of events. The time to delete fire event is not determined by some fixed number of events or a fixed temporal duration of events (as in the traditional count and time based windows) – rather it is ad-hoc. In QUARKS, we allow the application to control not only the insertion of KPs but also their deletion. The AMW is a set of triples derived from the event's KPs. Additionally, there are two functions, "ifunc" and "dfunc", which add and remove KPs from the AMW.

Incremental Query: Incremental queries (IQ) compute the incremental matches for a single incoming event in contrast to re-computing the entire match. IQ are implemented using parameterized SPARQL queries. See [5] for more on IQ.

Other windowing mechanisms: In addition to Application Managed Windows, count-based windows and time-based windows are supported. A *count-based window* specified as "COUNT N" maintains the last N KPs of a particular class in the working memory. A *time-based window* specified as "RANGE N [Time Unit]" maintains the KPs of a particular class that were added in the last N time units.

3   System Architecture and Event Processing

The system architecture is depicted in Figure 1. The client application makes calls to the Stream Reasoner API for adding or deleting a KP, and to register listeners for the queries. When a KP is added, it is sent to the Event Manager which consists of queues for KPs that are waiting to be scheduled for processing. When a KP is processed, its triples are added to the working memory (called a Memory Area). The working memory is an in-memory data structure containing known facts including the inferred facts. There are multiple Memory Areas – often one per application. After a KP is added to the working memory, multiple reasoners (such as rule-based reasoners, OWL reasoner, RDFS reasoner etc) act upon the facts to produce entailments.

The reasoners use both the facts in the dynamic knowledge (the KPs) and background knowledge. Our current assumption is that both the relevant parts of the background knowledge and the dynamic knowledge from the KPs fit into main memory. After the processing by the reasoners, the Event Manager calls the Query Runner module to run registered continuous queries for the KP being processed. Note that QUARKS processes the KPs as a single unit: inserting the KP into working memory and then running the continuous queries that are registered for the KP.

The results of running the continuous query are sent to "listeners" which are

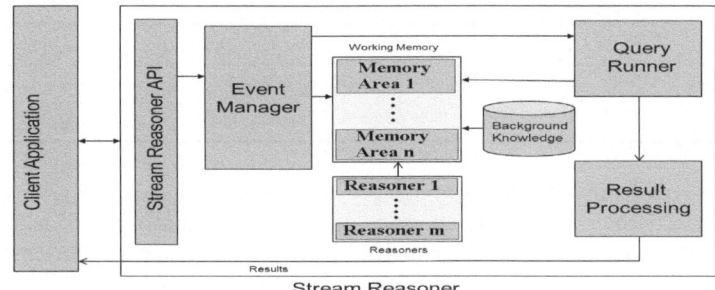

Fig. 1. System Architecture of QUARKS

Fig. 2. Event Processing in QUARKS

registered for the continuous query. The listeners are registered by the client application and return the results to the client application (formatting them if needed).

The event processing flow is depicted in Figure 2. First KP are queued for insertion into working memory (WM), then they are inserted into WM that triggers reasoners including rule based reasoners; finally registered continuous queries are run on the combined background knowledge and dynamic knowledge.

By default, a Rete-based rule reasoner [4] is used to process events – this is because Rete-based rule reasoner is a proven fast pattern matcher, and is one of the main reasons for good performance, but processing using only queries is allowed. Bulk of the logic should be written using rules to ensure good performance. We used Apache Jena framework for both Rete-based reasoning and queries. Note that our methodology of using a combination of rules and queries is not limited to a particular choice of rule engine or framework.

4   Experimental Evaluation and Conclusion

An experimental study was conducted to evaluate the stream reasoner. Four scenarios (Query 1, Query 2, Query 3, Query 4) from the experimental evaluation of CQELS [2] were evaluated using QUARKS. The results are presented in Table 1. Note that scenario Query 3 and Query 4 required two cascaded queries, but maintaining some logic in the client and using a single query instead of using two queries chained together performs better. The metric used was average processing time P defined as:
P = (Elapsed time to process N events) / N
(The elapsed time is adjusted for the first event insert time which is a one-time overhead, since the reasoner does some initializations).

From the result, it is clear that maintaining application logic and a single query instead of using two queries chained together performs better. The reason is that when

Table 1. Timing (in ms) for the scenarios using different methodologies

	Query 1	Query 2	Query 3	Query 4
Rule+Query	0.88	3.62	2.69	2.75
App Logic	-	-	0.98	0.98

the logic is simple, the overheads of using a query is more, and sometimes significant (as illustrated in the results). The above results are of the same order of magnitude as the state-of-the-art, as can be seen in [2]. The experiments were run on a system having Quad Core Intel Core i5 2.67 GHz CPU and 4GB memory.

Application optimizations: The ordering of the patterns in the rules had a significant effect on the performance. The rule pattern ordering guidelines [7] for the Rete engine Jess were found to be quite useful. Also, some of the rules had a subset of patterns that could be resolved from the background knowledge alone. So here an application optimization was to pre-compute these subsets of patterns with a separate rule which generates an entailment E, and replacing the subset of patterns in the original rule by the entailment pattern E. This gave significant performance benefits.

To conclude, in this paper we adopted a combination of Rete-based rule engine and a SPARQL query processor to implement a stream reasoner, QUARKS. Evaluation was done using the stream reasoning queries mentioned in [2]. The results produced are encouraging. The stream reasoner described also has some practical features such as Application Managed Windows, Knowledge Packets and Incremental Queries. In future work, we wish to explore automatically optimizing the ordering of patterns in the rule, automatically generating pre-computation rules, support for temporal operators and parallelization of processing (wherever possible).

Acknowledgments. We thank Dr. Dilys Thomas of TRDDC, Pune and Sounak Dey of TCS Innovation Labs, Kolkata for their comments on this work.

References

1. Barbieri, D., Braga, D., Ceri, S., Valle, E., Grossniklaus, M.: C-SPARQL: SPARQL for continuous querying. In: 18th World Wide Web Conference, pp. 1061–1062. ACM (2009)
2. Experimental evaluation of CQELS stream reasoner,
   http://code.google.com/p/cqels/wiki/Experiments
3. Le-Phuoc, D., Dao-Tran, M., Xavier Parreira, J., Hauswirth, M.: A native and adaptive approach for unified processing of linked streams and linked data. In: Aroyo, L., Welty, C., Alani, H., Taylor, J., Bernstein, A., Kagal, L., Noy, N., Blomqvist, E. (eds.) ISWC 2011, Part I. LNCS, vol. 7031, pp. 370–388. Springer, Heidelberg (2011)
4. Forgy, C.L.: Rete: A Fast Algorithm for the Many Pattern / Many Object Pattern Match Problem. Artificial Intelligence 19, 17–37 (1982)
5. Mukherjee, D., Banerjee, S., Misra, P.: Ad-hoc ride sharing application using continuous SPARQL queries. In: 21st International Conference Companion on World Wide Web (WWW 2012), pp. 579–580. ACM (2012)
6. Banerjee, S., Mukherjee, D., Misra, P.: 'What Affects Me?' A Smart Public Alert System based on Stream Reasoning. In: 7th International Conference on Ubiquitous Information Management and Communication (ICUIMC). ACM (2013)
7. Efficiency of rule-based systems,
   http://herzberg.ca.sandia.gov/docs/70/rete.html

From Theoretical Framework to Generic Semantic Measures Library

Sébastien Harispe, Stefan Janaqi, Sylvie Ranwez, and Jacky Montmain

LGI2P, Ecole des mines d'Alès, Parc Scientifique G. Besse, F-30035 Nîmes Cedex 1
`firstname.name@mines-ales.fr`

Abstract. Semantic Measures (SMs) are of critical importance in multiple treatments relying on ontologies. However, the improvement and use of SMs are currently hampered by the lack of a dedicated theoretical framework and an extensive generic software solution. To meet these needs, this paper introduces a unified theoretical framework of graph-based SMs, from which we developed the open source Semantic Measures Library and toolkit, a solution that paves the way for design, computation and analysis of SMs. More information at dedicated website: http://www.semantic-measures-library.org.

Keywords: Semantic Similarity Measures, Unifying Framework, Semantic Measures Library, Software for Semantic Measure Computation.

1 Introduction

Numerous initiatives take advantage of ontologies to characterize entities, such as scientific publications, people or genes. To exploit such knowledge for information retrieval and knowledge discovery, inexact searches have to be performed, which require measures that are capable of assessing the degree of likeness of entities. Semantic measures (SMs) are designed for this purpose: to capture the relatedness of concepts (and by extension semantically characterized entities), by taking into account the semantic space in which they are defined. This paper explores graph-based SMs, here denoted SMs for convenience.

Study of SMs involves various communities which have designed numerous measures for specific treatments and ontologies [1, 2]. However, no unifying theoretical framework has been proposed to explicitly characterize core elements of SMs through the spectrum of similarity and graph theory. Indeed, given the lack of contributions focusing on theoretical aspects of SMs, studies are often restricted to a specific community and do not benefit to a broader target audience.

Likewise, most of software dedicated to SMs are developed for particular ontologies (e.g. WordNet, UMLS, Gene Ontology, MeSH, Disease Ontology [3–6]). This diversity of software solutions has drawbacks given that SM evaluations rely exclusively on empirical studies. Therefore, the lack of an extensive software solution slows down studies of SMs as well as the sharing of new findings related to the domain.

Y.T. Demey and H. Panetto (Eds.): OTM 2013 Workshops, LNCS 8186, pp. 739–742, 2013.

This paper proposes a unified theoretical framework and a generic software solution to mutualize efforts and advance the increasing role of SMs in numerous fields. The second section introduces the framework which defines a reduced set of abstract primitive functions that are commonly used for SM design. The third section presents the Semantic Measures Library, an extensive open source library dedicated to the computation, development and analysis of SMs.

2   A Unifying Theoretical Framework for Semantic Measures

Most SMs are expressed reducing an ontology to a graph $G = (C, E, R)$, with C being the set of classes represented as vertices and E the set of edges representing the oriented pairwise relationships defined between two classes. G is assumed to contain a taxonomical sub-graph defining a partial order $\preccurlyeq$ on C with $x \preccurlyeq y$ if x is a subclass of y. Moreover, classical knowledge bases are composed of a collection of entities which are conceptually characterized through classes, e.g. genes annotated by concepts [1] or PubMed articles indexed by MeSH descriptors. SMs used to compare entities are extension of those designed to compare pairs of classes. We therefore focus on SMs estimating the similarity of pairs of classes, that is to say a function $\mu: C \times C \to \mathbb{R}^+$. Formulas of existing measures proposed in the literature are not presented, we orient the reader to the numerous surveys for detailed presentations [1, 2].

This section defines a unifying theoretical framework aiming to: (i) better characterize SMs at a theoretical level through the definition of the primitive abstract functions on which SMs rely, (ii) distinguish common and relevant features of SMs, (iii) analyse measures' characteristics and properties, (iv) design and optimize SMs in accordance with usage contexts. Presented results expand previous works on the characterization of SMs through abstract formulations [3, 7–9]. Their main goal was to establish links between various models of semantic similarity rather than distinguishing the primitive functions governing measures design. Our contribution focuses mainly on the definition of those primitive functions. It is therefore not constrained to a specific model of similarity (e.g. feature, information theory, geometric and transformation models).

The set of primitive functions which can be used to express most abstract formulations of SMs is:

- $\rho(a)$: semantic representation of a class a (denoted $\tilde{a}$). With $\mathbb{K}$ a set composed of paths, classes or any subset of G, we define $\rho: C \to \mathbb{K}$.
- $\Theta(\tilde{a})$: salience of the representation of a class, i.e. the amount of information carried by a semantic representation $\tilde{a}$, $\Theta: \mathbb{K} \to \mathbb{R}^+$.
- $\Psi(\tilde{a}, \tilde{b})$: commonalities of the pair $(\tilde{a}, \tilde{b})$, $\Psi: \mathbb{K} \times \mathbb{K} \to \mathbb{R}^+$.
- $\Phi(\tilde{u}, \tilde{v})$: differences of the pair $(\tilde{a}, \tilde{b})$, $\Phi: \mathbb{K} \times \mathbb{K} \to \mathbb{R}^+$.
- $\zeta(\tilde{a}, \tilde{b})$: amount of information defined in the semantic space, which is not found in the couple of representations $(\tilde{a}, \tilde{b})$, $\zeta: \mathbb{K} \times \mathbb{K} \to \mathbb{R}^+$.

Once the representation of a class and the corresponding operators used to estimate the commonalities and differences are defined, some abstract functions estimating similarity can be used. For instance, the similarity can be assessed based on an abstract expression of the *ratio model* (Sim_{RM}), initially proposed by Tversky to compare semantic elements represented as sets of features [9]:

$$Sim_{RM}(a,b) = \frac{\Psi(\tilde{a},\tilde{b})}{\alpha \cdot \Phi(\tilde{a},\tilde{b}) + \beta \cdot \Phi(\tilde{b},\tilde{a}) + \Psi(\tilde{a},\tilde{b})}$$

with $\tilde{a} = \rho(a)$, α and β two parameters defining the asymmetrical contribution of the operator Φ.

The unifying framework is not constrained to a specific measure but rather relies on primitive functions commonly used to define SMs. As an example, numerous similarity measure expressions rely on a function Θ estimating the amount of information carried by the representation of an element, e.g. the cardinality when compared elements are represented by sets. Such a function Θ enables the use of the abstracted form of two general expressions unifying binary measures: Gower & Legendre and Caillez & Kuntz parameterized measures [8]. Those abstract measures, among others, can be used to derive most of SMs through specific expressions of the abstract functions on which they rely (ρ, Θ, Ψ, Φ) [7, 8].

To define a concrete measure, SM designers should specify the primitive functions distinguished by the framework. As an example: (i) representing a class by the set of its subclasses, $\rho(b) = A(b)$; (ii) defining the commonality classes as a function of the Information Content (IC) carried by their Most Informative Common Ancestor (MICA), $\Psi(\tilde{u},\tilde{v}) = IC(MICA_{u,v})$; (iii) evaluating the difference of two classes by $\Phi(\tilde{u},\tilde{v}) = IC(u) - IC(MICA_{u,v})$; (iv) setting Sim_{RM} with α and β equal to 1 corresponds to the measure proposed by Pirró & Euzenat [3].

Research on SMs is driven by a cycle consisting of three aspects: theoretical studies, software development and empirical studies. Another important aspect for SM studies is therefore to provide ways to take advantage of theoretical contributions through software solutions.

3   The Semantic Measures Library

The Semantic Measures Library (SML) is a generic software solution dedicated to SM computation, analysis and development. By generic, we mean that the SML can be used to take advantage of SMs on a wide range of semantic graphs. Following the abstraction layers defined in the previous section, a large collection of SMs has been implemented. Moreover, thanks to the code base available (e.g. graph algorithms), new measures can easily be designed and evaluated. The SML is written in JAVA and open-sourced under the GPL-compatible CeCILL licence. In addition, the SML-Toolkit enables non-developers to benefit from functionalities provided by the SML through command-line interfaces. Documentation, tutorials and downloads of both the SML and the toolkit are available at http://www.semantic-measures-library.org.

4   Conclusion

This paper defines a unifying theoretical framework for SMs. By underlining close relationships between measures, we distinguish the primitive functions required for their design. Besides facilitating the definition of countless new measures, this new insight allows us to study SMs which are grouped in accordance with the expressions of the abstract functions they rely on. This leads us to draw interesting perspectives regarding the theoretical studies of SMs.

To address the handicapping lack of a generic, extensive and efficient software solutions dedicated to SMs, we developed the open source Semantic Measures Library (SML) and associated toolkit. The SML, both highly tuneable and not limited to a particular semantic graph, is suited for diverse application contexts. Downloads and documentation are available at http://www.semantic-measures-library.org.

References

1. Pesquita, C., Faria, D., Falcão, A.O., Lord, P., Couto, F.M.: Semantic similarity in biomedical ontologies. PLoS Computational Biology 5(7), e1000443 (2009)
2. Pedersen, T., Pakhomov, S.V.S., Patwardhan, S., Chute, C.G.: Measures of semantic similarity and relatedness in the biomedical domain. Journal of Biomedical Informatics 40(3), 288–299 (2007)
3. Pirró, G., Euzenat, J.: A Feature and Information Theoretic Framework for Semantic Similarity and Relatedness. In: Patel-Schneider, P.F., Pan, Y., Hitzler, P., Mika, P., Zhang, L., Pan, J.Z., Horrocks, I., Glimm, B. (eds.) ISWC 2010, Part I. LNCS, vol. 6496, pp. 615–630. Springer, Heidelberg (2010)
4. Pedersen, T., Patwardhan, S., Michelizzi, J.: WordNet:Similarity: measuring the relatedness of concepts. In: Proceedings of HLT-NAACL, Demonstration Papers, pp. 38–41 (2004)
5. Yu, G., Li, F., Qin, Y., Bo, X., Wu, Y., Wang, S.: GOSemSim: an R package for measuring semantic similarity among GO terms and gene products. Bioinformatics (Oxford, England) 26(7), 976–978 (2010)
6. Li, J., Gong, B., Chen, X., Liu, T., Wu, C., Zhang, F., Li, C., Li, X., Rao, S., Li, X.: DOSim: An R package for similarity between diseases based on Disease Ontology. BMC Bioinformatics 12, 266 (2011)
7. Sánchez, D., Batet, M.: Semantic similarity estimation in the biomedical domain: An ontology-based information-theoretic perspective. Journal of Biomedical Informatics 44(5), 749–759 (2011)
8. Blanchard, E., Harzallah, M., Kuntz, P.: A generic framework for comparing semantic similarities on a subsumption hierarchy. In: Proceedings of 18th European Conference on Artificial Intelligence, pp. 20–24 (2008)
9. Cross, V., Yu, X., Hu, X.: Unifying ontological similarity measures: A theoretical and empirical investigation. International Journal of Approximate Reasoning 54(7), 861–875 (2013)

Categorization of Modeling Language Concepts: Graded or Discrete?

Dirk van der Linden[1,2,3]

[1] Public Research Centre Henri Tudor, Luxembourg, Luxembourg
dirk.vanderlinden@tudor.lu
[2] Radboud University Nijmegen, Nijmegen, the Netherlands
[3] EE-Team, Luxembourg, Luxembourg*

Abstract. We investigate the category structure of categories common to conceptual modeling languages (i.e., the types used by languages such as actor, process, goal, or restriction) to study whether they more closely approximate a discrete or graded category. We find that most categories exhibit more of a graded structure, with experienced modelers displaying this even more strongly than the other participants. We discuss the consequences of these results for (conceptual) modeling in general.

Keywords: categorization, conceptual modeling, model semantics.

1 Introduction

We categorize the world around us in different ways depending on the subject matter. Some things we categorize more discretely, like natural things (e.g., fruits and plants), some things we categorize in a more graded way, such as artifactual things (e.g., tools, vehicles). These different categorization tendencies have been shown many times in research, starting around the time of Rosch et al. [7]. Also, they have been investigated by many others explicitly elaborating on the category structure for a number of natural and artifactual categories (cf. [2,1,4]). On the other hand, some work investigating this has had difficulties in finding significant differences in categorization tendencies between artifactual and natural categories (cf. [5]). Regardless of the debate whether particular kinds of categories are usually categorized in a particular way, it is clear that *we do not categorize everything in the same way.*

We aim to clarify whether the categories common to many modeling languages and methods (i.e., those types used by a language to instantiate domain concepts by) are categorized in a discrete or graded fashion. The implications of this for model creation and usage (particularly for models used to capture and document a certain domain) are important to be aware of. If a category from a language is typically judged in a discrete fashion, the semantics of models are likely easier to communicate, formalize, and keep coherent. However, if such a category is

---

* The Enterprise Engineering Team (EE-Team) is a collaboration between Public Research Centre Henri Tudor, Radboud University and HAN University of Applied Sciences (www.ee-team.eu).

Y.T. Demey and H. Panetto (Eds.): OTM 2013 Workshops, LNCS 8186, pp. 743–746, 2013.
© Springer-Verlag Berlin Heidelberg 2013

typically judged in a graded fashion, communicating it to others becomes more involved, requiring more explicit discussion, and the formalizations and tools we use need to explicitly support this structure.

2   Method

Participants: Fifty-six participants participated in the present study. Twenty-one of them were advanced (3rd or 4th year) students at an undergraduate university of applied science with a focus on computing science and modeling, thirty-five were employees at a public research center with a focus on IT and used modeling languages and tools to varying degrees. All participated voluntarily and received no compensation for their participation.

Materials: The materials used for the benchmark in the experiment were based on the list of exemplars reported on by Barr & Caplan [1]. We used 5 full, 5 partial and 5 non-members terms for both of the benchmarks. For the benchmark we included the categories FRUIT and VEHICLES. For the modeling part of the experiment we investigated the categories ACTOR, EVENT, GOAL, PROCESS, RESOURCE, RESTRICTION and RESULT. These categories result from an earlier performed analysis on modeling languages and methods [6]. The terms used for the members of the categories from the modeling languages are the terms used by the modeling language and methods, based on the official (or most-used) specification.

Procedure: The procedure was based on Estes' [3] setup. Participants completed the task through an on online survey. They were instructed to judge whether a list of given terms were either full, partial or non-members for the current category. Participants were informed beforehand that partial member scores meant that the exemplar belonged to the category, but to a less degree than others. This was first done for the two benchmark categories, and followed in the same way for each of the investigated categories from the modeling languages. The orders of the terms in each category were randomized for each participant.

3   Results

The proportion of graded membership judgments for the terms used in the benchmark which are partial members are shown in detail in Table 1. What was to be expected is that the typically discrete category (FRUIT) would show lower proportions of graded judgments compared to the typically graded category (VEHICLES). The given scores indicate the proportion of partial member judgments (e.g., 19% of students, 13% of beginning modelers, and 30% of expert modelers considered an avocado as a partial member of the FRUIT category). Shown are respectively the scores for students, beginning modelers, expert modelers, and the scores as reported by Barr & Caplan [1], and Estes [3].

A more detailed overview of the average amount of full, partial and non-member judgments for each investigated category is given in Table 2. The results

Table 1. Partial member proportions for the partial member terms of the benchmark

Category	Term	Student	Beginner	Expert	Ref. [1]	Ref. [3]
FRUIT	avocado	0.19	0.13	0.30	0.37	0.16
	coconut	0.24	–	0.05	0.38	0.37
	tomato	0.33	0.27	0.25	0.34	0.05
	cucumber	0.19	–	0.25	0.23	0.21
	rhubarb	0.14	0.20	0.15	0.45	0.26
VEHICLES	gondola	0.24	0.20	0.20	0.50	0.21
	tricycle	0.14	0.13	0.10	0.64	0.58
	wheelchair	0.29	0.27	0.50	0.70	0.63
	horse	0.48	0.27	0.55	0.54	0.50
	husky	0.38	0.27	0.55	0.27	0.21

are given for each investigated group (students, beginning modelers and expert modelers), and indicate the proportion of membership judgments. For example, students considered 47% of the presented terms for the ACTOR category to be full members, 18% to be partial members and 35% to be non-members. The primary points of interest here are the higher scoring partial and non-member results, as they indicate words actually used by modeling languages that are either only considered to be partially reflective of their category (e.g., a 'market segment' would be only considered somewhat an ACTOR), or are considered not to be exemplars of that category (e.g., a 'requirement unit' would not be considered an ACTOR).

Table 2. Average amount of membership scores (full, partial and non-members) for each group of investigated categories

Category	student (n = 20)			beginner (n = 15)			expert (n = 21)		
	full	partial	non	full	partial	non	full	partial	non
ACTOR	0.47	0.18	0.35	0.30	0.14	0.55	0.41	0.25	0.35
EVENT	0.46	0.14	0.41	0.39	0.16	0.45	0.29	0.19	0.51
GOAL	0.65	0.11	0.23	0.60	0.16	0.24	0.56	0.20	0.24
PROCESS	0.66	0.14	0.20	0.62	0.22	0.16	0.41	0.32	0.28
RESOURCE	0.59	0.19	0.22	0.62	0.19	0.20	0.54	0.22	0.24
RESTRICTION	0.50	0.21	0.29	0.55	0.18	0.27	0.39	0.24	0.37
RESULT	0.73	0.16	0.11	0.86	0.07	0.08	0.76	0.16	0.09
FRUIT	0.44	0.10	0.45	0.47	0.05	0.42	0.49	0.09	0.41
VEHICLE	0.48	0.14	0.37	0.49	0.13	0.37	0.51	0.20	0.29

It was expected that the partial member judgments for the natural and artifactual benchmark categories would show a difference, with the artifactual category displaying a higher proportion of graded judgments. Although compared to the results from Barr & Caplan [1] and Estes [3] the overall amount of graded judgments seems to be lower, the relative distribution still seems intact. This is the case for both the beginning and expert modelers (the proportion of some graded judgments for VEHICLES being at least twice as large compared to the ones for FRUITS). This is not the case for the student group, as the difference between the benchmark categories there was found to be much smaller. This could be explained by the lower amount of experience with (and exposure to) modeling (and modeling languages) students have.

On average the proportion of partial member judgments is 0.16 for students, 0.16 for beginning modelers, and 0.23 for expert modelers. When we compare these scores to the average proportion of partial member judgments for the discrete and graded benchmark categories in Table 2 (respectively 0.10 and 0.14 for the students, 0.05 and 0.13 for the beginning modelers and 0.09 and 0.20 for the expert modelers), we can see that for the two groups of modelers most scores shown for the categories from modeling languages more clearly reflect the graded benchmark category than the discrete one. Thus, as a careful first investigation we seem to have found support that most categories from modeling languages are of a graded nature. Given that the distribution of terms for these categories was not the same as the benchmark categories (i.e., the benchmark categories were made up of equal amounts of full, partial and non-members, while for the categories from the modeling languages we were unaware of this distribution, with them likely containing proportionally more full members) this makes it all the more acceptable to support the idea described in the introduction that *these categories can be seen as exhibiting a graded structure.*

Acknowledgements. This work has been partially sponsored by the *Fonds National de la Recherche Luxembourg* (www.fnr.lu), via the PEARL programme.

References

1. Barr, R., Caplan, L.: Category representations and their implications for category structure. Memory & Cognition 15(5), 397–418 (1987)
2. Diesendruck, G., Gelman, S.: Domain differences in absolute judgments of category membership: Evidence for an essentialist account of categorization. Psychonomic Bulletin & Review 6(2), 338–346 (1999)
3. Estes, Z.: Domain differences in the structure of artifactual and natural categories. Memory & Cognition 31(2), 199–214 (2003)
4. Estes, Z.: Confidence and gradedness in semantic categorization: Definitely somewhat artifactual, maybe absolutely natural. Psychonomic Bulletin & Review 11(6), 1041–1047 (2004)
5. Kalish, C.W.: Essentialism and graded membership in animal and artifact categories. Memory & Cognition 23(3), 335–353 (1995)
6. van der Linden, D.J.T., Hoppenbrouwers, S.J.B.A., Lartseva, A., Proper, H.A.: Towards an investigation of the conceptual landscape of enterprise architecture. In: Halpin, T., Nurcan, S., Krogstie, J., Soffer, P., Proper, E., Schmidt, R., Bider, I. (eds.) BPMDS 2011 and EMMSAD 2011. LNBIP, vol. 81, pp. 526–535. Springer, Heidelberg (2011)
7. Rosch, E., Mervis, C.B.: Family resemblances: Studies in the internal structure of categories. Cognitive Psychology 7(4), 573–605 (1975)

Author Index